Rethinking Society for the 21ˢᵗ Century

Report of the International Panel on Social Progress

Volume 1: Socio-Economic Transformations

This is the first of three volumes containing a report from the International Panel on Social Progress (IPSP). The IPSP is an independent association of top research scholars with the goal of assessing methods for improving the main institutions of modern societies. Written in accessible language by scholars across the social sciences and humanities, these volumes assess the achievements of world societies in past centuries, the current trends, the dangers that we are now facing, and the possible futures in the twenty-first century. It covers the main socio-economic, political, and cultural dimensions of social progress, global as well as regional issues, and the diversity of challenges and their interplay around the world. This particular volume covers topics such as economic inequality and growth, finance and corporations, labor, capitalism, and social justice.

The International Panel on Social Progress brings together more than 300 scholars from all disciplines of social sciences and the humanities, and from all continents. Since 2014, the mission of the Panel has been to gather expertise and disseminate knowledge on the perspectives for social progress around the world in the coming decades. The Panel is an independent initiative supported by more than 30 scientific or academic institutions and international foundations. With Amartya Sen as President, and Nancy Fraser, Ravi Kanbur, and Helga Nowotny as co-chairs of the Scientific Council, the Panel has been co-directed by Olivier Bouin and Marc Fleurbaey.

Rethinking Society for the 21st Century

Report of the International Panel on Social Progress

Volume 1: Socio-Economic Transformations

CAMBRIDGE
UNIVERSITY PRESS

CAMBRIDGE
UNIVERSITY PRESS

University Printing House, Cambridge CB2 8BS, United Kingdom

One Liberty Plaza, 20th Floor, New York, NY 10006, USA

477 Williamstown Road, Port Melbourne, VIC 3207, Australia

314–321, 3rd Floor, Plot 3, Splendor Forum, Jasola District Centre, New Delhi – 110025, India

79 Anson Road, #06-04/06, Singapore 079906

Cambridge University Press is part of the University of Cambridge.

It furthers the University's mission by disseminating knowledge in the pursuit of
education, learning, and research at the highest international levels of excellence.

www.cambridge.org
Information on this title: www.cambridge.org/9781108423120
DOI: 10.1017/9781108399623

First published 2018

Printed in the United Kingdom by TJ International Ltd. Padstow Cornwall

A catalogue record for this publication is available from the British Library.

Library of Congress Cataloging-in-Publication Data
Names: International Panel on Social Progress, author.
Title: Rethinking society for the 21st century : report of the International Panel on Social Progress. Other titles: Socio-economic
transformations. | Political regulation, governance, and societal transformations. | Transformations in values, norms, cultures.
Description: Cambridge, United Kingdom; New York, NY: Cambridge University Press, 2018. | Includes index. |
Volume 1. Socio-economic transformations – Volume 2. Political regulation, governance, and
societal transformations – Volume 3. Transformations in values, norms, cultures.
Identifiers: LCCN 2018003514 | ISBN 9781108399593 (Set of 3 hardback volumes) | ISBN 9781108423120 (vol. 1 : hardback) |
ISBN 9781108423137 (vol. 2 : hardback) | ISBN 9781108423144 (vol. 3 : hardback) | ISBN 9781108399579 (Set of 3 paperback volumes) |
ISBN 9781108436328 (vol. 1 : paperback) | ISBN 9781108436335 (vol. 2 : paperback) | ISBN 9781108436342 (vol. 3 : paperback)
Subjects: LCSH: Social change. | Progress. | Political science. | Civilization – 21st century.
Classification: LCC HN18.3.I568 2018 | DDC 306–dc23
LC record available at https://lccn.loc.gov/2018003514

ISBN 978-1-108-39959-3 Set of 3 hardback volumes
ISBN 978-1-108-42312-0 Volume 1 Hardback
ISBN 978-1-108-42313-7 Volume 2 Hardback
ISBN 978-1-108-42314-4 Volume 3 Hardback
ISBN 978-1-108-39957-9 Set of 3 paperback volumes
ISBN 978-1-108-43632-8 Volume 1 Paperback
ISBN 978-1-108-43633-5 Volume 2 Paperback
ISBN 978-1-108-43634-2 Volume 3 Paperback

This First Report of the International Panel on Social Progress is dedicated to Kenneth Arrow, Anthony Atkinson, Abdul Raufu Mustapha, and Klaus Rennings, who sadly passed away while the Report was being drafted

Contents

Introduction to Volume 1

Authors:[1]
Olivier Bouin, Marie-Laure Djelic, Marc Fleurbaey, Ravi Kanbur, Elisa Reis

---

[1] Affiliations: OB: RFIEA; MLD: Sciences-Po; MF: Princeton University; RK: Cornell University; ER: Federal University of Rio de Janeiro.

0.1 Why a Panel on Social Progress?

There are many expert panels on issues ranging from biodiversity to chemical pollution or nuclear proliferation, and the most famous is now the Intergovernmental Panel on Climate Change. A few years ago, a small group of academics started to wonder: Why is there no panel about the promotion of social justice, about the search for a general set of better policies and better institutions – in a nutshell, for a better society? Many policy issues examined by the existing panels have deep societal roots in the economy, in politics, and in cultures and values. Addressing these deeper factors would ease the search for solutions in many domains.

This questioning turned out to be widely shared among social scientists, and motivated the launch of the International Panel on Social Progress (IPSP), in its first congress in Istanbul in 2015. The IPSP is a purely bottom-up initiative, started by a group of researchers. It is complementary to many ongoing efforts by various groups and organizations with which it is collaborating. The United Nations are pushing the ambitious Agenda 2030 and its associated Sustainable Development Goals (SDG); the Organization for Economic Co-operation and Development (OECD) has launched multiple initiatives for a "better life," for "inclusive growth," as well as more technical efforts such as the fight against tax evasion; the World Bank has developed multiple approaches against poverty and inequality, and is not afraid of listening to the "voices of the poor" or of "rethinking the social contract"; the ILO articulates an agenda for the promotion of "decent work"; the Social Progress Imperative, also a bottom-up initiative of a few academics, seeks to promote social policies via a specific measurement approach meant to supplement economic indicators. These important efforts are just a few examples in a long list.

The International Panel on Social Progress distinguishes itself from other initiatives by combining three characteristics. First, it seeks to examine not just policy issues for the medium term but also structural and systemic issues for the long term. In other words, it is not afraid of asking existential questions about capitalism, socialism, democracy, religions, inequalities, and so on. A combination of intellectual caution, political conformism, and vested interests often prevent such existential questions from being explicitly discussed. But we should not be afraid to ask: What system should we aim for?

Second, the IPSP seeks to mobilize a uniquely wide set of perspectives, from all the relevant disciplines of social sciences and humanities as well as from all the continents. While the influence of the academic culture of developed countries remains strong in the Report, a substantial effort has been made to open the drafting effort to a global set of views and to present initiatives and case studies from developing countries. Social innovation is not a prerogative of the developed world, quite the contrary. The Global South has been widely influential on many occasions in the far or more recent past and today it still generates many ideas and initiatives that can inspire the world.

Finally, the IPSP does not talk exclusively to the policy-makers in charge of governmental action. Given its coverage of long-term structural issues, its ideas for innovative action also, and primarily, target the actors who are the real "change-makers" of society, namely, the many leaders and citizens who participate in public debates, who volunteer work in civil society organizations, and who push the official decision-makers out of their comfort zone. Social progress has always been, in the long run, a bottom-up affair, and ideas are a key fuel for its engine.

0.2 Social Progress in Sight

The focus on "social progress" in this Report deserves some explanations, as the notion of progress has suffered from use and abuse by a particular elite, who, since the Industrial Revolution, found it natural to lead the world according to its privileges and prejudices. The Panel refers to "social progress" to send a message. Social change is not a neutral matter, and, even if there are many conflicting views on how to conceive of a good or just society, this Panel takes the view that a compass is needed to parse the options that actors and decision-makers face. Moreover, the twentieth century and the beginning of the twenty-first century have successively made most observers of society lose their faith in socialism and their trust in capitalism, leaving a general sense of disarray and disorientation. The message of this Panel is a message of hope. We can do better, this is not the end of history.

If a main message emerges from this three-volume Report, it is indeed that: (1) considerable progress has been made in the past centuries and humanity is at a peak of possibilities, but it now faces challenges that jeopardize its achievements and even its survival; (2) addressing these challenges and mobilizing our current collective capacities to the benefit of a wider population require reforms that will hurt certain vested interests but rely on general principles that are readily available, involving an expansion of participatory governance and the promotion of equal dignity across persons, groups, and cultures; (3) there is not a unique direction of progress but multiple possibilities and many ideas that can be experimented, with variable adaptability to different economic, political, and cultural contexts.

0.3 Aims of the Report and Additional Resources on www.ipsp.org

The Report presented here is made of 22 chapters over three volumes. Every chapter is co-signed by a multidisciplinary team of authors and represents the views of this team, not necessarily the views of the whole panel. In total, more than 260 authors have been involved, with about 60 percent of contributors coming, in roughly equal proportions, from economics, sociology, and political science, and the remainder representing other disciplines. Each chapter starts with a long summary of its contents, so as to help readers navigate the Report.

The objective of the Panel was to have every chapter team write a critical assessment of the state of the art in the topic covered in the chapter, acknowledging the ongoing debates and suggesting emerging consensus points. The initial objective was also to conclude every chapter with multiple recommendations for action and reform, with a transparent link to the diverse values that underlie the recommendations. These two objectives were encapsulated in the expressions "agree to disagree" and "conditional recommendations." In the end, one can observe differences in the degree to which the chapters are able to cover all sides of the debates and to make concrete recommendations that relate to a diversity of possible values and goals. But this Report proves that a large group of specialists from different disciplines can work together and provide a synthesis that no single brain could alone produce. This Report provides the reader with a unique overview of the state of society and the possible futures, with a mine of ideas of possible reforms and actions. For scholars and students, it also offers an exceptional guide to the literature in the relevant academic disciplines of social sciences and the humanities.

The drafting process involved the collection of thousands of online comments. Nevertheless, this Report reflects, as planned, the voice of academia rather than a broader group of thinkers or stakeholders. This is the contribution of a group of people who specialize in research. They offer their expertise and thoughts to the public debate, without seeking to bypass the democratic confrontation of projects. The readers are invited to take this Report as a resource, as a mine for ideas and arguments, as a tool for their own thought and action. They are also invited to engage with the Panel members and share their views and experiences.

Some of the chapters have longer versions, with more detailed analysis, more data, or case studies, which are available in open access on the IPSP website (www.ipsp.org), along with videos of the authors and teaching resources. Visitors of the website are also invited to provide comments and to participate in surveys and forums.

0.4   Outline of the Report and of Volume I

The Report is divided into three parts, together with two introductory chapters and two concluding chapters. The introductory chapters lay out the main social trends that form the background of this Report (Chapter 1), and the main values and principles that form a "compass" for those who seek social progress (Chapter 2).

The first part of the Report deals with socio-economic transformations, and focuses on economic inequalities (Chapter 3), growth and environmental issues (Chapter 4), urbanization (Chapter 5), capitalist institutions of markets, corporations and finance (Chapter 6), labor (Chapter 7), concluding with a reflection on how economic organization determines well-being and social justice (Chapter 8).

The second part of the Report scrutinizes political issues, scrutinizing the ongoing complex trends in democracy and the rule of law (Chapter 9), the forms and resolutions of situations of violence and conflicts (Chapter 10), the mixed efficacy of supranational institutions and organizations (Chapter 11), as well as the multiple forms of global governance (Chapter 12), and the important role for democracy of media and communications (Chapter 13). It concludes with a chapter on the challenges to democracy raised by inequalities, and the various ways in which democracy can be rejuvenated (Chapter 14).

The third part of the Report is devoted to transformations in cultures and values, with analyses of cultural trends linked to "modernization" and its pitfalls, as well as globalization (Chapter 15), a study of the complex relation between religions and social progress (Chapter 16), an examination of the promises and challenges in ongoing transformations in family structures and norms (Chapter 17), a focus on trends and policy issues regarding health and life–death issues (Chapter 18), a study of the ways in which education can contribute to social progress (Chapter 19), and finally, a chapter on the important values of solidarity and belonging (Chapter 20).

The two concluding chapters include a synthesis on the various innovative ways in which social progress can go forward (Chapter 21) and a reflection on how the various disciplines of social science can play a role in the evolution of society and the design of policy (Chapter 22).

The present volume (Volume I) contains the two introductory chapters as well as the first part of the Report. Chapter 1 argues that humanity is at a peak of possibilities, given the tremendous achievements obtained through science and technology as well as the emergence of complex economic and political institutions, but it also identifies the considerable challenges and threats that need to be addressed in the coming decades, such as inequalities and development gaps, population growth and migrations, environmental degradation and climate change. Chapter 2 shows the list of relevant values and principles at the core of the ideal of social progress is long and deserves to be better known and debated, including in view of cultural variations that put different weights on them. It also puts human issues in perspective and argues for a broader view encompassing other forms of life in a comprehensive understanding of our stewardship of the planet.

Chapter 3 analyzes the trends and the determinants of economic inequalities, and provides a comprehensive discussion of the various ways in which inequalities and poverty can be reduced, emphasizing in particular that standard forms of redistribution are far from the only policy levers one should consider. Chapter 4 argues that growth can be made compatible with "planetary welfare," but that this requires shifting from an exploitative view of the relation between the economy and nature, toward a much more careful and collectively organized management of the many "commons," including global commons such as the climate and biodiversity, that are essential to our development and flourishing. Chapter 5 focuses on cities, which will be the habitat of most members of future generations, and it highlights how the various elements of urban design and urban policy have crucial consequences for the dialectic of exclusion and inclusion among social groups. A vision of the "just city" (or a set of visions, for various economic, social, and cultural contexts) has to be part of any concrete view of a just society. Chapter 6 lay bare some widespread misconceptions of the key institutions of capitalism, discusses a variety of important financial issues that impact beyond the economic sphere (e.g. lobbying), and provides compelling arguments for a reform of the corporation that would change both its governance and its social purpose. Chapter 7 dives into the world of work, emphasizing how important work is for the structuration of individual lives and social groups. It addresses the growing anxiety about the future of work in a digitalized age and argues for moderate optimism in this respect, without ignoring the observed worrisome trends in the quality of jobs. Chapter 8 takes a systemic perspective on well-being and social justice, and examines how cooperation and social cohesion have been and can be promoted through various economic institutions and social systems. In particular, it provides a thorough discussion of the qualities and limitations of social democracy, and a balanced assessment of the

Introduction

contribution of market competition and government intervention to social progress.

The fact that socio-economic issues are placed at the beginning of the Report does not reflect the view that they matter more than political and cultural issues treated in the other parts. This first part does point at the importance of issues of power and culture in socio-economic trends, and therefore invites the reader to abandon the mechanistic view that the economy is the basis that univocally determines the other components of the social fabric.

Acknowledgments

The preparation of this Report has benefitted from support by so many individuals and organizations that it is impossible to adequately pay tribute to them in short acknowledgments. While most individual contributions have come from people who have been duly invited to become members of committees or authors, the work of the Panel has also benefitted from people who spontaneously proposed to help. The cooperative spirit and enthusiasm of many participants, at all levels, has added a wonderful human touch to this intellectual endeavor.

We first gratefully acknowledge the decisive moral and scientific support from the members of the Honorary Advisory Committee, chaired by Amartya Sen: Kenneth Arrow, Anthony Atkinson, Manuel Castells, Kemal Dervis, James Heckman, Kumari Jayawardena, Inge Kaul, Ira Katznelson, Edgar Morin, Mustapha Nabli, Sunita Narain, Julian Nida-Rümelin, Michael Porter, Robert Reich, Youba Sokona, and Margot Walltröm. It is very sad that Kenneth Arrow and Anthony Atkinson passed away while this Report was being completed. Their contributions to social analysis and inequality studies have been seminal and extremely influential. This Report is dedicated to them.

The Scientific Council, co-chaired by Nancy Fraser, Ravi Kanbur, and Helga Nowotny, provided key input in the selection of authors and the review of the first draft of the Report: Bina Agarwal, Ash Amin, Ernest Aryeetey, Akeel Bilgrami, Tito Boeri, Gustavo Cardoso, Barbara Czarniawska, Veena Das, Gerald Davis, Ahmed Galal, Robert Goodin, Peter Hedström, Torben Iversen, Katsuhito Iwai, Hans Joas, Mary Kaldor, Alice Kessler-Harris, Ilona Kickbusch, Venni Krishna, Will Kymlicka, Claudio Lopez-Guerra, Nora Lustig, Jane Mansbridge, Aihwa Ong, Philip Pettit, Edgar Pieterse, Katharina Pistor, Deborah Posel, Elisa Reis, Annelise Riles, John Roemer, John Ruggie, Saskia Sassen, Kim L. Scheppele, David Schkade, Johan Schot, Seteney Shami, Petra Sijpesteijn, Theda Skocpol, Paul Slovic, Dennis Snower, Boaventura de Sousa Santos, Marcel Van der Linden, Philippe Van Parijs, Leela Visaria, Erik Olin Wright, and Xiaobo Zhang.

The Steering Committee, led by Olivier Bouin and Marc Fleurbaey, includes Ernest Aryeetey, Mamadou Diouf, Marie-Laure Salles-Djelic, Nancy Fraser, Katsuhito Iwai, Ravi Kanbur, Cécile Laborde, Vinh-Kim Nguyen, Helga Nowotny, Shalini Randeria, Elisa Reis, Leela Visaria, Elke Weber, Michel Wieviorka, Björn Wittrock, and Xiaobo Zhang. Efficient assistance with project management has been provided by Samira El-Boudamoussi, Fabiana di Paola, and Denise Zapecza.

Reviewers of the first draft have provided much useful feedback and included Kadri Aavik, Michel Aglietta, Diane-Laure Arjaliès, Kristin Bakke, Maria Balarin, Eudine Barriteau, Shrimoyee Bhattacharya, Kean Birch, Charles Cho, Sean Cleary, Boris Cournède, Gala Diaz, Jean Drèze, Nancy Folbre, Leonardo Garnier, Olivier Godechot, Nicole Hassoun, Miguel Jaramillo, Arne Jarrick, Pierre-Benoît Joly, Susanne Kadner, Girol Karacaoglu, Yann Kervinio, Pierre-Antoine Kremp, Eloi Laurent, Justin Leroux, Mari Martiskainen, Dominique Méda, Afshin Mehrpouya, Mustapha Nabli, Kristi Olson, Bob Pease, Fabienne Peter, Kopano Ratele, Valéry Ridde, Sean Safford, Maurice Salles, Remzi Sanver, Iva Šmídová, Bruce Smyth, Yamina Tadjeddine, Bruno Théret, Josselin Thuilliez, Anália Torres, Alain Trannoy, Laura Valentini, Christian Walter, and Stuart White. Very helpful feedback has also been collected in many events, including workshops coorganized with the FMSH and WZB, the Graduate Institute in Geneva, CIDE in Mexico, the European Commission, the OECD, the World Bank; lectures hosted by the Gulbenkian Foundation-Paris, the University of Vienna, the IFFS in Stockholm, the Universities of Leuven and Louvain-la-Neuve, the University of Oslo, Université Laval in Québec, UN-DPAD; and special sessions in academic congresses. Online comments have been received on the IPSP platform, but also on the Immanent Frame.

The work of many assistants has been essential to many facets of IPSP work: Chloé Bakalar, Mark Budolfson, Johannes Himmelreich, Anne Monier, Andreas Schmidt, Orri Stefansson, Alexander Stingl have served as scientific assistants; Austin Addison, Vinicius Amaral, Michael Anderson, Neeraj Bajpayee, Damien Capelle, Rene Chalom, Jason Choe, Axel Ehlinger, Hélène Fleurbaey, Mitchell Hamburger, Brian Jabarian, Shefali Jain, Isabella Lloyd-Damnjanovic, Colleen O'Gorman, Richard Peay, Melody Qiu, Julia Schorn, AJ Sibley, Amina Simon, Jessica Sims, Caleb South, Sol Taubin, Tien Tran, Tammy Tseng, Roxana Turcanu, Andrew Tynes, Flora Vourch, Jiemin "Tina" Wei, Karis Yi, and Yihemba Yikona have served as research assistants. Additional assistance for particular chapters has been provided by Robert Zimmerman (Chapter 3), Kristin Seyboth (Chapter 4), Emmanuelle Wiley and Sarah Larsen (Chapter 5), and Natalie Stelzer (Chapter 8).

Frédéric Schaffar, Caleb South, and especially Finn Woelm have provided great web development; Sofie Wolthers has heartily supervised social media and videos; Rose Kelly, Erika Karlsson, Nicolas de Lavergne, Justin Leroux, Christine Levavasseur, Gian Paolo Rossini, Annick Sardeing, Caleb South, Julien Ténédos, Bernard Tiélès, Sofie Wolthers, Finn Woelm, and many authors of the Panel have made great contributions to communication work; Hélène Fleurbaey, Johannes Himmelreich, Fernanda Marquez-Padilla, Kalea Power, Amina Simon, Olga Stepanova, Jiemin "Tina" Wei, and Yihemba Yikona have helped with translations.

Useful advice has also been generously provided at various stages by Diana Alarcon, Ramona Angelescu Naqvi, Anthony Appiah, Gustaf Arrhenius, François Bourguignon, James Burke, Françoise Caillods, Sean Cleary, John Danner, Mathieu Denis, Michael Green, Heide Hackmann, William Hirsch, Pierre Jacquet, Eileen Jerrett, Robert Keohane, Christopher Kuenne, Neil Pierre, and Benoît Rossel. Many people provided good advice and this list is very incomplete.

Many institutions have supported the Panel financially and/or in kind, in particular by hosting events such as workshops of the chapter teams. The key pillars of the Panel have been the Collège d'Etudes Mondiales (Foundation Maison des Sciences de l'Homme) in Paris, and the University of Princeton, especially the University Center for Human Values, as well as the Woodrow Wilson School. Important partners include the Institute for Futures Studies and the Riksbanken Jubileumsfond in Stockholm, Cornell University, the Friedrich Ebert Stiftung, the Centre for European Economic Research (ZEW, Mannheim), the Mercator Research Institute on Global Commons and Climate Change (MCC, Berlin), the Kiel Institute for the World Economy, the Social Progress Imperative. Other partners include the International Labor Organization (ILO), the Calouste Gulbenkian Foundation, Bilgi University (Istanbul), the Princeton Institute for International and Regional Studies, University of Miami College of Arts and Sciences & Department of Political Science, the International Social Science Council (ISSC), the University of Melbourne, the Network of European Institutes for Advanced Study (EURIAS), the Institute of Global Governance (University College, London), the UN Research Institute for Social Development (UNRISD), the Centro de Investigación y Docencia Económicas (CIDE, Mexico), the Volkswagen Stiftung, the University of Sussex Science Policy Research Unit (SPRU), the Graduate Institute in Geneva, the Swedish Collegium for Advanced Studies (Uppsala), the Centre de recherche en éthique (Montreal), BRAC University, the University of Vienna, the Swedish Research Council, ESSEC, Sciences-Po, the University of Manchester, the Institute for the Study of Labor (IZA), Dublin City University, the Center for Research and Studies in Sociology (University Institute of Lisbon), The FutureWorld Foundation, Wikiprogress, the Scholars Strategy Network, the Global Development Network (GDN), Southern Voice, Asociación de Investigación y Estudios Sociales (ASIES), MANZ Publisher, and the Russell Sage Foundation. The UN Committee for Economic and Social Affairs (ECOSOC), its Department of Economic and Social Affairs, the OECD and the World Bank have also coorganized events and participated in joint work, in particular within the T20.

Last but not least, we are grateful to the Cambridge University Press team, in particular Stephen Acerra, Kristina Deusch, and Karen Maloney, for their enthusiastic support during the preparation of this Report.

Introduction

Introductory Chapters

Social Trends and New Geographies

Coordinating Lead Authors:[1]
Marcel van der Linden, Elisa Reis

Lead Authors:[2]
Massimo Livi Bacci, Stephen Castles, Raul Delgado-Wise, Naila Kabeer, K.P. Kannan, Ronaldo Munck, Adrienne Roberts, Johan Schot, Göran Therborn, Peter Wagner

Contributing Authors:[3]
Tim Foxon, Laur Kanger

[1] Affiliations: MVDL: International Institute of Social History, Amsterdam; ER: Federal University of Rio de Janeiro.
[2] Affiliations: MLB: University of Florence; SC: University of Sydney; RDW: University of Zacatecas; NK: London School of Economics; KPK: Centre for Development Studies, Kerala; RM: Dublin City University; AR: University of Manchester; JS: University of Sussex; GT: Cambridge University; PW: Catalan Institute for Research and Advanced Studies (ICREA) and University of Barcelona.
[3] Affiliations: TF, LK: University of Sussex.

1

Summary

This opening chapter sets the scene for subsequent more detailed analysis of many of the issues raised here. We start by discussing in Section 1.1 the tension in the current era between humanity's simultaneously standing at "the peak of possibilities" while also, possibly, facing an abyss due to growing inequalities, political conflict and the ever-present danger of climate catastrophe. We turn in Sections 1.2 and 1.3 to the main social and spatial transformations that have characterized the last 25 years. Again we see advances and regressions, above all uneven and fragile development. These sections set the scene for a consideration of three specific challenges: the tension between capitalism and democracy (Section 1.4); that between production and reproduction with an emphasis on gender relations (Section 1.5); and that between demographic change and sustainability (Section 1.6). We then conclude with a sober appraisal of the prospects for the emergence of viable agents for social transformation (Section 1.7) before making some general remarks on the challenges and possibilities for social progress (Section 1.8).

The underlying hypothesis for social progress is that development is, and always has been, contradictory. Poverty amongst plenty, individual advancement versus collective regression, and repression intertwined with liberty. If the industrial era emerged through what Karl Polanyi called a "great transformation," are we headed toward, or do we need, a "new" great transformation? We posit a general need for the market to be reembedded in society if social progress is not to be halted or even reversed.

In terms of the political order we find that the recent transformations of democracy and capitalism have had hugely ambiguous features. It is not wrong to say that the planet is currently both more democratic and more affluent than it was three decades ago. But the ways in which such progress has come about endangers not only future progress, it even puts past progress at risk. In political terms, the increasing diffusion of democracy means that more people across the globe have a say on the collective matters that concern them. But under current circumstances, their participation may not be able to reach the kind of decisions that one would understand as collective self-determination. In economic terms, material affluence is being created in unprecedented forms and volume. But, first, this affluence is so unevenly generated and distributed that poverty and hardship do not disappear and are even reproduced in new and possibly more enduring forms. And second, the continuing production of this material affluence may/will endanger the inhabitability of the planet, or large parts of it, even in the short or medium term.

We have seen our task as one of offering a complex assessment of the current situation that has not been overdetermined by our own political preferences. The positive and negative components of the picture we offer are constitutive of the ambivalent nature of social progress. We are acutely aware that the world looks very different according to our standpoint geographically, socially and by our social and cultural identity. So we have not posited a false unity in terms of outlook. We consider it useful to pose the key questions as clearly as possible from a collective perspective that includes many diverse disciplinary and subject standpoints.

We also seek to avoid an analysis determined by either a depressed *Weltanschauung* that sees only catastrophe ahead given recent political developments or what some have called a Polanyian Pollyanna tendency that is emotionally committed to positive social transformation regardless of the evidence. Quite simply, neither pessimism nor optimism are adequate diagnostic tools. This is particularly the case when we turn to the possible agents of the "new" social transformation we advocate. While we show the decline of twentieth-century agents of social change we also try to bring to life the new potential actors for redistribution, social justice, and recognition.

1.1 On the Peak of Possibilities or Facing an Abyss?

At the beginning of the twenty-first century humankind is standing on a peak of capacity and possibilities, following from an unprecedented liberation from what Immanuel Kant called its "self-imposed immaturity." Many people have more options to express themselves and to build a better collective future. These positive outcomes were generated during the historical Great Transformation in a process of collective action producing public and collective benefits (Polanyi 1944). A wide range of actors from business, governments, labor movements, and social movements from across the globe struggled to construct, expand, and maintain spaces for human emancipation. It led to embedded markets which regulated social consequences. This process had an important science and technology component, as the political struggles for human emancipation and appropriation of benefits focused often on scientific and technological change. At the same time, humanity is facing an abyss of disasters, resulting from the unintended and sometimes intended consequences of the Great Transformation and its recent aftermath. New challenges, from steep inequalities to climate change and many others, captured recently in the 17 Sustainable Development Goals, threaten the opportunity for future gains and might diminish opportunities for human flourishing. The twenty-first century is in need of a new Great Transformation to embed and regulate markets yet again in social relations which in this second round should include our relationships with the environment.

Human history cannot be summed up in linear trend lines, as it is full of cycles, contingent shocks, unintended and unexpected consequences, and reversals, as well as being globally diverse. The history of the past, say, 200 years looks very different depending on from what part of the social world one looks at it. Social science and historiography need to fully recognize and take into account this diversity, with its important implications for ambiguous and contested meanings of concepts like progress, development, and evolution. However, human history is also not reducible to a series of random events. Patterns are discernible, and some social changes do appear most likely to be irreversible. For instance, the abolition of plantation slavery, of patrimonial states, of apartheid, or of certain aspects of male dominance (where it has occurred) seems to have a high threshold of reversibility. Perhaps this indicates that the world situation at the dawn of the twenty-first century is best approached from a perspective that focuses on the development of patterns.

The drive to control society and nature as embedded in modern science and technology has taken a new leap forward in recent times, comparable to the two industrial revolutions, of coal and steam and of electricity and the combustion engine. Even though social processes are irreducible to any technological determinism, scientific and technological changes do have a great social impact. We are living in a world of rapid and possibly accelerating technical change, driven by a quest for further control of society and nature. This quest is clearly visible in two major breakthroughs of knowledge and its applications. One is springing out of electronics, with electronic programming, communication, and monitoring. It has created not only the internet, search engines into gigantic data collections, e-commerce, and smartphones, but also new forms of design and artificial intelligence – now capable of beating human masters of the most difficult games, robotics, and driverless cars. The other is a biological revolution, following the discovery of the genetic code, the mapping of the human genome, the development of genetic manipulation and cloning, and the beginning of applications from stem cell research. However, the cognitive and technical advances of humankind cover a broader field. Our knowledge of space has expanded exponentially, from outer astronomic space to inner space navigated by nanotechnology. New energy sources have been created, by nuclear, solar, wind, wave, and fracking technology, the implications of which also illustrate the ambiguity of human creativity, the first having already proved its riskiness, the last being widely regarded as dangerous. Such ambivalent developments are also visible in other areas.

Between 1980 and 2011 income per capita increased 1.8 percent p.a. (in constant prices and at global purchasing power parity), compared to 1.2 percent p.a. for 1870–1913, and 2.9 percent p.a. for 1950–1972. The increase has been very unequally distributed, but from 1999 to 2012 about 840 million people got out of extreme poverty (defined as less than US$1.90 a day in income or consumption at purchasing power parities), including around 800 million in Asia, while extreme poverty still increased in Sub-Saharan Africa (by 13 million) (Cruz et al. 2015: 6). Massive middle-class aspirations of consumption are arising, most strongly in Asia (ADB 2011), but also in Latin America, and at least discernible in Africa. The improvement of the lot of poor people in big poor countries was large enough to produce, in the first decade of this century, some decline of income inequality among the inhabitants of the world, after a period of high plateau stability since the mid-twentieth century, and 150 years of continuous increase of inequality before that (Milanovic 2016: 120ff).

The biomedical revolution has led to a qualitative leap in humankind's self-emancipation, particularly in women's increased autonomy with regard to their bodies, through control of reproduction by effective contraception and safe abortions where they are available.[4] In some parts of the world – Sub-Saharan Africa being the main exception – women have gained greater control of their fertility. On a world scale, the total fertility rate is now down to 2.5 child per woman. Above this is Sub-Saharan Africa (more than 5), and the Arab states at 3.5 (UNFPA 2015: 127). Humans have also learnt to repair their bodies, by organ transplants, nanotechnological implants, and by stem-cell transfers. We have become able to change our sex, as well as to change our appearance through cosmetic surgery. However, human mastery of themselves does not extend to vulnerability to infectious diseases, as the epidemics of AIDS, SARS, Ebola, Zika, and as the return of old viral enemies thought defeated for good, like tuberculosis and polio, have recently demonstrated.

---

4   According to a survey of 196 countries based on 2013 United Nations data, approximately 26 percent of countries only allow abortions to save the life of the mother, an additional 42 percent allow abortion when the mother's life is at risk and one other specific reason applies (i.e. the pregnancy was the result of rape or incest or because of fetal impairment) and 3 in 10 countries allow them for any reason (before a certain point). Six countries do not allow abortions under any circumstances (Theodoru and Sandstrom 2015).

For all regions of the world, the United Nations Development Program's Human Development Index has continuously improved during the 1990–2014 period, and between development groups of countries there has also occurred some convergence, at a snail's pace, as the index increase has been consistently smaller the higher the degree of development (UNDP 2015: 215). Life expectancy (at birth) in the world increased from 64 to 71 years, with some convergence among regions and income group countries (WHO 2015: 52).

Global connectivity has also enormously increased, thanks to electronic media. Satellite television spreads worldwide, not only images and entertainment – which bring people together in some sense – but also information, including different perspectives and kinds of information. Social media, such as YouTube, Facebook, or Twitter are creating something of a global public. The United Nations, and its specialized agencies, have increasingly come to constitute a global agora – instead of a Cold War dueling place – where global development goals and climate change are being seriously at least talked about.

The last third of the twentieth century saw two epochal transformations of human social life, not universal, and far from complete, but in a world historical perspective of immense importance, which should not be diminished by myopic familiarity. The ancient hierarchies and exclusions of gender and race were shaken to their foundations. In some parts of the world they crumbled, while remaining as ruins, in others they cracked but kept standing, while opening fissures and crevices of evasion. Through all the persistent, in some respects aggravating, divisions, and conflicts among humankind, to which we shall turn below, the undermining of institutionalized racism, sexism, and male domination, where it has occurred, signals a profound process of social inclusion. They were processes of existential equalization, by which previously discriminated, marginalized, and/or excluded categories of people have been, at least officially, recognized as equal members of society.

The United Nations' Declaration of Human Rights proclaimed in 1948: "Men and women of full age, without any limitations to race, nationality or religion, have the right to marry and to found a family. They are entitled to equal rights as to marriage, during marriage, and its dissolution. Marriage shall be entered into only with free and full consent of the intending spouses." (Article 16) But this right was then embodied only in Scandinavian (and with a foreign nationality qualification Soviet) marriage codes and practices (Therborn 2004: 75). Starting in the late 1960s and gathering momentum in the l970s, male dominance and bans of interreligious or interracial marriages have been dismantled in large parts of the world, though not in most Muslim countries. Male dominance and sexism are still strong in India, several parts of Asia, and in Sub-Saharan Africa. More broadly, according to the World Bank's research, numerous legal and regulatory barriers prevent women from being able to interact with public authorities and the private sector, to manage, control, and inherit property, to access paid employment and credit, and to be protected from domestic violence and sexual harassment (World Bank 2013). Almost 90 percent of the 143 countries surveyed have, for instance, at least one legal difference restricting women's economic opportunities (World Bank 2013: 8). Yet, signaling progress, women's right to education and to participation in the public sphere is now very widely recognized. The

Third of the Millennium Development Goals, gender parity in education at all levels, was reached in the "developing" world as a whole, although with respect to tertiary education overall parity hid underrepresentation of males in East Asia, Latin America, and North Africa, and of women in South Asia and Sub-Saharan Africa (UN 2015a: 29).

The military smashing of the racist horrors of Nazism did not mean an end to institutionalized racism. Apartheid in South Africa actually developed after 1945. Racial segregation stayed as a rule of the American way of life until the second half of the 1950s. "Keep Australia White" was official Labor party policy until the early 1970s. The Civil Rights movement in the United States finally brought the right to vote to all African-American citizens in the late 1960s, and in the early 1990s the apartheid regime crumbled. Indigenous peoples of the settler states of the Americas and Oceania have been officially racially rehabilitated in the beginning of this century. The historical sea-change is highlighted by the fact that in the 1990s South Africa got a Black President, and in the 2000s Bolivia elected a President of native-American descent for the first time, and the United States an African-American.

Racism and misogynous sexism have certainly not disappeared from the planet, but the huge changes of the last half-century provide an important platform for meeting the challenges of today. The last decade has also witnessed a retreat of another sexism, homophobia, with a widespread, if by no means universal, recognition of the right to same-sex marriage. Since the first law allowing same sex marriage in modern times was passed in the Netherlands in 2001, it has been recognized in almost two dozen countries – though no country in Asia and no country other than South Africa on the African continent recognizes this right.

Less epochal than the partial dismantling of sexism and racism but also inclusive, was the late-twentieth-century spread of democracy, which may be taken as an institution of political inclusion. Democracy had its first breakthrough in the aftermath of World War I, but has had a dramatic twentieth-century history, with brutal reversals, violent contests, fraud, and difficult processes of redemocratization. For the time being, democracy appears more widespread and more stable than ever before, if not everywhere more trusted. In the late 1980s–1990s dictatorships of very different kinds fell or imploded for very different reasons, all over the world, though far from everywhere. A global wave started in Asia – Philippines, South Korea, Taiwan – continuing in Latin America and Eastern Europe, to reach Sub-Saharan Africa.

In the struggles against political exclusion and repression there developed a discourse which has come to constitute still another dimension of inclusive social developments, a discourse of human rights. While frequently instrumentalized in geopolitical conflicts, human rights constitute a principle of universal inclusion. The antislavery campaigners of the nineteenth century and before used the notion, but for a very minimalist human right, of not being enslaved. Now it is being used in reference to a large register of rights for each and everybody.

Very probably, new, unexpected challenges to human societies will appear later in this century, and there is already quite a number of difficult problems confronting human wisdom and creativity. But one issue is most likely to raise a paramount challenge to humankind of the twenty-first century: the ecological unsustainability of the current development path. Climate change and the threats from global warming, and from other human-made environmental hazards are issues generated by choices made in the past, such as the unlimited exploitation of fossil fuels.

While waiting for the fatal meltdown of global warming, other environmental problems are piling up, largely as effects of unplanned urbanization. Exposure to air pollution is increasing rapidly, with known dire effects, although no reliable mortality data seem to be available. From 2000 to 2013 the number of people in low and middle income countries exposed to polluted air above the World Health Organization's guidelines increased by 900 million (Cruz et al. 2015: figure 20). The number of people affected by natural hazards annually quadrupled between 1974–1984 and 1996–2005, largely because the number of people living in flooding, cyclone, or other disaster-prone areas has increased (Brecht et al. 2013: 2–3). The recurrent smog of Beijing and Delhi, and the annual inundations of Jakarta illustrate acute problems already in place.

Climate change challenges the whole world. In what measure can recent scientific-technological revolutions yield adequate cognitive-technical means to meet the challenge? Clearly, there has been a major boost for climate science, which has deepened its understanding of the extremely complex processes involved, although it too often ignores social dimensions. New sources of energy have been developed, and the concept of "sustainable development" has been inserted into urban planning and national political discourse.

The crucial issues seem to be two. First, how are the costs of limiting global warming to be allocated globally? An important part of this question is, to what extent do the polluters of the first industrial revolutions have to pay for past sins? To what extent is some sort of progressive international sharing of the global costs realistic? Another aspect is: who shall pay for a stop or strict limitation of fossil fuels production, only the coal and oil producers themselves? And how can the loss of jobs in the fossil sector be compensated for? Secondly, and decisively, what social forces can be envisaged to successfully redirect forms of consumption and reevaluate preferences, in the rising cities of Asia as well as in the North Atlantic area, which may be necessary for adopting a path of environmentally sustainable development?

The global human rights movements of the late twentieth century did spawn planetary ecological awareness and movements but not much of a political force. Environmentalist movements have emerged all over the world, but nowhere yet has any been near hegemony. How shall the climate scientists be able to convince national power holders with their conflicting national interests? The political sociology of eventual adequate and effective climate policies has to be clarified and laid out.

The scientific and technological advances of recent times have indeed increased human emancipation, but mainly of humans as individuals, whether as managers, designers, communicators, doctors or patients, little with respect to mastering collective problems and in providing common goods – Wikipedia is a rare exception. Technologies are usually developed to cater to individual needs, not collective needs (individual cars instead of public transportation, individually owned washing machines, individual instead of collective cooking, etc.). Except for a brief period in 1996–2004, technological innovations have not even increased labor productivity, at least not in the leading economy of the world, also the center of the electronic and biological revolutions (apart perhaps from productivity in the service sector). Rather, productivity growth has slowed down, after 1970 and again after 2004, and it has been forecast to decelerate further up to 2040 (Gordon 2016: 522ff, 637ff).

The Great Inclusions, of race, and gender, and sexuality, are most likely to stay, and rather likely to move forward – even during the US acceleration of economic inequality, the income position of women and of African-Americans tended to approximate, somewhat, that of their male/White superiors (Lindert and Williamson 2016: 222ff). However, in Europe and USA, in particular, they are getting overwhelmed by new rifts in social cohesion caused by rising intranational economic inequality, and by mounting divisions between the winners and the losers of national borders wide opened to trade and migration. The complex political repercussions of this have been a shake-up of the political landscape on the one hand and policy stalemates on the other. In spite of widespread anger as well as social scientific concern and criticism, not a single democracy has been able to do anything to change what has been called "the economy of 1%" (Oxfam 2016). Latin America's exceptional twenty-first century decade of equalization is breaking down in economic crisis and political acrimony.

The combination of severe planetary environmental challenges and galloping intranational inequality is explosive. Because ecological issues affecting all humankind will require panhuman cooperation, which in turn is deeply imperiled, if not impossible, under conditions of mounting inequality and exclusion, with the diverging priorities and increasing mistrust the latter tend to generate. As the 1 percent are the least likely to be affected by climate adversities, an adequate response put together by the increasingly interwoven global upper class appears even less likely. The significance of the (slight) overall global economic equalization due to the high growth of China, India, and others is diminished by these countries being internally more unequal and divided than both the United States and Europe. Current inequality is making it very difficult for humankind to make full use of its peak of capacity and possibilities in meeting the planetary challenges of this century. Economic resources are appropriated by a few, as underlined by the fact that 62 individuals have amassed as much wealth as the bottom half of humankind, 3.6 billion people (Oxfam 2017: 11), in other words, on average the former own 58 million times more than the latter. Stark inequalities tear societies and polities apart, which leads to bitter and violent conflicts or "at best" sociopolitical paralysis, rather than to resolute collective action.

Inequality is taking on very sinister implications, some returning, others new. These implications are likely to get increasing pressure from the upheavals of the world of work in the wake of coming automation. Inequality and poverty have to be seen as largely located inside increasingly hazardous environments, on barren vulnerable land, in peripheral urban areas, particularly vulnerable to storms, flooding, and landslides, in rich countries (USA: New Orleans), as well as in poor countries (Tschakert 2016). At the other end, the richest 10 percent of humanity produce about half of the CO_2 emissions of the world.

It has been known to scholars for some time that there has been a historical mid-to-late-twentieth-century tendency for the intra-national social gap of life expectancy in Europe to widen, but mainly because longevity among the privileged classes has grown faster. However, in recent years, instances of an absolute rise of mortality and decline of life expectancy have been found, e.g. among US White high-school dropouts (Case and Deaton 2015), and among the poor and the unemployed in Finland (Tarkiainen et al. 2013). The economic inequality tendencies have linked up with the inclusion of women into the labor force in an unexpected way, generating a new process of intergenerational exclusion. While coupling between well-educated, well-earning men and women is becoming more stable, with more time and money invested in their children, the opposite is occurring at the end of the precariat and the unemployed. There more family instability and more children growing up in relative poverty with a single parent under stress prevails (Putnam 215).

Today's humanity has an immense responsibility. It has inherited unprecedented capacities and possibilities, of knowledge, technology, communicability, and with much of an escape from the ancient racial/ethnic and gender confinements and divisions of humankind. It also is facing its share of the perennial problems of humankind, of finding its livelihood, staking out a path to a good life, resolving conflicts and issues of injustice, coping with the dialectics and the unintended consequences of evolution, the dialectics highlighted by, e.g. the rise of mortality among the marginalized in the midst of the biomedical revolution. On top of that humanity has to confront the unprecedented challenge of climate change and of creating sustainability amidst an inhabitable planetary environment.

We now address important recent social and spatial transformations and then analyze in detail three central tensions that need to be confronted in the "Next" Great Transformation.

1.2   Recent Social Transformations

Of all the complex issues, the one that may be said to loom largest over the idea of progress is the continuing reality of "poverty amidst plenty." Over the past four decades, there has been an unprecedented increase in material income, wealth and resources on a global scale along with the persistence of enormous deprivation for not less than one-third of human kind. Even when some material advancement has taken place for sections of the previously deprived segments of people, the role of structures of inequality can be seen as central to this paradox of poverty amidst plenty. What should be underscored as worrisome is the trend toward increasing inequality in a whole range of arenas that challenges the idea of social progress.

It is difficult to measure the development of inequality reliably. Central indicators of countries' success, such as the Gross Domestic Product (GDP), have many significant shortcomings (Fleurbaey and Blanchet 2013). The building of alternative indicators (composite indicators, subjective well-being indexes, capabilities, and equivalent incomes)

is under way, but still underdeveloped. Although the available figures suggest a precision that does not really exist, they nevertheless reveal significant trends. They tell us, for example, that between 1970 and 2013, global gross output of goods and services considerably exceeded the population increase, or in other words, that the output per person was rapidly growing. The extraordinary process of growth over the last decades is beyond doubt, with the sole exception of the so-called transitional economies that witnessed a catastrophic fall in their income between 1980 and 2000 but most notably during the last decade of the twentieth century.

The overall geography was marked by interesting, if not drastic, changes across the same period. The share in world output of the developed rich countries decreased from 70 to 59 percent after peaking to close to 79 percent in between. This decline was due to the ability of the "developing" countries to increase their share from 17 to 37 percent. The so-called BRIC group (Brazil, Russia, India, China) claims a share of a little more than one-fifth of global GDP, largely contributed by China. But there has been a more careful documentation of "developing" countries that demonstrated a greater potential for growth and development with significant shares of population beyond the BRIC group and they are referred to as "The Next 14" (Nayyar 2013). In the group of Next 14 are Argentina, Brazil, China, Chile, Egypt, India, Indonesia, South Korea, Malaysia, Mexico, South Africa, Taiwan, Thailand, and Turkey. This group comprises a little more than half the global population. Although this group is an analytical construct of economically dynamic countries with a significant share of world population, they are not a formal group in the international arena. Yet the emergence of these select 14 countries should count as a new trend in the global economic scenario since the Industrial Revolution, despite the recent deceleration in economic dynamism in some of them. This growth is the end result of a whole range of developments equally unprecedented. Global trade increased tremendously from $4.37 trillion to $45 trillion or from close to 36–60 percent of the world income between 1980 and 2013, creating a vast web of trade interdependencies across countries in different continents. Not only did foreign direct investment increase by 3.4 times between 1990 and 2013; through so-called "arms-length outsourcing," firms from "developed" countries increasingly contract out some or all of their production to nominally independent suppliers in "developing" countries while retaining control over the production process.

1.2.1   History Matters

The global geography of economic wealth has changed to a significant extent but given the highly unequal starting point of the players as well as the change in demographic trends the shift is relative. This is reflected in per capita income that could be roughly portrayed as a sign of economic clout if not self-perceived human welfare. Two groups of countries – the so-called low income and the low middle income "developing" countries – lost out in this process along with the transitional economies. Losing out implies that a country's per capita income as a share of the average per capita income of the "developed" countries is lower in 2013 as compared to 1970. For example, per capita income of Zimbabwe was 12.2 percent of the average per capita income of "developed" countries in 1970; it fell to 2.03 percent in 2013 leading to a wider gap than when it started.

What should be seen as a major setback is the fact that all the countries in the Low Income Developing Country group have been losing out in terms of this inequality measure despite the fact that 15 out of the 26 countries have managed to perform well during 1990–2013. This group has the highest incidence of various forms of human deprivation and is classified as countries with a "low human development index" by the UNDP. The second group of Lower Middle Income "developing" countries has a less pessimistic record but with two-thirds of the countries losing out.

The results are better for the next group of Upper Middle Income "developing" countries that includes China and other east and southeast Asian countries. China is a star performer here. Yet it has to go a long way to catch up. The exercise shows that the 1970–1990 period, especially the 1980–1990 was a period of losing out for a majority of the "developing" countries. The poorer a country, the greater was its decline relative to the developed country average (UNCTAD 2015). The crash in commodity prices and unfavorable terms of trade could be counted as some of the reasons for this relative decline. Given the remarkable recovery since 1990, it would be tempting to attribute that to the new regime of globalization. But the remarkable growth momentum within the group of "developing" countries, especially the Next 14, and consequent rise in commodity prices and a greater flow of migrant labor within the Global South need to be factored here. In short, there has been a great degree of economic interdependency among "developing" countries since 1990.

For the transitional economies the end of the 1980s witnessed not only political turmoil but also a concomitant collapse in economic growth. Most of them are on their way to recovery but there is a long way to close the gap, given the fact that they have seen a sharp decline in per capita income compared to the "developed" countries.

The best performers are the group of "developed" countries consisting mostly of the "old rich," i.e. the USA, Western Europe, and Japan. To a very large extent they now have a much shorter gap with the average per capita of their own group than four decades ago. What this shows is the convergence of income among the rich countries. But the lesson from the point of inequality is that the preexisting huge gap between the poorest and the richest group of countries has further widened.

The question of inequality is being discussed by scholars as well as several global civil society organizations and movements (see e.g. Piketty 2014; Oxfam 2017). However, inequality has many dimensions and a focus mainly on the economic one is bound to be too limited to understand the many social and political consequences of inequality. Therborn (2006) classifies these dimensions broadly as (a) resource inequality, (b) vital inequality, and (c) existential inequality. Resource inequality refers to inequality in income, assets, and in skills. Vital inequality refers to bodily health as well as a sense of well-being that transcends mere bodily health. Existential inequality is perhaps the most important one when it comes to social and political tensions and conflicts both within and across countries. It has to do with dignity or its absence, freedom, respects, rights, and sense of participation.

Given the fact that vital inequality refers to one dimension of human capability, it appears to be more appropriate to call it "capability inequality" by bringing in education including skills.

1.2.2   Enhancing Capabilities

Despite the enormous increase in wealth and income in the world as well as technological developments that can fulfill the basic requirements for a decent and dignified human existence, there are considerable deficiencies that impede social progress such as the opportunity to access basic capabilities, namely, education and health, to mention the most important ones. Some progress seems to have been made but the deficits are quite large and even formidable. Illiteracy may not be the most important problem now but the absence of a minimum of education is. Consider the proportion of people without at least a secondary level of education. It is a huge deficit in most "developing" countries. In many poor countries only a small fraction has attained this rather modest threshold in an age of digital communication, information sharing, and knowledge production. A similar picture emerges when the question of basic health conditions is flagged. There are several indicators but the robust one of Infant Mortality Rate (IMR) would indicate the state of affairs in most "developing" countries. While the High Human Development countries report an average IMR of five deaths under one year per thousand births, it is (at 64) 13 times greater in Low Human Development countries (see UNDP 2014).

There is a direct link between the absence of basic capabilities and income poverty. Low capabilities lead to considerably lower opportunities for gainful employment. Those with low capabilities also have very low assets or are asset poor, a fact that also reduces or denies opportunities for gainful self-employment. We highlight the importance of addressing capability-building and enhancement as a precondition for eliminating poverty and creating opportunities for broad-based growth. New and emerging inequality has to do with the development of Information and Communication Technologies (ICT). ICTs have been associated with increased possibilities for entrepreneurship, economic prosperity, democratization, political participation, social capital, access to plurality of information, better education, sustainable development, and the like. However, access to ICTs continues to be highly unequal with "developed" countries having a considerable lead. Moreover, this global digital divide seems to be relatively durable: for example, in comparison to 2010 the ICT Development Index (IDI) increased by 0.92 points for developed and 0.89 points for "developing" countries but only 0.56 points for the Least Developed Countries (ITU 2015: 56). These countries risk becoming the "black holes of informational capitalism" (Castells 2010), largely bypassed by global flows of information, power, and wealth.

The developmental significance of the digital divide is contested. Accounts of the rapid spread of mobile phone technology in Sub-Saharan Africa have led to speculation about "skipping stages" of development. For others the techno-economic vision of globalizing ICTs misses the nature of development and is insufficient (and even counterproductive) to address uneven global development.

The "digital divide" does not only pertain to differences between countries but is also reflected in other measures, e.g. gender, education, income, and place of residence. Males, highly educated, wealthy, and urban citizens have better access than females, less educated, poor, and rural population.

1.2.3 Intersecting Inequalities

Along with the material inequalities captured by such measures as income, wealth, and so on ("what you have") there are other forms of inequality that revolve around identity ("who you are"). The inequalities at work here are the product of social hierarchies which define particular groups in a society as inferior to others on the basis of devalued aspects of their identity. Group-based inequalities thus resonate with the above-mentioned idea of "existential inequality." Considering the multidimensional nature of inequality further involves consideration of how particular differences and divisions are produced through social structures and power relations. Gender relations, for instance, cannot be reduced to differences between "men" and "women," but rather reflect differences in the ways in which categories of "masculine" and "feminine" have been established and maintained, how the former is privileged over the latter, and how different types of women and femininities are valued differently, as are different types of men and masculinities (Connell 1995). These hierarchies are created and maintained through norms, values, and practices which serve to routinely disparage, stereotype, exclude, ridicule, and demean certain groups relative to others, denying them full personhood or the right to participate in society on equal terms with others.

It is quite possible to face discrimination on the basis of your identity without being materially deprived. Gender and sexual identity, for instance, cut across class so that to be a woman or LGBTQ (lesbian, gay, bisexual, transgender, queer) does not necessarily mean being poor. However, the most entrenched forms of inequality, those that have persisted over generations, occur when group-based inequalities intersect with material deprivation. In South Asia, members of the lowest castes and tribal groups have long been overrepresented among the very poorest. Indeed their disadvantage has remained unchanged on a range of indicators of wealth, capabilities, and well-being (Kannan 2014, 2016). In Latin America, it is generally Afro-descendants and indigenous peoples who have historically made up the very poorest sections of the population. In South Africa, the greater poverty of Black Africans persists, despite the rise of a black middle class, although the apartheid system has been formally dismantled. In China and Vietnam, it has been historically their ethnic minorities who have made up the poorest populations. In most of these cases, gender intensifies the disadvantage of those at the bottom of the economic hierarchy so that women from these groups tend to be poorer than the rest of the population, to earn less and to have lower levels of well-being and capabilities (Kabeer 2015).

1.2.4 Durable Inequalities

With regard to all the dimensions of inequality, one furthermore needs to ask how "durable" they are and how difficult it is to overcome them

(Tilly 1999). Taking both "developed" and "developing" countries, the most entrenched form of inequality of all kinds often is the one based on social identity such as race, caste, and ethnicity. More often than not it also reflects a class dimension with most of the excluded group of people experiencing the highest incidence of economic deprivation. It is so well entrenched that no coherent response to it has yet been undertaken from a global point of view. It is durable because it is based on distinctions between categories of human beings. Formation of categories of the types mentioned above has deep historical precedents. For Tilly, categorical inequality serves the objective of maintaining control over surplus generation. This is based mainly on exploitation and opportunity hoarding. Gender inequality could be said to upset this type of categorical inequality because of the disadvantaged position of women vis-à-vis men in the categorical groups mentioned here. However, this need not mean an overwhelming presence of gender inequality over this form of categorical inequality. What it does in fact is adding to the complexity of this inequality by a further layering of the gender dimension. That is to say, the inequality between the bottom group and the top group could be a more entrenched one than the inequality between men and women in each group or in general. Sometimes, gender inequality can be a mixed one especially at the top where women have come to attain a higher status than men as in the case of life expectancy or, in some contexts, average years of schooling.

Although inequality based on social identity has been a hallmark of most societies, research on this dimension is not as abundant as in the case of economic inequality between income groups. For some countries such as the United States (and to some extent India), a considerable amount of research has been done on the social inequality issues of the kind depicted here. In general, the evidence in the United States suggests a huge gap between the "whites" and "blacks" which in certain cases seems to be widening especially during periods of crisis (Levine et al. 2001). There is also evidence on widening wealth disparity between "whites" and "blacks" and "whites" and "Hispanics" (Kochhar and Fry 2014).

A similar picture of categorical inequality that has been well entrenched in terms of its durability is something that is also being faced by many "developing" countries. India is a prime example of this durable inequality. Although several religions coexist the dominant one is the Hindu religion and its caste system that has a deep hierarchical structure in a broad sense of upper, middle, and bottom. The bottom place is occupied by those classified as Scheduled Castes (who prefer to call themselves as *dalits* and constitute the ex-untouchable segment) and Scheduled Tribes (who prefer to call themselves *adivasis* or original inhabitants). In fact, the hierarchical structure has remained unchanged in a whole range of indicators of wealth, capabilities, and well-being (Kannan 2016).

1.2.5 The Increasing Power of the Multinational Corporations

Nation-states and their citizens are the principal focal points in the debates about global inequality. However, the increasing economic power of the multinational corporations (MNCs) should be seen as one of the principal factors contributing to the enormous inequality between the top and the bottom. One of the manifestations of this power is the increasing monopolization of finance, production, services, and trade, leaving every major global economic activity to be dominated by a handful of large multinational corporations. In the international political economy, large industrial and financial corporations have become, more than ever, the central players. Through mega-mergers and strategic alliances, this fraction of capital has reached unparalleled levels of concentration and centralization: in 2014 the top 500 largest multinational corporations acquired US$ 31.2 trillion in revenues (Fortune 2015), equal to 40 percent of the world's GDP (World Bank 2015). Overall, industrial and financial capital has undergone a profound restructuring process where:

First, is the ascendancy of finance capital over other fractions of capital. Finance capital began this ascendancy with the onset of an overproduction crisis in the late 1960s, when German and Japanese capital recovered from the devastation of World War II and began to compete with US capital on world markets (Brenner 2002). With the lack of profitable investment in production, capital began shifting toward financial speculation based on an unprecedented reserve of fictitious capital (McKinsey 2013). Another response to the overproduction crisis was the reduction of labor costs through global labor arbitrage. Moreover, with the downward pressure on real wages, a finance-led debt explosion sustained purchasing power for the realization of production. The end result has been the financialization of the capitalist class, of industrial capital, and of corporate profits.

Second, we see the configuration and expansion of global networks of large industrial and financial corporations as a restructuring strategy, which – through outsourcing operations and subcontracting chains – extend parts of their productive, commercial, financial, and service processes to the Global South in search of natural resources and abundant cheap labor. The strategy of global labor arbitrage – that is the substitution of high-wage workers in "developed" countries with like-quality, low-wage workers in the "developing" countries – is exemplified by the export platforms that operate as enclave economies in peripheral countries (Delgado Wise and Martin 2015). Moreover, an outstanding feature of contemporary global capitalism is the degree of network articulation and integration with the operations of large multinational corporations dominating international trade: at least 40 percent of all global trade is associated with outsourcing operations, including subcontracting and intrafirm trade, an estimated 85 million workers directly employed in assembly plants in the Global South, and over 3500 export processing zones established in 130 countries. This restructuring strategy has transformed the global geography of production to the point that now most of the world's industrial employment (over 70 percent) is located in the Global South.

Third, the restructuring of innovation systems through the implementation of mechanisms such as outsourcing (including offshoring) the scientific and technological innovation process, which allows multinational corporations to benefit from the research of scientists from the Global South. This restructuring reduces labor costs, transfers risks and responsibilities, and capitalizes on the advantages of controlling

the patent process. Four overarching aspects characterize this restructuring process:

(a) The increasing internationalization and fragmentation of research and development activities. In contrast to the traditional innovation processes occurring "behind closed doors" in research and development departments internal to large multinational corporations, this trend is known as open innovation.

(b) The creation of scientific cities – such as Silicon Valley in the United States and the new "Silicon Valleys" established in peripheral or emerging regions, principally in Asia – where collective synergies are created to accelerate innovation processes (Sturgeon 2003).

(c) The development of new methods of controlling research agendas (through venture capital, partnerships, and subcontracting, among others) and appropriating the products of scientific endeavors (through the acquisition of patents) by large multinational corporations.

(d) The rapidly expanding highly skilled workforce – particularly in the areas of science and engineering – in the Global South is being tapped by MNCs for research and development in peripheral countries through recruitment via partnerships, outsourcing, and offshoring.

Fourth, the renewed trend toward extractivism and land grabbing steered by the continuing overconsumption of the world's natural resources and the expansion of carbon-based industrial production. The increasing urbanization and industrialization in Asia, particularly China, has increased the demand for raw materials, which, combined with the transformation of commodities from a hedge asset to a speculative asset for finance capital, created a commodities boom since 2002 that has recently declined with the deaccelerating Chinese economy. High prices for commodities have driven the exploration for nonrenewable natural resources into remote geographies, deeper into the oceans and the jungles, in the process exacerbating social conflicts over land and water. This new extractivism has increased environmental degradation, not only through an expanded geography of destruction, but also by global extractive capital's strategy of environmental regulatory arbitrage (Xing and Kolstad 2002). Moreover, despite 25 years of increasingly dire warnings from the Intergovernmental Panel on Climate Change, the global consumption of fossil fuels continues to rise, "triggering a cascade of cataclysmic changes that include extreme heat-waves, declining global food stocks and a sea-level rise affecting hundreds of millions of people" (World Bank 2012). Given that the revenues of some of the world's most powerful and profitable multinational corporations depend on fossil fuel consumption, this pattern will likely continue, setting the world on a path toward a deepening ecological crisis.

The above trends are associated with the unprecedented commodification and private appropriation of tangible (through unrestrained extractivism and land grabbing) and intangible (through an exponential growth of patents and their overwhelming appropriation by multinational corporations) common goods. The cumulative effect is that contemporary capitalism is facing a profound multidimensional crisis (financial, economic, social, ecological crises) that undermines the main sources of wealth creation – labor and nature – to the point that it can be characterized as a civilizational crisis with a potentially catastrophic outcome.

1.3   New Spatial Configurations

The complex social transformations of the global order described in the previous section also have a spatial dimension. The Polanyi-inspired focus on the expansion of the free market and the related social countermovement to protect against the disembedding it creates is now widely accepted. However, a separate, sometimes unrelated, focus on the political economy of scale and the underlying notion that "space is a social construct" (Lefebvre 1991) also needs to be part of our reflexive lens. In brief, social relations cannot be understood without a firm focus on how they are grounded in particular places.

1.3.1   Time-Space Compression

Social and economic landscapes are not passive spectators, but are actively struggled over. A central notion here would be that of a "social-spatial dialectic" to underpin our analytical focus. This would direct us toward a reflexive and complex view of the contemporary order (and its possibilities for transformation) which understands social relations and spatial relations as mutually constructive. The spatial is thus not a mere reflection of social relations and requires explicit treatment here. We do this by critically examining the process(es) known as globalization and its impact.

Globalization as a "way of seeing" the world around us had become dominant amongst its supporters and detractors alike during the early 1990s. Then it was seen as epoch-making and signaling a transition to a brave new world, though with the crisis of 2008–2009 many argued that globalization had "gone too far." At first analysis was dominated by the optimistic globalization enthusiasts for whom the new communication technologies signaled a major shift to a new order in human history. Globalization in reality was/is more complex and contradictory than any technological determinism will allow for. Nor is it totally novel. We need to note that the phenomenon is not new, as the first wave of internationalization took place from around 1860 to 1914. And yet the world has changed dramatically compared to the postwar order and its particular social-spatial dynamic.

Globalization needs to be understood as a set of interlinked economic, political, social, and cultural processes. Its overarching theme has been that of connectivity or interconnectedness. We can no longer draw firm boundaries between the global and the local, the national and international or the economic and cultural dimensions of contemporary life. We cannot separate the "in here" of the city, community, or locality in which we live from the "out there" of global flows of money, capital, people, power, and dominance. Thus globalization is not an entity but a set of relationships. Our activities are all influenced by this complex and interrelated set of relationships that are "stretching" social relations to an unprecedented degree. This is not a "smooth" world where the overarching power differentials created by colonialism and imperialism are bound to disappear. Massive changes have occurred

since the international division of labor emerging in the postwar period was at its height in the mid-1970s but old inequalities persist and new ones have been created.

The concept of "time-space compression" proposed by David Harvey in the first wave of globalization studies seemed to capture well the processes in course (Harvey 1989). Spatial barriers – for example in relation to trade and communications – have been considerably undermined, though this does not mean the "end of geography" as the triumphalist globalizers of the 1990s declared. Time has also changed from being a reflection of a natural process (the day, the seasons) to being seen as instantaneous. We may not have reached the "distanceless" world that Heidegger once foretold, but the "shrinking" of the world greatly accelerated from the 1990s onwards. The qualities of time and space have been revolutionized and have changed the way we understand and represent the world. The elimination of spatial barriers and the compression of time do not, however, as we argue below, lead to a process of smooth and homogeneous social development. The changing spatiality of the global order is, if anything, more heterogeneous, differentiated and fragmented than it was in the past.

1.3.2   The Changing Role of the Nation-State

With the end of the Cold War and the rise of the most recent phase of globalization, many claimed that the Westphalian system of sovereign states was coming to an end. This included those who believed globalization to be driven by the information revolution and held a more or less optimistic view of the expansion of global interdependence and the notion that we all live in "one world." Some claimed that globalization had caused the state to wither away which was often perceived as a positive development. Kenichi Ohmae (1995), for instance, argued that the globalization of culture brought about by multimedia was key to undermining nationalism, which must be reduced (if not eliminated) in order to improve the quality of life of people globally. At the same time, he argued that the undermining of the nation-state was a positive development, as states were no longer the optimal geographical units for organizing economic activity, not least because of the rise of cross-border economic regions.

The "globalization skeptics" took a less enthusiastic approach to globalization and maintained an emphasis on the nation-state, arguing that claims about the erosion of borders and the undermining of state power were overstated (Reis 2004). Instead, it was argued that the state has continued to perform more or less the same functions that it had always performed and that there is nothing historically unprecedented about contemporary levels of economic interdependence. Some argued that though international economic conditions may work to constrain certain government actions, this does not mean that governments are immobilized. Rather, it was argued that the internationalization of capital does not merely restrict policy choices, but it expands them as well (Weiss 1998: 385). Rather than focusing on global interconnectedness, skeptics further emphasized the heightened levels of internationalization (or relations between nation-states) and the growing importance of regionalism, particularly in North America, the Asia-Pacific, and Europe.

While some were optimistic about the diffusion of authority attendant on the rise of globalization and the seeming decline of the nation-state, critics such as Susan Strange (1996) argued that the changes associated with globalization had limited the ability of states to exert influence over outcomes that matter most to people's well-being. Instead, the deepening and expansion of market structures enhanced the power of private actors, which were increasingly acting as political authorities over a growing range of activities (1996: 45). As seen above, multinational corporations, for instance, have become more important sites of authority over labor–management relations, undermining the spatially bounded authority of states. At the same time, the geography of taxation has been restructured as MNCs operating across multiple jurisdictions, along with wealthy individuals, have exploited "offshore" tax regimes.

The early debates about globalization also emphasized the changing nature of national security, which seemed to be moving away from a model based on the monopolization of the use of force by the state toward a new global cooperative security community. This partly reflected changes taking place in the spatial control over movement, such as that which occurred with the introduction of the Schengen Area which eliminated border controls between 26 European countries. It also reflected the widening of the scope of security under globalization, which increasingly came to include cross-border issues such as climate change.

A number of transformations taking place in the twenty-first century have shifted the context and the relevance of these debates dramatically. The geopolitics of state power has not been absorbed or subverted by economic globalization. Due primarily to a series of US interventions and miscalculations, virtually a whole region from Pakistan to Libya has become a seemingly permanent war zone with no peace in sight. A rivalry for influence between the US and Russia in the lands of the former Soviet Union has led to violent conflicts just short of all-out war. The spectacular rise of China has also led to geopolitical tensions in the South China Sea, not to mention the possibility of a trade war with the US. Whereas the likes of Francis Fukuyama (1992) had proclaimed the "end of history," with liberal capitalist democracies emerging as the final form of human government, it is now clear that forms of political organization have not been homogenized and globalization did not usher in a linear move toward greater democratic openness.

Claims about the shrinking of geography through cultural homogenization – i.e. through "Americanization" or "McDonaldization" – have not come to fruition and nationalist (often anti-Western) attitudes persist or reemerge in many places. While certain dimensions of security continue to be addressed at the global level (namely with regard to climate change), regional security agreements such as the Schengen Agreement have been undermined by state responses to the influx of refugees from Syria and elsewhere, which have included the deployment of new migration controls, the erection of fences and walls, and even the use of direct violence. The election of Donald Trump as President of the US has thrown the future of the NATO military alliance into doubt while states such as Turkey have moved toward increasingly authoritarian rule.

The ways in which many states responded to the most recent global financial crisis is another signal of the continued relevance of state power and authority. The geographical expansion of finance, which David Harvey (2003) has described as a "spatio-temporal fix" for the problems of profitability in the manufacturing sector, has brought with it recurring financial and economic crises. In the wake of the crisis of 2008, states in Europe and North America responded with massive (publicly funded) bailouts, up to and including the full or partial nationalization of banks, financial firms, and other industries (such as the American automotive and British steel industries). While there is little evidence to suggest a dramatic reregulation of global capital flows, there have been some moves toward greater oversight of finance and a number of countries in the Global North and South have introduced limited capital controls. At the same time, since the turn of the millennium, the BRICS states (Brazil, Russia, India, China, South Africa) have been engaged in renewed state-led developmentalist projects that do not sit easily with the market-led economics of the pro-market period and also, arguably, reflect a Polanyian countermovement process.

We also see a renewed emphasis on the nation-state in the political developments of 2016, and there is much talk of a "globalization backlash." The cycle that began in 1989 of a triumphant opening of borders and deregulation seemed to be coming to a close, or so did at least its acceptance as the common sense of the era. The basic tenets of globalization were challenged first in the UK through Brexit and then in the US through the Trump victory. Trade deals were questioned and the possibility of protectionism was back on the agenda. The free movement of people was rejected by many. This did not necessarily presage a return to the 1930s as some commentators in the heat of the moment suggested but it did, at minimum, point to the end of the early phase of globalization in the sense that it no longer held economic, political, and social hegemony. Fundamental pillars of the post 1989 order – the single market in Europe and the North American Free Trade Agreement (NAFTA) in North America – were now in question and fundamental building blocks for Globalization 2.0 – such as the Trans-Pacific Partnership (TPP) and the Trans-Atlantic Trade and Investment Partnership (TTIP) – looked increasingly unlikely to materialize.

1.3.3   New Spatialities of Development

In terms of the broader spatialities of development, the dominant postwar development theory – the modernization approach – maintained that there was just one true path to development and that was to "catch up" with the original industrializing countries. The economics of the free market, the politics of Western democracy and the forward-looking actors of Western culture would take us all to modernity along a teleological path. By the 1960s an alternative, more nationalist perspective had emerged based around the dependency paradigm. It turned modernization on its head in terms of advocating a delinking from the global economy but it shared a methodological nationalism with modernization theory even if its vision was of a socialist future. In the more radical versions of the dependency approach, the path of dependent countries pointed rather to the "development of underdevelopment" – things could only become worse. This prospect was amply disproven by the rise of the original NICs (newly industrializing countries) in the 1970s and 1980s particularly in South East Asia. The NICs were beginning to look like truly "developing" countries.

The 1990s were characterized by a new version of modernization theory, the so-called Washington Consensus building on the neoliberal creed inaugurated by the Pinochet dictatorship in 1973 and gaining momentum under the Thatcher and Reagan governments in the UK and US. The "discipline of the market" would create "investor confidence" as the state was forced to reduce its direct interventions and reframe its regulatory role. The new watchwords were liberalization, flexibilization, and privatization, designed to increase the power of capital and atomize organized social networks. Discipline in the workplace was deemed to be crucial to business confidence and the historic postwar balance between capital and labor incomes was dramatically altered in favor of the first. However a series of increasingly severe financial crises in Mexico (1994), across East Asia (1995), and Russia (1998) showed that this model was not sustainable. It reached its nadir in 2001 when Argentina's economy collapsed after religiously following the International Monetary Fund's precepts for over a decade. It was only a matter of time before a more systemic crisis would emerge.

The early years of the new millenniums also saw the rise of the association of BRIC, which account for nearly half of the world population, one-third of the world's land surface, and a quarter of the global economic output. The rise of the BRIC has fundamentally altered the sociospatial dynamic of global development and calls into question the current model of global governance. In 2003 this emerging South-East bloc was in a position to question the World Trade Organization's free trade model and led the walkout by the Group of 21 "developing" countries. When the 2008–2009 global crisis emerged from within the Northern economies this bloc was not brought down through financial disintegration, as had been the case in earlier financial crises. While there was massive capital flight, a partial degree of decoupling from the global financial system meant that there was little exposure to the toxic assets of the North Atlantic economic system. If the crisis was to lead to a rethinking of the Washington Consensus it was also to usher in a more polycentric world order.

We are now clearly at the cusp of the globalization wave which began in the 1990s. Probably the next wave will not see the same leading players (North Atlantic plus Japan) as other countries, regions, and cultures to the East and the South continue to contest the hegemonic order. The future is uncertain and contested; there will be no simple progress to a Western model of modernity (Munck 2016a). Reform measures may include debt reduction for low-income countries, controls in short-term capital movements, reforms of the international financial institutions, the curbing of financial speculation and a greater emphasis on domestic demand-led growth. In theory these measures might contribute to encouraging a Polanyian style countermovements to address the social and ecological harm done by the unregulated market.

1.3.4 New Geographical Mobilities

The recession of the mid-1970s was a major economic turning point, marking the end of the system of mass production in the old industrial countries. This had both social and spatial consequences. Migrant labor recruitment was replaced by capital outflows to new industrial areas in the Global South. These in turn precipitated large-scale flows

of workers, for instance from South Asia to the Gulf oil countries, and somewhat later from less developed parts of Asia to the new industrial tigers. Between the mid-1970s and the outbreak of the global financial crisis in 2008, a new global labor market based on neoliberal ideas developed. The governments of the old industrial countries expected that the outsourcing of manufacturing and the move to a postindustrial economy would eliminate the need for labor immigration. The new emphasis in the USA, Canada, Australia, and Western Europe was on facilitating the entry of highly skilled personnel and entrepreneurs. By the early twenty-first century, new industrial countries like South Korea, Hong Kong, Singapore, and even China were joining the global competition to attract skills.

International migration is today an integral part of the transformation that is reshaping societies and politics around the globe. In many cases migration takes place under favorable conditions and leads to positive outcomes, but where migration becomes an act of desperation driven by violence or poverty, it throws up substantial challenges for the migrants themselves, and for the populations of origin, transit, and destination countries.

The old dichotomy between migrant-sending and migrant-receiving countries is being eroded (Castles et al. 2014). Most countries experience both emigration and immigration, although one or the other often predominates. The USA, Canada, Australia, New Zealand, Argentina, and Brazil are considered "classical countries of immigration." Their current people are the result of population-building immigration – to the detriment of indigenous peoples. Today, migration continues in new forms, with an emphasis on meeting labor market demand. Virtually all of Northern and Western Europe became areas of labor immigration and subsequent settlement after 1945. Since the 1980s, Southern European states like Greece, Italy, and Spain, formerly zones of emigration, have also become immigration areas, although in recent years emigration has been increasing in response to the global economic crisis. Today Central and Eastern European states are experiencing both emigration and immigration.

The Middle East and North Africa region is affected by complex population movements. Some countries, like Turkey, Jordan, and Morocco, have been major sources of migrant labor, while Turkey is now also an immigration country. The Gulf Oil states experience large, officially temporary, inflows of workers. Iran has been a major receiving country for refugees from Afghanistan, along with Pakistan. In Africa, colonialism and European settlement led to the establishment of migrant labor systems for plantations and mines. Decolonization since the 1950s has sustained old migratory patterns – such as the flow of mineworkers to South Africa and Maghrebis to France – and started new ones, such as movements to Kenya, Gabon, and Nigeria, as well as to Europe. Although economic migration predominates, Africa has more refugees and internally displaced persons (IDPs) relative to population size than any other region of the world. Asia and Latin America have complex migratory patterns within their regions, as well as increasing flows to the rest of the world.

According to the United Nations Department of Economic and Social Affairs, the world total stock of international migrants (defined as people living outside their country of birth or citizenship) grew from about 100 million in 1960 to 153 million in 2000 and then to 244 million in 2015. This sounds a lot, but was just 3.3 percent of the world's 7.4 billion plus people. The number of international migrants has grown only slightly more rapidly than overall global population since 1960 (UN Population Division 2009; UNDESA 2013). However, falling costs of travel and communications have rapidly increased nonmigratory forms of mobility such as tourism, business trips, and commuting.

Thus nearly 97 percent of people live in their countries of birth, and internal migration is far greater than international migration. It is impossible to know exact numbers of internal migrants, although the UN Development Programme estimated some 740 million in 2009 (UNDP 2009). Internal and international migrations are closely linked. Both are often rural–urban movements, linked to processes of economic transformation, which erode rural livelihoods, leaving little choice but to migrate to rapidly growing cities in search of work. In the world's population giants where industrialization is concentrated in specific regions (like China, India, Indonesia, or Brazil) rural–urban migration is mainly internal; for smaller countries or those in which economic development is lacking, rural–urban migration often means moving across national borders.

Inequality is a major driver of migration, but often in conjunction with other factors that trigger the decision to embark on difficult and risky journeys, whether in the form of internal or international migration. In many cases, people decide to migrate because their existing livelihood has been destroyed or rendered unviable. For example, the "Green Revolution" (Glaser 1987) in less "developed" countries has increased agricultural outputs, while requiring significant capital outlays and larger farms. The benefits of the higher productivity are accrued by large landowners and transnational agribusiness, while small farmers and landless laborers often lose their livelihoods. Many move to burgeoning slums in emerging industrial cities. Manufacturing – often in the form of subcontracting for transnationals – has expanded, but job growth in the formal sector is inadequate for the growing urban population, so that many rural–urban migrants have to eke out a living in the informal sector.

"Migration crises," like those currently impacting in Europe, occur when conditions in origin areas become so bad that flight is essential. This may be because of civil war and sustained violence (as in the case of Syria) or because of a mix of poverty, lack of employment opportunities, and human insecurity. It follows from this that emergency migration flows are generally "mixed flows," which undermine the administrative distinctions made by governments and agencies like the United Nations High Commissioner for Refugees (UNHCR). Migrant's motivations are complex: they have to leave their place of origin, but also hope to build better lives for themselves and their families in another place.

Many people are today asking the question whether "migration crises" are merely a passing phenomenon or a "new normal" not just for Europe but for the world as whole? We are now able to answer this question: if global inequalities in incomes and human security continue to grow as they have in recent years, then crisis-driven migrations are indeed likely to become more frequent and larger in scope, presenting considerable challenges to potential destination-states.

Against the background of the preceding analysis of the current situation and the dominant social and spatial transformation, the following three sections will illustrate in exemplary form some of the key tensions in the present. The ways in which these tensions will be addressed in future action are crucial to determine the prospects for social progress and the risks of social regress.

1.4   Democracy and Capitalism

During the final decade of the twentieth century, expectations of democratization and economic globalization went hand in hand, raising hopes for reaching a fully democratic world in which all material needs would be satisfied and poverty overcome. To many observers it appeared as if the commitment to "human rights and democracy" would diffuse ever more widely, encountering ever less explicit opponents. Political institutions were transformed by apparently incessant "waves of democratization." After the end of authoritarian regimes in Southern Europe during the 1970s, similar processes had occurred in South East Asia; military dictatorships had been overcome in Latin America; the apartheid regime had crumbled in South Africa; and Soviet-style socialism had disappeared in Eastern Europe and in the states emerging from the fall of the Soviet Union.

But this was not to pass.

1.4.1   The Paradox of the Present

Given the strengths of the beliefs in liberal democracy and the free market and the power with which institutional changes inspired by those beliefs made an impact on societies in many regions of the globe, it seemed as if political and economic progress were both well defined and unstoppably on their way. However this situation was not to last. Economic progress was highly uneven. Economic growth was spectacular in parts of East Asia and somewhat later, during the first decade of the twenty-first century, also throughout much of Latin America. But the post-Soviet societies suffered considerably from the free-market "shock therapy," even with reductions in life expectancy in the former Soviet Union. "Structural adjustment policies" had similarly negative effects in African and Latin American countries. True, later economic growth in Latin America and in post-apartheid South Africa was accompanied by extended welfare policies and the rise of new middle classes. In other regions, however, it created increasing social inequality and worsening working conditions. Industrialization in so-called "emerging economies" goes along with dangerously reduced environmental quality in urban regions and intensified exploitation of nature, in particular through resource extraction. Despite deindustrialization in formerly so-called "advanced economies," such exploitation has increased the risks and dangers related with climate change. Furthermore, the whole period from the 1990s to the present was marked by financial crises, first regionally in several countries of Latin America and East Asia, in Russia, and in Turkey, then more widely diffused from the finance centers of the globe, since 2008.

In political terms, the picture is similarly ambiguous. There can be no doubt that democratic institutions are today much more widespread than, say, in 1980. In many cases, newly introduced democratic procedures have by now been operational over extended periods. In some countries, in particular in Latin America and South Africa, driven by the impetus of social movements, democracy has been highly innovative in facing social and environmental challenges. At the same time, it has become obvious that "democratization" is by far not a linear, evolutionary process. Attempts at "democracy promotion" from the outside have led to the destruction of state structures. The "Arab Spring" was successful in bringing down autocratic regimes but, with the exception of Tunisia, has failed in creating democratic institutions. State failure, in turn, has entailed increasing and uncontrollable violence in large regions of the globe and has provided territorial bases for groups to spread violence worldwide. Furthermore, even within procedurally functioning democracies the relation between citizens and political institutions has often become thin and weak. Many citizens have stopped believing that their participation can have an effect on policy outcomes. Key areas of decision-making, such as on monetary policy through central banks, have indeed been insulated against democratic deliberation. As a response, citizens either turn away from politics, such citizen disaffection becoming visible in declining participation in elections. Or they express their discontent by supporting political parties, mostly newly arising, that mainly express distrust in the existing institutions and the "political class."

For all those reasons, the diffuse optimism of the late twentieth century has waned. Then, the dominant view was that the existing obstacles to free political and economic action only had to be removed, and progress would emerge. Since then, however, many of those supposed obstacles have effectively been removed, but the outcome certainly was not the great progress that had been promised and expected. Even though there has been progress, there clearly has not only been progress. In some respects, there has clearly been regress, even regress that endangers much of earlier progress. Thus, we have today rather divided views about how to assess the political and economic transformations of the past few decades, and we live in great uncertainty with regard to the outlook for the future.

1.4.2   A Short Look at the Historical Experience

Why should expectations for social progress be connected with democracy, with capitalism and with a combination of the two in the first place? With regard to democracy, the answer to this question may seem to be self-evident for us today. But we tend to forget that the idea of democracy, forcefully proposed in the late eighteenth century, was largely rejected by the elites in Europe and North and South America because of the instability and unpredictability that were associated with it. Capitalism, in turn, is anyway better known for its critics than for its proponents. It is widely seen as carrying social inequality, exploitation, and alienation with it. Thus, it may sometimes seem as if proponents of democracy reject capitalism and that proponents of capitalism reject democracy.

There clearly is a tension between democracy and capitalism that needs to be better understood. But to do so, we first need to reconstruct the strong and clear arguments for both democracy and capitalism that

have historically been put forward. Ideas that closely tie the progress of humankind with the advance of democracy and capitalism arose in the seventeenth and eighteenth century, and they retain some of their relevance today.

The period from 1500 to 1800, which historians of Europe call the early modern times, was marked by events that shook all certainties about the moral and political order, most importantly the encounter between people who did not know about the other's existence, when Europeans set foot in America, and the intra-Christian religious wars after the Reformation. These events sparked a radical rethinking of the basis of human existence and of our ways of living together. The notion arose that individual human beings have inalienable rights and that any legitimate political order needs to emerge from the agreement between those rights-holders. By the late eighteenth century, this combination of natural rights and social contract was connected with a further assumption: when free human beings bring their knowledge and their reason into the processes of deliberation and decision-making, the outcome will be superior to decisions by autocrats or oligarchs. Thus, democracy was not merely the only legitimate regime, it was also functionally superior to all other political forms. The idea of democracy incarnated political progress.

At the end of the eighteenth century the future progress of humankind as a society was seen as based on free human beings able to communicate with each other on equal terms about their ways of living together and on trading with each other the products of their labor in a peaceful and mutually beneficial way. During the nineteenth century, these ideas remained on the horizon, to some extent even on the agenda. Freedom of commerce became part of the many new constitutions. Free-trade agreements were signed between some countries. Sometimes the nineteenth century is also described as the era of the gradual extension of suffrage, as the beginning of the age of democratization.

But it is quite misleading to read the nineteenth century in the light of the expectations for progress raised during the preceding period. Capitalist progress occurred more through industrialization than through market exchange. Class-divided societies emerged instead of market societies in which producers met each other on equal terms. Institutional political participation remained restricted to men and to tax-paying property owners for most of the century. Universal suffrage was introduced rarely earlier than the end of World War I, and even then women remained excluded in countries such as France and Italy. The formal abolition of slavery happened as late as the second half of the nineteenth century in some societies such as the United States of America and Brazil. Furthermore, large parts of the world lived under European colonial domination or, if not, under conditions of economic dependence from the leading powers. Attempts of elites to catch up with the leading powers and to emulate their path of progress, such as were undertaken in Japan, Russia, and the Ottoman Empire, were not inspired by notions of democratic popular sovereignty and market exchange as developed in the eighteenth century. Rather, progress was more and more identified with the rationalization and centralization of state structures and with industrialization that was either state-led or led by large capitalist companies, supported by a modern science more and more oriented toward industrial production. This was the image of progress that was widely advertised at World Fairs in the period around the turn of the century.

By 1900 the sociopolitical constellation was marked by a "persistence of the Old Regime" (Mayer 1985) in which domestic, colonial, or settler oligarchies dominated the majority population. The emergence of an industry-based economic order, marked by industrialization in the North Atlantic region increasingly supplied with raw materials and agricultural products from other parts of the world, mostly benefitted the dominating groups. But resistance to political and economic exclusion had increased. At the end of World War I, during which the elites had become dependent on the majority population for the military effort itself and for the continuity of production while many men were at war, rights to political participation and to workers' organization were widely extended in many societies. In parallel, the existing capitalist mode of industrial expansion reached a threshold, to be overcome later through mass consumption.

The combination of extension of democracy and capitalist crisis led to an explosive situation. The fact that democracy had become more widespread, at least in the procedural sense of equal universal suffrage, meant that demands by the population could not as easily be ignored or oppressed as during earlier periods. Economic crises, in turn, meant decline in production, rise in unemployment and increasing public deficits and, thus, entailed that material demands could not easily be satisfied either. The tension between democracy and capitalism that arose spelt the breakdown of democracy in many of the countries where it existed and the rise of authoritarian and totalitarian regimes.

1.4.3 Rethinking the Relation between Democracy and Capitalism

These experiences made it necessary to rethink the eighteenth-century ideas of perennial progress through the extension of democracy and capitalism. Facing the rise of industrial capitalism and the denial of democracy during the nineteenth century, emerging critical thinking had assumed that there was a basic contradiction between capitalism and democracy that could only be overcome by superseding capitalism. However, the experiences of industrial-economic growth during the late nineteenth and early twentieth centuries had suggested that capitalist organization of production could lead to social progress in terms of an improvement in the satisfaction of material needs. Social movements divided between those who continued to aim at overcoming capitalism and those who strove for reorienting capitalism toward social needs by embedding it politically into democratic frameworks. By the end of World War I, the Bolshevik revolution in Russia and the introduction of egalitarian-inclusive democracy in several countries marked the temporary success of linking economic and political progress. By the beginning of World War II, the breakdowns of democracy and the rise of Nazism and Stalinism marked their failure.

A significant conclusion from these experiences is that it is equally erroneous to think that democracy and capitalism are in basic harmony with each other as different expressions of human freedom and self-determination as it is to see them in basic and irreconcilable contradiction with each other. Rather, there is a fundamental tension between them, a tension that can explode in catastrophic terms. But there is no determinism at work.

Critical thinking had described the expansionism of capitalism as a tendency toward commodification, toward turning all relations between human beings into relations mediated by commodities. Thus, a thinking effort directed toward identifying ways and means for preventing the tension between democracy and capitalism from exploding may usefully explore the appropriate limits of commodification. Economic theory, indeed, had held that self-regulating markets would generate optimum collective outcomes assuming that what is exchanged on markets are commodities. But the original arguments about "sweet commerce" and "wealth of nations" did not entail that every aspect of social life was suitable for commercialization and commodification. Commodities are goods and services that are produced in view of being sold. Much of that which is being sold in the history and present of capitalism, however, has not been produced toward that end. Trying to understand "the rise and fall of market society," Karl Polanyi (1944) rightly underlined that labor, land and money are not produced to be sold. Thus, economic thought and economic policy are wrong in treating them as commodities like other goods that are indeed produced to be sold. As a consequence, a market economy needs to be consciously embedded into society, not disembedded from it, as much free-market thinking tended to hold.

Analyses of the experiences with industrial-economic development and with the breakdowns of democracy have often focused on the adequate relation between states and markets as modes of regulation in terms of their functional efficacy. However, the necessary embedding of markets into society is more than a matter of formal regulation. Thinking of the democratic embedding of markets means that the degree and form of commodification becomes a subject of collective self-determination, the outcome of which will vary both in the light of earlier experiences made and of the specific conditions in which a society finds itself (Casassas and Wagner 2016).

After World War II, the democratic capitalist nation-state was seen as the answer to the tension between democracy and capitalism. It would be democratic as the expression of the collective self-determination of a nation through equal universal suffrage. At the same time, it would moderate political passions by focusing on electoral competition between moderate parties and discouraging uncontrolled social movement activity. It would reap the benefits of the functional efficacy of a market economy. But it would do so by embedding the latter into the national framework through political regulation of external commerce, not least through the currency but also through import substitution policies, and through domestic demand management, often to be called Keynesianism. Furthermore, taxation would be used as a means for social redistribution, paying for the building of welfare states.

In this form, the democratic capitalist nation-state was regarded as the container of social progress, as a general achievement at which humankind had arrived through historical learning. While developed in the North, the framework was thought to be applicable worldwide through "modernization and development." Decolonization was an expression of collective self-determination of nations. And those new nations would embark on state-led policies of economic development. Such modernization was expected, over time, to close the gap between "First" and "Third World." Functional requirements of industrial organization, in turn, would lead to convergence between the "First" and the socialist "Second World."

1.4.4 The Current Challenge: Toward a Democratic Reembedding of the Economy

The political consequences of current economic policy-making regimes are a considerably limited reach of democratic decision-making: policies concerning taxation, industrial relations or working conditions enter directly into the global competition for capital and tend to be not pursued if they adversely affect the "business climate." Others such as those concerning welfare or education are dependent on state revenues, thus are indirectly but severely affected by restrictive fiscal policies. Governments dependent on electoral majorities normally tend to avoid policies that make domestic social inequality rise. That the latter happens across many – though not all – democratic societies across the world gives testimony to the self-limitation of the reach of democracy. The very notion of government by regulation spells a farewell to democratic self-understandings, though its full technocratic meaning is hidden behind new terms such as governance, "best practice," legitimation through efficiency, etc.

The combination of the extension of the reach of capitalist practices and the self-limitation of the reach of democratic practices is at the core of a key paradox of our time: while there have never been more societies in which politics is based on democratic procedures, the actual capacity for substantive collective self-determination is radically diminished compared to preceding periods of democratic practices. Given that the current capitalist economy that has been disembedded from democracy is more crisis-prone than the embedded one, such a situation is highly unstable. It is dysfunctional even for much capitalist enterprise, as the recurrent crises show; and it falls normatively far short from what is possible in terms of satisfaction of material needs, of social justice, and of collective autonomy.

Many democratic governments have succumbed to the notion that the pursuit of domestic social justice is no longer possible under conditions of global capitalist conditions. By now they are regularly – and increasingly – paying the price for such an attitude through citizen disaffection and populist protest votes. It is only a matter of time for this downward turn to let explicitly anti-democratic governments come to power in apparently consolidated democratic settings. Democracy is not sustainable under conditions in which the elected declare themselves incapable of pursuing the expressed policy choices of the electorate. This diagnosis, though, is so bleak only for parts of the current situation. Many new or reemerging democracies have been built on resistance to undemocratic and oppressive regimes through social movements. They keep being marked by intense political participation. And in many of them, such as Brazil and South Africa for much of the last two decades, economic policies have successfully been pursued in conjunction with expansive social policies. Significant poverty reduction and some decrease in social inequality

have been the effects (Wagner 2016). To maintain or foster the social cohesion of a society by connecting economic with social policy under democratic conditions can become an asset in the current global context, a step toward upward social competition replacing downward economic competition between societies.

In times of global extension of economic networks, furthermore, it also needs to be recalled that the normative argument for a commercial society, as mentioned above, was not a call for a capitalist economy based on wage-labor, even though this became the dominant historical trajectory for more than a century. Today, the Polanyian notion of "reembedding" should not be seen as limited to providing a statist frame for capitalism, given that this historical measure of "self-defense of society" is precisely what has been destroyed or at least considerably weakened in the recent disembedding of the economy from the democratic capitalist nation-state. Across the globe, today, alternative forms of economic activity exist and proliferate, not least due to the dysfunctions of the capitalist economy. They include time-honored forms such as cooperatives and associations, often now reconstituted to face global challenges; directly anti-capitalist forms such as factory recuperations, or formally illegal ones such as occupation of land and buildings; producer–consumer networks for local and ecological consumption; regional initiatives to practice and promote new understandings of economic development, such as *buen vivir* in the Andean countries. The new movement of "self-defense" against the ravages of capitalism would need to be built from the accumulated experiences of such economic reorganization with a view to building a global economy oriented toward social justice and ecological sustainability. Such economy is likely to include wage-labor as one of its forms, but no longer as the dominant one.

We need a new understanding of democracy, going both beyond mere individual "consumer" choice every four or five years between prefabricated political options and beyond the notion of an electoral majority imposing its preferences on the entire society. Political progress would be the building of a participatory democracy in which citizen involvement is a permanent feature. Furthermore, such involvement needs going beyond the mere choice between proposals made by instrumentally support-seeking elites, be it through elections or referenda, but should include serious deliberation about the issues at stake, the elaboration of policy options, and the evaluation of the consequences of all available options. Without such an understanding of democracy, the democratic form risks to remain an instrument in the hands of elites rather than the tool for collective self-determination.

The path toward the domestic economic and political progress sketched above is often described as unviable because of the current global context. Nation-states, even those of a considerable size, so the argument goes, face the global economic and political conditions as an unavoidable constraint. Such reasoning obviously contains a grain of truth under current conditions of global connectedness. However, it is also self-defeating since it rules out from the start the possibility of changing the global context. One may even surmise that the argument that nothing can be done serves a purpose: it exonerates business and government elites from responsibility for the consequences of their actions and inactions. And at the same time it helps justifying whatever actions they take by permitting to argue that this was the only possible action given the global constraints.

While the argument contains a grain of truth, it hides a larger untruth. There are at least two significant ways in which domestic actors, even from within smaller polities, can influence the global context: through aiming at international coordination and agreement, and through exemplary action. Under current conditions, polities are highly interdependent and much less in control of the effects of domestic policy choices than in earlier periods. At the same time, current means of information and communication also permit processes of international communication with a view to identifying problems and coordinating ways of addressing problems. The current debate over climate change is a case of intended coordination, with yet uncertain success. One also has to note, though, that common problem definition can have adverse effects, namely when a problem is misidentified and the solutions ill-designed. But if accompanied by intense ongoing communication, monitoring, and deliberation, international communication can mitigate the significance of the external constraint for national actors by building momentum for common policy innovation. Importantly, the persistent plurality of political actors on the globe, in contrast to a world government, can also facilitate policy innovation. It allows individual actors or groups of actors to elaborate exemplary forms of action when coordination and agreement cannot be achieved.

Over the past three decades, the intensification of global economic activity under conditions of disembedding from democracy may have a mixed overall record, but it has clearly had two radically negative effects of global significance: it has created new forms of misery due to deteriorating living and working conditions in, often urban, sites of high economic activity and due to neglect of the rural population. And due to the acceleration of emission of pollutants through industry, transport, resource extraction, and large-scale agriculture, it has endangered the very inhabitability of the planet or at least large regions of it. Both these effects have begun to be addressed in global terms: through poverty reduction programs; through widely publicized denunciation of slavery-like working and living conditions; and through the beginning of coordinated action to reduce climate-changing emissions. Such activity has been pursued by various actors, from social movements to international agencies and commissions. Such manifoldness is an asset, allowing exemplary action to emerge and to be propagated. What is largely missing, however, is an attempt to bring together the meaning of those actions toward the elaboration of a new understanding that would see economic development as necessarily embedded within global policy choices.

To achieve such global embeddedness requires an elaboration of the meaning of democracy at the global level. There are good reasons against the idea of a global state and against world government. On the one side, political communication and deliberation in a single global polity could only be extremely "thin," to use Michael Walzer's (1994) metaphor, and devoid of substance and meaning. On the other side, plurality is a value in its own right, and the idea of a global majority overruling a global minority is not very appealing. Thus, democratic deliberation and decision-making has its appropriate place

in political collectivities that have a history of close connectedness and have acquired forms of political communication that support collective decision-making.

1.5   Production and Reproduction

The process of economic internationalization of the last 25 years has generated an unprecedented expansion of the global labor force. Our focus here is on production and reproduction as inseparable elements in the transformation of society. Likewise, we need to conceive of transformation in the world of work in the Global North and the Global South as inextricably linked. We also need to bear in mind that the move toward disembedding the economy from social relations creates a countermovement through which society reacts in different ways to this process.

Due to the interlinked processes of globalization and informationalization, as well as the steady increase in the proportion of women in paid employment, we have seen a massive increase in the number of people working worldwide. Best estimates are that the global workforce stood at 1.7 billion in 1980 and that it had risen to 2.9 million in 2010 (not quite doubling in size) with a projected 3.5 billion workers for 2030. Despite all the current emphasis on financialization, work clearly continues to be of central importance to the global economy. It is the increase in workers that is driving social transformation, as much as the exponential increase in the number of personal computers. This world of production cannot be separated from the work of social reproduction which often takes place within households and communities, though the state and the market also play a role. The dominant economic policies of the last 25 years have severely impacted on household reproduction with a decline in welfare support and the negative impact of deregulation and privatization on low-income families.

In the 1960s the international development critique focused on the failure of economic growth to generate stable employment, with the underlying assumption that secure employment/livelihoods was essential to human flourishing. There was also a strong belief that bringing women into the labor market would loosen the structures of male dominance. However, as larger and larger numbers of women across the world enter the labor market, the labor market is becoming increasingly precarious in the North and the prospects for social protection/labor regulations is becoming increasingly remote in the Global South. A rise in the number of women entering the labor market has been accompanied by shifting labor market conditions that have rendered more and more jobs for all workers akin to the precarious and informal forms of work traditionally associated with women. Taken together these processes can be understood as the feminization of labor. Yet, the rise of the female breadwinner has not been accompanied by renegotiations of the gender division of unpaid reproductive labor within the domestic domain. Unpaid reproductive labor within the home remains invisible and largely uncounted. So, what we have seen is internal and international migration of mainly women from rural areas and poorer regions whose work plugs the care deficits in both wealthy and middle-class homes, which then have mixed effects for the children (and elderly) they leave behind. The 2008–2009 crisis resulted in what could be called a triple crisis of "food/fuel/finance" in some of the countries the Global South which has a profound and lasting impact on production and reproduction.

1.5.1 Deindustrialization and the "New" Economy

As some tendencies are diverging across regions, let us first look in some more detail at the North and then at the South. Over the last 25 years there has been a dramatic transformation in the world of work in the Global North or the developed world as some still call it. Economic internationalization and the new information technologies acted to transform production and reproduction in complex ways. In broad terms the period from the mid-1970s to the mid-1990s saw a significant shift away from manufacturing, once the distinguishing mark of what were called the advanced industrial societies. The steady decline of traditional manufacturing jobs (along with the agricultural sector) did not lead to a homogeneous postindustrial economic order or an informational society.

The social transformation of the world of production and reproduction was not unilinear with contradictory tendencies toward new "high tech" work on the one hand and deskilling/flexibilization on the other hand. Women gained a greater role in the new economy but also the gender division of labor became more oppressive for women for the reasons noted above. In the study of the shifting patterns of production since the 1950s much emphasis has been laid on the new information and communication technologies and the whole notion of automation. It would be too simplistic to say that new technologies simply replace workers. Notions of a "workless future" or the "death of the working class" have not come to fruition. Technological change more often lead to greater output demand thus increased production and a greater demand for labor. There is not, on the other hand, much empirical support for the notion that new technologies lead inevitably to social progress. New technologies are, most seemly, transforming everyday life and the whole area of production/reproduction social relations.

The new technologies hugely accelerated globalization and facilitated the emergence of the global supply chains. But there were also adverse effects such as the stagnation of median real incomes and the growth of long-term unemployment. That workers were the losers in this new global capitalism is shown by the historic shift in the share of the national income going to labor (rather than capital). In the countries of the Organization for Economic Co-operation and Development (OECD) this share had been steadily rising between 1950 and 1975 but then dropped from 66 percent in 1990 to 60 percent in 2010 and is now well below 1950 levels, showing a decisive shift in bargaining power away from workers.

Contrary to the rosy views of a modernization theory which sees a constant advance of social progress, the advanced societies are moving toward more precarious employment relations, once seen as the preserve of the developing world. This has been dubbed by "Brazilianization" of the West, as precarity, informalization, and marginality become the norm and disrupt the postwar social settlement (Beck 2000). For some workers in the North this is now an anachronism as countries like Brazil industrialize while their own countries deindustrialize and lead to the decomposition of stable working-class patterns

of production and reproduction. The new norm in terms of social relations of production is now becoming insecurity, informality, and precarity of employment. In particular, youth unemployment rates have shot upwards since the onset of the crisis and show no sign of abating. While we must always be wary of a unilinear analysis, because there are always countertrends, we would conclude that the once settled compromise between capital and labor in the advanced industrial societies is no longer the dominant pattern or a status quo that can easily be reverted to.

In the aftermath of the Great Recession of 2008–2009 what were the employment trends in the OECD? World trade slowed dramatically despite some temporary recoveries. We saw a steady increase of what we can call vulnerable employment (self-employed and family workers) which points toward working poverty which increased by 23 million between 2009 and 2012. Recovery was patchy and there were many setbacks after the initial coordinated fiscal and military stimulus policies in much of the North. Growing public deficits and sovereign debt problems in country after country (especially in Europe) led to so-called austerity policies in a vain attempt to reassure the capital markets. The Northern economy was steadily reducing its capacity to create new jobs. By 2012, compared to 2009, there were 30 million fewer people in the labor market compared to precrisis trends and projections. The system seemed to be running out of steam and capitalism's historical ability to bounce back from crisis through new technological breakthrough seemed in question.

1.5.2 Industrialization in the South and the New International Division of Labor

The perspective from the South, however, differs considerably. From the mid-1970s to the mid-1990s as the North deindustrialized, the Global South industrialized at a gradually increasing rate. Of the nearly doubling of the global labor force between 1980 and 2010, the large majority were accounted for by the "farm to factory" shift in the South. In China, we have seen the emergence of 120 million nonagricultural jobs since the turn of century, leading to a dynamic industrialization process. In India, a substantial 67 million jobs were added in the industrial and service sectors over the same period. In China, as is well known, this resulted in an unprecedented wave of urbanization and industrialization. In India, nearly half of all the new nonagricultural jobs were in the low-skill construction sector rather than the higher-value-added manufacturing end of the spectrum. Likewise, in Latin America it is mainly in Brazil where social transformation through industrialization was effective. Several other countries in the region remain linked into an extractive (agromining) economic model.

Development – defined as economic growth and social progress – is the main driver of transformation in the Global South which has led to a new international division of labor, predicted in the 1970s but only fully realized over the last decade or so. This shows that the North–South divide was not condemned to continue an industrial–agrarian divide. What industrialization across vast swathes of the Global South from the 1970s onwards did not produce, however, was a convergence of incomes. Put at its simplest, industrialization does not, in and of itself, lead to development. Industrial convergence from the 1980s onwards – as the North deindustrialized and the South industrialized – did not lead to a narrowing of the longstanding North–South divide. In terms of global social progress it is thus clearly essential to address intercountry inequalities as much as intracountry inequalities.

The overwhelming fact of production in the Global South is that it occurs primarily in the informal sector and sees the continuation – and even exacerbation – of precarious work (Munck 2016b). The model of the informal sector was a 1970s category which took the formal employment patterns of the North as the norm. There was an implicit expectation that this sector would help absorb the growing mass of people thrown off the land or out of urban jobs through the modernization process. The problem was an assumed dualism between formal and informal sectors when in fact they were perfectly complementary. In practice informalization, and what we today call precarization, continues to dominate and is a critical component of capitalist globalization. The notion of upgrading this sector and promoting "decent work" norms, while laudatory, continues to posit a past northern pattern (full employment and welfare state) against which to measure the present. Social progress in the Global South may take other forms and we need to be open to non-Northcentric solutions.

There was an initial perception that the Great Recession (2008–2009) did not impact as severely in the Global South as it did in the North, as briefly discussed above. This was mainly due to continued growth in the BRIC countries but by 2015 even China's counted economic vitality was called into question by a volatile stock market. Overall, we note that while in 1994, 39 percent of the developing world's workers lived in conditions of extreme poverty (defined as less than US$1.25 per day) this proportion had dropped to 25 percent in 2004 and 13 percent in 2014 (World Bank 2015). While on the surface an impressive achievement in terms of social progress (although questions remain over the methodologies used and measurement in China particularly) the quality of jobs in the "developing" countries leaves a lot to be desired. The barriers to female labor force participation continue to be very high, gender pay gaps persist, and in many cases, employment has not come with supports for domestic labor, leading to a double or triple burden. Youth unemployment rates continue to rise. More than half the workers in the developing world (1.5 billion) continue in so-called vulnerable employment and welfare rights are patchy at best. While the development imperative has driven up the number of workers in paid work across the Global South in terms of social progress we have a less than optimistic scenario.

1.5.3 Global Work and Gender

When debates emerged around the "feminization of labor" in the late 1980s, this drew attention to several interrelated shifts associated with the model of globalization we commented in previous pages. This model compelled greater numbers of women to enter the labor force while at the same time rendering labor markets increasingly precarious. One of the many paradoxes of this process is that insofar as there has been some erosion of gender inequality in labor markets this has largely happened as the result of the convergence of men and women at the lower rungs of the labor market rather than through the integration of women into the protected "inside." This is evidenced,

for instance, in the (slight) fall in the gender gap in labor force participation rates that has occurred over the past two decades and has as much to do with falling rates for men as it does with rising rates for women.

The 2008 global financial crisis has worsened whatever progress was being made toward reducing gender inequality in labor markets (Elson 2010). Several years after the crisis, it has become clear that while some of the initial impacts in the developed economies affected those industries dominated by men (such as the financial, manufacturing, and construction sectors), the impacts then spread to other sectors around the world, including into the service sectors that are dominated by women. Evidence from past and present crises suggests that where women are concentrated in export manufacturing (e.g. in Latin America and Asia), female job losses will probably be greater than male job losses. Women are also disproportionately affected by job losses in the textile and tourism sectors (e.g. in many parts of Africa and East Asia, including China). In the OECD countries, cuts in public sector jobs have had a drastic effect on women's employment. In the EU, where women constitute on average 69.2 percent of public sector workers, job losses, wage reductions, and pay freezes disproportionately affect women. Signaling a reversal of progress that had been made in women's position in the labor market, female employment rates in 2012 had fallen below or close to the 2005 level in 22 EU Member States. The gender pay gap also increased in nine Member States (European Women's Lobby 2012).

Despite these recent shifts, women have participated in large numbers in the massive increase in the global workforce since the 1980s. Yet, they have often gained jobs in contexts where male employment was either stagnant or declining. Women's growing share of the workforce, its so-called "feminization," has attracted a great deal of attention in the literature because of the view that the entry of women into the workforce would release them from patriarchal constraints within the home and lead to their emancipation. However, these theories flourished in an era when employment was associated with stable, full-time jobs in large-scale factory production systems that allowed workers to unionize to defend their rights. These are the jobs that the International Labor Organization (ILO) continues to describe as "typical." Yet a sizeable majority of women today are to be found in jobs that are considered "atypical" and whose emancipatory potential has become the subject of a great deal of debate.

There are various forces behind the rise of female labor force participation rates across the world. Falling fertility rates, rising levels of female education and changing aspirations have made it both possible and desirable for women to take up paid work. Women have also been "pushed" into the labor market by the declining importance of agriculture, growing landlessness, urbanization, economic recession, debt crisis, structural adjustment policies and accompanying declines in male employment prospects and wages.

In addition, we witness the changing nature of the global economy and the emergence of a female-specific demand for labor. The ascendancy of neoliberal ideologies across the world has made the pursuit of market-led growth the central driving force in shaping the pace and pattern of globalization, putting pressure on all countries to hone their international competitiveness through the deregulation of labor markets. Women have emerged as the flexible labor force par excellence within this new global regime: they are generally free of the "fixed costs" associated with organized labor; their continued responsibility for unpaid care work within the home combined with the gender-stratified occupational structure serve to curtail their options and weaken their bargaining power while hegemonic ideologies of the male breadwinner are used to justify paying them less than men.

Women have therefore increased their share of the labor market at a time when labor markets are increasingly deregulated and when jobs have become increasingly "atypical" for both men and women. At the same time, they continue to predominate in the lower ranks of the occupational hierarchy with more limited job opportunities than men and lower earnings. Within the OECD context, the gender wage gap has declined but women's continued responsibility for unpaid care and domestic work within the home means they are more likely to be in low-paid, flexible, and part-time work than men, with working mothers suffering an additional "motherhood penalty."

Elsewhere, globalization has contributed to women's labor force participation through two primary routes: the generation of jobs associated with the trade in commodities and of jobs associated with the movement of labor. The generation of jobs through increased trade in commodities has taken a number of forms. In some cases, technological change combined with the search for flexible labor arrangements in an increasingly competitive global environment has led multinational firms to locate different stages of labor-intensive manufacturing (garments, textiles, electronics) and services (call centers, back office processing) to different parts of the world in order to take advantage of differences in wage costs, factor endowments, or congenial investment climates. In other cases, countries seeking to earn foreign exchange have sought to exploit their location-specific comparative advantage to expand trade in tourism as well as traditional (coffee, cocoa, bananas) and nontraditional (flowers, fruits, organic crops) agricultural commodities.

1.5.4   Global Value Chains and the Gender Division of Labor

The concept of global value chains was developed to map the distribution of roles, activities, and value-addition of goods and services whose production, distribution, and consumption cut across national boundaries. Global value chains in labor-intensive manufacture of consumer goods, services, and nontraditional agricultural exports tend to be driven by large retailers, branded manufacturers, and supermarkets who draw their profits from high-value research, design, sales, and marketing stages, which are characterized by high barriers to entry. The production end of these global chains, on the other hand, is characterized by low barriers to entry and decentralized production networks, made up of highly competitive workshops, farms, and factories, generally located in the informal economies of low-wage countries. This is where most women workers producing for global markets are located.

The conditions in which they work vary considerably, depending on whether they are employed by multinationals or their direct suppliers or whether they are subcontracted based upon smaller workshop or home-based piece work. By and large, wages and working conditions are better, the more direct the relationship between multinationals and workers and not simply due to the higher levels of profit that characterize these organizations. It also reflects the pressure that has been brought to bear on these organizations. The nature of the linkages within these global value chains has allowed transnational activists to mobilize consumer support in affluent countries to force multinationals to adopt corporate codes of conduct to ensure minimum labor standards are observed.

There are, however, clear limits to what has been achieved – both in terms of the standards observed and of which suppliers are included. In particular, the right to association and collective bargaining remains one of the least enforced clauses of these codes of conduct and generally enforcement does not go beyond direct suppliers. These are sectors characterized by highly mobile capital and the constant threat of relocation serves to curtail the capacity of workers to mobilize for enforcement.

The other route through which globalization has generated jobs for women has been through the growing cross-border movements in search of jobs. By 2006, women represented almost half of the total number of international migrants, with many now migrating on their own rather than with other family members. They migrate because of lack of opportunities or social restrictions on their life choices in their own countries, as well as their awareness of opportunities in more affluent countries.

A significant proportion of these opportunities have been generated by the movement of women into paid work in affluent regions of the world. In the absence of much change in the gender division of unpaid care work and household chores, there is a growing demand for paid domestic workers by those women who can afford it. The availability of migrant labor provides a pool of low-cost labor to meet this demand. Restrictions on the mobility of labor, in stark contrast to the almost unfettered mobility of capital, has meant that legal migration is generally based on temporary contracts with fewer rights than other workers and little opportunity to engage in collective action to improve the terms of employment. At an even greater disadvantage are those who enter without documentation and have hardly any rights at all.

Contrary therefore to the more optimistic expectations, women's greater entry into the labor market has not been accompanied by their widespread emancipation. Some women have made it into the higher levels of management in some countries but most women continue to be concentrated in forms of work that do not hold out much transformative potential: part-time, low-paid work in the Global North and temporary, irregular, and informal employment in the Global South.

1.5.5   Global Care Chains and Migration

Changes associated with the global feminization of labor have meant that women's paid labor has become increasingly important to the survival of families and communities. This has helped to fuel women's labor migration, particularly in the areas of domestic and/or care work.

Migration may be from rural to urban areas, or from poorer to (relatively) richer countries. In both cases, the remittances sent home to families have become an important source of income.

In many advanced industrialized countries, demand for this work has been fueled by women's entry into the paid labor force not matched by a shift in the gender-based division of unpaid labor in the home or in state support for childcare. However, it has also been prompted by shifting demographics. The Japanese Ministry of Health, Labor and Wealth, for instance, projected that the country, which employed 1.77 million care workers in 2013, would need 2.53 million care workers in 2025 (Onuki 2016).

The demand for female domestic workers has also grown in middle-income and "developing" countries. In Asia, for instance, wealthier countries such as South Korea, Japan, Malaysia, and Taiwan have attracted large numbers of migrants from poorer countries in the region (Seol and Skrentny 2009). In many cases, bilateral labor agreements are designed in ways that support short-term (i.e. temporary) migration of sole workers, forcing them to leave families behind. These agreements also tend to make it difficult for workers to report violations of their working conditions or abuse from their employers, as visa status is often tied to employment with a particular employer. While domestic work may present the best option for women in poor countries and regions, the work is often low paid and highly exploitative, with nannies expected to work evening and weekends and to be on call at all times. It has also been found that in certain regions, domestic work relies on child labor. According to the ILO, approximately 175,000 children under 18 are employed in domestic service in Central America and more than 688,000 in Indonesia.

These "global care chains" (Hochschild 2000) further increase the amount of domestic work that is left to be done by those (mainly women) who care for the families left behind. As with much reproductive work, this work has been hidden and privatized. So too has the work done by those mothers that migrate, who engage in the paid work of social reproduction while simultaneously performing motherhood for their own children at a distance – what has been called "transnational motherhood" (Arat-Koç 2006).

Transnationalized relations of social reproduction also incorporate other dimensions of migration. For example, mothers may move to care for their children who have been sent abroad to receive education in places like Korea or Taiwan (Chee 2003; Kofman 2012: 10). Migrant domestic workers form a category of gendered and racialized labor that has expanded remarkably in virtually all advanced industrial economies (Anderson 2000, 2007; Cox 2006). Domestic and care work is marked by hierarchies of work tasks, of formal and informal modes of employment, and of groups with varied statuses (Huang, Thang, and Toyota 2012). For instance, Filipina domestic workers are preferred in some places due to their better education and English, but rejected in others because they are seen as too active in defending their rights. Domestic work by migrant women can be the result of increased opportunities of professional or white-collar employment for majority-group women: hiring foreign maids can free women in Italy, the USA or Singapore from housework and childcare (Iredale, Guo, and Rozario 2002; Huang, Yeoh, and Abdul Rahman 2005). Such transnational care

hierarchies sometimes go a stage further, when migrant domestic workers hire a maid in the home country to look after their own children. "Global care chains" may mean higher living standards and better education, but at a high emotional cost (Yeates 2012).

1.5.6 Global Social Policy

Among the global social policy proposals on the table to deal with the global financial crisis in the realms of production and reproduction one of the potentially most far reaching is the Social Protection Floor Initiative, led by the ILO and the World Health Organization. It sets out two broad elements to secure basic social services for the most needy: (1) A basic set of essential social rights and transfers, in cash and in kind, to provide a minimum income and livelihood security for all and to facilitate effective demand for and access to essential goods and services; and (2) The supply of an essential level of goods and social services such as health, water and sanitation, education, food, housing, life and asset-saving information that are accessible for all. There is clearly an urgent need for such a coordinated international effort to secure basic social protection for all now struggling to survive in the poorest countries. But we must note that in and of itself the social protection floor will not alter the architecture of a global political economy that produces extreme poverty and inequality even while it generates untold wealth and privilege for the few.

1.6 Demographic Change, Consumption, and Sustainability

The sustainability of the human way of life on our planet has been a rising concern for at least half a century. It was first raised with regard to the depletion of resources, then widened into a general ecological concern about risks for health and biological diversity, and reached its height with imminent climate change endangering living conditions in major parts of the world. The consequences of human interventions into the biology and geology of the earth have reached such dimensions that geologists started to speak of a new era, the Anthropocene, beginning at around 1800, as the era in which the main determinant of planetary changes is the human being.

Such impact results from various elements: the number of human beings living on the earth; their material way of life; and the kind of technology they use. An early attempt, at the beginning of this concern, to disaggregate different drivers of environmental impact was made in the "IPAT equation" of Ehrlich and Holden (1971). This identity states that environmental impact (I) is the product of population (P), the level of affluence (A), usually measured by GDP per capita, and the level of technology (T), measured by the impact per unit of GDP, so that

$$I = P \times A \times T.$$

So, for example, CO_2 emissions are the product of population, GDP per capita, and CO_2 emissions per unit of GDP. Though these factors are not independent, decomposing impacts in this way highlights the relative contribution of the different drivers. For global environmental impacts such as CO_2 emissions, though technological improvements and changes within sociotechnical systems have led to reductions in

T, i.e. lower impacts per unit of economic activity, this has been more than offset by growth in *P* and *A*, population and GDP per capita. Or in other words, a larger population and greater material affluence have increased environmental impact; they would continue to do so unless technological changes and changes in the way of life work to reduce such impact. In the following, we explore this tension in the current situation by looking first at the trends of population growth.

1.6.1   Population Growth and Consumption

Population growth is crucial when dealing with sustainable development. The wave of growth of the population of the world, initiated more than two centuries ago, is slowly on the wane. The speed of growth was just 3 per thousand per year during the eighteenth century, 5 per thousand during the nineteenth, 9 per thousand in the first half of the twentieth, peaking at 18 per thousand in the second half. Reliable current evaluations set the present rate of growth at 11 per thousand, and there is a widespread consensus among the experts that the decline will continue, approximating zero growth by the beginning of the next century. Recent UN projections set the world population at about 11 billion people by the year 2100, a tenfold increase since 1800, and double the size reached at the end of the twentieth century (UN 2015b). Oversimplifying a very complex history, this cycle is the result of the modern demographic revolution, due to the historical transition from high to low patterns of mortality and fertility; a revolution that in the rich countries in Europe and North America initiated in the first part of the nineteenth century saw its conclusion in the mid-twentieth century. The same revolution began more than a century later in the rest of the world and has still to run its full course.

The general mechanisms of the modern demographic revolution, or transition, are well understood: broadly speaking, they are the consequence of the rupture of the syndrome of poverty, both of resources and of knowledge, that have kept mortality at a very high level since the beginning of mankind. The rupture of the syndrome has increased survival and the expectation of life and, subsequently, with a gap of a few decades, brought about a gradual adjustment of fertility. The fall of the death rate has generally preceded that of the birth rate causing an acceleration of population growth that, subsequently, has slowed down with the fall of the birth rate. With modernity, survival, and reproduction cease to be conditioned by instinct, biology, and material constraints and are, more and more, the fruit of individual choice and behavior.

The relative inertia typical of population change makes a projection over a generation relatively reliable, at least at the world and regional level. Let us therefore consider the possible trends over the 2015–2050 period: according to the UN projections, world population will increase from 7.3 to 9.7 billion, or 2.4 billion over 35 years (the same number was added to the world population in the 29 years between 1986 and 2015, and in the 36 years between 1950 and 1986). In other words, there will be 2.4 billion more people on the earth to be fed, clothed, and housed; they will need energy and combustibles for heating, cooking, and transportation; they will need working tools, infrastructures, manufactured goods made with raw materials and energy; they will use and consume space. The economic system must be able to cope

with this additional aggregate demand, while the environment will undergo an accrued human impact. Almost 50 percent of the world population increase will take place in Africa and an additional 28 percent in the Indian subcontinent. In Europe, China, and Japan, population will initiate a declining course well before mid-century; urban population will continue to grow, while the rural population will continue to decline. Although comprehensive projections are missing, it can be confidently said that the population of the coastal areas – more fragile and more densely populated – will continue their fast growth, much faster than the areas of the interior. Finally there are concerns that the general population growth will accelerate the intrusion in other fragile areas, such as the pluvial forests.

The population question, central to the debate on development in the second part of last century, is slowly sliding out of the international agenda. In the background of the population conferences promoted by the United Nations in 1974, 1984, and 1994 stood the issue of the unsustainability of the rapid world population growth, particularly in what used to be called the less "developed" countries. Not least for diplomatic reasons, this central concern was not explicitly put on the table, but emerged in the discussions and in the documents whenever they dealt with the various aspects of population change. Population issues were still present in the solemn UN Millennium Declaration of the year 2000 and were addressed by some of the Millennium Development Goals (MDGs), but have almost disappeared from the debates leading to the approval, by the UN General Assembly, of the 2030 Agenda and of the Sustainable Development Goals (SDGs) for 2015–2030. Population growth is indeed slowing its pace, but this fact should not push into oblivion several major developments, of a demographic nature, that threaten the "sustainability" notion that informs the 2030 Agenda. Among these are the very rapid growth of the African continent, the very low fertility of eastern Asia and of Europe, the international migration flows, the unchecked human penetration in fragile or pristine areas, or the fact that population growth can be a major factor of global warming.

Given the moderate levels of mortality prevailing in a large majority of countries, the main driver of population growth is fertility, which, at the global level, has undergone a sustained decline. Sixty years ago, the number of children per woman for the entire world was around 5, reduced by half to 2.5 in 2010–2015. But given the unequal pace and timing of the demographic transition in the various areas of the world, there are, nowadays, populations with persistently high fertility, and populations where fertility remains well below replacement. In Sub-Saharan Africa the number of children per woman stands at 5.1 (2010–2015), more than triple the levels of China and Europe (1.5–1.6). If fertility of Sub-Saharan Africa remained unchanged (in Nigeria, the most populous country of Africa, fertility is close to 6), its population would treble by 2050, from 0.96 to 2.75 billion in 35 years. These numbers would require an extraordinary rate of economic growth in order to allow for sufficient investments in infrastructures, raise hundreds of million people out of extreme poverty, eradicate hunger, and improve the modest levels of consumption of the rest of the population. The environmental impact of these growing numbers of people, with an increased per capita income, would be very high if their ways of life followed the patterns set by Western Europe and North America earlier. If nothing else changed, this rapid population growth would threaten – if not make impossible – the viability of the sustainability paradigm in the region.

The transition from high to moderate fertility is linked to well-known developments, beside a general improvement of the economic conditions of the population. Chief among these are the improvement of health and a sustained decline of child mortality; primary education for all; empowerment of women over a wide range of issues; and the end of gender discrimination. More specifically, given the high proportion of women with unmet needs of contraception (globally, almost one in five), at the core of policies should remain the provision of a full range of safe, reliable, and good quality contraceptive services. For the countries where fertility is very low, there is a (tepid) consensus that current low levels will give way to a gradual recovery: this is the position of the institutions and researchers who venture demographic forecasts and projections. Why this should happen is not clear: some argue that since very low fertility generates negative economic externalities, states may react by channeling more resources to couples and families, inducing them to have more children. The problem is, however, how to solve the conflict between the negative externalities produced by low fertility and the economic benefits – for the parents – of having one child instead of two, or two instead of three.

A further threat to sustainability comes from the growing environmental impact of income growth, again for the moment assuming technology and way of life according to unchanged North-western models. Let's take the cases of Europe and Sub-Saharan Africa: while in the former region population will be almost stationary over the 2015–2050 period, in the latter the rate of growth will be approximately 2 percent per year. Let us further make the hypothesis that per capita income will grow, in the two areas, at the respective rates of 2 percent (a rather optimistic hypothesis for Europe) and 5 percent (a plausible pace in Sub-Saharan Africa for many economists). Since, without change in technology and way of life, the physical impact of mankind on Earth is a function of the combination of population and economic affluence (or income or product), the simple multiplicative algorithm, as introduced above, tells us that, over the next 35 years, such impact (assuming business as usual) would double in Europe and increase more than twelvefold in Sub-Saharan Africa.

There are other areas of the world, beside Africa, where fertility and the rate of growth are very high, taking account also of the density, distribution patterns of settlement, conformation of the land and other environmental characteristics. Population growth is also a powerful factor in the process of global warming; a determinant of the pressure on fragile or pristine territories; a determinant of human intrusion into vital areas such as pluvial forests and inland water reserves. For all those reasons, population growth must remain a central element in the debate on sustainability.

1.6.2 Sustainability

However, the issue of population growth needs to be seen within the wider challenge of achieving a sustainability transition that enhances human well-being for all, whilst ensuring that the impacts of human activity remain within planetary boundaries. We all know

that technology may decouple economic growth from unsustainable patterns of production and consumption. In other words, with different technology it is possible to lower the content of energy and non-renewable materials of every additional unit produced or consumed. Furthermore, changes in way of life – such as settlement patterns and intensity of transportation – may reduce resource use even with given technology.

In the 1970s, debates on sustainable development tended to focus on the challenges associated with population growth. Whilst population is often not headlined for political sensitivity reasons, several measures enshrined in the 2015 Sustainable Development Goals for 2030 will lead to reductions in fertility in poorer countries, including reducing child and maternal mortality, access to preprimary and primary education for all, and universal access to sexual and reproductive health and reproductive rights. But in recent years, furthermore, debates on sustainable development have increasingly centered on the question of the compatibility or otherwise of current levels of affluence and consumption with the need to reduce environment impacts so as to remain within planetary boundaries, including those relating to climate change, biodiversity loss, and nutrient cycling (Steffen et al. 2015). Two broad approaches have been proposed.

The more radical view argues that the previous positive relation between levels of GDP and measures of human well-being has broken down since the 1970s, so that continuing high rates of economic growth are no longer delivering improvements in human well-being in richer countries, even when these growth rates can be achieved. Combined with the need to reduce environmental impacts to within planetary boundaries, those who take this view argue that richer countries should pursue a strategy of "prosperity without growth" (Jackson 2009). Whilst this position is sometimes caricatured as proposing a zero level of GDP growth, more thoughtful proponents of this view argue that only a radical reconfiguration of current economic systems would be able to reconcile human well-being and environmental goals.

The more mainstream view, often characterized as green growth, argues that continuing high levels of GDP growth are in fact necessary to enable the high levels of investment needed in research and development and deployment of new technologies with much lower carbon emissions and other environmental impacts. In this way, growth in resource use and material consumption would be constrained to remain within environmental limits, whilst economic growth would continue, increasingly powered by activities within the "intellectual economy" (Bowen and Hepburn 2013). This would lead to an "absolute decoupling" of economic growth and environmental impact, as reduction in the T factor in the IPAT equation would offset continuing growth in affluence and population, until a stable population is reached.

Debates between these two views center on the aspirations of the new citizens growing up in extreme poverty in "developing" countries, as well as the political tractability of economic system change. Proponents of the more radical view argue that most citizens of "developing" countries aspire to the lifestyles of those in richer countries, as communicated globally through the internet and images from television and Hollywood movies. If this aspiration were to be achieved at current average levels of per capita consumption in richer countries, then this would lead to levels of resource use and environmental impact far exceeding global environmental limits. Under this view, the unprecedented levels of technological change needed to reduce impacts per unit of GDP are highly unlikely to be achieved under the current economic system, which prioritizes increasing consumption as the primary route to human well-being. Instead, they argue for a strategy of reducing wasteful levels of consumption in richer countries, whilst strengthening community-based routes to well-being, and focusing on more decentralized, resource-efficient, and locally owned technology solutions for "developing" countries.

Proponents of the more mainstream view argue that any constraints on economic growth in richer countries would undermine the opportunities for development to meet the aspirations of citizens in "developing" countries, as well as constraining investment in more resource-efficient technological solutions and being politically intractable in richer countries. Instead, they argue for much greater emphasis on improving and deploying new technologies in both richer and "developing" countries that would reduce global environment impacts, such as CO_2 emissions, whilst bringing local health, air quality, and economic benefits. Nevertheless, they recognize that even such a focus on green growth would require a significant reorientation of current political and economic priorities.

Whichever of these views, or more subtle new ideas, prevails in these debates on sustainable development, it is clear that achieving legitimate aspirations of those in "developing" countries for a better life, enacting measures to constrain fertility rates consistent with individual liberties and human rights, addressing current high levels of global inequality, and ensuring that the impacts of human activity remain within planetary boundaries are central to realizing social progress toward a better society.

1.6.3 Mobility

Mobility – domestic and international – is a structural capability of humans and a vital component of human capital, and is a powerful factor of social progress. But the absence of an even moderate global governance of international migration is a major threat to the political and social sustainability of social development. Among the SDGs (and targets) of the UN 2030 Agenda, there is almost no mention of international migration, except a reference (target 10.7, the only one on migration out of a total of 69 targets) to the need to "facilitate orderly, safe, regular and responsible migration and mobility of people," generic and ambiguous statement (who is going to facilitate? What does "responsible migration" mean?) and impossible to achieve without an embryo of international governance of flows. This summarizes the profoundly rooted unwillingness of states to deal with the issue, and to entrust even a small fraction of their sovereignty to an international institution in order to regulate international flows. There are strong forces generating global migration flows, because of the growing planetary interconnection between economies and cultures, the "shrinking" of the world, and, most of all, because of the still profound economic and demographic divide between rich and poor countries.

1.7 Actors for Social Progress

Social progress is full of ambiguities. The ways in which social progress has been produced in the past also puts further progress at risk. Among the problems discussed in the previous sections that need to be resolved are the following:

- climate change and the deterioration of the human environment;
- the fragmentation, downgrading, and exclusion of labor;
- racial, gender, and religious discrimination;
- increasing economic, social, and health inequality;
- regional disparities and shifting geographical divisions of labor;
- fundamental tensions between capitalism, democracy, and human rights;
- environmental consequences of economic growth and increasing population densities.

These obstacles are often interconnected; frequently, one issue cannot be solved without solving others. To bring back social progress calls for a new Great Transformation which would reembed market forces into society and nature. This time round the reembedding cannot just be accomplished through national government intervention, but needs new constellations of actors and new forms of conscious action as a precondition for regenerating expectations for social progress, but in the end its realization will depend on the emergence of a new governance model which relies less on the nation-state and more on nonstate actors, international institutions, and local action. To finish this opening chapter we provide a brief cross-section of collective action, which is central to bringing about the next Great Transformation.

1.7.1 Protest on the Rise

Dissatisfaction with injustices and inequities is widespread. During the last decade protests have grown in all regions of the world. Several research reports confirm that "despite the absence of exactitude in measurement, data from the past several decades do point to a fairly clear pattern of increasing frequency. Major protests multiplied in the second half of the 1980s and early 1990s, coinciding with what is commonly called the third wave of democracy, but then decreased significantly throughout the 1990s and the first half of the 2000s. Protests began to accelerate again in the second half of the 2000s and have reached a peak in the past five years [i.e. 2011–15]" (Carothers and Youngs 2015; see also Economist Intelligence Unit 2013; Ortiz et al. 2013).

The large majority of protest events address their grievances to their own national governments and demand that these governments develop economic, social, and environmental policies that are in the interest of the population at large, and not of only the wealthy and powerful. Social movement organizations are numerous and very heterogeneous, varying from the Occupy initiatives and the World Social Fora, via Via Campesina, the Zapatistas, the Brazilian Movimento dos Trabalhadores Sem Terra (MST), and the Argentinian Piqueteros, to the Self-Employed Women's Association and the New Trade Union Initiative in India. The demands put forward by protesters are generally sundry, and the forms protests take are heterogeneous. Protests oppose the elimination of subsidies on food and fuel; wage cuts; VAT increases on basic goods and services; the emaciation of social security; the reform of pension and health care systems; the flexibilization of labor; but also pollution, war, rape, and corporate influence. The lack of "real democracy" is a regular issue.

Naturally, social movements and social contestations do not fight for "social progress" as such, but focus on more specific issues. Their activities are not only numerous, but also extremely heterogeneous. Worldwide there are hundreds of thousands of unions, associations, and groups defending the interests of the disadvantaged and those discriminated against: workers, women, people of color, LGBTQ, etc. The number of environmentalist groups is impressive too, as are the initiatives against organized violence in its multiple shapes. In addition, the awareness has increased that lasting change for the better can no longer be realized only on a national scale. The number of transnationally organized social-movement organizations (TSMOs) has grown dramatically since the 1970s, from 183 in 1973, to 348 in 1983, 711 in 1993, and over a thousand in 2003 (Smith 2005: 266). The number of nongovernmental organizations is even vastly larger, while the number of international NGOs (INGOs) has in recent decades increased significantly as well.

There are huge tensions between these many institutional actors. INGOs and NGOs are mostly advocacy organizations without a proper membership structure, defending the interests of people, animals, or natural riches that are supposed not to "speak for themselves." They often compete with emancipatory movements of subaltern groups and minorities, and sometimes weaken these movements by recruiting talented leaders for their own purposes (Petras 1999). More importantly, the many actors in the field have notorious substantive differences, and sometimes work in opposing directions. NGOs and interest groups frequently focus on issues that may be mutually conflicting, e.g. environmental interests and labor interests. Even within separate movements incompatibilities may occur, for instance between workers in rich and poor countries. The majority of the TSMOs organize around issues of human rights, although especially in the low-income countries they often engage with multiple issues. And finally, the arrival of a new wave of globalization and its concurrent ideology of "free markets" has simultaneously weakened some actors, while it has strengthened others.

We live in a transitional period in which many challenges can no longer be dealt with by national authorities, and not yet (if ever) by supranational or world authorities. "In the contemporary global world, there is no equivalent of the nation-state at the world level that could implement fiscal and welfare policies, anti-trust controls, labor and environmental laws aimed at regulating markets and at correcting market failures. Nor is there a world independent judiciary which can control and sanction illegal behavior. Nor is there a democratic polity at the world level" (Martinelli 2005: 247). This helps to explain the "negative" attitude of many social movements that say "no" to certain developments and have no positive alternative, because this would require a world authority. Nevertheless, transnational action focused on states is even possible under these adverse circumstances – either by pressing national governments to coordinate policies across

borders, or by exemplary local activities that can inspire movements in other parts of the world (Ferrara 2008).

1.7.2 Movements in Decline

A comparison between some declining and rising social movements can illustrate uneven development. National liberation movements have been extremely important during a large part of the twentieth century, but have currently lost much of their impetus.

Labor movements are the "classical" social movements, but they have been severely enfeebled as well by the political and economic changes of the last 40 years. Their core consists of three forms of social movement organizations: cooperatives, trade unions, and workers' parties. All three organizational types played key roles in social progress, but are now in crisis.

After World War II, consumer cooperatives have lost much of their competitive advantages over other shop-owners: chain stores, central purchasing organizations, self-service stores, supermarkets, shopping centers and the like, resulting in increasing financial difficulties. A serious dilemma made itself felt: either they could merge with a regular capitalist business, become a limited liability company, or borrow substantial amounts from banks – in each case, they ceased to be autonomous cooperatives; or, they could counter the rising competition through modernization and operational expansion – thereby increasing the considerable social distance between members and administrators, as well as further reducing involvement among the members and thereby undermining the organization's cooperative nature (Van der Linden 2008).

Independent mass trade unions have been seriously weakened. Union density (union members as percentage of the total labor force) generally has been declining (see e.g. Van der Linden 2016). The largest umbrella organization, the International Trade Union Confederation (ITUC), estimated in 2014 that about 200 million workers worldwide belong to trade unions, and that 176 million of these are organized in the ITUC. The ITUC also estimates that the total number of workers is roughly 2.9 billion (of whom 1.2 billion are in the informal economy). Therefore, global union density currently amounts to no more than 7 percent (ITUC 2014: 8). The weakness of the unions has several causes.

Firstly, the composition of the working class is changing. Unions find it difficult to organize employees in the service or financial sector. The rapidly growing informal economy is complicating things further, since workers change jobs frequently and have to earn their income under often very precarious conditions. An additional factor is the "labor supply shock" (Freeman 2010) which has manifested itself since the early 1990s. Through the entry of Chinese, Indian, Russian, and other workers into the global economy, there has been an effective doubling of the number of workers producing for international markets over the past two decades.

Secondly, significant economic shifts have taken place. The growth of foreign direct investment in the core countries and the semi-periphery

1

of the world economy has been impressive, and multinational corporations and multistate trading blocs (EU, North American Free Trade Agreement, Mercosur, etc.) have multiplied. Brazil, India, and especially China are important new players who change the rules of the game. This is accompanied by new supranational institutions, such as the World Trade Organization, established in 1995.

Thirdly, in many countries there has been a strong neoliberal offensive against the old-style unions and their modus operandi: national legislation enfeebled trade unions, the dominant practice of collective bargaining has increasingly become decentralized, and individualized labor contracts have become much more widespread than before. Weakened trade unions therefore have to face more and more competition from alternative structures that are better adapted to the new-style labor relations. In Brazil, South Africa, the Philippines, or South Korea, militant workers' movements (social movement unions) have emerged (Scipes 2014). The ineffectiveness of old-style unions is underlined by the growing tendency on the part of international trade secretariats (now called Global Unions) to engage in the direct recruitment of members in the periphery. We may think, for example, of the activities of the Union Network International (the global union for the service sector) relating to IT specialists in India.

Labor, social-democratic, and communist parties are generally considered to be political representatives of the working class. The oldest parties, the social-democratic and labor parties, are not doing very well electorally. All "classical" parties of this type in Europe, Australia (and, in a sense, Brazil) have reached their apex in the past, at least for the time being, varying from the 1930s (Switzerland) to the early twenty-first century (Portugal and Brazil) (see Van der Linden 2016). More important is, though, that this family of parties is struggling with a fundamental identity problem. Social-democratic and labor policies have since the 1930s/40s been based on two pillars: social Keynesianism and a specific "red" party subculture with its own sports associations, women's clubs, organizations for nature lovers, consumer cooperatives, newspapers, theatre groups, and the like.

The sociocultural and economic reversal since the 1960s/70s toppled both "pillars" of the social Keynesian stage, as the parties' subcultural networks fell to pieces and social Keynesianism became less feasible. A great many challenges had to be met more or less simultaneously. Traditional centralism had to be reconciled with basic democratic movements and feminism with the conventional androcentric culture. Moreover, the environmental movement needed to be taken seriously without abandoning the pursuit of economic growth (the condition for social redistribution in a capitalist context). Generalized confusion resulted in a tremendous increase of floating voters; ageing and decreasing membership numbers; and the virtual disappearance of active proletarian members.

Communist parties are the second major political form. For most of them the high point was in the 1940s. Now, many communist parties are having a hard time. In quite a few countries the parties have been dissolved after electoral decline, splits, or financial bankruptcy. In other countries, formerly powerful parties have lost much of their influence.

Overall we can say that on a world scale, consumer cooperatives have either not been doing well, or they have morphed into retail industries without members democratically controlling the business. Trade unions are not only a weak force, but their power is also decreasing; and in many countries trade unions have lost their natural allies, the workers' parties, either because these parties have disappeared or because they have adopted a variant of neoliberalism. As a consequence, INGOs and NGOs have partly shouldered activities that traditionally would have been the responsibility of the international trade union movement, such as the struggle to regulate and abolish child labor.

1.7.3   Movements on the Rise

While globalization and pro-market tendencies weakened traditional labor movements, these same trends had a more ambiguous impact on some other movements. The so-called second wave of feminism which manifested itself since the 1960s had generally been abating from the late 1970s or 1980s, but received a new impetus from the 1990s. In quite a few countries – but certainly not in all – the impact of feminist activities has increased. While there have been many gains for the feminist movement, as Nancy Fraser (2013) points out, many of the "gains" have gone to support liberal (and pro-capitalist) feminist agendas that focus on women's empowerment through greater participation in the market. In contrast, some of the more radical critiques put forward by second-wave socialist feminists and others who criticized societies that overvalued paid labor and careerism, failed to acknowledge or remunerate caring labor, and imposed barriers to collective action in support of women's rights have been sidelined. At the same time, while a growing number of corporations have taken on certain aspects of the liberal feminist agenda, these initiatives are often at odds with the calls from postcolonial and other critical feminists in the Global North and South to recognize and challenge the ways in which the expansion of global "flexibilized" capitalism and the intensification of corporate power has perpetuated forms of gendered, class-based and racialized inequality (Roberts 2015).

This version of feminism is often espoused by elite Western women and is epitomized by Facebook Chief Operating Officer Sheryl Sandberg. In her bestselling book, *Lean In* (2013) Sandberg urges women to achieve advancement by "leaning in" to demand greater recognition and voice in the workplace. The movement linked to this campaign (coordinated through leanin.org) has received the support of hundreds of corporate "partners," including some of the world's largest corporations such as Coca-Cola and Pepsico, Wal-Mart, Google, Facebook, and others. While much second-wave feminism (at least in the Global North) was critical of the patriarchal welfare state, which was organized around the norm of the male-breadwinner, the new corporate feminism endorses dual-earning households and the new "flexibilized" capitalism, leaving issues of feminized care work largely unanswered and the retreat of the state from social provisioning largely unchallenged. These shortcomings take on a related but distinct form as this version of feminism is extended to the Global South where it manifests itself in terms of a business-friendly solution to the connected problems of gender inequality and poverty. Thus, while there are some progressive aspects to the notion endorsed by the World Bank (2011) and a growing number of public and private actors that gender equality is "smart economics," this has also created some foreclosures to progressive feminist action as corporate-driven development has effectively been removed as objects of critique (Roberts and Soederberg 2012).

Human rights movements have become widespread, and have enlarged their field by including economic justice and women's rights (e.g. the struggle against gender-based violence). Of special importance has been the spread of the internet: "Because the nature of human rights violations often necessitates rapid action, a tool like the internet that can provide immediate, cheap dissemination of information to a wide international audience is invaluable" (Forsythe 2009: 188). LGBTQ movements have been doing well, and since the beginning of the millennium same-sex marriages have been granted in an increasing number of countries or certain subjurisdictions.

Environmentalist movements have probably never been larger than in recent years. Climate change in general and global warming in particular have been a major stimulus for mobilization. "In the West environmental movements focus on consumption, productive use of natural resources and conservation or protection of natural resources." In other parts of the world, e.g. South Asia, "such movements are based on the use of, as well as control over, natural resources" (Puja Mondal: www.yourarticlelibrary.com/essay/environmental-movements-around-the-world/31425/).

Numerous are the movements that try to protect or improve social conditions on a local level, varying from the Bolivian "Water Wars" of 2000, and the massive South Asian campaign against the Narmada dam, to the Argentinian piqueteros, and the Brazilian Sem Terra movement. There are also interesting consciousness-raising initiatives such as the All India People's Science Network with a membership of 700,000, which takes up public issues that are intimately related to popular needs and aspirations, such as education, health, and the environmental impact of development projects and the idea of people's participation in development programs; it also fights superstition and threats to secular values.

In addition, there is, what one could perhaps call, a movement for small-scale self-organization and autonomy. Small workers' cooperatives are widespread nowadays. A report of the International Co-operative Alliance estimates that there are worldwide about 11 million workers who co-own the enterprise for which they work (Roelants, Hyungsik, and Terrasi 2014: 8). Many self-employed tried to protect themselves against sickness or other adversities by founding small mutual-aid societies with a common fund that is used to help members in need. Peer-to-peer exchange and collaborative consumption initiatives (sharing economy) seem to be on the rise.

But there are also rising movements that are not necessarily progressive, and may even deflect the struggle for progress. The social void, which especially labor organizations have allowed to emerge, is partly filled by religious and nationalist movements, which offer their supporters elementary forms of social security and trust networks, as well as self-esteem and clear life goals. Many poor people are drawn into such movements, in all their variants – from the Pentecostalist movements of Latin America and Sub-Saharan Africa, to Salafism in North Africa, the Middle East, and Central Asia. Precarious youth in

capitalist industrial cities likewise appear sometimes to be attracted to groups offering a new religious certainty. A typical example is the Hindu-fascist Shiv Sena movement, which gained influence after the defeat of the big textile workers strike in Bombay in 1980–1981. The social plagues of casualization, immiseration, increasing petty crime and trafficking made the Shiv Sainiks popular very fast. They offered the poor not only honor, status, and self-respect, but also cooperated with yellow "trade unions," which offered some protection (Heuzé-Briguant 1999).

1.7.4 Supranational Public Authorities

The so-called globalization process has contradictory effects on rights. Rights can be seen as claims enforced by public authorities. Unenforceable claims or claims that are privately enforced should not be considered as rights in a strict sense (Hohfeld 1978). Some scholars believe that the current changes "threaten all rights embedded in states, including workers' rights" (Tilly 1995: 6). Other scholars have stressed that globalization is not replacing the state. "If globalization has reduced the state's power in one respect, the process has made the state more indispensable in another, that is as the central mechanism for redistributing the social income between social classes and regions" (Hobsbawm 1995: 43). It has been pointed out that "the threats to workers' rights taking place in the high-income countries as a result of globalization are not necessarily paralleled in countries where the welfare state hardly has been built. Transnational investment in fact has thrived on the existing lack of workers' rights in export-processing zones" (Benería 1995: 47). Under certain circumstances globalization can even generate pressures in favor of workers' rights, for instance when workers in advanced countries feel threatened by the competition of their fellow workers in low-wage countries.

In any case, rights are only rights if a public (national or international) authority is capable and willing to enforce them. In the field of labor rights, for example, the ILO is a crucial institution. Its conventions, if ratified by member states, are guidelines for good practices at shopfloor level. However, two weak spots of the ILO have to be stressed. Not only is the ILO a relatively powerless organization; it is also rather slow in its response to new developments. The ILO could therefore use some streamlining, but more importantly, it could use additional competences. A necessary first step would be that the ILO should be given the possibility to further develop its monitoring and reviewing capacity. The ILO case illustrates that, because rights are publicly enforceable claims and states are losing some of their guaranteeing capacity, bigger innovations are required. We will then need more powerful international agencies as guarantors of social rights.

1.8 Challenges and Possibilities for Social Progress

Ever since it came onto the agenda the notion of social progress has been hotly contested and always controversial. Many people have had good reason to deny its pertinence, while others contest its assumed positivity. Current doubts and ambivalence are not unique: beliefs in the existence and/or the possibility of progress have always had their historical ups and downs. In contemporary history, a period of strong belief in social progress and high hopes for its continuance was the era running from about 1950 to 1980, in spite of being lived under the risk of a thermonuclear Third World War. It was the time of the arrival of mass consumption and of the extension of social rights in the well-off quadrant of the world. In Asia and Africa it was the time of national independence movements coming to fruition through the "New Emerging Forces" of the Bandung meeting. In Latin America it was the years when the high modernist capital city Brasilia was built, and when new futures were proclaimed, on the one hand by the Cuban revolution and on the other by the "Alliance for Progress." It was the moment of triumph and a peak of strength of mass social movements firmly believing in progress in the North, of national liberation movements in Asia and Africa, of trade unions and workers parties in the developed capitalist world, and of the Communist movement, for a while basking in the glory of the Sputnik and the spread to Asia and Latin America.

That world of the recent past, however, is now bygone. This is not the place to explain why, but we have to highlight how the stage for debates and struggles of progress has changed dramatically to give us the situation we face today. A historical conjuncture favorable for social progress includes four crucial pillars: a vision of a positively different society; inclusive institutions and/or mass movements for collective identity and action; widespread individual resources and freedom of action; and movements of the "damned of the earth," i.e. of the socially disadvantaged. A belief in progress needs a horizon of an achievable better world. It requires an inclusive social vehicle with room for the mass of the population to reach this better world. This belief is further strengthened and sustained by a large number of individuals experiencing a sense of empowerment. Finally, for social progress to be general, nobody should be left out, which requires individual empowerment and collective action by the most disadvantaged.

In the post-World War II period, there were the visions of coming mass consumption-cum-upward social mobility, of welfare states with extensive social rights, of national liberation, and of socialism. The national welfare and developmental states were inclusive institutions, and so were the labor and nationalist movements sustaining or fighting for them. The spread of education, at different levels in different parts of the world, urbanization, and industrialization provided individual opportunities. Labor movements, Feminism, Latin American populism, and national liberation and civil and human rights movements mobilized and organized the disadvantaged, including the most vulnerable.

Today socialism has largely disappeared from the horizon (except to some extent in Latin America) and the still existing welfare states are struggling to maintain themselves. Discretionary consumption and a middle-class life have become discernible to large, but still mostly minority populations of Asia, Latin America, and Africa, but outside East Asia it is not (yet) widely convincing. In Europe, North America, and Japan these prospects no longer inspire or hold out much hope for people. On the contrary, for a growing number of younger people in

particular, middle-class consumerism is appearing increasingly fragile or elusive.

The inclusivity of the nation-state is challenged, in different ways, from two sides, from the mobility of capital and from the mobility of labor. The former constrains the economic resources of the state, the latter complicates and sometimes disrupts the existing concept of citizenship. Many inclusive popular mass movements and organizations have been eroded or fragmented. Explicitly exclusivist movements and currents, ethnic and religious, have seen a considerable resurgence and even seize the state.

Significant minorities are holding two opposite and delimited visions of a different future. One is focused on technological advances only without any perspective of broad social progress, another is envisaging a society of no growth and of reduced consumption in the rich countries as the only way to avert a climate catastrophe. In this situation, what could be a realistic vision of social progress?

One credible and unifying vision of social progress might be that of *universalizing and advancing human capability*. We noticed at the outset of this chapter that because of revolutionary technological and biomedical advances, economic development, long-term social inclusion, through cutting down (if by no means doing away with) ancient institutionalized racism and sexism, and because of a huge growth of ecological and climate knowledge, humankind is standing at a historical peak of its possibilities. Social progress will mean realizing these possibilities.

The crucial inclusive institution has to be global in order to be able to face up to the challenges of the planetary ecosystem as well as of universalizing the capability of every human being. For the foreseeable future, this global institution is unlikely to look like a cosmopolitan world. Rather, it will be a human community of nations. Currently, however, not even that is a short-term realizable prospect. Nations are increasingly divided economically and are ideologically polarized. Most nations are in need of reconstitution and an awareness of global challenges might contribute to it. What will happen to the existing global climate agreements will be the most pertinent indicator of progress in this respect.

Global and regional international institutions are stronger and more influential than 50 or 25 years ago, the United Nations and its family of specialized organizations, the Group of Twenty, the European Union, the African Union, the Association of Southeast Asian Nations, the Community of Latin American and Caribbean States, etc. There is also a wider and denser net of globally networked social movements and of humanitarian and human rights NGOs. There are more NGOs working for global inclusion and public goods than ever before. But there are also new and increasingly active exclusivist currents in the world. Some global steps against international tax havens and money laundering are being discussed at international levels of power, but not even embryonically is there a global institution in sight for regulating the world economy – i.e. global capitalism – in a direction of human equality and the planetary common good.

Individual empowerment is expanding with extended education and extralocal digital connectivity, providing wider opportunities for women in most parts of the world, and generating international youth and children's cultures. But this empowerment is often hemmed in by increasing social segmentation and mounting employment crises.

New movements for collective empowerment of the most disadvantaged have emerged, of indigenous peoples, of informal workers, of urban slum-dwellers, for example. But they are usually much weaker than the great labor and liberation movements of the past. Indeed, the informalization and precarization of work, with their denial or minimization of workers' rights seems be the predominant tendency.

In conclusion, a relaunch of global social progress in tandem with technological and biomedical advances – i.e. a new Great Transformation – is not beyond the realms of possibility even though its short-term prospects look modest. Inclusive global institutions, sustained by inclusive global movements and networks, increased individual empowerment worldwide, by education, connectivity and stronger health, and organizational rights and possibilities for the world's most disadvantaged are prerequisites. They are all aimed at universalizing human capability. Both old and new social movements will be part of this seemingly utopian enterprise and there will be both national and regional tendencies also pointing toward social transformation.

References

Anderson, B. 2000. *Doing the Dirty Work? The Global Politics of Domestic Labor.* London: Zed.

Anderson, B. 2007. "A Very Private Business: Exploring the Demand for Migrant Domestic Workers," *European Journal of Women's Studies* 14/3: 247–264.

Arat-Koç, S. 2006. "Whose Social Reproduction? Transnational Motherhood and Challenges to Feminist Political Economy," in M. Luxton and K. Bezanson (eds.), *Social Reproduction: Feminist Political Economy Challenges Neo-Liberalism.* Montréal & Kingston: McGill-Queen's University Press.

Asian Development Bank 2011. The Role of the Middle Class in Economic Development: What Do Cross-Country Data Show. www.adb.org

Beck, U. 2000. *The Brave New World of Work.* Cambridge: Polity Press.

Benería, L. 1995. "The Dynamics of Globalization," *International Labor and Working-Class History* 47(Spring): 45–52.

Bowen, A., and C. Hepburn 2013. "Prosperity with Growth: Economic Growth, Climate Change and Environmental Limits," in R. Fouquet (ed.), *Handbook on Energy and Climate Change,* Cheltenham, UK: Edward Elgar.

Brecht, H., U. Deichmann, and H.G. Wang 2013. A Global Risk Index. Policy Research Working Paper 6506, Washington, DC: The World Bank.

Brenner, R. 2002. *The Boom and the Bubble: The U.S. in the World Economy.* New York: Verso.

Carothers, T., and R. Youngs 2015. *The Complexities of Global Protests.* Washington: Carnegie Foundation.

Casassas, D., and P. Wagner (eds.) 2016. "Modernity and Capitalism", special issue of *European Journal of Social Theory* 19/2.

Case, A., and A. Deaton 2015. "Rising Morbidity and Mortality among White Non-Hispanic Americans in the 21st Century," *PNAS* 12/49.

Castells, M. 2010. *End of Millennium, 2nd edn. with a New Preface.* Chichester, UK: Wiley Blackwell.

Castles, S., H. De Haas, and M. Miller 2014. *The Age of Migration: International Population Movements in the Modern World,* 5th edn. New York: Guilford Press.

Chee, M.W.L. 2003. "Migrating for the Children: Taiwanese American Women in Transnational Families. Wife or Worker?," in N. Piper and M. Roces (eds.), *Asian Women and Migration.* Lanham, MD: Rowman and & Littlefield.

Connell, R.W. 1995. *Masculinities.* Berkeley: University of California Press.

Cox, R. 2006. *The Servant Problem: Domestic Employment in a Global Economy.* London: I.B. Tauris.

Cruz, M., J. Foster, B. Quilinn, and Ph. Schellekens 2015. "Ending Extreme Poverty and Sharing Prosperity: Progress and Policies," World Bank Policy Research Note. www.worldbank.org

Delgado Wise, R., and D. Martin 2015. "The Political Economy of Global Labour Arbitrage," in K. van der Pijl (ed.), *Handbook of the International Political Economy of Production.* Cheltenham, UK: Edward Elgar.

Economist Intelligence Unit 2013. "Rebels Without a Cause: What the Upsurge in Protest Movements Means for Global Politics." London: Economist, www.eiu.com/ProtestUpsurge.

Ehrlich, P., and J. Holden 1971. "Impact of Population Growth," *Science* 171/3977: 1212–1217.

Elson, D. 2010. "Gender and the Global Economic Crisis in Developing Countries: A Framework for Analysis," *Gender and Development* 18/2: 201–212.

European Women's Lobby 2012. *The Price of Austerity: The Impact on Women's Rights and Gender Equality in Europe.* Brussels: European Women's Lobby.

Ferrara, A. 2008. *The Force of Example.* New York: Columbia University Press.

Fleurbaey, M., and D. Blanchet 2013. *Beyond GDP. Measuring Welfare and Assessing Sustainability.* Oxford: Oxford University Press.

Forsythe, D.P. (ed.) 2009. *Encyclopedia of Human Rights,* Vol. 5. Oxford: Oxford University Press.

Fortune 2015. Global 500, Retrieved from http://fortune.com/global500/ (last accessed December 21, 2017).

Fraser, N. 2013. *Fortunes of Feminism: From State-Managed Capitalism to Neoliberal Crisis.* London: Verso.

Freeman, R. 2010. "What Really Ails Europe (and America): The Doubling of the Global Labor Force," *The Globalist,* March 5.

Fukuyama, F. 1992. *The End of History and the Last Man.* New York: Avon Books.

Glaser, B. (ed.) 1987. *The Green Revolution Re-Visited: Critique and Alternatives.* London: Allen & Unwin.

Gordon, R.J. 2016. *The Rise and Fall of American Growth.* Princeton and Oxford: Princeton University Press.

Harvey, D. 1989. *The Condition of Postmodernity: An Enquiry into the Origins of Cultural Change.* London: Basil Blackwell.

Harvey, D. 2003. *The New Imperialism,* Oxford: Oxford University Press.

Heuzé-Briguant, G. 1999. "Populism and the Workers Movement: Shiv Sena and Labour in Mumbai," *South Asia: Journal of South Asian Studies* 22/2 (December): 119–148.

Hobsbawm, E. 1995. "Guessing about Global Change," *International Labor and Working-Class History* 47 (Spring): 39–44.

Hochschild, A.R. 2000. "The Nanny Chain," *American Prospect* 11/4: 32–36.

Hohfeld, W.N. 1978. *Fundamental Legal Conceptions as Applied in Judicial Reasoning,* ed. Walter Wheeler Cook. Westport, CN: Greenwood Press, c. 1919.

Huang, S., S.A. Yeoh, and N. Abdul Rahman 2005. *Asian Women as Transnational Domestic Workers.* Singapore: Marshall Cavendish Academic.

Huang, S., L.L. Thang, and M. Toyota (eds.) 2012. *Global Networks. Special Issue: Transnational Mobilities for Care: Rethinking the Dynamics of Care in Asia.* Oxford and Malden, MA: Blackwell.

ILO 2006. *Changing Patterns in the World of Work.* Geneva: International Labour Office.

ILO 2012. *The Global Employment Trends for Women.* Geneva: International Labour Office.

ILO 2014. *World of Work Report. Developing with Jobs.* Geneva: International Labour Office.

ILO 2015. *World Employment Social Outlook. The Changing Nature of Jobs.* Geneva: International Labour Office.

Iredale, R., F. Guo, and S. Rozario (eds.) 2002. *Return Skilled Migration and Business Migration and Social Transformation.* Wollongong: Centre for Asia Pacific Social Transformation Studies.

ITUC 2014. *Building Workers' Power. Congress Statement.* Berlin: International Trade Union Confederation.

Jackson, T. 2009. *Prosperity Without Growth, Economics for a Finite Planet.* London: Earthscan.

Kabeer, N. 2015. "Gender, Poverty, and Inequality. A Brief History of Feminist Contributions in the Field of International Development," *Gender and Development, special issue: Inequalities* 23/2: 189–205.

Kannan, K.P. 2014. *Interrogating Inclusive Growth: Poverty and Inequality in India.* Routledge: New Delhi and Oxon.

Kannan, K.P. 2016. "At the Bottom of Durable Inequality: The Status of India's Dalits and Adivasis." Paper presented at the Collective Book Workshop, Department of Anthropology, London School of Economics, June 30–July 1, London.

Kochhar, R., and R. Fry 2014. "*Wealth Inequality Has Widened along Racial, Ethnic Lines since the End of Great Recession.*" Pew Research Center, December 12.

Kofman, E. 2012. "Rethinking Care through Social Reproduction," *Social Politics* 19/1: 142–162.

Lefebvre, H. 1991. *The Production of Space.* Oxford: Blackwell.

Levine, R.S., J.E. Foster, R.E. Fullilove, M.T. Fullilove, N.C. Briggs, P.C. Hull, B.A. Husaini, and C.A. Hennekens 2001. "Black-White Inequalities in Mortality and Life Expectancy, 1933–1999: Implications for Healthy People 2010," in *Public Health Reports* 116, September–October: 474–483.

Lindert, P.H., and J.G. Williamson 2016. *Unequal Gains.* Princeton and Oxford: Princeton University Press.

Maddison, A. 2007. *Contours of the World Economy, 1-2030 AD.* Oxford: Oxford University Press.

Martinelli, A. 2005. "From World System to World Society?" *Journal of World-Systems Research*, 11/2: 241–260.

Mayer, A. 1985. *The Persistence of the Old Regime. Europe to the Great War.* New York: Pantheon.

McKinsey Global Institute 2013. *Financial Globalization. Retreat or Reset?* McKinsey & Co. (June). Retrieved from www.mckinsey.com/global-themes/employment-and-growth/financial-globalization (last accessed December 21, 2017).

Milanovic, B. 2013. "Global Income Inequality in Numbers: in History and Now," *Global Policy* 4/2: 198–208.

Milanovic, B. 2016. *Global Inequality.* Cambridge, MA: The Belknap Press of Harvard University Press.

Munck, R. 2016a. "Global Sociology: Towards an Alternative Southern Paradigm," *International Journal of Politics, Culture and Society* 29/3: 233–249.

Munck, R. 2016b. "Globalisation, Labour and the Precariat: Old Wine in New Bottles?" in C. Schierup and M.B. Jorgensen (eds.), *The Politics of Precarity. Migrant Conditions, Struggles and Experiences.* Leiden and Boston: Brill.

Nayyar, D. 2013. *Catch Up.* Oxford: Oxford University Press.

Ohmae, K. 1995. *The End of the Nation-State: The Rise of Regional Economies.* New York: Simon & Schuster Inc.

Olzhansky, S.J., T. Antonucci, L. Berkman, R.H. Binstock, A. Boersch-Supan, J.T. Cacioppo, B.A. Carnes, L.L. Carstensen, L.P. Fried, D.P. Goldman, J. Jackson, M. Kohli, J. Rother, Y. Zheng, and J. Rowe 2012. "Differences in Life Expectancy Due to Race and Educational Differences Are Widening, and Many May Not Catch Up," *Health Affairs* 31/8: 1803–1810.

Onuki, H. 2016. "The Neoliberal Governance of Global Labor Mobility: Migrant Workers and the New Constitutional Moments of Primitive Accumulation," *Alternatives* 41/1: 3–28.

Ortiz, I., S.L. Burke, M. Berrada, and H. Cortes 2013. World Protests 2006–2013. Initiative for Policy Dialogue and Friedrich-Ebert-Stiftung New York Working Paper No. 274.

Oxfam 2016. An Economy for the 1%. Oxfam Briefing Paper.

Oxfam 2017. An Economy for the 99%. Oxfam Briefing Paper.

Petras, J. 1999. "NGOs: In the Service of Imperialism," *Journal of Contemporary Asia* 29/4: 429–440.

Piketty, Th. 2014. *Capital in the Twenty-First Century.* Cambridge, MA: Harvard University Press.

Polanyi, K. 1944. *The Great Transformation,* New York: Farrar & Rinehart.

Putnam, R.D. 2015. *Our Kids.* New York: Simon & Schuster.

Ranis, G., F. Stewart, and A. Ramirez 2000. "Economic Growth and Human Development," *World Development* 28/2: 197–219.

Reis, E. 2004. "The Lasting Marriage between State and Nation Despite Globalization," *International Political Science Review* 35/3: 251–257.

Roberts, A. 2015. "The Political Economy of 'Transnational Business Feminism': Problematizing the Corporate-Led Gender Equality Agenda," *International Feminist Journal of Politics* 17/2: 209–231.

Roberts, A., and S. Soederberg 2012. "Gender Equality as Smart Economics? A Critique of the 2012 World Development Report," *Third World Quarterly* 33/5: 949–968.

Roelants, B., E. Hyungsik, and E. Terrasi 2014. *Cooperatives and Employment. A Global Report.* Brussels: International Co-operative Alliance.

Sandberg, S. 2013. *Lean in: Women, Work, and the Will to Lead.* New York: Random House.

Scipes, K. 2014. "Building Global Labor Solidarity Today: Learning from the KMU of the Philippines," *Class, Race and Corporate Power* 3/1: Article 4. http://digitalcommons.fiu.edu/classracecorporatepower/vol3/iss1/4 (last accessed December 21, 2017).

Seol, D.-H. and J.D. Skrentny 2009. "Why Is There So Little Migrant Settlement in East Asia?" *International Migration Review* 43/3: 578–620.

Smith, J. 2005. "Exploring Connections between Global Integration and Political Mobilization," *Journal of World-Systems Research* 11/2: 255–285.

Strange, S. 1996. *The Retreat of the State: The Diffusion of Power in the World Economy.* Cambridge: Cambridge University Press.

Sturgeon, T.J. 2003. "What Really Goes on in Silicon Valley? Spatial Clustering and Dispersal in Modular Production Networks," *Journal of Economic Geography* 3/2: 199–225.

Steffen, W., K. Richardson, J. Rockström, S.E. Cornell, I. Fetzer, E.M. Bennett, R. Biggs, S.R. Carpenter, W. de Vries, C.A. de Wit, C. Folke, D. Gerten, J. Heinke, G.M. Mace, L.M. Persson, V. Ramanathan, B. Reyers, and S. Sörlin 2015. "Planetary Boundaries: Guiding Human Development on a Changing Planet." *Science* 347, 1259855.

Tarkiainen, L.. P. Martikainen, and M. Laaksonen 2013. "The Changing Relationship between Income and Mortality in Finland, 1988–2007," *Journal of Epidemiology and Community Health* 67/1: 21–27.

Theodoru, A.E., and A. Sandstrom 2015. "*How Abortion is Regulated Around the World,*" Pew Research Center. www.pewresearch.org/fact-tank/2015/10/06/how-abortion-is-regulated-around-the-world/ (last accessed December 21, 2017).

Therborn, G. 2004. *Between Sex and Power. Family in the World, 1900–2000.* London: Routledge.

Therborn, G. 2006. *Inequalities of the World.* London: Verso.

Tilly, Ch. 1995. "Globalization Threatens Labor's Rights," *International Labor and Working-Class History* 47(Spring): 1–23.

Tilly, Ch. 1999. *Durable Inequality.* Berkeley: University of California Press.

Tschakert, P. 2016. "The Role of Inequality in Climate-Poverty Debates," World Bank Policy Research Working Paper 7677. www.worldbank.org

UN 2015a. The Millennium Development Goals Report. www.un.org

UN 2015b. *World Population Prospects. The 2015 Revision,* New York. http://esa.un.org/unpd/wpp/ (last accessed December 21, 2017).

UN Population Division 2009. *International Migrant Stock: The 2008 Revision.* New York: UN Population Division. www.un.org/esa/population/migration/UN_MigStock_2008.pdf (last accessed December 21, 2017).

UNCTAD 2015. *International Trade and Development Statistics.* United Nations, Geneva. Available online.

UNDESA 2013. Population Data Sets. United Nations, Department of Economic and Social Affairs, Population Division.

UNDP 2009. *Human Development Report 2009: Overcoming Barriers: Human Mobility and Development.* New York: United Nations Development Programme. http://hdr.undp.org/en/reports/global/hdr2009/ (last accessed December 21, 2017).

UNDP 2014. *Human Development Report 2014.* New York: United Nations Development Programme.

UNDP 2015. *Human Development Report 2015.* New York: United Nations Development Programme. www.undp.org

UNFPA 2015. *State of the World's Population 2015.* New York: United Nations Population Fund. www.unfpa.org

Van der Linden, M. 2008. *Workers of the World. Essays toward a Global Labor History.* Leiden and Boston: Brill.

Van der Linden, M. 2016. "Global Labour: A Not-So-Grand Finale and Perhaps a New Beginning," *Global Labour Journal* 7/2: 201–210.

Wagner, P. 2016. "Democracy and Capitalism in Brazil, South Africa and Europe," in G. Rosich and P. Wagner (eds.), *The Trouble with Democracy. Political Modernity in the 21st Century.* Edinburgh: Edinburgh University Press.

Walzer, M. 1994. *Thick and Thin: Moral Argument at Home and Abroad.* Notre Dame, IN: University of Notre Dame Press.

Weiss, L. 1998. *The Myth of the Powerless State.* Ithaca: Cornell University Press.

WHO 2015. *World Health Statistics 2015*. Geneva: World Health Organization. www.who.org

World Bank 2008. World Development Indicators Database. World Bank 2011. *World Development Report 2012: Gender Equality and Development*. Washington, DC: The International Bank for Reconstruction and Development/The World Bank.

World Bank 2012. *Turn Down the Heat: Why a 4°C Warmer World Must Be Avoided*. Washington, DC: World Bank. http://documents.worldbank.org/curated/en/2012/11/17097815/turn-down-heat-4%C2%B0c-warmer-world-must-avoided (last accessed December 21, 2017).

World Bank 2013. *World Development Indicators*. Washington, DC: World Bank.

World Bank 2015. *World Development Indicators*. Washington, DC: World Bank.

World Co-operative Monitor 2015. Brussels: International Co-operative Alliance. www.monitor.coop

Xing, Y., and C. Kolstad 2002. "Do Lax Environmental Regulations Attract Foreign Investment?" *Environmental and Resource Economics* 21/1: 1–22.

Yeates, N. 2012. "Global Care Chains: A State-of-the-Art Review and Future Directions in Care Transnationalization Research," *Global Networks* 12/2: 135–154.

1

2

Social Progress: A Compass

Coordinating Lead Authors:[1]
Henry S. Richardson, Erik Schokkaert

Lead Authors:[2]
Stefano Bartolini, Geoffrey Brennan, Paula Casal, Matthew Clayton, Rahel Jaeggi, Niraja Gopal Jayal, Workineh Kelbessa, Debra Satz

Contributing Authors:[3]
Gustaf Arrhenius, Tim Campbell, Simon Caney, John Roemer

---

[1] Affiliations: HR: Georgetown University; ES: University of Leuven.
[2] Affiliations: SB: University of Siena; GB: Australian National University; PC: Catalan Institution for Research and Advanced Studies, University of Pompeu Fabra; MC: University of Warwick; RJ: Humboldt University; NGJ: Jawaharlal Nehru University; WK: Addis Ababa University; DS: Stanford University.
[3] Affiliations: GA, TC: Institute for Futures Studies Stockholm; SC: Oxford University; JR: Yale University.

Summary

This chapter sets out the main normative dimensions that should be used in assessing whether societies have made social progress and whether a given set of proposals is likely to bring progress. Some of these dimensions are values, bearing in the first instance on the evaluation of states of affairs; others are action-guiding principles. Values can inspire and in that sense also guide actions. Principles aim to offer more specific guidance on how to rank, distribute, and realize values. Recognizing a multiplicity of values and principles is important not only to being respectful of the variety of reasonable views about what matters but also because it is difficult to reduce the list of dimensions that ultimately matter to a shorter one in a way that reflects all aspects of the phenomena in question. Many of the chapters that follow will explicitly address only a subset of these values and principles: the ones most salient for their issues or areas; but in principle, all remain relevant.

This chapter's principal contributions are its listing of basic values and principles (set out in Table 2.1), its interpretation of each of them, and its defense, so far as space permitted, of the suggestion that each of these has basic or nonderivative importance.

Any use of these basic values and principles in guiding or assessing social progress should be guided by respect for the equal dignity of all persons (Section 2.2). The values of well-being and freedom are each of pervasive importance; each has also been interpreted in importantly different ways, which the chapter distinguishes (Section 2.3). Other basic values relevant to social progress include values directly important in individuals' lives – nonalienation, esteem, solidarity, and security – and values embodied in the environment and in human culture.

Table 2.1 | Where to find the values and principles that define the compass

Cross-cutting considerations
The principle of equal dignity: Section 2.2.3.1
Respect for pluralism: Section 2.2.3.2
Basic values
Well-being: Section 2.3.1
Freedom: Section 2.3.2
Nonalienation: Section 2.3.3
Solidarity: Section 2.3.4
Social relations: Box 2.3
Esteem and recognition: Section 2.3.5
Cultural goods: Section 2.3.6
Environmental values: Section 2.3.7
Security: Section 2.3.8
Basic principles
Of general applicability:
Basic rights: Section 2.4.2
Distributive justice: Section 2.4.3
Beneficence and generosity: Section 2.4.5
Applicable to governments:
The rule of law: Section 2.6.2.1
Transparency and accountability: Section 2.6.2.2
Democracy: Section 2.6.2.3
Giving rights determinate reality: Section 2.6.2.4
Applicable to civil society:
Toleration: Section 2.6.3.1
Educating and supporting citizens: Section 2.6.3.2
Applicable to global institutions:
Global justice: Section 2.6.4

There are also principles of nonderivative importance in evaluating and fostering social progress (Section 2.4). We argue that respect for basic rights is the most uncontroversial principle of social justice. While libertarians argue that justice consists solely in respecting those rights, we present a set of distributive principles that go beyond respect for basic rights: equality of opportunity (luck), egalitarianism, prioritarianism, and maximin. We discuss the distributive implications of utilitarianism and the potential of other maximization approaches. Finally we argue that even if a society were perfectly just, it might still have to rely in cases of urgent need on the beneficence and generosity of individuals.

These values and principles can be used to assess the social progress of a variety of different institutions, groups, and practices that embrace different sets of agents (Section 2.5). They can apply to civil society groups, nations, and to the global human society. It is also possible to extend their reach to future generations and to nonhuman animals.

Attending to this variety of agents reveals the need to note additional principles that are not uncontroversially derivable from more generally applicable principles (Section 2.6). Some principles are especially applicable to governments, such as the rule of law and the rights of political participation. Other principles are of special significance for civil society or for global institutions and transactions.

Despite their multiplicity, these basic values and principles can be translated into a set of concrete indicators relevant for specific policy domains (Section 2.7). Concrete indicators will always give a narrowed interpretation of the underlying objectives. Evaluating whether a change does or would constitute social progress requires an intelligent conversation on how tradeoffs between different objectives should be handled and on how moral and feasibility constraints should be taken into account.

2

2.1   The Compass for This Report

This full Report is an ambitious attempt to assess social progress along many dimensions. The idea of social progress implies a positive development, a change for the better. Our Report is predicated on accepting that the idea of progress makes sense: e.g. that the abolition of slavery is a good thing. Nonetheless, a person can embrace the ideal of social progress without accepting it as a fact. That is, she can be skeptical about the extent to which current conditions constitute improvements over past conditions. She may also disagree with others with respect to what social progress consists in.

All views of social progress depend on identifying the dimensions along which progress is being measured or defined as well as the relevant indicators and benchmarks for comparison. For example, someone who thought that social progress should be assessed with respect to the standard of living might think that real consumption is the relevant measure of social progress. From our perspective, any such one-dimensional model is too simple, even if one thinks that the material standard of living is *an* indicator of progress. For there is a plurality of value dimensions along which social conditions differ – not only the standard of living, but also freedom, social inclusion, sustainability, and so on. Moreover, because these values are multiple, they can conflict and tradeoffs are often unavoidable.

This chapter provides what its authors take to be the most important normative dimensions for making comparisons. Our aim is to provide the key, nonderivative values and the important principles for guiding action that can be used to generate a "report card" for assessing social policies and institutions. The subsequent chapters of this overall Report further elaborate the various elements of social progress in ways appropriate to specific arenas of social life. Our hope is that this chapter contains the main elements from which these more specific elaborations take guidance. A second purpose of this chapter is to provide a framework for tracking improvements along the various evaluative dimensions. For example, what exactly is involved in an improvement in freedom or human well-being?

Further, the very idea of progress entails that we can identify a general line of direction. It is here that we hope the metaphor of a compass can be illuminating. A compass helps you understand where you are in the space around you. It locates your starting point relative to other points and thus provides an orientation for any journey you wish to take. While our map is complex and the destination is multifaceted, the goal of this chapter is to set the general line of travel. Users of this compass may disagree about details of a goal while agreeing that some changes mark improvements. But we cannot do without information about goals altogether if we are to assess social changes.

The best path forward is often a winding one. Sometimes you have to go south to get around the bay in order to eventually go further north. To know if going south should be viewed as positive or negative change, you need to see how this change relates to the direction you want to go in. You also need to know whether taking one path rather than another locks you in to a particular destination. Not all paths can be retraced. Indeed, some improvements may lie off all already given paths.

There are two caveats to note with respect to the role of our compass in this Report. First, to decide the best path to follow, you also need to assess how feasible any given path is. A compass cannot provide that information. A map will help, but sometimes even the best guidebook is out of date, and one is left uncertain which paths are passable. We may not yet have sufficient evidence for what policy measures best improve educational outcomes in poor countries or what system of global regulations best addresses climate change. In many cases we must make our decisions under conditions of risk – situations where we do not know the outcomes but can measure the probabilities (think of a coin toss). And sometimes we must make decisions under conditions of uncertainty, where we do not have enough information to even know anything about the probabilities. We often have no way to know whether heading south around the bay will get us to the north. Beyond this, what works best for going north in one context may not work best in a different one. Societies vary in the challenges they face and in their resources for meeting those challenges. Feasibility constraints also differ: what is possible in one society may not be possible in another.

Second, it is inevitable that people will disagree about the weightings of the various values with respect to each other, as well as about the best principles of action to use for policy purposes. Sometimes empirical evidence can help narrow the scope of disagreements but that is not always the case. Working out what to actually do under circumstances of disagreement, nonideal conditions, and risk and uncertainty is a complex exercise.

2.2   Building Blocks of the Analysis

In this section, we set out the most basic normative concepts we use in setting out our compass and the cross-cutting normative assumptions that guide how we develop it.

2.2.1   Values vs. Principles

The moral compass we set out rests on a distinction between values and principles. Values refer to those states of affairs, or aspects of states of affairs, that (other things equal) we have reason to realize. Human well-being, freedom, a nonalienated life, social solidarity, a healthy sustainable environment are items that ought to be promoted or respected. By contrast, principles give agents – individuals, civil society groups, political communities, and global institutions – more precisely specified norms to guide their conduct. For example, societies and global institutions ought to respect principles for the fair and efficient distribution of benefits and burdens; governments ought to be transparent, follow the rule of law, and respect citizens' rights. Before setting out the various values and principles that inform our compass, we offer some general remarks about the evaluation of states of affairs and the moral norms that limit our pursuit of them (2.2.1). We then draw a distinction between basic and derivative values (2.2.2) and specify two moral ideas – equal dignity and respect for pluralism – that are the foundation of the compass (2.2.3).

Box 2.1 | The History of the Idea of Progress

Our simple conception of progress as an improvement over time should not be confused with the Enlightenment conception of progress, which implied that history or social evolution builds in a deep *tendency* toward improvement. Progress, on this eighteenth-century European understanding, does not simply happen, but is the result of an ongoing and irresistible process.

This idea of progress's irresistible forward march arose from the idea that history has a meaning and a direction. This idea is found in many thinkers, including Kant, Hegel, and Marx. Although each of these thinkers described the driving force behind inexorable overall progress differently, each saw the dynamics of social change as embedding a "logic of history." The subject of progress, as they conceived it, was humanity or the human species as such; the inevitable progress was general, not local. This idea of a universal subject of progress underwrote a more general expectation that the world's different cultures and values would converge, while the Enlightenment's optimism supported the view that the outcome would realize moral progress and give everyone a fulfilling life.

Today we are confronted with a loss of trust in this Enlightenment idea of progress, leading some to talk about the "end of progress" (Allen 2015). Many doubt that world history is in fact inexorably following a single predicted path toward a convergent future in which developments in technology enable human needs to be satisfied and peoples to live peaceably together. The claim that progress is guaranteed by some deep dynamic underlying human affairs has become less plausible. For example, disastrous effects of growth on the environment have suggested that technological progress can go together with social or moral decline. Postcolonialist critics of the Enlightenment conception have highlighted the Eurocentrism of its linear model of progress and its purportedly unified view of history. Any discussion of progress in the twenty-first century needs to avoid Eurocentrism and claims to inevitability. Our compass takes on board a pluralism that allows for progress in one domain at the same time as regress in another domain.

2.2.1.1 States of Affairs

Assessing the nature and extent of social progress often takes the form of evaluating states of affairs, the way things are in the world. For example, other things equal, lower infant mortality is generally regarded as better than higher mortality, because infant deaths are bad. We typically judge different states of affairs by assessing the extent to which good items are present and bad things are absent.

Two observations are important in evaluating states of affairs. First, having a cardinal measure is useful in circumstances where we must make probabilistic calculations – for example, if an action may produce state A (better than the status quo S) or B (worse than S), but we are uncertain which, then we need to know the differences between A and S and between B and S to have a sense as to whether that action will be desirable. Second, it is important to acknowledge that, because certain items have such different characters, outcomes might be incommensurable (cannot be placed on a cardinal scale of overall value) or incomparable (cannot be given a determinate place in an ordinal ranking) (see Chang 1998).

2.2.1.2 The Need for Principles: Moral Constraints and Options

If the evaluation of states of affairs were all that mattered to judgments concerning progress, our task would be exhausted by providing a complete account of good and bad items – or different *aspects* of goodness and badness. Nevertheless, as important as it is to attempt to compare different states of affairs, we should not equate social progress with the realization of better states of affairs. For one thing, distinct histories can make a difference to how it is reasonable to promote social progress. The judgment that country A is better, all things considered, than country B, given their different social norms and different circumstances, does not necessarily imply that country B should try to be more like country A. It may be reasonable for country B instead to opt to improve things consonantly with maintaining its freely chosen path.

In addition, sometimes, although an outcome A is better than a different outcome, B, it would be a mistake to try to achieve A because doing so would violate *moral side-constraints* that forbid certain kinds of action. For example, although reducing infant mortality is an important goal, that does not imply that one is morally permitted to steal others' money to pay for medicines to serve that goal. Certain kinds of action are morally prohibited even if their performance would improve outcomes. This observation is particularly important for a theory of social progress, because it highlights the fact that realizing a better state of affairs via the only available means might be morally wrong.

To assess social progress solely by evaluating states of affairs would also be to overlook the importance of *moral options*. To give a simple example, many hold that a political community is sometimes morally permitted to choose not to pursue policies that it has most reason to pursue: it may host the Olympic Games even though it would do more good if its resources were spent on other projects. The idea of moral options suggests that even though an outcome would be best, all things considered, individuals or political communities might be entitled to act in ways that fail to realize it.[4]

Taking these thoughts about moral constraints and options together, we distinguish between two aspects of normative assessment. First, we can seek to evaluate states of affairs as good or bad, or better or worse than others, without attending to the question of how those states of affairs are produced. Call this the "substantive" level of normative assessment. Second, a normative assessment can focus not on states of affairs but rather on the manner in which those states are produced. This latter aspect, which we might call the "process" aspect, often involves an appeal to principles that bear directly on what individuals or collective agents do. Some schemes of normative assessment might be purely process-focused, in the sense that the only feature of evaluation is how the states of affairs were produced – e.g. whether they were the result of democratically adopted policies. Our view is that anyone assessing a society's progress should take into account both substantive and procedural elements. One wants to know both whether the society, and the individuals in it, are enjoying valuable outcomes and how well the processes and procedures of the society – its systems of justice, governance, economic regulation, mutual accommodation, and the like – are performing.

2.2.2   Basic vs. Derivative Values

We can collapse some parameters of evaluation into other aspects when those parameters are derivative from more basic ones. The economists' preoccupation with gross domestic product (GDP) per head, for example, is explained by a concern for individual well-being, the common view being that increased income means increased preference satisfaction and that preference satisfaction is the metric of well-being. On this view, it is individual well-being that matters, normatively, not GDP/head. If increased GDP/head involved *reduced* preference satisfaction, or increased preference satisfaction involved *reduced* individual well-being, there would be grounds for modifying the use of GDP/head as an evaluative tool for those cases.

It is helpful to distinguish between *nonderivative* values or principles – those that are sought or respected for their own sake – and *derivative* ones – those that are sought for the sake of something else. Of course, there are disagreements about which values and principles are derivative and which nonderivative. These debates are complicated by the fact that there are many causal and conceptual connections among them all. Our attempt in this chapter has been to limit ourselves to discussing values and principles that seem to us to have nonderivative normative importance. Thus, for example, we treat as distinct the basic liberty to choose one's diet and the health-related well-being that ensues from one's choice.

Many items that have derivative value are instrumentally valuable – valuable because they are productive of a basic value. The "free market" is a familiar case in point. We value the market order because (and to the

extent that) it produces greater material well-being and greater liberty (or perhaps over some periods of history and in some domains, greater equality). There is a proper distinction here between means and ends and we think it fetishistic to value the means independently of the ends which they promote. As Milton Friedman observed, disagreements about the free market are often not primarily disagreements about values but about facts – facts concerning how markets operate and the effects they have on well-being, liberty, or individual virtue. These are matters of fierce ideological contestation. But in principle they are matters resolvable by appeal to evidence and debate among people of goodwill.

Derivative values include not only items that are valuable instrumentally. For example, we might value equality neither for its own sake (that is, nonderivatively) nor because it is a means of promoting a different value such as well-being (i.e. for its instrumental value), but because it is a *constitutive* feature of a larger ideal, such as the ideal of a political community that displays fraternity or solidarity.

In addition to keeping in mind the distinction between nonderivative and different kinds of derivative value, it is important, when we evaluate social progress, to recognize that some items serve us as *proxies* or *indicators* of progress: they are *evidence* of the presence of those items that are valuable for social progress instrumentally, constitutively, or nonderivatively.

It seems clear that in the arena of action, these institutional pointers will occupy an important role. We assess societies by reference to whether they embody well-functioning democratic political systems or deliver tolerable economic outcomes for citizens. We do this recognizing that such assessment is partial, provisional, and always susceptible to challenge on factual grounds – and always answerable to the basic values and principles.

2.2.3   Two Foundational Ideas

2.2.3.1   Equal Dignity

Many declarations of human rights begin with an expression of the equal dignity of human beings. In the words of *The 2030 Agenda for Sustainable Development*, "the dignity of the human person is fundamental" (United Nations 2015). Two elements of equal dignity are worth spelling out. The first is the claim that every human being matters.[5] It is not enough for equal dignity for everyone to believe that *his or her own* life matters. Rather, the principle of equal dignity asserts that *everyone's life matters* and requires each to recognize and honor that fact.

The second is the idea that humans enjoy *equal* dignity. On the most demanding interpretations of equality our attention is *comparative*: however we treat individuals or groups, we must not treat some more favorably than others (Dworkin 2011). The more modest, rhetorical, reading makes the *noncomparative* claim that everyone is entitled to a certain kind of consideration: on this view, a person's entitlements do not depend on the extent of others' entitlements (Raz 1986).

---

4   The terms "moral constraint" and "moral option" were, so far as we are aware, coined by Kagan (1989).

5   This is not the claim that only human lives matter: see Section 2.3.6.

Affirming equal dignity does not deny that individuals have special obligations to particular others such as their own family or their co-citizens. Rather it serves to prohibit certain attitudes and activities – racism and sexism, for example – that cannot be reconciled with the equal importance of everyone. More controversially, it places certain demands on us, to ensure that everyone's basic needs are satisfied to the best of our collective ability.

2.2.3.2   Respect for Pluralism

Any account of social progress must acknowledge the fact that people and societies disagree about what makes outcomes good or bad and actions right or wrong. In the context of such disagreement, any conception of social progress will be controversial and must avoid the Eurocentrism of the Enlightenment conception of progress (Box 2.1). But how noncontroversial should our compass be? At one extreme, we might try to articulate a compass that is acceptable to as many as possible in the light of the distinctive convictions about ethics, religion, and morality they hold. However, a moment's reflection suggests that such a compass would be unattractive: there are very many people who hold deeply repugnant views and a conception of social progress that failed to challenge such views would itself be seriously inadequate.

But the other extreme must be avoided as well. At that end of the spectrum are conceptions that treat everyone's beliefs about religion, morality and ethics as fundamentally irrelevant to the project of identifying social progress. The worry about this approach is that it can be alienating. Part of the role of a compass is to give individuals a conception of social progress that they can understand and embrace as their own, and to provide a basis for social unity (see Rawls 2005). For these reasons, the values and principles of the compass should be ones that reasonable people can, in good faith, regard as their own – as ones that follow from or, at least, are not inconsistent with their deeply held convictions.

Steering a course between these two extremes is an account that takes people's distinctive beliefs seriously but avoids incorporating egregious moral mistakes (Nagel 1991). How that course is set out in detail is a matter of judgment. Plainly, our compass should acknowledge the equal moral worth of human beings regardless of race, ethnicity, gender, age, talent, and social position. Thus, racist views that deny this basic principle of equal dignity need not detain us in the design of our compass. But it would be wrong for our compass to be presented as mandating the acceptance of a particular religious doctrine, since people can reasonably differ in their religious beliefs and attitudes.

2.3   Basic Values

For many people, social progress just means an increase in average or total individual well-being (and perhaps an improvement in its distribution). But people also care about how their well-being is produced: they care about their freedom of choice and about their social standing. In this chapter, we treat such values as freedom and esteem as independent basic values.

2.3.1   Well-being

At the outset, it is helpful to distinguish between two different questions that relate to the value of well-being. First, when we ask "what does human well-being consist in?" we often mean to ask "what makes one's life go well?" According to some, a person's life going well can be aptly described in terms of the achievement of a single final end. Different theories of what that end is have been proposed. Hedonists argue that well-being consists in having the mental state of pleasure and lacking that of pain; others claim that an individual's life goes better to the extent that her preferences are satisfied; and still others claim that there is an objective list of goods to which we should refer to judge how well an individual's life has gone or is going (for a brief survey, see Parfit 1984, appendix I).

The second question concerns our metric for comparing different individuals for the purposes of making distributive decisions. If our aim is to reduce inequality in well-being or to give priority in decision-making to the most disadvantaged, we need to be able to compare the situations of different individuals in the right way, to identify the level of advantage of different individuals and how much more or less they would be advantaged by a particular policy. Some refer to this task as making "interpersonal comparisons of well-being."

It might seem natural to think that the idea of well-being used for making interpersonal comparisons just is well-being in the sense of what it means for an individual's life to go well and, indeed, some do take this view. But others believe that when making interpersonal comparisons for the purpose of guiding distributive decisions it would be wrong to adopt one's preferred conception of what fundamentally makes an individual's life go well; wrong, perhaps, because it would be a disrespectful response to the moral and religious disagreements prevalent in modern societies (Dworkin 2000; Rawls 2005).

2.3.1.1   Multidimensionality in Well-being

What dimensions of well-being should be included in our analysis of well-being, once we grant that there is a distinction between how the concept functions for an individual and how it is to be used for social assessment? The capability approach "concentrates on the capabilities of people to do things – and the freedom to live lives – that they have reason to value" (Sen 1999: 85). But which capabilities? Consider how proponents of that approach answer this question. Nussbaum (2000, 2006) proposes as universally valid a list of ten "central capabilities." Sen (1999, 2009), on the other hand, argues that the list should not be defined by theoreticians, but should be drawn up in a participatory process through public reasoning.

A difficult question is about the relationship among the different dimensions. Should they be seen as incommensurable or is it possible to aggregate them into one measure of individual well-being? If one takes the former position, how should one handle interpersonal comparisons involving a tradeoff between the different variables? If one takes the latter position, how should the aggregation across dimensions be conceived?

2.3.1.2 Different Conceptions of Well-being: Happiness, Capabilities, Preferences

In this section we compare four different conceptions of well-being: a resourcist conception, a hedonistic conception, the capability approach, and a preference-based conception. The first three of these are "objective" in that they offer substantive and unvarying components of well-being. The preference based view is "subjective" in that it gives only a formal characterization of an individual's well-being, allowing each individual to fill in the content differently. These relationships are summarized in Table 2.2.

Resources

Some argue that if all relevant commodities could be bought on a market, giving people equal resources would give them equal opportunities for well-being, while leaving them freedom to use these resources as they choose. There are a few difficulties with this equation of resources with well-being. In the first place, not all relevant dimensions of well-being can be bought on the market – think about health or the quality of the natural environment. Second, differences among people will mean that the same level of resources will not provide equal opportunity for well-being. For instance, how well-nourished people are depends not only on how much they eat, but also on the varying characteristics of their bodies and activities. Providing someone with serious disabilities with equal resources as someone without those disabilities is unlikely to result in their having equal opportunity for well-being.

Utility and Happiness

One of the most striking phenomena in the recent social science literature is the rapidly growing interest in the analysis of individuals' happiness at a given time and of their evaluation of their life satisfaction, as measured by simple questions in large opinion surveys. If one is willing to accept the answers from the surveys as an interpersonally comparable measure of well-being, one obtains from each of these sorts of data a ready-to-use one-dimensional measure expressed on a convenient scale.

Are the happiness and life satisfaction measures simply two ways of getting at the same thing? The suggestion that they are is contested by most psychologists. They see "subjective well-being" as a multifaceted experience with at least two components: feelings and cognitions. For the cognitive component, individuals have to take some distance when formulating a judgment over their life. Positive and negative emotions, on the other hand, come in a continuous flow and are related to pleasures and pains as understood by Jeremy Bentham (1970). We will accordingly take the two measures to suggest two alternative views: in basing the evaluation of individual well-being on feelings of happiness, it suggests "hedonic welfarism;" "preference welfarism," by contrast, starts from judgments about what is a valuable life.

In recent decades, important social philosophers such as Dworkin have criticized any approach that defines well-being solely on the basis of

Table 2.2 | Conceptions of well-being

Objective, state of mind	Objective, not state of mind	Subjective
Happiness	Resources	Preferences
	Capabilities and functionings	

mental states of either sort. Sen (1985a) elegantly summarized many of these arguments by pointing out that subjective welfarism suffered from two problems. The first he calls "physical-condition neglect": "A person who is ill-fed, undernourished, unsheltered and ill can still be high up in the scale of happiness or desire-fulfillment if he or she has learned to have 'realistic' desires and to take pleasure in small mercies" (Sen 1985a: 21). Interestingly, the recent work on subjective well-being has produced convincing empirical evidence that adaptation of this sort is indeed a pervasive real-world phenomenon.

The second problem is "valuation neglect." Valuing a life is a reflective activity in a way that "being happy" or "desiring" need not be (Sen 1985a: 29). If an acceptable approach to well-being should explicitly take into account this valuational activity by the persons themselves, then hedonic welfarism must be rejected. Feeling well is important to individuals, but it is not the only consideration entering their assessments of life.

Whatever the stance taken on welfarism, "it would be odd to claim that a person broken down by pain and misery is doing very well" (Sen 1985a: 17). In any multidimensional approach, how well or poorly someone is feeling is a relevant dimension, just not the only dimension.

Functionings and Capabilities

The origins of the capability approach are to be found in a series of influential papers and monographs, written by Amartya Sen and Martha Nussbaum. We have seen that Sen considers subjective welfarism unacceptable because of the problems of "physical condition-neglect" and "valuation neglect." On the other hand, focusing exclusively on income or on material resources would not do justice to the heterogeneity of human beings, either. As mentioned above, personal and environmental characteristics determine what people can achieve with a given amount of resources. According to Sen (1985a), these achievements, i.e. what the person manages to do or to be – such as being well-nourished, well-clothed, mobile, being able to appear in public without shame – are what really matter for well-being.

Sen further claims that a description of well-being in terms of achieved functionings is not yet sufficient, however, because it does not integrate the essential notion of freedom. His classic example involves the comparison between two individuals who are both undernourished (Sen 1985a). The first person is poor and cannot afford to buy sufficient food. The second person is wealthy and so capable of eating sumptuously but freely chooses to fast for religious reasons. While they achieve the same level of nourishment, it would be strange to say that they enjoy the same level of well-being. Therefore Sen suggests that well-being be understood in terms of capabilities (Sen 1985b: 200), defined as the set of functionings vectors that are accessible to the person, i.e. the set from which they can choose.

The capability approach is inherently multidimensional. In fact, many of its proponents (including Nussbaum) emphatically reject the idea that the different life dimensions are commensurable. But as soon as we are interested in the inequality of well-being, the possible interferences and complementarities among the different dimensions can no longer be neglected. Functioning in domains facing risk is associated with "corrosive disadvantage," where a disadvantage in one domain is likely to spread its effect to other domains – from hunger to unbearable debt for instance. By contrast, functionings are "fertile" when achievement in one domain carries over benefits to another domain. Friendship helps people to secure their health and also their jobs. The most disadvantaged in society are those who experience a clustering of several disadvantages and who therefore find it most difficult to get out of poverty unless the ties among these disadvantages are broken.

Preference-Based Well-being

The most popular version of preferentialism is the economic view of respect for (consumer) preferences as revealed in choice behavior. The booming literature on behavioral anomalies has undermined the attractiveness of this approach, however. People are often imperfectly informed or follow suboptimal decision heuristics when taking decisions. A more attractive version interprets "preferences" as reflecting people's well-informed and well-considered ideas about what is a good life. On this interpretation, preferences, in addition to reflecting desires, also have a strong cognitive "valuational" component.

It would be a mistake to think that a preference-based view of well-being necessarily coincides with that based in individual reports of happiness or subjective life satisfaction. Recall the earlier example of poor people who report high levels of satisfaction because their aspirations have adapted to their situation. A preference-based notion of well-being should respect individuals' well-informed ordinal preferences about what constitutes a good life, but correct for differences in aspirations. Here is one proposal (see e.g. Fleurbaey and Blanchet 2013; Decancq et al. 2015). The basic ideas are presented more formally in the box on preferentialism and equivalent income. Choose reference values for all the nonincome dimensions of life. Then define the "equivalent income" as the level of income that would make the individual indifferent (as judged by his own convictions) between his current situation and the hypothetical reference situation where he would be at these reference values for all nonincome dimensions. If the individual reaches these reference values, his income and his equivalent income coincide. In general, the difference between the income and the equivalent income measures the loss in well-being that results from deviations from that reference level, and this loss is dependent on individual preferences.

The attractiveness of preference-based approaches, including the idea of equivalent income, depends not only on the ethical assumption that idealized preferences are a good indicator of well-being, but also on it

being psychologically meaningful to suppose that individuals do have such idealized preferences. As psychological research has shown (e.g. Kahneman 2011), this is far from obvious.

2.3.2 Freedom

As we noted in Section 2.3.1.2, in connection with capabilities, people value not only the goods they achieve but also the freedom they enjoy in pursuing them. Because freedom relates to the processes by which we achieve goods, there are principles associated with it, which we come to in Sections 2.4 and 2.6; but freedom is also a basic value – and in fact it has been claimed over and over again that the realization of freedom is the normative core of modern societies (Honneth 2015).

However, quite different and to some extent incompatible ideas have been associated with the concept of freedom. We can make some initial headway by asking what the opposite of – or the key obstacle to – freedom is. Some possible candidates:

*   *Coercion*: I am unfree when someone coerces me or I am coerced to do something;
*   *Heteronomy*: I am unfree when I am not self-determined – when I do not govern my life autonomously or "by my own law";
*   *Alienation*: I am unfree if I am "foreign to myself" in anything I do, when I do not experience my own activities and plans *as* my own.

We can bring some order into this variety by turning to the famous distinction between negative and positive freedom (Berlin 1975). Negative freedom, for Berlin, is "freedom from" (in particular from external coercion and the interferences of others). Positive freedom, in contrast, refers to "freedom to" do certain things that are considered essential for individual self-determination or self-realization (Geuss 1995).

On the first (negative) conception, I am most free when I can do what I want with the least hindrance and obstruction by others. The goals I pursue are not up for judgment except insofar as they harm others or impede others' freedom – this is the liberal principle of non-intervention. A series of objections has been raised against this negative understanding of freedom: isn't who can do *what* also relevant? Mustn't we assess the goals and the relevant hindrances? Charles Taylor (1985b: 215–16) points out that there are not just external impediments to freedom, but also internal impediments, "when we are quite self-deceived, or utterly fail to discriminate properly the ends we seek." In these cases we have to introduce positive reference points in order to distinguish between hindrances and aspects of our personality: "You are not free if you are motivated, through fear, inauthentically internalized standards, or false consciousness, to thwart your self-realization." Moreover it is questionable whether we can speak of freedom without considering the material preconditions of realizing freedom and thus also the social conditions in which people act. Philip Pettit (2001) has argued that it is not enough that one happens not to be interfered with, for it matters that one would remain protected against interference even if others' attitudes toward one changed.

According to some philosophical perspectives, freedom is a more fundamental and demanding basis for assessing social progress than is well-being. To exemplify how a conception of freedom that could play such a role might be built up, we will briefly set out a multilevel analysis based loosely on Hegel. It casts negative and positive freedom as complementary aspects of a more complex ideal. We can build this idea up in a series of steps, understanding freedom, successively, as:

1. not being hindered from doing what I want (negative freedom, absence of external coercion);

2. doing what I want *most* (which already calls on us to set our valuational priorities and rules out manipulation and internalized coercion);

3. doing what I *really* want, i.e. which corresponds to who I really am (drawing in the idea of authenticity; see Taylor 1985a: 15–44);

4. doing what I can *rationally* want (an idea that may correspond to Kant's conception of freedom as rational autonomy or self-legislation);

Box 2.2 | Preferentialism and Equivalent Income

Figure 2.1 illustrates the distinction between respecting individual preferences and using subjective well-being measures. For this graphical representation, we restrict ourselves to two dimensions (income and health), but this is only for illustrative purposes. The indifference curves in the figure indicate which combinations of income and health are equally good in the light of the individual's conception of the good life.

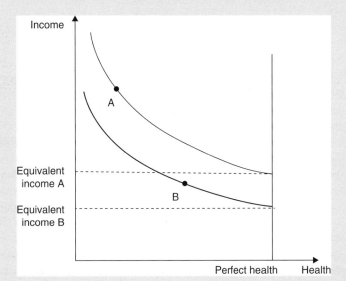

Figure 2.1 | Equivalent income.

In the situation depicted in this figure, both the individual in life A and the individual in life B agree that the life in A is better than the life in B. Yet it is possible that the individual in life A has high expectations and aspirations and therefore attaches low satisfaction scores to both situations, whereas the individual in B has low expectations and gives high satisfaction scores to both situations. In this case, it is possible that individual A scores her own life lower than individual B scores his own life.

The challenge is to formulate a measure of individual well-being that respects individual preferences when individuals have different ideas about what constitutes a good life. Such a situation is represented in Figure 2.2. Consider first the case where the two individuals are both in situation X, having precisely the same income and health. Despite the fact that they are in the same "objective" situation X, it can be argued that the individual with the "steeper" indifference curve is worse off than the individual with the "flatter" indifference curve: she cares more about her health outcomes and, hence, more strongly disvalues being sick. This illustrates the importance of taking into account the fit between situations and preferences.

However, it is possible to argue that in some comparisons of life situations differences in preferences do not matter for the measurement of well-being. This may occur when the two individuals both enjoy perfect health as the individuals in A' and B'. When both individuals are in perfect health, one can compare their well-being on the basis of their incomes irrespective of their preferences, the argument goes.

Box 2.2 | (continued)

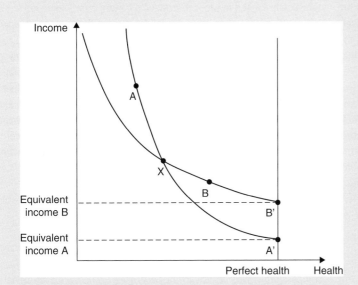

Figure 2.2 | The role of preferences.

Consider now the individuals in A and B in Figure 2.2. According to their preferences, the individual in A is equally well-off as in A' and the individual in B is equally well-off as in B'. Given that we can evaluate the lives A' and B' on the basis of the incomes, we can also evaluate A and B on the basis of these incomes. These hypothetical incomes for A and B have been called "equivalent incomes."

5. doing what accords with those social institutions and practices that I take part in, participation in which is essential for my self-understanding (social freedom as set out in Hegel 1973).

Whereas (1) describes negative freedom and (2) represents a transitional step, (3), (4), and (5) represent positive conceptions of freedom. On the fifth understanding, my freedom depends on realizing those desires of mine that accord with the social institutions that make the realization of my freedom possible in the first place. This fifth conception thus integrates individual and social perspectives on freedom. I am free in this role precisely because I can realize something that is important to the social institutions that undergird my freedom. Much more would need to be said about what it takes for social institutions to undergird freedom in this sense. It should be plain from this sketch of this conception, however, that the idea of freedom, so developed, states a demanding standard for assessing social progress.

Seen in the light of these arguments, a purely negative conception of freedom seems peculiarly thin. In response, advocates of liberalism such as Berlin and Taylor (1985b) object that the positive notion of freedom is not only vague but courts paternalistic if not authoritarian and totalitarian consequences. It would allow us to mask efforts to force people to live in accordance with reason as promoting their positive freedom. Advocates of a negative conception of freedom insist among other things that freedom also consists precisely in doing what does not agree with the demands of reason or of social convention. In response, it is urged that negative freedom is incomplete, because

there can be no adequate individual freedom in the mere coexistence of individuals alongside one another, but rather only in the context of a system of social cooperation in which social institutions adequately embody the idea of freedom (in ways set out in Section 2.6.2.4). The moral of this criticism of negative freedom cannot be that we should throw it overboard, but rather that we need to situate it in a broader context in which the complementary meaning of positive freedom can also emerge. We are deceiving ourselves if we think that we are already free merely in the absence of external hindrances: in these circumstances we can also be unfree if we are in thrall to our drives or involuntary impulses, or if we cannot relate to the social institutions that shape our own lives as ones that we can make our own and that can thus enable our freedom.

2.3.3 Nonalienation

Alienation is the inability to establish a minimally satisfactory relationship of identification with or personal engagement with other human beings, things, social institutions and thereby also – as the theory of alienation emphasizes – with oneself (Jaeggi 2014). An alienated world presents itself to individuals as insignificant and meaningless, as a world that is not "one's own," in which one is not "at home." For instance, Karl Marx argued that workers experience their labor as alienating. One can speak of alienation "wherever individuals do not find themselves in their own actions" (Habermas 1993). Thus understood, alienation does not describe the simple absence of something, but rather a defective relation.

Another characteristic of alienation is that one can be alienated only from those things or relations that are nonetheless in some sense "one's own." The social roles in which someone can be considered "alienated from themselves" are roles played by that same person. Desires that we doubt are really "ours" are so confusing, precisely because they are at the same time undoubtedly our desires. And the social institutions that seem alien to us are the same institutions that we have created and that we reproduce.

Alienation weaves together two different elements: firstly, a *loss of power*: alienated relations are relations in which we as subjects are – or at least experience ourselves to be – disempowered. And secondly, a *loss of meaning*: an alienated world is a senseless world, a world we don't experience as meaningful or relate to in a meaningful way. On this understanding of alienation, there is a direct conceptual connection to freedom: insofar as our freedom presupposes that we can take ownership of what we do and the conditions in which we do it, overcoming alienation is a precondition for realizing freedom.

2.3.4 Solidarity

As the African proverb reminds us, "rain does not fall on one roof alone" (Manser 2007). "Solidarity" refers to a certain sense of belonging or togetherness. If, with the sociologist Émile Durkheim (1964), we understand "solidarity" as "what prevents the breakdown of society," our compass need not include it, for the breakdown of society will register losses in many other values. If instead we understand "solidarity" as referring to widespread dispositions to act in a way that reflects one's mutual attachments, its significance is controversial. One could argue, for instance, that the transition away from reliance on community-based, solidaristic dispositions and toward welfare-state arrangements informed by principles of justice constitutes social progress. Yet some invoke solidarity as the motivational basis of welfare-state arrangements. And some notion of social cooperation seems to be in the background of any principle of distributive justice, even if this fact is seldom acknowledged (Brudney 1999; Rawls 1999a).

Without denying that solidarity can have such instrumental value, this section argues that solidarity can also be seen as a basic value, i.e. that an improvement in solidarity is an independent parameter of social progress. Solidarity so understood is associated with the widespread acceptance of the idea that we somehow "owe to each other" certain ways of acting.

Solidarity, so understood, is distinct from other kinds of social relations. Like friendship, solidarity can be based on a mutual and mutually recognized feeling of attachment, identification, and bonds of obligation. But friendship is a close face-to-face relation between individuals, whereas we can form solidaristic bonds with distant people, with large numbers of people, and even with strangers.

Consider solidarity as it evolves in social movements. Here solidarity is mediated through a common cause that unites a group of people because it stands for something they each identify with. The importance of identification demonstrates that solidarity should not be equated with the shallower common interest of a coalition. To be sure,

solidarity may be based on common interest, for example the common interest of workers during a strike. Yet solidarity seems to express a deeper commitment than is necessary for a coalition, which is opportunistically formed in order to achieve a certain goal. Moreover, many of the attitudes that we consider solidaristic don't seem to be directed to realizing individual self-interest.

Solidarity is something like mutual and mutually aware support among people as they work together in pursuit of common goals considered worthwhile and legitimate. Given this emphasis on the importance of a common goal, we can see that the existence of a common background among people relating face-to-face, such as we find in tight-knit communities, does not guarantee solidarity. On the contrary, small communities can be unsolidaristic. Conversely, there are many instances of the "solidarity of strangers." The decisive question is under which conditions the members – the "we" – of a certain community are able to relate to each other and to act in a solidaristic way.

If we think of solidaristic motivations as an expression of common goals, shared projects, or a common fate, they are also distinct from compassion in two significant respects (see Section 2.4.5 on beneficence and generosity). First, as we have indicated, solidarity, relying on inclusion, involves a kind of mutual awareness wherein one relates one's situation to the situation of the others. Acting out of solidarity means standing up for each other because one recognizes "one's own fate in the fate of the other." Pity or compassion for the other, in contrast, do not necessarily relate the other's to one's own situation, except in the very vague sense of being a vulnerable human being oneself. Most importantly, compassion and altruism are likely to mark the relation between unequals, the relation between those who need and those who provide help. In contrast, solidarity is, at its core, a symmetrical, mutual, and reciprocal relation.

This is not to deny that solidarity has an altruistic aspect. Solidaristic action generally expresses the belief that the success and well-being of others are important to ensuring the flourishing of projects with which I myself identify. Emphasizing the symmetrical and reciprocal character of solidarity thus does not imply denying or underestimating its altruistic dimension. Rather, the most distinctive, attractive, and challenging feature of solidarity is that it seems somehow to transcend the very dichotomy between altruistic and egoistic motivations. Despite its reciprocity, the motivation for solidarity cannot be reduced to the enlightened self-interest of rationally calculating, egoistic individuals. And despite the readiness-to-help involved, this is neither based on compassion alone nor on altruism as such. Neither is the symmetry involved in solidarity the self-interested symmetry and reciprocity of an insurance model, where everyone tries to lower his own risk by sharing it with others.

Solidarity is a shared set of attitudes or dispositions that individuals recognize or are aware of in one another, that motivate them to cooperate in a shared endeavor, and that involve a commitment to that cooperation for its own sake. Achieving solidarity, then, seems to be itself of irreducible value. Solidarity, in which people cooperate with others in ways that accept those others as equals and that jointly express that they care about this cooperation for its own sake, is one of humanity's highest achievements.

Box 2.3 | Social Relations

Confirming what we have learned from behavioral economics, neuroscience, epidemiology, and evolutionary biology, recent studies on human happiness have indicated that human beings are more pro-social than previously imagined. The happiness literature draws not only on the survey information about reported happiness and life-satisfaction mentioned in Section 2.3.1.2 but also on objective data on well-being (suicides, mental diseases, psychotropic drug use, and alcohol addiction). The message emerging from this literature is that several things matter for well-being, including material standards of life; but the quantity and, above all, the quality of social and intimate relationships play a major role in shaping people's happiness. "Relational goods" (Guy and Sugden 2005) are a component of social capital, which also encompasses measures of trust in institutions, voters turnout etc. Individuals with more and better relationships are happier (Helliwell and Putnam 2004; Helliwell 2006; Bruni and Stanca 2008).

In several important ways, economic growth can interfere with relational goods. In the long run, average well-being is more likely to increase in countries where relational goods are increasing rather than in countries where the economy is growing (Bartolini and Sarracino 2014). In contrast, the most celebrated exemplars of growth in recent decades – the US and China – share similar patterns of declining subjective well-being (Brockmann et al. 2009; Stevenson and Wolfers 2013), paralleled by a significant spread of mental illnesses, especially anxiety and depression (Twenge 2000; Diener and Seligman 2004; Wilkinson and Pickett 2009; Case and Deaton, 2015). In these countries, the decline of well-being is largely explained by two driving forces. The first arises from changes in human relationships: an increase in solitude, distrust, familial instability, and generational cleavages and a decrease in solidarity, honesty, and social and civic participation (Bartolini et al. 2013; Bartolini and Sarracino 2015). The second is the upsurge of social comparisons, i.e. the increasing dependency of one's satisfaction with one's economic achievements on the achievements of those with whom one compares oneself (Brockmann et al. 2009; Bartolini and Sarracino 2015). A social crisis can be an engine of economic growth. In fact, money offers many forms of protection – real or illusory – from relational poverty. If the elderly are alone and ill, the solution is a caregiver. If our children are alone, the solution is a babysitter. If we are afraid, we can protect our possessions with alarm systems, security doors, private guards, etc.

Responding to the decay of a society's relational goods and infrastructure by relying on such private goods can yield a vicious cycle. Becoming accustomed to enjoying more private goods induces us to work and produce more so as to be able to afford them, thereby generating economic growth. The economic growth generated by these mechanisms can in turn fuel relational decay. Indeed, more economic activity can result in less time, attention, and energy devoted to relationships. When growth does have this decaying effect, a process is generated in which growth fuels relational decay and this feeds growth. The outcome of this self-fueling mechanism is a growing affluence of what is private and an increasing scarcity of what is common: relations and the environment (Bartolini and Bonatti 2008).

There is thus a possible dark side to economic growth. Relational goods that are free for one generation become scarce and costly for the next generation and eventually luxury goods for the generation following that. From this perspective, it is crucial to account for the relational goods enjoyed in a society separately from accounting for its economic growth. Economic growth that seriously undercuts human social relations may not count as social progress overall.

2.3.5   Esteem and Recognition

People generally like to be approved of by others; and will do much to avoid being disapproved of. There is a family of related attitudes and statuses of this sort – esteem, approval, honor, glory, respect, repute; and their negatives – disesteem, disapproval, dishonor, disrespect, ill-repute. All depend (perhaps in slightly different ways) on the attitudes of others; and all are such that the positive versions are general objects of desire.

This being so, a preference-based notion of well-being (as set out in Section 2.3.1.2 above) would suggest that one aspect of social progress would be increases in the level of esteem within a society (and decreases in disesteem). However, esteem may be resistant to aggregate increase in this way. In many contexts, esteem seems to be indirectly "positional," because whether one does well or badly in some activity is typically assessed by reference to how well people do on average. So, if to be "honest as this world goes is to be as one picked out of ten thousand" (as Hamlet claims) then being reliably honest will earn considerable esteem. If, on the other hand, one lives in a very honest society then even modest lapses in truthfulness will tend to give rise to disesteem. If everyone increases her level of honesty then that simply tends to raise the prevailing standard and all receive much the same level of esteem as before. One might applaud the increased honesty; one might even think that it is an instance of social progress. But it is a contributor to social progress *in itself* and not because of a general increase in the esteem that people enjoy.

This observation suggests that the main contribution that esteem can make to social progress lies in creating incentives for better performance in arenas where performance contributes to social progress directly (Brennan and Pettit 2004). So, for example, the desire for esteem among their peers may make judges more scrupulous in upholding the requirements of the law. However, the desire for esteem and associated peer pressure may also work for ill. Much depends on the values that prevail within a society – and more especially within the "ponds" that people occupy. If it is routine in a given society to afford honor (esteem/respect) to individuals on the basis of their birth, or membership of a "class" or caste, then the forces of esteem seem objectionable on egalitarian grounds. In such cases, action might be appropriate on two fronts: on the one hand, to change the values on which the esteem in question depends; on the other, to undermine the operation of esteem itself (as one might through suppressing information about the attributes in question).

To be an object of esteem (or disesteem) one must be recognized as "qualifying" for evaluation. Esteem is an intrinsically human phenomenon. One might admire a view; but one doesn't esteem it. This inherently "human" property, and the idea of mutual recognition among persons on which esteem depends, is deeply linked to the fundamental ideal of equal moral standing set out in Section 2.2.3.1. Completely to lack such standing – to be treated routinely as "invisible" for the purposes of generating esteem (and disesteem) – is to lack moral recognition. There is something arguably even worse for someone than to be disesteemed: the situation in which one is nonestimable. The Dalits (formerly "untouchable castes") in India have historically suffered such an extreme fate, and despite punitive legal provisions against it, continue to suffer discrimination. Short of invisibility is failure to be recognized as an equal. While servants can sometimes be esteemed in some ways by those they serve, they are not treated as having equal moral standing. Recognition in this sense is, we think, an element in well-being, but it also a value that goes beyond its contribution to well-being. There is a basic moral requirement that each be afforded recognition of this kind. This requirement is basic not only for the moral reasons set out in Section 2.2.3.1, but also because it concerns the social mechanisms whereby one becomes the very person who one is (Hegel 1977). It will be a contribution to social progress if such recognition is more extensive rather than less (Honneth 1995).

Increasing recognition has two dimensions: one involves promoting the extension of the relevant kind of moral status to larger numbers in society; the other involves extending the *contexts* in which such recognition is afforded. This latter dimension involves the fact that recognition can be specific to domains. Women might be recognized at the food market but not in political discussion. Wider such recognition (in both dimensions) is something to be pursued under the social progress agenda.

2.3.6 Cultural Goods

The progress of human societies is not adequately measured solely by looking at the achievements of those currently alive. Cultural achievements – knowledge, insights, modes of creative and artistic expression, and means of understanding – deserve a separate place on the ledger of social progress because they contribute not only to present well-being but also to future well-being. And some authors contend that they are valuable in their own right, over and above the contribution they make to individual well-being (Taylor 1995). Consider religion, for example. Doubtless, religious activities contribute to the well-being of participants, at least as those participants perceive their well-being; but instead of treating these activities primarily as means to their own well-being, they typically treat them as ends in themselves. Or consider artistic pursuits. The thought is that the quality of a community's musical life, say, is an independent object of value, not to be assessed either in terms of the total amount of money people are prepared to spend on it, or the number of votes it can muster in determining government policies.

Recognizing the contribution of cultural achievements to the future is important in part because they are the fruits of many generations' work and cannot be remade overnight. Many cultural artifacts, along with cultures themselves, are fragile. To be sure, in the flux of human history, many specific forms of cultural expression and items of human knowledge will inevitably – and sometimes thankfully – be lost. The collective maintenance of human memory, however, seems necessary to meaningful human progress. In the words of the Kenyan novelist Ngugi wa Thiong'o (2003), "A people without memory are in danger of losing their soul." This is one reason for the kind of effort engaged in by UNESCO to designate and help protect sites and monuments around the globe as World Heritage Sites.

In addition to working to protect and preserve the knowledge and the cultural forms and achievements bequeathed to them by the past, societies must also work actively to cultivate and build upon their heritage. They must pass on to their descendants as full a range of knowledge and as broad and deep an acquaintance with and engagement in the tremendous variety of modes of human understanding and of expressions of the human spirit as they reasonably can. For the children now alive, the value of these efforts will show up, we may be confident, in the well-being and the freedoms that they enjoy; but for the children and grandchildren of those children, this kind of social effort has an importance that transcends its effects on those who are now alive.

2.3.7 Environmental Values

For most mainstream ethical traditions of the West, humans are the main focus of moral consideration. These ethical traditions often fail

Box 2.4 | Gender Equality

Esteem and recognition matter to everybody. They are, however, particularly important for undervalued groups – even those, like women, that are not numerical minorities. Members of such groups typically have to work harder to achieve a given level of recognition, and their activities, abilities, and achievements tend to be treated as unimportant. The cause of all this tends to be not just deliberate, self-serving bias on the part of the dominant group but also "implicit bias" (Brownstein 2016) on the part of anyone. This sort of bias can extend to members of the disvalued group itself. A lack of protest, then, is not always a sign that the group's current treatment is acceptable.

Women can suffer extreme forms of aggression, including battery, rape, trafficking, and slavery. More frequently, like other members of oppressed groups, they also suffer systematic "microaggressions" (Pierce 1970) such as interruptions, dismissive, disrespectful or aggressive replies, or mockery, which cause its recipients to feel they do not count. The resulting loss of self-esteem can in turn lead to the confirmation of stereotypes because people give up or because they underperform due to the impact the loss of confidence has on their performance (Wilkinson and Pickett 2009: chs. 3 and 8). Women are also paid less than men for equal work, are underrepresented in leadership positions, and bear disproportionate burdens in child-rearing.

Some argue that attempts to break this vicious cycle by deploying affirmative action or quotas are self-defeating, as it can cause everyone to think of the benefit of these policies as falling on the undeserving. However, the history of affirmative action *for men*, particularly white men, shows that it was extremely beneficial to them, and that the status quo is not and has never been a pure meritocracy (Gheaus 2015). As Catharine MacKinnon (1988: 36) famously put it: "Virtually every quality that distinguishes men from women is already affirmatively compensated in this society. Men's physiology defines most sports, their needs define auto and health insurance coverage, their societally designed biographies define workplace expectations and successful career patterns, their perspectives and concerns define quality in scholarship, their experiences and obsessions define merit, their objectification of life defines art, their military service defines citizenship, their presence defines family, their inability to get along with each other – their wars and rulerships – defines history, their image defines god, and their genitals define sex."

By contrast, affirmative action *for women* and other minorities has proven effective at creating new role models, challenging stereotypes, integrating elites, and incorporating their perspectives. Allowing women into traditionally male positions has also allowed us to see more clearly the difference between *sex*, the biological difference between males and females, and *gender*, a social construction including stark distinctions and stereotypes, differentiated roles, biased perceptions, power imbalances, and arbitrary allocations of resources and tasks (Haslanger 2012).

The arbitrariness of gendered divisions – which can be oppressive for both women and men trapped into rigid roles (Hearn 2015) – is perhaps more obvious than that of sexual distinctions. Men and women, however, cannot be neatly separated in two groups even from a purely biological, anatomical, hormonal, chromosomal, or behavioral perspective. Like sexual orientation, sexual identity can be a matter of degree, and such identity has varied across time and space.

Sexist biases are not only unjust, but deprive society as a whole from the contributions of many of its members. Research continues to show that policies of inclusion have benefits for problem solving (Page 2007).

2

to assign intrinsic value to the environment, to the extent that they advocate that the natural environment has instrumental value only. Similarly, although some scholars, institutions, and organizations have persuasively criticized mainstream economic growth theorists, who have defined development in economic terms, they themselves have adopted a human-centered approach to social progress. In 1969, the UN General Assembly stressed that "each Government had the primary role and ultimate responsibility of ensuring the social progress and well-being of its people" (Declarations on Social Progress and Development, Article 8).

What is obvious is that human societies cannot flourish in isolation from the environment. Robust social progress requires a healthy natural environment and the protection of different natural resources. Yet, respect for the natural environment should go beyond its instrumental value for human well-being.

Many contemporary environmental philosophers have defended the intrinsic value of various aspects of the natural environment. Some of these arguments build on human valuations; some do not. The latter arguments present an objectivist version of nonanthropocentric intrinsic value theory (Taylor 1986; Rolston 1988; Attfield 1994, 2003, 2016); the former arguments develop an intersubjectivist version (Callicott 1989).

Some of these philosophers argue that nonhuman animals, at least those with neurophysiological capacity for experiencing well-being and its opposite, have moral standing. On all versions of this nonanthropocentric view, nonhuman creatures have intrinsic value independently of human interests. On objectivist versions, this value is also seen as independent of human valuations. Biocentrists go farther, as they hold that all living beings have intrinsic value and that everything that is intrinsically valuable ought to be the object of moral concern. Creatures that lack feelings have the capacities to grow, flourish, reproduce, and self-repair. Other environmental ethicists have extended the attribution of intrinsic value even beyond living things. For ecocentrists all natural entities are morally considerable. Some of them ascribe nonanthropocentric intrinsic value also to species and ecosystems (e.g. Rolston 2002).

Eugene C. Hargrove (1992) doubted that ordinary people would accept the existence of intrinsic natural values unless such a belief was part of their cultural heritage. On this account, he suggested a strategic, temporary retreat to what he called "weak anthropocentrism," the view that the value of animals, plants, and nature is not merely instrumental (1992: 191). But Hargrove's pessimism now appears outdated. People's views have evolved since he made this suggestion; and today, many people (including animal welfarists and most environmentalists) do care about the good of animals and plants for their own sake.

This compass takes the view that the natural environment has both instrumental and intrinsic value. Unlike egalitarian biocentrists, however, we believe that living beings do not all have the same intrinsic value. There can be more and less intrinsic value, degrees and types of intrinsic value. Arguably, a monkey has more intrinsic value than an ant because of having more sophisticated capabilities. Indeed, it may be that some nonhuman animals have interests – a point to which we will return in Section 2.5.5. "Having interests" does not require having emotions or attitudes or other forms of higher consciousness. It is difficult to deny that creatures capable of health have interests (or an interest) in being healthy, and in not being injured or beset by disease. We of course concede that no nonhuman animals have the right to worship, to go to school, vote, or publish their own biographies and histories. Other animals may not think abstractly about their place in the natural environment and their relationship to others; but this fact provides no basis for holding that animals have no rights and interests. What it does suggest is that humans differ from other animals in having cumulative transmissible cultures of a degree and

kind found in no other species – a capacity that flows from our radically richer linguistic capacities. On this basis, what we may conclude is that a human is more valuable than a monkey.

In asserting the intrinsic value of other animals and ecosystems, we by no means mean to deny that they have instrumental value. The flourishing of nonhuman beings and of the natural environment contributes to human lives' value in many ways. There is no doubt that social progress requires an ecologically sustainable planet. We do think, however, that considering animals for their own sakes can also result in a better life for humans.

Various indigenous communities in the world have developed such a more respectful relationship to nature. They believe that humans are a part of nature. Accordingly, for them, it is obvious that the natural environment and ecosystems deserve moral consideration and protection, including those elements thereof that provide no economic value. These communities recognize both the instrumental and intrinsic value of the natural environment – a position that, as stated above, is perfectly consistent.

2.3.8   Security

In addition to caring about what goods they enjoy and which they are capable of enjoying, people care about the security of their enjoyment of basic goods and of their capabilities of enjoying them. "Security" is at least roughly the contrary of "vulnerability." We may think of it as consisting in there being a variety of protections in place that would enable people to hold on to the goods and capabilities that they need even when circumstances sour. So understood, as involving a kind of "counterfactual robustness" to the goods and central capabilities one enjoys, across possible variations in the circumstances, security is a good whose value does not wholly derive from that of these goods and capabilities. Establishing the security of a given type of good is not the same as maximizing people's chances of enjoying it; rather, security limits the kinds of risks people face by putting in place certain protections – potentially rejecting maximizing strategies that are too risky.

A wide range of thinkers agree that assuring security of this sort is a central function of government. Thomas Hobbes characterized it as "the end for which [the rulers were] entrusted with sovereign power," covering not merely "bare preservation, but also all other contentments of life" (1994, II.xxx.1: 219). Martha Nussbaum (2006) has argued that governments must put in place constitutional guarantees that secure each citizen's enjoyment of a decent minimum of each of ten central capabilities. Influentially, the *Human Security Report 2005* emphasized the importance to security of the "responsibility to protect" (Human Security Centre 2005). Given the variety of goods and capabilities whose security is important to us, the means to providing the relevant types of security are quite diverse. Whereas constitutional checks and balances are crucial to securing liberty, a whole panoply of other measures are needed to provide food and water security, of life-and-death concern to much of the world's population. Many of these issues are treated in the following chapters, which discuss many of these areas in which security is needed.

Here the point is that security with regard to important goods and capabilities is an important good in itself. It is one thing to supply a community with potable water and another thing to supply it with a secure source of potable water. The former can be done by regularly airlifting in bottled water – a practice that could be stopped at the whim of the authority funding the effort. It is another thing to provide a community with an adequate system of reservoirs and a reliable, sustainably operating filtration system. The relative security against shifting circumstances afforded by the latter is an instance of the good of security, in this case as something over and above the good of the water itself.

2.4 Basic Principles

Having elaborated the different values that we take as relevant to the assessment of social progress, we now turn to the relevant principles. As we argued in Section 2.2.1.2, principles need to be considered because they register the importance of moral side constraints and morally protected options and because they reflect the importance of process: of how decisions are reached, how these decisions affect the allocation of goods and ills, and how actions are carried out.

The principles set out in this section are not always compatible with one another in practice, but neither do they necessarily clash. One way that their potential clashing might be eased would be to see different ones of them as applying to different domains. For example, someone might hold that one principle holds across national borders, while another principle governs our relations with our fellow citizens (see Section 2.6.4 on global justice). It is also possible to hold that different principles apply to different types of social problems: the principles most relevant for dealing with climate change are not necessarily the principles most relevant for dealing with poverty. In practice, however, there is disagreement both about whether each of these principles is plausible and, if not, which of the principles is correct.

The principles relevant in a given context can have implications for which values are accorded weight, and how much weight they are accorded, if any. Therefore, identification of relevant principles is critical to the evaluation of social states.

2.4.1 Branches of Justice

Justice is generally understood to be about what people are owed in different contexts. *Reparative* justice aims to compensate people or to correct for past wrongs and/or their continuing legacies. *Criminal* justice considers the appropriate treatment for people who have wronged others. *Social* (or *distributive*) justice explores how at least some of the good things and bad things in life should be distributed among people.

Reparative justice and criminal justice each apply only in the context of wrongdoing. Only because there are wars, coercion, fraud, assaults, and corruption have societies developed systems of punishment and repair. By contrast, problems of distributive justice arise as an inevitable part of the human condition – specifically, that we cooperate to produce our lives together under conditions of moderate scarcity.

2.4.2 Basic Rights

The most uncontroversial principle for social justice can be understood in terms of the assertion that each individual has a claim on a set of resources and freedoms that would allow him or her to live a minimally decent life. The strongest language we have for expressing this assertion is the language of human rights. There are many theories about the bases of human rights, but it is not necessary for people to agree on these theories in order to agree that human beings have certain entitlements.

Since the adoption in 1948 by the United Nations of the Universal Declaration of Human Rights, every individual is seen as having a set of rights against his or her state, and the international community itself is seen as having obligations to ensure that human rights are respected if the state is unable or unwilling to do so.

Human rights are a powerful framework for evaluating social progress. There are two important points to note about using human rights as a metric of social progress. First, human rights set a threshold level of attainment. Once individuals cross the human rights threshold, this metric takes no further account of their relative positions. Thus a human rights perspective is indifferent between two societies whose members are all above its threshold, but where one society is twice as wealthy as the other. Second, while there is considerable overlap in the understanding of human rights among different societies, some rights seem more important than others. Ensuring that everyone has adequate nutrition, for example, appears to be much more important than ensuring the right to paid vacation time. It is thus difficult to use human rights as a principle of justice without having some way of differentiating the importance and relevance to practice of the various human rights.

2.4.3 Distributive Justice

Different theories of distributive justice articulate different conceptions of what distributions are acceptable as fair, as well as different conceptions of which values are to be distributed. Some theories of justice entail that a society needs to distribute liberties fairly between people; other theories see justice as obtaining when there is a fair distribution of human welfare; still others emphasize the distribution of resources (regardless of their welfare effects).

Theories of justice not only differ in their distributional metrics, they also differ in their conception of fairness. We will first discuss libertarianism and different variants of equality of opportunity. We then move to approaches that focus on outcomes. In that context we will return to how basic-rights approaches relate to the more demanding notions of justice and how they can be made operational. At the end of this subsection, considerations of efficiency and maximization enter the scene.

5

6

2.4.3.1 Libertarianism

Libertarians argue that securing basic rights (see Section 2.4.2) suffices to generate an adequate account of distributive justice, or "justice in holdings" (Nozick 1974: 150). They claim that justice consists in respecting people's rights, particularly rights to economic liberty – to hold, use, and transfer private property including the means of production – and, therefore, that taxation of the rich to benefit the poor is generally unjust. Within the libertarian family there is a distinction between those, such as Nozick, who hold that the right to private property is a fundamental moral right and those who argue for the protection of private property because of the beneficial consequences that arise from individuals securely holding, using and exchanging it (Friedman 1962; Tomasi 2012). Here we focus on the former, noninstrumental, defense of property rights.

For Nozick, each of us has a moral right of self-ownership: each individual owns herself in the sense that others are not morally permitted to use her body or mind without her consent. Self-ownership libertarians are less concerned with whether people enjoy certain goods; their emphasis is on preventing certain kinds of interference by the state or individuals. If an individual voluntarily works in exchange for income, then, provided the employer was entitled to her holdings of resources, the transfer is just. If the individual's income is now taxed, then, in effect, the government makes her work for someone else. On this extreme view, income taxation is equivalent to a kind of forced slavery (Nozick 1974, ch. 7). In fact, many libertarians would argue that there is no injustice in the fact that people starve, so long as their starving is not the result of anyone illegitimately interfering with their rights.

Perhaps somewhat surprisingly, self-ownership libertarianism also has a left branch (Vallentyne, Steiner, and Otsuka 2005). Left-libertarians insist on the importance of self-ownership, but state that natural resources should be considered as the common property of all human beings. This means that all human beings should share in the income that is generated by the use of these natural resources. This reasoning provides one justification for a so-called basic income: an income which is granted to everybody without any work condition.

2.4.3.2 Basic Needs and a Decent Minimum

A way of building on basic human rights that is quite different from the libertarian's is to hold that all people are entitled to a set of resources and freedoms that allow them to live a decent life. This general principle can be made operational for a multidimensional conception of a decent life such as the one that emerges from our account of basic values in Section 2.3. One can first define a sufficiency threshold for each dimension. One can then define "poverty" on the basis of not reaching the thresholds for the dimensions.

A threshold conception divides the population into two groups: those that have enough and those that do not, and claims that in a just society the latter group should be empty. This leaves a few important questions unanswered. First, how to rank individuals below the threshold? If it is not feasible to bring everybody above the sufficiency threshold, who should then get priority? Second, is sufficiency enough from the point of view of distributive justice; that is, are all situations in which everybody is above the sufficiency threshold equally good from the point of view of distributive justice? If not, then the sufficiency commitment can be seen as a constraint on other, more demanding principles. One could say, for instance, that distributive justice requires equality of outcomes, unless some inequality is needed to bring everybody above the threshold. Or that justice requires maximizing total well-being in society, under the constraint that everybody is above the threshold.

2.4.3.3 Equality of Opportunity, Luck Egalitarianism, Equality of Outcomes

There is near consensus that open discrimination cannot be tolerated in a good society. Nobody should be denied access to education, jobs, or health care on the basis of ethnic origin, gender, etc.

Nondiscrimination is the narrowest interpretation that can be given to the notion of equality of opportunity. It entails equality before the law. A more substantive interpretation would require that all children should get the same chances in life, independent of the socio-economic status of their parents. This notion of equality of opportunity is an "ex ante" concept: the ideal is to put all young adults in the same position at the starting gate of adult life without concern for the outcomes they will reach as adults.

Should society go further? For those, like Rawls, who put forward a principle of fair equality of opportunity that, like respect for basic rights and liberties, is supposed to constrain – rather than exhaust – the idea of justice in the distribution of advantages, it is enough to say that "those who have the same level of talent and ability and the same willingness to use these gifts should have the same prospects of success [at gaining jobs or offices] regardless of their social class of origin" (2001: 44).[6] For others, it is not obviously fair to allow those with greater talent and ability to reap greater rewards (an issue Rawls treats under the heading of the distribution of advantage).

Ronald Dworkin (1981a, 1981b) introduced a distinction between the goods or resources available to persons and their *choices*, which would lead to a degree of success in a plan of life. He argued that a person should be responsible for his choices, and hence it was important to equalize resources available to persons. However, Dworkin defined resource bundles comprehensively – to include not only transferable resources like money and wealth, but also nontransferable ones, like the family into which a person is born, or even his genetic make-up. So, equalizing resources consisted in finding the allocation of *transferable* resources (wealth) that would compensate persons properly for the inequalities in their bundles of *nontransferable* resources.

---

6 Rawls thus does not treat his principle of fair equality of opportunity as bearing on overall outcomes.

To decide on what the "right" compensation is, Dworkin proposed a thought-experiment. He imagined that a veil of ignorance denied persons of the knowledge of the resource bundles that they would be assigned in the "birth lottery," and that behind this veil they could purchase insurance against bad luck in that lottery. In this hypothetical insurance market, persons used their actual preferences over risk, but were endowed with an equal amount of money with which to purchase insurance. After the birth lottery occurs, and the "souls" who participated in the insurance market become persons located in families, transfers of wealth would occur to implement the insurance contracts that had been made.

Dworkin's scheme was ingenious, but it turned out to have a fatal flaw. John Roemer pointed out (in 1985) that unless everyone were very risk averse, the insurance market could result in the accumulation of more wealth by those who were "talented" – it could result in transferring wealth from the "handicapped" or disabled to the talented, or from the unlucky to the lucky.

In 1989, G.A. Cohen argued that Dworkin was correct to make a distinction between choice and resources, but that he had improperly placed the "cut" between the two. The right cut was between aspects of a person's situation for which he should not be held responsible and aspects for which he should be held responsible. In particular, a person should not be held responsible for choices that were induced by preferences that were induced by circumstances beyond his control.

Based upon this discussion, Roemer proposed (in 1993) a theory of *equality of opportunity*. He focuses on the distribution of final outcomes but distinguishes between factors for which individuals should not be held responsible ("circumstances") and factors for which they can be seen as responsible (their "effort"). The idea motivating the approach – which has also been called "responsibility-sensitive egalitarianism" or "luck egalitarianism" – is that individuals must be compensated for the effect of factors for which they are not responsible. This means that, somehow, it must be assured that super-intelligent individuals should get the same outcome as the less intelligent, provided they exert the same level of effort.

The list of circumstances could be quite comprehensive, or fairly small. A society could thus determine what equality of opportunity means by the choice of circumstances it wishes persons to be compensated for. Equality of opportunity is therefore a concept that is defined as *relative* to the conception of circumstances and responsibility that a society wishes to adopt. Formally mapping the possible answers to this question reveals that if one holds people fully responsible for their outcomes, one comes close to the libertarian position, on which inequality in outcomes is not morally problematic. By contrast, an equality-of-outcome position results if one does not hold people responsible for anything.

The sharpest criticism of this luck-egalitarian approach is formulated by philosophers like Elisabeth Anderson (1999), who argue that the concept of responsibility cannot bear the weight that luck egalitarians place on it. Even the negligent driver has a claim on society for aid in an accident. Other people have argued that ascribing some responsibility

to individuals is just the other side of the coin of acknowledging their freedom (Fleurbaey 2008).

2.4.3.4   Egalitarianism, Prioritarianism, and Maximin

Principles of distributive justice have also been developed independently of the idea of fairness of opportunity. One is a simple version of egalitarianism: distributive justice requires equality in some or all dimensions. Restricting ourselves to well-being as the relevant dimension, each of the different interpretations of well-being in Section 2.3 can be introduced into an egalitarian approach, yielding views with very different practical implications and different advantages and disadvantages.

Egalitarian views must settle on the relevant "currency" or "currencies" of equality (Sen 1980). Candidates for what is to be equalized include resources, subjective well-being, capabilities, and preference-satisfaction. Equalizing external resources means neglecting differences in needs and other differences in the personal conversion factors, as described in Section 2.3. We have seen that Dworkin (1981b)'s proposal to introduce internal resources (while making a distinction between preferences and handicaps) was one of the most important inspirations for responsibility-sensitive egalitarianism. Equality of subjective well-being (happiness) advocates redistributing from the happier to the less happy people, even if the former are happy because they were able to adapt to an awful objective situation or if the latter are unhappy because they have expensive tastes. The implications of equality of capabilities (if these are considered as commensurable) will depend on the procedure used to set the weights given to the different dimensions. If these are set "objectively," that might argue for redistribution from individual A to individual B, even if both individuals A and B take B to be better off. If the weights follow from collective deliberation, redistribution might be imposed on individuals who were dissenters in that deliberative process. In a preference-based approach, objective information is discarded to the extent that individual A can have a lower equivalent income than individual B, even if they reach a higher level on all the relevant dimensions. As we indicated in Section 2.3.1, each of these different notions of well-being has strong arguments in its support as well as having to face criticisms.

One can wonder if "equality" in itself is a good thing to strive for. In a seminal article, Parfit (1995) distinguished between "equality" and "priority." In the prioritarian view the relevant principle is that benefiting people matters more from the point of view of justice the worse off these people are. Fighting inequality can then still inspire action, but its value is merely instrumental: redistribution is defended because it may improve the fate of the worse-off, not because there is something intrinsically wrong about inequality. However, for policy evaluation the differences between prioritarians and egalitarians are minimal (Fleurbaey 2015).

A fundamental question arises if one aims at maximizing the advantage of the worst-off members of society and the working of society is such that accepting some inequality can improve the situation of these worst-off. One is then confronted with a tradeoff between "equality" and "efficiency" (interpreted as calling for maximizing the advantage of the worst-off). Rawls's "difference principle" (Rawls 1999a: 53) (which is also known as a maximin principle), maximizes the resources of those who occupy the lowest social position. Taking into account feasibility considerations, mainly related to incentives, the maximin criterion may lead to very different social policies than pure egalitarianism (Cohen 2008).

2.4.3.5   Utilitarianism's Distributive Implications

If individual well-being is measurable on a cardinal scale, the well-being levels of different individuals can be added and one can meaningfully define the sum and the average level of well-being. Utilitarianism, which has been extremely influential in economics, advocates maximizing this sum or this average.[7] The term "utilitarianism" is often loosely used in popular discourse, even to refer to all approaches that are consequentialist or that focus on material consumption only. As philosophers and economists (e.g. Sen and Williams 1982) use the term, however, utilitarians are defined (a) not merely as consequentialists, in that they evaluate policies and institutions on the basis of their outcomes, but also (b) as evaluating these consequences in terms of individuals' utilities and then (c) aggregating these individual utility levels by taking the simple sum or the average.

Some argue that maximizing aggregate well-being is a criterion of efficiency that has little to do with distributive justice. Others claim, however, that giving an equal (unit) weight to the well-being levels of all individuals embodies a degree of impartiality that reflects a conception of justice (e.g. Mill 1979: 60–61).

Utilitarianism has strong implications for the distribution of goods even though it is agnostic on the distribution of utilities. Disregarding feasibility constraints for the sake of the argument and assuming that the marginal utility of income (resources) is decreasing and that all individuals have the same utility function, maximizing the sum of utilities implies equally distributing incomes (resources) among individuals. It is clear that the assumptions needed to derive this outcome-egalitarian result are highly unrealistic.

2.4.4   Aggregate Maximization, Justice, and Efficiency

The multidimensional nature of the compass we have been developing seems to pose a challenge to the idea that having a rational basis for choice requires having something to maximize (a maximand). Yet maximization approaches may propose a large variety of maximands. Utilitarianism (Section 2.4.3.5) and maximin (Section 2.4.3.4) – or leximin, its lexicographic version (Rawls 1999a: 72) – are natural examples of maximands that have been amply discussed in the literature. Utilitarianism and leximin both satisfy the Pareto principle, in that an improvement in the well-being of one individual (keeping all the other well-being levels fixed) is taken to be a social improvement. Yet, they may both be seen as extreme, with utilitarianism only concerned about the sum of well-being, i.e. attaching the same weight to all well-being levels, and maximin only concerned about the minimum, i.e. attaching a positive weight to the worst-off and zero weights to

all the others. Welfare economists have proposed maximands (concave social welfare functions) that are in-between these two extremes, with marginal welfare weights that are declining if the well-being level increases. This idea of giving a relatively larger weight to the worse-off is close to prioritarianism. As long as an increase in an individual well-being level leads to an increase in social welfare, these functions, too, satisfy the Pareto criterion.

Until now we only focused on maximands that, in a certain sense, embody a tradeoff between efficiency and redistribution; but the idea of maximization or optimization can be interpreted more broadly. In fact, almost all approaches to distributive justice that have been discussed before can be reformulated as an optimization problem. Respect for basic needs can be made operational by minimizing the number of people below the threshold; egalitarianism by minimizing a measure of inequality, which can be variously defined (see e.g. Cowell 2011).

At an abstract level, such exercises in formulating a maximand simply register a social ordering of possible social states. Loosely formulated, optimization just means picking the "best" element. A shortcoming of formulating action principles as a maximization exercise is that it is not always easy to rephrase subtle ethical arguments in a form that is amenable to a mathematical formulation or to sum up the implications of potentially clashing values and principles in a single ordering of social states. Disregarding subtleties and unresolved tradeoffs may give a false feeling of precision and sweep important arguments in the debate under the carpet.

That said, one should not neglect the advantages of a maximizing approach. First, a maximization approach leads to an unambiguous formulation of the different criteria, which allows for a clear-cut comparison of their policy consequences. Second, as noted before, formulating a realistic compass for measuring social progress requires taking into account not only what is ideal, but also what is possible. Formulating a maximization problem makes it possible to introduce feasibility constraints into the exercise in a natural way.

2.4.5   Beneficence and Generosity

The duty of beneficence calls for action to assist and support others in need; the virtue of generosity keeps one open to doing so. Even a society with just institutions will sometimes need to rely on beneficence and generosity in cases of sudden and urgent need. Generous individuals and organizations function as a kind of moral capital, making a society's achievements less vulnerable to disaster and disruption.

Societies develop practices and institutions that help see to it that people are provided with urgently needed assistance. Many of these efforts – such as the establishment of fire and ambulance services – efficiently provide the public good of security (Section 2.3.8). At the same time, they relieve individuals of the burdens of obligations they would otherwise occasionally have to provide first aid or carry buckets of water. While these social measures vary from place to place, they usually include social safety nets, disaster assistance programs,

---

[7]   The two are of course equivalent if the population size remains constant. The thorny issue of the optimal population size is discussed further in Box 2.5.

and efforts at humanitarian relief. Globalization and the proliferation of charitably oriented nongovernmental organizations make it possible for individuals to contribute to extending urgently needed assistance of almost any kind to anyone at any time. The prevalence of such urgent needs reflects considerable injustice (as will be discussed in Section 2.6.4). Even if efforts at securing justice should displace much of the potential broad-scale work that beneficence might do, however, the ineliminability of accidents and natural disasters tells us that a role for beneficence – both individual and social – will remain. For that matter, the difficulty of eliminating injustice will also mean that there are more highly vulnerable and needy people than there should be. For these reasons, generous hearts and multiple organizations for helping those in need are necessary to supplement governmental schemes. Other things equal, the presence of such organizations and the individual motives that underlie them are significant elements in securing social progress more robustly.

2.5   Units of Assessment

A compass for guiding our deliberations about social progress must provide a sense of the entities on whose progress we must or may permissibly focus. This question about the units whose progress is being assessed should be distinguished from the question about who or what are the *agents* of social progress, the types of entities that can or should do something to promote social progress. In Section 2.6, we will come to the different types of agent that ought to act in ways that promote progress, and specifically to principles that apply specially to each of them. In the present section, our focus is on the former question, that of identifying the *objects of assessment* relevant to social progress – the units about which we ask whether social progress has been achieved on account, say, of an improvement in justice or an improvement in the well-being of its members.

The lives of individual human beings clearly matter. Do groups, religious communities, nations, and regions matter, and, if so, in what ways? To what extent do future generations matter within an account of social progress? An account of social progress must also take into account the interests of nonhuman animals. But in what ways?

Thus, in this section, we focus on the kinds of units whose progress we ought to be assessing when identifying whether overall social progress has occurred or might be realized. We take for granted that the global unit is one whose progress matters: we clearly must ask whether or in what way there has been human progress, and how or in what way human progress might be promoted.

2.5.1   Individuals

Social progress involves a number of improvements that take place primarily at a societal level. Such improvements, however, should be felt within individual lives, preferably all individual lives.

It can be entirely unobjectionable for an individual to sacrifice the enjoyment of goods for a period of time to obtain greater benefits later, even if the costs she imposes on herself are significant and long

lasting. But we cannot mechanically assume that there is no difference between an individual at two different times and one individual and another, so that whatever sacrifice is permissible in one case is also permissible in the other. Intrapersonal and interpersonal distributional decisions significantly differ because we are each distinct and separate individuals, each with her own life to lead (Nagel 1995).

Now, the most natural way to think about our separate lives as the units of distribution is to take our entire lifespan into account. To illustrate this point in relation to egalitarianism: some say that while an equal society is compatible with individuals having very different lives, with some having better childhoods and others a better old age, on the whole there should not be major net differences at birth among individual's total life prospects (Daniels 2008). Equality, thus understood, may sometimes require the reversal, rather than the elimination, of inequality for a period of time. For example, if a woman puts her career on hold to support her husband, it is better from the point of view of equality if he then puts his career on hold to support hers. If a decade where one flourishes while the other does not is replaced by a decade where they both flourish equally, total-lives equality would not be achieved (McKerlie 2012).

It is fairly uncontroversial to say that if, in a society or the world as a whole, people's lives improve in *length* and *quality*, social progress has, ceteris paribus, been achieved. However, difficult questions arise when length and quality compete. Suppose, for example, that A lives a shorter life than B but, on average, is more advantaged in terms of well-being or resources in each year of that life. According to the total-life view, it might be that we should regard A and B as having had an equally advantaged life.

While the total-life view is widely accepted, some find it insufficiently demanding, for example, because they think that nobody should have a childhood, or an old age, that falls below a certain threshold, even if this is compensated by a sufficiently good life in between. Another argument against focusing exclusively on total lives may be pressed by referring to societies stratified by age groups. Some of them exhibit many of the unattractive features of deeply inegalitarian societies even if the lives of their members are not unequal when taken as a whole, since everybody (who survives) eventually manages to belong to the council of the elderly, for example.

2.5.2   Civil Society Groups

While it is uncontroversial to claim that an account of social progress ought to attach fundamental moral importance to improving the lives of individuals, it is more contentious to think that organizations or groups have such importance except derivatively. Although we often use language that suggests that groups are unitary entities with lives of their own – we often say that such and such a policy would be bad for "the nation" or an "organization" – many believe it is more plausible that attending to the interest of a group is shorthand for acting in the shared interests of several individuals rather than the interests of a single "group-individual." According to one version of this view, although the interest of a single individual in having the opportunity to speak a particular language, for example, might not be sufficient to justify holding others under a duty to protect or promote that language, the fact that many individuals share an interest in speaking that language may be enough to generate a duty on the wider society to protect it. On this view, collectives have no interests that are separate from the interests of the individuals that comprise them (Raz 1986; Jones 2008).

At the present time, efforts at assessing social progress are mainly concerned with evaluating the performance of governments. Given that presumption, there is reason to limit the overall assessment to items that generate reasons for governments to act. Many doubt that there are nonderivative or instrumental reasons for governments to respond to the claims of particular communities or organizations within civil society or to treat them as having any claims that are distinct from the interests of individuals freely to express their convictions and to associate with others. Notwithstanding the different views in that debate, there is widespread agreement that the claims of such groups or communities warrant the attention of the wider political community only if their activities satisfy some threshold of reasonableness (Kymlicka 1995). Several standards for identifying reasonableness in this context have been proposed, which have included particular requirements for the treatment of women (Okin 1999), children (Feinberg 1992; Callan 1997), and nonhuman animals (Casal 2007).

If the purpose of assessing social progress is simply to assess government's performance, then this point of agreement argues for ignoring how civil-society institutions are doing, independently of assessing the effects on their members. The conclusion would be different, however, if the point of assessing progress were not simply to rate or guide governments, but to consider, overall, how well a society is faring. Basic liberties shield some civil society institutions – notably the religious ones – from government interference. What goes on in them may not be the business of governments to worry about. Still, because of their importance to esteem (Section 2.3.5), what goes on in them may be of intrinsic importance of a kind relevant to assessing social progress in this second way.

2.5.3 Nations

It is very common to assess the social progress of a nation or national state. Nations – apart from those that are sometimes referred to as "failed" – are well-structured human collectivities with a legal system and an effective written or unwritten constitutional structure. This makes it natural to assess nations on how well they are doing. To get a deeper understanding of why it makes sense to assess the progress of nations, rather than simply focusing on outcomes for individuals, it will be useful to take a brief look at the reasons that can be raised against an unrestricted right to freedom of movement.

Suppose we argue that we should allow the free international movement of people. Allowing such movement would certainly be appealing in many ways. It would allow people to move to wherever suited their needs and preferences. If some locations become too crowded, the market may help even things out. But although the effects of such a system are hard to predict, some problems are easy to envision. People may bring habits that are inappropriate to different

environments, there could be problems of brain-drain, and cultural confrontations may intensify.

More revealing of the normative importance of nations is that unrestricted freedom of movement would interfere with the ability of nations to pursue progress in their own distinctive ways. A nation may have decided to maintain high taxes to support public goods and assist the needy. Being forced to open their borders may jeopardize this ambition. Alternatively, a country's people may have decided to become environmental pioneers and invest massively in green technology, knowing that their commitment to environmentalism could involve major financial costs for them. Having made such a commitment, they would prefer the population to remain reasonably stable, so that the plan can be legitimately and successfully carried through.

Thus, we have reasons to allow some restrictions on the movement of people to create greater stability in the populations of a territory, and to allow different collective projects to be tried out, just like we have reasons to allow individuals to engage in what John Stuart Mill (1978: ch. 3) referred to as their diverse "experiments in living." Countries should be allowed to try out different tax systems and institutional designs, restrict certain benefits to their residents and enjoy most of the benefits of their wise policy choices, and bear the consequences of their poor choices too. Being restricted by the same democratically elected and mutually binding public rules and sharing certain institutions could create bonds and obligations between humans over and above those we have with all humans, and so some movement restrictions could be justified.

To be sure, we should remain critical of current international borders and willing to question them. After all, they are largely just the product of historical accidents and were often drawn arbitrarily by colonial powers. Moreover, many people around the world are fleeing serious repression and human rights violations. These people deserve to be taken in. The general reasons to preserve nation-states are not reasons to preserve the status quo and all state boundaries exactly as they are.

2.5.4 The Ethical Status of Future Generations

Suppose that we managed to eradicate all remaining poverty in the world over the course of the next two decades by embarking on an industrializing binge in which we exhaust all of the world's remaining fossil fuels. Suppose that this considerably improves average well-being and social justice and that the economic program builds in ways of mitigating the immediate effects of pollution on humans and other animals. Yet, finally, suppose that this effort dooms later generations to a world wracked by catastrophic climate change and a dearth of usable energy supplies. Should these ill effects on later generations be counted against the social progress that the globe, 20 years from now, should be assessed as having achieved?

Almost everyone believes that future generations have moral standing in the sense that their interests and claims limit what the present generation can permissibly do. It is uncontroversial to claim that the present generation ought to take steps to avoid or limit the damage we do to the Earth's atmosphere and the depletion of its resources. Beneath the surface of this consensus, however, lurk differences with respect to how we ought to understand the moral standing of future generations, and how demanding are our duties to them.

1.   At the threshold of these questions lies a stubborn conceptual obstacle to claiming that later generations can be harmed by anything we do. Doubts about whether those who are alive can harm future generations have arisen from a puzzle elaborated by Parfit, the so-called *nonidentity problem* (Parfit 1984: ch. 16). Given that each individual is the product of a particular pair of gametes that can combine only within a limited time period, it is plausible to assume that the way people live their lives affects the identity of future individuals. Had cheap travel by train, car, or airplane not developed, for example, very many present people would not have been born because their parents would not have met or procreated when they did. This fact appears to pose a problem for our usual *person-affecting* way of understanding our moral requirements according to which, for example, A ought not hit B because hitting B is bad for B; it *harms* him in the sense that, all things considered, it makes *him* worse off than he would be had A not hit him. The damage we do to the Earth's atmosphere by the emission of carbon from cars and planes, which leaves future generations with a worse environment than we enjoy, appears not to be harmful to future individuals in this sense, at least for those who have lives worth living. To see this consider an individual, Cari, whose existence depends on a previous generation's carbon-emitting lifestyles. She would not have existed had the previous generation led a more environmentally friendly lifestyle. If she has a life worth living we cannot say that the previous generation's emissions have harmed Cari in the sense of making her worse off than she would have been had it been more environmentally friendly; it appears that its emitting activity was not bad for her.

     Although a small minority holds that the nonidentity problem establishes that we have very few duties to future generations (e.g. Schwartz 1978), most hold that, the problem notwithstanding, future generations have moral standing. Parfit himself argues that the fact of nonidentity indicates that we ought to understand our concern for future generations in *impersonal* or *nonperson-affecting* terms. Other things being equal, if we can choose between producing one of two possible (nonoverlapping) future populations of the same size we ought to produce the one that enjoys the higher standard of living. (Matters become more complicated once we acknowledge that the choices of the present generation can affect the population size of future generations – see Box 2.5.) On this view, morality is not exhausted by a concern for the interests of identifiable individuals.

     Parfit's is not the only reasonable response to this problem. Several different views have been developed in defense of the claim that, contrary to appearances, facts about nonidentity do not show that a person-affecting moral concern for future generations is problematic (Shiffrin 1999; Meyer and Roser 2009). Some argue that cultural groups or nations can be harmed even if the nonidentity problem shows that future individuals are not (Page 2006). Others argue that depleting the Earth's resources *wrongs* future people even if it does not harm them; we wrong

them in the sense that we fail to recognize their legitimate claims to an environment of a certain sort (Kumar 2003).

2.   Assuming that we have reason to take future generations into account when assessing social progress, how stringent are these reasons? Do the distributive ideals that apply within generations (see Section 2.4.3) also apply intergenerationally? Certain defenses of equality, for example, regard it as an appropriate ideal only for those who reciprocate in a scheme of cooperation. Such defenses face difficulties in extending egalitarian norms intergenerationally, because of the absence of a reciprocal relationship between us and distant future generations.[8] By contrast, conceptions of threshold, egalitarian, or prioritarian justice that view justice in impersonal terms, or as unreliant on preexisting reciprocal relationships, appear to be applicable intergenerationally.

How ought our compass for evaluating social progress to be configured with respect to the demands of intergenerational justice? Two promising candidates are *respect for decent minima* and *sustainability*. The idea of sustainability – now so prominent in light of the sustainable development goals (see Box 2.8) – states that the present generation is entitled to use the Earth's resources as it chooses subject to the condition that it leaves future generations with as many resources or opportunities of equal value as it enjoyed (see Barry 1999). Guaranteeing a decent minimum to everyone may require doing more for them than this if, for example, without further saving or investment, enabling them to continue the present levels of consumption is insufficient to sustain a particular threshold of well-being or advantage for everyone (Meyer and Roser 2009). These ideas of sustainability and sufficiency can be well combined (see Casal, 2007) into a hybrid conception of our duties to future generations that includes a concern for both.

2.5.5   Humans and Other Animals

In Section 2.3.7, we noted that not only humans but also other animals and ecosystems have intrinsic value. In the case of other animals, at least, it is important to keep track of how well they are doing. In recent times, human activities have drastically reduced the number of existing species. We also impose much suffering on animals. We have moved from eating occasional animal prey to building factory farms that house animals in pitiful conditions. We also use many animals in all sorts of experiments and tests, including those performed for trivial purposes.

At the same time, humanity has come to realize that it is not only ourselves or our tribe that matters, and has begun to see that some ethical principles have validity across species boundaries. This realization appears to have been always present in some religions, such as in those of Indian origin, but not in others, such as those of Abrahamic descent. Nowadays, hardly anyone denies that animal suffering matters or claims we may disregard an individual's interests merely because of its species. The legal protection of nonhuman animals is now widely seen as part of social progress, and has reached the supranational level with, for example, the 2009 Lisbon Treaty affirming the legal relevance of animal suffering to European legislation.

---

8   Though see Mazor (2010) for an argument for demanding intergenerational duties that appeals to the fact of *overlapping* relationships between contiguous generations.

Box 2.5 | The Problem of Optimal Population Size

Optimal population size is the population size that maximizes value given constraints on available resources. In classical optimum population theory, the relevant value is economic output (Dasgupta 1969). Most contemporary discussions of this issue take the relevant value to be human welfare. The problem of optimal population size arises when policies that affect the welfare of future generations also affect the *number* of people that will exist.

If the current generation continues to consume resources at the expense of future generations, and population increases significantly, there could be an enormous population in which most lives are barely worth living. Suppose we could instead create a smaller population with very good lives. Intuitively, this smaller population with very high welfare levels is better than the much larger population with much lower welfare levels. However, many traditional moral theories violate this intuition. For example, per Classical Utilitarianism (CU) (see Section 2.4.3.5), we should maximize overall welfare. We can do this either by making people's lives better or by increasing the size of the population with lives worth living. So, per CU, an enormous population with lives barely worth living *could* be better than a smaller population with very good lives. In his seminal work on optimal population size, Derek Parfit (1984: 388) named this result "the Repugnant Conclusion" and considered it a reason to reject CU.

One might think that Average Utilitarianism (AU), which ranks populations according to average welfare per life in the population, fares better than CU, since it avoids the Repugnant Conclusion. However, AU implies, absurdly, that we can improve a population by adding lives not worth living (Parfit 1984: 422; Arrhenius 2000), for instance if the lives of those currently in the population are *even worse* than the added lives would be.

There are many ways to avoid the Repugnant Conclusion. They include: aggregating welfare differently; revising the notion of a life worth living; rejecting the transitivity of "better than"; and appealing to other values such as, for example, equality or desert (for overviews, see Broome 2004; Blackorby et al. 2005; Arrhenius et al. 2010). However, these ways of avoiding the Repugnant Conclusion have other counterintuitive consequences. In fact, several *impossibility theorems* demonstrate that no theory can fulfil a number of intuitively compelling adequacy conditions that, most agree, any reasonable theory of optimal population size must fulfil (Arrhenius 2000, 2011, forthcoming) – for example, the condition that one population is better than another if everyone is better off in the former than in the latter, and the condition that it is better to create people with a higher rather than lower level of well-being.

Therefore, it seems we must either abandon one or more of the adequacy conditions on which these theorems are based or become moral skeptics. There is no easy choice here.

These developments draw on and extend the values and principles we have so far listed as important for assessing and guiding social progress – most importantly the value of well-being and the idea of justice and the various principles under its umbrella. Arguably, animals have the lowest welfare levels, the lowest capabilities, and all too often have been deprived of their natural habitats (McMahan 2002; Vallentyne 2006).

Others however have resisted this kind of extension of our principles, or believe it needs to be qualified, because they think it overreaches. Not all living things, they argue, deserve consideration. For example, some hold that only higher functioning beings – persons – should be protected. On one construal, "persons" have a sense of themselves as intelligent creatures that persist over time and can think of themselves as existing in different moments and places (Locke 1998, II.xxvii: 9).

The set of individuals that can count as persons in this sense includes some highly intelligent and empathetic animals such as the great apes, some whales and dolphins, elephants, and perhaps some exceptionally intelligent birds, like the magpies, which are also capable of mirror self-recognition, forward planning, and empathy and practice tool use and death rituals. By contrast, some humans, such as anencephalic babies, are arguably not persons.

Death is particularly bad for persons because they typically have more to lose from losing their lives, they are more connected to their future and they are more connected to others who would also suffer from their death. By contrast, if a fish is not more connected to its future than it is to another fish, and a fish is never missed by others, it is hard to explain why it is better that a fish lives 20 years than if a fish that lives ten is replaced by another who lives ten. Imprisonment is also particularly bad for persons as they can imagine themselves elsewhere, resent being captured, have a sense of time, and may worry about others missing them or suffering a similar fate. A fish that cannot distinguish between the pond where it is captive and another pond where it is not, cannot miss others and keeps on seeing the limits of the pond as if for the first time, does not suffer comparably.

Although the above-mentioned capacities explain why death or confinement may be worse for persons than for some nonhuman animals, it does not settle the question of whether there is any reason to judge pain of the same kind, intensity, and duration, as worse for persons than for any animals which can feel such pain. Even if there was such a reason, pain will still be bad for them, and so at least an important range of other animals come under the scope of moral concern. This being so, a complete reckoning of social progress will take account of the lives of individuals of at least some other species.

2.6 Principles Specially Applicable to Certain Types of Agent

The previous section developed the idea that, when assessing social progress, we must keep track of how well agents at various different levels are faring: not only individuals, but also civil society, nations, future generations, and nonhuman animals and ecosystems. In this section we turn to principles specially applicable to this or that type of agent and indicate what they ought to do. These principles are not reducible to the fully general principles set out in Section 2.4. That is in part because they take account of the distinctive circumstances faced by differently embodied or realized human collectives. Because these principles state or imply obligations, the agents that we canvass in this section do not fully coincide with those discussed in Section 2.5. That is because the idea of moral requirements does not seem applicable to all of those agents. While we humans have obligations with regard to other animals and to ecosystems, it is implausible to say that these other animals have any obligations, let alone that ecosystems would.

In laying out principles applicable specially only to this or that type of agent, we will first cover a variety of agents that are institutionally structured (governments, civil society institutions, the global system), if only on the basis of quite informal institutions (or, if you prefer, on the basis of social practices). A full development of these principles of special application would consider how they interact (see Box 2.6).

2.6.1 The Normative Relevance of Institutions

Human institutions are important for social progress both for their structural properties and for their motivational implications. We explicate each of these two features in turn.

"Institutions" serve to structure the relations among individuals – either by creating incentives for individuals to act in ways that are in the interests of others (with "interests" here broadly construed); or by

coordinating the actions of individuals in ways that minimize conflict (or perhaps fail to do so); or by determining the distribution of benefits and costs across those who interact under that institution. These functions involve processes or procedures (see Section 2.2.1.2) that are "structural" in the sense that they operate in a way that is definite and yet interacts with the ends of the individuals in them at any given time. Some institutions, at least, operate according to a conventional set of rules that assign rights and obligations that are internal to the institution, thereby defining their procedures in a relatively explicit way (Rawls 1999a: 47).

For example, as economists have long argued, the competitive market serves such a structural role by creating incentives for participants to operate in the interests of others – at least in relation to so-called "private" goods – yielding efficient cooperation with a minimum of governmental encroachment on freedom of choice. In cases where goods are not fully private, such as that of carbon emissions, where an individual's action affects many other people, other arrangements need to be sought.[9]

As an example of the redistributive aspects of institutional structures, consider the effect of democratic processes on redistributive policies. One possibility is that because voting power is distributed more equally than economic power, the effect of democratic processes will be to give rise to government policies that redistribute economic resources away from the richer toward the poorer. Equality of political influence may of course be something that is valued in itself, but these structural effects on transfers of economic power are also normatively significant. An opposite possibility is that inequalities in the distribution of wealth can give some disproportionate influence over government policies, leading to further advantages for the wealthy.

The structural effects of institutions are often analyzed in abstraction from the motivations of the agents who are subject to them. But there are two reasons not to consider that abstraction as a firewall. First, the effects institutions have will likely be influenced by what motivations agents have. How well the market works depends on how extensively participants have internalized norms of trustworthiness. And how redistributive an equal franchise turns out to be seems likely to depend on the proportion of low-income individuals who actually vote. Second, it seems likely that institutional arrangements will affect motivations in various ways, and so will mold the people that grow up with them.

Adam Smith (in a manner echoed later by Durkheim 1964) thought that the division of labor would tend to make people "as stupid and ignorant as it is possible for a human creature to become ..." (Smith 1994: V.i.f.50). In a somewhat similar spirit, many market critics have thought that commercial society encourages greed – and indeed seem to have thought that this effect was so obvious that it does not require any empirical support.

Such motivational effects may be of concern in their own right. Any normative scheme that admits some element of concern for virtue as an end in itself will be concerned about the effects of institutions on human character. Additionally, any motivational changes are likely to

---

9   These new arrangements may include market-based mechanisms such as the creation of a market for emission permits.

Box 2.6 | Division of Labor among Principles

Some argue that the multiplicity of moral values and principles is merely apparent or superficial, and that a sound understanding will allow us to operate with a single principle. This is a controversial view. Taking a cautious approach, this compass-setting chapter has proceeded on the assumption that it is better to mention all of the values and principles that seem on reflection to be intrinsically important, lest crucial considerations be overlooked.

Assuming, then, that those seeking to promote or to assess social progress should take account of a plurality of principles, two further questions will arise. First, are all of the principles equally relevant in all contexts? And if not, are there important ways in which combinations of principles could work together across different contexts? The analogy, here, is to the division of labor. Perhaps pairs or trios of principles work together in complementary ways, such that if each were honored in its own domain (the relevant) society would be just or would flourish (Scheffler 2005). Being open to considering such possibilities is important to thinking concretely about how honoring moral principles can help promote social progress.

Two of the best-known proposals about such a division of moral labor are found in John Rawls's theory of justice. The first Rawlsian proposal is that we distinguish between "the basic structure of society," which "comprises the main social institutions – the constitution, the economic regime, the legal order and its specification of property and the like, and how these institutions cohere into one system," on the one hand, and the transactions that occur within it, on the other (Rawls 2005: 301). Here, the idea is that the institutions of the basic structure affect individual transactions by settling the rules of the game, as it were. The elements of the basic structure settle, at least in outline, under what conditions claims to property-ownership will be recognized, contracts honored, or basic rights protected. The basic structure, Rawls argued, must satisfy principles concerning the basic liberties, equal opportunity, and distributive fairness. If it does, he controversially held, then individual economic freedom (a nonbasic liberty) can be given more sway at the level of individual transactions (Rawls 1999a: 73–8). The point of this moral division of labor is to allow a plurality of moral concerns to be well satisfied by giving different ones sway in different domains.

Rawls's second proposal for a moral division of labor invokes the more common distinction between those features of a society's public life that are settled by constitutional law and those that are not. Just as a society's basic structure frames what can go on within it, so too does a society's constitutional law (Rawls 1999a: 174). Rawls characterized the "constitutional essentials" as including not only the "general structure of the political process" but also the "equal basic rights and liberties" (Rawls 2005, 227). He argued (again, controversially: see e.g. Barry 1973) that a more just society would result if legislative efforts to implement distributive justice were effectively constrained by constitutionally secured basic liberties than if these two elements were left to compete with one another in an unstructured way, without any division of moral labor (Rawls 1999a: 179).

have implications for the structural effects of other institutions. For example, if markets drive out altruistic behavior, that might have effects on our willingness to support democratic institutions.

In this way various institutional arrangements may be at odds, or may work in complementary fashion. Sometimes one institution may serve to moderate excesses in another, as in the example about how democratic processes may moderate the worst possible distributional excesses of markets. Sometimes one institution may support (or undermine) the motivational background that helps another institution to work well. Normative analysis must be attentive to the relations among institutions. And these include not just direct effects, but also those effects mediated by any motivational changes that institutional arrangements induce.

When scholars talk of the structural properties of institutions, they typically have in mind the two basic institutional forms of markets and politics (usually democratic politics). To be sure, there is a range of other organized activities, not fully reducible to either market or politics (or some combination), that might plausibly contribute to well-being in a way that we have not otherwise captured or that have a normative importance not fully exhausted by their contribution to well-being. One such institution is the corporation, which is not a market institution as such. Another range of activities that we have in mind are things like artistic pursuits, religious activities, sports, academia – a heterogeneous collection of activities that together constitute "civil society." This term is familiar from the literature on democracy, where much is written about all that a vibrant civil society contributes to democratic objectives, both directly and indirectly. Yet in addition, each location in civil society represents, at least in principle, a location for independent assessment of social developments of the kind that characterize a vibrant political life.

2.6.2 Principles Applicable to Governments

2.6.2.1 The Rule of Law

The rule of law distinctively enshrines the principle of formal civic equality and makes it possible to restrain the exercise of arbitrary power by enabling citizens to hold public officials accountable. The original notion of the "rule of law" (Dicey 1915 and Aristotle and Cicero in antiquity) seems to have focused on the idea that lawmakers should be subject themselves to the laws they make. The thought is that, so constrained, lawmakers would be disposed to legislate in the common interest rather than exploit their powers to promote their own interests. But the idea is typically generalized to embody a requirement of equality before the law for all. This requirement implies an absence of discrimination of all kinds, and can have both a procedural and a substantive aspect. The procedural aspect requires that individuals will be entitled to due process before legal institutions: they will have equal standing before the courts and be treated with appropriate respect. Further, individuals will not be held without charge or be peremptorily carted off in the middle of the night. In criminal cases, individuals will be treated as innocent until proven guilty; and the onus of proof in such cases will lie with the accuser. The substantive aspect relates to the law itself: the law will not be applied retroactively and individuals will not be held in custody without charge beyond minimal limits.

An effective rule of law will require certain institutional features: a judiciary that is independent (an aspect of the so-called separation of powers) and noncorrupt, and compliance by the executive with the courts' determinations. Since these features of the legal process are normatively desirable for a vast variety of reasons, it is sensible to count their effective realization as a point on the social progress compass. But we might ask what institutional supports might be helpful in making it more likely that these features will be realized, because these supports then become appropriate indicators that the rule of law is in place and secure. For instance, we might attend to the procedures whereby judges are selected, what pool the judges are selected from and who does the selection (and what interests or biases those selectors might have).

While legal scholars tend to focus on courts and judicial procedures and political theorists on the content of laws, criminologists and legal sociologists tend to focus on the delivery of the rule of law. They

emphasize the crucial role of the police. Here too there are dangers – for corruption, for discrimination among different classes of putative violators, for the exercise of brutality – and these can exist even where the law itself is decent and judicial procedures impeccable. Much depends on the culture of the police: the extent to which professional standards are appropriate and are enforced by both peer pressure and institutional incentives (such as promotion). And this depends in turn on a certain degree of transparency and answerability for conduct in appropriately public forums.

2.6.2.2 Transparency and Accountability

"Sunlight" so the aphorism goes "is the best antiseptic." When there are cameras that photograph police treatment of arrestees there is less danger of police brutality. When there is full disclosure of politicians' asset portfolios, there is less danger that policy decisions will be made in politicians' private interests. The mere fact that scrutiny is possible in such cases is sufficient to inhibit indefensible practices. In part, the inhibition arises from the fact that people care directly about the extent to which they are esteemed or disesteemed by the general public, a value on which we commented already in Section 2.3.5. In the case of politicians, these public attitudes are buttressed by the fact that candidates who behave "badly" as perceived by the general public can expect to suffer electoral consequences; and in the case of the police, because there is oversight by political agents who are likely to be held responsible if nothing is done.

The transparency that needs to be maintained is not a merely passive property. It is often not enough that the relevant activities are not secret. In many contexts, we also need institutions of publicity: avenues whereby the relevant failures are liable to be publicized. A free and independent media is clearly critical in this regard. Even democratically elected governments need to prove that they are responsive to the needs of their citizens and representative of their interests and preferences. They must be held accountable on an ongoing basis, with all the necessary safeguards to ensure that an unresponsive or unrepresentative government cannot continue in power indefinitely.

Sometimes, to be sure, full public disclosure is not desirable, either because public opinion does not track what is normatively desirable or because the release of information would undercut the desirable effects of policy. The intentions of central banks in relation to monetary policy, much like the battle plans of the military hierarchy, cannot be made available prior to action. Sometimes secrecy is positively valuable. For example, the secret ballot is regarded as a cornerstone of best democratic practice precisely because voters should not be liable to intimidation or undue influence from employers or marriage partners or authority figures. Equally, the proceedings of jury deliberations are insulated from public scrutiny precisely because it is felt that public opinion should have no influence.

Even where there is appropriately no accountability to the general public, there should generally be some kind of accountability. How jurors actually deliberate is rightly subject to scrutiny by other jurors;

indeed, in many jurisdictions, final voting is not secret within the jury. If the absence of a secret ballot in these arenas is desirable, it is because the importance of having jurors answerable *to each other* overrides the risk of intimidation.

No principle of transparency would be acceptable if it rode rough-shod over the value of privacy, which is something else that matters to people for its own sake. People can value their privacy even where they have nothing in particular to hide. Therefore, invasions of people's privacy in the interests of detecting criminal or terrorist activity imposes a loss on ordinary citizens. How much secrecy should shield the "secret police" is a question that ought to be an issue of public judgment and public knowledge.

The upshot of these thoughts is that a requirement of effective transparency applies at least to public institutions, bearing in mind that:

1. there is a presumption in favor of privacy where the information does not impact on public roles;
2. sometimes mechanisms of publicity and accountability can be rendered more effective by focusing on a targeted audience rather than an open-ended one;
3. transparency is a more effective tool when buttressed by broadly democratic institutions – although it may be more needed where democratic constraints are weak or absent.

2.6.2.3   Democracy

Amartya Sen (2009: 329–332) has noted that while institutionalized systems involving the election of legislators may have originated in Europe and North America, many other cultures, including Emperor Ashoka's India and some African cultures, had independently developed the idea that government should rest on open discussion among free and equal citizens. He quotes Nelson Mandela's recollections of local council meetings in Mqhekezweni (Mandela 1994: 21):

> Everyone who wanted to speak did so. It was democracy in its purest form. There may have been a hierarchy of importance among the speakers, but everyone was heard, chief and subject, warrior and medicine man, shopkeeper and farmer, landowner and laborer … The foundation of self-government was that all men were free to voice their options and equal in their value as citizens.

An elaborate democratic system – including checks and balances – was developed by the Oromo people of Ethiopia (Legesse 2000). The Oromo constitution had imposed a system of checks and balances long before the emergence of the so-called modern democracies. Unlike in the Western democratic traditions, power is distributed across generations and age groups in the Oromo *gadaa* government. Elected leaders are required to test their knowledge before assuming power. The *gadaa* national assembly can remove the *gadaa* leader from power if he commits serious mistakes that endanger the peace of the Oromo people.

There are strong reasons to support the principle that all governments should be democratic, in a way that combines democracy's "purest" elements, as singled out by Mandela – discussion among citizens treated as free and equal – with its institutionalization via the election of representatives who make the laws of the jurisdiction in question. Modern representative democracy gives equal political rights to all (honoring the principle of one person one vote), but affords no forum wherein all citizens can gather to deliberate on the common good. Nevertheless, it is viewed as the best way to honor their equal standing as citizens while respecting their basic liberties. At their best, modern democratic arrangements allow citizens to arrive at decisions regarding the common good without doing violence to the diversity of views they hold.

Already, this defense of representative democracy can be seen to respond to several of the general values and principles set out above in Sections 2.3 and 2.4. It has been argued, for instance, that implementing democracy will enhance citizens' well-being by tending to lead to more reliably sensible decisions (Estlund 2008; Landemore 2013), by broadening citizens' sympathies and otherwise enhancing their characters (Mill 1991), or by helping avert famines (Sen 1999: 178–180) and wars – at least with other democratic nations (Rawls 1999b: sec. 5). Others have aimed to ground democracy as necessary for equality (Christiano 2008) or freedom (Pettit 2012). Moreover, understood as involving rule by the people, or collective self-rule, democracy is a political instantiation of the basic value of autonomy (Rousseau 1968, I: 8; Richardson 2002).

Each of these broadly instrumental modes of arguing for democracy has strong merits. However, it is doubtful that any one of them suffices as a complete justification of the principle that governments should be democratic. As noted, this principle calls for combining the element of respectful and reasoned discussion, the element of treating citizens as free and equal, and a set of electoral mechanisms. Accounts appealing just to one basic principle or value seem unable to account for all of these elements of democracy. A more complete justification of democracy may require characterizing it as a distinctive principled response to a number of basic values and principles (Richardson 2002). On such an account, democracy has intrinsic importance and, therefore, normative significance of its own. For that reason, it is important to list the principle of democracy here, as a principle specially applicable to governments.

The democratic principle that we have framed states that all governments should be democratic. There are two ways that this principle might be extended. Each builds on the observation that the core arguments for democracy center on the fact that governmental institutions have power and authority over individuals. First, at the global level, while there is not now a global government, there are many international organizations that wield authority. Working out how to adapt democratic ideals to cover these institutions is an urgent and ongoing effort (Archibugi et al. 2012; Valentini 2012). The second extension would make a case for democracy, or something like it, within a commercial firm or corporation – either by stressing the value of participation (Dewey 1969) or, again, by highlighting resemblances between a corporation's power and authority and a government's (Dahl 1985; Walzer 1983).

2.6.2.4 Giving Rights Determinate Reality

All agents must respect human rights and the equal dignity of persons; it falls specially to governments, however, to give them determinate reality for their own citizens and residents. When they do that, they must exercise diligence, intelligence, and creativity in giving these rights shape in a way that is both robust and suitably tailored to local circumstances.

In describing this duty of governments, we do not need to settle the long-disputed question of whether human rights have determinate content and objective validity that is independent of the establishment of any government. If there are such so-called "natural rights," then governmental efforts to give reality to rights should respect these objective contours. Even absent such an agreement, however, there is, as we noted in Section 2.4.2, broad consensus on the moral importance of many human rights, despite disagreement about how best to justify them. Whatever their ultimate normative source, these rights will need to be given an effective reality by concrete institutions. This effort will inevitably shape them in specific ways that are not determinately fixed by their general justifications.

This need for governments to give rights concrete reality has been most obvious to people in the case of so-called "positive rights." Take, for example, the right to work. Article 23 of the *Universal Declaration of Human Rights* states that "Everyone has the right to work, to free choice of employment, [and] to just and favorable conditions of work and to protection against unemployment." Without appropriate governmental institutions, this declaration would be, as it is pejoratively put, merely aspirational. To take an extreme case, in a so-called "command economy," an individual's choice of employment is not free. More generally, the right to work is ill realized without some form of social guarantee of employment security.

Governments must also take affirmative steps to give concrete reality to the core human rights, including the negative ones. In order for anyone meaningfully to enjoy a right not to be assaulted, a police force, a criminal justice system, and perhaps street lights need to be in place (Shue 1996: 37–38). As common as these measures are, they are not strictly necessary means to realizing these rights, but time-tested sufficient means of effectively realizing these rights.

As it deploys such means, the state will also, unavoidably, be engaged in settling the precise contours of the relevant rights. Immanuel Kant (1996) argued that getting the contours of rights definitely settled is the key reason why individuals have a duty to submit to political rule. Consider, for example, whether the right to bodily integrity should be interpreted as generating an objection to someone taking photographs of one's body, perhaps for advertising use (cf. Pallikathayil 2010). Does it imply that it is wrong for medical scientists or police detectives to make use of someone's bodily fluids or tissues for research, investigative, or commercial purposes (cf. Skloot 2010)? More broadly, the specific contours of privacy rights not only vary in different cultures but are now constantly being forced to shift in reaction to shifting information technologies (Allen 2011).

2.6.3 Principles Applicable to Civil Society

We have already characterized civil society as a heterogeneous collection of institutions, associations, and practices that are not properly characterized either as the market or as political institutions (Section 2.6.1). This subsection elaborates additional principles that could be seen as applying distinctively to the domain of civil society and its treatment by political institutions, with many of these also reinforcing the basic principles set out in Section 2.4.

2.6.3.1 Toleration

Requiring peaceably accepting differences with others, such as religious ones, toleration is a principle most appropriately applied to the realm of civil society. Honoring principles of toleration is a prerequisite for any more robust and valuable respect for others' cultures and beliefs. Toleration presumes the existence of practices or beliefs that people consider wrong or perhaps even bad, but that they are voluntarily willing to accept under certain conditions. In societies marked by strong cultural differences, for example, states can and do make laws and policies to promote multiculturalism, mostly with a view to securing harmony and peaceful coexistence among members of different cultures, races, and religious communities living in a bounded political community. Legislated multiculturalism however will remain fragile unless individuals and groups in societies learn to value pluralism and diversity, and attitudes of toleration are fostered in civil society (Maclure and Taylor 2011).

In all free and democratic societies, there will be a plurality of incompatible, but reasonable, religious, philosophical, moral, and political doctrines that individuals and groups subscribe to, and that are comprehensive in their scope. These belong to what Rawls calls the "background culture" of civil society, expressed in its daily life, its associations, its universities, and churches (Rawls 2005: 14). How then, despite these deep divisions, can people live together as free and equal citizens of a stable, just, and well-ordered society? The challenge is to elaborate a political conception of justice that even a diverse citizenry holding a plurality of deeply opposed but reasonable doctrines can collectively affirm.

Toleration should not merely be a matter of the powerful choosing to be indulgent or of people merely facing the necessity of getting along (Forst 2003). Rather, despite holding incompatible ethical beliefs and subscribing to different cultural practices, people can still respect each other as moral equals, making it possible for them to come together to define a framework for their collective life that is governed by norms that they all accept but that do not go in favor of any one "ethical community" (Forst 2003, 74). The limits to justifiable toleration would flow from two criteria: reciprocity, which prevents us from claiming for ourselves a resource that we deny to others; and generality, which requires that the reasons we offer in support of certain norms should be acceptable as valid to everyone involved as free and equal persons (Forst 2003, 76).

A plurality of conceptions of the good thus applies, *pace* Rawls, not only in societies that meld people from different cultures but in every society where individuals have the freedom to frame and pursue their own conceptions of the good. Conceptions of the individual and the common good will clash even in a culturally homogeneous society, so long as it respects basic liberties. These are discussed and arbitrated, through the exercise of public reason in the public sphere – itself an important institution (Habermas 1989; Richardson 2002: ch. 13).

Configured as a realm where citizens, of equal moral standing, recognize themselves as social beings and give expression to this recognition through mutual cooperation, civil society thus provides crucial conditions for democracy. Within a public sphere, bolstered by protection of the freedoms of association and expression, civil society's many associations can fruitfully interact, making possible the articulation of the common or public good. Civil society is thus a "source of both value and values" (Edwards 2011: 5) or, as Michael Walzer described it, a space where all visions of the good life are included but none is privileged (Walzer 2007: 123). It is in civil society that the preliminary negotiations among these multiple and competing visions takes place, though the final determination of the vision that will guide society occurs through processes of democratic decision-making.

2.6.3.2   Educating and Supporting Citizens

It is therefore preeminently in civil society that citizens are prepared for participation in public activity. Citizenship entails more than simply voting every few years, presuming a commitment to some notion of the common good that can motivate active participation in public affairs. This could take many forms: debate and disagreement; forming or joining associations that represent one's particular vision of the common good; or seeking public office. A society's educational institutions play a central role in creating citizens, especially in a democracy (Gutmann 1987).

Rights that are formally guaranteed by the basic structure, but remain substantively unavailable to citizens, may also be claimed through practices of "insurgent citizenship" (Holston 2008), making civil society a site of contestation over citizens' entitlements. In the extreme case of an unresponsive state, this may require movements and practices of civil disobedience that are viewed as legitimate if undertaken publicly and nonviolently, with the willingness to suffer punishment for violating the law (e.g. Walzer 2007).

Associations in civil society complement the work of the institutions of representative democracy in giving basic rights and liberties determinate reality (see Section 2.6.2.4). While it is formal democratic institutions that provide the mechanisms enabling a society to chart its path to progress, as its citizens understand and define it, the many elements of civil society play a complementary role in setting social norms and maintaining a democratic political culture that is respectful of core values and principles such as freedom and justice.

2.6.4   Global Justice

We began our discussion of the different units whose progress is to be assessed (Section 2.5) by stating that we may take for granted that

among these is the global unit. For some dimensions of assessing global progress, shifting from the national to the global level of assessment is a simple matter of aggregating the indicator data. That shift is considerably more complex when the dimension under assessment is justice. Under the heading of justice, we have discussed different distributive principles (such as equality and sufficiency) (Section 2.4.3), and also different accounts of the metric of distributive justice, such as resources and capabilities (Section 2.3.1.2). In addition to articulating these aspects of the relevant principles, accounts of justice must also specify among whom such principles apply. Who is included within the scope of justice? This section looks specifically at the extent to which principles of justice should apply to the world as a whole. Are there global principles of justice? Or do principles of justice apply only within units like the state or nation? Or do some principles apply globally and others within the state or nation?

2.6.4.1   The Geographical Scope of Justice

Traditionally, theories of justice have taken the nation or the state to define the scope of principles of distributive justice. However, increasingly political philosophers have argued that they apply – also or instead – at the global level.

We can divide arguments for global justice into "associational" and "nonassociational" approaches. The former hold that principles of justice apply to, and regulate, "associations," where an association is a catch-all term for human cooperative groupings, including various different kinds of social or economic system. The latter, nonassociational approach, by contrast, holds that principles of justice can apply to a set of persons regardless of whether or not its members share membership in some preexisting social or economic or political association. Though these two approaches differ in their starting points, they tend to converge in their conclusions.

Consider associational approaches first. A leading exponent of an associational approach is Rawls's *A Theory of Justice* (1999a), which develops principles of justice that apply to the "basic structure" of a society (see Box 2.6). Now, although every nation-state has a basic structure, many have argued that thinking only of the basic structure of nations is no longer tenable. Charles Beitz (1999: 143–153) has argued that, given the nature and extent of global interdependence, one must conclude that there is a global basic structure, and hence should endorse global principles of justice. His argument draws attention to the extent of the global trade of resources, goods, and services; the existence of multinational corporations; and the influence of the international financial system, comprising numerous transnational and global regulatory frameworks and regimes and institutions such as the World Trade Organization, the World Bank, and the International Monetary Fund. All of these affect people throughout the world. This position receives further support once we consider global environmental interdependence, dramatic in the case of climate change. Drawing on these kinds of economic, political, and environmental linkages, we can see that in a globalized world, there is a powerful case for endorsing global principles of distributive justice, and that confining principles of justice to states is implausible.

A related reason for endorsing global principles of justice has been proposed by Thomas Pogge. Pogge's argument has two key elements. First, he holds that "any institutional design is unjust when it foreseeably produces an avoidable human rights deficit" (2008: 25). He then adds that agents have a strict duty not to uphold and support such unjust schemes. If they do uphold them they are violating their duty not to harm others by acting in a way that sustains a system that foreseeably and avoidably denies people their rights.

The second step in Pogge's argument is that the governments of wealthy countries are, in fact, violating this duty and are responsible for global poverty. They do so by imposing unjust global trade rules that enable them to further enrich themselves, often by colluding with unjust and repressive states (Pogge 2008: 119–121; Wenar 2016). The governments of affluent countries thus have a duty of justice to eradicate poverty, where this should not be understood as having an amorphous duty to aid the global poor, but rather as a strict duty of justice not to collude in causing their poverty.

Notwithstanding their differences, Beitz and Pogge's arguments rest on a shared normative assumption and a shared empirical one. Both assume that justice applies within systems characterized by at least a certain level of interdependence. Second, their arguments assume that the level of interdependence and economic integration required for the application of principles of distributive justice is met at the global level.

In contrast, the nonassociational arguments for global justice do not depend for their force on empirical claims about the extent of global interdependence. They hold that principles of justice can apply even if persons do not share membership in any preexisting association.

One example of this kind of approach is Henry Shue's defense of basic rights to a minimally decent human life (1996). Shue argues that persons have a basic right to have their basic needs met, where a basic right is a right that a person must enjoy if he or she is to enjoy other rights. Since humans all need food, water, and shelter to enjoy other rights, they have, on Shue's argument, a basic right to this minimum standard of living. Shue then reasons that this entails not only a duty not to cause poverty but also two more affirmative duties – a duty "to protect from deprivation" and a duty "to aid the deprived" (1996: 68).

Others go further. Some think that Rawls's Difference Principle should be applied at the global level, and thus that global inequalities should be arranged so as to maximize the condition of the world's least advantaged (Beitz 1999: part III). Or they adopt an egalitarian approach, and hold that global inequalities are unjust (Caney 2005). Luck egalitarians hold that "it is bad – unjust and unfair – for some to be worse off than others through no fault of their own" (Temkin 1993: 13). If this is right then it would suggest that it is bad for some to be worse off than others because they come from one country rather than another, and thus that luck egalitarianism should apply at the global level (see Section 2.5.3).

Yet in all these approaches the central cosmopolitan point remains: the core tenets underlying standard accounts of justice – whether associational or nonassociational – suggest that those accounts should apply at the global level.

2.6.4.2   Three Kinds of Association

Some, not accepting this point but not willing to jettison the category of global justice, either, hold that whilst there are some global principles of justice, there are others that apply only within the nation or state. Many, for example, have argued that egalitarian principles apply only within the state (e.g. Miller 2007), but that a threshold based conception of justice applies globally.

First, some reason that principles of egalitarian justice apply within schemes of reciprocity. They further argue that the state is a realm of reciprocity but that there is no global scheme of reciprocal cooperation. They infer from this that egalitarian principles apply within the state, but not at the global level (Sangiovanni 2007).

Second, some argue that the state is a morally distinctive kind of relationship because it exercises coercion. Michael Blake (2013), for example, starts from a commitment to autonomy, and then argues that this has two implications. First, since autonomy is centrally valuable it is important that everyone enjoys the decent minimum standard of living necessary to be an autonomous agent (so a principle of sufficiency should apply at the global level). Second, however, when a state coerces its citizens in ways that purport to put them under legal duties, it owes them a justification for that restriction of their autonomy. And this, Blake contends, can be met only by the state applying egalitarian standards to its citizens. Since he believes that there is no analogous coercive framework at the global level, he concludes that there is no case for equality at the global level.

However, even if equality applies in schemes of reciprocity, it does not follow that it *only* applies in such schemes. The argument from autonomy and coercion is similarly vulnerable. Some will argue that the global order is indeed relevantly coercive (Valentini 2011: 115ff); but waiving that objection, that equality applies in a coercive framework does not show that it applies *only* in such a context. (For further discussion and references see Caney 2011.)

2.6.4.3   Different Principles for Different Issues?

One further question needs to be addressed. At the global level there are very many issues that might plausibly be thought to be subject to principles of justice. These include (among others) the nature of global trade, the distribution of burdens and benefits in combatting climate change, migration, and free movement, the regulation of international financial markets, international labor rights, and rules concerning sweatshop labor. This heterogeneous list raises the question of whether there should be different principles of justice for different issues. Such a diversity of principles could mirror to some extent the diversity of global institutions, which include institutions concerned with trade (like the WTO), climate change (the United Framework Convention on Climate Change [UNFCCC]), the Ozone layer (the Montreal Protocol), the use of the sea (United Nations

Convention on the Law of the Sea), labor rights (the International Labor Organization), and so on.

However, although the issues dealt with by global institutions are heterogeneous, it would be implausible to treat any of them in isolation, as they are profoundly causally interdependent. For example, trade (by facilitating fossil-fuel-intensive economic growth) can contribute to climate change; tackling climate change by using biofuels instead of fossil fuel energy can lead to a spike in food prices in developing countries, thus affecting rights to food. Given this extensive interdependence among all of the issues dealt with by international institutions, there is a need for an overarching set of principles that regulates the ways in which they interact. This is especially so, given that the different policy areas often bear on the same interests of individuals, such as health and the capacity to lead the life of one's choice.

2.7   Looking Ahead: Using the Compass

This chapter has aimed to set out the key values and principles relevant to assessing social progress. These are relevant to all social domains, albeit in differing degree and with greater or lesser directness. We have concentrated on values and principles that have a claim to nonderivative importance – normative significance that is not clearly derivable from any other value or principle. Even with this restriction, we have generated a long list of values and principles that must be taken into account in assessing social progress (see Table 2.1).

To bring these values and principles to bear in assessing social progress and in guiding policy proposals in any given social domain, it will often be necessary and apt to do more work in interpreting and specifying them in a way suitable to that domain. Sincere efforts at doing so will respect the values and principles in question.

Assessing progress – achieved or expected – and designing policies are different but related activities. In this concluding section we discuss briefly how to bring these relatively abstract values and principles usefully to bear on specific issues. We first discuss the idea of using report cards to value policy outcomes (has there been social progress?). We then comment on the link between outcomes and specific policy actions (what policy measures should be taken?). Here we are using the term "outcomes" broadly, to include whether or not the principles' requirements on process have been or will be satisfied over the relevant period.

2.7.1   Evaluating Social Progress and Regress

Social progress is an overarching concept that integrates many social domains. An overall accounting of social progress would need to consider the causal interactions among these different domains and how to integrate these in an overall normative perspective. The examples abound, but let us just mention the well-known relationship between health and the distribution of material welfare. Yet, for all practical purposes, there is a division of labor with different

actors responsible for action in different domains (Section 2.4 *init.*; Box 2.6). These specific actors often cannot meaningfully focus on overall social progress as such, and instead need guidance tailored to their specific domain. Moreover, while ultimately all values and principles may be relevant in all domains, some will be essential in some domains and largely negligible in others. We therefore illustrate how to apply our normative framework with a specific domain in mind (e.g. climate change, income distribution, gender relations, democracy).

The *first* challenge is then to determine which of the *values and principles are (most) relevant for the specific issue at hand*. To do so well is an art, not a science, and will benefit from input from a wide range of perspectives.

After selecting the relevant values and principles, one must answer two follow-up questions. First, at what level should the values and principles be applied and evaluated (see Section 2.5)? At the local, the regional, the national, the world level? Including future generations and nonhuman animals or not? The decisions in this regard will affect how the relevant values and principles should be interpreted and made operational. For example, the content of distributive justice might reasonably be thought to depend on the level at which it is evaluated. One may be egalitarian at a lower level and aim at a decent minimum at the world level (see Section 2.6.4.2). One may have a preference-based concept of well-being when thinking about actual generations but use a more objective well-being concept for future generations, whose preferences are unknown (Karnein 2016). One might accept a preference-based concept of well-being for humans (who have a sophisticated valuational capacity), but understand well-being in a hedonist way for other animals. These choices matter and must be made explicit at the start.

The second follow-up question is who the relevant actors are, whose past or expected contributions to social progress are to be assessed? As noted in Section 2.6, certain principles apply specially to certain types of actors, such as governments, individuals, or social organizations. More generally, it is common to look to different sets of actors to take the lead in realizing different values and principles. Here, too, complex interactions may be expected. For instance, within a well-organized society, even if acts of generosity and beneficence should come in the first place from individuals, government policy can facilitate these actions both by providing tax incentives, say, and by providing social safety nets that prevent such generosity from being overwhelmed. We will return to this second question in the following subsection.

Suppose now that someone concerned with progress in a given social domain has selected and interpreted a set of relevant values and principles and specified at which level and to which actors they should be applied. To go further, one will have to make the analysis still more specific and operational. *How can one move from the relatively abstract values and principles set out in this chapter toward a more specific set of indicators?*

The first step in this process is to make explicit how one interprets the principle. It is not enough to say that one is in favor of "distributive justice" or of "freedom," because the ideals of distributive justice or freedom can be interpreted in different ways. And these different interpretations will have consequences when we apply them to devise policies. Yet even where we have offered a single interpretation of a given value or principle – such as of *esteem* in Section 2.3.5 or *the rule of law* in Section 2.6.2.1 – we do not suppose or suggest that the work of interpretation is done. It may be necessary to specify the relevant values and principles further so as to bring out their full relevance to the domain, level, and actors in question. For instance, open-minded evaluation of the effect of evolving social media on social progress will not tendentiously specify the value of *relational goods* either as being fully achieved by being someone's online "friend" or as registering only face-to-face encounters; but, as technology continues to evolve, it will need to consider revised interpretations of this value that appropriately take account of new obstacles to and opportunities for human interrelationship that the newest social media provide.

Once an adequately interpreted and specified set of values and principles is in hand, one's aim is to evaluate, on their basis, whether a move from situation A to situation B is a case of social progress or not. This requires that we can structure and interpret the facts so that they can be evaluated in the light of each of the relevant values and principles. Suppose we care about the environment (Section 2.3.7). How to determine in which social state it is better honored and protected? And the same problem arises even for defining indicators for a seemingly straightforward concept such as *income inequality*. It is not always obvious how to define income; and even if it were, different inequality measures may evaluate a change in the income distribution differently.

In most cases one will therefore need a set of complementary indicators adequately to capture each interpreted value or principle; and even then care is needed. The task of bridging indicators to the underlying values and principles is even more delicate if we want to evaluate a development over time or compare the performance of different countries, since an apt selection of indicators will depend on the context. This difficulty has nothing to do with the degree of quantification of the indicators (to which we will return). Even if we restrict ourselves to ordinal indicators, each specific choice thereof will unavoidably be restrictive.

Once one has selected a set of indicators of the satisfaction of the relevant values and principles, one can set up a *report card*, monitoring, say, the yearly changes in the indicators or comparing the values of the indicators for different evaluation units (e.g. countries). Such a report card should be set up separately for each value and principle (see Table 2.3). If the full set of report cards reveals that some indicators show improvement and other indicators show disimprovement, an intelligent conversation is needed to come to an overall judgment; but the set of report cards should contain the information that is needed to feed that intelligent conversation.

To arrive at an *overall evaluation of social progress (or regress)*, requires two further steps. First, evaluating progress within any chosen domain will likely require taking account of various values and principles that may be at play. For example, inequality, freedom, and esteem may each be relevant to evaluating changes in the income distribution. Assessing progress in that domain will then require looking at this trio of values and principles. Second, *evaluating overall social progress requires*

Table 2.3 | Example of domain report card

PRINCIPLE OR VALUE X	Evaluation unit and period	...	Evaluation unit and period
Indicator 1			
Indicator 2			
...			
Indicator n			
Summary evaluation			

bringing together the results in the various social domains (e.g. income distribution, health, respect for political rights).

Similar methodological questions arise regarding each of these two steps. Let us first look at the overall evaluation within one domain. This is easy in situations of dominance, i.e. if there is progress (of regress) for all values and principles at the same time. It is also easy if one decides to give absolute (or "lexicographic") priority to one principle or value over the others and therefore is willing effectively to disregard the performance on the other dimensions. Setting aside these extreme approaches, however, one has to confront the issue of how to trade off a better performance ("progress") on one principle for a worse performance ("regress") on another principle.

The most radical solution is to apply weights. This basically requires that all the relevant indicators be quantitative. Simple weighted measures of social progress, aggregating at the same time over values or principles and over domains, have become very popular in recent years. They have the apparent advantage of transparency. However, their uncritical use may be dangerously misleading. Users of these measures are strongly tempted to look only at the resulting final score. This means neglecting both the potential weakness (or at least narrowness) and the informational richness of the underlying indicators. This danger can be exacerbated by the temptation to choose indicators based on how easy it is to define them quantitatively and to find data corresponding to them. Moreover, looking only at the score resulting from the exercise also means accepting uncritically the relative weights that are used to specify the tradeoffs. For lack of a better alternative, index designers all too often use an equal weighting procedure, but without having any good arguments for this choice. Finally, most simple measures assume that the set of weights is constant over time or in between-country comparisons. There are good reasons to question this assumption, as it seems natural to assume that the differing evaluative perspectives of the people in these different societies or the different circumstances of these societies – or both – will provide grounds for varying the weight ascribed to different objectives.

Weighting may be more or less acceptable if the items to be weighted are expressed in commensurable units. After all, the concave social welfare functions described in Section 2.4.4 in some sense exemplify sophisticated weighting the well-being of different individuals. However, when we have to consider very different objectives (esteem, cultural heritage, freedom, and the distribution of material consumption), all attempts at explicit weighting will necessarily do violence to the qualitative distinctions among the values and principles in question. This does not necessarily mean, however, that we cannot say

Table 2.4 | Synthetic report card

SOCIAL PROGRESS IN DOMAIN X	Evaluation unit and period	...	Evaluation unit and period
Summary evaluation principle 1			
Summary evaluation principle 2			
...			
Summary evaluation principle k			
Summary evaluation			

anything at all. Intelligent conversation can elucidate the tradeoffs and ultimately contribute to some definition of social progress in a given domain, perhaps by refining and enriching the underlying concepts. Provisional attempts to set up some formal weighting scheme can spur intelligent discussion even if they do not end up being accepted as definitive. They may indeed serve as a starting point for that discussion and perhaps even help in structuring it. Techniques of multicriteria decision-making can be useful in this respect. However, one should never take their outcomes simply at face value.

If desired, one can bring together the summary evaluations from the report cards on each different value and principle into one overall report card on social progress in domain X that could look as in Table 2.4.

Similar methodological questions arise in the last step, which is the *aggregation of the outcomes in the different domains to arrive at an overall social assessment*. Of course it can be informative to show that a nation – or the world – is doing better on life expectancy but worse on mental health and equality. But what are we to make of its "social progress" (or regress) "*all things considered*"? Here also, explicit weighting is an extreme solution. And here also it is not meaningful to accept uncritically the findings of any mechanistic weighting procedure. Even without explicit weighting one can get interesting insights by exploiting the assumption that a specific outcome becomes relatively less important as we have more of it. We illustrate this possibility further in Box 2.7. Yet, the ultimate evaluation of whether there has been social progress will have to follow from an informed and democratic deliberation procedure.

A complication arises if, as is likely, the same values or principles are relevant in more than one domain, giving rise to two distinct ways of proceeding. For instance, well-being and freedom will surely be affected by the situation in many domains: income, health, political institutions. It may then be misleading to first formulate an evaluation for each of the domains (with a narrowed down concept of well-being and freedom) and then "aggregate" over the different domains, for this will ignore the effects on well-being and freedom of interactions among the domains. An alternative option would be to first aggregate the effects of changes in the different domains on each of the basic normative dimensions, and then in a second step decide about the relative weighting thereof. The latter option is more difficult, but is better suited to take into account the interactions among the various domains, though perhaps less well suited to take into account interactions among the values and principles.

2.7.2 From Principles and Values to Action

In the previous subsection we introduced the idea of report cards for evaluating the outcomes (or the performance) of individual countries or of the whole world on the relevant dimensions of social progress. Evaluating outcomes is important and relevant, but one would hope that a compass could also be useful prospectively, i.e. to choose among different policy options.

It is clear, however, that a compass is not sufficient to find the best way forward. At the very least, one also needs a map. While we deliberately remained in this chapter at the level of normative principles, for policy analysis one also needs empirical knowledge about the facts and (even more difficult) about the causal relationships between actions and outcomes. Indeed, while mere correlations may be useful in a descriptive endeavor, they can be highly misleading when deciding about policies.

Thinking about policies requires taking into account feasibility. In this chapter, we have set out many values and principles that have a claim to nonderivative importance. Policy-makers can use this list of values and principles to help guide them toward a clearer understanding of what they seek to accomplish in any given context. The limits of feasibility always take shape in relation to some idea of what one is trying to do. Conversely, one's ideas about what one is trying to do often come to take more definite shape as one struggles with the limits of feasibility. In this regard, it is important to remember that it can make sense to think about what one seeks for the sake of what. For instance, macroeconomic policy might sensibly treat the capability to work as a central capability worth promoting for its own sake, while at the same time viewing this capability as a means to allowing individuals not only to earn income but also to realize their full potential (Sen 1975; Richardson 2015).

Interacting with one's evolving sense of the aims of policy are at least three types of constraints. First, there are resource constraints. Suppose that policy-makers could effect the social changes they want in the light of the ideals introduced earlier; i.e. suppose that they have an almost unlimited ability at social engineering. They accordingly would be able to select a "first best" policy option, to use the economics jargon. Even so, they would nonetheless be unable to achieve everything in a finite world with a limited set of (both natural and human) resources. They would still have normatively difficult choices to make.

Of course, the supposition that policy-makers could effect any social change they wanted is highly unrealistic. Society is not perfectly malleable. Governments do not have all the information needed to implement "first best"-policies – often because they lack knowledge about the true productive capacities of individuals (needed to implement a just scheme of income taxes) or about their preferences for public goods (needed to avoid free-rider behavior). Since individuals' behavioral choices will not necessarily be guided by the social principles that the government would like to pursue and since their behavior cannot be controlled by the government (because of informational asymmetries) and probably should not fully be controlled by the government even if it could (because of respect for human freedom), policy proposals will have to take into account incentive constraints. We then move in what economists call a "second

Box 2.7 | Weighing and Convexity

Even without explicit weighting, one could exploit the notion of convexity in any defensible aggregation function to induce something about how the relative priority of different elements is changing over time, or how it might differ between places. The idea of convexity is rather like the principle of diminishing marginal value of each specific element. It says that the appropriate terms of trade between elements reflect how much of each element is present. It does not tell you what the relative weights between elements are, but it does permit two kinds of comparisons: intertemporal and international.

Suppose we have very strong evidence for believing that there has been significant material progress since say 1700. We believe, say, that average income per head in the world has increased by about a factor of ten over the last three centuries. We do not know so much about equality except in the recent past; but suppose we focus on just the period from 1950 to the present. Within the US, GDP/head has almost tripled since 1950; and inequality has worsened since 1950. What do these facts suggest? They suggest that whatever the value of additional equality in terms of additional growth forgone (the "appropriate terms of trade") was in 1950, those relative values will have changed significantly over the last 70 years: increased equality should now be worth more than 70 years ago and increased average income should be worth less. The claim is a normative one, not a descriptive one.

Consider a different application: the tradeoff between mental health and longevity. We know that for every decade of the twentieth century, life expectancy in the West rose for virtually every category of persons by about two years per decade. Accordingly, the proper terms of trade between actions designed to increase longevity and any element that has remained roughly constant ought to increase the relative priority attached to the latter. Treating suicide as an indicator of mental health suggests that, relative to increasing longevity, reducing suicide should be a considerably higher priority now than it was in 1900.

The crucial overarching claim here is that in weighting the various elements of social progress to achieve an overall measure the weighting function is properly convex; other things equal, it ought to treat any given element as being of less significance relative to others, the more extensively that element is achieved vis-à-vis others. This is necessarily a normative claim because social progress is necessarily a normative concept: "social progress" is something that, other things equal, we ought to promote. Convexity is a substantive normative property and perhaps needs more defense than it receives here. But it is surely a weaker assumption than a full specification of weights; and it does allow us to say some things and to suggest some priorities in settings where we would otherwise have to be silent.

best"-setting. Note that we do not argue here for an adjustment of the ideal (e.g. from equality to maximin); we simply draw attention to the obstacles on the way to the ideal. Note also that one has to interpret "incentives" broadly: human beings are not driven only by materialistic motives.

While incentive constraints are the main focus of economists, we mentioned already in Section 2.2.1.2 that policy choices can also be constrained by moral considerations. This is a third way that policy choices can be constrained. In the case of some of the principles mentioned in this chapter, such as respect for basic rights, these constraints will ordinarily take the form of taking certain options off the table. For instance, policy-makers should simply not consider what they might be able to do if they could arbitrarily lock up or surreptitiously sterilize members of a small but obstreperous minority group. When dealing with tensions among principles or with the margins of their interpretation, however, it can be reasonable to take into account feasibility and incentive constraints (Rawls 1999a: part III). Consider, for example, what exactly should be done to implement an adequate system of transparency and accountability or how to implement religious liberty in a way that respects the freedom to exercise one's religious beliefs yet avoids allowing discrimination. When moral principles enter policy discussions, this may take the form of a requirement that some principles can never be subject to tradeoffs. In some cases, however, moral constraints must be introduced in the analysis explicitly.

Only a thorough empirical analysis, taking into account these constraints and incorporating the best available knowledge, may in the end lead to a well-supported set of specific policy proposals, linked to the different outcome goals. Remember, moreover, that different actors – and not only governments – are at play. The actions they each should take will differ, but will influence each other and must therefore be considered together.

Box 2.8 | Sustainable Development Goals

SUSTAINABLE DEVELOPMENT GOALS (United Nations 2015)	IN THIS CHAPTER
[Sustainability as itself a goal]	See Environmental values (2.3.7) and The ethical status of future generations (2.5.4)
1. End poverty in all its forms everywhere	Basic needs (2.4.3.2)
2. End hunger, achieve food security and improved nutrition, and promote sustainable agriculture	Basic needs (2.4.3.2)
3. Ensure healthy lives …	Basic needs (2.4.3.2)
… And promote well-being for all at all ages	Well-being (2.3.1)
4. Ensure inclusive and equitable quality education and promote lifelong learning opportunities for all	Equality of opportunity (2.4.3.3)
5. Achieve gender equality and empower all women and girls	Equality of opportunity (2.4.3.3); Gender Box 2.4
6. Ensure availability and sustainable management of water and sanitation for all	Basic needs (2.4.3.2)
7. Ensure access to affordable, reliable, sustainable, and modern energy for all	Basic needs (2.4.3.2)
8. Promote sustained, inclusive, and sustainable economic growth,	(this is a mere means)
… [and] full and productive employment and decent work for all	Giving rights determinate reality (2.6.2.4), including the right to work
9. Build resilient infrastructure, promote inclusive and sustainable industrialization, and foster innovation	(these items are mere means)
10. Reduce inequality within and among countries	Distributive justice (2.4.3)
11. Make cities and human settlements inclusive, safe, resilient, and sustainable	Basic needs (2.4.3.2)
12. Ensure sustainable consumption and production patterns	(these are means to sustainability)
13. Take urgent action to combat climate change and its impacts	(urging the importance of taking means)
14. Conserve and sustainably use the oceans, seas and marine resources for sustainable development	(these are means to sustainability)
15. Protect, restore, and promote sustainable use of terrestrial ecosystems, sustainably manage forests, combat desertification, halt and reverse land degradation, and halt biodiversity loss	(these are means to sustainability)
16. Promote peaceful and inclusive societies for sustainable development, provide access to justice for all, and build effective, accountable and inclusive institutions at all levels	Solidarity (2.3.4); Justice (2.4.1, 2.4.3, 2.6.4)
17. Strengthen the means of implementation and revitalize the global partnership for sustainable development	(these are means to sustainability)

Table 2.5 | Toolkit table

	Policy-makers	International organization	NGOs	Citizens
Goal 1	Policy a	Action A	Action A'	Action A"
Goal 2	Policy b	Action B	Action B'	Action B"
…				

This sort of analysis may finally result in a "toolkit table" that could look as in Table 2.5.

One could of course go further and add policy targets – e.g. a minimal share of GDP that should be devoted by the government to health care, or a minimal number of local medical units that should be set up by a NGO. Policy targets will necessarily depend on the specific situation and have to be adapted continuously. They can act as motivating and coordinating focal points. It may be convenient for actors to concentrate on a specific action target, rather than always to have to think in terms of a broader concept of social progress. On the other hand, there is also a danger of confusion between policy targets and normatively significant outcomes. What ultimately matters for social progress are the outcomes that are summarized on the report cards, which reflect values and principles of nonderivative importance. The distinction between outcomes that matter normatively for their own sakes and policy targets that may reflect mere means to those ends is

not always made explicitly in the lists of criteria that play a prominent role in actual policy debates. We illustrate this in Box 2.8.

Two important concluding remarks. First, decisions have to be taken under risk and/or uncertainty. Using the traditional distinction (Knight 1921) adverted to in Section 2.1, a situation of risk is a situation where we can attach probabilities to the possible events on the basis of evidence; a situation of uncertainty is one in which one cannot do this. Situations of risk can reasonably well be handled using traditional criteria of rational choice, although there is no consensus about whether one should take an ex ante or an ex post approach. Situations of uncertainty raise more challenging problems. It is important to think explicitly about risk and uncertainty when devising policies. Shifts in risk assessments should lead to policy adjustments. Moreover, in evaluating policies retrospectively, it is crucial to recognize that the decisions had to be taken in considerable ignorance about the actual state of the world. Even a policy that was optimal in the light of the knowledge that was available at the moment of taking the decision can be seen in retrospect to have had disastrous consequences, perhaps because unlikely possibilities ended up being realized. It is even possible that all the policy targets are reached but that the (normatively more significant) outcome targets are not. Even though Machiavelli (1995: ch. 18) was surely right that people commonly judge political events by the outcomes, policy-makers should neither be blamed for having been merely unlucky nor praised when unwise policies turn out well by sheer good luck.

Social Progress: A Compass

Box 2.9 | The Limits of Markets

Societies have always drawn limits on the kinds of things that can be bought and sold. While there is universal agreement that human beings should not be bought and sold (although in practice human trafficking remains an urgent problem) the morality of many other trades is debated. Table 2.6 uses the values detailed in this chapter to understand the issues at stake in some contested markets. The values we have highlighted here are inequality, understood as inequality not just in income and wealth but also in social standing; setbacks to individual welfare or autonomy; and harms to background social institutions and practices, including culture (Satz 2010).

For example, markets in child labor are problematic because of the harms to the child laborer, because of the inequality and vulnerability they produce between children and families, and because they undermine democratic institutions and lead to low productivity and growth. By contrast, a market in apples is unlikely to have such effects.

As can be seen in this chart, problematic markets can differ in what makes them so. This can be important for policy. For example, because the main reason for concern about markets for addictive drugs is harms to the users, effective regulation may remove the principal objections to such markets. For the same reason, banning certain addictive drugs may result in greater net harm to individuals and to society. This is arguably the case with current drug policy in the United States. Banning child labor looks to be highly justified given the above analysis, but care must be taken that such bans do not drive child labor underground with worse consequences for children and their families. That is why the best way of addressing some problematic markets is to provide resources and empowerment to the poor and vulnerable. This is particularly the case for an issue such as prostitution, where the principal problem is the marginalization and exploitation of the sex workers. By contrast, in the case of some problematic markets such as trade in antiquities, where what is most problematic is not the treatment of the purveyors but the fate of the items traded, policies should be instead driven by broader social values. These distinctions are illustrated in Table 2.6.

Table 2.6 | Different reasons for limiting markets

Contested or banned markets	Inequality	Harms to individual well-being	Harms to society
Child labor	X	X	X
Prostitution	X	–	–
Antiquities		–	X
Blood diamonds	–	X	X
International arms		X	X
Addictive drugs	–	X	–

X signifies a high score; – signifies a possible problem

Second, much of our discussion in this section assumed a setting with given institutions, with policy-makers taking decisions within a given structure. This perspective on its own does not sufficiently take into account the possibility of changing those decision-making structures, which is sometimes essential to social progress. If institutional changes need to be made, who is going to implement them? For instance, which actors can legitimately contribute to making the political process in a country more democratic, if those in power resist such change? Which actors can make steps in the direction of a better-functioning market? While feasibility constraints loom large in this context, the normative framework that has been introduced in this chapter can also be used to motivate and evaluate institutional change.

In Box 2.9 we illustrate this for one specific but highly relevant issue: the limits to be imposed on markets.

References

Allen, A. 2015. *The End of Progress: Decolonizing the Normative Foundations of Critical Theory*. New York: Columbia University Press.

Allen, A.L. 2011. *Unpopular Privacy: What Must We Hide?* Oxford: Oxford University Press.

Anderson, E. 1999. "What Is the Point of Equality?" *Ethics* 109: 287–337.

Archibugi, D., M. Koenig-Archibugi, and R. Marchetti (eds.) 2012. *Global Democracy: Normative and Empirical Perspectives*. Cambridge: Cambridge University Press.

Arrhenius, G. 2000. "An Impossibility Theorem for Welfarist Axiologies," *Economics and Philosophy* 16: 247–66.

Arrhenius, G. 2011. "The Impossibility of a Satisfactory Population Ethics," in E.N. Dzhafarov and L. Perry (eds.), *Descriptive and Normative Approaches to Human Behavior, Advanced Series on Mathematical Psychology*. Singapore: World Scientific Publishing Company.

Arrhenius, G. Forthcoming. *Population Ethics: The Challenge of Future Generations*. Oxford University Press.

Attfield, R. 1994. *Environmental Philosophy: Principles and Prospects*. Aldershot: Avebury.

Attfield, R. 2003. *Environmental Ethics: An Overview for the Twenty-First Century.* Cambridge: Polity Press.

Attfield, R. 2016. *Wonder, Value and God.* New York: Routledge.

Barry, B. 1973. "John Rawls and the Priority of Liberty," *Philosophy and Public Affairs* 2: 274–290.

Barry, B. 1999. "Sustainability and Intergenerational Justice," in A. Dobson (ed.), *Fairness and Futurity: Essays on Environmental Sustainability and Social Justice.* Oxford University Press.

Bartolini, S., and L. Bonatti 2008. "Endogenous Growth, Decline in Social Capital and Expansion of Market Activities," *Journal of Economic Behavior and Organization* 67: 917–926.

Bartolini, S. and F. Sarracino 2014. "Happy for How Long? How Social Capital and GDP Relate to Happiness over Time," *Ecological Economics* 108: 242–256.

Bartolini, S. and F. Sarracino 2015. "The Dark Side of Chinese Growth: Declining Social Capital and Well-being in Times of Economic Boom," *World Development* 74: 333–351.

Bartolini, S., E. Bilancini, and M. Pugno 2013. "Did the Decline in Social Connections Depress Americans' Happiness?," *Social Indicators Research* 110: 1033–1059.

Bartolini, S., L. Bonatti, and E. Sarracino 2014. "The Great Recession and the Bulimia of U.S. Consumers: Deep Causes and Possible Ways Out," *Cambridge Journal of Economics* 38: 1015–1042.

Beitz, C.R. 1999. *Political Theory and International Relations.* Princeton: Princeton University Press.

Bentham, J. 1970. *An Introduction to the Principles of Morals and Legislation.* J.H. Burns and H.L.A. Hart (eds.). Oxford: Oxford University Press.

Berlin, I. 1975 (1958). "Two Concepts of Liberty," in *Four Essays on Liberty.* Oxford: Oxford University Press.

Blackorby, C., W. Bossert, and D.J. Donaldson 2005. *Population Issues in Social Choice Theory, Welfare Economics, and Ethics.* New York: Cambridge University Press.

Blake, M. 2013. *Justice and Foreign Policy.* Oxford: Oxford University Press.

Brennan, G., and P. Pettit 2004. *The Economy of Esteem: an Essay on Civil and Political Society.* Oxford: Oxford University Press.

Brockmann, H., J. Delhey, C., Welzel, and H. Yuan 2009. "The China Puzzle: Falling Happiness in a Rising Economy," *Journal of Happiness Studies* 10: 387–405.

Broome, J. 2004. *Weighing Lives.* Oxford: Oxford University Press.

Brownstein, M. 2016. "Implicit Bias," in E.N. Zalta (ed.), *The Stanford Encyclopedia of Philosophy.* http://plato.stanford.edu/archives/spr2016/entries/implicit-bias/ (last accessed December 23, 2017).

Brudney, D. 1999. *Marx's Attempt to Leave Philosophy.* Cambridge, MA: Harvard University Press.

Bruni, L. and L. Stanca 2008. "Watching Alone: Relational Goods, Television and Happiness," *Journal of Economic Behavior and Organization* 65: 506–528.

Callan, E. 1997. *Creating Citizens: Political Education and Liberal Democracy.* Oxford: Clarendon Press.

Callicott, J.B. 1989. *In Defense of the Land Ethic.* Albany, NJ: SUNY Press.

Caney, S. 2005. *Justice Beyond Borders.* Oxford: Oxford University Press.

Caney, S. 2011. "Humanity, Associations, and Global Justice: In Defence of Humanity-Centred Cosmopolitan Egalitarianism," *The Monist* 94: 506–534.

Casal, P. 2007. "Why Sufficiency Is Not Enough," *Ethics* 117: 296–326.

Case, A. and Deaton, A. 2015. "Rising Morbidity and Mortality in Midlife among White Non-Hispanic Americans in the 21st Century," *Proceedings of the National Academy of Sciences* 112/49: 15078–15083.

Chang, R. 1998. "Comparison and the Justification of Choice," *University of Pennsylvania Law Review* 146: 1569–1598.

Christiano, Th. 2008. *The Constitution of Equality: Democratic Authority and Its Limits.* Oxford: Oxford University Press.

Cohen, G.A. 1989. "On the Currency of Egalitarian Justice," *Ethics* 99: 906–944.

Cohen, G.A. 2008. *Rescuing Justice and Equality.* Harvard: Harvard University Press.

Cowell, F. 2011. *Measuring Inequality,* 3rd edn. Oxford: Oxford University Press.

Dahl, R.A. 1985. *A Preface to Economic Democracy.* Berkeley: University of California Press.

Daniels, N. 2008. *Just Health.* Cambridge: Cambridge University Press.

Dasgupta, P.S. 1969. "On the Concept of Optimum Population," *The Review of Economic Studies* 36: 295–318.

Decancq, K., M. Fleurbaey, and E. Schokkaert 2015. "Inequality, Income and Well-being," in A. Atkinson and F. Bourguignon (eds.), *Handbook of Income Distribution, Vol. 2A.* New York: Elsevier.

Dewey, J. 1969. "The Ethics of Democracy," in J. Boydston (ed.), *John Dewey, The Early Works, 1882–1898, vol. 1.* Carbondale: Southern Illinois University Press.

Dicey, A.V. 1915. *Introduction to the Study of the Law of the Constitution,* 8th edn. London: Macmillan & Co.

Diener, E., and M. Seligman 2004. "Beyond Money: Towards an Economy of Well-being," *Psychological Science in the Public Interest* 5: 1–31.

Durkheim, E. 1964 (1893). *The Division of Labor in Society,* trans. G. Simpson, New York: Macmillan.

Dworkin, R. 1981a. "What Is Equality? Part 1: Equality of Welfare," *Philosophy and Public Affairs* 10: 185–246.

Dworkin, R. 1981b. "What Is Equality? Part 2: Equality of Resources," *Philosophy and Public Affairs* 10: 283–345.

Dworkin, R. 2000. *Sovereign Virtue.* Cambridge: Cambridge University Press.

Dworkin, R. 2011. *Justice for Hedgehogs.* Harvard: Harvard University Press.

Edwards, M. 2011. "Introduction: Civil Society and the Geometry of Human Relations," in M. Edwards (ed.), *The Oxford Handbook of Civil Society.* Oxford: Oxford University Press.

Estlund, D. 2008. *Democratic Authority: A Philosophical Framework.* Princeton: Princeton University Press.

Feinberg, J. 1992. "The Child's Right to an Open Future," in *Freedom and Fulfilment: Philosophical Essays.* Princeton: Princeton University Press.

Fleurbaey, M. 2008. *Fairness, Responsibility and Welfare.* Oxford: Oxford University Press.

Fleurbaey, M. 2015. "Equality versus Priority: How Relevant Is the Distinction?" *Economics and Philosophy* 31: 203–217.

Fleurbaey, M., and D. Blanchet 2013. *Beyond GDP: Measuring Welfare and Assessing Sustainability.* Oxford: Oxford University Press.

Forst, R. 2003. "Toleration, Justice and Reason," in C. McKinnon and D. Castiglione (eds.), *The Culture of Toleration in Diverse Societies: Reasonable Tolerance.* Manchester: Manchester University Press.

Friedman, M. 1962. *Capitalism and Freedom.* Chicago: University of Chicago Press.

Geuss, R. 1995. "Auffassungen der Freiheit," *Zeitschrift für philosophische Forschung* 49: 1–14.

Gheaus, A. 2015. "Three Cheers for the Token Woman!" *Journal of Applied Philosophy* 32: 163–176.

Gutmann, A. 1987. *Democratic Education.* Princeton, NJ: Princeton University Press.

Guy, B., and R. Sugden (eds.) 2005. *Economics and Social Interaction.* Cambridge: Cambridge University Press.

Habermas, J. 1989. *The Structural Transformation of the Public Sphere: An Inquiry into a Category of Bourgeois Society,* trans. T. Burger, Cambridge: MIT Press.

Habermas, J. 1993. *Justification and Application: Remarks on Discourse Ethics,* trans. C. Cronin, Cambridge: MIT Press.

Hargrove, E.C. 1992. "Weak Anthropocentric Intrinsic Value," *Monist* 75: 183–207.

Haslanger, S. 2012. *Resisting Reality: Social Construction and Social Critique.* Oxford: Oxford University Press.

Hearn, J. 2015. *Men of the World. Genders, Globalization, Transnational Times.* London: Sage.

Hegel, G.F.W. 1973 (1821). *The Philosophy of Right,* trans. T. M. Knox. Oxford: Oxford University Press.

Hegel, G.F.W. 1977. *The Phenomenology of Spirit,* trans. A. V. Miller. Oxford: Oxford University Press.

Helliwell, J. 2006. "Well-being, Social Capital and Public Policy: What's New?," *The Economic Journal* 116: 34–45.

Helliwell, J., and R. Putnam, R. 2004. "The Social Context of Well-being," *Philosophical Transactions of the Royal Society of London Series B: Biological Sciences* 359: 1435–1446.

Hobbes, Th. 1994 (1651). *Leviathan,* ed. E. Curley. Indianapolis: Hackett.

Holston, J. 2008. *Insurgent Citizenship: Disjunctions of Democracy and Modernity in Brazil.* Princeton, NJ: Princeton University Press.

Honneth, A. 1995. *The Struggle for Recognition: the Moral Grammar of Social Conflicts.* Cambridge: MIT Press.

Honneth, A. 2015. *Freedom's Right: The Social Foundations of Democratic Life.* New York: Columbia University Press.

Human Security Centre. 2005. *Human Security Report 2005: War and Peace in the 21st Century.* Oxford: Oxford University Press.

Jaeggi, R. 2014. *Alienation.* New York: Columbia University Press.

Jones, P. 2008. "Group Rights," in E.N. Zalta (ed.), *The Stanford Encyclopedia of Philosophy*, Spring 2014 edn. http://plato.stanford.edu/archives/spr2014/entries/rights-group/ (last accessed December 23, 2017).

Kagan, S. 1989. *The Limits of Morality.* Oxford: Oxford University Press.

Kahneman, D. 2011. *Thinking, Fast and Slow.* New York, Farrar, Straus & Giroux.

Kant, I. 1996. *Metaphysics of Morals*, ed. & trans. M. Gregor. Cambridge: Cambridge University Press.

Karnein, A. 2016. "Can We Represent Future Generations?" in A. Gosseries and I. Gonzalez (eds.), *Institutions for Future Generations*. Oxford: Oxford University Press

Knight, F.H. 1921. *Risk, Uncertainty, and Profit, Hart, Schaffner, and Marx Prize Essays, no. 31*. Boston and New York: Houghton Mifflin.

Kumar, R. 2003. "Who Can Be Wronged?" *Philosophy and Public Affairs* 31: 99–118.

Kymlicka, W. 1995. *Multicultural Citizenship.* Oxford: Oxford University Press.

Landemore, H. 2013. *Democratic Reason: Politics, Collective Intelligence, and the Rule of the Many.* Princeton, NJ: Princeton University Press.

Legesse, A. 2000. *Oromo Democracy: An Indigenous African Political System.* Lawrenceville, NJ: The Red Sea Press.

Locke, J. 1998 (1689). *An Essay Concerning Human Understanding.* London: Penguin.

Machiavelli, N. 1995 (1513). *The Prince*, trans. D. Wootton. Indianapolis: Hackett Publishing.

MacKinnon, C.A. 1988. *Feminism Unmodified: Discourses on Life and Law.* Cambridge: Harvard University Press.

Maclure, J., and Taylor, Ch. 2011. *Secularism and Freedom of Conscience.* Cambridge: Harvard University Press.

Mandela, N. 1994. *Long Walk to Freedom.* Boston, Mass. and London: Little, Brown, & Co.

Manser, M.H. 2007. *The Facts on File Dictionary of Proverbs.* New York: Infobase Publishing.

Mazor, J. 2010. "Liberal Justice, Future People, and Natural Resource Conservation," *Philosophy and Public Affairs* 38: 380–408.

McKerlie, D. 2012. *Justice Between the Young and the Old.* New York: Oxford University Press.

McMahan, J. 2002. *The Ethics of Killing.* Oxford: Oxford University Press.

Meyer, L. and Roser, D. 2009. "Enough for the Future," in A. Gosseries and L. Meyer (eds.), *Intergenerational Justice*. Oxford: Oxford University Press.

Mill, J.S. 1978 (1859). *On Liberty.* Indianapolis: Hackett Publishing.

Mill, J.S. 1979 (1863). *Utilitarianism.* Indianapolis: Hackett Publishing.

Mill, J.S. 1991 (1861). *Considerations on Representative Government.* New York: Prometheus Books.

Miller, D. 2007. *National Responsibility and Global Justice.* Oxford: Oxford University Press.

Nagel, Th. 1991. *Equality and Partiality.* New York: Oxford University Press.

Nagel, Th. 1995. "Personal Rights and Public Space," *Philosophy and Public Affairs* 24/2: 83–107.

Nozick, R. 1974. *Anarchy, State and Utopia.* New York: Basic Books.

Nussbaum, M. 2000. *Women and Human Development: The Capabilities Approach.* Cambridge: Cambridge University Press.

Nussbaum, M. 2006. *Frontiers of Justice: Disability, Nationality, Species Membership.* Cambridge, MA: Harvard University Press.

Okin, S.M. 1999. *Is Multiculturalism Bad for Women?* Princeton, NJ: Princeton University Press.

Page, E. 2006. *Climate Change, Justice and Future Generations.* Cheltenham: Edward Elgar.

Page, S. 2007. *The Difference: How the Power of Diversity Creates Better Groups, Firms, Schools and Societies.* Princeton, NJ: Princeton University Press.

Pallikkathayil, J. 2010. "Deriving Morality from Politics: Rethinking the Formula of Humanity," *Ethics* 121: 116–147.

Parfit, D. 1984. *Reasons and Persons.* Oxford: Clarendon Press.

Parfit, D. 1995. *Equality or Priority?* Lindley Lecture: University of Kansas.

Pettit, Ph. 2001. *A Theory of Freedom: From the Psychology to the Politics of Agency.* Oxford: Oxford University Press.

Pettit, Ph. 2012. *On the People's Terms: A Republican Theory and Model of Democracy.* Cambridge: Cambridge University Press.

Pierce, C. 1970. "Offensive Mechanisms," in F. Barbour (ed.), *The Black Seventies.* Boston, MA: Porter Sargent, 265–282.

Pogge, T. 2008. *World Poverty and Human Rights*, 2nd edn. Cambridge: Polity Press.

Rawls, J. 1999a. *A Theory of Justice*, rev. edn. Cambridge: Harvard University Press.

Rawls, J. 1999b. *The Law of Peoples with "The Idea of Public Reason Revisited."* Cambridge, MA: Harvard University Press.

Rawls, J. 2001. *Justice as Fairness: A Restatement.* Cambridge, MA: Harvard University Press.

Rawls, J. 2005. *Political Liberalism*, expanded edn. New York: Columbia University Press.

Raz, J. 1986. *The Morality of Freedom.* Oxford: Clarendon Press.

Richardson, H.S. 2002. *Democratic Autonomy: Public Reasoning about the Ends of Policy.* New York: Oxford University Press.

Richardson, H.S. 2015. "Using Final Ends for the Sake of Better Policy-Making," *Journal of Human Development and Capabilities* 16: 161–172.

Roemer, J. 1985. "Equality of Talent." *Economics and Philosophy* 1, 151–187.

Roemer, J. 1993. "A Pragmatic Theory of Responsibility for the Egalitarian Planner," *Philosophy and Public Affairs* 22: 146–166.

Rolston, H.III. 1988. *Environmental Ethics: Duties to and Values to Nature.* Philadelphia: Temple University Press.

Rolston, H.III. 2002. "Values in and Duties to the Natural World," in D. Schmidtz and E. Willott (eds.), *Environmental Ethics: What Really Matters and What Really Works.* New York and Oxford: Oxford University Press.

Rousseau, J.-J. 1968. *The Social Contract*, trans. M. Cranston. London: Penguin.

Sangiovanni, A. 2007. "Global Justice, Reciprocity, and the State," *Philosophy and Public Affairs* 35: 3–39.

Satz, D. 2010. *Why Some Things Should Not Be For Sale: The Moral Limits of Markets.* Oxford: Oxford University Press.

Scheffler, S. 2005. "Egalitarian Liberalism as Moral Pluralism," *Proceedings of the Aristotelian Society*, suppl. vol. 79: 229–253.

Schwartz, T. 1978. "Obligations to Posterity," in R.I. Sikora and B. Barry (eds.), *Obligations to Future Generations*. Philadelphia: Temple University Press.

Sen, A. 1975. *Employment, Technology and Development: A Study Prepared for the International Labour Office within the Framework of the World Employment Programme.* Oxford: Oxford University Press.

Sen, A. 1980. "Equality of What?," in *The Tanner Lectures on Human Values*, I, 197–220. Cambridge: Cambridge University Press.

Sen, A. 1985a. *Commodities and Capabilities.* Amsterdam: North-Holland.

Sen, A. 1985b. "Well-being, Agency, and Freedom: The Dewey Lectures 1984," *The Journal of Philosophy* 82: 169–221.

Sen, A. 1999. *Development as Freedom.* New York: Knopf.

Sen, A. 2009. *The Idea of Justice.* Cambridge, MA: Harvard University Press and London: Allen Lane.

Sen, A, and Williams, B. (eds.). 1982. *Utilitarianism and Beyond.* Cambridge: Cambridge University Press.

Shiffrin, S. 1999. "Wrongful Life, Procreative Responsibility, and the Significance of Harm," *Legal Theory* 5: 117–148.

Shue, H. 1996. *Basic Rights: Subsistence, Affluence, and U.S. Foreign Policy*, 2nd edn. Princeton, NJ: Princeton University Press.

Skloot, R. 2010. *The Immortal Life of Henrietta Lacks.* New York: Random House.

Smith, A. 1994 (1776). *The Wealth of Nations.* New York: Modern Library.

Stevenson, B., and J. Wolfers 2013. "Subjective Well-being and Incomes: Is There Any Evidence of Satiation?," *American Economic Review: Papers and Proceedings* 103: 598–604.

Taylor, Ch. 1985a. *Human Agency and Language.* Cambridge: Cambridge University Press.

Taylor, Ch. 1985b. *Philosophy and the Human Sciences.* Cambridge: Cambridge University Press.

Taylor, Ch. 1995. *Philosophical Arguments.* Cambridge, MA: Harvard University Press.

Taylor, P. 1986. *Respect for Nature: a Theory of Environmental Ethics.* Princeton, NJ: Princeton University Press.

Temkin, L. 1993. *Inequality.* New York: Oxford University Press.

Thiong'o, N. 2003. *Consciousness and African Renaissance: South Africa in the Black Imagination*. 4th Steve Biko Annual Lecture at University of Cape Town: http://ccs.ukzn.ac.za/files/NGUGI-BIKO.pdf (last accessed January 27, 2018).

Tomasi, J. 2012. *Free Market Fairness.* Princeton: Princeton University Press.

Twenge, J. 2000. "The Age of Anxiety? The Birth Cohort Change in Anxiety and Neuroticism, 1952–1993," *Journal of Personality and Social Psychology* 79/6: 1007–1021.

United Nations, General Assembly 2015. *Transforming Our World: The 2030 Agency for Sustainable Development.* A/70/L.1 (September 25, 2015).

https://sustainabledevelopment.un.org/post2015/transformingourworld (last accessed December 23, 2017).

Valentini, L. 2011. *Justice in a Globalized World: A Normative Framework.* Oxford: Oxford University Press.

Valentini, L. 2012. "Assessing the Global Order: Justice, Legitimacy, or Political Justice?" *Critical Review of International Social and Political Philosophy,* 15: 593–612.

Vallentyne, P. 2006. "Of Mice and Men: Equality and Animals," in K.L. Rasmussen and N. Holtug (eds.), *Egalitarianism: New Essays on the Nature and Value of Equality.* Oxford: Oxford University Press.

Vallentyne, P., H. Steiner, and M. Otsuka 2005. "Why Left-Libertarianism Is Not Incoherent, Indeterminate or Irrelevant: a Reply to Fried," *Philosophy and Public Affairs* 33: 201–215.

Walzer, M. 1983. *Spheres of Justice: A Defense of Pluralism and Equality.* New York: Basic Books.

Walzer, M. 2007. *Thinking Politically: Essays in Political Theory.* New Haven: Yale University Press.

Wenar, L. 2016. *Blood Oil: Tyrants, Violence, and the Rules that Run the World.* New York: Oxford University Press.

Wilkinson, R., and K. Pickett 2009. *The Spirit Level: Why More Equal Societies Almost Always Do Better.* London: Penguin.

Socio-Economic Transformations

3

Economic Inequality and Social Progress*

Coordinating Lead Authors:[1]
Stephan Klasen, Giovanni Andrea Cornia, Rebeca Grynspan, Luis F. López-Calva, Nora Lustig

Lead Authors:[2]
Augustin Fosu, Sripad Motiram, Flora Myamba, Andreas Peichl, Sanjay Reddy, Eldar Shafir, Ana Sojo, Ingrid Woolard

Contributing Authors:[3]
Shai Davidai, Michael Förster, Rahul Lahoti, Judith Sutz, Rainer Thiele

---

*   Acknowledgments: Note that all authors have contributed to this chapter in their personal capacity and any views expressed here should not be attributed to the organizations the authors are affiliated to. A much longer online version of this chapter is available at www.ipsp.org. The authors would like to thank Marc Fleurbaey, Paul Hufe, John Roemer, Martin Ungerer, participants at meetings at the OECD, the Graduate Institute in Geneva, at two IPSP lead author meetings, and other commentators for helpful comments and suggestions on earlier versions of the chapter. We thank Sol Taubin, Jessica Sims, the IPSP team in Princeton, and Samantha Lach for research support.

[1]   Affiliations: SK: University of Göttingen, Germany; GAC: University of Florence, Italy; RG: Ibero-American General Secretariat, Madrid, Spain; LLC: World Bank, Washington, DC, USA; NL: Tulane University, USA.

[2]   Affiliations: AF: University of Ghana, Accra, Ghana; SM: University of Massachusetts, Boston, USA and Indira Gandhi Institute of Development Research, Mumbai, India; FM: REPOA, Dar es Salaam, Tanzania; AP: ifo institute and University of Munich, Munich, Germany; SR: The New School, New York, USA; ES: Princeton University, USA; AS: Independent consultant, Santiago, Chile; IW: University of Cape Town, South Africa.

[3]   Affiliations: SD: The New School, New York, USA; MF: OECD, Paris, France; RL: Azim Premji University, Bengaluru, India; JS: University of the Republic, Montevideo, Uruguay; RT: Kiel Institute for the World Economy, Germany.

Summary[4]

Much of the literature on inequality has focused on economic inequality, usually measured through income, but there are many dimensions of inequality. Often interacting, these include inequality in freedoms, opportunities, and capabilities. One might also distinguish between interhousehold and intrahousehold inequality, vertical and horizontal inequality. One should also make a distinction between static and intertemporal assessments and address the issue of mobility. One should differentiate between unidimensional and multidimensional measures of inequality, objective versus subjective measures, absolute versus relative inequality, inequality versus polarization, and various indicators of inequality that emphasize the various dimensions of inequality.

Wide income and wealth inequality retards social progress intrinsically and instrumentally by inhibiting improvements in welfare and the promotion of social cohesion. While some social and economic differentiation is tolerable and even desirable, substantial inequality in resources, opportunities, or capabilities runs counter to most theories of justice. In addition, a wide inequality gap reduces overall well-being, increases poverty, lowers the impact of economic growth on poverty reduction, affects behavior that can trap poor people in poverty and promotes social conflict. There is, however, no consensus on the impact of income redistribution on economic growth.

Most data suggest that between-country inequality has narrowed somewhat since the 1980s. Meanwhile, within-country income inequality has been widening in many countries since the 1980s and now contributes a significantly larger share of global inequality. Since the late 1990s, trends in within-country income inequality have been more heterogeneous across regions of the world, with deceleration or stabilization in Asia, the OECD and transition countries, decrease in Latin America, and heterogeneous trends in Africa. The findings on the nonincome dimensions of inequality point generally to narrowing global inequality in health care and education, and substantial heterogeneity in the trends in within-country inequality.

There is considerable uncertainty and debate about the findings on the trends in inequality. This is associated partly with differences in the definitions of inequality, but also with poor data quality, lack of comparable data, and the irregular, incomplete, and inconsistent collection of data, especially in developing countries.

The key drivers of trends in inequality between and within countries and groups can be distinguished into two kinds: deep-seated causes and more immediate determinants. The drivers and determinants are often country-specific: contexts, policies, and institutions matter. Deeper causes in OECD countries include skill-biased technological change, the swelling trade in labor-intensive manufactured products with emerging countries, the rise in the incomes of top earners in the expanding financial sector, the declining redistributive role of the state, and labor market policies, especially on unionization, the minimum wage, and low-wage sectors. In developing countries, inequality trends are affected by the earnings distribution of employees, but also by differences in inequality across regions and between rural and urban areas. Greater trade with rich countries has not met expectations of narrowing inequality, but has often served to widen inequality. The substantial narrowing in inequality in Latin America more recently has been caused by positive economic conditions and favorable policies on taxes and fiscal redistribution, labor markets, and social protection.

Many of the drivers of the trends in inequality are deep-rooted, change only slowly, and therefore reproduce themselves. This reproduction of inequality leads to substantial path dependency in inequality, aided by entrenched social stratification that causes persistent inequalities across population groups. Deep drivers of inequality dynamics are also related to the influence of social movements, long-standing norms and attitudes affecting the degree in redistribution, the strong link between economic and political inequality, and demographic dynamics.

As recent trends in inequality in Latin America or the heterogeneity in trends among OECD countries suggest, policy can have a substantial influence on inequality. Policies focusing on inequality can be grouped into (1) policies to improve the conditions among the poor, the vulnerable, and the marginalized; (2) policies that promote the growth and sustainability of a strong middle class; and (3) policies that seek to curb the excessive concentration of income and wealth at the top. Among the first group, relevant policies should concentrate on building physical and

---

[4]   The content of the summary is based on the sections that follow. For expediency, the corresponding references appear in the sections themselves and were not repeated here.

human assets among the poor through, for example, land reform and pro-poor education policies; enhancing economic opportunities through, for instance, better access to markets, more progressive tax-expenditure systems, and cash transfer programs to cope with shocks; and promoting social inclusion through, for example, antidiscrimination policies, legal reforms, and improved access among disadvantaged groups to the courts and the legal system.

Among the second group, policies should focus on the middle class by promoting labor-intensive growth, fostering competition, favoring micro and small enterprises, addressing shocks through universal access to social protection, and enhancing employment and a living wage.

Policies in the third group should focus on the top of the distribution by supporting greater progressivity in the tax system including inheritance taxes, addressing tax avoidance and evasion, and establishing codes of practice to limit pay raises at the top of the distribution.

Macroeconomic policies and appropriate international action can play a supporting role. Macroeconomic and fiscal policies can also expand the revenue base available for redistribution, especially in countries with low ratios of tax to gross domestic product (GDP), for example, through resource taxes and more progressive income and consumption taxes.

International cooperation can support countries in designing and implementing pro-poor policies. It could also help narrow inequality by focusing on combating tax avoidance and evasion by wealthy individuals and multinational corporations, controlling illicit financial flows, regulating financial markets, and favoring more orderly and less costly international migration regimes.

The potential for implementing policies to narrow inequality in countries depends crucially on political economy issues within countries, and these are affected by the size and voice of the middle class, the power and incentives available to entrenched elites, the nature of political alliances, and the role of popular and social movements.

3

3.1 Introduction

3.1.1 Motivation

The concern to explain and to justify inequalities in society goes back at least to Rousseau in the European Enlightenment, and indeed had its predecessor in the form of episodic criticisms of the distribution of goods in society in various world civilizations. Nevertheless, after a long period of relative neglect, economic inequality and its effects on societies have become increasingly prominent in debates among economists and social scientists and in policy circles over the past three decades. Among the many recent ways this has become clear are the inclusion of the reduction of inequality as a separate goal among the seventeen Sustainable Development Goals (SDGs) recently adopted by the United Nations and the much greater attention being paid to inequality in academic literature and in the policy analyses of the International Monetary Fund (IMF), the Organization for Economic Co-operation and Development (OECD), the United Nations system, the World Bank, and other leading international organizations and financial institutions.

The focus in the 1980s and 1990s was on issues in economic inequality in industrialized countries. This was largely because of the sharply rising income inequality observed in many OECD countries beginning in the early 1980s aided by increasing availability of comparable data on income inequality. More recently, a debate in industrialized countries has revolved around inequalities in education and health. New information is also emerging on the advantages accruing to people at the top of the income and wealth distribution, which is usually poorly captured in standard household survey tools. This has extended the debate to include more about this segment of the distribution in the overall assessment of income and wealth inequality. Whereas earlier economic thinking had often involved the presumption that inequalities were relatively stable in developed countries, it came to be recognized that major shifts in such distributions are possible, and are in fact occurring.

In developing countries, the interest in and debates on inequality issues have been long-standing and have related, for example, to the well-known Kuznets curve or inverse U hypothesis of rising and then falling inequality in the development process. Until the early 1990s, however, comparable and consistent data to assess inequality trends across countries and over time were largely lacking. As many more, more reliable, and more frequent household surveys were run in a larger number of countries, the picture changed dramatically, allowing detailed assessments of trends in inequality for the first time. Analyses thus began to reveal that within-country income inequality has been widening in many parts of the developing world, especially since the 1980s. The 1990s and 2000s saw the emergence of a debate on global income inequality, which is related to both inequality within and inequality between countries. Similarly, supported by the availability of more data, growing attention is being paid to measuring inequality in other dimensions of well-being, such as education, health, and access to water, sanitation, and adequate housing.

This chapter surveys the literature in economics and the social sciences on inequality over the past three decades. While it includes a brief discussion on global inequality, the chapter focuses mainly on inequality within countries. Inequality between countries, especially in income, is principally an issue of differences in economic growth rates across countries, a subject covered in detail in Chapter 4.

The chapter discusses inequality in many dimensions, but a greater emphasis is inevitably placed on economic (and in particular income) inequality, simply because there is more information on this dimension, and much of the literature has dealt with it. The chapter also dwells on measures of the trends in and determinants of inequality, offers a detailed examination of the impact of inequality on the well-being of people now and in the future and, therefore, of the effect of inequality on social progress.

3.2 Concepts and Measures of Inequality

3.2.1 Inequality of What?

In his influential work *Inequality Reexamined*, Amartya Sen (1992) argues that equality can be measured on many different dimensions which he terms "focal variables." Human beings differ in terms of their characteristics (e.g. gender, race) and in terms of their endowments, ownership etc. Given these differences, privileging equality in one domain may result in tolerating inequality in another, e.g. equality in incomes may result in inequality in well-being given that different individuals may have different needs. In light of these considerations, Sen argues persuasively that, the question of what the focal variable should be is important. He then proceeds to evaluate different philosophical traditions (utilitarianism, Rawlsian justice) to make a case for focusing on the capabilities of individuals to achieve desirable functionings. Chapter 2 (Section 2.3) describes the capability approach in greater detail, arguing that it provides an objective approach to conceptualize well-being, unrelated to the states of mind of individuals.

In practice, the choice of focal variables has been dictated by several considerations, including the imperatives of a particular context/policy, availability of data, and ease of measurement. Based on these considerations, a substantial focus in the literature has been placed on inequality of incomes or expenditures among individuals and households. More recently wealth has emerged as an important focus variable, and studies have attempted to measure wealth inequality at both the individual and household levels (e.g. Davies and Shorrocks 2000; Jayadev et al. 2007).

Two other inequalities that have received some attention have been in the domains of education and health. Although techniques and concepts used in the measurement of income inequality have been applied here, the issues, nature of the data, limitations of data are different (see e.g. O'Donnell et al. (2008) on health, and Ferreira and Gignoux (2011a) on education).

One domain that has received considerable attention in recent times is that of opportunities. Chapter 2 (Section 2.4) discusses equality of opportunity as a part of a broader discussion of distributive justice. In the context of economic inequality, there has been substantial interest in the nature and extent of inequality of opportunity, particularly in the space of incomes, i.e. inequality of opportunity as a driver of (inequality in) incomes and earnings. The main inspiration for this agenda has been the work of John Roemer (e.g. 1998, 2008). Broadly speaking, Roemer has argued that what individuals achieve depends upon two sets of factors: those beyond their control (*circumstances*), and their *efforts*. It is unjust to hold individuals responsible for factors beyond their control (i.e. their circumstances) and societies should therefore try to reduce these disadvantages to the extent possible (or compensate individuals for suffering from such inequalities in circumstances). As Chapter 2 (Section 2.4) points out, this could be categorized as "responsibility-sensitive egalitarianism" or "luck egalitarianism." Roemer's formulation is simple, intuitively appealing, and (most importantly) amenable to empirical analysis. As a result, a large and growing body of literature has emerged that has tried to estimate the inequality of opportunity in various countries (e.g. de Barros et al. 2009; Checchi and Peragine 2010; Ferreira and Gignoux 2011b; Singh 2011). Some of the circumstance variables that have been identified are parental education, caste, gender, religion, and rural–urban location. Both parametric (regression-based) and nonparametric approaches have been suggested (see Singh 2011 and Kanbur and Wagstaff 2014 for details).

Even as the empirical literature on inequality of opportunity is gaining ground, there are serious critiques and unresolved philosophical questions. Chapter 2 (Section 2.4) presents a discussion of some of these, e.g. the role of preferences and the idea that the distinction between efforts and circumstances poses a threat to self-esteem and solidarity. Kanbur and Wagstaff (2014) present a discussion of these issues. Briefly put, some of these concern the difficulties in separating justifiable and unjustifiable sources of inequality, the treatment of luck, accounting for talent, and inequality of opportunity of children. To take one example, studies hold people responsible for their luck. This is problematic because one has to distinguish between "brute luck" (e.g. the case of someone who is involved in a road accident for no fault of his/her own) and "option luck" (e.g. the loss in the stock market to a calculating investor) – an argument can be made that it is unfair to treat both of these in a similar manner. Moreover, the treatment of absolute poverty needs to be addressed better – it is morally reasonable to argue that the concerns of the truly destitute need to be addressed *even if* their destitution is a result of their actions and/or risks that they have taken. There are also questions of how to interpret differences in information access or cognitive limitations that might affect outcomes and might erroneously be considered effort.

Despite the above limitations, the agenda of inequality of opportunity is promising and has the potential for influencing policies that promote equity. Circumstance variables could include (and have included) membership of groups, and in this sense, the literature on inequality of opportunity has shed light on differences among groups. However, philosophically, and to a large extent in its empirical application, the thrust of this literature has been on individuals. This is also true of the welfare economics tradition inspired by Sen's capability approach. The question of group-based, or horizontal, inequality is addressed in Section 3.2.3.

3.2.2 National Inequality, Global Inequality, Regional/Local Inequality

The frame of reference matters greatly for measurement, the assessment of the relevance of inequality, and related policy issues. Inequality in whichever dimension (e.g. income, wealth, education, health, etc.) can be studied in a very local context, within a small geographic area, a particular group of people, or even within households. At the other extreme, one can study global inequality. For people's well-being, behavior, and sense of equal treatment, local inequality may matter more than global inequality; but improved access to information may increase the relevance of national and global inequality for one's own assessment of well-being (e.g. Lohmann 2015). For much of policy-making that tends to be done at the national level within-country inequality is of particular importance. Moreover, to assess perceptions of inequality, it is often important to discern the relevant reference group that people use for comparisons which may differ according to context (Boyce et al. 2010; Stutzer 2004).

When considering global inequality, Milanovic's (2005b) influential classification into three types of global inequality is very useful. The first type refers to inequality between countries, treating each country as a single, equal-weighted observation. Such an analysis is useful to study inequalities in living standards across countries, differentials in economic power, and international inequality from a policy perspective where countries are usually the unit of observation and action (e.g. at UN fora). From a policy perspective, the only way to reduce global inequality using this concept in, say, the income dimension, is for the poorer countries of the world to grow faster than richer ones, so essentially this is an issue of differential growth rates which is taken up in detail in Chapter 4.

The second measure of global inequality weights the mean achievement of each country (e.g. per capita income) by population and then considers global inequality in these population-weighted terms. This measure more accurately reflects global inequality since now each person receives the same weight in the assessment of inequality but it still ignores within country inequality. The third measure addresses this last point and considers inequality between world citizens. Such an approach closely aligns with cosmopolitan positions on global justice. However, on its own, it is a statistic that is hard to interpret and from which to derive clear policy conclusions as it reflects inequality within countries as well as between countries, and gives more weight to populous countries. It is therefore useful to decompose global inequality into within- and between-country inequality; some of the inequality measures allow such decompositions.[5] An important and robust empirical finding on measuring global inequality in this way has been that over the past 30 years the contribution of between-country inequality to global inequality, while still the larger component, has been falling while the contribution of within-country inequality has been rising (e.g. Bourguignon 2015; Klasen, Scholl et al. 2016). See, for example, Figure 3.1, based on data from the Global Consumption and Income Project;

---

[5]   See the appendix of the online version of Chapter 3 (available at www.ipsp.org) for a discussion of inequality measures.

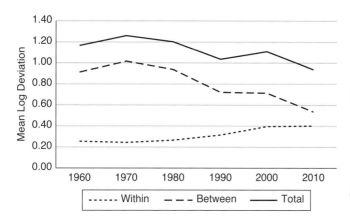

Figure 3.1 | Within and between country income inequality contribution to global inequality.
Source: Global Income and Consumption Database.

analyses in Bourguignon (2015), based on partly different data and methods, confirm these findings.

3.2.3   Horizontal versus Vertical Inequality

Horizontal inequality refers to inequality among groups, e.g. ethnic groups or race groups. This has to be contrasted with vertical inequality which concerns inequality among individuals or households (Stewart 2010). Horizontal inequality has been relatively underresearched and neglected. Severe inequalities among groups threaten social stability and can result in violent conflict and civil war. Moreover, individuals belonging to disadvantaged groups may advance their own well-being and the well-being of the society in a suboptimal manner. Also, it may be easier to address deep social problems (e.g. unemployment, poverty) by focusing upon groups that carry a disproportionate burden of these problems. An important group-based inequality is inequality between men and women (Klasen 2007). It differs from other group-based inequalities in that the two groups typically live together and share resources in households, while groups based on ethnicity, caste, religion, or region often inhabit different households. Thus *intra*household inequality between males and females is an important indicator of this type of group-based inequality, while *inter*household inequality between other groups such as ethnicity, race, caste, religion, or region capture most of the group-based inequality.

While these are indirect reasons for considering groups, Akerlof and Kranton (2000) and others have argued that group identity is important for individuals and directly affects them. Giving serious consideration to the welfare of disadvantaged groups could, therefore, enhance the welfare of individuals belonging to them. At the same time, all societies are diverse: people have many identities and can therefore belong to many different groups. But the illusion of singularity that constrains individual choices and assumes that any person belongs to a single collectivity that fuels an overarching, all-encompassing

identity, by placing a rigid line of segregation (Sen 2006), combined with severe inequality among such rigidly defined groups can create conditions for conflict.

Lastly, the study of horizontal inequalities has close linkages to inequality of opportunities. Often "circumstances" that cause inequality of opportunities relate to group membership (e.g. ethnicity, race, gender) so that horizontal inequality is a form of inequality of opportunities if circumstances are defined in such a way.

The measurement and conceptualization of horizontal inequality raises several complications since group membership could be fluid and inequality among groups (like among individuals and households) could exist on multiple dimensions. While the literature has acknowledged the former issue, it has taken the group definitions in a particular context as given. Stewart (2010) identifies economic, social, political, and cultural status as the relevant broad dimensions. Each dimension in turn comprises of several elements, e.g. economic: asset ownership; social: education; political: control over government; and cultural status: recognition of cultural practices. For empirical purposes, it has been suggested (Stewart 2002) that it is useful to arrive at an index for each element/dimension, but not aggregate over the elements. This is because the differences across elements may be interesting and have consequences, e.g. a situation of *consistency* where one group is uniformly disadvantaged could be different from one where it is disadvantaged in only some dimensions. It is also worth pointing out that it is not just "objective" horizontal inequalities that matter – perceptions play an important role too.

The empirical literature examining the impact of horizontal inequalities has used two different methodologies: case studies (Stewart 2008) and statistical/econometric analysis within and across countries (e.g. Mancini 2008; Østby 2008; Wimmer et al. 2009; Brown 2010; Motiram and Sarma 2014b). The latter studies suffer from severe data limitations. Stewart (2010) summarizes the broad conclusion that emerges from this agenda that horizontal inequalities "increase the risk of violent conflict, especially when they are consistent in the economic, social, political and cultural status spheres."

3.2.4   Individual versus Household-Based Inequality

(Income) inequality (and income poverty) is usually studied at the level of households. This choice is largely dictated by the available data, which measures total resources (income or consumption) a household has at its disposal and then only adjusts these total resources by household size or some equivalence scales which take into account different needs of members (e.g. children need fewer resources than adults) and economies of scale within the household (e.g. Buhmann et al. 1988). The construction of appropriate scales is controversial, can affect levels and trends of inequality, and there is no consensus on the right scales (Deaton and Zaidi 2002), although some scales are quite commonly used.[6] An important implicit assumption of these household-based analyses is that distribution within households is

---

[6]   Common scales used are the modified OECD scales (which give a weight of 1 to the first adult, 0.5 to all other adults, and 0.3 to children below 16) or the LIS scales which use the square root of household size. In developing countries, different scales tend to be used, see Deaton and Zaidi (2002).

equal (or according to needs in the case of an equivalence scale). To the extent that the distribution of resources within households is unequal, this will underestimate inequality and poverty (Haddad and Kanbur 1990). In the income/consumption dimension, it is very difficult to move to an individual assessment as incomes are shared within households and a considerable share of consumption expenditures is used to finance household-specific public goods (e.g. housing, durable goods, utilities) which cannot be easily ascribed to individual members (Klasen and Lahoti 2016). Some recent attempts have been made to study intrahousehold resource allocation by gender or other groups, but they usually rely on strong assumptions to identify allocation rules (e.g. Dunbar, Lewbel, and Pendakur 2013; Chiappori and Meghir 2015) As a result, it is very difficult to discern the role of gender inequality or inequality between age groups on aggregate income poverty and inequality, as the intrahousehold dimension is neglected. Using nonincome measures, however, there is more scope for an individual assessment (Klasen and Lahoti, 2016).

Assessments of wage inequality are often based on individual data. The link between levels and trends in wage, earnings, and overall household income inequality is not as close as one might expect since it strongly depends on how earners are distributed across households which, in turn, is affected by the distribution of unemployment or of female economic participation across the income distribution as well as marriage and household formation patterns (e.g. Gottschalk and Danziger 2005).

3.2.5   Functional Inequality

Another way to study inequality (especially income inequality) is to link it to the distribution of production factors and their returns. Since capital (including land) and labor (including human capital) are the two factors of production, the share of incomes accruing to capital and labor can also be one way to describe inequality. The relationship between the capital and labor shares and vertical inequality is close but far from perfect. For example, Piketty (2014) shows that the capital share has been rising in many countries but also that the labor earnings of some individuals (e.g. superstars, top earners in finance, and CEOs) have also risen and both have contributed to increased income inequality among households. Measuring these shares is not easy, particularly in developing countries where self-employment in agricultural and the informal sector employs a large share of the population, and income from self-employment combines capital income (from land and productive assets) with labor income (Trapp 2015).

3.2.6   Unidimensional versus Multidimensional Inequality

Most of the standard literature on welfare or inequality focuses on one dimension (often income or consumption). As also discussed in Chapter 2, Section 2.6, in many conceptions of well-being, including for example Sen's capability approach (Sen 1992), well-being itself is, however, seen as a multidimensional concept that cannot easily be reduced to a single dimension (or index). For example, the capabilities to be educated, healthy, and socially integrated, may all be very

valuable but cannot be reduced to one dimension (as prices or other weights cannot easily be assigned to them). If those capabilities are treated as the ultimate well-being outcomes, income will only be a highly imperfect proxy to capture these capabilities, related to the inherent heterogeneity of humans in their ability to translate incomes into capabilities, and the externality and public good aspects of health and education (where provision of quality health and education services depends more on public action than private incomes, Drèze and Sen 1989).

Also, the overlapping disadvantage of people suffering deprivations in several dimensions can be of particular interest as these might point to more structural and deep-seated inequalities and may also relate to horizontal inequality. Studying multidimensional inequality (or multidimensional poverty) might be a way to uncover those overlapping disadvantages (and advantages, see Ferreira and Lugo 2012).

When it comes to the measurement of multidimensional inequality, however, a number of complex conceptual and empirical difficulties arise (e.g. Aaberge and Brandolini 2014). They relate, among others, to whether different well-being dimensions can be considered as substitutes or complements, whether transfers of compensation between dimensions are possible, whether one should first measure inequality within a dimension across people and then aggregate across dimensions, or aggregate dimensions within people and then aggregate across people, and whether one has continuous or discrete variables at one's disposal. These difficulties arise in addition to the "usual" questions in multidimensional well-being measurement, such as the choice of dimensions and their relative weights (e.g. Muller and Trannoy 2012; Aaberge and Brandolini 2014; Bosmans et al. 2015). As a result, there is no consensus to date on appropriate summary measures of multidimensional inequality.

It is, of course, possible to study multidimensional inequality without such a summary measure. On the one hand, one can rely on a dashboard approach and study inequality in each dimension separately using well-known unidimensional inequality measures (see Ravallion 2011). While such an assessment provides a more complete assessment of inequality than reliance on a single dimension, such an approach does not allow for a complete ordering or ranking of multidimensional inequality of the units considered (e.g. groups, countries); nor does it say anything about overlapping disadvantages. One approach to address this problem studies whether one multidimensional distribution dominates another one, i.e. is certainly more unequal based on the assumption of some dominance criteria. To facilitate such comparisons, compensation and transfers can be conceptualized to help compare multidimensional distributions (e.g. Aaberge and Brandolini 2014). Another approach is to use standard inequality measures, dimension by dimension, and then aggregate them. An example is the Inequality-Adjusted Human Development Index (UNDP 2010), which adjusts achievements in the three human development dimensions (education, health, incomes) by a penalty for inequality within these dimensions. The gap between the HDI, which measures average achievements, and the IHDI, can then be seen as a measure of the welfare loss due to multidimensional inequality. While this nicely illustrates the extent of inequality within dimensions, it cannot say anything about overlapping disadvantages suffered by individuals in these dimensions (because the dimensions are considered separate). An alternative proposal has been by Harttgen and Klasen (2012) to first create an HDI at the household level and then study inequality in that HDI across people (and across countries). There, overlapping disadvantages are explicitly considered, but there are serious data issues and the aggregation of overlapping disadvantage across dimensions is based on a range of debatable normative assumptions.

To conclude, the literature on multidimensional inequality is still in its infancy. Clearly studying multidimensional inequality and overlapping disadvantages is important but the best ways to do this are still being debated.

3.2.7   Income versus Wealth Inequality

Wealth data are collected less frequently than income in household surveys and there are difficult measurement issues. For example, wealth can include pension wealth in a public or private pension system which depends on complex pension rules (and may be uncertain), it can include wealth in capital accumulating life insurances, it can include assets that are difficult to value due to absence of liquid markets for them (e.g. shares in privately held companies or housing in rural areas of poor countries), among many other issues. Also, since many households have no or even negative wealth, standard inequality measures that require positive numbers (such as the Theil measure or mean log deviation) cannot be used. As a result, most empirical analyses, especially those comparing inequality across space and time, focus on income inequality.

But this perspective is limiting in several ways. Wealth allows households to smooth over temporary shocks, households with wealth can use that wealth as collateral for credit for investments, and households can draw on income streams from their wealth as a long-term source of income. In fact, income streams from wealth form a large part of incomes of the richest households in advanced countries (Alvaredo et al. 2013; Piketty 2014). Wealth inequality is everywhere much more unequal than income inequality. In fact, in most countries, the poorest 60 percent of the population own little wealth at all (and many may be in debt), and most wealth is concentrated in the top decile (and sometimes even the top percentile holds the majority of wealth, Alvaredo et al. 2013). Also across countries, most of the world's wealth is concentrated among the very rich in rich (and some emerging) countries while many poor countries have only a tiny share of global wealth at their disposal (Davies et al. 2008). Thus, it is important to consider wealth inequality as an important driver of income inequality, and policies that reduce wealth inequality (such as inheritance taxes or taxes on capital income, or direct wealth taxes) are likely to affect income inequality.

3.2.8   Absolute versus Relative Inequality

Relative inequality is the most commonly used notion of inequality. Many studies of income inequality use the relative Gini coefficient,

usually without the "relative" qualifier. Measures of relative inequality satisfy the property of "scale invariance" wherein inequality is unaffected if the distribution is scaled by the same nonzero factor; i.e. the measure is unitless.

In two seminal articles, Kolm (1976a,b) argued that this convenience is obtained at a cost: "convenience could not be an alibi for endorsing justice." To illustrate: When all the incomes double, relative inequality stays the same even though the absolute difference between the incomes of the rich and the poor increases. Kolm thus characterized relative measures as "rightist" and contrasted them with "leftist" measures which satisfy the property that inequality is unaffected if all the incomes increase by the same absolute amount. Kolm argued that in his experience, this property (which we can refer to as "translation invariance") conforms to the notions that people have about inequality. An example of an absolute measure is the Absolute Gini, which is the Relative Gini multiplied by the mean. Is it possible to arrive at a tradeoff between convenience and ethics? "Intermediate" or "Centrist" measures strive to do this by increasing when all the incomes are scaled up by the same factor, and decreasing when all the incomes increase by the same absolute amount.[7]

Studies that have used measures other than relative ones have been sparse. Subramanian and Jayaraj (2013) examine inequality in consumption and find that, using relative measures, increases in consumption inequality in India since the 1990s have been modest. However, both intermediate and absolute measures show sharp increases. Atkinson and Brandolini (2010) examine absolute inequality in the context of the world distribution of income. Bosmans et al. (2011) use absolute, relative, and intermediate perspectives to analyze world inequality and argue that the choice of perspective matters.

Relative and absolute approaches also appear when studying the distributional impact of growth or "pro-poor growth" (Ravallion and Chen 2003; Klasen 2008a; Grosse et al. 2008). If the income growth rate of poorer groups exceeds that of the nonpoor, relative inequality will fall, but absolute inequality will often still increase as the absolute increments of the poor are smaller than those of the nonpoor. Related to this, Grosse et al. (2008) and Klasen (2008a) argue that considering absolute inequality is particularly appropriate for nonincome dimensions such as education or health where absolute increments are a much more commonly accepted metric than proportionate changes.

3.2.9   Inequality versus Polarization

Over the past two decades, a literature has emerged that has conceptualized the phenomenon of "polarization," which is broadly: "the appearance (or disappearance) of groups in a distribution" (Chakravarty 2009: 105). Several measures have been proposed and some scholars have argued that these are more closely linked to conflict and other social ills than measures of inequality. An old idea that can be traced back to Aristotle (Motiram and Sarma 2014b) is that societies with a

---

[7]   An example is the Intermediate Gini, which is the product of the Relative and Absolute Gini. This measure obeys "unit consistency," which ensures that two income distributions are ranked in the same manner irrespective of the units, i.e. the ranking of two distributions is unaffected if they are scaled by the same nonzero factor, e.g. which is seen as desirably. See Zheng (2006) Subramanian (2013), Subramanian and Jayaraj (2013) for some more details.

strong middle tend to prosper, be stable, and are less prone to conflict. Measures of bipolarization (e.g. Foster and Wolfson 1994; Wolfson 1994; Wang and Tsui 2000) are motivated by this idea. They conceptualize the middle in terms of the median and divide the population into groups below and above the median and measure the distance between these groups. At an intuitive level, one can see the connection of this with the formation of poles on either side of the median. Also, while a progressive transfer decreases inequality, it could increase polarization.

Distinct from the idea of bipolarization that artificially forms groups out of an existing distribution, Esteban and Ray (1993) consider a situation where there are several identifiable, preexisting income groups. Individuals belonging to a particular group identify with one another and are alienated from those belonging to the other groups. The effective antagonism among individuals depends upon identification and alienation and Esteban and Ray propose the sum of all effective antagonisms in a society as an index of polarization. Duclos et al. (2004) extend this analysis to a continuous income distribution where income groups are identified endogenously. While the above measures deal with one dimension (income), Zhang and Kanbur (2001) consider polarization in a context where individuals can be distinguished on two dimensions – income and nonincome group membership. They decompose overall income inequality into two components: inequality between nonincome groups and inequality within nonincome groups, and argue that polarization can be measured by considering the ratio of the former to the latter. Such multidimensional polarization indices are also a way of measuring horizontal inequality (Stewart 2002).

Do the polarization measures provide different results and insights compared to inequality measures? The evidence on this question is mixed. Zhang and Kanbur (2001) use data from China during 1983–1995 to conclude that they do not. Using their measure, they show that rural–urban polarization is quite high, whereas inland-coastal polarization is low, but rising. Motiram and Sarma (2014b) use consumption data from India to find that at the all-India level, polarization and inequality measures show similar increasing trends since early 1990s. However, state-level comparisons and trends display some differences. They find that group-based polarization has increased on many fronts: state, geographic regions, and rural–urban. Duclos et al. (2004) use data from the Luxembourg Income Study for 21 European countries to demonstrate that inequality and polarization rankings differ. Ravallion and Chen (1997) consider data from developing and transition countries and find close correspondence.

3.2.10 Subjective Measures: Perceptions of Inequality and Mobility

Most of the literature is focused on objective, quantifiable measures of inequality. But there are, of course, other ways to consider inequality, including subjective measures. Three different literatures can be subsumed under this heading. The first considers subjective outcome indicators such as "happiness" or "life satisfaction" which has been used as an important alternative indicator of well-being and is also discussed in Chapter 2, Section 2.3. While there is a very large and mature literature concerned with measuring the levels and determinants of happiness and life satisfaction, inequality in happiness

has been much less studied. This is partly related to data issues as happiness and life satisfaction is usually measured on a 4, 5, or 10 point Likert scale from which it is no easy to derive valid, credible, and comparable inequality measures. Kalmijn and Veenhoven (2005) recommend using the standard deviation as an inequality measure. When using a 10-point scale for life satisfaction, the measured inequality in life satisfaction is quite small (as to be expected) and generally falls with high mean levels of life satisfaction (Ott 2005). Given the conceptual and measurement challenges, it is not clear what robust conclusions emerge from this rather small literature on inequality in subjective well-being.

A second literature uses subjective perceptions to derive objective metrics. Examples of this are the formulation of "subjective poverty lines" in which households are asked what level of income they would require to not be poor (e.g. Pradhan and Ravallion 2000), or surveys that ask households to subjectively place themselves in the income distribution. Such measures can be a useful complement to objective inequality measures and yield interesting insights. For example, as shown by Cruces et al. (2013), poor people tend to overestimate their rank in the income distribution while rich people underestimate it, which is related to their perceptions being based on comparisons with relatively homogeneous reference groups. As a result, subjective inequality tends to be lower than objective inequality, but the difference is not uniform and depends on circumstances (see also Engelhardt and Wagener 2014).

A third (closely related) literature asks about people's perception of the level of income or wealth inequality and mobility in a society (irrespective of their own position) and perhaps one could use these subjective perceptions as measures of inequality. As is to be expected from the discussion above, income inequality is estimated to be much smaller than is objectively the case. This biased perception seems to be even larger for estimates of the wealth distribution (Norton and Ariely 2011). Similarly, perceptions of social mobility tend to be higher than actual social mobility, and there are important international differences, with people in the US believing that mobility is substantially larger than in Europe (e.g. Alesina and Glaeser 2004), even though it appears that mobility is lower in the US than in most European countries (Corak 2013). This literature has also shown, theoretically and empirically, that perceptions of inequality and of mobility affect preferences for redistribution (e.g. Benabou and Ok 2001; Cruces et al. 2013; Engelhardt and Wagener 2014).

All three literatures show that subjective assessment of inequality (and mobility) are generally a poor proxy for objective measures of inequality, and are affected by various systematic biases. Thus, as short-cut proxies for inequality or mobility, they are of limited use. Instead, however, these subjective measures provide important complementary information that sometimes can be as important or more important for subjective assessments of well-being in societies or preferences for political or social change.

3.2.11 Static versus Dynamic Inequality, Mobility

Most inequality analyses focus on current incomes. This does not consider dynamic issues such as shocks or life-cycle movements of incomes.

Inequality in current incomes may be larger than in lifetime incomes if, for example, today's poor include poor students who will ultimately earn much more over their lifetime, or include those who suffered a negative shock this year. Panel studies that study short-term income dynamics tend to find that inequality in average multiyear incomes tends to be substantially smaller than inequality in annual incomes, suggesting that shocks and/or measurement error are responsible for the higher reported static inequality at any point in time (e.g. Woolard and Klasen 2005; Grimm 2007; Burger, Klasen, and Zoch 2016).

More generally, we are also concerned about mobility, i.e. how individuals or groups fare over time. We might be interested in interpersonal mobility – how easy or difficult it is for individuals to move from one income or occupational group to another, or intergenerational mobility – how likely or unlikely it is for children to fall in the same group (income quantile, occupational class, educational level, etc.) as their parents. Panel data or data tracking different generations is needed for understanding mobility. Given the relative paucity of such data in developing countries, the empirical literature on mobility there is sparse – two recent exceptions are Hnatovska et al. (2011) and Motiram and Singh (2012). In contrast, the literature from developed countries is richer and there are studies from several countries, e.g. Björklund and Jäntti (2000); Bowles et al. (2005); Corak (2013); and Blanden et al. (2014).

Mobility is closely linked to the notion of equality of opportunity. As already discussed above, an influential view (due to Roemer 1998) holds that individuals should not be held responsible for factors that influence their performance, but which are beyond their control. The larger the influence of such variables, labeled as circumstances, the lower is the equality of opportunity. From this perspective, societies with low intergenerational mobility are likely to witness low equality of opportunity since parental background plays an important role in shaping the lives of the current generation.

3.2.12   Measures and Measurement Challenges

The online version of the chapter includes a detailed discussion of different inequality measures as well as measurement challenges and data issues associated with the measurement of inequality.

3.3   Why Inequality Matters

3.3.1   Introduction

A lot of the empirical literature on inequality, especially within economics, has focused on a purely economic perspective that tends to examine the relationship between economic inequality – usually proxied by income inequality – and other economic variables such as economic growth, savings, labor market performance, and the like. These relationships are important. In the analysis of the relevance of inequality, however, moving beyond an economic perspective is critical. Both in the larger social science literature and in the public discourse, inequality is considered also a moral issue linked to justice and human rights. It is also viewed as a political issue that affects the

operation of political systems, and it is likewise seen as a social issue that influences social stratification. Moreover, there is interaction in the inequality across these and other spheres. For example, economic and social inequality is likely to affect political inequality, which may have repercussions on economic and social inequality. Documenting the levels, the trends, and the interactions in this wider inequality and examining how they matter are therefore important.

It is important to also note that some inequality may be tolerable either because it is, in some ethical conception, considered acceptable, or because it leads to other beneficial outcomes. For example, one might interpret the Kuznets inverted U-shaped relationship between income inequality and economic growth – inequality initially rises along with economic growth, but then eventually falls – as an illustration of the phenomenon of tolerable or unavoidable inequality. In effect, inequality rises naturally as individuals, even those with the same initial allocation, behave differently in the implementation of investment schemes because of variations in rates of time preference and other preferences or possibly purely because of chance. This initial level of inequality may be considered tolerable. However, at a certain point, the inequality may become intolerable if it reduces economic performance, other desirable outcomes, or otherwise becomes intrinsically problematic.

3.3.2   Intrinsic Concerns

To what extent is a concern about inequality mandated by a concern about social justice? Social justice has been conceived in diverse ways, including as the embodiment of a regard for procedural rights and liberties, as the absence of absolute deprivation, and as the maintenance of inequality within tolerable limits or the eradication of inequality if it is deemed intolerable. The distinction between inequality in initial endowments and inequality in final outcomes has also figured prominently in recent debates, for example, debates involving luck egalitarians, who emphasize the existence of initial or starting gate equality in relevant endowments, such as Gerald A. Cohen, Ronald Dworkin, John Rawls, John Roemer, and many others. A plausible case has also been made that one should consider all theories of social justice egalitarian in the sense that they answer the question "equality of what?" (see Section 3.2.1; Sen 1979). For instance, libertarian theories, such as those of Nozick (1974), equal rights are central. From such a perspective, a spotlight on inequality is always mandated because of social justice even if the specific area of inequality, the focal variable, is associated with a particular theory of social justice. In addition, the extent to which an area of inequality is problematic may depend on the specifics of the theory. For example, the difference principle advanced by Rawls famously tolerates inequality as long as it demonstrably advances a specific good, namely, the advantages of the least advantaged members of society. The perspective on social justice that calls for a focus on equality of outcomes has not been especially influential since the 1970s, but it is now gaining more attention. Anderson (1999), for instance, argues that social justice demands a felt solidarity with others not merely because of a reasoned commitment to correcting injustice, but also for evaluative and empirical purposes. This may lead to a concern with equality of outcomes as well as with equality of starting points. It seems unreasonable to be indifferent about outcomes in assessing social justice, while feeling concern for others as an integral component of the demand for social justice.

If inequality refers only to a concern about a relative relationship and not to a concern about an absolute advantage or disadvantage, then the case for disvaluing inequality within a theory of social justice becomes weaker. The two kinds of inequality are, of course, empirically linked and deeply interconnected. Inequality between the rich and the super-rich may have arisen because of the facts of birth or luck in the availability of opportunities, but, in this case, the demand for corrective action from the standpoint of social justice may be thin. The distinction between disvaluing inequality absolutely and disvaluing inequality for some other reason, including the impact on absolute advantages and disadvantages, is important (Parfit 1997). However, in our world, relative inequalities are closely linked to low and even unacceptably low levels of absolute advantage; so attempting to separate the two is of doubtful utility.

3.3.2.1 Inequality of Opportunity, Capabilities, and Access to Primary Goods

The issue of whether to focus on ex ante inequality of endowments or ex post inequality of outcomes is important in contemporary discussions. The appropriate corrective action – to attempt to equalize resource endowments or educational opportunities versus taxation and transfers, for instance – would partly depend on what is considered the appropriate focus. Another, distinct concern has been the focus on space. For instance, if one is concerned about inequality of endowments, one may confine the focus to the resources possessed by individuals, but external to individuals, or one may take a more capacious view that includes natural endowments, such as athletic ability or intelligence. Though the latter cannot be redistributed directly, their inclusion among morally relevant considerations may influence the corrective actions one undertakes in other dimensions in which such actions are feasible. Similarly, one may be concerned about all outcomes, such as health and wealth, or only some outcomes, such as wealth. The choice to focus on specific outcomes may be based on, for example, the special relevance of these outcomes to human well-being or the role of social factors versus individual decision-making in determining individual outcomes.

Rawls (1971) advanced the idea of using primary goods as an index of the diverse social and individual resources relevant to an ex ante assessment of the opportunities available to a person to realize a chosen life plan. The concept of primary goods is inherently plural and extends beyond economic resources. However, it is also squarely focused on the means to achieve outcomes rather than the outcomes realized.

Sen (1992 and elsewhere) has emphasized the contrast between this Rawlsian conception and an alternate perspective, one based on capabilities, which takes account of the freedom to achieve specific outcomes. One aspect of the subtlety of the capability perspective

resides in the major role of freedom. The perspective is thus focused on opportunities rather than outcomes; yet, it reflects an awareness of the distinctions among outcomes by especially valuing the freedom to achieve those outcomes that the individual has reason to value. In this way, it mutes the differences between the ex ante and ex post approaches. The capability perspective also reflects an awareness of interpersonal variations in the ability to translate resources into outcomes. Whether it is morally appropriate to take account of such variations is a matter of debate.[8]

These perspectives all consider particular forms of inequality morally problematic and requiring corrective action. They differ in approach, and evaluations associated with them also differ in approach. An element of evaluative judgment is inescapable.

3.3.2.2 Inequality and Its Impact on Well-being

A large body of research in psychology, economics, and political science demonstrates that people are inequality averse, that is, they react negatively to the unequal distribution or allocation of resources, regardless of whether this leaves them at an advantage or a disadvantage, although they are more comfortable if they are left at an advantage (Loewenstein, Thompson, and Bazerman 1989; Fehr and Schmidt 1999). Indeed, the aversion to inequality seems to be universal (Henrich et al. 2006). People are willing to incur personal costs to reduce inequality and do so even as neutral third-party observers of inequality (Camerer and Thaler 1995; Fehr and Fischbacher 2004; Johnson et al. 2009). In recent studies using functional magnetic resonance imaging, researchers have documented the neural activation of reward processing areas – associated with positive affect – in response to fair allocations of resources and the activation of an area associated with specific negative emotions, such as anger and disgust, in response to unfair allocations of resources (Sanfey et al. 2003; Tabibnia, Satpute, and Lieberman 2008; Tricomi et al. 2010). People's aversion to inequality may be deep-rooted, emerging at a young age. Children as young as age seven years exhibit aversion to the unequal allocation of resources, and even five-year-olds apparently show a preference for the egalitarian distribution of rewards (Sutter 2007; Fehr, Bernhard, and Rockenbach 2008; Gummerum et al. 2010; Kogut 2011).

The empirical literature of the effect of income inequality on subjective well-being confirms these findings. At the micro level, income is associated with higher rates of happiness, but that the relationship is concave, suggesting that wider inequality reduces aggregate well-being (Deaton and Kahnemann 2010). This literature is somewhat less clear on whether income inequality in a society has an additional direct impact on well-being, apart from one's own position within the income distribution. While a majority of studies find such a link, others do not (Blanchflower and Oswald 2003; Sanfey and Teksöz 2007; Ferrer-i-Carbonell and Ramos 2012; Gruen and Klasen 2013). Particularly in developed and transition countries, most studies find negative effects of inequality, while in emerging and developing countries the effect is less clear.

---

[8]   See Pogge (2002) and Roemer (1998) for two contrasting views on this.

Given that people are overwhelmingly averse to even small, inconsequential economic inequalities in the laboratory, how may one explain people's acquiescence to larger, more consequential inequalities in everyday life? One possible explanation is that people simply do not appreciate how wide the disparities are (Norton and Ariely 2011; Norton et al. 2014; Kiatpongsan and Norton 2014). Nonetheless, although people tend to underestimate the amount of wealth inequality in their countries, they still prefer their countries to be more equal than they perceive them to be (Norton and Ariely 2011; Norton et al. 2014, Kiatpongsan and Norton 2014).

A second reason may be the belief in upward social mobility. According to the dominant ideology in the United States and many Western countries, people accept inequality as long as they believe that hard work pays off (Kluegel and Smith 1986). For example, in a cross-national survey of 25 countries, Shariff, Wiwad, and Aknin (2016) find a positive correlation between social mobility and acceptance of inequality. However, as demonstrated by Davidai and Gilovich (2015), people's perceptions of economic mobility may be as distorted as their perceptions of economic inequality. The mistaken belief in the broad scope of upward mobility may be an example of a general tendency to consider that institutional, judicial, and economic systems are fair (Jost and Banaji 1994). Because people need to believe that the prevailing economic system fosters a society in which individuals get what they deserve and deserve what they get, they glorify the well off as highly competent and industrious, and they vilify the poor as incompetent and lazy (Fong 2001; Mandisodza, Jost, and Unzueta 2006). Indeed, merely thinking about people's ability to choose for themselves increases their belief in personal responsibility, decreases their concern with wealth inequality, and, consequently, diminishes their support for redistributive measures (Savani, Stephens, and Markus 2011; Savani and Rattan 2012).

Underlying these beliefs about social mobility and the attribution of positive traits of the wealthy (and negative traits of the poor) is the distinction between inequality, which is uneven resource distribution, and inequity, which is resource distribution that does not offset relevant differences in ability, effort, need, and so on. People are generally averse to inequality and more concerned about procedural justice, that is, fairness in allocation processes, than about distributional justice, the fairness of allocations (Tyler 2011). People tend to be more egalitarian toward others who are perceived to expend as much effort as they expend or even more effort, but are less egalitarian toward others who are perceived to expend less effort than they do (Hoffman et al. 1994; Cherry, Frykblom, and Shogren 2002; Oxoby and Spraggon 2008). To the extent that people perceive large wealth and income discrepancies as indicative of underlying differences in effort and competence, they are likely to accept these as relatively benign manifestations of inequity rather than unacceptable instances of inequality.

People are also less concerned about economic inequality if it appears more remote and less personal. People care more about their local relative standing than their absolute position (Frank 1985; Norton 2013). For example, the incomes of individuals relative to the incomes of others around them are better predictors of life satisfaction and physical health than the absolute incomes of these individuals (Boyce, Brown, and Moore 2010; Daly, Boyce, and Wood 2015). Likewise,

people are more concerned about local inequality rather than global inequality, and they tend to apply more rigorous standards of fairness and egalitarianism within small communities than within large ones (Deutsch 1975; Pfeffer and Langton 1988). They are more likely to compare themselves with similar others and to be disturbed by inequality involving similar others as opposed to dissimilar others (Baron and Pfeffer 1994). People do not generally experience vast economic inequalities within a local context. While interactions between the rich and the poor occur routinely, they often occur in a context that favors equity over equality, such as the case of a waiter serving a wealthy patron. Only in the relatively rare cases in which inequality is locally substantial or occurs in contexts that are not associated with equity, such as if wealth inequality is clearly linked with unequal health outcomes, might people become more resistant to ongoing economic inequality.

These concerns about the impact of inequality on well-being can also be found in the economics literature. In the utilitarian tradition, the presumption of the declining marginal utility of income, derived essentially from the declining marginal utility of each good, is strong. This is reflected in concave money-metric social welfare functions, which will, for the same mean incomes, deliver lower aggregate well-being in more unequal societies. This is a formulation of inequality aversion (Atkinson 1970). Related arguments have been made by Dagum (1990) and Sen (1973), whereby well-being depends not only on one's own income, but also on one's rank in the income distribution. The key distinction with respect to the declining marginal utility view is that the relational aspect of inequality is emphasized in the sense that the difference in well-being to a reference group, rather than the absolute level of well-being, is particularly important.

These arguments have been incorporated, respectively, in the welfare measures of Atkinson (the "equally distributed equivalent income") and of Sen (welfare equals mean income, multiplied by 1 minus the Gini coefficient). Empirical applications include Jenkins (1997) and Gruen and Klasen (2001, 2003, 2008, 2012, 2013) and show that the welfare penalty of inequality, using plausible ranges of inequality aversion, can be large, sometimes reducing the welfare associated with an existing unequal income distribution – such as the income distribution prevailing in Latin America today – by 50 percent or more relative to a case in which the same income was distributed equally.

Income inequality can also exert an impact on the nonincome dimensions of well-being. For example, it can affect average health and education outcomes. Thus, Pickett and Wilkinson (2015) find that income inequality leads to lower average health outcomes. Widening inequality and the associated unemployment and social dislocation also contributed to sharply falling life expectancy during the early years of the transition in Eastern Europe and the former Soviet Union; the effects were more persistent in the latter (Cornia 2016b).

3.3.2.3   The Impact on Power Relations

Inequality may be economic, or it may be related to social differences, differences in political power or influence, or differences in cultural prestige. The various advantages and associated inequalities are distinct and

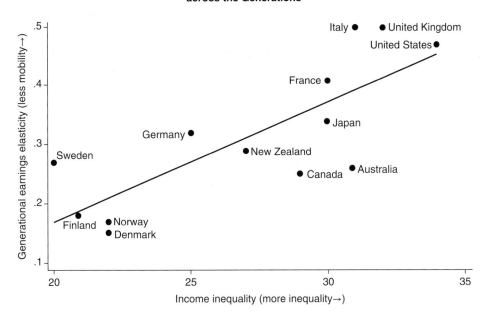

The Great Gatsby Curve: More Inequality is Associated with Less Mobility across the Generations

Figure 3.2 | The Great Gatsby Curve, selected OECD countries, 1960s and 1990s.
Source: Corak 2013.

may each also be tied to deep-seated differences based on gender, race, caste, or other factors. The day-to-day psychological and social experience of individual well-being or ill-being may be crucially shaped by inequalities in noneconomic dimensions. However, inequalities in these dimensions are often causally and symbolically linked to economic inequalities. The deep links make analysis of the historical background or the operation of a single dimension of advantage and disadvantage difficult.

One of the most pernicious effects of economic inequality is the impact on power relations in a society. This may take various forms. For instance, the greater influence of the privileged directly through the economic resources the privileged command and indirectly through their social status can cause institutional arrangements and policy choices to favor the interests of these people. Institutions may thus become instruments for extending and cementing inequality, leading to a vicious circle. A great deal of the literature on political economy and political sociology focuses on these connections (Mann 1986–2012; Winters 2012). For example, economic resources can be used to buy votes in elections or in legislative processes, buy the time and influence of the media or opinion makers, coerce or threaten to coerce people through economic sanctions or by commanding muscle power, and so forth (Bowles and Jayadev 2006). Such mechanisms may have predictable effects, leading, for instance, to oligarchs protecting their wealth from taxation or to lower levels of taxation for the privileged as suggested by the median-voter theorem (Meltzer and Richard 1981; Rodriguez 2004). There may be limits to such processes, however, especially if there are entrenched democratic institutions or active and politically mobilized groups such as a middle class pursuing their own collective projects. Economic inequality may give rise to inequality in politics, but nothing is fated.

Another, more subtle possibility is that economic privilege might become overlaid with markers of social and cultural privilege or

become associated with particular traits such as supposed economic knowledge or worldliness, leading others to defer to those who are better off. Such deference may be reflected in biases about who knows best how the world really works or about who should best command respect. Large numbers of legislators and leading politicians in many countries have great personal wealth, though this may also reflect the independence wealth provides. In a democratic age, there is also skepticism of the role of wealth in political life and an appropriate spotlight on the inappropriate influence of the relatively prosperous.

3.3.2.4 The Impact on the Intergenerational Transmission of Inequality

Inequality may be considered tolerable if people believe there is great intergenerational mobility and thus the opportunity to improve the position in the distribution. The empirical evidence, however, points to the opposite conclusion: wide inequality is associated with lower intergenerational mobility. This relationship has been popularized in the Great Gatsby Curve (Krueger 2012; Corak 2013). Figure 3.2 illustrates the relationship between intergenerational earnings mobility of fathers in the 1960s and sons in the late 1990s and inequality in disposable incomes in selected OECD countries. Clearly, more inequality is associated with less intergenerational mobility across the countries. Less data are available on other countries, but these findings have been replicated on a larger set of countries (Corak 2013). Among the mechanisms that may account for this relationship is the ability of the more well off to invest more heavily in their offspring; conversely, the difficulties the poor face in investing in their children; an association between the greater redistributive role of the state and more state investment to promote mobility; the direct role of inheritance; capital market imperfections that make investment difficult for the poor;

the ability of the more well off to help secure better employment for their children; and the greater access to networks enjoyed by the rich more generally. The relative importance of these various transmission channels has only been partially explored. It thus appears difficult empirically to justify wide inequality based on the prospects for greater intergenerational mobility.

3.3.3   The Instrumental Role of Inequality

3.3.3.1   Impact of Inequality on Poverty

Inequality has a direct impact on absolute income poverty. At a given mean income and a fixed absolute poverty line, wider inequality will invariably be associated with higher poverty rates (Bourguignon 2003). Less immediately obvious is the link between inequality and the poverty impact of growth, that is, the impact of inequality on the poverty elasticity of growth. Determining this relationship is useful for policy-makers because the relationship governs the extent to which the poor benefit from overall economic growth. Empirical studies generally find that the growth elasticity of poverty reduction has been quite low in Sub-Saharan Africa and substantially larger in Asia (Adams 2004; Kalwij and Verschoor 2007; Bresson 2009; Fosu 2009, 2010, 2011, 2015a).

Bourguignon (2003) shows that there is a mathematical relationship linking growth, inequality levels and trends, and absolute poverty reduction. Indeed, he shows that this elasticity decreases with widening initial inequality, but increases as income rises relative to the poverty line. While these results are all derived mathematically under an assumption of a lognormal income distribution, Bourguignon also tests these results empirically and finds that they fit the data well. An important implication is that the impact of growth on absolute poverty reduction is smaller in many Sub-Saharan African countries because these countries show wide initial inequality, and the ratio of mean income to the poverty line is low. So, the evidence on the small impact of growth on poverty reduction in Africa is purely mathematical, rather than a sign of policy failure, as is often lamented. Conversely, the rapid poverty reduction in Asia in recent decades is linked to the narrower initial inequality and a high ratio of mean income to the poverty line.

A weakness of the indicator of the growth elasticity of poverty reduction is that it considers percent changes, rather than percentage point changes; for example, a reduction in the poverty rate from 50 percent to 40 percent is a 20 percent reduction, but a 10 percentage point reduction. Policy-makers are generally interested in the percentage point reduction. Klasen and Misselhorn (2008) therefore extend Bourguignon's work by using absolute poverty measures, or the growth semi-elasticity of poverty reduction, that is, by how many percentage points does the poverty headcount change in response to a 1 percent increase in growth? They find that this semi-elasticity also decreases with widening initial income but decreases as income rises relative to

the poverty line. Both Bourguignon (2003) and Klasen and Misselhorn (2008) concur that higher growth rates, narrowing inequality, and more narrow initial inequality lead to greater poverty reduction.

3.3.3.2   The Impact on Economic Performance

One of the most controversial effects of inequality is its impact on economic performance. Two mechanisms suggest that wider inequality can promote economic growth. The first argument is that income inequality has a favorable effect on economic growth because the rich, in neoclassical and in Keynesian models, are assumed to have a higher propensity to save than the poor. Hence, an increase in income inequality triggers higher aggregate savings, which generate higher levels of investment and economic growth (Kaldor 1955).[9]

The second argument revolves around incentives. Two aspects are of special interest here. One aspect is that inequality itself provides incentives to work hard and invest because the returns tend to be higher in such context than in a more equal setting. These greater efforts and investments increase output generally. The other aspect relates to redistribution by the state. Redistribution can reduce inequality, but may also affect incentives negatively through, for instance, substantial marginal taxation on labor incomes. Li and Zou (1998) provide empirical support for the above hypothesis in a political economic setting whereby more equal income distribution triggers higher income taxation, which then produces lower economic growth. This outcome is underpinned by the assumption that such taxation finances mainly public consumption rather than productive services.[10]

Debates focus less on the potential plausibility of these mechanisms and more on their empirical relevance. For example, few economists doubt that a marginal tax rate at close to 100 percent would negatively affect effort and that, for example, one of the problems associated with the socialist system in Eastern Europe and the former Soviet Union was that earnings were not closely tied to effort (Kornai 1992). It is less clear whether the marginal tax rates commonly observed today have this effect or whether these effects are outweighed by the countervailing benefits of less inequality (Diamond 1998; Diamond and Saez 2011). Similarly, it is largely an empirical question whether inequality promotes domestic savings because the rich may not save more than the middle class and may take their money out of the country (Ray 1998; Ndikumana 2014).

There is a large literature suggesting, conversely, that high inequality reduces economic growth. Following Voitchovsky (2009), the theoretical channels of the influence of inequality on the size of the pie, that is, income levels and income growth rates, can be broadly grouped into four depending on the different parts and aspects of the income distribution: (1) the circumstances of the poor, (2) the overall distance between individuals, (3) wealth concentration, and (4) the size and circumstances of the middle class.[11]

---

[9]   Countering this view are scholars who worry about under-consumption and the resulting stagnation because of low and shrinking purchasing power among the majority. See, for example, Bleaney (1976) for a survey. The recent debate over secular stagnation has revived under-consumption as a potential cause of a growth slowdown. For example, see Teulings and Baldwin (2014).

[10]   This theory is, however, at variance with the findings of Alesina and Rodrik (1994), who assume that the taxation finances mainly productive services by the government.

[11]   Castells-Quintana and Royuela Mora (2014) and Erhart (2009) provide alternatives for structuring the transmission channels between inequality and growth.

The poor face credit constraints, which leads to forgone investment opportunities and, hence, forgone economic growth (Ghatak and Jiang 2002; Birdsall 2006). Credit constraints among the poor are particularly detrimental if they hinder investments in education, which may lead to long-term forgone economic opportunities and to intergenerational poverty traps (Galor and Zeira 1993; Grossmann 2008; Piketty 1997).

If earnings are low at the bottom end of the distribution, the opportunity costs of having children tend to be low, which can lead to higher fertility among the poor, as well as lower investment in each child, which hurts the poor but also overall economic growth. Similar to most discourses on the circumstances of the poor, the self-reinforcing mechanism of the large unskilled labor force squeezes wages at the low end of the distribution, which lowers the opportunity costs of children among the unskilled even more (Kremer and Chen 2002). The empirical analyses of Barro (2000), de la Croix and Doepke (2003), and Perotti (1996) support the fertility channel of the impact of inequality on growth.

Generally, greater socioeconomic polarization has been shown to lead to wider income and wealth inequality (Mogues and Carter 2005). Ferroni, Maeto, and Payne (2007) explore the links between trust, inequality, and social cohesion in Latin America and find that social cohesion is positively linked to economic growth and growth-enhancing institutions and negatively associated with inequality and low social capital in the form of trust. Similarly, it is argued that greater inequality leads to more crime. In particular, it makes property crimes more attractive. There is a lower opportunity cost attached to crime because the lower the wages, the less there is to gain at the bottom of the distribution. Meanwhile, the expected gains from crime are greater because there is more to steal from the top of the distribution (Chiu and Madden 1998; Josten 2003). That crime and social capital are interconnected is widely recognized in the literature, and several authors have found that crime adversely affects social capital, and this has additional implications for economic growth and development (Liska and Warner 1991; Messner, Baumer, and Rosenfeld 2004).

The economic distance between individuals or groups in a society can have major repercussions on growth through the formation of social capital and trust. A large recent literature has established that social capital and trust can help overcome the dilemmas in prisoner's dilemma games, thereby increasing overall cooperation within a society, which can have positive impacts on a wide range of outcomes, including business transactions, the adoption of technology, and enhanced health and education (Ostrom 1990).

If large, the distance between individuals can also have explicit negative consequences for growth through social unrest and socio-political polarization in society (Easterly 2001; Keefer and Knack 2002). A polarized political landscape can have adverse macroeconomic consequences such as political stalemates in efforts to achieve major policy reforms and political budget cycles as well as greater uncertainty leading to a less favorable investment climate.

Unequal income distribution that is characterized by heavy concentration of wealth at the top can be detrimental to growth by making the capture of institutions easier for elites and encouraging bias in the economy in the favor of elites (Glaeser, Scheinkman, and Shleifer 2003). An example is the establishment of exceptions favoring the most well off in the contributions to public goods and services such as health care and education. Such an unequal distribution is also detrimental to the process of democratization, thereby perpetuating the link across weak institutions, inequality, and low growth.

Domestic demand is a crucial factor in determining economic growth at least in the short to medium term. It is typically associated with a strong middle class. This implies a relatively equal income distribution, relatively few poor, who are able to cover their basic needs and do not require technologically sophisticated products, and relatively few rich, who primarily require luxury goods (Murphy, Sleifer, and Vishny 1989; Zweimüller 2000; Foellmi and Zweimüller 2006). In this context, redistribution from the rich to the poor would be growth enhancing because it would boost demand (Erhart 2009).

Another well-known channel linking inequality and growth through the middle class is analyzed through the median voter theorem and related political economy arguments. According to these, the wider the inequality in a society, the lower the income of the median voter relative to the average income and the greater the preference of the median voter for redistribution, thereby lowering growth and reducing the incentives for effort through high marginal taxation (Alesina and Rodrik 1994; Bertola 1993; Perotti 1993). This channel would only function in a democracy, which is also a reason to distinguish between democratic and nondemocratic countries in empirical analyses.

The median voter theorem has been challenged not only on empirical grounds, but also theoretically (Perotti 1996; Deininger and Squire 1998; Milanović 2000). For example, Benabou (2000, 2002) argues that, if the rich have more political power than the poor, they may lobby against redistribution measures even if these may be efficient. A recent report of the IMF (2014) – one of the few studies examining inequality, redistribution, and growth simultaneously – challenges this proposition using newer data and finds that wider inequality is associated with more redistribution, but concludes that redistribution is nonetheless not harmful to growth. Indeed, redistribution leads to both higher growth and longer duration in the growth spells. Notwithstanding, one ought to consider the peculiarities of the underlying data and the fact that the literature, as shown below, is far from conclusive about the overall effects on economic growth associated with redistribution.

3.3.3.3   The Empirical Impact on Growth

In the mid-1990s, the empirical debate was significantly enhanced by the availability of a much broader set of data on inequality across the world. Since then, many studies and reviews of the subject have appeared (Neves and Silva 2014). Cross-sectional studies generally tend to find a negative relationship between inequality and growth, whereas panel analyses yield mostly positive or insignificant results (Alesina and Rodrik 1994; Persson and Tabellini 1994; Clarke 1995; Perotti 1996; Deininger and Squire 1998).

Ensuing debates have focused on weaknesses in the data. Thus, Atkinson and Brandolini (2001) show that the comparability and consistency of the often-used Deininger and Squire (1996) dataset are questionable. Likewise, Knowles (2005) argues that most of the evidence on the growth and inequality relationship in cross-sectional studies is derived from inequality data that are not fully comparable. Once the heterogeneity in the underlying income concepts is accounted for, he concludes that there is no remaining relationship between income inequality and growth, but that inequality in expenditure is still negatively correlated with growth.

The World Income Inequality Database (WIID) has since appeared and significantly enhanced the coverage, but also the transparency of the data on inequality, although concerns and criticisms remain (Atkinson and Brandolini 2009). More recently, Solt (2016) has, based on the latest version of WIID, used imputation techniques to attempt to address data gaps and consistency issues in his SWIID dataset. Jenkins (2015) criticizes this approach, but the data have been used in a number of subsequent studies (Ostry et al. 2014; Scholl and Klasen 2015).

Endogeneity, that is, a problem caused by reversed causality or a spurious correlation related to an omitted third variable (unobserved heterogeneity), is a problem in these cross-sectional studies. The only cross-sectional study that explicitly addresses the endogeneity problem is the study of Easterly (2007), who instruments inequality through a country's wheat-sugar ratio, which is a function of the share of land suitable for growing wheat over the share of land suitable for growing sugarcane.[12] Easterly shows that wider inequality is associated with lower income, worse institutions, and less educational attainment. Most of the cross-sectional results should be viewed with caution because they may contain substantial omitted variable bias, given that any unmeasured factors associated with both inequality and growth can be wrongly attributed to an effect of inequality on growth.

Although the availability of panel data does not help perfectly resolve this issue, the possibility of introducing fixed effects allows the removal of at least the time-invariant portion of the omitted variable bias, which is also the main explanation for the divergence in findings between cross-sectional and panel studies.

Forbes (2000) used a panel approach to address unobserved heterogeneity through fixed effects and endogeneity through the use of generalized method of moments-type approaches. Her fixed effects specification that exploits the within-variation is also the more policy-relevant approach because policy-makers are interested in whether changes in inequality will promote or hurt subsequent growth. This approach came at the cost of rather short panel periods of only five years, which may be too short for the mechanisms discussed above to work. Forbes finds that widening inequality is associated with greater subsequent growth, although the result is not significant if ten-year periods are used.

The paper by Forbes has attracted a lot of debate and commentary, related to data, functional form, and econometric methodology (Banerjee and Duflo 2003; Knowles 2005; Roodman 2009). The effects of inequality on growth in a panel setting remains largely an open question. In another widely cited study, Barro (2000) finds that greater inequality leads to lower growth in poor countries and higher growth in rich countries, but there is little overall relationship between income inequality and growth. Deininger and Olinto (2000) focus on asset inequality instead of income inequality in their panel of 60 countries, and find a negative and significant relationship with subsequent growth rates. Ezcurra (2007) looks at annual regional growth across the European Union over 1993–2002 and concludes that greater inequality is associated with lower growth. Ostry et al. (2014), in an IMF study, examine the simultaneous impact of initial inequality and redistribution on subsequent growth in a panel setting. They find that initial inequality is associated with reduced growth in the subsequent five years, that redistribution has no impact on growth, and that greater inequality shortens the duration of growth spells. Insufficient information is provided on the details of their system generalized method of moments methodology to fully assess the robustness of their findings. Cingano (2014) focuses only on OECD countries and, using particularly good inequality data, also finds that initial inequality is associated with lower subsequent growth and that the effect of inequality at the bottom of the distribution is especially pronounced. Scholl and Klasen (2015) reexamine the data and the approach of Forbes (2000) using an expanded and updated panel dataset, including many more and arguably improved data on inequality and advanced econometric methods and tests. They find that inequality has a small positive impact on growth, but that this is entirely driven by the experience of transition countries in the 1990s; if one controls for this characteristic, no significant effect emerges.

Other approaches have used time series methods to assess the link between inequality and growth and several find that inequality reduces growth (e.g. Herzer and Vollmer 2012, 2013). Andrews, Jencks, and Leigh (2011) test the trickle-down hypothesis and find that a rise in top incomes is associated with a slightly higher growth in the following year, while Herzer and Vollmer (2013) find the opposite.

The results of reduced-form panel studies based on different methods are heterogeneous and, despite the continuous improvement of the inequality data since Deininger and Squire (1996), data issues and concerns about the functional form and appropriate estimation techniques are still being raised in the literature. While more panel studies seem to have found a negative effect of inequality on growth in recent years, these results are often driven by particular methodological choices, data, time periods, and lag structures. It appears clear, meanwhile, that the initial finding of a positive effect of inequality on growth is an outlier and related to a particular empirical approach. Thus, on average, there does not appear to be a uniform tradeoff between inequality and growth. It is quite plausible that these average effects hide substantial variation. In line with the theoretical literature,

---

12   The idea is based on the hypothesis of Engerman and Sokoloff (2002) that agricultural endowments are predictors of the institutional environment. Thus, growing sugarcane is more likely to involve large-scale farming and poor working conditions at low pay, which leads to extractive institutions and wider inequality, whereas wheat production involves family farming and is associated with less inequality and the emergence of a middle class.

it may well be the case that certain changes in inequality, such as deriving from investments in the human resources of the poor, will promote growth, while others, such as arbitrary seizures of assets, might hurt growth. The empirical literature on these various mechanisms is currently insufficient.

3.3.3.4   Inequality and Financial Stability

In the wake of the global financial crisis that started with the crisis in the US subprime mortgage finance sector, the question on whether inequality promotes unsound financial practices that can promote financial crises with negative growth and welfare implications has received attention. One argument is that widening inequality promoted the development of the subprime mortgage market to ensure that poorer people were able to purchase homes despite their stagnant or falling incomes. Some observers indeed argue that widening inequality, particularly in the United States, was a key cause of the global financial crisis. Kumhof and Ranciere (2011), Lysandrou (2011), Peragine et al. (2015), Rajan (2010), and Stockhammer (2015) argue that this is the case, while Bordo and Meissner (2012) dispute the link. Even if rising inequality facilitated the emergence of unsound financial practices that ultimately caused the crisis, the failure of financial market regulation and the politically driven deregulation in the financial sector played an important role in allowing these unsound practices to develop. It is difficult to assess to what extent this failure of regulation is related to rising inequality, for example, because of the push for deregulation by the rich.

3.3.3.5   The Impact on Conflict

There are two main theoretical lines of argument on the impact of inequality on conflicts: the relative deprivation hypothesis and the resource mobilization hypothesis (Muller 1985). According to the relative deprivation hypothesis, many forms of deprivation-induced discontent are positively associated with political violence. Most empirical research relies on polarization measures as a proxy for relative deprivation (Thorbecke and Charumilind 2002). Such measures tend to be positively related to the risk of conflict (Bueno de Mesquita 1978; Keefer and Knack 2002; Montalvo and Reynal-Querol 2005). Thus, to the extent that it may lead to polarization, income inequality could indirectly result in conflict.

The resource mobilization hypothesis draws attention to the discontent generated by the inequality of resources that could then lead to conflict. An offshoot of this hypothesis is the land maldistribution hypothesis, which posits that the discontent arising because of the highly concentrated distribution of land and the lack of land ownership in agrarian societies are significant determinants of mass political violence (Thorbecke and Charumilind 2002). There is evidence in support of the view that land inequality tends to raise the incidence of conflict (Russett 1964; Huntington 1968; Midlarsky and Roberts 1985; Binswanger et al. 1995). However, Muller and Seligson (1987) find that inequality in the distribution of income rather than inequality in the distribution of land primarily explains the rates of political violence across countries. André and Platteau (1998) fault both land inequality

and income inequality for provoking violence, particularly in the 1994 Rwandan genocide.

Although horizontal inequality may not be associated directly with conflict, it stimulates grievances that intensify the likelihood of rebellion (Gurr and Moore 1997). In certain cases, it facilitates the outbreak of conflict (Østby 2008). However, empirical research has not yet established a substantial relationship between vertical inequality and the risk of the outbreak of war (Fearon and Laitin 2003; Collier and Hoeffler 2004). Instead, the literature tends to find a stronger relationship between the polarization of groups and conflict, suggesting that the type of inequality matters significantly for conflict (Esteban and Ray 2011).

3.3.3.6   The Relationship between Inequality and Social Movements

Does the starkness of an inequality spur a disposition to organize social movements against inequality? Sociologists and political scientists have long considered the question whether absolute disadvantages or relative disadvantages may act as a trigger of social protest (Runciman 1972). This question may be reduced to a question about whether the level of disadvantage conceived in any way or a change in the nature of the disadvantage matters most in causing social protest. The literature is inconclusive. An important reason why this is so is because unequal situations that persist may tend to generate a cultural and ideological framework – for instance, adaptive preferences – that tends to rationalize inequality and repress social discontent (Elster 1985; Sen 2002). Another important reason is that, in a context of inequality, those who benefit from the inequality, such as political parties or nonparty political formations, including persuasive or coercive forces, may invest in strengthening the political actors that help sustain or widen the inequality, and, by definition, these factions possess more resources to accomplish such an outcome. Inequality may also tend to promote a society with more heterogeneous interests in the face of which collective action is more difficult (Bardhan, Ghatak, and Karaivanov 2007). Among those who share a common interest, the incentive for collective action may also become stronger, but, in most contemporary societies, individuals, even in large numbers, often have no ready method of joining together to support their shared interests, rendering collective action difficult (Bates 1981; Olson 1965). The impact of inequality on the sense of fellow feeling and the absence of widely accepted social standards and values are also relevant, but poorly understood factors that may influence the potential for collective action, including against inequality.

Examination of the empirical relationship between inequality and social movements reveals a clear link. For instance, the mobilization of new social movements promoted in Latin America beginning in the mid-1990s was a reaction to the sharp widening in inequality recorded during the previous decades that were dominated by liberalization and structural adjustment. Indeed, in Latin America, the steep decline in income inequality in 2002–2014 coincided with a major shift in the political landscape that was the culmination of a gradual return to and consolidation of democracy. This included a turn to the left in the political orientation of most incumbent governments. The

3

number of countries run by center-left administrations rose from two to thirteen between 1998 and 2009 and remained almost unchanged until 2013. This and the revival of social movements helped repoliticize the issues of inequality and social justice and bring distributive and redistributive policies back to center stage after the oblivion of the 1980s and 1990s.

As suggested in opinion polls of the Latinobarómetro survey, a major factor behind this political turnaround was growing frustration with the disappointing results of the policies of the Washington Consensus implemented in the 1980s and 1990s. These policies and the world recession and debt crisis of the 1980s led to a contraction in manufacturing and public services, rising unemployment, an enlargement of the informal sector, a severe reduction in GDP, sluggish growth throughout the 1980s, and widening inequality.

As Panizza (2005) notes, the political coalitions supporting the new center-left governments included social movements of the urban and rural poor, unemployed, and informal sector workers, indigenous groups, and local and decentralized organizations. These were now at the forefront of social mobilization, where they had replaced the historical trade unions and the parties on the left. The new coalitions included also representatives of the business community and professional middle class who had traditionally voted for conservative parties, but had switched political allegiance after experiencing a decline in the level and share of incomes during the two previous decades. There is little doubt they had been instrumental in raising awareness of redistributive issues and repoliticizing the entrenched inequalities in Latin America (Roberts 2014).

The role of social movements and their relationship to inequality is quite different in Africa. Although social movements for independence abounded in the 1950s and 1960s in Africa, these movements were primarily concerned with the transfer of political power from the colonialists, rather than against economic inequality. However, the structural adjustment supported by the Washington Consensus in the late 1970s through the 1990s under the Bretton Woods Institutions (mainly, the IMF and the World Bank) led to widening in inequality in many African countries. This occurred directly because of reductions in government subsidies on basic commodities and indirectly through depreciations of national currencies, resulting in higher prices for the commodities. This represented an attack on living standards, particularly among the urban poor, leading to food riots in the late 1970s and early 1980s (Zghal 1995). More recently, attempts by governments to reduce direct or indirect subsidies on essential commodities have been met with unrest because such policies invariably raise the prices facing many, including especially the poor, and widen inequality.

During the colonial period, South Asia witnessed anticolonial and nationalist movements. Using the language of inequality, one might frame these movements as the reflection of a desire to redress iniquities in the political environment, that is, transfer power from the colonial rulers. Since independence, South Asian countries have witnessed various social movements emerge in response to inequalities. One set of movements strived for more equitable land distribution to curb the power of the landed elite and to give a fairer share to small, low-income landholders and hired agricultural laborers

(Dasgupta 1975; Banerjee 1980). Agriculture continues to provide the raw material for movements, agitation, and mobilization such as in the protests among farmers in certain parts of India today (see Balamatti 2017; Langa and Sriram 2017).

Another dimension on which social movements have focused is caste, an important social division in South Asia. There is considerable debate on the nature of the caste system and how it was shaped by colonial rule (Srinivas 1998; Gupta 2000; Dirks 2001; and the references therein). Movements against the injustices of the caste system have arisen during various periods in the history of South Asia. After the end of colonial rule in countries that have become democracies, such as India, caste groups have relied on the state through affirmative action, for instance, and electoral politics to improve their disadvantaged status.

3.3.3.7 The Impact on Behavior

A fundamental aspect of inequality is that people are affected differentially. The better off have one set of experiences, and the less well-off have a different set of experiences, with substantially different impacts on behavior. An increasing body of knowledge points to developmental and biological disruptions occurring because of exposure to early childhood adversity (Shonkoff, Boyce, and McEwen 2009; McEwen and Gianaros 2010; Shonkoff et al. 2012; see also Chapter 18). Besides the effects on child development, there are important behavioral repercussions in adulthood associated with adverse circumstances.

A central feature in the lives of people with low incomes is that they must juggle their spending to coincide with sporadic income, and they must constantly weigh difficult and often expensive tradeoffs (Collins et al. 2009; Edin and Shaefer 2015; Morduch and Schneider 2017). Financial services, including at banks, informal lenders, and rent-to-own stores, as well as landlords, utility companies, and health care providers, impose high interest rates and steep late payment penalties. A substantial share of the annual incomes of the poor goes for such expenses (Edin and Lein 1997; Mullainathan and Shafir 2009; M. Barr 2012). It can be expensive to be poor.

The lack of sufficient funds leads to a drain on cognitive resources. It means needing to devote substantial time and mental resources to juggling: organizing payments for essentials, phone calls with providers, negotiations with creditors, and hits to credit scores. The constant budgetary concerns impose severe demands on the cognitive system, the human bandwidth (Miller 1956; Baddeley and Hitch 1974; Neisser 1976; Luck and Vogel 1997). This is bound to distract from other important duties, leading to diminished resources and reduced performance (Mullainathan and Shafir 2013). The cognitive overload and diminished mental bandwidth affect basic cognitive capacity, that is, the ability to solve problems, retain information, engage in logical reasoning, and so on. They can also affect executive control, the ability to direct cognitive activities, such as overseeing the allocation of attention, planning, remembering to perform important functions, self-monitoring, and impulse control (Mani et al. 2013; Mullainathan and Shafir 2013).

Other correlates of poverty may contribute to diminished bandwidth, including dysfunctional institutions, dangerous neighborhoods, physical pain, noise, pollution, and sleep deprivation. Poverty also correlates with depression and anxiety disorders, negative affects that narrow cognitive scope, and stress, which is the reaction of individuals to environmental demands that exceed their regulatory capacity (WHO 2001; Haushofer and Fehr 2014).

These constant and severe impositions on cognitive bandwidth may lead to short-sighted, risk-averse decision making, including favoring habitual behaviors at the expense of goal-directed behaviors (Haushofer and Fehr 2014). This may include a greater inclination to take out high-interest, short-term loans or becoming more impulsive in making dietary choices (Shiv and Fedorikhin 1999; Shah et al. 2012).

The challenges associated with poverty have long been observed to correlate with an excess of counterproductive behaviors (Mullainathan and Shafir 2013). Thus, the participation of the poor in the financial mainstream may be limited and is often misguided (Caskey 1994; Bertrand, Mullainathan, and Shafir 2006). The poor also fail to take advantage of the entitlement programs despite eligibility (Currie 2006). They do not undertake preventive health care and fail to adhere to drug regimens (Katz and Hofer 1994). They are less likely to keep appointments and are more often tardy, and they are less attentive parents (Neal et al. 2001; Karter et al. 2004; Lee and Bowen 2006).

The stigma and stereotyping of poverty impact perception and behavior. The poor tend to be scorned, perceived as incompetent, and disrespected (Kerbo 1976; Fiske 2011). This view is often coupled with a belief that the poor are a burden on society, lazy, and unmotivated. This can lead to cognitive distancing and to welfare stigma, which purportedly causes many among the poor to forgo important benefits offered in the public and the nonprofit sectors (Horan and Austin 1974; Bisset and Coussins 1982; Rogers-Dillon 1995; Kissane 2003; Reutter et al. 2009).

If the self-worth of the poor is threatened, the poor may consume executive resources, leading to executive function disorder. Thus, if certain situations prove stigmatizing or intimidating, the defensive responses required and the stress about being judged according to stereotypes, along with efforts to suppress negative thoughts and emotions, can disrupt cognitive performance (Steele 1997; Spencer, Steele, and Quinn 1999; Schmader, Johns, and Forbes 2008). In striving to provide products and services that might help the poor, poverty advocates may thus be confronted by the additional hurdle of impaired performance arising because of the reaction of the poor to the stereotype threat.

A theoretical advance in the interpretation and manipulation of stigma and stereotype threat is self-affirmation theory, which posits that people can be motivated to sustain a sense of self-worth and integrity (Steele 1988). For example, if positive aspects of the self, even those unrelated to the threat, are affirmed, the need to sustain one's sense of self-worth is met, and people respond less defensively to situations that otherwise would appear threatening (Aronson, Cohen, and Nail 1999; Sherman and Cohen 2006). Self-affirmation manipulations have been found to improve fluid intelligence and cognitive control performance among the poor and to enhance the willingness of the poor to take advantage of social benefits programs (Hall, Zhao, and Shafir 2013).

3.3.3.8   The Impact on Political Participation

A mechanism through which economic inequality may have a substantial impact on society is political participation, which can create a feedback loop relevant to the production and reproduction of economic inequality. The decision to participate in political processes by voting, seeking to persuade or mobilize others to stand for office, and so on may well be systematically shaped by economic inequality. This is so especially if the more well off are able to deploy their greater resources in the political process openly or covertly. The extent to which the more well off are permitted to shape the political process differentially may have an effect on individual political outcomes, but also influence the institutions that govern day-to-day political decision-making. Some of these institutions are open to public view, such as national electoral processes, and others are well hidden, such as the administrative procedures regulating specific industries, about which the general public may have limited awareness. Public financing versus private financing in the election campaigns of individual politicians and political parties, the remuneration of politicians that allows them to participate in politics without being either wealthy or paid off after their turn in politics, and other institutional and policy factors may help determine whether the more well off are able to shape political outcomes (Roemer 2006).

The low rates of voting and other forms of political participation in many countries, including wealthy countries with established democracies, are illustrative. Some voters may fail to vote because of their calculation that their votes are unlikely to be decisive. There are also other reasons. Some potential voters may believe, for instance, that the political options are already substantially set by powerful economic or social interests, thus rendering their votes meaningless. That the amount of trust in electoral democracy and in democratic institutions has been shrinking in some countries even as inequality has been widening is suggestive. This seems to be occurring in the United States, though the experience of European countries appears somewhat different.[13] Economic inequality may also interact with gender and social inequality to influence who is able to stand for public office, the messages that are advanced most forcefully, and the arguments that are able to succeed in public policy-making.

3.3.3.9   The Impact of Gender Inequality on Growth

The literature has been expanding on the causes of gender inequality in education and employment and the consequences on economic growth. Some theoretical papers have emphasized that gender

---

[13]   See, for instance, the results reported at "Beyond Distrust: How Americans View Their Government; 1. Trust in Government: 1958–2015," Pew Research Center, Washington, DC, November 23, 2015, www.people-press.org/2015/11/23/1-trust-in-government-1958-2015/.

inequality in education and employment can reduce economic growth (Galor and Weil 1996; Lagerlöf 2003; Rees and Riezman 2012; Teignier and Cuberes 2016). A number of empirical studies have argued that gender inequality in education reduces economic growth (Klasen 2002; Knowles et al. 2002; Yamarik and Ghosh 2003; Klasen and Lamanna 2009). The evidence appears to be quite robust, although most of it is drawn from cross-country econometric studies. There is also evidence that gender inequality in employment can reduce economic growth (Esteva-Volart 2009; Klasen and Lamanna 2009; Teignier and Cuberes 2016). The literature on this outcome is smaller and less conclusive. The quantitative importance of gender gaps for economic performance and the precise transmission channels for the effects of gender gaps on economic growth are less clear. Some argue that the growth costs of gender gaps are large, while others suggest that these gaps do not have substantial consequences, may not have a clear impact, or may be beneficial for growth (King, Klasen, and Porter 2009; Duflo 2012; Bandiera and Natraj 2013; Tertilt and Doepke 2014; Teignier and Cuberes 2016). A segment of the literature finds that gender gaps in the access to land and other resources in agricultural production reduce agricultural productivity in some settings (Goldstein and Udry 2008; Udry 2006).

3.3.3.10 The Relationship among Income Inequality, Education, and Health Inequality

As discussed in greater detail in Chapters 18 and 19 on health and education, because there are well-documented causal relationships in both directions between income, education, and health, income inequality likely promotes inequality in education and health unless steps, often involving public action, are taken to break the links. This calls for an investigation into the empirical importance of these links. The literature generally addresses this issue using two approaches. One approach is to study the correlations. The large literature on this topic finds that there is substantial correlation across income inequality, educational inequality, and health inequality (Checchi 2001; Deaton 2003). This correlation is hardly disputed, and there are good theories to explain the causal links in both directions. Less obvious is the impact of income inequality on average health or education outcomes. Most evidence points to the conclusion that wider income inequality leads to worse average health and education outcomes. For example, Pickett and Wilkinson (2015) find that the literature points to the strong causal impact of income inequality on average health outcomes.

The other approach is to study the joint distribution of income, health care, and education. In the cross-country context, this is the approach, for example, of Grimm et al. (2008, 2010); and Harttgen and Klasen (2012). These researchers find a strong correlation between income inequality, educational inequality, and health inequality. They also find that inequalities in nonincome dimensions are narrower, the greater the overall achievements in these dimensions. The conceptual and empirical literature on multidimensional inequality measures also discusses ways to capture the joint distribution of income, education, and health inequality (Aaberge and Brandolini 2014).

3.4 Global Inequality

The estimation of global income inequality requires two basic types of data, namely, data on incomes in all countries and data on the distribution of incomes within each country. Data on incomes and the distribution of incomes have only recently become available for a sufficient number of countries to make an estimation of global inequality a possibility. Calculating global inequality over the long run by going back 60 or more years is far more difficult because of the lack of data and thus involves making many assumptions with unreliable data.[14] Figure 3.3 presents estimates of global inequality and the between-country contribution to total inequality as calculated in various studies from 1820 to 2013. These estimates are not always comparable because the data and assumptions vary across studies, but they are the best available estimates of global inequality over the long run.

The estimates from 1820 to 1992 are from the seminal work of Bourguignon and Morrisson (2002). The Global Consumption and Income Project (GCIP) database includes data on global inequality in 1960–2013. Household income or consumption surveys that have become more frequent across countries only recently have been used to estimate global interpersonal inequality. Anand and Segal (2014); Bourguignon (2015); Jayadev, Lahoti, and Reddy (2015); Lakner and Milanović (2016); and Milanović (2002, 2005, 2012) use household survey information on income and consumption trends and distribution to estimate global interpersonal inequality. Other studies use survey data to develop distribution information, but scale the within-country distributions to national account estimates of mean income or consumption (Schultz 1998; Dowrick and Akmal 2005; Sala-i-Martin 2006; Chotikapanich et al. 2012).

The trends and the rate of change in global inequalityand its components may vary substantially depending on whether the estimates are based on household survey means or scaling up national accounts means, although the broad trends are similar (Deaton 2005). Anand and Segal (2008) find that the confidence intervals of global inequality measures are large because of various sources of uncertainty in the estimates arising from measurement and estimation problems. These facts make conclusions difficult about trends in global inequality in 1970–2000. Apart from the standard survey sampling errors, global estimates are also prone to errors arising from PPP measurements that are not quantified. Table 3.1 presents global estimates based on various studies to give a sense of the range in global inequality estimates in 1988–2008.

3.4.1 Trends in Between- and Within-Country Income Inequality

The shape of overall global income distribution was unimodal and basically log normal in 1820–1913. By 1950, the unimodal distribution had shifted to a bimodal distribution. Twin peaks became pronounced thereafter up to the 1980s. There was another gradual shift to a

---

[14] The lack of data has arisen because of the lack of household surveys or tax records data before the 1950s and, more crucially, the lack of purchasing power parity (PPP) estimates to convert incomes expressed in national currencies into a single international currency prior to the 1990s.

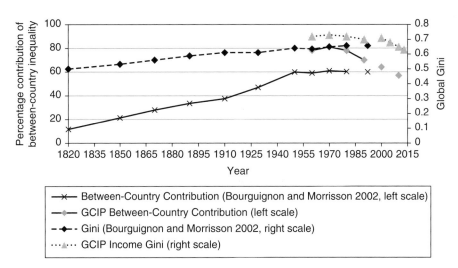

Figure 3.3 | Long-term trends in global inequality, 1820–2015.
Source: Bourguignon and Morrisson 2002; Jayadev, Lahoti, and Reddy 2015.

Table 3.1 | Comparison of global inequality estimates, various studies, 1988–2008

Source study	1988	1993	1998	2003	2005	2008
GCIP, income	69.6	69.6	69.2	70.6	68.4	66.6
Anand and Segal (2014), with top incomes	72.6	72.7	72.2	73.5	72.7	
Anand and Segal (2014), without top incomes, survey means	70.5	70.7	69.8	71.1	70.1	
Anand and Segal (2014), without top incomes, household consumption, national accounts	73.9	72.1	71.1	70.6	69.8	
Lakner and Milanović (2016), national accounts mean + top-heavy Pareto imputation	76.3	76.1	77.2	78.1		75.9
Lakner and Milanović (2016), national accounts means	71.5	70.5	70.6	70.7		67.6
Lakner and Milanović (2016), survey means	72.2	71.9	71.5	71.9		70.5
Milanović (2012)	67.8	69.3	68.8	70.1		
Milanović (2005)	61.9	65.2	64.2			
Milanović (2002)	62.5	65.9				
Bhalla (2002), income	67.0		65.0			
Bhalla (2002), consumption	66.0		63.0			
Bourguignon and Morrisson (2002)		66.0				
Chotikapanich et al. (1997)	65.0					
Dikhanov and Ward (2002)	69.0		68.0			
Dowrick and Akmal (2005), Geary-Khamis PPP US dollar		64.0				
Dowrick and Akmal (2005), Afriat efficiency index		71.0				
Sala-i-Martín (2006)	65.0	64.0	64.0			
Bourguignon (2012)	71.0		69.0			66.0

Note: GCIP = Global Consumption and Income Project (database), World Bank, Washington, DC, http://gcip.info/.
Sources: Based on Lakner and Milanović 2016; additional data compiled by Klasen et al. 2016.

unimodal distribution by 2010 (van Zanden et al. 2014; Jayadev, Lahoti, and Reddy 2015).

Global interpersonal inequality estimates based on historical data show that inequality was wide – the Gini coefficient was at about 0.5 – even in the early nineteenth century, during the first stages of the Industrial Revolution in the West.[15] Inequality widened substantially until World War I (1913) with the spread of industrialization and rapid growth in Western Europe, the Americas, and the Western offshoots (Australia, Canada, New Zealand, and the United States), while other regions were falling behind. An important feature of this period was a sharp increase in the between-country component of global inequality (the inequality that would exist if all individuals had the mean incomes of their countries, Milanović, 2011; Pritchett, 1997). Global inequality stabilized until World War II. It widened thereafter, but at a slower pace and peaked in the 1980s. The between component of global inequality showed an increase until 1955, when it peaked and accounted for 60 percent of total inequality. It was then stable until the late 1980s according to the national accounts data analysis of Bourguignon and Morrisson (2002).

---

[15]   The estimates are similar across the three studies that calculate a measure of global inequality in this period: 0.5 according to Bourguignon and Morrisson (2002); 0.48 according to van Zanden et al. (2014); and 0.54 according to Milanović (2011).

According to the GCIP estimates, consumption inequality was at around 0.69 Gini points in 1960 and held steady until 2005, when it was 0.68, but declined to 0.63 in 2013 based on household survey data. Lakner and Milanović (2016) also estimate similar trends in inequality in 1988–2008 (0.72–0.70), with only a slight decline overall.[16] The within-country component of inequality and total inequality increase by 2–4 Gini points if the data in household surveys are augmented by information on top incomes, but the trends remain similar (Anand and Segal 2015). The changes in the recent period seem small and insubstantial relative to the increase in global inequality during the nineteenth and early twentieth centuries.

Within-country inequality has expanded rapidly recently. Population-weighted average within-country income inequality widened from 0.42 in 1990 to 0.47 in 2010 according to the GCIP. In contrast, the between-country component of total inequality narrowed during the same period because of the faster pace of growth in China since the 1980s and in most developing countries in the first decade of the 2000s. Estimating global inequality and between-country inequality without China eliminates most of the decline in both these measures.

3.4.2 International Inequality in Education and Health

Human well-being is a multidimensional phenomenon that is often correlated with incomes, though the correlation is far from perfect (Drèze and Sen 1995). Several dimensions, including health, education, and income, have been combined to create composite indexes of well-being, of which the HDI of the United Nations Development Program is among the most widely applied. Prados de la Escosura (2015) uses historical data on health (life expectancy), education (adult literacy and enrollment rates), and income (per capita income) to create an historical HDI spanning 1870–2007. The index increased sixfold over the period, though there was up and down movements. In 1870–1913, there was steady, but moderate progress, which accelerated in 1913–1970, followed by sustained deceleration until 1990 and a rise thereafter. Prados de la Escosura (2015) shows that the gap between OECD countries and the rest of the world was stable until 1913, and the rest of the world slowly converged on the West up to 1970. After 1970, the pace of the catch-up of the rest of the world slowed. World regions vary in the timing and speed of the catch-up with OECD countries in human development. Latin America converged until the 1980s and then continued the convergence later, in the 2000s. Africa was catching up until the 1970s, but, since then, Sub-Saharan Africa has not caught up further. Asia witnessed a period of convergence until the 1970s, dominated by improvements in education and health in China, and – driven by China and India – has rapidly caught up since 1990. The Soviet Union exhibited substantial gains in human development between the 1920s and 1960s, leading to a substantial catch-up of Central and Eastern European countries with the OECD. Since the late 1960s, however, the gaps have widened again between the OECD and Eastern Europe, which has been stagnating since the mid-2000s, mainly because of the absolute stagnation and decline in life expectancy in many transition countries at the start of the transition process (Cornia 2016).

To take account of the within dimensions of inequality, the United Nations Development Program introduced the IHDI. The IHDI is based on indexes proposed by Foster, López-Calva, and Székely (2005) that are among the Atkinson family of inequality measures. The IHDI discounts the average value of each dimension of the HDI across the population according to the level of inequality. The gap between the HDI and the IHDI widens as inequality rises. Though not a perfect measure, the IHDI can be useful in gauging the losses in human development because of inequality. In 2015, IHDIs were calculated for 151 countries. The results indicated a global loss of 22.8 percent in human development because of inequality.[17] The loss was largest in Sub-Saharan Africa (33.3 percent) and smallest in Europe and Central Asia (13.0 percent).

3.4.2.1 Inequality in Education

Using the Atkinson index (with an inequality aversion coefficient of 1), the *Human Development Report* estimates inequality in mean years of schooling in 2015 at 26.8 percent globally. South Asia is the most unequal region on this measure (41.5 percent). Using mathematics and science scores among eighth graders in 49 mostly rich countries, Sahn and Younger (2007) estimate within- and between-country inequalities in learning achievement. They find that slightly more than half of all inequality among this group of countries arises because of within-country differences in achievement. Using data of the 2006 round of the Program for International Student Assessment survey, Ferreira and Gignoux (2014) calculate inequality in educational achievement in 57 countries. Slightly over one-third of total inequality in educational achievement in these countries is caused by inequality of opportunity.

3.4.2.2 Inequality in Health

Various health indicators – child height, adult height, life expectancy, infant or under-five mortality, morbidity, and so on – have been used to measure inequality in health and have led to differing conclusions (see Chapter 18). Pradhan et al. (2003) use the height of preschool-age children, which is supposed to be comparable across the world, to analyze global inequality in health. They find considerable variation in intrahousehold inequality across countries. Decomposing health inequality within and between countries, they find that more than two-thirds of health inequality can be attributed to within-country variation. This contrasts with income inequality, where most of the contribution to global inequality arises from the between component.

Studying life expectancy across world regions, Joerg et al. (2014) find that, though life expectancy at birth increased by about 30 years in all regions of the world, the trend shows large variations. Globally, they find that life expectancy diverged in the late nineteenth and early twentieth centuries and then converged in the late twentieth century

---

[16] Given the substantial uncertainty and estimation errors in various sources in the measurement of global inequality, this small change is likely insignificant.

[17] See "Table 3: Inequality-adjusted Human Development Index," United Nations Development Program, New York, http://hdr.undp.org/en/composite/IHDI (last accessed September 2016).

because of rapid gains in non-OECD countries. But in the two decades up until about 2000, life expectancy diverged across countries in several regions, and between-country inequality on this measure widened (Goesling and Firebaugh 2004). This outcome was closely linked with sharply rising AIDS mortality and substantial overall mortality rates in crisis-prone Sub-Saharan Africa. Recent years have seen large gains in life expectancy and declines in under-five mortality in these regions, thereby contributing to a return to converging trends in life expectancy globally.

3.5 Trends in Within-Country Inequality

3.5.1 Empirical Trends, by Outcome

3.5.1.1 Income Inequality

Data on income inequality often suffer from problems associated with incomparability across countries and across time, the lack of regularity in surveys, and from missing data. Although the situation is improving, the data problems remain severe, and the findings reflected in different datasets on levels and trends in inequality across countries and regions are frequently inconsistent, and trends are often sensitive to the start and end-point of the analysis. The data used in this subsection are taken from studies that have carefully combined comparable data.[18]

Within-country income inequality was long considered a stable feature of every economy (Deininger and Squire 1996). Yet, already in the late 1970s, there were signs of widening inequality in many advanced economies (Piketty 2014). In the 1980s, inequality also started moving upward in developing and transition countries, and this tendency continued in the 1990s (Gruen and Klasen 2001). As a result, over 1980–2000, 69 percent of the 109 countries on which data are available recorded a systematic widening in income inequality, while only 23 percent recorded a decline (Table 3.2, top panel). The greatest number of increases was recorded in the transition economies, Latin America, the OECD, and Southeast Asia.

Since the early 2000s, there has been a slowdown in the frequency and intensity of the rises in inequality. Indeed, in 2000–2010, Gini trends diverged (Table 3.2, bottom panel). Income inequality narrowed in practically all of Latin America. Consumption inequality narrowed in 13 of the 21 Sub-Saharan African countries on which consistent data are available. Income inequality also narrowed in Korea, Malaysia, the Philippines, and Thailand (Cornia and Martorano 2012). In contrast, though at a slower pace than during the previous two decades, inequality continued on an upward trend in most OECD countries and several European and Asian transition economies, while the widening accelerated in China and most of South Asia. Overall, during this period, 47 percent of the countries recorded an inequality decline and 41 percent an increase.

Table 3.3 presents unweighted average Gini coefficients by region and income category in 2000–2010, when regional inequality trends

diverged, and inequality widened in most cases more slowly than during the previous two decades. In 2010, average inequality across the world was moderate: the average Gini was slightly less than 0.4. The level of inequality in the advanced economies, Eastern Europe and Central Asia, and South Asia was below the world average. It was above the world average in Latin America and the Caribbean and in Sub-Saharan Africa. Inequality in East Asia was roughly at the world average. Latin America and the Caribbean showed the widest regional inequality. Inequality in low-income countries is well below the world average. The most unequal income group is the upper-middle-income countries, a reflection of the influence of unequal Latin America. Trends in inequality confirm many of these conclusions: slight increases in inequality in advanced economies and in East Asia, large reductions in Latin America, small reductions in South Asia, and little change in other regions, leading to the overall impression of slightly falling average within-country inequality in the world in 2000–2010.

There is evidence of a slight decline in average country-level inequality in the world in 2000–2010. In particular, Latin America and the Caribbean – the most unequal regions – experienced a significant decline in inequality. Low-income countries showed a slight increase. Inequality in middle- and high-income countries narrowed slightly. Convergence is graphically apparent in Figure 3.4, which also illustrates that declining inequality was more frequent in the 2000s. Of the 78 countries included in the figure, 45 showed a decline, 30 an increase, and 3 no change.

These data all refer to within-country income or consumption inequality. Inequalities in education and health can follow a separate dynamic. Educational inequality, if measured in terms of schooling outcomes, tends to be larger in poorer countries than in richer countries. As education expands, the inequality may first widen, but, as average educational attainment rises, inequality usually narrows as the less well educated groups slowly catch up to in years of schooling with more highly educated groups (Breen et al. 2010; Harttgen and Klasen 2012; Ram 1990). There is less information on trends in health inequality because many studies focus on health inequality at a specific point in time. This subject is covered in detail in Chapter 18.

3.5.1.2 Inequality in Access to Environmental Resources and in Risk Exposure

Access to environmental resources is typically unequally distributed within countries. For example, a report of the World Health Organization (WHO 2012) focusing on Europe finds that perceived access to green spaces varies across socio-economic groups identified by income, education, or other characteristics. In the United States, considerable evidence has been gathered that the poor share a disproportionate burden of polluted air, polluted water, and toxic waste (Bullard 1993; Eligon 2016).

A key environmental resource is land. In urban areas, inequality in the distribution of landownership is usually construed and understood

---

18   In the online version of the chapter, we also provide alternative estimates based on the Global Consumption and Income Project (GCIP), which are broadly similar, esp. regarding trends.

Table 3.2 | Trends in the Gini coefficient, countries per region, 1980–2000 and 2000–2010

	OECD	Transition Economies – Europe	Transition Economies – Asia	Latin America	MENA	Southeast Asia	South Asia	SSA	World
					Circa 1980s and 1990s				
Trend	*1980–2001*	*1990–1998*	*1980–2000*	*1980–2002*	*1980–2000*	*1980–1995*	*1980–2000*	*1980–1995*	
Rising inequality	14	24	2	14	2	5	3	9	73 (69%)
No change	1	0	1	1	3	0	0	2	8 (8%)
Falling inequality	6	0	0	3	3	2	2	8	24 (23%)
Total	21	24	3	18	8	7	5	19	105 (100%)
					Circa 2000–10				
	2000–2010	1998–2010	2000–2009	2002–2010	2000–2007	1995–2009	2000–2010	1995–2007	
Rising inequality	9	13	2	2	4	3	4	7	44 (41%)
No change	4	5	1	1	0	0	1	1	13 (12%)
Falling inequality	8	6	0	15	4	4	0	13	50 (47%)
Total	21	24	3	18	8	7	5	21	107 (100%)

Note: Countries were assigned to the rising, no change, or falling inequality groups on the basis of an analysis of time trends and of the difference between the initial and final Gini coefficients in each of the two subperiods. MENA = Middle East and North Africa. SSA = Sub-Saharan Africa.
Source: Cornia and Martorano 2012.

Table 3.3 | Average inequality, by region and income, 2000–2010

	Gini coefficients, five-year averages		
Region, income	2000	2005	2010
Region			
World	0.390	0.385	0.380
Advanced economies	0.298	0.302	0.304
East Asia and Pacific	0.380	0.391	0.389
Eastern Europe and Central Asia	0.331	0.329	0.333
Latin America and the Caribbean	0.551	0.532	0.502
Middle East and North Africa	–	–	–
South Asia	0.354	0.351	0.328
Sub-Saharan Africa	0.445	0.434	0.440
Country income category			
Low income	0.316	0.32	0.323
Lower middle	0.421	0.412	0.399
Upper middle	0.442	0.436	0.428
Total, middle	0.431	0.423	0.413
High	0.397	0.386	0.386

Note: The data are unweighted averages based on IDD (Income Distribution Database), Organisation for Economic Co-operation and Development, Paris, www.oecd.org/social/income-distribution-database.htm; PovcalNet (online analysis tool), World Bank, Washington, DC, http://iresearch.worldbank.org/PovcalNet/; SEDLAC (Socio-Economic Database for Latin America and the Caribbean), Center for Distributive, Labor, and Social Studies, Facultad de Ciencias Económicas, Universidad Nacional de La Plata, La Plata, Argentina and Equity Lab, Team for Statistical Development, World Bank, Washington, DC (accessed July 22, 2013), http://sedlac.econo.unlp.edu.ar/eng/statistics.php. The income concepts used for the computation of the Gini coefficients vary from region to region. – = not available.
Source: Lustig 2016a.

with respect to housing. For a description of the relevant issues and theories, particularly in developed countries, see Bruckner (2011). In developing countries, a phenomenon that has received recent attention is the expansion of slums (Davis 1999). A larger literature has focused on agricultural land that is typically unequally distributed, although the breadth of inequality varies across the regions of the world (Griffin et al. 2002). In the developing world, the countries of

Latin America and southern Africa have typically been characterized by greater land inequality. In certain contexts, historically disadvantaged groups, such as the scheduled castes in India, are suffering from deficiencies in landownership. Inequality in landownership can be linked to the existence of various agricultural institutions (Ray 1998). Land inequality has also been linked to lower growth and conflict (Alesina and Rodrik 1994; Deininger and Squire 1998). Since the early 2000s, access to land among poor farmers has been increasingly threatened by foreign land deals in which customary land users are evicted (Nolte et al. 2016). At the same time, improvements in the certainty of rights over land use have been gradually achieved in Sub-Saharan Africa and elsewhere since the mid-1990s (Cotula et al. 2004).

3.5.1.3   Levels and Trends in Inequality of Opportunity

As already discussed above, Roemer (1993, 1998) proposes a concept of inequality of opportunity that accounts for the source of the unequal distributions of outcomes (Roemer and Trannoy 2015, 2016). According to this notion, individual outcomes may be influenced by circumstances and efforts. Circumstances are defined as all factors that are beyond the control of the individual – such as parental education, gender, or ethnic origin – and for which individuals should not be held responsible. Effort, however, describes all actions and choices that are within the control of individuals for which individuals should be held at least partially responsible. Taking account of its origin, inequality may be decomposed into morally acceptable and morally unacceptable inequality. Hence, income differences because of effort are considered more acceptable, while income differences because of circumstances are not. Equality of opportunity occurs if the chances enjoyed by individuals to achieve a given outcome are influenced only by individual effort, irrespective of individual circumstances.

Empirical studies have measured the extent of inequality of opportunity in the achievement of various outcomes, such as incomes,

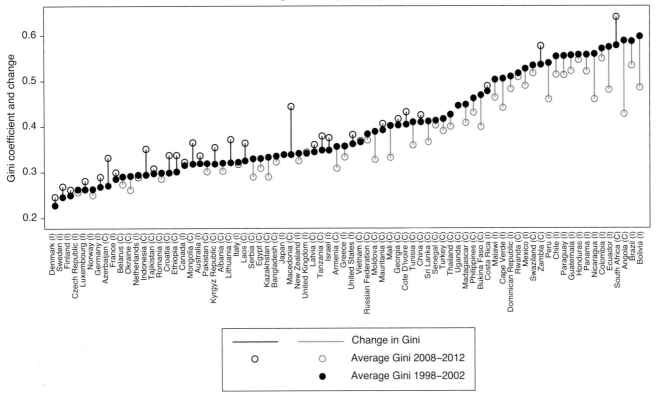

Figure 3.4 | Trends in the Gini coefficient, by country, 2000–2010.
Note: See Table 3.2 for additional data sources. Dark lines and dots refer to observations showing widening inequality between 1998–2002 and 2008–2012. Lighter lines and dots refer to observations showing inequality narrowing.
Source: Lustig 2016a.

wages, and health, in a variety of countries (Table 3.4). In European countries, inequality of opportunity accounts for about 5 to 25 percent of income inequality (Checchi et al. 2010). In a recent follow-up study, these authors show that these estimates were rather stable between 2005 and 2011. Pistolesi (2009) finds that, in the United States in 1968–2001, 20 to 43 percent of earnings inequality derived from inequality of opportunity. Results on less developed countries are usually somewhat higher than shares from European countries (Cogneau and Mesple-Somps 2008; Ferreira and Gignoux 2011b).

However, the empirical assessment of inequality of opportunity is complicated by the fact that datasets rarely account for all individual circumstances. Because the effect of omitted circumstances appears as an effect of effort, the measurements of inequality of opportunity are downward biased. Balcázar (2015) suggests that about three-quarters of inequality of opportunity is unexplained by the standard lower-bound estimator. This has led critics to question the relevance of inequality of opportunity for policy-makers altogether (Kanbur and Wagstaff 2014). In particular, it is argued that these studies could be used to play down the problematic nature of inequality because most inequality appears to be ethically acceptable from the perspective of equal opportunity. A strategy to address the downward bias involves the use of detailed datasets that contain broader information on circumstance variables. Björklund et al. (2012) use intelligence tests from military records to obtain a better measure of individual ability, which, indeed, emerges as one of the strongest contributors

to inequality of opportunity in Sweden. Hufe and Peichl (2016) use data with genetic information to move the lower-bound estimator in the direction of its true value. Another strategy is the use of panel data to estimate individual fixed effects with respect to the outcome of interest (Niehues and Peichl 2014). Scholars can thus measure the effect of all time-invariant circumstances. Such studies show that inequality of opportunity accounts for up to 75 percent of income inequality. However, this estimator is only an upper bound given that some components of individual effort are also constant over time. Both strategies are rather data intensive. Fruitful avenues for further research include the narrowing of the range between upper- and lower-bound estimators, increasing the comparability of inequality of opportunity estimates across countries and time, and the reconciliation of inequality of opportunity with other normative values (Foguel and Veloso 2014; Brunori et al. 2016).

3.5.1.4   Levels and Trends in Mobility and Intergenerational Inequality

As already discussed in Section 3.3.2.5, there appears to be a robust negative relationship between levels of inequality and levels of intergenerational mobility in a cross-section of countries. Few studies have investigated the issue of the development of intergenerational mobility over time. Most such studies have focused on the United States. Studies focusing on older cohorts tend to find little change

Table 3.4 | Overview of studies measuring inequality of opportunity

Author	Outcome	Data source	Circumstances	Country	IEO, index
Aaberge et al. (2011)	Permanent income	Statistics Norway, 1967–2006	Birth cohort, parental education, urban birth, household size	Norway	28
	Period-specific income	Statistics Norway, 1967–2006	Birth cohort, parental education, urban birth, household size	Norway	23–26
Björklund et al. (2012)	Permanent income	Statistics Sweden, 1955–67	Parental income, parental education, household type, number of siblings, intelligence quotient, body mass index	Sweden	13–41
Brunori et al. (2016)	Household per capita consumption	EIM, 2004	Birthplace, parental education, parental occupation	Comoros	30–42
		ECM, 2010	Birthplace, parental education, parental occupation	Congo Dem. Rep.	47
		GLSS, 2013	Birthplace, parental education	Ghana	35–56
		EIBEP, 2003	Birthplace, parental education, parental occupation	Guinea	35–37
		EPM, 2005	Birthplace, parental education, ethnicity	Madagascar	28–56
		IHS3, 2010	Birthplace, parental education, mother tongue	Malawi	43–56
		ECVM, 2011–12	Birthplace, ethnicity	Niger	33–40
		GHS, 2010–11	Birthplace, parental education, parental occupation, ethnicity	Nigeria	38–42
		GHS, 2012–13	Parental education, parental occupation	Nigeria	37–43
		EICV, 2000	Birthplace, parental education, parental occupation	Rwanda	26–42
		NPS, 2009–10	Birthplace, parental education, parental occupation	Tanzania	43–49
		NPS, 2010–11	Birthplace, parental education, parental occupation	Tanzania	41–46
		UNPS, 2009–10	Birthplace, ethnicity	Uganda	39–48
		UNPS, 2010–11	Birthplace, ethnicity	Uganda	40–53
Checchi and Peragine (2010)	Gross earnings	SHIW, 1993, 1995, 1998, 2000	parental education, sex, region	Italy	20
Pistolesi (2009)	Annual earnings	PSID, 1968–2001	Age, race, parental education, region, father's occupation	United States	20–43
Ferreira and Gignoux (2011)	Household per capita income	ECV, 2003	Sex, race, parental education, region	Colombia	23
Checchi and Peragine (2010)	Gross earnings	ENAHO, 2001	Sex, race, parental education, region	Peru	28
Pistolesi (2009)	Annual earnings	ENCOVI, 2000	Sex, race, parental education, region, father's occupation	Guatemala	33
Ferreira and Gignoux (2011)	Household per capita income	PNAD, 1996	Sex, race, parental education, region, father's occupation	Brazil	32
		ECV, 2006	Sex, race, parental education, region, father's occupation	Ecuador	26
		ENV, 2003	Sex, race, parental education, region, father's occupation	Panama	30
Niehues and Peichl (2014)	Annual income	SOEP, 1984–2009	Sex, country national, father's education and occupation, urban birth, height, birth year, born in German Democratic Republic or Federal Republic of Germany	Germany	47–62
		PSID, 1981–2007	Sex, country national, father's education and occupation, urban birth, height, birth year, birth in southern United States, race	United States	33–36
Peichl and Ungerer (2014)	Total net income	SOEP, 1992–2012	Sex, country national, father's education and occupation, urban birth, height, birth year, born in German Democratic Republic or Federal Republic of Germany	Germany	35 (1991)–24 (2011)
Cogneau and Mesple-Somps (2008)	Household per capita consumption	EPAMCI, 1985–8 GLSS, 1998 EICVM, 1994 EPAM, 1993 NHIS, 1992	Father's education and occupation, region (Colombia, Peru without father's occupation)	Côte d'Ivoire Ghana Guinea Madagascar Uganda	13 11 13 21 9
Checchi et al. (2010)	Net individual earnings	EU-SILC, 2005	Parental education and occupation, sex, nationality, region	Austria Belgium Cyprus Czech R. Denmark Estonia Finland France Poland Greece Hungary Ireland Portugal Latvia Lithuania Luxemburg Netherlands Slovak R. Slovenia Spain Sweden UK	22 17 30 11 14 11 10 13 9 17 10 22 12 12 15 24 19 14 5 19 11 21

Note: EU-SILC = European Union Statistics on Income and Living Conditions (database), Eurostat, European Commission, Luxembourg, http://ec.europa.eu/eurostat/web/microdata/european-union-statistics-on-income-and-living-conditions. Other data sources are generally national household surveys. IEO = inequality of economic opportunity index.

in relative mobility – that is, the correlation in incomes between parents and children – among cohorts born in the 1950s and the 1970s in the United States (Lee and Solon 2009). Meanwhile, widening inequality and slower economic growth have ensured that absolute mobility – that is, the likelihood that incomes of children exceed the incomes of parents – has fallen sharply among cohorts born after 1960, including especially among middle-income groups (Chetty et al. 2017).

3.5.1.5   Inequality in Political Participation and Power

Broadly, two distinct kinds of societies exist today. In the first, traditionally considered dictatorships, a small group controls political power and the institutions of the state and is mostly unaccountable to the citizenry. In the second, usually considered democracies, there is more accountability to the people and stronger checks and balances (such as through elections) on the actions and powers of the state and those who control the state. However, in both kinds of societies, disproportionate power may be wielded by certain individuals and groups. A vast literature has appeared on the state and nature of democracies and dictatorships (Poulantzas 1974; Moore 1993; Therborn 2006; Acemoglu and Robinson 2009).

One useful distinction that has been made is between inequality among individuals and inequality among groups (Stewart 2002). Studies on the vertical inequality (among individuals) have largely centered on consumption and income and virtually ignored political participation. This is despite the fact that some scholars have argued that certain individuals (the rich) have more power and are also more likely to vote, so that it is not the median voter who is decisive, and this has implications for redistribution (Benabou 2000). By contrast, studies on the horizontal inequality (across groups) have explicitly focused on politics and power. Stewart (2002) argues that inequality among groups is multidimensional and that the political dimension is crucial, along with the economic and social dimensions. Differences in political participation across groups may exist on several fronts, including government ministers, parliament, the civil service, and so on. Several studies have documented inequalities among groups in various contexts (Mancini 2008; Østby 2008; Wimmer et al. 2009; Brown 2010; Motiram and Sarma 2014a; Hufe and Peichl 2016). This literature argues that such inequalities are unfair and also lead to severe instability and conflict.

Gender is an important dimension on which differences in political participation and power are grounded. Only about 23 percent of parliamentarians in 2016 were women, although this represents an increase of 12 percentage points from 1993 (UN Women 2016). Wide variations in the share of women's parliamentarians exist across geographical regions; the Nordic countries are at the top, and the Pacific countries are at the bottom (UN Women 2016).

The literature on horizontal inequalities argues that various kinds of policies can be adopted to address these issues: affirmative action, antidiscrimination, and nation building (Stewart 2002). One option for addressing the issue of power and political participation is to reserve positions for disadvantaged groups. This policy has been tried in various

contexts; evidence suggests that it can produce desirable outcomes (Pande 2003; Chattopadhyay and Duflo 2004; UN Women 2016).

3.5.2   Group-Based Inequalities in Outcomes: Gender, Race, Ethnicity, Spatial

An extensive literature exists on levels and trends in gender inequality across the world. The literature highlights that gender gaps in educational enrollments, years of schooling, and completion rates are extremely large in the Middle East and North Africa, in South Asia, and in parts of Sub-Saharan Africa, but much smaller in East Asia, Latin America and the Caribbean, OECD countries, and Southeast Asia. Even in regions with large gender gaps in schooling, these have been reduced sharply in the last two decades (World Bank 2011; Klasen 2016). In contrast, the sizable gaps in labor force participation have closed much more slowly; most of the progress has occurred in OECD countries, such as France, the Nordic countries, and the United States. Progress has been much more uneven in other parts of world. For example, female labor force participation has been declining in India and stagnating in many other Asian economies, while it has increased sharply in Latin America (Gaddis and Klasen 2014; Klasen and Pieters 2015). Progress has been even slower in closing gender wage gaps. This is related to highly persistent gendered occupational and sectoral segregation (World Bank 2011; Borrowman and Klasen 2017).

The results in other group-based inequalities such as race or ethnicity are highly country- and context-specific so that it is impossible to present generalized results. Spatial disparities have been an important feature particularly in developing countries, and spatial inequalities remain sizable there (Kanbur and Venables 2005).

3.6   Accounting for Within-Country Inequality Trends

3.6.1   Trends and Drivers of Income Inequality in OECD Countries

3.6.1.1   Income Inequality Trends

For the period between the mid-1980s and 2013, household surveys show that the majority of the OECD countries experienced a widening in disposable household income inequality with Gini coefficients rising in 17 of the 22 OECD countries for which long-term data are available (OECD 2015, Figure 3.5).

The rise in income dispersion was stronger between the mid-1980s and the mid-1990s compared with later decades. A dominant pattern in this period was a widening in inequality in market income (OECD 2008). From the mid-1990s to the mid-2000s, the income distribution continued to widen on average, with some countries including the United States experiencing strong increases in income inequality, while it narrowed in ten other OECD countries. Since 2000, income inequality has increased substantially in Germany, Israel, Denmark, Sweden, and the United States and, to a lesser degree, in Australia, Finland, and France. It has fallen in Belgium, Greece, Mexico, and

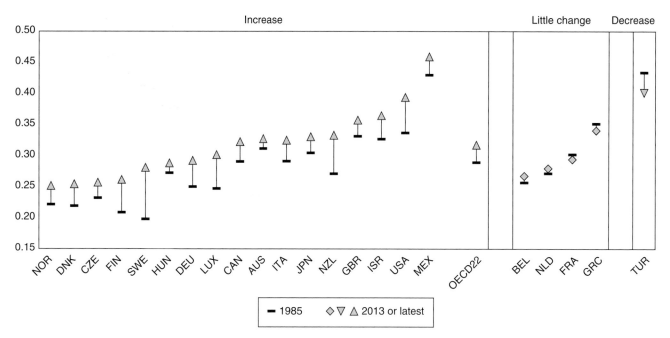

Figure 3.5 | Gini coefficients of income inequality, OECD, mid-1980s and 2013.
Note: Income refers to disposable household income, corrected for household size.
Source: OECD Income Distribution Database (IDD), www.oecd.org/social/income-distribution-database.htm.

Turkey, and, to a smaller extent, in the Netherlands and the United Kingdom. During the economic recovery following the global financial crisis of 2008–2009, income inequality before taxes and benefits rose again, while the cushioning effect of taxes and benefits has become weaker. As a result, a continued moderate upward trend in disposable income inequality has been observed in the most recent years (OECD 2015).

3.6.1.2   Drivers of Inequality Change

A large literature has analyzed the drivers of changes in inequality in OECD countries.[19] This subsection provides a brief summary of the drivers that have been analyzed in greatest detail (see also Figure 3.6).

Gross labor earnings make up the largest share of total household incomes and are an important driver of income inequality. Between the mid-1980s and mid/late 2000s, wage disparities among full-time workers in the OECD have widened by between 20 percent and 25 percent. Common explanations for this polarization in wages include changes in the supply and demand among skills and labor tasks and changes in labor market institutions (Atkinson, 2008, Acemoglu and Autor 2011). These considerations highlight that the drivers of widening wage inequality are multifaceted and particular to different segments of the wage distribution.

Changes in demographic structure, household size, and household compositions are important co-determinants of observed inequality patterns in OECD countries. All OECD countries have experienced

a gradual shift away from the typical family structure of the past resulting in a decline in average household size, a corresponding loss in economies of scale, and an expansion in the need for greater monetary income to assure the same level of well-being. For instance, Peichl et al. (2012) quantify how the trend toward smaller households has influenced the change in income distribution in Germany. The results show that the income gap would have increased regardless of the demographic trend, but at a lower rate. Furthermore, total disposable household income depends on the characteristics of the individuals forming the households. Within the OECD, the growth in female labor force participation has exerted a moderating influence on the observed upward trend in inequality (OECD 2015). This is consistent with findings of Cancian and Reed (1998) who have studied the role of women's earnings in inequality. By contrast, the correlation between the earning of men and the earnings of women within households – assortative matching – has tightened in recent decades. This has magnified existing inequalities across households (Burtless 2009; Schwartz 2010).

Tax-benefit systems represent an important means to cushion the effects of widening market inequalities. As shown by Immervoll and Richardson (2011), the redistributive effect of tax-benefit systems, measured as the difference in inequality between market and disposable incomes, has increased in OECD countries in recent decades. However, this rise has been outpaced by increases in market inequality. Evidently, tax-benefit systems comprise a multitude of instruments with differential distributional implications. For example, Fuest et al. (2010) show that, among selected European countries, personal income taxes and social insurance contributions

---

[19]   For a more detailed discussion summarizing drivers of inequality change, see for instance Förster and Tóth (2015).

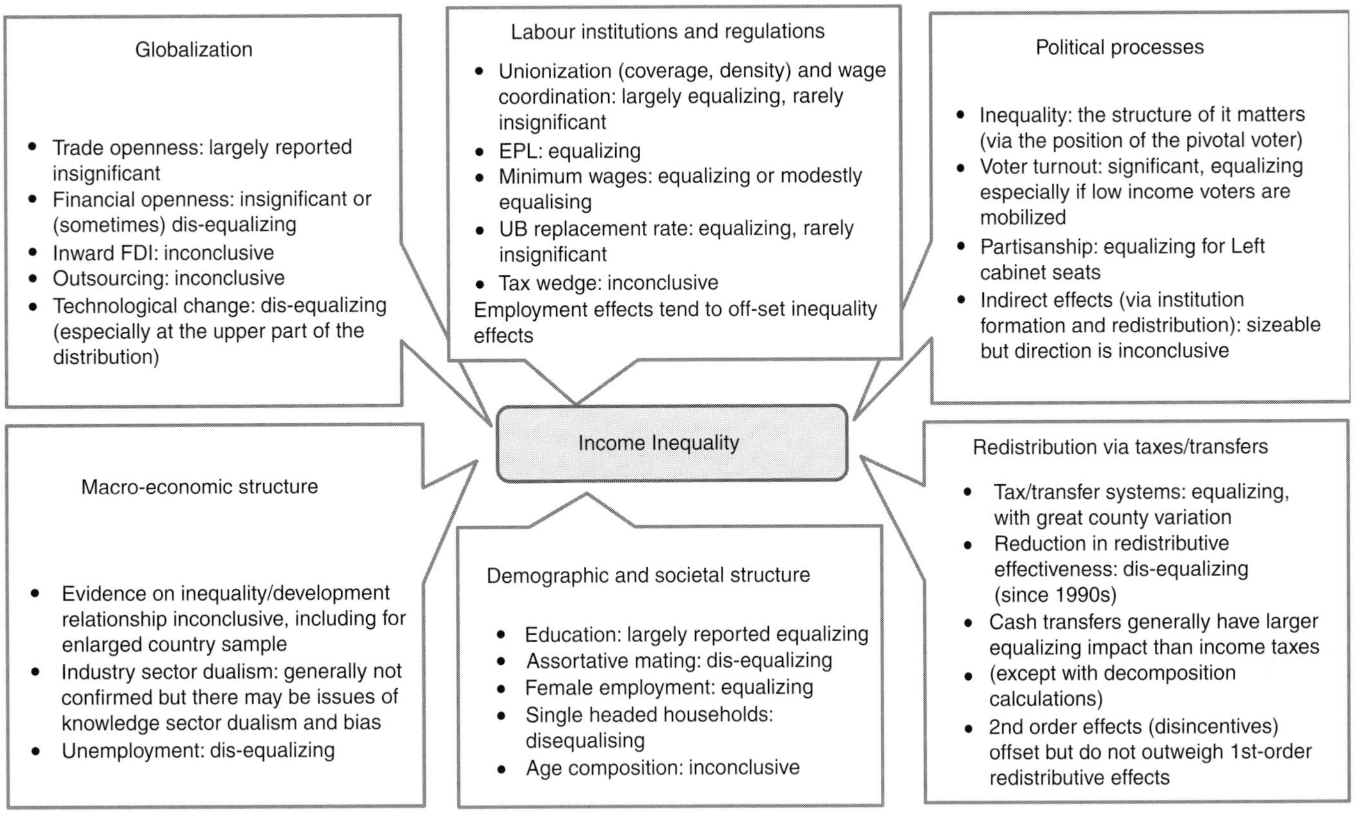

Globalization	Labour institutions and regulations	Political processes
• Trade openness: largely reported insignificant • Financial openness: insignificant or (sometimes) dis-equalizing • Inward FDI: inconclusive • Outsourcing: inconclusive • Technological change: dis-equalizing (especially at the upper part of the distribution)	• Unionization (coverage, density) and wage coordination: largely equalizing, rarely insignificant • EPL: equalizing • Minimum wages: equalizing or modestly equalising • UB replacement rate: equalizing, rarely insignificant • Tax wedge: inconclusive Employment effects tend to off-set inequality effects	• Inequality: the structure of it matters (via the position of the pivotal voter) • Voter turnout: significant, equalizing especially if low income voters are mobilized • Partisanship: equalizing for Left cabinet seats • Indirect effects (via institution formation and redistribution): sizeable but direction is inconclusive

Income Inequality

Macro-economic structure	Demographic and societal structure	Redistribution via taxes/transfers
• Evidence on inequality/development relationship inconclusive, including for enlarged country sample • Industry sector dualism: generally not confirmed but there may be issues of knowledge sector dualism and bias • Unemployment: dis-equalizing	• Education: largely reported equalizing • Assortative mating: dis-equalizing • Female employment: equalizing • Single headed households: disequalising • Age composition: inconclusive	• Tax/transfer systems: equalizing, with great county variation • Reduction in redistributive effectiveness: dis-equalizing (since 1990s) • Cash transfers generally have larger equalizing impact than income taxes • (except with decomposition calculations) • 2nd order effects (disincentives) offset but do not outweigh 1st-order redistributive effects

Figure 3.6 | Drivers of inequality change, OECD countries.
Note: "Significance" has to be understood here as a statistically significant association, notwithstanding the relative size of a coefficient. "Inconclusive" means that roughly as many studies report (significantly) positive as negative effects. EPL refers to employment protection legislation, FDI to foreign direct investment, and UB to unemployment benefit.
Source: Förster and Tóth (2015: 1804).

have a strong redistributive impact, whereas social benefits are less effective at redistribution because they are largely unconnected to the market income of the recipient. OECD (2016) shows that redistribution via cash benefits and income taxes cushions income inequality among the working-age population by some 27 percent on average in OECD countries. Two-thirds of this redistributive effect reflects the effect of benefits, with taxes accounting for the remaining third. As a consequence of the economic crisis, many OECD countries have been forced to cut back redistributive programs to achieve fiscal consolidation (OECD 2015). One may therefore expect dispersions in market income to prevail to a greater extent among disposable incomes in these countries in the future.

Recent cross-country work by the OECD has been aimed at providing a comprehensive overview of the potential causal drivers of inequality change among OECD countries (OECD 2011). This work has confirmed the role of skill-biased technological change, rising unemployment, eroding minimum wages, shrinking unionization, assortative matching, and reductions in the redistribution efforts of the state as significant drivers (Figure 3.6). However, there is no consensus on the respective size of these influences, and the results are inconclusive in many areas that have been examined (Förster 2016).

Most analyses of income inequality in OECD countries are based on standard household surveys that systematically underreport top incomes. Using tax records and other information, recent work has documented the levels of and trends in the top incomes (Atkinson and Piketty 2007; Piketty 2014). This work has shown that the share of the top incomes in total incomes has been rising substantially in most OECD countries since the 1970s, leading to further widening in inequality that is not captured in standard surveys. The rising market income share of top income-earners is mostly related to disproportionately rising compensation among top managers and top employees in finance, growing wealth inequality, and the rapidly rising returns to wealth among top income-earners. Inherited wealth plays a crucial role in the transmission of top incomes. Falling taxation on wealth and high incomes has exacerbated this trend toward rising income shares of top earners (Piketty 2014).

3.6.2 Changing Inequality Trends and Drivers in Three Asian Subregions

3.6.2.1 South Asia and Indonesia: Rising Inequality amid Rapid Growth

During the last two decades, the region recorded an unprecedented growth acceleration that contributed to a rapid reduction in the incidence of poverty. Yet, in South Asia, income inequality widened in most cases (Table 3.5).

Table 3.5 | Trends in the Gini index, selected South, East, and South East Asian countries

Country (years of reference)	First year	Second year
Bangladesh (1991–2010)	27.6	32.1
India (1993–2010)	32.5	37.0
Nepal (1995–2010)	35.2	32.8
Pakistan (1990–2011)	33.2	30.6
Sri Lanka (1990–2006)	32.5	40.3
China (1990–2008)[a]	32.4	43.4
Cambodia (1994–2008)	38.3	37.9
Indonesia (1990–2011)	29.2	38.9
Malaysia (1992–2009)	47.7	46.2
Philippines (1991–2009)[b]	43.8	43.0
Korea, Rep. (1998–2011)[a]	37.5	31.1
Thailand (1990–2009)	45.3	40.0
Vietnam (1992–2008)	35.7	35.0

[a]. Data of WIID (World Income Inequality Database), United Nations University–World Institute for Development Economics Research, Helsinki, www.wider.unu.edu/project/wiid-world-income-inequality-database.
[b]. Data of Li (2015).
Source: Kanbur et al. 2014.

In India, the Gini index rose over 1993–1994/2008–2009. A key factor behind this surge was the growing wage gap between the organized and unorganized sectors, as well as between urban and rural areas (Datt and Ravallion 2002, 2009; Ghosh 2015). At the same time, the remuneration of managers and capital owners grew rapidly (Ghosh 2015). The wages of unskilled workers in minority groups were additionally penalized by social norms (Ghosh 2015).

In the case of other South Asian countries and Indonesia, Kanbur et al. (2014) argue that inequality widened because of the skill-biased technological change. Decompositions suggest that growing educational inequality explains up to 45 percent of the increase in income inequality. Other factors that contributed to the rise of earnings inequality include weak labor institutions (minimum wages and collective bargaining), a commodity boom that favored only parts of populations, large and highly regressive fuel subsidies, and limited public expenditure on health care and education. In addition, there was an increase in the capital share and a decline in the bargaining power of organized labor (Miranta et al. 2013; Kanbur et al. 2014; Yusuf et al. 2015). A second explanation of the rising inequality is the increase in migration (IMF 2007). This has depressed the unskilled wage rate in both countries of origin and countries of destination. Trade liberalization has been increasing inequality in most cases because it increased the demand for skilled workers and for the reallocation of labor across regions and sectors. Such reallocation has been hampered, however, by low labor mobility (Koujanou-Goldberg and Pavcnik 2007). Similar effects were generated by foreign direct investment allocated to capital- and skill-intensive industries, consisting of mergers and acquisitions or replacing the output of labor-intensive local firms. An even more forceful impact was caused by the opening in the capital account (Prasad et al. 2003).

Claus et al. (2014) show that fiscal policy barely reduced market income inequality. In the region, corporate income taxes, social security payments, sales taxes, excise taxes, and custom duties were all regressive, on average. Only the personal income tax was progressive, though, in many countries, high exemption thresholds and generous deductions reduced the redistributive potential of this tax. Meanwhile, public expenditure on social protection and housing was regressive, though it is progressive in other regions. Only public expenditure on health care and education was progressive. Thus, in the absence of explicit social policies targeting the poor, the inequality of market incomes was little affected by the tax-and-transfer system.

3.6.2.2 Moderate Inequality Decline in Southeast and East Asia after the 1997 Crisis

After the Asian crisis of 1997, Korea, Malaysia, the Philippines, and Thailand experienced a moderate decline in income inequality (see Table 3.5). The impact of improvements in terms of trade appears to have been limited while a pragmatic and prudent pro-growth macroeconomic policy seem to have reduced inequality (Cornia and Martorano 2012). These countries also invested massively in public education, strengthened labor policies, and developed social insurance and assistance policies and institutions. As a result, average income inequality narrowed by 2 or 3 Gini points in the 2000s.

3.6.2.3 China: A Sharp Rise in Inequality until 2008 and a Modest Decline Thereafter

Despite the country's regional diversity, China showed a low Gini coefficient in 1978: 0.32 economy-wide and 0.21 in rural areas. The distributive impact of the post-1978 reforms varied markedly over time. The egalitarian agricultural reforms of 1978–1984 generated only a modest increase in both rural and urban inequality. In contrast, income concentration grew rapidly over 1985–2000 as the second wave of reforms focused on the urban industrial sector, with the result that the national Gini coefficient reached 0.43 in 2000. This surge in income disparity was caused by several factors, including a rise in the urban–rural income gap, mounting interprovincial inequality, widening rural inequality arising from widening earnings inequality in township and village enterprises, and increasing urban inequality because of the mass exploitation of rural workers who were without appropriate *hukou*, the household record indicating where people are allowed to live (Selden and Wu 2011). Because of pressures on the wages of migrant workers, earnings inequality, and corporate profits rose in line with the increase in the skill premium in the modern sector. Despite mounting concern among central authorities and the launch of programs such as Go West and the Harmonious Society during the third phase of reform, which focused on export-led growth during the 2000s, the Gini coefficient rose from 0.43 in around 2000 to 0.49 in 2007 (Li Shi 2015). The success of the export–led model depended, in fact, on labor policies that lowered wages and raised private, corporate, and public savings to finance rapid capital accumulation. It is unclear whether 2008 marks the beginning of a fourth phase in the trends in inequality in China. Data show that the overall Gini coefficient declined from 0.49 to 0.45 between 2007 and 2013, following a narrowing in the urban–rural gap in income per capita from 3.3 to 3.0 points because of the rapid rise in the wages of rural migrants and in the remittances of migrants to rural areas. The fall in the urban–rural income gap was facilitated

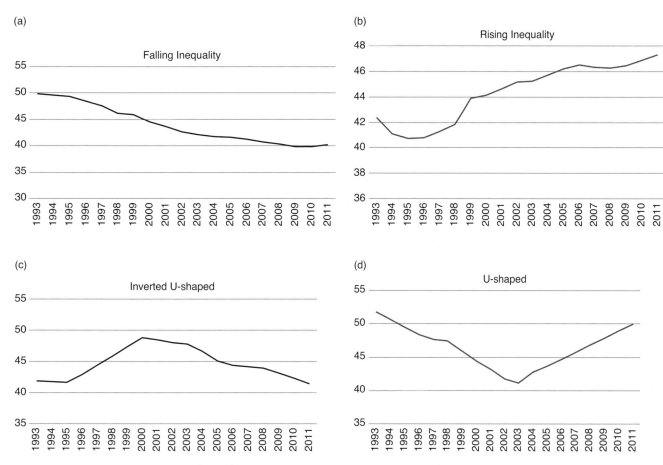

Figure 3.7 | Trends in the unweighted Gini coefficient of per capita consumption expenditure in Sub-Saharan Africa, 1993–2011.
a. Falling Gini: Burkina Faso, Cameroon, Ethiopia, The Gambia, Guinea, Guinea Bissau, Lesotho, Madagascar, Mali, Niger, Senegal, Sierra Leone, Swaziland
b. Rising Gini: Botswana, Côte d'Ivoire, Ghana, Kenya, Mauritius, South Africa, Uganda
c. Inverted U–shaped Gini: Angola, Mauritania, Mozambique, Rwanda
d. U-shaped Gini: Republic of Congo, Malawi, Nigeria, Tanzania, Zambia
Source: Cornia 2016.

by the introduction of pro-rural policies such as tax exemptions, the abolition of school fees, agricultural subsidies, and new health care, pension, and antipoverty schemes made possible also by the rise of the ratio of taxes to GDP from 12.2 in 1996 to 22.5 in 2010 (Selden and Wu 2011). However, inequality within urban areas and within rural areas continued to widen (Li Shi 2015).

3.6.3   The Bifurcation in Inequality Trends in Sub-Saharan Africa

3.6.3.1   Trends in Consumption Inequality

There are few analyses of inequality changes in Sub-Saharan Africa, not least because of limited data availability. Fosu (2015b) presents evidence of changes in inequality in 39 countries based on the PovcalNet database.[20] Table 3.2 shows that inequality declined in 21 of these 39 countries in 1995–2007. An analysis by Anyanwu et al. (2016) based

on a panel of 17 West African countries in 1970–2011 identified a nonmonotonic inverted U-shaped inequality trend. According to Cornia and Martorano (2017), over 1993–2011, the average unweighted Gini coefficient of the 29 countries in their data fell by 3.4 points, and the average population-weighted Gini fell by 2.0 points. Yet, a country-by-country analysis shows that such an average decline conceals more than it reveals. Indeed, this result is the sum of diverging falling, rising, inverted U-shaped, and U-shaped inequality trends (Figure 3.7). By restricting the analysis to the 2000s, one obtains a steadily declining trend in 17 countries (the two left panels in Figure 3.7) and a steadily rising trend in 12 countries (the two right panels). In West Africa, inequality narrowed steadily in 9 mostly agricultural economies out of 12, while a modest decline was recorded also in East Africa. In contrast, Central Africa and Southern Africa recorded a rise beginning around 2003, in line with the increase in the world prices of oil and minerals. These trends point also to growing intraregional divergence in inequality, as many low-inequality nations experienced a drop in the Gini, while high-inequality nations showed a rise or stagnation.

---

[20]   See PovcalNet (online analysis tool), World Bank, Washington, DC, http://iresearch.worldbank.org/PovcalNet/. See also Fosu (2015a), who presents similar data on 23 Sub-Saharan African countries.

3.6.3.2 Factors Explaining the Bifurcation in the Trends in Consumption Inequality

Inequality rose in countries that experienced a value added shift toward sectors characterized by high asset concentration (such as the resource sector), capital- and skilled-labor intensity (such as mining, oil extraction, and finance-insurance-real estate), the public sector, or unequal informal services (Anyanwu et al. 2016). In contrast, inequality fell or remained stable in countries in which growth occurred in agriculture, manufacturing, construction, and a number of service subsectors (Cornia 2016).

Educational policy affects inequality. Yet, while average primary-school enrollments grew by over 20 points between 1998 and 2012, secondary-school enrollments increased by only half that amount. Cogneau et al. (2007) show that, especially in urban areas, the skill premium rose because of a rapid expansion in the demand for skilled labor. An econometric analysis confirms that the number of workers with secondary or higher educational attainment relative to the number with lower educational attainment affects inequality (Cornia 2016). Anyanwu et al. (2016) find that greater access to secondary education and lower age dependency ratios are associated with more equal incomes in West Africa.

Persistently high population growth and ensuing rising population density have raised inequality (Anyanwu et al. 2016). Rapid population growth increases inequality because of its impact on the ratio between land and population, the extent of forest cover, distress migration to the urban informal sector, growing differentials in the dependency ratio between rich and poor households, falling wages among the unskilled, and reduced social spending per capita.

Inequality also narrowed in places where a stable, competitive effective exchange rate shifted production toward the labor-intensive tradable sector that also offers protection to import-competing domestic production. The opposite also occurred. With trade liberalization, average tariffs fell from about 15 percent to 8 percent. This led to deindustrialization and a rise in inequality and confirms the findings of Koujianou-Goldberg and Pavcnik (2007) about the increase in inequality for several years after trade liberalization. Anyanwu et al. (2016) find similar results on a panel of 17 West African countries.

Since the early 2000s, the region recorded an average increase in the ratio of taxes to GDP and, in some countries, in the share of direct taxes in the total. Regression analysis shows that this increase was equalizing (Cornia 2016). In several countries, expanding tax revenue and the cancellation of foreign debt allowed public social spending to be raised. Where this occurred, the effect was equalizing. Where social spending stagnated, despite a growing fiscal space, the Gini tended to rise (Cornia 2016).

Changes in global economic conditions affected inequality in a variety of ways. Overall, gains in the terms of trade in extractive industries had a disequalizing effect. Rising remittances in Sub-Saharan Africa were equalizing. Gains in international terms of trade were also equalizing,

except in mineral-rich countries. Inward foreign direct investment was disequalizing (Anyanwu et al. 2016; Cornia 2016). Foreign aid rose from $15 billion over 1990–2001 to about $40 billion by 2006–2007. Despite the doubts of several authors about the impact, an examination of the allocations of official development assistance since 2000 shows that this assistance was distributed according to criteria that were sensitive to the Millennium Development Goals (Hailu and Tsukada 2012).

Since the mid-2000s, the incidence of HIV/AIDS has slowly declined, and regression analysis shows this has exerted a modest equalizing impact in those countries affected (primarily in East and Southern Africa). The 2000s also witnessed the endogenous diffusion of low-cost and highly-divisible technologies, such as cell phones, the internet, and solar panels, that might have helped marginalized producers and consumers integrate into the market. While the growth effect of such shocks was favorable, the effect on inequality was likely to be concave. The new technologies were thus initially being acquired by the middle class. Meanwhile, the number of conflicts in the region fell from 25 in 1993 to 10 in 2010. The decline favorably affected growth and inequality (Anyanwu et al. 2016; Cornia 2016).

3.6.4 Declining Inequality in Latin America

3.6.4.1 Inequality Trends

Latin America has been characterized as a high-inequality region for a long time. After rising in the 1980s and 1990s, however, income inequality declined rapidly in the region until 2012 (Gasparini and Lustig 2011; López-Calva and Lustig 2010; Figure 3.8). During the same period, the incidence of total poverty fell from 42.0 percent to 25.3 percent. Applying a Datt–Ravallion (1992) decomposition reveals that an average of 39 percent of the reduction in poverty was derived from the decline in inequality.

3.6.4.2 Determinants of Declining Inequality in Latin America

There is no clear link between the decline in inequality and economic growth. As discussed in Lustig et al. (2016), inequality narrowed in countries that experienced rapid economic growth, such as Chile, Panama, and Peru, and in countries with low-growth spells, such as Brazil and Mexico. Nor is there a clear link between falling inequality and the orientation of political regimes: inequality declined in countries governed by regimes on the left, such as Argentina, Bolivia, Brazil, Chile, and Venezuela, and countries governed by centrist and center-right parties, such as Mexico and Peru. However, while inequality fell in countries of different political orientations, the most rapid decline was recorded under the social-democratic regimes (Cornia 2014a). Most studies point to two main explanations for the decline in inequality: (1) a reduction in hourly labor income inequality and (2) more robust and progressive government transfers. The former contributes the lion's share (Figure 3.9).[21] An average of 54 percent of the decline in the Gini

---

[21]   For example, see Azevedo et al. (2013b); Cornia (2014a); de la Torre et al. (2013); López-Calva and Lustig (2010); and Lustig et al. (2016). Microsimulation techniques suggest that a more rapid fertility decline observed among poor households over 1990–2012 reduced the Gini coefficient by between 0.7 points in Chile and 2.0 points in Peru (Badaracco 2014).

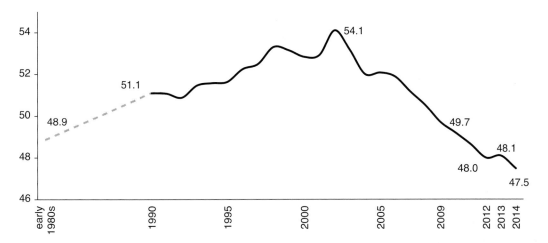

Figure 3.8 | Trends in the average unweighted regional Gini, Latin America, 1980s–2014.
Sources: Cornia 2014a; data of SEDLAC (Socio-Economic Database for Latin America and the Caribbean), Center for Distributive, Labor, and Social Studies, Facultad de Ciencias Económicas, Universidad Nacional de La Plata, La Plata, Argentina, and Equity Lab, Team for Statistical Development, World Bank, Washington, DC (accessed on June 10, 2016), http://sedlac.econo.unlp.edu.ar/eng/statistics.php.

coefficient can be attributed to changes in the distribution of hourly labor income (Azevedo et al. 2013a).

What explains the reduction in hourly labor income inequality? The available evidence suggests that a common factor in practically all countries was a fall in the returns to human capital, or, more precisely, in the relative returns to secondary and tertiary education.[22] Several authors underscore supply factors, such as an increase in the relative supply of workers with secondary and tertiary educational attainment, a result of the significant educational upgrading that took place in the region during the 1990s.[23] Other authors have emphasized demand factors or a combination of both demand and supply factors.[24]

Ferreira et al. (2014) conclude that, in the case of Brazil, the rising minimum wage and a substantial reduction in gender, race, and spatial wage gaps explain the lion's share of the decline in earnings inequality. Cornia (2014a) finds that macroeconomic conditions and a rising minimum wage played a role in a number of countries.

The determinants of the decline in nonlabor income inequality include returns to capital (interest, profits, and rents), private transfers (for example, remittances), and public transfers (for instance, CCTs, and noncontributory pensions). Azevedo et al. (2013a) show that the contribution of changes in the returns to capital in Argentina, Brazil, and Mexico, for example, tended to be small and unequalizing. However, household surveys are known to underestimate income from capital. So, the unequalizing effect may have been larger than current estimates indicate. Esquivel et al. (2010) show that, in Mexico, remittances proved to be equalizing and became even more so in the 2000s because they closed the gap in household per capita incomes between rural and urban areas.

Azevedo et al. (2013a) find that, on average, government transfers account for 21 percent of overall inequality decline. Lustig and Pessino (2014) show that, in Argentina, the large expansion in noncontributory pensions was fundamental in the reduction in inequality in 2006–2009. In the case of Brazil, Barros et al. (2010) find that, in 2001–2007, changes in the size, coverage, and distribution of public transfers accounted for 49 percent of the decline in inequality, while, in the case of Mexico, Esquivel et al. (2010) find that these factors accounted for 18 percent of the decline in inequality in 1996–2006.

3.6.5 Cross-cutting Issues Emanating from All or Most Regional Trends

Inequality is widening in many countries. This is especially true in developed countries and in some quickly rising Asian economies. Meanwhile, inequality trends have been more mixed in other developing countries and in emerging economies. Some countries, especially in Latin America, are experiencing narrowing inequality. However, even in these countries, inequality in access to finance, education, and health care is still substantial, while labor market and social protection institutions remain underdeveloped.

3.6.5.1 Access to Credit and Financial Markets

The literature on financial development and inequality finds a link between better financial development and narrower inequality (Beck et al. 2007; Clarke et al. 2006). Lo Prete (2013) suggests that a key variable in determining whether the poor are able to benefit from improved access to financial markets is literacy. Agnello et al. (2012) show that

---

[22] For example, see Azevedo et al. (2013b); Barros et al. (2010); Campos et al. (2014); Cornia (2014a); de la Torre et al. (2013); Ferreira et al. (2014); Gasparini and Cruces (2010); López-Calva and Lustig (2010).

[23] See Azevedo et al. (2013b); Cornia (2014a); López-Calva and Lustig (2010). Similar results were obtained for Argentina, Brazil, and Mexico (Barros et al. 2010; Esquivel et al. 2010; Gasparini and Cruces 2010; Campos et al. 2014).

[24] See, for example, de la Torre (2013); Gasparini et al. (2011).

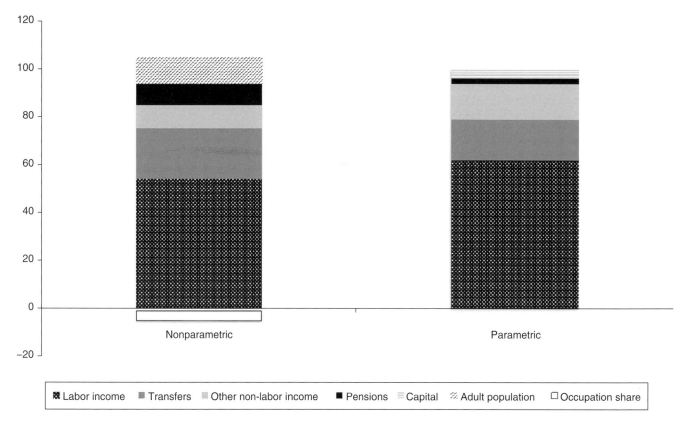

Figure 3.9 | Percent contributions of proximate determinants to inequality decline, Latin America, circa 2000–2010.

Note: The positive (negative) sign indicates an equalizing (unequalizing) effect of each determinant. The results shown are averages for 14 countries in the case of the nonparametric decomposition and 12 countries in the case of the parametric decomposition. The sum of the contributions of each determinant is, as expected, 100 percent.

Sources: Nonparametric results: Azevedo et al. (2013a); parametric results: Center for Distributional, Labor, and Social Studies, Universidad de La Plata, Argentina.

the removal of directed credits, lowering high reserve requirements, and the development of a more efficient securities market represented ways to broaden access to credit and reduce inequality.

While the literature on financial development mainly focuses on developing countries, the literature on financial deregulation focuses more on developed countries. For example, Tanndal and Waldenström (2016) find that Big Bang financial deregulation in Japan and the United Kingdom has led to an increase in top income shares. Beck et al. (2010) analyze an intrastate branch banking reform in the United States that boosted competition in the banking sector. They show that the reform led to less income inequality by increasing the incomes of low-wage workers. So, whether financial deregulation increases or decreases inequality seems to depend on the specific policy change that is implemented. Another strand in the literature investigates the effect of asset price changes on inequality. For example, Adam and Tzamourani (2015) show that equity price increases lead to increases in wealth inequality in the euro area, while bond price increases leave wealth inequality largely unchanged.

3.6.5.2   Human Capital Formation and Access to Education and Health Care

Income inequality depends on the distribution of human capital across households. Inequality in education has declined significantly in most

countries over the last 50 years or more. Especially in developing countries, this has been mostly driven by improvements in the access to human capital at the bottom of the income distribution, though large differences exist across regions (Castello-Climent and Domenech 2014). Most Latin American countries have substantially reduced the secondary-school enrollment gap (Cruces at al. 2014). Nonetheless, education outcomes remain much worse among disadvantaged groups (Dabla-Norris and Gradstein 2004). In some advanced economies, rising university costs have contributed to reduced access to education among the poor. In the United States, for instance, the cost of tertiary education has been growing much more quickly than the incomes of most households since 2001.

Inequality in health is a key determinant of educational and income inequality. In 2000–2015, average health status improved universally, including in the poorest developing countries. Yet, inequality in health outcomes is still widespread in developing economies. For instance, in developing countries, the infant mortality rate is two times higher among poor households than among rich households. Inequality in health care access is even more pronounced in developing countries (Gwatkin et al. 2007). However, even in advanced economies, income inequality is increasingly being reflected in lower life expectancy. This is particularly striking in the United States, where income today is a stronger predictor of life expectancy than it was a generation ago (Murray, Lopez, and Alvarado 2013).

3.6.5.3   Demographic Change and Inequality

Other determinants of inequality include demographic changes (such as in child and old-age dependency ratios) and patterns of household formation and composition. Using decomposition methods Jenkins (1995); Martin (2006); and Peichl et al. (2012) quantify how the trend toward smaller households has influenced the change in income distribution in the UK, US, and Germany. While trends toward smaller household size have worsened income distribution, they only account for a small part of total rise in inequality (OECD 2008).

Cancian and Reed (1998, 1999) study the role of women's earnings in overall inequality and find an equalizing effect associated with increasing female labor force participation. Burtless (1999, 2009) and Schwartz (2010) find that the growing correlation between the earnings of husbands and wives and the rising share of single-person households have contributed to more inequality.

In low- and middle-income countries, the increase in life expectancy and the old-age dependency ratio tends to generate unequalizing effects. The lack of pension coverage is often a source of poverty and upward pressure on overall inequality, especially if the elderly live alone (ILO 2014). Means-tested and universal noncontributory pension schemes are, however, being expanded, including in Southern Africa and Latin America, and these have been shown to have a strong effect on poverty reduction and equality (Niño-Zarazúa et al. 2011). Rapid aging may also represent a drag on economic growth and, indirectly, on inequality because of the large amount of private and public resources being allocated to pensions, health care, and the care of the elderly (Vos et al. 2008).

In developing countries, fertility decline often has initially a disequalizing effect as the rich and well-educated reduce their fertility first and are able to invest much more in their fewer children. As fertility decline reaches poorer segments, it should be equalizing. As most of Sub-Saharan Africa in in early stages of fertility decline, it tends to be disequalizing (Canning et al. 2015), while in East Asia and South America it is far advanced and more equalizing. For example, Badaracco (2015) shows that the most rapid relative decline in the fertility rate and in the child dependency ratio among poor households over 1990–2012 reduced the Gini by 0.7 and 2.0 points, respectively, in Chile and Peru.

3.6.5.5   Taxation, Social Protection, and Inequality

The progressivity of tax systems has declined in some advanced economies over the past few decades though it has improved in some developing regions, most notably Latin America (Cornia, Gomez Sabaini, and Martorano 2014; Lustig 2016c). In low and middle income countries, success in fiscal redistribution is driven primarily by redistributive efforts – the share of social spending in GDP in each country – and the extent to which transfers are targeted on the poor and direct taxes are targeted on the rich.[25]

Rising pre-tax income concentration at the top of the distribution in many advanced economies has coincided with declining top marginal tax rates. Conditional and unconditional cash transfers, and noncontributory social pensions have become an important policy tool for directing resources toward the lower end of the distribution in developing countries, but their redistributive impact varies widely across countries, reflecting differences in both the size and the progressivity of these transfers (IMF 2014). Overall, Doerrenberg and Peichl (2014) show that that government policies are capable of reducing income inequality despite countervailing behavioral responses. The effect is stronger for social expenditure policies than for progressive taxation.

3.6.5.6   Labor Markets

Skill-biased technological change and the resulting rise in the skill premium, together with the erosion in labor market institutions, have contributed to the widening inequality in both advanced and developing economies. This is because technological change can disproportionately raise the demand for capital and skilled labor relative to low-skilled and unskilled labor by eliminating many jobs through automation or upgrading the skill level required to attain or keep jobs (Acemoglu 1998; Card and Dinardo 2002). Indeed, technological advances have contributed the most to rising income inequality in OECD countries, accounting for nearly one-third of the widening gap between the 90th and the 10th percentile earners over the last 25 years (OECD 2011). Evidence from developing economies shows a similar trend: a growing earnings gap between high- and low-skilled workers in many countries, despite a large rise in the supply of highly educated labor. Changes in the skill premium have been found to contribute to the rise or fall in earnings and income inequality in Asia, Latin America, and several African countries in the 1990s (Cogneau et al. 2007; Kanbur et al. 2014; Keifman and Maurizio 2014).

Globalization has played a smaller, but reinforcing role. This has led to a shrinking middle class in many advanced economies and some large emerging market economies (Autor, Katz, and Kearney 2006). In developed countries, the most important driver has been the declining share of middle-skilled occupations relative to low- and high-skilled occupations (Autor, Kerr, and Kugler 2007; Goos, Manning, and Salomons 2009). In developing countries, this result has come about more because of income polarization (Duclos, Esteban, and Ray 2004; Fan, Kanbur, and Zhang 2011).

While evidence suggests that labor market regulations, such as the minimum wage, unionization, and social security contributions, tend to improve the income distribution, these institutions have been declining in many countries (Calderón and Chong 2009; OECD 2011). This has led to additional expansion in inequality.

Less well regulated labor markets, financial deepening, and technological progress have contributed to the rise in income inequality in many countries. Improvements in health and education outcomes at the low end of the distribution and the emergence of more noncontributory cash transfer programs have mitigated some of the

---

[25]   See analyses from Commitment to Equity Institute (www.commitmentoequity.org/) as well as the online version of this chapter for more details.

increases or led to declines. Demographic shifts and changes in taxation have also affected inequality trends. The relative importance of these factors varies across groups of countries.

3.7 Deep Drivers of Inequality

3.7.1 History and the Path Dependence of Inequality

The current level of income inequality is influenced by any asset inequality that may have prevailed in the past. This is especially so in developing countries that have not undergone a transition to democracy, carried out any asset redistribution, introduced progressive tax reforms, or broadened the access to land, education, and credit. Historically high asset concentration in some countries is determined by hierarchical social systems and the associated land concentration (such as in much of continental Europe, India, and the United Kingdom), the dispossession by colonial rulers of the land and natural resources of indigenous populations (as in East Africa, southern Africa, and Latin America), and social and cultural values that involve discrimination against women and specific groups such as lower castes and religious and ethnic minorities.

For example, the substantial inequality experienced at independence in Latin America was the legacy of the high concentration of land and political power inherited from colonial times (Engerman and Sokoloff 2005). This led to the development of institutions that maintained the privileges of an agrarian and commercial oligarchy until well after World War II by facilitating the diversification of the land and mining assets of the oligarchs into industry and financial assets (Torche and Spilerman 2006). Control over the political system and the army ensured that such dominance continued until the emergence of democracy and wider access to education. Evidence from Sub-Saharan Africa likewise supports the hypothesis of the path dependence of current inequality and of the relationship between current inequality and past property rights regimes over land with an important distinction between more egalitarian communal tenure systems and the highly unequal dualistic white settler regimes (Frankema, 2009).

A key issue is the persistence of such path dependence. Indeed, the relationship between the initial asset concentration and subsequent income inequality may be eroded by several factors, including structural transformation of the economy. The path dependence may not survive the withering away of the agricultural share in GDP. Its survival requires imperfect financial markets, such that only households with strong initial wealth are able to borrow and invest in new sectors. Its survival also requires that the initial conditions in asset inequality map into low and unequally distributed human capital accumulation and that political democratization is postponed.

Yet, democracy (or revolution) alone is no guarantee that inequality will narrow, as is demonstrated in the case of the recent political liberalization in the former centrally planned economies of Europe, where inequality widened appreciably during the transition process (Gruen and Klasen 2012). This also holds for the liberalization in formerly authoritarian regimes in Latin America in the 1980s and 1990s. There, inequality remained wide and, in some cases, widened additionally in the 1980s and 1990s. It began to narrow only around 2000, and the narrowing was generally more substantial in countries run

by center-left administrations that placed social justice at the core of their electoral and governmental agenda.

The path dependency hypothesis may break down also because of growing conflicts between old and new elites. History provides counterexamples to the thesis that a unified oligarchic interest creates a smooth pathway between agrarian and industrial asset inequality. The most notable of these counterexamples is the nineteenth-century debate in the United Kingdom over the Corn Laws that pitted the old agrarian elite against the new industrial interests, given that cheap food was a major determinant of industrial wages (Williamson 1990). Newly created industrial elites may find themselves sooner or later involved in a power struggle with the rural elite. In Chile, for instance, a peasant–capitalist alliance overcame agrarian elite opposition to land reform. Generally, a transformation in elites may weaken path dependence over time.

External factors may also affect the persistence of path dependence. Thus, Prados de la Escosura (2007) emphasizes that the gains in the international terms of trade experienced during the globalization of 1870–1914 in Latin America, which had become a major world supplier of agricultural commodities, exacerbated the asset inequality that was a legacy of the colonial period. Indeed, globalization raised the returns to land that benefited a tiny class of large landowners. But this also depends on the political orientation of governments. For example, while, over 1870–1914, the gains in the terms of trade exacerbated inequality, the period 2002–2012 leads to an opposite conclusions because the distribution of the benefits of the recent gains in the terms of trade led to the region's increased capacity to tax land and mining rents and the establishment of new redistributive institutions (Cornia 2015).

3.7.2 Demography, Fertility, and Inequality

Demographic dynamics, including the dynamics of fertility, mortality, and migration, can affect overall economic performance, but also inequality. The impact of fertility on inequality depends on the stage of the demographic transition and on how fertility and incomes are related (Lam 1986). In countries that have not entered a demographic transition and are therefore characterized by high fertility and mortality rates, there is usually a positive relationship among income, social status, and fertility and an even stronger relationship among income, social status, and surviving children, leading to a generally weak relationship between fertility and inequality (Colleran et al. 2015; Vogl 2016). In countries in which the fertility rate has started to decline, the rate tends to decline first and more quickly among wealthier and better educated groups, leading to a substantial fertility differential between these groups and poorer and less well educated groups. As a result of this dynamic, poorer households with many children cannot invest as intensively in each child because they are poorer and need to divide their smaller investments among more people (Lanjouw and Ravallion 1995). The large differential in investments in children between rich and poor households can lead to widening inequality depending on the associated mechanisms (Kremer and Chen 2002; de la Croix and Doepke 2003; Cordobia, Liu, and Ripoll 2016; Vogl 2016).

Empirical evidence strongly supports the existence of the large fertility differential between richer and poorer households during a demographic transition (Kremer and Chen 2002; de la Croix and Doepke 2003; Chiavegatto and Kawachi 2015; Vogl 2016).

The models suggest that, as the demographic transition proceeds and reaches poorer households, inequality will narrow once more. An acceleration of this effect through, for example, efforts to broaden educational access among the poor could help reduce inequality more rapidly (Kremer and Chen 2002).

Most OECD countries and many emerging Asian economies have already reached the final stage in the demographic transition in which overall fertility rates are low and no longer differ much across the income distribution (Vogl 2016). In contrast, in most of Latin America and southern Africa and among poorer Asian countries, the fertility differential, though closing, is still sizable, thereby sustaining inequality. The situation in much of Sub-Saharan Africa, especially Central, East, and West Africa, is described by overall high fertility rates and a sizable and, in some cases, still widening fertility differential that can put a break on economic performance and increase inequality. The fertility rate decline in these subregions is proceeding slowly and has stalled in some places, suggesting that the unfavorable inequality dynamics may play out over an extended period (Klasen 2016).

3.7.3   Links between Economic and Political Inequality

Economic inequalities are likely to be expressed partly in the greater influence of the relatively economically privileged in the political system (see Sections 3.3.2 and 3.3.3). This influence can lead to resistance to taxation, redistributive transfers, worker representation, and so forth. The character of the state is determined considerably by such influence. This may be reflected in the internal and external actions of a government. The attitude of developed-country governments toward international redistributive obligations also appears also to have been appreciably shaped by such domestic factors. Governments with a more social-democratic character often also adopt a more positive stance towards providing international development aid or otherwise undertaking to combat international inequalities directly. Strategic considerations may also be important in determining the magnitude and nature of development assistance. Similarly, the attitude of states toward other features of the international regime bearing on international inequalities – including loopholes in the international financial system enabling the outward flow of capital for purposes of tax avoidance or evasion – may also be shaped by self-interest, making it difficult to reach a straightforward analysis based on the nature of internal politics.[26]

3.7.4   The Link between Economic Inequality and Social Stratification

Deep ties are likely between economic inequality and social stratification. It has long been understood that, in many societies, race, caste, regional origin, and other factors define the social experiences

of people and influence their ability to develop and use productive capabilities in ways that are economically remunerative. Outright discrimination is crucial in limiting access to educational and employment opportunities. However, there may be more subtle mechanisms that revolve around aspirations. Thus, the lack of objective opportunities may lead to more restrained subjective appreciation of the objective opportunities that do exist or of the likelihood of succeeding in pursuing them because of discouragement or anxiety-induced poor performance.[27] Discrimination that is attached to attributes that are presumed based on class or other social constructs, particularly to phenotypic or physiognomically identifiable differences, such as aspects of race, may be among the most difficult types of discrimination to address through policies because they reflect deep-seated social attitudes. Moreover, such everyday attitudes are reproduced or reinforced by media representations and may be reflected in the operations of public institutions in ways that may be corrected through specific policies. This might include, for example, racial profiling by police, differential sentencing by the courts, differential admissions rates to educational institutions, and differential hiring rates.

3.7.5   Globalization and Inequality

The last two decades have seen the emergence, consolidation, and diffusion of an economic paradigm that emphasizes domestic financial liberalization, the removal of barriers to international trade and financial flows, and technology transfer. While the free circulation of labor across borders is not part of this paradigm, the demographic imbalances existing in the world and the spread of information made possible by the information and communication technology revolution have increased formal and informal migrant flows substantially.

The diffusion of this influential paradigm and the extraordinary development of information and communication technology foster rapid economic integration. In 1980–2002, average import tariffs fell by 70 percent to 80 percent (Table 3.6). Likewise, capital accounts were liberalized substantially except in Sub-Saharan Africa, South Asia, and the Asian economies in transition. Domestic financial liberalization – a precondition for the success of free capital flows – also recorded rapid progress. The world stock of migrants rose from 154.2 million in 1990 to 244.0 million in 2015 (UN DESA 2016). Of these, 138.0 million reside in advanced economies (mainly in Europe) and 75.0 million in Asia (especially the Middle East). Over 2000–2015, there was an acceleration in South–North migration.

3.7.5.1   Trade Liberalization

As suggested by neoclassical trade theory, the rationale behind trade liberalization is that free trade leads to greater specialization in sectors that use more intensely the factors of production with which each country is endowed, and that this generates mutual growth benefits for all trading partners. In developing countries with a strong supply of

---

26   See Boyce and Ndikumana (2012) and Ndikumana and Boyce (2001) on outward capital flows from Sub-Saharan Africa.

27   On aspirations and economic development, see Appadurai (2004); Flechtner (2014, 2016, 2017); Ray (2006). On discrimination and anxiety, see Hoff and Pandey (2012).

Table 3.6 | Policy changes, domestic and external liberalization, 1982–2010

Region	1982–1990	1991–1997	1998–2002	2002–2010
Average import tariff				
South America	40.0	19.0	12.2	10.6
Central America and Mexico	46.6	18.1	8.8	7.2
Sub-Saharan Africa	26.7	24.9	14.5	13.2
Middle East and North Africa	29.7	21.9	17.3	16.2
South Asia	62.9	52.9	20.8	14.9
East Asia and Southeast Asia	20.3	16.7	7.6	6.9
Asian economies in transition	44.5	38.9	15.5	12.6
Eastern Europe and former Soviet Union	—	11.0	9.0	6.0
Advanced economies	8.5	7.1	3.3	4.2
Kaopen index of capital account openness				
South America	−0.78	−0.17	0.76	1.00
Central America and Mexico	−0.84	0.29	1.18	1.67
Sub-Saharan Africa	−0.91	−0.82	−0.59	−0.56
Middle East and North Africa	−0.64	−0.35	0.02	0.36
South Asia	−1.29	−0.74	−0.93	−0.90
East Asia and Southeast Asia	0.85	0.96	0.50	0.57
Asian economies in transition	−1.73	−1.31	−1.07	−1.00
Eastern Europe and former Soviet Union	−1.84	−0.53	0.01	0.65
Advanced economies	0.83	1.89	2.28	2.32
Frazer index of domestic financial liberalization				
South America	5.1	6.8	6.9	7.7
Central America and Mexico	6.7	7.3	7.5	8.4
Sub-Saharan Africa	4.5	5.1	6.6	7.4
Middle East and North Africa	3.6	4.6	5.8	6.5
South Asia	4.7	5.6	6.4	7.4
East Asia and Southeast Asia	5.9	6.9	6.6	8.2
Asian economies in transition	0.0	2.9	4.6	8.0
Eastern Europe and former Soviet Union	0.5	3.2	7.4	8.7
Advanced economies	7.6	8.2	8.6	8.8

Note: Kaopen index of capital account openness: −2.5 for closure; +2.5 for complete openness. Frazer index of domestic financial liberalization: between 0 and 10; 10 = total liberalization.
Source: Cornia 2014c.

unskilled labor, trade liberalization involves shifting production from nontradables and capital-intensive import substitutes toward unskilled labor–intensive exports, thereby generating favorable distribution effects. In contrast, in the advanced countries specialized in the production of goods requiring more capital and skilled labor, inequality is expected to widened.

These predictions were validated in Europe and the United States during the trade liberalization of 1870–1914 and during the export drive of the Asian tigers (Wood 1994). Bourguignon and Morrisson (1990) find similar results for 35 small and medium developing countries. Yet, an equally important literature reaches opposite conclusions. For instance, a meta-analysis of the empirical evidence found that trade liberalization generated adverse distributive effects (Koujianou-Goldberg and Pavcnik 2007). An analysis of 21 liberalization episodes over the 1980s and 1990s shows that inequality rose in 13 cases, remained constant in 6, and fell only in 2 (Taylor 2004). Indeed, as shown also by the case of Latin America and Sub-Saharan Africa, trade liberalization has led to deindustrialization and the reprimarization of production (Ocampo 2012; Cornia 2016).

What other factors might explain the discrepancy between the theory and empirical evidence? First, developing countries often export goods that incorporate natural resources and the labor of semiskilled and skilled workers rather than much unskilled labor, such as mining and oil extraction. Land-intensive agricultural exports have equalizing effects only in the case of low land concentration.

Second, the advantages of trade liberalization are less evident in countries exporting raw materials, which are subject to large price variations (Erten and Ocampo 2012). If commodity prices fall, the ability of these countries to import goods for the leading sector falls, and employment and incomes decline.

Third, in middle-income countries, free trade may turn out to be unequalizing if exports are also liberalized in other countries that have more favorable factor endowments and production structures. The best example is offered by the decision of China and other low-wage East Asian economies to assign to labor-intensive exports the role of key growth driver. Their decision undoubtedly lowered the international price of labor-intensive goods, but also eroded the comparative advantages of the middle-income countries of Latin America and Southeast Asia relative to the developed countries. In addition and contrary to the findings of Wood (1994) on the first wave of the Asian tigers, the phenomenal growth and export performance of Bangladesh, China, Indonesia, and so on were accompanied by a rapid widening in domestic inequality because of a variety of factors, including wage suppression, growing dispersion between advanced regions integrated into world markets and more backward regions, imports of capital-intensive investment goods complementary to skilled labor, and a rising capital share.

Fourth, inequality may widen if trade liberalization does not occur simultaneously among all trading partners. For instance, the developing countries exporting agricultural goods opened up to foreign imports and so recorded job losses in the formerly protected sector, but achieved unsatisfactory export growth because of their internal problems and persistent protectionism in the advanced countries.[28]

3.7.5.2   Capital Account Liberalization

Mainstream theory has maintained until recently that the liberalization of portfolio investments – that is, purchases of bonds, shares, and securities by nonresidents in local stock markets; foreign bank lending to domestic banks; borrowing abroad by domestic firms, families, and the state; and derivatives – raises investment, growth, employment, productivity, and equity in countries with low savings, but high rates of return on capital and an abundant supply of cheap labor. Subsequent analyses have shown, however, that such gains were illusory because growth did not accelerate, and instability increased (Prasad et al. 2003). There is now a consensus on the usefulness of capital controls.

Indeed, the evidence points to a consistent deterioration in income equality and growth prospects associated with the liberalization of portfolio inflows and outflows, particularly in countries with weak labor institutions and weak social safety nets. The discrepancies between mainstream theory and the evidence suggest the following: (1) Left to themselves, deregulated financial systems do not perform well owing to problems of incomplete information, markets, and contracts, herd behavior, pure panics, weak supervision, and asset price speculation. Much of the recent instability and recession, including the recession of 2008–2013, derives from the deregulation of domestic and external financial transactions. (2) Large portfolio inflows can cause an appreciation of the real exchange rate, reduce employment and growth in the export sector, and encourage subcontracting and wage cuts in the tradable sector to preserve profit margins (Taylor 2004). (3) Portfolio investments are often directed not at agriculture and labor-intensive manufacturing, but at capital- and skill-intensive firms in finance, insurance, and real estate (Taylor 2004). (4) The disciplining effects accompanying the liberalization of the capital account have mostly had a deflationary impact by reducing tax revenue, public spending, and national income. (5) Bailouts of bankrupt financial institutions have involved transfers through taxes and inflation from poor nonparticipants in the financial sector to middle- and upper-income

participants, including large depositors, big borrowers, and financial institutions (Honohan 2005). Overall, an empirical analysis of the distributional impact of neoliberal policies in Latin America during the 1990s concludes that external financial liberalization was the component of the Washington Consensus package that had the strongest negative distributional impact (Behrman et al. 2000).

3.7.5.3   Technology Transfer

Globalization has been accompanied by a rapid transfer of costly state-of-the-art technology to developing countries and acceleration in technological change in the advanced economies. The skill-biased technical change hypothesis suggests that, in the industrialized countries, the new technologies generate a greater demand for skills and a more skewed distribution of earnings relative to technologies. Unless the educational system quickly provides an adequate supply of workers with new skills, the demand for and wages of unskilled workers will decline, while the demand for and the wages of skilled workers will rise more quickly than the supply of these workers. As a result, wage dispersion will increase in the sectors using the new technologies. Information technology also reduces the cost of monitoring unskilled workers and minimizes labor shirking, while lowering the wage premium needed to ensure the efficient performance of these workers. Especially in the service sector and in a few industrial branches, new technologies replace unskilled labor through physical capital, thereby pushing up the capital share and overall income concentration.

In developing countries, import liberalization has increased the access to labor-saving technologies produced in the West that are complementary to skilled labor, thus reducing the demand for unskilled labor, a change that has worsened income distribution. This negative short-term effect may be offset over the medium term by the benefits of more rapid industrial modernization.

3.7.5.4   Migration and Migrant Remittances

During the globalization of 1870–1914, when 60 million mostly unskilled workers migrated from the European periphery to the New World, migration reduced income inequality in Europe because the ratio of unskilled wages to farm rents rose following a drop in the labor supply deriving from the migration (Lindert and Williamson 2001). However, migration is now tending to widen inequality in the countries of origin because the unskilled poor are less likely to migrate than middle-class workers whose families are able to finance the high costs of informal international migration. Remittances are therefore generally received by households in the middle of the income distribution, often bypassing the people on the lowest rung. At the same time, the emigration of workers with rare skills may raise the wages of such workers in the countries of origin, leading to a rise in the wage premium and greater overall inequality. This is particularly true of the migration of highly skilled professionals – such as doctors and nurses

---

[28]   See also Box 3.6 in the online version of this chapter.

from Ghana – that represents a clear case of an unequalizing drain of human resources.

Yet, there are discrepancies between theoretical predictions and the results of a review of the empirical literature. Docquier and Rapoport (2003), for instance, argue that standard theory does not provide conclusive evidence on whether international migration widened or narrowed economic inequality in the countries of origin. They suggest that migration may not be unequalizing in countries of origin if it is state sponsored or if large migrant networks emerge in the countries of destination, as have been observed in El Salvador and Mexico during the last two decades (Cornia 2014a). Remittances may stimulate overall long-term growth in countries of origin by lessening the balance of payments constraint, permitting the import of capital goods, facilitating the formation of human capital because children remaining behind have a greater chance of graduating from school, and allowing poorer households to acquire productive assets and complementary inputs (McCormick and Wahba 2001).

Overall, the evidence shows that remittances have a favorable effect on poverty, volatility, and current consumption, but little effect on the investment rate, school enrollment rates, and the long-term growth rate of GDP (IMF 2005). The effect of migration in the countries of destination is controversial. There is limited evidence that migrants displace low-skilled local workers in manual jobs. Rather, the evidence points to a replacement effect. There seems to be, however, an positive effect on the wages of skilled workers.

3.7.6   Inequality, Knowledge, and Policy

3.7.6.1   Knowledge-Based Inequalities

Inequality is a multidimensional and multicausal phenomenon. Knowledge-based inequality is not new within or across countries. What is new is the recognition of knowledge, technology, and innovation as major causes of inequality.

One way of analyzing the type of causality that relates inequality to knowledge production and use is through the typology of social exclusion proposed by Sen (2000). Differentiating between active and passive, and constitutive and instrumental exclusion, four cells represent (1) active and constitutive exclusion, (2) active and instrumental exclusion, (3) passive and instrumental exclusion, and (4) passive and constitutive exclusion. Each of these social exclusion cells is connected to relative deprivation and relates to the type of knowledge that is produced and the way this knowledge is used and distributed. Cell one may be exemplified by the Agreement on Trade-Related Aspects of Intellectual Property Rights (TRIPS) and the exclusion it implies in accessing basic medicines (Stiglitz 2007). Cell four reflects the same type of problems from a passive perspective. In the realm of health care, for example, terms such as neglected disease or the 90/10 gap, coined by the World Health Organization, express a form of exclusion that is not actively pursued, but that nonetheless inhibits a great part of the world's population to benefit from better health offered by new knowledge. Knowledge-related exclusion in cell

two can be exemplified by the possibilities in choosing people to hire for jobs, to gain access to insurance, to receive fellowships, or to be accepted at educational institutions based on a wealth of personal data, including intimate data on DNA. Cell three includes the more widely recognized type of social exclusion derived from the unequal capabilities among people, organizations, and even whole societies to produce and use modern knowledge to solve problems. Freeman (1992) coined the term voluntary underdevelopment to describe the systematic preference for importing technical solutions over the effort to provide technical solutions from within based on efforts to develop local capabilities in science, technology, and innovation. Inequality arises in these situations because of the small share of highly qualified people in total employment and the associated low wages and weak stimulus for personal investment in education.

Each cell represents a particular feature of the prevailing knowledge-based inequality that may arise between countries or within countries. Each cell reflects a specific type of power that is exercised through different actors and mechanisms over global or national regulations, over research and innovation agendas, and over economic structures. The intertwined manifestations of social exclusion hinder major progress in such an agenda unless a more systemic and global perspective is pursued. However, precisely because of the specific nature of the various types of knowledge-based inequalities, it is important to identify the characteristics of the power influencing more directly each type of exclusion as well as the actors able to build alternatives.

3.7.6.2   The Production of Knowledge and Inequality

The nature of knowledge-based inequality is rooted partly in the kind of knowledge that is produced and partly in the knowledge that is not produced. Academic research agendas are molded by diverse influences internal and external to the academic world.

"The prioritization of research tends to create huge pockets of undone science that result in the systematic nonexistence of selected fields of research" (Hess 2007: 22). However, external influence may have quite different meanings in peripheral countries and in knowledge-based and innovation-driven economies (de la Mott and Paquet 1996). In the latter, terms such as academic capitalism describe the external influences that are considered more powerful in shaping academic agendas (Slaughter and Rhodes 2004). Meanwhile, in the peripheral countries, more often than not, undone science is characterized by a lack of knowledge demand rather than a biased demand for knowledge.

Undone science may also be a consequence of forces that operate within academia. Researchers are workers within institutions who build their professional environment – postgraduate studies, tenure, and the other rungs on the academic ladder – following unspoken rules as well as quite explicit rules. The impact of the academic evaluation system on the science that is effectively carried out has been an object of close scrutiny (Hicks 2004; Martin and Whitley 2010; de Rijcke and Rushforth 2015).

3.8   Affecting Inequality: The Scope and Limits of Policy

3.8.1   National Policy Issues in Addressing Within-Country Inequality

By adopting the SDGs in September 2015, countries worldwide committed to making the world a fairer place. The SDGs include a new goal when compared to the previous Millennium Development Goals, one that focuses explicitly on reducing inequality (SDG 10). As discussed in Section 3.3, concerns about inequality have arisen out of notions of justice and fairness, but also because of the negative consequences that wide inequality has on other outcomes that are crucial to development and well-being (Rawls 1971). As discussed extensively in this chapter, substantial inequality can lead, for instance, to higher absolute poverty, lower economic growth, policies biased in favor of the rich, persistently low social mobility, fewer incentives for cooperation and coordination, political polarization, and the weakening of the social contract (Coleman 1974; Bourguignon 2003; World Bank 2005, 2017; Esteban and Ray 2006; Stiglitz 2012; Ostry et al. 2014).

Societies possess various means to affect inequality in opportunities and outcomes. While there are policies that seek to influence inequality directly, policies that have other aims, such as overall macroeconomic and fiscal policies aimed at achieving growth and stability, can also have important distributional consequences. The focus here is, first, on policy actions to influence inequality and, second, the distributional consequences of other policies.

As indicated by Lustig (2016c), some policy actions designed to reduce inequality need to focus on improving the conditions of the poor, the vulnerable, and the socially excluded, that is, on increasing the assets (particularly, human capital), the opportunities, and the living standards of those at the bottom of the social ladder (Atkinson 2015; Basu 2013; Lustig 2016c; World Bank 2001). A second set of policies are geared to supporting the growth and sustainability of a strong middle class (Ferreira et al. 2013; Atkinson 2015; Lustig 2016c). Given the large and, in many countries, increasing concentration of income and wealth at the top, a third set of policies are aimed at curbing the excesses of such concentration (Piketty 2014; Atkinson 2015; Lustig 2016c).

Actions need to be centered on leveling the playing field, setting boundaries on market outcomes, and redistributing income and wealth through taxes and transfers, including the provision of services. In all three instances, the power of the state (individually and through multilateral mechanisms) to redistribute assets, income, opportunities, and power through laws, regulations, and fiscal policy can be crucial (Atkinson 2015; Lustig 2016c). Policies that focus on the poor and the middle class must also include measures designed to protect the losers from the undesirable consequences of economic progress – such as labor being displaced by new technologies (Lustig 2000; Lustig 2016c). While globalization and technological change may promote higher rates of growth, improve the lot of the poor, and reduce between-country inequality, they may also generate significant dislocation and downward mobility among vast segments of the population. Development is always uneven and generates tensions and demands for the redistribution of resources and power (Ray 2016; World Bank 2017).

Policies aimed at changing the distribution of assets, such as inheritance laws, land reform, minimum inheritance regulations, anti-discrimination, and affirmative action, are likely to be controversial and face political obstacles. Governments need to reach collectively supported decisions on how to allocate the resources to reduce poverty in an efficient and equitable manner, while supporting a sustainable social contract.

3.8.1.1   Building Assets, Enhancing Opportunities, and Promoting Social Inclusion

Increasing the assets that individuals have, the ways they can make use of them, and the returns they obtain is a central aspect of improving the distribution of productive opportunities. (World Bank 2000/2001; Atkinson 2015).[29] Policies can contribute to the redistribution of productive opportunities through the provision of public goods and services "before the market," or ex ante, as well as by enhancing access to markets. Policies can also contribute to the redistribution of income directly through the fiscal system of taxation and transfers (ex post redistribution). Improving the way that institutions function can have effects on the redistribution of opportunities and the reduction of inequality in outcomes. In particular, through the design of policies and the allocation of resources, for example, the responsiveness of the system to the needs of actors who tend to be left out of the bargaining process can be enhanced to have an impact on current and intergenerational inequality.[30]

Expanding the human, physical, natural, and financial assets that poor people own or can use may be accomplished through various mechanisms, for example, land reform, programs to distribute to the population the shares from the privatization of public enterprises, and the reform of inheritance laws. One key way of leveling assets across a population involves establishing a minimum inheritance capital endowment that is paid to all individuals when they reach adulthood (Atkinson 2015). The provision of housing subsidies among low-income groups can also serve to provide the poor with an important asset. Efforts to reduce inequalities in access to education and training and to upgrade the skills of the poor are also key to enhancing critical assets. It is key to make it as easy as possible for the poor to improve nutrition, receive preventive health care, and keep their children in school. Interventions that might work include delivering preventive health care and education for free and even rewarding households

---

[29]   Box 3.1, in the online version of this chapter, describes a framework, based on the assets approach, to organize the discussion around the types of redistribution instruments available to policy makers

[30]   For syntheses of these ideas see, for example, the World Development Reports devoted to poverty, inequality, and governance: World Bank 2001, 2005, and 2017, respectively.

for using these services (as conditional cash transfers do); setting up free chlorine dispensers next to water sources; rewarding parents for immunizing their children; distributing free deworming medicines and nutritional supplements to schoolchildren; and investing in water and sanitation infrastructure (Banerjee and Duflo 2011).

Building human capital begins within the household. The provision of information and access to reproductive health so that household members can make informed decisions about the desirable number of children and prevent unwanted teenage pregnancies are principal ingredients in human capital development (Banerjee and Duflo 2011; Azevedo et al. 2012). Human capital accumulation may also suffer if the infants and young children in poor households are malnourished. Crucial are early childhood intervention programs in health care and nutrition, for example, mother and child health programs and vaccination programs, as well as basic infrastructure investment in water supply and sanitation, electricity, and transportation because of the synergies among sound nutrition, health care, and people's ability to use new learning technologies. Ensuring that the poor have access to these services should be a key aspect of reforms in social service delivery (World Bank 2003). Improving service quality requires the participation of poor communities and households in choosing, implementing, and monitoring services to hold providers accountable. Community-based schemes to protect water resources and other elements of the natural environment should be supported.

Perhaps as important in building the human capital of the poor are programs that serve to increase the demand of households for health care and education services. Actions to boost demand include improvements in the quality and availability of social services and compensation of the poor through direct transfers for the associated costs of transportation, school materials, and so on as well as the opportunity costs of the participation of household members in school or in health care facilities. They include giving parents additional incentives to invest in the education and health of their children. Evidence shows that unconditional cash transfers and CCTs linked to stay-in-school programs, human development programs, and so on can help increase the demand of households for education and health services among offspring (Fiszbein and Schady 2009). Through their short-term effects as well as their longer-term impacts, they can also contribute to reducing inequality, including gender inequality.[31]

Poor people tend to have less access to infrastructure and are more likely to experience the impact of environmental degradation (World Bank 2000/2001; Banerjee and Duflo 2011; Hallegate et al. 2016). Thus, local efforts to improve living conditions, from investment in water and sanitation to neighborhood improvement programs and environmental clean-ups, can benefit especially the poor. Better housing, transportation, and service provision can enhance the quality of life, health, and productive opportunities of households directly. To the degree that investment raises the value of property and land (if ownership can be appropriately documented), it has the potential to boost household collateral and access to credit. The cost of such investment may be considered a direct transfer to the poor (World Bank 2000/2001).

Policies that promote access to market opportunities among the poor might involve the provision of infrastructure, such as roads to connect remote and underserved regions, programs to reduce crime and violence and thereby ensure a safe environment for living and working, expanding the access of households to technology, or reforms in land titling to facilitate the ability of households to use assets as collateral. They also might include addressing market failures more directly, such as in the credit market; and constraining discriminatory practices in the judiciary system or the labor market. Improving market access leads to an increase in the bargaining power of the poor (World Bank 2000/2001).

Idiosyncratic shocks such as illness, death of breadwinner, and unemployment as well as aggregate shocks such as economic crises, natural disasters, and epidemics can make the poor temporarily poorer. However, they can also generate poverty traps and dampen growth. To survive, the poor may pare their productive and human capital or stop investing in this resource. Access to subsidized forms of insurance can help the poor by replacing costly strategies – such as distressed sales of assets or borrowing at prohibitive interest rates – to mitigate the impact of adverse shocks and encouraging the use of more productive – but also more risky – technologies (Banerjee and Duflo 2011). Safety nets can encourage the poor to save. Microcredit can help small businesses to survive. For aggregate shocks, coping successfully requires a mix of measures to deal with economy-wide risks and to help people address adverse shocks. The proper mechanisms can cushion the damage of crises on human capital development. These include arrangements to protect pro-poor public spending if austerity policies must be implemented. Rather than improvising after a crisis has occurred, countries need to be able to scale up social safety nets, such as temporary employment, early childhood programs, and cash transfer programs quickly (Lustig 2000; World Bank 2000/2001).

Gender inequality, a persistent values-based social inequity, requires specific attention. Even though gender gaps have been narrowing, unequal gender relations remain pervasive around the world. In nearly all countries, most women encounter disadvantages related to the control of material resources through marital, inheritance, property, and land tenure rights, which, in developing countries, are often conferred exclusively on men, and women also frequently face greater insecurity relative to men (Deere et al. 2013). The limited autonomy of women can have important negative effects on children's education and health. Thus, in addition to normative concerns, improving gender equity can have instrumental benefits in poverty reduction. Progress has been achieved, such as in education and health, but there are still critical gaps. Approaches that integrate legal, political, and direct public action tend to be effective.

As discussed in Section 3.7.4, weaknesses or strengths in social structures are associated with much of the dynamics of poverty generation or reduction. Exclusionary social structures, such as class stratification or gender divisions, limit upward mobility. These structures

---

[31]   For details on how cash transfers can improve gender equity, see Box 3.2 in the online version of this chapter.

may involve explicit or implicit discrimination in access to housing and land based on ethnic, racial, religious, or sexual identity. Policies that support the participation of socially excluded individuals, including by fostering discussions on exclusionary practices, can help remove these obstacles. Affirmative action policies can help groups that face systematic discrimination. Forums that bring groups together can be helpful in mitigating fragmentation and guiding dissatisfaction away from social conflict and toward political processes. Tackling ethnic, racial, gender, or sexual bias in discriminatory laws and regulations and in the operation of the legal system is central to addressing inequality, as is promoting the representation of excluded groups in community and national organizations (World Bank 2000/2001). Because poor people lack the resources to access the legal system, measures such as legal aid and information dissemination are especially powerful for creating more inclusive and accountable legal systems. State action can also be essential to changing the social norms that contribute to the perpetuation of socially based inequalities.[32]

Rooted in norms and networks, social capital is an important asset among individuals seeking to exit poverty. It can be promoted by supporting existing social networks and providing broader links to markets, institutions, and organizations. Enhancing the legal or regulatory institutional framework supporting groups that represent the interests of poor households may boost the potential of the associated social networks. Additionally, given that poorer households tend to organize locally, their ability to advocate for state, regional, national policies should also be enhanced.

To combat exploitative forms of child labor and discrimination and foster fair practices in labor markets, governments should adhere to the core labor standards set out in the International Labor Organization's Declaration on the Fundamental Principles and Rights at Work. These include freedom of association and the right to collective bargaining, the elimination of forced labor, the effective prevention of child labor, and the elimination of discrimination in employment and professional occupations.

Governments should design tax and transfer systems so that the incomes or consumption of the poor after taxes and transfers are not lower than their incomes or consumption before the fiscal interventions. Evidence shows that, although the combination of taxes and transfers is equalizing to varying degrees, the payments of the poor in direct taxes and, especially, consumption taxes surpass the cash transfers they receive, particularly in low- and lower-middle- income countries (Lustig 2016a,b,c). Government spending on education and health should also support adequate coverage and the quality of basic services among the poor.

3.8.1.2 Building a Strong and Resilient Middle Class

The middle class flourishes in an environment of labor-intensive economic growth. Growth in jobs and labor incomes has two main sources: (1) the accumulation of resources, that is, investment, and

(2) efficiency, that is, how well resources are put to use, which is largely driven by technological innovation. Private investment can be promoted by reducing risk through stable fiscal and monetary policy, healthy financial systems, and a reliable and transparent business environment. It also requires a sound institutional environment in which rules are applied objectively and systematically and in which there are established incentives to tackle corruption, including the corruption associated with vested business interests, such as special dealing and kickbacks (World Bank 2017). Public investment, particularly in infrastructure, communication, and skills, complements private investment in the creation of productive opportunities and efficiency enhancement.

Microenterprises and small businesses face more risk of bureaucratic badgering and unequal treatment because the well-connected are favored. Measures that reduce the sources of market failures can contribute to the effective participation of such enterprises in the market by, for example, promoting access to credit through financial deepening or by reducing the transaction costs of reaching international markets, such as through export fairs, enhanced access to technology, or specialized training. Institutional reforms, such as lowering restrictions on the informal sector, addressing land tenure, or enabling regulation that encourages smaller investments, can also contribute to providing a conducive business environment for these firms.

International markets offer important opportunities for job and income growth in agriculture, industry, and services. Most countries that have experienced major reductions in income poverty and expansions in the middle class have made use of international trade. But opening up to trade and investment can create losers as well as winners, and it yields substantial benefits only if countries have the infrastructure and institutions to underpin a strong supply response. Thus, the opening up needs to be well designed, with special attention to country specifics and to institutional and other bottlenecks. The sequencing of policies should encourage job creation and manage job destruction. Explicit policies should offset the transitory costs among the groups that lose out as a result of globalization. The opening of the capital account has to be managed with utmost prudence and in step with domestic financial sector development to reduce the risk of high volatility in capital flows.

While globalization and technological progress appear to have reduced between-country inequality, their impact on within-country inequality has been unequalizing in many countries. Moreover, the associated forces have led to dislocation and downward mobility among significant segments of the middle class and the working poor. The benefits of globalization and technological progress have been disproportionately reaped, dramatically so in some cases, by those at the top of the social ladder. Raising the skill level of a labor force renders a country more able to benefit from globalization and technological progress. Indeed, the building of harmonious societies requires the introduction of drastic corrections in the outcomes markets produce. There is increasing evidence that markets do not and will not generate sufficient employment at a living wage for all (Atkinson 2015). Markets will continue to make the rich richer if left unchecked. Given this

3

---

[32] For a discussion on how social norms can hinder policies designed to expand opportunities, see the synthesis in the World Development Report 2017 (World Bank 2017). Also, see Box 3.3 on shifting social norms in the online version of Chapter 3.

background, it is essential now more than ever for societies to implement and, in some cases, reintroduce boundaries on market outcomes.

The first boundary on market outcomes should be placed on employment. A key determinant of employment growth is the nature of technological change, whether labor intensive or labor displacing, and whether intensive in skilled labor or low-skilled labor. Even if feasible, it may not be desirable to direct technological change away from labor-saving technologies. After all, the latter are at the core of which allowed mankind to enjoy increasing and diverse forms of well-being. The problem is that, if the income derived from the capital used to produce goods and services is not widely distributed, labor-saving technological change may leave vast portions of a population unemployed or underemployed, that is, working for fewer hours or in low wage jobs. To tackle this problem, countries should consider the implementation of some form of guaranteed work as proposed by Atkinson (2015: 140–142).

A second boundary on market outcomes should be placed on wages. According to economic theory, supply and demand do not fully determine the market wage; they only place bounds that allow scope for bargaining over the division of the surplus. However, the bargaining process is not merely a matter of individuals acting isolated from one another. Trade unions and collective bargaining can be crucial in helping produce a fairer distribution of the surplus and a more equitable distribution of wages. Labor unions have been losing their grip (Acemoglu et al. 2001). Unionization rates have been declining in practically all countries. Governments should support union-friendly legislation that does not foster egregious inefficiency and, above all, clientelism and corrupt practices. Particularly important are the rules that govern collective bargaining and the resolution of labor disputes. Setting the minimum wage at levels corresponding to a living wage is also an important instrument in establishing a lower bound for the division of the surplus.

Successful welfare states rely on universal programs (Chapter 8). However, universal should not be equated with providing everybody the same lump-sum transfer (Lustig 2016b). It means that everybody has the same right to the insurance aspect of universal welfare spending.[33] Thus, if one of the commitments of a welfare state is that all individuals should enjoy a minimum income, the insurance aspect implies that those individuals whose prefiscal income is less than the minimum, not the entire population, are entitled to receive transfers. Universalism means that every individual, whether rich or poor, should have access to free or affordable education, health care of acceptable quality, and social insurance to cope with idiosyncratic shocks, such as unemployment, illness, the death of a breadwinner, and so on. Universalism, however, is achieved over time. Today's most exemplary welfare states did not have universal programs from the start (Lindert 2004). Moreover, poor countries cannot be expected to provide universal coverage through all programs on day one given the limitations on their resource and institutional capacity. Nonetheless, to be politically sustainable and contribute to equalizing opportunities, the welfare state needs to award adequate social protection to all. It also needs to provide services of sufficient quality so that the middle class does not feel compelled to opt out.[34]

3.8.1.3 Curbing the Excesses of Income and Wealth Concentration at the Top

Evidence of the substantial and, in many countries, growing concentration of income and wealth at the top has led to discussions about the imposition of boundaries on market outcomes among the rich. This consideration arises not only because more resources collected from the rich could be used to support the universal welfare state. It also arises from a belief that the excessive concentration is the result of political rent-seeking given that the incomes of the rich do not reflect the contributions of the rich to society and that the high incomes foster political and social instability.

The high incomes and wealth at the top could be curbed along three main channels. The two most typical involve taxation: increase the progressivity of the tax system by applying high inheritance taxes and taxes on inter vivos gifts for the rich. The third measure is more unconventional: adopt a code of practice for pay. This is advocated by Atkinson (2015). The approach can be taken even further by punishing those who do not abide by the rule. For example, the city of Portland, Oregon, adopted, in December 2016, a tax penalty on corporations that pay their chief executives more than 100 times what they pay typical workers (Anderson 2016).

3.8.1.4 Macroeconomic Policies for the Reduction of Poverty and Inequality

Appropriate macroeconomic policies can facilitate the reduction of inequality and poverty under normal conditions and when countries are hit by external shocks. There is now a widespread consensus that macroeconomic policies should minimize the likelihood of crises triggered by external shocks, that short-term stabilization should not be contractionary and sustain the provision of essential public goods (Klasen 2004), and that higher than targeted inflation rates should be tolerated (Lustig 2000). The experience of the 1980s and 1990s in the developing countries and 2008–2014 in the advanced economies shows that growth will remain elusive and that inequality will rise unless fiscal and monetary policy are countercyclical, the real exchange rate is stable and competitive, real interest rates are low, and the financial sector is adequately regulated.

Measures to Prevent Macroeconomic Crises

Research suggests that the most unequalizing and destabilizing effect of recent policy reforms arose from the liberalization of portfolio flows and the poor regulation of the domestic financial sector (Prasad et al. 2003; Taylor 2004, Honohan 2004). Several measures can be introduced to control

---

[33] For a discussion on the insurance components of the welfare state, see Barr (2012b).

[34] For a discussion of the challenges faced to contend with fragmentation and exclusion in Latin America's social protection systems, see ECLAC (2014, 2015) and Sojo (2017). Also see Box 3.4 in the online version of Chapter 3.

portfolio inflows, including Chile's *encaje*, limiting the foreign indebtedness of domestic banks, sterilization, temporary capital controls (as in Colombia, Singapore, and Taiwan, China), or the closure of the capital account (China). Improvements in banking regulation and oversight are also important, as shown by Latin America in the 2000s (Rojas Suarez 2010).

A second key issue concerns the ex ante choice of an exchange rate regime that minimizes the risk of over- and undershooting. With the exception of large countries and of small economies (where dollarization may work), a pro-poor macro policy must focus on introducing a stable and competitive real exchange rate (Cornia 2004). Rodrik (2007) finds that such approach was instrumental in kick-starting growth in several exporting countries.

Other measures to prevent crises involve stabilization funds and fiscal rules that sustain public finance from the fluctuation in the world demand and prices of the commodities exported by developing countries. As tax revenue and capital markets behave pro-cyclically, policy should encourage the creation of stabilization funds, as in the case of the Chilean copper fund that sets aside resources during bonanzas and transfers them back into the public budget during crises, thereby functioning as intertemporal self-insurance.

Measures to Be Adopted If External Crises Cannot Be Avoided

Counties can basically follow two adjustment approaches (Stiglitz 2002). The monetarist approach emphasizes the defense of the nominal exchange rate, high interest rate, and fiscal austerity to attract foreign capital to cover foreign deficits caused by macro-shocks. Its impact on inflation is modest, while that on inequality is generally unfavorable. The Keynesian alternative consists in devaluing the nominal exchange rate and in a fiscal expansion which involves an increase in budget deficits and inflation, but also an increase in exports. Devaluation could also have adverse effects in countries with large dollar exposures. Given these different effects, the choice of the adjustment package may obey the "least costly approach" principle. This compares the extent of output contraction (greater in the monetarist approach), inflation (higher in the Keynesian approach), changes in the current account balance (more favorable for the latter), the capital account balance (the opposite), and the distribution of bankruptcies and moral hazard, which affect most domestic firms in the monetary approach and foreign firms in the devaluation-based approach.

A countercyclical fiscal policy is key if crises cannot be avoided. Deficits should be tolerated during crisis years and reduced gradually as the economy recovers. There is no evidence that temporary deficits are costly, while sharp expenditure cuts have a short- and long-run contractionary effect. Moreover, because tax revenue is endogenously determined by the level of output, a rapid reduction of the deficit involves a drop in revenue that leads to a new widening of the deficit. Adam and Bevan (2005) suggest that deficit reductions of up to 1.5 percent of GDP a year can help reestablish fiscal balance with a minimal impact on growth, while larger reductions hurt growth.

The standard monetary policy consists in achieving a one-digit inflation through the manipulation of the policy rate. Yet, the evidence compiled by Bruno and Easterly (1998) shows that reducing inflation below 40 percent does not lead to faster growth. Evidence also shows that the high interest rate needed to achieve single-digit inflation entails a high "sacrifice ratio." This point has been agreed by the IMF Institute which accepts that an inflation rate of 10 percent is acceptable in developing countries affected by longstanding structural distortions. In view of all this, money supply must be accommodating, as happened in several Latin American countries during the 2008–2009 crisis.

One way to stabilize the twin deficits consists in reducing the cost of servicing the domestic and international debt. Measures include automatic debt standstills, debt rescheduling, debt haircut and securitization (as in Greece in 2012–2014), debt for development swaps, and debt defaults, repudiation, or cancellation. Debt cancellation under the Heavily Indebted Poor Countries Initiative had a beneficial effect in terms of inequality (Cornia 2016).

Expenditure cuts are typically introduced to reduce deficits, but this may reduce the provision of public goods needed for long-term growth. A more equitable solution is to increase progressive taxation and channel the resources of stabilization funds into the public budget. In the African and Central American countries with low tax–GDP ratios, raising taxation of the middle class and the rich would help stabilize the budget deficit and reduce inequality. South America followed such approach during the 2000s (Lustig et al. 2013; Cornia et al. 2014).

The sectoral distribution of public spending cuts during adjustment significantly influences the well-being of the poor. Proportional cuts across sectors are easier to implement politically, but are not efficient as the rates of return of investments in health care, education, public works, and infrastructure rehabilitation are higher than in other sectors, while their benefits' incidence is progressive. The allocations to these sectors should thus be protected. In addition, public transfers to the poor ought to be increased to offset the impact of shocks and recessive stabilization. By 2010, around 800 million people worldwide already benefitted from such transfers.

3.8.2 International Actions to Support Inequality Change

So far, the focus has been on national policies to affect inequality. As shown throughout the chapter, national policies can have a substantial effect on inequality, and, in general, there is substantially more scope for national actors, compared with foreign or international actors, to affect within-country inequality. Nonetheless, initiatives can be taken in multilateral fora or by advanced nations bilaterally that affect inequality between countries by boosting growth in poorer countries, as well as support policies to affect inequality within countries. International organizations and advanced countries can contribute to improving the lot of the poor in developing countries through four main channels. First, richer nations can make capital available for poor countries through grants and long-term loans at concessional rates; reduce current official debt levels, such as through the Highly-Indebted Poor Countries Initiative; provide financial safety nets in the face of shocks; and supply direct bilateral aid. The specific role that aid can play in affecting within country inequality is highlighted in Box 3.1. Second,

Box 3.1 | Can Aid Help Reduce Inequality?

Foreign aid can help mitigate inequality within recipient countries if two conditions are met. Donors have to allocate aid in line with their rhetoric on pro-poor growth, targeting the most disadvantaged population groups. At the same time, authorities in recipient countries have to ensure that aid actually reaches the poor. Both conditions are likely to be violated at least to some extent. The literature shows that donors pursue a mix of motives, including developmental concerns and commercial and political self-interest (Hoeffler and Outram 2011). Likewise, aid may be used to buy the political support of the local elites, thereby favoring the rich over the poor. On the recipient side, aid may induce rent-seeking, which tends to be inequality-increasing as rents are captured by local elites (Reinikka and Svensson 2004; Angeles and Neanidis 2009).

The empirical evidence is limited and ambiguous. Herzer and Nunnenkamp (2012) suggest that aid exerts an inequality-increasing effect on the income distribution. Chong et al. (2009) do not find a robust association between aid and inequality, while Shafiullah (2011) and Hirano and Otsubo (2014) find that aid reduces income inequality. Hirano and Otsubo suggest that the mixed results may be connected to the heterogeneity of impacts across aid sectors. Specifically, aid given to the social sector has the largest inequality-reducing effect. These results are in line with findings on the impact of social sector aid on development outcomes. Dreher et al. (2008) show that aid for education has increased primary school enrollment and completion rates, while Mishra and Newhouse (2009) show that aid for health has lowered infant mortality. Two recent studies on Malawi and Uganda corroborate these findings (De and Becker 2015; Odokonyero et al. 2015).

Incentive problems among both donors and recipients notwithstanding, the part of foreign aid dedicated to the social sector appears to be effective. Further improvements in targeting may be seen as a realistic next step toward increasing the inequality-reducing potential of foreign aid.

opening markets to agricultural products and promoting freer trade or extending preferential agreements can help boost developing-country exports, improve access to modern technology, and encourage private capital inflows.

Third, international policy coordination can be important in promoting resource mobilization in countries by unmasking tax evasion, tax avoidance, and illicit financial flows among wealthy individuals, multinational corporations, and criminal actors. Success in these ventures can improve the fiscal space for redistribution and also put a fair tax on excessive incomes at the top.

Fourth, multilateral institutions can assist countries in the design of and advocate for policies and resource allocations that target the poor more effectively, establish appropriate boundaries in market outcomes, and curb the excesses of income concentration and wealth accumulation at the top.

3.8.3   The Political Economy: Governance, Policy Making, and Implementation[35]

Despite their potential to boost productivity and growth and strengthen the social contract, governments often fail to adopt pro-equity policies. If they do, these policies often fail to reach the desired goal. Why? Part

of the answer has to with the fact that, while the policies have the potential to increase efficiency, they may affect certain groups unfavorably, particularly in the short term.

Policy making occurs through a process whereby individuals and groups that possess different amounts of power interact within changing rules as they pursue what may be different interests. Actors who might be negatively affected by pro-equity policies in terms of rents, income, their ability to maintain influence, and so on may try to block the adoption or implementation of the policies. Potentially affected groups may attempt to undermine policies that seek land reform. Or public officials may undermine administrative reforms aimed at improving public services if the reforms promise to cut into the discretionary control of the officials over resources.

Entry barriers and the distribution of power among actors from policy makers, bureaucrats, civil society groups, and the private sector to individual citizens determine who gets to participate in the policy arena and whose voice is heard. The bargaining power that actors have emanates from an assortment of sources such as social norms, formal rules, control over resources, or the ability to mobilize others. In unequal societies, the capacity of various actors to influence decision-making tends to be uneven as well, feeding back into inequality.

---

[35]   This section draws closely on World Bank (2017).

A common manifestation of power asymmetries is clientelism, whereby benefits are exchanged in return for political support, which can undermine the effectiveness of pro-equity policies. Clientelism occurs if the relationship between public officials and voters becomes distorted, such that, instead of a dynamic wherein public officials are the agents of voters (who can sanction agents), the former buy the latter's vote in exchange for (usually) short-term benefits. In other cases, public officials become responsive to groups, such as the providers of public services, who are key to their political survival. Favoring the interests of these groups can have detrimental effects on the delivery of key services such as education, health care, or infrastructure, as providers wield their influence, withholding effort (for example, through absenteeism) or engaging in low-quality provision. Another cornerstone of the effectiveness of pro-equity polities is the importance of cooperation, particularly the willingness of individuals to contribute to the funding of public goods. In the absence of credible systems of rewards and penalties, citizens may have incentives to behave opportunistically, enjoying public services without paying taxes. The perception that others are free riding weakens the incentives to comply. Other factors debilitate compliance. Actors excluded from the benefits of policies or those who receive low-quality services tend to be unwilling to contribute to the necessary funding. Lack of compliance undermines the social contract. Conversely, solving cooperation problems can contribute to the effectiveness of policies.

The policies that are optimal on paper, but that do not reflect political equilibriums can be inefficient to adopt and implement if there are powerful actors who gain from the status quo. In these cases, second-best, but feasible policies may be preferable. Indeed, successful reforms often go beyond best practices, address incentives, and adapt to solve specific problems that are obstacles to development.

References

Aaberge, R., and A. Brandolini 2014. "Multidimensional Poverty and Inequality." Bank of Italy Discussion Paper No. 976.

Aaberge, R., M. Mogstad, and V. Peragine 2011. "Measuring Long-Term Inequality of Opportunity," Journal of Public Economics 95: 193–204.

Acemoglu, D. 1998. "Why Do New Technologies Complement Skills? Directed Technical Change and Wage Inequality," Quarterly Journal of Economics 113: 1055–1089.

Acemoglu, D., and D.H. Autor 2011. "Skills, Tasks and Technologies: Implications for Employment and Earnings," in D. Card and O. Ashenfelter (eds.), Handbook of Labor Economics. New York: Elsevier.

Acemoglu, D., and J. Robinson 2009. Economic Origins of Dictatorship and Democracy. Cambridge: Cambridge University Press.

Acemoglu, D., P. Aghion, and G.L. Violante 2001. "Deunionization, Technical Change, and Inequality," Carnegie-Rochester Conference Series on Public Policy 55: 229–264.

Adam, C.S., and D.L. Bevan 2005. "Fiscal Deficits and Growth in Developing Countries," Journal of Public Economics 89: 571–597.

Adam, K., and P. Tzamourani 2015. Distributional Consequences of Asset Price Inflation in the Euro Area. Working Paper. University of Mannheim.

Adams, R.H. 2004. "Economic Growth, Inequality and Poverty: Estimating the Growth Elasticity of Poverty," World Development 32: 1989–2004.

Agnello, L., S.K. Mallick, and R.M. Sousa 2012. "Financial Reforms and Income Inequality," Economics Letters 116: 583–587.

Akerlof, G.A., and R.E. Kranton 2000. "Economics and Identity," The Quarterly Journal of Economics 115: 715–753.

Alesina, A., and E. Glaeser 2004. Fighting Poverty in the US and Europe: A World of Difference. Oxford: Oxford University Press.

Alesina, A., and D. Rodrik 1994. "Distributive Politics and Economic Growth," Quarterly Journal of Economics, 109: 465–490.

Alvaredo, F., A.B. Atkinson, T. Piketty, and E. Saez 2013. "The Top 1% in International and Historical Perspective," Journal of Economic Perspectives 27: 3–20.

Anand, S., and P. Segal 2008. "What Do We Know about Global Income Inequality?" Journal of Economic Literature, 46: 57–94.

Anand, S., and P. Segal 2015. "The Global Distribution of Income," in A.B. Atkinson and F. Bourguignon (eds.), Handbook of Income Distribution, Vols. 2A–2B. New York: Elsevier.

Anderson, E. 1999. "What Is the Point of Equality?" Ethics 109: 287–337.

Anderson, S. 2016. "Historic CEO Pay Tax Proposal Passes in Portland," Institute for Policy Studies. www.ips-dc.org/historic-ceo-pay-tax-proposal-passes-portland/ (last accessed December 23, 2017).

André, C., and J-P. Platteau 1998. "Land Relations under Unbearable Stress: Rwanda Caught in the Malthusian Trap," Journal of Economic Behaviour and Organisation, 34: 1–47.

Andrews, D., C. Jencks, and A. Leigh 2011. "Do Rising Top Incomes Lift All Boats?" B.E. Journal of Economic Analysis and Policy, 11, Contributions Article 6.

Angeles, L., and K.C. Neanidis 2009. "Aid Effectiveness: The Role of the Local Elite," Journal of Development Economics 90: 120–134.

Anyanwu, J.C, A.E.O. Erhijakpor, and E. Obi 2016. "Empirical Analysis of the Key Drivers of Income Inequality in West Africa," African Development Review 28: 18–38.

Appadurai, A. 2004. "The Capacity to Aspire: Culture and the Terms of Recognition," in V. Rao and M. Walton (eds.), Culture and Public Action, Palo Alto: Stanford University Press.

Aronson, J., G. Cohen, and P.R. Nail 1999. "Self-Affirmation Theory: An Update and Appraisal," in J. Mills and E. Harmon-Jones (eds.), Cognitive Dissonance: Progress on a Pivotal Theory in Social Psychology, Washington, DC: American Psychological Association.

Atkinson, A.B. 1970. "On the Measurement of Inequality," Journal of Economic Theory 2: 244–263.

Atkinson, A.B. 2008. The Changing Distribution of Earnings in OECD Countries. New York: Oxford University Press.

Atkinson, A.B. 2015. Inequality: What Can Be Done? Cambridge, Mass.: Harvard University Press.

Atkinson, A.B., and A. Brandolini 2001. "Promise and Pitfalls in the Use of "Secondary" Data-Sets: Income Inequality in OECD Countries as a Case Study," Journal of Economic Literature 39: 771–799.

Atkinson, A.B., and A. Brandolini 2010. "On Analyzing World Distribution of Income," World Bank Economic Review 24: 1–37.

Atkinson, A.B., and T. Piketty 2007. Top Incomes over the Twentieth Century. Oxford: Oxford University Press.

Autor, D., L. Katz, and M. Kearney 2006. "Measuring and Interpreting Trends in Economic Inequality," AEA Papers and Proceedings 96: 189–194.

Autor, D., W.R. Kerr, and A.D. Kugler 2007. "Does Employment Protection Reduce Productivity? Evidence from US States," The Economic Journal 117: 189–217.

Azevedo, J.P., M. Favara, S.E. Haddock, L.F. Lopez-Calva, M. Muller, and E. Perova 2012. Teenage Pregnancy and Opportunities in Latin America and the Caribbean: On Teenage Fertility Decisions, Poverty and Economic Achievement. Washington, DC: World Bank.

Azevedo, J.P., G. Inchauste, and V. Sanfelice 2013a. "Decomposing the Recent Inequality Decline in Latin America." Policy Research Working Paper 6715, The World Bank.

Azevedo, J.P., G. Inchauste, V. Sanfelice, M.E. Dávalos, C. Diaz-Bonilla, B. Atuesta, and R.A. Castañeda 2013b. "Fifteen Years of Inequality in Latin America: How Have Labor Markets Helped?" Policy Research Working Paper 6384, The World Bank.

Badaracco, N. 2015. "Fecundidad y Cambios Distributivos en América Latina," Working Paper 173, CEDLAS-Universidad Nacional de La Plata, November.

Baddeley, A.D., and G. Hitch 1974. "Working Memory," The Psychology of Learning and Motivation, 8: 47–89.

Balamatti, A. 2017. "Demonetization and Agriculture: Lessons for Extension and Advisory Services." www.researchgate.net/publication/318224619_Demonetization_and_Agriculture_Lessons_for_Extension_and_Advisory_Services (last accessed August 18, 2017).

Balcázar, C.P. 2015. "Lower Bounds on Inequality of Opportunity and Measurement Error," Economics Letters 137: 102–105.

3

Bandiera, O., and A. Natraj 2013. "Does Gender Inequality Hinder Development and Economic Growth? Evidence and Policy Implications," *World Bank Research Observer* 28: 2–21.

Banerjee, A.C. 1980. *The Agrarian System of Bengal*, Calcutta: K.P. Bagchi.

Banerjee, A.V., and E. Duflo 2003. "Inequality and Growth: What Can the Data Say?" *Journal of Economic Growth* 8; 267–299.

Banerjee, A.V., and E. Duflo 2008. "What Is Middle Class about the Middle Classes around the World?," *Journal of Economic Perspectives* 22: 3–28.

Banerjee, A.V., and E. Duflo 2011. *Poor Economics: A Radical Rethinking of the Way to Fight Global Poverty*, New York: Public Affairs.

Bardhan, P., M. Ghatak, and A. Karaivanov 2007. "Wealth Inequality and Collective Action," *Journal of Public Economics* 91: 1843–1874.

Baron, J.N., and J. Pfeffer 1994. "The Social Psychology of Organizations and Inequality," *Social Psychology Quarterly* 57: 190–209.

Barr, M.S. 2012a. *No Slack: The Financial Lives of Low-income Americans*. Washington, DC: Brookings Institution Press.

Barr, N. 2012b. *Economics of the Welfare State*, Fifth Edition. Oxford: Oxford University Press.

Barro, R.J. 2000. "Inequality and Growth in a Panel of Countries," *Journal of Economic Growth* 5: 5–32.

Barros, R.J., M. De Carvalho, S. Franco, and R. Mendonca 2010. "Markets, the State and the Dynamics of Inequality in Brazil," in L.F. Lopez-Calva and N. Lustig (eds.), *Declining Inequality in Latin America: A Decade of Progress?* Washington, DC: Brookings Institution Press and UNDP.

Basu, K. 2013. "*Shared Prosperity and the Mitigation of Poverty: In Practice and in Precept*," World Bank Policy Research Working Paper No. 6700. Washington, DC: The World Bank.

Bates, R. 1981. *Markets and States in Tropical Africa*, expanded edition 2014. Berkeley: University of California Press.

Beck, T., A. Demirgüc, and R. Levine 2007. "Finance, Inequality and the Poor," *Journal of Economic Growth* 12/1: 27–49.

Beck, T., R. Levine, and A. Levko 2010. "Big Bad Banks? The Winners and Losers from Bank Deregulation in the United States," *The Journal of Finance* 65: 1637–1667.

Behrman, J., N. Birdsall, and M. Székely 2000. "Economic Reform, and Wage Differentials in Latin America," *Working Paper of the Research Department* no. 435, Washington, DC: Inter-American Development Bank.

Benabou, R. 2000. "Unequal Societies: Income Distribution and the Social Contract," *American Economic Review* 90: 96–129.

Benabou, R., and E. Ok 2001. "Social Mobility and the Demand for Redistribution: The POUM Hypothesis," *The Quarterly Journal of Economics* 116: 447–487.

Bertola, G. 1993. "Factor Shares and Savings in Endogenous Growth," *American Economic Revie*, 83: 1184–1198.

Bertrand, M., S. Mullainathan, and E. Shafir 2006. "Behavioral Economics and Marketing in Aid of Decision Making among the Poor," *Journal of Public Policy & Marketing*, 25: 8–23.

Bhalla, S. 2002. *Imagine There's No Country: Poverty, Inequality, and Growth in the Era Globalization*. Washington, DC: Peterson Institute.

Binswanger, H., K. Deininger, and G. Feder 1995. "Power, Distortions, Revolt and Reform in Agricultural Land Relations," in J. Behrman and T.N. Srinivasan (eds.), *Handbook of Development Economics*, Vol. 3. Elsevier Science B.V., Amsterdam.

Birdsall, N. 2006. "Rising Inequality in the New Global Economy," *International Journal of Development Issues* 5: 1–9.

Bisset, L., and J. Coussins 1982. *Badge of Poverty: A New Look at the Stigma Attached to Free School Meals*. London: Child Poverty Action Group.

Björklund, A., and M. Jäntti 2000. "Intergenerational Mobility of Socioeconomic Status in Comparative Perspective," *Nordic Journal of Political Economy* 26/1: 3–32.

Björklund, A., M. Jäntti, and J.E. Roemer 2012. "Equality of Opportunity and the Distribution of Long-Run Income in Sweden," *Social Choice and Welfare* 39: 675–696.

Blanchflower, D., and A. Oswald 2003. "Does Inequality Reduce Happiness? Evidence from the States of the USA from the 1970s to the 1990s" (unpublished manuscript, Warwick University).

Blanden, J., R. Haveman, T. Smeeding, and K. Wilson 2014. "Intergenerational Mobility in the United States and Great Britain: A Comparative Study of Parent–Child Pathways," *Review of Income and Wealth* 60: 425–449.

Bleaney, M.F. 1976. *Underconsumption Theories: A History and Critical Analysis*. New York: International Publishers.

Bordo, M., and C. Meissner 2012. "Does Inequality Lead to a Financial Crisis?" *Journal of International Money and Finance* 31: 2147–2161.

Borrowman, M., and S. Klasen 2017. Drivers of Gendered Sectoral and Occupational Segregation in Developing Countries. Courant Research Center Discussion Paper No. 222.

Bosmans, K., K. Decancq, and A. Decoster 2011. "The Evolution of Global Inequality: Absolute, Relative and Intermediate Views." Discussion Paper, Centre for Economic Studies, Catholic University, Leuven. Available at SSRN: http://ssrn.com/abstract=1806875 or http://dx.doi.org/10.2139/ssrn.1806875 (last accessed December 23, 2017).

Bosmans, K., K. Decancq, and E. Ooghe 2015. "What Do Normative Indices of Multidimensional Inequality Really Measure?" *Journal of Public Economics* 130: 1–120.

Bourguignon, F. 2003. "The Growth Elasticity of Poverty Reduction: Explaining Heterogeneity across Countries and Time Periods," in T. Eicher and S. Turnovsky (eds.), *Inequality and Growth: Theory and Policy Implications*, 1st edn. Cambridge, Massachusetts: MIT Press.

Bourguignon, F. 2012. *La mondialisation de l'inégalité*. Paris: Seuil et La République des Idées.

Bourguignon, F. 2015. *The Globalization of Inequality*. Princeton: Princeton University Press.

Bourguignon, F., and C. Morrisson 1990. "Income Distribution, Development and Foreign Trade," *European Economic Review* 34: 1113–1132.

Bourguignon, F. and C. Morrisson 2002. "Inequality among world citizens: 1820–1992," *American Economic Review* 92: 727–744.

Bowles, S. and A. Jayadev 2006. "Guard Labor," *Journal of Development Economics* 79: 328–348.

Bowles, S., H. Gintis, and M. Osbourne-Groves (eds.) 2005. *Unequal Chances: Family Background and Economic Success*. Princeton, NJ: Princeton University Press.

Boyce, C.J., G.D.A. Brown, and S.C. Moore 2010. "Money and Happiness: Rank of Income, Not Income, Affects Life Satisfaction," *Psychological Science* 21: 471–475.

Boyce, J.K., and L. Ndikumana 2012. "Capital Flight from Sub-Saharan African Countries: Updated Estimates, 1970–2010." Political Economy Research Institute Research Report, University of Massachusetts Amherst.

Breen, R. R. Luijkx, R. Müller, and R. Pollak 2010. "Long-Term Trends in Educational Inequality in Europe," *European Sociological Review* 26: 31–48.

Bresson, F. 2009. "On the Estimation of Growth and Inequality Elasticities of Poverty with Grouped Data," *Review of Income and Wealth* 55: 266–302.

Brown, G.K. 2010. "Inequality, Ethnicity and Violent Secessionism: A Mixed-Level and Survival Analysis Approach to Disaggregating the Study of Civil War." Centre for Research on Inequality, Human Security and Ethnicity, Oxford. Working Paper No. 80.

Bruckner, J. 2011. *Lectures on Urban Economics*. Cambridge, MA: MIT Press.

Bruno, M., and W. Easterly 1998. "Inflation Crises and Long Term Growth," *Journal of Monetary Economics* 41/1: 3–26.

Bueno de Mesquita, B. 1978. "Systemic Polarization and the Occurrence and Duration of War," *Journal of Conflict Resolution* 22/2: 241–267.

Buhmann, B., L. Rainwater, G. Schmaus, and T.M. Smeeding 1988. "Equivalence Scales, Well-being, Inequality, and Poverty: Sensitivity Estimates across Ten Countries Using the Luxembourg Income Study (LIS) Database," *Review of Income and Wealth* 34: 115–142.

Bullard, R. 1993. "Distributive Justice in the United States," *Yale Journal of International Law* 18: 319–335.

Burger, R., S. Klasen, and A. Zoch 2016. "Estimating Income Mobility when Income Is Measured with Error: The Case of South Africa." Economic Research Southern Africa Working Paper No. 607.

Burtless, G. 1999. "Effects of Growing Wage Disparities and Changing Family Composition on the U.S. Income Distribution," *European Economic Review* 43: 853–865.

Burtless, G. 2009. "Demographic Transformation and Economic Inequality," in W. Salverda, B. Nolan, and T.M. Smeeding (eds.), *The Oxford Handbook of Economic Inequality*. Oxford: Oxford University Press.

Calderón, C., and A. Chong 2009. "Labor Market Institutions and Income Inequality: An Empirical Exploration," *Public Choice* 138: 65–81.

3

Camerer, C., and R.H. Thaler 1995. "Anomalies: Ultimatums, Dictators and Manners," *Journal of Economic Perspectives* 9: 209–219.

Campos, R., G. Esquivel, and N. Lustig 2014. "The Rise and Fall of Income Inequality in Mexico, 1989–2010," in G.A. Cornia (ed.), *Falling Inequality in Latin America: Policy Changes and Lessons*, UNU-WIDER Studies in Development Economics. Oxford: Oxford University Press.

Cancian, M., and D. Reed 1998. "Assessing the Effects of Wives' Earnings on Family Income Inequality," *Review of Economics and Statistics* 80: 73–79.

Cancian, M., and D. Reed 1999. "The Impact of Wives' Earnings on Income Inequality: Issues and Estimates," *Demography* 36: 173–184.

Canning, D, S. Raja, and A. S. Yazbeck (eds.) 2015. *Africa's Demographic Transition: Dividend or Disaster?* Africa Development Forum. Washington DC: The World Bank.

Card, D., and J.E. DiNardo 2002. "Skill Biased Technological Change and Rising Wage Inequality: Some Problems and Puzzles," No. w8769. *National Bureau of Economic Research.*

Caskey, J.P. 1994. *Fringe Banking: Check-Cashing Outlets, Pawnshops, and the Poor.* New York: Russell Sage Foundation.

Castello-Climent, A., and R. Domenech 2014. *Capital and Income Inequality: Some Facts and Some Puzzles (Update of WP 12/28 published in October 2012)* (No. 1228). BBVA Bank, Economic Research Department.

Castells-Quintana, D., and V. Royuela Mora 2014. "Tracking Positive and Negative Effects of Inequality on Long-Run Growth," *IREA–Working Papers, IR14/001.*

Chakravarty, S. 2009. *Inequality, Polarization and Poverty: Advances in Distributional Analysis.* New York: Springer.

Chattopadhyay, R., and E. Duflo 2004. "Women as Policy Makers: Evidence from a Randomized Policy Experiment in India," *Econometrica* 72: 1409–1443.

Checchi, D. 2001. Education, Inequality, and Income Inequality. Sticerd Discussion Paper No. 52, London: LSE.

Checchi, D., and V. Peragine 2010. "Inequality of Opportunity in Italy," *Journal of Economic Inequality* 8: 429–450.

Checchi, D., V. Peragine, and L. Serlenga 2010. Fair and Unfair Income Inequalities in Europe. IZA Discussion Paper No. 5025.

Cherry, T.L., P. Frykblom, and J.F. Shogren 2002. "Hardnose the Dictator," *American Economic Review* 92: 1218–1221.

Chetty, R., D. Grusky, M. Hell, N. Hendren, R. Manduca, and J. Narang 2017. "The Fading American Dream: Trends in Absolute Income Mobility since 1940," *Science* 356: 398–406.

Chiappori, P.A., and C. Meghir 2015. "Intrahousehold Inequality," in A.B. Atkinson and F. Bourguignon (eds.), *Handbook of Income Distribution*, Vol. 2b. Amsterdam: Elsevier.

Chiavegatto Filho, A., and I. Kawachi 2015. "Income Inequality is Associated with Adolescent Fertility in Brazil: A Longitudinal Multilevel Analysis of 5565 Municipalities," *BMC Public Health* 15: 103–120.

Chiu, W.H., and P. Madden 1998. "Burglary and Income Inequality," *Journal of Public Economics* 69: 123–141.

Chong, A, M. Gradstein, and C. Calderon 2009. "Can Foreign Aid Reduce Income Inequality and Poverty?" *Public Choice* 140: 59–84.

Chotikapanich, D., W.E. Griffiths, D.S. Prasada Rao, and V. Valencia 2012. "Global Income Distributions and Inequality, 1993 and 2000: Incorporating Country-Level Inequality Modeled with Beta Distributions," *Review of Economics and Statistics* 94: 52–73.

Chotikapanich, D., R. Valenzuela, and D.P. Rao 1997. "Global and Regional Inequality in the Distribution of Income: Estimation with Limited and Incomplete Data," *Empirical Economics* 22: 533–546.

Cingano, F. 2014. Trends in Income Inequality and its Impact on Economic Growth. OECD Social, Employment and Migration Working Papers, No. 163, OECD Publishing. http://dx.doi.org/10.1787/5jxrjncwxv6j-en (last accessed December 23, 2017).

Clarke, G.R.G. 1995. "More Evidence on Income Distribution and Growth," *Journal of Development Economics* 47: 403–427.

Clarke, G.R.G., L.C. Xu, and H.F. Zou 2006. "Finance and Income Inequality: What Do the Data Tell Us?" *Southern Economic Journal* 72: 578–596.

Claus, I., J. Martinez-Vasquez, and V. Vulovic 2014. "Government Fiscal Policies and Redistribution in Asian Countries," in R. Kanbur, C. Rhee, and J. Zhuang (eds.), *Inequality in Asia and the Pacific: Trends, Drivers, and Policy Implications,* Asian Development Bank and Routledge.

Cogneau, D. and S. Mesplé-Somps 2008. "Inequality of Opportunity for Income in Five Countries of Africa," *Research on Economic Inequality* 16: 99–128.

Cogneau, D., T. Bossuroy, Ph. De Vreyer, C. Guénard, V. Hiller, P. Leite, S. Masplé-Somps, L. Pasquier-Doumer, and C. Torelli 2007. *"Inequalities and Equity in Africa,"* Agence Française de Développement, Paris.

Coleman, J. 1974. "Inequality, Sociology, and Moral Philosophy," *American Journal of Sociology,* 80: 739–764.

Colleran, H., G. Jasienska, I. Nenko, A. Galbarczyk, and R. Mace 2015. "Fertility Decline and the Changing Dynamics of Wealth, Status, and Inequality," *Proceedings of the Royal Society B* 282: 20150287.

Collier, P., and A. Hoeffler 2004. "Greed and Grievance in Civil War," *Oxford Economic Peace Research* 45: 143–62.

Collins, D., J. Morduch, S. Rutherford, and O. Ruthven 2009. *Portfolios of the Poor: How the World's Poor Live on $2 a Day.* Princeton, NJ: Princeton University Press.

Corak, M. 2013. "Income Inequality, Equality of Opportunity and Intergenerational Mobility," *Journal of Economic Perspectives* 27: 79–102.

Cordoba, J., X. Liu, and M. Ripoll 2016. "Fertility, Social Mobility and Long Run Inequality," *Journal of Monetary Economics* 77/C: 103–124.

Cornia, G.A. 2004. *Inequality, growth and Poverty in an Era of Liberalization and Globalization.* Oxford: Oxford University Press.

Cornia, G.A. (ed.) 2014a. *Falling Inequality in Latin America: Policy Changes and Lessons,* UNU-WIDER Studies in Development Economics. Oxford: Oxford University Press.

Cornia, G.A. 2014b. Income Inequality in Latin America: Recent Decline and Prospects for its Further Reduction. Number 149, July, CEPAL Working Papers Series *Macroeconomia del Desarrollo.*

Cornia, G.A. 2014c. "The New Structuralist Macroeconomics and Income Inequality," in G.A. Cornia and F. Stewart (eds.) *Towards Human Development: New Approaches to Macroeconomics and Inequality.* Oxford: Oxford University Press.

Cornia, G.A. 2015. "The Political Economy of Falling (& Now Rising) Inequality in Latin America, 2002–2013," Powerpoint presentation at the conference on Political and Economic Inequality: Concepts, Causes and Consequences, ETH, Zurich 29-1-2016, www.cis.ethz.ch/news-and-events/CISEvents/Workshops/inequalityworkshop/speakers0.html (last accessed December 23, 2017).

Cornia, G.A. 2016a. *An Econometric Investigation of the Causes of the Bifurcation of Within-Country Inequality Trends over 1991–2011 in Sub-Saharan Africa.* UNDP, Regional Bureau for Africa, Working Paper Series on Inequality N.4, New York.

Cornia, G.A. 2016b. "The Mortality Crisis in Transition Economies," *IZA World of Labor* 2016: 298.

Cornia, G.A. 2017. "Is Latin America's Recent Inequality Decline Permanent or Temporary?," *Development and Change,* forthcoming.

Cornia, G.A., and B. Martorano 2012. Development Policies and Income Inequality in Selected Developing Regions, 1980–2010. UNCTAD Discussion Paper 210.

Cornia, G.A., and B. Martorano 2016. *Building the IID-SSA Inequality Dataset and the Seven Sins of Inequality Measurement in Sub-Saharan Africa.* UNDP, Regional Bureau for Africa, Working Paper Series on Inequality N.2, New York.

Cornia, G.A., J.C. Gomez Sabaini, and B. Martorano 2014. "Tax Policy and Income Distribution During the Last Decade," in G.A. Cornia (ed.), *Falling Inequality in Latin America: Policy Changes and Lessons,* Oxford: Oxford University Press.

Cotula, L., C. Toulmin, and C. Hesse 2004. *Land Tenure and Administration in Africa: Lessons of Experience and Emerging Issues.* February 2004, International Institute for Environment and Development, London.

Cruces, G., C. Garcia Domench, and L. Gasparini 2014. "Inequality in Education: Evidence from Latin America," in G.A. Cornia (ed.), *Falling Inequality in Latin America: Policy Changes and Lessons.* Oxford: Oxford University Press.

Cruces, G., R. Perez-Truglia, and M. Tetaz 2013. "Biased Perceptions of Income Distribution and Preferences for Redistribution: Evidence from a Survey Experiment," *Journal of Public Economics* 9: 100–112.

Currie, J. 2006. "The Take-up of Social Benefits," in A. Auerbach, D. Card, and J.M. Quigley (eds.), *Public Policy and the Income Distribution,* New York: Russell Sage.

Dabla-Norris, E., and M. Gradstein 2004. The Distributional Bias of Public Education: Causes and Consequences. IMF Working Paper 04/214.

Dagum, C. 1990. "On the Relationship between Income Inequality Measures and Social Welfare Functions," *Journal of Econometrics* 43: 91–102.

Daly, M., C. Boyce, and A. Wood 2015. "A Social Rank Explanation of How Money Influences Health," *Health Psychology* 34: 222–230.

Dasgupta, S. 1975. "Caste Dominance and Agricultural Development in Village India," *Human Organization* 34: 400–403.

Datt, G., and M. Ravallion 2002. "Is India's Growth Leaving the Poor Behind?" *Journal of Economic Perspectives* 16: 89–108.

Datt, G., and M. Ravallion 2009. Has India's Economic Growth Become More Pro-Poor in the Wake of Economic Reforms? World Bank Policy Research Working Paper 5103.

Davidai, S., and T. Gilovich 2015. "Building a More Mobile America – One Income Quintile at a Time," *Perspectives on Psychological Science*, 10: 60–71.

Davies, J., A. Sandström, A. Shorrocks, and E. Wolff 2008. *The World Distribution of Household Wealth*. Helsinki: UNU Wider.

Davies, J.B., and A.F. Shorrocks 2000. "The Distribution of Wealth," in A.B. Atkinson and F. Bourguignon (eds.), *Handbook of Income Distribution Vol 1*. Amsterdam: Elsevier.

Davis, M. 1999. *The Planet of Slums*, London: Verso.

De, R., and C. Becker 2015. The Foreign Aid Effectiveness Debate: Evidence from Malawi. AidData Working Paper 6.

Deaton, A. 2003. *Health, Income and Inequality*. NBER Research Summary.

Deaton, A. 2005. "Measuring Poverty in a Growing World (or Measuring Growth in a Poor World)," *The Review of Economics and Statistics* 87: 1–19.

Deaton, A., and D. Kahnemann 2010. "High Income Improves Evaluation of Life but Not Emotional Well-being," *PNAS* 107: 16489–16493.

Deaton, A., and S. Zaidi 2002. Guidelines for Creating Consumption Aggregates for Welfare Analysis. Living Standards Measurement Study Working Paper No. 135.

de Barros, R., F.H.G. Ferreira, J.R.M. Vega, and J. Chanduvi 2009. *Measuring Inequality of Opportunities in Latin America and the Caribbean*. Washington DC: The World Bank.

de la Croix, D., and M. Doepke 2003. "Inequality and Growth: Why Differential Fertility Matters," *American Economic Review*, 93: 1091–1113.

de la Motte, J., and Paquet, G. (eds.) 1996. *Evolutionary Economics and the New International Political Economy*. London: Pinter.

de la Torre, A., E. Levy-Yeyati, and S. Pienknagura 2013. *Latin America and the Caribbean as Tailwinds Recede: In Search of Higher Growth*. Semiannual Report, Regional Chief Economist Office, Latin America and the Caribbean, The World Bank.

Deere, C.D., L. Boakye-Yiadom, C. Doss, A.D. Oduro, et al. 2013. Women's Land Ownership and Participation in Agricultural Decision-Making: Evidence from Ecuador, Ghana and Karnataka, India. The Gender Asset Gap Project, Research Brief Series: No. 2.

Deininger, K., and P. Olinto 2000. Why Liberalization Alone Has Not Improved Agricultural Productivity in Zambia: The Role of Asset Ownership and Working Capital Constraints. Policy research working paper, World Bank.

Deininger, K., and L. Squire 1996. "A New Dataset Measuring Income Inequality," *The World Bank Economic Review*, 10: 565–591.

Deininger, K., and L. Squire 1998. "New Ways of Looking at Old Issues: Inequality and Growth," *Journal of Development Economics* 57: 259–287.

de Rijcke, S., and A. Rushforth 2015. Researcher Meets Indicator: Effects of Evaluative Metrics on Research Groups. Paper presented at the Atlanta Conference on Science and Innovation Policy, September 2015.

Deutsch, M. 1975. "Equity, Equality, and Need: What Determines Which Value Will Be Used as the Basis of Distributive Justice?" *Journal of Social Issues* 31: 137–149.

Diamond, P. 1998. "Optimal Income Taxation: An Example with a U-Shaped Pattern of Optimal Marginal Tax Rates," *American Economic Review* 88: 83–95.

Diamond, P., and E. Saez 2011. "The Case for a Progressive Tax: From Basic Research to Policy Recommendations." CESifo Working Paper No. 3548.

Dikhanov, Y., and M. Ward 2002. "Evolution of the Global Distribution of Income 1970–99," 53rd Session of the International Statistical Institute, Seoul, Republic of Korea, pp. 22–29.

Dirks, N.B. 2001. *Castes of Mind. Colonialism and the Making of British India*, Princeton, NJ: Princeton University Press.

Docquier, F., and I. Rapoport 2003. Remittances and Inequality: A Dynamic Migration Model. IZA Working Paper 808. June 2003.

Doerrenberg, P., and Peichl, A. 2014. "The Impact of Redistributive Policies on Inequality in OECD Countries," *Applied Economics* 46/17: 2066–2086.

Dowrick, S., and M. Akmal 2005. "Contradictory Trends in Global Income Inequality: A Tale of Two Biases," *Review of Income and Wealth* 51: 201–229.

Dreher, A., P. Nunnenkamp, and R. Thiele 2008. "Does Aid for Education Educate Children: Evidence from Panel Data," *World Bank Economic Review* 22: 291–314.

Drèze, J., and A.K. Sen 1989. *Hunger and Public Action*, Oxford: Clarendon Press.

Drèze, J., and A.K. Sen 1995. *India: Economic Development and Social Opportunity*, New York: Clarendon Press.

Duclos, J-Y., J-M. Esteban, and D. Ray 2004. "Polarization: Concepts, Measurement and Estimation," *Econometrica* 72: 1737–1772.

Duflo, E. 2012. "Women Empowerment and Economic Development," *Journal of Economic Literature* 50: 1051–1079.

Dunbar, G., A. Lewbel, and K. Pendakur 2013. "Children's Resources in Collective Households: Identification, Estimation, and an Application to Child Poverty in Malawi," *American Economic Review* 103: 438–471.

Easterly, W. 2001. "The Middle Class Consensus and Economic Development," *Journal of Economic Growth* 6: 317–335.

Easterly, W. 2007. "Inequality Does Cause Underdevelopment: Insights from a New Instrument," *Journal of Development Economics* 84: 755–776.

ECLAC (Economic Commission for Latin America and the Caribbean) 2014. *Social Panorama of Latin America 2013*, Santiago.

ECLAC (Economic Commission for Latin America and the Caribbean) 2015. *Inclusive Social Development. The Next Generation of Policies for Overcoming Poverty and Reducing Inequality in Latin America and the Caribbean*, Santiago.

Edin, K., and L. Lein 1997. *Making Ends Meet: How Single Mothers Survive Welfare and Low-Wage Work*, Russell Sage Foundation.

Edin, K., and H.L. Shaefer 2015. *$2.00 a Day: Living on Almost Nothing in America*. New York: Houghton Mifflin Harcourt.

Eligon, J. 2016. "A Question of Environmental Racism in Flint," *New York Times*, Jan. 21.

Elster, J. 1985. *Sour Grapes: Studies in the Subversion of Rationality*. Cambridge: Cambridge University Press.

Engelhardt, C., and A. Wagener 2014. Biased Perceptions of Income Inequality and Redistribution. Hannover Discussion Paper No. 526.

Engerman, S.L., and K.L. Sokoloff 2002. Factor Endowments, Inequality, and Paths of Development among New World Economics. *National Bureau of Economic Research*, No. w9259.

Engerman, S.L., and K.L. Sokoloff 2005. Colonialism, Inequality and Long Run Paths of Development. Working Paper 11057, NBER, Cambridge, MA.

Ehrhart, C. 2009. The Effects of Inequality on Growth: A Survey of the Theoretical and Empirical Literature. ECINEQ Working Paper 107.

Erten, B., and J.A. Ocampo 2012. Super-Cycles of Commodity Prices since the Mid-Nineteenth Century. DESA Working Paper No. 110ST/ESA/2012/DWP/110, February 2012.

Esquivel, G., N. Lustig, and J. Scott 2010. "Mexico: A Decade of Falling Inequality: Market Forces or State Action?" in L.F. Lopez-Calva and N. Lustig (eds.), *Declining Inequality in Latin America: A Decade of Progress?* Brookings Institution Press and UNDP.

Esteban, J., and D. Ray 1993. "On the Measurement of Polarization," *Econometrica* 62: 819–851.

Esteban J., and D. Ray 2006. "Inequality, Lobbying, and Resource Allocation," *American Economic Review* 96: 257–279.

Esteban, J., and D. Ray 2011. "Linking Conflict to Inequality and Polarization," *American Economic Review* 101: 1345–1374.

Esteva-Volart, B. 2009. *Gender Discrimination and Growth: Theory and Evidence from India*. Mimeographed, University of York, Canada.

Fan, S., R. Kanbur, and X. Zhang 2011. "China's Regional Disparities: Experience and Policy," *Review of Development Finance* 1: 47–56.

Fearon, J.D., and D.D. Laitin 2003. "Ethnicity, Insurgency, and Civil War," *American Political Science Review* 97: 75–90.

Fehr, E., and U. Fischbacher 2004. "Third-Party Punishment and Social Norms," *Evolution and Human Behavior* 25: 63–87.

Fehr, E., and K.M. Schmidt 1999. "A Theory of Fairness, Competition, and Cooperation," *Quarterly Journal of Economics* 114: 817–868.

Fehr, E., H. Bernhard, and B. Rockenbach 2008. "Egalitarianism in Young Children," *Nature* 454: 1079–1083.

Ferreira, F.H.G., and J. Gignoux 2011a. The Measurement of Educational Inequality: Achievement and Opportunity. Discussion Paper No. 6161, Bonn: Institute for the Study of Labor.

Ferreira, F.H.G., and J. Gignoux 2011b. "The Measurement of Inequality of Opportunity: Theory and an Application to Latin America," *Review of Income and Wealth* 57: 622–657.

Ferreira, F.H.G., and J. Gignoux 2014. "The Measurement of Educational Inequality: Achievement and Opportunity," *The World Bank Economic Review* 28: 210–246.

Ferreira, F.H.G., and A. Lugo 2012. "Multidimensional Poverty Analysis: Looking for a Middle Ground," *World Bank Research Observer* 28: 220–235.

Ferreira, F.H.G., S. Firpo, and J. Messina 2014. A More Level Playing Field? Explaining the Decline in Earnings Inequality in Brazil, 1995–2012. IRIBA Working Paper: 12, The University of Manchester.

Ferreira, F.H.G., J. Messina, J. Rigolini, L.F. López-Calva, M.A. Lugo, and R. Vakis 2013. *Economic Mobility and the Rise of the Latin American Middle Class*. Latin America and Caribbean Studies; Washington, DC: World Bank.

Ferrer-i-Carbonell, A., and X. Ramos 2012. Inequality and Happiness: A Survey. GINI Discussion Papers 38, AIAS, Amsterdam Institute for Advanced Labour Studies.

Ferroni, M., and J.M. Payne 2007. "Development under Conditions of Inequality and Distrust: Social Cohesion in Latin America. IFPRI Discussion Paper, 777.

Ferroni, M., M. Mateo, and M. Payne 2008. Development under Conditions of Inequality and Distrust – Social Cohesion in Latin America. IFPRI Discussion Paper, 00777. Washington DC: IFPRI.

Fiske, S.T. 2011. *Envy Up, Scorn Down: How Status Divides Us*. New York: Russell Sage Foundation.

Fiszbein, A., and N. Schady 2009. *Conditional Cash Transfers: Reducing Present and Future Poverty*. World Bank: Washington, DC.

Flechtner, S. 2014. "Aspiration Traps: When Poverty Stifles Hope," *World Bank Inequality in Focus* 2/4: 1–43.

Flechtner, S. 2016. *Aspirations and the Persistence of Poverty and Inequalities*, Ph.D. dissertation, Europa-Universität Flensburg Internationales Institut für Management und ökonomische Bildung.

Flechtner, S. 2017. "Inequality, (Unmet) Aspirations and Social Protest," in H. Hanappi and S. Katsikides (eds.), *Evolutionary Political Economy in Action. A Cyprus Symposium, Part 1: Political Economy in Action*. Abingdon/New York: Routledge.

Foellmi, R., and J. Zweimüller 2006. "Income Distribution and Demand-Induced Innovations," *Review of Economic Studies* 73: 941–960.

Foguel, M.N., and F.A. Veloso 2014. "Inequality of Opportunity in Daycare and Preschool Services in Brazil," *Journal of Economic Inequality* 12: 191–220.

Fong, C. 2001. "Social Preferences, Self-Interest, and the Demand for Redistribution," *Journal of Public Economics* 82: 225–246.

Forbes, K.J. 2000. "A Reassessment of the Relationship between Inequality and Growth," *American Economic Review* 90: 869–887.

Förster, M. 2016. Rising Inequalities in OECD Countries: Trends, Consequences, Drivers, and Policies how to Curb Them. Paper presented at 2016 APPAM Conference, London.

Förster, M., and I. Tóth 2015. "Cross-Country Evidence of the Multiple Causes of Inequality in the OECD Area," in F. Bourguignon and A.B. Atkinson (eds.), *Handbook of Income Distribution*. New York: Elsevier.

Foster, J.E., and M.C. Wolfson 1994. Polarization and the Decline of the Middle Class: Canada and the US. Working Paper No. 31, Oxford Poverty & Human Development Initiative.

Foster, J.E., L.F. López-Calva, and M. Székely 2005. "Measuring the Distribution of Human Development: Methodology and an Application to Mexico," *Journal of Human Development* 6: 5–29.

Fosu, A.K. 2009. "Inequality and the Impact of Growth on Poverty: Comparative Evidence for Sub-Saharan Africa," *Journal of Development Studies* 45: 726–745.

Fosu, A.K. 2010. "Inequality, Income, and Poverty: Comparative Global Evidence," *Social Science Quarterly* 91: 1432–1446.

Fosu, A.K. 2011. Growth, Inequality, and Poverty Reduction in Developing Countries: Recent Global Evidence. CSAE Working Paper WPS/2011-07, Centre for the Study of African Economies, Department of Economics, University of Oxford.

Fosu, A.K. 2015a. "Growth, Inequality and Poverty in Sub-Saharan Africa: Recent Progress in a Global Context," *Oxford Development Studies* 43: 44–59.

Fosu, A.K. 2015b. Growth and Poverty Reduction in Africa: The Context and Evidence. Background Paper submitted to the African Development Bank for the African Development Report 2015 on "Growth-Poverty Nexus: Overcoming Barriers to Sustainable Development."

Frank, R.H. 1985. *Choosing the Right Pond: Human Behavior and the Quest for Status*, Oxford: Oxford University Press.

Frankema, E. 2009. "The Colonial Roots of Land Inequality: Geography, Factor Endowments, or Institutions?," *The Economic History Review* 63: 418–451.

Freeman, C. 1992. "Science and Economy at the National Level," Chapter prepared for the OECD Experimental Working Session on Science Policy, reprinted in C. Freeman (ed.) *The Economics of Hope*. London: Pinter Publishers.

Fuest, C., J. Niehues, and A. Peichl 2010. "The Redistributive Effects of Tax Benefit Systems in the Enlarged EU," *Public Finance Review* 38: 473–500.

Gaddis, I., and S. Klasen 2014. "Economic Development, Structural Change, and Women's Labor Force Participation Rate: A Re-examination of the Feminization U-Hypothesis," *Journal of Population Economics* 27: 639–681.

Galor, O., and D. Weil 1996. "The Gender Gap, Fertility, and Growth," *American Economic Review* 86: 374–387.

Galor, O., and J. Zeira 1993. "Income Distribution and Macroeconomics," *Review of Economic Studies* 60: 35–52.

Gasparini, L., and G. Cruces 2010. "A Distribution in Motion: The Case of Argentina," in L.F. Lopez-Calva and N. Lustig (eds.), *Declining Inequality in Latin America: A Decade of Progress?* Brookings Institution Press and UNDP.

Gasparini, L., and N. Lustig 2011. "The Rise and Fall of Income Inequality in Latin America," in J.A. Ocampo and J. Ros (eds.), *Oxford Handbook of Latin American Economics*. Oxford: Oxford University Press.

Gasparini, L., G. Cruces, L. Tornarolli, S. Galiani, and P. Acosta 2011. Educational Upgrading and Returns to Skills in Latin America. Evidence from a Supply-Demand Framework, 1990–2010. Policy Research Working Paper 5921, The World Bank.

Ghatak, M., and N.N.H. Jiang 2002. "A Simple Model of Inequality, Occupational Choice, and Development," *Journal of Development Economics* 69: 205–226.

Ghosh, J. 2015. "Growth, Industrialization and Inequality in India," *Journal of the Asia Pacific Economy*, 20: 42–56.

Glaeser, E., J. Scheinkman, and A. Shleifer 2003. "The Injustice of Inequality," *Journal of Monetary Economics* 50: 199–222.

Goesling, B., and G. Firebaugh 2004. "The Trend in International Health Inequality," *Population and Development Review* 30: 131–146.

Goldstein, M., and C. Udry 2008. "The Profits of Power: Land Rights and Agricultural Investment in Ghana," *Journal of Political Economy* 116: 982–1022.

Goos, M., A. Manning, and A. Salomons 2009. "Job Polarization in Europe," *American Economic Review* 99: 58–63.

Gottschalk, P., and S. Danziger 2005. "Inequality of Wage Rates, Earnings, and Family Income in the United States, 1975–2002," *Review of Income and Wealth* 51: 231–254.

Griffin, K., A.R. Khan, and A. Ickowitz 2002. "Poverty and the Distribution of Land," *Journal of Agrarian Change* 2: 279–330.

Grimm, M. 2007. "Removing the Anonymity Axiom in the Measurement of Pro-Poor Growth," *Journal of Economic Inequality* 5: 179–197.

Grimm, M., K. Harttgen, and M. Misselhorn 2008. "Human Development Index by Income Groups," *World Development* 12: 2527–2546.

Grimm, M., K. Harttgen, S. Klasen, M. Misselhorn, T. Munzi, and T. Smeeding 2010. "Inequality in Human Development: An Empirical Assessment of 32 Countries," *Social Indicators Research* 97: 191–211.

Grosse, M., K. Harttgen, and S. Klasen 2008. "Measuring Pro-Poor Growth using Non-Income Indicators," *World Development* 36: 1021–1047.

Grossmann, V. 2008. "Risky Human Capital Investment, Income Distribution, and Macroeconomic Dynamics," *Journal of Macroeconomics* 30: 19–42.

Gruen, C., and S. Klasen 2001. "Growth, Income Distribution and Well-being in Transition Countries," *Economics of Transition* 9: 359–394.

Gruen, C., and S. Klasen 2003. "Growth, Inequality, and Well-being: Intertemporal and Global Comparisons," *CESIfo Economic Studies* 49: 617–659.

Gruen, C., and S. Klasen 2008. "Growth, Inequality, and Welfare: Comparisons across Space and Time," *Oxford Economic Papers* 60: 212–236.

Gruen, C., and S. Klasen 2012. "Has Transition Improved Well-being?" *Economic Systems* 36, 11–30.

Gruen, C., and S. Klasen 2013. "Income, Inequality, and Subjective Well-being: An International and Intertemporal Perspective Using Panel Data," *Jahrbuch für Wirtschaftsgeschichte/ Economic History Yearbook* 2013/1: 15–36.

Gummerum, M., Y. Hanoch, M. Keller, K. Parsons, and A. Hummel 2010. "Preschoolers' Allocations in the Dictator Game: The Role of Moral Emotions," *Journal of Economic Psychology* 31: 25–34.

Gupta, D. 2000. *Interrogating Caste: Understanding Hierarchy and difference in Indian Society*. Penguin Books India.

Gurr, T.R., and W.H. Moore 1997. "Ethno-political Rebellion: A Cross-Sectional Analysis of the 1980s with Risk Assessment for the 1990s," *American Journal of Political Science* 41: 1079–1103.

Gwatkin, D, S. Rutstein, K. Jonhson, E. Suliman, A Wagstaff, and A. Amouzou 2007. *Socio-economic Differences in Health, Nutrition and Population within Developing Countries: An Overview*. Country Report on PHN and Poverty. Washington, DC: The World Bank. http://siteresources.worldbank.org/INTPAH/Resources/IndicatorsOverview.pdf (last accessed December 23, 2017).

Haddad, L., and R. Kanbur 1990. "How Serious Is the Neglect of Intra-Household Inequality?," *Economic Journal* 100: 866–881.

Hailu, D., and R. Tsukada 2012. Is the Distribution of Foreign Aid MDG-Sensitive? DESA Working Paper No. 111, February 2012, United Nations, New York.

Hall, C.C., J. Zhao, and E. Shafir 2013. "Self-Affirmation among the Poor: Cognitive and Behavioral Implications," *Psychological Science* 25: 619–625.

Hallegatte, S., M. Bangalore, L. Bonzanigo, M. Fay, T. Kane, U. Narloch, J. Rozenberg, D. Treguer, and A. Vogt-Schilb 2016. *Shock Waves: Managing the Impacts of Climate Change on Poverty. Climate Change and Development*. Washington, DC: World Bank.

Harttgen, K., and S. Klasen 2012. "A Household-based Human Development Index," *World Development* 40: 878–899.

Haushofer, J., and E. Fehr 2014. "On the Psychology of Poverty," *Science* 344: 862–867.

Henrich, J., R. McElreath, A. Barr, J. Ensminger, C. Barrett, A. Bolyanatz, J.C. Cardenas, M. Gurven, E. Gwako, N. Henrich, C. Lesorogol, F. Marlowe, D. Tracer, and J. Ziker 2006. "Costly Punishment across Human Societies," *Science* 312: 1767–1770.

Herzer, D., and P. Nunnenkamp 2012. "The Effect of Foreign Aid on Income Inequality: Evidence from Panel Cointegration," *Structural Change and Economic Dynamics* 23: 245–255.

Herzer, D., and S. Vollmer 2012. "Inequality and Growth: Evidence from Panel Cointegration," *The Journal of Economic Inequality* 10: 489–503.

Herzer, D., and S. Vollmer 2013. "Rising Top Incomes Do Not Raise the Tide," *Journal of Policy Modeling* 35: 504–519.

Hess, D. 2007. *Alternative Pathways in Science and Industry. Activism, Innovation, and the Environment in an Era of Globalization*. Cambridge: The MIT Press.

Hicks, D. 2004. "The Four Literatures of Social Science," in H. Moed, W. Glänzel, and U. Schmoch (eds.), *Handbook of Quantitative Science and Technology Research*. Dordrecht: Kluwer Academic Publishers.

Hirano, Y., and S. Otsubo 2014. Aid is Good for the Poor. World Bank Policy Research Working Paper 6998.

Hoeffler, A., and V. Outram 2011. "Need, Merit, or Self-Interest: What Determines the Allocation of Aid," *Review of Development Economics* 15: 237–250.

Hoff, K., and P. Pandey 2012. *Making Up People – the Effect of Identity on Preferences and Performance in a Modernizing Society*. Policy Research Working Paper No. WPS 6223. Washington, DC: World Bank.

Hoffman, E., K. McCabe, K. Shachat, and V. Smith (1994), "Preferences, Property Rights, and Anonymity in Bargaining Games." *Games and Economic Behavior* 7: 346–380.

Honohan, P. 2004. Financial Sector Policy and the Poor. World Bank Working Paper 43.

Honohan, P. 2005. Banking Sector Crises and Inequality. *Policy Research Working Paper Series 3659*, The World Bank.

Horan, P.M., and P.L. Austin 1974. "The Social Bases of Welfare Stigma," *Social Problems* 21: 648–657.

Hufe, P., and A. Peichl 2016. Beyond Equal Rights: Equality of Opportunity in Political Participation. Mimeo.

Huntington, S. 1968. *Political Order in Changing Societies*. New Haven, CT: Yale University Press.

ILO 2014. *World Social Protection Report 2014–5*. Geneva: ILO.

International Monetary Fund (IMF) 2005. *World Economic Outlook*. Washington, DC: IMF.

International Monetary Fund (IMF) 2007. *World Economic Outlook*. Washington, DC: IMF.

International Monetary Fund (IMF) 2014. *Fiscal Policy and Income Inequality*. IMF Policy Paper, Washington, DC.

Immervoll, H., and L. Richardson 2011. Redistribution Policy and Inequality Reduction in OECD Countries: What Has Changed in Two Decades? LIS Working Paper No. 571.

Jayadev, A., R. Lahoti, and S.G. Reddy 2015. Who Got What, Then and Now? A Fifty Year Overview from the Global Consumption and Income Project. https://papers.ssrn.com/sol3/papers.cfm?abstract_id=2602268 (last accessed December 23, 2017).

Jayadev, A., S. Motiram, and V. Vakulabharanam 2007. "Patterns of Wealth Disparities in India During the Era of Liberalization," *Economic and Political Weekly* 42: 3853–3863.

Jenkins, S.P. 1995. "Accounting for Inequality Trends: Decomposition Analysis for the UK, 1971–86," *Economica* 62: 29–63.

Jenkins, S.P. 1997. "Trends in Real Income in Britain: A Microeconomic Analysis," *Empirical Economics* 22: 483–500.

Jenkins, S.P. 2015. "World Income Inequality Databases: An Assessment of WIID and SWIID," in F. Ferreira and N. Lustig (eds.), *Special Issue, Appraising Cross-National Income Inequality Databases, Journal of Economic Inequality* 13: 629–671.

Joerg, B., M.D.E. Marco, R. Auke, and T. Marcel (eds.) 2014. *How Was Life? Global Well-being since 1820: Global Well-being since 1820*. OECD Publishing.

Johnson, T., C.T. Dawes, J.H. Fowler, R. McElreath, and O. Smirnov 2009. "The Role of Egalitarian Motives in Altruistic Punishment," *Economics Letters* 102: 192–194.

Jost, J.T., and M.R. Banaji 1994. "The Role of Stereotyping in System Justification and the Production of False Consciousness," *British Journal of Social Psychology* 33: 1–27.

Josten, S.D. 2003. "Inequality, Crime and Economic Growth. A Classical Argument for Distributional Equality," *International Tax and Public Finance* 10: 435–452.

Kaldor, N. 1955. "Alternative Theories of Distribution," *Review of Economic Studies* 23: 83–100.

Kalmijn, W., and R.E. Veenhoven 2005. "Measuring Inequality of Happiness in Nations: In Search for Proper Statistics," *Journal of Happiness Studies* 6: 357–396.

Kalwij, A., and A. Verschoor 2007. "Not by Growth Alone: The Role of the Distribution of Income in Regional Diversity in Poverty Reduction," *European Economic Review* 51: 805–829.

Kanbur, R., C. Rhee, and J. Zhuong 2014. *Inequality in Asia and the Pacific: Trends, Drivers and Policy Implications*, Co-published by the Asian Development Bank and Routledge.

Kanbur, R., and T. Venables 2005. *Spatial Inequality and Development*, Oxford: Oxford University Press.

Kanbur, R., and A. Wagstaff 2014. How Useful Is Inequality of Opportunity as a Policy Construct? Research Working Paper WPS6980, World Bank.

Karter, A.J., M.M. Parker, H.H. Moffet, A.T. Ahmed, A. Ferrara, J.Y. Liu, and J.V. Selby 2004. "Missed Appointments and Poor Glycemic Control: An Opportunity to Identify High-Risk Diabetic Patients," *Medical Care* 42: 110–115.

Katz, S.J., and T.P. Hofer 1994. "Socioeconomic Disparities in Preventive Care Persist despite Universal Coverage: Breast and Cervical Cancer Screening in Ontario and the United States," *Jama* 272: 530–534.

Keefer, P., and S. Knack 2002. "Polarization, Politics and Property Rights: Links between Inequality and Growth," *Public Choice* 111: 127–154.

Keifman, S., and R. Maurizio 2014. "Changes in Labour Market Conditions and Policies, and Their Impact on Wage Inequality During the Last Decade," in G.A. Cornia (ed.), *Falling Inequality in Latin America: Policy Changes and Lessons*, Oxford: Oxford University Press.

Kerbo, H.R. 1976. "The Stigma of Welfare and a Passive Poor," *Sociology & Social Research* 60: 173–187.

Kiatpongsan, S., and M.I. Norton 2014. "How Much (More) Should CEOs Make? A Universal Desire for More Equal Pay," *Perspectives on Psychological Science* 9: 587–593.

King, E., S. Klasen, and M. Porter 2009. "Women and Development," in B. Lomborg (ed.), *Global Crises, Global Solutions*, 2nd edn. Cambridge: Cambridge University Press.

Kissane, R.J. 2003. "What's Need Got to Do With It? Barriers to Use of Nonprofit Social Services," *Journal of Sociology & Social Welfare* 30: 127–148.

Klasen S. 2002. "Low Schooling for Girls, Slower Growth for All? Cross-Country Evidence on the Effect of Gender Inequality in Education on Economic Development," *World Bank Economic Review* 16: 345–373.

Klasen S. 2003. "Malnourished and Surviving in South Asia, Better Nourished and Dying Young in Africa: What Can Explain this Puzzle?," in FAO (eds.), *Measurement and Assessment of Food Deprivation and Undernutrition.* Rome: FAO.

Klasen, S. 2004. "In Search of the Holy Grail: How to Achieve Pro-Poor Growth?" in B. Tungodden, N. Stern, and I. Kolstad (eds.), *Toward Pro Poor Policies-Aid, Institutions, and Globalization.* New York: Oxford University Press.

Klasen, S. 2007. "Gender-Related Indicators of Well-being," in M. McGillivray (ed.), *Human Well-Being: Concept and Measurement.* Basingstoke: Palgrave Macmillan.

Klasen, S. 2008a. "Economic Growth and Poverty Reduction: Measurement Issues in Income and Non-Income Dimensions," *World Development* 36: 420–445.

Klasen, S. 2008b. "The Efficiency of Equity," *Review of Political Economy* 20: 257–274.

Klasen, S. 2016. Gender, Institutions and Economic Development. Courant Research Center Discussion Paper No. 211.

Klasen, S., and R. Lahoti 2016. How Serious Is the Neglect of Intra-Household Inequality in Multi-dimensional Poverty Indices? Courant Research Center Discussion Paper.

Klasen, S., and F. Lamanna 2009. "The Impact of Gender Bias in Education and Employment on Economic Growth: New Evidence for a Panel of Countries," *Feminist Economics* 15: 91–132.

Klasen, S., and S. Lange 2016. How Narrowly Should Anti-poverty Programs Be Targeted? Courant Research Center: Poverty, Equity and Growth – Discussion Paper No 213.

Klasen, S., and M. Misselhorn 2008. "Determinants of the Growth Semi-Elasticity of Poverty Reduction. Ibero America Institute for Econ. Research (IAI) Discussion Papers 176, Ibero-America Institute for Economic Research.

Klasen, S., and J. Pieters 2015. "What Explains the Stagnation of Female Labor Force Participation in Urban India?" *World Bank Economic Review* 29: 449–478.

Klasen, S., and C. Wink 2003. "Missing Women: Revisiting the Debate," *Feminist Economics* 9: 263–299.

Klasen, S., T. Krivobokova, F. Greb, R. Lahoti, S. Hidayat Pasaribu, and M. Wiesenfarth 2016. "International Income Poverty Measurement: Which Way Now?" *Journal of Economic Inequality* 14: 199–225.

Klasen, S., N. Scholl, R. Lahoti, S. Ochmann, and S. Vollmer 2016. Inequality-Worldwide Trends and Current Debates. Courant Research Centre: Poverty, Equity and Growth-Discussion Papers 209.

Kluegel, J.R., and E.R. Smith 1986. *Beliefs about Inequality: Americans' Views of What Is and What Ought to Be.* Hawthorne, NY: Aldine de Gruyter.

Knowles, S. 2005. "Inequality and Economic Growth: The Empirical Relationship Reconsidered in the Light of Comparable Data," *Journal of Development Studies* 41: 135–159.

Knowles, S., P.K. Lorgelly, and P.D. Owen 2002. "Are Educational Gender Gaps a Brake on Economic Development? Some Cross-Country Empirical Evidence," *Oxford Economic Papers* 54: 118–149.

Kogut, T. 2011. "Someone to Blame: When Identifying a Victim Decreases Helping," *Journal of Experimental Social Psychology* 47: 748–755.

Kolm, S.C. 1976a. "Unequal Inequalities I," *Journal of Economic Theory* 12: 416–442.

Kolm, S.C. 1976b. "Unequal Inequalities II," *Journal of Economic Theory* 13: 82–111.

Kornai, J. 1992. *The Socialist System.* Cambridge, MA: Harvard University Press.

Koujianou-Goldberg, P., and N. Pavcnik 2007. *Distributional Effects of Globalization in Developing Countries.* NBER Working Paper 12885. Cambridge, MA: National Bureau of Economic Research.

Kremer, M., and D.L. Chen 2002. "Income Distribution Dynamics with Endogenous Fertility," *Journal of Economic Growth* 7: 227–258.

Krueger, A. 2012. The Rise and Consequences of Inequality. Presentation made to the Center for American Progress, January 12. www.americanprogress.org/events/2012/01/12/17181/the-rise-and-consequences-of-inequality (last accessed December 23, 2017).

Kumhof, M., and R. Rancière 2011. Inequality, Leverage and Crises. IMF Working Paper 10/268.

Lagerlöf, N. 2003. "Gender Equality and Long-Run Growth," *Journal of Economic Growth* 8: 403–426.

Lakner, C., and B. Milanovic 2016. "Global Income Distribution: From the Fall of the Berlin Wall to the Great Recession," *World Bank Economic Review* 30: 203–232.

Lam, D. 1986. "The Dynamics of Population Growth, Differential Fertility, and Inequality," *American Economic Review* 76: 1103–1116.

Langa, M., and J. Sriram 2017. "Farmers' Protest: Fault Lines in the Fields," *The Hindu*, 10.06.2017. www.thehindu.com/news/national/other-states/fault-lines-in-the-fields/article18951520.ece (last accessed December 23, 2017).

Lanjouw, P., and M. Ravallion 1995. "Poverty and Household Size," *Economic Journal.* 105/433: 1415–1434.

Lee, C.I., and G. Solon 2009. "Trends in Intergenerational Income Mobility," *Review of Economics and Statistics* 91: 766–772.

Lee, J.S., and N.K. Bowen 2006. "Parent Involvement, Cultural Capital, and the Achievement Gap among Elementary School Children," *American Educational Research Journal* 43: 193–218.

Li, H., and H. Zou 1998. "Income Inequality Is Not Harmful for Growth: Theory and Evidence," *Review of Development Economics* 2: 318–334.

Li Shi 2015. "The Latest Changes in Income Inequality in China." Video presentation made at UNU-WIDER 2015 Annual Development Conference, September 17, 2015, Helsinki. www.wider.unu.edu/video/trends-and-prospects-global-inequality (last accessed January 27, 2018).

Lindert, P.H. 2004. *Growing Public: Social Spending and Economic Growth since the Eighteenth Century, Volume I: The Story.* New York: Cambridge University Press.

Lindert, P.H., and J.G. Williamson 2001. *Globalization and Inequality: A Long History.* World Bank.

Liska, A.E., and B.D. Warner 1991. "Functions of Crime: A Paradoxical Process," *American Journal of Sociology*, 96: 1441–1463.

Loewenstein, G.F., L. Thompson, and M.H. Bazerman 1989. "Social Utility and Decision Making in Interpersonal Contexts," *Journal of Personality and Social psychology* 57: 426–441.

Lohmann, S. 2015. "Information Technologies and Subjective Well-being: Does the Internet Raise Material Aspirations?" *Oxford Economic Papers* 67: 740–59.

López-Calva, L.F., and N. Lustig (eds.) 2010. *Declining Inequality in Latin America: A Decade of Progress?* Brookings Institution Press and UNDP.

Luck S.J., and E.K. Vogel 1997. "The Capacity of Visual Working Memory for Features and Conjunctions," *Nature* 390: 279–281.

Lustig, N. 2000. "Crises and the Poor: Socially Responsible Macroeconomics," *Economía, The Journal of the Latin American and Caribbean Economic Association* 1/1: 1–45.

Lustig, N. 2016a. The Sustainable Development Goals, Domestic Resource Mobilization and the Poor. Background Document for WDR 2017.

Lustig, N. 2016b. "Fiscal Policy, Income Redistribution and Poverty Reduction in Low and Middle Income Countries," in N. Lustig (ed.), *Commitment to Equity Handbook: A Guide to Estimating the Impact of Fiscal Policy on Inequality and Poverty.* Brookings Institution and CEQ Institute (available online).

Lustig, N. 2016c. "Inequality and Fiscal Redistribution in Middle-income Countries: Brazil, Chile, Colombia, Indonesia, Mexico, Peru and South Africa," *Journal of Globalization and Development* 7: 17–60.

Lustig, N., and R. Deutsch 1998. *The Inter-American Development Bank and Poverty Reduction: An Overview.* Washington, DC: Inter-American Development Bank, May.

Lustig, N., and C. Pessino 2014. "Social Spending and Income Redistribution in Argentina in the 2000s: the Rising Role of Noncontributory Pensions," *Public Finance Review* 42: 304–325.

Lustig, N., and D. Teles 2016. Inequality Convergence: How Sensitive Are Results to the Choice of Data? Tulane University Economics Working Paper 1613.

Lustig, N., L.F. Lopez-Calva, and E. Ortiz-Juarez 2016. "Deconstructing the Decline in Inequality in Latin America," in K. Basu and J.E. Stiglitz (eds.), *Proceedings of IEA roundtable on Shared Prosperity and Growth.* Basingstoke: Palgrave Macmillan.

Lysandrou, P. 2011. "Global Inequality as One of the Root Causes of the Financial Crisis: A Suggested Explanation," *Economy and Society* 40: 323–344.

Mancini, L. 2008. "Horizontal Inequality and Communal Violence: Evidence from Indonesian Districts," in F. Stewart (ed.), *Horizontal Inequalities and Conflict: Understanding Group Violence in Multiethnic Societies,* Basingstoke: Palgrave Macmillan.

3

Mandisodza, A.N., J.T. Jost, and M.M. Unzueta 2006. "'Tall Poppies' and 'American Dreams' Reactions to Rich and Poor in Australia and the United States," *Journal of Cross-Cultural Psychology* 37: 659–668.

Mani, A., S. Mullainathan, E. Shafir, and J. Zhao 2013. "Poverty Impedes Cognitive Function," *Science* 341: 976–980.

Mann, M.l (1986–2012, three volumes). *The Sources of Social Power.* Cambridge: Cambridge University Press.

Martin, B., and R. Whitley 2010. "The UK Research Assessment Exercise: A Case of Regulatory Capture?" in R. Whitley, J. Gläser, and L. Engwall (eds.), *Reconfiguring Knowledge Production: Changing Authority Relationships in the Sciences and their Consequences for Intellectual Innovation.* New York: Oxford University Press.

Martin, M.A. 2006. "Family Structure and Income Inequality in Families with Children, 1976 to 2000," *Demography* 43: 421–445.

McCormick, B., and J. Wahba 2001. "Overseas Work Experience, Savings and Entrepreneurship amongst Return Migrants to LDCs," *Scottish Journal of Political Economy* 48/2: 164–178.

McEwen, B.S., and P.J. Gianaros 2010. "Central Role of the Brain in Stress and Adaptation: Links to Socioeconomic Status, Health, and Disease," *Annals of the New York Academy of Sciences* 1186: 190–222.

Meltzer, A.H., and S.F. Richard 1981. "A Rational Theory of the Size of Government," *Journal of Political Economy* 89: 914–927.

Messner, S.F., E.P. Baumer, and R. Rosenfeld 2004. "Dimensions of Social Capital and Rates of Criminal Homicide," *American Sociological Review* 69: 882–903.

Midlarsky, M.I., and K. Roberts 1985. "Class, State, and Revolution in Central America: Nicaragua and El Salvador Compared," *Journal of Conflict Resolution* 29: 163–193.

Milanovic, B. 2000. "The Median-Voter Hypothesis, Income Inequality, and Income Redistribution: An Empirical Test with the Required Data," *European Journal of Political Economy* 16: 367–410.

Milanovic, B. 2002. "True World Income Distribution, 1988 and 1993: First Calculation Based on Household Surveys Alone," *Economic Journal* 112: 51–92.

Milanovic, B. 2005a. "Can We Discern the Effect of Globalization on Income Distribution? Evidence from Household Surveys," *World Bank Economic Review* 19: 21–44.

Milanovic, B. 2005b. *Worlds Apart: Measuring International and Global Inequality.* Princeton, NJ: Princeton University Press.

Milanovic, B. 2011. "A Short History of Global Inequality: The Past Two Centuries," *Explorations in Economic History* 48: 494–506.

Milanovic, B. 2012. "Global Inequality Recalculated and Updated: The Effect of New PPP Estimates on Global Inequality and 2005 Estimates," *Journal of Economic Inequality* 10: 1–18.

Milanovic, B. 2016. *Global Inequality: A New Approach for the Age of Globalization.* Cambridge, MA: Harvard University Press.

Miller, G.A. 1956. "The Magical Number Seven, Plus or Minus Two: Some Limits on Our Capacity for Processing Information," *Psychological Review* 63: 81–97.

Mishra, P., and D. Newhouse 2009. "Does Health Aid Matter?" *Journal of Health Economics* 28: 855–872.

Mogues, T., and M.R. Carter 2005. "Social Capital and the Reproduction of Economic Inequality in Polarized Societies," *Journal of Economic Inequality* 3: 193–219.

Montalvo, J., and M. Reynal-Querol 2005. "Ethnic Polarization, Potential Conflict, and Civil Wars," *American Economic Review* 95: 796–816.

Moore, B. 1993. *Social Origins of Dictatorship and Democracy: Lord and Peasant in the Making of the Modern World.* Boston: Beacon Press.

Morduch, J., and R. Schneider 2017. *The Financial Diaries: How American Families Cope in a World of Uncertainty.* Princeton, NJ: Princeton University Press.

Motiram, S., and K. Naraparaju 2014. "Growth and Deprivation in India: What does Recent Evidence Suggest on 'Inclusiveness'?" *Oxford Development Studies* 43:145–164.

Motiram, S., and N. Sarma 2014a. "Polarization, Inequality and Growth: The Indian Experience," *Oxford Development Studies* 42: 297–318.

Motiram, S., and N. Sarma 2014b. "The Tragedy of Identity: Reflections on Violent Social Conflict in Western Assam," *Economic and Political Weekly* 49: 45–53.

Motiram, S., and A. Singh 2012. "How Close Does the Apple Fall to the Tree? Some Evidence on Intergenerational Occupational Mobility from India," *Economic and Political Weekly* 47: 56–65.

Mullainathan, S., and E. Shafir 2009. "Savings Policy and Decision-Making in Low-Income Households," in M. Barr and R. Blank (eds.), *Insufficient Funds: Savings, Assets, Credit, and Banking among Low-Income Households.* New York: Russell Sage Foundation Press.

Mullainathan, S., and E. Shafir 2013. *Scarcity: Why Having Too Little Means So Much.* New York: Henry Holt Times Books.

Muller, C., and A. Trannoy 2012. "Multidimensional Inequality Comparisons: A Compensation Perspective," *Journal of Economic Theory* 147: 1427–1449.

Muller, E.N. 1985. "Income Inequality, Regime Repressiveness, and Political Violence," *American Sociological Review* 50: 47–61.

Muller, E.N., and M.A. Seligson 1987. "Inequality and Insurgency," *The American Political Science Review* 81/2: 425–452.

Murphy, K.M., A. Shleifer, and R. Vishny 1989. "Income Distribution, Market Size, and Industrialization," *Quarterly Journal of Economics* 104: 537–564.

Murray, C., A. Lopez, and M. Alvarado 2013. "The State of US Health, 1990–2010: Burden of Diseases, Injuries, and Risk Factors," *The Journal of the American Medical Association* 310: 591–606.

Ndikumana, L. 2014. "Capital Flight and Tax Havens: Impact on Investment and Growth in Africa," *Revue d'Economie du developpement* 22: 99–124.

Ndikumana, L., and J.K. Boyce 2001. "Is Africa a Net Creditor? New Estimates of Capital Flight from Severely Indebted Sub-Saharan African Countries, 1970–96," *Journal of Development Studies* 38: 27–56.

Neal, R.D., D.A. Lawlor, V. Allgar, M. Colledge, S. Ali, A. Hassey, C. Portz, and A. Wilson 2001. "Missed Appointments in General Practice: Retrospective Data Analysis from Four Practices," *British Journal of General Practice* 51: 830–832.

Neisser, U. 1976. *Cognition and Reality: Principles and Implications of Cognitive Psychology.* New York: WH Freeman/Times Books/Henry Holt & Co.

Neves, P.C., and S.M.T. Silva 2014. "Inequality and Growth: Uncovering the Main Conclusions from the Empirics," *Journal of Development Studies* 50: 1–21.

Niehues, J., and A. Peichl 2014. "Upper Bounds of Inequality of Opportunity: Theory and Evidence for Germany and the US," *Social Choice and Welfare* 43: 73–99.

Niño-Zarazúa, M, A. Barrientos, D. Hulme, and S. Hickey 2011. *Social Protection in Sub-Saharan Africa: Getting the Politics Right.* Brooks World Poverty Institute, University of Manchester.

Nolte, K., C. Wytske, and M. Giger 2016. International Land Deals for Agriculture. Fresh Insights from the Land Matrix: Analytical Report II. Bern, Montpellier, Hamburg, Pretoria: Centre for Development and Environment, University of Bern; Centre de coopération internationale en recherche agronomique pour le développement; German Institute of Global and Area Studies; University of Pretoria; Bern Open Publishing.

Norton, M.I. 2013. "All Ranks Are Local: Why Humans Are Both (Painfully) Aware and (Surprisingly) Unaware of Their Lot in Life," *Psychological Inquiry* 24: 124–125.

Norton, M.I., and D. Ariely 2011. "Building a Better America – One Wealth Quintile at a Time," *Perspectives on Psychological Science* 6: 9–12.

Norton, M.I., D.T. Neal, C.L. Govan, D. Ariely, and E. Holland 2014. "The Not So Common Wealth of Australia: Evidence for a Cross-Cultural Desire for a More Equal Distribution of Wealth," *Analyses of Social Issues and Public Policy* 14: 339–351.

Nozick, R. 1974. *Anarchy, State and Utopia.* New York: Basic Books.

Ocampo, J.A. 2012. *The Development Implications of External Integration in Latin America.* UNU/WIDER Working Papers 48/2012. Helsinki, UNU/WIDER.

Odokonyero, T., A. Ijjo, R. Marty, T. Muhumuza, and G.O. Moses 2015. Sub-National Perspectives on Aid Effectiveness: Impact of Aid on Health Outcomes in Uganda. AidData Working Paper 18.

O'Donnell, O., E. van Doorslaer, A. Wagstaff, and A. Lindelow 2008. *Analyzing Health Equity Using Household Survey Data: A Guide to Techniques and Their Implementation.* Washington, DC: The World Bank.

OECD 2008. *Growing Unequal?: Income Distribution and Poverty in OECD Countries.* Paris: OECD Publishing.

OECD 2011a. *Divided We Stand: Why Inequality Keeps Rising.* Paris: OECD Publishing.

OECD 2011b. *Growing Income Inequality in OECD Countries: What Drives it and How Can Policy Tackle it?* OECD Forum on Tackling Inequality, Paris, May 2.

OECD 2015. *In It Together: Why Less Inequality Benefits All.* Paris: OECD Publishing.

Olson, M. 1965. *The Logic of Collective Action: Public Goods and the Theory of Groups.* Cambridge, MA: Harvard University Press.

Østby, G. 2008. "Inequalities, the Political Environment and Civil Conflict: Evidence from 55 Developing Countries," in F. Stewart (ed.), *Horizontal Inequalities and Conflict: Understanding Group Violence in Multiethnic Societies*, Basingstoke: Palgrave Macmillan.

Ostry, J., A. Berg, and C. Tsangarides 2014. Redistribution, Inequality, and growth. IMF Staff Discussion Note 14/02.

Ostrom, E. 1990. *Governing the Commons: The Evolution of Institutions for Collective Action.* Cambridge: Cambridge University Press.

Ott, J. 2005. "Level and Inequality of Happiness in Nations: Does Greater Happiness of a Greater Number Imply Greater Inequality in Happiness?," *Journal of Happiness Studies* 6: 397–420.

Oxoby, R.J., and J. Spraggon 2008. "Mine and Yours: Property Rights in Dictator Games," *Journal of Economic Behavior & Organization* 65: 703–713.

Pande, R. 2003. "Can Mandated Political Representation Increase Policy Influence for Disadvantaged Minorities? Theory and Evidence from India," *American Economic Review* 93: 1132–1151.

Panizza, F.E. 2005. "Unarmed Utopia Revisited: The Resurgence of Left-of-Centre Politics in Latin America," *Political Studies* 53: 716–734.

Parfit, D. 1997. "Equality and Priority," *Ratio*, 10: 202–221.

Peichl, A., and M. Ungerer 2015. Equality of Opportunity: East vs. West Germany. SOEP Paper No. 798.

Peichl, A., N. Pestel, and H. Schneider 2012. "Does Size Matter? The Impact of Changes in Household Structure on Income Distribution in Germany," *Review of Income and Wealth* 58: 118–141.

Perotti, R. 1993. "Political Equilibrium, Income Distribution, and Growth," *Review of Economic Studies* 60: 755–776.

Perotti, R. 1996. "Growth, Income Distribution, and Democracy: What the Data Say," *Journal of Economic Growth* 1: 149–187.

Persson, T., and G. Tabellini 1994. "Is Inequality Harmful for Growth?" *American Economic Review* 84: 600–621.

Pfeffer, J., and N. Langton 1988. "Wage Inequality and the Organization of Work: The Case of Academic Departments," *Administrative Science Quarterly* 33: 588–606.

Pickett, K., and R. Wilkinson 2015. "Income Inequality and Health: A Causal Review," *Social Science and Medicine* 128: 316–326.

Piketty, T. 1997. "The Dynamics of the Wealth Distribution and the Interest Rate with Credit Rationing," *Review of Economic Studies* 64: 173–189.

Piketty, T. 2014. *Capital in the Twenty-First Century.* Cambridge, MA: Harvard University Press.

Pistolesi, N. 2009. "Inequality of Opportunity in the Land of Opportunities, 1968–2001," *Journal of Economic Inequality* 7: 411–433.

Pogge, T. 2002. "Can the Capability Approach Be Justified?" *Philosophical Topics* 30: 167–228.

Poulantzas, N. 1974. *Fascism and Dictatorship.* London: Verso.

Pradhan, M., and M. Ravallion 2000. "Measuring Poverty Using Qualitative Perceptions of Consumption Adequacy," *Review of Economic and Statistics* 82: 462–471.

Pradhan, M., D.E. Sahn, and S.D. Younger 2003. "Decomposing World Health Inequality," *Journal of Health Economics* 22: 271–293.

Prados de la Escosura, L. 2007. "Inequality and Poverty in Latin America: A Long Run Exploration," in K.H. Hatton, K. O'Rourke, and A.M. Taylor (eds.), *The New Coparative Economic History: Essays in Honour of Jeffrey Williamson.* Cambridge, MA: MIT Press,.

Prados de la Escosura, L. 2015. "World Human Development: 1870–2007," *Review of Income and Wealth* 61: 220–247.

Prasad, E., K. Rogoff, S.J. Wei, and M. Kose 2003. Effects of Financial Globalisation on Developing Countries: Some Empirical Evidence. *IMF Occasional Paper* 220, Washington, DC: IMF.

Prete, A.L. 2013. "Economic Literacy, Inequality, and Financial Development," *Economics Letters* 118: 74–76.

Pritchett, L. 1997. "Divergence, Big Time," *Journal of Economic Perspectives* 11: 3–17.

Rajan, R. 2010. *Fault Lines.* Princeton, NJ: Princeton University Press.

Ram, R. 1990. "Educational Expansion and Schooling Inequality; International Evidence and Some Implications," *Review of Economics and Statistics* 72: 266–274.

Ravallion, M. 1998. "Does Aggregation Hide the Harmful Effects of Inequality on Growth?" *Economics Letters* 61: 73–77.

Ravallion, M. 2001. "Growth, Inequality and Poverty: Looking Beyond Averages," *World Development* 29: 1803–1815.

Ravallion, M. 2003. "Inequality Convergence," *Economics Letters* 80: 351–356.

Ravallion, M. 2011. "Mashup Indices of Development," *The World Bank Research Observer* 27: 1–32.

Ravallion, M. 2015. "The Luxembourg Income Study," in F. Ferreira and N. Lustig (eds.), *Special Issue, Appraising Cross-National Income Inequality Databases Journal of Economic Inequality* 13: 527–547.

Ravallion, M., and S. Chen 1997. "What Can New Survey Data Tell Us about Recent Changes in Distribution and Poverty," *World Bank Economic Review* 11: 357–382.

Ravallion, M., and S. Chen 2003. "Measuring Pro-Poor Growth," *Economics Letters* 78: 93–99.

Ravallion, M., S. Chen, and P. Sangraula 2007. "New Evidence on the Urbanization of Global Poverty," *Population and Development Review* 33: 667–701.

Rawls, J. 1971. *A Theory of Justice.* Cambridge, MA: Harvard University Press.

Ray, D. 1998. *Development Economics.* Princeton, NJ: Princeton University Press.

Ray, D. 2006. "Aspirations, Poverty and Economic Change," in A. Banerjee, R. Benabou, and D. Moookherjee (eds.), *Understanding Poverty.* Oxford: Oxford University Press.

Ray, D. 2016. "Aspirations and the Development Treadmill," *Journal of Human Development and Capabilities* 17: 309–323.

Rees, R., and R. Riezman 2012. "Globalization, Gender and Growth," *Review of Income and Wealth* 58: 107–117.

Reinikka, R., and J. Svensson 2004. "Local Capture: Evidence from a Central Government Transfer Program in Uganda," *Quarterly Journal of Economics* 119: 679–705.

Reutter, L., M. Stewart, G. Veenstra, D. Raphael, R. Love, and E. Makwarimba 2009. "'Who Do They Think We Are, Anyway?' Perceptions of and Responses to Poverty Stigma," *Qualitative Health Research* 19/3: 297–311.

Roberts, K. 2014. "The Politics of Inequality and Redistribution in Latin America's Post-Adjustment Era," in G.A. Cornia (ed.), *Falling Inequality in Latin America.* Oxford: Oxford University Press.

Rodriguez, F. 2004. "Inequality, Redistribution and Rent-Seeking," *Economics and Politics* 16: 287–320.

Rodrik, D. 2007. *One Economics, Many Recipes: Globalization, Institutions, and Economic Growth.*, Princeton, NJ: Princeton University Press.

Roemer, J.E. 1993. "A Pragmatic Theory of Responsibility for the Egalitarian Planner," *Philosophy and Public Affairs* 22: 146–166.

Roemer, J.E. 1998. *Equality of Opportunity.* Cambridge, MA: Harvard University Press.

Roemer, J.E. 2004. "Equal Opportunity and Intergenerational Mobility: Going Beyond Inter-generational Income Transition Matrices," in M. Corak (ed.), *Generational Income Mobility in North America and Europe.* Cambridge: Cambridge University Press.

Roemer, J.E. 2006. Party Competition under Private and Public Financing: A Comparison of Institutions. Cowles Foundation Paper No. 1191, Yale University.

Roemer, J.E. 2008. "Equality of Opportunity," in S. Durlauf and L. Blume (eds.), *The New Palgrave Dictionary of Economics.* London: Macmillan.

Roemer, J.E. 2015. "On the Importance of Circumstances in Explaining Income Inequality," *Revue Economique* (forthcoming).

Roemer, J.E., and A. Trannoy 2015. "Equality of Opportunity," in A.B. Atkinson and F. Bourguignon (eds.), *Handbook of Income Inequality.* Elsevier, New York.

Roemer, J.E., and A. Trannoy 2016. "Equality of Opportunity: Theory and Measurement," *Journal of Economic Literature* 54: 1288–1332.

Rojas Suarez, L. 2010. The International Financial Crisis: Eight Lessons for and from Latin America. CGD, Working Paper 202, 1/27/10.

Rogers-Dillon, R. 1995. "The Dynamics of Welfare Stigma," *Qualitative Sociology* 18: 439–456.

Runciman, W.G. 1972. *Relative Deprivation and Social Justice: A Study of Attitudes to Social Inequality in Twentieth Century England.* London: Pelican.

Russett, B.M. 1964. "Inequality and Instability: The Relation of Land Tenure to Politics," *World Politics* 16/3: 442–454.

Sahn, D.E. and S.D. Younger 2007. Decomposing World Education Inequality. *Cornell Food and Nutrition Policy Program*, Working Paper 187.

Sala-i-Martin, X. 2006. "The World Distribution of Income: Falling Poverty and… Convergence, Period," *Quarterly Journal of Economics* 121: 351–397.

Sanfey, P., and U. Teksöz 2007. "Does Transition Make You Happy?" *Economics of Transition* 15: 707–731.

Sanfey, A.G., J.K. Rilling, J.A. Aronson, L.E. Nystrom, and J.D. Cohen 2003. "The Neural Basis of Economic Decision-Making in the Ultimatum Game," *Science* 300: 1755–1758.

Savani, K., and A. Rattan 2012. "A Choice Mind-Set Increases the Acceptance and Maintenance of Wealth Inequality," *Psychological Science* 23: 796–804.

Savani, K., N.M. Stephens, and H.R. Markus 2011. "The Unanticipated Interpersonal and Societal Consequences of Choice Victim Blaming and Reduced Support for the Public Good," *Psychological Science* 22: 795–802.

Schmader, T., M. Johns, and C. Forbes 2008. "An Integrated Process Model of Stereotype Threat Effects on Performance," *Psychological Review* 115: 336–356.

Scholl, N., and S. Klasen 2015. Re-estimating the Relationship between Inequality and Growth. University of Goettingen, mimeo.

Schultz, T.P. 1998. "Inequality in the Distribution of Personal Income in the World: How It Is Changing and Why," *Journal of Population Economics* 11: 307–344.

Schwartz, C.R. 2010. "Earnings Inequality and the Changing Association between Spouses' Earnings," *American Journal of Sociology* 115: 1524–1557.

Selden, M., and J.M. Wu 2011. "The Chinese State, Incomplete Proletarianization and Structures of Inequality in Two Epochs," *The Asia-Pacific Journal*, 9: 1–35.

Sen, A. 1976. "Real National Income," *Review of Economic Studies* 43/1: 19–39.

Sen, A.K. 1979. *"Equality of What."* The Tanner Lectures on Human Values delivered at Stanford University.

Sen, A.K. 1982. "Real National Income," in A.K. Sen, *Choice, Welfare and Measurement*. Oxford: Basil Blackwell.

Sen, A.K. 1992. *Inequality Reexamined*. Cambridge, MA: Harvard University Press.

Sen, A.K. 2000. Social Exclusion: Concept, Application and Scrutiny. Social Development Papers No. 1, Asian Development Bank.

Sen, A.K. 2002. *Rationality and Freedom*. Cambridge, MA: Harvard University Press.

Sen, A.K. 2006. *Identity and Violence. The Illusion of Destiny*. New York: W.W. Norton & Company.

Shafiullah, M. 2011. "Foreign Aid and its Impact on Income Inequality," *International Review of Business Research Papers* 7: 91–105.

Shah, A.K., S. Mullainathan, and E. Shafir 2012. "Some Consequences of Having Too Little," *Science* 338: 682–685.

Shariff, A.F., D. Wiwad, and L.B. Aknin 2016. "Income Mobility Breeds Tolerance for Income Inequality Cross-National and Experimental Evidence," *Perspectives on Psychological Science* 11: 373–380.

Sherman, D.K., and G.L. Cohen 2006. "The Psychology of Self-Defense: Self-Affirmation Theory," in M.P. Zanna (ed.), *Advances in Experimental Social Psychology* 38. San Diego, CA: Academic Press.

Shiv, B., and A. Fedorikhin 1999. "Heart and Mind in Conflict: The Interplay of Affect and Cognition in Consumer Decision Making," *Journal of Consumer Research* 26: 278–292.

Shonkoff, J.P., W.T. Boyce, and B.S. McEwen 2009. "Neuroscience, Molecular Biology, and the Childhood Roots of Health Disparities: Building a New Framework for Health Promotion and Disease Prevention," *Jama* 301/21: 2252–2259.

Shonkoff, J.P., A.S. Garner, B.S. Siegel, M.I. Dobbins, M.F. Earls, L. McGuinn, and Committee on Early Childhood, Adoption, and Dependent Care 2012. "The Lifelong Effects of Early Childhood Adversity and Toxic Stress," *Pediatrics* 129: e232–e246.

Singh, A. 2011. "Inequality of Opportunity in Earnings and Consumption Expenditure: The Case of Indian Men," *Review of Income and Wealth* 58: 79–106.

Slaughter S., and G. Rhoades 2004. *Academic Capitalism and the New Economy: Markets, State and Higher Education*. Baltimore, MD: The Johns Hopkins University Press.

Sojo, A. 2017. *Protección social en América Latina: la desigualdad en el banquillo*. Libros de la CEPAL 143, Santiago.

Spencer, S.J., C.M. Steele, and D.M. Quinn 1999. "Stereotype Threat and Women's Math Performance," *Journal of Experimental Social Psychology* 35: 4–28.

Srinivas, M.N. 1998. *Village, Caste, Gender, and Method*. Oxford: Oxford University Press.

Steele, C.M. 1988. "The Psychology of Self-Affirmation: Sustaining the Integrity of the Self," in L. Berkowitz (ed.), *Advances in Experimental Social Psychology* 21. San Diego, CA: Academic Press.

Steele, C.M. 1997. "A Threat in the Air: How Stereotypes Shape Intellectual Identity and Performance," *American Psychologist* 52: 613–629.

Stewart, F. 2002. Horizontal Inequality: A Neglected Dimension of Development. QEH Working Paper Series – QEHWPS81.

Stewart, F. (ed.) 2008. *Horizontal Inequalities and Conflict: Understanding Group Violence in Multiethnic Societies*. Basingstoke: Palgrave Macmillan.

Stewart, F. 2010. *"Horizontal Inequalities as a Cause of Conflict: A Review of CRISE Findings,"* No. 1, January 2010, Centre for Research on Inequality, Human Security and Ethnicity, Oxford.

Stiglitz, J.E. 2002. *Macro-Policy Issue: Dealing with an Economic Downturn*. New York: Initiative for Policy Dialogue, Columbia University.

Stiglitz, J.E. 2007. Give Prizes Not Patents. Accessible at: www.project-syndicate.org/commentary/prizes--not-patents (last accessed January 4, 2016).

Stiglitz, J.E. 2012. *The Price of Inequality: How Today's Divided Society Endangers Our Future*. New York: W.W. Norton & Company.

Stockhammer, E. 2015. "Rising Inequality as a Cause of the Present Crisis," *Cambridge Journal of Economics* 39: 935–958.

Stutzer, A. 2004. "The Role of Income Aspirations in Individual Happiness," *Journal of Economic Behavior & Organization* 54: 89–109.

Subramanian, S. 2013. "Assessing Inequality in the Presence of Growth: An Expository Essay," *The Review of Black Political Economy* 42: 179–199.

Subramanian, S., and D. Jayaraj 2013. "The Evolution of Consumption and Wealth Inequality in India: A Quantitative Assessment," *Journal of Globalization and Development* 4: 253–281.

Sutter, M. 2007. "Outcomes versus Intentions: On the Nature of Fair Behavior and Its Development with Age," *Journal of Economic Psychology* 28: 69–78.

Tabibnia, G., A.B. Satpute, and M.D. Lieberman 2008. "The Sunny Side of Fairness Preference for Fairness Activates Reward Circuitry (and Disregarding Unfairness Activates Self-Control Circuitry)," *Psychological Science* 19: 339–347.

Tanndal, J., and D. Waldenström 2016. Does Financial Deregulation Boost Top Incomes? Evidence from the Big Bang. IZA Discussion Paper No. 9684.

Taylor, L. 2004. "External Liberalization, Economic Performance and Distribution in Latin America and Elsewhere," in G.A. Cornia (ed.), *Inequality, Growth, and Poverty in an Era of Liberalization and Globalization*. Oxford: Oxford University Press.

Teignier, M., and D. Cuberes 2016. "Aggregate Costs of Gender Gaps in the Labor Market: A Quantitative Exercise," *Journal of Human Capital* 10: 1–32.

Tertilt, M., and M. Doepke 2014. Does Female Empowerment Promote Economic Development? NBER Working Paper No. 19888.

Teulings, C., and R. Baldwin 2014. Secular Stagnation: Facts, Causes, and Cures. VOX. http://voxeu.org/content/secular-stagnation-facts-causes-and-cures (last accessed December 23, 2017).

Therborn, G. 2006. *What Does the Ruling Class Do When it Rules: State Apparatuses and State Power under Feudalism, Capitalism and Socialism*. London: Verso.

Thorbecke, E., and C. Charumilind 2002. "Economic Inequality and Its Socioeconomic Impact," *World Development* 30: 1477–1495.

Torche, F., and S. Spilerman 2006. Household Wealth in Latin America. UNU-WIDER, Research Paper No. 2006/114.

Trapp, K. 2015. Measuring the labour income share of developing countries. UNU-WIDER Working Paper 41/2015.

Tricomi, E., A. Rangel, C.F. Camerer, and J.P. O'Doherty 2010. "Neural Evidence for Inequality-Averse Social Preferences," *Nature* 463: 1089–1091.

Tyler, T. 2011. "Procedural Justice Shapes Evaluations of Income Inequality: Commentary on Norton and Ariely," *Perspectives on Psychological Science* 6: 15–16.

Udry, C. 2006. "Gender, Agricultural Productivity, and the Theory of the Household," *Journal of Political Economy* 104:1010–1046.

UN DESA 2016. *International Migration Report 2016*. United Nations, New York.

UN Women 2016. www.unwomen.org/en/what-we-do/leadership-and-political-participation/facts-and-figures (last accessed October 14, 2016).

UNDP 2010. *Regional Human Development Report for Latin America and the Caribbean 2010: Acting on the Future: Breaking the Intergenerational Transmission of Inequality*. New York: United Nations Development Programme.

van Zanden, J.L., J. Baten, P. Foldvari, and B. van Leeuwen 2014. "The Changing Shape of Global Inequality 1820–2000: Exploring a New Dataset," *Review of Income and Wealth* 60/2.
doi: 10.1111/roiw.12014

Vogl, T. 2016. "Differential Fertility, Human Capital, and Development," *Review of Economic Studies* 83: 365–401.

3

Voitchovsky, S. 2009. "Inequality and economic growth," in T. Smeeding, B. Nolan, and W. Salverda (eds.), *The Oxford Handbook of Economic Inequality*. Oxford: Oxford University Press.

Vos, R., J.A. Ocampo, and L. Cortez 2008. *Aging and Development*. London and New York: Zed Books and the United Nations.

Wang, Y.Q., and K.Y. Tsui 2000. "Polarization Orderings and New Class of Polarization Indices," *Journal of Public Economic Theory* 2: 349–363.

Williamson, J. 1990. "The Impact of the Corn Laws Just Prior to Repeal," *Explorations in Economic History* 27: 123–156.

Wimmer, A., L.E. Cederman, and B. Min 2009. "Ethnic Politics and Armed Conflict: A Configurational Analysis of a New Global Data Set," *American Sociological Review* 74: 316–337.

Winters, J. 2012. *Oligarchy*. Cambridge: Cambridge University Press.

Wolfson, M.C. 1994. "When Inequalities Diverge," *American Economic Review* 84: 353–358.

Wood, A. 1994. *North-South Trade, Employment and Inequality*. Oxford: Clarendon Press.

Woolard, I., and S. Klasen 2005. "Determinants of Income Mobility and Household Poverty Dynamics in South Africa," *Journal of Development Studies* 41: 865–897.

World Bank 2000/2001. *World Development Report 2000/2001: Attacking Poverty*. New York: Oxford University Press.

World Bank 2003. *World Development Report 2004: Making Services Work for Poor People*. Washington, DC: World Bank.

World Bank 2005. *World Development Report 2006: Equity and Development*. Washington, DC: World Bank.

World Bank 2011. *World Development Report 2012: Gender Equality and Development*. Washington DC: The World Bank.

World Bank 2017. *World Development Report 2017: Governance and the Law*, Washington, DC: World Bank.

World Bank/FAO/IFAD (Food and Agricultural Organization/International Fund for Agricultural Development) 2009. "Module 4: Gender Issues in Land Policy and Administration," in *Gender in Agriculture Sourcebook*, Washington, DC and Rome: World Bank/FAO/IFAD.

World Health Organization 2001. *The World Health Report 2001: Mental Health: New Understanding, New Hope*. World Health Organization.

World Health Organization 2012. *Environmental Inequalities in Europe*, World Health Organization European Centre for Environment and Health, Bonn.

Yamarik, S., and S. Ghosh 2003. *Is Female Education Productive? A Reassessment*. Mimeograph. Medford, MA: Tufts University.

Yusuf, A.A., A. Sumner, and A.R. Irlan 2015. "Twenty Years of Expenditure Inequality in Indonesia, 1993–2013," *Bulletin of Indonesian Economic Studies* 50: 243–254.

Zghal, A. 1995. "The 'Bread Riot' and the Crisis of the One-Party System in Tunisia," in M. Mamdani and E. Wamba-dia-Wamba (eds.), *African Studies in Social Movements and Democracy*, 99–129. Dakar & Oxford: CODESRIA Book Series.

Zhang, X., and R. Kanbur 2001. "What Difference Do Polarization Measures Make: An Application to China," 37: 85–98.

Zheng, B. 2006. "Unit Consistent Decomposable Inequality Measures," *Economica* 74: 97–111.

Zweimüller, J. 2000. "Schumpeterian Entrepreneurs Meet Engel's Law: The Impact of Inequality on Innovation-Driven Growth," *Journal of Economic Growth* 5: 185–206.

3

4

Economic Growth, Human Development, and Welfare

Coordinating Lead Authors:[1]
Purnamita Dasgupta, Ottmar Edenhofer

Lead Authors:[2]
Adriana Mercedes Avendano Amezquita, Antonio Bento, Simon Caney, David De la Croix, Augustin Fosu, Michael Jakob, Marianne Saam, Kristin Shrader-Frechette, John Weyant, Liangzhi You

Contributing Authors:[3]
Gian Carlo Delgado-Ramos, Marcel J. Dorsch, Christian Flachsland, David Klenert, Robert Lempert, Justin Leroux, Kai Lessmann, Junguo Liu, Linus Mattauch, Charles Perrings, Gregor Schwerhoff, Kristin Seyboth, Jan Steckel, Jessica Strefler

Chapter Management:[4]
Kristin Seyboth

---

[1] Affiliations: PD: Institute of Economic Growth, Delhi, India; OE: Mercator Research Institute on Global Commons and Climate Change (MCC) and the Potsdam Institute for Climate Impact Research.

[2] Affiliations: AMAA: Universidad Pedagogica y Tecnologica de Colombia; AB: University of Southern California; SC: University of Warwick; DDLC: Université catholique de Louvain; AF: University of Ghana; MJ: MCC; MS: ZEW; KSF: University of Notre-Dame; JW: Stanford University; LY: IFPRI.

[3] Affiliations: GDR: National Autonomous University of Mexico; MD, DK, GS, JSteckel: MCC; CF: MCC and Hertie School of Governance; RL: Rand Corporation; JL: HEC Montreal; KL, JStrefler: Potsdam Institute for Climate Impact Research; JL: Southern University of Science and Technology, China; LM: University of Oxford; CP: Arizona State University; KS: KMS Research and Consulting.

[4] KMS Research and Consulting.

Summary

Economic growth is often much lauded, but it also has its critics (Section 4.1.1). It may be viewed as a double-edged sword. On the one hand, it may be viewed as a narrative of liberation, lifting people out of poverty. On the other, it may be viewed as one of alienation, increasing inequality, and associated with environmental degradation.

Although Gross Domestic Product (GDP) is used dominantly as a measure of economic growth, there are many competing definitions of the more general concept of economic development and also competing indicators proposed as alternatives to GDP in measuring economic growth (Section 4.1.2). There are many linkages between economic growth, sustainable development, and social welfare (Section 4.1.5). The Industrial Revolution, which was a milestone in economic growth, led to increasing per-capita incomes, but also fundamental transitions in the way societies are organized, including changed fertility patterns, increasing investment in education, and rapid urbanization (Section 4.1.3). Determinants of economic growth and stagnation include population and demography (Section 4.2.1), education and human capital (Section 4.2.2), technological change (Section 4.2.3), resource endowments, geography, and environment (Section 4.2.5) and various actors, institutions, and politics (Section 4.2.6).

Welfare/well-being[5] is an overarching goal for policymakers. It is multidimensional in the sense that it includes poverty, inequality, the environment and other public goods such as health and education. It is normative in the sense that there are multiple perspectives on what matters to society (happiness, capabilities to function, etc.). Economic growth is important in that it positively impacts welfare along some dimensions and negatively along others. Growth in income per capita in itself is viewed to matter in itself in that it contributes to other goods, such as preference satisfaction (Section 4.3.1.1), happiness (Section 4.3.1.2), capabilities to function (Section 4.3.1.3), and the meaning of life (Section 4.3.1.4).

There is a debate as to whether economic growth should be judged in terms of its contribution to maximizing happiness or preference satisfaction (Section 4.3.2.1), ensuring economic equality (Section 4.3.2.2), raising people above a certain threshold (Section 4.3.2.3), or giving priority to the least advantaged (Section 4.3.2.4), each of which has arguments pro and against.

Economic growth has been correlated with fundamental transitions in the way societies are organized, changed fertility patterns, an increase in manufacturing and service sectors as well as energy and material consumption, increasing investment in education and rapid urbanization (Section 4.4.1).

It has been shown to be associated with a widening gap in the control of global income/wealth, suggesting that the gains of economic growth have not been evenly distributed. Economic growth in recent decades has decreased inequality at the global level, but has led to increasing inequality within countries.

Economic growth has also been correlated with environmental damage, such as climate change (Section 4.4.2.3), water scarcity and pollution (Section 4.4.2.5), and species extinction (Section 4.4.2.7). Climate change and other environmental damages impact the poor disproportionately, and may also increase inequality within and between countries. Economic growth has also been linked to air pollution (Section 4.4.2.4) and harmful impacts to nature and animals, which are argued to have an intrinsic value in themselves (Section 4.3.1.6).

Welfare is a broader concept than the income per capita status of the economy, and is measured by multidimensional indicators including health, education, political voice, environment, etc. (Section 4.4.3.2). Several improved welfare measures have been developed over the last decades, classified into monetary and nonmonetary measures. Indicators may be measured in a disaggregated way (i.e. a dashboard) or via a single indicator (Section 4.4.3.2).

Economic growth has been shown to have adverse effects on the global commons, which need to be protected to ensure that any use is sustainable over time (Sections 4.5.1, 4.5.2, and 4.5.3). Governing the global commons requires institutions that enable and facilitate collective action at international, national, and subnational levels.

---

[5]   Welfare or well-being in this chapter may be defined as the level of prosperity or standard of living of individuals or groups of people. Welfare is more often used when referring to groups of people, implying that individual well-being has to be added up in some way.

The challenge for policy-makers is to mitigate the negative effects of economic growth while preserving the positive effects. An integrated perspective on growth and capitalism allows for an evaluation of its costs and benefits, and also provides pathways for the transformation of contemporary capitalism, maintaining its driving forces, but addressing inequalities and protecting natural resources. Well-designed and implemented regulation of environmental and other externalities[6] leads to increasing welfare, without necessarily impeding economic growth. Environmental regulation creates assets for society.

Key Recommendations

1. Public policy needs to be formulated for the purpose of achieving social objectives. These social objectives involve intra- and intergenerational synergies and tradeoffs.
2. Economic growth is not a social objective in itself, but it can promote social objectives and help to overcome tradeoffs. It can also exacerbate conflicts among social objectives.
3. Economic growth has led to increasing welfare. However, the quality of growth matters.
4. To achieve the desired social objectives, appropriate policy instruments are needed.

---

[6] An externality is a positive or negative impact on an unrelated third party that results from the production or consumption of a given good.

4.1   Introduction

The purpose of this chapter is to evaluate the compatibility of human development and planetary welfare with economic growth. It does so by reviewing the theoretical and empirical literature on the two-way interface between economic growth on the one hand, and human development and planetary welfare on the other.

The chapter begins by introducing different narratives of economic growth (Section 4.1), discussing different definitions and determinants of economic growth and providing historical context (Section 4.2). Section 4.3 then examines the various normative criteria that can be used to evaluate economic growth, showing that growth matters in that it contributes to other goods. Section 4.4 examines the effects of economic growth in the framework of social and natural wealth. The chapter concludes by discussing how the global commons may be governed in order to prevent the adverse effects economic growth has had in the past (Section 4.5).

4.1.1   Narratives

Economic growth can be understood in multidimensional terms, though is defined here as "the process by which the amount or quality of goods and services one can earn with the same amount of work increases over time" (see Section 4.1.2).

There are two major narratives about economic growth: the first emphasizes the benefits such as material prosperity and poverty eradication. The second is concerned with the detrimental effects: unfair distribution and environmental destruction. Both narratives have influenced current theories and debates on economic growth. This section provides an overview of these two narratives and then discusses the synthesis – or "third way" – proposals, which attempt to find pathways to move ahead, bringing together the positives of both narratives. This framing is applied throughout the chapter to explain the compatibility of human development and planetary welfare with economic growth.

Capitalism, which has been credited with unprecedented economic growth, is an economic system based on three institutions: private property rights, markets, and firms. These institutions are developed to different degrees in different countries, which leads to a wide variety of capitalist systems. Capitalism can create externalities on the environment and on society. The balance of power between the government, markets, firms, and civil society determines the degree to which these externalities are accounted.

The two major narratives about capitalism and growth are as follows (Randazzo and Haidt 2015): In the first narrative, economic growth is viewed as a process of liberation. It provided an abundance of material goods after centuries of life at the subsistence level for almost the entire population. It brought along dramatic improvements in life expectancy, health care, education, and cultural development.

In the second narrative, economic growth is viewed as a process of alienation or exploitation. Capitalism's success in efficiently providing goods and services for individual consumption created a mindset that tends to underestimate resulting environmental problems, biasing distribution of gains toward owners and managers of resources and against workers, and causing uncompensated harm to nature while at the same time neglecting long-term sustainability concerns. When left unregulated, capitalism can create exploitation and large inequalities and threaten human existence by putting adequate environmental conditions at risk.

The popularity of the narratives of capitalism as "liberation" and "exploitation" with different segments of society raised a concern about finding a more integrated perspective in order to forge a welfare enhancing and socially progressive pathway for economic growth.[7] In recognition of this, third way approaches emerged to highlight the potential of capitalism (and its limitations) in order to move the discussion forward. Such a broad theoretical framework allows for an evaluation of the costs and benefits of capitalism but also provides pathways for the transformation of contemporary capitalism: making growth more equitable and sustainable. The common idea is to maintain the driving forces of capitalism for innovation, diversity, and democratic institutions and to address inherent problems such as inequality and environmental degradation by suitable policies.

4.1.1.1   Economic Growth as a Process of Liberation

In the eighteenth century Thomas Malthus described economic growth as an endless cycle of small technological improvements and ensuing small increases in population (Malthus 1798). Toward the turn of the nineteenth century, however, the previous pattern of stagnation changed into a quite stable process of exponential economic growth that still continues today. This was driven mainly by technological change (Solow 1956; Swan 1956), which shifted the trend of having a large number of children to educating children. This allowed the escape from the Malthusian "trap" (Galor and Weil 1999, 2000; Hansen and Prescott 2002).

Exponential growth could take off once inventors were rewarded adequately by receiving a share of the benefits that accrued from their invention. This link between the effort and the reward was established with the first modern patent system in England in the sixteenth century (MacLeod 1988).

The patent system demonstrates the pattern that good institutions foster economic growth. Institutions here are understood as the social and legal norms and rules that underlie economic activity (Rutherford 2001). Acemoglu et al. (2005) use the Korean peninsula as an example. When the Korean peninsula gained independence after World War II it was extremely homogeneous. The political division into a northern and a southern part, however, installed very different types of institutions. The democratic South Korea embarked on a process of rapid growth while the repressive North Korea stagnated. Hall and Jones (1999)

---

[7]   Mattauch (2015) argues that neoclassical growth theory is dominated by the narrative that capitalism is liberation, and proposes building a public economic theory that unifies both narratives.

confirm this with a sophisticated econometric analysis: differences in productivity can be explained by differences in institutional quality.

What is it about institutions that make them so powerful in generating economic growth? Easterly (2013) argues that the decisive element is that they grant individual rights. Individuals with rights can essentially solve their own problems, in particular that of poverty. Rights, enforced by functional institutions, help individuals to claim the benefits of their work. Ultimately, they provide incentives to innovate and develop technology. These incentives create a positive externality that allows the economy as a whole to grow.

The remarkable stability and persistence of economic growth was famously observed by Kaldor (1961). While capital per worker had increased, the real interest rate and the ratio of capital to output were stable in the long run. Most remarkably, however, labor productivity grew at a sustained rate, implying that inventions and productive new ideas had not run out. Jones and Romer (2010) confirm the stability and persistence of economic growth. They show that institutions have an undisputed central role for economic growth.

The recognition that freedom generates wealth fueled a process of liberalizing international trade (Williamson 1993). Over time it was realized that globalization requires careful regulation (Rodrick 1997; Stiglitz 2002; Cetorelli and Goldberg 2012), but there is a lot of empirical evidence on positive effects of international trade (Wacziarg 2001; Winters 2004). Even concerns about higher unemployment and brain drain turned out to be unfounded (Felbermayr et al. 2011; Docquier and Rapoport 2012). Once countries open to trade, they converge toward the most developed economies (Sachs and Warner 1995; Ben-David 1996).

4.1.1.2   Capitalism as Alienation or Exploitation

Capitalism also has had several adverse effects, which threaten to destroy some of its greatest achievements. There are four major inherent problems of growth-focused capitalism: (1) increased wealth inequality; (2) overuse of natural capital; (3) unrestricted corporate power; and (4) too narrow a focus on material consumption.

Recently, wealth inequality increased strongly in several industrialized countries: the gap between the top 1 percent and the rest of the population has increased significantly over the course of the last three decades (Piketty 2014; Piketty and Zucman 2014). This development also results in an increasing wealth/income ratio during the same period (Piketty and Zucman 2014).[8]

The increase in wealth inequality can be attributed to different drivers. Stiglitz (2015a) and Piketty, Saez, and Stantcheva (2014) see political changes that facilitate the appropriation of economic rents[9] by wealthy economic agents among the main drivers of wealth inequality. This includes monopoly rents (which can result from excess market power) and political rents (which occur when economic agents also

have political influence). Several types of exploitation rents occur in the financial sector, for instance through predatory lending practices and market manipulation (Stiglitz 2015a).

Technological change is the main driver behind economic growth. However, it can have adverse distributional effects since it is biased toward high-skill workers (Brynjolfsson and Mcafee 2014; Autor 2015). Autor (2015) argues that technological change is a two-edged sword: there is both a substitution effect between machines and human labor and a complementary effect between the two. The substitution effect has outweighed the complementary effect in the last decades to some extent, but this will not prevail in the longer term. Journalists and even expert commentators are argued to overstate the substitution effect.

Piketty (2014) identifies reduced growth of economic output and population as a further driver of inequality: Slower growth means that less wealth is newly created. The wealth created in the past, however, is more concentrated than newly generated wealth due to inheritance. While the individual's right to retain created wealth provided the basis for growth, it also causes increasing inequality in a situation of slow growth.

For a long time, growth-focused policy-makers ignored that, if natural capital stocks are left unregulated, they tend to be overexploited. Apart from climate change, other forms of environmental degradation have occurred over the years, affecting the sustainability of economic growth and welfare of regions and subpopulations within countries (see Section 4.4.2). The historical use of fossil fuels demonstrates this point. Fossil energy is an important economic input – its deployment, however, releases greenhouse gases into the atmosphere, which cause climate change (IPCC 2013). An individual's use of fossil energy enhances total output, but has an impact on the economic activity of others. It hence creates an externality that cannot be addressed if the market is left to its own devices.

The strong correlation between economic growth, greenhouse gas emissions (Edenhofer et al. 2014a), and natural capital depletion in general has led some authors to the conclusion that economic growth causes more harm than good. Schneider et al. (2010), Jackson (2009), and Kallis (2011) argue that economic growth is so strongly associated to the destruction of natural capital that de-growth, the deliberate halt or reversal of economic growth, is the only feasible approach to maintain the natural capital. This line of reasoning has been questioned mostly for the premise that the depletion of natural capital and economic growth are inseparable (Jakob and Edenhofer 2014), but has gained significant popular support. This is reinforced by concepts such as the circular economy, which aims at reducing waste and pollution by recycling industrial and biological waste in production (EMAF 2016).

A major concern behind a more globalized economy is the enormous market power and political influence of large (multinational) corporations, which often exceeds the protective power of nation-states. These corporations exercise their power through lobbyism,

---

8   A large part of this increase, however, can be attributed to a change in land prices (Homburg 2015).
9   An economic rent is the share of income received by a factor owner that exceeds the cost of providing the factor in production (Wessel 1967; Segal 2011).

trade regulations, and liberal financial markets (Stiglitz 2006). Large corporations can move abroad to avoid strict local regulations such as environmental policies and labor rights (Stiglitz 2006). They can even erode beneficial health, environmental, and labor regulations by suing governments in front of international courts (see e.g. Sud et al. 2015). An increase in corporate power is also linked to a decrease in collective bargaining. According to Mishel et al. (2015), between one-fourth to one-third of the growth in wage inequality between 1973 and 2007 in the US can be attributed to the erosion of collective bargaining ("de-unionization"). Furthermore, some multinational corporations have been accused of complicity in cases of violations against human rights, for example through collaborations with repressive regimes (Ramasastry 2002).

The drive for private profit, which is at the heart of capitalism, has also been identified as a threat to economic growth itself. Tollison (1982) identifies two forms of rent-seeking: rent-seeking for natural rents, which is a productive search for profitable activities, and rent-seeking for artificial rents, which is the unproductive competition for existing rents. The second type of rent-seeking has been identified as harmful for economic growth by Murphy et al. (1993) and Mohtadi and Roe (2003) since it consumes resources, but does not create additional value for the society.

A final criticism of current growth patterns concerns the usefulness of growth in consumption for increased well-being. Hirsch (1977), for instance, points out that there may be "social limits to growth" if people use their income predominantly to pursue status seeking behavior. Further, Frederick and Loewenstein (1999) and Layard (2011) show that consumers overestimate the pleasure they will derive from new purchases, misjudging the rapid psychological adaptation to new goods. This effect is often reinforced through advertising (Layard, 2011). Both effects explain a rather weak positive effect of personal income on subjective well-being (Kahneman and Deaton 2010).

4.1.1.3 The "Third Way" Alternatives

Economic policies that allow for a "third way" (preserving the benefits of capitalism while addressing its inherent problems) are organized around making growth more equitable and environmentally sustainable. There are four essential elements to such a model: (1) increased public investment, (2) environmental policy, (3) international cooperation, (4) redistribution without harming growth.

First, public capital, in a broad sense that includes energy, transport, health, and education infrastructure, is crucial for both economic growth and equity, but tends to be underfinanced in most developed economies (Estache and Fay 2007; Romp and Haan 2007; Bom and Ligthart 2014). Increasing public investment has the potential to address several of capitalism's inherent problems: First, an increase in education investment can supply workers with the skills necessary to flourish in a labor market that increasingly focuses on skills which are complementary to machines (Autor 2015). This increased public investment should be financed preferably through nondistortionary taxes on externalities and less distortionary taxes

on rents or bequests to reduce adverse growth effects. Second, depending on the financing mechanism, public investment has the potential to decrease inequality (Chatterjee and Turnovsky 2012; Klenert et al. 2016).

Second, the destruction of natural capital can be countered, conceptually, by investing in natural capital. This can be achieved in a straightforward manner by obliging individuals to pay the social cost for natural capital. The alignment between individual and social costs can be achieved by Pigouvian taxation. By increasing Pigouvian taxes to very high or prohibitive levels even concepts of strong sustainability can be realized (Edenhofer et al. 2014b). Problems such as biodiversity loss can also be addressed in this way, for example through prohibitive taxes on deforestation. Additionally, complementary measures such as subsidies for renewable technologies (Acemoglu et al. 2012; Mattauch et al. 2015), public investment into sustainable infrastructure (Guivarch and Hallegatte 2011) and direct restoration of natural capital (through the removal of pollutants for example) are needed for transition toward an environmentally sustainable economy.

Third, the problems generated by abusive corporate power can be addressed by global cooperation (Finkelstein 1995). The tendency for pollution intensive firms to produce in countries with the weakest regulation can be addressed through international environmental agreements like the 2015 Paris Agreement (UNFCCC 2015). Similarly, the race to the bottom in social protection and labor standards can be addressed through the International Labour Organization (ILO). Strengthening international cooperation between governments can generally reduce the risk of corporations playing countries off against each other. To address the ability of corporations to start well-funded legal attacks, Stiglitz (2006) suggests that "advanced industrial countries finance strong legal assistance for the developing countries."

Fourth, there is an important distinction to be made between inequality in returns to efforts (which has a generally positive effect on growth) and inequality in factors that go beyond the personal responsibility ("inequality of opportunity"), which can have detrimental growth effects (Roemer 1993; Marrero and Rodriguez 2013). We propose three pathways toward reducing inequality of opportunity: (1) inheritance taxation (Piketty and Saez 2013), (2) public investment, as proposed in point one, and (3) policy changes to reduce rent income. Other ways of reducing inequality such as the taxation of aggregate wealth might have adverse growth effects and are hence less desirable (Judd 1985; Chamley 1986). Finally, alternative forms of industrial organization such as labor-managed firms have been proposed to enhance workplace democracy and to reduce inequality (Meade 1972).

4.1.2 Concepts and Measurements of Growth

Economic development today is understood in multidimensional terms. Income continues to be an important component, though there are several other dimensions to defining an acceptable notion of development in an economy such as health, education, people empowerment, gender equality, etc.

Nowadays, economic growth covers a very precise and narrow notion, which comes from growth theory (a branch of macroeconomics):

> *Definition*: Economic growth is the process by which the amount or quality of goods and services one can earn with the same amount of work increases over time.
>
> *Example*: Almost everything people buy today requires fewer days of work than it did in the past. A classic example is provided by Nordhaus (1996, table 1.6) in his history of lighting. According to him, 10 minutes of work today buys 3 hours of reading light each night of the year, while it only bought 10 minutes of light per year two centuries ago.

The most widespread empirical measure of economic growth is GDP per capita. It should be noted, however, that historically GDP was not developed with the primary aim of measuring long-term economic growth, but that this use of GDP numbers became a practice over time (Coyle 2014). As GDP is the sum of all primary incomes distributed by resident production units, GDP per capita is a broad measure of income per person in an economy. Economic growth generally implies that income per person rises over time, unless hours of work fall steadily.

The above definition has the merit of stressing that economic growth is rooted into productivity improvements. Rising GDP per capita is just one possible manifestation of these improvements. The productivity based view is consistent with most of the theories of growth developed so far. Later in this chapter, we consider the multidimensional measures of human development and discuss the relationship to economic growth (both positive and negative aspects).

The above definition stresses also that economic growth is not necessarily quantitative (like buying more goods with one hour of work), but can be qualitative (buying higher quality goods with one hour of work).

The definition, relevance, and measurement of economic growth has been challenged from many sides. Since GDP is an indicator of economic activities which lead to monetary transactions it cannot act as an accurate measure of welfare (Fleurbaey 2009; Stiglitz et al. 2009).[10] The reasons for this can be structured into three groups (Afsa et al. 2008; Fleurbaey 2009): First, being an aggregate monetary measure, GDP neglects distributional issues as well as determinants of well-being which have no direct or indirect market value such as health, longevity, social relations, and personal safety. (Different conceptions of well-being relevant for assessing the social impact of economic growth are discussed in Section 4.3.) Second, it is a measure of productive flows and hence by design does not account for the impact of economic activities on stocks, in particular on stocks of natural capital. Third, it does not include household production of services. In some cases, events generally considered detrimental to well-being can lead to an increase in GDP. For instance, an increase in traffic jams may lead to higher gasoline consumption which increases GDP, but reduces well-being and has adverse effects on the environment (Stiglitz et al. 2009).

Several improved welfare measures have been developed over the last decades, which can be classified as monetary and nonmonetary measures. The monetary measures can be seen as a generalization of GDP, which take national income as a starting point and then correct it for factors such as nonmarket aspects of well-being and sustainability. Nonmonetary approaches aim at including more subjective factors such as happiness (see Section 4.4.3.1 for a definition of some determining factors of nonmonetary measures). Nonmonetary measures may capture determinants of well-being which are difficult to conceive with a monetary approach. For instance, the Social Progress Index does not incorporate GDP directly, it rather combines different indicators for three dimensions of well-being: basic human needs, foundations of well-being, and opportunity (Stern et al. 2016). However, one of the major shortcomings of nonmonetary measures is the arbitrary weighting of different determinants of well-being. Due to this subjectivity they are not able to provide a comprehensive measure of well-being, but they can be valuable components of synthetic indicators. In the following we thus focus on monetary measures.

There are several measures of national productivity that are closely related to GDP. Gross national product (GNP) counts production by all citizens of a country, at home and abroad, while GDP counts all production occurring within a country. Gross domestic income (GDI) is basically GDP measured by the income method. GNI is GDI plus income received from outside the country, minus income payments leaving the country. Fourth, the previous measures are all gross indicators, which means that they do not account for depreciation. Both, the net domestic product (NDP), and the national income (NI) factor in depreciation. The NI metric additionally subtracts indirect taxes such as sales taxes. Finally, some authors argue that gross output (GO), i.e. the sum of all sales both final and intermediate, is a "natural measure for the production sector" that is complementary to GDP (Jorgenson et al., 2006).

The accepted view on the relationship between economic growth and other aspects of development has appreciably widened over the years. It now accounts for the multiple factors that impact growth, from the role of natural, social, political, and institutional capital, to the challenges of sustaining economic growth in terms of distributional concerns across people, societies, and time.

Several alternate measures have been proposed in place of the GDP-type definitions to account for the environment, such as the Measure of Economic Welfare (MEW) (Nordhaus and Tobin 1972) and the Index of Sustainable Economic Welfare (ISEW) (Daly and Cobb 1989). In addition, the quest for better capturing human progress have led to the emergence of a number of viewpoints in which the dimensions of human development are intricately linked with economic growth. There are many illustrations of these such as the propagation of the capabilities approach, and the multidimensional poverty index for policy planning purposes in developing countries.

The following sections elaborate on the evolution of definitions and narratives on economic growth. Specific measurements of sustainability are discussed in Section 4.1.4, and aggregate indicators that integrate aspects of social and natural wealth appear in Section 4.4.3.

---

[10] Even though some say that it actually can be used as a proxy for welfare (see e.g. Jorgenson et al. 2006).

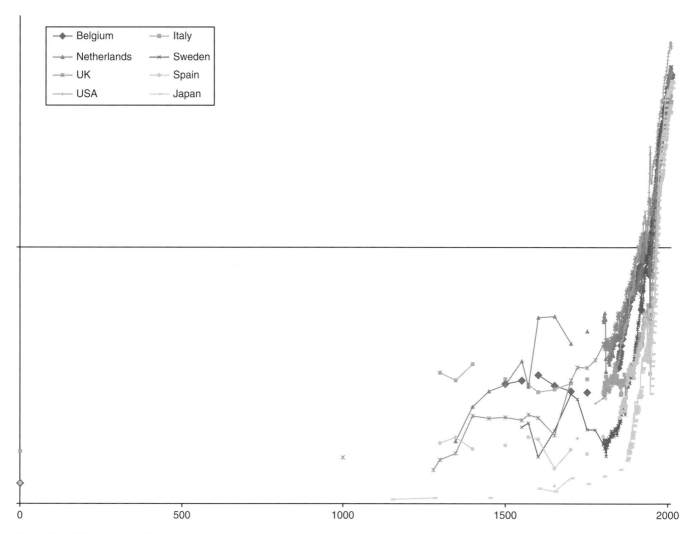

Figure 4.1 | GDP per capita in selected countries, 1-2010CE.
Logarithmic scale. Horizontal line = 5000 dollars (1990 International US$).
Source: Bolt and van Zanden, 2013.

4.1.3 The Great Acceleration/Transition from Stagnation to Growth

Measuring economic growth is difficult, especially for periods for which little information is available. Harmonized National Accounts were set up in most countries after World War II. They provide different ways to measure aggregate production, either through summing the added values of all resident production sectors, or through summing all the incomes distributed by those sectors. Making data comparable across countries requires correcting for differences in price levels to obtain estimates that capture the real purchasing power of income. The most comprehensive database so far is the Penn World Tables version 8.0 (Feenstra et al. 2013) which provides information on relative levels of income, output, inputs, and productivity, covering 167 countries between 1950 and 2011. Based on a broad set of historical studies, Maddison (2003) reconstructed income per capita data over the past two centuries, and added some point estimates for earlier periods (in 1 Common Era (CE), 1000 CE, 1500 CE, 1600 CE, and 1700 CE). Such estimates very often require educated guesses on unobservable trends – nonetheless, they show the best information given what is known at one point in time. Very recently, Bolt and van Zanden (2013) have revised and complemented Maddison's work (the "Maddison project"). Figure 4.1 presents the latest estimates for GDP per capita for selected countries.

Over the past millennium, income per capita in the selected countries has increased 32-fold, from $717 per person per year around the year 1000 to $23,086 in 2010. This contrasts sharply with the previous millennia, when there was almost no advance in income per capita. The figure shows that it started rising and accelerating around the year 1820 and it has sustained a steady rate of increase over the last two centuries. One of the main challenges for growth theory is to understand this transition from stagnation to growth and in particular to identify the main factor(s) that triggered the takeoff.

Is the finding that there was stagnation in the standard of living until 1820 truly robust? This claim is particularly striking given that mankind experienced significant technological improvements that would have been expected to increase productivity and income per person, from the Neolithic revolution to the invention of the printing press. Three facts corroborate the idea that there was indeed stagnation over the most part of human history: first, estimates of life expectancy computed on specific groups across time and space do not display any trend before 1700 CE (de la Croix and Licandro 2015). Second, body height computed from skeletal remains does not display any trend either, while height is known to depend very much on nutrition when young (Koepke and Baten 2005). This indicates that there was no systematic improvement in nutrition over time. Third, real wages computed from historical sources did not tend to rise in any sustained way before the Industrial Revolution (Allen 2001).

The Industrial Revolution led not only to increasing per capita incomes, but fundamental transitions in the way societies are organized, including changed fertility patterns, increasing investment in education, and rapid urbanization (Galor 2005) (see Section 4.4.1.3). Industrialization also implies structural change in economic activity with increased specialization and division of labor. As a consequence, the emergence of new constituencies and interest groups also results in fundamental changes in the political system, such as an expansion of the franchise (Acemoglu and Robinson 2000) (see Section 4.4.1.4).

This increase in economic activity in one part of the world has led to what has been described as "the Great Divergence" (Pomeranz 2000). Countries that successfully embarked on a course of industrialization, i.e. Europe and its offshoots (the US, Canada, Australia, and New Zealand) dominated the global economy, giving them geopolitical weight to shape global institutions to their advantage. After World War II, Japan was the first Asian country to industrialize. Only recently, coinciding with the acceleration of the "second wave of globalization" (Baldwin and Martin 1999), industrialization has become more widespread in poor countries.

Economic integration into global market by means of trade and investment across national borders gives poor countries the opportunity to specialize in activities for which they enjoy a comparative advantage (e.g. labor-intensive activities, such as textiles and assembly of electronic products). Hence, trade openness has often been a central feature of newly industrializing countries' development strategies (Rodrik 2005). China's spectacular growth performance is a salient case in point for such "export-led growth" (Rodrik 2006). Yet, these countries did not simply liberalize trade and foreign direct investment, but also employed an array of specifically tailored industrial policies to overcome market failures, such as financial frictions and coordination failures (Rodrik 2005).

Whereas successful growth takeoffs have occurred predominantly in Asia (Hausmann, Pritchett, and Rodrik 2005), it has been argued that about one billion people are still mired in extreme poverty, especially in Sub-Saharan Africa. It seems rather unlikely that this "bottom billion" living in resource-rich, landlocked, badly governed and conflict-ridden countries will achieve decent living standards in the near future (Collier 2008).

4.1.4 Sustainable Development

The idea of sustainable development encompasses various aspects – from that of sustainable development as development that meets the needs of the present without compromising the ability of future generations to meet their own needs (WCED 1987), to preserving ecosystem services, and coevolution of the three pillars of economic, social, and environmental objectives (Fleurbaey et al. 2014).

The Millenium Development Goals (MDGs) became widely associated as sustainability indicators (UN 2006, 2012). Several other indicators have also emerged, ranging from measures of green GDP (see Section 4.4.3.1 for discussion on green accounting) to measuring footprints such as those of carbon or water. Other developments include the Measure of Economic Welfare (MEW) (see Section 4.1.2; Nordhaus and Tobin 1972), the extension of the system of national accounts (SNA) to incorporate the use, augmentation, and depletion of natural resources through building satellite accounts (SEEA), and the extension of the concept of capital to include natural capital. More recently, the Sustainable Development Goals (SDGs) relate to the availability and management of water and sanitation, access to affordable and modern energy for all, ensuring a quality education, achieving gender equality, and ending poverty and hunger, while achieving food security and improved nutrition (UN 2016).

In order to find an improved measure of sustainability, several investment measures have been proposed which separate consumption from net investment and which correct prices whenever necessary and feasible. In these frameworks different methods are used to impute prices on nonmarketed goods and services. Genuine savings (GS) is among the most common such measures and its development goes back to Hamilton (1994) and Pearce et al. (1996). Hamilton and Clemens (1999) demonstrate that GS are negative in many developing countries, in particular in Sub-Saharan Africa, while they tend to be positive in high-income industrial countries.

GS as a measure of sustainability has been extended as well as criticized on several aspects: Considering extensions, Arrow et al. (2003) analyze the role of varying population in measuring genuine savings and find that including population as a type of capital is the only consistent approach. Pillarisetti (2005) argues that GS is flawed as a measure of sustainability and can lead to erroneous policy implications for several reasons: (1) GS is GDP-based and industrialized countries appear to have positive GS, even though they have a substantial ecological footprint,[11] (2) many externalities manifest themselves on a global scale and national indicators are hence futile, (3) it is empirically redundant since education expenses have a strong influence on the numerical value of GS, (4) it is based on the concept of weak sustainability, which assumes a perfect substitutability between different types of capital such as health, physical, and natural capital.

The right way to measure sustainable development continues to invoke much debate. While a framing in terms of threshold levels of attainment is endorsed by countries (as in the case of the SDGs to eliminate poverty) it fails to address the issue of sustainability in a holistic manner (for instance, questions of adequacy in terms of intergenerational equality as discussed in Section 4.3.2.2).

---

[11] The ecological footprint measures how much land is required for the generation of consumption within a country. This includes land needed for waste disposal and land-based climate change mitigation options (CO_2 sequestration). The world economy is considered unsustainable if the ecological footprint of all countries exceeds the amount of available land. One major problem with this measure is how to aggregate over different types of land uses (Smulders 2008).

Critics of sustainable development argue that economic growth cannot be green (Alier and Muradian 2015).[12] The concern of whether growth is radically incompatible with sustainability depends to a large extent on the definition of growth and the extent to which its distributional aspects matter to society (see Sections 4.3.1 and 4.3.2). The decoupling of material resource consumption and economic growth is considered to be one way of bringing compatibility between economic growth and sustainable development, with particular emphasis being laid on the decoupling of fossil fuel energy use with growth in GDP. However, the evidence on this is not clear, since in most countries the growth in per capita consumption clearly overrides any gains from the lowered intensity of resource use in production (see for instance the discussion in Fleurbaey et al. 2014). Amartya Sen proposes a more complex and multidimensional perspective (see Section 4.3.1.3) (Sen 2000). An integrative approach calls for more complexity in operationalization of the concept of sustainable development, which recognizes the multiple linkages between growth, development, and social welfare as emphasized through the different sections of this chapter. The idea of sustainability thus is inherently problematic to operationalize and its articulation in a functional way as "sustainable development" does not provide an unequivocal answer as to its implications for economic growth, or vice versa.

4.1.5 Global Commons

The United Nations Environmental Programme defines "global commons" in jurisdictional terms to be "resource domains or areas that lie outside of the political reach of any one nation-state" (UNEP 2017: 1). Classical global commons from this perspective include the High Seas (including the sea bed, Antarctica, the atmosphere, and outer space (Buck 1998). The lack of authority to comprehensively regulate the global commons creates great challenges for their governance, which we will turn to in Section 4.5. Historically, some global commons have been regulated "guided by the principle of the common heritage of humankind" (UNEP 2017). Frequent overuse and the importance of global commons for well-being and economic growth require that principles of justice for their governance are established.

Economic growth has a relationship with the "global commons" in at least two ways. First, economic growth can have adverse effects on the global commons. For example, economic growth has historically involved high emissions of greenhouse gases and thereby brought about the prospect of dangerous anthropogenic climate change (UNFCCC Article 2; see also Section 4.4.2.3). In addition, economic growth can lead to high emissions of CFCs which damage the ozone layer, and thus increase the prospects of skin cancer and eye cataracts. Other impacts of economic growth include pollution of the high seas and the depletion of resources (see Sections 4.4.2.4 and 4.4.2.1). All of these effects may be deemed to increase threats to health, food, or water – thereby viewed as "bads," which should, other things being equal, be minimized and distributed equitably.

A second interrelation is the source of resources and environmental services that global commons provide, which in themselves can facilitate or enable economic growth. For example, the sea beds are rich with resources such as cobalt, copper, manganese, and iron (Buck 1998: 90 and, more generally, pp. 88–91). In addition, Antarctica contains mineral resources (such as copper, gold, iron, silver, and petroleum) (Franck 1995: 401–405).

There is a need for principles of justice to protect the global commons and ensure that any use is sustainable over time. There is also a need to regulate access to the natural resources and environmental services contained with the "global commons" (Caney 2012). In particular, since the atmosphere, Antarctica, the high seas, and space exist beyond the confines of states there is a need for principles of global justice. Furthermore, since current economic behavior affects the standard of living of future generations there is a need for principles of intergenerational justice to regulate the global commons.

This raises a methodological question of how to treat the global commons within a theory of justice. Some propose principles designed to treat the global commons on their own (Risse 2012: part II), whereas others argue that the issues surrounding the global commons (like the use of the atmosphere) should be treated in light of people's overall rights (such as their rights to develop and promote a reasonable standard of living) (Caney 2012).

4.2 Determinants of Economic Growth and Stagnation

Determinants of economic growth include changes in demographics (Section 4.2.1), accumulation of human capital (Section 4.2.2), endogenous technological innovation (Section 4.2.3), resource endowments, geography, and the environment (Section 4.2.4) the existence of institutions (Section 4.2.5), and cultural and social movements and social capital (Section 4.2.6).

4.2.1 Population and Demography

The growth takeoff was systematically accompanied by a demographic transition. (See Figure 4.2, demonstrating this transition as took place in Sweden.)[13] Birth and death rates were systematically high before the takeoff, then mortality went down, while fertility stayed high for some time. During this period, population size increased fast. Then fertility dropped quickly and population growth decelerated. Once economic growth had taken off, both birth rate and death rate were low, and population growth became negligible (or even negative in some cases). The demographic transition took two centuries in England and other European countries. In East Asia, it was much faster, of the order of half a century. Causality between

---

12 According to The Organization for Economic Co-operation and Development (OECD), *green growth* seeks to promote growth and economic development while ensuring that natural assets continue to provide the resources, and the environmental services on which our welfare depends. This is a development approach that seeks to achieve long-term Sustainable Development Goals from concrete axes of action.

13 Sweden is the only country with more than 250 years of population censuses.

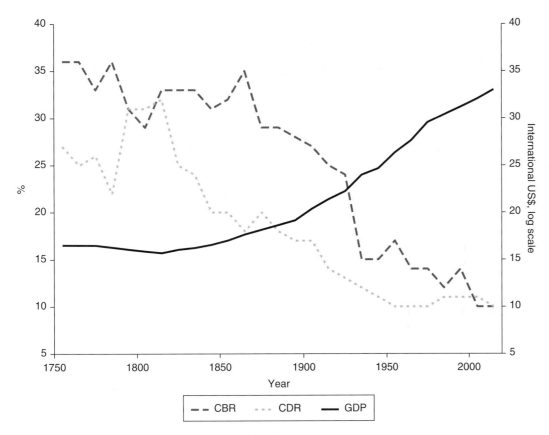

Figure 4.2 | Correlation of economic growth and demographics in Sweden.
Note: Left axis: crude birth rate (CBR) (dark gray dashes) and crude death rate (CDR) (light gray dots) in Sweden per 1000. Right axis: GDP per capita. Logarithmic scale
(1990 International US$).

the two transitions goes both ways: the demographic transition was triggered by the income takeoff, at least as far as the drop in mortality is concerned. At the same time, the economic takeoff was made possible by the demographic transition, because investment in the education and health of a smaller number of children was made possible.

The link between the demographic transition and the takeoff of economic growth is a process of "quality-quantity trade-off" (Cervellati and Sunde 2005; Galor 2011). This originates in a simple budget constraint, which holds both at the individual level and at the country level:

Total spending on children = number of children x spending per child

Keeping the total spending constant, enhancing the "quality" of children by spending more on each child requires reducing their number. Consequently, the drop in fertility observed during the demographic transition allows for an increase in spending on education and health, thereby making the accumulation of human capital from one generation to the next easier. For the case of Sweden, Figure 4.3 shows that the drop in fertility comes with a sharp increase in formal education, with a rise in adult longevity, and with a rise in people's height, which signals better nutrition and a lower exposition to disease when young (see de la Croix and Licandro 2015).

In a neoclassical growth model, the quantity of capital ("machines") per worker is key to determine income per worker. Keeping this

capital-labor ratio high is more difficult when population grows rapidly, because every new investment is "diluted" in a fast rising number of workers. This establishes a negative link between grows of population and income per person.

Demographics also matter for growth by means of the "demographic dividend" (see Lee and Mason 2006). According to this view, countries face a window of opportunity to grow just after fertility has gone down. At that moment, the population is mostly composed of working-age persons, and the burden of dependent (both young and old) is small. This view is confirmed by the empirical literature, which finds that the correlation between the age-composition of the population and economic growth is stronger than between a global measure of population growth and economic growth (see e.g. Kelley and Schmidt 1995). The composition of the population, as well as age-specific variables, is relevant to growth. A decrease in the death rate of workers in particular does not have the same effect as a decrease in the death rate of dependents, young or old (Lindh and Malmberg 2007). From these studies, it is also clear that the impact of population growth has changed over time and varies with the level of development.

4.2.2 Education and Human Capital

The accumulation of human capital (the combination of education, experience, and health) is one way to sustain economic growth.

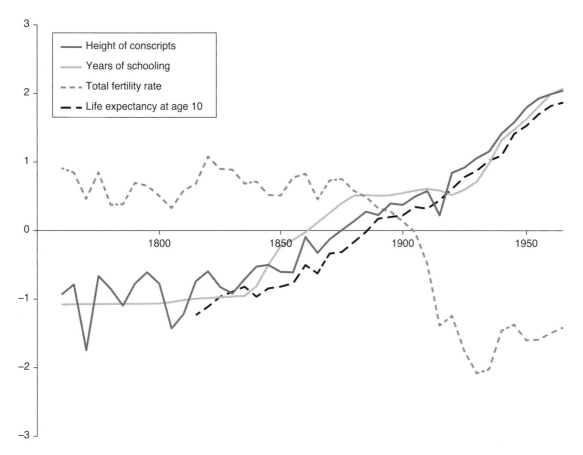

Figure 4.3 | The quantity-quality tradeoff for 1760–1965 birth cohorts in Sweden.
Note: Three measures of quality (body height, years of schooling, life expectancy at age 10), vs. total fertility rate. All data normalized.

Even if a country cannot increase its supply of labor indefinitely, it can enhance the quality of labor. Human capital can be accumulated in two ways: (1) by education during the early stage of life; and (2) by accumulating experience (learning-by-doing) during the working life or on-the-job training. Investment in formal education has increased substantially all over the world. In England for example, the number of years spent at school went from two on average in 1820 to more than fourteen in 2000 (Maddison, 2007). In developing countries, school enrolment grew rapidly between 1960 and 2000.

Several explanations for the takeoff toward modern growth rely on incentives to accumulate human capital. If, for some reason, it becomes profitable for households to invest in education, growth can be sustained thanks to the human capital externalities stressed in the endogenous growth model literature. Two types of shocks are considered here. The first is based on Ben-Porath's (1967) idea that the return on investment in education depends on the length of time during which education will be productive, implying that a longer active life makes the initial investment in human capital more profitable. Provided that human capital is an engine of growth, an initial increase in longevity (for exogenous biological/climatic/medical reasons) may in turn sustain the permanent accumulation of human capital and income growth (see e.g. Cervellati and Sunde 2005). The second type of shock triggering education can be institutional. For

example, Engerman and Sokoloff (2002) identify conditions under which a country will introduce public education early, favoring a skilled workforce and a rapid industrial revolution. One key condition is to have a relatively equal distribution of land among the population (such as nineteenth-century Canada and USA), avoiding the case where a land rich elite would oppose education reform, fearing more skilled workers and more taxes (such as in Latin America).

Human capital accumulation may run into the problem of diminishing returns. Even without diminishing returns, its accumulation may be limited by the finite lifetime available for learning and the fact that, though institutions and social conditions may affect the productivity of learning, each generation has to accumulate its human capital anew. Recent literature stresses that the quality of education matters more than its quantity (OECD 2010).

It is however fair to recognize that many poor countries experienced an educational boom without an accompanying takeoff in economic growth. Empirical studies stress the lack of correlation between educational attainment and growth. As Maloney and Valencia (2014) explain, "Empirically, documenting the impact of even very basic measures of human capital on growth or relative incomes has proved surprisingly complex." The accumulation of human capital is a necessary condition for growth, but it does not seem to be a sufficient condition.

4.2.3 Technological and Structural Change

In economics, technology is generally understood as "the utilization of natural phenomena and regularities for human purposes" (Mokyr 2008). In a more abstract sense, it also includes the utilization of social phenomena, e.g. through the design of organizations or the creation of brand value. In economic theory, technology is often assumed to be simply the functional relation between inputs and output. Technological change can in this sense be understood as the process by which people are looking for ways to produce more or better output from inputs. Its meaning is thus closely related to that of innovation. When empirically assessing innovation, the distinction between technological innovation (based mainly on research and development) and nontechnological innovation (based on organization, design, training, etc.) is often made, which refers to a narrower definition of technology, restrained to the realms of natural sciences and engineering. In sociology, technology is also understood to embrace "all forms of productive techniques" (Abercrombie et al. 2000). The fields of analysis related to technology, however, differ from those of economics, focusing i.a. on the social processes underlying technical change, on the influence of technology on work situation, work morale and alienation and on the role it plays in conflicts between employees and management (Lawson and Garrod 2001). Technological change in this chapter is discussed primarily from the point of view of economic research.

Technological change as the invention of new production methods is in a trivial sense the central engine of growth in the long term. If there are limits to producing more output using given methods, the only way to sustain growth over a long period is to invent better methods. Over shorter periods, given methods can be exploited in more productive ways by more investment, better education, greater availability of land, improvement in institutions, and many other factors. But ultimately these increases in productivity hit limits (economist speak of "diminishing returns") and higher productivity is possible only with new or better methods to produce goods and services.

Technological progress has always been present in human history, but it led to sequence of waves of innovation and a sustained increase in standard of living only during the last few centuries. Mokyr's explanation of the takeoff of modern economic growth with the Industrial Revolution sees the main driving force in a new culture of knowledge developing with the enlightenment (Mokyr 2005).

Five features are central for understanding the way in which technological change increases economic growth: (1) nonrivalry of technology; (2) partial tacitness and (3) partial excludability of knowledge related to technology; (4) the existence of large R&D organizations; and (5) the process of creative destruction.

1. Nonrivalry means that technological (as well as other) knowledge can be used by many agents simultaneously without anyone's individual use of it being diminished. One far-reaching prediction implied by the nonrivalry of knowledge is that a larger population generating new ideas based on existing ideas will lead to faster technological progress and faster growth in income per capita. This prediction is, however, hard to test because the international diffusion of knowledge makes it difficult to define the set of knowledge generated and used by a particular population (Jones 2005). Externalities (spillovers) play a central role here and they are related to the nonrivalry of knowledge. If, when a firm or an individual invests, this investment has positive spillovers on other firms or individuals, the private return of the investment (to the firm or the individual) is smaller than the social return (to all firms or individuals together). Free availability of knowledge for further knowledge creation is one kind of externality associated with technological change. Another externality occurs in learning-by-doing, when better production methods are developed as part of the practical use of technology. Nonrivalry does not imply that technological ideas can diffuse across individuals, firms, regions, and countries without cost.

2. The development and use of technology involves not only codified but also to a large extent tacit knowledge, which "has not been stated or measured in explicit form" (Freeman and Soete 1997). Skills acquired through learning on the job often represent tacit knowledge. In many cases, tacit knowledge is necessary to make productive use of codified knowledge. The importance of tacit knowledge, but also local infrastructure, demand patterns institutions, and culture are factors that make transfer of technologies across firms, industries, and countries costly and in some cases impossible despite the nonrivalry of knowledge.

3. Partial economic excludability means that it is possible to exclude others from some of the economic benefits of knowledge (e.g. via a patent), but not from all benefits, since knowledge that has been made available at some point can always serve as a basis for creating new, useful knowledge. This applies in particular to codified knowledge, which can be written down using language or other symbols.

4. While part of technological knowledge emerges as by-product of practical experience with available technologies, much of technological change in advanced economies is the result of purposeful research and innovation activities. Modern R&D has been increasingly moved to large organizations. As Freeman and Soete (1997) point out: "During the twentieth century the main locus of inventive activity shifted away from the individual inventor to the professional research and development (R&D) laboratory, whether in industry, government and academia" (p. 197). This implies that the assessment of risks and benefits of R&D activities have to be advantageous with regard to the objectives of the specific organization for technological change to take place.

5. Technological change is not a smooth, continuous process but has, since the work of Kondratieff and Stolper (1935) and Schumpeter (1942), been recognized to occur in waves of "creative destruction," which make old products and processes obsolete. Each wave is associated with a particular "general purpose technology" (Bresnahan and Trajtenberg 1995), a technology that differs in a fundamental way from previous technologies. General purpose technologies diffuse in many industries and offer much scope for internal improvement and secondary innovation. The diffusion also operates though firm entry and exit. While the exact delineation of general purpose technologies and of the associated long waves of variations in rates of economic growth are subject to debate, frequently listed candidates of GPTs are the

4

steam engine, electricity, the internal combustion engine, mass production, computer technology, the internet.

Technological change at the macroeconomic level has always been intertwined with structural change. Structural change refers to the reallocation of production activity and employment across the broad economic sectors agriculture, manufacturing, and services. In many advanced countries (including the EU-15 countries, the United States, and Japan), employment in agriculture fell with rising GDP from more than three-quarters in the nineteenth century to below 10 percent at the end of the twentieth century. The share in manufacturing peaked between 30 and 45 percent in most countries and has been declining. The share in services exceeds 60 percent today. In developing countries, a similar relation between GDP and sectoral employment shares is observed (Herrendorf et al. 2014).

Economic theory distinguishes two main drivers of structural change. One is associated with uneven technological change across sectors. When technological change is higher than average in one sector, less labor is needed to produce a given level of output and falling relative prices increase the demand for this sector's output. The second is associated with the dependence of consumer preferences on income. At a low income, demand is relatively high for agricultural goods and other goods are often home-produced or not consumed at all. With rising income, nutritional needs are largely satisfied and the demand for manufactured goods such as household appliances, automobiles, and entertainment devices rises. Once consumption of manufactured goods approaches satiation, it increasingly moves toward personal services, such as health services, education, entertainment services, coaching and counselling or financial services. Overall these two driving forces have led in advanced countries to a declining share of employment and value added in agriculture and to an evolution of the shares of manufacturing following an inverted U-shape (Herrendorf et al. 2014).

The forces of creative destruction and structural change have on average hugely increased GDP per capita in many countries. Phases of downturn in particular regions or industries where processes and skills became obsolete have, however, had temporary or permanent negative consequences for some groups. Technological and structural change have moreover radically transformed the boundaries between private and professional life and different roles played by men and women in their economic lives. Before the industrial revolution, most men and women worked on the family farm or in small, family-owned business. A gendered division of work tasks existed, but in many cases it did not lead to women and men working in different economic sectors. With industrialization, many men moved to factory work, whereas married women increasingly stayed at home. Home production was still an extremely time-consuming activity, involving e.g. the carrying of water, the baking of bread, and the making of clothes. With the spread of running water, indoor plumbing, and electricity and with the diffusion of household appliances such as refrigerators and dishwashers the time needed for household work has been greatly reduced (a further important innovation was contraception). This offered the possibility for women to increasingly enter the labor market without men being obliged to share a large amount of household work

(Gordon 2016). On the other hand, the sphere of R&D organizations has developed in many parts as a male-dominated world, where women are underrepresented compared to their overall presence on the labor market.

The move of economic activity to the service sector has meant that an increasing share of economic output and investment has become intangible and knowledge-based. Knowledge-based services as an input into production, such as software or R&D, have continued to fuel productivity growth in conventional goods production, e.g. in the production of automobiles. As a final good, e.g. as movies, counselling services, medical services, or legal services to final consumers, their productivity growth is in many cases more qualitative than quantitative. In some areas, the quantitative progress in terms of longevity or survival rates for severe diseases has been impressive (Gordon 2016).

Processes of structural change and industrialization continue to be important for economic growth in developing countries. The fact that many technologies have already been invented in advanced countries offers much scope for technology diffusion and catching up. In the recent past, Asian countries have largely built their fast economic growth on increasing shares of their manufacturing sectors. In other regions, such Latin America and Sub-Saharan African countries, a premature deindustrialization is feared to limit future growth opportunities (Rodrik 2016). While economists worry about the future of the pace of technological change in advanced countries (see Section 4.2.8), a lack of technological opportunities is not the most pressing concern when it comes to poor countries, where factors discussed in the other sections of this chapter (such as education, institutions, geography) represent larger obstacles to productivity growth and to taking advantage of better technologies. Foreign direct investment (FDI; see Section 4.2.4) and higher education gained abroad are important channels for transfer of technological knowledge to developing countries and for building up intangible capital.

4.2.4 Globalization, Trade, and International Capital Flows

Economic theory emphasizes that welfare gains can be achieved if countries specialize in the production of goods and services for which they enjoy a "comparative advantage." Sources of such comparative advantage can be due to technological advantages (Ricardo 1817) or a relative abundance of production factors, e.g. labor or natural resources (Heckscher and Ohlin 1991). Hence, a country can export products that it can produce relatively cheaply and import those from the world market which would be more costly to produce domestically. In addition, recent theories show that countries may also trade in quite similar, but differentiated products (such as cars or computers of different brands; see Krugman 1979; Melitz 2003).

Empirical evidence demonstrates that trade-openness, defined as the sum of imports and exports divided by GDP, is positively related to economic growth (Wacziarg 2001). In a similar vein, trade liberalization has been found to increase plant productivity, arguably by increasing market size as well as competitive pressures to innovate

4

(Bustos 2011; Lileeva and Trefler 2010). However, even though more profound integration into the global economy can be beneficial at a certain stage of economic development, trade liberalization is not a silver bullet to spur economic growth, but needs to be employed selectively (Rodríguez and Rodrik 2000). That is, trade openness has often been a central feature of newly industrializing countries' development strategies (Rodrik 2005). Yet, these countries did not simply liberalize trade and foreign direct investment, but also employed an array of specifically tailored industrial policies to overcome market failures, such as financial frictions and coordination failures (Rodrik 2005).

Even though trade results in overall economic gains, the associated benefits and losses are not evenly distributed (Stolper and Samuelson 1941). In particular, trade openness is likely to increase inequality in earnings and may result in higher unemployment (Helpman, Itskhoki, and Redding 2010), which may explain the recent backlash against already existing as well as planned free-trade agreements.

Similar to trade in goods and services, the literature on FDI suggests positive effects on firms in recipient countries by means of so-called "technology spill-overs" (Blalock and Gertler 2008). Yet, whether these benefits materialize depends on numerous factors, including host country conditions and the type of FDI inflows (Javorcik 2008; Crespo and Fontoura 2007). Finally, financial globalization also takes place in the form of equity flows, as investors in one country acquire, say, company stocks or government bonds from another country. Even though theoretical considerations suggest that easier access to finance should be expected to spur investment and economic growth in countries that receive financial inflows, empirical evidence suggests that relatively rich countries have benefited, whereas poorer ones often did not have the absorptive capacities to employ those inflows effectively (Prasad, Rajan, and Subramanian 2007). Moreover, the link between openness to financial flows and the onset of financial crises, in which currency and banking crises mutually reinforce each other, is well documented in the literature (Reinhart and Kaminsky 1999).

4.2.5 Resource Endowments, the Resource Curse, Geography, and Environment

A growing body of literature that relies on cross-country comparisons is increasingly pointing to the critical importance of resource endowments, geography, and the environment (Rodrik 2002). Several competing theories attempt to explain the channels through which resource endowments affect economic growth and its distribution. Easterly and Levine (2003) emphasize that resource endowments affect the policies and institutions that emerge in different countries. It has also been argued that in resource-rich countries colonization has resulted in extractive institutions, which, in turn, have hampered economic development in recent times (Acemoglu et al. 2002). Kim (1999) argues that factor endowments determine the geographical distribution of manufacturing over time, potentially facilitating the exploitation agglomeration benefits. Auty (1997, 2001) documents an empirical link between resource endowments, landholding systems, the type of political state, the choice of development strategy, and the overall economic performance of a country.

4.2.5.1 The Resource Curse

Empirical evidence has established a so-called curse from natural resources. (Sachs and Warner 2001; Frankel 2010). The "curse" refers to an observation that countries endowed with richer natural resources systematically grow slower than resource-poor countries. Frankel (2010) speculates about possible links that lead to the curse, and examined the effects of resource endowments on long-term trends in world commodity prices, volatility, crowding out of manufacturing, civil war, poor institutions, and the Dutch disease. Isham et al. (2005) provide empirical evidence that many oil, mineral, and plantation crop-based economies experienced a substantial deceleration in growth following the boom and bust of the 1970s and 1980s. Isham et al. (2005) further attributes the curse to the fact that in resource-rich countries economic activity is developed along a narrow geographic and economic base, and is predisposed to social divisions and weak institutions. As a consequence, these countries don't have the ability to respond to shocks. Bilion (2001) examined theories of relationships between resources and armed conflicts, and puts forwards a clear argument where, in the presence of rich natural resource endowments, capital is misallocated toward the production of criminal-style activities.

Ploeg (2011) argues that volatile resource revenues are a major factor for political instability and hence bad economic performance. He also points out that "resources are not destiny" and that some countries, such as Norway and Botswana, have successfully used their resource endowments to promote economic development. According to Mehlum et al. (2006), sound institutions have been a key element behind this outcome.

The literature identifies a variety of institutional settings appropriate to counter the resource curse. Enhancing transparency (e.g. via the Extractive Industries Transparency Initiative) can help to keep corruption in check and contribute to sound spending policies. In addition, sovereign wealth funds can smooth volatile revenues and provide a buffer to maintain public spending in times of low commodity prices (Sala-i-Martin and Subramanian 2003).

4.2.5.2 Geography and the Environment

Geography impacts on economic development either directly (e.g. by factors related to climate and the disease environment) as well as indirectly (e.g. by its effect on trade via transportation costs (Gallup et al. 1999)).

Some authors (Easterly and Levine 2003) note that by shaping diseases, geographical endowments can constitute a limit to growth. Gallup et al. (1999) demonstrate the effects that location and climate have on income levels and income growth, attributing these to channels such as transportation costs, disease burdens, and agricultural productivity. Geography appears to limit growth in tropical regions, since these bear a heavy burden of disease. These geographical barriers to growth are likely to become increasingly problematic, since most of the expected population growth will occur in these disadvantaged regions (Sachs and Warner 1997), and can further be exacerbated by climate change (IPCC AR2).

4

Some geographic areas have been conducive to agglomeration of population and the development of cities and ideas that lead to increased growth through learning and agglomeration. Geography can limit growth in regions located far from coasts or navigable rivers, where transportation costs are high and, as a consequence, possibilities for trade are limited. Redding and Venables (2004) provide convincing evidence that access to markets and sources of supply explain cross-country variation in per capita income.

4.2.6　Actors and Institutions

Institutions can be defined as "commonly known rules used to structure recurrent interaction situations that are endowed with a sanctioning mechanism" (Voigt 2009: 8). They are often blamed or praised for their role in promoting growth with the argument "that it is the way that humans themselves decide to organize their societies that determines whether or not they prosper" (Acemoglu et al. 2005: 397). Key institutions for economic growth are property rights, markets (including labor and capital markets) and rules of government revenue collection and spending.

Democratic political institutions also offer a large potential for growth because they foster equal opportunity and collective decisions over the resources of the state. But there are examples of strong economic growth without democracy (China).

In assessing their potential effect on economic growth, it is important to verify whether the sanctions prescribed by an institutionalized rule are actually enforced (Voigt 2009). It is difficult to detect a robust additional effect of short-run policies (e.g. in the area of trade or monetary policy) on economic growth when controlling for institutions that often change only slowly (Easterly 2005). One reason might be that poor policies often reflect poor institutions.

Emphasizing the persistent influence of institutions over a long period, Acemoglu et al. (2002) argue that relatively rich countries colonized by European powers in the 1500s are now relatively poor and vice versa. They explain this "reversal of fortune" by the types of institutions imposed by European settlers. "Extractive" institutions were introduced in the relatively rich countries. They were characterized by an absence of protection of property rights and rule of law for the local population and focused on appropriation of the countries' natural wealth by the settlers. In the relatively poor areas, there were fewer incentives to plunder, and so to prevent the development of investment-friendly institutions. As a result, the decline or rise of those countries is rooted in a major – exogenous – institutional change linked to colonization.

A number of authors have also linked the poor performance of many developing countries with governance issues: corruption, ethnic fragmentation, civil wars, etc. (Mauro 1995; Easterly and Levine 1997; Bloom et al. 1998; Collier and Hoeffler 2002). Mere political pluralism is often associated with more internal conflicts and political disorder. It appears that the implementation of institutions protecting private property and contracts as well as the rule of law and increasing the quality of bureaucracies does not only have a direct effect on economic activity but also helps attenuating ethnic conflicts. Still it is not obvious how to foster these developments (Fosu 2017).

Institutions supporting innovation are of particular importance for growth. Interactions of many actors at the micro level, which are governed by markets as well as nonmarket institutions, result in innovation at the aggregate level (Soete et al. 2010). Actors crucial for innovation include the following: "(1) governments and related agencies supporting innovation through regulation, standard setting, public private partnerships, and funding of basic research, (2) sectors and industries comprised of firms which generate commercial innovations through experimentation, R&D, and product improvement, (3) universities which conduct basic research and train a technical and scientific workforce, and (4) other public and private organizations that engage in education oriented activities" (Watkins et al. 2015).

In addition to national actors and international nonprofit organizations, multinational corporations are actors that play an important and sometimes ambiguous role in fostering innovation and growth in developing countries (Watkins et al. 2015).

4.2.7　Culture, Social Movements, and Social Capital

Social movements are multidimensional and are mediated by cultural values (sets of identities and practices) – they have been led by workers, peasants, indigenous groups, women, and others. They may take place through their forms of expression in social media, educational processes to promote critical thinking, strengthen the democratic system and exert sociopolitical pressure.

Such movements have played a fundamental role in economic growth because they have manifested dissatisfaction and demanded improvements in different dimensions of human development. For example, social movements have covered quality of education, comprehensive health systems, wage improvements, and other dimensions that seek to raise social welfare through equity and social justice. In the second half of the twentieth century, the degradation of natural resources caused in part by economic growth has led to the emergence of environmentalist social movements (Leff 1983).

4.2.8　On the Possibility of Slowed Future Growth

Is it possible to imagine a situation where technical progress would come to a rest, or would only pertain to marginal and useless aspects of technology? For example, if the state of the art turns so complex that it becomes beyond human capacities to push further the frontier of knowledge. Or it could be that the required technologies to achieve the needed ecological and energy transitions remain without reach. Such a pessimistic view is defended by Gordon (2016) who, after a careful analysis of productivity measures, claims that the enormous productivity-enhancing innovations of the last century and a half cannot be equaled.

Such a halt to progress seems unlikely, in particular given mankind history of permanent improvements since the Neolithic revolution (see Mokyr et al. 2015 for a brief history of the idea of progress and some arguments against technophobia). Hence the primary engine of growth is likely to stay on for the next centuries. It is not the case however of the secondary engines. In the developed world, years of schooling and longevity are bounded above by limits to the length of human life. Even if one can break some biological limits, the gains in terms of growth of further improvements along this dimension will remain low. About education, there might remain some reserves for improvement on the side of quality. Still in developed countries, the urbanization process, which was so key for generating the takeoff to modern growth of the nineteenth century, is now completed. The same remark applies to the fertility transition: demographic dividends are over for developed countries (and for most of the developing world too).

This extinction of the secondary engines of growth does not apply to developing countries, which still have several decades of bonuses to obtain from them, in particular in Africa which has just started its demographic transition.

Slowed future growth seems thus a true possibility for the rich countries. The implications of such a situation are still very poorly understood. Certainly, it would put the social protection systems of rich countries under stress. It will make any redistribution policy more difficult to implement within the existing institutions, and the whole policy debate more tense. The usual tradeoff between equality and efficiency will be tougher. Indeed, relying exclusively on productivity gains to generate income growth requires the economy to work as efficiently as possible, which, in some cases, may restrict the scope for redistribution policies. It is the case for example of capital taxation policies, including bequest taxations. Higher capital taxes are needed to help redistribution resources and contain the rise in wealth inequality (Piketty 2014), but the cost of such policies in terms of loss of efficiency is likely to be more severe in a slowly growing economy.

Beyond the debate on the advent of slower growth, some authors have argued in favor of halting growth on purpose. Jackson (2009), for example, argues that "for the advanced economies of the Western world, prosperity without growth is no longer a utopian dream. It is a financial and ecological necessity." Jackson's approach is based on a formal model of Keynesian inspiration – hence designed to tackle short-run issues – where growth is driven by demand (consumption, investment). This approach contrasts strongly with the classical approach relating growth to technical progress. For Jackson, stopping growth amounts to fighting consumerism, probably not to fighting progress.

4.3   Evaluation of Growth, Welfare, and Human Development

As discussed in Section 4.1.1, economic growth is often much lauded, but it has its critics too. Such positive and critical evaluations rest on both empirical and normative commitments. In this section we consider various normative criteria that can be used to evaluate growth. These normative criteria have been introduced in Chapter 2.

Here we focus on the normative standards *specifically as they apply to economic growth*. The section is divided into two halves. First, Section 4.3.1 identifies different accounts of what should be deemed to be a benefit and what a burden. Its focus is on "what matters" – happiness, preference satisfaction, or something else. There is widespread recognition that analyses of economic growth that assess it simply by appealing to GDP are unsatisfactory since GDP does not *in itself* matter. It matters because, and to the extent that, it contributes to other goods (Stiglitz, Sen, Fitoussi 2010). Section 4.3.1 considers some accounts of what they might be. Once we have an account of what matters, the next question is what is the right rule concerning those benefits. Should economic growth be judged in terms of its contribution to maximizing the good, or ensuring equal amounts of it, or raising people above a threshold, or some other criterion? These issues are explored in Section 4.3.2. Not all of the goods to be discussed in Section 4.3.1 (such as political stability) are easily treated as goods to which distributive principles can be applied. Some (such as benefits like happiness, preference satisfaction, or capabilities), however, are, and thus a discussion of what rule should govern the distribution of those goods is required.

4.3.1   What Matters

4.3.1.1   Preference Satisfaction

Some hold that what matters is that people's preferences are satisfied. To evaluate economic growth or the lack of it one must, on this view, determine what impacts it has for the satisfaction of people's preferences as a measure of their well-being.

Is it valid to appeal to preference satisfaction to evaluate economic growth? One challenge is posed by Amartya Sen, who argues that preferences formed in unjust social circumstances might reflect this (Sen 1987: 11). The appeal of the preference satisfaction approach is lost if the account simply reflects unjust circumstances set up by the powerful in ways that advantage them.

A second concern arises from the phenomenon that J.K. Galbraith referred to as the "dependence effect" in his classic *The Affluent Society* (1958: ch. 11). His claim was that if people had exogenously given preferences then the fact that an economic system satisfied them would count in its favor, but since economic systems create preferences they deserve little credit for satisfying people's preferences.

Advocates of a "preference satisfaction" view can respond to some of these objections. For example, in response to Sen's critique they might stipulate that a person's good is what he or she would desire in a situation in which – as well as having full information and being fully rational – they have genuine choice and are not subject to the

4

manipulation of others (Brandt 1979). This might also help respond to Galbraith's challenge for the emphasis would then be *not* on satisfying preferences produced and created by the existing economic system, but rather preferences that a well-informed nonmanipulated rational agent would choose. This takes us far from actual desires to desires formed in rather idealized circumstances (Griffin 1986: ch. 1, esp. pp. 10–15).

4.3.1.2   Happiness

A second criterion that might be used to evaluate economic growth equates individual well-being with happiness, where happiness is defined in terms of pleasant mental states. Some argue convincingly that economic growth does not promote happiness (e.g. Easterlin 2010: 13–45: originally published in 1974). (See Chapter 8 for a full discussion of the Easterlin paradox.)

Should we then judge economic growth in terms of its impact on happiness? Several objections have been pressed against this criterion. For example, Robert Nozick argues that it would not be desirable to be plugged into an "experience machine" that provides wonderful pleasant mental states for life, indicating that there is more to life than pleasant mental states (Nozick 1974: 42–45). A second objection argues that happiness is not a reliable criterion as to what matters. Dan Moller, for example, reasons that other goods matter and that economic growth has value to the extent that it furthers these goods (Moller 2011: 186–189).

4.3.1.3   Capabilities to Function

A third concept of well-being by which one might judge economic growth is the "capabilities" approach pioneered by Amartya Sen (1987, 1999, 2009, part III) and Martha Nussbaum (2006: 69–81), which is discussed in depth in Chapter 2. Unlike the preference satisfaction and happiness theories, it takes a more objective approach. It identifies human functionings and evaluates social, economic, and political institutions (and so economic growth) in terms of their effects on people's capability to enjoy these functionings.

One might assess economic growth (or its absence) in terms of its impacts on capabilities. For example, economic development that lifts people out of poverty will, of course, promote several key capabilities (Sen 1999; Alkire 2002b). At the same time, growth can also result in harms to other capabilities. In particular, environmental externalities (such as climate change and biodiversity loss) will have adverse effects on some capabilities, most notably the capability for good health as well as control over one's environment.

This approach is, however, not without critics (Fleurbaey and Banchet 2013: 225ff). One question concerns the issue of how one identifies "capabilities" – is one list of capabilities more plausible than another? These concerns notwithstanding, the capabilities approach provides a useful and intuitive framework for evaluating growth.

4.3.1.4   Meaning of Life

Some might argue that the previous three criteria do not constitute an exhaustive basis on which to judge economic growth. They might, thus, appeal to the idea of a "meaningful" life to evaluate economic growth. Human beings do not exclusively strive for happiness, but a sense of meaning also matters for the conception of individual targets in life. Some correlates of happiness and meaning, such as religion, friends, and family overlap. Others, however, point in opposite directions. For instance, one recent cross-country study (Oishi and Diener 2014) found that people in poor countries on average enjoy a greater sense of meaning in life than people in rich countries. Likewise, one recent study in the US (Baumeister et al. 2013) points out that "concerns with personal identity and expressing the self contribute[s] to meaning but not happiness," concluding that one can lead an unhappy, but nevertheless a meaningful life.

Living a good life can mean living in accordance with one's values, i.e. that one's identity is constituted by adhering to these values. This perspective is closely related to the ancient concept of virtue ethics, which states that leading a good life means striving for fundamental virtues, such as wisdom or justice.

4.3.1.5   Status Consumption

People assess their economic well-being not only in absolute terms, but also relative to others ("keeping up with the Joneses," Gali 1994). This phenomenon of "status consumption" can be defined as:

> the motivational process by which individuals strive to improve their social standing through the conspicuous consumption of consumer products that confer and symbolize status both for the individual and surrounding significant others   (Eastman, Goldsmith, and Flynn 1999: 42; Eastman and Eastman 2011: 10).

The importance of status consumption increases with income, as people use higher shares of their income to acquire scarce goods (such as houses or works of art) that convey social status (Hirsch 1977).

Does it matter that economic growth promotes status consumption, and, if so, in what ways? For a preference satisfaction theory, it matters whether status consumption aids in satisfying people's desires. If it does not, or if it just generates further insatiable desires, then status consumption does not advance someone's good. Similarly, for a happiness-based theory status consumption has value because, and to the extent that, it results in happiness; but if acquiring the goods turns out not to result in the pleasant mental states then it will not count as advancing people's good.

A capability approach will take a different tack. For example, status consumption could matter only insofar as it contributes to an "affiliation" capability (forming associations with others and being treated with equal respect) (Nussbaum 2006: 77).

Whilst it might be rational for an individual to seek status consumption to keep up with others, society as a whole may benefit little from economic growth if increasing incomes turn into a zero-sum game in which one individual's gain is the other's loss (Frank 2005). In this case, every member of society could be made better off by collectively agreeing on restricting consumption and benefit from the reduced effort (in terms of labor, natural resources, etc.) needed to produce this consumption in the first place (Scitovsky 1976: 120; Howarth 2006; Frank 2008).

4.3.1.6 Nonanthropocentric Values, Intrinsic Value of Nature and Animal Welfare

The focus so far in Section 4.3.1 has been on ways in which economic growth impacts human beings, though economic growth may also impact the environment or nonhuman animals in adverse ways.

Does the impact on the environment and nonhuman animals matter, if it does not also have an impact on human beings? Anthropocentric concerns have been the primary values that traditional Western philosophers have recognized, though in the latter half of the twentieth century, environmental ethics emerged as a separate philosophical discipline. (See Chapter 2, Section 2.3.7 for a full discussion of the intrinsic value of nature debate.) One of the thorniest ethical issues that remain is how to balance human and nonhuman welfare (Singer 1975; Regan 1983; Taylor 1986). Whatever the ultimate theoretical account of human–nonhuman balancing, in many cases human-and-nonhuman goods are aligned. Of course, some situations embody genuine conflict between human survival and biotic or abiotic welfare. Yet because both humans and nonhumans rely on the same biotic and abiotic systems for survival and well-being, many cases of human–environment conflict are avoidable. As Thomas Pogge suggests, many such conflicts have arisen from colonialism, greed, imperialism, and the desperation and human inequality that they cause (Blackstone 1974; Pogge 2002; Singer and Mason 2006; Shrader-Frechette 2007; Bob and Bronkhorst 2010).

4.3.1.7 Political Stability and Legitimacy

A further criterion for the evaluation of economic growth concerns its impact on political stability and legitimacy. Some authors have explored whether economic growth furthers political stability (Paldam 1998), and there is an established literature on how economic growth – and the rate of change of growth – impacts both political stability and political legitimacy (Hirschman 1973; Huntington 1968; Przeworski, Alvarez, Cheibub, and Limongi 2000). There is, in addition to this, a literature on whether political stability promotes economic growth (Alesina, Özler, Roubini, and Swagel 1996).

Political instability should not be confused with mere "political change" (Przeworski, Alvarez, Cheibub, and Limongi 2000: 188), and so political stability should not be understood as a lack of political change. Political stability can instead be understood as an absence of major "political upheavals" (Przeworski, Alvarez, Cheibub, and Limongi 2000: 189ff). Political stability can also be defined as "the state in which a political object exists when it possesses the capacity to prevent contingencies from forcing its non-survival" (Dowding and Kimber 1983: 238–239).

Political legitimacy can be distinguished into "normative" notions of political legitimacy (which claim that a political institution has legitimacy if it meets some moral standards) and "descriptive" notions of political legitimacy (which claim that a political institution has legitimacy if those subject to it recognize it as being entitled to govern) (Peters 2010).

The values of political order and political legitimacy are, to some extent, derivative values. That is, they have value, in part, because, and to the extent that, the social and political institutions that are in place are valuable ones that should be stabilized and legitimized. So before knowing whether stabilizing and legitimizing a regime is valuable it is necessary to know whether it is worth preserving, or whether there is a more just and less oppressive alternative available.

Bernard Williams has argued that the question of how to secure order and political stability is the "first political question," meaning that "the securing of order" is necessary to pursue other ideals (like social justice) (Williams 2005: 3). However, this is consistent with thinking that its value derives from the realization of these other goals. An evaluation of the effect of economic growth on stability and legitimacy must therefore be conducted together with its effects on justice and the standard of living.

4.3.2 How Is It Distributed?

The previous section considered some of the metrics that might be used to evaluate economic growth, and specified various benefits (happiness, preference satisfaction, capabilities, meaning of life, etc.) and various burdens (pollution) that need to be borne in mind. There is a further question concerning how the goods in question (whether happiness or capabilities or some other good) should be distributed. This section turns to those questions.

4.3.2.1 Maximizing the Good

One familiar view of distributive criteria is that the good should be maximized. The best-known version of this is utilitarianism, which takes utility (understood either as happiness or as preference satisfaction) as its good and then calls for its maximization (Sidgwick 1981 [1907]). See Chapter 2, Section 2.4.3.5 for a full discussion of utilitarianism's distributive implications.

Since our focus is on economic growth and thus the standard of living of people in the future, it is worth noting that an additional set of questions arise when we apply a maximizing approach to future generations. Derek Parfit has argued that if the aim is to maximize total utility then this might lead to what he calls "the repugnant conclusion" – a world with very many people, all of whom have a low (but positive) standard of living (Parfit 1984: ch. 17). Others object that applying a maximizing approach might impose very demanding obligations on current generations who are required to sacrifice their consumption in order to create greater benefits for future generations. This has led some to embrace "discounted utilitarianism" (which

4

applies a positive pure time discount rate), and for others to abandon maximizing views (Parfit 1984: 484–485; Rawls 1999: 262).

4.3.2.2   Equality

An alternative distributive principle by which to evaluate economic growth would be to assess it in terms of its impact on the realization of equality. (See Chapter 2 for a discussion of different kinds of egalitarianism.)

One question that is very relevant when evaluating economic growth is whether the focus should be just on inequality within a country or whether it should concern global inequalities. The issue at stake is that of the scope of egalitarian justice. Given that economic growth often has implications beyond the borders of any given state, it is important to consider whether egalitarian principles apply globally or not (for a discussion see Chapter 2).

On one view, inequality matters only within a state. This view holds that there is something special about the state that entails that egalitarian principles apply there but not elsewhere. This might be because the state exercises coercion over its citizens (Blake 2013) or because the state is a scheme of cooperation (Sangiovanni 2007). A contrasting, cosmopolitan, view maintains that it is arbitrary to apply equality within one country. Luck egalitarians, for example, will hold that egalitarian principles should apply at the global level, and thus criticize global inequalities as unjust (Caney 2011).

A second question concerns the application of this principle over time. Given the effects of economic growth on future generations it is necessary to enquire whether egalitarian principles – or some other principles – should be applied over time. One concern about maintaining that equality should apply across time is that it would seem to prohibit one generation from making future generations better off. As such it seems vulnerable to a particularly acute version of the "leveling down" objection (Parfit 1997: 210–211). It would seem implausible to limit growth if and because it would result in an intertemporal inequality.

In light of this, one might consider an alternative view, voiced by Brian Barry, who argued that "those alive at any time are custodians rather than owners of the planet, and ought to pass it on in at least no worse shape than they found it in" (Barry 1991: 258). On this view, one generation may not leave future ones worse off but may leave them better off.

Related approaches claim that members of each generation have a right to an equal standard of living on the grounds that it is objectionable for some to have less or more purely because of when they are alive. However, they argue, each generation has a right to leave future generations better off, and in line with this preference governments should maximize the standard of living of current generations subject to leaving future generations better off (thereby honoring what they term "growth sustainability" (Llavador, Roemer, and Silvestre 2015: 4 and 34)). For this argument see Llavador, Roemer, and Silvestre (2015: 1–5 and 34–38; also Roemer 2011, 2013).

4.3.2.3   Sufficiency and Meeting Core Needs

As noted above, one rationale for reducing inequalities is that it is necessary for reducing human misery and suffering. This argument is not deeply committed to equality (Scanlon 1997: 2). It implies that inequality is acceptable so long as people's standard of living is above some designated level. This takes us to sufficientarianism, "the doctrine that what is morally important with regard to money is that everyone should have enough" (Frankfurt 2015: 7). Sufficientarianism insists that there is a threshold standard of living, below which no one should fall. This could be quite a minimal standard, calling for meeting everyone's basic needs. Or it could be something more demanding, requiring a higher standard of living.

At the global level, many endorse a sufficientarian threshold. One version of this, for example, is couched in terms of rights and it holds that all persons throughout the world have rights to have their basic needs met (Shue 1996). This approach contrasts with purely aggregative approaches which seek to promote the good of the whole, and it emphasizes the rights of everyone not to fall beneath a minimum standard.

Such a sufficientarian approach can also inform intergenerational justice and thus be employed to judge the value of economic growth over time. On one widely held view, current generations have a duty not to act in ways that result in future generations being unable to enjoy a basic standard of living.

One difficult issue surrounding sufficientarianism is the question of how to define the sufficiency threshold and where to draw the line (Casal 2007). It is also unclear why differences just below any designated threshold have immense moral significance but benefits above it lack any. It would be implausible to insist on a policy that improves the standard of living of someone below the threshold at the cost of imposing considerable losses on everyone else leaving them just above the threshold (Casal 2007). As she notes, a sufficientarian approach to evaluating economic growth – whilst important – cannot be the full story: it needs to be supplemented with additional principles, such as equality or prioritizing the least advantaged (Casal 2007).

4.3.2.4   Priority for the Least Advantaged

This takes us to a fourth distributive principle that might be applied when evaluating economic growth – the principle of prioritizing the least advantaged. Parfit, defines "the Priority View" as follows: "Benefiting people matters more the worse off these people are" (Parfit 1997: 213). This is importantly distinct from egalitarian views for whereas egalitarian views are concerned with how people fare relative to others, prioritarian views, by contrast, are concerned only with people's absolute level, and not with how well one person does in comparison to another (Parfit 1997: 214).

Some apply prioritarianism to the global level, and thus would evaluate global economic growth in light of Parfit's Priority View. The reasons given in defense of the Priority View, if sound, would seem to apply with equal force at the global level as well as within the state (Caney

2005: ch. 4). Similarly, to the extent that it is a valid principle at all there is no reason to think that it should apply solely within one generation. An intertemporal priority view would thus evaluate economic growth in terms of its effects on current and future generations, giving more weight to persons the worse off they are, though it would have to address the complicated issues raised by population ethics (Holtug 2010: ch. 9).

The Priority View is not without critics, however. Some have argued that whatever appeal it has, it has none when all are above a high sufficiency threshold. In a society where some have very high levels of wealth but others have even more, there seems, they argue, little reason to attribute greater weight to the interests of the first group (Crisp 2006: 157). Rather, it gets its force from cases where people are severely disadvantaged.

4.3.2.5   Environmental Justice

The previous sections have discussed the general principles of distributive justice normally applied to the economy as a whole. In this section, a specific focus is given to environmental justice, or injustice, which occurs whenever a vulnerable group of people faces disproportionate environmental risks, has less-than-equal access to environmental goods, or has less opportunity to participate in environmental decision-making.

Children represent a minority victimized by environmental injustice because they are more sensitive to the same doses of virtually all forms of environmental pollution. Studies consistently show that socio-economically deprived groups are more likely to be subject to environmental injustice, as are people in developing nations – these people tend to be less able to prevent and to remedy such inequities. Members of communities facing such threats typically are too poor to "vote with their feet" and move elsewhere (e.g. Boer, Kastor and Sadd 1997; Ringquist 1997; Maher 1998; and NAACP 2016).

Critics of environmental justice typically claim that, on balance, victims of alleged environmental insults may benefit from living near noxious facilities because of factors such as cheaper housing costs (Baker 1993; Starkey 1994; Hayward 2013). Such claims ignore the fact that those living amid environmental injustice likely have not consented to it, but instead can afford nothing better. This supposed consent is not genuine consent if people have no other options. Environmental injustice need not be deliberate, albeit a serious concern for many members of society.

4.4   Social and Natural Wealth

The previous section has shown that economic growth matters in that it contributes to other goods, though there is debate as to how economic growth should be judged in terms of different distributive principles. This section examines the effects of economic growth in the framework of social and natural wealth, and clarifies the positive and negative impacts it has had historically, which contribute to the two overarching narratives introduced in Section 4.1.1: liberation and exploitation.

4.4.1   Social Wealth

In the framework of social wealth, this section discusses the relationship of economic growth with health and poverty (Section 4.4.1.1), inequality (Section 4.4.1.2), urbanization (Section 4.4.1.3), political change and democracy (Section 4.4.1.4), and consumption patterns more generally (Section 4.4.1.5). Social wealth can be understood as the set of established social practices (including practices in private production, governmental institutions, and people's daily lives) that affect the potential for generating human well-being in a society. Much of the section provides support for the first narrative of economic growth – liberation.

4.4.1.1   Health and Poverty Reduction

Historical changes (see Volume 3 of this Report, Chapter 18, Section 2 on the rise in longevity) show that improvements in average health and reduction in its variability have been made possible by economic growth. Many scientific discoveries, medical advances, and public health initiatives that have produced enormous health gains in the most advanced countries would not have occurred outside the context of industrialization and growth (Weil 2014).

The impact of economic growth on poverty reduction is not straightforward. Dollar et al. (2016) argue that, overall, "growth is good for the poor." That is, even though the relationship between countries' growth performance and poverty reduction shows quite some variance, on average every percentage point of economic growth increases the income of the two poorest quintiles by about 1 percent. The finding that economic growth seems to "lift all the boats" is confirmed by more recent developments. Absolute poverty, defined as the number of people with daily income below US$ 1.90 (measured in year 2011 US$ at purchasing power parity),[14] has dropped from about 2 billion in 1990 to less than 800 million in 2013. Most of this decline can be attributed to East Asia and the Pacific, i.e. the region that displayed the highest rate of economic growth during the respective period (see Figure 4.4). However, even though poverty rates have fallen considerably in all regions of the developing world (from 40 percent in 1990 to 11.5 percent in 2013), the progress when measured by the number of people in absolute poverty is less impressive. For example, the number of people in poverty has increased in Sub-Saharan Africa (SSA), and now stands at about almost 400 million, even though the poverty rate has fallen slightly from 54 percent in 1990 to 41 percent in 2013 (WDI 2016).

The responsiveness of poverty to economic growth differs substantially across regions, with a lower level of initial inequality associated with a

---

[14]   Such low thresholds have frequently been criticized as constituting a mere subsistence level (Pritchett 2006), suggesting that poverty itself may go much beyond this measure.

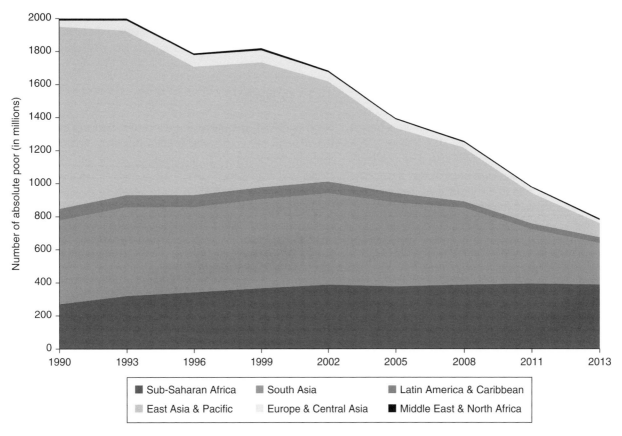

Figure 4.4 | Development of absolute poverty over the period 1990–2013.
Note: Poverty is defined as disposable income below 1.90 US$ per day (vertical axis in millions).
Source: WDI (2016)

higher rate of transformation (Fosu 2010). In particular, SSA has generally exhibited less impressive progress on poverty, compared with the rest of the developing world, even during the more recent period of substantial growth resurgence. This is not only due to relatively high levels of inequality, but also to the low levels of income, which tend to reduce the rate at which growth is translated into poverty reduction relative to the rest of the world (Fosu 2009). Nevertheless, on average, economic growth has been the main force behind the recent progress on poverty in SSA (Fosu 2015).

Growth therefore doesn't automatically reduce poverty. The disconnect is due to weak institutions, policy-making, research capacity, and to insufficient public investment.

Another major reason, in particular in SSA, is slow agricultural growth and rural development (Diao et al. 2012). Most of the poor are to some degree dependent on farming and so fostering agricultural growth is often seen as a strategy to support pro-poor development (Thrittle, Lin, and Peisse 2003). Agricultural growth rates in many African countries are less than one-third of the nonagricultural sector's growth rates, and per capita agricultural income increased at less than 1 percent per year from 2000 to 2015 (World Bank 2016). Consequently, the rural–urban divide in Africa continues to widen. Diao et al. (2012) found that improving agricultural productivity in most African countries is essential to achieving inclusive,

pro-poor growth. Staple-food crop and livestock production must be expanded because they have the scale and linkages to poor households needed to reduce national poverty within a reasonable period of time.

Poverty alleviation is not exclusively a matter of disposable income, but a matter of development possibilities in a broader sense. This includes access to physical and social infrastructures necessary to satisfy basic human needs. Examples include health, education, and social security, as well as expansion of physical infrastructure (Alkire 2002a). This view is further buttressed by the recent finding that poverty is persistent, in that the level of poverty prevailing in an earlier period tends to promote further poverty in the future (Ravallion 2012).

Economic growth can therefore support poverty alleviation and provide the means to physical foundation for human well-being, such as basic infrastructure. Yet, there is no automatic link between economic growth and access to development opportunities. In order to ensure that growth is indeed good for the poor, accompanying policies can support societal transformations during the process of industrialization (Drèze and Sen 2013). Vice versa, even with low rates of economic growth, governments can take measures to address poverty by strengthening social inclusion. For instance, the Indian state of Kerala is often cited as a good example of how good development outcomes

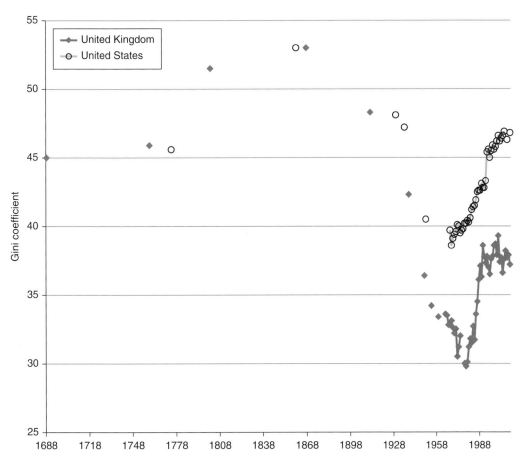

Figure 4.5 | Long run inequality trends: income Gini coefficients.
Source: Roine and Waldenström 2015.

can be achieved even with comparatively low per capita incomes (Kannan 1995).

4.4.1.2   Inequality

The "Kuznets curve" suggests that inequality first increases and then decreases in the course of the growth process (see Figure 4.5). The rising part of the curve is true mechanically, as growth proceeds a gap tends to emerge between leaders and laggards, but the decreasing part is dubious in light of the rise in inequality observed in both the more advanced countries as well as the emerging economies in the last 30 years. A detailed analysis of within-country inequality trends is provided in Chapter 3.

Among-nation or international inequality may have begun because of variations – in climate, environment, and geography, including different amounts of natural resources and available farmland – that contributed to western European agricultural, technological, and immunological advantages (Diamond 1997). As a result of these disparities in natural advantages, international gaps in economic development increased. These gaps, in turn, made possible colonialism, slavery, and imperialism, which includes the murder

or socio-economic, political, or military subjugation of millions of people (Bartolome de las Casas 1992; Howe 2002; Cooper 2005; Hobsbawm 2008).

As a result, the income of the average Angolan or Ethiopian is only 2 percent of that of the average American. An American with the average income of the bottom 10 percent in the country is nevertheless better off than two-thirds of the world's population. Hence within-nation inequality is dwarfed by among-nation inequality (Frieden 2001; Milanovic 2002; World Bank 2006).

Among-region inequality increased partly because of colonialism, as Western Europe has been mainly a colonizer and not its victim, whereas Latin America and Africa have been predominantly victims and not perpetrators of colonialism. Some regimes likewise tend to have victimized regions rich in natural resources and hence created and exacerbated regional inequalities.

Beyond the causal effect of growth on inequality, we can also wonder whether income inequality is good or bad for growth? Most of the existing literature on inequality and growth concentrates on the accumulation of physical capital. In countries with large numbers of poor, there is a high demand for redistribution policies, which in turn lead to tax distortions that slow growth. Inequality can also influence growth because of its effects on the accumulation of human capital, in particular if the poor are subject to credit constraints, preventing them from investing enough in human development (e.g. education, health, and skill formation).

Demographic variables must be taken into account in order to assess the effects that economic growth may have on income distribution (differential fertility and mortality). When inequality is high, fertility of the poor is very high as compared to that of the rich, making it more difficult to accumulate human capital in the economy (de la Croix and Doepke 2003).

4.4.1.3   Social Transitions

Urbanization is the increase in the proportion of households living in cities. High urbanization levels always accompany high income per person. Urbanization is necessary for growth, but is not sufficient to spur growth in itself. Advanced societies without a large proportion of their members living in cities are not observed. But poor or stagnant societies with high urbanization rates (from the Roman Empire to some developing countries today) do exist. Gollin, Jedwab, and Vollrath (2015) develop the idea of premature urbanization, which arises in particular in resource-exporting countries, with "consumption cities" having a larger fraction of workers in nontradable services, high poverty rates, and extensive slums.

Urbanization directly contributes to growth by moving people from low efficiency sectors to more productive ones (McMillan and Rodrik, 2011). Part of the growth observed in developed countries today came from this reallocation. Now that this movement is coming to an end, one of the "engine" of growth is no longer operating.

Beyond its direct effect on productivity, urbanization is also very much related to the increase in human capital. Indeed, cities are the place where people acquired secondary and tertiary education, and where upper tail human capital was developed, through institutions tightly linked to cities, such as academies, museums, universities, libraries, etc. More generally, cities generate agglomeration externalities, by allowing private resources to generate social benefits (Fujita and Thisse 2002).

Urbanization is also an inevitable component of "modernization," and is related to many other features of development, such as democratization, secularization, individualization, rising standard of living and the emancipation of women (see Volume 3 of this Report, Chapter 17). Modernization is also intrinsically linked to what demographers call the second demographic transition (van Bavel and Kok, 2010). Beyond the drop in fertility arising from this second transition, modernization implies significant family transformations. Wealthier societies introduced the possibility of divorce (de la Croix and Mariani 2015). Highly educated couples may now decide to remain childless, introducing a wedge between marriage and parenthood (Baudin et al. 2015). New forms of marriage are on the rise, and people who marry have become more and more similar in terms of income and education (rise in homogamy). At the same time, endogamy and marriage between close kin is on the decline.

4.4.1.4   Political Change and Democracy

Income per person is strongly correlated with social institutions that are usually considered positive for welfare, such as democracy and gender equality. Most countries were not democracies before the modern growth process took off at the beginning of the nineteenth century. Democratization came gradually together with income growth. However, there is no one-directional causality between institutions and economic development. Economic and political change can therefore probably best be understood as a process of co-evolution, in which economic changes affect political power structures, which in turn can promote or delay economic change. This view can be traced back to Marx (1867), who predicted the demise of capitalism, which, as a consequence of its internal contradictions, will be overthrown by the exploited working class and replaced by socialism. A similar perspective is also exposed by Schumpeter (1942), who expected capital accumulation to result in huge bureaucratic structures, which will increase demand for more democratic control and result in a socialist regime.

Sen (2013) discusses three channels through which economic growth interacts with political factors. These include, first, provision of public goods by the government, second, credible commitment to potential and current investors that it will not expropriate their profits, and, third, overcoming coordination failures. He also emphasizes that these political factors may be of different importance in the stage of transitioning from a phase of economic stagnation to growth acceleration and the stage of maintaining stable long-term growth, respectively.

Recent literature has frequently emphasized the importance of robust institutions, such as secure property rights, free media, accountable government, and democracy as an important foundation for economic development (Rodrik, Subramanian, and Trebbi 2004). However, it has also been argued that in numerous cases improvements in democracy have only occurred after a phase of building up industrial production structures, as in the case of state-led industrialization in numerous Asian countries (Chang 2007).

Regarding the role of the state, Hall and Soskice (2001) identify major differences between liberal market economies, such as the UK and the US, on the one hand and controlled market economies, such as France, Germany, and Scandinavia, on the other. Whereas for the former, the market is employed as the main device to guide economic decisions, the latter adopt a more corporatist model, in which business associations and labor unions play more important roles in political decision making. In a similar vein, even though industrial policy has frequently been criticized due to the impossibility of "picking winners" (Pack and Saggi 2006), some authors argue that it might have an important role in facilitating coordination between different sectors, in particular in economies and facing a large array of political and institutional constraints (Hausmann and Rodrik 2003). Hence, in such cases, industrial policy does not amount to actively picking winners, but rather removing barriers to create conditions that allow for "self-discovery." In such a setting, the state would aim at simultaneously addressing multiple market failures facing an uncertain and politically constrained second-best setting, not unlike the process of robust policy-making outlined in Section 4.5.4.

4.4.1.5 Consumption Patterns

The effect of economic growth on changes in consumption patterns is closely related to the process of structural change discussed in Section 4.2.3. Gordon (2016) described the evolution of consumption patterns in the USA since the onset of the Industrial Revolution in a way that is exemplary for advanced countries, but that also reflects patterns witnessed in emerging and developing countries. Between 1870 and 1970, American's consumption drastically changed in many respects: Homes became more comfortable in terms of size, lighting, and protection from extreme temperatures, humidity, and insects. The quality and variety of the diet increased – decreasing in terms of consumption of meat (but becoming more varied) and corn, and increasing in terms of consumption of fruits, milk products, eggs, fats and oils, and sugar. The share of processed food and fabricated clothing increased relative to home-made products. Household appliances increased the productivity of home production. The innovations eased the work burden on wives and daughters whose task in the household had been to carry water, to bake bread and to make clothes. Access to many networks became available such as electricity, running water, trains, paved roads, and automobiles to drive on them, daily mail delivery extending to rural areas, telegraphs and telephones, radio and television. After 1970, the internet was the most important new network. Raising incomes allowed people to consume more and new goods and services beyond the basic needs of food and shelter. The share of consumption on perishable goods declined from 52 percent in 1869 to 9 percent in 2013. The share of semi-durable goods remained stable at around 15 percent but changed its compositions to new goods motor vehicle fuels and pharmaceuticals. The same applied to the share of durables of around 10 percent, where new goods such as telephones and motor vehicles became available. The share of consumption of services rose from 24 percent to 66 percent. This evolution, especially also the diffusion of network access, has been widespread throughout the population and not concentrated to rich classes.

4.4.2 Natural Wealth

In the framework of natural wealth, this section discusses the relationship of economic growth with the depletion of exhaustible resources (Section 4.4.2.1), planetary boundaries (Section 4.4.2.2), climate change (Section 4.4.2.3), air and water (Sections 4.4.2.4 and 4.4.2.5), food security (Section 4.4.2.5), biodiversity (Section 4.4.2.6), and socio-economic metabolism (Section 4.4.2.7). Much of the section provides support for the second narrative of economic growth – alienation.

4.4.2.1 Depletion of Exhaustible Resources

Historically, the economists' view was that there is a finite stock of resources available to humans (Hotelling 1931). This model predicts that resource use declines over time and resource prices increase exponentially. Empirical tests of the Hotelling model, however, fail without exception, due to the geology of resources (Halvorsen and Smith 1991; Lin and Wagner 2007; Hart and Spiro 2011; Atewamba and Nkuiya 2017).

While the exact figure varies between resources, current consumption of exhaustible resources can be maintained for centuries with the resources available in the Earth's crust (Nordhaus 1974; Krautkraemer 1998). As the most accessible deposits get exhausted, further deposits become increasingly difficult to reach. At the same time, technology advances and keeps pace with the difficulty of reaching the deposits (Managi et al. 2004; Hart 2016; Stürmer and Schwerhoff 2016), thus allowing increasing resource consumption.

Exhaustible resources do indeed produce rents, but these rents are rents from market power, not scarcity (Ellis and Halvorson 2002; Hansen and Lindholt 2008; Huppmann and Holz 2012; Nakov and Nuno 2013).

The abundance of exhaustible resources is no reason to be unconcerned, however. The carbon emissions embodied in fossil fuel reserves are at least ten times higher than the remaining disposal space in the atmosphere (Jakob and Hilaire 2015). If dangerous climate change is to be avoided, the majority of fossil fuels must remain unburned. In addition, mining of all kinds of resources causes significant local pollution. As a consequence, sustainability is not threatened by the sheer availability of resources, but rather by the side-effects of producing and using them; in other words by the planetary boundaries (Section 4.4.2.2) and climate change (Section 4.4.2.3).

4.4.2.2 Planetary Boundaries

The Industrial Revolution stimulated unprecedented economic growth (see Section 4.1.3). Since that time, human activities have become the main driver for earth system changes, pushing the system beyond a stable natural state and introducing substantial environmental problems such as air and water pollution (Sections 4.4.2.4 and 4.4.2.5), climate change (Section 4.4.2.3), soil pollution by heavy metals, a hole in the ozone layer, wetland retreat, and loss of biodiversity (Section 4.4.2.7) (Hudson 1992; Crutzen 2002; Steffen et al. 2007; and Rockström 2009a).

The damage to environment and resources threaten both current and future generations. Therefore, there is an inevitable conflict between short-term and long-term development as well as local and global development.

Rockström et al. (2009a,b) proposed a framework to quantify the planetary boundary within which we can safely operate. This framework identifies nine biogeochemical classes: climate change (Section 4.4.2.3), ocean acidification, stratospheric ozone depletion, nitrogen (N) cycle, phosphorus (P) cycle, global freshwater use (Section 4.4.2.5), land system change, biodiversity loss (Section 4.4.2.7), atmospheric aerosol loading and chemical pollution. The baseline of all the calculations is the beginning of the Industrial Revolution. Three of these classes have transgressed their limit: climate change, nitrogen cycle, and biodiversity loss. Global P and N cycles, atmospheric aerosol loading, freshwater use, and land use change are close to their limits. It is worthwhile to note that if one boundary is transgressed, other boundaries are under serious risk. For example, land use in the Amazon could change water resources on the Tibetan Plateau (Snyder

Table 4.1 | Economic analysis of health impacts of climate change in Europe.

Diseases	Coverage	Year	Economic model	Annual cost or savings	Reference
Health impact cost studies (attributed to climate change)					
Cardio-respiratory	EU	2050	CGE	€38 billion savings	Bosello et al.
	FSU			€4 billion savings	
Heat related, Salmonellosis, Flooding	EU	2080	Bottom-up	€46–147 billion cost	Kovats et al.
Heat-related	EU	2080	Bottom-up	€50–118 billion cost	Watkiss et al.
Salmonellosis		2011–40		€70–140 million cost	
Heat-related	Skopje, FYRM	2005–10	Bottom-up	€1 million cost	WHO Regional Office for Europe
Heat-related	Rome, Italy	2020	Bottom-up	€281 million cost	Alberini et al.
Heat-related	Germany	2071–2100	Bottom-up	€300–€700 million (hospital admissions) cost	Hübler et al.
				€2.5–€10.3 billion (productivity) cost	
Cardio-respiratory	EU	2050	Bottom-up	€125 billion cost	Holland et al.
Pollution	OECD Europe, Eastern Europe	2100	CGE	0.02% of GDP cost	Nordhaus and Boyer
Adaptation cost studies (attributed to climate change)					
All health-related adaptations	Europe and Central Asia	2010–2050	Bottom-up	€1.18 (CSIRO) – €4.32 billion (NCAR) cost	World Bank
Diarrheal cases	WHO European Region	2030	Bottom-up	€148 million cost	Ebi
Disease treatment	Western Europe	2060	Bottom-up	€0.68 billion savings	Agrawala et al.
	Eastern Europe			€0.06 billion savings	

Source: Hutton and Menne 2014

et al. 2004). Change of the nitrogen–phosphorus boundary can influence ecosystems, absorption of CO_2 and therefore impact the climate boundary (Rockström 2009a). Climate change will influence the local monsoon climatic system, subsequently altering local energy and precipitation patterns, and eventually freshwater accessibility and ecosystems services.

This framework of planetary boundary – even if subject to further research and future insights – provides a blueprint of where human beings' position is in different dimensions of natural boundaries. This can also guide us to take measurements to maintain and support sustainable development. Within these nine planetary boundaries, humanity can continue to develop and thrive for generations to come – while crossing them could generate abrupt or irreversible environmental changes.

4.4.2.3 Climate Change

About half of cumulative anthropogenic CO_2 emissions between 1750 and 2010 have occurred in the last 40 years – this increase has been driven by growth in economic activity. Climate change also poses risks to economic growth as it is likely to have far-reaching consequences across sectors, impacting human well-being in multiple ways.

The currently observed impacts of climate change, the projected risks for the future, and the challenges and opportunities for adaptation and mitigation under alternative scenarios have been documented in the recently published IPCC reports (IPCC 2014: Summary for Policy Makers WG II and WG III, Synthesis Report). Impacts occur across components of natural wealth including biodiversity, water, and land,

with adverse consequences for ecosystem services, whether regulatory, provisioning, or cultural. Social and economic consequences arise for food security, human conflict, and loss of economic assets (MEA 2003; MEA 2005; Atkinson et al. 2012).

Climate change impacts health in direct and indirect ways: direct impacts on morbidity and mortality include the impacts from floods, droughts, extreme heat, and cyclones, while indirect impacts can occur from disruptions and changes in ecological processes impacting spread of disease vectors, food production and under nutrition, and displacement of populations, disruptions in provisioning of health care services, and damages to health infrastructure among others (see Table 4.1). Human health is impacted adversely by climate related occurrences, and many of these impacts are seen to be distributed unequally, often disproportionately affecting the poorest and those facing current deficits in water, sanitation, and basic health care services (Smit et al. 2014; Watts et al. 2015; Dasgupta 2016).

For resource constrained, low- and middle-income economies, where multiple co-stressors such as poverty, malnutrition, lack of basic amenities, and health care services exist, accounting for climate change implies new demands on resources and prioritization within a development agenda, to ensure that the gains from sustainable development are not eroded in the near or longer term due to climate change impacts.

Conventional ways of understanding the relationship between economic systems and ecosystems are no longer adequate and create challenges for the long-run sustainability of the process of economic growth. It reinforces the idea that economic systems and ecosystems are both complex adaptive systems, and the need for economic policy

4

interventions that can lead to increased resilience and robustness (Arrow et al. 2014; Chopra and Dasgupta 2016). Expert judgments are required about the elasticity of substitution between natural wealth and other modes of wealth for long-run sustainability and innovative methods for economic valuation of the ecosystem assets and services that would get adversely impacted due to climate change (Atkinson et al. 2012).

4.4.2.4 Air Pollution

Air pollution is a problem for much of the globe, especially particulate matter. PM sources include electric-power plants, industrial facilities, automobiles, trucks, trains, ships, biomass burning, and fossil fuels used for heating (Rohde and Muller 2015).

The impact of air pollution on economic growth is dominated by health effects like higher mortality, higher health expenditures, and lower production. Air pollution is estimated to cause between 3 and 7 million of the 9 million annual preventable deaths. Other economic losses may arise from crop losses attributable to air pollution, acidification, eutrophication, and the discouragement of tourism (IEA 2016).

Pollution control has been shown to drive growth, and also to save more in benefits than is required for regulation (US EPA 2011).

4.4.2.5 Water

Population growth, urbanization, rapid economic growth, and climate change have put increasing stress on our planet's water resources. Both water scarcity and declining water quality are global concerns. Water shortage is connected to food security, poverty, public health, conflict, energy production, and ecosystem management (WWAP 2015; Liu et al. 2017). A lack of sanitation is linked to malnutrition, poverty, and disease – roughly 2.4 billion people worldwide do not have access to safe, affordable sanitation. An estimated 645,000 children younger than five years of age perish every year from diarrhea – a preventable, sanitation-related disease (WHO 2016). To complicate the issue, global water demand is expected to increase by 55 percent by 2050. Though agriculture is anticipated to remain the largest user of water (currently around 70 percent), water demand for manufacturing is expected to increase by 400 percent, for electricity by 140 percent and for domestic use by 130 percent (OECD 2012; UN-Water 2015).

Water quality has been impacted by human activities, which impact Biochemical Oxygen Demand (BOD), as well as Nitrogen (N) and Phosphorus (P) levels. Globally, 1 in 8 people are at high risk of water pollution from organic compounds, affecting BOD; 1 in 6 people are at high risk of N pollution, and 1 in 4 people are at high risk of P pollution. Most of these people live in developing countries in Asia (Veolia and IFPRI 2014).

The frequency and intensity of local water crises have been increasing, which have had severe impacts on food security, economic development, and environmental sustainability. Solutions to these potential crises are available, including enhancing the resilience of the water system for irrigation, domestic, and industrial purposes through highly selective and efficient investments in infrastructure and in water governance. Even more important are water conservation and water use efficiency improvements in existing irrigation and water supply systems through water management reform, policy changes, and investment in advanced technology. The investments, policy reforms, and the water institutions must be tailored to local conditions, both ecologically and socio-economically (Rosegrant, Cai and Cline 2005). There is enough water available to meet the world's growing needs, but not without dramatically changing the way water is used, managed, and shared. The global water crisis is one of governance, much more than of resource availability. To allow water resources to enable rather than limit economic growth and sustainable development, this is where the bulk of the action is required (WWAP 2015).

4.4.2.6 Food Security

Food security has been theorized, analyzed, and measured in different ways. It is a contested, evolving, and multidimensional construct (Foran et al. 2014). Its early conceptualization relates to the "right to food." Within the context of the Green Revolution, the idea evolved to "food self-sufficiency" (Chaifetz and Jagger 2014), meaning the improvement of infrastructure, innovation, and institutional governance. The imbalance between population growth and food availability was considered the main threat. Consequently, since the 1970s focus has been paid to agricultural productivity: the priority has been to meet demand.

A much broader understanding of food security was adopted by the World Food Summit in Rome in 1996, which included, in addition to availability, access to affordability and utilization of food. The "stability" dimension was later added to the definition, given the recognition of resource scarcity (such as for phosphorus; Cordell and Neset 2014) and the exacerbation of the environmental and climate change crises. The implications of which include crop productivity reduction, food safety, incidence and prevalence of foodborne diseases, rising food costs, and the potential unrest for land and resources (Ericksen, Ingram and Liverman 2009; Tirado et al. 2010; Lobell and Burke 2010; Allouche 2011; Brooks and Loevinsohn 2011; McCann 2011; Smith et al. 2014).

Globally, the percentage of undernourished has gone from 18.6 percent in 1990–1992 to 10.9 percent in 2014–2016 – equivalent to an absolute decline of about 216 million during a time when the population increased by 1.9 billion (FAO, IFAD, and WFP 2015). Currently, up to one-third of total calories in developed countries are of animal origin (Kastner et al. 2012). Growing demand for meat and dairy products, particularly in emerging economies, is expected to be between two to three times its current levels, which means greater pressure on productivity and land demand (Kastner et al. 2012).

Food insecurity under existing socio-economic and environmental conditions could be reduced through a portfolio of policies and interventions, from improving transport, storage, and communications infrastructure, to market incentives, trade regulation, social protection programs, resource efficiency, resilience increasing, and coping strategies strengthening. Urban and peri-urban agriculture may be an additional strategy for food security and climate change mitigation, particularly in low-income countries (Barthel and Isendahl 2013; Magnusson and Bergman 2014; Poulsen et al. 2015). More profound transformations would need to review issues of land property and use; seed ownership and sharing; preservation of crops biodiversity and its associated knowledge; a reconsideration of the most convenient types of food production systems in socioecological and productive terms (including modern agroecology versus genetically modified organisms) while avoiding food waste (about 1.3 billion tons of wasted food are generated annually) and attaining aspects of reducing food demand by promoting diet changes.

4.4.2.7   Biodiversity

Biodiversity conservation, in the traditional sense, refers to the preservation of wild living species in protected areas and remnant wild lands, and the economic value of biodiversity is frequently conflated with the economic value of wildlife tourism. But biodiversity covers much more than endangered wild species, and biodiversity change covers much more than traditional conservation efforts. Biodiversity has changed as a result of people's decisions about which species to promote, and which to control, which gene stocks to build, and which to run down. The value of biodiversity to people lies in its role in the production of foods, fuels, and fibers, on the moderation of environmental threats, on disease and disease control, on the recreational, aesthetic, scientific, and educational benefits it offers, and on many other things. All "ecosystem services" depend either positively or negatively on the composition of species. In some cases, more biodiversity is better for people. Erosion control on hill slopes, for example, tends to be increasing in the number of grass species. On the other hand, the health of people living in the humid tropics tends to be decreasing in the number of disease vectors, parasites, and pathogens. Similarly, the production of foods, fuels, and fibers depends on reducing the number of crop competitors (weeds), crop predators (pests), and crop diseases (pathogens).

The impact of biodiversity on economic growth is mixed. In countries that are home to charismatic megafauna or flora (African savannas, pacific coral reefs, tropical rainforests) biodiversity is the basis for ecotourism – the most rapidly growing sector worldwide. In 2015, travel and tourism contributed US$7.2 trillion or 9.8 percent of global GDP. In countries subject to climatic or geophysical extreme events (subtropical coastal areas in particular), the species richness of coastal and inland forests reduces the damage done by storms, floods, and tsunamis. We do not have estimates of the impact on Global GDP, but we do have estimates of the impact of individual events. The Indian Ocean Tsunami of 2004, for example, is thought to have caused damage of $15 billion, mostly in areas without coastal protection. The production of foods, fuels, and fibers in agriculture, aquaculture, forestry, and fisheries all depend on the conversion of habitat and the reduction of biodiversity. These industries together currently account for around 10 percent of global GDP. As with tourism, the importance of these industries varies widely.

4.4.2.8   Socio-economic Metabolism

Modern economic growth has led to entirely new and intense forms of consumption, which include the rising use of fossil fuels, the emergence of novel technologies, the expansion of infrastructures, and industrialization. Other changes include standardization process, mass production, just-in-time production, and more recently the outsourcing of production within a context of a globalized market, the expansion of urban infrastructure, transportation, and logistics, and of technologies such as the automobile, air transportation, petrochemicals, electronic communications, among others.

The amount, variety, and intensity of goods and services consumption has changed drastically in the course of economic development. Analyses of historical consumption patterns of energy and materials show an increasing use of resources over time. The "metabolic profile," or the energy and material average consumption patterns in biophysical terms, for hunter-gatherers has been estimated in about 10–20 Gj/cap/yr of energy and 0.5–1 ton/cap/yr of materials; for agrarian societies within 40–70 Gj/cap/yr and 3–6 ton/cap/yr; and for the industrial society between 150 to 400 GJ/cap/yr and 15 to 25 ton/cap/yr (Haberl et al. 2009).

The metabolic intensity of industrial societies, mainly, since the second half of the twentieth century, or what has been called the Great Acceleration (Steffen et al. 2011), has resulted in a growing transgression of planetary boundaries, taking us further apart from the Holocene-like conditions which support human life, as well as other forms of life (Steffen et al. 2015). Data show that during that period, material and energy use increased 5.6 times faster than population (Schaffartzik et al. 2014). Yet, per capita consumption patterns were asymmetrical as they are associated to purchasing power and therefore to income levels. Hence, by the year 2000, 10 percent of world population consumed about 40 percent of energy and 27 percent of materials (Steinberg, Krausmann and Eisenmenger 2010).

Energy and material consumption patterns, which reached a total consumption of 70.1 billion tons in 2010, or 10.1 tons per capita (UNEP 2016), have been coupled with economic growth during the last century (Csereklyei and Stern 2015); while the human population increased fourfold and the economy grew about twenty times, material and energy use increased an average of tenfold: biomass consumption increased 3.5 times, energy consumption 12 times, ores and industrial minerals 19 times and construction minerals up to 34 times (case of cement) (Krausmann et al. 2009; UNEP 2011a). From 2000 to 2010 all material consumption, except for biomass, increased further: fossil fuels by 2.9 percent, metal ores by 3.5 percent and nonmetallic minerals by 5.3 percent on average (UNEP 2016) (see Figure 4.6).

A business as usual scenario may lead to an extraction of about 150 billion tons of resources annually by 2050 or almost three times the amount of the year 2000 (UNEP 2011a); other estimations even consider a scenario of up to 180 billion tons (Schandl et al. 2016). Material stock, mainly urban infrastructure, utilities, and vehicle fleet, will be of particular relevance as they increased 23-fold from 1900 to 2010,

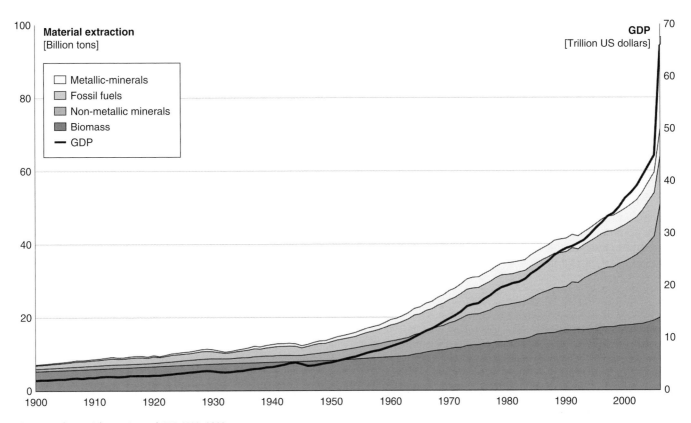

Figure 4.6 | Material extraction and GDP, 1900–2010.
Source: based on Krausmann et al. 2009; The World Bank data (http://data.worldbank.org/indicator/NY.GDP.MKTP.CD); and UNEP data (http://environmentlive.unep.org/)

reaching 792 billion tons of which two-thirds were added since 1980 (Krausmann et al. 2017). Since 82 percent of all in-use material stock is 30 years or younger, pathways to reuse and recycling materials will be central; only by 2030 about 35 percent, or 274 billion tons of materials, of the stock in-use in 2010 will be discarded (Krausmann et al. 2017).

Opportunities for decoupling material consumption and stock formation from economic growth are already being explored through, for example, more efficient production technologies and practices, renewable energies, urban sustainable planning and development, behavioral and consumption adjustments, material substitutions and light weighting, extension of service lifetimes, or the reuse and recycling of materials (two key actions to additionally confront material supply risk and reserves depletion). For policy orientation, a sustainability corridor of material consumption patterns has been suggested at "10-2-5 target" of abiotic, biotic, and used biotic and abiotic materials (UNEP 2016).

4.4.3 Measuring Sustainability: Social and Natural Wealth

This section gives an overview of different methods for measuring wealth. Building on the introduction of GDP and GDP-based indicators in Section 4.1.2, Section 4.4.3.1 begins with a discussion of measurements of welfare that include nonmarketed assets into the calculation of a GDP-like indicator, such as the net national product and genuine savings. The advantages of a whole dashboard of indicators for well-being are

discussed in Section 4.4.3.2. Section 4.4.3.3 shows how public policy decisions can be drawn from such a dashboard of economic and well-being indicators by using the welfare diagnostics approach.

4.4.3.1 Aggregate Indicators

As discussed in Section 4.1.2, GDP is only one aggregate measure of national productivity. In spite of its wide acceptance, measuring economic activity through GDP has several drawbacks. A number of alternative measurements of income and sustainability were presented in Section 4.1.2 and 4.1.4 respectively. This section is focused on indicators that incorporate a number of social and natural wealth measures, reflecting those discussed in Sections 4.4.1 and 4.4.2 respectively.

Green accounting is a form of accounting that extends national income measures to include different concepts of sustainability, with a focus on the environment (Smulders 2008). It develops a broader welfare base and allows welfare to depend on factors such as health, pollution levels, or environmental quality. Altruistic preferences that account for inter- (and to a lesser extent intra-) generational inequality are also allowed. Several monetary measures for green accounting have been developed such as the (green) net national product (NNP), genuine savings (GS), and the index of sustainable economic welfare (ISEW).

The NNP takes the intertemporal component into account and factors in depreciation of physical capital and depletion of natural capital stocks (Weitzman 1976). Nonmarketed goods such as health and the environment are assigned values by using their shadow prices. These shadow prices can be interpreted as the opportunity cost in foregone consumption of investing in a nonmarketed good.

The theoretical result that, if there are no externalities, or if all externalities are internalized by appropriate policy instruments, NNP is proportional to social welfare is sometimes called the Weitzman principle (Weitzman 1976, 2003).[15] Some sustainability concepts are related to this principle, such as the Hartwick (1977) rule that states that investing all profits and rents from exhaustible resource extraction into physical capital allows a society to maintain a constant level of utility. This is equivalent to green net investment being zero (Smulders 2008). In reality, however, several externalities are likely not to be internalized and factors such as exogenous technological change and changing global prices invalidate the finding that zero green net investment implies sustainability (Asheim et al. 2007).

NNP is theoretically neat and has inspired some practical approaches to define wealth in a broader way, see Section 4.3.1. However, NNP has several shortcomings and two major lines of criticism have emerged: The first is the difficulty of implementing it in practice. The second is that it suffers from some of the same conceptual shortcomings as GDP like ignoring the unequal distribution of wealth in society and not considering the possibility of changing preferences.

Putting NNP into practice requires determining the value of variables other than consumption. In simple cases the value of capital stocks other than private capital is given by the marginal rate of substitution between consumption and the other variable. How many units of consumption would society be willing to sacrifice for one unit of improvement in the state of nature for example? The marginal rate of substitution is difficult to measure with precision.

Fleurbaey and Blanchet (2013, Section 4.3.5) identify two additional difficulties in measuring the prices required for the calculation of NNP. The first is that many individuals cannot freely choose the exact consumption bundles they would prefer, in particular concerning exactly how many hours they would like to work. In this case market prices (like wages) do not reflect the true appreciation for goods (like leisure). The second is that individuals appreciate goods like leisure differently so that there is no unique market price for these goods. In order to replace market prices, which do not reflect the value of a good in society when markets work imperfectly, Fleurbaey and Blanchet (2013) propose the use of the willingness-to-pay, which reflects the true appreciation of individuals for a good.

NNP thereby offers an improvement over GDP in two important ways. It identifies variables other than consumption that contribute to the wealth of society and it gives a guideline on their importance relative to GDP. Like GDP, however, it does not address inequality. NNP is concerned only with aggregate values and is blind to the distribution of wealth in society. Monetary aggregates often implicitly assume that the measured aggregate quantities are distributed equally. If this condition is not met, welfare can be improved by improving the allocation without changing the aggregate

quantities. Refinements to monetary aggregates such as presented in Jorgenson (1990) can take inequality into account, but even those lead to problematic results when personal abilities and needs are unequal (Fleurbaey, 2009).

4.4.3.2   A Disaggregated Dashboard of Welfare Indicators

In 2008, a commission was created to assess how to improve the statistical information about the status of the economy and society – the "Commission on the Measurement of Economic Performance and Social Progress" (CMEPSP). The commission's report comes to several important conclusions, which can be summarized as follows (Stiglitz et al. 2009): First, the perspective should shift from production-based indicators to indicators of well-being. Second, well-being is multidimensional (and in large parts subjective), it includes material living standards, health, education, personal activities including work, political voice and governance, social aspects, environment (present and future conditions), and insecurity (economic and physical). Third, measuring sustainability involves the future and hence always requires taking normative assumptions. Sustainability should be examined separately from well-being, since a high current level of well-being can be achieved at the cost of low sustainability, while increased sustainability today may imply lower levels of current well-being. In order to measure sustainability several indicators are needed that measure changes in the quality and quantity of stocks that matter for future well-being such as natural, human, and physical capital.

Regarding the third point, the measurement of sustainability, Stiglitz et al. (2009) discuss the advantages and the shortcomings of using a set of indicators, instead of aggregating the indicators into one number. Both monetary and nonmonetary measures would be necessary for deriving sound policy advice from such a dashboard of indicators. Such a set of indicators can be interpreted as analogous to a car's dashboard: If all the indicators in the dashboard of a car such as gasoline level, speed, and revolutions per minute would be aggregated into one single indicator, this indicator would not be very helpful.

The CMEPSP made great progress in providing tools for the measurement of social progress, it did not, however, develop recommendations on how to draw public policy decisions from such a set of indicators.

4.4.3.3   Welfare Diagnostics

As discussed above, there is a broad spectrum of possible perspectives on how one can define well-being (see Section 4.3). For this reason, a flexible approach that encompasses the concept of social welfare from the perspective of multiple policy objectives is required as a basis for policy-making.

Even though public policy cannot optimize social welfare, it can nevertheless aim at removing the most serious obstacles to human well-being (Jakob and Edenhofer 2014). This so-called "welfare

---

[15]   Asheim and Weitzman (2001) evaluate under which conditions the Weitzman principle holds when NNP is measured in monetary rather than utility terms.

diagnostics" aims to identify factors that are essential for human well-being – i.e. basic needs – and correcting deficiencies. Welfare diagnostics can be understood as a process that includes the following three steps:

1. Identify the relevant dimensions of welfare (e.g. consumption possibilities and their distribution, or capabilities) as well as the tradeoffs between them. Define minimum thresholds for environmental quality and human development.
2. Establish limits regarding the use of natural resources in line with the feasibility set from step 1 by means of fiscal policies, such as Pigouvian taxes, tradable permit schemes, or resource rent taxes. Appropriate the associated rents to the public budget.
3. Use the revenues from step 2 to invest in infrastructure required to meet the minimal thresholds for human development defined in step 1. That is, revenues from e.g. carbon pricing could be used to finance water or electricity access.

As public deliberation is crucially important to determine which factors matter for social welfare, how basic needs are to be defined, how tradeoffs between them should be assessed, and how individual indicators of well-being are added up to a social indicator (see also Chapter 3), welfare diagnostics is also closely related to the capabilities approach discussed in Section 4.3.1.3.

Welfare diagnostics identifies determinants of well-being that are considered essential (basic goods such as access to clean water and hygiene) (Jakob and Edenhofer 2014). It then aims at increasing the supply of these basic goods. Large groups of individuals with potentially different views about social welfare could agree to such policies. Not all factors of well-being have to be at their optimal levels to enhance social welfare (Hausman et al. 2005). Therefore, a more pragmatic approach that aims at correcting major deficiencies already leads to large increases in social welfare.

Minimum thresholds (so-called "guardrails") can be established for capital stocks essential to welfare. Welfare diagnostics can provide some guidance on how to simultaneously address overuse of natural resources and underprovision of access to infrastructure services (such as water, sanitation, electricity, health, education, etc.) that are fundamental for human development. The central task for public policy is then to ensure the attainment of these minimum thresholds for sustainable development.

In order to successfully carry out welfare diagnostics, policy-makers need accurate scientific information on environmental limits as well as the economic, technological, and institutional requirements to remain within these boundaries. For instance, for the case of climate change, the benefits of slowing down global warming would need to be compared with mitigation costs and potential risks of key technologies to reduce emissions, such as use of bio-energy, carbon capture and sequestration, or nuclear power (Jakob and Steckel 2016).

However, defining thresholds and deciding what constitutes a socially acceptable risk is an inherently normative question that cannot be answered by scientists but requires public deliberation (Edenhofer

and Kowarsch 2015). For this reason, participative democracy is a fundamental cornerstone to express social preferences and guide policy decisions aiming to find the right balance between short-term exigencies of human development and long-term considerations to safeguard environmental quality.

Measures such as those proposed above may have important distributional impacts across time and income groups. For instance, infrastructure access will likely be obtained only after a certain time period needed for construction, but higher energy prices are experienced immediately. For this reason, well-designed policy packages that prevent adverse distributional impacts and compensate political losers need to be devised (IMF 2013).

4.5 Governing the Commons: Overcoming the Underprovision of Social Commons and Avoiding the Exploitation of Natural Commons

Economic activity often involves the utilization of natural resources such as oceans, forests, and the atmosphere. Governance is needed to keep the exploitation of these natural commons in check (Section 4.1.1.2), and is a key ingredient of the "third way" of creating economic growth without environmental degradation (Section 4.1.1.3). At the global level, the overuse of natural commons is particularly severe because international treaties have proven a poor and difficult substitute for the absent global authority (Section 4.5.1). Learning from successes in managing local common-pool resources (Section 4.5.2) could be the foundation of a polycentric governance of global commons (Section 4.5.3).

4.5.1 The Problem of Collective Action

4.5.1.1 Tragedy of the Commons

The definition of global commons and their influences by and on economic growth were discussed in Section 4.1.5. Commons problems usually relate to common-pool resources (CPRs), or underprovided and impure public goods.

Garrett Hardin's (1968) influential analysis of the "tragedy of the commons" had established the perception that CPRs are prone to overuse and collapse unless either private property or central state solutions are implemented. However, subsequent research particularly by Elinor Ostrom (1990) clarified that Hardin's analysis more specifically addressed a "tragedy of open-access." Ostrom finds empirically that humans routinely devise complex governance arrangements to transform open-access situations into regulated commons regimes. Strategies for ensuring the sustainable use of CPR systems often focus on strengthening the degree of excludability, i.e. assigning property rights to ensure enclosure of the resource system or parts of its output. Successful commons governance in these cases works through establishing a private good or club good, often including decisions on distribution or exclusion. Commons management also

4

often involves the provision of public goods, such as technologies that reduce the costs of protecting the commons (for example, low-carbon energy technologies in the case of protecting the atmospheric commons). It is important to clarify that there is no single "right" governance or property regime for goods or resource systems with CPR or public good characteristics. An unregulated forest has the characteristics of a CPR, but its sustainable use can be organized via privatization, state property or any other form of mixed property rights assignment including common ownership. The choice of governance often has severe implications regarding the distribution of wealth, and should be guided by principles of justice.

Governance of commons is not about a blunt call for implementing common property regimes wherever possible, but a specification of complex rules and property rights. In the context of commons governance property rights refer to a bundle of rights including the authority to undertake particular actions, including rights of access, withdrawal, management, alienation (i.e. sale), appropriation of value, or exclusion from a resource (Ostrom 2000; Barnes 2006). The private owner of a forest, for example, may choose to delegate access or harvesting rights to other individuals or group agents. Addressing questions of commons governance often includes addressing highly controversial questions of inclusion and exclusion, of initial entitlement and legitimate ownership.

A key challenge of global commons governance is that they are either situated outside national jurisdiction or their conservation and sustainable use conflicts with national sovereignty and regulation. Their use may affect different levels of governance in distinct ways, often requiring global cooperation. Yet, policies to govern the global commons will often conflict significantly with existing patterns of resource use, sovereignty rights, and other related well-established interests. Additionally, most global commons interact with other global resource systems, i.e. management of one common will most likely also impact the use of others.

4.5.1.2 Global Perspective without World Government

The management of global commons, however, cannot be delegated to a central authority but involves negotiation and agreement by up to 200 sovereign states and other stakeholders such as industry and civil society groups. Managing global commons thus becomes a collective action challenge: while it is in everybody's interest that some management scheme is implemented, there are strong free riding incentives for the individual state (or actor) not to comply (cf. Sandler 2004; Barrett 2007).

Thus a key approach to manage global commons has been establishing multilateral institutions through international agreements (Barrett 2007), and to make participation as broad and as ambitious as possible. However, achieving this turns out to be difficult. For the case of environmental commons, Barrett (2003) reviews more than 300 treaties but observes that most of the treaties do not succeed in making a difference. The academic game theory literature that investigates the underlying causes for this cooperation failure (Heal 1992; Carraro and Siniscalco 1993; Barrett 1994), pinned down

strong free riding incentives as the culprit for low cooperation and/or little ambition of international environmental agreements. An extensive body of literature explored designs of environmental treaties to overcome the cooperation failure, which included minimum participation clauses (Carraro et al. 2009), sanctions (Nordhaus 2015) and rewards or transfer payments (Lessmann et al. 2015). These studies were summarized in Benchekroun and Van Long (2014) and Carraro (2014).

4.5.2 Successful Management of the Commons

4.5.2.1 Taxes, Property Right, and Regulation

The neoclassical economic tradition has long since come up with solutions for a strong central state to prevent an overuse of natural commons. Overuse of commons is driven by the social costs of utilizing a commons exceeding the individual costs. Taxing the individual for accessing the commons at the marginal social costs, as suggested by Arthur C. Pigou, will therefore align individual and social interests. The so-called Pigouvian tax will thus trigger the socially optimal utilization of the commons (Pigou 1920).

The same can, however, be achieved with (arguably) less intervention by the state: If the state merely establishes property rights, i.e. access rights to the commons, and if these permits can be traded at no cost, then bargaining among private agents for these permits will achieve the same socially optimal utilization (Coase 1960).

Although theoretically equivalent in the outcome, the Coasean perspective has emphasized the benefits of a smaller role of the state and the informational problems for the state to know the socially optimal utilization. By contrast, the Pigouvian perspective has pointed out that trading permits is hardly without costs, and thus Coasean bargaining is therefore likely inefficient in situations with large numbers of agents (Hovenkamp 2009).

Beyond arguments of political economy and transactions costs, the equivalence of price and quantity instruments (here: Pigouvian tax vs. Coasean bargaining) frequently breaks down when the restrictive idealized assumptions are relaxed. Weitzman (1974) showed that under uncertainty, the ratio of marginal costs and marginal benefits of accessing the commons is distinctive for the superiority of one instrument over the other, sparking a branch of literature on "prices vs. quantities" (cf. Hepburn 2006 for a survey). For the specific case of the uncertainties associated with climate change, for example, a price instrument has been shown to be superior (Newell and Pizer 2003).

Contrary to the intuition that additional instruments improve welfare, the efficiency of Pigouvian taxes is undermined if private actors additionally engage (uncoordinated) in Coasean bargaining (Buchanan and Stumblebine 1962; Turvey 1963). But again, this result is turned on its head if (ex ante) transaction costs of bargaining are high (MacKenzie and Ohndorf 2016). Lehmann (2012) identifies a range of situation where a mix of multiple instruments improves over the outcome with a single pricing instrument.

Applied to global commons, the choice between price or quantity instruments translates to choosing between a global tax on the utilization (e.g. harvesting or polluting) or a global trading scheme for rights to utilize or pollute (Stavins 2011). According to Stavins, in the final analysis only few differences between a tax and a permit trading scheme remain, and even among environmental economists preference for one instrument over the other is unsettled (Goulder and Schein 2013). There is, however, overwhelming consent that it is essential to (a) establish a price for accessing commons, and (b) in doing so, rely on one of the market based instruments, i.e. a tax or a permit trade system.

One asymmetry between tax and trading identified in recent research with particular relevance in the context of polycentric global commons management concerns their different properties in enabling heterogeneous actors to express diverging preferences for the commons (Goulder and Stavins 2011; Williams 2012; IPCC 2015, Chapter 15). For example, in the context of a greenhouse gas (GHG) cap-and-trade system unilateral efforts to enhance mitigation efforts by states or other actors, e.g. via additional policies such as renewable feed-in tariffs, have been shown to have no impact on carbon emissions. Still, additional policies can be merited to address other externalities, such as those related to learning-by-doing in new technologies. By contrast, with a price instrument (e.g. a GHG tax or minimum price in an ETS[16]) unilaterally enhanced abatement can increase the overall amount of emission reductions, if the price signal for other covered emission sources remains unchanged.

4.5.2.2   Political Economy and Rent-Seeking

Even if an ideal policy to manage externalities exists, implementing it successfully requires overcoming political hurdles. Environmental policies to manage a common are bound to generate winners (e.g. occupants of vulnerable sites and future generations) and losers (e.g. businesses and sometimes consumers). In addition to the political-economy problem of garnering sufficient support from the population, policy changes are subject to rent-seeking, whereby political actors aim to steer policy for their private benefit. The problem is even more pronounced when several tiers of government interact (national, state, and maybe even municipal). These challenges can be illustrated using the example of carbon pricing, as outlined in Section 4.5.2.1.

Carbon pricing affects the entirety of the population, who sees, e.g., the price of gasoline and electricity rise as a result. In some low- and middle-income countries, this may actually be progressive, meaning that the poor suffer disproportionately less (Brenner et al. 2007; Datta 2010; Nurdianto and Resosudarmo 2016). This is but a mild consolation, considering that this progressivity occurs, in particular, where the income distribution is so unequal that the poorest are unable to afford energy-intensive goods. By contrast, high-income countries tend to experience regressive distributional impacts (Sterner 2012; Flues and Thomas 2015). Significant carbon pricing (and ambitious climate policy more generally) also distributes costs and benefits unevenly across groups with asymmetric political influence. While costs are concentrated on the present and particularly affect well-organized interest groups such as the fossil resource industry, the benefits of climate change mitigation (reduced climate change impacts) accrue to future generations and the dispersed global population, which is hardly politically organized at all (Victor 2011). These concerns help explain why, when priced, carbon is priced far below most estimates of the "social cost of carbon" (World Bank and Ecofys 2016), which is the price that would yield an optimal reduction in GHG emissions.

Even if set below the social cost of carbon, a carbon price (tax or permit auctions) could generate sizeable government revenues. Should the political-economy challenges to raise revenues from climate policy be overcome, a government faces another set of challenges in how funds should be allocated. Both sets of challenges cannot be completely disentangled because public support for carbon pricing depends on revenue usage. More support is given to revenue recycling that is geared toward environmental projects or returned to the population in a revenue neutral way than when usage is unspecified or destined to national debt reduction (Kallbekken et al. 2011; Amdur et al. 2014). Support could also be garnered by lowering taxes for those who would be more adversely affected by the climate policy – or who would oppose it the most – in a sort of "double dividend" fashion, but with an emphasis on redistribution (Klenert et al. 2017; see also Dissou and Siddiqui, 2014). Alternatively, revenues may be earmarked for financing specific projects, e.g. building social commons such as public infrastructure. Earmarking, however, is controversial. As there is no relation between the amount of revenue generated by climate policy and the revenue that should be spent on any given project, it is not clear how much should be allocated to each project (Parry 2016). Hence, infrastructure funding is best done nationally rather than through earmarks that target specific infrastructures separately (Marron and Morris 2016). Moreover, the funds available for such projects will have to be what remains after transfers and programs benefitting the political losers – transfers for the general population, especially the poor, and retraining programs for the displaced workforce – are made.

4.5.2.3   Social Norms, Informal Institutions, and Social Movements

Prospects of commons management via self-organization of local communities may be more promising (Ostrom 1990; Ostrom 2009). Successful local CPR management via different forms of cooperative management regimes is possible, though success depends on a number of design principles (Ostrom 2000). Humans do self-organize and succeed in problem-solving even in situations with weak individual incentives for cooperation – but not always. Facilitative formal and informal institutions enable people to carry out their management roles (Ostrom 2010b), including mechanisms such as effective monitoring, conflict-resolution or sanctioning for noncompliance, and devising rights to organize and to participate in rule-setting (Dietz et al. 2003).

Findings in experimental (behavioral) economics in recent decades have provided the empirical and theoretical underpinnings for this

---

[16]   Minimum prices in cap-and-trade systems have e.g. been implemented in California, Quebec, the Northeastern US RGGI trading system, and some Chinese provincial ETS (Acworth et al. 2017).

understanding of human capacities for successful cooperation despite pervasive incentives for free-riding by self-interested agents (Ostrom and Walker 2003; Carlsson and Johansson 2012; Fehr and Fehr 2016). It can be shown that humans are conditional cooperators, especially in reciprocal settings. Many humans are not purely self-interested but have other-regarding preferences. Face-to-face communication and trust are particularly conducive to such behavior. As the perception of fairness matters for the agents' willingness to cooperate, burden-sharing, and transfer mechanisms among asymmetric players can further facilitate cooperation. This is in stark contrast to the neoclassical perspective on the homo economicus and explains the divergence of neoclassic pessimism and the optimistic message from Ostrom's research.

4.5.3 Up-scaling to the Global Level: Polycentric Governance of Global Commons?

Sustainable governance of global commons is increasingly important to maintain global prosperity and human well-being in the twenty-first century, e.g. related to problems of climate change (see Section 4.4.2.3), biodiversity loss (see Section 4.4.2.7) or access to and conservation of other ecosystem services. Compared to local commons, global commons problems face a set of additional difficulties, especially due to challenges of scale, diversity, and complexity (Ostrom et al. 1999; Stern 2011; Ostrom 2014). Research following Ostrom can offer at least two useful directions to mitigate and partly overcome global collective-action challenges: applying lessons to international negotiations (Section 4.5.3.2) and taking a polycentric perspective for global problems (Section 4.5.3.3).

4.5.3.1   Upscaling Local Lessons to the International Level

Lessons may be taken from successful local commons management to enhance cooperation among states on the international level. Some have argued that the community of international negotiators may exhibit dynamics similar to CPR settings with low number of participants ("small-N"), and applying lessons from smaller scale CPR and experimental research may be applicable in this context (Messner et al. 2013; LeVeck et al. 2014). For example, research has shown that repeated communication affects trust levels, which themselves substantially determine levels of cooperation (Cole 2015). Positive experience of cooperation can further enhance mutual reputation and trust, potentially resulting in even higher cooperation levels. Graduated sanctions and rewards through transfers, and monitoring and compliance mechanisms can also catalyze trust-building and help deter free-riding. It remains an open question if lessons from small-N settings can indeed be applied to the international level where negotiators are embedded in principal–agent relationships with their governments and population (Putnam 1988) that are critical for structuring their behavior.

4.5.3.2   A Polycentric Approach

Local lessons may also be applied where the harsh dichotomy between top-down and bottom-up approaches to global commons governance is transcended in efforts that include the broad array of subinternational actors (Ostrom 2010a; Ostrom 2010c). Many problems with global commons properties need some kind of international action to be properly addressed – they all are also dependent on implementation, compliance, or even structural changes on several subsidiary policy levels. As there is no first-best monocentric governance architecture for global commons problems, polycentric theory stresses the benefits and needs of an adaptive and decentralized system of multiple self-governing and interacting units of different scale across policy levels (Dorsch and Flachsland 2017). Recognizing site-specific conditions, i.e. heterogeneous preferences as well as heterogeneous competencies and constraints of different actors, enables policy design to realize site-specific co-benefits and to mitigate costs (Dalmazzone 2006). Participation in smaller units can foster self-organization and trust-building, while the interaction between units can foster mutual learning and diffusion of norms (Shobe and Burtraw 2012; Hoffmann 2011; Hulme 2009). Externalities between subsidiary groups can be addressed in larger organizational settings, i.e. to avoid conflicting policies.

The prevalent task for real-world multilevel governance arrangements is then to mobilize collective action at several scales by organizing this interplay of interests, capabilities, and externalities productively. Also, transfer schemes among different groups with asymmetric preferences can be used to enable higher levels of ambition by providing compensation for increased policy ambition on behalf of those particularly able and willing to provide such compensation.

4.5.3.3   Polycentric Climate Governance Architecture

Empirically, most global commons problems like climate change mitigation are to a large extent already addressed via polycentric policy approaches, encompassing international agreements as well as a multitude of subsidiary policies, institutions, and civil engagement on the local, national, and regional level all over the globe (Paavola 2011; Jordan et al. 2015). These arrangements include traditional state-led and market instruments as well as other forms of climate action by different state and nonstate actors.

Still, national governments remain key actors not only for international multilateralism. Many nation-states adopt a growing number of unilateral climate policies and strategies (Dubash et al. 2013; Nachmany et al. 2015), coordinate and mutually foster their climate policies in bi- and minilateral agreements (like US-CHN, G7/G20, EU; see Falkner 2015), but also provide various support functions for nonstate initiatives (Hale and Roger 2014; Hickmann 2016).

In many cases, regardless of the specific interests of their national governments, subnational entities such as states and cities can also be policy drivers (e.g. for California, Rabe 2010 and Urpelainen 2009; for cities, Hakelberg 2014). In transnational networks such as the C40 Cities Climate Leadership Group, the ICLEI Local Governments for Sustainability network or the World Mayors Council, subnational governments as well as nonstate actors self-organize to commit to specific climate and energy targets, introduce review schemes and foster policy transfer through information sharing or capacity building (Hoffman 2011; Bulkeley et al. 2014).

4

Additionally, a broad range of climate action by nonstate actors is evident – from business self-regulation, civil society groups, universities, foundations or individuals (e.g. UNEP 2015; Partzsch and Ziegler 2011). Given the encyclical intervention Laudato Si by Pope Francis, even religious groups contribute to the eclectic but increasingly meaningful emerging global climate governance landscape (Edenhofer et al. 2016).

Efforts at achieving such international agreements remain necessary to address international free-riding incentives, but they are already characterized and complemented by polycentric governance structures aiming not only at ensuring implementation but also at harnessing decentralized potentials for mitigation.

4.5.4 Robust and Context Specific Policies

Strategies for governing the commons should prove robust, able to meet multiple near- and longer-term goals even in the face of deep uncertainty regarding the efficacy of specific actions and how the future might evolve. In some cases, identifying a robust strategy can prove simple. But as systems come under increasing stress, identifying and implementing robust strategies can prove more difficult, in particular considering the ethical implications of many management choices. In recent years, the processes and tools for providing quantitative, evidence-based, multiobjective, multiscenario decision support have grown sufficiently mature to help identify robust strategies for addressing complex challenges of managing the commons.

In laying the context for such processes and tools it proves useful to frame two broad approaches to social choice in polycentric governance systems, described by Sen (2009) as transcendental and relational reasoning. The former seeks to first envision a common vision of a perfectly just world, which can then be used to inform our near-term choices (Rawls 1971). This approach infuses much climate policy and its supporting quantitative analysis. Among its virtues, transcendental reasoning provides a clarity of purpose that may add in communication and coordinating diverse action across a polycentric society.

Relational reasoning posits that two fundamental attributes of our world include irreducible uncertainty about the consequences of our actions and a diversity of priorities, goals, and values. With such attributes, no transcendental vision of the type envisioned by Rawls would be possible because the level of agreement it presupposes does not (and ideally should not) exist in a diverse society. Neither would any common transcendental vision prove sufficient to inform near-term choices, because the uncertainties are too deep to chart an unambiguous path to the ideal. Relational reasoning thus envisions an iterative process of deliberative social choice that seeks to distinguish more just choices from less just choices in the face of imperfect knowledge and conflicting goals. A variety of literatures also embrace this view as both an apt description of reality as well as a normative ideal, including concepts of risk governance (Renn 2008), democratic experimentalism (Ansell 2011), and the broadly inclusive sociotechnical experiments (Stilgoe 2015) envisioned in the science policy literature.

Policy frameworks such as the Paris Agreement include both transcendental and relational elements, the former in its temperature targets and the latter in its iterative pledge and review process of national pledges.

A key challenge for relational reasoning is assuring that an iterated set of choices converges to acceptable near and longer-term outcomes. To prove successful, such processes should result in policy choices that prove robust and adaptive, that is, meet multiple objectives over a wide range of plausible scenarios (Lempert and Schlesinger 2001; Lempert et al. 2003; Walker et al. 2010). This can prove particularly challenging in contexts of polycentric governance that involve complex systems with path dependence and threshold behaviors.

As one means to address this challenge, quantitative tools for multiobjective robust optimization (Kasprzyk et al. 2013), scenario discovery (Lempert 2013), and exploratory modeling (Bankes 1993) have increasingly been combined to support iterative, participatory decision processes similar to the "pragmatic-enlightened model" (PEM) approach (Edenhofer et al. 2015) described in Section 4.4.3.3. The most advanced examples involve adapting to the impacts of climate change. For instance, four neighboring cities in North Carolina, USA – Raleigh, Durham, Chapel Hill, and Cary – have linked their previously independent water supply systems to improve risk management in the face of increased climate variability, in particular an increased prevalence of drought (Zeff et al. 2014, 2016) Examples of such multijurisdictional robust strategies for reducing greenhouse gas emissions are harder to find. Some jurisdictions have begun to link carbon price regimes, which should increase efficiency, but without any guarantees that multidecadal reduction goals will be met in the face of many uncertainties. Some analyses have examined how emission reduction goals depend on alternative definitions of social welfare (Drouet et al. 2015; Adler et al. 2016; Garner et al. 2016) or the long-term policy persistence (Patashnik 2014) of alternative carbon pricing compensation schemes (Isley et al. 2015). But such analyses have not yet been incorporated into polycentric decision processes that seek robust near-term actions in the face of deep uncertainty about the consequences of human choices regarding greenhouse gas emissions and a diversity of views on how to value those consequences.

4.6 Conclusions and Action Toolbox

Economic activity clearly is not a complete measure of social welfare. For this reason, economic growth cannot be characterized as "only good" or "only bad," as the two polar narratives in the introduction suggest. Rather, social welfare includes a number of social and environmental dimensions in addition to material consumption. Similarly, the wealth of a given society cannot exclusively be measured in terms of physical capital, but also includes social and environmental capital as reflected in Section 4.4. Protecting and growing social and environmental capital requires a much better management of the global commons as described in Section 4.5.

So how can this fundamental insight be translated to policy action? Section 4.3 gives a wealth of ideas on how welfare can be measured

Table 4.2 | Overview of how policy-makers, international organizations, and civil society can participate in the definition of welfare indicators, identification of bottlenecks and implementation of policies

Action	Policy-makers	International organizations	NGOs and individual citizens
Definition of welfare indicators	Monitoring and reporting of indicators.	Data collection; harmonization and comparison of indicators.	Elicitation of social preferences; holding governments accountable for reporting
Identification of bottlenecks	Design roadmaps to guide reforms	Link the identification of a bottleneck to policy design	Identify bottlenecks and communicate them to the public sector
Implementation of policies	Implement policy instruments; overcome political resistance	Gather data on best practices	Provide feedback on the experiences with policy; draw attention to problems and adverse side-effects

in better ways than in GDP. These can be used as a starting point for three blocks of action (summarized in Table 4.2).

First, governments would have to define a set of welfare indicators that can be used to assess how far implemented or proposed policies either have contributed or are expected to contribute toward social objectives. While scientist can generate knowledge and communicate policy options it is the responsibility of politicians to make value judgments. A welfare indicator is a way of making these value judgments transparent and justify policy choices. International organizations could perform important tasks in collecting the information necessary to establish welfare indicators (for example by measuring social and environmental capital), help to transfer knowledge across jurisdictions, and make different indicators comparable. By elicitation of social preferences, civil society and citizens could contribute to the choice of which welfare dimensions should be included in the respective indicators. NGOs may also have an important role to ensure that the reporting is conducted in a transparent and objective manner.

Second, the welfare indicators can then be used to identify bottlenecks. Bottlenecks in this context are those policy changes or government actions that would achieve the greatest improvements in social welfare. For instance, in countries with high levels of poverty, the bottleneck might be a reform policy to increase economic performance, measured in an increase in GDP, whereas in a country where pollution threatens human health, environmental regulation might be the most important bottleneck. NGOs and citizens could create demand for reforms of public policies by identifying bottlenecks and communicating them to the public sector. Governments would need to design roadmaps to guide bold long-term reforms that can address the most important bottlenecks. International organizations could provide technical expertise to link the identification of a bottleneck to the design of responding policy.

Third, governments would need to seek to actively learn how to implement robust and effective policy instruments and overcome political resistance, e.g. by means of appropriate compensation schemes. This requires policy-makers to engage in an ongoing process of innovating, evaluating, comparing, and refining policies. The basis of evaluation would be the welfare indicator selected in the first step. International organizations could support the process by gathering data on best practices and by offering technical expertise in the design of policies for given objectives defined by the government. NGOs and citizens would need to provide feedback on the experiences with implemented

policy and to draw attention to dysfunctional aspects and adverse side-effects of adopted policies.

References

Abercrombie, N., S. Hill, and B.S. Turner 2000. "Technology," in *The Penguin Dictionary of Sociology*, 4th edn. London: Penguin.

Acemoglu, D., and J.A. Robinson 2000. "Why Did the West Extend the Franchise? Democracy, Inequality, and Growth in Historical Perspective," *Quarterly Journal of Economics* 115/4: 1167–1199.

Acemoglu, D., and J. Robinson 2012. *Why Nations Fail: The Origins of Power, Prosperity, and Poverty*. New York: Crown Publishers.

Acemoglu, D., P. Aghion, L. Bursztyn, and D. Hemous 2012. "The Environment and Directed Technical Change," *American Economic Review* 102/1: 131–136.

Acemoglu, D., S. Johnson, and J. Robinson 2002. "Reversal of Fortune: Geography and Institutions in the Making of the Modern World Income Distribution," *Quarterly Journal of Economics* 117: 1231–1294.

Acemoglu, D., S. Johnson, and J. Robinson 2005. "Institutions as a Fundamental Cause of Long-run Growth," in P. Aghion and S.N. Durlauf (eds.), *Handbook of Economic Growth*, vol. 1A. New York: North-Holland.

Acworth, W., J. Ackva, D. Burtraw, O. Edenhofer, S. Fuss, C. Flachsland, C. Haug, N. Koch, U. Kornek, B. Knopf, and M. Montes de Oca 2017: *Emissions Trading and the Role of a Long Run Carbon Price Signal: Achieving Cost Effective Emission Reductions under an Emissions Trading System*. Berlin: ICAP.

Adler, M.D., D. Anthoff, V. Bosetti, G. Garner, K. Keller, and N. Treich 2016. *Priority for the Worse Off and the Social Cost of Carbon*. CESifo Working Paper No. 6032.

Afsa, C., D. Blanchet, V. Marcus, M. Mira d'Ercole, P.A. Pionnier, G. Ranuzzi, L. Rioux, and P. Shreyer 2008. Survey of Existing Approaches to Measuring Socio-economic Progress. Background paper for the first meeting of the CMEPSP.

Agrawala, S., F. Bosello, C. Carraro, and E. De Cian 2009. *Adaptation, Mitigation and Innovation: A Comprehensive Approach to Climate Policy*. Venice: Department of Economics, University of Venice. Working Paper No. 25/WP/2009.

Alberini, A., A. Chiabai, and G. Nocella 2006. "Valuing the Mortality Effects of Heat-waves," in B. Menne and K. Ebi (eds.), *Climate Change Adaptation Strategies for Human Health*. Germany: Springer.

Alesina, A., S. Özler, N. Roubini, and P. Swagel 1996. "Political Instability and Economic Growth," *Journal of Economic Growth* 1/2: 189–211.

Alier M.J., and R. Muradian 2015. *Handbook of Ecological Economics*. Cheltenham: Edward Elgar.

Alkire, S. 2002a. "Dimensions of Human Development," *World Development* 30/2: 181–205.

Alkire, S. 2002b. *Valuing Freedoms: Sen's Capability Approach and Poverty Reduction*. New York: Oxford University Press.

Allen, R. 2001. "The Great Divergence in European Wages and Prices from the Middle Ages to the First World War," *Explorations in Economic History* 38: 411–447.

Allouche, J. 2011. "The Sustainability and Resilience of Global Water and Food Systems. Political Analysis of the Interplay between Security, Resource Scarcity, Political Systems and Global Trade," *Food Policy* 36/suppl. 1: S3–S8.

Amdur, D., B.G. Rabe, and C. Borkk 2014. "Public Views on a Carbon Tax Depend on the Proposed Use of Revenue: A report from the National Surveys on Energy and Environment," *Issues in Energy and Environmental Policy*, 13.

http://closup.umich.edu/issues-in-energy-and-environmental-policy/13/public-views-on-a-carbon-tax-depend-on-the-proposed-use-of-revenue/ (last accessed December 2, 2016).

American Public Health Association (APHA) 2015. *Health in All Policies.* Washington, DC: APHA.

Ansell, C.K. 2011. *Pragmatist Democracy: Evolutionary Learning as Public Philosophy.* Oxford: Oxford University Press.

Arrow, K., P. Dasgupta, and K. Mäler 2003. "The Genuine Savings Criterion and the Value of Population," *Economic Theory* 21: 217–225.

Arrow K., P. Ehrlich, and S. Levin 2014. Some Perspectives on Linked Ecosystems and Socioeconomic Systems. http://mahb.stanford.edu/wp-content/uploads/2013/08/Some-Perspectives-on-Linked-Ecosystems-and-Socio-Economic-Systems-Arrow-Ehrlich-and-Levin-20131.pdf (last accessed December 23, 2017).

Asheim, G.B., and M.L. Weitzman 2001. "Does NNP Growth Indicate Welfare Improvement?" *Economics Letters* 73: 233–239.

Asheim, G.B., W. Buchholz, and C. Withagen 2007. "The Hartwick Rule: Myths and Facts," in G. Asheim (ed.), *Justifying, Characterizing and Indicating Sustainability.* Dordrecht, The Netherlands: Springer.

Atewamba, C., and B. Nkuiya 2017. "Testing the Assumptions and Predictions of the Hoteling Model," *Environmental and Resource Economics* 66/1:169–203.

Atkinson, G., I. Bateman, and S. Mourato 2012. "Recent Advances in the Valuation of Ecosystem Services and Biodiversity," *Oxford Review of Economic Policy* 28/1: 22–47.

Autor, H. 2015. "Why Are There Still So Many Jobs? The History and Future of Workplace Automation," *Journal of Economic Perspectives* 29: 3–30.

Auty, R. 1997. "Natural Resource Endowment, the State and Development Strategy," *Journal of International Development* 9/4: 651–663.

Auty, R. 2001. "The Political Economy of Resource-Driven Growth," *European Economic Review* 45/4: 839–846.

Baker, J.S. 1993. "*Dissent,*" in *Louisiana Advisory Committee to the US Commission on Civil Rights, The Battle for Environmental Justice in Louisiana.* Kansas City: US Commission on Civil Rights.

Baldwin, R.E., and P. Martin 1999. Two Waves of Globalisation: Superficial Similarities, Fundamental Differences. NBER Working Papers 6904. National Bureau of Economic Research, Inc. https://ideas.repec.org/p/nbr/nberwo/6904.html (last accessed December 23, 2017).

Bankes, S.C. 1993. "Exploratory Modeling for Policy Analysis." *Operations Research* 41/3: 435–449.

Barnes, P. 2006. *Capitalism 3.0: A Guide to Reclaiming the Commons.* Oakland, CA: Berrett-Koehler Publishers.

Barrett, S. 1994. Self-enforcing International Environmental Agreements. Oxford Economic Papers, New Series 46, 878–894.

Barrett, S. 2003. *Environment and Statecraft: The Strategy of Environmental Treaty-Making.* Oxford: Oxford University Press.

Barrett, S. 2007. *Why Cooperate? The Incentive to Supply Global Public Goods.* Oxford: Oxford University Press.

Barry, B. 1991. "Justice between Generations," in *Liberty and Justice: Essays in Political Theory,* Volume 2, 242–258. Oxford: Clarendon Press.

Barthel, S., and C. Isendahl 2013. "Urban Gardens, Agriculture and Water Management: Sources of Resilience for Long-term Food Security in Cities," *Ecological Economics* 86: 224–234.

Baudin, Th., D. de la Croix, and P.E. Gobbi 2015. "Fertility and Childlessness in the US," *American Economic Review* 105/6: 1852–1882.

Baumeister, R.F., K.D. Vohs, J.L. Aaker, and E.N. Garbinsky 2013. "Some Key Differences between a Happy Life and a Meaningful Life," *Journal of Positive Psychology* 8/6: 505–516.

Ben-David, D. 1996. "Trade and Convergence among Countries," *Journal of International Economics* 40/3: 279–298.

Ben-Porath, Y. 1967. "The Production of Human Capital and the Life Cycle of Earnings," *Journal of Political Economy* 75: 352–365.

Benchekroun, H., and N. Van Long 2014. "Game Theoretic Modeling in Environmental and Resource Economics," in *Handbook of Regional Science,* 951–971. New York: Springer.

Bilion, P. 2001. "The Political Ecology of War: Natural Resources and Armed Conflicts," *Political Geography* 20/5: 561–584.

Blackstone, W. 1974. "Ethics and Ecology," in W. Blackstone (ed.), *Philosophy and Environmental Crisis.* Athens, GA: University of Georgia Press.

Blake, M. 2013. *Justice and Foreign Policy.* Oxford: Oxford University Press.

Blalock, G., and P.J. Gertler 2008. "Welfare Gains from Foreign Direct Investment through Technology Transfer to Local Suppliers." *Journal of International Economics* 74/2: 402–421.

Bloom, D.E., J.D. Sachs, P. Collier, and C. Udry 1998. "Geography, Demography, and Economic Growth in Africa." *Brookings Papers on Economic Activity*, 1998/2: 207–295.

Bob, U., and S. Bronkhorst 2010. "Environmental Conflicts:Key Issues and Management Implications," *African Journal on Conflict Resolution* 10/2: 9–30.

Boer, J., M. Kastor, and J.L. Sadd 1997. "Is There Environmental Racism?" *Social Science Quarterly* 78/4: 793–810.

Bolt, J., and J.L. van Zanden 2013. The First Update of the Maddison Project; Re-Estimating Growth Before 1820. Maddison Project Working Paper 4.

Bom, P.R.D., and J.E. Ligthart 2014. "What Have We Learned from Three Decades of Research on the Productivity of Public Capital?," *Journal of Economic Surveys* 28/5: 889–916.

Bosello F., R. Roson, and R.S.J. Tol 2006. "Economy-Wide Estimates of the Implications of Climate Change: Human Health," *Ecological Economics* 58: 579–581.

Brandt, R. 1979. *A Theory of the Good and the Right.* Oxford: Clarendon Press.

Brenner, M., M. Riddle, and J.K. Boyce 2007. "A Chinese Sky Trust?" *Energy Policy* 35: 1771–1784.

Bresnahan, T.F., and M. Trajtenberg 1995. "General Purpose Technologies 'Engines of Growth'?" *Journal of Econometrics* 65: 83–108.

Brooks, S., and M. Loevinsohn 2011. "Shaping Agricultural Innovation Systems Responsive to Food Insecurity and Climate Change," *Natural Resources Forum* 35/3: 185–200.

Bruni, L., and R. Sugden 2013. "Reclaiming Virtue Ethics for Economics," *Journal of Economic Perspectives* 27/4: 141–164.

Brynjolfsson, E., and A. Mcafee (2014). *The Second Machine Age: Work, Progress, and Prosperity in a Time of Brilliant Technologies.* New York: Norton & Company.

Buchanan, J.M., and W.C. Stubblebine 1962. "Externality," in *Classic Papers in Natural Resource Economics.* New York: Springer.

Buck, S. 1998. *The Global Commons: An Introduction.* Washington, DC: Island Press.

Bulkeley, H., L. Andonova, M.M. Betsill, D. Compagnon, T. Hale, M.J. Hoffmann, P. Newell, M. Paterson, S.D. VanDeveer, and C. Roger 2014. *Transnational Climate Change Governance.* Cambridge: Cambridge University Press.

Bustos, P. 2011. "Trade Liberalization, Exports, and Technology Upgrading: Evidence on the Impact of MERCOSUR on Argentinian Firms," *American Economic Review* 101/1: 304–340.

Caney, S. 2005. *Justice Beyond Borders: A Global Political Theory.* Oxford: Oxford University Press.

Caney, S. 2011. "Humanity, Associations, and Global Justice: In Defence of Humanity-Centred Cosmopolitan Egalitarianism," *The Monist* 94/4: 506–534.

Caney, S. 2012. "Just Emissions," *Philosophy & Public Affairs* 40/4: 255–300.

Carlsson, F., and O. Johansson-Stenman, O. 2012. "Behavioral Economics and Environmental Policy," *Annual Review of Resource Economics* 4: 75–99.

Carraro, C. 2014. "International Environmental Cooperation," in *Handbook of Sustainable Development,* 418. Cheltenham, UK: Edward Elgar Publishing.

Carraro, C., and D. Siniscalco 1993. "Strategies for the International Protection of the Environment," *Journal of Public Economics* 52: 309–328.

Carraro, C., C. Marchiori, and S. Oreffice 2009. "Endogenous Minimum Participation in International Environmental Treaties," *Environmental and Resource Economics* 42: 411–425.

Casal, P. 2007. "Why Sufficiency Is Not Enough," *Ethics* 117/2: 296–326.

de las Casas, B. 1992. *A Short Account of the Destruction of the Indies,* ed. N. Griffin and A. Pagden. New York: Penguin.

Cervellati, M., and U. Sunde 2005. "Human Capital Formation, Life Expectancy and the Process of Development," *American Economic Review* 95: 1653–1672.

Cetorelli, N., and L. Goldberg 2012. "Banking Globalization and Monetary Transmission," *Journal of Finance* 67/5: 1811–1843.

Chaifetz, A. and P. Jagger 2014. "40 Years of Dialogue on Food Sovereignty: A Review and a Look Ahead," *Global Food Security* 3: 85–91.

Chamley, C. 1986. "Optimal Taxation of Capital Income in General Equilibrium with Infinite Lives," *Econometrica* 54/3: 607–622.

Chang, H.-J. 2007. *Institutional Change and Economic Development.*

Chatterjee, S., and S.J. Turnovsky 2012. "Infrastructure and Inequality," *European Economic Review* 56: 1730–1745.

4

Chopra, K., and P. Dasgupta 2017. "Economic Systems and Ecosystems," in H. Sandhu (ed.), *Ecosystems Science, Valuation and Management: Theory and Practice*. New York: Springer.

Coase, R.H. 1960. *The Problem of Social Cost*. New York: Springer.

Cole, D.H. 2015. "Advantages of a Polycentric Approach to Climate Change Policy," *Nature Climate Change* 5: 114–118.

Collier, P. 2008. *The Bottom Billion: Why the Poorest Countries Are Failing and What Can Be Done About It*. Oxford: Oxford University Press. https://ideas.repec.org/b/oxp/obooks/9780195374636.html (last accessed December 23, 2017).

Collier, P., and A. Hoeffler 2002. "On the Incidence of Civil War in Africa," *Journal of Conflict Resolution* 46/1: 13–28.

Cooper, F. 2005. *Colonialism in Question*. Berkeley: University of Caliornia Press.

Cordell, D., and T. Neset 2014. "Phosphorus Vulnerability: A Qualitative Framework for Assessing the Vulnerability of National and Regional Food Systems to the Multi-dimensional Stressors of Phosphorus Scarcity," *Global Environmental Change*. 24/2014: 108–122.

Coyle, D. 2014. *GDP: A Brief but Affectionate History*. Princeton, NJ: Princeton University Press.

Crespo, N., and M.P. Fontoura 2007. "Determinant Factors of FDI Spillovers – What Do We Really Know?" *World Development* 35/3: 410–425.

Crisp, R. 2006. *Reasons and the Good*. Oxford: Clarendon Press.

de la Croix, D., and M. Doepke 2003. "Inequality and Growth: Why Differential Fertility Matters," *American Economic Review* 93: 1091–1113.

de la Croix, D., and O. Licandro 2015. "The Longevity of Famous People from Hammurabi to Einstein," *Journal of Economic Growth* 20: 263–303.

de la Croix, D., and F. Mariani 2015. "From Polygyny to Serial Monogamy: A Unified Theory of Marriage Institutions," *Review of Economic Studies* 82/2: 565–607.

Crutzen, P.J. 2002. "Geology of Mankind: The Anthropocene," *Nature* 415: 23.

Csereklyei, Z., and D. Stern 2015. "Global Energy Use: Decoupling or Convergence?" *Energy Economics* 51: 633–641.

Dalmazzone, S. 2006. "Decentralization and the Environment," in E. Ahmad and G. Brosio (eds.), *Handbook of Fiscal Federalism*. Cheltenham: Edward Elgar.

Daly, H., and J. Cobb 1989. *For the Common Good*. Boston, MA: Beacon Press.

Dasgupta, P. 2004. *Human Well-Being and the Natural Environment*. New York: Oxford University Press.

Dasgupta, P. 2016. *Climate Sensitive Adaptation in Health: Imperatives for India in a Developing Economy Context*. New York: Springer. www.springer.com/in/book/9788132228226 (last accessed January 27, 2018).

Dasgupta, P., J.F. Morton, D. Dodman, B. Karapinar, F. Meza, M.G. Rivera-Ferre, A. Toure Sarr, and K.E. Vincent 2014. "Rural Areas," in C. Field V. Barros, and D.J. Dokken, et al. (eds.)]*Climate Change 2014: Impacts, Adaptation, and Vulnerability, Part A. Contribution of Working Group II to the Fifth Assessment Report of the Intergovernmental Panel on Climate Change*, 613–657. Cambridge and New York: Cambridge University Press. https://ipcc-wg2.gov/AR5/images/uploads/WGIIAR5-Chap9_FINAL.pdf (last accessed December 12, 2015).

Datta, A. 2010. "The Incidence of Fuel Taxation in India," *Energy Economics* 32: 26–33.

Deaton, A. 2013. *The Great Escape: Health, Wealth and the Origins of Inequality*. Princeton, NJ: Princeton University Press.

Diamond, J. 1997. *Guns, Germs, and Steel*. New York: W.W. Norton.

Diao, X., J. Thhurlow, S. Benin, and S. Fan 2012. *Strategies and Priorities for African Agriculture: economywide perspectives from country studies*. Washington, USA: International Food Policy Research Institute.

Dietz, T., E. Ostrom, and P.C. Stern 2003. "The Struggle to Govern the Commons," *Science* 302: 1907–1912.

Dissou, Y., and M.S. Siddiqui 2014. "Can Carbon Taxes Be Progressive?" *Energy Economics* 42: 88–100.

Docquier, F., and H. Rapoport 2012. "Globalization, Brain Drain, and Development," *Journal of Economic Literature* 50/3: 681–730.

Dollar, D., and A. Kraay 2002. "Growth is Good for the Poor," *Journal of Economic Growth* 7/3: 195–225.

Dollar, D., T. Kleineberg, and A. Kraay 2016. "Growth Still Is Good for the Poor," *European Economic Review* 81: 68–85.

Dorsch, M.J., and C. Flachsland 2017. "A Polycentric Approach to Global Climate Governance," *Global Environmental Politics* 17/2: 45–64.

Dowding, K., and R. Kimber 1983. "The Meaning and Use of 'Political Stability'," *European Journal of Political Research* 11/3: 229–243.

Drèze, J., and A. Sen 1989. *Hunger and Public Action*. Oxford: Oxford University Press.

Drèze, J., and A. Sen 2013. *An Uncertain Glory: India and Its Contradictions*. Princeton, NJ: Princeton University Press.

Drouet, L., V. Bosetti, and M. Tavoni 2015. "Selection of Climate Policies under the Uncertainties in the Fifth Assessment Report of the IPCC," *Nature Climate Change, Letters* 5: 937–940.

Dubash, N.K., M. Hagemann, N. Höhne, and P. Upadhyaya 2013. "Developments in National Climate Change Mitigation Legislation and Strategy," *Climate Policy* 13: 649–664.

Easterlin, R. 2010. *Happiness, Growth, and the Life Cycle*, ed. H. Hinte and K.E. Zimmermann. New York: Oxford University Press.

Easterly, W. 2005. "National Policies and Economic Growth: A Reappraisal," in P. Aghion and S. Durlauf (eds.), *Handbook of Economic Growth*, Volume 1, Part B. Amsterdam: Elsevier.

Easterly, W. 2013. *The Tyranny of Experts: Economists, Dictators, and the Forgotten Rights of the Poor*. New York: Basic Books.

Easterly, W. and R. Levine 1997. "Africa's Growth Tragedy: Policies and Ethnic Divisions," *Quarterly Journal of Economics* 112/4: 1203–1250.

Easterly, W. and R. Levine 2003. "Tropics, Germs, and Crops: How Endowments Influence Economic Development," *Journal of Monetary Economics*, 50/1: 3–39.

Eastman, J. and K.L. Eastman 2011. "Perceptions of Status Consumption and the Economy," *Journal of Business & Economics Research* 9/7: 9–20.

Eastman, J., R.E. Goldsmith, and L.R. Flynn 1999. "Status Consumption in Consumer Behavior: Scale Development and Validation," *Journal of Marketing Theory and Practice* 7/3: 41–52.

Ebi, K. 2008. "Adaptation Costs for Climate Change-Related Cases of Diarrhoeal Disease, Malnutrition, and Malaria in 2030," *Global Health* 4: 1. [PMC free article] [PubMed]. www.ncbi.nlm.nih.gov/pmc/articles/PMC2556651/ (last accessed January 27, 2018).

Edenhofer, O., and M. Kowarsch 2015. "Cartography of Pathways: A New Model for Environmental Policy Assessments." *Environmental Science & Policy* 51 (August): 56–64.

Edenhofer, O., C. Flachsland, M. Jakob, and K. Lessmann 2014a. The Atmosphere as a global commons–challenges for International Cooperation and Governance, in W. Semmler and L. Bernard (eds.), *The Oxford Handbook of the Macroeconomics of Global Warming*. Oxford: Oxford University Press.

Edenhofer, O., C. Flachsland, and B. Knopf 2016. "Science and Religion in Dialogue over the Global Commons," *Nature Climate Change* 5: 907–909.

Edenhofer, O., S. Kadner, C. von Stechow, G. Schwerhoff, and G. Luderer 2014b. Linking Climate Change Mitigation Research to Sustainable Development. *In Handbook of Sustainable Development: Second Edition*. Cheltenham, UK: Edward Elgar Publishing.

Edenhofer, O., L. Mattauch, and J. Siegmeier 2015. "Hypergeorgism: When Rent Taxation Is Socially Optimal," *FinanzArchiv: Public Finance Analysis* (July 2014), 1–35.

Edenhofer, O., R. Pichs-Madruga, R., Sokona, Y., Kadner, S., Minx, J., Brunner, S., … and Minx, J. (eds.) 2014c. *Climate Change Mitigation of Climate Change. Contribution of Working Group III to the Fifth Assessment Report of the Intergovernmental Panel on Climate Change*. Cambridge: Cambridge University Press.

Edenhofer, O., C. Roolfs, B. Gaitan, P. Nahmmacher, and C. Flachsland 2017. "Agreeing on an EU ETS Minimum Price to Foster Solidarity, Subsidiarity and efficiency in the EU," in H. Volleberg, I. Parry, and K. Redanz (eds.), *Energy Tax and Regulatory Policy in Europe: Reform Priorities*. Cambridge, MA: MIT Press.

Ellis, G.M., and R. Halvorsen 2002. "Estimation of Market Power in a Nonrenewable Resource Industry," *Journal of Political Economy*, 110/4: 883–899.

EMAF (Ellen MacArthur Foundation) 2016. "Circular Economy Overview." www.ellenmacarthurfoundation.org/circular-economy/overview/concept (last accessed January 27, 2018).

Engel, E. 1857. Die Productions- und Consumtionsverhältnisse des Königreichs Sachsen, Zeitschrift des statistischen Bureaus des Königlich Sächsischen Ministeriums des Inneren, Nr. 8 und 9.

Engerman, S., and K. Sokoloff 2002. Factor Endowments, Inequality, and Paths of Development among New World Economies. NBER Working Paper No. 9259.

Ericksen, P., J. Ingram, and D. Liverman 2009. "Food Security and Global Environmental Change: Emerging Challenges," *Environmental Science & Policy* 12/4: 373–377.

4

Estache, A., and M. Fay 2007. Current Debates on Infrastructure Policy. World Bank Policy Research Working Paper 4410.

Falkner, R. 2015. A Minilateral Solution for Global Climate Change? On Bargaining Efficiency, Club Benefits and International Legitimacy. Grantham Research Institute on Climate Change and the Environment Working Paper No. 197.

FAO 1996. Rome Declaration on World Food Security. *World Food Summit.* November 13–17, 1996. Rome, Italy. www.fao.org/docrep/003/w3613e/w3613e00.HTM (last accessed December 23, 2017).

FAO, IFAD, and WFP 2012. *The State of Food Insecurity in the World 2012.* Rome: Food and Agriculture Organization.

FAO, IFAD, and WFP 2015. *The State of Food Insecurity in the World 2015.* Rome: Food and Agriculture Organization.

Feenstra, R., R. Inklaar, and M. Timmer 2013. *The Next Generation of the Penn World Table.* www.ggdc.net/pwt www.ggdc.net/pwt (last accessed December 23, 2017).

Fehr-Duda, H., and E. Fehr 2016. "Sustainability: Game Human Nature," *Nature* 530: 413.

Felbermayr, G., J. Prat, and H. Schmerer 2011. "Globalization and Labor Market Outcomes: Wage Bargaining, Search Frictions, and Firm Heterogeneity," *Journal of Economic Theory* 146/1: 39–73.

Finkelstein, L.S. 1995. "What Is Global Governance?," *Global Governance* 1/3: 367–372.

Fleurbaey, M. 2009. "Beyond GDP: The Quest for a Measure of Social Welfare," *Journal of Economic Literature* 47/4: 1029–1075.

Fleurbaey, M., and D. Blanchet 2013. *Beyond GDP: Measuring Welfare and Assessing Sustainability.* New York: Oxford University Press.

Fleurbaey, M., and G. Gaulier 2009. "International Comparisons of Living Standards by Equivalent Incomes," *Scandinavian Journal of Economics* 111/3: 597–624.

Fleurbaey M., S. Kartha, S. Bolwig, Y.L. Chee, Y. Chen, E. Corbera, F. Lecocq, W. Lutz, M.S. Muylaert, R.B. Norgaard, C. Okereke, and A.D. Sagar 2014. "Sustainable Development and Equity," in O. Edenhofer, R. Pichs-Madruga, Y. Sokona, E. Farahani, S. Kadner, K. Seyboth, A. Adler, I. Baum, S. Brunner, P. Eickemeier, B. Kriemann, J. Savolainen, S. Schlömer, C. von Stechow, T. Zwickel, and J.C. Minx (eds.), *Climate Change 2014: Mitigation of Climate Change. Contribution of Working Group III to the Fifth Assessment Report of the Intergovernmental Panel on Climate Change.* Cambridge and New York: Cambridge University Press.

Flues, F., and A. Thomas 2015. The Distributional Effects of Energy Taxes. OECD Taxation Working Papers 23. www.oecd-ilibrary.org/taxation/the-distributional-effects-of-energy-taxes_5js1qwkqqrbv-en (last accessed December 13, 2016).

Foley, J.A., R. DeFries, G.P. Asner, C. Barford, G. Bonan, S.R.., Carpenter, S.R. … P.K. Snyder 2005. Global Consequences of Land Use. *Science* 309: 570–574.

Foran, T., J. Butler, L. Williams, W. Wanjura, A. Hall, L. Carter, and P. Carberry 2014. "Taking Complexity in Food Systems Seriously: An Interdisciplinary Analysis," *World Development* 61: 85–101.

Fosu, A.K. 2009. "Inequality and the Impact of Growth on Poverty: Comparative Evidence for Sub-Saharan Africa," *Journal of Development Studies* 45/5: 726–745.

Fosu, A.K. 2010. "Inequality, Income and Poverty: Comparative Global Evidence," *Social Science Quarterly* 91/5: 1432–1446.

Fosu, A.K. 2015. "Growth, Inequality and Poverty in Sub-Saharan Africa: Recent Progress in a Global Context," *Oxford Development Studies* 43/1: 44–59.

Fosu, A.K. 2017. Governance and Development in Africa: A Concise Review. Global Development Institute Working Paper Series 2017-008, University of Manchester, UK.

Franck, Th.M. 1995. *Fairness in International Law and Institutions.* Oxford: Clarendon Press.

Frank, R.H. 2005. "Positional Externalities Cause Large and Preventable Welfare Losses," *American Economic Review, American Economic Association,* 95/2: 137–141. https://ideas.repec.org/a/aea/aecrev/v95y2005i2p137-141.html (last accessed December 23, 2017).

Frank, R.H. 2008. "Should Public Policy Respond to Positional Externalities?" *Journal of Public Economics* 92/8–9: 1777–1786. https://ideas.repec.org/a/eee/pubeco/v92y2008i8-9p1777-1786.html (last accessed December 23, 2017).

Frankel, J. 2010. The Natural Resource Curse: A Survey. National Bureau of Economic Research, Working Paper 15836.

Frankfurt, H. 2015. *Inequality.* Princeton and Oxford: Princeton University Press.

Frederick, S., and G. Loewenstein 1999. "Hedonic Adaptation," in D. Kahneman, E. Diener, and N. Schwarz (eds.), The Foundations of Hedonic Psychology. New York: Russell Sage Foundation.

Freeman, C., and L. Soete 1997. *The Economics of Industrial Innovation.* Cambridge, MA: MIT Press.

Frey, B., and A. Stutzer 2002. *Happiness and Economics.* Princeton, NJ: Princeton University Press.

Frieden, J. 2001. "Inequality, Causes and Possible Futures," *International Social Science Review* 2/1: 33–40.

Fujita, M., and J.F. Thisse 2002. *Economics of Agglomeration.* Cambridge: Cambridge University Press.

Galbraith, J. 1958. *The Affluent Society.* New York: Houghton Mifflin.

Galbraith, J. 1967. *The New Industrial State.* New York: Houghton Mifflin.

Gali, J. 1994. "Keeping Up with the Joneses: Consumption Externalities, Portfolio Choice and Asset Prices," *Journal of Money, Credit and Banking* 26/1: 1–8.

Galloway, J.N. and Cowling, E.B. 2002. "Reactive Nitrogen and the World: Two Hundred Years of Change," *Ambio* 31: 64–71.

Gallup, J.L., Sachs, J. and Mellinger, A. 1999. "Geography and Economic Development," *International Regional Science Review* 22/2: 179–232.

Galor, O. 2005. "From Stagnation to Growth: Unified Growth Theory," in P. Aghion and S. Durlauf (eds.), *Handbook of Economic Growth.* Oxford: Elsevier.

Galor, O. 2011. *Unified Growth Theory.* Princeton, NJ: Princeton University Press.

Galor, O., and D. Weil 1999. "From Malthusian Stagnation to Modern Growth," *The American Economic Review,* 89/2: 150–154.

Galor, O., and D. Weil 2000. Population, Technology, and Growth: From Malthusian Stagnation to the Demographic Transition and Beyond. *The American Economic Review,* 90/4: 806–828.

Garner, G., P. Reed, and K. Keller 2016. "Climate Risk Management Requires Explicit Representation of Societal Trade-offs." *Climatic Change* 134/4: 713–723.

Gollin, D., R. Jedwab, and D. Vollrath. 2015. Urbanization With and Without Industrialization." *Journal of Economic Growth* 21/1: 35–70.

Gollin, D., D. Lagakos, and M.E. Waugh 2014. The Agricultural Productivity Gap. *Quarterly Journal of Economics* 129: 939–993.

Gordon, R.J. 2000. "Does the 'New Economy' Measure up to the Great Inventions of the Past?," *Journal of Economic Perspectives* 14/4: 49–74.

Gordon, R.J. 2012. *Is US Economic Growth Over? Faltering Innovation Confronts the Six Headwinds.* CEPR Policy Insights.

Gordon, R.J. 2016 *The Rise and Fall of American Growth: The U.S. Standard of Living since the Civil War.* Princeton, NJ: Princeton University Press.

Goulder, L.H., and A. Schein 2013. "Carbon Taxes vs. Cap and Trade: A Critical Review," *Climate Change Economics,* 4/03. www.worldscientific.com/doi/pdf/10.1142/S2010007813500103 (last accessed January 27, 2018).

Goulder, L.H., and R.N. Stavins 2011. Challenges from State-Federal Interactions in US Climate Change Policy. *The American Economic Review* 101: 253–257.

Griffin, J. 1986. *Well-Being: Its Meaning, Measurement and Moral Importance.* Oxford: Clarendon Press.

Guivarch, C., and S. Hallegatte 2011. "Existing Infrastructure and the 2 C Target," *Climatic Change* 109/3–4: 801–805.

Haberl, H., M. Fischer-Kowalski, F. Krausmann, J. Martínez-Alier, and V. Winiwarter 2009. "A Socio-metabolic Transition towards Sustainability? Challenges for Another Great Transformation." *Sustainable Development* 19(2011): 1–14.

Hakelberg, L. 2014. Governance by Diffusion: Transnational Municipal Networks and the Spread of Local Climate Strategies in Europe. *Global Environmental Politics* 14, 107–129.

Hale, T., and C. Roger 2014. Orchestration and Transnational Climate Governance. *The Review of International Organizations* 9, 59–82.

Hales, S., S. Kovats, S. Lloyd, and D. Campbell-Lendrum 2014. *Quantitative Risk Assessment of the Effects of Climate Change on Selected Causes of Death, 2030s and 2050s.* Geneva, Switzerland: World Health Organization http://apps.who.int/iris/bitstream/10665/134014/1/9789241507691_eng.pdf (last accessed October 14, 2014).

Hall, P.A., and P. Soskice. 2001. *Varieties of Capitalism: The Institutional Foundations of Comparative Advantage.* Oxford: Oxford University Press.

Hall, R., and C. Jones 1999. "Why Do Some Countries Produce So Much More Output Per Worker Than Others?," *The Quarterly Journal of Economics,* 114/1: 83–116.

4

Halvorsen, R., and T.R. Smith 1991. "A Test of the Theory of Exhaustible Resources," *The Quarterly Journal of Economics*, 106/1: 123–140.

Hamilton, K. 1994, "Green Adjustments to GDP," *Resources Policy* 20/3: 155–168.

Hamilton, K., and M. Clemens 1999. "Genuine Savings Rates in Developing Countries," *The World Bank Economic Review* 13/2: 333–356.

Hansen G., and E. Prescott 2002. "Malthus to Solow," *American Economic Review* 92: 1205–1217.

Hansen, P.V. and L. Lindholt 2008. "The Market Power of OPEC 1973–2001," *Applied Economics*, 40/22: 2939–2959.

Hardin, G. 1968. "The Tragedy of the Commons," *Science* 162: 1243–1248.

Hart, R. 2016. "Non-renewable Resources in the Long Run," *Journal of Economic Dynamics and Control* 71: 1–20.

Hart, R., and D. Spiro 2011. "The Elephant in Hotelling's Room," *Energy Policy* 39/12: 7834–7838.

Hartwick, J. 1977. "Intergenerational equity and investing rents from exhaustible resources. *American Economic Review* 67: 972–974.

Hausmann, R., and C.A. Hidalgo 2011. "The Network Structure of Economic Output," *Journal of Economic Growth* 16/4: 309–342.

Hausmann, R., and D. Rodrik. 2003. "Economic Development as Self-Discovery." *Journal of Development Economics* 72/2: 603–633.

Hausmann, R., L. Pritchett, and D. Rodrik (2005). "Growth Accelerations," *Journal of Economic Growth* 10/4: 303–329.

Hausmann, R., D. Rodrik, and A. Velasco 2005. "Getting the Diagnostics Right," *Finance and Development* 43/1. www.imf.org/external/pubs/ft/fandd/2006/03/hausmann.htm (last accessed January 27, 2018).

Hayward, S. 2013. *Environmental Justice, EPA Style.* Washington, DC: American Enterprise Institute.

Heal, G. 1992. International Negotiations on Emission Control. *Structural Change and Economic Dynamics* 3: 223–240.

Heckscher, E.F., and B. Ohlin. 1991. *Heckscher-Ohlin Trade Theory.* Cambridge: MA. MIT Press.

Helpman, E., O. Itskhoki, and S. Redding. 2010. "Inequality and Unemployment in a Global Economy." *Econometrica* 78/4: 1239–1283.

Hepburn, C. 2006. "Regulation by Prices, Quantities, or Both: A Review of Instrument Choice. *Oxford Review of Economic Policy* 22: 226–247.

Herrendorf, B., R. Rogerson, and Á. Valentinyi 2014. Growth and Structural Transformation, in P. Aghion and S. Durlauf (eds.), *Handbook of Economic Growth.* Elsevier, Amsterdam.

Hickmann, T. 2016. *Rethinking Authority in Global Climate Governance: How Transnational Climate Initiatives Relate to the International Climate Regime.* Abingdon, UK: Routledge.

Hidalgo, C.A. and R. Hausmann 2009. "The Building Blocks of Economic Complexity," *Proc. Natl. Acad. Sci.* 106: 10570–10575.

Hidalgo, C.A., B. Klinger, A.-L. Barabási, and R. Hausmann 2007. "The Product Space Conditions the Development of Nations," *Science* 317: 482–487.

Hirsch, F. 1977. *Social Limits to Growth.* London and Henley: Routledge and Kegan Paul.

Hirschman, A. 1973. "The Changing Tolerance for Income Inequality in the Course of Economic Development," *Quarterly Journal of Economics* 87/4: 544–566 (with a mathematical appendix by M. Rothschild).

Hobsbawm, E.J. 2008. *On Empire: America, War and Global Supremacy.* New York: Pantheon Books.

Hoffmann, M.J. 2011. *Climate Governance at the Crossroads: Experimenting with a Global Response after Kyoto.* Oxford: Oxford University Press.

Holland, M., M. Amann, C. Heyes, et al. 2011. "The Reduction in Air Quality Impacts and Associated Economic Benefits of Mitigation Policy." Technical Policy Briefing Note 6. Summary of results from the EC RTD ClimateCost project. In P. Watkiss (ed.), *The ClimateCost Project.* Sweden: Stockholm Environment Institute (Final Report. Volume 1: Europe).

Holtug, N. 2010. *Persons, Interests, and Justice.* New York: Oxford University Press.

Homburg, S. 2015. "Critical Remarks on Piketty's Capital in the Twenty-first Century," *Applied Economics* 47 (February): 1401–1406. http://doi.org/10.1080/00036846.2014.997927 (last accessed on January 27, 2018).

Hotelling, H. 1931. "The Economics of Exhaustible Resources," *Journal of Political Economy* 39/2:137–175.

Hovenkamp, H. 2009. "Coase Theorem and Arthur Cecil Pigou," *The Arizona Literary Revew* 51: 633.

Howarth, R.B., 2006. "Optimal Environmental Taxes under Relative Consumption Effects," *Ecological Economics* 58/1: 209–219. https://ideas.repec.org/a/eee/ecolec/v58y2006i1p209-219.html (last accessed December 23, 2017).

Howe, S. 2002. *Empire*, New York: Oxford University Press.

Hübler, M., G. Klepper, and S. Peterson 2008. "Costs of Climate Change: The Effects of Rising Temperatures on Health and Productivity in Germany," *Ecological Economics* 68/1–2: 381–393.

Hudson, P. 1992. *The Industrial Revolution.* London: Edward Arnold.

Hulme, M. 2009. *Why We Disagree about Climate Change: Understanding Controversy, Inaction and Opportunity.* Cambridge: Cambridge University Press.

Huntington, S. 1968. *Political Order in Changing Societies.* New Haven and London: Yale University Press.

Huppmann, D., and F. Holz 2012. "Crude Oil Market Power – a Shift in Recent Years?," *The Energy Journal* 33/4: 1–23.

Hutton, G. and B. Menne 2014. "Economic Evidence on the Health Impacts of Climate Change in Europe," *Environmental Health Insights* 8: 43–52.

IEA 2016. *Energy and Air Pollution: World Energy Outlook Special Report.* Paris: OECD/IEA.

IMF 2013. Energy Subsidy Reform: Lessons and Implications. www.imf.org/external/np/pp/eng/2013/012813.pdf (last accessed December 23, 2017).

IPCC 2013. Climate Change 2013: The Physical Science Basis. *Contribution of Working Group I to the Fifth Assessment Report of the Intergovernmental Panel on Climate Change*, T.F. Stocker, D. Qin, G.-K. Plattner, M. Tignor, S.K. Allen, J. Boschung, A. Nauels, Y. Xia, V. Bex, and P.M. Midgley (eds.). Cambridge, UK and New York: Cambridge University Press.

IPCC 2014. "Summary for Policymakers," in *Climate Change 2014: Impacts, Adaptation, and Vulnerability. Part A: Global and Sectoral Aspects. Contribution of Working Group II to the Fifth Assessment Report of the Intergovernmental Panel on Climate Change*, 1–32. Cambridge, UK and New York: Cambridge University Press. http://ipcc-wg2.gov/AR5/images/uploads/WG2AR5_SPM_FINAL.pdf (last accessed October 4, 2015).

IPCC 2015. *Climate Change 2014: Mitigation of Climate Change.* Cambridge: Cambridge University Press.

Isham, J., M. Woolcock, L. Pritchett, and G. Busby 2005. "The Varieties of Resource Experience: Natural Resource Exports Structures and the Political Economy of Economic Growth," *World Bank Economic Review* 19/2: 141–174.

Isley, S.C., R.J. Lempert, S.W. Popper, and R. Vardavas 2015. "The Effect of Near-Term Policy Choices on Long-Term Greenhouse Gas Transformation Pathways," *Global Environmental Change* 34: 147–158.

Jackson, T. 2009. *Prosperity without Growth. Economics for a Finite Planet.* USA and UK: Earthscan.

Jakob, M., and O. Edenhofer 2014. "Green Growth, Degrowth, and the Commons," *Oxford Review of Economic Policy*, 30/3: 447–468.

Jakob, M., and O. Edenhofer 2015. "Welfare with or without Growth? Do We Need to Reduce Economic Activity to Protect the Environment and Increase the Quality of Life?," *GAIA* 24/4: 240–242.

Jakob, M. and J. Hilaire. 2015. "Climate Science: Unburnable Fossil-Fuel Reserves," *Nature* 517/7533: 150–152.

Jakob, M., and J.C. Steckel 2016. "Implications of Climate Change Mitigation for Sustainable Development," *Environmental Research Letters* 11/10: 1–9.

Jakob, M., C. Chen, S. Fuss, A. Marxen, and O. Edenhofer 2015. "Development Incentives for Fossil Fuel Subsidy Reform," *Nature Clim. Change* 5/8: 709–712.

Jakob, M., C. Chen, S. Fuss, A. Marxen, N. Rao, E. Edenhofer 2016. "Using Carbon Pricing Revenues to Finance Infrastructure Access," *World Development* 84: 254–265.

Javorcik, B.S. 2008. "Can Survey Evidence Shed Light on Spillovers from Foreign Direct Investment?," *The World Bank Research Observer* 23/2: 139–159.

Jones, C. 2005. "Growth and Ideas," in P. Aghion and S.N. Durlauf (eds.), *Handbook of Economic Growth*, vol. 1B. New York: North-Holland.

Jones, C., and P. Romer 2010. "The New Kaldor Facts: Ideas, Institutions, Population, and Human Capital," *American Economic Journal: Macroeconomics* 2/1: 224–245.

Jordan, A.J., D. Huitema, M. Hildén, H. van Asselt, T.J. Rayner, J.J. Schoenefeld, J. Tosun, J. Forster, E.L. Boasson 2015. "Emergence of Polycentric Climate Governance and Its Future Prospects," *Nature Climate Change* 5: 977–982.

Jorgenson, D. 1990. "Aggregate Consumer Behavior and the Measurement of Social Welfare," *Econometrica* 58/5: 1007–1040.

Jorgenson, D.W., J.S. Landefeld, and W.D. Nordhaus 2006. *A New Architecture for the U.S. National Accounts.* Chicago: The University of Chicago Press.

Judd, K.L. 1985. "Redistributive Taxation in a Simple Perfect Foresight Model," *Journal of Public Economics* 28/1: 59–83.

Kahneman, D., and A. Deaton 2010. "High Income Improves Evaluation of Life but Not Emotional Well-Being." Proceedings of the National Academy of Sciences 107/38: 16489–16493.

Kaldor, N. 1961. "Capital Accumulation and Economic Growth," in F.A. Lutz and D.C. Hague (eds.), *The Theory of Capital.* New York: St. Martins Press.

Kallbekken, S., S. Kroll, and T.L. Cherry 2011. "Do You Not Like Pigou, or Do You Not Understand Him? Tax Aversion and Revenue Recycling in the Lab," *Journal of Environmental Economics and Management* 62/1: 53–64.

Kallis, G. 2011. "In Defence of Degrowth," *Ecological Economics* 70/5: 873–880.

Kannan, K.P. 1995. "Declining Incidence of Rural Poverty in Kerala," *Economic and Political Weekly* 30/41–42: 2651–2662.

Kasprzyk, J.R., S. Nataraj, P.M. Reed, and R.J. Lempert 2013. "Many-Objective Robust Decision Making for Complex Environmental Systems Undergoing Change," *Environmental Modeling and Software* 42: 55–71.

Kastner, T., M.J. Ibarrola, W. Koch, and S. Nonhebel 2012. "Global Changes in Diets and the Consequences for Land Requirements for Food," *PNAS* 109/ 18: 6868–6872.

Kelley, A.C., and R.M. Schmidt 1995. "Aggregate Population and Economic Growth Correlations: The Role of the Components of Demographic Change," *Demography* 32/4: 543–555.

Kim, S. 1999. "Regions, Resources, and Economic Geography: Sources of U.S. Regional Comparative Advantage, 1880–1987," *Regional Science and Urban Economics* 29/1: 1–32.

Klenert, D., L. Mattauch, O. Edenhofer, and K. Lessmann 2016. "Infrastructure and Inequality: Insights from Incorporating Key Economic Facts about Household Heterogeneity," *Macroeconomic Dynamics* 1–32.

Klenert, D., G. Schwerhoff, O. Edenhofer, and L. Mattauch 2017. "Environmental Taxation, Inequality and Engel's Law: The Double Dividend of Redistribution," *Environmental and Resource Economics*, forthcoming. http://link.springer.com/article/10.1007/s10640-016-0070-y (last accessed December 23, 2017).

Koepke N., and J. Baten 2005. "The Biological Standard of Living in Europe during the Last Two Millennia," *European Review of Economic History* 9: 61–95.

Kondratieff, N.D., and W.F. Stolper 1935. "The Long Waves In Economic Life," *The Review of Economics and Statistics* 17: 105–115.

Kovats, S., S. Lloyd A. Hunt, and P. Watkiss 2011. "The Impacts and Economic Costs on Health in Europe and the Costs and Benefits of Adaptation." Technical Policy Briefing Note 5. Results of the EC RTD ClimateCost Project. In P. Watkiss (ed.), *The ClimateCost Project.* Sweden: Stockholm Environment Institute (Final Report. Volume 1: Europe).

Krausmann, F., S. Gingrich, N. Eisenmenger, K-H. Erb, H. Haberl, and M. Fischer-Kowalski 2009. "Growth in Global Material Use, GDP and Population during the 20th Century," *Ecological Economics* 68: 2696–2705.

Krausmann, F., D. Wiedenhofer, C. Lauk, W. Haas, H. Tanikawa, T. Fishman, A. Miatto, H. Schandl, and H. Haberl 2017. "Global Socioeconomic Material Stocks Rise 23-fold over the 20th Century and Require Half of Annual Resource Use," *PNAS* 114/8: 1880–1885.

Krautkraemer, J. 1998. "Nonrenewable Resource Scarcity," *Journal of Economic Literature* 36/4: 2065–2107.

Krugman, P.R. 1979. "Increasing Returns, Monopolistic Competition, and International Trade." *Journal of International Economics* 9/4: 469–479.

Kuznets, S. 1934. "National Income, 1929–1932," *NBER Bulletin* 49: 1–12.

Kuznets, S. 1973. "Modern Economic Growth: Findings and Reflections," *Am. Econ. Rev.* 63: 247–258.

Lawson, T., and J. Garrod 2001. "Technology," in *Dictionary of Sociology.* London: Routledge.

Layard, R. 2011. *Happiness: Lessons from a New Science,* 2nd edn. London: Penguin.

Lee, R., and A. Mason 2006. "What is the Demographic Dividend?," *Finance and Development* 43/3.

Leff, E. 1983. "Notas para un análisis sociológico de los movimientos ambientalistas. Nuevos elementos para el análisis sociológico de los movimientos sociales," in M. Cárdenas (ed.), *Política ambiental y desarrollo: un debate para América Latina.* Bogotá: Fescol Inderena.

Lehmann, P. 2012. "Justifying a Policy Mix for Pollution Control: A Review of Economic Literature," *Journal of Economic Surveys* 26: 71–97.

Lempert, R. 2013. "Scenarios that Illuminate Vulnerabilities and Robust Responses," *Climatic Change* 117: 627–646.

Lempert, R.J., and M.E. Schlesinger 2001. "Climate-change Strategy Needs to be Robust," *Nature* 412/6845: 375–375.

Lempert, R.J., S.W. Popper, and S.C. Bankes 2003. *Shaping the Next One Hundred Years: New Methods for Quantitative, Long-term Policy Analysis.* Santa Monica, CA: RAND Corporation.

Lessmann, K., U. Kornek, V. Bosetti, R. Dellink, J. Emmerling, J. Eyckmans, … Z. Yang 2015. "The Stability and Effectiveness of Climate Coalitions: A Comparative Analysis of Multiple Integrated Assessment Models," *Environmental and Resource Economics* 62: 811–836.

Lessmann, K., R. Marschinski, M. Finus, U. Kornek, and O. Edenhofer 2014. "Emissions Trading with Non-signatories in a Climate Agreement – an Analysis of Coalition Stability," *The Manchester School* 82: 82–109.

LeVeck, B.L., D.A. Hughes, J.H. Fowler, E. Hafner-Burton, and D.G. Victor 2014. "The Role of Self-interest in Elite Bargaining," *Proceedings of the National Academy of Sciences* 111: 18536–18541.

Lileeva, A., and D. Trefler. 2010. "Improved Access to Foreign Markets Raises Plant-Level Productivity… for Some Plants," *Quarterly Journal of Economics* 125/ 3: 1051–1099.

Lin, B. 2011. "Resilience in Agriculture through Crop Diversification: Adaptive Management for Environmental Change," *BioScience* 61/3: 183–193.

Lin, C.-Y. C. and G. Wagner 2007. "Steady-State Growth in a Hotelling Model of Resource Extraction," *Journal of Environmental Economics and Management* 54/1: 68–83.

Lindh, T., and B. Malmberg 2007. "Demographically based Global Income Forecasts up to the Year 2050," *International Journal of Forecasting* 23: 553–567.

Liu, J., A.J.B. Zehnder, and H. Yang 2009. "Global Consumptive Water Use for Crop Production: The Importance of Green Water and Virtual Water," *Water Resources Research* 45/5: 1–15.

Liu J., H. Yang, S.N. Gosling, M. Kummu, M. Flörke, M. Pfister, N. Hanasaki, Y. Wada, X. Zhang, C. Zheng, J. Alcamo, T. Oki, 2017. Water scarcity assessments in the past, present, and future. *Earth's Future* 5: 545–559.

Llavador, H., J.E. Roemer, and J. Silvestre 2011. "A Dynamic Analysis of Human Welfare in a Warming Planet," *Journal of Public Economics* 95/11: 1607–1620.

Llavador, H., J.E. Roemer, and J. Silvestre 2015. *Sustainability for a Warming Planet.* Cambridge, MA: Harvard University Press.

Lobell, D., and D. Burke 2010. *Climate Change and Food Security. Adapting Agriculture to a Warmer World.* USA: Springer.

Mace, G., Masundire, H., Baillie, J., et al. 2005. "Biodiversity," in H. Hassan, R. Scholes, and N. Ash (eds.), *Ecosystems and Human Wellbeing: Current State and Trends,* 79–115. Washington, DC: Island Press.

MacKenzie, I.A., and M. Ohndorf 2016. "Coasean Bargaining in the Presence of Pigouvian Taxation," *Journal of Environmental Economics and Management* 75: 1–11.

Mackenzie, F.T., L.M. Ver, and A. Lerman 2002. "Century-Scale Nitrogen and Phosphorus Controls of the Carbon Cycle," *Chemical Geology* 190: 13–32.

MacLeod, C. 1988. *Inventing the Industrial Revolution: The English Patent System, 1660–1800.* Cambridge: Cambridge University Press

Maddison, A. 2003. *The World Economy, a Millennial Perspective.* Paris: OECD.

Maddison, A. 2007. *Contours of the World Economy: Essays in Macro-economic History.* Oxford: Oxford University Press.

Magnusson, U. and K. Bergman 2014. *Urban and Peri-urban Agriculture for Food Security in Low-income Countries.* Upsalla, Sweden: Swedish University of Agricultural Sciences (SLU Global).

Maher, T. 1998. "Environmental Oppression," *Journal of Black Studies* 28/3: 357–368.

Maloney, W.F., and F. Valencia Caicedo 2014. Engineers, Innovative Capacity and Development in the Americas. World Bank Policy Research Working Paper No. 6814.

Malthus, T. 1798. *An Essay on the Principle of Population,* London: Johnson.

Managi, S., J. Opaluch, D. Jin, and T. Grigalunas 2004. "Technological Change and Depletion in Shore Oil and Gas," *Journal of Environmental Economics and Management* 47/2: 388–409.

Marrero, G.a., and J.G. Rodríguez 2013. "Inequality of Opportunity and Growth," *Journal of Development Economics* 104: 107–122.

Marron, D., and A. Morris 2016. How to Use Carbon Tax Revenue. Urban-Brookings Tax Policy Center, Policy Brief. www.brookings.edu/research/how-to-use-carbon-tax-revenues/ (last accessed December 2, 2016).

Martínez, A. 2015. Desarrollo Sostenible es una contradicción. Interview with El Espectador, November 15, 2015.

Marx, K. 1867/1990. *Capital – A Critique of Political Economy*. London: Penguin Classics.

Mason, A. 2001. "Egalitarianism and the Leveling Down Objection," *Analysis* 61/3: 246–254.

Mattauch, L. 2015. Rent and Redistribution. The welfare implications of financing low-carbon public investment. PhD thesis. Technical University of Berlin.

Mattauch, L., F. Creutzig, and O. Edenhofer 2015. "Avoiding Carbon Lock-In: Policy Options for Advancing Structural Change," *Economic Modelling* 50: 49–63.

Mauro, P. 1995. "Corruption and Growth," *The Quarterly Journal of Economics* 110/3: 681–712.

McCann, J. 2011. "The Political Ecology of Cereal Seed Development in Africa: A History of Selection," *IDS Bulletin* 42/4: 24–35.

McMillan, M.S., and D. Rodrik 2011. Globalization, Structural Change and Productivity Growth. Working Paper 17143. *National Bureau of Economic Research*.

MEA 2003. *Ecosystems and Human Well-being- A Framework for Assessment*. Millennium Ecosystem Assessment. Washington, DC: Island Press.

MEA 2005. *Ecosystems and Human Well-being: Our Human Planet, Summary for Decision-Makers*. Millennium Ecosystem Assessment. Washington, DC: Island Press.

Meade, J. 1972. "The Theory of Labour-Managed Firms and of Profit Sharing," *The Economic Journal* 82/325: 402–428.

Mehlum, H., K. Moene, and R. Torvik 2006. "Institutions and the Resource Curse," *The Economic Journal* 116/508: 1–20.

Melitz, M.J. 2003. "The Impact of Trade on Intra-Industry Reallocations and Aggregate Industry Productivity," *Econometrica* 71/6: 1695–1725.

Messner, D., A. Guarín, and D. Haun 2013. The Behavioural Dimensions of International Cooperation. Global Cooperation Research Papers.

Milanovic, B. 2002. "True World Income Distribution, 1988 and 1993," *The Economic Journal* 112/476: 51–92.

Mishel, L., E. Gould, and J. Bivens 2015. *Wage Stagnation in Nine Charts*. Economic Policy Institute, January 6.

Mohtadi, H., and T.L. Roe 2003. "Democracy, Rent Seeking, Public Spending and Growth," *Journal of Public Economics* 87/3: 445–466.

Mokyr, J. 1992. *The Lever of Riches*. Oxford: Oxford University Press.

Mokyr, J. 2005. "Long-Term Economic Growth and the History of Technology," in P. Aghion and S.N. Durlauf (eds.), *Handbook of Economic Growth*, vol. 1B. New York: North-Holland.

Mokyr, J. 2008. "Technology," in *The New Palgrave Dictionary of Economics*, 2nd edn. Basingstoke: Palgrave Macmillan.

Mokyr, J., C. Vickers, and N.L. Ziebarth 2015. "The History of Technological Anxiety and the Future of Economic Growth: Is This Time Different?," *Journal of Economic Perspectives* 29/3: 31–50.

Moller, D. 2011. "Wealth, Disability and Happiness," *Philosophy & Public Affairs* 39/2: 177–206.

Murphy, K.M., A. Shleifer, and R.W. Vishny 1993. "Why is Rent-Seeking So Costly to Growth?," *The American Economic Review* 83/2: 409–414.

Murphy, R., A. Schleifer, and R.W. Vishny 1989. "Industrialization and the Big Push. *J. Polit. Econ.* 97: 1003–1026.

NAACP 2016, Environmental and Climate Justice Program, Baltimore, National Association for the Advancement of Colored People.

Nachmany, M., S. Fankhauser, J. Davidová, N. Kingsmill, T. Landesman, H. Roppongi, P. Schleifer, J. Setzer, A. Sharman, C.S. Singleton, et al. 2015. *The 2015 Global Climate Legislation Study: A Review of Climate Change Legislation in 99 Countries: Summary for Policy-makers*. London: Grantham Research Institute on Climate Change and the Environment, GLOBE International.

Nakov, A., and G. Nuno 2013. "Saudi Arabia and the Oil Market," *The Economic Journal* 123/573: 1333–1362.

Newell, R.G., and W.A. Pizer 2003. "Regulating Stock Externalities under Uncertainty," *Journal of Environmental Economics and Management* 45: 416–432.

Nordhaus, W. 1974. "Resources as a Constraint on Growth," *American Economic Review* 64/2: 22–26.

Nordhaus, W. 1996. "Do Real-Output and Real-Wage Measures Capture Reality? The History of Lighting Suggests Not," in T. Bresnahan and R. Gordon (eds.), *The Economics of New Goods*. Chicago: University of Chicago Press.

Nordhaus, W. 2015. "Climate Clubs: Overcoming Free-Riding in International Climate Policy," *The American Economic Review* 105: 1339–1370.

Nordhaus, W., and J. Boyer 2000. *Warming the World: Economic Models of Global Warming*. Cambridge, MA: MIT Press.

Nordhaus, W., and J. Tobin 1972. *Is Growth Obsolete?* New York: Columbia University Press.

North, D.C., 1990. *Institutions, Institutional Change and Economic Performance*. Cambridge: Cambridge University Press.

North, D.C., and B.R. Weingast 1989. "Constitutions and Commitment: The Evolution of Institutions Governing Public Choice in Seventeenth-Century England," *Journal of Economic History* 49: 803–832.

Norton, B. 1982. "Environmental Ethics and the Rights of Nonhumans," *Environmental Ethics* 4/1982: 17–36.

Nozick, R. 1974. *Anarchy, State, and Utopia*. Oxford: Basil Blackwell.

Nurdianto, D.A., and B.P. Resosudarmo 2016. "The Economy-Wide Impact of a Uniform Carbon Tax in ASEAN," *Journal of Southeast Asian Economies* 33: 1–22.

Nussbaum, M.C. 2006. *Frontiers of Justice: Disability, Nationality and Species Membership*. Cambridge, MA: Harvard University Press.

OECD 2010. *The High Cost of Low Educational Performance*. OECD Publishing.

OECD 2012. *OECD Environmental Outlook to 2050*, OECD Publishing.

OECD 2014. *OECD Pensions Outlook 2014*. OECD Publishing.

Offer, A. 2006. *The Challenge of Affluence: Self-Control and Well-Being in the United States and Britain since 1950*. New York: Oxford University Press.

Oishi, S., and E. Diener 2014. "Residents of Poor Nations Have a Greater Sense of Meaning in Life Than Residents of Wealthy Nations," *Psychological Science* 25/2: 422–430.

Orum, P., R. Moore, M. Roberts, and J. Sanchez 2014. *Who's In Danger? Race, Poverty, and Chemical Disasters*. Brattleboro, VT, Environmental Justice and Health Alliance for Chemical Policy Reform.

Ostrom, E. 1990. *Governing the Commons: The Evolution of Institutions for Collective Action*. Cambridge: Cambridge University Press.

Ostrom, E. 1998. "A Behavioral Approach to the Rational Choice Theory of Collective Action: Presidential Address, American Political Science Association, 1997," *American Political Science Review* 92: 1–22.

Ostrom, E. 2000. "Reformulating the Commons," *Swiss Political Science Review* 6: 29–52.

Ostrom, E. 2009. *Understanding Institutional Diversity*. Princeton, NJ: Princeton University Press.

Ostrom, E. 2010a. "A Multi-scale Approach to Coping with Climate Change and Other Collective Action Problems," *Solutions* 1: 27–36.

Ostrom, E. 2010b. "Beyond Markets and States: Polycentric Governance of Complex Economic Systems," *American Economic Review* 100: 641–672.

Ostrom, E. 2010c. "Polycentric Systems for Coping with Collective Action and Global Environmental Change," *Global Environmental Change* 20: 550–557.

Ostrom, E. 2012. "Nested Externalities and Polycentric Institutions: Must We Wait for Global Solutions to Climate Change before Taking Actions at Other Scales?," *Economic Theory* 49: 353–369.

Ostrom, E. 2014. "A Polycentric Approach for Coping with Climate Change," *Ann. Econ. Finance* 15: 71–108.

Ostrom, E. 2015. *Governing the Commons*. Cambridge: Cambridge University Press.

Ostrom, E., and C. Hess 2010. "Private and Common Property Rights. Property Law and Economics," in B. Bouckaert (ed.), *Encyclopedia of Law and Economics*, 2nd edn. Cheltenham: Edward Elgar.

Ostrom, E., and J. Walker 2003. *Trust and Reciprocity: Interdisciplinary Lessons for Experimental Research: Interdisciplinary Lessons for Experimental Research*. New York: Russell Sage Foundation.

Ostrom, E., J. Burger, C.B. Field, R.B. Norgaard, and D. Policansky 1999. "Revisiting the Commons: Local Lessons, Global Challenges," *Science* 284: 278–282.

Ostrom, E., T.E. Dietz, N.E. Dolšak, P.C. Stern, S.E. Stonich, and E.U. Weber 2002. *The Drama of the Commons*. Washington, DC: National Academy Press.

Ostrom, E., R. Gardner, and J. Walker 1994. *Rules, Games, and Common-Pool Resources*. Ann Arbor, MI: University of Michigan Press.

Ostrom, E., J. Walker, and R. Gardner 1992. "Covenants with and without a Sword: Self-governance Is Possible," *American Political Science Review* 86: 404–417.

4

Ostrom, V. 2014. "Polycentricity: The Structural Basis of Self-Governing Systems," in *Choice, Rules and Collective Action: The Ostrom's on the Study of Institutions and Governance*, 45. Colchester: European Consortium for Political Research Press.

Ostrom, V., C.M. Tiebout, and R. Warren 1961. "The Organization of Government in Metropolitan Areas: A Theoretical Inquiry," *American Political Science Review* 55: 831–842.

Paavola, J. 2011. "Climate Change: The Ultimate 'Tragedy of the Commons,' " in D.H. Cole and E. Ostrom (eds.), *Property in Land and Other Resources*. Cambridge, MA: Lincoln Institute of Land Policy.

Pack, H., and K. Saggi. 2006. "Is There a Case for Industrial Policy? A Critical Survey," *The World Bank Research Observer* 21/2: 267–297.

Paldam, M. 1998. "Does Economic Growth Lead to Political Stability?," in S. Borner and M. Paldam (eds.), *The Political Dimension of Economic Growth*. Basingstoke: Macmillan.

Parfit, D. 1984. *Reasons and Persons*. Oxford: Clarendon Press.

Parfit, D. 1997. "Equality and Priority," *Ratio* 10/3: 202–221.

Parry, I. 2016. "Choosing among Mitigation Instruments: How Strong Is the Case for a US Carbon Tax?," in I. Parry, A. Morris, and R. Williams (eds.), *Implementing a US Carbon Tax: Challenges and Debates*. New York: Routledge.

Partzsch, L., and R. Ziegler 2011. "Social Entrepreneurs as Change Agents: A Case Study on Power and Authority in the Water Sector," *International Environmental Agreements: Politics, Law and Economics* 11: 63–83.

Patashnik, E.M. 2014. *Reforms at Risk: What Happens after Major Policy Changes Are Enacted*. Princeton, NJ: Princeton University Press.

Pearce, D.W., K. Hamilton, and G. Atkinson 1996. "Measuring Sustainable Development: Progress on Indicators," *Environment and Development Economics* 1/1: 85–101.

Peters, F. 2010. "Political Legitimacy," in *Stanford Encyclopedia of Philosophy*. http://plato.stanford.edu/entries/legitimacy/ (last accessed December 23, 2017).

Pigou, A.C. 1920. *The Economics of Welfare*. London: Macmillan.

Piketty, T. 2014. *Capital in the Twenty-first Century*, trans. A. Goldhammer. Cambridge, MA: Harvard University Press.

Piketty, T., and E. Saez 2013. "A Theory of Optimal Inheritance Taxation," *Econometrica* 81/5: 1851–1886.

Piketty, T., and G. Zucman, G. 2014. "Capital Is Back: Wealth–Income Ratios in Rich Countries, 1700–2010," *The Quarterly Journal of Economics* 129/3: 1255–1310.

Piketty, T., E. Saez, and S. Stantcheva 2014. "Optimal Taxation of Top Labor Incomes: A Tale of Three Elasticities," *American Economic Journal: Economic Policy* 6/1: 230–271.

Pillarisetti, J.R. 2005. "The World Bank's 'Genuine Savings' Measure and Sustainability," *Ecological Economics* 55: 599–609.

Ploeg, F. van der 2011. "Natural Resources: Curse or Blessing?," *Journal of Economic Literature* 49/2: 366–420.

Pogge, T. 2002a. "Responsibilities for Poverty-Related Ill Health," *Ethics & International Affairs* 16/2: 71–79.

Pogge, T. 2002b, *World Poverty and Human Rights*. Cambridge: Polity Press.

Pomeranz, K. 2000. *The Great Divergence: China, Europe, and the Making of the Modern World Economy*. Princeton, NJ: Princeton University Press.

Poulsen, M., P. McNab, L. Clayton, and R. Neff 2015. "A Systematic Review of Urban Agriculture and Food Security Impacts in Low-Income Countries." *Food Policy* 55: 131–146.

Prasad, E.S., R.G. Rajan, and A. Subramanian. 2007. "Foreign Capital and Economic Growth." *Brookings Papers on Economic Activity* 38/1: 153–230.

Pritchett, L. 2006. "Who Is Not Poor? Dreaming of a World Truly Free of Poverty," *World Bank Research Observer* 21/1: 1–23.

Przeworski, A., M.E. Alvarez, J.A. Cheibub, and F. Limongi 2000. *Democracy and Development: Political Institutions and Well-Being in the World, 1950–1990*. Cambridge: Cambridge University Press.

Rabe, B.G. 2010. "Introduction: The Challenges of US Climate Governance," in *Greenhouse Governance: Addressing Climate Change in America*, 3–23. Washington, DC: Brookings Institution Press.

Ramasastry, A. 2002. "Corporate Complicity: From Nuremberg to Rangoon – An Examination of Forced Labor Cases and Their Impact on the Liability of Multinational Corporations," *Berkeley J. Int'l Law.* 20: 91–159. http://scholarship.law.berkeley.edu/bjil/vol20/iss1/4 (last accessed December 23, 2017).

Randazzo, A. and J. Haidt 2015. "The Moral Narratives of Economists," *Econ. Journal Watch* 12/1: 40–57.

Ravallion, M. 2012. "Why Don't We See Poverty Convergence?" *American Economic Review* 102/1: 504–523.

Rawls, J. 1971. *A Theory of Justice*. Cambridge, MA: Harvard University Press.

Rawls, J. 1999. *A Theory of Justice*. Revised edition. Oxford: Oxford University Press.

Redding, S., and A. Venables 2004. "Economic Geography and International Inequality," *Journal of International Economics* 62/1: 53–82.

Regan, T. 1983. *The Case for Animal Rights*. London: Routledge & Kegan Paul.

Reinhart, C.M., and G.L. Kaminsky. 1999. "The Twin Crises: The Causes of Banking and Balance-of-Payments Problems," *American Economic Review* 89/3: 473–500.

Renn, O. 2008. *Risk Governance: Coping with Uncertainty in a Complex World*. London: Earthscan.

Ricardo, D. 1817. *On the Principles of Political Economy and Taxation*.

Ringquist, E. 1997. "Equity and the Distribution of Environmental Risk," *Social Science Quarterly* 78/4: 811–829.

Risse, M. 2012. *On Global Justice*. Princeton, NJ and Oxford: Princeton University Press.

Robinson, J.A., and D. Acemoglu. 2000. "Political Losers as a Barrier to Economic Development," *American Economic Review* 90/2: 126–130.

Rockström, J., W. Steffen, K. Noone, A. Persson, F. Chapin, E. Lambin, T. Lenton, M. Scheffer, C. Folke, H. Schellnhuber, B. Nykvist, C. de Wit, T. Hughes, S. van der Leeuw, H. Rodhe, S. Soerlin, P. Snyder, R. Costanza, U. Svendin, M. Falkenmark, L. Karlberg, R. Corell, V. Fabry, J. Hansen, B. Walker, D. Liverman, K. Richardson, P. Crutzen, and J. Foley 2009a. "A Safe Operating Space for Humanity," *Nature* 461: 472–475.

Rockström, J., W. Steffen, K. Noone, Å. Persson, F.S. Chapin, III, E. Lambin, T.M. Lenton, M. Scheffer, C. Folke, H. Schellnhuber, B. Nykvist, C. A. De Wit, T. Hughes, S. van der Leeuw, H. Rodhe, S. Sörlin, P. K. Snyder, R. Costanza, U. Svedin, M. Falkenmark, L. Karlberg, R.W. Corell, V.J. Fabry, J. Hansen, B. Walker, D. Liverman, K. Richardson, P. Crutzen, and J. Foley 2009b. "Planetary Boundaries: Exploring the Safe Operating Space for Humanity," *Ecology and Society* 14/2: 1–36.

Rockström, J., L. Karlberg, S. Wani, J. Barron, N. Hatibu, T. Oweis, A. Bruggeman, J. Farahani, and Z. Qiang 2010. "Managing Water in Rainfed Agriculture – The Need for a Paradigm Shift." *Agricultural Water Management* 97/4: 543–550.

Rodríguez, F., and D. Rodrik. 2000. "Trade Policy and Economic Growth: A Skeptic's Guide to the Cross-National Evidence," *NBER Macroeconomic Annals* 15: 261–338.

Rodrik, D. 1997. "Has Globalization Gone Too Far?," *California Management Review* 39/3: 29–53.

Rodrik, D. 2002. *Institutions, Integration, and Geography: In Search of the Deep Determinants of Economic Growth*. Cambridge, MA: Harvard University Publication.

Rodrik, D. 2005. "Growth Strategies," in P. Aghion and S. Durlauf (eds.), *Handbook of Economic Growth*. New York: Elsevier.

Rodrik, D. 2006. "What's So Special about China's Exports?," *China and World Economy* 14/5: 1–19.

Rodrik, D. 2016. "Premature Deindustrialization," *Journal of Economic Growth* 21/1: 1–33.

Rodrik, D., A. Subramanian, and F. Trebbi. 2004. "Institutions Rule: The Primacy of Institutions Over Geography and Integration in Economic Development," *Journal of Economic Growth* 9/2: 131–165.

Roemer, J.E. 1993. "A Pragmatic Theory of Responsibility for the Egalitarian Planner," *Philosophy and Public Affairs* 22/2: 146–166.

Roemer, J.E. 2011. "The Ethics of Intertemporal Distribution in a Warming Planet," *Environmental and Resource Economics* 48/3: 363–390.

Roemer, J.E. 2013. "Once More on Intergenerational Discounting in Climate-Change Analysis: Reply to Partha Dasgupta," *Environmental and Resource Economics* 56/1: 141–148.

Rohde, R, and R.A. Muller 2015. "Air Pollution in China: Mapping of Concentrations and Sources," *PLoS ONE* 10/8: e0135749.

Roine, J., and D. Waldenström 2015. "Long-run Trends in the Distribution of Income and Wealth," in A.B. Atkinson and F. Bourguignon (eds.), *Handbook of Income Distribution*, vol. 2A. Amsterdam: North-Holland.

Romer, P. 1990. "Endogenous Technological Change," *Journal of Political Economy* 98/5 pt 2: S71–S102.

Romp, W., and J. De Haan 2007. "Public Capital and Economic Growth: A Critical Survey, *Perspektiven der Wirtschaftspolitik* 8/S1: 652.

Rosegrant, M., X. Cai, and S. Cline 2005. *World Water and Food to 2025: Dealing with Scarcity*. Washington, DC: International Food Policy Research Institute.

Rutherford, M. 2001. "Institutional Economics: Then and Now," *The Journal of Economic Perspectives* 15/3: 173–194.

Sachs, J. 1999. "Resource Endowments and the Real Exchange Rate: A Comparison of Latin America and East Asia," in T. Ito and A.O. Krueger (eds.), *Changes in Exchange Rates in Rapidly Developing Countries: Theory, Practice, and Policy Issues*. Chicago: University of Chicago Press.

Sachs, J., and A. Warner 1995. "Economic Reform and the Process of Global Integration," *Brookings Papers on Economic Activity* 1995/1: 1–118.

Sachs, J., and A. Warner 1997. "Fundamentals Sources of Long-Run Growth," *American Economic Review* 87/2: 184–188.

Sachs, J. and A. Warner 2001. "The Curse of Natural Resources," *European Economic Review* 45/4–6: 827–838.

Sala-i-Martin, X., and A. Subramanian 2003. Addressing the Natural Resource Curse: An Illustration from Nigeria. NBER Working Papers 9804.

Sandler, T. 2004. *Global Collective Action*. Cambridge: Cambridge University Press.

Sandler, T. 2010. "Overcoming Global and Regional Collective Action Impediments," *Global Policy* 1: 40–50.

Sangiovanni, A. 2007. "Global Justice, Reciprocity, and the State," *Philosophy and Public Affairs* 35/1: 3–39.

Scanlon, T.M. 1997. The Diversity of Objections to Inequality. The Lindley Lecture (Department of Philosophy, University of Kansas, February 22, 1996).

Schaffartzik, A., A. Mayer, S. Gingrich, N. Eisenmenger, C. Loy, and F. Krausmann 2014. "The Global Metabolic Transition: Regional Patterns and Trends of Global Material Flows, 1950–2010," *Global Environmental Change* 26: 87–97.

Schandl, H., S. Hatfield-Dodds, T.O. Wiedmann, A. Geschke, Y. Cai, J. West, D. Newth, T. Baynes, M. Lenzen, and A. Owen 2016. "Decoupling Global Environmental Pressure and Economic Growth: Scenarios for Energy Use, Materials Use and Carbon Emissions," *Journal of Cleaner Production* 132: 45–56.

Schneider, F., G. Kallis, and J. Martinez-Alier 2010. "Crisis or Opportunity? Economic Degrowth for Social Equity and Ecological Sustainability. Introduction to This Special Issue," *Journal of Cleaner Production* 18/6: 511–518.

Schumpeter, J.A. 1942. *Capitalism, Socialism and Democracy*. New York: Harper & Brothers.

Scitovsky, T. 1976. *The Joyless Economy: An Inquiry into Human Satisfaction and Consumer Dissatisfaction*. Oxford: Oxford University Press.

SDR 2015. *Global Sustainable Development Report, Advance Unedited Version*. Economic and Social Affairs, United Nations https://sustainabledevelopment.un.org/content/documents/1758GSDR%202015%20Advance%20Unedited%20Version.pdf (last accessed December 23, 2017).

Segal, P. 2011. "Resource Rents, Redistribution, and Halving Global Poverty: The Resource Dividend," *World Development* 39/4: 475–489.

Sen, A. 1987. *The Standard of Living*. Cambridge: Cambridge University Press.

Sen, A. 2000. *Development as Freedom*. New York: Anchor Books.

Sen, A. 2004. 'Capabilities, Lists, and Public Reason: Continuing the Conversation', *Feminist Economics* 10/3: 77–80.

Sen, A. 2009. *The Idea of Justice*. London: Allen Lane.

Sen, K. 2013. "The Political Dynamics of Economic Growth," *World Development* 47: 71–86.

Shobe, W.M., and D. Burtraw 2012. "Rethinking Environmental Federalism in a Warming World," *Climate Change Economics* 3: 1250018.

Shrader-Frechette, K. 2007. *Taking Action, Saving Lives*. New York: Oxford University Press.

Shrader-Frechette, K., and A. Pusateri 2015. "Flawed Scientific-Evidence Standards and Diesel Regulations," *Accountability in Research* 22/3: 162–191.

Shue, H. 1996. *Basic Rights: Subsistence, Affluence, and U.S. Foreign Policy*, 2nd edn. with a new afterword. Princeton: Princeton University Press. Sidgwick, H. 1981 (1907). *The Methods of Ethics*, 7th edn., with a foreword by John Rawls. Indianapolis: Hackett Publishing Company.

Singer, P. 1972. "Famine, Affluence and Morality," *Philosophy & Public Affairs* 1: 229–243.

Singer, P. 1975. *Animal Liberation*. New York: Random House.

Singer, P., and J. Mason 2006. *Eating*. London: Arrow Press. Smith, K.R., A. Woodward, D., Campbell-Lendrum, D.D. Chadee, Y. Honda, Q. Liu, J.M. Olwoch, B. Revich, and R. Sauerborn 2014. "Human Health: Impacts, Adaptation, and Co-benefits," in *Climate Change 2014: Impacts, Adaptation, and Vulnerability. Part A: Global and Sectoral Aspects. Contribution of Working Group II to the Fifth Assessment Report of the Intergovernmental Panel on Climate Change*.

Smith, P., M. Bustamante, H. Ahammad, H. Clark, H. Dong, E.A. Elsiddig, ... F. Tubiello 2014. *Agriculture, Forestry and Other Land U7se (AFOLU). In: Climate Change 2014: Mitigation of Climate Change. Contribution of Working Group III to the Fifth Assessment Report of the Intergovernmental Panel on Climate Change*. Cambridge and New York: Cambridge University Press.

Smulders, S. 2008. "Green National Accounting," in S.N. Durlauf and L.E. Blume (eds.), *The New Palgrave Dictionary of Economics*, 2nd edn. Palgrave Macmillan, The New Palgrave Dictionary of Economics Online. April 8, 2016.

Snyder, P.K., J.A. Foley, M.H. Hitchman, and C. Delire 2004. "Analyzing the Effects of Complete Tropical Forest Removal on the Regional Climate Using a Detailed Three-Dimensional Energy Budget: Application to Africa. *J. Geophys. Res. Atmos.* 109: D21.

Soete. L., B. Verspagen, and B. Ter Weel 2010. "Systems of Innovation," in B.H. Hall and N. Rosenberg (eds.), *Handbook of the Economics of Innovation*, vol. 1, New York: North-Holland.

Solow, R. 1956. "A Contribution to the Theory of Economic Growth," *The Quarterly Journal of Economics* 70: 65–94.

Solow, R. 1987. "We'd Better Watch Out," *New York Times Book Review*, July 12: 36.

Sonak, S., M. Sonak, and A. Giriyan 2008. "Shipping Hazardous Waste: Implications for Economically Developing Countries," *International Environmental Agreements* 8/2: 143–159.

Starkey, D. 1994. "Environmental Justice," *State Legislature* 20/ 3: 27–31.

Stavins, R.N. 2011. "The Problem of the Commons: Still Unsettled after 100 Years," *American Economic Review* 101: 81–108.

Steffen, W., P.J. Crutzen, and J.R. McNeill. 2007. "The Anthropocene: Are Humans Now Overwhelming the Great Forces of Nature?," *Ambio* 36: 614–621.

Steffen, W., A. Persson, L. Deutsch, J. Zalasiewicz, M. Williams, K. Richardson, C. Crumley, P. Crutzen, C. Folke, L. Gordon, M. Molina, V. Ramanathan, J. Rockstroem, M. Scheffer, H.J. Schellenhuber and U. Svendin 2011. "The Anthropocene: From Global Change to Planetary Stewardship," *Ambio* 40/7: 739–761.

Steffen, W., K. Richardson, J. Rockström, S.E. Cornell, I. Fetzer, et al. 2015. "Planetary Boundaries: Guiding Human Development on a Changing Planet," *Science* 347/6223: 1259855.

Steinberg, J., F. Krausmann, and N. Eisenmenger 2010. "Global Patterns of Material Use: A Socioeconomic and Geophysical Analysis," *Ecological Economics* 69: 1150–1157.

Stern, P. 2011. "Design Principles for Global Commons: Natural Resources and Emerging Technologies," *International Journal of the Commons* 5/2: 212–232.

Stern, S., A. Wares, and T. Hellman 2016. Social Progress Index 2016. Methodological Report.

Sterner, T. 2012. "Distributional Effects of Taxing Transport Fuel," *Energy Policy* 41: 75–83.

Stiglitz, J.E. 2002. *Globalization and Its Discontents*. New York: Norton.

Stiglitz, J.E. 2006. *Making Globalization Work*. New York: Norton.

Stiglitz, J.E. 2015a. "The Origins of Inequality and Policies to Contain it," *National Tax Journal* 68/2: 425–448.

Stiglitz, J.E. 2015b. In interview during the UNU-WIDER 30th Anniversary Conference "Mapping the Future of Development Economics."

Stiglitz, J.E., A. Sen, and J.P. Fitoussi 2009. Report by the Commission on the Measurement of Economic Performance and Social Progress. http://ec.europa.eu/eurostat/documents/118025/118123/Fitoussi+Commission+report (last accessed January 27, 2018).

Stiglitz, J.E., A. Sen, and J.P. Fitoussi 2010. *Mismeasuring our Lives: Why GDP Does not Add Up*. New York: The New Press.

Stilgoe, J. 2015. *Experiment Earth: Responsible Innovation in Geoengineering*. Abingdon, UK: Earthscan, Routledge.

Stolper, W.F., and P.A. Samuelson. 1941. "Protection and Real Wages." *The Review of Economic Studies* 9/1: 58–73.

Stone, C. 1972. "Should Trees Have Standing?," *Southern California Law Review* 45: 450–501.

Stürmer, M., and G. Schwerhoff 2016. Non-Renewable Resources, Extraction Technology, and Endogenous Growth. Conference Paper, NBER Summer Institute, 2016.

Sud, S.R., J.E. Brenner, and E.R. Shaffer 2015. "Trading Away Health: The Influence of Trade Policy on Youth Tobacco Control," *The Journal of Pediatrics* 166/5: 1303–1307.

Swan, T.W. 1956. "Economic Growth and Capital Accumulation," *The Economic Record* 32/2: 334–361.

Taylor, P. 1986. *Respect for Nature*. Princeton, NJ: Princeton University Press.

Thrittle, C., L. Lin, and J. Piesse 2003. "The Impact of Research-led Agricultural Productivity Growth on Poverty Reduction in Africa, Asia and Latin America," *World Development* 31/12: 1959–1975.

Tirado, M.C., R. Clarke, L.A. Jaykus, A. McQuatters-Gollop, and J.M. Frank 2010. "Climate Change and Food Safety: A Review," *Food Research International* 43/7: 1745–1765.

Tollison, R.D. 1982. "Rent Seeking: A Survey," *Kyklos* 35/4: 575–602.

Turvey, R. 1963. "On the Divergence between Social Cost and Private Cost," *Economica* 30: 309–313.

UN 2006. *The Millennium Development Goals Report*. Economic and Social Affairs, United Nations, New York. http://mdgs.un.org/unsd/mdg/Resources/Static/Products/Progress2006/MDGReport2006.pdf (last accessed December 23, 2017).

UN 2012. Review of the Contributions of the MDG Agenda to Foster Development: Lessons for the Post-2015 UN Development Agenda; Discussion Note, UN system task team on the post 2015 UN development agenda.

UN 2015. Transforming Our World: The 2030 Agenda for Sustainable Development. https://sustainabledevelopment.un.org/post2015/transformingourworld/publication (last accessed December 23, 2017).

UN 2016. Sustainable Development Goals : 17 Goals to Transform Our World. www.un.org/sustainabledevelopment/sustainable-development-goals (last accessed December 23, 2017).

UN-Water 2015. Compendium of Water Quality Regulatory Frameworks: Which Water for Which Use? UN Water. www.iwa-network.org/which-water-for-which-use (last accessed December 23, 2017).

UNEP 2011a. *Decoupling Natural Resource Use and Environmental Impacts from Economic Growth*. Paris, France.

UNEP 2011b. *Towards a Green Economy. Pathways to Sustainable Development and Poverty Eradication. United Nations Environment Programme*. Nairobi, Kenya.

UNEP 2015. *Climate Commitments of Subnational Actors and Business: A Quantitative Assessment of Their Emission Reduction Impact*. United Nations Environment Programme, Nairobi.

UNEP 2016. *Global Material Flows and Resource Productivity*. Assessment Report for the UNEP International Resource Panel. Nairobi, Kenya www.resourcepanel.org/file/423/download?token=Av9xJsGS (last accessed January 27, 2018).

UNEP 2017. International Environmental Governance of the Global Commons, http://staging.unep.org/delc/GlobalCommons/tabid/54404/Default.aspx (last accessed December 23, 2017).

UNFCCC 2015. "Adoption of the Paris Agreement," in *FCCC/CP/2015/L.9/Rev.1* (ed.), United Nations Office at Geneva, Geneva (Switzerland), 12/12/2015. http://unfccc.int/resource/docs/2015/cop21/eng/l09r01.pdf (last accessed January 10, 2016).

UNTT Working Group on Sustainable Development Financing 2013. "UN System Task Team on the Post-2015 UN Development Agenda Working Group on 'Financing for Sustainable Development'. Executive Summary." https://sustainabledevelopment.un.org/content/documents/2091Executive%20Summary-UNTT%20WG%20on%20SDF.pdf (last accessed December 23, 2017).

Urpelainen, J. 2009. "Explaining the Schwarzenegger Phenomenon: Local Frontrunners in Climate Policy," *Global Environmental Politics* 9: 82–105.

US EPA 2011. The Benefits and Costs of the Clean Air Act: 1990 to 2020. Final Report of US Environmental Protection Agency Office of Air and Radiation.

Van Bavel, J., and J. Kok 2010. "Pioneers of the Modern Life Style? Childless Couples in Early Twentieth Century Netherlands," *Social Science History* 34: 47–72.

Veolia and IFPRI 2014. The Murky Future of Global Water Quality: New Global Study Projects Rapid Deterioration in Water Quality. A White Paper by Voila and IFPRI (international Food Policy Research Institute).

Victor, D.G. 2011. *Global Warming Gridlock: Creating More Effective Strategies for Protecting the Planet*. Cambridge: Cambridge University Press.

Voigt, S. 2009. How (Not) to Measure Institutions. Joint Discussion Paper Series in Economics, No. 2009, 37.

Wacziarg, R. 2001. Measuring the Dynamic Gains from Trade. *The World Bank Economic Review* 15/3: 393–429.

Walker, W., V. Marchau, and D. Swanson 2010. "Addressing Deep Uncertainty Using Adaptive Policies," *Technology Forecasting and Social Change* 77: 917–923.

Watkins, A., T. Papaioannou, J. Mugwagwa, and D. Kale 2015. "National Innovation Systems and the Intermediary Role of Industry Associations in Building Institutional Capacities for Innovation in Developing Countries: A Critical Review of the Literature," *Research Policy* 44/8: 1407–1418.

Watkiss, P., L. Horrocks, S. Pye, A. Searl, and A. Hunt. 2009. *Impacts of Climate Change in Human Health in Europe PESETA-Human Health Study*. Luxembourg: European Commission Joint Research Centre and Institute for Prospective Technological Studies.

Watts, N., W.N. Adger, P. Agnolucci, J. Blackstock, P. Byass, W. Cai, S. Chaytor, T. Colbourn, M. Collins, A. Cooper, P. Cox, J. Depledge, P. Drummond, P. Ekins, V. Galaz, D. Grace, H. Graham, M. Grubb, A. Haines, I. Hamilton, A. Hunter, X. Jiang, M. Li, I. Kelman, L. Liang, M. Lott, R. Lowe, Y. Luo, G. Mace, M. Maslin, T. Oreszcyzn, S. Pye, T. Quinn, M. Svensdotter, S. Venevsky, K. Warner, B. Xu, J. Yang, Y. Yin, C. Yu, Q. Zhang, P. Gong, H. Montgomery, A. Costello 2015. "Health and Climate Change: Policy Responses to Protect Public Health," *The Lancet*. 386/10006: 1861–1914. Published online June 23, 2015. http://dx.doi.org/10.1016/S0140-6736(15)60854–6 (last accessed July 11, 2015).

WDI 2016. World Development Indicators Database. Available at: http://databank.worldbank.org/data/reports.aspx?source=world-development-indicators (last accessed January 27, 2018).

WEF 2016. *The Future of Jobs Employment, Skills and Workforce Strategy for the Fourth Industrial Revolution*. World Economic Forum.

Weil, D. 2014. "Health and Economic Growth," in P. Aghion and S. Durlauf (eds.), *The Handbook of Economic Growth*, Vol. 2B. Amsterdam: North-Holland.

Weitzman, M.L. 1974. "Prices vs. Quantities," *The Review of Economic Studies* 41: 477–491.

Weitzman, M.L. 1976. "On the Welfare Significance of National Product in a Dynamic Economy," *The Quarterly Journal of Economics* 90/1: 156–162.

Weitzman, M. 2003. *Income, Wealth, and the Maximum Principle*. Cambridge, MA: Harvard University Press.

Wessel, R.H. 1967. "A Note on Economic Rent," *The American Economic Review* 57/5: 1221–1226.

WHO 2002. *The World Health Report*. Geneva, Switzerland: World Health Organization.

WHO 2003. *Summary Booklet: Climate Change and Human Health – Risks and Responses*. Geneva, Switzerland: World Health Organization.

WHO 2009. *Global Health Risks: Mortality and Burden of Disease Attributable to Selected Major Risks*. World Health Organization, Geneva.

WHO 2013. Regional Office for Europe Climate Change and Health: A Tool to Estimate Health and Adaptation Costs. www.euro.who.int/en/health-topics/environment-and-health/Climate-change/publications/2013/climate-change-and-health-a-tool-to-estimate-health-and-adaptation-costs (last accessed December 23, 2017).

WHO 2014. *WHO Guidance to Protect Health from Climate Change through Health Adaptation Planning*. World Health Organization. http://apps.who.int/iris/bitstream/10665/137383/1/9789241508001_eng.pdf?ua=1 (last accessed December 23, 2017).

WHO 2016. Reinventing the Toilet for 2.5 Billion in Need. www.who.int/bulletin/volumes/92/7/14-020714/en/ (last accessed February 2016).

Williams, B. 2005. "Realism and Moralism in Political Theory," in G. Hawthorn (ed.), *In the Beginning was the Deed: Realism and Moralism in Political Argument*. Princeton and Oxford: Princeton University Press.

Williams, R.C. 2012. "Growing State–Federal Conflicts in Environmental Policy: The Role of Market-Based Regulation," *Journal of Public Economics* 96, 1092–1099.

Williamson, J. 1993. "Democracy and the 'Washington consensus,'" *World Development* 21/8: 1329–1336.

Winters, L. 2004. "Trade Liberalisation and Economic Performance: An Overview," *The Economic Journal* 114/493: F4–F21.

Woodward, J. 1986. "The Non-Identity Problem," *Ethics* 96/4: 804–831.

4

World Bank 2006. *World Development Report 2006: Equity and Development.* Washington, DC: World Bank

World Bank 2010. *The Cost to Developing Countries of Adapting to Climate Change. New Methods and Estimates. The Global Report of the Economics of Adaptation to Climate Change Study.* Washington, DC: World Bank.

World Bank 2011. *The Changing Wealth of Nations: Measuring Sustainable Development in the New Millennium.* Washington, DC: World Bank.

World Bank 2012. *Hidden Harvest, The Global Contribution of Capture Fisheries.* Washington, DC: World Bank.

World Bank 2015a. *Shock Waves: Managing the Impacts of Climate Change on Poverty* Washington, DC: World Bank. https://openknowledge.worldbank.org/handle/10986/22787 (last accessed December 23, 2017). License: CC BY 3.0 IGO.

World Bank 2015b. *World Development Indicators 2015.* Washington, DC: World Bank. http://data.worldbank.org/data-catalog/world-development-indicators (last accessed December 23, 2017).

World Bank 2016a. *Agriculture, Value Added (% of GDP).* http://data.worldbank.org/indicator/NV.AGR.TOTL.ZS (last accessed 2016).

World Bank 2016b. *World Development Indicators.* Washington, DC: World Bank. www. worldbank.org (last accessed February 2016).

World Bank & Ecofys 2016. *Carbon Pricing Watch 2016: An Advance Brief from the State and Trends of Carbon Pricing 2016 Report.* www.ecofys.com/en/publications/carbon-pricing-watch-2016/ (last accessed December 2, 2016).

World Commission on Environment and Development 1987. *Our Common Future.* Oxford: Oxford University Press.

WWAP (United Nations World Water Assessment Programme) 2015. *The United Nations World Water Development Report 2015: Water for a Sustainable World.* Paris, UNESCO.

Zeff, H., J. Herman, P. Reed, and G. Characklis 2016. "Cooperative Drought Adaptation: Integrating Infrastructure Development, Conservation, and Water Transfers into Adaptive Policy Pathways," *Water Resources Research* 52/9: 7327–7346.

Zeff, H.B., J.R. Kasprzyk, J.D. Herman, P.M. Reed, and G.W. Characklis 2014. "Navigating Financial and Supply Reliability Tradeoffs in Regional Drought Management Portfolios," *Water Resources Research* 50/6: 4906–4923.

5 Cities and Social Progress

Coordinating Lead Authors:[1]
Saskia Sassen, Edgar Pieterse

Lead Authors:[2]
Gautam Bhan, Max Hirsh, Ana Falú, Hiroo Ichikawa, Luis Riffo, Pelin Tan, Doris Tarchopulos

---

[1] Affiliations: SS: Columbia University, USA; EP: University of Cape Town, South Africa.
[2] Affiliations: GB: Indian Institute for Humane Studies, India; MH: Hong Kong Institute for the Humanities and Social Sciences; AF: National University of Argentina in Córdoba; HI: Meiji University, Japan; LR: CEPAL, Chile; PT: Mardin Artukli Üniversity, Turkey; DT: Pontificia Universidad Javeriana, Colombia.

Summary

Today's cities confront a range of particular challenges that were not faced (at least knowingly) by cities in past periods. We focus on several of these in order to understand how cities can be enabled to become more viable and just. The question of cities and social progress has a long history of thought and multiple debates. The first section examines some of this. The second section provides a few conceptual anchors adopted by the authors to conduct the analysis and explore potential recommendations. The third section focuses on the multiple ways in which the urban condition materializes in diverse parts of the world and under diverse constraints. The examinations range from continental Africa to specific instances – Turkey's refugee crisis. This section concludes with a discussion of megacities and the global geography of power of global cities. The fourth section provides a counterpoint to the general trends by exploring the fact that built environments are not neutral – they benefit some sectors of the urban population more than others. It examines the case of women in cities as one instance of an array of disadvantages that affect them generally more than other population groups. We need to unpack the barriers and challenges of urban space. The sixth section examines how technology can be made to work for people and systems in cities. The seventh section explores the connection between social justice and cities through the prism of an emerging discourse – the right to the city. The final section revisits some of these issues through the lens of recommendations that can contribute to more just cities over the short, medium, and long term.

The urbanizing of people and of societies has become one of the major trends of the last few decades. This urbanizing has long generated a diversity of formats. But the available evidence suggests that today this variability has become even greater. Besides the familiar formats we have known across time and place, there is now a proliferation of novel formats – private cities, gated communities, office parks that pretend to be cities and are experienced by many as such, and more. This proliferation of diverse "urban" types ranges from cities occupying a territory so vast it is barely governed to small and fully managed towns.

This chapter focuses on the diverse dynamics shaping urbanization across the world in order to understand how cities can become more just. In today's world justice denotes environmental sustainability, well-being, access to basic services, cultural autonomy, gainful employment, and more. Given the massive budget deficits in most countries, especially in the Global South, achieving justice demands a radical shift in the patterns of economic development. Cities can and must play a central role in this urgent sociotechnical process. It is impossible to cover the extraordinary variability of the urban condition in this chapter. But one vector all cities share is the making of urban space. Urban Space makes visible injustice as well as positive potentials. The question then is how can we maximize urban space as a positive in the lives of the billions of marginalized citizens, the discriminated, and the persecuted.

5.1   Introduction

The urbanizing of people and of societies has become one of the major trends of the last few decades. This urbanizing has long generated a diversity of formats. But the available evidence suggests that today this variability has become even greater. Besides the familiar formats we have known across time and place, there is now a proliferation of novel formats – private cities, gated communities, office parks that pretend to be cities and are experienced by many as such, and more. This proliferation of diverse "urban" types ranges from cities occupying a territory so vast it is barely governed to small and fully managed towns.

This chapter focuses on the diverse dynamics shaping urbanization across the world in order to understand how cities can become more just. In today's world justice denotes environmental sustainability, well-being, access to basic services, cultural autonomy, gainful employment, and more. Given the massive budget deficits in most countries, especially in the Global South, achieving justice demands a radical shift in the patterns of economic development. Cities can and must play a central role in this urgent sociotechnical process. It is impossible to cover the extraordinary variability of the urban condition in this chapter. But one vector all cities share is the making of urban space. Urban Space makes visible injustice as well as positive potentials. The question then is how can we maximize urban space as a positive in the lives of the billions of marginalized citizens, the discriminated, and the persecuted.

A second vector that can cut across this enormous diversity is the special city of each urban epoch. In today's world, cities confront a range of particular challenges not faced (at least knowingly) by cities in past periods. Climate change is shorthand for a mix of negative conditions that today's cities will face sooner or later – and cities in the past, mostly, did not. The expulsion of millions each year, mostly from rural areas due to the development of mines and plantations, is an old history, but it has reached extreme levels today. The city becomes one of the few places where the growing numbers of the displaced can find a patch to put their bodies down. The rise of asymmetric war has meant the urbanizing of war; today, when a conventional army goes to war the enemy is mostly an irregular combatant who benefits from urbanizing war. One key tactic is attacks in cities that are not part of the "theater of war," as we saw in a long list of cities over the last decade, from Bali and Casablanca to New York and Paris.

A third challenge is the evident difficulty of generating and focusing attention and material resources on the urgent need of redistribution to combat exclusionary urbanism. Today's major actors and dynamics in cities worldwide too often are generating inequalities of all sorts and escalating concentrations of power and advantage. Highly valued Western frameworks – democracy, rights, social justice, and more – are not as useful, even in the West, as we often think. While inequality has always been a feature of cities, today we are seeing the ascendance of economies that generate distributions far more extreme than in the recent past: massive benefits to some and shrinking options to growing majorities.

In today's world, then, the city is becoming one of the spaces that make visible the extreme trends that mark our epoch. Smaller towns and urban settlements may still be somewhat protected from this increasing maldistribution of resources and benefits, but this might soon be changing. Here we examine major challenges facing cities and what conditions can enable cities to be more just. The just city is not simply a perfect city. This is unachievable given the diversity of elements that constitute a city. But it is a city that enables all its residents, and that is marked by a serious engagement with social justice for all.

The text is organized as follows. After the Introduction, the second section provides a few conceptual anchors guiding the analysis. The third section focuses on the multiple ways in which the urban condition materializes across the world. The examination ranges from continental Africa to specific instances, such as Turkey's refugee crisis and Tokyo's urban innovations. This section concludes with a discussion of megacities and the new geographies of power constituted through the proliferation of global cities. The fourth section provides a counterpoint to general trends by exploring the fact that built environments are not neutral – they benefit some more than others. Women with small children, for instance, often experience disadvantages invisible to the rest of the population. The sixth section examines how technology can be made to work for people and systems in cities. The seventh section examines the connection between social justice and cities through the prism of an emerging discourse – the right to the city. The final section develops recommendations to achieve more just cities over the short, medium, and long term.

But first a brief set of specifications as to what is a city at a time when vast private office parks and gated communities with their own guards, are proliferating across the world.

5.2   Conceptual Anchors

Cities and urban life are profoundly heterogeneous and complex conditions. A city is a unique blend of landscape infused morphologies, people, cultures, histories, conflicts, sociotechnical interfaces, and constant flows of resources, data and ideas (Pieterse and Simone forthcoming). This complicates the task of exploring the link between cities and social progress. We need to identify a few conceptual anchors.

5.2.1   Beyond Density: What Is a City?

Cities are complex systems. But they are incomplete systems (Sassen 2014). In this mix lies the possibility of making – making the urban, the political, the civic, a history, an economy. It is also because of these features that we can work at making cities, developing cities in particular directions that make them more socially just. And this possibility of making holds even for those who do not have power: poor immigrants, refugees, and slum dwellers can transform a degraded part of the city into a thriving neighborhood with its own subeconomy. This form of dynamic agency cannot happen in an office park, even if they work there.

These constitutive features – incompleteness, complexity, and the possibility of making – take on urbanized formats that can vary enormously across time and place; it points to a unique and ever-present potentiality. Such formats often originate in deep histories of place. This also explains why every city is distinct, even when that distinctiveness is more in the cultures and memories of locals than in the design of its buildings or the predictable form that shape movement and interactions. The urban may not be alone in having these characteristics, but these characteristics are a necessary part of the DNA of the urban. It also holds the key to advancing social progress.

A second key feature of cities is that this mix of complexity and incompleteness has allowed cities to outlive more formal and closed systems such as republics, kingdoms, banks and corporations. Cities are simply more adaptive. Consider any major city with a long life: its authority systems, its big old firms, its power regimes, are all likely to be gone. But the city itself and its neighborhoods are there, even after centuries.

A third feature of cities is that across time and place cities – not a fortress or palace dressed as a city – have enabled a broad range of contradictory outcomes. They are a place where the oppressor and the oppressed have multiple encounters, where the claims of the poor can, at some point, get a hearing, or at least become visible. We can think of it as the capacity of a city to make us all into urban subjects – moments when the multiple differences of religion, class, culture, ethnicity, and more, are suspended. This potential and occasional lived reality constitutes the speech of the city. To these older familiar intersections we must now add the range of challenges generated by environmental destruction. Rising waters, desertification, pollution, are all likely to be felt by both the rich and the poor (think air pollution in Beijing), even if the poor are going to suffer far more. The city embodies and enables forms of entanglement that are inconceivable in nonurban space.

A fourth feature is that in today's world the frontier is increasingly inside cities. Mostly it is no longer at the edges of empire as it was over the last few centuries. We can think of the frontier as a space where actors from different worlds have an encounter for which there is no established rules of engagement. In the historic frontier of the West, this encounter was marked by imperial powers usually slaughtering the indigenous people. Today, the fact that the frontier is in the city gives the weaker party some power – the power to make claims, to demonstrate, in short the power of voice, or at least subversion.

These, and several other marking conditions we examine in this Report, are critical to understand the specific capacities of cities as sites for dynamic change and progress. Further, conceiving of cities in these terms means that much of today's dense built-up terrain is not necessarily a city in the constitutive senses outlined. It might

be a gated community, an expanded or mini strip mall, or a private office complex with guards controlling access. It is built density, but it lacks "cityness" and its capabilities. Cityness derives from the cultural interactions generated by intense diversities, which thrives on incompleteness, complexity, and potentiality.

5.2.2 Urbanity and Social Progress

A dominant narrative of urbanization and development held that national growth rises with growing urbanization, and, indeed, is driven by it.[3] It clearly leaves out earlier urban epochs and urbanizing geographies across the world. The modernity marked by shifts from agriculture to urban manufacturing and services comes with social shifts around questions of membership. Citizenship, subjectivity, personhood shaped urban selves that tended to mirror the cities they inhabited. Modernity and modernization became both economic and sociospatial projects.

Even if, for a moment we take this narrative at its word,[4] it is important to remember that growth is not development. "Social progress" – our shared ground of investigation in this Report – is perhaps precisely the bridge that tries to hold the two together, determining the form of their relation. It is the current configurations of this relation inside the urban that is the object of investigation in this chapter.

This is a difficult task. Urbanization is a spatial, social, and economic transition with deeply local and distinct histories in different regions. Within each, layers and geographies of inequalities and exclusions lie alongside significant improvements in both core human development and prosperity over the past century. Diverse older inequalities persist even as newer constraints (e.g. ecological limits of urban life and form) arise.

Our reading is made all the more complex because urbanization's patterns and histories neither were nor are autonomous. They are, in fact, constitutive of each other. This is true of the colonial systems of the eighteenth or twentieth century where growth and development in one region came at the expense of extractions and destructions in another. Such disjunctions also exist today: in the current global system cities function as economic networks that are structurally dependent on making their own "outsides" and peripheries. This is most starkly illustrated by the fact that 600 urban economies account for 60 percent of global GDP (UN-Habitat 2016a; Sassen 2017). How then do we assess urbanization and social progress is predicated on tradeoffs – what one site gains, another loses.

---

[3]   This is a contested narrative in academic circles, but in policy and international development circles, is largely accepted as gospel. See, on the empirical relationship between urban agglomerations and growth, Bettencourt, L. and West, G. (2010) "A unified theory of urban living," *Nature*, 467: 912–913. For a popular narrative, see Glaeser, E. (2011) *Triumph of the City: How our Greatest Invention makes us Richer, Smarter, Greener, Healthier, and Happier*. London: Macmillan. For international policy articulations, see McKinsey (2010) "Lions on the move: The progress and potential of African economies," McKinsey Global Institute, Available: www.mckinsey.com/insights/africa/lions_on_the_move (last accessed January 5, 2016) and McKinsey (2012) "Urban World: Cities and the rise of the consuming class," McKinsey Global Institute, Available: www.mckinsey.com/insights/urbanization/urban_world_cities_and_the_rise_of_the_consuming (last accessed January 5, 2016). For international development agencies, see UN-Habitat (2016) Habitat III: The New Urban Agenda, Available: www.habitat3.org (last accessed January 6, 2016).

[4]   For a good and current review of this relationship and its evidence, see Turok, I. (forthcoming 2017) "Urbanisation and Development: Reinforcing the Foundations" in Bhan, Srinivas and Watson (eds) (forthcoming 2017) *The Routledge Companion to Planning in Cities of the Global South*. Routledge: London.

Social progress must be structured to mediate the relation between growth and development. Across regions and across periods, this relation has at times bent toward equity and inclusion, or toward exclusions divisions. Our task is to document the diversity of these relations and their geographies, and seek to find ways of moving toward equity and inclusion – even if any gains will constantly have to be protected, sustained, and, perhaps, reinvented.

5.2.3   Redesigning the Built Environment and Social Progress

Now more than ever, the city is all we have. (Koolhaas 1995)

Historically, the physical form of the city has reflected the society it hosts, its structure and functioning. Its geometry expresses and explains the city's aesthetic, technical, tactical, political, religious, economic, cultural, and, of course, social values. Since ancient times the city has been a designed object. In the West, Theseus' synoecism, which led to the Greek polis, was an ideal living space. Aristotle saw it as meeting essential human needs, as expressed in the acropolis, the agora, the theatre, the network of streets, the houses, the fields for crops and grazing, and the walls. From this idea, Hippodamus of Miletus created the grid to found cities, in keeping with the development of the concept of polis and in accordance with the idea of symmetry, logic, functionality, and rationality reflecting the ideal society (Mumford 1961).

Renaissance aesthetics sought to change the structure of the medieval village and project new cities that focused on human beings, to ensure the proper setting, or "stage," for a new, classical architecture. Later, Thomas More's utopia envisaged a society in an ideal location, based on a new political, economic, and cultural organization that would allow for the inhabitants' well-being in equal conditions. In a sense, philosophical and theological imaginations always had distinct physical expression.

The rapid growth of cities during the Industrial Revolution gave rise to movements like social hygiene in the late nineteenth and early twentieth centuries. It was preoccupied with the ways in which deficiencies in the physical and social environment caused epidemic, endemic, and occupational illnesses. Therefore, the solution to health problems and new technologies demanded radical spatial and social reforms. This led to the creation of modern urbanism, an epistemic field linked to science and public service and aimed at achieving the common good through a new urban structure predicated on changing urban forms and operations.

Since then, models of the ideal twentieth-century city have proliferated, aiming at overcoming health problems and social injustice, and rectifying the imbalance of living conditions imposed by the Industrial Revolution. In the West, these models include Baron Haussmann's plan to transform preindustrial Paris (1854); Cerdá's General Theory of Urbanization and Barcelona Extension (1867); Ebenezer Howard's Garden City movement (1898), Wright's Broadacre City (1932), and Mumford and Osborn's New Towns (1942, 1951). Colonial incursions in much of the rest of the world, brought racially based adaptations of these ideologies to the building and regulation of urban cores serving colonial administrations.

An emblematic and influential twentieth-century model is the Athens Charter (1943), based on the postulates of Le Corbusier and the Congrès International d'Architecture Moderne, CIAM (1928–1959). The charter proposed a city that ensured citizen justice and equality through a uniform composition and structure that would contribute to social homogenization. In theory, application of these guidelines would solve the problems of the industrial city through functional relationships grounded in a new idea of circulation and standardized serial housing construction.

However, consistency between the principles that inspired the charter and the problems they were intended to solve was never achieved politically. These values were invariably molded to suit the political and economic interests of elites who sought to use regulation as an instrument to secure their interests and discipline potential dissent from the poor and working classes. Furthermore, urban planning and regulatory regimes were used to safeguard and promote real-estate driven accumulation which demanded a system of land speculation through zoning linked to the construction, automobile, and appliance industries. The democratic and inclusionary potential of planning was usurped to ensure a specific mode of accumulation.

Functionalist urbanism led to the instrumentalized modern city.[5] It negated the benefits of a dense, compact city. It subordinated the street and public life to buildings. It repudiated the public in favor of the private, and went for large-scale gated high-rise housing complexes. Urban transformation was dictated by highways, a loss of regional scale, and the proliferation of suburbs. These features were also evident in Latin America given a rather early onset of colonial independence. In contrast, much of Africa and Asia remained marked by truncated and bifurcated colonial regulatory regimes until World War II. Inevitably, the contemporary city is a heterogeneous mix of parts of the traditional city, its historical center, modern bits, contemporary global corporate headquarters, disconnected parts, abandoned areas, marginalized peripheries, settlements devoid of urbanity, urbanized rural sections, urban fractions scattered throughout the countryside, autonomous or dependent suburbs, and more. This contributes to a constitutive heterogeneity and incompleteness, but it also explains why the built environment generates inequality, marginalization, segregation, immobility, and unsustainability. The scale of these negative features raises the question as to whether urban planning can possibly solve urban problems, make cities that benefit all, and remain within environmental guardrails (WBGU 2016).

We must recognize the duality of the city. On the one hand, it has contributed to the evolution of society as a whole, while simultaneously

---

[5]   A paradigm internationalized for decades, in the reconstruction of cities devastated by World War II – via international agencies that financed the development such as the World Bank (IBRD), the Inter-American Development Bank (IADB), and the United Nations (UN).

remaining a major obstacle to social equity. A quick scan of urban challenges in both developed and developing contexts shows us that all cities inherit problems and today confront a host of new and interrelated challenges – rising inequality, climate change, and a considerable lack of social progress for many residents (Sassen 2014, 2017).

In response to these dynamics, growing numbers of scholars, professional urbanists, activists, and practitioners experimenting with alternatives, are determined to understand and address these challenges. The global policy and research discussions that informed the "2030 Sustainable Development Goals" and "The 2015 Paris Agreement" have brought cities to the fore. Urban actors from diverse sectors and interest groups now share a strong focus on urban sustainability[6] as the core imperative to address the legacies of extractive and functionalist urbanism. This translates into research and policy focused on the compact city – dense, mixed, intensive, open, and diverse, with a positive impact on society and sustainability.[7] This is an agenda that speaks to urban form and mixity, and to the efficient use of resources. Sustainable urbanism will vary enormously given the distinct histories of cities across the world.

5.3   Differential Urbanization and Regional Trends

How do we understand the patterns and trends of urbanization globally? A comprehensive review is impossible and therefore we adopt a different method – a multiscalar reading. First, we open with macro-data at the global level that speaks of urbanization across regions. Then, we choose one example – Africa – to show that the "region" itself as a scale of analysis hides tremendous variation. We shift scales again to the nation, and use the example of Turkey to highlight patterns of urbanization that are often omitted in macro-understandings by looking at the refugee as an urban resident. We also focus on a major highly developed megacity, Tokyo, for a brief examination of how a wealthy city can engage exiting technical capabilities.

Each of these modes allows us insights into urbanization trends and patterns while reminding us of the limitations of data.

5.3.1   Global Trends

Across the world, urbanization has taken different spatial and historic trajectories (see Figure 5.1). The regions broadly described

as the Global North went from predominantly rural to predominantly urban between 1750 and 1950 in lockstep with modernization and industrialization (Satterthwaite 2007). Latin America saw its urban expansion in the first half of the twentieth century, with many large countries becoming 60–80 percent urban by the 1970s. South America is possibly the most urbanized region on the planet; the Caribbean's relatively lower urbanization lowers the region's average. An equivalent demographic and territorial transition now unfolds in Sub-Saharan Africa (1950–2035) and in Asia (1960–2050) (UN-DESA 2015).

Urbanization is now the dominant settlement form in LAC, North America, Europe, and Oceania. But the fastest growth in the twentieth century has been in East Asia (led by China and India). But by the twenty-first century, Africa (especially Sub-Saharan Africa) will lead, along with India and China. South Asia remains one of the less urbanized regions in the world, signaling that its urbanization is yet to come.

How do we understand the character of this urbanization and its relation to social progress? The answer is complex. Certainly, in Africa, India and – to some extent – China, urbanization is rising rapidly at low, low-middle or, at best, middle income status. Even controlling for the colonial forms and legacies of urban development, this points to critical challenges to the assumed relationships between urbanization and development. Urban expansion is not necessarily being led by a strong, embedded, and employment-generating economic structure in low and low-middle income countries. To this we must add persistent poverty, which in turn brings segmented consumption and labor markets, low tax and revenue bases, deficient and inadequately expanding infrastructure, and uncertain state capacity to direct resources and investments. Urbanization at this pace becomes an arena of significant struggles for social progress. Many of the urban challenges in Africa and South Asia – slums, widespread economic informality, unequal rights to the city, weak fiscal structures, and diminished local governments – are evidence of this struggle.

Latin American urbanization points differently to the ability of cities to expand opportunity and human development through strong local government after a period of economic expansion. Yet a new set of challenges – of scale, altered consumption, and persistent inequality – remain. In Europe and North America, after decades of growth, the sustainability of urban economic development has come into question as intracity inequalities often marked on identity-based exclusions have become political contestations, demographic shifts with falling

6   This coincides with the appearance of the term Sustainable Development in the Brundtland Report (1987), which was included in Agenda 21, produced in the United Nations Earth Summit in Rio de Janeiro in 1992 and then transferred to the Second Conference of the United Nations on Human Settlements (HABITAT II) held in Istanbul in 1996, where its use spread to the discourse on human settlements. Recently, the term Sustainable Urban Development has melded with the term Sustainable Urban Transformations, which refers to the progress, evolution, or modification of the city without affecting the economic, social, physical and environmental issues that guarantee a certain long-term welfare for the population, which implies intelligent urban planning and development. UN-habitat. 2010 State of the World's Cities 2010/2011: Bridging the Urban Divide. Earthscan.

7   There is a vast literature on this subject: Williams, Jenks and Burton, 2000; Burgess and Jenks, 2002; Burton, 2000; Burton, 2001; Burton, Jenks and Williams, 2003; Burdett and Sudjic, 2007; Rogers, 2008; Rogers, 1999; Lynch, 1984; Sennett, 2006; Van der Ryn and Calthorpe, 1991; Gehl 1989; Gehl, 2013; de Solà-Morales, 2008, de Solà-Morales, 2013; Bohigas, 2003; Bohigas, 2004; Fudge and Nyström, 1999.

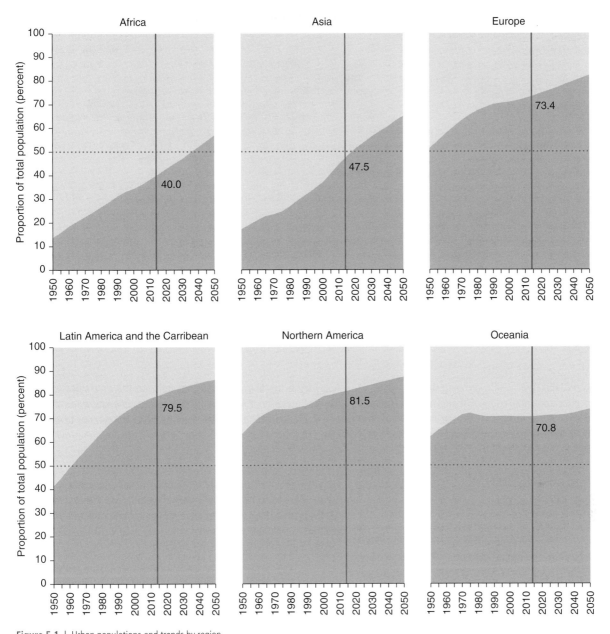

Figure 5.1 | Urban populations and trends by region.
Source: United Nations, Department of Economic and Social Affairs, Population Division (2014). World Urbanization Prospects: The 2014 Revision, Highlights (ST/ESA/SER.A/352)

birth rates and changing immigration patterns are altering the composition of cities.

5.3.2   Settlement Structures: Megacities

The formats of this urbanization also matter. Figure 5.2 shows one end of the settlement structures of world urbanization: the mega-city. We argued above that rapid urbanization in low and low-middle income countries comes with risks and opportunities for the relation between growth and development. This holds especially for the ways this urbanization spatializes. One such case is the proliferating megacity.

Continuous urban agglomerations of 10 million residents or more, with settlements that extend beyond any administrative

boundaries in the city-region, exemplify the gains of agglomeration and economies of scale. It can signal resilience against economic fluctuations given strong and diverse local economic circuits; and it can create a reliant base for redistribution. But if they grow with a mostly poor population, such areas also create enormous challenges regarding governance, infrastructure, management, and equity. In both cases, they generate problems regarding food, ecological footprints, and sustainable growth. According to the UN Population Division's World Urbanization Prospects (2014), there are 28 "megacities" in the world today with over 10 million inhabitants, amounting to 453 million people or 12 percent of the world's urban population. A large number of the world's megacities already are in the Global South – and will be in even greater numbers by 2050.

5

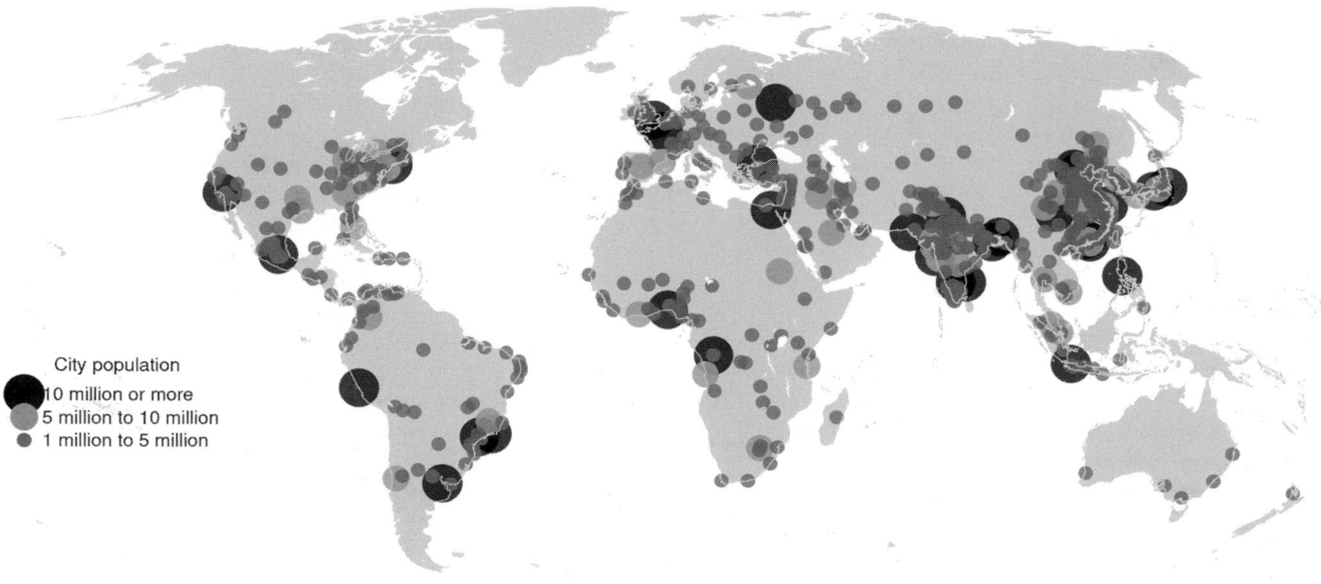

Figure 5.2 | Share and location of megacities, 2016.
Source: UN-DESA, 2016

Beyond the megacity, urbanization is also growing through vast and changing peri-urban interfaces and edges. Urbanization in Africa is most rapid and prevalent in what the OECD calls the urban–rural interface zones marked by a continuum of rural areas, villages, towns and cities of fewer than 500,000 inhabitants. This is particularly evident in the agrarian and late urbanizing countries. Drawing on UN-DESA data, the OECD calculates that 83 percent of Africa's population lives in such rural–urban interfaces (UN-DESA 2015).

Academic and policy studies are highly skewed toward the larger cities – megacities, large cities and capital cities even when the predominant urban experience is small-scale. The size of a city holds important implications for the potential to transform urban life toward more sustainable patterns.

5.3.3   Within the Region: Disaggregating African Urbanization

Regional data on Africa obscures enormous variation across the Continent. These differences are best captured by the acute intraregional differences. Thus, both North and Southern Africa are well past the 50 percent urbanization mark, whilst East Africa is at the 20 percent level (UN-DESA 2015). West Africa contains some more urbanized countries, with 50 percent urban Nigeria (largest African country by population) and 39 percent urban Ghana.

Information from the Africa Economic Outlook 2016 (OECD/AfDB/UNDP 2016) offers a novel typology for categorizing countries in terms of urbanization, fertility transitions, and level of economic development (as indicated by the changing role of agriculture and the economic importance of natural resource extraction). See Table 5.1.

Apart from the five countries that fall into the diversifiers category, the vast majority of African countries reflect very low levels of wealth as reflected in GDP per capita data revealing the relative level of economic development, which in turn speaks to the enormous needs these societies face. Furthermore, the fertility rates provide an insight into the growth of demand for basic services (education, health care, social security) and infrastructure systems (energy, mobility, water, sanitation, waste, ICT, and so forth). Low levels of wealth, and the accompanying relatively small tax bases, eroded further by predominantly informal economies, reduces the pool of resources that African governments can draw on to meet expanding demand.

Understanding what social progress might mean in this context calls for an empirics of urbanization that includes specific scalings. The metrics we use must themselves capture the diversity of major urban processes within a city, within a country, and across the world. It is not enough to focus simply on the statistics describing economic, population, and built environment conditions.

5.3.4   Refugees and Urbanization: The Case of Turkey

Shifting focus to the city allows us to see further specificities in urbanization and to contextualize its historical modes and processes. Twentieth-century urbanization in Turkey was centered on industrialization, especially after the turn from empire to nation-state. This in turn generated urban migrations, especially to Istanbul and Ankara. And it generated vast urban peripheries – "Gecekondu," a term similar to the English "slum" yet different in that the migrants built the housing themselves (Özler 2000). This type of self-organized work often enters in conflict with existing rules, notably building on state land. A good number of these urban settlements were legalized by the state in the 1980s in response to effective claims and populist struggles. As is the case in other parts

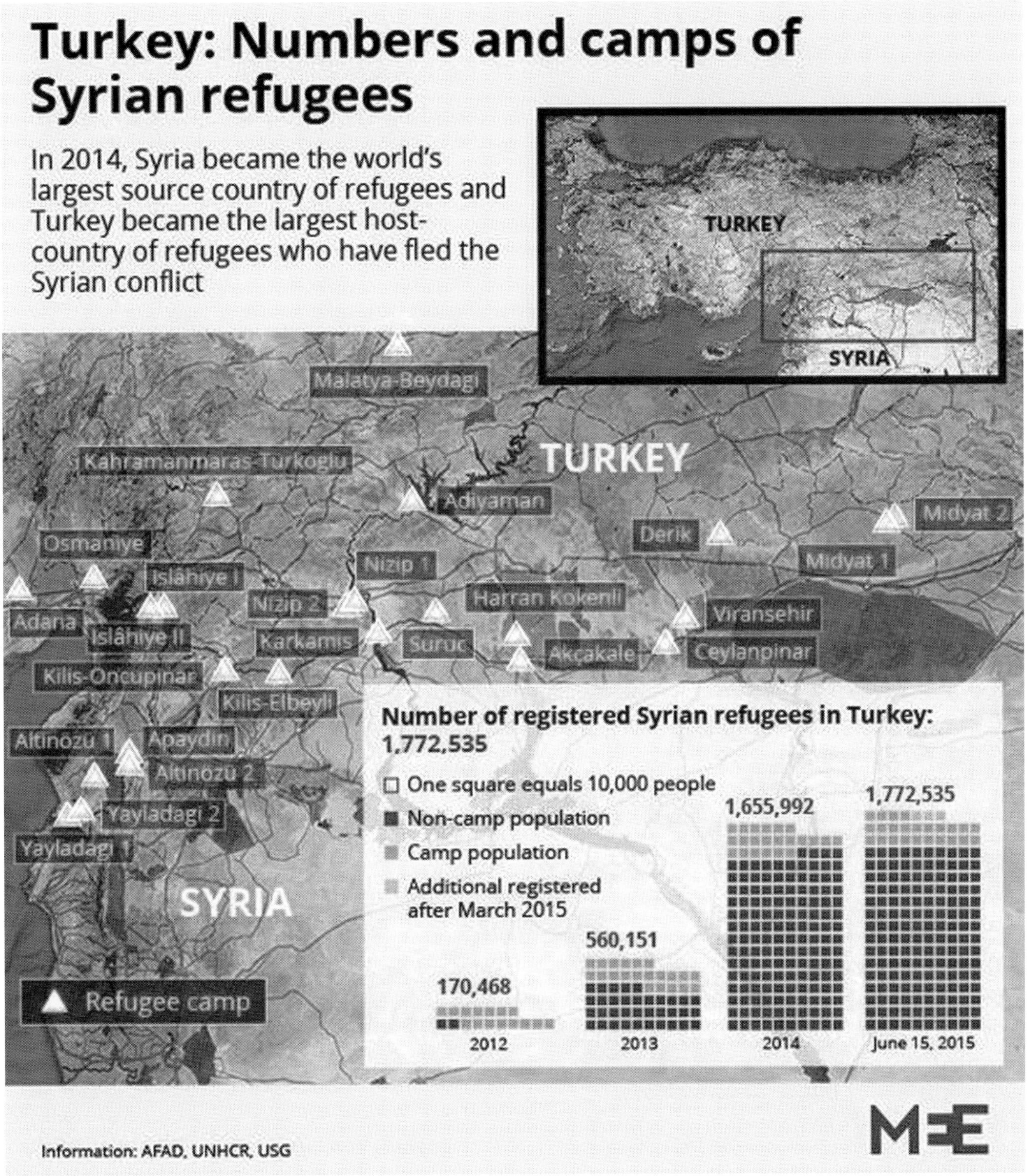

Figure 5.3 | Visualization of refugees in Turkey.
Source: Middle East Eye (AFAD, UNHCR, USG)

Box 5.1 | The Future of the Rich Mega-City: Tokyo

Today, Tokyo's metropolitan area is the largest city in the world with more than 35 million people, with an economy almost equivalent to the size of Brazil. Tokyo, the oldest megacity after New York, is expected to remain the largest of all the megacities in 2030. It faces a plethora of challenges that many other emerging megacities are experiencing or have yet to experience.

Tokyo thus can serve us well as natural experiment: it is a megacity, its infrastructure and people are aging fast, but unlike many other megacities, it has resources and a long, well-established central planning tradition. The rapidly aging and declining population is pressuring the city to move away from the conventional growth model of the post-World War II decades and to seek a new model of shrinkage or contraction. By carefully examining the future of this megacity, we could be able to imagine the future of megacities, that is, the future of cities that will be home for a good share of the urban population in the world.

Among the questions we must ask are (1) How can we envision the future of a city? (2) What are the key factors in shaping the future of the city? (3) What would be the key strategies ensure the survival of the city and people in the future? In 2011, Hiroo Ishikawa led a research project on the future of Tokyo as vice-chairman of its steering committee. The research, entitled "Tokyo Future Scenario 2035," aimed to formulate possible urban strategies for the city in the face of unprecedented demographic, economic, and political challenges. The research employed a technique called "scenario planning," in which multiple future scenarios for the next 25 years were set up to describe corresponding strategies.

The approach to the city's future was by setting up seven interrelated sectors of human activity: International Relations / Diplomacy, Economy, Environment, Technology, Urban Space, Life/Society/Culture, and Administration. With the collaboration of a broad range of experts in these sectors and the collection of wide-ranging data to analyze the current situations of the city, three key factors were identified to set up possible scenarios of the future.

Although all of major sectors are highly relevant to the prediction of the future trajectory of a city, three of them, Environment, Technology, and Urban Space, seem to have a direct influence on the shape of the future city. In what follows we use the case of Tokyo to explore its possible futures through these three dimensions.

(a) Environment: Tokyo will face major challenges when it comes to the environment. There are several possible future scenarios that await Tokyo. None of these concerns the energy consumption structure in Tokyo and the city's efforts to reduce the energy consumption and carbon emission. Despite the low per capita energy consumption (half the national average), Tokyo's energy consumption has gradually been increasing. The city now seeks to develop low carbon emission buildings for homes and offices and replace the conventional vehicles with energy-efficient cars. The multiple scenarios suggested that the willingness to invest in the energy saving cost is one of the key factors that affect the city's future trajectory. There are, clearly, other major issues: Nonfossil energy, reduction, and optimization of final disposal amount, restoration of ecological system, civil activism, and government leadership.

(b) Technology: The technological innovations in the next few decades allow us to imagine some aspects of the future of city life in Tokyo. Of special interest is the way the locally specific demands in Tokyo arising from a shrinking population, disaster prevention, and elderly health care will lead to a particular technological development-assisted lifestyle. This subject is further developed in the section on Technology and the City.

(c) Urban Space: A particular issue that Tokyo will face in the near future is the simultaneous "aging" of the population and of its infrastructure. According to the estimates of the Japanese Government, the proportion of maintenance costs to the overall social infrastructure investment of the country will increase from 20 percent in 2002 to 32–46 percent in 2025. A large part of Tokyo's urban infrastructure was built in the era of rapid economic expansion (1950s–1980s) and its future maintenance and renovation cost will double the current cost. With a rapidly declining population, low economic development, and a high risk of natural disasters, Tokyo will need to find the possible public–private initiatives to maintain and renovate the old infrastructure.

Other issues to be considered are the reduction of natural disaster risks, the making of attractive space, efficient mobility, universal design, sustainable infrastructure, sustainable buildings, and countermeasures against heat-island phenomena.

Table 5.1 | African countries categorized by urbanization, fertility transition, and economic transformation

Category	Features
Diversifiers	Their urbanization levels of diversifiers range between 40% and 65%. They are also close to completing their fertility transition with total fertility ratios of three or fewer children per woman. These countries are Egypt, Mauritius, Morocco, South Africa, and Tunisia. This group has Africa's highest level of income (above USD 10,000 gross national income [GNI] per capita in 2013 with the exception of Morocco) and of human development (with a Human Development Index [HDI] value above 0.60).
Early urbanizers	Nine countries fall into this category distinguished by progress in their urbanization and fertility transition without having been able to diversify their economic base. Mostly found in West Africa, they include Côte d'Ivoire, Ghana, and Senegal. These countries are about 35–50% urbanized and have total fertility ratios of about five children per woman. They are typically low- to lower-middle income countries (USD 1000–4000 GNI per capita in 2013), with low-to-medium levels of human development (HDI values between 0.40 and 0.57).
Late urbanizers	The 11 countries that fall into this category are predominantly rural yet have begun their urbanization and fertility transition and structural transformation more recently. In contrast to the early urbanizers, they are located in East Africa and include Ethiopia, Kenya, and Tanzania. Less than one-third of their population typically lives in urban areas. Their total fertility rates are four to six children per woman. Income levels are low (USD 1000–2200 GNI per capita in 2013), and levels of human development are low-to-medium (HDI values between 0.38 and 0.54). Interestingly, two relatively authoritarian countries, Ethiopia and Rwanda have demonstrated an impressive capacity to diversify their economic base over the past decade, albeit off a low basis.
Agrarians	Here we include 11 countries that are at an early urbanization stage and early fertility transition – on average women have six children. About one-third of the population resides in urban areas, incomes are low, and so are human development indicators. These are mostly landlocked countries – e.g. Niger, Chad, and Malawi – with economies dominated by agriculture and natural resources. Generally manufacturing stands at 4–12% of the economy. Urbanization has partly been driven by the profits from natural resources, which have also drawn labor out of agriculture. Compared with other countries at similar income levels, these 11 countries show a higher degree of urbanization (40–78%) and a high degree of urban primacy, with the capital usually disproportionally bigger than a country's other cities.
Natural resource-based economies	These countries have sharp variations in income levels, in the types of natural resources they produce (e.g. hydrocarbons, minerals, and metals) and in their geographies (e.g. Libya is predominantly arid while Nigeria is mostly rain-fed). The overreliance on natural resources makes them extremely vulnerable to international market swings, and hence complicates the development role of the state.

of the world, one effect of this legalizing is speculation in land and housing markets.

Some of these neighborhoods became part of the urban pattern and economic cycles of cities. Thus as Istanbul shifted from a "self- service" city to neoliberal urbanization, "Gecekondu" residents became a significant source of low-wage workers for the new economic centers. For example, Maslak district, a key site in Istanbul's northwestern expansion, relied on "Gecekondu" workers for the building of skyscrapers, and for security, cleaning, and other service jobs (Özler 2000). Istanbul's "globalization" was centered in privatization, financial speculation, construction, and the raising of local municipal power. From 2001 onwards, Istanbul and most major cities/towns in Turkey, found in cities and construction a key space of capital accumulation. It reshaped urban policy and the production of space (public space, infrastructure, housing).

Gated Communities emerged in the 1990s as yet another urbanization pattern as the upper classes (both secular and from Islamist and conservative groups) sought to withdraw from urban centers. The first waves were led by middle and upper middle-class from secular as well from Islamist and conservative groups. A second wave after 2010 saw the building of gated communities in urban centers, with new architecture and design projects that include public and commercial facilities. The history of gated communities from the 1990s onward points to the relation of class structure and urban spaces in Turkey (Agier 2002, 2016).

In the midst of this urbanization pattern for the rich, another type of urbanization has now emerged. It is linked to the current refugee crisis. Future cities will increasingly confront the effects of massive displacements due to war, climate change, and the loss of rural land due to the accelerated expansion of mines, plantations, and water grabs (Sassen, 2014: ch. 2, 2016a). Refugee flows bring

with them new economies, housing, security policies in urban space and everyday life, and more. This is a whole new type of urban complex that will proliferate in the next decade and more. Urbanization marked by significant numbers of refugees is evident in cities as diverse as Istanbul, Paris, or Berlin. Camps near cities and towns (such as in Paris or in South Eastern Anatolia) create new spatial relation in terms of transportation, economy, and human relations. Are the cities ready for this? What kind of liquid infrastructures are created? How will it shape infrastructures like housing, water sources, and public spaces? These influences will become important in the near urban future. For example, the cost of a rent of one tent in a camp in France creates its own micro-economy connected to larger towns in terms of human trafficking. At the other hand, the self-organized solidarity networks in Istanbul, Berlin or Athens becoming stronger in urban spaces that influences the urban knots of public spaces and usage of technology such as mobile phones. The rent and housing market influenced by middle-class refugees or refugees who can effort renting spaces.

These new patterns of forced migration are built upon long histories of refugee urbanization. Existing refugee camps are important elements in urban life especially in Lebanon, Jordan, or West Bank where they created another archetype in the definition of "city" and "urban." Urbanized camps (or future urbanized camps) are their own form of a city that in many ways can be superior. Zaatari camp (Jordan) is one of the examples of a camp that has somehow created its own active social and economic networks. According to Agier (2016), "Campsvilles": "the camps gradually become the sites of an enduring organization of space, social life and system of power that exist nowhere else. These are paradoxical devices, hybrids that, for lack of an appropriate term, I shall call city-camps (camps-villes)." Agier defines the refugee camp as a sociospatial entity; the space of a heterogeneous everyday life; and as a biopolitical space that embodies networks of practices of the actors and agencies.

Urbanized refugee camps are facing similar processes as cities, for example types of gentrification. If a camp can remain in a city center, it can face gentrification and housing value speculation. Property is often a challenge as most residents in refugee camps do not have legal ownership. But renting a house can be done even if outside the law. One fact that emerges from these trajectories of displaced peoples is the fact of multiple forms of urbanization, within and across cities.

5.3.5 Today's Geography of Power: Global Cities across the World

Our final scale of analysis looks at cities as basic units but compares them on a global scale. The Global Power City Index of The Mori Foundation (Tokyo) is one way to do this. It was formulated in an effort

to better organize and understand the complex system of attraction that exists for certain cities in a global economic system that makes them compete with each other as nodes. By measuring and tracking a comprehensive list of specific indicators, the GPCI provides valuable data that can be utilized by policy-makers, researchers, businesses, or even potential residents. Defining "attractiveness" can be difficult, however, as what constitutes an attractive destination is dependent on a multitude of perspectives from different actors. It is for this reason that in addition to measuring functions for economy, research and development, cultural interaction, accessibility, livability, and environment, the GPCI also includes an "actor-specific ranking," which evaluates cities based on the interests of specific individuals.

The GPCI was first developed and introduced by the Mori Memorial Foundation's Institute for Urban Strategies in 2015. Its rankings have been updated yearly since. The index measures and evaluates the

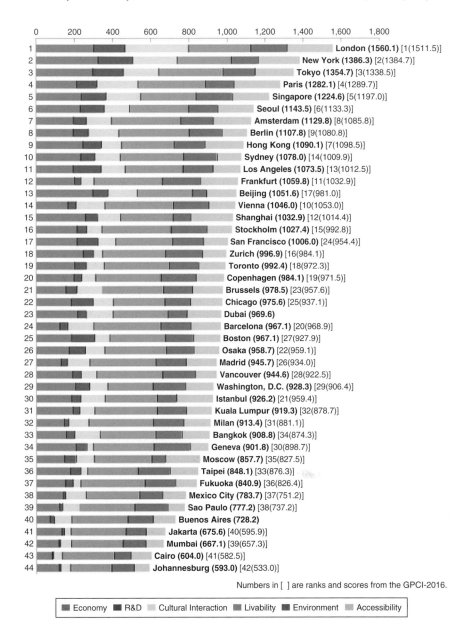

Numbers in [ ] are ranks and scores from the GPCI-2016.

Figure 5.4 | GPCI ranking 2015.

comprehensive power of 40 of the world's leading cities according to six primary functions – economy, research and development, cultural interaction, livability, environment, and accessibility – across 70 unique indicators.[8] The most recent ranking is summarized in Figure 5.4.

The Introduction section made a case for cities as constitutively complex, incomplete, and filled with potentiality. This serves as a reminder that cities need to be understood historically, spatially, and the product of culturally driven practices to forge a built environment in unique geo-ecological settings. In this section those starting points were further illustrated with a multiscalar description of different dimensions of urbanization. Across these immense diversities, it is nonetheless possible to observe a number of important convergences and consistencies. In the next section, we explore the "performance" of cities in terms of normative horizons rooted in human rights, social justice, and environmental sustainability.

5.4   The Right to the City, for Whom?

Forty-five years after the publication of the first edition of Henri Lefebvre's influential work on *The Right to the City* (*Le droit à la ville*, 1968), its core concerns still offer a critical lens for understanding the urban. In recent decades, globalization, and neoliberal policies have generated nonstop changes in more and more cities, altering urban life and raising questions about how to plan and manage these spaces (Falú 2009). Lefebvre helps us think through what these changes mean for everyday life in the city.

Lefebvre posits that the city, and urban space generally, are best understood not only in terms of territory but also as a series of social relations. All that is produced in our cities results from our collective making of the social, even if it encompasses a process that is never autonomous from the political economy that envelops the urban. This way of conceiving the urban provides a political perspective that emphasizes citizens' needs. It rescues us, humans, from erasure within the cities that we build and inhabit. Thus, socially produced urban space goes beyond the materiality of the city to include its social dimensions: the lives we are able to live, our relationships with others, the choices we make, our engagement with the political, our experiences in the local arena, our cultural expressions, our actions, and, overall, the matter of "what happens" in the physical city (Lefebvre 1968 [1978]: 105–110).

Here we explore who has the right to the city? As David Harvey has asked: What rights are we talking about, and about whose city? Or perhaps stated in a different manner: Who defines and builds the city? Who benefits from its public goods and diverse services (Falú 2013)? Further, given the current aggressive financializing of buildings in major cities, we must ask, "Who Owns the City?" (Sassen 2015b).

Interrogating the urban condition along these critical lines goes to the core of any notion of equity and social progress. We consider one illustrative identity – gender. It is marked by a kind of exclusion that defines everyday life for many urban citizens. It illuminates the relationship between cities and social progress.

Scholars have used diverse conceptual instruments to understand discrimination, exclusion, segregation, fragmentation, and more. There are multiple other axes we can use: sexuality, religion, ability, age, race, ethnicity, language, or nationality. Here we want to focus on a few specifics to address the urban question. The aim is to underline the importance of recognizing identity-based exclusions to understand cities. This helps identify modes of inquiry and analysis that render such exclusions visible, and thus open to challenge.

In segregated, exclusionary cities, the urban is in tension with citizens' rights; not all citizens are equal, have the same opportunities, or experience the city in the same way. Differences arise regarding socioeconomic standing, gender, age, race, sexuality, etc. And these compromise one's access to the material and/or symbolic resources we need to feel at home or empowered in a city. The concept of the Right to the City has the potential to work across these differences and inequalities due to the shared experience of inhabiting a common space. Yet, such a seemingly simple notion still needs to be enabled.

5.4.1   Omitted Subjects

Conceptualizing the "city" through socially constructed categories entails engaging how a city is built, represented, and experienced by its residents. These aspects vary across historical contexts, power relations, dominant ideologies, and more. To keep in mind omitted subjects means we must be attentive not only to who is left out in cities, but also to the consequences of their exclusion. "Gender" is an identity marker useful for assessing these questions. Next we focus on how gender intersects with urban space, time, and economic growth in a city.

5.4.1.1   Women in the City: Gendering Urban Space and Time

Numerous disciplines have produced theory and research about gender[9] dynamics. These efforts have brought to light the subordinate positions and conditions confronting women in cities due to powerful and ongoing gender-based divisions of labor. Women are relegated to the private home environment out of the public eye. In contrast, "men [are] linked to productive work – income generators – and women [are] seen as responsible only and exclusively with regard to domestic and reproductive tasks: caring for the children and running the household" (Falú 1998).

---

8   For access to all the data and reports, see: www.mori-mfoundation.or.jp/english/ius2/gpci2/#press
9   Gender itself is not a category reducible to women. We understand and note that it equally concerns and impacts transgender people as well as men, and that the category of "woman" itself requires disaggregation into its intersections with race, class, ethnicity, age, sexuality and caste, among others. We are focusing here on using women as a strategic essentialism, to use Gayatri Spivak's useful phrase, given constraints of space.

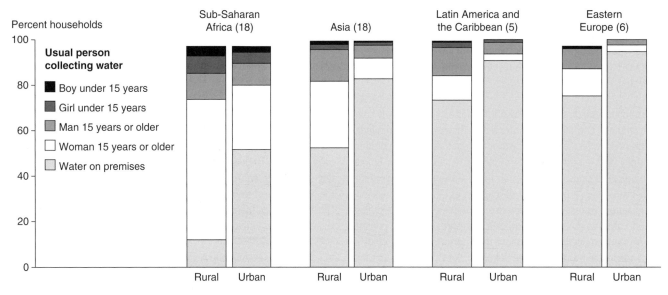

Figure 5.5 | Household responsibilities for water collection, by region and urban/rural areas, 2005–2007.
Source: (The) World's Women 2010. Trends and Statistics. UN-DESA 2010

Changes are happening. But it is still the case that in many urban contexts, women often perceive and experience the city differently than men. Due to their responsibilities in the home, women use cities in specific ways. If they combine work with family life, their journeys to work are often short. They use time in fragments: there is no full day at work and no full day away from their children. During daylight hours, public spaces are more likely to be women's spaces. Women often spend time in nearby parks and neighborhood streets, mixing with children, people with disabilities, and senior citizens. And yet, those spaces are often built and designed according to what are assumed to be men's needs and perspectives. Since its modern incarnation, urban design and planning have operated on the basis of the universal or unmarked citizen. But in concrete everyday life, there are no unmarked users: there are often profoundly gendered roles and actors.

The patriarchal framework extends beyond public spaces. It affects access to systems, services, and infrastructures for those living in the city, precipitating inequalities with deeply gendered impacts. For example, inadequate access to water for households in poor urban communities directly affects women as they are often in charge of collecting water (particularly in Africa and South Asia) (see Figure 5.5).

This pattern recurs across different urban services and infrastructure. There is a solid body of research confirming women's disadvantages in the use of urban space – be it safely walking the streets, claiming space in public parks, accessing or transportation, and adequate sanitation. Further, while there is much good research on cities, much of it assumes gender neutrality – whether in the household, transportation, or business districts. If our understanding of cities and potential policy reforms are to enhance social progress, it is critical to revisit urban planning from a gender-based perspective. We need to recognize

the practical and strategic needs of women. And we need to act on them. Moser (1993) acknowledged this fact decades ago, along with researchers and practitioners across the world.

5.4.1.2   Gendering Time

A useful way to address these issues is to gender our understanding of time itself. Inconvenient distances for accessing shops, schools, health services, and possibly jobs, all entail a significant appropriation of women's time (Falú and Segovia 2007; Falú 2008, 2013). For instance, traffic systems are geared mostly toward the pattern of men's commutes to and from their work to city centers, albeit with significant differences in quality and frequency according to an area's income level. Women who want to combine work and family need short trips to work.

These urban patterns indicate an appropriation of women's time and a devaluing of their economic contribution in both their homes and paid jobs. Ana Falú (2013) takes this analysis further by arguing that the different significance assigned to women's activities constitutes the central gender system for organizing urban space. Thus, the public sphere is marked mostly as masculine, so it acquires economic and social value. The private sphere, marked mostly as feminine, is given only symbolic value – not even women's reproductive work is recognized. Studies of time use indicate not only a gendered difference in how women and men use their hours, but also the impacts of these patterns on time allocation.

Deepening the data on this pattern would require "time-use" surveys and time-budget analyses in many diverse cities and at diverse urban scales. As noted by experts (e.g. Durán, Aguirre, Batthyany, and Scuro 2010)[10] on these approaches, two trends are worth

---

10   Some studies serve as reference for this issue: Aguirre, Rosario (2009) "Uso del tiempo y desigualdades de género en el trabajo no remunerado," in: Rosario Aguirre (editor) Las bases invisibles del bienestar social. El trabajo no remunerado en Uruguay. INE/INMUJERES/ UDELAR, FCS, DS/UNIFEM/UNFPA. Montevideo. Batthyany, Karina and Scuro, Lucía "Desafíos de Uruguay y la región"en Revista de Ciencias Sociales • Departamento de Sociología • Año XXIII / N° 27 • Diciembre 2010. Uso del tiempo, cuidados y bienestar.

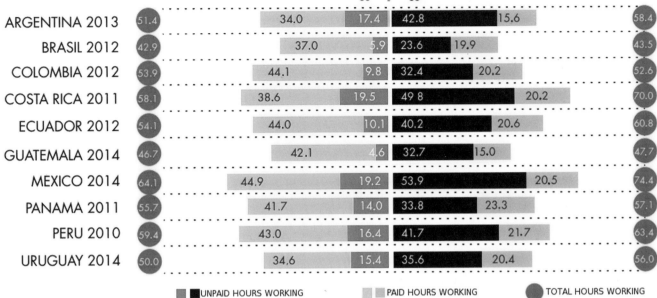

PAID AND UNPAID TIME SPENT
WORKING, IN WEEKLY HOURS

MEN | WOMEN

	Total (M)	Unpaid (M)	Paid (M)	Paid (W)	Unpaid (W)	Total (W)
ARGENTINA 2013	51.4	34.0	17.4	42.8	15.6	58.4
BRASIL 2012	42.9	37.0	5.9	23.6	19.9	43.5
COLOMBIA 2012	53.9	44.1	9.8	32.4	20.2	52.6
COSTA RICA 2011	58.1	38.6	19.5	49.8	20.2	70.0
ECUADOR 2012	54.1	44.0	10.1	40.2	20.6	60.8
GUATEMALA 2014	46.7	42.1	4.6	32.7	15.0	47.7
MEXICO 2014	64.1	44.9	19.2	53.9	20.5	74.4
PANAMA 2011	55.7	41.7	14.0	33.8	23.3	57.1
PERU 2010	59.4	43.0	16.4	41.7	21.7	63.4
URUGUAY 2014	50.0	34.6	15.4	35.6	20.4	56.0

■ UNPAID HOURS WORKING   ■ PAID HOURS WORKING   ● TOTAL HOURS WORKING

Figure 5.6 | Total time spent on paid and nonpaid work, disaggregated by sex, hours per week.
Source: ECLAC (2016)

mentioning: women devote most of their time to unpaid work and, further, typically work longer hours than their male counterparts. Time-budget studies highlight women's contributions to invisible, unremunerated labor, amounting to around 20–30 percent of the GDP of cities. A study conducted in ten countries in South America revealed that women devote, on average, 4.76 more weekly hours to both paid and unpaid work as compared to their male counterparts. In the cases of specific countries, the time deficit between male and female labor was found to be as high as nearly 12 hours (ECLAC 2016). Such approaches help us understand spatial and economic inequalities at the core of the sexual division of labor. Figure 5.6 provides a summary of these trends.

This is not new knowledge. Jane Jacobs (1961) taught us about the significance of the proximity of services and equipment for society in general and for women in particular. Gaps in knowledge about omitted subjects are also part of a larger epistemological question about the subjects deemed worthy of study. Such knowledge asymmetries are central to systemic inequality and its reproduction. We must address knowledge gaps when exploring productive and inclusive urban forms. Debates surrounding compact versus diffused cities, or the impact of new, urban spatial fragmentation, must address specific identity-based exclusions, mobility patterns of the marginalized, and more. We must focus on urban socio-economic plans that put

child-care and flexible working hours for women at the center of planning.

In brief, progressive urban design and planning must include omitted subjects.

5.4.1.3 Gendering Economic Growth

Another instance of how the study of omitted subjects can high-light barriers to social progress is how we measure growth. The Latin American case is helpful here. The State of the World's Cities[11] reaffirms ECLAC's findings (2012, 2014) regarding inequality in Latin America and the Caribbean (LAC). The study, led by the Global Urban Observatory of UN-Habitat, includes analyses of inputs, consumption, and expenditure in cities, Gini coefficient data for 101 cities in 47 countries, including 19 in LAC. It shows an index of 0.55 for LAC, making it the most unequal region in the world; any score above 0.4 is considered problematic.

However, this aggregate score hides further differences, especially by gender. Women with the same qualifications as men consistently earn less at all education levels; most women work in the low-end service sector. ECLAC finds that working women mostly do not receive social

Aguirre, Rosario, "Los cuidados entran en la agenda pública." Durán, María Ángeles (1999) Los costos invisibles de la enfermedad. Madrid, Fundación BBV. Falú, Ana (ed. 2002) "Ciudades para Varones y Mujeres. Herramientas para la acción." Falú, Ana; Morey, Patricia and Rainero, Liliana (ed. 2002) "Uso del tiempo y del espacio: asimetrías de género y de clase" en Ciudad y Vida Cotidiana. Asimetrías en el uso del tiempo y del espacio. Córdoba, Argentina. Informe Observatorio GENERO CEPAL 2012.
11   State of the World Cities 2008/2009. Harmonious Cities. UN Habitat, Earthscan, London. Sterling. Va.

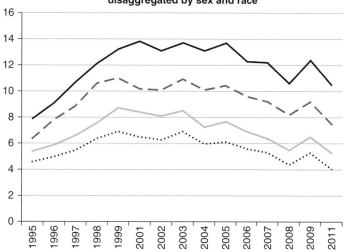

Unemployment rates for populations over 16 years of age, disaggregated by sex and race

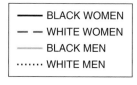

Figure 5.7 | Unemployment rate, disaggregated by sex and race.
Source: Based on PNAD (2013)

benefits nor do they match men's minimum wage. This is illustrated by the fact that 71 percent of caregivers are female domestic workers. Afro-descendant and indigenous populations evince even sharper inequalities, showing how race and gender intersect in complex ways (see Figure 5.7).

These income differentials need to be factored into analysis showing economic growth. According to ECLAC, GDP growth averaged 4.3 percent for the LAC region. Yet a paradox persists: Even as overall poverty declined during this period 45.6 to 25.4 percent, it increased among women in general and, particularly, women heads of households – the latter accounting for 38 percent of poor households and 43 percent of indigent households. The Argentine Institute for Social Development (IDESA 2014) finds, for example, that 80 percent of young Argentine mothers are poor.

Women's overloaded work burden is generating a paradox: the more women work, the poorer they are. Between 1990 and 2008, female participation in the work force increased by 21 percent, totaling over 100 million women in the LAC region. Also in this period, the region registered significant economic growth and a decrease in poverty. But poverty did not decrease among women. In 2002, there were 109 poor women for every 100 poor men; in 2012 the ratio rose to 118:100. Further, poor women have high fertility rates, giving birth to twice as many children than their rich counterparts. Accessing sexual, health, and reproductive rights is severely limited due to their low social and economic status (Falú 2013). It suggests we must link socio-economic patterns to age, education, and reproduction to understand how poverty functions for women.

These trends point to disjuncture between economic growth and overall social progress. The nature and quality of women's work, as well as its remuneration, does not automatically change with economic growth. Even when an economy grows, as was the case in the LAC region, most women remain unemployed; when they

work, they constitute the majority of the lowly paid service sector; thus 71 percent of domestic workers are women, most of whom are indigenous and/or black. Linking sexual division of labor to issues of poverty, household type, and access to services and equipment, it is important to note that 45 percent of mothers who work outside the home in Brazil do not have any support for childcare (ECLAC 2015).

Figure 5.8 analyzes the gendered trends between age and education level in garnering employment. The figure reveals the ways in which women's socio-economic development, in this case evident in higher rates of schooling, does not necessarily correlate with overall upward mobility and socio-economic well-being as is the case for their male counterparts.

One of the striking features of home-based work is its gendered construction. Because it makes it easier to perform childcare, cooking and other household duties, more women choose to work from home as compared to men. While we focused on the Latin American case, these patterns are evident throughout the world. Thus, data on the informal sector in India shows that home-based workers, constituting 23.5 million people, are mostly women. In the South Asian context, women's choices regarding the location of work are often dictated by social and cultural constraints on mobility. As a result, home-based work is often the best (and sometimes the only) option for many women in accessing income (Edwards and Field-Hendrey 2002; Kantor 2003; Sudarshan and Sinha 2011). But as in Latin America, this concentration of women in home-based work is unlikely to change even in times of robust development, such as India saw over the past two decades.

In addition to focusing on material considerations of space and income, we must consider the impact of noneconomic and social factors on social progress. Here the question of violence is, perhaps, the most urgent.

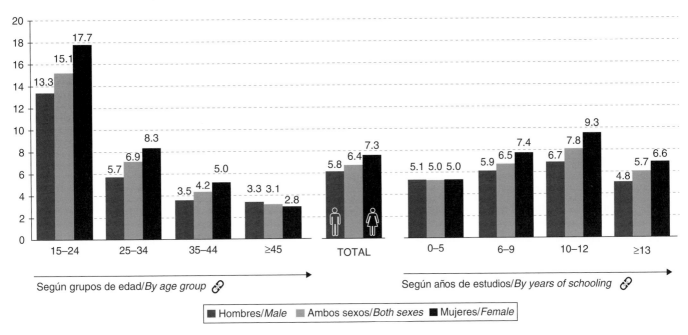

Figure 5.8 | Unemployment rates, disaggregated by age group and years of schooling.
Source: ECLAC (2014)

5.4.1.4   Increasing Violence in Cities

Violence is persistently inflicted upon the bodies of women. This crisis has found its way onto governmental and societal agendas. Diverse tools have been adopted and explored across the world: promotion of protocols, participatory planning, and gender responsive budgeting. But progress is slow. Violence persists in both public and private domains. But as with all policy measures, political will and adequate resourcing are key to achieve impact. This has not necessarily been forthcoming.

In order to advance women's agency, ECLAC's Equal Opportunity Observatory speaks of physical autonomies and the autonomies of political and economic decisions. Building on this approach, one can add the idea of autonomy in the use of urban space. Women and girls experience multiple and various forms of violence and harassment in public spaces: from leering to stalking and sexual assault. Certain types of harassment and violence, such as aggressive staring and passing comments, have been normalized as part of urban life in many cities. One study of four cities across the globe, found that almost 60 percent of women reported feeling unsafe in urban spaces.[12] Insecurity and the threat and reality of violence prevent women and girls from participating as full and equal citizens in community life. The Universal Declaration of Human Rights states that women and girls have a "right to the city." When this right is violated, women and girls can face significant obstacles to educational, economic, and political opportunities. Vera Malaguti Batista (2005) found that in the case of Rio de Janeiro, the undertow of structural violence naturalizes segregation, leading to hierarchical spaces and tangible and intangible lines of circulation to the disadvantage of women and girls.

This violence generates fear and inhibits life in the city. Kessler (2008) notes that this fear regulates social life and establishes the grounds for othering, conjuring stigmatization. This is acutely evident in the historical neglect of women's right to the public sphere. In short, compared to men, women lack the material and symbolic resources for enhancing their relative positioning in the city. Women experience a poverty of rights when it comes to political participation, bodily autonomy, equal access to work, infrastructure, transportation, and security (Falú 2009).

Invariably, for women and other invisible subjects, cities are a political territory. The city becomes a territory for confrontation, forcing all kinds of risk-taking in hopes of activating and achieving urban rights (Pitch 2008). While this risk-taking breeds a growing confidence in terms of advocacy, it nonetheless requires significant economic, cultural, and symbolic resources (Falú 2013).

5.5   Barriers to Accessing Urban Space

Social injustice in cities is made visible by particular deprivations across diverse domains – employment, transport, basic services, housing, public space, security, environmental destruction, and more. Affected social groups are often victims of diverse systemic inequalities; one example is women and indigenous populations, as explored in the previous section. More generally, regardless of socio-economic standing, all city residents are susceptible to inconvenient or negative situations such as breakdowns of basic infrastructure. But this does not amount to social injustice, a condition marked by multiple and interlocking deprivations across years, and often lifetimes.

---

12   Women in Cities International, "Learning from Women to Create Gender Inclusive Cities," 2009, UN Women, NY. CAFSU (2002). Women's Safety: From Dependence to Autonomy, Acting Together for Women's Safety. Montreal: www.femmesetvilles.org/pdfgeneral/cafsu_fiches_en.pdf. CISCSA (2006). Tools for the Promotion of Safe Cities from the Gender Perspective. Argentina: www.redmujer.org.ar/pdf_publicaciones/art_18.pdf.

Space can define city contexts, making visible power asymmetries. Particular classes and interest groups often have the economic and political weight that privileges their ambitions in shaping, designing, and reproducing a city (Logan and Molotch 1987; Sassen 2015b). This power often rests on the exclusion and oppression of certain demographics (Young 1990; Fainstein 2011).

Such vectors turn cities into ambiguous spaces. While a city is the locus of forces that feed its complexity and incompleteness (creativity, innovation, cooperation, solidarity), it also harbors and reproduces vile excesses, injustice, violence, and large-scale deprivations. Degraded and dangerous slums exemplify this reality (Davis 2006; UN-Habitat 2016a, 2016b). However, the inhumane conditions of basement bed-renting and overcrowding in well-run cities, such as London or Tokyo, signal routinized brutality. The accelerated growth of luxurious, often gated, residential, and consumption spaces further deepen spatial inequality. Rapid urbanization and the rise of inequalities are increasingly evident across the world (Piketty 2014; Oxfam 2016; Credit Suisse 2014). A growing number of major cities are becoming the visible expressions of concentrated wealth and power. These and other economic, political, and cultural factors, fuel distrust, anger, and frustration (Wilkinson and Pickett 2009). This mix is also increasingly motivating collective action in cities across the globe (Castells 2012). The growth of the rich 30–40 percent of the population in major cities is increasingly experienced as a massive loss of habitat by the poor and by the modest middle classes (Sassen 2014: chs. 1 and 3, 2015b).

These negative trends threaten the future of cities regarding rights, citizenship, and democracy (Harvey 2008; Schmid 2012). A rights-based approach may be necessary to understand how social progress can be achieved amidst these structural constraints in cities. Emphasizing the experiences of excluded and invisible urban populations invites us to ask how capitalist market forces can be regulated to attenuate the social effects of urban accumulation?

Next we explore four general processes that constitute major barriers or challenges to justice in cities: (a) the new logics underpinning urban capitalist production; (b) the unstable world of employment; (c) people on the move and urban space; (d) democracy, citizenship, and rights in the city.

5.5.1   The Production of Uneven Urban Space

The production of space in cities has historically been a deeply contested issue. The material and nonmaterial dimensions underlying these production processes result from convergent and disputed decisions made by diverse groups and mediated through institutions, culture, and technologies (Hall 1988; Soja 2000; Lefebvre 2003).

Many cities in the world did not result from formal state design and plans. They were built by residents and communities in, often, painfully slow increments. These processes involved a variety of strategies and tactics, requiring people of different skills and occupations, and diverse forms of land and property ownership (Simone 1994; Bayat 2010; Buechler 2014; Weinstein 2014). Such modes of urban development are particularly common in the Global South: *favelas* in Rio, *bastis*

in Delhi, *colonias populares* in Mexico City, *musseques* in Luanda, *amchi wastis* in Pune, *ashwa'iyyat* in Cairo, shacks or *mjondolos* in Durban, *sukumbhashi bastis* in Dhaka, *katchi abadis* in Karachi, *kampung liars* or *hak miliks* in Kuala Lumpur, and the *sahakhums* in Phnom Penh. Teresa Caldeira (2015) refers to a shared history of "auto-construction" – the production of the city by residents and communities building their own homes and neighborhoods. Auto-construction is marked by "transversal engagements with official logics of legal property, formal labor, colonial dominance, state regulation, and market capitalism."

Some actors are clearly more powerful than others in terms of resources and capacities to shape a city toward their own interests (Logan and Molotch 1987; Ren 2011; Lloyd 2010; Sassen 2015b, 2017). To forge a just urban society requires mapping the differential powers of people and groups as they drive urban dynamics. This knowledge is essential in assessing whether urban policies and investments are advancing or hindering more inclusive and sustainable pathways for cities (Davis 2006).

In today's world, cities and urban life cannot be disentangled from capitalist developments. Nonetheless a city is also legible through land markets, master plans, governance codes, norms, and laws. Further, capitalism itself functions through highly variable dynamics. The city has long been a locus of economic capitalism in Western modernity (Mumford 1961; Soja 2000). Over time, urban experiences, spaces, and lifestyles have been partly or wholly commodified (Schmid 2012: 55). This has been enabled by novel capacities (financialization, rapid technological change), increasing wealth concentration, ongoing environmental exploitation, and crisis tendencies (Harvey 2010; Piketty 2014; Streeck 2014; De Mattos 2016; Pieterse and Simone forthcoming). We can expect ongoing concentration of wealth, power, and influence.

In this context, Young's (1990) notion of the structural organization of decision-making and Molotch's (1976) concept of the City as a Growth Machine have evolved into a much wider and complex web of interactions. Much of it is geared toward the extraction and appropriation of urban value via combinations of new technologies and financial products, sophisticated scientific models, and regulatory frameworks (Sassen 2014: ch. 3, 2017). This has exacerbated wealth concentration, therewith precipitating wider implications for urban futures – e.g. large-scale purchases of building stock and land by powerful, footloose global groups operating in about 100 cities globally (Sassen 2015b). These processes carry risks – e.g. the loss of a city's social complexity and diversity, shifts from public to privatized spaces, the undermining of urban democracy and rights, and more.

Cities that attract the super-rich (e.g. London, New York, Miami, Frankfurt, Hong Kong, or Singapore) have long been different from the major cities of the Global South. But more recently the latter have seen the sharp expansion of high-end centers and neighborhoods for the rich and new types of economic sectors; this holds especially for the richer Latin American and Asian countries. These expanded rich zones coexist with poor migrants from rural areas – mostly small-holders increasingly expelled from their land by new modes of development (e.g. plantations, mining, expansion of urban areas, etc.). This feeds into a rapidly growing labor force that cannot find jobs. Combined with a lack of sound urban policies, the result is expanding slum urbanism. Notable examples include Dharavi in India, Manshiet in Egypt, Kibera in Kenya, Organi Town in Pakistan, Makoko in Nigeria or Villa El Salvador in Peru. Here, informality effectively constitutes a mode of urbanization (Roy 2009; Buechler 2014; Weinstein 2014).

Who produces the city and for which purposes? We can address this via two competing logics. The first regards the city, and space more generally, as a source of profit. The second logic deems the city as a potential source for achieving a dignified life and a thriving habitat. This logic has dominated the past three decades. And it has worked for many residents and firms, even if it has also brought sharper inequalities and losses for the modest middle classes (Fainstein 2011; Santos Junior et al. 2015; Sassen 2016b, 2017). This approach breaks from earlier spatial Keynesianism or social-democratic welfare regimes focused on distributive policies to promote spatial balance and equity (Sassen 1991/2001; Brenner 2004).

These tensions are evident in national and urban planning, regulatory frameworks, and urban laws that regulate how conflictive approaches are mediated. The New Urban Agenda adopted at the Habitat III (Quito, November 2016) explicitly confronts this issue pushing away from neoliberal orthodoxy in favor of more redistributive approaches rooted in The Right to the City.[13] These shifts are partly driven by recent collective actions in cities across the world. Significant increases in public protest and direct action push urban policy frameworks and institutions toward more inclusive and sustainable models. Habitat III signals a tipping point in global urban policies toward more just cities.

5.5.2 The Uncertain World of Work

A second key barrier to achieving a just city, especially in the developing world, is the limited capacity for job creation. It has also become an issue in developed countries regarding youth, with unemployment at 20–30 percent. Recent projections by the International Labor Organization confirm a bleak outlook across most world regions (ILO 2016). Growing automation further threatens a variety of occupational categories.

The economies and cities of the Global South show high rates of informal employment, concentrated in diverse unskilled activities with low productivity, irregular and low wages, and limited social safety nets. A recent study found that informal work in urban Latin America accounts for 46 percent of jobs, but is over 60 percent in Bolivia, Ecuador, Colombia, and Peru (ECLAC 2015). The Economic Commission for Africa (ECA) finds that in "recent years, African countries have experienced remarkable economic growth, but this has not generated sufficient decent jobs for the millions of young persons who enter the labor market each year. While it is estimated that there are 122 million new entrants annually, African countries created only 37 million jobs over the last decade, out of which only 28 percent were in wage-paying formal jobs" (ECA 2015: 2). Another significant share of

informal employment is increasingly linked to illegal economies, which means dangerous, unhealthy, and criminal jobs; this may account for 10 percent of global GDP (Carrión 2013). These trends materialize in frontiers and in cities, even though both are linked to wider global networks; the most common activities for illegal networks are in urban-based economic sectors such as real estate, commerce, and tourism (Carrión 2013).

Several causal factors help explain the difficulties in generating adequate employment levels. They vary across continents, countries, regions, cities: population growth, migration patterns, labor saving technologies, aging societies, and discrimination. However, one fundamental, underlying factor is the logic of capitalist development, today increasingly driven by the financialization of growing sectors of the economy; this produces extreme wealth concentration, recurrent crises, and low growth. We saw this mix most recently in the 2008 crisis: one example for the US is the bankruptcy of over 14 million households (Sassen 2014: ch. 3), and for Europe, massive job losses (Harvey 2012; Mendez 2014; Hadjimichalis 2013; BLS 2010). Wealth concentration can contribute to low growth because aggregate demand stagnates due to sharp differences in saving rates among diverse social groups (Stiglitz 2012; Dabla-Norris et al. 2015). Stagnation or decline in real wages means households and workers are unable to save, or save less.

Public policies aimed at reversing these trends must aim at expanding equality of opportunities. This includes tackling the discriminations faced by specific demographics (gender, age, race, etc.) as argued in the previous section. And they must reduce actual income differences across employment categories by capping upper-end earnings, raising minimum income levels, and introducing universal income grants. According to experts this is the only way to achieve equity in occupational and class positions (Dubet 2013); urban justice in developing market economies means generating jobs that are able to satisfy two objectives: level and quality. Emerging debates about technological innovation should include conditions for sustainable economies. And they should address the social question in its many manifestations, one of which is the importance of expanding social, solidarity, circular, and care economies. These economies are vital for rethinking employment modes that support modest communities in cities through urban justice, place-making, and new bases for network economies (UNEP 2014; Mason 2015; WBGU 2016).

5.5.3 People on the Move: Unequal Cities

Throughout history, cities have been sites of both expulsion and shelter. Regarding shelter, urban economic, social, cultural, and political infrastructural landscapes must be able to accommodate sudden inflows of people. The current rise of refugee flows into Europe has made visible the difficulties this entails.

Worldwide, migrations will escalate further due to a massive loss of habitat generated by climate change the escalation of land grabs for mining, plantations, and water extraction; these are migrations best understood as resulting from particular modes of "economic development" (Magdoff 2013; Arboleda 2015; Sassen 2016a, 2018). Some of the factors influencing massive land grabbing are free trade agreements, relaxing of foreign investment regulations in Global South countries, financialization of the global economy, higher prices of food, increasing interest in biofuels, and depletion of water reserves (Magdoff 2013; Sassen 2014: ch. 2, 2017). Climate change and conflicts around loss of habitat could both generate violence leading to further migrations (Reuveny 2007; IPCC 2013).

There are 740 million internal migrants, 50 percent of which are concentrated in the cities of ten highly industrialized countries; and there are over 230 million international migrants (IOM 2015). By far the largest share of migrants is hosted by cities and camps in Africa, a fact mostly overlooked in the debate in Europe. Also Asia is also a far larger host of refugees than the West. There is also an increased South–South migration in response to rapid economic growth in China and a few other Asian countries. The critical degradation of air, earth, and water has significantly impacted poor communities, leading to evacuations of an estimated 800 million people worldwide.

These diverse flows have transformed urbanization patterns (IOM 2015: 37; see also Liu-Farrer 2011), notably a major expansion of informal housing and commerce, to the point that the regular economy is so remote that it becomes almost inaccessible for people with limited mobility. This also makes it almost impossible for citizens and refugees to access and exercise social and civic rights. The cumulative character of these dynamics across years or decades is producing overlapping slum urbanisms (IOM 2015: 45).

5.6   Technology and the City

The last two decades have seen a noticeable interest in the potential of digital technology to save the city from congestion, pollution, waste, crime, uneven service provision, information gaps, and more. Most of it has been via the marketing version of smart cities. However, across time and place, people and social conditions have complicated the straightforward implementation of technologies. And they do so also today. The specific materialities of daily life and people's cultures of use are not easily predictable. Such a mix can unsettle or disrupt the best technical designs – and has done so in past eras and in today's digitally driven world. This holds at many levels – from advanced complex systems to daily applications of standard technologies.

5.6.1   Digitization: Cities No Longer Matter?

Back in the 1980s, massive developments in telecommunications and the ascendance of information industries led analysts and politicians to proclaim the end of cities. Cities, they told us, would become obsolete as economic entities. The growth of information industries would allow firms and workers to remain connected no matter their locations. The digitizing of both services and trade would shift many economic transactions to electronic networks, where they could move instantaneously around the globe or within a country. Many, though not all, of these predictions have taken place. From the 1970s onward, there have been large-scale relocations of offices and factories to areas less congested and cheaper than central cities. And the growth of computerization meant that clerical work could be located anywhere – in a clerical "factory" in the Bahamas or China or a home in a nearby suburb.

But the end of cities as key economic centers has not happened. Already back in the early 1990s, Sassen (1991) argued that the globalization and digitization of economic activity would in fact strengthen the role of major cities in national and global operations. While large national corporations had until the 1980s basically executed most of their functions in-house, once deregulation and globalization took off, the knowledge inputs of these firms were going to escalate dramatically. A firm operating in 20 or 30 or more countries would need specialized bits of knowledge of all sorts: it might range from a need of 85 hours of Chinese lawyering and accounting, 25 hours of Argentinian investment preferences, and so on. It would not make sense to hire full-time staff to execute these tasks. Out of these needs came the making of a vast, state of the art, and innovative intermediate sector.

In short, the global city function refers to a growing number of cities worldwide becoming "production" sites for some of the most complex and advanced inputs needed by firms operating globally – whether these were firms in mining, engineering, entertainment sectors, finance, and more.

Contesting the widespread notion in the 1980s that place no longer mattered to global firms in a digital era, Sassen argued that while old-style cities were in fact dying, a new type of complex operational space was installing itself in a growing number of major cities across the world (Sassen 2016a, 2017). For Sassen the "Global City function" is an extreme space for the production and/or implementation of very diverse and very complex intermediate capabilities. This did not refer to the whole city; she posited that the Global City was a complex, highly variable, and creative production function addressing the complex needs of firms operating globally. She did also warn that this intermediation function would have a large shadow effect on the cities where it operated. We have clearly seen this effect in the sharp rise of housing prices and the massive buying of properties in global cities across the world.

The much announced spatial dispersion of economic activities is only half of today's digital age. The other half is the sharpened spatial concentrations of major economic sectors in cities – whether in the shape of "Silicon Valleys" or of major financial centers. Globalization and digitization brought with them a rapidly growing expansion of state-of-the-art knowledge sectors in a rapidly expanding number of cities across the world. Sassen's "global city functions" are now evident in almost 100 major and minor (global) cities.

These trends of the 1980s, 1990s, and onward went against the major models emphasizing territorial dispersal. That was not an unreasonable proposition, especially considering the high cost of locating a business in a major downtown area. While major cities saw a sharp growth of smaller, highly specialized, and high-profit firms from the 1980s onwards, they also saw the departure of large, and more routinized, commercial banks, insurance firms, and corporate headquarters. In fact, these departures were far more visible and received far more media attention than the arrival of small highly specialized, many foreign, intermediate firms. This all complicated the understanding of the role of cities in the emerging new global economy.

A second major trend that went against predictions of the demise of cities as core economic centers was the arrival and employment of a rapidly growing low-wage workforce. They served in the new emerging firms and in the households of the growing numbers of high-income young specialized experts. As the middle classes in many major cities across the world escaped impoverished cities losing the large traditional firms, the low-wage labor market expanded rapidly given escalating demand from the new type of economy installing itself in these cities.

This new phase in old cities made visible the fact that even the most advanced information industries, such as global finance and specialized corporate legal and accounting services, have a production process that is partly place-bound: not all of the activities of these industries circulate in electronic networks. Secondly, it made visible the growth of bi-modal labor markets, where demand was centered on high-income specialized professionals and very low-wage workers. Out were the vast middle sectors that had been the core workforce in large traditional corporations and now had become obsolete. It also meant the decline of the thriving middle classes and the rise of a very high-income upper middle class.

Thus emerges an economic configuration quite different from that suggested by the concept of information economy. Examining these transformations via a focus on the city allows us to capture a whole range of trends that are far less visible if we focus on national level data. Further, we recover the material conditions, production sites, and place-boundedness that are also part of globalization and the digitized economy. To understand the new digitized elements in our economies, we actually need detailed examinations of a broad range of activities, firms, markets, and physical infrastructures that go beyond images of global electronic networks and the new globally circulating professional classes.

Digital technologies have not made cities obsolete, but they have altered the economic function of cities (Greenfield 2017). The notion of a global economy has become deeply entrenched in political and media circles all around the world. Yet its dominant images – the instantaneous transmission of money around the globe, the information economy, the neutralization of distance through telematics – are partial, and hence profoundly inadequate, representations of what globalization and the rise of information economies actually entail for the concrete life of cities.

Missing from this abstract model are the actual material processes, activities, and infrastructures crucial to the implementation of globalization. And if this is so, what does it tell us about the importance of place and its far greater mix of diverse economic sectors and social groups than is suggested by the prevalent imagery of high-level corporate economic globalization and information flows? Is there a new and strategic role for major cities, a role linked to the formation of a truly global economic system, a role not sufficiently recognized by analysts and policy-makers? Economic globalization is not only about massive dispersal of operations across the world but also about thick places where key activities concentrate as is the case with all major global cities?

Overlooking the spatial dimension of economic globalization and over-emphasizing the virtual information dimensions have served to distort the role played by major cities in the current phase of economic globalization. A focus on cities almost inevitably brings with it recognition of the existence of multiple social groups, neighborhoods, contestations, claims, and inequalities. In view of this, we move the discussion into a critical exploration of the "promise" and challenges of technology in the city.

5.6.2 The Planned and Unplanned City: Can the Formal and Informal Work Together?

Note: This section draws heavily on Hyman and Pieterse forthcoming.

Contemporary studies on urban development tend to focus on large-scale megaprojects such as airport hubs, satellite towns, and master-planned university campuses in rapidly developing cities in Asia, Africa, and the Middle East. It makes one think of "megastructure porn." Insufficient attention has gone to how such megaprojects have eventually been appropriated by the public for purposes that diverge from – and often negate – their intended uses. Here we examine the informal, creative, and unsanctioned reconfigurations of urban megaprojects in order to rethink some of our fundamental assumptions about the aesthetic, social, and spatial dimensions of urbanization. The informal uses of formal infrastructure projects do not stand in opposition to one another, but rather need to be understood as mutually beneficial processes.

African cities are arguably postnetworked cities, simply because swathes of urban settlements and the built environment do in fact function. Yet, they have somehow bypassed the conventional notion of the modern networked city supported by the "modern infrastructural ideal" (Graham and Marvin 2001) or the "integrated urban ideal" (Gandy 2004). Modern configurations of conventional service delivery modalities are not uniformly appropriate for cities of the Global South.

Yet insufficient attention has gone to the innovative and transient systems extended as hybrid provisional solutions in the debate on service delivery in impoverished urban settlements (Harris 2016). Harris (2016: 155) explains that hybrid systems "defy easy categorization or generalization" as a result of their context specific emergence, "impacted by specific technical, social and institutional realties," which Jaglin (2014) refers to as sociotechnical dispositifs. By embracing sociotechnical hybridization, diversity, and permanently heterogeneous assemblages, it is no longer necessary to remain yoked to the traditional urban growth trajectory of prenetworked to the postnetworked city (Jaglin 2016). Robust decentralized hybrid networks are constituted by technological interventions, the devolution of management authority, and failing local urban policy reform. These networks ensure daily reproductions, providing services in unconventional ways. It is in this way that Jaglin (2016) raises the possibility of "off-network cities."

Hybrid delivery arrangements can be used for more than delivering basic services to the urban poor. Informal operators, alternative suppliers, and small-scale providers, who operate alongside, or as an appendage to, conventional utilities, recognize the demand and spending power of urban societies. They have taken it upon themselves to deliver services where there is a lack of conventional modes (Jaglin 2014). The socio-economic and spatial dynamics that determine demand include the emerging middle class as well as unregulated, mushrooming urban sprawl. Thus some dispositifs can be characterized as modern, and delivered with a degree of sophistication while others are makeshift, and generally low-cost (Jaglin 2016). Conventional operators, relying on conventional delivery modes, are unable to contend with these socio-economic and spatial specificities. Examples of hybrid configurations are dotted across Africa's urban settlements. These bring the argument to life and offer a taste of the imagination of Africa's urban residents and the diverse possibilities for service delivery.

An exemplary case is M-Kopa, a Kenyan based private company, which provides reliable electricity to households unconnected from the grid (Tracy and Jacobson 2012), and households who are unsatisfied with existing, interrupted services. A combination of decentralized solar power and telecommunication technologies provide consumers with access to clean and affordable electricity while circumventing the need for central delivery networks and accommodating income volatility (Rolffs et al. 2014). Consumers pay a deposit on a decentralized solar system[14] via the mobile payment platform, M-PESA, which allows the frequency and size of balance repayment to be distributed over time depending on cash flow and income. Daily repayments are designed to be less than the average spent on alternative fuels such as kerosene, offering economic and environmental dividends. The upfront deposit is considered to be relatively high, because it incentivizes a long-term commitment; this limits competition and flexibility by locking consumers into a particular service provider. The challenge of lock-in associated with large-scale industrial infrastructure systems is a feature of conventional services and can also apply in certain cases to hybrid systems as discussed by Ahlers et al.'s (2013) with regard to Greater Maputo.

The M-Kopa case provides a useful indicator for how medium-tech innovations can be deployed to enhance organic, affordable practices. These may not be the most technologically advanced, but provide a basis from which to integrate systems in the future, whilst also being able to make a material difference in the lives of those who are most marginalized and excluded from urban opportunities.

5.6.3 When Technology Alters Urban Space

Technology has the ability to promote social change and advance urban development in numerous positive ways. In theory, these ways also include substantial improvements in the urban environment and

how we interact with the natural world. The history of technology innovation demonstrates that with each major shift there are profound social and cultural adaptations that follow in tow (Ahlers et al. 2013). Technology sociologists suggest that we are on the cusp of a number of significant technological convergences that could herald very different forms of mobility, service provision, living arrangements and socialities. In order to appreciate the potential scope of these advances, we will take a brief detour through the anticipated "internet of things" and "smart city" potentialities. These agendas incorporate new transportation systems, robotics, virtual reality, and health breakthroughs that could lead to significant improvements in urban livability, convenience, and efficiency.

While the benefits and application of technology can vary depending on location, access, affordability, and the people using it, in general terms thoughtfully deployed technological innovations can result in positive development of urban areas. Moreover, technological innovation has the potential to improve the day-to-day lives of city residents across the world. In practice we are more likely to see these experiments going from prototype to deployment in developed societies, especially wealthy cities and a substantial market for automated intelligent services.

A few examples are worth mentioning. In transportation, new advances in autonomous vehicles could change the ways people move in cities as they can navigate busy streets using advanced GPS technology. Sensors and on-board computer systems provide continuous feedback between the exterior environment and the vehicle's actions. Passengers can opt to focus on other issues and avoid the stress of commuting in dense urban environments. This could be of considerable use to the elderly, who might be uncomfortable handling stressful driving situations. There are also safety benefits as such systems can react quickly to sudden changes by sensing a speeding car in the opposite lane, or detecting erratic driving behavior in other vehicles. If an accident does occur, AVs equipped with automated connections to emergency services can share life-saving information over a network (National Highway Traffic Safety Administration 2016).

Another projected technological advance is that of personal rapid transit, which would take the form of personal pods seating 1–2 people (Skytran 2016). These could be stored on the roofs or sides of buildings and offer on-demand transportation through a network of rails, removing the need for large roadways near living areas. For longer distances and greener commuting, maglev pods offer cross-country travel. Such advances will radically change how people move and interact with the city. Such benefits should be available to all sectors of society regardless of sociocultural and economic conditions.

The shift from human-led to computer-led actions extends to homes. Future homes will be enabled to execute daily activities for occupants. Houses managed by centralized systems that oversee electricity, water and gas, waste disposal, and more. Networks can oversee blocks and

---

14   This includes PV panels, ceiling lights, and charging outlets for mobile phones and a radio.

city levels in order to optimize resource consumption and regulate demand/supply.

Elements of such systems have already been introduced in Songdo, South Korea (Songdo IBD, 2015). Designed from the beginning as a "Smart City," waste is ferried directly from houses to purification facilities through hidden pipelines, and computer systems are integrated throughout the city – in homes, roads, light fixtures, and buildings. Environmentally sustainable living practices could become much more commonplace and easy to manage. Monitoring of functions could cover neighborhoods within a wider city-network, and further enable monitoring city-wide environmental policy.

Daily tasks – cleaning, cooking, and shopping – can become easier for both rich and poor households, both young and old. Rooms could be adaptive, changing shape or design based on time-of-day, or even physical parameters. If several guests arrive for dinner, the room dimensions and furniture could automatically open up space. Such applications have already been developed for smaller levels with "Exobuilding" – a large tent-canopy that changes based on physical factors. We stress again that this technology should be available to all demographic sectors, without price or location barriers.

Buildings themselves can benefit from new technology – improving urban environments rather than disrupting it. Living buildings, which can be "living," "regenerative," and "adaptive" offer unique possibilities (Nugent et al. 2011). In the first option, buildings are powered by their natural environment, harnessing rain for water and wind/sun for power. Regenerative structures actually improve their environment by using biotic coating and materials to increase plant life and habitats. They also produce more energy than required and can share it with nearby structures. Adaptive buildings are open and able to be moved or changed to fit the needs of a location or climate, and can be repurposed much more easily than traditional buildings.

From a macro perspective of smart homes and smart cities can offer an all-encompassing integration of technology and urban space/development. These integrated systems at the city-level provide a way to manage infrastructure and keep residents "connected to the city." People could be directly integrated as part of the city system, allowing more accurate planning and more speedy responses to individual and community needs (Malecki 2014) – whether fixing a communal tennis court or adding security in a disadvantaged community.

Overall, technological advancements have a surplus of positive benefits for city life. As long as they remain inclusive, and account for sociocultural differences, they can improve urban life for residents anywhere in the world.

As discussed earlier, it is not necessarily the case that just and inclusive decisions will be taken in future developments of cities. It is therefore imperative to locate the smart city agenda within a larger matrix of policy design, negotiation, prioritization, and sequencing that should mediate the allocation of scarce resources. Beyond the ideal of extending technological innovations in mobility, construction, and household functioning to everyone, the reality is that currently these

innovations are reinforcing the intensification of urban inequalities. Put differently, smart city solutions are commodified as elite offerings for gated living and business parks; these formats essentially eliminate cityness and further raise the barriers to full urban inclusion. It is important to remain open to the potential of technological innovations, especially when it forms parts of a larger agenda for universal access to basic services. These innovations require explicit forums where the implicit tradeoffs can be aired, debated, and resolved. Another important dimension of the role and function of technology is its meaning and use-value, usually very different from the engineers' perspective.

5.6.4   Deploying Technical Capabilities in the City

Urban policy-makers have identified new technologies as motors of urban development and social change. Yet there is often a distinct gap between the deployment of high-tech "solutions" and the technical acumen and cultural expectations of the urban population. The result is that these new technologies are poorly utilized, and often serve more as an aesthetic rather than functional purpose. We need more productive approaches to the use of technology. An effective example is the formulation of low- and "middle"-tech approaches that celebrate the transformative power of new technologies while also acknowledging the social, technical, and financial limitations of urban dwellers, especially in developing countries.

We must consider the importance that rapidly developing cities are placing on information technology as motors for urban development and social change. Southeast Asian cities such as Bangkok, Kuala Lumpur, and Singapore, evince distinct gaps between the introduction of sophisticated technologies, the technical acumen of the urban population, and the ability of local economies and education systems to produce tech-related employment opportunities. A concrete example is in the many taxis outfitted with a GPS system and the many taxi drivers that do not know how to operate them. Similarly, most new buildings in Southeast Asia are outfitted with touchscreen information panels, but they are often inoperable, and thus serve more of an aesthetic rather than functional purpose. Finally, quite a few cities have devoted considerable resources to developing technology-focused innovation districts to house firms from IT, biotechnology, and other such fields. Yet many of these districts fail to attract enough companies. They deploy their "high-tech" image as a real estate development strategy aimed at selling condominiums and filling shopping centers in the immediate surroundings of "high-technology zones," which themselves suffer from very low tenancy rates.

How can we devise a more productive approach to the use of technology in rapidly developing cities, and in rapidly developing world regions such as Southeast Asia? A more appropriate response might be to devise low-tech, or "middle-tech" approaches that acknowledge both the transformative power of new technologies, and the social, technical, and financial limitations of urban dwellers in developing countries. In this regard the investigations of Filip de Boeck (2012) and Sylvy Jaglin (2014, 2016) into hybrid infrastructure

5

architectures in poor African cities provide useful tools and entry points.

5.6.5 Digital Ecologies of Meaning

Cities are particularly complex and mixed settings. The enormous variety of urban issues makes cities both a key site for the implementation of an extremely broad range of technologies, and a lens to detect what all else might benefit from developing applications.[15] The city becomes a site for both implementation and discovery of what else is needed. It allows us to understand a range of diverse interactions between users (whether systems, organizations, or people) and digital technologies (more precisely, the design and implementation of these technologies).

The city can bring to the fore features of electronic interactive domains that remain insufficiently examined. The technical properties of these domains deliver their utility to users through complex ecologies that include more, often much more, than the technical capacities in play (Sassen 2012, 2017). Such ecologies include: (a) "nontechnological" variables – the social, the subjective, the political, all variables that characterize users more so than technology; (b) the fact that these "nontechnological" variables can and do shape technical developments signals that they could do much more of this, and thereby broaden the range of cultures and social differences in play; and (c) they could include the cultures of use of many very different users. It is this intermediation that brings in the social, the political, the economic, the cultural, and more, into a technical space.

The importance of including such variables is made clear in so-called smart city development. Here, technology inputs are mostly run centrally by big firms; this is good for handling standardized needs. But it leaves users' capacities and at least some needs out of the picture. Users are limited to choosing from predesigned options, but cannot contribute to those choices (and thereby experience a technical learning curve). In short, one key dimension of a genuinely smart city is open-sourcing the pertinent systems (Sassen 2015a).

As we add intelligence to tools and systems we must enable human intelligence to move as well, to be part of it. This is not confined to programming. Critical are forms of knowledge that bring in the social, the cultural, and the political into the digital as it instantiates in diverse settings. If we do not introduce these, admittedly messy, components we delegate the making of knowledge about these technologies to the engineers and software designers. From the social perspective this would mean we simply fall back onto basic mechanizing, where the machine takes over and our role disappears or is routinized. Instead, we should recognize that at least some of these technologies, when used by people, can be constituted/experienced partly in social terms.

Considering electronic interactive domains as part of larger ecologies, (rather than as merely technology) we make conceptual and empirical

room for the broad range of social logics driving users and the diverse cultures of use through which digital interactive spaces acquires meaning. Each of these logics and cultures activates an ecology. Such activating features tend to be absent in much of today's technically driven analysis of digital capabilities and their capacity to address human needs (and whims). And herein lies a vast research and theorization agenda.

5.7 Just Urban Societies and the Right to the City

There is growing interest in bringing social justice into questions of development to achieve an expanded understanding of human well-being. The contributions of thinkers like John Rawls, Amartya Sen, Nancy Fraser, Iris Marion Young, Achille Mbembe, among others come to mind. It is in this intellectual context that urban justice has emerged as an important perspective to think about actual and future urban trajectories. However, the profound challenges associated with intensifying inequality, privatization of the commons, urbanization of poverty, rising insecurity, and acute gender inequality have also played a major role in exploring the relevance of urban justice. These issues are central to the debate about the Right to the City.

5.7.1 Notions of Urban Justice

Fainstein (2011: 3) argues that the instinctive notion of injustice "consist of actions that disadvantage those who already have less or who are excluded from entitlements enjoyed by others who are no more deserving." Thinking in urban terms, justice also entails the capacities of citizens to create and use urban spaces. Increasing income inequalities and the social exclusion of significant groups, generate negative effects for social interactions. The making of unjust cities has specific negative impacts on integrating vulnerable social groups into a thriving urban polity (e.g. Sennett 2018).

Across the world, spatial fragmentation and intensified separation of functions are sharpening existing social divides and inequalities – access to places of employment, social services, and public spaces. This is particularly discriminating against social groups with constrained mobility, e.g. the elderly, disabled, and chronically poor groups, women responsible for dependent populations, including children. Increasingly we should add sharp increases in travel times between home and work; estimates for large cities show average travel time on public transport can be two times more than for private cars. Residents of poor suburbs can spend three or four hours a day travelling, with significant impacts in quality of life (CAF 2011).

A key feature in most Global South cities is spatial illegality – with its direct and indirect barriers to securing urban justice. It includes insecure tenure through the threat and reality of forced evictions. It deeply affects household investment patterns and individual and collective

---

15   For instance in one project we have found an acute shortage of applications that might enable the life of low-income workers both at the job and in their neighborhoods (see, e.g. Sassen 2015a).

social development. Forced evictions affect millions of households annually (Sassen 2016a).

But even without eviction, spatial illegality represents a condition of terminal delay. Communities who live with this uncertainty also experience delayed provision of public services. Sustained political contestation and struggle are often the only way of getting basic services. Invariably, basic human development outcomes are thus delayed or denied. This exposes the tension between enforcing legal and regulatory rules versus providing basic services to address fundamental human rights.

Most slum, makeshift, and peripheral communities live in this limbo between victimization and recognition. Individual lives are marked by a combination of insecure tenure and informal employment. It constrains a life as equal citizens and legitimate stakeholders in urban development. These constraints are both formal – with the lack of a legal address or work contract – as well as affective, including the difficulty of being considered a full legal resident. "Encroachment" or "trespassing" become operative designations. Thus urban development interventions aimed at improving slum conditions must go beyond economic and spatial interventions. They must also confront the core questions of legitimate and legal urban residence. Legitimate rights to land and tenure are key for urban justice.

We must recognize the societal and individual costs of high levels of inequality. The deterioration in the quality of social relations can lead to violence, anger, malaise, depression, loneliness, and distrust (Wilkinson and Pickett 2009). In political cultural terms, inequality can also fuel growing levels of distrust and disaffection with democracy. Thus recently we have seen massive urban collective action against the causes and manifestations of urban injustice; this has put enormous pressure on democratic institutions charged with regulating social tensions (Latinobarómetro Database; Castells 2012; Hadjimichalis 2013; Ruiz 2015).

How can urban institutions help improve the quality of social relations? How might cities become spaces for cooperation and solidarity? These questions pose a big challenge for urban planners. It calls for improving their efficacy to produce just urban spaces that foster inclusiveness, sociability, cooperation, and autonomy.[16] An important challenge is how to deal with increasingly conflictive approaches about what a city is for: a place for capital accumulation versus a place for human development? We must go beyond the commodification of urban space (Schmid 2012) and ask "Who Owns the City?" (Sassen 2015b).

5.7.2 Urban Justice via the Right to the City

This wide range of issues raises the concept of "The Right to the City," now also a movement. Diverse global, national, and local initiatives

are growing around this notion, e.g. the World Charter for the Right to the City, the European Charter for Human Rights in the City, the City Statute of Brazil, the Montreal Charter of Rights to the City, and the Mexico City Charter for the Right to the City (Moura and Azevedo 2016; Purcell 2013).

The World Charter for the Right to the City broadens the traditional focus on improving the quality of life based on housing and the neighborhood, and going beyond the city to encompass its rural surroundings. The city becomes a protective mechanism for its population. This implies a new way of respecting, defending, and fulfilling the civic, political, economic, social, cultural, and environmental rights guaranteed in regional and international human rights instruments.[17]

In the Mexican case, the Right to the City is defined as:

> … the equitable use of cities within the principles of sustainability, democracy, equity, and social justice. It is a collective right of the inhabitants of cities, conferring to them legitimacy of action and organization, based on respect for their differences, expressions, and cultural practices, with the objective to achieve full exercise of the Right to Free Determination and to an adequate level of life. The Right to the City is interdependent of all the integrally-conceived, internationally recognized human rights, and therefore includes all the civil, political, economic, social, cultural and environmental rights regulated in the international human rights treaties (México City Charter for the Right to the City 2010).[18]

The progressive character of this notion is evident in seeing the City as a collective good and recognizing the multiple rights for its inhabitants. Nevertheless, as a concept and political claim it remains the focus of robust debates among academics, urban movements, and politicians. At stake is whether the concept can produce actions that transform urbanization patterns.

The Right to the City is contested because, on the one hand, it can be a liberal-democratic framework focused on rights in relation to liberties, and, on the other, can ensure legal protections for those who lack full rights and thus use urban political struggles to achieve those rights (Purcell 2013).

That struggle is part of executing the right to the city as a collective right. The progressive interpretation of the right to the city does not accept the liberal proposition that when a legal right is "granted," political actions come to a close (Purcell 2013: 142). This draws on Lefebvre, who sees the Right to the City as an active and ongoing transforming of the actual existing city, opening up possibilities for active involvement in the production of new urban landscapes, institutions, and social relations (Lefebvre 1996; Harvey 2008; Schmid 2012; Purcell 2013).

---

[16] One highly innovative experience is the Theatrum Mundi Project, led by Richard Sennett that interrogates how urban design or urban landscapes could foster cooperation, respect, encounters, and so forth. See www.thetro-mundi.org
[17] Retrieved from www.urbanreinventors.net/3/wsf.pdf
[18] Retrieved from www.hicgs.org/content/Mexico_Charter_R2C_2010.pdf

5

211

5.7.3 Who Is the Citizen? Membership and Its Instabilities

The Right to the City is closely connected with broader conceptions of citizenship. We can "think of citizenship as an incompletely theorized contract between the rights-bearing individual and her state. It is in this incompleteness of citizenship that lies the possibility for its long and mutating life" (Sassen 2008: ch. 5). This signals that the "citizen" is made and remade: and this includes making by those who do not belong, whether the foreigner outside or the foreigner inside a country.

Historically, outsiders have been a key factor for ensuring this incompleteness of citizenship. They are the ones who have subjected the institution to new types of claims across time and place, whether it is nonproperty owners in England's 1800s claiming rights to citizenship or gays and lesbians in 2000 claiming the same rights as other citizens. Women, minoritized citizens, asylum seekers, immigrants, all have contributed to expand the rights of all citizens in often multigenerational trajectories. They may not have gained much power in this process, but their powerlessness became complex – they made a history, a politics.

Making by the powerless has a very different temporality from that of making by the powerful. It can take decades and even centuries, but in the long run of history the powerless are always the majority. And when their demands for expanded inclusions succeeded, they strengthened the institution of citizenship partly by making it more complex and incomplete, a mix that enables adjustments in the meaning of membership across diverse historical epochs and their specific modes of making the spaces for belonging.

Today the meaning itself of the national state and national membership are becoming unstable, and either neutralize nationhood or distort it into a visceral prepolitical passion. Over the last few decades, we have seen the emergence of a larger operational space for human mobilities that cuts across all sorts of borders and tends to reposition experiences of membership away from the national container. Experiences of membership shift to other types of entities. These include transnational oppositional politics – of identity, sexual preferences, feminisms, environmental, liberation struggles, and many more. Cities, not nation-states, are often the spaces where these counterpolitics instantiate. We also see this ascendance of cities in the formation of new types of geographies of power that cut across old divides – North/South, East/West – and across interstate borders of all sorts and materialize in a sequence of major cities. One enabling tool for these new types of geographies of privilege is the proliferation of specialized visas enabling firms to hire what are de facto immigrant workers but are pointedly referred to as "foreign professionals."[19] The powerless are also creating such new geographies that cut across borders and are shaped through very specific routings and instruments: we can think of refugees, certain types of small-traders, cultural circuits, and more. Again, cities are critical anchors in these geographies.

Increasingly, for today's mobile global class of the very rich, citizenship or formal state-authorized membership has diminished meaning – they do not need it to gain access to foreign national territories. In contrast, for the dispossessed, citizenship can be a critical tool for survival, though it rarely delivers. Citizens are losing rights in Western neoliberalized countries and economic corporate actors are gaining rights (Sassen 2008: ch. 6). Ironically, it is the claims by those who have barely been recognized in law – a broad mix of minoritized subjects, including immigrants and refugees – that have given new life to the meaning of citizenship. And historically Europe, especially, has shown us how the claims by outsiders for access to hospitals, schools, transport, and more, contributed to strengthen the publicness of such facilities, thereby also benefitting citizens. But today these victories are under major attack in almost all Western countries. One question this raises is whether the current influx of refugees and migrants might serve once again to expand the meaning of citizenship by adding elements. We have already seen this in the case of same-sex marriage, cross-caste, or cross-tribal marriage, etc.

This possibility of expanding the meaning of citizenship is to a large extent furthered by urban conditions. Cities function as a kind of natural experiment enabling new mixes of meanings, and the unsettlement of older convictions strengthen the publicness of major facilities in the long run (even if not immediately). The interesting historically strategic role of "the foreigner" – especially the disadvantaged poor immigrant and asylum seeker – is to generate claims for an expanding domain of the public good because it is their space for survival. The growing numbers of citizens who are losing ground given the new politics of "austerity" can also benefit from these claims by the outsiders, because they are becoming outsiders in their own countries.

Can we learn something from this European history of multiple microintegrations alongside, often, murderous hatred of the outsider? It is a fact that the immigrant groups of the past are today reasonably well absorbed, notwithstanding their differences. They have given us many of today's citizens. They are not at issue in today's debates. But in their time, they were the issue.

Anti-immigrant sentiment and attacks happened in each of the major immigration phases in all European countries. No labor-receiving country managed to avoid such xenophobic sentiments, even when the foreigner was the same phenotype, religion, or culture as the native – in short, even when the outsider was basically your cousin. No European country has a spotless record. French workers killed Italian workers in the salt mines in the 1800s and objected to German and Belgian workers hired for Haussmann's rebuilding of Paris, in both cases invoking that they were the wrong types of Catholics.

History and demography suggest that those fighting for incorporation in the long run won, even though only partly. The "wrong Catholic" of yesterday's Europe still lives on dressed in a variety of new

---

19   One instance of these high-end bordered spaces are the private financial trading network that are estimated to account for up to 70 percent of financial trading worldwide according to the US Federal Reserve Bank, which refers to them as "dark pools in finance." Though digital, they depend on massive infrastructures, and these tend to be in cities, close to or in the financial centers; neither the state nor existing national law plays much of a role in these types of spaces (Sassen 2014, Chs. 1 and 3).

identities: perhaps today it is the newly arrived Muslim. But what the past does tell us is that we fool ourselves if we think that differences of phenotype, religion, and culture are the issue, and that these are obstacles built in stone and hence insurmountable.

Migration hinges on a move between two worlds, even if within a single region or country – such as East Germans moving to West Germany who were seen as a different ethnic group and one with undesirable traits. Misplaced fear and prejudice are key players and so is today's European "austerity" politics, one that benefits the rich corporate sector and hurts the middle and working classes, who then see in the foreigner yet another threat. Social membership takes time, and struggle. But it can eventually feed into more formal meanings of membership. At its best, our diversities, our foreignness, feed into dynamics that value this complexity of membership and its inevitable incompleteness.

It is with this historical perspective in mind that we want to combine the normative horizon of urban justice, as captured in the Right to the City, and, on the other, everyday practices of space-making by ordinary citizens struggling to retain a foothold in the city. Thus we move on to a series of "modest interventions" from around the world that show us the agency of exploited and marginalized social groups in the city. These vignettes also serve as a bridge to the final chapter where we explore more practical multiscalar recommendations to advance social progress in the city of the twenty-first century.

5.7.4 Modest Interventions Also Matter

Here we focus on efforts aiming at supporting women's needs and efforts. These are just some of the multiple and mostly modest organizations that are multiplying across the world.

5.7.4.1 Initiatives by Women for Women

Here we present a series of very modest interventions aimed at enabling women. There are many more such interventions across the world. But they are still not enough. A significant difference could be achieved toward a more just city if these kinds of interventions are multiplied across the cities of the world.

Foreign Domestic Worker Rights, Hong Kong

Hong Kong relies heavily on migrants to meet the demands of the local labor market. In 2012, some 230,000 foreign women – mostly Filipino, Thai, and Indonesian – worked in the city as live-in cooks, nannies, and maids (Stanton 2012). Under Hong Kong's immigration law, foreign domestic workers (FDWs) are bound exclusively to their employers by two-year contracts. The contracts require FDWs to live in their employer's home, and should they be fired, they have just two weeks to find new employment or be deported (Hong Kong Immigration Department 2012). The ever-present threat of deportation is a significant constraint on FDWs' ability to report abuse or mistreatment, and many employers take advantage. Indeed, of Indonesian domestic

workers in Hong Kong, 42 percent were paid less than they agreed on with their employers (Varia 2007). In 2001, more than 25 percent of FDWs reported verbal or physical abuse, with a high prevalence of sexual abuse (Hong Kong Human Rights Monitor 2001).

The Bethune House Migrant Women's Refuge was founded in 1986 to help migrant women in need, especially those fired by their employers or who have fled their abuse. The refuge's goal, beyond freeing women from unsafe or abusive working conditions, is to develop their ability to advocate for themselves – both in society and in a court of law. The refuge provides legal aid and arranges for FDWs to observe legal proceedings so that they can become familiar with the process and empower themselves as self-advocates. Some former FDWs use the skills and knowledge they gained through the Bethune House to advocates for other migrant workers (Santon 2012).

Female Youth Employment Initiative, Afghanistan

Afghanistan has been racked by more than three decades of war, and the damage to its human capital, especially of women and girls, has been devastating. In 2006, the United States Educational, Scientific and Cultural Organization estimated that the literacy rate among adolescents ages 15–24 was at most 20 percent (World Bank 2009). During the Taliban's rule (1996–2001), women were excluded from the education system, and literacy for rural women fell to as low as 10 percent. In 2007, six years after the fall of the Taliban, women made up less than one-third of students in school (World Bank 2009). With the US military's withdrawal on the horizon, along with the rollback of international aid, Afghanistan needs to maximize its human capital to integrate into the global economy.

To help tackle this challenge, the World Bank, the Nike Foundation, and the Government of Denmark have partnered to fund the Afghanistan Female Youth Employment Initiative. The pilot program, launched in 2009, targets women ages 15–27 living in Mazar-e Sharif, the capital of Balkh Province, and seeks to equip them with nontraditional skills so that they can participate in export opportunities made possible by the city's proximity to Tajikistan, Turkmenistan, and Uzbekistan (World Bank 2009). Urban Afghanistan has received disproportionately little aid money for education; the pilot seeks to redress this imbalance and give Afghan women not just education but also marketable skills. As of 2012, the pilot project had created opportunities for some 1300 young women to receive education and occupational training from private nongovernmental organizations in Afghanistan (Afghanistan Ministry of Education n.d.).

Childcare for Factory Workers, Bangladesh

Bangladesh's booming export economy is built in part on the backs of working women. Discounting associated industries, garment factories produce 10 percent of the country's GDP and employ 3 million workers, 80 percent of them women (German and Pyne 2010). Each year, roughly 500,000 Bangladeshis migrate from the countryside to Dhaka, the capital, to find work (Akter 2010). And even if they find work, their struggles are far from over. In 2010, 67 percent of people living in Mohammadpur slum, one of the city's oldest and largest, earned less than 5000 *taka* a month (roughly $60). The average household spent 3232 *taka* a month on food, and 933 *taka* a month on rent (Akter 2010). Low wages and high prices of basic foods make it nearly impossible for mothers to stay home with their children, even in families where fathers are the primary wage earners. Children are often left unattended in dangerous conditions while their mothers work to support the family. If possible, older children stay home to care for their younger siblings – but at the expense of their education (Phulki 2012). In any case, poor women struggle to care for themselves and their families as they integrate into the urban workforce.

Many humanitarian and international organizations have provided significant aid to Bangladesh. The nongovernmental organization Phulki, however, identified a key problem – breastfeeding is all but impossible for mothers working in factories (Phulki 2012). Options available to working women in the developed world, such as expelling milk throughout the day and storing it in sterile, refrigerated containers, is not possible due to a lack of infrastructure and education. Given Bangladesh's high food insecurity and malnutrition, the discomfort that lactating women experience when they cannot discharge their milk, and breastfeeding's many health benefits for both mothers and children, solving that problem alone would have been extremely valuable. But Phulki's solution has grown to address other struggles that working migrant mothers face. Working directly with factory owners and employees, Phulki established factory-based daycare centers for children aged six weeks to two years. The organization establishes the centers, provides start-up support, and then turns their management over to factory owners. Factory employees gain access to affordable childcare and can breastfeed nursing children (Phulki 2012). Moreover, many of the factory owners take advantage of their relationship with Phulki to offer adult education classes on topics like family planning, literacy, and nutrition (Global Fund for Women 2003). Over 20 such factory-based childcare centers have been established.

Juntos Program: Conditional Cash Transfer Targeting Women in Peru

Poverty in Latin America remains highly influenced by gender. But inequality is not static across the region. As many countries narrowed their wage, poverty, and education gaps, Peru fell behind. Despite a constitution that provides for equal rights, women hold only about 25 percent of land titles (SIGI 2012). Also, the legal tradition of "informal ownership" allows husbands to sell their wives' property without permission, women earn about 46 percent less than men, and 38 percent of women report being victims of domestic violence (SIGI 2012).

Juntos, a conditional cash transfer government aid program established in 2005, has made significant headway not only in reducing family poverty and malnutrition but also in empowering women. Like other conditional cash transfer programs, Juntos pays needy families a small monthly stipend (about $33) in exchange for participating in health and education programs and obtaining government identification documents (Holmes et al. 2010). Mothers of eligible families

(women with children younger than 14 or pregnant women) are paid directly. Women who receive these payments are required to attend weekly training sessions that focus on basic reading and writing and are introduced to other programs that focus on empowerment, equality, and legal aid (Holmes et al. 2010). A primary goal of these time-consuming training sessions is to hold Peruvian men responsible for household work and to change their attitudes toward the gendered division of labor. Women in the program have reported some success in this endeavor, with both men and women reporting that changes were taking hold. According to one man interviewed, "Before only men were the boss … Now it is different, we are changing … Previously, my wife did what I said, she didn't give her opinion. Now she does, one can tell, and we reach a solution. Women's opinions were less important. Now she gives her opinion regarding how to progress in life" (Holmes et al. 2010: 4). Women also saying "We now have reached an agreement, we go alone to the bank. [Previously] men did not understand, they got annoyed even when we attended meetings. We were afraid and even had to miss meetings" and that "Out of jealousy, sometimes they asked us 'why do you go? You leave your house unattended' … Now they don't" (Holmes et al. 2010: 4). Juntos, with its strong impact on gender relations in Peru, are creating more links for women to integrate themselves into mainstream society, advancing greater gender equity.

Mother Centers International Network Empowerment

The Mother Centers International Network for Empowerment grew out of social research conducted by the German Youth Institute in Munich in the early 1980s (Jaeckel, Laux, and Bryant 2002). Staff members discovered that preventative policies that enabled families to access community assets were much more effective than intervening after families fail (MINE 2012). To facilitate this, they opened family-oriented, grassroots community centers (Mother Centers) to recreate family and community networks that had been damaged by socio-economic dislocation. The main tenet of the organization is participation: everyone has something to contribute to the community, and the centers exist to facilitate that interaction (Laux and Kolinska 2004: 5). Many social service providers project the message that individuals seeking help have some kind of deficit ("You have a problem. Come to us, the experts, for help"), but at Mother Centers, everyone is a participant and a contributor, and the message is that they are needed ("You are good at least at one thing. Come to the Mother Center and contribute to the community") (Laux and Kolinska 2004).

The fall of totalitarian governments in Eastern Europe created a huge demand for community infrastructure and social services that had disappeared in a sea of unemployment, violence, upheaval, and decay. Mothers at home with children faced severe isolation – not just from goods and services but also from human contact and social networks. The Mother Center initiative spread quickly through peer visits and exchanges in the postsocialist world (MINE 2012) and helped restore the contact points that are the foundation of coherent society.

The Mother Centers movement has continued to expand though grassroots peer exchanges and individual initiative. Today, there are more than 850 centers worldwide (not only in the United States,

Germany, and the former socialist regimes of the European Union but also in countries like Rwanda and Cameroon) (Laux and Kolinska 2004: 7). The centers are self-managed public spaces in neighborhoods that offer peer networks and drop-in childcare, facilitate access to community and employment resources, and expand children's positive social space. They revolve around a drop-in coffee shop or other shared space where childcare is provided. And they offer adult education classes and services, such as hair cutting, secondhand shops, sewing classes, computer training, and job retraining. When possible, women are paid hourly for services, providing them with much-needed income and a sense of ownership and empowerment (MINE 2012). Centers usually reach between 50 and 1000 families per neighborhood. They supplement the usual social safety net – and in some cases replace it (Jaeckel, Laux, and Bryant 2002).

5.7.4.2   Resisting Urban "Renewal"

In many cities across the world municipalities are aggressively promoting "urban renewal" or "urban transformation" policies to attract foreign direct investment and enhance real estate markets. This often entails destroying neighborhoods that fall within the catchment of the renewal efforts, and postindustrial zones popular with underground groups and long-term working class occupants. These neighborhoods have diverse geographical conditions, social structures, and community identities; they also contain variable numbers of poor residents. Here we focus on two such evictions in Istanbul and the resistance of the inhabitants.

Ayazma, established in 1980, is an ethnically diverse neighborhood, partly resulting from forced migration. It is situated near the Olympic Stadium, built in 2001. Most inhabitants were forced to leave the area when the municipality began destroying houses on February 1, 2007. Nearly 880 houses have been destroyed, and 650 families were forced to move to another housing project, built by TOKÌ, called Bezirganbahçe. Other families moved back to their homelands, others returned to their relatives in Istanbul, and yet others tried to survive in the tents set up to handle the displaced in Ayazma.

In contrast, the Gülensu neighborhoods on the east side of Istanbul are arguably an example of successful resistance against the local municipality. Many of these migrant families had moved to Istanbul in the 1970s. As a former gecekondu area, the district was included in an "urban transformation projects" list of the municipality. But then an official letter from the municipality informed inhabitants they had to leave. They collected 7000 signatures and brought 32 court cases to say "no" to urban transformation. They established the Gülsüyü-Gülensu Neighborhood Association along with the Platform of Istanbul Neighborhoods Association. These are neighborhoods under threat of state-led urban transformation. But the recent generation is strongly united as a leftist political community. And they succeeded in stopping the new development plan.

5.7.4.3   Public Space and Urban Justice Movements

A more visible form of resistance – occupying public spaces – has also become frequent in various cities around the world. It is of course one example of a larger repertoire targeting authoritarian local regimes and the larger capitalist logics they privilege. Invoking Lefebvre's "revolutionary moment," David Harvey (2012: 7) posits that "reinventing the city inevitably depends upon the exercise of a collective power over the processes of urbanization." Harvey continues in direct reference to urban centers that "there is an impulse toward, and longing for its restoration which arises again to produce far-reaching political effects." Visible collective actions in urban space create their own heterotopic urban space: the moment when the public reclaims urban space as a collective space despite their differences.

We saw this in Gezi Park (Istanbul): it exemplifies a new urban space of conflict where collective power reshapes its meaning: it becomes a commons, a space that contests privileged urban formats. The heterogeneity of the public, the types of passive resistance against police force, and the shared consciousness of claiming everyday life via occupying the park resonates with other urban movements, notably the K21 (Stuttgart 21) protest, or the anti-nuclear protest after the 2011 tsunami in Meiji Shrine Park in Tokyo. The spontaneous "coming together" in Gezi Park began to function as a code for other possible local movements, bringing a sort of temporary coherence across neighborhoods. For example, the anti-nuclear protests in Turkey, protests by the Istanbul Chamber of Architects and the Istanbul Chamber of Urban Planners against urban destruction of modest spaces, and against centralized top-down projects such as 3.Bridge for Istanbul, the redevelopment of Taksim Square, and other related movements. Gezi Park was a call to Turkish authorities for a more participatory grassroots urban decision-making approach. In this sense, Gezi Park became a form of radical democracy, and a space for the radical formation of citizenship whereby a heterogeneous public appears spontaneously.

Thus, echoing Lefebvre, the possibilities and power of collective action represent a desire to create something radically different. With the benefit of hindsight, one can see that the Gezi event became an instance of the right to the city because it politicized numerous other demands for rights across Turkey's multiple social levels.

5.8   Recommendations

Urban governments confront challenges that extend well beyond providing core municipal services such as water, sanitation, energy, transport, primary health care, and so on. Many urban governments remain profoundly constrained by narrow-minded legislative frameworks that treat the different tiers of the state as fundamentally hierarchical and subject to the ultimate authority of national governments. With these challenges, one must also consider the path dependency of infrastructural systems embedded in particular land-uses and the pernicious problem of institutional inertia.

Cities are assemblages of layers and layers of continuous investment in the built urban fabric – infrastructures, buildings, and common spaces. While value lies in land markets and the materialization of citizenship and the commons, these have been eclipsed by the incessant desire for private expansion. There is a profound temporal momentum to these processes. At any given moment, deliberate urban intervention has to contend with the aggregate value and path-dependent directionality consolidated over decades and centuries. In any given fiscal year, the resources available to a public authority will be miniscule compared to the aggregate value of the built environment and the logics that drive its relentless reproduction (Sassen 2017). In other words, even with the most radical or progressive intensions, the scope for shifting the machinic dynamics (Amin and Thrift 2002) of the city is highly circumscribed.

This directional force is compounded by the problem of institutional inertia. Regardless of the political system, public bureaucracies are marked by a tendency to reproduce what it understands and control, thus neutralizing everything else beyond its purview or influence. Ensuring stability, predictability and continuity, is instinctive for public institutions. To address deeper issues, institutions need extraordinary leadership, sustained external pressure and deep cultural work across all domains of a society. To tackle the challenges that cities face, one needs institutional understandings and responses that go against the rationality of modern governments that thrive on sectoral specialization, control, and fragmentation.

For example, the ecological crisis that stalks economic viability and social cohesion has brought to the fore the profound interdependency of natural and social systems. It has also shown how inadequate the Westphalian system of sovereignty, linked to hierarchical Weberian bureaucracies, is to deal with multidimensional and complex urban problems. One response to this institutional crisis has been to promote greater supranational and subnational regionalism. It is within this shift of territorial focus that the role of city governments is being promoted as the only viable institutional and political response to increased and unpredictable risks (à la Beck). A notable example is the C40 Coalition of urban governments that insist that cities will take the lead in figuring out more effective policy responses to questions of climate change adaptation and mitigation whilst nation-states fiddle.[20] This is a significant political-institutional movement but one must question whether a more nuanced reflection might be lost along the way.

There is clearly a need to establish a much more refined understanding of the spatiality of the economy, labor, consumption, infrastructure, and power. This is especially true as the global economy continues to convulse with more rapid boom and bust cycles, and shifting centers of value creation and concentration. For example, with technological and cultural changes there is more scope than ever to actively promote very small polities. At the neighborhood scale, this operates almost autonomously in terms of food production, energy generation, water management, recreation, and leisure. Simultaneously, there is an urgent need to regionalize the management of key infrastructures to ensure distributional justice and create administrative consumption patterns in step with ecological cycles. However, where reasonably strong local governments do exist, their jurisdictional authority cannot accommodate the neighborhood. Thus, they actively resist regional coordination or integration, undercutting the possibility of sustainable and just urban governance. We should also keep in mind that in large swathes of Africa, the Middle East and Asia, there is no substantive local governments to speak of. Democratic decentralization remains

a deferred political dream. Keeping these dynamics in mind, we now draw the chapter to a close by reflecting on a number of fields of action.

5.8.1 The Right to the City Rests on Social and Environmental Justice

Urban space is currently structured to ensure optimum extraction of economic value for elites and business owners who dominate the ownership of private companies and real estate. Often urban governments act against their own populations to guarantee these class interests. This constitutes a violation of universal human rights and precious environmental resources. The international policy discussions that have circulated around the formulation of the seventeen SDGs for 2030, the Paris Agreement, and the forthcoming New Urban Agenda all recognize that the current modalities of capital accumulation and discounting of social and environmental externalities are untenable (GCEC 2014). Urban areas account for 80 percent of economic value generated (in GDP terms) and a similar amount of greenhouse gas emissions and resource exploitation. Thus, it is crucial that cities be rethought and reorganized in order to address the interlocked crises of economic development, employment, environmental destruction, and growing social divides and prejudices.

Considering the scale and complexity of the challenge, it is essential to put the well-being and rights of city dwellers at the core of this transformation agenda. The international groundswell toward the right to the city provides the most promising entry point to build a shared vision of prosperity that is both inclusive and just. Ideally, all cities should adopt their own unique Right to the City Charter democratically agreed upon at the local level. Each charter should implement global agreements such as the SDGs, the climate agenda, and the New Urban Agenda. The promising experiments underway in European cities and across various Latin American countries provide important reference points for comparative research, exchange, and learning.

5.8.2 Spatial Justice

One of the complexities of a rights-based approach to social progress in cities is that rights can be in competition and the interests of the most marginal can suffer as a result. Thus spatial justice should be prioritized to ensure that abuses be directly and legally confronted. Spatial justice means that land-use development at the expense of the poor are halted and systematically reversed in favor of a more inclusive approach. This requires legal mechanisms to secure the power of collective and common use over private use rights as established in law in Brazil and other Latin American countries. It can arrest speculative and wasteful investment policies. Public authorities can maximize returns on collective investments in infrastructure, public space, and green open space systems essential for public

---

[20]   See this piece just published: www.theguardian.com/commentisfree/2016/may/05/mayorsnew-york-paris-rio-climate-action-cities

health. Once the binding constraint of urban space is removed it becomes easier to advance social progress in other domains of urban life.

5.8.3   Well-being and Dignity

The absence of tenure security is often a reason why public authorities do not provide access to infrastructure and services to urban populations who live in makeshift and peripheral settlements. Thus, the focus on spatial justice needs to be connected to related socio-economic rights to housing, water, sanitation, and safe energy. In view of the extreme deprivations experienced in especially poorer cities, it is imperative that urban governments guarantee access to a minimum level of services irrespective of income or status. This means that even migrant, refugee, and other iterant groups qualify for access. There is evidence from various world regions that such measures can be financed through intergovernmental transfers and intra-urban redistribution to ensure that the employed population covers the cost of universal access for everyone. This will lead to the overall well-being and productivity of the entire urban economy and restore vital ecosystem services that everyone depends on. For example, if peripheral communities do not have to rely on scavenging for wood, ecosystems can be regenerated. Universal access to basic services will also reduce the insecurity that stalks popular neighborhoods and contribute to the overall sense of stability and safety in the city, increasing social interactions and solidarity citywide.

5.8.4   Democratic Control of Lifeworlds

Note: This concept is drawn from Normal Long (2001: 241) who explains lifeworlds as the: " 'lived-in' and largely 'taken-for-granted' social world centring on particular individuals. Such worlds should not be viewed as 'cultural backcloths' that frame how individuals act, but instead as a product of an individual's own constant self-assembling and reevaluating of relationships and experiences. Lifeworlds embrace actions, interactions and meanings, and are identified with specific socio-geographical spaces and life histories."

The provision of a minimum level of basic services will require some form of contribution from the residents of poor and peripheral neighborhoods. If a household cannot make a monetary contribution toward the provision of essential municipal services, it is foreseeable that these households contribute in other forms, especially labor. Poorer cities need to be encouraged to adopt labor intensive methods and utilize opportunities offered by low-cost technology systems to advance environmentally friendly approaches to infrastructure

deployment. For example, micro-energy grids that rely on renewable energy sources that can be combined with mobile phone convenience, creating scope for microsocial enterprises rooted in these communities. These enterprises can be enrolled to perform essential maintenance services to ensure that access and utilization is optimized through ongoing community awareness programs. In fact, it is possible to think of these sociotechnical interfaces with neighborhood level infrastructure systems as the core of urban citizenship that produces full inclusion and access to the city as whole. We return to this point when we discuss recommendations pertaining to the institutionalization of radical democracy.

5.8.5   Economic Inclusion and Infrastructural Resilience

Note: This section draws heavily on Pieterse and Simone forthcoming.

Swilling and Annecke (2012) suggest that progressive urbanists can build broad-based coalitions for radical urban transformation around two social justice benchmarks: CO_2 emissions per capita and resource consumption per capita. Their argument works with the scientific consensus established through the International Panel on Climate Change (IPCC), which recommends that total carbon emissions per capita per annum should average 2.2 tons. This would be just and equal allocation. The protracted negotiations of the IPCC that seek to restrict overall temperature increases to below 2 degrees Celsius translate into this measurement. We can disaggregate the proportional contributions of countries, cities, and within cities different income groups. Thus a per capita envelope of 2.2 tons per annum can be a powerful rallying call for environmental social justice (Swilling 2006).

Swilling and Annecke (2012) also argue for working with the analysis and recommendations of the International Resource Panel (IRP) established by UNEP. The IRP follows a similar methodology as the IPCC, and arrived at the conclusion that a sustainable and equitable global metabolic rate would depend on contracting material extraction to an average of 6 tons per capita per annum (Fischer-Kowalski and Swilling 2011). Rich countries and wealthy classes sharply overshoot this level of consumption.

These two metrics potentially open up a discussion about the tensions between continued unsustainable economic growth, ensuring access to basic services for all, and taking the necessary policy decisions to reduce carbon emissions. The technocratic nature of these indicators provide a sound basis to get large firms to engage in these debates as part of their professed commitments to good corporate citizenship as ensconced in various globalized "ethical business" standards, including life-cycle accounting.[21]

---

[21]   It is easy to dismiss the various green washing forums, standards, protocols, and policy frameworks of the ethical business movement that come together in the World Business Council of Sustainable Development or like-minded forum of Davos. However, these institutions are important in that they create a set of norms and standards that often lead to the formulation of legal dispensations that regulate the practices of the private sector. One of the topics that are increasingly being driven by international NGOs such as Oxfam and their partners is the issue of tax evasion and tax havens. There can be little doubt that the scope of development investment can be much greater if these resources can be captured more effectively. Defining and institutionalizing new norms with legal effect in these domains are unlikely to come about without the discursive role of the plethora of "ethical business" institutions.

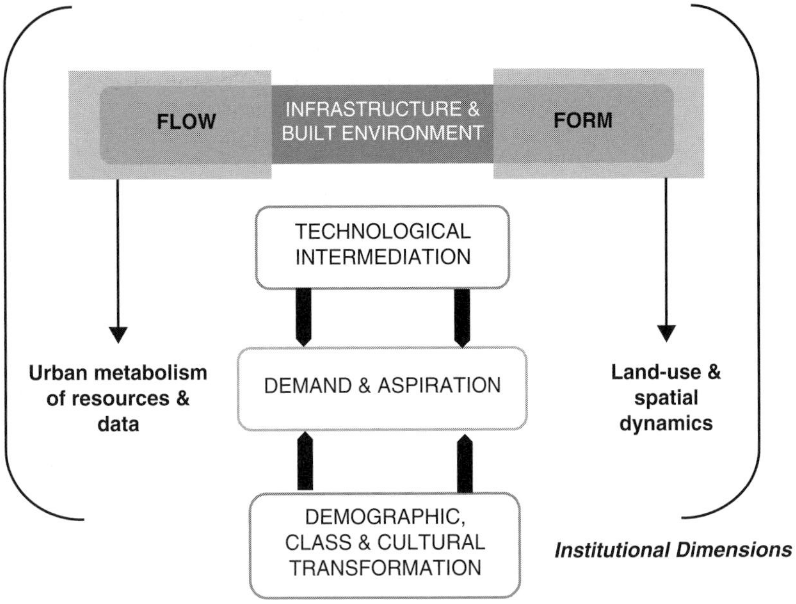

Figure 5.9 | Dimensions of material reproduction of territories.
Source: Pieterse and Simone forthcoming

Figure 5.9 isolates the structural elements of a broader analysis about how to change the "carbon intensity" and "resource efficiency" of a given city. These factors are determined by the aggregate resource consumption of the city, which in turn is shaped by its infrastructure and resource efficiency regarding urban flows. The nature of land-uses and associated markets (formal and informal), mobility systems and relative densities drive the form of the urban system as explored below. Thus, if a group of urban actors latches on to proxy indicators of resource efficiency, it potentially creates a broad platform for claims about how urban infrastructure systems, land-use provisions and planning regulations need to be changed to systematically move a city to a more just position.

Furthermore, such a perspective is also consistent with an aggressive argument for a transition to a green economy that is: resource efficient, low carbon, economically and socially inclusive, and spatially just. This definition of the green economy extends the approach promoted by UNEP in their influential green economy report of 2011 (UNEP 2011). However, by adding the spatial dimension to their framing, it becomes possible to connect the mediating role of sociotechnical systems (i.e. infrastructure networks) to the broader concerns with the substance and flows of the economy. The literature on dematerialization or decarbonizing the economy is often apolitical, aspatial, and mainly focused on technological innovations coupled with incentive systems promoted through public policy and regulatory reform. The spatiality of resource flows, emissions, and social inclusion is what effectively politicizes the green economy discourse. Unfortunately this broader perspective is usually lost in the claim-making politics of progressive actors who tend to focus on a sector (e.g. energy or movement or water), or a specific piece of city at the micro level. It is imperative to figure out how best to articulate specialist claim-making and resistance with a larger political-policy canvass.

Urban justice cannot be achieved without addressing the politics of spatial injustice and access to essential services and the commons.

Most high income and middle-income cities will have overshot their sustainable endowment of resources consumption per unit of economic output. They will also demonstrate a degree of inequality, which shows that a considerable proportion of the population are well below the average – those living in slum and popular neighborhoods (Swilling 2006). Furthermore, disaggregated analysis of most cities in Africa and Asia reveal that the urban poor endure untenable residential densities in precarious settlements whereas the middle classes and elites enjoy overly generous densities that skew the average for the city (Angel 2012). Put differently, spatially blind infrastructure modernization can worsen class divisions and exclusions in the city even when it is framed as inclusive city development. Politically astute perspectives are needed to highlight connections between the need for infrastructure investment, its resource efficiency, distributional effects and impact on the unsustainable, and unjust path-dependency of the operating systems of the city.

This line of political reasoning opens up every single infrastructural system and economic investment to close public scrutiny. Does it contribute to aggregate resource efficiency and does it deal with differential densities in a way that can foster spatial justice for all? It is precisely in such a political arena that the contextualized imperatives of adaptive urbanism can come to fore and be translated into spatially specific claims for sociotechnical reforms. Furthermore, new ICT-based tracking applications also equip coalitions with accessible tools to ensure that the politics around these metrics remains in the public eye and the basis of continuous debate. For example, the Peta Jakarta program mobilizes social media to crowdsource real-time data on flooding in the city, which is also underpinned by a continuous tracking of water flows across the city cross-referenced to indexes of land ownership. All of this information is then provided as open-source data. Similar mechanisms and information cultures are manifesting in numerous cities across the world (UN-Habitat 2015).

5.8.6 Spatial form

The search for a sustainable urban form extends beyond the policy trope of a compact city, and takes into account the variety of urban patterns that already exist in diverse cities, that are to varying degrees marked by planned and unplanned elements. However, it is possible to recast the compact city fetish to incorporate a number of attributes: density, which should be in close relationship with another attribute, continuity. In tandem, density and continuity allows for formal and social integration of the city by connecting its different parts and creating a sequence of dynamic, accessible places that can easily be traversed on foot and connected at a larger scale through public transportation. This is the ideal evoked by Richard Sennett (2006, 2018) as the open city.

However, density and continuity is not enough. A mixture of diverse and overlapping housing types, along with various urban activities, is also required. In other words, a rich diversity of residential stock that is embedded in an equally rich grain of shops, small businesses, services, public facilities, and ideally substantial modern nonpolluting industries. The street-level interactions should foster a dynamic environment marked by robust interaction and numerous opportunities for encounters among local residents and visiting sojourners. Thus, the street becomes the connective tissue between housing, shops, services, and numerous public facilities such as schools, health centers, and transportation. It is this intense complex and unfinished mixture that generates the attributes of urbanity or cityness, as well as the formal definition of the city such as temporality (De Solà-Morales et al. 2008) or the readability (Bohigas 2004) of public space and its link with the private realm.

At the local and larger regional scale of the city this approach calls for a focus on intensity nodes that can fulfill complementary functions within a polycentric framework (Salat 2016). The key to making such a spatial form and set of dynamics work is intensification – which is the result of density, continuity, and the mixture of urban activities and housing types. It refers to the number of functions and their characteristics in relation to the qualities of the urban form where these functions take place. In other words, this concept is related to the dynamism, vitality, and diversity at a local level (Jacobs 1961; Sennett 1992) essential for individual and collective life. Given the inherited legacies of urban form and built stock, it also calls for more intensification. This denotes urban transformation in two ways: one, the process of recycling existing urban areas in the city and compacting it by increasing housing density and population; and two, introducing new activities and complementary functions into existing and new ones. This obviously implies land use changes to include or increase social, commercial, and service activities, in the said nodes and/or along streets (Burton et al. 2003; Williams 2004).

5.8.7 New Urban Knowledge Systems and Innovation

The agenda for urban transformation is profoundly complex and deeply steeped in politics. There are a number of uncertainties and unknowns in terms of how best to reorient urban infrastructural systems, land-use patterns and consumption patterns away from the predominant patterns of exclusion, exploitation, and inequality. In the context of the potential of a sustainability technological wave (Ahlers et al. 2013;

Perez 2014), it is clear that the economies that gravitate around the built environment and infrastructure networks can offer an important, if not the most significant, leverage to effect the anticipated technological wave. However, this requires explicit research, experimentation, ongoing advocacy, and vibrant radical democratic forums and processes.

Clarifying how best to transition from the status quo to sustainable operating systems requires considerable data and analysis, deliberative forums between technology companies, public sector investors, citizens, diverse interest groups that will be affected, knowledge partners and strategic intermediaries that can create effective communication between these actors and domains. The detailed work of defining the terms, pace, and priorities of such urban transitions toward more inclusive and sustainable pathways boils down to defining new ways of investing and managing the urban realm – innovation. This demands radically altering national innovation systems that continue to operate on industrial-era sectoral obsessions that are disconnected from the space-economy and social justice imperatives of the twenty-first century. However, universities are coming to terms with the new imperatives of national and regional innovation systems and can be essential partners in fostering the local innovation systems that must cohere around the development imperatives of city-regions.

In this sense it is best to define regional innovation systems in relation to city-regions (or smaller scale town-centered agglomerations) that are committed to low-carbon, resource-efficient, and inclusive growth paths working together to champion a new economic and social vision for the world. In this sense, some of the hyperbole about Mayors ruling the world and this being an urban century has some validity. City-based regionalism is strengthened by key environmentally sensitive infrastructure systems for energy, water management, mobility, and ICT. These sectors are also the core drivers of the urban (and national) transition to sustainable green economies, which are: low-carbon, resource-efficient, ecologically regenerative, and spatially integrated. The trend toward city-based international networks reflects an important institutional form to engage within democratic oversight.

The key point is that if these regionally anchored innovation systems take root and flourish it can dramatically shorten the time-frames of learning, and figuring out policy approaches that work on the ground in the world regions with the greatest need and the least resources to address them.

5.8.8 Institutionalization of Radical Democracy

There is a real danger that the recommendations and policy perspectives in this section become technocratic jargon. In closing, it is imperative to stress that the beginning and end-point of an urban agenda for social progress has to be vibrant radical democratic passions and processes. Despite the enormous variation across world regions and cities, it is possible to offer a few guidelines on how democratic cultures can be nurtured that will be conducive to the formulation and implementation of radical urban reforms as intimated before.

Table 5.2 | Co-governance instruments at the local level

Building blocks	Potential co-governance mechanisms
1. Strategy and planning	• Macro long-term strategic plans, e.g. CDS, growth management strategy, climate change mitigation, and adaptation strategy • Spatial development frameworks • Medium-term income and expenditure frameworks • Local and neighborhood levels plans, including prescient level plans to promote sustainable human settlements
2. Service delivery innovations	• Participatory service delivery planning, budgeting, management, and monitoring • Joint delivery systems at the local level • Public auditing mechanisms to ensure contract compliance and recourse for dissatisfied citizens • Digital crowdsourcing of service delivery problems and bottlenecks to improve responsiveness and effectiveness • Digital feedback mechanisms (e.g. sensors) to improve the overall coordination and management of the service • Dedicated financial and training resources to boost the capacity of community organizations to fulfill these roles
3. Advocacy and agitation	• Ensure that formal invited spaces for public consultation and engagement are open for a wide range of civic and private organizations and voices • Ensure legal protection for civic actors to establish their own political and practice spaces that may be critical or oppositional to official deliberative spaces • Ensure legal and moral fealty to the principle of the right to information, a free press, and freedom of expression
4. Social learning mechanisms for innovation	• Establish and support regional innovation systems that connect green businesses, universities, think-tanks, social movements, public policy entrepreneurs, and state-owned enterprises • Promote a culture of innovation labs focused on critical systemic questions that present obstacles to the medium- and long-term sustainability of the city or town • Promote a culture of public debate through exhibitions and learning fairs that draw in all age groups and foster a shared dialogue about good practice and lifelong learning • Encourage festivals of democratic achievement driven by nongovernment actors, to promote and celebrate key milestones on the urban transformation journey. These events can build onto established culturally significant rituals and festivals

In the first instance it is essential that the core of democratic local authorities are in place and vibrant, i.e. elected councils are in place to legally mediate competing social interest and demands and hold the executive authority to account. Second, strong local government leadership is in evidence either in the form of executive Mayors (that may or may not be directly elected), working closely with the council and representative bodies of civil society and the private sector. In an era where every urban management decision can have far-reaching long-term consequences, it is essential that political leaders can offer vision and direction on how the tough tradeoffs and imperatives will be addressed during her/his term of office. Institutionally, this ought to translate into the adoption of various techniques (that have unique cultural inflections in different regions, countries, and cities) identified in Table 5.2.

Third, there should be an institutional commitment to subject as many aspects of urban management and service delivery to democratic engagement and oversight. In a time of ubiquitous technology and mobile connectivity, even among poor classes, a vast portfolio of participatory techniques and applications are available for adoption to suit local contexts (Friedmann 2002; Narayan and Kapoor 2008; Mitlin 2008). These are especially important when service delivery models can be differentiated to satisfy diverse income groups' demands and to accommodate the possibility of community co-production where the residents might not be in a position to pay for user charges. During the 1990s participatory budgeting was emerging as a powerful instrument to facilitate participation, democratize prioritization, and improve service delivery efficiency. Today, these measures are complemented by social auditing techniques that allow citizens to scrutinize and monitor the contracts between municipalities and service providers. And in contexts where social auditing is not allowed, citizens can use various mobile applications that can empower them to lodge complaints, take photographs of poor service, and expose bureaucratic neglect. It is particularly young people who are drawn to these forms of citizenship.

Fourth, it is vital that local authorities and city leaders (mayors and leaders from other sectors) commit to fostering atmospheres of vibrant democratic engagement, social learning and innovation. Local authorities need to be confident in their own identities, premised on clear legal mandates, but also invest in the establishment of strategic deliberative forums to debate long-term imperatives of sustainable urban development alongside participatory techniques to continuously improve service delivery. Furthermore, local authorities need to actively encourage constructive critical opposition by civil society, both formal and informal, and project their own perspectives and visions into the public domain. Such tolerance enhances political capital and it creates sufficient political diversity for true innovation to emerge.

The scope and complexity of the demographic, economic, environmental, and cultural challenges that impinge on cities demands step-change innovation. This can be induced through intentional research and development laboratories that bring together diverse expertise and interests to produce novel insights and applications. With the recent appreciation of the power and importance of design thinking, cities around world are experimenting with these formats. This is an important addition to the practice of creative urban governance. However, design thinking, especially "spatial literacy," has enormous potential to revolutionize the ways in which poor and informal neighborhoods are routinely planning, upgraded, managed and transformed into fully urban spaces. It is beyond the scope of this chapter to delve into this, but suffice to underscore that it is potentially the linchpin that can connect bottom-up innovations with top-down renovations of urban management and service delivery.

References

Afghanistan Ministry of Education. 2012. "Terms of Reference: Conducting Social Marketing Survey, Providing Job and Life Skills Trainings, and Job Placement

Service." *Islamic Republic of Afghanistan*. www.worldbank.org/projects/P116036/adolescent-girls-initiative-afghanistan?lang=en (last accessed December 23, 2017).

Agier, M. 2002. "Between War and City: Towards an Urban Anthropology of Refugee Camps," *Ethnography* 3: 317–341.

Agier, M. 2016. *Borderlands: Towards an Anthropology of the Cosmopolitan Condition*. Malden: Polity Press.

Ahlers, R., V. Perez Güida, M. Rusca, and K. Schwartz 2013. "Unleashing Entrepreneurs or Controlling Unruly Providers? The Formalisation of Small-Scale Water Providers in Greater Maputo, Mozambique," *The Journal of Development Studies* 49/4: 470–482.

Akter, T. 2010. "Migration and Living Conditions in Urban Slums Implications for Food Security," *Unnayan Onneshan*. http://unnayan.org/reports/Migration.and.living.conditions.in.urban.slums.pdf (last accessed January 28, 2018).

Angel, S. 2012. *Planet of Cities*. Cambridge, MA: Lincoln Institute of Land Policy.

Arboleda, M. 2015. "Spaces of Extraction, Metropolitan Explosions: Planetary Urbanization and the Commodity Boom in Latin America," *International Journal of Urban and Regional Research* 40: 96–112.

Batthyany, K. and L. Scuro 2010. "Desafíos de Uruguay y la región," *Revista de Ciencias Sociales* 23 : 7–9.

Bayat, A. 2010. *Life as Politics: How Ordinary People Change the Middle East*. Stanford, CA: Stanford University Press.

Bohigas, O. 2003. *Realismo, urbanidad y fracasos*, Publicaciones ETSAB – Escuela de Arquitectura de Barcelona (last accessed December 23, 2017).

Bohigas, O. 2004. *Contra la Incontinencia Urbana / Against the Urban Incontinence: Reconsideracion moral de la arquitectura y la ciudad / Moral Reconsideration of the Architecture and the City*. Sociedad Editorial Electa Espana.

Brenner, N. 2004. *New State Spaces. Urban Governance and the Rescaling of Statehood*. Oxford: Oxford University Press.

Buechler, S.J. 2014. *Labor in a Globalizing City: Economic Restructuring in São Paulo, Brazil*. Switzerland: Springer.

Burdett, R. and D. Sudjic. 2007. *The Endless City: An Authoritative and Visually Rich Survey of the Contemporary City*. London: Phaidon Press.

Bureau of Labor Statistics (BLS) 2010. Metropolitan Area Employment and Unemployment. News Release, December 2009.

Burton, E. 2000. "The Potential of the Compact City for Promoting Social Equity," *Achieving Sustainable Urban Form*: 19–29. http://journals.sagepub.com/doi/abs/10.1080/00420980050162184 (last accessed January 28, 2018).

Burton, E. 2001. The Compact City and Social Justice. A paper presented to the *Housing Studies Association Spring Conference, Housing, Environment and Sustainability*, University of York.

Burton, E., M. Jenks, and K. Williams 2003 *The Compact City: A Sustainable Urban Form?* London: Routledge.

Caldeira, T. 2015. "Social Movements, Cultural Production, and Protests. São Paulo's Shifting Political Landscape," *Current Anthropology* 56: 126–136.

Carrión, F. 2013. "Mercados ilegales: nueva arquitectura institucional y su expresión territorial en Latinoamérica," in F. Carrión (ed.), *Asimetrías en la Frontera Ecuador-Colombia: Entre la complementariedad y el sistema*. Quito: FLACSO.

Castells, M. 2012. *Networks of Outrage and Hope: Social Movements in the Internet Age*. Malden: Polity Press.

Cerdá, I. 1867. *Teoría general de la urbanización, y aplicación de sus principios y doctrinas a la reforma y ensanche de Barcelona*. Imprenta Española.

Corporación Andina de Fomento (CAF). 2011. *Desarrollo Urbano y Movilidad en América Latina*. Panamá: CAF.

Credit Suisse. 2014. *Global Wealth Report 2014*. Zurich: Research Institute Credit Suisse A.G.

Dabla-Norris, E., K. Kochhar, N. Suphaphiphat, F. Ricka, and E. Tsounta 2015. *Causes and Consequences of Income Inequality: A Global Perspective, Staff Discussion Note 15/13*. Washington, DC: International Monetary Fund.

Davis, M. 2006. *Planet of Slums*. London: Verso.

De Boeck, F. 2012. "Infrastructure: Commentary from Filip De Boeck." *Curated Collections, Cultural Anthropology Online*. November 26, 2012, http://culanth.org/curated_collections/11-infrastructure/discussions/7-infrastructure-commentary-from-filip-de-boeck

De Mattos, C. 2016. "Lógica nanciera, geografías de la nanciarización y crecimiento urbano mercantilizado," in A. Orellana, F. Link, and J. Noyola (eds.), *Urbanización Planetaria y la Reconstrucción de la Ciudad*. Santiago de Chile: RIL Editores.

de Solà-Morales, M. 2013. "Four Paradigms for a Course on Urbanism Ethics." *QRU: Quaderns de Recerca en Urbanisme* 2: 12–27.

de Solà-Morales, M., K. Frampton, and H. Ibelings 2008. *A Matter of Things*. Rotterdam, NAi Publisher.

Dubet, F. 2013. *Porqué preferimos la desigualdad?* Buenos Aires: Siglo XXI.

Durán, M.Á. 1999. *Los costos invisibles de la enfermedad*. Madrid, Fundación BBV.

Durán, M.Á., R. Aguirre, K. Batthyany, and L. Scuro 2010. "Uso del tiempo, cuidados y bienestar Desafíos de Uruguay y la region," *Revista de Ciencias Sociales* XXIII/27, December 2010.

ECLAC (United Nations Economic Commission for Latin America and the Caribbean) 2012. Informe Observatorio de Igualdad de Género de América Latina y El Caribe. www.cepal.org/es/publicaciones/35401-observatorio-igualdad-genero-america-latina-caribe-oig-informe-anual-2012-bonos (last accessed December 23, 2017).

ECLAC (United Nations Economic Commission for Latin America and the Caribbean) 2014. Panorama social de América Latina y El Caribe. www.cepal.org/es/publicaciones/37626-panorama-social-america-latina-2014 (last accessed December 23, 2017).

ECLAC (United Nations Economic Commission for Latin America and the Caribbean) 2015. Latin America and the Caribbean: looking ahead after the Millennium Development Goals Regional monitoring report on the Millennium Development Goals in Latin America and the Caribbean. http://repositorio.cepal.org/bitstream/handle/11362/38924/S1500708_en.pdf (last accessed December 23, 2017).

ECLAC (United Nations Economic Commission for Latin America and the Caribbean) 2016. Observatorio de igualdad de género. Trabajo no remunerado de las mujeres, un aporte a la economía. Infografía. http://oig.cepal.org/es/infografias/trabajo-no-remunerado-mujeres-un-aporte-la-economia (last accessed December 23, 2017).

Edwards, L.N., and E. Field-Hendrey 2002. "Home-Based Work and Women's Labor Force Decisions," *Journal of Labor Economics* 20/1: 170–200.

Fainstein, S. 2011. *The Just City*. Ithaca: Cornell University Press.

Falú, A. 1998. "Propuestas para mejorar el acceso de las mujeres a la vivienda y el hábitat," in Moncada y Ponce Falú (Coord.), *Cuarto Cuaderno de Trabajo: Género, Hábitat y Vivienda, Propuestas y Programas*. Consejo Nacional de las Mujeres. Presidencia República del Ecuador.

Falú, A. 2002. Ciudades para Varones y Mujeres. Herramientas para la acción, Red Mujer. www.redmujer.org.ar/pdf_publicaciones/art_31.pdf (last accessed December 23, 2017).

Falú, A. 2008. *Mujeres en la Ciudad, de violencias y derechos*. SUR, Chile: Red Mujer y Hábitat.

Falú, A. 2009. "Ciudades de derechos o el derecho a la ciudad?," in P.M. Cristina (ed.), *Derecho a la ciudad: por una ciudad para todos y todas*. Buenos Aires: Ministerio del Interior.

Falú, A. 2013. *Anales de la II Cumbre Iberoamericana sobre Agendas Locales de Género de la Unión Iberoamericana de Municipalistas*. Aguas Calientes, México, September 23–27.

Falú, A., and O. Segovia (eds.) 2007.*Ciudades para convivir: sin violenciashacia las mujeres*. Santiago de Chile: Ediciones sur / unifem, aecid, Red Mujer y Hábitat.

Falú, A., P. Morey, and L. Rainero 2002. "Uso del tiempo y del espacio: asimetrías de género y de clase en Ciudad y Vida Cotidiana. Asimetrías en el uso del tiempo y del espacio," Córdoba, Argentina. Informe Observatorio Genero, CEPAL.

Fischer-Kowalski, M. and M. Swilling 2011. Decoupling: Natural Resource Use and Environmental Impacts from Economic Growth. United Nations Environment Programme, Switzerland.

Friedmann, J. 2002. *The Prospect of Cities*. Minneapolis and London: University of Minnesota Press.

Fudge, C. and L. Nystrøm. 1999. *City and Culture: Cultural Processes and Urban Sustainability*. Boverket.

Gandy, M. 2004. "Rethinking Urban Metabolism: Water, Space and the Modern City." *City* 8/3: 363–379.

GCEC (Global Commission for the Economy and Climate). 2014. *Better Growth Better Climate: The New Climate Economy Report: The Synthesis Report*. Washington, DC: The Global Commission on the Economy and Climate.

Gehl, J. 1989. "A Changing Street Life in a Changing Society," *Places* 6/1: 9–17.

Gehl, J. 2013. *Cities for People*. Washington, DC: Island Press.

Global Fund for Women 2003. Impact Report No. 1: Economic Opportunity Initiative.

German, E. and S. Pyne 2010. The Dreams of Dhaka's Garment Girls, *Global Post*. September 9, 2010. www.pri.org/stories/2010-09-08/dreams-dhakas-garment-girls (last accessed January 28, 2018).

Graham, S. and S. Marvin 2001. *Splintering Urbanism: Networked Infrastructures, Technological Mobilities and the Urban Condition*. New York: Routledge.

Greenfield, A. 2017. *Radical Technologies: The Design of Everyday Life*. London: Verso.

Hadjimichalis, C. 2013. "From Streets and Squares to Radical Political Emancipation? Resistance Lessons from Athens during the Crisis," *Human Geography* 6: 116–136.

Hall, P. 1988. *Cities of Tomorrow: An Intellectual History of Urban Planning and Design in the Twentieth Century*. Oxford: Blackwell Publishing.

Harris, R. 2015. "International Policy for Urban Housing Markets in the Global South since 1945," in F. Miraftab and N. Kudva (eds.), *Cities of the Global South*. New York: Routledge.

Harvey, D. 2008. "The Right to the City," *New Left Review* 53: 23–40.

Harvey, D. 2010. *The Enigma of Capital and the Crisis of Capitalism*. London: Prole Books.

Harvey, D. 2012. *Rebel Cities. From the Right to the City to Urban Revolutions*. London: Verso.

Haussmann, G.E. 1854. *Mémoire sur les eaux de Paris présenté à la Commission Municipale par M. le Préfet de la Seine*. Paris: Vinchon.

Holmes, R., N. Jones, R. Vargas, and F. Veras 2010. Cash Transfers and Gendered Risks and Vulnerabilities: Lessons from Latin America. Overseas Development Institute. www.odi.org/sites/odi.org.uk/files/odi-assets/publications-opinion-files/6042.pdf (last accessed January 28, 2018).

Hong Kong Human Rights Monitor. 2001. Shadow Report to the United Nations Committee on the Elimination of Racial Discrimination Regarding the Report of the Hong Kong Special Administrative Region of the People's Republic of China. *Hong Kong Human Rights Monitor*. http://hkhrm.org.hk.

Hong Kong Immigration Department. 2012. Quick Guide for the Employment of Domestic Helpers from Abroad (ID 989). *The Government of Hong Kong Special Administrative Region*. www.immd.gov.hk/pdforms/ID(E)989.pdf (last accessed January 28, 2018).

Howard, E. 1902. *Garden Cities of Tomorrow (original 1898 title: Tomorrow: A Peaceful Path to Real Reform)*. London: Swan Sonnenschein. University Press.

Hyman, K. and Pieterse, E. forthcoming. "Infrastructure Deficits and Potential in African Cities," in R. Burdett and S. Hall (eds.), *The SAGE Handbook of Urban Sociology: New Approaches to the Twenty-first Century City*. London: Sage Publishers.

IDESA 2014. Que es IDESA. *Instituto para el desarrollo social argentino*. www.idesa.org/QueEsIDESA (last accessed December 23, 2017).

Institute for Urban Strategies, The Mori Memorial Foundation 2013. *Tokyo Future Scenario 2035 – Four Scenarios and Urban Strategy Proposal*. Tokyo: Nikkei Printing Inc.

Institute for Urban Strategies, The Mori Memorial Foundation 2015. *Global Power City Index – Yearbook 2015*. Tokyo: Nikkei Printing Inc.

Intergovernmental Panel on Climate Change (IPCC) 2013. "Summary for Policymakers," in T.F. Stocker, D. Qin, G.-K. Plattner, M. Tignor, S.K. Allen, J. Boschung, A. Nauels, Y. Xia, V. Bex, and P.M. Midgley (eds.), *Climate Change 2013: The Physical Science Basis. Contribution of Working Group I to the Fifth Assessment Report of the Intergovernmental Panel on Climate Change*. Cambridge and New York: Cambridge University Press.

International Labor Organization (ILO) 2016. *World Employment Social Outlook. Trends 2016*. Geneva: ILO.

International Migration Organization (IOM) 2015. *World Migration Report, 2015. Migrants and Cities: New Partnerships to Manage Mobility*. Geneva: IOM.

Jacobs, J. 1961. *The Death and Life of Great American Cities*. New York: Vintage Press.

Jaeckel, M., A. Laux, and G. Bryant 2002. "Mothers in the Center: Mother Centers." Self published. www.scribd.com/document/166954203/THE-CITY-AS-A-COMMON-GOOD-URBAN-PLANNING-AND-THE-RIGHT-TO-THE-CITY (last accessed January 28, 2018).

Jaglin, S. 2014. "Rethinking Urban Heterogeneity," in *The Routledge Handbook on Cities of the Global South*. London: Routledge.

Jaglin, S. 2016. "Is the Network Challenged by the Pragmatic Turn in African Cities? Urban Transition and Hybrid Delivery Configurations," in O. Coutard and J. Rutherford (eds.), *Beyond the Networked City. Infrastructure Reconfigurations and Urban Change in the North and South*, London, New York: Routledge.

Kantor, P. 2003. "Women's Empowerment through Home–Based Work: Evidence from India," *Development and Change* 34/3: 425–445.

Kessler, G. 2008. "Inseguridad subjetiva: un nuevo campo de investigación y políticas públicas," in A. Álvarez (ed.), *Estado, democracia y seguridad ciudadana. Aportes para el debate*. Buenos Aires: PNUD.

Koolhaas, R. 1995. *Whatever Happened to Urbanism?* Cambridge: MIT Press.

Latinobarómetro Database. www.latinobarometro.org/.

Laux, A., and R. Kolinska 2004. "Building Bridges with the Grassroots: Scaling Up through Knowledge Sharing." *World Urban Forum*, Barcelona. https://practicalaction.org//docs/shelter/wuf04_building_bridges.pdf (last accessed January 28, 2018).

Le Corbusier. 1943. *La charte d'Athènes*. Paris: Plon.

Lefebvre H. 1968. *Le Droit à la ville [The Right to the City]* (2nd edn.). Paris: Anthropos.

Lefebvre, H. 1996. "The Right to the City," in E. Kofman and E. Lebas (eds.), *Writing on Cities*. Oxford: Blackwell.

Lefebvre, H. 2003. *The Urban Revolution*. Minneapolis: University of Minnesota Press.

Liu-Farrer, G. 2011. *Labour Migration from China to Japan: International Students, Transnational Migrants*. London: Routledge.

Lloyd, R. 2010. *Neo-Bohemia: Art and Commerce in the Postindustrial City*. New York: Routledge.

Logan, J., and H. Molotch 1987. *Urban Fortunes. The Political Economy of Places*. Berkeley: University of California Press.

Lynch, K. 1984. *Good City Form*. Cambridge, MA: MIT Press.

Magdoff, F. 2013. "Twenty-First Century Land Grabs. Accumulation by Agricultural Dispossession," *Monthly Review* 66: 1–18.

Malaguti Batista, V. 2005. *Dificeis Ganhos Faceis: Drogas e Juventude Pobre no Rio de Janeiro*. Revan: Medicina e Saœde edition.

Malecki, E.J. 2014. "Connecting the Fragments: Looking at the Connected City in 2050," *Applied Geography* 49: 12–17.

Mason, P. 2015. *Tourism Impacts, Planning and Management*. Abingdon: Routledge.

Méndez, R., and J. Prada-Trigo 2014. "Crisis, desempleo y vulnerabilidad en Madrid," *Scripta Nova Revista Electrónica de Geografía y Ciencias Sociales* 8: 474.

Middle East Eye 2015. "Syrian Refugees in Turkey." AFAD, UNHCR, USG. www.middleeasteye.net/multimedia/infographics/syrian-refugees-turkey-317392719 (last accessed December 23, 2017).

MINE (Mother Centers International Network for Empowerment) 2012. www.mine.cc/.

Mitlin, D. 2008. "With and Beyond the State: Co-production as the Route to Political Inuence, Power and Transformation for Grassroots Organizations," *Environment and Urbanisation* 20: 339–60.

Molotch, H. 1976. "The City as a Growth Machine: Toward a Political Economy of Place," *American Journal of Sociology* 82/2: 309–332.

Moser, C. 1993. *Gender Planning and Development: Theory, Practice and Training*. New York and London: Routledge.

Moura, R. and T. Azevedo 2016. "Estatuto de la metrópolis: perspectivas y desafíos para la (des)gobernanza metropolitana brasilera," in A. Orellana, F.Y. Link, and J. Noyola (eds.), *Urbanización Planetaria y la Reconstrucción de la Ciudad*. Santiago de Chile : RIL Editores.

Mumford, L. 1951. *Introduction. Towards New Towns for America. By Clarence Stein*. Chicago: Public Administration Clearing House.

Mumford, L. 1961. *The City In History – Its Origins, Its Transformation, and Its Prospects*. New York: Harcourt Brace Jovanovich, Inc.

Narayan, D. and S. Kapoor 2008. "Beyond Sectoral Traps: Creating Wealth for the Poor," in C. Moser and A. Dani (eds.), *Assets, Livelihoods and Social Policy*. Washington DC: World Bank.

National Highway Traffic Safety Administration 2016. *Automated Vehicle Technologies*. NHTSA.

Nugent, S., A. Packard, E. Brabon, and S. Vierra 2011. "Living, Regenerative, and Adaptive Buildings." *Whole Building Design Guide*. www.wbdg.org/resources/living-regenerative-and-adaptive-buildings (last accessed January 28, 2018).

OECD/AfDB/UNDP 2016. *African Economic Outlook 2016: Sustainable Cities and Structural Transformation*. Paris: OECD Publishing.

Osborn, F.J. 1942. *New Towns after the War*. London: J. M. Dent & Sons Ltd.

Oxford Committee for Famine Relief (OXFAM) 2016. *An Economy For the 1%: How Privilege and Power in the Economy Drive Extreme Inequality and How This Can Be Stopped*. Oxfam.

Özler, Ş.İ. 2000. "Politics of the Gecekondu in Turkey: The Political Choices of Urban Squatters in National Elections," *Turkish Studies* 1: 39–58.

Pesquisa Nacional por Amostra de Domicílios (PNAD) 2013. Instituto Brasileiro de Geografia e Estatística (IBGE).

Phulki. 2012. "About Phulki" www.phulkibd.org/about.php (last accessed December 23, 2017).

Pieterse, E. and A. Simone forthcoming. *City Secrets: A Polemic for Emergent Urbanisms.* Cambridge: Polity Press.

Piketty, T. 2014. *Capital in the Twenty-First Century.* Cambridge: Harvard University Press.

Pitch, T. 2008. *El género de la seguridad urbana.* Santiago de Chile: CEPAL.

Promotion Committee of the Mexico City Charter for the Right to the City 2010. "Mexico City Charter for the Right to the City." www.hic-gs.org/content/Mexico_Charter_R2C_2010.pdf (last accessed December 23, 2017).

Purcell, M. 2013. "Possible Worlds: Henri Lefebvre and the Right to the City," *Journal of Urban Affairs* 36: 141–154.

Rede de Desenvolvimiento Humano – Redeh - Centro de intercambio y servicios para el Cono Sur Argentina – CISCSA 2016. *Pra lá e Pra cá: El Derecho de Las Mujeres a Las Ciudades.* Brasília: Redeh.

Ren, X. 2011. *Building Globalization: Transnational Architecture Production in Urban China.* Chicago: The University of Chicago Press.

Reuveny, R. 2007. "Climate Change-Induced Migration and Violent Conflict," *Political Geography* 26: 656–673.

Rogers, R.G. 1999. *Towards an Urban Renaissance.* London: Spon.

Rogers, R.G. 2008. *Cities for a Small Planet.* New York: Basic Books.

Rolffs, P., R. Byrne, and D. Ockwell 2014. Financing Sustainable Energy for All: Pay-As-You-Go vs. Traditional Solar Finance Approaches in Kenya. STEPS. Working Paper 59. Brighton: STEPS Centre.

Roy, A. 2009. "The 21st-Century Metropolis: New Geographies of Theory," *Regional Studies* 43(6): 819–830.

Ruiz, C. 2015. *De Nuevo la Sociedad.* Santiago de Chile: LOM.

Salat, S. 2016. "The Break-even Point. Impact of Urban Densities on Value Creation, Infrastructure Costs and Embodied Energy," *SBE 16 Turin Conference Proceedings.*

Santos Junior, O., L. De Queiroz, and C. Gaffney 2015. "Brasil. Os Impactos da Copa do Mundo 2014 e das Olimpiadas 2016." Río de Janeiro, *Observatorio das Metropoles,* 23 April 2016. Web. www.observatoriodasmetropoles.net/index.php?option=com_k2&view=item&id=1175%3A"brasil-os-impactos-dacopa-2014-e-das-olimp%C3%ADdas-2016"&Itemid=163.

Sassen, S. 1991/2001. *The Global City. New York, London, Tokyo,* 2nd edn. Princeton: Princeton University Press.

Sassen, S. 2008. *Territory, Authority, Rights: From Medieval Authority to Global Assemblages.* Princeton, NJ: Princeton University Press.

Sassen, S. 2012. 'Interactions of the technical and the social: digital formations of the powerful and the powerless.' *Information, Communication & Society* 15: 455–78.

Sassen, S. 2014. *Expulsions: Brutality and Complexity in the Global Economy,* Cambridge, MA: Belknap Press of Harvard University Press.

Sassen, S. 2015a. 'Digitization and Work: Potentials and challenges in low-wage labor markets' (Position Paper). *Open Society Foundation.* www.saskiasassen.com/PDFs/publications/digitization-and-work.pdf

Sassen, S. 2015b. "Who Owns The City?" November 24, 2015. *The Guardian.* www.theguardian.com/cities/2015/nov/24/who-owns-our-cities-and-why-this-urban-takeover-should-concern-us-all

Sassen, S. 2016a. "A Massive Loss of Habitat: New Drivers for Migration" *Sociology of Department* 2(2): 204–33. http://saskiasassen.com/PDFs/publications/SS%20Massive%20Loss%20Habitat.pdf

Sassen, S. 2016b. "The Global City: Enabling Economic Intermediation and Bearing Its Costs" *City & Community* 15(2): 97–108. http://onlinelibrary.wiley.com/doi/10.1111/cico.12175/abstract

Sassen, S. 2017 "Predatory Formations Dressed in Wall Street Suits and Algorithmic Math." *Science, Technology & Society* 22(1): 6–20.

Satterthwaite, D. 2007. "The transition to a predominantly urban world and its underpinnings," *International Institute for Environment and Development Human Settlement.* Group Discussion Paper.

Schmid, C. 2012. "Henri Lefebvre, the Right to the City and the New Metropolitan Mainstream," in N. Brenner, P. Marcuse, and M. Mayer (eds.), *Cities for people, not for prot: critical urban theory and the right to the city.* London: Routledge.

Sennett, R. 1992. *The uses of disorder: Personal identity and city life.* New York: WW Norton & Company.

Sennett, R. 2006. *The open city.* Urban Age, 1–5.

Sennett, R. 2018. *Making and Dwelling: Ethics for the City.* London: Penguin.

SIGI (Social Institutions and Gender Index). 2012. "Peru." Web. www.genderindex.org/country/peru.

Simone, A.M. 1994. "In the mix: remaking coloured identities." *Africa Insight* 24.3: 161–173.

Skytran 2016. "Skytran – About," Skytran. www.skytran.com/

Soja, E.W. 2000. *Postmetropolis: Critical Studies of Cities and Regions,* Oxford: Blackwell.

Songdo IBD 2015. "*Songdo IBD – About,*" Songdo IBD.

Stanton, C. 2012. "The Global Fund for Women Impact Report: Gender Equality In Asia & The Pacic." *Global Fund For Women,* San Francisco. Web. www.globalfundforwomen.org/wp-content/uploads/2012/04/Global_Fund_for_Women_Impact_Report_Breaking_Through.pdf (last accessed January 28, 2018).

Stiglitz, J. 2012. *The Price of Inequality: How Today's Divided Society Endangers Our Future.* New York: W.W. Norton & Company.

Streeck, W. 2014. "How Will Capitalism End?" *New Left Review* 87: 35–64.

Sudarshan, R., and S. Sinha 2011. *Making Home-Based Work Visible: A Review of Evidence from South Asia.*

Swilling, M. 2006. "Sustainability and Infrastructure Planning in South Africa: a Cape Town case study." *Environment and Urbanization* 18/1: 23–50.

Swilling, M., and E. Annecke 2012. "Rethinking Urbanism," in M. Swilling and E. Anneke, *Just Transitions: Explorations of Sustainability in an Unfair World.* New York: United Nations University Press.

Thrift, N., and A. Amin 2002. *Cities: Reimagining the Urban.* Cambridge: Polity Press.

Tracy, J., and A. Jacobson 2012. The True Cost of Kerosene in Rural Africa. Lighting Africa Report. www.lightingafrica.org/wp-content/uploads/2016/07/40_kerosene_pricing_Lighting_Africa_Report.pdf (last accessed January 28, 2018).

United Nations Economic Commission for Africa (ECA) 2015. *Contribution to the 2015 United Nations Economic and Social Council (ECOSOC) Integration Segment.*

United Nations Environment Programme (UNEP) 2011. Towards a Green Economy: Pathways to Sustainable Development and Poverty Eradication. www.unep.org/greeneconomy

United Nations Environment Programme (UNEP) 2014. *Decoupling 2: Technologies, Opportunities and Policy Options.* Nairobi: UNEP.

United Nations Human Settlements Program (UN-Habitat) 1996. Report of the United Nations Conference on Human Settlements (Habitat II). Istanbul, June 3–14, 1996. www.un.org/ruleoflaw/wp-content/uploads/2015/10/istanbul-declaration.pdf (last accessed January 28, 2018).

United Nations Human Settlements Program (UN-Habitat) 2010. State of the World's Cities 2010/2011: Bridging the Urban Divide. http://mirror.unhabitat.org/pmss/listItemDetails.aspx?publicationID=2917&AspxAutoDetectCookieSupport=1 (last accessed December 23, 2017).

United Nations Human Settlements Program (UN-Habitat) 2012. State of the World's Cities 2012/2013. Prosperity of Cities, Nairobi: UN-Habitat.

United Nations Human Settlements Program (UN-Habitat) 2015. E-Governance and Urban Policy Design in Developing Countries. https://unhabitat.org/books/e-governance-and-urban-policy-design-in-developing-countries/ (last accessed December 23, 2017).

United Nations Human Settlements Program (UN-Habitat) 2016a. Habitat III: The New Urban Agenda. www.habitat3.org (last accessed December 23, 2017).

United Nations Human Settlements Program (UN-Habitat) 2016b. Urbanization and Development: Emerging Futures. World Cities Report 2016, Nairobi: UN-Habitat.

United Nations Statistics Division 2015. *Millennium Development Goals Indicators.* United Nations MDG Indicators. http://mdgs.un.org/unsd/mdg/SeriesDetail.aspx?srid=655&crid (last accessed December 23, 2017).

United Nations, Department of Economic and Social Affairs (UN-DESA), Population Division 2014. *World Urbanization Prospects: the 2014 Revision, Highlights.* New York and Geneva: United Nations.

United Nations, Department of Economic and Social Affairs (UN-DESA) 2015. "2014 Revision of World Urbanization Prospects." ed. P.D. *Department of Economic and Social Affairs.* New York: UN.

5

United Nations, Department of Economic and Social Affairs (UN-DESA) 2016. *The World Cities in 2016. Data Booklet.* Department of Economic and Social Affairs. New York: UN.

Van der Ryn, S., and P. Calthorpe 1991. *Sustainable Communities.* Gabriola Island, BC: New Catalyst Books.

Varia, N. 2007. "Sanctioned Abuses: The Case of Migrant Domestic Workers," *Human Rights Brief* 14: 17–20.

WBGU – German Advisory Council on Global Change 2016. *Humanity on the Move. Unlocking the Transformative Power Of Cities.* Berlin: WBGU.

Weinstein, L. 2014. *The Durable Slum: Dharavi and the Right to Stay Put in Globalizing Mumbai.* Minneapolis: University of Minnesota Press.

Wilkinson, R. and K. Pickett 2009. *The Spirit Level: Why More Equal Societies Almost Always Do Better.* London: Allen Lane.

Williams, K. 2004. Can Urban Intensication Contribute to Sustainable Cities? An International Perspective. http://citeseerx.ist.psu.edu/viewdoc/download?doi=10.1.1.565.6770&rep=rep1&type=pdf (last accessed January 28, 2018).

World Bank 2009. "Project Information Document: Adolescent Girls Initiative – Afghanistan." *The World Bank.* http://documents.worldbank.org/curated/en/421511467995355571/pdf/Project0Inform1cument1Concept0Stage.pdf (last accessed January 28, 2018).

Wright, F.L. 1932. *"Broadacre City," An Architect's Vision.* New York: The New York Times Company.

Young, I.M. 1990. *Justice and the Politics of Difference.* Princeton: Princeton University Press.

6

Markets, Finance, and Corporations: Does Capitalism have a Future?

Coordinating Lead Authors:[1]
Simon Deakin, Fabian Muniesa, Scott Stern, Lorraine Talbot

Lead Authors:[2]
Raphie Kaplinsky, Martin O'Neill, Horacio Ortiz, Kerstin Sahlin, Anke Schwittay

[1]   Affiliations: SD: University of Cambridge; FM: Mines ParisTech; SS: MIT; LT: University of Birmingham.
[2]   Affiliations: RK: University of Sussex; MON: University of York; HO: CNRS, Université Paris Dauphine; KS: Swedish Research Council; AS: University of Sussex.

Summary

This chapter provides an overview and a critique of modern capitalism focusing on the core institutions of finance and the corporation. It considers the degree to which they foster or inhibit social progress. For the purposes of this chapter we see social progress as the removal of inequalities in wealth and power and the facilitation of innovation and technological progress from which all people can benefit. The chapter acknowledges that capitalism, corporations, and finance have developed over time, within nation-states and in relation to institutions in other nation-states. Their contribution to social progress, or in the alternative, social regression, varies according to historical, political, and geographical context. We show that while globalization has significantly impacted capitalism, corporations, and finance, making them global as well as national in scope, they continue to be grounded within nation-states. Throughout the chapter we aim to show the integration of the state and the capitalist economy and the dependence of the institutions of capitalism on the state.

The first substantive section provides a brief narrative about the nature and scope of modern capitalism. We show how attributes of the capitalist market economy, including its tendency to expand, and to create high levels of productivity driven by labor saving innovations, have created huge wealth. We note, however, that this type of capitalism has also produced massive inequalities between people and groups and has caused environmental problems which disproportionally effect developing nations. Social progress is also inhibited by the control which powerful market actors can exercise over regulation and innovation opportunities. Not only does this restrict access by new and potentially brilliant players to realize their vision, it ensures that products are made only for profit. As society becomes more unequal, innovation becomes increasingly focused on the desires of the wealthiest.

We then go on to consider the corporate form as an institution of capitalism and a legal mechanism which has enabled economic progress and innovation but has also enhanced inequality and social regression. We suggest that in a period where there has been scant economic recovery after the global financial crisis, social regression is likely to be the dominant outcome of corporate activity. The chapter considers the historical emergence of the company as a legal person and the development of the share as a fungible and transferable property form, enhanced by the institution of limited liability. Our analysis notes that shareholders do not own the firm: they emerged historically as outside investors akin to bondholders, and their continued claim to control rights in the company came to be justified in the modern period as a device for reducing monitoring and other transaction costs. However, in terms of social progress, the idea that it is the duty of managers to deliver value for shareholders has enhanced inequality and stymied innovation. Increasing value for shareholders has been achieved through lowering pay and conditions for workers in most developed countries, particularly the US and the UK, and through utilizing low cost and often unprotected labor from developing countries in an increasingly globalized corporate economy. A catalogue of human tragedies in the factories of countries such as Bangladesh testify to this, as does the huge and growing disparity between the global wealthiest 1 percent – mainly based in the global North (Lakner and Milanovic 2016) – and the rest of the world. We show how extracting value from developing countries is achieved by multinational corporations through subsidiaries and through contractual networks. Both forms generally protect the parent or lead company from liabilities arising from industrial accidents such as the Rana Plaza factory collapse. Corporations at the top of global value chains claim the most valuable part of the value creation process, which are also those most strongly protected by intellectual property rights and other legal mechanisms. We consider, among others, the case of large pharmaceutical companies. We show that innovation is being stymied in their case by the pressure to deliver shareholder value, resulting in more profit being utilized for dividends and share buy-backs rather than research and development.

In addition, we examine financial institutions, which have become increasingly important in national economies and also increasingly global. Corporations rely on access to finance and incorporate financial businesses in their own operations. Global wealth is centered around global financial hubs and it is those centers that essentially decide who will have access to funds. Financial institutions rely on extracting a portion of global wealth and do not extend finance by reference to criteria of social progress. The chapter also notes the growing role of finance in the delivery of public goods and the regressive effects of this shift. The institutions of finance have come to inhibit social progress because as intermediaries between global production and finance they reflect power imbalances within and between nation-states and thereby reinforce global inequalities.

Intrinsic to capitalism, corporations, and finance, is the state. At a fundamental level, the state protects private property and market exchange. It also constitutes the corporate form as a mode of economic organization in which capital hires labor, not the reverse. In the middle decades of the twentieth century this intrinsic inequality was tempered by the operation of the welfare state. Since the 1980s, mechanisms of risk-sharing and redistribution, which were characteristic of the welfare state, have been weakened in many countries. There has been a shift away from the publicly instituted regulation of the postwar decades, in favour of forms of "governance" suitable for more liberalized and less welfare-orientated economies (Supiot 2015). In part this is happening because states see themselves as competing with one another for investments and corporate relocations. International agencies, which previously operated to contain the destabilizing effects of cross-border flows of goods and resources, now actively promote the removal of social and environmental protections which are described as "nontariff barriers" to trade.

These developments will require, in due course, a systematic legal and political response, which will place limits on markets and reset the relationship between trade and the state. We cannot cover all aspects of the process here, for reasons of space, and because it is still unfolding (indeed, in some respects has yet to begin). To illustrate what might be done in one of the areas which form part of our remit, we conclude the chapter by looking at how reforms to the legal institution of the company could help reverse the trends we have identified in the earlier parts of the chapter. We discuss reforms to tackle tax evasion and the obfuscation of wealth which have been enabled by multinational corporate networks gaming regulation and tax law. Our analysis also discusses reforms to protect productive companies from rent-seeking by shareholders. We consider the problems which arise when corporate regulation shifts from public control to soft law and voluntary social responsibility practices. We propose a radical restructuring of corporate decision-making which would see the removal of certain control rights from shareholders. We suggest ways in which inclusive innovation could be promoted.

The chapter concludes in arguing that global corporate capitalism has come to depend upon the perpetuation of inequality both within and between nation-states, and as such is inhibiting progress which is truly social. The slow growth which has proceeded from the global financial crisis has enhanced these problems. We conclude that reform which delivers for all people is now both an economic and social imperative.

6.1   Introduction

The financial crisis which began with the credit crunch of 2007 and climaxed the following autumn with the failure of leading financial institutions in the USA and Britain is far from unique in the long run of capitalism. While the toll of the years 1772, 1825, or 1873 (and many others) may not ring as clearly as 1929 or 2008 in the modern imagination, their impact on the participants of the day was equally profound. Indeed, as Marx first noted, and others including Kondratieff later confirmed, cycles of growth, stagnation, and collapse were endogenous to capitalism. During the 1990s it was possible to believe that business cycles were a thing of the past. We now know (again) that this is not the case. In addition, the dramatic wealth inequalities that exist in capitalist economies and are expanding in the face of rapid technological change no longer seem to be transitory, but rather represent a systematic feature of capitalism. With the rise of moguls, oligarchs, and princelings, there is a growing discussion of the distortions to the broader social order that arise with massive wealth disparities. Scientific awareness of the multiple links that exist between capitalist organization of the economy and the ecological crisis – conducive to the formulation of the Anthropocene as a new subdivision of geological time – have also pointed the debate in new, critical directions. The capitalist system might suffice for the creation of a plethora of material goods, but it pays scant attention to the fair distribution of these goods and to the unintended consequences of their proliferation. Any economic system must be judged by not only what it delivers but also by how sustainably, responsibly, and democratically it does so – in particular by the degree to which it delivers the capacity for all individuals in a society to achieve safety, dignity, and the potential to thrive.

While there are many reasons to question the soundness of the fundamental foundations of capitalism, it has been more successful than any other economic system in generating wealth. Some argue that capitalism has been beneficial at all levels of society. In 2013, *The Economist* reported that nearly 1 billion people were now living at the poverty line of $1.25 a day per person, a 50 percent reduction from 1990. Others, however, take issue with the $1.25 baseline. The World Bank (2013) maintains that the poverty line should more realistically be set at $5 a day. Oxfam (2016) has pointed to growing wealth disparities and the huge wealth inequality between most of the Global South and Global North, and to the increasingly wealthy elite which is pulling away from the rest of the world. Furthermore, the fall in the number of people affected by absolute poverty since the 1990s is almost entirely down to the results of economic growth in China, and here, as elsewhere, such growth is associated with the emergence of a new, super-rich elite, and growing pressure on the social fabric.

The divisive nature of wealth distribution under contemporary capitalism is played out in many forms. The 1999 WTO conference, the site for the advancement of the world capitalist order, was accompanied by national and international protest movements against it. A growing group of protestors across the globe have questioned whether the capitalist system fosters the right type of growth: whether the types of exploitation by international corporations observed in Bangladeshi factory collapses, Foxconn suicides, the many other scandals that have not reached similar, international attention, and the vast global differentials in wealth, mean that capitalism should not have a future. These abuses as well as the myriad environmental disasters that have been documented since Rachel Carson's *Silent Spring* – and before – have called into question the long-run trajectory of capitalism.

We do not have a complete theoretical or empirical understanding of the (in)capacity of institutions to respond to persistent inequalities and inequities across and between nations. What is clear is that the interests of the financial elite were protected at the cost of those of the mass of taxpayers in the last worldwide financial crisis. This has only sharpened contemporary critiques of capitalism. Whether the problems associated with capitalism, particularly in its current form which sees a prominent role for financial interests and for finance as a mode of governance, mean that capitalism cannot promote social progress, is an open question.

Our discussion focuses on how capitalism operates and whether it delivers or inhibits social progress. In the sections below, we provide a historically focused account of the emergence of the key interlinked phenomena of the current capitalist system. The meaning of "capitalism" is contentious: definitions of the concept abound that revolve around a series of recurring themes, but with notable variations. Citing a series of notable classics (Sombart, Weber, Schumpeter, Keynes, Marx), Streeck (2016) observes how different definitions of capitalism emphasize different elements of its configuration, depending on the claim being made. In what follows we aim to follow Streeck in decomposing capitalism into a series of elements which contemporary social science has come to see as critical for the understanding of the capitalist way of organizing economic processes and social life. Capitalism is here understood as a moving, unstable reality, with different modes or varieties of capitalism being historically and geographically identifiable (see Chapter 8 for a discussion of varieties of capitalism). The elements that are discussed in what follows do not constitute an exhaustive list of necessary conditions for capitalism. In fact, capitalist configurations can be identified that do not meet all of them. They nonetheless appear in a number of accounts that are relevant to the subject matter. These elements are: (1) price systems, international trade, and the expansion of markets; (2) corporations, shareholder value, and capital control; and (3) financial institutions, credit, and the banking system. The purpose of this chapter is to provide a pluralistic compass for understanding capitalism, finance, and corporations, their relation to social progress, and the changes necessary to make capitalism deliver progress for the well-being of all. Our contribution is underpinned by the question of whether it is ultimately possible for capitalism to deliver a socially progressive future.

6.2   Capitalism: A Market Economy

6.2.1   Introduction: The Nature of the Market

The "market" is a mechanism of allocation which allows for goods, services, information, or resources to be exchanged between transacting parties at a price, that is, through the mediation of monetary payment. There is no unique model of what a market is or should be, and different types of market mechanisms, rules and institutions are recognizable in both theoretical modeling and empirical history (Hodgson 2009). These differences may correspond, in theoretical debate, to varying criteria of allocative efficiency or distributive justice. In practical reality, they are generally related to the characteristics of exchanged goods, the idiosyncrasies of institutional settings, and their dependence on historical processes and the politics of the situation.

In this chapter we refer to the market as an essential institution of capitalism. This approach commonly features in such terms as "market society," "market capitalism," or "market-based capitalism"; that is, as a distinctive feature of the organization of an entire productive system and, moreover, as the key element in the social order of a particular historical configuration. The market, in this approach, is an allocation mechanism, but is also much more than that: it is the organizing principle for the functioning not just of the economy, but of society at large. The highly normative aspect of academic debates around the problem of a market society is best exemplified in the confrontations that took place in the 1940s on the interpretation of the links between liberalism, socialism, and the rise of fascism in Europe. The critique of the governmental control of economic processes and the praise for the social virtues of a free market offered by Friedrich A. Von Hayek (1944) provides a sharp contrast with the analysis of fascism as a catastrophic reaction to the dismantlement of social cohesion by free market policies given by Karl Polanyi (2001). Today, discussions on the social damage that "market fundamentalism" may prompt are still marked by this crucial debate (Block and Somers 2014; see also Chapter 1). The notion of "neoliberalism" refers, in these contemporary discussions, to a doctrine that sees in the principle of a free market the guarantee for the development of a virtuous social order and of the policies that serve it – which include deregulation, privatization, free trade, and austerity (Springer, Birch, and MacLeavy 2016).

Considered as an element of contemporary global capitalism, markets feature most distinctively through the development of international trade and of competition policies, which constitute in turn crucial aspects of globalization (Kaplinsky 2005). The notion of competitiveness has indeed been signaled abundantly as a key ingredient of neoliberal governance (Davies 2014). It refers to the capacity of economic actors to perform satisfactorily in a market that constitutes the prime medium of economic life and that is perceived at once as a source of threats and as a vehicle for opportunities. Although they find justification in liberal doctrines of free trade, competitive markets evidently require, in order to just be competitive, a complex regulatory apparatus. Competition law plays an essential role, for example through the development of antitrust schemes, in the establishment of global competition as a key factor in the shaping of economies and societies worldwide (Gerber 2010). The field of international commercial arbitration has also been identified as an area in which a particular legal order is essential to the formation of an institutional environment favorable for international business and global trade (Dezalay and Garth 1998). International trade agreements are also critical for the understanding of the terms in which a competitive world market has been constructed in recent decades. Trade agreements such as NAFTA (the North American Free Trade Agreement, established in 1994 between Mexico, Canada, and the United States) are not just concerned with the flow of goods and services, but in establishing regulatory regimes which impact on modes of production and have consequences for distribution.

Capitalism operates through markets which have developed historically and reflect the balance of power both within nations and globally. In the following section, we examine the nature and development of capitalism starting from its essential elements; the relationship of capital to labor and the drive to innovate and increase productivity.

6.2.2   Capitalism and Labor

As noted in the introduction, there are many extant types of capitalist society, and at least as many theories of the nature of capitalism. What we take to be pertinent to our understanding of capitalism and to identifying its link to social progress is the way in which capitalism treats workers and the way it treats wealth that is connected to worker's productive activity, that is, capital itself. Capitalist production is based on wage labor and a specific variant of finance, identified with equity capital. Integral to this mode of production is the drive to maximize profits. This creates a dynamic for innovation which increases the productivity of labor. In the process of profit-seeking, capitalism veers from periods of high growth and development to periods of economic crisis and slumps in production, which adversely affect workers (Piketty 2014).

The rise of a market in wage labor can be more or less precisely dated to a process which began in the economies of Western Europe in the early modern period, that is, in the long transition from feudalism which began in the fourteenth century, and came to fruition in the nineteenth-century "age of industry." The institution of wage labor implies the "subordination" of the worker within the capitalist firm and, more generally, the social stratification associated with the appearance of a working class, a proletariat, with no direct access to the traditional means of production and subsistence (the land and the family). The members of a working class, so defined, are required to sell their labor power under conditions of inequality: in a capitalist labor market, "capital hires labor," not the reverse. While this basic institutional feature of capitalism is well understood on all sides of the debate about the nature of market economy, what is not so well understood, and which needs to be emphasized here, is that the emergence of wage labor was not a natural or spontaneous process, but one which, at every stage, involved the creation of an apparatus for governing labor market relations associated with the rise of nation-states with significant regulatory and tax-raising capacities (Deakin and Wilkinson 2005).

In a capitalist economy, "capital" takes a particular form. "Debt" may be as old as human society itself (Graeber 2011) but equity finance is a modern phenomenon, which is traceable to the first appearance, in seventeenth-century Europe, of the institution of joint stock. Equity capital enables the surplus generated by production to be freed from its connection to material assets and to human labor. Through the creation of forms of intangible property, that is, shares and similar corporate securities, the surplus becomes fungible, that is, tradable in a market setting. This makes possible its redistribution across different uses, hence the allocative role of the "capital market." Again, the point we wish to stress here, and which generally does not receive enough attention across the social sciences, is that none of this would have been possible without a series of legal and regulatory innovations (Harris 2000).

The conjunction of wage labor markets and capital markets is underpinned by the state through the legal system as well as complementary institutions including systems of taxation and public finance. Over time, the employment contract had attached to it various social rights beginning with the right to workers' freedom of association and extending to characteristic institutions of the "welfare" or "social state" including social insurance and labor legislation in the areas of health and safety, employment protection, and equal treatment. This process was the result of the extension of the democratic franchise to the working class and was more generally coterminous with the emergence and stabilization of the institutions of liberal democracy including the practice of legal autonomy or the "rule of law." Labor rights were massively expanded in the high-growth postwar period, often referred to as the "golden age." Since then labor rights, particularly in their collective form, have been significantly eroded, together with the security provided by the welfare state. Since the 2008 crisis, austerity policies have continued to bite into welfare provision. Social rights are seen to be a charge on the capitalist firm, so even if firms collectively benefit from the provision of public goods including orderly industrial relations, individual profit-seeking enterprises will take whatever opportunities they can to minimize or avoid social or fiscal commitments.

As capitalist labor and capital markets expand globally, the paradoxical effects of capitalism on social progress are amplified. Global corporations and supply chains can take advantage of labor located in the Global South to change the basis of the social contract in the North. The wealth they create is increasingly captured by elites in all countries, with those in part of the Global South enjoying, if anything, an even clearer advantage over the rest of the society than elsewhere (Palma 2011). Thus the extension of capitalism to virtually all parts of the world economy since the fall of the Berlin Wall in 1989 is very far from ensuring the equal enjoyment by all elements of society of the fruits of technological and scientific progress.

6.2.3   Innovation: A Driver of Capitalism

Whatever the merits or demerits of capitalism from the point of view of social progress, it has proved more effective than any other system to date in promoting innovation. Innovation should be understood as a dynamic internal to capitalism which drives and harnesses technological progress.

The expansion of private capital is principally generated by firms introducing new production processes, new products, new business models, new forms of work organization, and new forms of relationships between firms in value chains – that is, by innovating. Highlighting the central role played by innovation in capitalist development, Schumpeter showed how new technologies rendered existing forms of production obsolete, resulting in "waves of creative destruction," with massive implications for production, employment, firm-survival, the sectoral composition of output and for society at large (Schumpeter 1942).

The profit maximizing imperative of capitalism is actualized through rising labor productivity, and this is achieved through innovations in work practices and technologies. A pervasive feature of innovation

under capitalism has been the consolidation of management power over labor. This can take the form of organizational innovations – the way Amazon's warehouses are run, with workers being fitted with pedometers to ensure that they worked at the required (and intense) pace, is a modern expression of an established process of control. Innovation in technology and mechanization leading to organizational change not only provided inanimate energy to increase productivity, but it also provided the capitalist with greater control over the labor process.

Most innovation since the Industrial Revolution has occurred in advanced economies where wages are relatively high by global standards and where finance capital is relatively cheap. Capitalist innovation is labor-saving in the short run, but creates new demands for labor over the longer run. As a pervasive trend, innovation has substituted machinery for labor in the quest to reduce production costs. This reinforces the tendency for innovation to favor control of labor by capital. But it has also generated entirely new occupations and professions, and it is too early to say that radical innovations of today such as artificial intelligence or blockchain will not work in the same way in the future.

The state has always played a key role in facilitating capitalist innovation. First, the state is needed to protect property rights in knowledge. Without some form of intellectual property protection, the rents generated by innovation will not flow back to knowledge producers. Second, the state underpins the corporate structures which drive accumulation. Third, the state provides the macro-institutional framework which sustains opportunities for capitalist development.

The structure of markets plays an important role in the character of innovation paths. Focusing on the demand side, since innovation responds to purchasing power, and since the overwhelming share of global demand has emanated from high income consumers, innovation has resulted in products which predominantly meet the needs of the wealthy rather than those excluded from the fruits of growth. For example, in pharma, innovation has targeted the needs of higher income consumers such as dementia and cancer, rather than on neglected diseases such as malaria which affect the lives of hundreds of millions of the human population. Moreover, since capitalist innovation involves the private appropriation of rewards, it has favored the development of curative pharmaceutical formulations protected by intellectual property rights, rather than preventive public goods such as immunization whose benefits are difficult to capture by innovating firms.

So, while innovations have the potential to impact the lives of all participants, innovation which targets wealthy individuals creates a potentially self-sustaining wedge of inequality that market mechanisms have no means of overcoming (Jaravel 2016). Any market with liquidity constraints will favor ideas with the largest potential for profit, that is to say, those focused on the wealthy, even if there are, in principle, profitable innovations available which would help the less well-off.

Time preference is an important shaper of innovation in capitalism. Many innovations involve costly investments in R&D and are a long time in the making. Their returns may also accrue over long time periods, and may build up gradually. These time profiles may be especially extended in the case of technologically complex or risky innovations. Hence, innovating firms with high rates of time preference (that is, utilizing high discount rates on their investments) will tend to steer away from these types of innovations, and prefer to invest in more trivial innovations with a shorter payback period. This will have a cost to society at large, but also to the long-run profitability of the firm.

One of the dominant characteristics of contemporary capitalism has been the tendency for rapid returns to senior management and shareholders to be prioritized over long-term gains which are also more widely shared across different corporate constituencies and by wider society. This tendency is dulling the incentive to invest in innovations which are risky and have long gestation periods. The state can play a role not just in funding and supporting innovation, but in altering the time horizon for returns, and in ensuring that they are more equitably shared. In recent decades the myth has been propagated that virtually all innovation arises from investments by the private sector and that the state should withdraw from this realm of economic activity. However, we now know from recent research that virtually all recent technological developments of significance have arisen from prior investments in the state sector. The core developments in the IT, bio-tech, nanotech and green-tech sectors all had their origins in state-sponsored R&D (Mazzucato 2013). The long gestation periods and uncertainties involved in these types of innovation are such that the private sector would have been incapable of supporting them without significant financial and regulatory support from government (Lazonick 2014).

So while capitalism contains an intrinsic drive to innovate and to increase productivity, and so has the potential to deliver huge opportunities for social progress and for the meeting of material needs, innovation is a complex process which is very far from spontaneous and may also have socially regressive outcomes. At present there is a danger that the most advantaged in the world economy are reaping the lion's share of the increase in wealth generated by innovation. The pursuit of innovations which maximize profits runs the risk of sidelining those with greater potential for social progress (Jaravel 2016).

6.2.4   The Socially Regressive Tendencies of Innovation under Contemporary Capitalism

Under current conditions, the drive toward labor-saving technological progress has profound social implications. Unemployment is high in the developing world and formal employment relatively low. At a conservative estimate, the informal economy accounts for more than 70 percent of work in Africa and South Asia (Charmes 2012). Unemployment is an endogenous feature of capitalism and thus is prevalent in the high-income economies too. Once capitalism in the global North was provided with access to a reserve army of labor from the 1990s – China, India, and Eastern Europe – unemployment, coupled with a growing degree of precarious work, once again became a feature of many high and middle income economies, not least in sectors being disrupted by radical and revolutionary technological change.

The diffusion of information and communication technologies ("ICTs") and the arrival of the so-called gig-economy have put working conditions under pressure in many countries. New forms of organizing transport such as those associated with Uber may provide for more efficient use of resources; cars which were previously idle are now used more intensively. However, this is also leading to the casualization of work and to a reduction in the share of the surplus from production going to wages. In the hospitality sector, AirBnB provides some property owners with good incomes but is also leading to speculative investments in property while reducing incomes and wages in the hotel industry and eroding the taxes which governments previously garnered from the hospitality sector.

Closely aligned to the progressive elements of innovation in meeting material needs are the regressive elements of innovation when captured within a capitalist framework. These include the mechanisms used to protect the entrepreneurs' benefits from innovations through forms of price fixing such as oligopolies, or intellectual property rights. This can exclude further development of essential medicines or exclude use of the patented product through price, even though free or cheaper products could alleviate pressing social problems.

Underemployment, informal employment, casual employment, and unemployment are an intrinsic characteristic of capitalism and delivered in large part by capitalist innovations. This negative impact on work increases economic inequalities and decreases security and personal progression. Coupled with this is the tendency for investment in innovation to be linked to purchasing power thus increasing innovation in products focused on high income purchasers. Capitalist innovation (particularly under the corporate form) can often have short-term horizons, where a rapid return of profit is preferred over the development of innovations that provide the maximum social benefits.

6.2.5   Capitalism and Globalization

In the pursuit of productivity savings, capitalist business organizations, mostly constituted as corporations, tend to expand globally. The power of the major corporations in North America and Europe who sought to gain access to external markets led to a series of multilateral initiatives (initially under the aegis of the GATT and subsequently the WTO) to reduce the barriers to the exchange of goods and services across national borders.

Until the 1970s, economic growth in the major individual economies had largely resulted from a combination of domestic firms producing for domestic consumption, foreign-owned firms producing for the domestic market in their overseas operations, and trade between economies in finished products. New technologies and new markets transformed this picture of domestically focused production and consumption and trade in finished products, and gave rise to a new form of business organization – the Global Value Chain (GVC).

GVCs arose from a strategy in which firms, operating in increasingly competitive global markets and in an environment of increasingly knowledge-intensive production, began to focus on their core competences (Hamel and Prahalad 1994). Core competences are those capabilities which have a value in the final market, are unique to the firm and are difficult to copy. Any other activities were outsourced to suppliers and customers. The greater the competition in these outsourced activities, the greater the share of chain rents that the lead outsourcing firm was able to capture. Initially outsourcing occurred in the domestic economy, but as innovation in ICTs and logistics innovations unfolded, so outsourcing assumed an increasingly global character. Lead firms, and their lead suppliers increasingly "sliced-up" their value chains and sought to encourage links with suppliers and users across the global economy.

GVCs now dominate global trade and much of global production. The World Trade Organization estimated that in 2012, two-thirds of global trade occurred within the framework of GVCs (UNCTAD 2013). A substantial (but unmeasured) share of this trade in GVCs is controlled ("governed") by one or more parties. This may involve control over logistics, the division of labor in the chain, technology and innovation, property rights, branding, and other determinants of competitive positioning in final markets and the distribution of returns in GVCs (Gereffi and Korzeniewicz 1994; Kaplinsky and Morris 2001). In a global world dominated by GVCs, governance of these chains involves a complex interplay between private and public sector actors exercising power – firms within value chains, civil society, nation-states, and international regulatory bodies (Davis, Kaplinsky, and Morris 2017).

The advance of globalization through the medium of GVCs has a number of important implications for social progress. It has enhanced productivity and provided cost savings. Larger markets provided the opportunity for lead firms to gain from economies of scale and to specialize in their core competences in which barriers to entry provided the scope for rent generation and appropriation. Importantly, the spread of GVCs provided a much enlarged and much cheaper global labor force for global firms to draw on, with production relocated to low-wage environments in Asia, Central America, North Africa, and elsewhere. On the one hand this reduced the costs of inputs for lead firms. It also resulted in major employment growth in several low-income economies. After the mid-1980s, China became a particularly important source of outsourced production, initially in low wage unskilled tasks but increasingly also in technology-intensive intermediates and final products. As noted earlier, this has resulted in a massive reduction in extreme poverty.

An important consequence of the deepening of globalization through the spread of GVCs was the spread of values and consumer preferences across the globe. This has had contradictory consequences. On the one hand it promoted values relevant to social progress such as respect for human rights, labor standards, and gender equality. On the other hand, and particularly in recent years, it has led to cultural dissonances, with a rowback against these global values, particularly amongst communities marginalized from the fruits of globalizing growth (Kaplinsky 2005). The dominant growth paradigm has been characterized by the growing separation of production and consumption on a global scale, involving the foreign ownership of productive capital, where the owner organization dwarfs the host state.

The rise of GVCs has allowed transnational corporations to transfer-price rents by shifting the tax-take from the source to the residence principle. This affects the ability of states to tax transnational companies and it also impacts on the global distribution of wealth. GVCs enhance firms' capacity to source inputs (particularly labor) from the least-cost global sources. This has considerable implications for the distribution of income within the firm (capital and labor), and within individual countries (for example, managerial salaries are often influenced by global rates rather than living standards in the economy in which production occurs). This has led to adverse impacts on labor in the North, as jobs and wages have been undercut by competition from labor in the Global South, and the capacity to regulate the firm is diminished as firms operate and optimize on a global scale, whereas governments operate on a national scale. With regard to markets, trade and market entry are no longer governed solely or principally by states but increasingly by the corporate sector itself, which imposes standards and which governs access to niche markets. The capacity of corporation-generated regulation to deliver in terms of enabling (or at least not inhibiting) social progress is very limited. In contrast, corporations have a huge capacity to influence regulation in their interests and to sideline social progress issues such as environmental protection and labor issues.

Finally, globalization has led to adverse environmental impacts that are over and above those that would have emerged through more locally focused forms of capitalist development. By their nature, GVCs that outsource their supply chains across the globe make demands on energy intensive and polluting logistical systems, with massive environmental externalities.

6.2.6   Conclusion

Capitalism is a dynamic economic system, with an intrinsic drive to produce innovation and an increase in material wealth. It may do so, however, at great cost to social progress. In today's world the gains of innovation are not being equally shared, and too often we are seeing technological progress married to a deterioration in working conditions and in the erosion of the tax base. To understand why this is occurring we need to take a closer look at the core institution of contemporary capitalism, the corporation.

6.3   The Corporation

6.3.1   The Nature of the Corporate Form

For current purposes we define corporations as legally structured entities engaging in production for the purpose of profit. Most of our discussion will focus on larger corporations operating on a transnational basis. The term "corporation" or "company" is ambiguous and can be taken to refer both to the juridical form which is used, among other things, to attribute legal personality to productive activities, or to the organizational structure through which production occurs (for discussion see Aoki 2010; Robé 2011). The relationship between the emergence of the corporate form in its juridical sense and the rise of capitalism is a complex one but there is no doubt that there is a close link between them and that the attribution of legal personality to business firms was a historically momentous step.

The idea that the business firm should operate as a legal person separate from the shareholders and endowed with a "permanent" existence emerged alongside the identification of the "share" as an item of property which could be traded in its own right. The first judicial decisions to identify the share as a personal right consisting of a title to revenue, as distinct from a beneficial interest in the underlying business, were reported in the 1830s (Williston 1888). Judges at this time conceptualized the shareholder as a money investor with an interest in the surplus produced by business, rather than as a co-owner of the physical assets of the firm. This legal innovation allowed the firm to retain control over its working capital while providing investors with liquidity. The effect was to shield equity capital from risk, a trend reinforced when, in a related development, it became normal (from the mid-nineteenth century onwards) to recognize shareholders' limited liability (that is, shareholders' immunity from suit, except to the extent of any unpaid equity, for the trading debts of the entities in which they held stock).

Today, the legal institutions of corporate personality and limited liability for shareholders are justified as devices for reducing monitoring and other transaction costs, lowering the cost of capital, and facilitating the trading of shares (Armour, Hansmann, Kraakman, and Pargendler 2017). Corporate personality is not confined to these broadly capital-protective functions, however. "Asset partitioning," it is suggested, by shielding the firm's working assets against direct control by shareholders and creditors, supplies the institutional basis for corporations to become enduring organizational forms (Hansmann, Kraakman, and Squire 2006). The resulting "capital lock-in" provided the basis for the innovations associated with the network industries of the "second industrial revolution" of the final decades of the nineteenth century (Blair 2004). During this period the corporate form also became the basis for modern enterprise liability, and hence for a legally recognized form of corporate responsibility, in areas including accident liability and environmental law, and for the treatment of corporate profits as taxable income for the purposes of fiscal law, so assisting the financing of the regulatory state (Deakin 2003). Entities of various kinds, including nonprofits and cooperatives owned by customers and workers as well as industrial firms constituted as companies limited by share capital, benefited from the availability of the corporate form, and continue to do so (Adams and Deakin 2017), although business models such as the mutual building society have largely failed to flourish via the corporate form (Talbot 2010).

The multifunctional nature of company law means that the solution to the abusive exercise of corporate power is unlikely to be found in the simple abolition of the corporate form. However, it does not follow that measures cannot be taken to limit abuses of the right to incorporate. Techniques for "lifting the corporate veil" are well understood, and can be applied in the context of fiscal law to limit artificial asset partitioning (as we shall explore in further detail below). In numerous jurisdictions, the law provides that the firm's shareholders may lose immunity from suit in the case of environmental or labor violations, and parent companies have been made liable for the

human rights violations of their subsidiaries. There is no shortage of legal techniques for countering tax evasion and regulatory avoidance; the failure to deploy them is much more the result of lobbying by vested interests than the inadequacy of legal mechanisms (Blumberg and Strasser 2011).

6.3.2   The Evolution of the Corporate Function

In the mid-1960s, most US corporations stated their mission in terms of producing value for communities, workers, and the public at large; virtually none referred to maximizing shareholder value as their goal (Jacoby 2005). In the UK, while the law itself was heavily shareholder orientated, as a matter of practice corporate decision-making was undertaken in consultation with trade unions and government (Talbot 2016). Today, the unhindered promotion of shareholder value is almost universally considered to be the purpose of corporate activity, and even references in corporate annual reports to the need to be socially responsible are often presented as a means of further enhancing shareholder value. The current salience of the shareholder interest in the thinking of executives in listed US and British companies is the result of three decades of concerted institutional effort to align the interests of managers and shareholders. The need for such an alignment is the premise of agency theory, the cornerstone of modern corporate finance, and the guiding principle of corporate governance codes, which, from the early 1990s, have spread the essentials of this model, which originated in the USA and Britain, to the rest of the world (Aguilera and Cuervo-Cazurra 2009).

There is some elision in the idea that shareholders are the owners of the corporation and that the managers are, as a result, their agents. Lawyers know that it is misleading to talk of the shareholders owning the firm as such (Ireland 1999; Robé 2011), but recognize, at the same time, that the standard corporate contract grants shareholders voice, income, and control rights which are unique to them as a group and are not shared with workers or creditors (Armour, Hansmann, Kraakman, and Pargendler 2017). Directors have a duty to promote the corporate interest, which in principle may not mean the same thing as maximizing shareholder value, but in practice often does. English case law has tended to respect the principle of shareholder primacy except, on occasion, when it threatens the ability of the company to produce future value. Boards are generally free to take a range of interests into account when setting corporate strategy and may choose to prioritize investment over dividends, for example. However, there are many pressures for directors to pursue shareholder value above all other considerations, such as the need to raise or maintain share price to appease the equities market, and pressure from their own activist shareholders, personal incentives such as performance-related remuneration (Talbot 2016).

Shareholder primacy, although not in general mandated by law, has come to be seen as common sense. In some areas of law, the requirement to prioritize the shareholder interest can be more explicitly spelled out. When a change of control is imminent, through a takeover or restructuring, directors' room for maneuver tends to narrow down to a duty to safeguard the financial concerns of the shareholders, at least in the English and American common law; countries with a French or

German civil-law tradition, on the other hand, tend to give less priority to the shareholder interest (Adams and Deakin 2018; Johnston 2007).

The corporation is inevitably an exercise in delegation, but it does not follow that a policy of empowering the presumed principals, the shareholders, at the expense of managers and workers, necessarily results in improved corporate performance (Deakin 2014). For example, proponents of agency theory have argued that independent boards would be better placed to represent the interests of the shareholders than boards consisting wholly or mainly of executives. Companies with independent boards should be able to access capital at lower cost and should be better run. These improvements should be reflected in higher levels of profitability. However, there is mixed evidence on the relationship between board independence and corporate profitability. Independent directors on British and American boards appear to be effective, on the whole, in reminding executives of the importance of maintaining investor confidence. They are less effective in setting strategy and in assessing corporate risks, a failing which became apparent in the course of the financial crisis of 2008. In countries with limited experience of independent boards, such as Japan, external directors are confined to an advisory role, and monitoring is internalized at the level of largely autonomous senior management teams. This model, while far from best practice as recommended by international corporate governance norms, has remained largely unaffected by global trends, and has proved resilient in the face of attempts to introduce features of shareholder-centric corporate governance, including hostile takeovers and confrontational hedge fund activism, into Japan (Buchanan, Chai, and Deakin 2011).

The standard corporate governance model in countries such as the USA and Britain has no role for employees other than as contractual counterparties and potential creditors, a view which assumes that labor inputs

can be completely contracted for (Easterbrook and Fischel 1991). This view not only goes against the grain of modern institutional economics, which recognizes the open-endedness and asymmetry of the employment relation (Coase 1988; Williamson 1999), but fails to explain the widespread managerial practice of recognizing that employees make firm-specific inputs that are at risk if the firm fails, and granting them voice and income rights that go some way to protecting their interests (Adams and Deakin 2018). In other countries, mostly influenced by German practice, with two-tier boards and a role for employee-nominated directors, employee involvement in corporate governance is not simply a matter for firm practice, but has a legal underpinning. Virtually all legal systems recognize a role for employment protection legislation in protecting employees' investments in firm-specific skills and knowledge, although on the whole the degree of such protection is lower in common law countries than those of civil law origin.

It seems, then, that there is no single or uniform view on the issue of corporate purpose (Veldman, Gregor, and Morrow 2016). However, the recent trend in both labor and company law has been to elevate the interests of shareholders over those of other corporate groups, and as we shall see, this has affected all systems no matter which variant of capitalism they have, historically, been associated with.

6.3.3 Contemporary Trends in Corporate Governance: Shareholder and Worker Rights in Advanced and Emerging Economies

Since the early 1990s, two global trends in corporate governance laws and regulations can be identified. The first is an increase in the enactment of legal protections for shareholders (see Figure 6.1). This trend is consistent across common law and civil law systems,

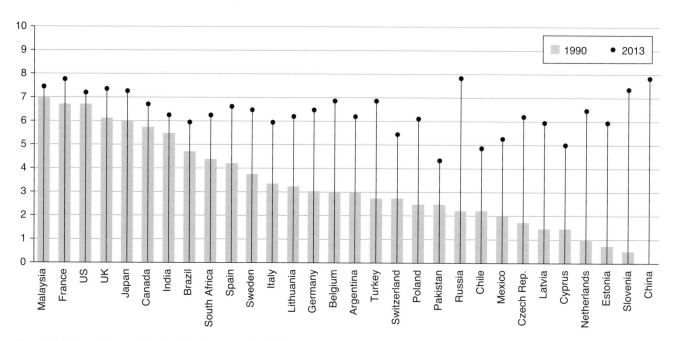

Figure 6.1 | Shareholder protection through law in 30 countries, 1990 and 2013.
Note: The left-hand column indicates the score attributed to shareholder protection on a 1–10 scale, using leximetric coding methods.
Source: Katelouzou and Siems (2015)

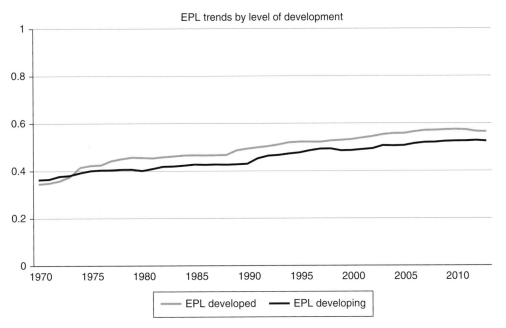

Figure 6.2 | Trends in employment protection legislation (including co-determination laws), 1970–2013, for 117 countries. Developed' countries are defined as those in OECD membership in 2017, "developing" countries are those not members of the OECD in 2017.
Source: Adams et al. (2018)

and across countries by reference to their level of development, although the overall level of legal protection remains higher in common law countries and in developed economies. The second trend is one of relative stability in the laws governing employee protection and co-determination rights, with a small decline after 2008 (see Figure 6.2). Thus the picture is one of stagnation in labor rights worldwide, while the rights of capital were being significantly strengthened. The global crisis which began in 2008, although originating in the financial sector rather than in the labor market, has not led to a reversal of this trend; if anything, with the recent fall in labor protection, it has intensified it.

The intention behind these policies was that shareholder protection would lead to increased efficiency in capital markets, while restricting or retrenching worker rights would lead to an improvement in labor market outcomes, as measured by increases in employment and productivity. The recent development of methods for consistent and transparent coding of changes in corporate and labor laws (Armour, Deakin, and Siems 2017) makes it possible to assess whether these policies have been successful.

In cross-national panel regressions, after controlling for GDP growth and for differences in the institutional environments of countries, a rise in shareholder protection does not consistently lead to a higher level of financial development. There is a correlation, which in some models can be interpreted as a causal relationship, between increased shareholder rights and the level of stock market capitalization in common law countries. In civil law countries there appears to be no similar effect, which suggests that a model of shareholder protection that originated in the common law (or "liberal market") countries has not translated well into the civil law (or "coordinated market") systems (Deakin, Sarkar, and Singh 2012).

It also appears from econometric analysis that legal reforms are more likely to have an impact on stock market indicators in developing markets than in developed ones (Deakin, Sarkar, and Singh 2012). This suggests that there may be less leeway for shareholder-centric reforms to change financial outcomes in systems with already mature stock markets.

The deregulation of labor law, meanwhile, has no consistent relationship to improved labor market outcomes. Instead, emerging evidence suggests that a higher level of employment protection is correlated with improved productivity and employment outcomes, and also with a higher level of innovation, as proxied by patenting activity (Acharya et al. 2014). There is also evidence to suggest that strengthening shareholder rights leads to a reduction in reported levels of innovation, measured in the same way (Belloc 2013). Meanwhile, an increase in worker rights is correlated with greater equality (proxied by a higher share of national income taken in the form of wages and employee benefits) (Deakin, Malmberg, and Sarkar 2014), and increased shareholder protection with its opposite (a lower labor share) (Sjoberg 2009). The bolstering of shareholder rights, together with the reduction of employee rights, would seem to have a direct and negative impact on social progress.

We are learning that the recent global consensus on the need to protect the rights of capital while attenuating those of labor has not worked entirely as planned. Shareholder-centric corporate governance was meant to lead to more transparent and responsive management, and to improved corporate profitability. In systems where this model has been taken the furthest, it has succeeded in tilting the balance of power in favor of shareholders and against both managers and workers. Executives are more sensitive to capital market pressures and the disciplinary effect of hostile takeovers and hedge fund activism is tangible.

However, this system has not led to the expected increase in equity capital as a source of investment to drive growth. Since the 1980s, in the USA and the UK (but not elsewhere), outflows of capital from listed firms to shareholders, in the form of dividends and share buybacks, have been outstripping equity flowing into the corporate sector in the form of IPOs and new share subscriptions from already listed firms (Henwood 1998; Lazonick 2014). It would seem that much of the capital released from the corporate sector through takeovers and restructurings, coupled with regular shareholder pressure for dividends and buybacks, did not support productive investment, but was used to sustain asset prices in shares, until those bubbles finally burst with the onset of the global financial crisis.

Also revealing is growing evidence of an inverse relationship between shareholder protection and innovation (Belloc 2013). This appears to be related to managers' reluctance to commit to long-term investment in research and development when faced with growing pressures to maintain shareholders' returns.

The conclusion to emerge from the empirical literature on corporate governance, then, is that the strengthening of shareholder rights has effects which are not uniform across different national or regional varieties of capitalism, or by reference to levels of development. More generally, though, this evidence tells us that increasing shareholder protection does not necessarily lead to more corporate investment in production and increased growth. Particularly in the developed world, it is more likely to lead to asset price inflation and financial turbulence.

6.3.4   The Impact of Shareholder Value Maximization Strategies on Innovation

There are two key points to be made about innovation in a corporate setting where shareholder maximization strategies dominate, and one proviso. First, in such a setting, shareholder maximization strategies will tend to inhibit investment in innovation. Corporations will prefer financial strategies such as share buybacks to maintain shareholder value and will shy from long-term investment in R&D. The second is that investment will be made with a view to profit rather than social need. As we shall see, financialized pharma firms are increasingly using speculative strategies and their monopoly position as holders of IP rights to push up the price of curative drugs, in the process restricting patients' access to life-saving drugs and shifting costs on to public health care systems.

The proviso is that this aversion to investment is not entirely down to laws and policies that drive shareholder value maximization. It also flows from the tendency for firms to find it increasingly difficult to deliver shareholder value from the ordinary process of production (Talbot 2016). This is the result of the slowing of growth in the global economy, which is particularly acute in developed countries.

Case Study: Innovation in Pharma

The disease Hepatitis C has infected approaching 170 million people globally and kills around 700,000 persons each year. The disease disproportionately affects low-income and marginalized groups including those co-infected with HIV and imprisoned individuals. Since 2013 new drugs have come on to the market with the potential to achieve cure rates of over 90 percent.

Among these new therapies are the drugs Sovaldi and Harvoni, which are manufactured by Gilead Sciences (for the research on which this case study is based, see Roy and King 2016). In countries where they have been made available at low or no cost (which include some developing countries, such as Egypt, and developed ones, such as Iceland), public health authorities have been able to develop strategies for eliminating Hepatitis C completely. In other countries, such as the USA, where Gilead charges what it regards as a market price for the drugs, access has been more limited. In 2014 the US Medicaid program paid over $1 billion to fund Hepatitis C treatments that reached only 2.4 percent of eligible patients. In the US, Gilead was charging around $90,000 for each course of Hepatitis C treatment.

Companies such as Gilead maintain that they need to charge the price the market will bear for curative treatments in order to fund future research and development. However, most of the funding that supported the research which led to the development of Hepatitis C cures was supplied by government. After the Hepatitis C virus was discovered in 1989, the problem facing those seeking to develop a cure was that the virus could not be grown in a cell culture, complicating the process of testing for anti-viral effects. Publicly funded scientific research in the USA and Germany in the following decade led to the development of a research tool known as the subgenomic replicon, which made it possible to generate parts of the Hepatitis C virus for testing. A university spin-off based in New York, Apath, commercialized the replicon using funding supplied by the US National Institute of Health's Small Business and Innovation Research Program (SBIR). A company called Pharmasset, a spin off from a lab at Emory University that received financing via SBIR as well as venture capital funding, went on to develop the compound known as sofosbuvir, which became the basis for the new generation of drugs addressing the need for a Hepatitis C cure.

Pharmasset spent a total of $62 million on the development of the sofosbuvir compound from the preclinical research stage to the point of phase II trials, and identified a budget of a further $126 million for phase III testing which would bring the drug to market. In 2011 Pharmasset was bought by Gilead Sciences for $11 billion. Gilead was one of a number of companies investing in Hepatitis C therapies at this point and assessed sofosbuvir as superior to its own products. Gilead was able to combine sofosbuvir with a number of its own therapies to create a new treatment regime capable of curing Hepatitis C within an eight-week period. Gilead reported clinical trial research costs of $880 million between 2012 and 2014 in developing these treatments.

Gilead's purchase of Pharmasset and the IP rights it thereby acquired gave it a near monopoly in the Hepatitis C drugs market. Between the launch of its new drugs in 2013 and the first quarter of 2016, Gilead accrued over $31 billion in revenues from its Hepatitis C medicines, nearly three times the cost of the purchase of Pharmasset. In 2015 Gilead's revenue from Hepatitis C drugs was $19 billion, which was equivalent to around two-thirds of the national budget for the US

National Institutes of Health in the same period. In the first quarter of 2016, Gilead had cash balances of $21 billion.

Although pharma firms argue that the surpluses they accrue from drug sales are needed to fund future research, in practice they are being used for share buybacks (repurchases of stock which enable profits to be distributed to shareholders) and dividends. In 2015 Gilead announced over $27 billion in share buybacks. Between 2015 and 2016 Gilead's R&D budget rose from $2 billion to $3 billion.

Gilead's story is not unique. In the past decade, Pfizer has spent $139 billion on share buybacks and $82 billion on R&D. Gilead's model is, nevertheless, a new development in the industry, as it suggests that a strategy of targeted acquisitions of start-ups, coupled with the capacity to exploit monopoly rents from ownership of life-saving therapies, can generate supra-normal returns for shareholders. These returns are in the nature of windfall gains made at the expense of public finances, as public health budgets are diverted to meet the high costs of life-saving treatments largely financed by government in the first place. The losers from the system include the patients whose access to life-saving treatments is rationed by high prices. Additionally, long-term investment in R&D loses out to short-term financial speculation.

6.3.5 The Impact of Shareholder Value Maximization Strategies: Hiding Corporate Wealth and Tax Avoidance

The ability to create a new legal person in the form of a corporation or company that can have a legal existence anywhere in the world has enabled individuals and companies to engage in huge wealth-hiding activities. This trend exacerbates already huge wealth inequalities, as the super-rich pay increasingly less tax. It reduces the tax available to the state for public welfare and reduces the capital available for innovation and investment.

Gabriel Zucman (2015) estimates the total amount of wealth that is legally hidden to be $7.6 trillion. Company law provides the structures that enable this secrecy. These include shell companies defined by the US Securities and Exchange Commission to refer to a publicly held company with no or nominal assets other than money. Shell companies have no fixed business assets, but exist as a front for the operations of other entities. Company law also permits the construction of nominee directors and shareholders to keep secret the identity of those who actually control and own companies. In addition, it enables companies to incorporate in low tax jurisdictions by having a figurehead director who signs forms and appears to be engaging in management while the real decisions are made outside this jurisdiction. Obfuscation is a thriving business. A routine Google search in 2016 revealed that there are thousands of agencies offering to set up nominee directors or shareholders (Talbot 2018a). The standard rate is around £400 in the UK. The US state of Delaware alone hosts millions of such operations. A single building in Delaware will routinely act as the registered office for hundreds of thousands of these companies.

The issue here is not just the hiding of wealth. It is also about evading and avoiding tax. Tax evasion, the nondeclaration of assets and earnings in order to pay less or no tax, is a crime. However, corporate tax avoidance, structuring corporate networks in order to reduce tax liability is legal, but is so endemic and enabled by global corporate capitalism that it has become a highly publicized global scandal.

Taxation within nation-states is based on one of two principles (Davis, Kaplinsky, and Morris 2017). First is the "source" principle, according to which a state will tax on the basis of the location of an actual economic activity. The second is the residence principle, according to which persons pay tax in the jurisdiction in which they are resident. Because multinationals will have economic activity in many places in which they are not resident, it was recognized from an early stage that such companies could be taxed twice, which was considered likely to retard global growth. A double tax convention was drafted in 1927, by which time thousands of tax treaties were in place to ensure that incomes were only taxed once. However, it soon became apparent that this measure could be used to ensure that tax was not paid *either* at source *or* at residence. For example, companies incorporated in the United States, where tax is based on residence (place of incorporation), could transfer valuable assets to countries where tax was based on economic activity (determined by seat of management). The use of complex corporate groups has enabled multinational corporations to organize the business across the globe so as to avoid or reduce tax. Jurisdictions with low or zero corporate taxes have been pivotal to such schemes.

The use of complex corporate groups has enabled multinational corporations to geographically locate the most profitable part of their value chain in regimes with low corporate tax. The LuxLeaks tax avoidance scandal, revealed in 2014, showed that up to 340 multinational corporations, ranging from Ikea to Pepsi, had funneled profits through Luxemburg, thereby reducing their tax to as little as 1 percent. Another well-known example is that of Boots after it was acquired by Kohlberg, Kravis Roberts & Co LP (KKR). The company through which KKR purchased the company was reincorporated in Switzerland. The purpose of this restructuring was to locate the profitable parts of Boots in a low tax regime, while the debt incurred by the company in acquiring Boots was located in the higher tax regime of the UK. Estimates on tax avoidance in the UK ranges from the Tax Justice Network's of £30bn a year to HMRC estimates of £120bn a year.

Transferring valuable assets within corporate networks is very difficult to regulate. Asset transfer is particularly easy for IT corporations whose value in intellectual properties is easy to move and difficult to evaluate. Monitoring thousands of transfers of this kind has proved impossible. Microsoft, Hewlett-Packard, Apple and Google are just some of the corporations that have cropped up as massive tax avoiders. Using figures from 2013, Zucman calculated that one-third of corporate profits in the US are made abroad and 55 percent of that total are "made" (through asset transfers) in zero or low tax countries (the Netherlands, Bermuda, Luxemburg, Ireland, Singapore, and Switzerland). This puts corporate tax avoidance in the US at about $130 billion every year.

One of the most significant revelations about the hiding of assets and tax evasion in offshore havens has come from the Panama Papers. An anonymous source provided an estimated 11.5 million documents from the Panama-based, German law firm Mossack Fonseca, which specializes in providing offshore accounts to its clients. It revealed details from thousands of clients and implicated nearly 10,000 UK and 3000 US companies and nearly 2000 UK financial intermediaries including banks and accountants. 500 banks and their subsidiaries registered nearly 15,600 shell companies with Mossack Fonseca. HSBC accounted for over 2300 companies, UBS 1100, Société Générale, 979, the Royal Bank of Canada 378, Commerzbank 92, and Credit Suisse 1105. Oxfam's Report of April 11, 2016 showed that of the 68 companies that were lent money by the World Bank's private lending arm (IFC) in 2015, to finance investments in Sub-Saharan Africa, 51 used tax havens with no apparent link to their actual business.

The scale of the scandal is global. The Panama Papers name over 70 states, and heads of state in Argentina, Iceland, Saudi Arabia, Ukraine, and United Arab Emirates are personally identified. In some cases political leaders who had been active in maintaining the status quo were identified. The British prime minister at the time of the disclosures, David Cameron, was seen to have benefited from an offshore investment fund, Blairmore, controlled by his father. The then executive chair of the UK tax authority HMRC, Edward Troup, was a partner of Simmons & Simmons, the city law firm which acted for Blairmore when he was still a partner. In the late 2000s Troup led the opposition to reforms put forward by the then prime minister Gordon Brown to curb corporate tax avoidance. The integration of politicians' self-interests and their role as policy-makers is also demonstrated by then prime minister Cameron's lobbying for trusts to be excluded from the EU Anti Money Laundering Directive.

The problem of corporate tax evasion and avoidance is well known and politicians have discussed a number of initiatives, outlined in Section 6.5. It is however, on the increase. At a national level it has the most detrimental effect on poorer working people, who routinely pay their taxes via employment or consumption but who rely on a welfare state that is increasingly denied taxes from the wealthiest corporations and persons. At an international level, tax evasion and avoidance have the most detrimental effect on developing countries. Oxfam estimates that the loss of tax revenue to developing countries is at least $100 billion per year (Oxfam 2016). This hits the poorest while the indigenous wealthy hold their wealth in offshore tax havens. Oxfam's analysis of the 200 biggest global corporations (who are also World Economic Forum's strategic partners) showed that 9 out of 10 "have a presence in at least one tax haven" and that in "2014, corporate investment in these tax havens was almost four times bigger than it was in 2001" (Oxfam 2016: 20). The combination of the capacity of the company's legal form to inhabit different jurisdictions and to hide wealth coupled with the inability of sovereign states to adopt a uniform tax policy makes tax avoidance an entrenched social problem.

6.3.6 The Impact of Shareholder Value Maximization Strategies: Leveraging and "Going Private"

The control rights in the company possessed by shareholders under company law are extensive. They enable shareholders to make decisions about the use and disposal of corporate assets and finance.

In practice, however, in large companies these control rights are rarely used, and control is vested in, and exercised by, directors. Shares are treated as tradable investments and shareholders claim a return on those investments. Mostly they are nonactive, rentier capitalists, not unlike bondholders. The passivity of most shareholders underpins the expectations behind company law. Activist shareholders subvert this expectation and the law, by continuing to connect share ownership with control rights, makes it possible for a person or group of persons to exercise complete control over the company's assets and business by purchasing of the company's shares and exercising those legal rights. Such a large purchase is generally made through financing, that is, loans secured on the company's assets. By holding shares these individuals and groups can begin to take apart the valuable parts of the company and extract its accumulated value. In short, the company form enables the most financially well positioned to take assets from the company, close down the business and put employees out of work. In social progress terms it is a process that increases economic inequality, diminishes production and the possibility of innovation, and removes the capacities of workers.

This process is further enabled by the law which allows shareholders to reregister a public company as a private company thereby reducing the regulative oversight applicable to most large companies with many employees.

In most jurisdictions there is a difference between a public company in which the public can buy shares and a private company in which there is no share market and shares are held by a close-knit group of persons, often within families. Public companies are subject to much greater scrutiny, they are required to make more disclosures, and are subject to more stringent laws, particularly in respect of the company's capital. Many key principles in company law are based on the assumption that shareholders and directors are different people, the latter owing a fiduciary duty to the company (which is either implicitly or explicitly understood to mean shareholders), the former possessing a self-interested, decidedly nonfiduciary role. Directors' duties are built on the assumption that directors are representing the interests of others. It is a breach of duty to represent their own interests at the expense of those they are meant to be acting for. The assumption of separateness between shareholder and director reflects the reality of most public companies. However, if, as is common in a private company, shareholder and director are one and the same, keeping those roles separate becomes problematic. A director must be sure not to treat company funds as their own and to observe the corporate veil. This legal distinction is not especially problematic if the private company is small, does not involve many other people and is essentially a quasi-sole trader or partnership. It becomes highly problematic if the private company is large in terms of assets and workers, with many competing stakeholders. The law continues to assert that the director has a duty to promote shareholders' interests even when the director is the only shareholder, but this will often be to the detriment of many other stakeholders.

This situation can typically arise when a public company with many stakeholders is bought out by a single person or small group of persons and reregisters as a private company (Talbot 2018a). By these means the law effectively allows big business to use the less exacting regulation intended for small business. As a result, businesses are increasingly opting to register or reregister as private companies. In the UK, 37,000 private companies have assets worth more than £18 million and 2200 have more than 1000 employees (compared to only 340 quoted companies with over 1000 employees). Large companies becoming private happens in the context of leveraged buyouts, when many shareholders are replaced very few, who are also directors. In such a situation, control resides with a few people in their capacity as voting shareholders and/or as directors. Those individuals then usually take the company private, thus enabling them to use the governance system developed for small companies. They often achieve the buyout through debt secured against the company's assets, which must be repaid from corporate earnings or assets. For those commentators who consider leveraged buyouts to be a good thing, the leverage part is beneficial, an essential mechanism for pressurizing management to profit maximize and thus enhance efficiencies (Kaplan 2010). The buyout will also result in directors owning much of the equity which, according to agency theory, incentivizes them to profit maximize. They are under a legal duty to act in shareholders' interest, and they are the shareholders. Private equity firms will often seek out industry specific management as part of the buyout package. For advocates of leveraged buyouts, they are effective mechanisms to strip out unproductive parts of an underperforming business creating a leaner and more profitable business after around 5–7 years that will be reregistered as a public company and floated on the share market, or "go public" again. It is the association of shareholder value with a good economic and social outcome that justifies this activity.

However, a close analysis of what actually occurs in leveraged buyouts reveals a picture of value extraction, which is shared between the new shareholders, directors, deal makers, and lenders, to the detriment of other stakeholders. Valuable and productive company assets are frequently sold and then leased back to the company. The profit from the sale can be declared as a dividend. Workers lose their jobs or have to accept wage cuts and less favorable terms and conditions. Assets can be revalued and enjoyed as dividends paid for by loans. Shareholders/directors can lend the company money on terms which are not scrutinized. Bit by bit, all that is valuable in the company is drained away. And it happens within the law. The recent UK case of BHS Plc is typical of the abuse enabled by the law and where the net result was that a few billionaires made hundreds of millions in profit in a couple of years while nearly 20,000 people lost their pensions and jobs, some after a lifetime of service in the business.

British Homes Stores was first established in the UK in 1928. When it was bought out by a group headed by millionaire Philip Green, BHS Plc had 164 stores, 11,000 employees and was valued at just under £400 million. The shares in BHS Plc were purchased for the bargain price of £200 million. This discount arose because the company was considered to have an "old fashioned" image. The bargain was accounted for by offsetting the assets with "negative goodwill" of over £300 million. Green borrowed £1.7 million for this transaction. After the sale, BHS Plc was reregistered as a private company, and renamed BHS Ltd.

In 2002, Green as director, declared a dividend of £166.5 million for the shareholders, who were Green and other members of the Green family. The profits were on paper only and were mainly composed of the value of the negative goodwill, in other words, via an accounting device. Negative goodwill is obviously not actual money and so the dividends were funded with additional borrowing together with the sale of property for £105 million to Green's other companies which were then leased back by BHS Ltd. By 2004, an additional £256 million in dividends had been declared. BHS Ltd now had debts of over £250 million. For the remaining years of its existence, the company languished in debt. No more dividends were declared but companies owned by the Green family charged BHS Ltd an estimated £124 million for rent of properties which BHS had previously owned. BHS Ltd was eventually put into administration, owing over £1.2 billion including £517 million in pension obligations.

The shareholder orientated legal system which is evident to different levels in most capitalist economies encourages and condones corporate decision-making that delivers value to shareholders. As a director of BHS Ltd, Philip Green successfully represented the interests of shareholders. Those shareholders were himself and his family. By reregistering the company as a private he was able to declare profits under a much less exacting regime to that of public companies, far in excess of actual profitability, funded by crippling loans, which destroyed the ongoing profitability of BHS Ltd. The accumulated value of nearly 80 years of trading, company property, and the pensions of over 20,000 people were legally extracted by Green because the law decrees that companies exist to make value for shareholders and that private companies (including those that were public companies) are free from strict oversight.

6.3.7 The Impact of Shareholder Value Maximization Strategies on Inequality

A growing body of evidence links certain features of the contemporary corporate form to rising inequality. Econometric analysis suggests that laws and regulations strengthening shareholder protection lead to increases in inequality, as indicated by a fall in labor's share of national income and a related increase in the share taken by dividends and profits (Adams and Deakin 2018). Restructurings resulting in hostile takeovers and hedge fund activism are diminishing the capacity of firms to provide stable employment linked to seniority, as was common until the 1980s in the USA and other developed countries. More generally, the strengthening of shareholder rights, when coupled with declining levels of union membership and collective bargaining coverage in many industrialized economies, has, as might be expected, led a reduction in the relative bargaining powers of shareholders and workers, and has undermined the power of organized labor to capture part of the surplus from production. Thus, the labor share has been going down even while labor productivity has been increasing. Between 1973 and 2014 labor productivity in the US grew by 72 percent but wages for the average worker increased by just 9 percent (Oxfam 2016).

A feature of inequality not captured by data on the labor share is that even within the diminishing portion of national wealth taken by wages rather than profits, an increasing amount is taken by very high earners in corporations, whose pay and benefits are linked to share prices through the use of stock options and bonuses. The theory behind executive pay which became influential in the 1980s and 1990s was that linking pay to performance as measured by share prices would help mitigate agency costs. There is little evidence of this (Bebchuk and Fried 2003), as even adherents of the theory have surmised (Baker et al. 1988), but the pay of senior executives has multiplied exponentially as financialized modes of executive pay have become the norm. Between 2000 and 2014 the median total earnings of CEOs of companies in the FTSE 100 (that is, the top 100 companies by market value listed on the London stock exchange) increased by 278 percent, while the rise in total earnings for full-time employees was only 48 percent. In 2000, a FTSE CEO earned 47 times more than an average full-time employee; by 2014 they earned 120 times more. The pay of US CEOs has increased by 54 percent since 2009, while that of ordinary workers has been stagnant (Incomes Data Services 2014). High executive pay, in and of itself, is not the cause of greater economic inequality, but policies that privilege capital do cause inequality between those who possess capital or whose income is linked to capital (such as executives) and those who do not possess it (Piketty 2014).

A related feature driving inequality is the rise of the financial industry. This has exacerbated the general trend toward earnings inequality which has been a feature of the US economy since the 1970s and of Europe since the 1980s. The rise of the financial sector is driving inequality between professions, and also causing geographic disparities, both within and between states. Wealth is increasingly concentrated in global financial centers, most prominently London, New York, Tokyo, Singapore, Hong Kong, and Shanghai.

Although business firms ultimately depend for their existence on national legal systems which grant them entity status and provide state protection for corporate assets, including intellectual property rights, globalization has created new opportunities for corporate power to transcend the nation-state. Global production is dominated by multinational corporations which often have subsidiaries in dozens of nations and operate through supply chains sometimes involving thousands of strategic "partners." However, these multinational businesses are not always the networks they are often supposed to be, but vertically integrated structures in which power is vested in the parent company. Corporate law is used to offload risk on to subsidiary companies in low-wage economies, with courts in industrialized countries only rarely "lifting the veil" of corporate personality to find the parent liable for health and safety breaches and other labor violations.

The rise since the 1980s of retailer or "merchant" corporations echoes the legal form and mode of operation of the charter companies of the early modern period, which used layers of vertical contractual relations to extract value from foreign trading while avoiding ultimate legal liabilities for their activities overseas. Today, a company like Nike does not engage in production of its own; it contracts with producers, mostly in low-wage markets (Nike suppliers operate in over 600 factories in South and East Asia), to supply the goods which it markets and sells (Harvey 2010).

It is part of the strategy of global garment brands to ensure that suppliers compete on price, so directing them into a strategy of making savings through low wages, job insecurity, and hazardous working conditions. The Rana Plaza disaster, discussed below, is simply one of the more visible results of this business model. The brands which used the products made at factories such as Rana Plaza are customers at the end of a long chain and are not legally responsible for working conditions on overseas sites.

6.3.8   Conclusion: The Corporation and Social Progress

The corporate form, particularly with its current shareholder orientation, amplifies the tendencies within capitalism itself to undermine social progress. The corporate form allows investors protection from risk through limited liability, and the transferable money form which is the company share allows shareholders to opt out of an investment with ease. Employees, in contrast, are grounded in the productive enterprise and subject to the negative impacts of shareholder maximization strategies. We have seen how financialized methods to increase share value increasingly morph into straightforward asset stripping, leading to layoffs and losses to pension funds. Shareholder maximization strategies result in an aversion to investing in innovation, a trend which is particularly pronounced in the current post global crisis period, or to the introduction of innovations which enhance the power of management over labor. This tends to result in loss of quality in the work available, the rewards which accrue to it, and job security. Management, in contrast, increasingly enjoys more security and extraordinary remuneration. The corporate form thereby increases inequality and decreases quality of life for the majority of people. To the degree that it is the corporate form that reduces social progress in these ways – as opposed to the inevitable workings of capitalism itself – reforms to the corporation can be effective. We set out a number of such reforms in Section 6.5 (see Chapter 8 for a discussion of corporate tax reforms).

6.4   Finance

6.4.1   The Notion of Finance in Capitalism

The notion of finance is overtly ambiguous. It can denote a particular body of technical knowledge or academic science concerned with the valuation of economic assets, the assessment of investment strategies or the development of financial instruments and techniques (this is the meaning of finance found in expressions such as "financial analysis," "corporate finance," "quantitative finance," or "financial engineering"). The notion of finance can also refer to the actual organization of the banking system, and to the processes, actors, and institutions that shape money provision policies (as in "financial institutions," "financial regulation," or "financial markets"). This meaning can be extended to governmental budgetary processes and the management of public money (as in "public finance"). The notion of finance can finally convey the mundane meaning of handling money for household life (as in "personal finance"). Finance can therefore be considered as a multifaceted set of institutions, mechanisms, practices, actors, instruments, and ideas whose common feature would lie in their relation to the distribution of money in society.

For the purpose of assessing its impacts on social progress – and without abandoning a comprehensive understanding thereof – we focus here on a definition of finance that corresponds to what has been often termed the "global financial industry," that is, the set of interconnected financial institutions (commercial and investment banks as well as other financial establishments such as insurance companies and international financial institutions such as the World Bank or the International Monetary Fund) that control today the largest portion of the circuits of credit and investment worldwide. Finance encompasses both the actual organization of this set of interconnected financial institutions, and the worldviews, policies, and measures that they produce and inform.

Finance has a long history. An assessment of the present situation certainly requires awareness of the multiple and changing forms in which money, credit, debt, funding, or capital have functioned in humanity (Graeber 2011). There is however considerable agreement on two broad facts that define the present situation. The first fact is that the capitalist economy, understood as a system in which the means of economic activity largely rely on private ownership and profit, has progressively come to play a dominant role in the organization of society worldwide (Braudel 1992; Polanyi 2001). From commercial banking and credit institutions to investment management and insurance, the financial services industry has come to play accordingly a crucial role in economic life in advanced liberal democracies and, to a lesser extent, in so-called "emerging economies." The second fact is that the contemporary evolution of the financial services industry is characterized by the emergence of what has been labeled "global finance," and which consists in an internationalized network of financial institutions characterized by a tendency to capital-intense oligopolistic concentration (Fligstein 2001; Abdelal 2007; Ouroussoff 2010; Woll 2014). This correlates with observable shifts in the organization of power relations, in the form, for example, of the formation of global financial elites or the importance of phenomena of regulatory capture and regulatory oversight in the financial sector.

6.4.2   Contemporary International Financial Dynamics

From the perspective of international dynamics, the global expansion of the financial industry and its increasing role in the organization of the distribution of monetary resources are subject to controversy so as to their contribution to economic growth. Countries that have embarked on the expansion of their financial industries nationally – in particular rich countries in Europe, the US, and Japan – have not only known little GDP growth in the last 30 years, but have also experienced growing inequalities. A similar situation has derived from the "lost decade" of the 1990s for developing countries that opened their economies to global financial flows, in the former Soviet bloc, in South-East Asia and in Latin America. India is somewhat an exception, since the expansion of stock markets accompanied a high level of growth since the early nineties, but this has occurred within an economy that is notoriously disconnected from global financial flows. At the other side of the spectrum, China, with a nationalized financial industry under explicit control of the government and of the Communist Party of China, has experienced drastic reductions of poverty and unmatched levels of long-term GDP growth (Aglietta and Bai 2012). It is still under debate whether finance played a negative or positive role in each case, and whether these developments are not mostly independent of the financial structure. The answers lie most likely in a nuanced combination

of positive and negative effects and on the acknowledgment of the impact of several interdependent and independent variables.

In Europe and the US, in the 1970s and 1980s, regulatory changes (often designated by the name of "deregulation") contributed to the expansion of the role of the financial industry in the distribution of monetary resources without the guidance of government (Aglietta 2000; Coriat, Petit, and Schméder 2006; Abdelal, 2007; Mehrling 2010; Krippner 2011). This was followed by similar changes in Japan and most of the low and middle income countries, in Latin America, Africa, South-East Asia, and the former Soviet bloc. For the latter, except Japan, the aim of the transformation was to partake in global financial flows that were expected to enhance growth and reduce inequalities. The several crises of the 1990s and early 2000s, in Mexico, Russia, South-East Asia, Argentina, Turkey, and in the US with the Internet bubble, to name a few, did not necessarily stem the regulatory trend. The expansion of global regulatory bodies, in particular around the Basel agreements (Baud and Chiapello 2017), was structured around the main principles guiding this regulatory trend: the creation of markets where the financial industry would be able to operate freely, albeit with certain rules of transparency and risk management, the latter most often based on the industry's own standards (Huault and Richard 2012). The financial crisis of 2007–2008 was the occasion of a temporary revision of this trend, in particular of the lack of separation between investment banking and the rest of the banking system, and in general concerning the inability of governments to control the risk exposure of industry actors (Tett 2009; Engelen et al. 2011; MacKenzie 2011; Admati and Hellwig 2013; Woll 2014; Stockhammer 2015). Yet, the obvious negative economic consequences of the last crisis, for almost a decade now, have not really stemmed this trend, as the minor regulatory changes in the US and Europe attest. In many developing countries, the focus has shifted from accessing global financial flows as a primary source of growth to profiting from the economic expansion of China by participating in its global trade circuits. The consequences of this on regulation and government are still to be seen, with varying cases in Latin America, Africa, and South-East Asia. In any case, the debates about regulation do consider as a premise that the current financial organization has been mainly fostered by regulatory changes since the demise of the Bretton Woods agreements, and that it remains a political issue how to deal with the role taken up by the financial industry since then. Authors such as Stiglitz (2002, 2006, 2010) have aptly emphasized in this regard the damaging role that the global financial industry in general (and international financial institutions such as the World Bank and the International Monetary Fund in particular) has had, in part, in the stability of fiscal and monetary policy in both the developing world and higher income countries. The necessity of accessing capital tends to translate indeed, paradoxically, into the weakening of the conditions for stable growth and productive focus (see Stiglitz et al. 2006).

6.4.3   Contemporary Issues: Financialization and Austerity

A number of researchers in economics, management science, political science, sociology and anthropology have used the notion of "financialization" in order to characterize the growing role of finance in the organization of the firm and in economic conduct at large. This term covers three partly interrelated, partly independent processes (Van der Zwan 2014): a particular organization of the economic system where the financial industry occupies a central role in the distribution of monetary resources among firms and between firms and the rest of society (see also Epstein 2005; Krippner 2011); an orientation of business management that gives priority to shareholder value above other concerns, such as labor rights, human rights and environmental and social responsibilities (see also Fligstein 1990; Froud et al. 2006); and the growing presence of credit and financial pressures in the everyday life of the majority of the population, as exemplified by the extension of mortgages before the US "subprime crisis," but also by the extension of microcredit, among others (see also Martin 2002; Langley 2008; Schwittay 2014; Deville 2015; Mader 2015). These phenomena have an impact not only on the concrete distribution of monetary resources, among firms, between firms, and between companies and the rest of social activities, but also on the legitimacy of different discourses about the organization of society, limiting social and political imagination to models where finance occupies a central role.

The concept of "austerity" is essential for an assessment of the role of finance in the present situation. The doctrine of restraint in public spending – and the concomitant "downsizing" of public services and public administrations – gained political prominence with the "neoliberal" revolution in the US and the UK in the 1980s, stressing the need to limit the economic size of state-funded activities, through programs of privatization of public resources (see Blyth 2013; Davies 2014; Streeck 2014; Birch 2015). The specific notion of "austerity" emerged more specifically, with these broad aims, in the context of post-2008 political strategy. Several analyses have highlighted the expansion of such type of rationale through the notion of "New Public Management," and the negative impact of these policies in the quality of public services such as health, transport, and education in the UK, for instance (Hood et al. 2004; Pollitt and Bouckaert 2011).

Since its initial application in the UK and the US, the concept became central in the redefinition of the notion of development standing at the center of the programs funded by the World Bank and the International Monetary Fund. Since the 1980s, financial crises, in particular related to government debt default and currency collapses in poor or middle income countries, led to help by these organizations that was tied to the condition of applying "structural adjustment programs" consisting in state budget reduction and privatizations. This led to the "lost decade" of the 1990s in most of the countries where these programs were applied, in Latin America, South-East Asia, and Africa, and to a lesser legitimacy of the concept in the early 2000s, in particular after the South-East Asian crisis of 1997 and the Argentinean crisis of 2001, in countries that had avowedly followed strictly IMF conditions. The growth of the early 2000s in countries that detached from these policies, notably profiting from the extremely high growth rates of China, further discredited the concept. The case of India offers a rare example of the application of IMF policies ensuing in high levels of growth since the early 1990s, in a context where these policies where nevertheless applied along with a strong presence of the state, which virtually owned until recently almost all the banking system, and with growing levels of inequality. Yet, the concept has reappeared to decry or justify the policies proposed or imposed by the IMF and the European Union to help financially the countries of the Eurozone that were affected by

the 2007–2008 crisis, in particular Ireland, Portugal, Spain, and, most notably, Greece (Streeck 2014).

6.4.4 Finance and Social Progress: Financial Power, Inequality and Sovereignty

It is evident that, thus broadly defined and contextualized, finance entertains a crucial, yet complicated relationship with social progress. On the one hand, the provision of credit within society certainly stands as a central requirement for the progress of human life, social cohesion, personal liberty, environmental sustainability, and world development. Money is thus featured, in a number of liberal and progressive philosophies, as part of a project aiming for a society of equal and independent individuals (Hart and Ortiz 2014). Contemporary financial institutions, which stand as crucial intermediaries that facilitate the circulation of monetary credit and the allocation of capital, are thus expected to fulfil a crucial role in the attainment of social progress. On the other hand, financial rationales translate into the establishment of hierarchies between what is deemed financially valuable and what is not, which ultimately results in the establishment of social hierarchies and power cleavages. Money thus does also appear, in a number of critical accounts, as the prime vehicle for inequality and domination, and the global financial industry is indeed often signaled, more precisely, as a threat to social progress.

The expansion of finance in the last 30 years is indeed marked by the difficulty of assessing its impact on social progress. On the one hand, it is considered that whatever benefits of the massive global integration of trade circuits exist for global social progress, these benefits depended partly on the availability of globally circulating funds that have been mainly managed by the private-sector financial industry. At the same time, the countries with higher economic growth and poverty reduction, i.e. China and India, have not participated in the expansion of the financial industry which has been mainly directed from the US and Europe. And those who have participated in this expansion (e.g. Europe, the US, and Japan) have experienced low growth and growing inequality. The many countries that integrated global financial flows since the late 1980s and early 1990s in Latin America, South-East Asia, and the former Soviet bloc, experienced a severe contraction in growth and so reversed this trend in the 2000s mainly through commodity exports and their participation in Chinese economic growth. On the other hand, it is possible to claim that indeed finance allows the Global North – and particular the US – to maintain its position in the global order while developing countries have to accept what finance they can get on whatever terms they are given (Norfield 2016).

Recent analyses of growing inequality in income distribution, in particular in the US and Europe, have shown that the expansion of the financial industry has been accompanied by a very rapid increase of income for the higher levels of management in that sector. The statistical impact of this trend on total income inequality is actually very significant, and it attests to the magnitude of the change (Atkinson and Bourguignon 2000, 2015; Godechot 2012; Piketty 2014; Piketty and Zucman 2014; Saez and Zucman 2016). This income inequality is not just between professional groups, but also geographical, within states and between states. Global financial centers have continued to accumulate wealth, in London, New York, Tokyo, Singapore, Hong Kong, or Shanghai. This has contributed to geographical inequalities, between the countries hosting financial centers and those that do not, and inside the countries and even the cities where these centers are hosted, between their locations and the rest of the territory. In many cases, this has contributed to reinforcing geographical inequalities inherited from the eighteenth and nineteenth centuries' colonial distribution of financial centers. In other cases, it has allowed certain locations to rise as regional financial centers, such as Johannesburg, Singapore, Hong Kong, Shenzhen, and Shanghai. Managing these inequalities implies a complex balance between local and global politics (Leyshon and Thrift 1997; Sassen 2006, 2012).

The major potential impact of finance for social progress comes from the concentration of monetary resources in the hands of the financial industry since the 1980s. Managing pensions in the US, and savings of middle classes in most rich countries, the financial industry has the capacity to impose hierarchies and orientations in economic activity, by granting credit at different levels of cost, potentially all around the world. Professional methodologies of valuation, analysis, and investment are today gathered in a common body of officially sanctioned rules of practice often referred to as "financial economics" or "quantitative finance," which have gained scientific legitimacy in part due to the fact that some of their authors have obtained reputable academic awards such as the Nobel Memorial Prize in Economic Sciences (Bernstein 1992; MacKenzie 2006). The debates concerning the role of this type of finance techniques oppose two views. That favored by regulation in most rich countries, by mainstream academics and by the industry itself, considers that these methods render financial markets close to informational efficiency, thereby allowing financial prices to convey accurate information to other economic actors, and ensuing in a distribution of monetary resources that most approaches social optimality. The other view considers that these methods only give priority to investments that have a short-term monetary profitability, which is incompatible with the need for long-term investment in public utilities that offer low or even no monetary profit, such as education, health, and heavy infrastructure, such as roads and communication networks. Yet the latter are a prerequisite for economic growth and social progress. The development of public–private partnerships has aimed at bridging this gap, giving rise to concerns about the possibility that this would be public subvention for private profits without further gains in efficiency. The debates remains locked in the fact that, since the financial industry needs short-term profitability to survive in the long term, it has serious limitations in addressing long-term social investment. The very small scope of experiments with impact bonds, microfinance, and social or ethical investment only highlights these limitations.

Since the creation of bond and stock markets in the wake of European colonial expansion, the growth of the financial industry has been also closely tied to its capacity to collect private capital to finance sovereign debt. In the US, Europe and many countries of Africa, Latin America, and Asia, the Bretton Woods agreements provided the frame for a growing issuance and international circulation of sovereign debt instruments. For most countries in the world, state budgets are unthinkable without the use of government debt. Yet, there are different scenarios that do not allow for a clear-cut assessment of the impact of this symbiosis between private finance and public management concerning

social progress (Kolb 2011; Lienau 2014). The US stands as a unique case, the global prominence of the US dollar giving it the ability to fund the federal budget by issuing debt beyond the means affordable by any other country. Its financial strength has enabled it to force developing countries to open their borders for trade or risk being cut off from finance. The Japanese state could issue debt reaching a ratio to GDP unmatched by any other rich country, but which is funded almost exclusively by Japanese big banks and insurance companies, thereby isolating government budgetary decisions from foreign, i.e. not nationally elected, pressure. The Chinese and Indian economies, which have almost closed off their sovereign bond markets to international investors, are in a similar situation. Most other countries lie in the middle, and while some manage to find cheap funding to orient their budgetary decisions per internal political aims, in line with the idea of democracy, other governments find their policies directed by global private creditors, which are then accused of countering democratic will. In general, this lack of democratic scope is most prevalent in the poorest countries, i.e. those in most need of investment to alleviate poverty and inequality. The impact of finance in these countries is therefore most often criticized as being negative both for long-term investment and for the democratic process itself.

The role of finance in the distribution of monetary resources is the object of several controversies concerning the fairness and legitimacy of the social hierarchies that it contributes to create by allocating credit in selective and therefore unequal ways. The rise of finance since the 1980s, in the US, Europe, Japan, Latin America, South-East Asia, India, Africa, the former Soviet bloc, and even, to a lesser extent, China, was premised on the general idea that it would allow for a distribution of credit close to social optimality, due to the free interplay of maximizing investors in markets that regulation needed to ensure would be informationally efficient. Thus, social progress was at the center of the project, at least in discourse, and the explicit shift of political power from states to the financial industry was legitimized accordingly. In particular, after the end of the Cold War, finance was presented for several years as a major tool for the adoption of an economic system based on competitive markets that was itself supposed to be a central foundation of political democracy. Three decades later, the results of this call to finance have had mixed results at best.

In the US and Europe, the negative effects of the last financial crisis have been obvious and undisputed, but did not lead to a major revision of the role of finance in the allocation of monetary resources, except for the policies of quantitative easing which were partly aimed at bailing out the financial industry itself, while the lower and middle classes continued to experience a relative loss of income and higher inequality. This has led to the accusation that the financial industry has captured regulatory bodies and central banks, which cannot propose radical policies that would go against the industry's interests (Varoufakis 2011; Huault and Richard 2012; Streeck 2014). The role of the financial industry in the political fragilities of poor countries and the return to mild forms of dictatorship in most of South-East Asia and in Russia, for example, have put into question the ability of finance to claim political legitimacy. In the Eurozone, the IMF has been accused of overriding the results of elections and even referendums in Greece, in the name of financial rationales. According to some analysts, just as in the 1930s, the rise of anti-democratic sentiments can therefore be itself blamed on the insistence of the financial industry to obtain short-term returns from sovereign debts against the will of the electorate. In all these cases, the case for finance being a factor of democratic governance is being jeopardized to quite an extent.

6.4.5   Finance and Social Progress: Basic Human Needs

The global financial industry connects with the issue of human needs in general only as far as the latter can be the object of monetary profit. The concern is, thus, whether human needs are best addressed through non-for-profit or through for-profit economic management, irrespective of whether this latter occurs in competitive markets or through state-backed oligopolies or monopolies, as is often the case. International institutions have developed the field of "project finance" as a way to draw for-profit managerial methods, deemed more efficient, to conduct the development of basic infrastructures concerning human needs such as health, food, and water. Yet, this only concerns minor volumes compared to those managed by the financial industry at large, and they fall within the same limits highlighted above: either the projects are profitable, or they must be made profitable through state support, which means a transfer of taxes that requires close democratic scrutiny. The lack of investment in poor and middle-income countries as compared to rich countries, where most of the financial markets are concentrated, attests to the difficulty for the financial industry to venture into risky areas, deeming it more prudent to invest hundreds of billions of US dollars in the US subprime mortgage market, which can eventually be bailed out by the Federal state, than in war-torn Democratic Republic of the Congo, for instance, where much smaller amounts could have a much bigger impact in terms of access to health, education, food, water, and, ultimately, peace.

Agricultural production is increasingly being perceived as an asset class by the financial industry, treated with the same methods of valuation and investment used for stocks, bonds, and derivatives (Cheng and Xiong 2014). This has led to the massive purchase of land and the reorientation of production toward profitable and, especially, standardized markets that can be monitored at a distance by fund and asset managers (McMichael 2009, 2012; Russi 2013; Clapp 2014; Fairbairn 2014; Isakson 2014). This has favored forms of production, such as the use of GMOs, and choices of crops that may hamper local access to basic commodities and that may not always take into account the need for less intensive agriculture in order to sustain the quality of the land in the long term. The expansion of agriculture land and logging at the expense of tropical forests, following this same logic, may also create environmental and social problems in the future. The development of carbon-credit markets has been proposed as a palliative, where state regulation and limits to investment can be traded to preserve land that would otherwise fall into this short-term investment perspective.

Food distribution also raises a number of issues for the understanding of the impact of finance in addressing human needs. The first issue concerns the management of distribution of food through global markets for commodities that are today inherently linked to global financial markets through the massive use of options and futures. This has been shown to lead to sometimes rapid and strong swings in food prices, depriving poor populations of access to basic commodities. The

food riots of 2007–2008 around the world were a stark reminder of the limits of the current pricing system and its dependence on short-term valuation methods developed by the financial industry (McMichael 2009). The second partly related issue concerns the tendencies to obesity in rich countries and in the middle and upper classes of middle income and poor countries, while about one person in eight, or roughly a billion people, live under the threat of malnutrition according to FAO standards. The financial industry could have an impact in the orientation of funding for a better distribution of better food. Yet, this would only be possible with clear return expectations or with state guarantees. So far, finance has followed the strategies of big corporations and even increased their need for short-term return, with lobby and investment more oriented toward sales than toward healthy and evenly spread access to food. State regulation seems to be the only check on this trend so far.

Finance also plays a role in the way a basic human need such as peace is addressed. The concern with tangible short or at best mid-term monetary returns has rendered the financial industry very weary of engaging in terrains with high uncertainty. The professional difference between "risk," deemed calculable, and "uncertainty," deemed unforeseeable, has justified the eviction of entire regions of the planet from the "investment universe" of the industry, and the imposition of prohibitively high rates of return for regions marked by war and strong social conflicts. On the other hand, the industry has continued to finance corporations deemed able to obtain returns in those regions, such as the weapons industry, the oil industry, and mining. These latter are often themselves part of the factors leading to conflicts, and in that sense the financial industry has not contributed to peace, except for the marginal disinvestment strategies of ethical funds, for instance.

However, the last 30 years have experienced a massive global financial integration. The central case in point is the accumulation of US-dollar denominated reserves by the People's Republic of China. This has led to a fundamental interdependency of the two biggest economic powers in the world, which seem on the other hand increasingly pitched against each other for the control of resources around the world, a trend that has obvious military components in the South-East China Sea, but that has already implied political instability and the support of authoritarian governments in Africa, South-East Asia, Sri Lanka, and elsewhere. In this confrontation, financial interdependency, mediated by the production and management of financial securities, may be considered a factor of peace and stability, which was for instance absent in the opposition between the two blocs during the Cold War. Besides this case, this financial integration, fostering global trade relations, can be considered to have mixed results. On the one hand, it has fostered a global interdependency that pushes governments to negotiate. On the other hand, through the policies of the IMF, the World Bank, and now through funding by the Chinese Development Bank and other Chinese banks, certain authoritarian governments, and the conflicts they sustain, have found renewed funding.

6.4.6   Finance and Innovation

Finance has almost become a synonym for innovation, at least in high-value potential sectors such as biomedicine and technology, and through the constant reference to notions of "value creation" in dominant policy discourse in that area (Muniesa 2017). Such notions do accompany ventures that are often presented in terms of progress. Venture capitalism and innovation investment at large appear today, in many accounts, as the "bright side" of financial capitalism: concerned with "long term" futures and concentrating on "value creation" in the real world. That said the literature points toward two limits: finance may partly fail from sorting desirable from less desirable innovations according to social progress criteria, and fail also from putting sustainability into the equation. An assessment of this problem can benefit from a focus on biomedical and pharmacological innovation.

A most critical link between biomedical and pharmaceutical innovation on the one hand and social progress on the other resides in the capacity to tackle urgent global problems, such as neglected diseases (tuberculosis, malaria, HIV/AIDS, and Neglected Tropical Diseases or NTDs), that can offer the currently dominant system of innovation policy and its alternatives. The current system is characterized, to quite a large extent, by a patent regime of intellectual property protection and by financial techniques of project valuation and investor protection. Both aspects have received abundant attention in the literature, and are marked by scientific and policy controversy. In legal and economic scholarship, patents are commonly considered as more efficient than other approaches to innovation policy. As a form of property rights, patents act as channels between potential customers or users, potential innovators, and potential investors, guiding investment toward projects with the prospect of value creation, and securing return. A number of scholars have nonetheless identified problems and failures of this system from both an allocative perspective and from the viewpoint of social progress, and explored alternatives that could provide efficient alternatives but which tend to fail from proving viable in a context dominated by the patent system (Fisher and Syed 2006; Kapczynski and Syed 2013; Lezaun and Montgomery 2015; Van Overwalle 2015). The standard methodologies of financial valuation that determine the value of a pharmaceutical innovation from the point of view of an investor have been also criticized in the literature, with particular attention to the drawbacks of discounted cash flow (DCF) analysis, which tend to devalue exploratory innovation (Hartmann and Hassan 2006; Christensen, Kaufman, and Shih 2008). Overall, the imperative of economic viability that any innovation faces, including innovations that may fall within the domain of neglected diseases (malaria, tuberculosis, NTDs, etc.), for example, is today heavily marked by the requirements of finance, that is, of a mode of distribution of monetary resources that, in order to function, needs to contribute to the maximization of return on investment.

6.4.7   Challenges to Mainstream Models of Finance

Recent evolutions of contemporary financial capitalism have been characterized in the literature by a turn to moral values as a possible palliative to the threats posed to social progress by the excesses of financial rationalities, with a focus on rules of good practice and economic activism in financial services. Notions such as "corporate social responsibility" (CSR) and "socially responsible investment" (SRI) have permeated today mainstream corporate cultures, both inside and outside the financial industry. These are scrutinized in the relevant

literature as vehicles for the development of a socially and environmentally virtuous rationale in capitalistic enterprises but also, critically, as stratagems to legitimatize forms of corporate conduct that are in reality still driven by profit maximization (Banerjee 2008; Gond and Crane 2010; Fleming and Jones 2013; Ghadiri, Gond, and Brès 2015). Comparable considerations can be observed in the case of Islamic banking and finance (Maurer 2012; Pitluck 2012), microfinance (Schwittay 2014) or corporate philanthropy (McGoey 2015). And a similar logic can be identified in debates around the development of ethics curricula and measures in business education (Ortiz and Muniesa 2018). Ultimately, discussions revolve around whether the financial industry can integrate moral and political aims in its operations that do not infringe on its need to obtain profits to survive and that impact the distribution of monetary resources in the sense of greater social progress. Given the varieties of actors, in these debates, the definitions of morality and social progress are diverse and not always compatible. In parallel to these developments a literature has also emerged that emphasizes the difficulties of challenging the dominant scientific culture in finance and the mainstream (that is, Brownian) paradigm in financial modeling in the last decades (de Bruin and Walter 2016; Chiapello and Walter 2016).

Overall, the global financial industry seems to be confronted today to a series of moral and political critiques that locate in its most defining rationales the engine of both the widening of social inequalities and the endangering of democratic order (Piketty 2014). It is also confronted to scientific epistemic critiques that accuse it of relying on probabilistic assumptions and calculative methods that favor the emergence of blank spots and unforeseen dangers. Responses to the moral and political quandaries of finance that emerge from within the financial field proper have provided only limited insights. Responses to the scientific limitations have rather contributed to the escalation in the widening of the expertise "silos" in which financial knowledge operates (Tett 2011).

6.5   Enabling Social Progress through Reform of the Corporation

To this point we have set out a number of examples of how capitalism fails to meet social progress outcomes. We have seen that intrinsic to the capitalist system as whole, at least in its contemporary form, is the perpetuation of regressive social outcomes such as inequality and powerlessness. Capitalism is having these effects today because of the way the corporation is constituted in law and practice and because of the way finance works. Reforming the corporation, the organization within which the large part of both financial and nonfinancial market exchange takes place, will be critical if capitalism is not to suffer a system-wide failure. While such reforms cannot by their nature address more fundamental tendencies within capitalism toward social regress, they may be able to counter some of the more egregious characteristics of the financially orientated capitalism of today.

Corporate decision-making driven by the goal of shareholder value maximization has led to the marginalization of labor, the reduction of investment in production and innovation, and the stripping of value from productive corporate enterprises. It has also facilitated the avoidance of fiscal liabilities and regulatory responsibilities.

6

The policy implication of the critique we have offered is that it is essential, and urgent, to find ways to reduce shareholder power and to enable more inclusive and socially progressive decision-making. This means tackling leverage and asset stripping while developing policies to enhance innovation with the potential to advance social progress. As part of this policy analysis we need to consider how far corporate social responsibility initiatives offer possibilities for making businesses more socially progressive. For space reasons we cannot consider all the issues that must be addressed, but we can explore the potential for social science analysis to address problems arising from the current corporate model, and to help identify alternatives to the contemporary orthodoxy (see Chapter 8 for a discussion of corporate tax reforms).

6.5.1 Corporate Governance: Changing Board Composition

In certain historical periods and in some jurisdictions, the tendency of the institution of the corporation to lead to social regress has been qualified by socially orientated policies, including extensive welfare state provision and regulation. The current focus on producing shareholder value as the principal goal of the company is derived from the way in which the law conceives shareholders' legal rights, as well as in corporate governance initiatives aimed at extending shareholder influence over corporate decision-making, including those that use the language of "stewardship" (Talbot 2013). The policy of enhancing shareholder control rights increases the drive to maximize profits by displacing risks on to other stakeholders. It discourages long term productive investment in favor of asset stripping and short-term value extraction. Thus it is important to identify find mechanisms to reduce the drive to shareholder value maximization and to support the voice and income rights of workers in the firm and citizens beyond it.

Increasing the power of other stakeholders, particularly employees, while decreasing the power of shareholders, would substantially change the way corporate governance operates. Clearly, shareholders require some forum in which to make their views known, but so too do other stakeholders. A stakeholder board, which represented employees, shareholders, consumers, and creditors among others, would enable a diverse range of voices to influence the conduct of management. While the shareholders' interest is liquid and easily transferable, employees' interests tend to be bound to the productive entity. While shareholders will seek immediate returns, employees will have a longer term commitment to the company. The distinct and often conflicting interests of investors and workers need to be held in balance if the company is to produce value over the medium to long term. The stakeholder board could be in the form of a separate supervisory board as in the German model, or could be constituted a subcommittee; the precise form will vary from one context to another and may be country-specific. The key concern is that a range of interests should be able to assert real power over the orientation of the company. To that end, devolving the legal powers possessed by shareholders to stakeholders in general would enable a more representative board to exercise such power. Not all legal powers would need to be transferred to stakeholder boards, as many relate specifically to issues relating to the property rights vested in shares. However, many legal powers relate to the general governance of the company, such as section 168 of the UK Companies Act,

which currently gives shareholders the power to remove directors. Provisions such as this should be exercised by stakeholder boards.

6.5.2 Policy Implications: Leveraging and "Going Private"

The implications of our analysis on registering a public company as private is that the process should be much more strictly regulated and in some cases straightforwardly prohibited. Currently, reregistration is allowed for, following a shareholder vote. This gives power to individuals who stand to profit to the detriment of other stakeholders, particularly past and present employees. Thus the law should be changed to ensure that any decision to reregister the form of a business should be considered by those who will be affected, in this case the nonfinancial stakeholders. This is a key decision to which a stakeholder board would be ideally suited.

If agreement is reached on "going private," regulation should be devised to inhibit assets stripping and to ensure that the new private company protects assets and pensions. Dividend law should be reexamined to deal with the loopholes which enable artificial transactions to constitute "realized" profits. These currently include the transfer of revalued assets to other entities within a group, and the creation of paper profits, such as negative goodwill.

The BHS case shows that the pendulum has swung too far toward shareholder empowerment and too far away from management and employee control. The result is to undermine the corporate veil. The law understands that shares are a title to dividends and not to the company's assets. The corporate veil is the legal outcome of this. However, the corporate veil can become flimsy at best in a situation where a single person or group of linked individuals stands in for the entire body of shareholders. The corporate veil between the company and its shareholders/directors needs to be more firmly drawn in order to protect the underlying productive entity. The current emphasis on empowering shareholders and increasing their control rights runs counter to this suggestion, and must be addressed. The purchase of shares, which are often undervalued, should not give the purchaser an entitlement to the company in its entirety.

Colluding in this de facto veil piercing is the auditing business. Auditing is dominated by the "Big Four"; auditors to nearly all FTSE 100 and 250 companies. These auditors do what their clients want and the reduced controls over private companies make their job easier. Their incentive to comply with the spirit of regulations is very weak. Furthermore, the leading auditing firms are part of the regulation of their own profession. A radical rethink of how to make these firms accountable is required. This could range from stronger legal controls to making auditing a public function. This would produce much-needed revenue for governments and would help ensure that pensions were protected. It would also increase trust in the pension system and reduce the public cost of the squandering of pension funds as occurred with BHS.

A further reform would be to subject large private companies, both those originally constituted as such and those which were previously listed on a stock exchange, to an effective corporate governance code of the kind applicable to companies with a listing. This change was proposed in the UK government Green Paper on corporate governance reform of November 2016. We have a number of concerns with proposals such as these. First, the "comply or explain" method of compliance in the corporate governance codes has been successful in respect of listed companies precisely because they are subject to the listing requirements of the relevant stock exchange. Furthermore, as public companies, their value is determined by the market and part of that determination is based on the adequacy of their reporting. None of these imperatives or incentives apply to private companies and without them, compliance becomes a cursory exercise. Inadequacies in reporting, more explaining than complying, have no practical consequences for the private company. The second problem is with the lack of oversight in the process and immediate outcome of going private, such as leverage. This can change the entire capital structure of the company to the detriment of employee's work and pensions. The third problem is with the content of corporate governance codes. They necessarily do not address the issues covered by law such as rules relating to the company's capital. Indeed, it is precisely the lighter touch legal rules applicable to private companies that motivates reregistration as noted above. In short, the corporate governance codes do not address the social progress problems inherent in "going private." If applicable to large private companies, they would not have inhibited a situation like BHS.

6.5.3 Corporate Social Responsibility: Does It Have a Role in Enabling Social Progress?

The practice of corporate social responsibility has grown exponentially over the last 20 years, pushed in large part by the work of human rights groups, NGOs and academic researchers in highlighting the exploitative and dangerous working conditions in the developing countries that provide the goods for many global brands. Corporations in turn have shown an increased enthusiasm for demonstrating their adherence to social concerns as well as meeting their legal obligation to act to enhance shareholder value; a shift known as pursuing the "triple bottom line" rather than the "bottom line." A new profession of CSR experts and consultants has emerged. Companies compete to be the most CSR cognizant, proudly displaying any award for good CSR activities on their websites. Even the most inherently unsocially responsible companies, such as those selling tobacco (a product with surely no social benefits), boast glossy CSR reports from their own CSR committees of CSR experts. The British American Tobacco Corporation's last CSR committee's report reviewed its activities in addressing human rights risks and promoting the interests of tobacco farmers, sustainable agriculture, and the success and global reach of its Youth Smoking Prevention initiative.

In contrast to Milton Friedman's famous claim that the social responsibility of companies was to make profit for shareholders and not to consider the wider community (responsibility for which lay elsewhere), companies are finding that good CSR means good business. Many corporations market products accredited as socially responsible, such as those certified by the FairTrade Association, because consumers increasingly prefer products with a CSR pedigree. A good CSR image

protects corporate reputation and brand, that part of the GVC which claims the majority of the profit. The value of brands makes the corporate watchers and activists particularly strong, enabling them to pressurize corporations to adopt socially responsible policies. Reports of human rights abuses, child labor, or environmental destruction can have a have a direct impact on consumer preferences and thus the bottom line.

CSR is widely embraced by the largest national corporations and global corporations. Nearly 75 percent of global corporations report on their corporate responsibility. Emerging economies like Malaysia, India, and Indonesia have CSR reporting in nearly 100 percent of their publicly owned companies, as it is mandatory. They recognize that it is a necessary part of demonstrating their business credibility. Reports will often follow similar formats covering key concerns, so that 78 percent of global companies that report refer to the Global Reporting Initiative guidelines.

CSR projects are often applied in developing countries in which most global production takes place where there is little actual protection of labor, or indeed the environment, even where there are laws that purport to do so. For example, although Bangladesh has labor laws that in principle provide high levels of protection for workers, the near impossibility of an employee being able to enforce the law and the poor socio-economic position they find themselves in mean that the law is unable to actually protect labor in practice (Talbot 2018b).

Many advocates of CSR argue that it is necessary when the state itself cannot, or will not, protect labor. This is particularly so in "captured states," that is, those states where the politicians are frequently the owners and employers of their country's businesses and employees. Such a state of affairs is not uncommon in developing states.

Within global chains, CSR has the advantage of reaching through the chain into various jurisdictions. So while typically the parent company will be located where there are some labor and environmental standards and mechanisms through which to enforce them, other parts of the chains, consisting of subsidiaries companies or other associations will not. They are simultaneously legally distinct from the parent and fully integrated in the value chain which is created to profit the parent company's investors. Workers involved in production of the tangible product will suffer on two accounts. First, although they are the value producers, the parent company's ownership of "rents," means they will not enjoy that value. Second, they tend to be located in areas with traditionally poor labor and environmental standards and/or enforcement.

In the case of garment workers in Bangladesh, the majority of the value is captured not by the garment producer but by the lead (merchant) company that claims value through its "unique" branding and high street presence. The producer organization claims a small part of the overall value created while labor claims only a small wage. The producers are the cheapest part of the value chain. At the same time garment workers have few institutional mechanisms through which to enforce their rights. In this context, CSR may be the only protection for workers. So, where the law of the parent company's jurisdiction does not apply to its global subsidiaries and business affiliations, CSR acting "beyond the law" may provide workers with some protection. It may be in the company's interest to apply, or to be seen to apply, business ethics that are closer to those of its domestic jurisdiction and those of its main consumers. There may be a strong business case for adopting policies that benefit the producers' workers and provide visibility and proof of good corporate citizenship.

This justification for CSR reveals the failure of the law in this respect. In construing the relationship as arms-length contracting the law radically misconstrues and misrepresents the real relationship of power between suppliers and purchasers. The buyers are global retail brands, some of which are the largest in the world. They are heavily integrated into the production process and have a powerful hold over the conditions and pay of the producers' workers. They can ensure that producers cut costs to the bone, suppress wages, enforce overtime, and ignore health and safety problems.

Increasingly, corporations might evidence their social responsibility through the adoption of Codes provided by global institutions or private accreditations systems which are largely created, promoted, and monitored by civil society groups (those groups that are not affiliated to government or business). On the former, there is a history of global institutions colluding with corporations in the creation of codes of conduct in order that they will have minimal impact on profit-making. Following an initiative launched at Davos in 1999 between Kofi Annan and the CEO of Nestlé, the UN and the largest corporations launched a "principle-based" human rights initiative called the Global Compact. Designed to usurp the more stringent UN "Norms," the Global Compact is based on self-monitoring of voluntary action (Talbot 2013). Corporations can voluntarily sign up to the Compact and thereby commit to observe ten principles which are based around human rights, labor, the environment, and anti-corruption. The corporations that sign up to this must produce an annual Communication on Progress (COP), a self-certifying document that shows how they think they are observing the ten principles. That document is publicly available on the Global Compact website. The website reports that it has "more than 12,000 participants, including over 8,000 businesses in approximately 145 countries around the world." It is popular with business. They get the credit for signing up and being aligned to UN-endorsed human rights commitments without having to evidence any of their claims, without being monitored by any external body and without committing to any binding obligations. Similarly, the UN convened Principles for Responsible Investment sets out aspirations and involves no external monitoring. The UN's Ruggie "Framework" sets out a corporation's "*responsibility* to respect human rights" in contrast to a state's *duty* under international law to protect its citizens against human rights abuses. Corporations' "responsibilities" should be met by having a human rights policy which is publicly available and a human rights due diligence process to identify and then to prevent or mitigate adverse human rights impacts that are directly linked to their operations, products, or services. This process of monitoring must be ongoing and should ideally involve dialogue with affected persons (but doesn't have to). Like the Compact, this is essentially a self-monitoring process although Ruggie clearly anticipated the engagement of a wider stakeholder community as well as the reputational effects of corporate social responsibility.

Corporations have also established their own guidelines. The Ethical Trading Initiative is an industry derived code that requires members to submit annual reports to the ETI board showing how they are dealing with labor conditions in their supply chains and how they have complied with ETI base principles. International Standardization Organization 26000 (ISO 26000), designed to promote CSR in corporations, requires no monitoring, provides no certification, and only gives guidance on best CSR practice. It aims to "clarify social responsibility." In both of these initiatives there is no external monitor and no persons or mechanism to ensure these standards are maintained.

Other initiatives that go further in conforming to a basic standard of specificity and engagement have found monitoring and enforcement difficult. Social Accountability 8000 (SA 8000), originally developed by Social Accountability International (an international accreditation body) in 1998 to reduce sweatshop practice, requires detailed social auditing to ensure that its very specific standards and requirements are met and are verifiable. Corporations will not be certified without this. The veracity of monitoring is ensured through announced or unannounced audits to certify compliance, and corporations which have signed up to SA8000 must keep appropriate records to show compliance and to continue to be certified. Social Accountability International reports that SA8000 is currently certifying 3388 facilities in 71 countries, over 65 different industries, employing a total of 2,019,193 workers. However, a recent report evidenced that many of the agencies which were supposed to be qualified to monitor businesses as SA8000 compliant, were themselves negligent and poorly trained. Good standards have not been enforced, corporations have not been properly monitored and factories in developing countries continue to be dangerous and exploitative. The system of training and funding means that the auditors invest in their (not inexpensive) training. They then can earn from the companies they audit. Without companies choosing to have this audit there are no customers so audits are unlikely to be so exacting as to put off future clients. These are all problems inherent in voluntary systems. Both the monitors and the monitored become mutually dependent (Talbot 2018b).

However, it is clear that corporations will only adopt binding agreements in respect of corporate responsibility when not to do would compromise their bottom line. The Bangladesh Accord 2013 is the most striking example of this. This initiative legally binds the retail corporations which buy garments from the hundreds of producers in Bangladesh in agreements to improve the safety of the working environment and to commit to this for a fixed period of years. Corporations were driven to adopt this because of commercial threats to their particular rents, in this case their brand. The instance of the Accord was the Rana Plaza tragedy from which the corporate brands sought to distance themselves claiming to be mere customers who were equally shocked by the deaths and injuries caused by the hazardous conditions. However, the truth was that global garment brands ensured that suppliers competed on price, making savings through low wages, job insecurity and hazardous working conditions. They were often the sole customers of these factories, making specific requirements of management is respect of the workforce and often managing directly. Local people, trade unions, and local and international activists challenged this version of events, forcing the brands to show contrition through a more stringent CSR program. Global retailers accepted the Accord and its greater specificity and enforceability because their brand needed to be rehabilitated.

This initiative legally binds companies that sign up to the Accord (signatory companies) to various agreements to improve the safety of the working environment and to commit to a fire and building safety program for five years. Currently, the Accord covers 215 signatory companies, 1600 factories and around two million workers in Bangladesh. The agreement covers all suppliers of signatory companies and the signatory companies.

However, the mechanism to ensure compliance with the Accord does not take account of the power relationship between a factory which is dependent on the large retailer's order and the large retailer who can find a supplier elsewhere. Supplier factories are therefore highly unlikely to risk losing their main or only buyer by pursuing a dispute. It falls to the corporate retailer's choice to comply or not. What this means is that for all the Accord's attempts to be more hard law, as with all CSR initiatives it relies on the corporation's assessment about what is good for business (Talbot 2018b). If fulfilling their obligation is good for business they will do it, if it isn't, they won't.

Furthermore, the Accord has a limited scope, dealing only with safety in the workplace. It does not extend to improved wages and job security. The largely female workforce remains employed until they have children and are then quickly replaced with more cheap female labor. As Oxfam (2016) notes, "firms are consistently using their dominant position to insist on poverty wages. Between 2001 and 2011, wages for garment workers in most of the world's 15 leading apparel-exporting countries fell in real terms."

As these examples show, in order to begin to be effective, from a social progress perspective, CSR strategies must address the social needs that the corporation detrimentally affects, rather than vanity projects that look attractive in their Annual Report. Commitments must be clear and specific. There is a growing perception that general principles which are open to numerous interpretations, such as are found in Global Compact, ETI, and the Ruggie Guidelines, serve only the corporations to which they are meant to be addressed. The effectiveness of corporate self-monitoring (again a feature of Global Compact, ETI, and the Ruggie Guidelines) cannot be relied upon. Self-monitoring is the preferred method of compliance for corporations. Hence the rejection of the Norms. Self-monitoring provides corporations with a shield to resist external regulation. For monitoring to be effective it must be performed by independent external people and organizations that can understand the intricacies of compliance and enforcement. The lesson of SA8000 is that this is difficult to achieve. There is also a danger of capture as Social Accountability International is a charity dependent on funds, much of which comes from its corporate members.

For rules to be effective there must also be behavior-changing sanctions. When dealing with global corporations this would have to be substantial amounts, impossible to enforce without a prior legal agreement which CSR, by its voluntary nature, eschews. The strength of CSR, such as it is, remains with the corporation's reliance on reputational issues. When death and injury on the scale of Rana Plaza can be connected with corporate policies then those corporations are forced to take such measures that will repair their image with customers.

But the Accord is only about safety and it doesn't even include such safety issues as those that arise from long working hours, or working close to full term pregnancy, for example. The everyday exploitation of billions of workers falls outside the remit of CSR. Highlighting the everyday exploitation of workers in developing countries (as many NGOs so expertly do) keeps us informed, but in terms of what can be done there, we believe that it is only through organized labor that workers can claim better pay and conditions.

6.5.4 Corporations and Innovation

The story of Hepatitis C that we reviewed earlier may represent an extreme case of the tendency for a financialized model of innovation to turn in on itself, enabling profit-orientated companies to use government funding and legal protection for intellectual property rights to extract rents from the public sector and ration access to technologies with major potential for improvements in human well-being. However, it could also be that it is a straw in the wind, and a warning of how financialization and shareholder value maximization strategies, supported by shifts in the institutional framework of corporate governance, are undermining the potential of the capitalist system to promote social progress. Corporate-led innovation of the kind we currently see is favoring the current generation at the cost of future ones, particularly with regard to the environment. The failure to internalize environmental externalities in innovation has led to critical stresses to the climate and the biosphere chronicled by the IPCC.

The immediate responses to the problems raised by the Hepatitis C case include proposals for value-based pricing (Bach and Pearson 2015) and the public funding of clinical trials (Baker 2008), both of which have recently been discussed by a high-level panel on access to medicines convened by the United Nations Secretary General. These developments go some of the way to addressing the specific problems arising in pharma, but do not address the wider structural issue of the relationship between a financialized form of capitalism and the innovation system. How should we respond to the wider challenge this poses?

Two core initiatives can be identified, which can lead to enhanced forms of social progress and which involve the reformulation of the way in which corporations operate, their access to appropriate forms of finance, and the market structures that help to determine their innovation trajectories. The first is to foster more inclusive patterns of innovation; the second is to foster the introduction of more environmentally friendly sociotechnical systems.

More inclusive trajectories of innovation need to target both process and product innovation. On the process side, there is a greater need for more labor-friendly innovation, both in terms of the quantum of employment and in the character of work. Process innovation also needs to be more environmentally friendly, since a disproportionate share of environmental externalities are thrust on the shoulders of the poor. On the product front, innovation needs to focus on the needs of

6

the poor, with a greater emphasis on low-price functional products and lesser emphasis on differentiated, overpackaged, nonrecyclable, and throwaway products. Perhaps of greatest importance is the need to respond to the fact that corporate-driven innovation underinvests in the public goods which have disproportionate welfare implications, such as neglected tropical diseases. A third prong of the inclusive innovation agenda is to develop processes which lead to the greater involvement of other stakeholders in innovation, particularly in those currently excluded from the fruits of growth and innovation. The introduction on a stakeholder board, as discussed above, would assist in actualizing these goals. State-based incentives such as tax incentives would also help encourage inclusive innovation.

Innovation occurs at a number of levels, incremental, radical, and "revolutionary." In this latter category are a series of historically transformational technologies, including steam power, iron and steel, the railways, the internal combustion engine, and ICT. Each of these transformational technologies affects and diffuses through a myriad of economic activities. In each case, the core technology is embedded in a socio-economic system with associated residential patterns, social attitudes, and patterns of productive organization and consumption. The most recent paradigm is one associated with the globalization of the mass production paradigm, driven by the diffusion of cheap energy and the internal combustion engine. It has resulted in an increasing divorce between production and residence, and production and consumption and, as we have seen, the systemic production of environmentally damaging technologies.

An alternative sociotechno-economic paradigm is needed to enable innovation to foster both more inclusive outcomes, and more environmentally friendly outcomes. One of the major lessons of historical experience is that a new "revolutionary" technological paradigm has the potential to provide a growth opportunity and to provide a different trajectory to social and economic systems. Because it is new it also provides the scope for profit-driven corporations to develop and exploit innovation rents. It is here that a green-technology revolution may hold out the prospect of a better, more inclusive and more sustainable future. The vision here is one which brings production and consumption, and work and residence, closer together. It is one that provides for reduced environmental inputs, and involves a world of less inequality and greater harmony. This need not be a noncapitalist social order, but it will inevitably involve a different type of capitalism, one that requires some changes in the nature of the corporation and in the role played by the financial sector.

6.6   Conclusion: Modern Capitalism and the Limits of Reform

In this chapter we have set out some key characteristics of modern capitalism, with the focus on markets, finance and the corporation, which directly impact on social progress. In analyzing the key institutions of modern capitalism we have attempted to ground them in an understanding of their historical origins and development. Early capitalism in developed countries was characterized by laws and institutions that supported the expansion of capital but, conversely,

did little to protect the growing labor force, thereby creating distinct social classes. Organized labor gradually achieved some legal rights and protections but it was not until the end of World War II that states in the global North opted to promote substantive equality and social security. For a brief period of a few decades, financial markets operated under strict regulation, equity markets were relatively inactive, and organized labor had legal powers and political credibility.

In contrast, today's capitalism is characterized by a pervasive ideological commitment, held by governments and transnational organizations alike, which identifies social progress with the success of business. Listening and responding to business, through varied forums and lobbying, has become one of the roles of government. One of the consequences is that governments no longer have an overriding commitment to the well-being of their own citizens. Social security, progressive taxation, collective labor rights, and public regulation were the means states once used to protect citizens' interests. Treating human welfare as a cost to business has resulted in a world in which corporate taxation is seen as optional and compliance with regulation a matter of choice.

Governments claim to be advancing social progress while engaging in activities that achieve the opposite. The result, not surprisingly, has been an increase in inequality within countries, a trend common to both the developed world and the developing one. That this trend has gone hand in hand with a global reduction in absolute poverty does not make it any less destabilizing or, ultimately, any more sustainable. It is not only that labor's share in national income has been falling; there has been a downward trajectory in profitability for most of the last 40 years (see Figure 6.3).

Contemporary capitalism is vulnerable to a renewed financial crisis which, if it occurred any time soon, would result in harsh economic consequences for many and most likely in severe political turmoil. Underconsumption, allied to unemployment and underemployment, is giving rise to social tensions and to the rise of authoritarian politics. Overlaying all of this, with profound implications for humankind, is the threat of climate change and climate chaos.

In this chapter we have put forward legal reforms to corporate structure which have the aim of producing a more socially inclusive form of corporate governance. These reforms, although initially focused on the corporation, have the potential for a wider impact on the institutions of capitalism. The thread uniting them is the idea that the process of entrenching the rights of capital over the past 30 years has unbalanced capitalism itself.

The rise of shareholder value maximization was a legal and political reaction to declining profitability in the 1970s (Talbot 2016). Attacking the rights and material expectations of labor might have worked, for some, for a while, but did not address the root problem of an economy which can only achieve innovation at the cost of social cohesion. Whether a different type of reform will do better remains to be seen. Reforming the corporation to enable social progress may well mean that capitalism in any form is no longer possible. A reformed corporate form, one that delivers social progress, will also deliver a lower level of

Figure 6.3 | World rate of profit, 1869–2007.
Source: Maito (2017)

profit. Shareholders will not easily accept a reduction in their control rights (Talbot 2013). Perhaps capitalism can only flourish in a world in which a super-rich elite continues to thrive, while inequalities and social dislocation increase.

This will be our fate if governments continue to elevate the role of the private sector in the delivery (and removal) of public services and in economic governance nationally and globally. A political and economic system that is skewed to the interests of capital necessarily increases inequality within and between nations. For governments to divest powers to corporations, or to a partnership between corporations, transnational, and supranational organizations, is necessarily to undermine democracy. Under this arrangement it becomes natural for those in control of corporations to use the legal mechanisms at their disposal to extract value, hide liabilities, and avoid tax.

And yet, despite the huge power corporations possess to shape the business environment, capitalism today is characterized by falling commodity prices, low growth, and low returns on investments. Money is pouring out of emerging economies, and their debts are huge. Corporate profit is low in all but the largest of multinational enterprises. Global investment in production is one-third of what it was before the financial crisis. Stock markets are falling in real terms everywhere despite extraordinary financial measures such as quantitative easing and ubiquitous share repurchase programs. The resulting squeeze on the labor share reduces demand while household debt continues to rise.

In the current state of capitalism, a sobering possibility is that profits will only be generated in the future if corporations remain free to extract value, hide liabilities and avoid tax, and if they retain the right to exploit the global division of labor in ways that undermine human well-being. Reforming the corporation to advance social progress is incompatible with the survival of the shareholder-value maximizing corporation. So, does capitalism have a future? Yes, but in its current form, almost certainly not one that enhances social progress. Thus, it may be that in the pursuit of social progress, capitalism itself will have to evolve into another economic form.

References

Abdelal R. 2007. *Capital Rules: The Construction of Global Finance*. Cambridge, MA: Harvard University Press.

Acharya, V., R. Baghai-Wadji, and K. Subramanian 2014. "Labor Laws and Innovation," *Journal of Law and Economics* 56: 997–1037.

Adams, Z. and S. Deakin 2017. "Enterprise Form, Participation and Performance in Mutuals and Cooperatives," in J. Michie (ed.), *The Oxford Handbook of Mutuals and Co-owned Business*. Oxford: Oxford University Press.

Adams, Z. and S. Deakin 2018. "Corporate Governance and Employment Relations," in J. Gordon and W.-G. Ringe (eds.), *The Oxford Handbook of Corporate Law and Governance*. Oxford: Oxford University Press.

Adams, Z., L. Bishop, S. Deakin, C. Fenwick, S. Martinsson, and G. Rusconi 2018. The Economic Effects of Laws Relating to Employment Protection and Different Forms of Employment: Analysis of a Panel of 117 Countries, 1990–2013. Forthcoming, Centre for Business Research Working Paper Series, University of Cambridge.

Admati, A.R. and M. Hellwig 2013. *The Bankers' New Clothes: What's Wrong with Banking and What to Do about It*. Princeton, NJ: Princeton University Press.

Aglietta, M. 2000. *A Theory of Capitalist Regulation: The US Experience*. London: Verso.

Aglietta, M. and G. Bai 2012. *China's Development: Capitalism and Empire*. London: Routledge.

Aguilera, R. and A. Cuervo-Cazurra 2009. "Codes of Good Governance," *Corporate Governance: An International Review* 17: 376–387.

Aoki, M. 2010. *Corporations in Evolving Diversity: Cognition, Governance and Institutions*. Oxford: Oxford University Press.

Armour, J., H. Hansmann, R. Kraakman, and M. Pargendler 2017. "What Is Corporate Law?," in R. Kraakman et al. (eds.), *The Anatomy of Corporate Law: A Comparative and Functional Approach*, 3rd edn. Oxford: Oxford University Press.

Armour, J., S. Deakin, and M. Siems (eds.) 2017. *CBR Leximetric Datasets (Updated)*. Cambridge: Apollo Repository, https://doi.org/10.17863/CAM.9130 (last accessed December 23, 2017).

Atkinson, A.B. and F. Bourguignon (eds.) 2000. *Handbook of Income Distribution: Volume 1.* Amsterdam: Elsevier.

Atkinson, A.B. and F. Bourguignon (eds.) 2015. *Handbook of Income Distribution: Volume 2.* Amsterdam: Elsevier.

Bach, P. and S. Pearson 2015. "Payer and Policy Maker Steps to Support Value-Based Pricing for Drugs," *Journal of the American Medical Association* 30: 1–3.

Baker, D. 2008. "The Benefits and Savings from Publicly Funded Clinical Trials of Prescription Drugs," *International Journal of Health Services* 38/4: 731–750.

Baker, G.P., M.C. Jensen, and K.J. Murphy 1988. "Compensation and Incentives: Practice vs. Theory," *The Journal of Finance* 43: 593–616.

Banerjee, S.B. 2008. "Corporate Social Responsibility: The Good, the Bad and the Ugly," *Critical Sociology* 34/1: 51–79.

Baud, C., and Chiapello, E. 2017. "Understanding the Disciplinary Aspects of Neoliberal Regulations: The Case of Credit-Risk Regulation under the Basel Accords," *Critical Perspective in Accounting.* https://doi.org/10.1016/j.cpa.2016.09.005 (last accessed December 23, 2017).

Bebchuk, L.A., and J.M. Fried 2003. Executive Compensation as an Agency Problem. Working Paper 9813. National Bureau of Economic Research. www.nber.org/papers/w9813 (last accessed January 17, 2018).

Belloc, F. 2013. "Law, Finance and Innovation: The Dark Side of Shareholder Protection," *Cambridge Journal of Economics* 37: 863.

Bernstein, P.L. 1992. *Capital Ideas: The Improbable Origins of Modern Wall Street.* New York: The Free Press.

Birch, K. 2015. "Neoliberalism: The Whys and Wherefores … and Future Directions," *Sociology Compass* 9/7: 571–584.

Blair, M. 2004 "Locking in Capital: What Corporate Law Achieved for Business Organizers in the Nineteenth Century," *UCLA Law Review* 51: 387–455.

Block, F., and M.R. Somers 2014. *The Power of Market Fundamentalism.* Cambridge, MA: Harvard University Press.

Blumberg, P., and K. Strasser 2011. "Legal Form and Economic Substance of Enterprise Groups: Implications for Legal Policy," *Accounting, Economics and Law: A Convivium* 1: 1–30.

Blyth, M. 2013. *Austerity: The History of a Dangerous Idea.* Oxford: Oxford University Press.

Braudel, F. 1992. *Civilization and Capitalism, 15th-18th Century* (Vols. I, II and III). Berkeley: University of California Press.

Buchanan, J., D.-H. Chai, and S. Deakin 2011. *Hedge-Fund Activism in Japan: The Limits of Shareholder Primacy.* Cambridge: Cambridge University Press.

Charmes, J. 2012. "The Informal Economy Worldwide: Trends and Characteristics," *Margin: The Journal of Applied Economic Research* 6: 103–132.

Cheng, I.-H. and W. Xiong 2014. "Financialization of Commodity Markets," *Annual Review of Financial Economics* 6: 419–441.

Chiapello, E. and C. Walter 2016. "The Three Ages of Financial Quantification: A Conventionalist Approach to the Financiers' Metrology," *Historical Social Research* 41/2: 155–177.

Christensen, C.M., S.P. Kaufman, and W.C. Shih 2008. "Innovation Killers: How Financial Tools Destroy Your Capacity to Do New Things," *Harvard Business Review* 86/1: 98–105.

Clapp, J. 2014. "Financialization, Distance and Global Food Politics," *Journal of Peasant Studies* 41/5: 797–814.

Coase, R.H. 1988. *The Firm, the Market and the Law.* Chicago: University of Chicago Press.

Coriat, B., P. Petit, and G. Schméder 2006. *The Hardship of Nations: Exploring the Paths of Modern Capitalism.* Northhampton, MA: Edward Elgar Publishing.

Davis, D., R. Kaplinsky, and M. Morris 2017. *Rents, Power and Governance in Global Value Chains.* PRISM Working Paper, 2, March 2017. www.prism.uct.ac.za (last accessed January 27, 2018).

Davies, W. 2014. *The Limits of Neoliberalism: Authority, Sovereignty and the Logic of Competition.* Thousand Oaks, CA: Sage.

De Bruin, B. and C. Walter 2016. "Research Habits in Financial Modelling: The Case of Non-normality of Market Returns in the 1970s and the 1980s," in E. Ippoliti and P. Chen (eds.), *Methods and Finance: A Unifying View on Finance, Mathematics and Philosophy.* New York: Springer.

Deakin, S. 2003. "'Enterprise-Risk': The Juridical Nature of the Firm Revisited," *Industrial Law Journal* 32: 97–114.

Deakin, S. 2014. The Legal Framework Governing Business Firms and its Implications for Manufacturing Scale and Performance: The UK Experience in International Perspective. *Future of Manufacturing Project: Evidence Paper 5.*

London: Foresight Programme. www.ukirc.ac.uk/collaboration/the-foresight-programme (last accessed December 23, 2017).

Deakin, S. and F. Wilkinson 2005. *The Law of the Labour Market: Industrialisation, Employment, and Legal Evolution.* Oxford: Oxford University Press.

Deakin, S., J. Malmberg, and P. Sarkar 2014. "How do Labour Laws Affect Unemployment and the Labour Share of National Income? The Experience of Six OECD Countries, 1970–2010," *International Labour Review,* 153: 1–27.

Deakin, S., P. Sarkar, and A. Singh 2012. "An End to Consensus? The Selective Impact of Corporate Law Reform on Financial Development," in M. Aoki, K. Binmore, S. Deakin, and H. Gintis (eds.), *Complexity and Institutions: Norms and Corporations.* London: Palgrave.

Deville, J. 2015. *Lived Economies of Default: Consumer Credit, Debt Collection and the Capture of Affect.* London: Routledge.

Dezalay, Y., and B.G. Garth 1998. *Dealing in Virtue: International Commercial Arbitration and the Construction of a Transnational Legal Order.* Chicago, IL: University of Chicago Press.

Easterbrook, F., and D. Fischel 1991. *The Economic Structure of Corporate Law.* Cambridge, MA: Harvard University Press.

Economist 2013 "Towards the End of Poverty," and "Not Always with Us," *The Economist,* June 1, 2013.

Engelen, E., I. Erturk, J. Froud, S. Johal, A. Leaver, M. Moran, and K. Williams 2011. *After the Great Complacence: Financial Crisis and the Politics of Reform.* Oxford: Oxford University Press.

Epstein, G.A. (ed.) 2005. *Financialization and the World Economy.* Cheltenham: Edward Elgar.

Fairbairn, M. 2014. "'Like Gold With Yield': Evolving Intersections between Farmland and Finance," *Journal of Peasant Studies* 41/5: 777–795.

Fisher, W.W. and T. Syed 2006. "Global Justice in Healthcare: Developing Drugs for the Developing World," *UC Davies Law Review,* 40: 581–678.

Fleming, F. and M.T. Jones 2013. *The End of Corporate Social Responsibility: Crisis and Critique.* Thousand Oaks, CA: Sage.

Fligstein, N. 1990. *The Transformation of Corporate Control.* Cambridge, MA: Harvard University Press.

Fligstein, N. 2001. *The Architecture of Markets: An Economic Sociology of Twenty-First-Century Capitalist Societies.* Princeton, NJ: Princeton University Press.

Froud, J., S. Johal, A. Leaver, and K. Williams 2006. *Financialization and Strategy: Narratives and Numbers.* London: Routledge.

Gerber, D. 2010. *Global Competition: Law, Markets and Globalization.* Oxford: Oxford University Press.

Gereffi, G., and M. Korzeniewicz (eds.) 1994. *Commodity Chains and Global Capitalism.* Westport, CT: Greenwood.

Ghadiri, D.P., J.-P. Gond, and L. Brès 2015. "Identity Work of Corporate Social Responsibility Consultants: Managing Discursively the Tensions Between Profit and Social Responsibility," *Discourse and Communication* 9/6: 593–624.

Godechot, O. 2012. "Is Finance Responsible for the Rise in Wage Inequality in France?" *Socio-Economic Review* 10/3: 447–470.

Gond, J.-P. and A. Crane 2010. "Corporate Social Performance Disoriented: Saving the Lost Paradigm?" *Business and Society* 49/4: 677–703.

Graeber, D. 2011. *Debt: The First Five Thousand Years.* New York: Melville House.

Hansmann, H., R. Kraakman, and R. Squire 2006. "Law and the Rise of the Firm," *Harvard Law Review* 119: 1333–1403.

Harris, R. 2000. *Industrializing English Law: Entrepreneurship and Business Organisation 1720–1844.* Cambridge: Cambridge University Press.

Hart, K., and H. Ortiz 2014. "The Anthropology of Money and Finance: Between Ethnography and World History," *Annual Review of Anthropology* 43: 465–482.

Hartmann, M. and A. Hassan 2006. "Application of Real Options Analysis for Pharmaceutical R&D Project Valuation: Empirical Results from a Survey," *Research Policy* 35/3: 343–354.

Harvey, D. 2010. *The Enigma of Capital.* Oxford: Oxford University Press.

Henwood, D. 1998. *Wall Street: How It Works and for Whom.* London: Verso.

Hodgson, G. 2009. "On the Institutional Foundations of Law: The Insufficiency of Custom and Private Ordering," *Journal of Economic Issues* 43: 143–166.

Hood, C., O. James, G. Peters, and C. Scott (eds.) 2004. *Controlling Modern Government: Variety, Commonality and Change.* London: Edward Elgar.

Huault, I. and C. Richard (eds.) 2012. *Finance: The Discreet Regulator, How Financial Activities Shape and Transform the World.* New York: Palgrave Macmillan.

Incomes Data Services 2014. www.incomesdata.co.uk/wp-content/uploads/2014/10/IDS-FTSE-100-directors-pay-20141.pdf (last accessed December 23, 2017).

Ireland, P. 1999. "Company Law and the Myth of Shareholder Ownership," *Modern Law Review* 62: 32–57.

Isakson, S.R. 2014. "Food and Finance: The Financial Transformation of Agro-Food Supply Chains," *Journal of Peasant Studies* 41/5: 749–775.

Jacoby, S. 2005. *The Embedded Corporation: Corporate Governance and Employment Relations in Japan and the United States*. Princeton: Princeton University Press.

Jaravel, X. 2016. "The Unequal Gains from Product Innovations," SSRN Scholarly Paper. http://ssrn.com/abstract=2709088 (last accessed December 23, 2017).

Johnston, A. 2007. "Takeover Regulation: Historical and Theoretical Perspectives on the City Code," *The Cambridge Law Journal* 66: 422.

Kapczynski, A., and T. Syed 2013. "The Continuum of Excludability and the Limits of Patents," *Yale Law Journal* 122: 1900–1963.

Kaplan, S. 2010. "Method over Magic: The Drivers behind Private-equity Performance," in R. Finkel and D. Greising (eds.), *The Masters of Private Equity and Venture Capital*. New York: McGraw Hill.

Kaplinsky, R. 2005. *Globalization, Poverty and Inequality: Between a Rock and a Hard Place*. Cambridge: Polity.

Kaplinsky, R., and M. Morris 2017. *A Handbook for Value Chain Research*, Vol. 13. IDRC Ottawa. www.prism.uct.ac.za/Papers/VchNov01.pdf (last accessed December 23, 2017).

Katelouzou, D. and M. Siems 2015. "Disappearing Paradigms in Shareholder Portection: Leximetric Evidence for 30 Countries, 1990–2013," *Journal of Corporate Law Studies* 15: 127–160.

Kolb, R.W. (ed.) 2011. *Sovereign Debt: From Safety to Default*. Hoboken, NJ: John Wiley & Sons.

Krippner, G.R. 2011. *Capitalizing on Crisis: The Political Origins of the Rise of Finance*. Cambridge, MA: Harvard University Press.

Lakner, C.. and B. Milanovic 2016. "Global Income Distribution: From the Fall of the Berlin all to the Great Recession," *The World Bank Economic Review* 30: 203–232.

Langley, P. 2008. *The Everyday Life of Global Finance: Saving and Borrowing in Anglo-America*. Oxford: Oxford University Press.

Lazonick, W. 2014. "Profits without Prosperity," *Harvard Business Review*, September 2014. https://hbr.org/2014/09/profits-without-prosperity (last accessed January 17, 2018).

Leyshon, A. and N. Thift, N. 1997. *Money/Space: Geographies of Monetary Transformation*. London: Routledge.

Lezaun, J. and C.M. Montgomery 2015. "The Pharmaceutical Commons: Sharing and Exclusion in Global Health Drug Development," *Science, Technology, and Human Values* 40/1: 3–29.

Lienau, O. 2014. *Rethinking Sovereign Debt: Politics, Reputation, and Legitimacy in Modern Finance*. Cambridge, MA: Harvard University Press.

MacKenzie, D. 2006. *An Engine not a Camera: How Financial Models Shape Markets*. Cambridge, MA: The MIT Press.

MacKenzie, D. 2011. "The Credit Crisis as a Problem in the Sociology of Knowledge," *American Journal of Sociology* 116/6:1778–1841.

Mader, P. 2015. *The Political Economy of Microfinance: Financializing Poverty*. London: Palgrave Macmillan.

Maito, E. 2017. "The Tendency of the Rate of Profit to Fall Since the 19th Century and a World Rate of Profit," in G. Carchedi and M. Roberts (eds.), *The World in Crisis*. London: Zero Books.

Martin, R. 2002. *Financialization of Daily Life*. Philadelphia, PA: Temple University Press.

Maurer, B. 2012. "The Disunity of Finance: Alternative Practices to Western Finance," in K. Knorr Cetina and A. Preda (eds.), *The Oxford Handbook of the Sociology of Finance*. Oxford: Oxford University Press.

Mazzucato, M. 2013. *The Entrepreneurial State: Debunking Public vs. Private Sector Myths*. New York: Anthem.

McGoey, L. 2015. *No Such Thing as a Free Gift: The Gates Foundation and the Price of Philanthropy*. London: Verso.

McMichael, P. 2009. "A Food Regime Analysis of the 'World Food Crisis'," *Agriculture and Human Values* 26/4: 281–295.

McMichael, P. 2012. "The Land Grab and Corporate Food Regime Restructuring," *Journal of Peasant Studies* 39/3–4: 681–701.

Mehrling, P. 2010. *The New Lombard Street: How the Fed Became the Dealer of Last Resort*. Princeton, NJ: Princeton University Press.

Muniesa, F. 2017. "On the Political Vernaculars of Value Creation," *Science as Culture* 26: 445–454.

Ortiz, H., and F. Muniesa 2018. "Business Schools, the Anxiety of Finance and the Order of the 'Middle Tier'," *Journal of Cultural Economy* 11: 1–19.

Ouroussoff, A. 2010. *Wall Street at War: The Secret Struggle for the Global Economy*. Cambridge: Polity.

Oxfam 2016. *An Economy for the 1%*. London: Oxfam.

Norfield, T. 2016. *The City: London and the Global Power of Finance*. London: Verso.

Palma, G. 2011. "Homogeneous Middles vs. Heterogeneous Tails, and the End of the 'Inverted-U': It's All About the Share of the Rich," *World Development* 42: 87–153.

Piketty, T. 2014. *Capital in the Twenty-First Century*. Cambridge, MA: Harvard University Press.

Piketty, T., and G. Zucman 2014. "Capital is Back: Wealth-Income Ratios in Rich Countries, 1700–2010," *Quarterly Journal of Economics* 129/3: 1255–1310.

Pitluck, A.Z. 2012. "Islamic Banking and Finance: Alternative or Façade?" in K. Knorr Cetina and A. Preda (eds.), *The Oxford Handbook of the Sociology of Finance*. Oxford: Oxford University Press.

Polanyi, K. 2001. *The Great Transformation: The Political and Economic Origins of Our Time*. Boston, MA: Beacon Press.

Pollitt, C., and G. Bouckaert (eds.) 2011. *Public Management Reform: A Comparative Analysis*. Oxford: Oxford University Press.

Robé, J.-M. 2011. "The Legal Structure of the Firm," *Accounting, Economics and Law: A Convivium* 1/1: Article 5.

Roy, V., and L. King 2016. "Betting on Hepatitis C: Financial Speculation on Shareholder Value in Drug Development, Pricing and Profitability," *British Medical Journal* 354: i3718.

Russi, L. 2013. *Hungry Capital: The Financialization of Food*. Hants: Zero Books.

Saez, E., and G. Zucman 2016. 'Wealth Inequality in the United States since 1913: Evidence from Capitalized Income Tax Data', *Quarterly Journal of Economics* 131: 519–578.

Sassen, S. 2006. *Territory, Authority, Rights: From Medieval to Global Assemblages*. Princeton, NJ: Princeton University Press.

Sassen, S. 2012. *Cities in a World Economy*. Thousand Oaks, CA: Sage.

Schumpeter, J.A. 1942. *Capitalism, Socialism and Democracy*. Hove, E. Sussex, UK: Psychology Press.

Schwittay, A. 2014. "Designing Development: Humanitarian Design in the Financial Inclusion Assemblage," *PoLAR* 37: 29–47.

Sjoberg, O. 2009. "Corporate Governance and Earnings Inequality in OECD Countries 1979–2000," *European Sociological Review* 5: 519.

Springer, S., K. Birch, and J. MacLeavy (eds.) 2016. *The Routledge Handbook of Neoliberalism*. Abingdon: Routledge.

Stiglitz, J. 2002. *Globalization and its Discontents*. New York: W.W. Norton & Company.

Stiglitz, J. 2006. *Making Globalization Work*. New York: W.W. Norton & Company.

Stiglitz, J. 2010. *Freefall: America, Free Markets, and the Sinking of the World Economy*. New York: W.W. Norton & Company.

Stiglitz, J., J.A. Ocampo, S. Spiegel, R. Ffrench-Davis, and D. Nayyar 2006. *Stability with Growth: Macroeconomics, Liberalization and Development*. Oxford: Oxford University Press.

Stockhammer, E. 2015. "Rising Inequality as a Cause of the Present Crisis," *Cambridge Journal of Economics* 39/3: 935–958.

Streeck, W. 2014. *Buying Time: The Delayed Crisis of Democratic Capitalism*. London: Verso.

Streeck, W. 2016. *How Will Capitalism End?: Essays on a Failing System*. London: Verso.

Supiot, A. 2015. *La gouvernance par les nombres*. Paris: Fayard.

Talbot, L. 2010. "Keeping Bad Company: Building Societies a Case Study," *Northern Ireland Legal Quarterly* 60/4: 443–470.

Talbot, L. 2013. "Why Shareholders Shouldn't Vote: A Marxist-Progressive Critique of Shareholder Empowerment," *Modern Law Review* 76/5: 791–816.

Talbot, L. 2016. "Changing the World with Company Law? Some Problems," *Legal Studies* 36: 513.

Talbot, L. 2018a. "Capitalism: Why Companies are Unfit for Social Purpose and How they Might be Reformed," in N. Boeger and C. Villiers (eds.), *Shaping the Corporate Landscape: Towards Corporate Reform and Enterprise Diversity*. Oxford: Hart Publishing.

Talbot, L. 2018b. "Reclaiming Value and Betterment for Bangladeshi Women Workers in Global Garment Chains," in I. Lynch-Fannon and B. Sjafell

6

(eds.), *Creating Corporate Sustainability: Gender as an Agent of Change.* Cambridge: Cambridge University Press.

Tett, G. 2009. *Fool's Gold: How Unrestrained Greed Corrupted a Dream, Shattered Global Markets and Unleashed a Catastrophe.* London: Little Brown.

Tett, G. 2011. "Silos and Silences: The Role of Fragmentation in the Recent Financial Crisis," in C. de France and C.O. Meyer (eds.), *Forecasting, Warning and Responding to Transnational Risks.* New York: Springer.

UNCTAD 2013. *World Investment Report 2013. Global Value Chains: Investment and Trade for Development.* New York and Geneva: United Nations.

Van der Zwan, N. 2014. "Making Sense of Financialization," *Socio-Economic Review* 12/1: 99–129.

Van Overwalle, G. 2015. "Inventing Inclusive Patents: From Old to New Open Innovation," in P. Drahos, G. Ghidini, and H. Ullrich (eds.), *Kritika: Essays on Intellectual Property*, vol. 1. Cheltenham: Edward Elgar.

Varoufakis, Y. 2011. *The Global Minotaur: America, the True Origins of the Financial Crisis and the Future of the World Economy.* London: Zed Books.

Veldman, J., F. Gregor, and P. Morrow 2016. *Corporate Governance for a Changing World: Report of a Global Roundtable Series.* London: Frank Bold/Cass Business School. www.purposeofcorporation.org/corporate-governance-for-a-changing-world_report.pdf (last accessed December 23, 2017).

Williamson, O. 1999. *The Mechanisms of Governance.* Oxford and New York: Oxford University Press.

Williston, S. 1888. "History of the Law of Business Corporations before 1800 – Part II," *Harvard Law Review* 2: 149.

Woll, C. 2014. *The Power of Inaction: Bank Bailouts in Comparison.* Ithaca, NY: Cornell University Press.

Zucman, G. 2015. *The Hidden Wealth of Nations: The Scourge of Tax Havens.* Chicago: University of Chicago Press.

The Future of Work – Good Jobs for All*

Coordinating Lead Authors:[1]
Werner Eichhorst, André Portela Souza

Lead Authors:[2]
Pierre Cahuc, Didier Demazière, Colette Fagan, Nadya Araujo Guimarães, Huiyan Fu, Arne Kalleberg, Alan Manning, Frances McGinnity, Hillel Rapoport, Phil Scranton, Johannes Siegrist, Kathleen Thelen, Marie-Anne Valfort, Jelle Visser

* We are grateful to external discussants who provided valuable comments on earlier versions of this draft, at a workshop in Paris (April 2016), a panel at the SASE Annual Meeting in Berkeley (June 2016) and discussants at presentations in Geneva, at the OECD in Paris (September 2016), Sao Paulo (October 2016), and Brussels (January 2017) as well as comments received online. Travel support by the Friedrich Ebert Foundation for a chapter workshop held in Paris in April 2016 is gratefully acknowledged as is support by IZA and the University of Manchester. In this chapter the sections were drafted by the following authors: (i) New technology and globalization: Alan Manning and Phil Scranton; (ii) Demographic change as a driving force: André Portela Souza and Fran McGinnity; (iii) Changes and prospects on employment relations: Arne Kalleberg, Huiyan Fu, including work by Nadya A. Guimaraes and Didier Demazière; (iv) More flexible workplaces and working time?: Colette Fagan; (v) Diversity and discrimination in the labor market: Fran McGinnity, Hillel Rapoport and Marie-Anne Valfort; (vi) The impact of work and employment on health and well-being: Johannes Siegrist; (vii) Collective bargaining: Jelle Visser; (viii) Skill formation and the labor market: André Portela Souza; and (ix) Protection against labor market risks: employment protection, unemployment benefits, and active labor market policies: Pierre Cahuc, Werner Eichhorst, and Kathleen Thelen.

[1] Affiliations: WE: IZA Institute of Labor Economics (IZA), Germany; APS: São Paulo School of Economics, Fundação Getulio Vargas, Brazil.

[2] Affiliations: PC: CREST-ENSAE, Malakoff, and Ecole Polytechnique, France; DD: Sciences Po CSO, France; CF: University of Manchester, UK; NAG: University of São Paulo, Brazil; HF: Regent's University London, UK; AK: University of North Carolina, Chapel Hill, USA; AM: London School of Economics, UK; FM: The Economic and Social Research Institute (ESRI), Ireland; HR: University of Paris I Panthéon-Sorbonne, Paris School of Economics, France; PS: Rutgers University, USA; JS: University of Duesseldorf, Germany; KT: Massachusetts Institute of Technology (MIT), USA; MAV: University of Paris I Panthéon-Sorbonne, France; JV: University of Amsterdam, The Netherlands.

Summary

This chapter assesses the global evidence on major factors influencing the future of work. It has become evident that there is a large variation in national developments, yet, there are shared issues of general relevance that make it possible to tell a global story.

First, technology and globalization are intimately related forces driving permanent structural change in employment and affecting the global distribution of economic activities and jobs. While there has been permanent technological change, its implications differ with respect to levels of development and speed of adjustment around the globe. Global integration has become stronger, not least facilitated by modern IT and other technological innovation, leading to declining costs of international transactions, but also by political decisions to remove barriers. This points at the importance of political decisions in shaping the impact globalization can have on the further development of employment patterns. Looking at most recent changes, workers in different parts of the world have been affected quite asymmetrically by technology and globalization. Winners and losers of change can be identified, with a certain tendency toward employment polarization in many developed countries, creating societal and political challenges in compensating for losses while not foregoing the potential wins – and by preparing societies to reap the benefits of technological advancements and global integration through forward-looking, preventive strategies.

Second, demographic change is a major driving force in the world of work around the globe. Diversity in the labor market, induced by demographic factors, is on the increase, with rising employment of women, older workers and migration, although significant gaps regarding the labor market integration of women, older workers as well as migrants, continue to exist in some regions of the world. Empirical studies into the effects of diversity create a nuanced picture, pointing at the many dimensions of diversity and its consequences. But diversity is also often linked to discrimination. In fact, there is empirical evidence on discrimination in the labor market based on ethnicity, gender, age, disability, sexual, or religious orientation – this is not only creating barriers for individual careers but also implying a loss of productive potentials in the economy. Anti-discrimination rules and systematic awareness raising, monitoring and enforcement are therefore justified as are positive strategies to change actual practices in the labor market.

When looking at different types of employment types we can identify a large variety of contracts, deviating more or less from a permanent, full-time dependent employment status in the formal sector, which is often taken as a benchmark to assess the quality of a job. Part-time work, fixed-term contracts, temporary agency work, but also different forms of self-employment or own-account and crowd work as well as informal employment differ regarding core parameters such as employment stability, earnings, and inclusion into social protection from standard employment. Institutional changes, but also changes in the structure of demand and supply for certain skills have opened up this broad diversity of contractual relationships in the world of work around the globe, not least the creation of highly flexible demand patterns and complex value chains in today's economies. Virtually all labor markets exhibit some forms of segmentation, with barriers to mobility between the segments. From a policy perspective, narrowing the regulatory gaps as well as inequality regarding inclusion into social protection between different contract types is a pressing issue, with concrete challenges depending on the national context. Moving to the margins of the labor market, different forms of under-, non- or unemployment continue to exist, pointing at a full or partial exclusion of some groups from paid work. Patterns of exclusion and boundaries of the labor market are structured by institutional rules defining certain status forms, and in particular only the existence of a welfare state and social policies make unemployment a useful category and indicator in some regions of the world.

While there is a fragmentation of labor markets characterized by different forms of "external" flexibility, firms have also become more flexible "internally," i.e. as regards their internal processes of working, but in particular regarding working time and mobile working. In general, patterns of working time and workplace flexibility can be in the interest of employers, of workers or both. Over time we have seen many new and diverse arrangements emerging, potentially reconciling productivity and flexibility interests of employers and work/life preferences of workers. There has been an improvement in many cases. Still, there are many issues that can be perceived as problematic from a social progress point of view, in particular very short, very long, and unpredictable working time requirements or ill-designed shift work arrangements which have negative effects on workers' health and families. This is also observed in poorly regulated informal employment or in segments of formal labor markets where working time standards have eroded due to a lack of collective bargaining and appropriate legislation and enforcement.

Work is intimately related to individual health and well-being. While unemployment is definitively harmful in terms of well-being and health, being employed can help raise individual well-being and health. However, there are also some health risks attached to work. Precarious forms of work can have negative effects on mental health. Industrial work was particularly at risk of physically hazardous working conditions as regards occupational injuries or work-related diseases caused by chemical substances, but as a matter of fact, in many low- and medium-income countries these risks are still very much a present phenomenon. However, in many developed countries recent changes in the modern world of work have created new mental and psychological demands on individuals, creating stressful psychosocial work environments and working-time related stress. Evidence indicates that jobs defined by high demands and low control, and by high effort in combination with low reward, increase the risk of stress-related disorders, such as cardiovascular disease or depression. While this evidence has clear implications for work practices so that employers have to meet their responsibilities, there is a role for public policies as regards the prevention of health risks at the workplace.

Collective bargaining is an important institutional mechanism to establish negotiated standards regarding pay, working time, and other working conditions. It also has a role in settling distributional conflicts. Compared to legislation, collective agreements can be more flexible as they take into account sectoral or firm-specific issues. Empirical research can show that multi-employer collective bargaining can lead to lower earnings inequality and that coordinated or centralized bargaining is beneficial to a positive economic development. Yet, bargaining systems are quite diverse around the globe, with huge differences in bargaining coverage, union density, and employer organization, as well as a tendency to decline in collective bargaining coverage and increased decentralization; similar differences can also be observed inside individual countries. While collective bargaining is a voluntary system, public policies such as extension clauses and minimum wages can also contribute to shape wage structures in systems with low organizational density.

Human capital is a core element of individual life chances and employment potentials. It is also crucial for economic productivity and societal wealth. Empirical research points at the fact that skill formation has a peculiar pattern over the life course with educational investments at different stages building upon each other. Education in early childhood has the strongest returns and a clear potential of reducing ability gaps across children from different backgrounds. Schooling enrolment is far from complete, in particular in medium and low income countries, but is essential in securing individual chances of independent living outside of poverty. Comparative research also gives hints at the specific contribution of vocational education and training for a smooth transition from school to work, in particular if combined with structured learning in firms. Higher education is important for societal progress and innovation. As with schooling also higher education tends to operate under credit constraints so that support through public subsidies is an important measure to mitigate inequality in access to higher education. Finally, continuous training on the job is needed to update skills in a changing economic environment.

Policies regarding employment protection, unemployment protection, and reemployment have direct influence on stability and mobility on the labor market. In many countries, institutional rules governing permanent contracts in the formal sector stabilize open-ended employment relationships, but may hamper entry into the core labor market for some groups in the labor force as they tend to reinforce a segmentation of employment. Furthermore, in many countries both formal and effective coverage by unemployment benefits is very limited, leading to a double disadvantage of those in more temporary or informal employment as their access to unemployment protection is also limited. Hence, employment and unemployment protection often privilege certain groups over others, creating gaps in protection for the most vulnerable people. Active labor market policies can help promote the reentry into employment after phases of unemployment, and in fact, there are many options of effective reemployment measures – however, taking a global perspective, the delivery of such policies is quite unequal given institutional, administrative, and fiscal constraints. All in all, relaxing employment protection while strengthening unemployment benefit systems and active labor market policies can help support individuals in a dynamic economic environment where transitions between jobs need to be secured. This, of course, requires fundamental institutional change and capacity building in many countries.

Based on our assessment of the global evidence on core employment issues, we derived some main principles to guide policy-making:

1. Opportunity for economic growth should be provided in accordance with ecological sustainability.
2. Full and fair employment in the formal sector should be made a central aim.
3. Good jobs should be defined by as jobs with the following essential features: jobs that are free of any form of precariousness; that enable the workers to exert come control on their time and tasks; that provide fair employment relation and job security; that offer opportunities to stimulate individual development; that prevent any form of discrimination; and reconcile work and extra-work demands well.

4. Inclusive institutions including collective bargaining are needed to provide equitable opportunities for all.

5. We recognize that technological change and globalization generate new jobs while undercutting existing employment is essential. If programs addressing job displacement are implemented, efforts to facilitate reskilling are preferable to cash compensation, though either must come with access to public and health services. Using public funds to shape technologies that generate more employment than they destroy should be a priority for regions, nation-states, and transnational institutions.

6. Globalization cannot be framed as a race to the bottom, but rather as a process founded on minimum standards for employment everywhere. Of course, policies toward strengthening full and fair employment for all may vary according to the level of economic and social development in different regions of the world as well as according to institutional arrangements at national level.

Against this backdrop, we see a core set of policies that are essential:

- Rules regarding employment protection should allow for flexibility while avoiding a deeper segmentation of the labor market.

- Social protections should cover all types of work, yielding no particular hidden advantage of choosing one or another type of work.

- Skill formation at different stages of the life course is essential, in particular ensuring the acquisition of skills that can be used in the labor market as well as access to education also for vulnerable groups.

- Inclusive labor markets need effective policies to make the most out of diversity and ensure nondiscrimination. Anti-discrimination legislation is important but it is not enough to combat discrimination as it is not "self-enforcing." A combination of proactive policies to promote equal opportunities in employment, and sanctions for noncompliance or discriminatory behavior is essential.

- Legislative and collectively agreed standards regarding working conditions are fundamental to ensure a fair distribution of economic gains as well as to guarantee working conditions that are compatible with health and extra-work demands.

- Capacities to bargain collectively are seen as a major complement to legislation. Vital social partnership in old and new sectors and forms is therefore important. Institutions to protect workers from insecurity and uncertainty, as well as to facilitate the creation of good jobs, must be created by political forces.

7.1   Introduction

Work and employment are core activities for individuals and society. Participation in the labor market determines a wide range of life chances that are mediated through earned income. Employment also confers differential social status through the occupational hierarchical arrangements of society. Moreover, paid work contributes to the realization of important human needs of performance, agency, skill development, and personal control, of reward, recognition, and related self-esteem, and of participating in wider social networks providing support and a sense of belonging. Under favorable conditions these experiences contribute to working people's health and well-being, strengthening their sense of social identity and their motivation toward striving for purpose in life. Yet, exclusion from paid work and poor quality employment are powerful threats to human health and well-being. These opportunities and threats are unequally distributed across the globe, between and within societies, leaving poor people, those with less education, skills and capabilities in more disadvantaged conditions.

The world of work is constantly changing. Demographic shifts, technological innovations, institutional reforms, and global economic integration affect the way people work. Both the demand and the supply of labor are fundamentally different from earlier times. Over the last decades, the global labor force has increased, and it has become more diverse in terms of age, gender, and ethnicity. Technological innovations have a major impact on occupations and industries, changing the ways economies in different world regions, in both developed and developing countries, work along with new division of labor that are facilitated by global economic integration.

Taking a global perspective we can also see growing diversity in terms of job types ranging along the whole continuum from permanent formal employment to different forms of nonstandard work, in particular part-time work, fixed-term contracts, and temporary agency work, to on-call work, different forms of self-employment, and the large segment of informality. Increasing flexibility and diversity can (also) be observed with respect to working time and mobile working patterns. While today's labor markets can probably create more jobs than in earlier decades, the issues of hazardous working conditions, unemployment, inactivity, long-term unemployment, worklessness, exclusion, and discrimination are far from being solved.

Against this backdrop, policy choices at the global, national, regional, or sectoral level are essential, taking into account the different context conditions. Core policy areas such as education and training at different stages in life, collective bargaining and wage setting, and also the role of labor market regulation, social protection, and active labor market policies need to be addressed, trying to strike a new balance between flexibility and security in order to stimulate the creation of more good jobs for all.

In our understanding and with respect to the sphere of employment, social progress means a fair chance of inclusion and productive activity as well as good or better jobs for all, taking into account the potentials and restrictions of global employment dynamics and national paths of institutional adaptation and economic development.

In many respects, this chapter refers to global initiatives such as the employment aspects in Goal 8 of the UN's 2030 Sustainable Development Goals (SDG) and the related ILO Decent Work agenda, pointing at the goal of decent work for all, aiming at full and productive employment for all women and men, ensuring equal pay for work of equal value and an improved labor market access for young people and the disabled, furthermore creating safe and secure work environments, social protection as well as ensuring proper labor rights and social dialogue, issues that are also addressed by this chapter.

Based on a comprehensive assessment of the existing evidence, our chapter suggests some policy principle and concrete policy options that might further those objectives, not ignoring some tensions that might exist between flexibility and security in the different labor markets. The ultimate direction of reforms in line with an idea of social progress lies in institutional arrangements that facilitate the reconciliation of flexibility and productivity with access to decent jobs and social protection. We argue that distinct productive policy options are available that can be implemented more globally in order to achieve these goals simultaneously. Furthermore, we can also see from a comparative perspective that institutions, i.e. public policy decisions, make a difference with respect to the functioning of labor markets and the quality of jobs that can be created.

7.2   New Technology and Globalization

7.2.1   Introduction

Main drivers influencing the future of work are technology, globalization, and demography. While demographic issues are addressed further below, this section concerns the impact of new technology and globalization on labor markets and what, if anything, can be done to ensure that the potential benefits are widely and equitably shared.

New technology allows people to accomplish some task in a new way or to do something that was previously impossible. Globalization, broadly defined, means that interactions between people become easier. Both types of developments offer opportunities for progress. Across the broad sweep of history, new technology and increasing interactions between ever larger numbers of people have been important drivers of what is commonly thought of as progress.

New technology and globalization offer potential progress but cannot guarantee its emergence. After all, technical advances can yield new, more powerful weapons to destroy others more effectively. Moreover, new technology can benefit some groups at the expense of others. More intensive interactions produced by globalization can be used by some to harm others, even as they offer opportunities for people to help one other. Channeling new technology and globalization into policies for progress is important.

As technology and globalization are the products of human action, they do not have the inevitability that is sometimes claimed for them. Innovation does not fall from the sky, but results from conscious attempts to push back the frontier of human knowledge. People in industry, universities, and government prioritize research areas, although progress cannot be guaranteed. The role of human action in globalization is even clearer. Globalization partly derives from new technology that reduces communication costs, but it also results from lower barriers to interaction whether reductions in tariffs through trade agreements or China's political decision to become integrated into the world economy. Different historical periods have been associated with falling or rising barriers to interaction – despite a recent trend toward more interaction, there is now a backlash in many parts of the world. So both new technology and globalization represent choices that affect the scope and nature of social progress.

Some analysts claim that new technology and globalization constrain the policies that firms and nations can pursue and thus potentially limit social progress. For example, some believe increased competition leaves no choice but to cut social welfare provisions and taxes. It is important to engage these arguments.

In this section we aim to address the following questions:
- How is technical progress and globalization affecting labor markets throughout the world. In what regards are they fostering or hindering progress?
- How can the forces driving innovation and globalization be influenced so that the possibilities for progress that they offer are turned into realities?
- How do innovation and globalization affect the policies that can be used to pursue social progress?

7.2.2   The Impact of New Technology on Labor Markets

New technology always reduces demand for some types of labor and increases demand for other types. Most current discussion is about the impact of ICT, but machines have been displacing human labor for a very long time. There have typically been winners and losers from this process.

Those disadvantaged have typically been workers with specific skills where those jobs can now be more cheaply done by machines. They are often very visible as their skills may be made worthless and the affected workers may be reduced to destitution. Hence, there have been periodic predictions and serious concerns that new technology leads not just to adverse impacts for some groups of workers but to a large-scale decline in the demand for labor, e.g. the "automation anxiety" of the 1960s and the renewed "automation anxiety" of today.

Who seem to be those advantaged and harmed by contemporary new technology? Changes in the structure of employment point to job polarization, rapid growth in the employment share of high-wage occupations (e.g. managers and professionals), more modest but still positive growth in the share of low-wage positions (e.g. shop workers and care assistants) and declines in the share of jobs in the middle of the distribution (e.g. clerical and manufacturing jobs). The most compelling explanation for these trends is the routinization hypothesis (Autor, Levy, and Murnane, 2003): machines and algorithms come to replace people on tasks for which a program of manageable length can be written to perform the work well. Skilled craftsmanship in

manufacturing often involves precise but repetitive work, which it is entirely possible to design a machine to do. Similarly, being a bank clerk used to require the ability to do arithmetic fast and accurately (these were not low-skilled jobs) but computers can do this faster and without error. The demand for both types of jobs has been falling. But it is not – as yet – easy to design a computer that will manage people, telling them what to do and motivating them. So in management people still have a comparative advantage over machines. And, a job like cleaning (that we think of as being unskilled because doing it requires no special aptitude) is currently quite beyond the capability of computers. Humans do tasks like cleaning without any seeming effort but the amount of information processing involved is actually huge.

What about the impact of new technology on the overall demand for labor? Past concerns about the "end of work" have been proved wrong – the average worker has gained from new technology, not suffered from it – real wages have risen and unemployment rates show no clear long-term trend. Why have so many commentators got things so wrong? One explanation is that the workers who benefit from new technology are often diffuse and invisible. New technology results in prices for affected goods falling; thus consumers can buy what they did before and have money left over to spend on other things. As they buy more haircuts, for example, the employment of hairdressers will rise and, absurd though it sounds, such newly employed hairdressers owe their jobs to new technology in some distant part of the economy. Many past and present accounts of technology's impact completely overlook these indirect effects, but they have been the most important.

However, there is no guarantee that the current impact of new technology will echo past patterns; and there are a wide variety of views without the evidence being clear-cut. There are those who argue that we are living through a "second machine age" based on developments in ICT (Brynjolfsson and McAfee 2014), yielding very rapid technical progress leading to a fall in the demand for labor; while others argue that progress has slowed to a crawl (Gordon 2016).

All this discussion has been about the impact of new technology at the frontier. But it is important to recognize that in many countries, technological change centers on the new application of "old" technology (Edgerton 2006), now being adopted because the diffusion of knowledge is far from perfect or because economic incentives have changed. And those changing incentives are often because of globalization.

7.2.3   The Impact of Globalization on Labor Markets

The most dramatic factors behind globalization in recent decades have been China's shift from inward- to outward-looking practices, partly mirrored by India and other developing countries, aided by reductions in man-made trade barriers. Developing countries' main advantage over developed countries is access to cheaper labor, so they tend to specialize in labor-intensive production. The export-oriented, often autocratic, path of industrial development followed by Japan in the 1950s, South Korea from the 1960s, and, more recently China, requires them to upskill as the economy grows and incomes rise. Sectors like

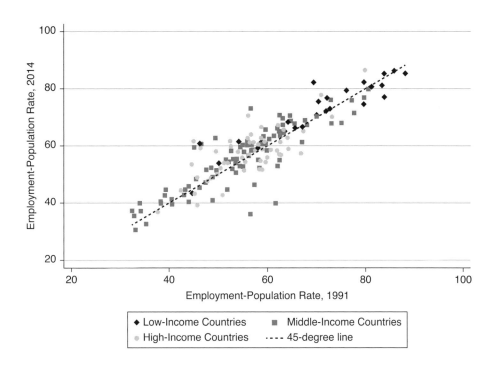

Figure 7.1 | Employment-population rates in 2014 and 1991.
Source: World Bank

apparel are forever moving shop as comparative labor costs alter. So, globalization, like technology, involves constant change.

Such constant change also leads to winners and losers. In the developed world, evidence has accumulated that industrial sectors where competition with China has been fiercest have seen the largest reductions in employment (Autor, Dorn, and Hanson, 2016). Indeed, most advanced economies have their version of America's Rust Belt. Those damaged are often very visible and increasingly vocal, arguing that the changes result from unfair competition with China. But, consumers' selection of Chinese manufactured goods is largely because they are cheaper. And those who benefit from these lower prices have more money to spend on other goods and services, thus stimulating employment elsewhere. The workers who produce such goods and services are the gainers from globalization, though they are often hard to identify.

In the developing world, globalization is often a mixed blessing. Globalization has surely created millions of jobs in the Global South, though innovation and technological change have mostly been involved indirectly. Advances in jet propulsion, aircraft design, and international communications underlie the expansion of tourism globally, but the vast majority of jobs created at Southern destinations are low- or no-tech positions – cleaning and personal services in lodgings, local food supply/preparation, or visitors transport. Rapid, reliable air links are the foundation for reverse flows as well, with millions of (chiefly) women relocating long distances for low-paid service jobs (especially from Southeast Asia to the Middle East) which fund family-supporting remittances through electronic fund transfers (Odama 2004; Bahramitash 2005). In addition, sex tourism has swelled the number of sex workers across the Global South from Costa Rica

to Kenya to Cambodia (Hoefinger 2014). Another innovation, containerization, when paired with the economic advantages of export processing zones, generates large-scale employment in assembly, packing, and shipping, drawing workforces from rural districts whose traditional farm and craft livelihoods are crumbling (George et al. 2012). Heth and Mobarak (2015) argue that clothing factories in Bangladesh have increased women's education, delayed marriage, and reduced fertility, all positive outcomes. But, at the same time, deadly factory collapses and the continued exploitation of children cannot be ignored. Such outcomes illustrate a combination of opportunity and hazard, the unevenness of which some have termed "the asymmetries of globalization" (Yotopoulos and Romano 2007).

7.2.4 An Overview of the Impact of New Technology and Globalization on Labor Markets

Little clear evidence of the "end of work" surfaces in official statistics as yet. Figure 7.1 plots the employment-population rate for those aged 15–74 in 2014 against that in 1991, using World Bank Data. These figures may not capture all forms of employment, and are also influenced by changing demographic patterns, educational enrolments for younger workers and retirement for older workers. Very large variation in employment-population ratios exists across countries, but there is no clear trend over time. This is the case for all stages of economic development.

But what about the quality of jobs on offer? One way to consider this is to look at the occupational structure of employment. Table 7.1 presents estimates of the decadal changes in the shares of employment in

Table 7.1 | Estimated decadal changes in employment shares of major occupation groups, 1998–2014

	ISCO major groups	All countries	Low-income countries	Middle-income countries	High-income countries
1	Managers	0.3	−1.9	0.1	0.5
2	Professionals	2.6	−0.1	3.2	2.1
3	Technicians and associate professionals	1.2	5.3	−2.0	2.1
4	Clerical support workers	−1.3	−8.7	0.5	−1.8
5	Services and sales workers	1.9	6.7	4.1	1.3
6	Skilled agricultural, forestry and fishery workers	−0.6	−0.6	−1.7	−0.2
7	Craft and related trades workers	−3.3	−5.5	−3.7	−3.2
8	Plant and machine operators and assemblers	−0.8	−2.1	0.0	−1.0
9	Elementary occupations	0.1	7.0	−0.4	0.2

Note: these are estimated changes in percentage points from an unbalanced panel for 1998–2014 in which the weights are designed to add to total employment in the world and to correct for the probability of data on the occupational structure being observed.
Source: World Bank.

1-digit occupations, for the world as a whole and low-, middle- and high-income countries.

For the world as a whole, decline in shares of clerical workers and skilled workers in agriculture and manufacturing is evident. But professionals, associate professionals, and service/sales workers have rising shares. These trends are not exactly the same in countries at different levels of development but all have a fall in craft workers, while most have a drop in clerical workers and a rise in service/sales workers. There is some element of polarization here but the overall trend seems to be toward better jobs.

However, statistics on the stable fraction of people working and their types of work may not do justice to a growing sense of insecurity felt by many workers. Changes produced by new technology and globalization have consequences for individuals. But progress is not just measured in employment rates; incomes are also important. New technology and globalization may have large effects on the distribution of earnings. There are a number of aspects to these concerns.

First, is it plausible that new technology and globalization primarily benefit the owners of capital relative to labor – that machines are increasingly competitive with labor, and that globalization is more to the advantage of footloose capital and increased financialization than to labor, which remains less mobile? Some studies argue for a fall in labor's share in income in most countries at all stages of development (Karabarbounis and Neiman 2014). Others argue that the impact is much less dramatic once one takes one includes things like health insurance costs and pension contributions in total labor costs (Pessoa and van Reenen 2013).

Next, consider the distribution of income among workers. This has many aspects – the evolution of wage inequality within countries, both at the bottom and the top of the wage distribution, alongside the evolution of between-country inequality. The overall consensus (Bourguignon 2015; Milanovic 2016) is that the recent period has seen rising inequality within many countries, with especially large gains for the top 1 percent (Piketty 2014). Still, this may have accompanied the largest fall in inequality between countries since the Industrial Revolution, so that the impact of new technology and globalization cannot be accurately summarized as "rising (or falling) inequality."

Milanovic estimates how people at different points in the world income distribution fared, ca. 1988–2008 (see Figure 7.2). He finds a 65 percent increase in real incomes for the top 1 percent but – perhaps surprisingly – those at the world median did even better, primarily because of rapid real income growth in China and other large developing countries. In contrast those groups that have fared worst are at the 80th percentile of the world income distribution, a position that corresponds to the average citizen in the richest countries. Average workers in the richest countries have experienced stagnation or even decline in real living standards. McKinsey (2016) estimates that 65–70 percent of households in advanced economies have had flat or falling incomes, 2005–2014, vs. only 2 percent in 1993–2005. Whether this derives from globalization, new technology, or the financial crisis remains subject to debate; but these trends pose serious challenges for the richest and most politically stable countries.

7.2.5 Innovation and Globalization for Social Progress

Because innovation and globalization result from decisions, choices have to be made about creating forms and practices that are most conducive to social progress. Market-based economies will not automatically deliver efficient innovations or even the right types of innovation. As knowledge is a public good, expecting self-interested individuals to produce it will not deliver efficiency.

Large actors like states play a big role in influencing decisions, thus influence is possible. For example, although many think innovation largely flows from self-interested companies and individuals, Mazzucato (2013) shows that states have been vital in pursuing high-risk investments. Resources also can be directed toward activities deemed important for social progress – for example, Atkinson (2015) argues for more research about new, efficient ways to deliver care services, but this remains quite a challenge in states with weakly developed welfare institutions.

There are dangers that countries may retreat into "beggar thy neighbor" policies, injuring others while attempting to protect their citizens. The rise in tariffs during the 1930s only served to intensify the Great Depression, with world trade falling more than

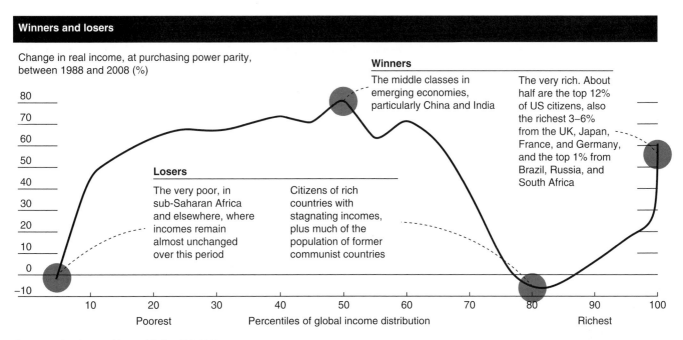

Figure 7.2 | Gainers and losers globally, 1988–2008.
Source: Milanovic (2016)

total output. Cooperation at the global level is needed to prevent a repeat. Yet many worry that new free trade deals are unduly influenced by special interest groups capable of mobilizing large-scale lobbying. In this case, extending globalization extracts rents for powerful interest groups rather than benefiting the world as a whole. As there always are likely to be both gainers and losers within countries, a need continues for policies that deliver widely shared economic growth.

7.2.6   Innovation and Globalization as Constraints on Policies for Progress

If change produces losers, then policies might well compensate those affected. Of course preventing change through preventing job loss or protectionist trade policies can be attractive. However, there is a cost – as change is slowed, there may be fewer losers but also fewer gainers. As change may not be so easy to deflect, it's better to implement policies that compensate losers.

Although some argue that new technology and globalization obstruct such compensation, this is not the case. Labor market institutions like those embodied in the Danish "flexicurity" model, which aims to make people comfortable with change by supporting them when their jobs disappear (providing relatively generous welfare benefits and helping them to find new opportunities) are a model unthreatened by innovation or globalization.

And redistribution through taxation remains viable and important. So large has been the increase in the share of income going to the top 1 percent that taxing them more heavily would only return them to earnings levels they had a few short years ago. It is simply not credible that slightly higher taxes will drastically reduce work effort

among high-earners, as has long been claimed. Wealth taxation is needed to break down asset concentrations. This will be all the more important if "robotization" means that capital's share of income rises. New technology can be an ally: it can be used to record ownership of wealth and to fight tax evasion. International cooperation is equally important.

7.3   Demographic Change as a Driving Force

Demographic change is a major driving force behind the structural changes of labor supply composition in the world. The world population is around 7.4 billion people in 2016. It is expected to reach around 9.85 billion in 2050. Table 7.2 shows the population figures for regions of the world in 2016 and 2050.

Asia and Africa are the most populated regions in the world and are the ones where the population growth is expected to be the most rapid ones. Europe is expected to have a decrease in its population size in the next three decades. Latin America, North America, and Oceania will grow but more slowly.

The world population is not only expected to grow but also to age faster. Figure 7.3 presents the older population forecast for the world and regions.

The population 60 years old and above is expected to grow from above 500 million to 2000 million individuals by 2050. The trend in aging occurs across all regions in the world but it is more rapid in less developed regions. The forces behind this trend are the decline in fertility and the increase in longevity. This trend poses strong pressures on labor markets, provisions for goods and services, particularly health care, and family structures.

Table 7.2 | Population by regions

Region	Population mid-2016 (millions)	Population mid-2050 (millions)
World	7.417	9.868
Africa	1.203	2.527
Asia	4.437	5.327
Europe	740	728
Latin America and the Caribbean	637	775
North America	360	445
Oceania	40	66

Source: www.worldpopdata.org

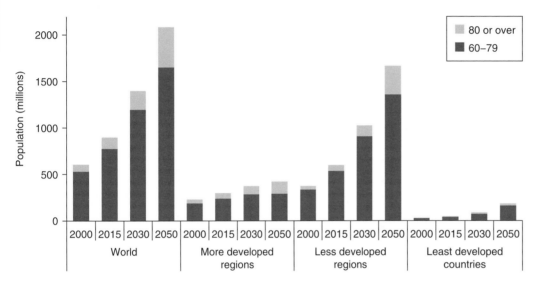

Figure 7.3 | Population aged 60–79 and 80 over time.
Source: United Nations (2015a): World Population Prospects: The 2015 Revision

This section aims to give a flavor of world variation and change over time connected to demographics in three key elements of labor market diversity: the proportion of older workers; migrants and nonmigrants; and participation rates of men and women. They are based on data from the International Labor Organization (ILO) and cover 11 world regions (see OECD 2016 for regional groupings).

7.3.1 Older Workers

There has been much recent concern about youth unemployment, particularly in Europe (Bell and Blanchflower 2011), and indeed some suggestion that early retirement of older workers might reduce youth unemployment in some European countries (Zimmermann et al. 2013).[3] In fact there is an increasing trend toward an ageing workforce. Figure 7.4 presents the proportion of the labor force aged 50 or over by continent in 1995 and 2015, and shows a rise in the proportion

of over 50 year olds in almost all regions. The increase between 1995 and 2015 is particularly marked in North America, Latin America, and Oceania (see Figure 7.4). By contrast in Africa the proportion of the labor force aged 50 and more has remained low. A number of factors underlie this general trend toward an older workforce. In some countries, particularly in Europe and the US, the population itself is ageing, so there is a lower proportion of younger workers. There has also been an increase in education participation among under 25s in many countries, reducing this age group's labor market participation. It does raise issues about the treatment of older workers in the labor market in terms of age discrimination, and health issues, which are more prevalent among older workers, also come to the fore (see also Sections 7.6.3 and 7.7).

Additionally, it raises two set of policy questions related to labor demand and supply. First, how technology will respond and evolve so that it is adaptable to an aging workforce? Second, how education and

---

[3]   In fact Zimmermann et al. (2013) in their analysis find that there is no competition between younger and older workers in the European countries they examined.

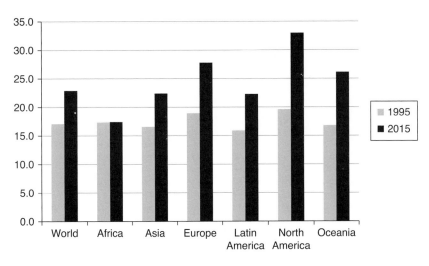

Figure 7.4 | Proportion of the labor force aged 50 or over, 1995 and 2015.
Source: Own calculations from the ILO dataset EAPEP World Regions 1990–2020. These data cover 191 countries

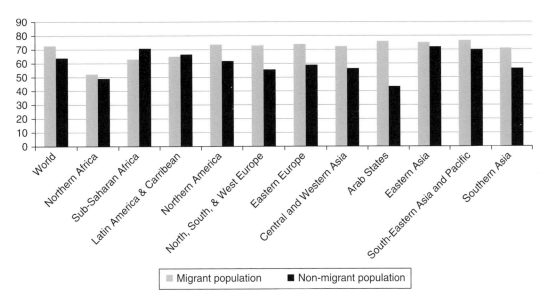

Figure 7.5 | Labor force participation rates by world region for migrant and nonmigrant populations, 2013.
Source: ILO Global Estimates on Migrant Workers, 2015d, Table 2.8

training will change and adapt over the life-cycle of an individual that may stay longer in the labor market?

7.3.2   Migrant Workers

Another important trend in the world demographics is the flows of labor force across countries. According to recent ILO estimates, there were around 232 million migrants in the world, of which 150 million were migrant workers (ILO 2015d). Estimating the number of migrants is challenging, particularly when there are large population fluctuations or difficulties carrying out large-scale surveys (ILO 2015d). According to the International Organizational for Migration the share of international migrants in the global population has become steady around

3 percent in the last three decades. However, the number of refugees has increased recently and has reached 15.1 million refugees in 2015.

Labor market prospects are one of the main reasons that people migrate. And indeed, they are the ones that are more likely to participate in the labor market. Figure 7.5 presents labor market participation rates for migrant and nonmigrant populations in world regions. In most regions of the world, migrants' labor market participation is higher than that of nonmigrants, partly because of the younger age profile of migrants but also because many migrants migrate in order to work. Of course the proportion of migrant workers in the workforce also varies across countries – from less than 3 percent in much of Africa, Latin America, and South and East Asia, to around 20 percent in Northern America, 16 percent in Northern, Southern, and Western Europe and 35 percent in the Arab states (ILO 2015d). The definition

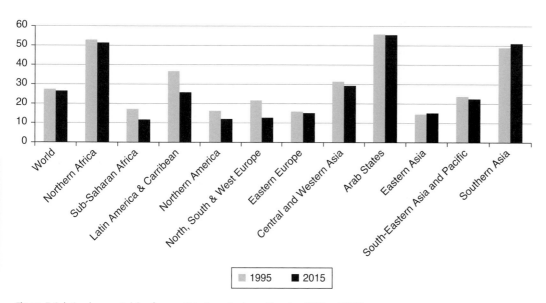

Figure 7.6 | Gender gaps in labor force participation rates by world region, 1995 and 2015.
Note: The gender gap is measured as the male participation rate minus the female participation rate. The data cover 178 countries. Source: ILO Key Labor Market Indicators, derived from Trends Econometric Models, November 2015

used here is migrants, that is those born abroad, some of whom may be from ethnic minorities, but does not capture second-generation ethnic minorities. Ethnic minorities typically show lower labor market participation in European countries (Heath and Cheung 2007).

Migration in the age of globalization is likely to increase in the coming decades. How migrants fare in the labor market and how they affect the performance of the markets and well-being of society are important issues to be understood. They are discussed in a subsection below.

7.3.3   Labor Market Participation of Men and Women

Finally, another important structural change in the labor market is the role of women. Women have increased their labor market participation but still they are lower than that of men. Figure 7.6 presents gender gaps in labor force participation rates by region, 1995 and 2015. In all regions, women's participation is lower than men's, though the gap in participation varies considerably across regions. There are very high gender gaps in Northern Africa, the Arab States, and Southern Asia. The reasons for women's lower participation are myriad, and include their role in unpaid labor and childrearing, policies around parental leave, childcare and working-time flexibility, taxation, gender differences in education in some countries, and also cultural norms and attitudes to women's employment and women's roles (Jaumotte 2003).

In North America and Northern, Southern, and Western Europe, the gender gaps have fallen somewhat in the past 20 years. In these countries women's participation rose steadily over the twentieth century, particularly in the United States (Blau et al. 2006). But in the past 20 years the gap has narrowed because men's participation has fallen in the recession more than women's participation (see Karamessini and Rubery 2014).

In general the gender gap is lowest in higher income countries, though with some notable exceptions: the Arab States, where income is higher but the gap very large, and also in Sub-Saharan Africa, where the gap is among the lowest of the world regions. ILO (2016) attributes this low gap in the Sub-Saharan Africa to the lack of social protection income and persistent poverty, leaving women with no alternative but to work. And of course the nature of employment is important: in Sub-Saharan Africa and Southern Asia, most working women are self-employed and a large proportion of them work as contributing family workers (34.9 percent in Sub-Saharan Africa and 31.8 percent in Southern Asia) (ILO 2016).

Sectoral and occupational segregation – the type of jobs men and women do – contribute considerably to gender gaps in job quality and the gender wage gap (Blau and Kahn 2007; Burchell et al. 2014). Agriculture employs most women in low to middle income countries; in high income countries women are concentrated in health and education, wholesale and retail trade sectors. To the extent that women are disproportionately concentrated in lower quality jobs, this may be additional source of inequality in the workplace.

An important reason for differences in paid work is that women do much more unpaid work, in the form of childcare, eldercare, housework, and collecting fuel and water. Globally women spend two and a half times as much as men on unpaid labor (United Nations 2015b, from time-use data); in India and Pakistan women spend ten times as much as men on unpaid work (McKinsey Global Institute 2015).

Increasing rates of paid employment by women, an ageing workforce, and migration have led to a growing debate and research interest in labor market diversity: some implications of this are discussed in Section 7.6. One issue is whether diversity in the labor market is good or bad for economic and social outcomes. Another important question relates to individual outcomes and how individuals from different groups – women, men, immigrants, natives, ethnic minorities, old, young, those with a disability, or a different sexual orientation – fare in the labor market. Do modern labor markets offer "good jobs for all" – or just for those with the "right" skin color, gender, or age? Having access to a paid job is crucial for financial security of the individual and their family.

7.4   Changes and Prospects on Employment Relations

7.4.1   Introduction

Employment relations provide the link between individuals and their employing organizations. They specify the reciprocal expectations and obligations connecting employers and employees and can be either implicit or explicit contractual arrangements that describe how work is organized, governed, evaluated, and rewarded. Employment relations differ in their scope, ranging from broadly defined relational exchanges that are often open-ended in duration and provide training and welfare supports for employees, to narrowly defined transactional ones that are more instrumental, entailing little commitment and often for work performed within a fixed time-frame (see Kalleberg and Marsden 2015).

Employment relations differ in more developed, industrialized countries from those in developing countries. Relatively rich countries are characterized by a formal economy in which employment relations are regulated in varying degrees, depending on a country's political and labor market institutions. Developing countries, by contrast, are dominated by an "informal" economy (also referred to as the "black," "gray," "underground," or "shadow" economy) in which enterprises, employment relationships, and work are partially or fully outside of government regulation and taxation and are not covered by labor laws or other social protections. While developed countries also have informal economies to some degree, in developing countries the informal economy *is* the economy.

7.4.2   From Standard to Nonstandard Employment Relationships

A useful starting point for assessing changes in employment relations is the SER, which involves relational exchanges between employers and employees. The SER was the employment norm in industrial nations for the middle of the twentieth century and was a central part of the social contract that accompanied the spread of Fordist mass production and the ascendancy of large organizations. Nevertheless, the SER was far from universal and characterized only a minority of employment relations; it was found mainly in larger organizations and was concentrated among white-collar employees (usually men) in managerial occupations and blue-collar workers in certain highly organized industries.

The SER was generally typified by the performance of work on a preset schedule at the employer's place of business and under the employer's control and direction. It often, but not always, involved full-time employment and a shared expectation of continued employment assuming satisfactory employee performance. SERs were associated with a psychological contract in which employees exchanged their commitment to employers in exchange for earnings and often the possibility of careers within firm internal labor markets having job ladders, with entry restricted to the bottom rungs and upward movements associated with the progressive development of skills and knowledge. SERs were also the normative foundation in industrial countries of a variety of labor laws and regulations such as protections against unsafe working conditions and the right to bargain collectively, as well as welfare benefits such as social insurance and pensions (Stone and Arthurs 2013). The institutions supporting the SER presumed models of employment relations and the family having a full-time, primary-breadwinner husband, and a wife who cared for children and the home.

Changing political, social, technological, and economic conditions in the last quarter of the twentieth century in all industrial countries prompted governments and employers to seek greater flexibility in their employment systems than was available through the SER (Cappelli 1999; Kalleberg 2011). Growing price competition and more fluid capital markets put pressure on firms to maximize profitability and respond to rapidly changing consumer tastes and preferences. Slow economic growth triggered high unemployment and made it difficult for economies to generate enough jobs to assure all workers of full-time wage employment. Rapidly proliferating computer-based technologies and communication and information systems made quick adaptation to changing market opportunities both possible and necessary. Corporations outsourced many of their functions, leading to the "fissuring" of organizations and the proliferation of subcontracting relationships (Weil 2014). The expansion of the service sector made it necessary for some employers to staff their organizations on a 24/7 basis. New legal regimes contributed to the growth in nonstandard work by allowing employers to avoid the mandates and costs associated with labor laws that provide protection for permanent employees. So too did demographic shifts in labor force composition involving growth in worker groups – such as married women and older people – who sometimes prefer the flexibility that nonstandard arrangements offer, though not necessarily the associated insecurity.

Together, these changes made the fixed costs and overhead obligations associated with the SER less viable for employers and led to the rise of a new normative form of employment relations often referred to as *nonstandard employment relations* (Kalleberg 2000); other labels include alternative work arrangements, market-mediated arrangements, nontraditional employment relations, flexible staffing arrangements, atypical employment, precarious employment, disposable work, and contingent work.

While nonstandard employment relations take several distinct forms, they generally differ from the SER in one or more ways (see also ILO 2016). In particular, they tend to involve more transactional exchanges and provide less employment security than the SER. Some nonstandard work arrangements, including self-employment and independent contracting, collapse the employer–employee distinction. In these situations, workers administer and direct their own

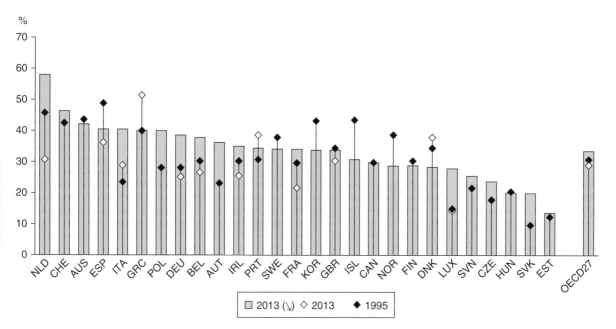

Figure 7.7 | Shares of nonstandard employment in total employment, 1985–2013.
Source: OECD, 2015a: Figure 4.6, p. 144

activities and are paid by clients for services performed or goods provided. By hiring independent contractors, employers avoid many of the regulations (such as the requirement to pay taxes and benefits of various kinds) associated with the employment and so the issue of misclassifying employees as independent contractors has become a matter of considerable dispute.

Nonstandard employment relations are not new in developed countries. Unstable jobs, temporary work, and peripheral labor force attachment, and many employment relations that do not involve full-time work or open-ended employer–employee commitments have dominated industrial societies historically (see Jacoby 1985). For instance, under the "inside contracting" system in nineteenth-century United States manufacturing, management engaged contractors, provided them with machinery and factory space, supplied raw material and capital, and sold products, while the contractors were responsible for organizing production and for hiring, paying, and directing the actual workers. Indeed, the efficiencies associated with SERs and internal labor markets in the post-World War II period are the historical anomaly, not the use of nonstandard employment relations. Nonetheless, the latest incarnation of nonstandard employment relations does have novel features that distinguish it from earlier ones: for example, contemporary nonstandard employment relations increasingly involve labor market intermediaries; and advances in technology and communication enable employees to be spatially very distant from their employers.

The ILO (2015a) reports that 75 percent of all workers in countries for which data are available (covering 84 percent of the global workforce) are employed on temporary or short-term contracts, in informal jobs, are "own account" workers who are technically self-employed but do not have any employees, or have unpaid family jobs. Since 1985, a large proportion of all employment across OECD countries

was in nonstandard employment relations (i.e. self-employed, full-time temporaries, part-time temporaries, part-time permanent) (OECD 2015a; see Figure 7.7). The percent of nonstandard work arrangements across these 27 countries in 2013 varies from a low of 13.5 percent in Estonia to 57.9 percent in the Netherlands. In over half the countries, the percent of nonstandard employment was greater in 2013 than in previous years.

The types of nonstandard arrangements are not homogenous: for example, permanent part-time workers have different employment relations and contracts from temporary workers. The characteristics of particular nonstandard arrangements also differ among countries: in the Netherlands, for example, part-time work is regulated and relatively well rewarded, as compared to the more precarious position of part-timers in the US and UK. Thus, the relative attractiveness of nonstandard work depends on how such employment relations are protected, regulated, and rewarded. In some countries, working in temporary or part-time work (or even being unemployed) may constitute an appealing alternative to regular, full-time employment.

7.4.3   Part-Time Work

The ILO (2015a) estimates that about 17 percent of the global workforce work less than 30 hours per week (the generally accepted cut-off for defining part-time work) and that in most countries, the number of part-time jobs has grown faster than full-time jobs since the recent economic crisis. Women are far more likely to work part-time globally than men (24 percent vs. 12.4 percent; ILO 2015a). Part-time work has expanded, reaching 16.7 percent of total employment in 2014 within OECD countries, and 38.5 percent in the Netherlands or 26.9 percent in Switzerland.

The quality and nature of part-time work varies considerably among countries (see Fagan et al. 2014). Indeed, there is some debate as to whether all part-time work should be considered nonstandard work at all, because in some countries many less-than-full-time jobs incorporate all other features of the SER (such as part-time work in the Netherlands, for example). In addition, some part-time arrangements represent employer accommodations to employee preferences for reduced hours and more flexible schedules. Many other part-time jobs, however, are highly insecure, lacking enhancements such as benefits, training opportunities, and the expectation of continuity. Part-timers are more likely than full-timers to hold two or more jobs in order to make a living. Countries differ considerably in their regulation of part-time work, though the ILO (2015a) reports increases in protections regarding equal treatment and equal dismissal rights in both OECD and emerging countries (but not in developing countries) since the early 1990s.

Workers' preferences and needs must also be taken into account when considering the desirability of part-time work. Some women work part-time because their time is constrained by childcare or eldercare responsibilities; other men and women work part-time while they are students, approaching retirement or because of chronic ill-health. Much of the part-time work in developing and transition countries is involuntary part-time, in which workers would prefer full-time work in order to obtain an adequate income. The proportion of involuntary part-time workers is less in developed countries, though these percentages have increased since the recent economic crisis due to the relative scarcity of full-time jobs (Fagan et al. 2014). Involuntary part-time employment accounted for 4.1 percent of total employment within OECD in 2014, and 21 percent of total part-time employment.

7.4.4   Temporary Agency Work and Fixed-Term Contracts

Temporary work includes both persons hired on a fixed-term temporary basis and workers procured via labor intermediary organizations such as contract companies and temporary help agencies. Fixed-term contracts have become particularly important in countries where employment protections make it difficult for employers to terminate open-ended contracts, such as France, Germany, Italy, and Spain.

Temporary agency work (TAW), in particular, illustrates a major shift in employment relations, which is here mediated via a third party rather than being a bilateral relation. TAW is characterized by a distinct triangular employment structure where workers are typically employed and dispatched by private employment agencies while working at the facilities, and under the authority, of user firms on limited-term contracts, normally ranging from one day to a few months. The shift from a bilateral to trilateral arrangement has fundamentally changed the nature of the employment relationship: the worker's de jure employer is an intermediary organization rather than the de facto employer that pays for and directs the use of the worker's labor.

Over the past two decades, TAW has not only registered exponential growth but also become a globalizing service industry with considerable geographic expansion and industrial diversification; leading agencies have taken up some functions of human resource management and

extended their services to a number of new areas including search and placement, recruitment process outsourcing, outplacement and online recruitment. According to the latest report produced by CIETT (2016), the global trade body of private employment services, in 2014, approximately 71.9 million people gained access to the labor market through a private employment agency and the average growth of agency work between 2013 and 2014 is 3 percent (Indian figures excluded). The growth and expansion of TAW indicates that the industry has gained considerable political acceptability among all of the social partners – governments, businesses, and labor unions – that create new regulatory conditions favorable for employment agencies and businesses. Much has been said about how public policies are geared toward a reregulation, rather than a deregulation, of employment relations in the interests of capita. The corollary is that many of the protective coverings that postwar "embedded liberalism" allowed and occasionally nurtured are stripped away; as Harvey (2005: 168) avers, "the individualized and relatively powerless worker then confronts a labor market in which only short-term contracts are offered on a customized basis."

A large body of empirical research shows that agency workers are subject to precarious work and unequal treatment (e.g. Kalleberg 2000). Except for a handful of high-status and affluent knowledge workers, a great many are excluded from – or differentially included in – the same array of pay and benefits that are available to full-time workers in some countries including job security, bonus payments, social security and protection, childcare, sick leave, and paid holiday. To a great extent, the contemporary "temp revolution" reflects a shift toward labor precarity and inequality. Although often characterized by promises of flexibility, individuality, and freedom, TAW constitutes an important element of social division, intersecting with other axes of inequality such as gender, age, region, ethnicity, and race.

It is noteworthy that the triangular employment relations involving TAW are prone to legal ambiguities, making it difficult for the law to tackle exploitation and manipulation on the part of agencies and user firms. The situation is especially grave in emerging TAW markets that generally lack broad regulatory support and effective enforcement measures. For example, in China, in addition to tens of millions of migrants from rural villages who account for the vast majority of agency workers, vocational student interns have also become constrained labor, being subject to double control of teachers and schools, who act as labor-dispatching agencies, and factory managers (Smith and Chan 2015).

Besides temporary agency work, fixed-term contracts are another form of temporary employment. By definition, the continuation of such jobs is less secure and more contingent upon firm, individual, and economic conditions.

While fixed-term contracts can create entry positions for people seeking access to paid work, allowing employers to screen such entrants, in particular after leaving school or graduating or after phases of unemployment or inactivity, in strongly regulated and segmented labor markets with strict dismissal protection for permanent jobs this often leads to longer chains of temporary jobs with low probabilities to move to a permanent job. The situation looks more favorable in more flexible labor markets. Empirical evidence further suggests that vocational training, based on temporary contracts with an employer providing training, helps overcome the barrier between fixed-term and permanent contracts, making a temporary job more of a "stepping stone" than a "dead end" (Eichhorst 2014; ILO 2016).

7.4.5   Self-Employment and the "Gig" Economy

The so-called "gig" economy – consisting of self-employed persons such as independent contractors or freelancers who often work on discrete projects that are managed by online platforms that broker work between employers and workers and often customers – has attracted much recent attention. The term originated in the United States to refer to short-term, "on demand" work arrangements between persons or between a person and an organization and has since been used to describe the situation in industrial countries more generally. The rise of the gig economy recalls the small-scale entrepreneurship of the eighteenth century. The gig economy also takes a number of forms, including transportation platforms such as Uber and Lyft that connect drivers with riders, "crowdsourcing" arrangements in which people group their efforts to achieve particular outcomes, and freelance platforms (such as Upwork.com) that match skilled workers to jobs. Technological advances in communication and information systems have made it easier for organizations to specialize their production, assemble temporary workers quickly for projects, and rely more on outside suppliers. "Gigs" are also becoming more common offline, as in short-term engagements in which persons contract with other persons or organizations for specific activities.

Estimates of the size of the "gig" economy vary widely. In the United States, for example, the estimates range from 600,000 workers (or 0.4 percent of total US employment) who work with an online intermediary to one-third of the workforce (Harris and Krueger 2015). Statistics on the size of the gig economy in other industrial countries are equally scarce. Part of the reason for the lack of information on this group is the difficulty in distinguishing independent contractors, for example, from employees. Employers receive financial advantages from hiring independent contractors (such as not needing to pay them benefits or assume liability for their actions) and so are often motivated to avoid counting them as employees, thus creating a form of "hidden employment" (e.g. De Stefano 2016) that circumvents labor laws and other obligations. In the United States, there is a lively and still unsettled legal battle over whether Uber drivers should be considered employees of the company – since Uber exerts considerable control over their actions and remuneration – or as independent contractors. In the United Kingdom, courts recently ruled that Uber drivers are workers and thus covered by some aspects of labor law.

Work in the gig economy is heterogeneous, with considerable differences in the quality of jobs. Certain high-skilled workers can garner higher economic rewards as independent contractors or consultants than they might as employees in SERs, for example. In these instances, nonstandard arrangements allow workers to capitalize on abundant market opportunities and demands for their skills,

despite the insecurity and instability associated with any particular "gig." Workers with fewer marketable skills, on the other hand, do not benefit as much from the flexibility afforded by the gig economy.

7.4.6   The Informal Economy

The informal sector is an enterprise-based concept that refers to organizations that are not regulated, don't register their employees, and have informal bookkeeping practices. By contrast, informal employment denotes jobs that do not provide basic social or legal protections, employment benefits or any compensation for job loss. Informal jobs may be found in both informal enterprises and in informal arrangements in the formal sector (e.g. undocumented workers working in restaurants) (see ILO 2012) and encompasses those who "by law or in practice, are not covered by national legislation, taxation or social protection" (ILO 2013a: 4). Hence, the forms of nonstandard work discussed above (such as part-time work or temporary jobs) may be regarded as informal in countries where such nonstandard work arrangements are not regulated or receive social protections. Informal workers comprise both wage employment and "own account" workers. Informal economy work represents an extreme form of precarious work, as it is unregulated and more uncertain and insecure.

The notion of an informal economy emerged in the 1970s as a way of describing unregulated and unprotected work activities in the developing world. It received little scholarly attention for many years, as it was widely believed that processes of modernization would replace informal work activities with formal ones. However, recent trends toward the casualization of work and nonstandard work arrangements have expanded the informal economy: formal industrial and service sector jobs have been accompanied by unstable and insecure employment practices as production moves from large, registered enterprises in the formal sector into smaller units in the informal sector via subcontracting, including relocation to regions where labor or other production costs are cheaper.

The majority of employment is informal in most developing countries, and so is a sizeable proportion of employment in many developed countries. Sixty percent of the global workforce is in the informal sector (Williams 2014). An ILO (2012) study of 47 countries found that six countries (India, Brazil, Mexico, Vietnam, Pakistan, and the Philippines) accounted for three-quarters of informal employment in 2011. Informal employment made up at least two-thirds of nonagricultural employment in fifteen other countries. The lowest percentages were found in central and eastern European countries. Figure 7.8 shows the share of persons employed in the informal economy for selected countries.

The rise of nonstandard work arrangements has produced greater informality in developed countries as the pressures toward flexibility described above have led to removal of social and legal protections in the formal sector. Williams (2014) classifies the 27 member states of the European Union by the degree of informality of their workforces and finds that countries on the eastern and southern side of the EU-27 have more informal, wage-based employment, while those on

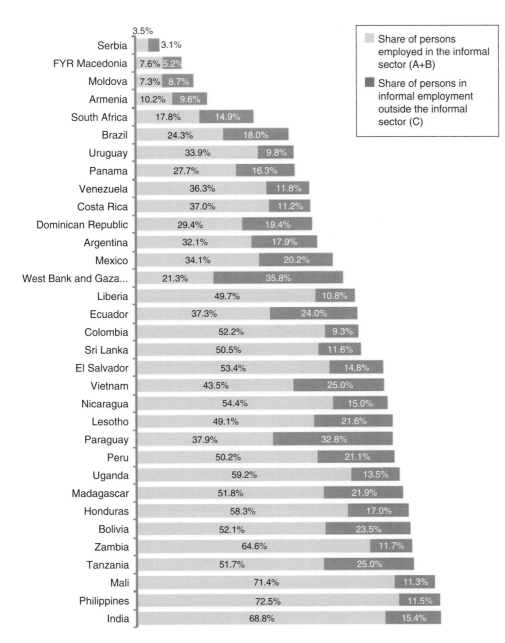

Figure 7.8 | Informal employment.

Note: The data refer to nonagricultural employment and the latest year available for each country.

Source: ILO, Statistical Update on Employment in the Informal Economy, June 2012

the western and Nordic side are less likely to be have informal wage employment and more apt to include own-account informal sectors. He suggests that these patterns of informality are related to western and Nordic countries being wealthier, more equal, and exhibiting greater labor market intervention, social protection, and social transfers.

An extreme form of informal economy is *child labor*, which refers to work done by young people, especially hazardous work (such as those in many manufacturing, mining and construction as well as agricultural jobs). The ILO (2015b) estimates that in 2012, there were 47.5 million adolescents aged 15–17 years working in hazardous jobs, accounting for 40 percent of all those employed in this age group and over a quarter

of all those in child labor. The proportion of child laborers is greatest in Africa, followed by Asia and Latin America. Child labor is outside the regulations of the formal economy for those countries that have laws defining legal working ages and protecting young workers who meet these criteria. This is especially a problem in newly developing countries, as the growing opportunities provided for working in manufacturing industries encourage the use of young workers. Girls are particularly vulnerable to child labor given prevailing social norms about marriage and children and are likely to be exposed to the vilest forms of child labor such as sexual trafficking and exploitation and working as domestics in homes. While still pervasive, the ILO reports that there has been a decline in the number of child laborers in recent years.

7.4.7   Unemployment

Unemployment, according to the ILO's standard definition that is used worldwide in national labor force surveys, refers to the situation whereby people do not have paid jobs but are actively searching for work and are able to start immediately if offered a suitable job. The number of unemployed worldwide by this definition in 2014 is estimated at 201,300,000 people, a rate of 5.9 percent (ILO 2015c). Unemployment levels are highly diverse across the world. It is highest in Europe (10.2 percent in 2014), North Africa (12.5 percent) and the Middle East (11 percent), and lowest in Asia (3.9 percent to 4.6 percent depending on subregions) and to a lesser extent the emerging economies within the G20 (5 percent).

This impressive range of variation raises questions about the validity of the ILO concept of unemployment and its measurement for most countries (Bescond et al. 2003). For example, in socialist and centrally planned economies the unemployment was certainly underestimated in the 1980s (less than 1 percent or even 0.5 percent). This full employment situation was just an appearance since unemployment was hidden within companies, where a relevant fraction of the labor force remained almost unoccupied, while the productivity was very low (Linotte 1994). Moreover, the ILO definition has never captured precisely labor market dynamics in less developed countries where a large part of employment has remained informal and unofficial. Here, the low official unemployment rates mainly result from the weight of informal work (OECD 2015b: 256), which underestimates unemployment because individuals are forced to accept poor quality activities in order to survive: in India, for example, the unemployment rate is much lower than in the OECD (3.6 percent in 2014) but more than one-third of the active population receives extremely low wages (OECD 2015b: 249). In those cases, it would be more accurate to register people as unemployed who are unable to obtain any paid work or who have a job that pays less than a living wage. Even for developed countries, the ILO concept now appears more insufficient now than it was when the current definition was adopted in 1982, before the diversification of nonstandard forms of employment.

The boundaries among unemployment, paid work, and inactivity are increasingly blurred, since employment deprivation can take a variety of forms, that of: officially recognized unemployment, sometimes with benefits; an aspiration to work more; a combination of job search and more or less informal activities; nonemployment characterized by discouragement and giving up the job search; a more or less pronounced withdrawal toward professional inactivity; a resourcefulness marked by the flow of heterogeneous activities; and an exclusion from the sphere of production and economic exchanges. Two typical and polar configurations describe the diversity of employment relations and labor market regimes:

• First, the social configurations characterized by a strong codification of the statuses concerning paid work and nonwork: work is a formal wage employment, unemployment is a job deprivation compensated and framed by public policies, inactivity is a set of situations potentially supported by social protection. In this case, despite the heterogeneity of welfare regimes, societies at least

aim to protect the unemployed against social marginalization and poverty (Ganssmann 2000).

• Second, the social configuration characterized by a weak regulation of statuses encompassing all situations, in and out the labor market: work is informal and unofficial, unemployment means a lack of paid work and is weakly differentiated, and inactivity means the absence of social protection in some countries. In such contexts the individuals have the responsibility to mobilize their available social resources to deal with the lack of work and to avoid the more exacerbated forms of exclusion (Demazière et al. 2013).

Unemployment is generally associated with a high risk of poverty and social exclusion (because of lack or exhaustion of unemployment benefits). According to Eurostat, the risk of poverty in the EU was 16.6 percent for adults (15 or older) in 2013 and 46.6 percent for those in unemployment. In addition, almost a quarter of these are exposed to risks of poverty and social exclusion (ILO 2015c: 36). Long-term unemployment (a period of 12 months or more) is especially problematic in Europe. It has increased in recent years: in 2014, this represented 50 percent of unemployment in the European Union against 38.5 percent five years earlier (ILO 2015). Within the OECD this level reaches 35.2 percent. Long-term unemployment often leads to exclusion and marginalization (Gallie 2004). Indeed, when the duration of unemployment lengthens, job search weakens, becomes more faltering and more erratic. This discouragement process may result in a complete renunciation of job search.

The risks of unemployment, long-term unemployment, economic precariousness, and social exclusion are very unevenly distributed among the population. Despite variations between countries, these groups tend to be women, immigrants and their descendants, and individuals with the lowest levels of skills and education. Younger workers, but also older workers to a somewhat lesser extent, tend to be in a worse position than the prime-age group. This shows that both ends of working life are particularly vulnerable to unemployment in all its forms. While women's unemployment rates (and long-term unemployment shares) are now at equivalent levels with men's, gender hierarchy continues to persist within the labor market. Women occupy significantly more precarious positions: involuntary part-time (6.1 percent of active women against 2.5 percent of active men in 2014 in OECD), lower wages, and slower professional careers (Maruani 2013).

7.5   More Flexible Workplaces and Working Time?

Since the late 1970s working-time has been restructured, particularly in developed economies, where more diverse working-time arrangements have emerged (Messenger 2004). This restructuring was driven largely by employers' operational requirements for more flexible work practices and extended operating hours in an increasingly connected global economy. Technological developments, including the spread of the internet have been used to propagate an increased reliance on remote working, instantaneous communication, and handover across different time zones, and so forth, which have eroded previous boundaries to the working day. Some employers have reformed work schedules to accommodate workers' preferences for certain forms of flexibility, such as flexitime or some types of part-time work as part of workforce recruitment and retention strategies. This included adjusting to the working-time availability of women with young children who constituted a growing proportion of the labor force in some economies.

The outcome has been a stall in the negotiated reduction of full-time hours, an expansion of part-time employment, work schedules which are more diverse and often less predictable and some improvements in reconciliation measures in some countries. Workforce inequalities in working-time conditions persist that are associated with the segmented structure of labor markets. The gender division of household labor is one fundamental axis that produces inequalities in women and men's working-time conditions. Gender differences intersect with other characteristics that affect employment opportunities and working time conditions. In particular, workers with higher levels of human capital (education, training, experience) and social capital (networks) are the most likely to gain the better paid, more secure jobs with decent working time arrangements.

7.5.1 The Gender Division of Household Work and Employment

Women do the majority of the unpaid household work across the world, including the time involved in looking after children, elderly parents and other relatives (European Commission 2016b; OECD 2016; Miranda 2011; ILO 2016). This unpaid work constrains women's availability for employment. It is one of the reasons why the labor force participation rate for women is lower than that for men in all regions of the world, even if the gender gaps have narrowed over the last decade in some regions. By 2015 the gender gap in participation rates was most pronounced in Northern Africa, Southern Asia, and the Arab States and narrowest in Eastern Asia, Europe, North America, and Sub-Saharan Africa (Section 7.3.3).

The time demands of unpaid work are particularly onerous for women in low-income households that rely on women's labor for subsistence farming and fetching fuel and water in regions with poor physical infrastructure. This is prevalent in many parts of Africa, Asia, the Arab States, Latin America, and the Caribbean. As a consequence many women are channeled into informal, part-time or other forms of non-standard employment (Section 7.4) in order to obtain paid working hours that can be combined with the demands of their household work. While some informal sector employment involves long working hours, the incidence of short hours working is higher for informal than formal employment for women in all regions of the world except Africa; and a similar pattern applies for men (ILO 2017, forthcoming).

As a result, even if women work shorter hours in employment, once unpaid work time is added in the total working time of employed women is much longer than that of employed men. This applies even in European countries with the smallest gender inequalities in time spent on unpaid work, which typically are those where government policy has established high standards of labor rights and gender equality, exemplified by the Nordic countries (Eurofound 2013b; European Commission 2016b).

7.5.2 Working-Time Quality and the Impact on Work–Life Balance

The volume of hours worked, when they are scheduled and the workers' control over their working-time arrangements impact on the quality of life or "work–life balance," which refers to the quality of the fit between employment, unpaid family work, and personal life.

Long working hours have a pronounced negative impact on men and women's self-assessment of the quality of their working-time and their "work-life balance," and on health outcomes (Tucker and Folkard 2012; Fagan et al. 2012, 2014). When the work is physically arduous, or involves working at speed to meet tight deadlines this compounds the fatigue caused by long working hours.

Regular schedules during daytime weekday hours generally make it easier for workers to plan and coordinate their employment and private lives. So do work practices that give workers some autonomy, by which we mean discretion and control, to decide when and where they do their work. Such autonomy reduces the negative effects of long hours but it does not eradicate them (Fagan and Burchell 2002; Burchell et al. 2007).

Employed men and women are more likely to report a good work-life balance if they do not work long full-time hours and if they work daytime, weekday and predictable schedules (Fagan et al. 2012; Eurofound 2012; Nijp et al. 2012; Ingre et al. 2012). Part-timers are more likely than full-timers to report that they have a good work–life balance but they are less likely to consider they have good career prospects (Eurofound 2012). Men and women employed full-time and caring for children or other relatives are less likely to report a good work–life balance than full-timers without these additional demands on their time. When parents have variable and unpredictable schedules there is a negative impact on their child(s) educational development (e.g. Economic Policy Institute 2015).

European, North American, and Australian surveys reveal that a large proportion of full-time and part-time employed workers report a mismatch between their actual and preferred working hours (Fagan 2004). In general those who work long full-time hours in jobs with high or medium level earnings are the most likely to prefer shorter working hours in exchange for a pay cut, and those working short part-time hours are the most likely to want to increase their hours (Fagan et al. 2014).

7.5.3 Full-Time and Part-Time Employment Hours

Full-time hours declined during the twentieth century, particularly in the developed economies of North America, Australia, and Europe (Bosch et al. 1994; Messenger 2004) and in some developing economies (Lee and McCann 2007). This was produced through the introduction of regulatory limits in some countries and sectors through a combination of international agreements (ILO Conventions, EU Directives), national legislation, and collective agreements between employers and trade unions. However, long full-time working hours remain widespread, particularly in developing economies but also some affluent economies such as Japan, the USA, and the UK (Figure 7.9).

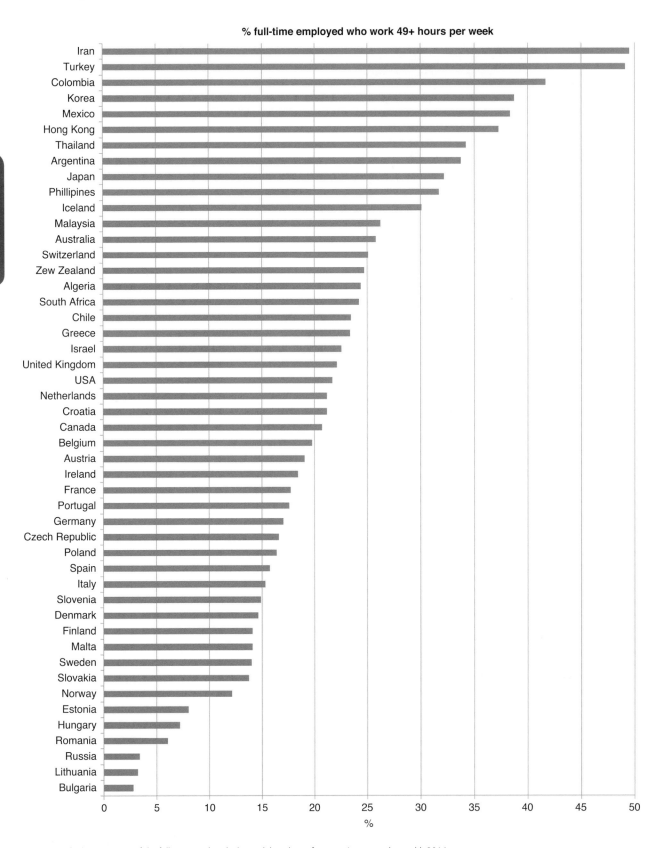

% full-time employed who work 49+ hours per week

Figure 7.9 | The proportion of the full-time employed who work long hours for countries across the world, 2014.
Full-time employment defined as 35+ hours per week. Data for all countries is for 2014 apart from the USA where data is for 2013.
Source: ILO database

The rate of part-time employment for the employed, and hours worked

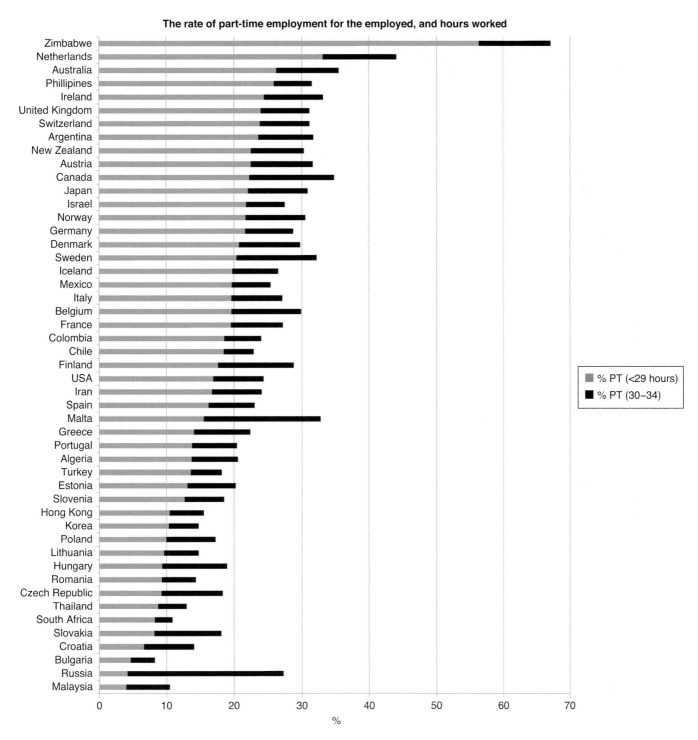

Figure 7.10 | The rate of part-time employment for the employed for countries across the world, 2014.
Data for all countries is for 2014 apart from the USA where data is for 2013.
Source: ILO database

Part-time employment has increased in many countries from the 1970s onwards (Fagan et al. 2014). Figure 7.10 shows that one-fifth or more of the employed are part-time in most of the countries shown from across the world. In most countries the majority of part-timers are women, usually combining employment with the time demands of family and household work which falls disproportionately to women (Section 7.5.1). Some men and women also work part-time voluntarily because they are in education, approaching retirement or have chronic ill-health. Involuntary part-time – the percentage of part-timers who are underemployed because that have been unable to obtain full-time employment – is common when there is a high unemployment rate. Thus in the aftermath of the 2008 recession the rate of involuntary part-time work increased in developed economies, for example by 2014 in the EU27 40 percent of male part-time employment and

26 percent of female part-time employment was involuntary. In developing economies much of the casual part-time employment in the informal economy is involuntary underemployment because those involved have been unable to obtain full-time work (either as an employee or in self-employment). Furthermore, the gender division of family care responsibilities produces another form of underemployment in countries where women are constrained to work part-time because this is the only feasible option in the context of limited childcare and eldercare services.

Most part-time employment is a category of nonstandard employment. However, it is important to differentiate between the quality of marginal and integrated forms of part-time employment (O'Reilly and Fagan 1998). Integrated part-time employment refers to those part-time jobs where the principles of the standard employment relationship have been extended through the implementation of equal treatment, and where part-time employment is available at a wide range of occupational levels, and the primary distinction is that the job involves reduced hours.

Across the world many workplaces operate on the basis of long full-time working hours. If part-time employment exists it involves short, fragmented or irregular schedules in a narrow set of low status and low-paid jobs. In this type of workplace workers have little scope to reduce or adjust their schedules because of their low wages, limited job security, and weak bargaining power.

There are workplaces which offer better quality working time arrangements: full-time hours are shorter part-time jobs are organized on the principles of equal treatment and standard employment conditions and are available in a wider range of occupations; full-time and part-time schedules are largely regular and predictable; and workers have some discretionary control over work-time (such as the ability to refuse to work overtime, flexibility in when or where they do their work, or entitlements to take time off for certain personal or domestic reasons). The latter type of workplaces is more prevalent in countries with a social-democratic tradition of working-time standards set by effective working-time regulation and innovation established through the collective bargaining and legislation which is characteristic of the "European Social Model"; notably the Nordic countries, France, Germany, the Netherlands, and Belgium (Berg et al. 2014; Fagan et al. 2014; Eurofound 2016). In some countries the comparatively low incidence of long full-time hours reflects regulated working-time in the formal economy but underestimates actual hours of work once multiple jobs in the formal and informal economy are aggregated, for example in some of the Central Eastern European countries shown in Figure 7.10, such as Bulgaria and Romania.

In many developed and developing countries across the world unions and governments have introduced initiatives to curb very long full-time hours (Messenger 2004; Lee and McCann 2007), and some have sought to promote the expansion of better quality part-time employment in the formal economy, where part-time employment is rare, such as South Korea, China, and Japan (Fagan et al. 2014). However, where progress has been made it has also stalled or been eroded in the current era; with laws repealed, diluted, or ineffectively implemented in some countries and the decline in union coverage and bargaining power in many parts of the world.

7.5.4 Work Schedules

Nonstandard work schedules – which involve shiftwork and other work in the evening, at night, at weekends have always been prevalent in developing economies and have gone hand-in-hand with long full-time hours or casual part-time jobs. Nonstandard work schedules expanded in many developed economies during the 1990s and subsequently stabilized despite the spread of the global 24-hour economy (Evans et al. 2001; Eurofound 2007, 2012, 2015b).

While night work and many forms of shiftwork have negative effects on health and do not fit well with the day-to-day rhythms of family life; it is primarily the volume of hours worked and the workers' control over their schedule which impacts on their self-assessment of work–life balance.

Fixed schedules offer the advantage of predictability, and this is still a common work arrangement in many countries. For example, in 2010 in the EU27 43 percent of employed men and 49 percent of employed women worked a fixed schedule (the same daily start and finish times and the same number of days per week). In contrast another third had unpredictable schedules, including 19 percent of employed men and 13 percent of employed women whose schedules changed regularly with no more than 24 hours' notice (Eurofound 2012). Unpredictable schedules include short-notice overtime or schedule changes, some forms of annualized hours agreements, and extreme forms of on-call work such as "zero hours" contracts. The latter are a stark form of casualization which has, for example, expanded in the UK in retail, hospitality and home care services. Such unpredictability and short notice changes in work schedule requirements is unconducive to work–life balance.

When workers have some flexibility to adapt their working hours this provides the means to secure a better fit between employment, domestic responsibilities, and other activities. Access to such flexibility remains uneven. For example, in 2011–2012 in the EU around six out of ten of the employed had no flexibility in their working hours (Eurofound 2012b).

7.5.5 Workers' Flexibility through Reconciliation Entitlements and Negotiated Flexibility

Statutory family-related leave entitlements (maternity, paternity, parental, domestic emergencies, etc.) have improved in many countries. However, there are pronounced national differences in the amount and flexibility of the leave, and the amount of earnings or benefits provided during the leave period, and the proportion of the workforce who meet the eligibility conditions (Plantenga and Remery 2005; Ray 2008; ILO 2014). Furthermore, the implementation of leave entitlements remains uneven. Workers may lose their jobs, or encounter discrimination if they take leave, revealed, for example, in a recent UK survey of maternity leave (Equality and Human Rights Commission 2016). Men remain less likely to use parental leave entitlements, although their take-up increases in national systems which provide an individual entitlement to paid and flexible parental leave options (Moss 2015).

Since the late 1970s there has been some expansion in the coverage of working-time options in developed economies which provide workers with some discretion and flexibility in their schedule, such as flexitime and other types of working time accounts, and teleworking options (Golden and Figart 2001; Riedmann et al. 2006; Chung et al. 2007). Likewise some part-time schedules are designed to make it easier for workers to better combine employment with family or other commitments (Fagan 2004; Anxo et al. 2007; Fagan et al. 2012, 2014). A number of countries have introduced a statutory "right to request" an individual adjustment to working-time; usually to switch to part-time hours but some also make provision for other adjustments to when or where hours are worked (Fagan et al. 2014).

In Europe at least, the research evidence shows that flexible working options for employees (such as flexitime, opportunities to switch to part-time hours, to work from home etc.) are more developed and used by workers in affluent economies, particularly in the public sector and in large private sector workplaces, where a union is recognized or where more than half of the workforce is female (Anxo et al. 2006; Riedmann et al. 2010).

7.5.6   Flexible and Mobile Working

The home has always been the primary workplace for homeworkers and many own-account workers, as has the street for many vendors in the informal sector. Remote working by other workers has increased, facilitated by advances in information technologies and the spread of the internet.

Eurofound (2012) estimates that a quarter of European workers are "e-nomads" who use ICT for their work and who do part of their work at sites other than their employer's or their own work premises. E-nomads are mainly highly educated professionals and knowledge workers. Digital working makes it more difficult for workers or employers to estimate actual work time; which may undermine the accuracy of trends in working time recorded in standard survey questions.

Setting up and running a workspace at home comes at a cost, many of which are borne by the worker. For a low-income home-based worker this can place a burden on housing conditions and living arrangements which may already be cramped, and where work has to be completed under conditions of inadequate heating, lighting, storage space, or equipment.

For other workers the opportunities for telework and mobile work patterns provide some flexibility in principle to enhance work–life balance. This working arrangement also provides an opportunity for employers to save costs by reducing office space. However, there are

risks and downsides to this trend as well. Firstly, the reduction in office space may impact negatively on the workforce's working conditions (Lewis et al. 2017). Secondly, the costs incurred from remote working may be less burdensome than those faced by homeworkers but they are rarely covered in full by the employer, or by tax relief. Thirdly, it can become more difficult to create boundaries between work and personal time, whether it is a homeworker compelled to work to a tight deadline in order to be paid (Felstead and Jewson 2000; Felstead et al. 2002) or a professional who operates under an explicit or normative expectation that remote working means constant "online" availability to respond to clients, co-workers and their line manager. This can be exacerbated when workloads are unmanageable and work is "taken home" in order to keep up.

7.5.7   Working-Time Quality: A Social Progress Assessment

Working time arrangements impact on workers' health and well-being, and their ability to fulfil family care responsibilities and participate in other civic, voluntary and leisure activities. Long working hours, poorly designed shift work, and working time requirements which are variable or unpredictable all have negative effects on the worker. The impact extends beyond their personal health and well-being; it can impact on their children's development, the care they are able to provide for elder and other family members, the time and energy they have left to contribute to their community.

There are efficiency gains to be made from working-time innovations. Empirical studies show that well-designed reductions in working hours are accompanied by productivity gains (Golden 2012). Some workers are willing to trade a wage reduction for shorter hours, which is more feasible for the better paid or when real wages are rising (Fagan 2004). Significant working time reductions can also promote work sharing if the reduction means the work team has to be expanded. A particular type of work sharing is temporary reductions in working-time in order to avoid lay-offs in economic downturns, which operates, for example, in Germany's manufacturing industries.

Likewise reconciliation measures and other working time options also bring economic benefits to firms through improved workforce recruitment and retention, enhanced staff morale and loyalty, and other productivity gains from innovation in work schedules (Eurofound 2006; Cranfield University School of Management and Working Families 2008; Smeaton et al. 2014). Cost benefit analysis of such interventions has been a powerful tool in campaigns for the introduction of family leave at the federal state level in the USA (Sarna et al. 2013) and in enterprise-level innovations (Rapoport et al. 2002; Kossek 2005; Bailyn 2006; Kelly et al. 2008). At the macroeconomic level a well-designed and coherent set of reconciliation measures are a social investment which improves the well-being and quality of life of workers and their families. When such measures are widely available they temper social class inequalities between households and help to progress gender equality by supporting women's employment options.

Working time conditions have improved in many countries over many decades; but across the globe the poor quality of working time for many men and women is evident. This is particularly acute in poorly regulated parts of the economy. Long full-time working hours remain widespread. For low wage workers this is often a stark economic necessity. Many well-paid managers and professionals jobs also require long working hours due to heavy workloads and to compete for career progression. Much part-time employment is in poor quality and insecure jobs and is undertaken involuntarily because full-time employment is not available or by women with care responsibilities in the context of a lack of childcare and eldercare services. Where better quality part-time employment exists the opportunities for career progression are, on average, curtailed compared to those for full-time workers. Workers generally prefer jobs where the schedules are predictable or where they have some scope to vary when and where they work, but many have little control over their hours of work. There are significant occupational differences in the quality of working time. Managers and professional having more control over their work schedules, more predictable schedules and the quality of part-time work in these occupations is vastly superior to that of manual art-time work.

The dominance of the informal economy in many developing countries, combined with the erosion of working-time standards which had been introduced in the formal sector in some developed countries (e.g. the roll back of the French legislation for a 35 hour week) and the decline in coverage by collective agreements presents challenges for progressing working-time standards, as for any employment condition. Historically the primary drivers for progress in working-time standards have been regulations and innovations introduced by collective bargaining and legislation, secured by powerful unions in the context of industrial growth and productivity gains (Bosch et al. 1994). Additional policy instruments are needed to secure progress in working-time standards in the political and economic conditions of the current global era.

7.6   Diversity and Discrimination in the Labor Market

7.6.1   Introduction

While diversity in the labor market is not new, increasing rates of paid employment by women, migration, an ageing workforce and a focus on disability have led to a growing research interest in labor market diversity. One issue is whether diversity in the labor market is good or bad for economic and social outcomes. Another important question relates to individual outcomes and how individuals from different groups – women, men, immigrants, natives, ethnic minorities, old, young, those with a disability, or a different sexual orientation – fare in the labor market. Do modern labor markets offer "good jobs for all" – or just for those with the "right" skin color, gender, or age? Having access to a paid job is crucial for financial security of the individual and their family. There will always be differences in access to good jobs due to differences in individual's skills. Yet some groups experience discrimination: they are treated differently in access to jobs and in their working conditions not because of their productivity, that is "what they can do," but because of their group membership, that is "who they are." To the extent that some groups are discriminated against, this is inimical to social progress. Having individuals assigned jobs below their potential is also economically inefficient (OECD 2008).

7.6.2   Diversity and Economic Outcomes

A population can be diverse along a number of dimensions: age, gender, ethnicity, birthplace, genetic makeup, religion, or any other physical or cultural trait. The main dimensions of diversity that have been considered in the literature on diversity and growth are ethno-linguistic diversity and, more recently, genetic and birthplace diversity. While the first two are quite persistent (i.e. evolve very slowly over time) at the level of countries, the last one can be changing more rapidly in a context of sustained immigration. And indeed, population heterogeneity in terms of birthplaces is increasing in virtually all advanced economies due to immigration. Theory suggests that diversity has both positive and negative economic effects. The former are due to complementarities in production, diversity of skills, experiences, and ideas. The latter arise from disagreements about public policies, animosity between different groups and conflict.

7.6.2.1   Measuring Diversity

Diversity is usually measured through fractionalization indices such as the Herfindahl index, computed as one minus the sum of the square shares of each subgroup in the population. The index ranges between zero (in case there is only one homogenous group) and one (in case the population at hand consists of a myriad of small subgroups) and in effect gives the likelihood that two randomly drawn individuals from the population belong to different subgroups. Such Herfindahl indices have been proposed for ethnic fractionalization (Easterly and Levine 1997; Alesina et al. 2003; Fearon 2003), linguistic diversity (Desmet et al. 2012), or birthplace diversity (Alesina, Harnoss, and Rapoport 2016).

7.6.2.2   A Macro View on Diversity

Ethnic Fractionalization and Racial Diversity

The literature on ethnic diversity and economic performance has generally found a negative relationship between ethno-linguistic fractionalization and growth/development. For example, Easterly and Levine (1997), show that ethnic fragmentation is associated with lower economic growth, especially in Africa. Collier (1999, 2001) adds that ethnic fractionalization is less detrimental in the presence of democratic institutions. It is, however, unclear if this observation is not a corollary of higher income, as shown in Alesina and La Ferrara (2005). Fearon and Laitin (2003) add that ethnic diversity alone is not sufficient to explain the outbreak of civil war.

At lower levels of aggregation, Putnam (1995), and Alesina and La Ferrara (2000, 2002) stress the role of trust, showing that individuals in racially diverse cities in the US participate less frequently in social activities and trust their neighbors to a lesser degree. The authors also find evidence that preferences for redistribution are lower in racially diverse communities. This also extends to the provision of productive public goods (Alesina et al. 1999).

Birthplace Diversity

Most recently, Alesina, Harnoss, and Rapoport (2016) propose a new index of diversity based on people's birthplaces. People born in different countries are likely to have different productive skills because they have been exposed to different life experiences, different school and value systems, and thus have developed different perspectives that allow them to interpret and solve problems differently. If early preworking age years are formative for one's own values, perspectives, and problem-solving skills, these differences are more likely to be complementary and lead to higher overall productivity gains than for other dimensions of diversity. The authors find that, empirically, ethno-linguistic, genetic, and birthplace diversity are almost completely uncorrelated. Most importantly, they differ economically in that ethno-linguistic fractionalization turns out either negative or nonsignificant while birthplace diversity remains robustly positively related to long-run income even after controlling for many covariates. This positive relationship is stronger for skilled migrants in richer countries and is economically, not just statistically significant. Increasing the diversity of skilled immigrants by 1 percentage point is shown to raise long-run output by about two percentage points. Moreover, Alesina et al. (2016) address endogeneity issues by specifying a gravity model to predict the size and diversity of a country's immigration; finally, they allow the effect of diversity to vary with bilateral cultural distance between immigrants and natives, the results being suggestive of optimal diversity at intermediate levels of cultural distance.

7.6.2.3   A Micro View on Diversity

This mostly macro literature is completed by a series of studies especially in the field of management at the "team" level and, more recently, in the field of the economics of firms and productivity. For example, a study on productivity in the airline industry, by Hambrick et al. (1996), found that management teams which are more heterogeneous in terms of education, tenure, and functional background react more slowly to a competitor's actions, but also obtain higher market shares and profits than their more homogeneous competitors. In a recent experimental study, Hoogendoorn and van Praag (2012) set up a randomized experiment in which business school students are assigned to manage a fictitious company. They find that more diverse teams (defined by parents' countries of birth) consistently outperform more homogeneous ones when the majority of team members are foreign. Finally, Kahane et al. (2013) use data on team composition of NHL teams in the US and find that teams with higher shares of foreign (European) players tend to perform better. They attribute this finding both to skill effects (better access to foreign talent) and to skill complementarities among the group of foreign players; however, when players come from too large a pool of European countries, team performance starts decreasing.

Turning to economic analyses of diversity at the firm or plant level, it is fascinating to see that their results tend to support the conclusions from the cross-country studies on ethnic vs. birthplace diversity, with generally negative outcomes for the former and positive ones for the latter. For example, Hjort (2014) analyzes the productivity of teams working at flower production plants in Kenya and uses quasi-random variation in ethnic team composition to identify productivity effects from ethnic diversity in joint production. He finds evidence for taste-based discrimination between ethnic groups, suggesting that ethnic diversity, in the context of a poor society with deep ethnic cleavages, affects productivity negatively. Brunow et al. (2015) analyze the impact of birthplace diversity on firm productivity in Germany. They find that the share of immigrants has no effect on firm productivity while the diversity of foreign workers does impact firm performance positively (as does workers' diversity at the regional level). These effects appear to be stronger for manufacturing and high-tech industries, suggesting the presence of skill complementarities at the firm level as well as regional spillovers from workforce diversity. Parrotta et al. (2014) use a firm level dataset of matched employee-employer records in Denmark to analyze the effects of diversity in terms of skills, age, and ethnicity on firm productivity. They find that while diversity in skills increases productivity, diversity in ethnicity and age decreases it. They interpret this as showing that the costs of ethnic diversity outweigh its benefits. Interestingly, they also find suggestive evidence that diversity is more valuable in problem-solving oriented tasks and in innovative industries.

7.6.3   Discrimination in the Labor Market

Discrimination in the labor market is defined as a situation in which equally productive individuals are rewarded differently due to their membership to different groups.[4] It can be "taste-based," to the extent that the taste or distaste of economic agents (consumers, workers, employers) toward various groups influences recruiters' hiring decision (Becker 1957). It can also be "statistical:" in the absence of precise information about candidates' productivity, recruiters rely on their group membership as soon as it correlates with not easy-to-observe productive characteristics (Phelps 1972; Arrow 1973). This section considers the evidence on the extent to which such discrimination occurs.

The salience of group membership in the labor market is not constant over time or across space. What it means to be Black or Muslim or female or an older worker can be very important in some countries and irrelevant in others. Why is this the case? Recent studies have highlighted the importance of symbolic boundaries to distinguish between "us" and "them" (Bail 2008). Wimmer (2008) argues that boundary making is not fixed, but a result of a struggle between social actors, influenced by institutions, the distribution of power, and political networks. Past practices, legal rules, social attitudes, the media portrayal of certain groups and the actions of political elites can all contribute to this "boundary making." Yet even when group boundaries and group identity are very important, whether this translates into labor market discrimination is not given. Actors operate in social settings, so country-level policies and practices may contribute to the systematic disadvantage of certain groups, or alternatively to "levelling the playing field" (Pager and Shepherd 2008, see Section 7.6.4).

---

[4]   We focus here on "unfair" discriminations, as opposed to "fair" discriminations that are part of national affirmative action programs and aim to compensate historically discriminated groups (e.g. Blacks in South Africa). See Section 6.5 for a brief discussion of affirmative action.

Discrimination in the labor market is challenging to measure. The typical approach is to compare the wages or jobs of majority and minority populations, statistically controlling for differences in education and experience (human capital characteristics). The remaining difference between groups is often attributed to discrimination, though this is problematic given that some relevant human capital differences may be incompletely measured. Using surveys to ask people directly about their experience of discrimination is another method, though here reports of discrimination can vary depending on the perspective of the respondent, their expectations and the information available to them (McGinnity and Lunn 2011). Legal cases may represent the "tip of the iceberg" in terms of how many incidents of discrimination actually make it to court and are successful (OECD 2013).

Field experiments, by contrast, provide direct observations of discrimination. They retain key elements of the laboratory experiment (matching, random assignment) and apply them to real-world contexts (such as job applications). In experiments to test discrimination in recruitment, typically two (or more) matched fictitious candidates – one from a minority group, another from the majority – apply for the same job, and differences in responses are recorded. In audit studies, whereby actors apply for jobs either by telephone or in person, and/or attend interview, matching candidates can be challenging (Heckman and Sigelman 1993). In correspondence tests, where fictitious applicants respond to job vacancies with written applications, the equivalence of candidates is easier to demonstrate (Riach and Rich 2002). As Rooth (2014) notes, correspondence tests to not provide general evidence of discrimination in the labor market as they are limited to a particular time and space and jobs that permit written applications; they also raise ethical issues (Riach and Rich 2004).Yet they do provide compelling evidence in the areas they test.

7.6.3.1 The Extent of Discrimination in the Labor Market: Evidence from Correspondence Tests

Gender

Two regularities can be drawn from correspondence studies designed to identify gender-based discrimination (Riach and Rich 2002; Azmat and Petrongolo 2014; and Rich 2014). First, men are typically discriminated against when they apply for a "female" job (such as secretary or receptionist) and women are discriminated against when they apply for a male job, such as motor mechanic (Riach and Rich 2002).

Second, women are discriminated against for high status jobs, particularly when they are at "risk" of pregnancy or when they face family constraints. A US study by Correll et al. (2007) found that childless women received twice as many callbacks to interview as mothers with equivalent CVs. Fathers were not penalized. Petit (2007) finds that discrimination varies according to skills level. Comparing single and childless male and female applicants, she finds that women are discriminated against in their access to high-skilled jobs when they are 25, but are treated similarly to men when they apply for low-skilled jobs.

Age

Correspondence studies point to substantial discrimination against older applicants, where "old" can range from late thirties to late fifties. This result does not only prevail in studies that tend to overestimate age-based discrimination by endowing younger and older applicants with similar work experiences (Bendick, Jackson, and Romero 1997). It is also robust to experimental setups that rely on work experiences commensurate with age (Neumark, Burn, and Button 2015). Based on an unprecedented number of job applications (more than 40,000), the study by Neumark, Burn, and Button offers the richer set of results. Notably, older women are found to be more discriminated against than older men.

Race or ethnicity

Studies of labor market discrimination by race or ethnicity have been by far the most common application of correspondence testing to date, and present overwhelming evidence of discrimination on the basis of race/ethnicity in the countries and occupations tested. As Bertrand and Duflo (2016) note, evidence has been accumulated from nearly all continents: Latin America (e.g. Galarza and Yamada (2014) compare Whites to indigenous applicants in Peru), Asia (e.g. Maurer-Fazio (2012) compares Han, Mongolian, and Tibetan applicants in China), Australia (e.g. where Booth, Leigh, and Varganova (2012) compare Whites to Chinese applicants), the United States and Canada, and in many European countries.

Zschirnt and Ruedin (2016) perform a meta-analysis based on 43 correspondence studies conducted in OECD countries between 1990 and 2015 to measure unequal treatment of racial and ethnic minorities. Their results indicate that, on average, minority applicants have to send 50 percent more applications to be invited for an interview than majority applicants. They also reveal that discrimination is typically highest for people of North African and Middle Eastern origin in European correspondence tests, though ethnic differences in discrimination are sensitive to time and place (Zschirnt and Ruedin 2016). The authors find no systematic differences between the discrimination of minority men and minority women, nor is there a clear link between the economic cycle (boom/recession) and discrimination against minorities. In terms of cross-sectoral variation, Zschirnt and Ruedin (2016) report lower discrimination against ethnic minorities in the public than in the private sectors, which may be linked to differences in the recruitment process, though this issue remains underexplored.

Religion or Belief

The particularly strong discrimination directed at people of North African and Middle Eastern origin in OECD countries suggests that the penalty they experience is not only due to their extra-European origin but also to their perceived religious affiliation, Islam. This surmise raises a more general question: are religious minorities discriminated against in Christian-heritage societies? Three correspondence studies in France compare the callback rates of applicants who differ in their perceived religion but are identical in every other respect, including national origin. Adida, Laitin, and Valfort (2010) and Pierné (2013) reveal strong religious discrimination: the probability of candidates being called back is much lower when they are perceived as Muslim rather than Catholic. Valfort (2016) includes both female and male applicants (of Lebanese origin), as well as a second minority religion, Judaism and finds the probability of Catholics being invited to an interview is 30 percent higher than it is for Jews and 100 percent higher than it is for Muslims. But, in line with Bursell (2014) and Arai, Bursell, and Nekby (2016), discrimination against Muslims varies strongly by gender. While the callback rate for Catholic women is "only" 40 percent higher than that for Muslim women, the callback rate for Catholic men is four times higher than that for Muslim men. Indeed the intensity of the discrimination faced by male Muslim applicants in France is six times as high as the discrimination directed at male African-American applicants (relative to their White counterparts) in the US (Bertrand and Mullainathan 2004).

Sexual Orientation

Correspondence studies that aim to test sexual orientation discrimination usually indicate homosexuality through the volunteer engagement of the applicant in a gay/lesbian organization. Overall, they reveal a significant penalty experienced by homosexual men and women in the labor market. To be sure, this way of signaling same-sex sexual orientation may confound homosexuality with political activism. A recent trend in the literature on anti-gay/lesbian discrimination involves signaling sexual orientation by stressing the sex of the candidate's partner (Weichselbaumer 2015). Studies that have implemented these adjustments leave the previous conclusion unaffected: gays and lesbians are discriminated against in their access to employment.

Disability

The design of tests to detect disability discrimination is challenging, as some disabilities are related to the applicants capacity to do the job, and there are only a limited number of correspondence tests (Riach and Rich 2002). A recent study by Baert (2016) compares the callback rates of male applicants without and with disability (blindness, deafness, or autism). The results reveal that the disabled candidate is only half as likely to be invited to a job interview as his nondisabled counterpart. Yet, given the seriousness of some of the featured disabilities, this gap might not only reflect discrimination but also differences in observed productive characteristics.

This concern leads Amari et al. (2015) to focus on two disabilities that should not limit productivity in the accounting positions their fictitious male candidates apply for (spinal cord injury and Asperger's Syndrome). Their findings point to a moderate level of discrimination against the disabled applicants: their probability of being called back is 26 percent lower than that of the nondisabled applicants.

7.6.4 Policies to Counter Discrimination and Promote Diversity

There are a large variety of policies and actions that can potentially contribute to tackling discrimination against disadvantaged groups in the labor market. These range from antidiscrimination legislation, to equal employment policies, affirmative action and other strategies to promote diversity. At an international level, the Universal Declaration of Human Rights provides the most fundamental framework for antidiscrimination (OECD 2013). All OECD countries have integrated anti discrimination provisions into their national legal framework (OECD 2008). Each antidiscrimination or equal opportunity law provides for the creation of agencies to monitor its application and implement its programs. The powers of these equality bodies vary across countries but can be far-reaching – typically activities range from awareness-raising, coordinating equality policies, receiving complaints and in some countries conducting legal actions, investigations, and imposing sanctions.

A key problem with antidiscrimination law in all countries is that legal rules are not self-enforcing: they rely on the actions of individuals who feel discriminated against (OECD 2008). And taking legal action can be costly, complex, time-consuming, and is often an adversarial process in the workplace, even with financial support and advice from equality bodies. The outcomes vary considerably across countries depending on the legal framework and efficiency of the legal system.

The legal framework is complemented by more proactive or positive strategies to influence practice and processes in the labor market. Affirmative action, which originated in the US, is typically defined as a set of policies that make specific efforts to advance the economic status of minority groups and women (Holzer 2010). Typically the policies monitor the representation of minority groups and take active steps to address underrepresentation, such as introducing a fixed quota, which generally implies preferential treatment of the target group (that is positive discrimination). The legitimacy and efficiency of quotas have been debated in the United States for many years: as a policy tool, hard affirmative action and quotas by race have generally been discontinued in the United States (OECD 2013).[5] Equal opportunities programs have similar goals to affirmative action but typically use targets, which do not imply preferential treatment. Equal opportunities programs with targets continue, for example in the European action plan against racism (OECD 2013). However, evaluating the effectiveness of such policies has proven difficult. In terms of recruitment and personnel practices, there is an urgent need to assess initiatives to see if they do indeed have the desired effect (Bertrand and Duflo 2016).

7.7 The Impact of Work and Employment on Health and Well-being

Exclusion from paid work and exposure to hazards and poor quality employment are powerful threats to human health and well-being. These threats are unequally distributed across the globe, between and

---

[5] The impact of affirmative action quotas has not been uniformly positive: one negative by-product of quotas is they may increase stereotypes if such measures are associated with lower standards for the groups concerned (Holzer 2010).

within societies, leaving poor people, those with less education, skills, and capabilities in more disadvantaged conditions. Although any estimate is imprecise, roughly 195 million people of the world's population of employment age are *unemployed*. In low- and middle-income countries, a majority of those working are employed in the *informal economy*, often lacking any statutory regulation, protection against occupational hazards, and social security benefits. Large parts of those working in the informal sector do not earn enough to lift themselves and their families above the poverty line, with more women than men affected. Even worse, despite international proscription, several millions of children are still exposed to *child labor*, and more than 10 million of adults are suffering from *forced or bonded labor*, specifically in Africa, South America, and the Pacific region (Benach et al. 2007).

In high income countries, as well as in some rapidly developing countries, the nature of work and employment underwent significant changes in recent past, mainly due to the far-reaching impact of digitalization and economic globalization. These changes resulted in impressive progress of the quality of employment and the provision of safety and social security, and hence, contributed to improved work-related health. Yet, with growing economic competition and augmented pressure for cost-containment, workload and work intensity increased in large parts of the workforce in these countries, often in combination with job instability and threats to job loss (Gallie 2013). These threats of a stressful psychosocial work environment are becoming more widespread with a growing transnational labor market and with the expansion of nonstandard employment relations, and they are *exacerbated by major economic downturns*, financial crises, and related fiscal austerity measures. There is now solid scientific evidence on adverse health effects of stressful psychosocial work environments resulting from these conditions (see Section 7.7.2).

To date, large *differences in the quality of work and employment* still persist even in socio-economically most advanced regions, such as Europe (WHO 2014). However, at each level of development, we observe consistent social gradients of the quality of work and employment. Poor quality is not confined to the poorest members of society. Rather, with each step one moves up on the social latter of a country's social structure, one observes gradually less poor work. Therefore, related policy efforts should aim at improving health-conducive work and employment across the whole of the social structure, but targeted progressively more toward those with higher levels of need (Marmot 2015). The current worldwide situation of work and employment with its far-reaching afflictions of people's health and well-being contrasts sharply with an important goal of the United Nation's recently endorsed SDG agenda: "Promote sustained, inclusive and sustainable economic growth, full and productive employment and decent work for all" (United Nations 2015c). *It is therefore important to demonstrate the best scientific evidence on associations of working conditions with health in order to motivate responsible stakeholders and the wider public to develop evidence-based policies to reduce adversity and to promote healthy work.*

7.7.1 Work, Employment and Health: Summarizing the Evidence

Broadly speaking, *four categories of unhealthy work* can be distinguished, in addition to the afflictions resulting from job loss

and precarious employment: (1) occupational injuries and exposure to "traditional" (physical, chemical, biological) occupational hazards; (2) physically strenuous work; (3) work-time related stressors (e.g. shift work, long work hours); (4) stressful psychosocial work environments (e.g. work pressure, job insecurity, harassment). In many occupations, diverse combinations of these conditions are observed, often resulting in an *accumulation of disadvantage*. As mentioned, this is most often the case among working people in lower socio-economic positions. It should be emphasized that these categories reflect the general recognition that the importance of work for health goes beyond traditional occupational diseases and beyond traditional occupational safety approaches toward preventing accidents and injuries, thus requiring a more comprehensive, interdisciplinary approach toward dealing with occupational health.

In the following paragraphs a brief summary of substantial scientific research findings is given. As the majority of empirical studies were conducted in industrialized countries there are obvious gaps of knowledge, in particular with regard to informal work, agricultural work, and a variety of precarious jobs in the formal sector in economically less developed countries (Benach et al. 2007).

7.7.1.1 Unemployment, Precarious Employment, and Health

The causal link of associations between *unemployment* and health has long been debated, given powerful selection factors and evidence on reverse causation which means that people with poor health are more likely to lose their job. Valid findings are restricted to prospective epidemiologic cohort studies based on individual data that control for baseline health and important confounding factors. Several such studies have been analyzed in systematic reviews and meta-analyses. The main results indicate that *long-term unemployment* is associated with a statistically significant, but moderate *increase of relative risks of suffering from depression, suicide, or cardiovascular disease*. Moreover, according to several studies, all-cause mortality following long-term unemployment is elevated (Donkin et al. 2014). These associations should be interpreted with some caution as protective factors such as strong social support, psychological resilience (e.g. self-efficacy, optimism), and the provision of comprehensive social protection policies at national level reduce their strength. On the other hand, long-term unemployment substantially increases the risk of adopting health-adverse behaviors, including addiction, thus aggravating morbidity and mortality risks.

Precarious employment has been defined as a condition of high job instability and lack of alternative employment opportunity, often combined with low wage and low social protection. Accordingly, a wide spectrum of employment arrangements in the formal economy is considered precarious, including involuntary part-time jobs, fixed-term contracts, temporary agency work, freelance, and some forms of self-employment. Research on potential effects of precarious work on health is still limited, not least due to methodological difficulties. However, *job instability and job insecurity* in the face of business restructuring or downsizing are clearly *associated with reduced mental health* (Cooper et al. 2012). In line with these findings preliminary evidence indicates that the recent *great economic crisis adversely* affects the *health* of populations at working age, partly due to stressful effects of labor market disadvantage and financial strain, partly due to restrictions in access to health care (Karanikolos et al. 2013).

7.7.1.2 Occupational Diseases and Injuries, Physical, Chemical, and Biological Occupational Hazards

Globally, 2.3 million deaths occur annually due to work-related diseases (mainly cancer and cardiovascular diseases) and occupational injuries (Takala et al. 2014). Almost one thousand workers lose their life every day due to *occupational accidents*, most of them in low- or middle-income countries. Failures in developing and controlling basic standards of *occupational safety measures* and training are the major determinants of a high burden of occupational injuries, especially so in low-income countries (WHO 2014). Importantly, there is a strong link between a country's overall level of economic progress and competitiveness on one hand and the total occupational accident rate on the other hand: the higher economic progress the lower the rates of accidents (Takala et al. 2014).

While substantially reduced in high-income countries, exposure to *"traditional" occupational hazards* remains high in developing countries. As an example, in rapidly developing countries it was estimated that 125 million workers are still exposed to *asbestos* (WHO 2008), and the incidence of *cancers caused by occupational exposures* is likely to increase in most regions of the world. Other occupational diseases are due to dangerous workplace exposures such as biological agents, mutagenic substances, skin and airways sensitizers, noise, heat, cold, or vibration, causing high societal costs, for instance in case of occupational asthma or hearing impairment (Montano 2014).

7.7.1.3 Physically Strenuous and Repetitive Work

Work in the agricultural sector and in certain industries is associated with *heavy lifting, tiring and painful positions, and repetitive movements*. Although these conditions are more frequent in less developed countries and among unskilled or semi-skilled workers certain biomechanical and posture-related risks (e.g. repetitive hand or arm movements in computer work) prevail in the service and IT sectors of advanced societies. For instance, about half of the European workforce exerts repetitive movements on the job, mainly due to computer work (Eurofound 2015). In the long run, *back pain and musculoskeletal disorders* (MSD) result from these exposures. MSD of the neck, lower back, lower and upper limbs are the second most frequent medical cause underlying disability benefit claims in OECD countries, and they define the most frequent occupational disease and the highest self-reported work-related health complaint in Europe, where strong social gradients are observed (OECD 2010). *Sedentary work* is a further occupational health risk, widely prevalent among white-collar occupations.

7.7.1.4 Shift Work, Long Working Hours

In economically advanced countries (e.g. Europe), shift work affects more than 20 percent of the workforce (Eurofound 2015). Research

on *shift work* documents *elevated risks of cardiovascular disease and metabolic syndrome*, in particular after chronic exposure (Siegrist et al. 2015). However, it is difficult to disentangle work-related influences from those related to a disturbed work–life balance, changes in circadian rhythms, and health-adverse behaviors.

A further health risk at work relates to *long working hours*. In Europe, every tenth male worker reports to work regularly more than 60 hours per week. For special service occupations and professions, persons performing on-call jobs, freelancers, and several groups having atypical jobs, it has become increasingly difficult to clearly distinguish work from nonwork periods in their daily life. Long working hours (e.g. >55 h/week) were associated with *moderately increased relative risks of depression, coronary heart disease, and stroke* (Bannai and Tamakashi 2014). For instance, a large-scale study observed a dose–response relationship between number of working hours and risk of stroke (see Figure 7.11 (Kivimäki et al. 2015).

7.7.1.5 Stressful Psychosocial Work Environments

A collective increase in competition, work pressure, and job demands occurred in the context of significant changes in work and employment mentioned above. In relevant parts of the labor force work intensification was associated with increased job insecurity resulting from economic or sociopolitical transformation or from far-reaching organizational restructuring (Eurofound 2015). High levels of stressful experience are observed under these conditions. *Psychosocial stress* occurs if a person is exposed to a threatening demand (stressor) that taxes or exceeds her or his capacity of successful response. Furthermore, stress results from experiences of severe injustice, unfairness, and threats to one's physical or psychological integrity. Threats to personal control and appreciation elicit sustained negative emotions of anxiety and anger, paralleled by "stress responses" originating from the organism's innate physiologic alarm mechanisms. While potentially beneficial in acute life-threatening situations chronic stress in the long run impairs the functioning of distinct bodily systems and increases the risk of developing a *stress-related mental or physical disorder*, such as *depression, cardiovascular, or metabolic disease*.

Recurrent psychosocial stress at work acts as a major determinant of these developments, but the variety and complexities of work and employment characteristics provide a challenge to scientific research. In fact, *theoretical concepts* are needed to delineate particular stressful aspects within these complexities that can be identified at a high level of generalization. Among several approaches two such concepts were widely applied in international occupational stress research, "demand–control," and "effort–reward imbalance." The *demand–control (or job strain) model* identifies stressful work in terms of job task profiles defined by high psychological demands and a low degree of control or decision latitude (Karasek and Theorell 1990). The *effort–reward imbalance model* was developed as a complementary approach with a primary focus on the work contract; the principle of social reciprocity being at the core of the model (for review Siegrist and Wahrendorf 2016). Rewards received in return for efforts expended at work include fair wage or salary, recognition, and career opportunities (promotion, job security). The model asserts that lack of reciprocity (high effort in

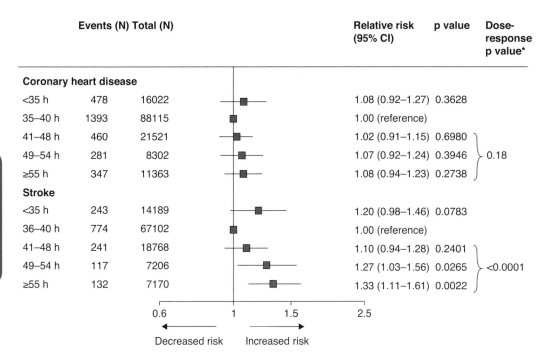

	Events (N)	Total (N)		Relative risk (95% CI)	p value	Dose-response p value*
Coronary heart disease						
<35 h	478	16022		1.08 (0.92–1.27)	0.3628	
35–40 h	1393	88115		1.00 (reference)		
41–48 h	460	21521		1.02 (0.91–1.15)	0.6980	
49–54 h	281	8302		1.07 (0.92–1.24)	0.3946	0.18
≥55 h	347	11363		1.08 (0.94–1.23)	0.2738	
Stroke						
<35 h	243	14189		1.20 (0.98–1.46)	0.0783	
36–40 h	774	67102		1.00 (reference)		
41–48 h	241	18768		1.10 (0.94–1.28)	0.2401	
49–54 h	117	7206		1.27 (1.03–1.56)	0.0265	<0.0001
≥55 h	132	7170		1.33 (1.11–1.61)	0.0022	

0.6   1   1.5   2.5

← Decreased risk   Increased risk →

Figure 7.11 | Association of categories of weekly working hours with incident coronary heart disease and stroke. Estimates adjusted for age, sex, and socioeconomic status.*
*For trend from standard to long working hours.
Source: Kivimaki et al. (2015)

combination with low reward) occurs frequently and generates strong negative emotions and psychobiological stress responses with adverse long-term effects on health. The utility of these two theoretical models is due to the fact that they are based on two core stress-theoretical notions, "control" and "reward" and that their measurement in terms of psychometrically validated questionnaires is available in a variety of languages, thus enabling cross-country comparisons. Moreover, strong social gradients of both forms of stressful psychosocial work were documented, leaving those in lower positions at higher risk (Donkin et al. 2014).

Several *systematic reviews* summarize the current state of knowledge in this rapidly expanding field of occupational health research that is mainly based on *prospective observational cohort studies*, supplemented by experimental research and intervention studies. Strong evidence indicates that the *risk of* incident *depression* is almost twice as high among workers exposed to job strain or effort-reward imbalance compared to workers with low or no stress at work. Moreover, *relative risks of coronary heart disease* are increased by 30–60 percent under these conditions. The burden of work-stress related disease is even larger as additional risks are associated with stressful work, such as metabolic disorders, alcohol dependence, sleep disturbances, sickness absence, reduced health functioning, and disability pension, thus generating substantial economic loss in addition to human suffering (Schnall et al. 2017; Siegrist and Wahrendorf 2016). As depression is one of the leading disorders worldwide and as it has been observed as a main cause of disability pension, at least in high income countries (OECD 2010), evidence of the contribution of stressful psychosocial work environments to this latter development is warranted. Figure 7.12 provides some of this evidence, documenting a linear relationship of stressful work with risk of disability pension due

to depression, based on a large longitudinal study in Finland (Juvani et al. 2014).

Although the majority of studies were conducted in high-income countries, there is accumulating evidence that these *work stress models* are *valid in rapidly developing countries* as well, specifically in China and Latin America, an observation of particular interest in times of economic globalization (Siegrist and Wahrendorf 2016; Schnall et al. 2017).

7.7.1.6   National Labor and Social Policies

National labor and social policies can influence the quality of work and employment within respective workforces by setting rules and regulations which protect workers' health, by investing in active labor market policies including rehabilitation services, and by offering financial support in case of job loss and other income shocks. It is therefore assumed that the mean *quality of work and employment* is *more favorable in countries* that developed *comprehensive welfare state measures* than in countries with poor welfare state investments. In addition, favorable policies to some extent may mitigate the adverse effects of stressful work on the health of workers. There is some *preliminary evidence* along these lines. For instance, concerning the first assumption, a comparative cross-country study of older workers in Europe analyzed the association of a summary measure of work stress per country with two indices of each country's amount of offering compensation (or social protection) and integration (or active labor market) policies respectively. Figure 7.13 displays the scatter plots of this association. To interpret the results one should note that scores of stressful work range from 0 (no stress) to 48 (high stress) and that each one of the two policy indices developed by OECD ranges from 0

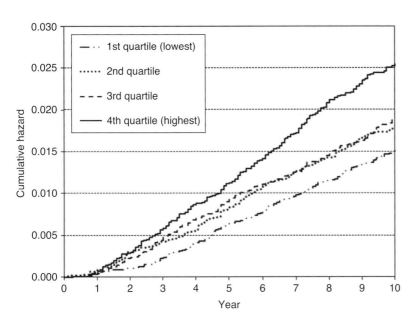

Figure 7.12 | Cumulative hazard curves of disability pension due to depression by psychosocial stress at work (quartile of effort-reward imbalance).
Note: Finnish Public sector study; N= 51.874 employees; 75% women.
Source: Juvani et al. (2014)

(poorest policy) to 50 (best policy). In case of the compensation index, associations are slightly less pronounced. In contrast, an almost linear association is observed in case of the integration index where more pronounced integration policies are related to lower levels of stressful work (Wahrendorf and Siegrist 2014).

7.7.2 Work and Health: Two Causal Directions

The previous section demonstrated selective evidence on how adverse working and employment conditions affect the health of people in the labor market. This evidence is based on the assumption of a *causal link between adverse work and subsequent poor health*. Despite an ongoing methodological debate this assumption is supported by crucial quality criteria of epidemiological research, such as the strength and consistency of prospectively documented associations between exposure and health in occupational cohorts, the dose–response relationship of this association, the demonstration of biological pathways explaining the link, and the reduction of risk following removal of the exposure.

With a major focus on noxious aspects of work and their risks for morbidity and mortality, the *positive, health-promoting aspects of modern working conditions* are disregarded. However, in keeping with the theoretical models mentioned, we can conclude that jobs that offer options of personal control, skill development, and recurrent experience of self-efficacy, and employment relationships characterized by just exchange, fairness, and appropriate material and nonmaterial rewards, including promotion prospects and job security, are conducive to the health and well-being of workers. In fact, a broader approach stressing the protective, health-promoting features of work has been proposed as guidance to public policies related to workers and the workplace (Schulte et al. 2015). Moreover, several *intervention studies* that improved working conditions along these principles demonstrated *beneficial effects* on workers' health and well-being.

A *second causal direction* between work and health is of similar importance: *Sickness and disability can impair access or return to work as well as adequate performance on the job*. In view of a globally ageing workforce and economic pressures toward postponing pension age chronic diseases and disabilities are increasingly perceived as challenges to maintain the workability and productivity of older people (OECD 2010). In most countries people with chronic disease or disability experience barriers to employment in terms of prejudice and discrimination, lack of vocational rehabilitation, employers' fear of reduced productivity, or absence of national integration policies. For instance, while most people with spinal cord injury can work to some extent, the average global employment rate among people with this type of disability is as low as 37 percent (WHO 2013). Large variations between countries are mainly due to the development of appropriate medical and vocational rehabilitation and the implementation of antidiscrimination policies. Mental illness, and specifically depression, is another case of concern. Rates of return to work after disease onset are low and occur late, and stigmatization of depressed people within proximal social environments and the society at large is still a major obstacle. Programs of early, stepwise return to work, applying individual placement and support models as well as continued medical and psychological treatment were shown to be successful and cost-effective (Marmot 2015). The fact that people with disability or long-term sickness are disadvantaged in their opportunities of fair participation in social life, and specifically of access to paid work, contradicts basic human rights. Therefore, policy initiatives are needed that aim at reducing discrimination and at widening fair opportunities of social participation.

7.7.3 Policy Implications

To strengthen fair work and employment globally major policy efforts are required at different levels. The provision of safe work and

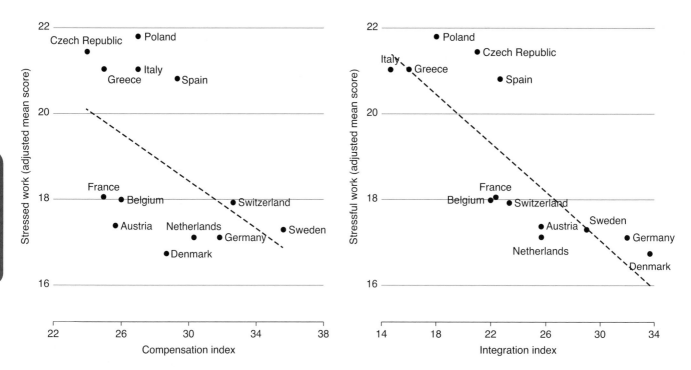

Figure 7.13 | Adjusted mean scores of stressful work among older male and female employees (N=11181) and policy indices.
Notes: Mean scores of stressful work are adjusted for sex, age, retirement age, periods of disability, job absence due to disability, childhood circumstances (occupational position of main breadwinner, number of books, housing conditions, and overcrowding) and labor market disadvantage (occupational position in main job, involuntary job loss (laid off and plant closure) and period of unemployment).
Source: Wahrendorf and Siegrist (2014). The figure is available under the terms of the Creative Commons Attribution License (https://creativecommons.org/licenses/by/4.0/)

basic social protection to employed people is a key responsibility of *employers*. However, respective commitments need to be controlled by authorities, based on national laws and regulations. Despite some binding international conventions, most importantly the convention on fundamental rights that has meanwhile been endorsed by the member states of the *International Labor Organization* (ILO 2013b), many countries in less developed parts of the world still lack basic safety, health, and social protection measures of working people, they are deprived of occupational health and safety services, and their social security system fails to meet even basic needs of working people and their families (Benach et al. 2007; WHO 2008). With the diffusion of neoliberal policies stimulated by economic globalization, the impact of national legislation, of social protection and active labor market programs has been weakened. Against this background, it has become increasingly difficult to achieve progress in negotiations on fair employment and working conditions between employers, trade unions and governments, given their restriction to the national context. Therefore, efforts are needed toward *establishing effective supranational regulation* to ensure basic human rights at work internationally.

Several such initiatives have been proposed, such as the ILO's *"Social Protection Floor Initiative."* Amongst others, this initiative recommends the introduction of *minimal wages*, of *health- and unemployment-insurance*, and of reliable *pension systems*, thus *extending formal employment contracts* at the expense of the informal sector. Moreover, *national labor market programs* are proposed to reduce youth

unemployment and adult long-term unemployment. *Transnational corporations* are asked to apply the same employment standards for their employees in high-income and low-income countries, and to refrain from relocating their production sites to countries with minimally regulated workforce. There is now some evidence that the *World Trade Organization* (WTO) recognizes the importance of occupational health and safety standards and related social protection measures in transnational trade and investment treaties. Finally, the *World Health Organization* (WHO) has fostered a global movement to promote health equity, including work-related health (WHO 2008). Based on these initiatives several recommendations are proposed (see below).

In conclusion these policy efforts at different levels directed toward responsible stakeholders, political and financial decision-making bodies, and professional and civil organizations involved in occupational affairs should result in substantial progress of developing and preserving fair, just and healthy working and employment conditions and in reducing social inequalities in health.

7.8   Collective Bargaining*

7.8.1   Introduction

Collective bargaining – negotiations between trade unions and employers or employers' organizations to set wages and working

---

*   Section drafted by Jelle Visser

conditions – is a key labor market institution and fundamental right, recognized by the international community. The relevant convention (C98, adopted in 1949) of the ILO has been ratified by 164 countries and calls on governments for support. For workers, collective bargaining provides *protection* (ensuring adequate pay and working conditions), *voice and empowerment* (collective expression of grievances and participation in the success of the enterprise), and *distribution* (fair share of benefits of training, technology, and productivity growth). For employers, collective bargaining aims at *conflict management*, providing for dispute resolution and legitimizing managerial control through joint rules. Collective bargaining relieves the state from the complex task of *setting standards* and *solving coordination problems* in an area where the risk of conflict and noncompliance is high.

Like the statutory minimum wage, collective agreements establish a floor in the labor market and provide a level playing field for fair competition. Unlike a national minimum wage, collective bargaining makes can tailor this floor to varying conditions in an occupation or industry. In many countries it is possible, moreover, to derogate by collective agreement from legal minimum standards on wages, working time, and employment protection. This regulatory flexibility can be an important advantage.

Collective agreements, fixing wages and hours for a larger group of workers and over a longer period, can have a stabilizing function for the economy, help firms to plan their operations and workers to plan their lives, reduce uncertainty and stimulate investment. On a microeconomic plane, collective bargaining can make allocation and price setting in the labor markets more efficient by addressing coordination and market failures due to asymmetry of information and unequal bargaining power between workers and employers, and by reducing transaction costs involved in individual bargaining. By ensuring that workers' request for pay updates in line with productivity increases are heard, collective bargaining limits costs of litigation and excessive staff turnover. It may thus improve the quality of the employment relation, improve allocation and motivation, and contribute to productivity. However, collective bargaining can also introduce distortions ('rent seeking') at the expense of outsiders and consumers.

7.8.2   Effects on Productivity, Earnings, and Employment

In "Two Faces of Unionism" Freeman and Medoff (1984) envisage a pro-productive role for unions through aggregating worker preferences in the provision of workplace public goods and facilitating efficient contracting where there is a long-term relation between worker and firm, but employers' ex ante promises to take workers' interests into account are not credible. Research on productivity effects is mostly from the US and UK, and the findings are not overwhelming. Most survey-based studies indicate that the effects are minimal. More promising results are reported for Germany, where collective bargaining over pay takes place outside the firm for entire sectors but is combined with workplace co-determination within firms. Dual representation and multilevel bargaining with general principles and guidelines negotiated outside the firm tend to limit the possibility of "hold-ups." Single-union representation and, in case of multiple unions, joint bargaining platforms, central union

control over strikes improve governability. Sequential declines in the "disadvantages of unionism" have been reported for Britain in combination with changes in the collective bargaining system away from the conflictual multiunionism model of the 1970s (for a summary of recent literature: Addison 2016).

The monopoly side of unions has been studied in connection with wage rigidity in times of high and rising unemployment. Recent studies using European firm-level data collected at the onset of the Great Depression of 2008–2009 suggest that unions and collective agreements constrain the adjustment of wages, but also that unions encourage the use of alternative cost-cutting strategies, such as a temporary reduction in working hours, part-time employment, and the limitation of extras and bonuses, in order to temper the adverse effects on employment (*Labor Economics* 19/5, 2012). If there is a harmful effect of unions showing in higher unemployment rates or larger fluctuations in unemployment, this is mitigated when collective bargaining is coordinated across unions, firms and sectors. The effectiveness of coordination is enhanced with trust and cooperation in labor relations (Blanchard, Jaumotte, and Loungani 2013). Cooperation, as assessed by senior business executives in a 2014 survey published by the World Economic Forum, correlates with trust in unions and is highest in some of the continental and Northern European countries with high bargaining coverage (OECD 2017).

Collective bargaining is associated with higher earnings and lower profits. A study based on ISSP survey data for 1995–1999 covering seventeen countries found a wage advantage for workers covered by collective bargaining from less than 1 percent, negative or insignificant in Sweden, Italy or the Netherlands, 4 percent in Germany, 7 percent in Norway and Spain, rising to more than 20 percent in Japan (Blanchflower and Bryson 2003). A recent study of German wage data found that the gap between mean wages of covered and uncovered workers had risen from 1 to 10 percent between 1999 and 2010, if controlled for firm size (Felbermayr et al. 2014). Addison et al. (2014), controlling for employee heterogeneity, report a smaller wage gap of 3–4 percent. Workers whose firms abandoned the sectoral collective agreement experienced a loss, whereas workers whose firms joined the agreement enjoyed a gain.

7.8.3   Bargaining Coverage

The bargaining coverage rate – the share of employees covered by collective agreements – is the key indicator for assessing the relative strength of collective bargaining. Coverage rates vary massively across countries (Figure 7.14), from less than 5 percent in Egypt, Ethiopia, El Salvador, Guatemala, Panama, Paraguay, Peru, Malaysia, the Philippines, and Thailand and to about 90 percent or more in Iceland, Sweden, Finland, Uruguay, France, Belgium, and Austria. Collective bargaining plays a marginal role in low-income countries with a large informal labor market. However, the relationship with industrialization, development or income is not straightforward. In some of the richest countries, after decades of union decline collective bargaining plays a marginal role, with coverage rates having dropped in 2015 to 11.8 in the USA (7.4 percent in the private sector) and 16.8 percent in Japan.

Within countries, the highest coverage (and unionization rate) is in the public sector, in manufacturing, and transport, whereas collective bargaining tends to be less widespread in market services and agriculture. Large firms are more likely to be covered than small firms, explaining part of the sectoral variation. Workers with open-ended employment contracts, those with full-time jobs, and older workers are more likely to have access to collective bargaining than temporary, part-time, and younger workers (OECD 2017). These variations mirror differences in unionization. Bargaining coverage (and union density) rates between men and women have converged, with female unionization and coverage rates overtaking those of men in some Northern and Eastern European, Anglo-Saxon, and African countries.

7.8.4   Unions and Collective Bargaining

As a *voluntary* process between *independent* and *autonomous* parties, collective bargaining presupposes independent employee representation. Usually representation is expressed through the trade union and one should expect that where unions are weak (few members, few resources, limited strike capacity) collective bargaining is weak. Negotiating the terms of employment for their members is a core union activity besides lobbying for labor-friendly laws and managing common (insurance) funds. Unions need members to claim representation and recognition as bargaining agents, and they need members, loyalty and money to back up claims with strike action. Are therefore more workers covered by collective agreements when more are unionized?

Figure 7.14 addresses this question in a cross-country comparison, showing union density and bargaining coverage rates, calculated as a proportion of *employed* wage earners. It turns out that differences in union density account for less than half the differences in bargaining coverage (R^2=.44; 85 countries). In most countries bargaining coverage is much broader than union membership. The opposite, with smaller coverage rates, applies in countries, mostly in Africa, Asia, and Central America, where unions are present in the state sector but collective bargaining is restricted (as wages are set by public authorities) and unions fail to gain recognition in the private sector.

Bargaining coverage can exceed union density for two main reasons. Firstly, collective agreements are often applied *erga omnes* ("toward everybody"). Even if agreements are legally binding only for union members, employers often apply the same terms to nonmembers, either because they do not know who is a member or they want to limit rivalry, maintain social peace, and limit union incentives for organizing. Works councils, elected by and from the company's staff are in many European countries charged with supervising the implementation of the collective agreement for all, union and nonunion employees. This tends to create a "free rider" problem for the unions, which is sometimes mitigated by a small payroll tax used for reducing union membership dues or lowering union bargaining costs. This is often regulated, not by law, but by agreement between unions and employers. In the USA, however, legislation has moved in the opposite direction, with most states having "right to work" laws allowing employees to opt out from paying union dues in unionized workplaces. Secondly, the administrative extension of sectoral agreements to firms that are not members of the signatory employers' association(s) increases inclusiveness.

7.8.5   Extension and Employers' Organization

Extension is a public policy act based on legislation mandating the government, a public agency or the court to declare a collective agreement binding on all employers operating in a sector or occupation. Extension serves several purposes, like (1) promoting collective bargaining; (2) furthering industrial peace; (3) creating common standards or funds for apprenticeship and vocational training; (4) establishing and enforcing minimum wages and terms of employment; (5) binding foreign service providers to domestic standards; and (6) protecting wages and rights of migrant and posted workers. Extension had been used since the nineteenth century but became widespread during the 1930s Depression (Hamburger 1939). The legal possibility of extending collective agreements exists in well over 50 countries (Hayter and Visser 2017).

What makes extension different from other forms of state regulation, such as a statutory minimum wage, is that it is based on a concurrence – a negotiated agreement. It thus retains some of the flexibility and self-regulatory features of collective bargaining, but like the law in democratic societies it binds the minority to majority decisions. In order to prevent particular groups or large firms imposing their conditions on others, many countries require that the collective agreement must cover a majority of employees before it can be extended and sometimes they allow small or struggling firms to be (temporarily) exempted. The use of extension varies from quasi-automatic application (for instance in France, Spain, or Belgium) to being extremely rare or having fallen in disuse (Japan, Canada, Poland, the Baltic states). During the Great Recession, extension was ended or restricted in Greece, Romania, and Ireland, reregulated in Portugal, and eased in Germany.

Extension presupposes multi-employer bargaining. Where there is no sectoral (or occupational) agreement, there is nothing to be extended. When collective bargaining takes place only or mostly at enterprise level, coverage will be low even if agreements apply *erga omnes*. The current maximum is less than one-fourth of all private sector employees. Under conditions of enterprise bargaining employees in small firms and in sectors dominated by small firms will have no access to collectively bargaining even if they want it, either because there is no union or employers impose conditions unilaterally, with individual bargaining only for those whose experience and skills are in demand.

Where unions and employers' associations negotiate at sectoral level, coverage rates are always higher, upwards from 50 percent with an average around 75 percent. Presence or absence of multi-employer bargaining accounts for three-quarters of the difference in coverage rates (R^2 = .77, 78 countries). Sectoral agreements will cover also workers in small firms where unions have few members. This inclusion is guaranteed when agreements are extended but can also be achieved through union pressure (boycotts and secondary picketing) on nonmember firms to apply the "common rate," as is practiced in Sweden and Denmark.

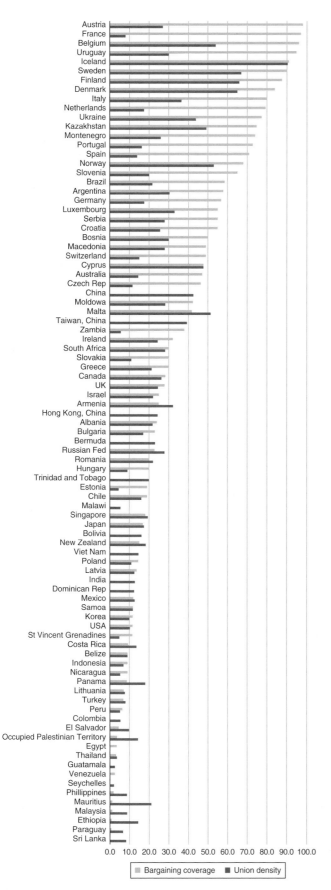

7

For obvious reasons, multi-employer bargaining depends on employers having organized and willing to negotiate. Unfortunately, reliable data on the extent of employer organization is scarce and exists only for European countries. From data covering the last decade or two, we find that on average employer associations are far more stable than unions and that the level of organization, measured as the share of employees working in member-firms, doubles that of unions (OECD 2017). Developments in Central and Eastern Europe since 1989 show that it has been extremely difficult to create employers' organizations where they did not exist and that the frailty and disunity of such organizations has translated in weakness of collective bargaining.

7.8.6 Decentralization and Union Decline

Technological and organizational changes, decline of manufacturing, privatization, outsourcing, and scaling down of public sector employment, together with the increase of unemployment and contingent employment have been the main drivers behind union decline. Whether the same factors are behind the observed long-term decline in strike participation rates (in the private sector) and indicate a growing difficulty to express collective worker power and social solidarity is plausible but not undisputed, also because strike data are notoriously hard to compare. Globalization and increased pressures to relocate production have narrowed the margins of worker bargaining power.

These trends have been accompanied by changes in the content and organization of collective bargaining. Stabilizing the employment relationship through collective standard setting was the norm for about half a century since the 1930s Great Depression. This corresponded with the ascent of sectoral collective bargaining and pattern setting by large firms, with high and stable coverage rates reaching the majority even in countries and industries where unions organized only the minority of skilled, dominantly male workers. Since the 1980s employers and governments have advocated more pay and contract flexibility, leaner or no agreements at the sectoral level, and more room for variable pay at enterprise level. The state and international organizations, like IMF and OECD, have advocated labor market reforms including lower employment protection and weakening or ending national and sectoral bargaining, as occurred in Central America, Chile, East Asia, Britain, and Turkey, throughout Central and Eastern Europe, as well as in Greece and Romania during the Great Recession.

In the 1980s the United Kingdom was the first and only European country where the government was determined to end multi-employer bargaining and roll-back union power – a process that has been coined "disorganized centralization" (Traxler 1995). This approach had been preceded in the USA, found followers in New Zealand and Australia, but not in Europe at that time. Reestablishing free unions and collective bargaining after 1989, the postcommunist European countries made explicit room for sectoral collective bargaining, though the practical effects were minimal. In Northern Europe, collective bargaining was gradually reorganized into a two-level bargaining model with leaner and broader sectoral agreements that left more to decide at enterprise level. Unlike the "unorganized" variant, such "organized decentralization" was not associated with declining coverage, even though unions lost members and bargaining clout. Finally, in a number

Figure 7.14 | Bargaining coverage rates across 85 countries in 2014–2015.
Source: ICTWSS Database (Visser 2015); Industrial Relations Indicators, ILO, available at: www.ilo.org/ilostat [Industrial Relations]

Figure 7.15 | Time trends in bargaining coverage and union density rates, 1960–2013, by country groups.
Source: ICTWSS Database (Visser 2015)

of countries both centralizing and decentralizing tendencies tended to block each other (Italy, Finland, Spain, or France), while in Germany collective bargaining coverage eroded with the disaffiliation of small firms from their employers' associations and greater scope for using opening clauses by large firms.

Figure 7.15 shows the changes in union density and bargaining coverage rates in 32 industrialized high-income countries with (annual) data between 1960 and 2014. Around 1980s the mean level of unionization starts to decrease, one decade later followed by a decline in bargaining coverage. Decomposing the average in three groups – fifteen Western European countries with mainly sectoral and two-level bargaining systems; nine non-European countries (USA, Canada, Australia, New Zealand, Japan, Israel, Turkey, Mexico, and Chile) with dominantly enterprise bargaining: eight postcommunist countries in Central and Eastern Europe (CEE) with failed sectoral and limited enterprise bargaining – we gain some insight as to what has been going on.

In the non-European part of the OECD unionization and coverage rates have fallen since the early 1980s. The mean coverage rate in 2015 was below 20 percent compared to 50 percent in 1980; this matches with a mean unionization rate of 16 percent today compared to 36 percent in

1980. In Central and Eastern Europe both unionization and coverage rates have dropped year after year since free unions and free collective bargaining were restored. In Western Europe union decline began around 1980 but was milder and bargaining coverage remained close to 80 percent until 2008, with lower and declining coverage rates in the UK, Ireland, and Switzerland, and slow but continuous decline in Germany.

7.8.7   Sectoral and Enterprise Bargaining

Enterprise bargaining (US, Canada, Mexico, Chile, Turkey, most Asian and Central Eastern European countries, the UK, and Ireland) is associated with declining union density and coverage, and bargaining coverage is as exclusive as union membership. Multi-employer bargaining (as in continental Western Europe, but also in Argentina, Uruguay, Brazil, or South Africa) allows both rates to diverge, with inclusive bargaining coverage rates in spite of union decline. Employers face different choices under enterprise and sectoral bargaining. Under conditions of enterprise bargaining they may withhold or withdraw union recognition as a credible threat in seeking a cheaper or less constraining contract, or else relocate employment to a nonunion environment. Newly established firms may refuse recognition to begin with and base the choice of where to invest on how easy it is to avoid unions. Union contracts tend to become associated with older firms and investments, and coverage and unionization rates decrease together with declining employment in older firms and sectors. Legally mandated union recognition procedures, based on elections in which workers must choose between offers from the union and threats issued by the employer, as in the USA and since 2000 in the UK, have done nothing to stop the erosion in bargaining coverage and union representation.

When collective agreements apply to whole branches of the economy, employers seeking a change in the contract face a different choice. They cannot easily escape collective arrangements by switching to a nonunion environment, at least not when staying in the same sector and country. They can outsource activities to firms and subcontractors located in branches with cheaper collective agreements; make greater use of "flexible employment"; discontinue membership in employers' associations; or work hard to obtain a change in the sector agreement, for instance transforming it into a framework for local negotiations. All of these strategies have been used and are visible in the data, but the overall impact on coverage rates is not a priori clear. The change to less-prescribing sectoral agreements in Scandinavia, combined with local wage negotiations, tends to have increased or stabilized bargaining coverage. Outsourcing to cheaper contracts and greater use of flexible employment has been matched by an increase of bargaining coverage in industrial cleaning, catering and security, and for temporary agency and part-time workers in the Netherlands.

7.8.8   Minimum Wages

To offset decreasing union and bargaining coverage, many countries, among them all the postcommunist countries in Central and Eastern Europe, as well as Britain, Ireland, Israel, and most recently Germany, have introduced a statutory minimum wage. In the eight European countries without a statutory minimum, high bargaining coverage rates supported by union action (Sweden and Denmark), extension of sectoral agreements (Finland, Iceland, Norway, Austria, Switzerland), judicial action (Italy) or special mandates for setting minimum wages in nonunionized sectors (Switzerland) assure minimum standards in most sectors. The USA and Canada introduced minimum wage legislation as far back as in the 1930s, later followed by most countries in Central and South America. China adopted a minimum in 1994, which was strengthened in 2004; South Africa did so after the end of apartheid; Brazil strengthened its system of regional minimum wages in 1995 with further increases in 2005; the Russian Federation complemented its national minimum wage with regional floors in 2007; In South east Asia, after Korea and Japan, the latest countries to introduce a statutory minimum are Malaysia, Myanmar, and Laos, in Africa Cabo Verde recently introduced a national minimum.

Besides issues of monitoring and law enforcement, legislation cannot match the flexibility of collective bargaining, not does it provide for participation and involvement of people affected by the outcomes. Not only the level but also the setting of the minimum wage varies across the word, and so will the effects on collective bargaining. Its adjustment may be an autonomous political decision, as in the USA; the

result of expert consultation (UK) or a national agreement between the social partners (Belgium); adjustments may follow changes in contractual wages (Netherlands, Germany) or occasionally overtake sectoral minima and contractual changes (France, Portugal). Whether the minimum wage complements or replaces collective bargaining depends on such features. In its recently published policy guideline the ILO recommends broad legal coverage, full consultation, or direct participation of the social partners, and setting the minimum wage at a level that ensures a living wage for working people and takes account of the effect on employment (ILO 2016). Most countries have fixed the minimum wage somewhere between 45 and 60 percent of the median, with outliers below 40 or even 30 percent in Estonia, the Czech Republic, Vietnam, Mali, or India, and a higher minimum wage above 65 percent in France, Indonesia, and the Philippines. The relative high minimum wage in some developing countries (measured by the distance to the median) reflects the much larger wage inequality (relatively flat at the bottom, with large spikes at the top) in these countries (ILO 2017).

7.8.9   Wage Inequality

Unions, collective bargaining, and minimum wages tend to reduce wage inequality. The size and shape of the effect depends on how collective bargaining is organized. The minimum wage tends to compress wages at the lower end. By raising wages within the lowest-paying firms it tends to decrease between-firm inequality, in part by truncating low-pay employment. Enterprise bargaining tends to reduce inequality within firm. When collective bargaining takes place at national or industry level, not only are more workers covered but inequality tends to be reduced both within and across firms, and differences between union and nonunion members tend to be smaller. Decentralization, such as the change from national to sectoral bargaining in Sweden or the increased use of opening clauses in sectoral agreements in Germany have been associated with increases in wage inequality.

Across countries, wage inequality tends to be lower where collective bargaining is inclusive, as indicated by higher coverage rates and sectoral rather than enterprise bargaining (Hayter 2015). The highest inequality is found in countries in which sectoral and national wage bargaining has disappeared and is inexistent. Jaumotte and Buitron (2015), using a panel regression analysis of 20 advanced economies from 1980 to 2010, found that union (and bargaining) decline is strongly related to rising incomes (not just wage) inequality *at the top* of the distribution. Three potential mechanisms might account for this: stagnation of the "middle class" and of wages at the lower and middle end, which "mechanically" increases the "top" share; changes in firm behavior and less influence of unions on (sharply rising) executive pay; declining power and voice of unions in politics influencing redistributive policies and taxation.

7.8.10   Conclusion

Collective bargaining, as an established practice and institution which has existed well over 100 years, is under pressure. In many parts of the world it is an institution in retreat, alongside the decline in union organization. This weakening is bad news for workers, especially for those with little individual bargaining power. Collective bargaining is for them the main tool to provide protection, voice, empowerment, and fair participation in the process and proceeds of labor. Governments may step in and in most countries they do provide basic protection, at minimum levels, on wages, working hours, and workers' rights. The recent Great Recession combined with "the longer-running trend of rising inequality have added momentum to minimum-wage debates" (OECD 2015a: 1). Will it turn trends in collective bargaining and union organizing?

To counter decline, unions have attempted to build new membership and networks in hitherto unorganized sectors and seek representation and recognition for contingent and part-time workers, the self-employed and migrant workers. Collective bargaining for the dependent self-employed is now on the agenda of European trade unions, requiring changes in competition law and extension of social insurance coverage. In Brazil and India, to name only two countries with a large informal economy, millions of workers in the informal sector, without social insurance and employment protection, have organized. The Self-Employed Women's Association in India, which operates as trade union, cooperative, and bank, has inspired similar organizations elsewhere. Since 2000 international framework agreements between global union federations and leading multinational corporations, mostly with their home basis in Europe, have proliferated and currently some 200 agreements are in operation. Their aim is to secure core labor rights across multinational corporations' global supply chains. As "soft law" instruments they cast a public spotlight on the normative significance of fundamental social standards and workers' rights. By promising to respect core labor right as defined by the ILO and not obstruct worker efforts to organize, such initiatives may help workers in subsidiaries, including those located in the USA, to seek representation and recognition.

7.9 Skill Formation and the Labor Market

Since the seminal works of Schultz (1961) and Becker (1962), the role of human capital formation has become central to all discussions about the development of individual potentials and their performance in the labor market, and more broadly, on the success of societies to improve the overall well-being of their citizens. By human capital formation it is understood the process of investment and accumulation of a set of skills, abilities, and productivity characteristics that an individual acquire along her life-cycle. Although investments in human capital encompass several dimensions of skills and ability acquisition we concentrate this section on the issues of investment on formal education and training.

Human capital can be divided into general human capital and specific human capital (Becker 1993). General human capital is the stock of skills and knowledge that can be used productively by the individual in any economic activity or task. It is a generic knowledge or skills that are transferable across tasks, sectors, or firms. For instance, being literate or able to perform analytical reasoning are skills that are transferable from one task to the other. Specific human capital is the stock of knowledge or skills that are useful in a specific task or company

only. The knowledge to operate a specific technology, for example, is valuable to perform that particular task but not very valuable for other tasks or activities. General education is an investment in general human capital and vocational education can be investment in either general or specific human capital.

Human capital theory predicts that individuals with higher human capital have higher earnings. Mincer (1974) developed an empirical model based on human capital theory to estimate the rewards of the productivity characteristics in the labor market and, under certain hypothesis, the returns to schooling. In general, the returns to one extra year of schooling estimated ranged from 5 to 15 percent among the higher income countries (Card 1999).

Another important aspect of the empirical literature is the issue of measurement of human capital. The proxy that is widely used is the number of completed years of schooling of the individuals in cross-sectional studies and the average completed years of schooling in cross-country studies (Barro 1997). More recently, this measure has been called into question. Hanushek and Woessmann (2015) argue that the average years of schooling in a population is not a good proxy for the stock of human capital of a country. More important is the level of cognitive skill of the people, indicated by cognitive ability measures such as test scores.

7.9.1 The Technology of the Life-Cycle Skill Formation

Cunha and Heckman (2007) and Cunha et al. (2006), based on several studies of individual's skill formation, develop a very useful analytical framework to discuss the technology of individual's investment in human capital through her life-cycle. Skill formation is a life-cycle process. Skills are multidimensional and their acquisitions occur in several periods from childhood to adulthood. The process of skill formation exhibits two main properties, self-productivity, and complementarity. Self-productivity is the property that a skill obtained in one stage of life augments the subsequent attainment of other skills later in life. For instance, self-control learned early in life can boost the learning of cognitive skills later on. Complementarity is the property that a skill attained in one period increases the productivity of the human capital investment in future periods. For instance, children exposed to storytelling early on improve their vocabulary so that the investments on learning later on are more productive. Thus self-productivity and complementarity generate multiplier effects in skill formation. Skill investments at different stages boost each other and earlier investment must be complemented by later investment in order for the early investment to be productive.

These two properties have some important implications. First, it implies that the skill formation has critical periods and sensitive periods. A critical period of a skill is a stage of life when such a skill must be attained; otherwise it will not be acquired anymore. The sensitive period is the stage when a skill is obtained at the lowest cost or effort. Second, it implies that there is no equity-efficiency tradeoff in the early life investments. The returns to remediation policies for disadvantaged adolescents are lower than the returns to investments at early childhood among children from disadvantaged background.

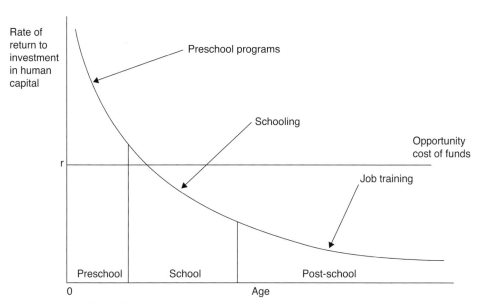

Rates of return to human capital investment initially setting investment
to be equal across all ages

Figure 7.16 | Rates of return to investment in human capital.
Source: Cunha et al. (2006)

The technology of skill formation has a dynamic implication for how human capital investment should be distributed across the life-cycle. Figure 7.16 depicts the summary of the findings of this large empirical literature that suggests that earlier age investments has greater marginal returns compared to later life investments. The horizontal axis represents the individual's age. The vertical axis represents the returns to investment in human capital. Assuming (1) that the amount invested in each period is the same, (2) the cost of the investment is constant and exogenous, and (3) the individual has enough funds to finance the investments, investments in human capital presents decreasing marginal returns and the individuals will invest up to the point that the marginal gain (represented by the curved line) is equal the marginal cost r of funds.

7.9.2 Cognitive and Socio-emotional Abilities

The recent literature on life-cycle skill formation has emphasized the fact the skills are multidimensional and both cognitive and socio-emotional abilities are important for a successful adult life. Several studies have documented that cognitive abilities are important determinants of schooling, wages, and other socio-economic outcomes in the adult life (Heckman 1995; Murnane, Willett, and Levy 1995).

There are also evidences that socio-emotional abilities have important direct effects on adult outcomes. Abilities such as perseverance, motivation, time preference, risk aversion, self-esteem, and self-control have direct impacts on schooling as well as on wages and crime behavior (over and above schooling) (Borghans, Duckworth, Heckman, and ter Weel 2008; Bowles, Gintis, and Osborne 2001; Heckman, Stixrud, and Urzua 2006).

7.9.3 The Role of the Early Childhood Investments

Abilities are malleable and can be strongly influenced by the environment. Abilities attained during early childhood are crucial to the development of an individual's lifetime skills. Ability gaps across individuals of different family and economic background appear at early ages and remains later in life (Cunha and Heckman 2006).

There are evidences, however, that appropriate early childhood interventions can be very effective in reducing or even closing the ability gaps across children of different socio-economic backgrounds. For instance, the Perry Preschool Program, an early childhood program at Chicago targeted at disadvantaged children and which was evaluated experimentally, has significant impacts on several dimensions in adult life such as cognitive tests, employment, earnings, crime behavior, and others (Schweinhart et al. 2005).

7.9.4 Schooling in the Developing World: The Role of Credit Constraints

Improvements in the human capital of the individuals are crucial to the development process. Lower income countries exhibit less average years of schooling compared to higher income countries. Figure 7.17 presents the average years of schooling of the adult population of 187 countries in 2012.

Barro and Lee (2013) compile these figures using the available data for most of the countries. The average years of schooling across all countries is around eight years of schooling. The lowest is Burkina Faso with 1.8 and the highest is Germany and the US with 12.9.

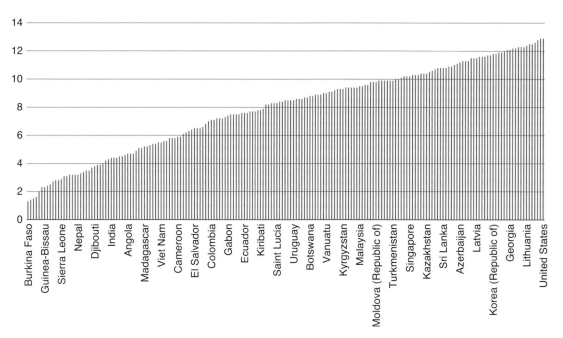

Figure 7.17 | Average years of schooling of adults by countries, 2012.
Source: Barro and Lee (2013)

The interaction between low income and low education perpetuates the situation characterized as a poverty trap. Many channels can generate poverty traps. One central channel is the role of credit markets in the financing of human capital investments. Poor individuals cannot afford to pay for their education. If they cannot borrow from the credit market, they do not invest in their human capital. In general, poor families lack resources or assets that are used as collaterals for loans. In the absence of a developed credit market which accepts higher future earnings as collaterals for the loans, poor families would invest less in the education of their offspring. Having less education, they would remain poor. On the other hand, richer families are able to invest more in human capital and thereby to earn more in the future. The presence of credit constraints can explain why individuals have different levels of schooling and income within a country (Orazem and King 2008) or why countries differ in their levels of income and human capital (Ljungqvist 1993).

Several policies have been implemented to improve the human capital accumulation in developing countries. From the demand side, conditional cash transfer programs, school subsidies, and voucher programs have been experimented with in many countries. On the other hand, improvement in school access and school quality and teachers' training are examples of policies in the supply side. The results are mixed. Many policies aimed to increase school enrollment have been successful although improving learning is still a challenge (Glewwe and Kremer 2006). The effectiveness of the educational policies seems to depend on the appropriate policy design that is well-adjusted to the context (Behrman 2010).

7.9.5   Vocational Education and Training

An alternative to the general education path is vocational education and training (VET). This form of education seeks to provide practical

experience in a particular occupational field, thereby often breeding specific human capital. VET programs are usually known for easing the school to work transition, increasing workers' productivity and helping provide the market with demanded specific skilled labor. Nonetheless several aspects of this form of education are still unclear: The long term benefits of vocational education, who should pay for it or which system to use, for example, are still up to debate.

7.9.5.1   The Tradeoffs between General and Specific Human Capital Investments

On that aspect, one of the first works to assay the tradeoffs of specific human capital investments was Becker (1962). Becker defines general human capital as the type of human capital that increases a worker's productivity in all firms. Opposed to it, there is the specific human capital which is a form of capital that increases productivity by different amounts in each firm. For example, a doctor trained internally in a hospital can use her skills in other hospitals and hence it is considered a general skill. The ability to operate special equipment used in one firm only can be considered a specific skill.

One advantage of vocational education programs is that they are able to provide workers with both types of skills. Technical schools for example are known for breeding general human capital that can be used throughout an entire industry. On-the-job training programs, on the other hand, provide workers with a specific human capital for a particular firm.

7.9.5.2   Short-Term and Long-Term Benefits

One common claim about specific human capital investments is that it eases the school to work transition by decreasing the

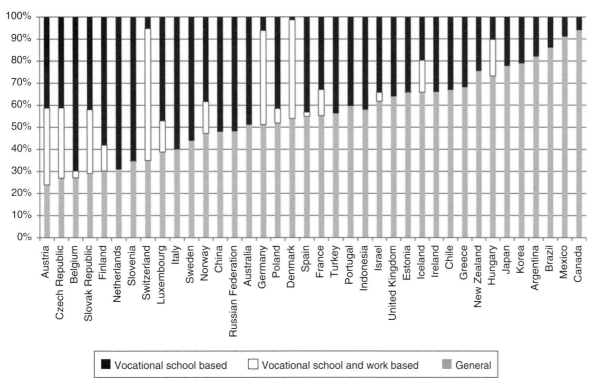

Figure 7.18 | Shares of general, vocational and "dual" vocational education enrollment at upper secondary level in selected countries in 2011.
Source: Zimmermann et al. (2013)

probability of unemployment after high-school. Hanushek et al. (2011) provides an interesting analysis of life-long benefits of this different type of education. After carefully examining unemployment trends in several countries Hanushek et al. (2011) concludes that even though vocational education paths may lead to an increase in employability on the short term after graduation, this effect tends to be dissipated over time. In fact, at later stages of life, general education programs seem to contribute more to an increase in worker's employability.

Although varying considerably by country Hanushek et al. (2011) argues that one reason for this difference is that individuals with general education are more likely to take a career-related training than individuals with a specific education. That means that general education generally puts workers in a better position to update their skills, an important asset in dynamic economies.

7.9.5.3   Firms' vs. Individuals' Investments

Becker (1993) argues that since in competitive markets wages are equal to marginal productivity, firms would have no incentives to make general human capital investments because any marginal productivity increase would be offset by an equal increase in wages. A firm will only offer training if its costs are paid by its employees, who ultimately are the ones that will benefit from the higher wages. Since specific human capital is defined as the type of training that increases productivity for one specific firm only the wage assumption does not hold. That is, the individual cannot find a higher wage elsewhere and hence the firm can benefit from retaining the services of the trained worker.

The practical implications of this theory is that firms tend to pay for specific human capital training since they benefit from the higher productivity of workers while workers pay for general human capital formation since in this case they benefit from the higher wages. Although purely specific and purely general human capitals are rare in practice, Becker's model is considered to be an important insight on the forms of financing the investments on human capital.

7.9.5.4   "In Class" Training vs. "On the Job" Training

Countries differ significantly on the relative amount of investment in general and vocational education. Additionally, VET systems vary significantly across countries. Figure 7.18 shows the proportion of workers by type of education across selected countries. Some countries rely heavily on general education such as Canada and others rely more on VET such as Austria. As noticed in Eichhorst et al. (2015) three main categories stand out: the vocational and technical schools, the formal apprenticeship programs and the dual system. The vocational and technical schools are more typical of Southern European countries. This system relies on the educational system to provide the practical skills demanded by specific occupations. Although still considered vocational education, vocational and technical schools deal with a highly transferable form of knowledge when considering the Becker model and thus can be used to increase the productivity of an entire industry and not only a particular firm.

Second, in the formal apprenticeship programs, most commonly found on the United States, United Kingdom, and in Australia, human capital is acquired mostly on the workplace, with institutional instruction serving merely as a complement. Unlike the previous system, apprenticeships teach a very specific type of skill.

Finally, there is the dual system. Typical of Germanic countries such as Austria, Switzerland, and Germany this system is in a middle ground between apprenticeship and vocational and technical schools. Displaying a high degree of formalization and a strong involvement of the social partners, this system relies on both vocational schools and employers to provide vocational training. While knowledge from this system is considerably more transferable than in the previous one, governments usually bear the costs of training in schools, while institutional framework allows companies benefit from trained workers.

7.9.5.5 The Challenges of the Matching between the Structure of the Supply of the Vocational Training and the Structure of the Occupations in the Labor Market

Another common argument about vocational education, or about more specific types of human capital, is that it leads to higher horizontal mismatches. That is, since the vocational education demands very specific skills then the chances of mismatches between the field of training and the job structure are higher. This correlation between specific human capital and horizontal mismatch was first noticed in Robst (2007) at the college level but can also be applied to VET courses. In a recent article however, Eymann and Schweri (2015) finds no evidence that this mismatch leads to a wage penalty in a highly vocational education oriented country like Switzerland.

On the other hand Mavromaras et al. (2012) finds that vocational educational workers are less prone to vertical mismatches when compared to other workers with more general degrees. That is, workers in vocational tracks have a lower probability of being considered overskilled or underskilled for the job they hold. Although the final impacts of vocational training on mismatches is still open to debate (Kahn 2015), it seems clear that school-based VET are more effective when a proper match can be made between the vocational training and the future occupation of employment (Zimmermann et al. 2013; Eichhorst et al. 2015).

Although vocational education increases the chances of employment, there are two concerns about it. First, there is a broader concern about the right mix of general and specific knowledge a young individual should acquire. General skills that include a minimum amount of culture that allows individuals to become an engaged good citizen are desired. Too early entry in the vocational track may hamper the acquisition of this type of general skills. Second, the rapid changing technologies increase the risks skill obsolescence. The challenge is to design a training system that allows individuals be retrained frequently.

7.9.6 Tertiary Education

Higher education is an important path for many students There are several evidences for many different countries that the college wage premium is high (Peracchi 2006). However, countries differ significantly concerning access to higher education. For instance, around two-thirds of high school graduates access some form of postsecondary education in the US (McPerson and Schapiro 2006), whereas this figure is less than 15 percent in Brazil.

Given that it is highly specialized, higher education is very costly. This fact raises several questions regarding efficiency and equity issues. On one hand, even among higher income countries, there are credit-constrained families that cannot afford its cost. Some of these potential students could profit from going to college beyond its cost. Moreover, higher education can generate positive externalities on societies. It can help, for instance, promote technological change and generate better-informed public debate. Additionally, if selection into college is merit-based only, it can raise inequalities and perpetuate low diversity among higher education population. If the provision is left to the market alone, it can create inequities (Chapman 2006).

Countries have tackled the higher education access issue in different ways. There are cases where the supply of higher education is public and fully subsided to the students (some European and Latin American countries) and other that the supply are public or private but it is subsidized through student loans (USA, UK). Clearly, there is no silver bullet to the best way to provide higher education. Fully subsidized and free access to higher education has the advantage of allowing a greater access but with high costs that may lead to overeducation (Groot et al. 2000). Credit and students loans may be a better way to enable self-selection by individuals into college but in order to be effective it has to be well designed and implemented (Chapman 2006).

The challenge is that the increase of life expectation and the expansion of the technological frontier push for higher education expansion and the societies have to find creative ways to provide affordable access to the new generations.

7.9.7 On the Job Training

Individuals can continue to accumulate human capital after they have completed their formal education through further investments in on the job training. Training on the job can occur through learning by doing or through formal training programs at or away from the workplace. The costs of such investments include the reduced productivity of the trainees during the learning process and the time devoted by the trainers. The benefits for the worker are the gains in productivity later on. These investments can be in general or specific human capital. Generally, employees and employers share their costs. The greater the investment there is in specific human capital the greater the cost share born by employers.

There is empirical evidence that on the job training increases worker's productivity. Haelermas and Borghans (2011) conduct a meta-analysis of the wage effects of on the job training and find that it increases wages, on average, by 2.6 percentage points. Adjusting for hours spent on the job training and schooling, and assuming the rate of return to schooling is 8 percent, the authors estimate that training courses are profitable until the age of mid-50.

Of course, there is great heterogeneity across training courses. Knowledge about the expected wage returns of a specific program is important for a firm to decide which investments on the job training to provide. Moreover, if well designed, on the job training can be a helpful policy for those that missed the earlier opportunity to invest in their human capital and need to catch up later in life. For instance, Heinrich et al. (2013) find positive impacts on earnings and employment of the two primary adult workforce support and training programs under the US Workforce Investment Act (WIA).

7.9.8   Concluding Remarks

There is accumulated evidence about the importance of investments in human capital for an individual's productive and successful adult life. The correct human capital investments in the appropriate time along the life-cycle of the skill formation can have lasting effects. And well-designed interventions can mitigate or even compensate those less fortunate individuals that did not have the appropriate human capital investment early on.

There are some clear policy recommendations from this literature. First, appropriate early childhood investments are crucial for an individual's success in life and are the most cost-effective way to reduce inequalities of opportunities. Thus, governments should create opportunities for early childhood investments for all and appropriate interventions for those less fortunate children in order to avoid potential future risks for their human capital accumulation process.

Second, skills beget skills. Thus, later life investments should be made so that the development of abilities and skills be fully realized. Governments should provide opportunities for the continuation of the human capital investment process. Special attention should be given to mobility between different educational tracks, and avoiding early selection and dead ends.

Third, even if an individual reach adult life with lags and gaps on their human capital, there are appropriate policies that can mitigate or compensate for these gaps. In these cases, government can provide appropriate policies that need to be well designed and contextualized in order to bear their full fruits.

Finally, since the technology and occupation changes are increasingly becoming facts of life, appropriate institutions of training and retraining workers should be put in place with sufficient fluidity so that demand and supply of skills are adjusted appropriately.

7.10   Protection against Labor Market Risks: Employment Protection, Unemployment Benefits, and Active Labor Market Policies

The welfare state has a major influence on the functioning of the labor market through different types of benefits, work incentives, and active labor market policies, but these institutions also interact with other labor market institutions such as employment protection, human capital formation, or wage setting. From the perspective of social progress in times of constant economic change, technological innovations, and globalization, it is an important empirical research topic and a policy issue to understand and adapt labor market institutions and welfare state features in order to balance flexibility and security in line with a progressive orientation. Therefore, the different pillars of protection against labor market risks need to be analyzed – employment protection, unemployment benefits, and active labor market policies – but special attention has to be paid on design issues that relate to the interaction of the three pillars.

7.10.1   Where Do We Stand and What Are the Trends in Employment Protection?

Employment protection legislation (EPL) is a set of norms governing the dismissal and the hiring of employees. The rules of employment protection can have several objectives: protecting employees against the abusive behavior of employers, limiting dismissals to reduce the social costs of reorganizing the productive apparatus, stabilizing the total volume of employment, increasing employment, etc.

Figure 7.19 displays the OECD indicator of the strictness of EPL for workers on regular contracts, which focuses on the conditions for terminating employment and the consequences if a dismissal is found to be unfair. The OECD indicator goes from 0, for the less strict regulation, to 5 for the most stringent. Figure 7.19 shows that there is a strong heterogeneity across OECD countries in 2013. The stringency of regulation is low in English-speaking and common law countries whereas it is high, above the OECD average, in the Czech Republic, Portugal, France, the Netherlands, and Germany. EPL is also an issue in many developing countries which are featuring stringent EPL in their formal sector.

The actual heterogeneity in the strictness of employment protection may be even more pronounced than that displayed in Figure 7.19 because the OECD only reports the mandatory legislative restrictions governing recruitment and dismissal. In practice, employment protection can be specified in legislation, collective agreements, or individual employment contracts. It also depends on the interpretation of rules by courts or tribunals and the effectiveness of enforcement that are not accounted for by the OECD indicator.

Economic analysis indicates that EPL mainly has an ambiguous impact on unemployment and employment. Of course, employment protection reduces the destruction of permanent jobs. However, on the other hand, it reduces employment creation, as the additional costs induced by maintaining an unprofitable workforce reduces the anticipated profitability of new jobs. Furthermore, EPL can increase the stability of some jobs and increase the instability of other jobs not concerned by the most restrictive provisions, leading to more dualism or segmentation in the labor market. EPL also has an ambiguous impact on productivity: on one hand it can improve the experience of workers because it increases their job tenure, but on the other hand it may weaken the necessary reallocation of the labor force toward more productive jobs.

Many empirical studies have been devoted to EPL over the last two decades, exploiting natural experiments provided by reforms of EPL.

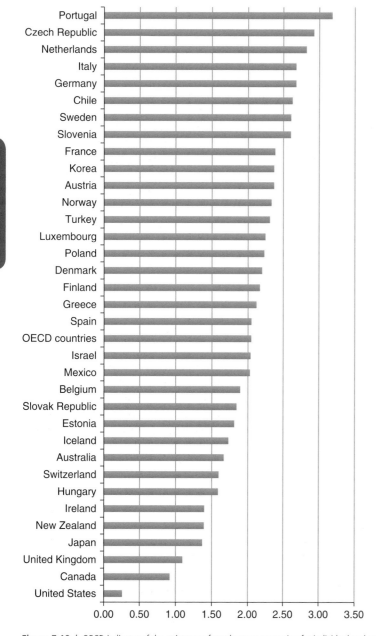

Figure 7.19 | OECD indicator of the strictness of employment protection for individual and collective dismissals (regular contracts) in 2013.
Source: OECD Indicators of Employment Protection database

The empirical literature which relies on microeconomic data with proper identification strategies finds that more stringent EPL reduces labor turnover of permanent workers, but has adverse effects on overall employment and increases the instability of temporary jobs (see Boeri et al. 2015, for a recent survey). EPL also reduces labor productivity and lengthen unemployment spells.

All in all, EPL has strong redistributive implications. It protects those who already have a job, notably a permanent contract in the formal sector. Unemployed individuals and workers with temporary contracts generally suffer in the presence of strict EPL rules for permanent contracts and therefore gain from labor market flexibility enhancing reforms, notably when they are implemented uniformly across the board rather than being confined to new hires in new types of contracts. Two-tier regimes that allow for the coexistence of very rigid and very flexible contract types indeed increase labor market segmentation, preventing the outsiders from having access to the primary labor market of permanent contracts. Therefore, EPL does not appear to be an efficient tool to protect workers against economic uncertainty.

7.10.2 What Do Principles of Justice Suggest?

7.10.2.1 Protecting Employees against Abusive Dismissals

The need to protect employees against abusive dismissals constitutes an objective of employment protection in Europe. It is the doctrine of the "just cause," which states that employers cannot fire their employees without invoking a proper reason. This doctrine is not applied everywhere. For example, the United States, which have the lowest degree of strictness of job protection among OECD countries, have adopted the doctrine of employment at will, which states that an employer can terminate a work contract for good reasons, bad reasons or without reason, as long as it does not infringe fundamental human rights. This doctrine, which does have a few exceptions in the United States, is justified by the idea that imposing constraints on the choice of work contracts is more of an inconvenience than an advantage for employees. They are free to negotiate redundancy payments, even for lower salaries, if they want. However, according to this doctrine, imposing legal redundancy payments would have negative effects on salaries or other benefits that an employee would get out of the employment relationship, which an employee does not necessarily want.

This doctrine is valid in an environment where the labor market works in a perfectly competitive manner without information asymmetry between employers, employees, and public authorities. This is obviously not the case in general. As such, the doctrine of the just cause needs relevant justification. For example, an employer can fire employees because they demand the application of costly regulations, even if they are useful for the entire company, like regulating work accident prevention. This kind of dismissal is clearly abusive: it goes against a regulation that is justified by efficiency and fairness.

7.10.2.2 Providing Insurance against Dismissals

Besides justifying EPL by the need to protect workers from arbitrary actions by employers, it can be argued that employment protection can provide insurance to workers when the lack of public employment insurance or imperfection of financial markets limit the possibilities for workers to insure themselves against dismissals. However, job protection inhibits the ability of firms to adapt their manpower and hinders the reallocation of workers toward more productive jobs. More stringent protection of open-ended contract also induces firms to use more temporary jobs, which increases job turnover and labor market segmentation. From this perspective, job protection is clearly not the best policy to provide insurance against dismissals. Unemployment insurance accompanied by active labor market policies aiming at facilitating the reallocation of workers from low to high productive jobs is much more efficient than job protection.

7.10.2.3 Job Protection and the Social Value of Employment

The decision to destroy a job can have repercussions that go far beyond just the interests of the company and the employee concerned. In this case, the value of a job for the whole economy – its social value – is different from its private value.

An important reason for the gap between the social value and private value of a job resides in the design of the tax system. A very large majority of tax revenues come from people who have a job. The unemployed and the inactive contribute very little to financing collective goods and transfers. This results in a difference between the social value and private value of a job, measured by the loss of obligatory contributions and the additional costs in the form of social transfers induced by the passage of the status of employee to that of unemployed or nonworking.

In this context, an employer that fires one of its employees counts on the other employees and employers to finance the benefits of the dismissed employee. This employer also does not taken into account the fact that the job they destroyed will no longer help finance unemployment insurance. By neglecting the fiscal consequences caused by their behavior when they dismiss someone, companies only take into account the personal costs of what they suffer and not the actual cost of this dismissal for the group. In situations where this actual cost exceeds the personal costs, companies will have a tendency to destroy too many jobs. As stressed by Blanchard and Tirole (2007), a tax on layoffs, proportional to the social cost induced by layoffs can constitute a form of EPL that incentivizes employers to take socially efficient layoff decisions.

7.10.2.4 Major Obstacles and Opportunities

Governments carry out reforms to increase the flexibility of the labor market. Nevertheless, most frequently, these reforms essentially made the labor market flexible at the fringe by facilitating the use of temporary jobs without significantly modifying the protection of permanent jobs. In many European countries, this evolution has resulted in a strong segmentation of the labor market, with a market for temporary jobs, reserved as a priority for labor market entrants and reentrants (youth, women who have to stop working to deal with care responsibilities, immigrants, and less qualified employees), and a market for permanent jobs, reserved as a priority to the most qualified employees with good professional experience. In this context, temporary jobs act as an adjustment variable, and it is the most precarious populations that are systematically the most affected by recessions.

The segmentation of the labor market between temporary and permanent jobs raises more issues than just those of fairness. It also causes an ineffective rotation of the workforce on many levels. Firstly, it translates into a rotation excess of the workforce, as companies avoid transforming temporary jobs into permanent jobs when the costs of parting with the employee are different. Consequently, the employees in temporary jobs that stay with the company for a limited time benefit less often from professional training programs and have more problems building up a professional career. Moreover, the strong protection of permanent jobs, characteristic of highly segmented labor markets, limits the reorganization possibilities of a large part of the productive apparatus.

In order to complete labor market reforms, as a priority, governments should reduce the segmentation between temporary and permanent jobs and align the social and the private values of employment. A foreseeable strategy consists in substituting Pigouvian layoff taxes (setting incentives to avoid negative external effects) to the rules that limit the dismissals for economic causes. The details of implementing this strategy depend of course on each national context (Garcia Pérez 2015). These reforms should be part of a comprehensive package that

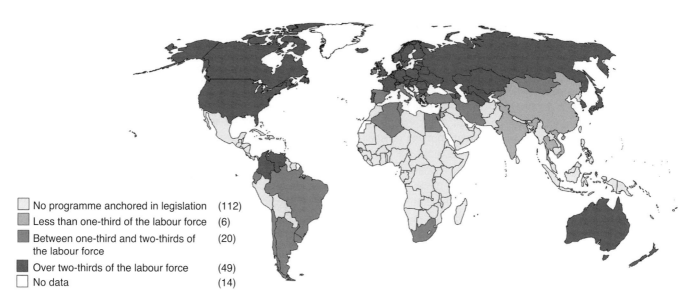

No programme anchored in legislation   (112)
Less than one-third of the labour force (6)
Between one-third and two-thirds of   (20)
the labour force
Over two-thirds of the labour force   (49)
No data   (14)

Figure 7.20 | Unemployment protection schemes worldwide by extent of legal coverage of the labor force, latest available year.
Note: Figures in brackets refer to the number of countries in each group. Data from 2009–2013; for most countries, 2012/13.
Source: ILO World Social Protection Report 2014/2015

promotes a better safety net and the reallocation of labor toward more productive jobs relying on effective unemployment insurance and reemployment services (Scarpetta 2014; Eichhorst, Marx, and Wehner 2016), effectively linking the functioning of the different pillars of protection so that they support each other in providing flexibility and security at the same time and in a fair and balanced way.

7.10.3   Unemployment Benefits and Active Labor Market Policies

Welfare state elements such as unemployment benefits and active labor market policies can provide security of income and adaptability via better reemployment chances in a flexible and turbulent labor market. This understanding of unemployment protection allows for the reconciliation of security objectives with a flexible labor market that depends on successful transitions from job to job.

Most countries with unemployment benefits have a two-tier system based on (a) unemployment insurance linked to contributions during employment that provides earnings-related benefits for a limited duration; and (b) means-tested income support schemes for those unemployed people with no or insufficient entitlements to insurance benefits. Figures 7.20 and 7.21 however show the huge differences in formal and effective coverage by unemployment benefit systems. In many low- and medium-income countries access to benefits is very limited.

The effects of benefit systems on income, employment trajectories, and other indicators have been analyzed intensively. First, it can be shown that unemployment benefits play a stabilizing role at the level of the individual or household as well as at the level of the economy. On the one hand, they compensate for part of the individual income loss due to unemployment, and on the other hand, as they kick in quickly in a

recession with increasing unemployment, they can effectively stabilize domestic demand (Dolls, Fuest, and Peichl 2012). Hence, well-designed and accessible benefits can help avoid poverty, social exclusion, and an aggravation of economic slumps.

Second, unemployment benefits, in particular regarding earnings-related unemployment benefits collected in the initial phase of unemployment, can help protect acquired human capital as the unemployed are not forced to take up the first best jobs, but can afford some time to find the best available job match. At the individual level, this can lead to better labor market transitions, more productive employment and higher earnings, while, at the aggregate level, better job matches imply a more productive employment of those in the labor force. More generally speaking, unemployment benefits systems can serve as a mechanism to ensure the acceptance of a flexible and dynamic labor market (with less rigid EPL) that is characterized by creative destruction and job turnover associated with labor turnover that requires an adaptable and productive labor force. If employment protection becomes dysfunctional to the extent that it stabilizes obsolete jobs and tends to slow down structural change by hampering mobility to more dynamic sectors, well-designed unemployment benefits (articulated with effective ALMPs) can ensure a more mobility-friendly, dynamic labor market. However, in particular, insurance benefits can lead to a double disadvantage for those that have only relatively short employment records such as young people, women who have interrupted participation due to care responsibilities, labor market entrants.

Unemployment benefits also interact with alternative benefits such as disability insurance or early retirement options that may lead to early withdrawal from the labor market. In general, designing unemployment benefits in a way to minimize disincentives to work and avoid long-term benefit dependency is a core issue. Benefit systems allow the public employment service to remain in contact with their clients, but to

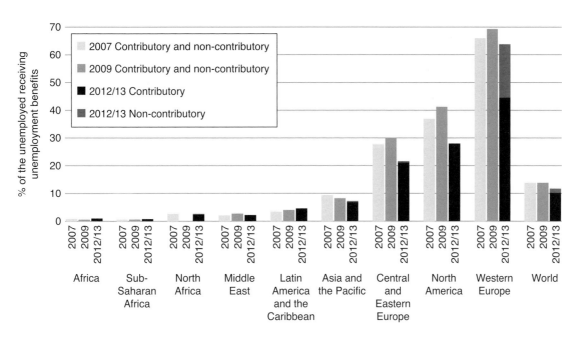

Figure 7.21 | Effective coverage of unemployment benefits, 2007, 2009, and 2012/2013
Notes: Numbers of unemployed receiving unemployment benefits collected from national social security unemployment schemes. Global average weighted by the labor force.
Source: ILO World Social Protection Report 2014/2015

counter potentially long-lasting benefit dependency many OECD countries have turned toward activation over the last two or three decades. Making benefit receipt conditional upon active job search and participation in active labor market policy measures has been the major change in this respect; this implies stricter monitoring and enforcement on the one hand, providing better targeted and tailor support on the other hand. Of course, this could not be achieved without changes to the mode of operation of public employment services and making them more effective (see also Martin 2014; Martin and Grubb 2001; Eichhorst, Kaufmann, and Konle-Seidl 2008; Graversen and van Ours 2008; Rosholm 2014).

When looking at the development of unemployment benefits and ALMPs in major world regions, in particular after the crisis, one major trend has been to try to buffer the impact of the crisis through some benefit expansion, in particular toward vulnerable groups such as fixed-term employees, freelancers, or young people – however, in times of austerity this was oftentimes counterbalanced by retrenchment measures (ILO 2015c; European Commission 2016b). The same holds for ALMPs where both expansionary and curtailing steps could be observed. Hence, there is the challenge of unequal or limited protection and support in some countries, not only developing countries, as regards insurance for labor market entrants, unemployed with short employment spells and in case of exhaustion of insurance benefits.

The evaluation of ALMP has made major progress both in terms of data, methods and establishing a significant body of evidence, mostly for developed countries (Card, Kluve, and Weber 2010, 2015; Carling and Richardson 2004; Jespersen, Munch, and Skipper 2008; Sianesi 2008; Greenberg, Michaloupoulos, and Robins 2003). While micro studies analyze the effects of measures on participants in comparison to similar nonparticipants, macro studies can also take into account

potentially significant side effects such as deadweight losses, displacement, and substitution effects. Apart from that, medium and long-run effects might differ significantly from short-run outcomes of ALMPs.

In general, direct job creation schemes fully funded by the public sector are seen as rather problematic with respect to later entry into the regular labor market. However they may play a certain role for the hardest-to-place, but this requires proper targeting and selection. Publicly sponsored training has been proven to show positive medium- and long-run effects on employment probabilities and subsequent careers, once the lock-in effect during the training period is overcome. Again, carefully designing training programs that prepare for actual work experience is crucial. Subsidizing employment with private employers through temporary hiring incentives is costly and has potential side effects on nonsubsidized workers and firms, but they can lead to higher employment probabilities of those who would not have entered the labor market so quickly. Finally, job search assistance and placement have been identifies as effective and cost-efficient measures. However, there is now also a broad consensus that mainly demanding, work-first interventions based on counseling and strict activation are effective in shortening unemployment, but they work only in such a way for unemployed close to the labor market, but not for others as regards access to decent and sustainable jobs. If there are individual barriers to employment, highly individualized support is preferable, including a broad repertoire of measures, including major training. However, this is quite demanding as regards PES capacities and funding needed.

Active labor market policies are not unaffected by broader institutional arrangements and economic conditions. In rigid labor markets with heavily regulated permanent contracts and other barriers to mobility the role of ALMPs in stimulating entry and career advancement is more limited than in more permeable or "flexible" constellations. And in a situation of weak labor demand, the capacity of the labor market to absorb job searchers is more difficult, even if supported, trained, and advised. In difficult economic situations with high or increasing unemployment, effective delivery of services at high quality might be more problematic due to a lack of appropriate delivery infrastructure and funding possibilities as well as limited labor demand – which implies also that labor market problems cannot be solved through ALMPs. However, there is also some evidence that ALMPs have a larger impact in bad times (Kluve 2010).

Despite many reforms in the labor market, many countries continue to suffer from a high share of long-term unemployed people or otherwise excluded working-age persons. Long-term unemployment can be combatted with tailored supportive services as many studies show particular effectiveness of ALMPs with regard to those at risk of long-term unemployment (ideally at an early stage) (see also Lalive, Morlok, and Zweimüller 2011). However, this requires major fiscal and administrative effort, in particular to deliver appropriate packages of tailored support, including training and other forms of ALMP. For the most difficult to place, some well-targeted forms of subsidized employment may be the only realistic option once all other efforts have failed and when one still wants to ensure social inclusion.

Unemployment benefits and active labor market policies have a long tradition in developed countries, designing proper benefit systems and ALMP delivery structures is an unsolved issue in many developing countries and emerging economies, in particular when there is a high share of informal workers and self-employed. In the formal sector, employment protection and severance pay often ensure against income losses. Noncontributory schemes can play a role here as can steps to establish conditional income support schemes that help move to the formal sector (Robalino 2014). On the ALMP side, public works programs can act as a partial replacement for income support in these cases. All in all, a benefit system combined with active labor market policies generates significant demand for fiscal resources as well as administrative capacities to ensure proper delivery.

Unconditional basic income has been proposed as an alternative to existing conditional benefit schemes with a view of simplifying administration, removing the punitive element of activation policies and facilitating innovation and creativity. However, unconditional basic income is a contested issue as some think that unconditional basic income support would be a plausible option for a future characterized by a decline in paid work while other see this as a risky break with a welfare state and society based on paid work as a major mechanism of societal inclusion, a division of labor and public revenues. In any case, an unconditional basic income would imply a massive change in social policies with fiscal and economic implications that are hard to assess at the outset.

7.10.4   Flexicurity and the Political Economy of Reforms

Linking the institutional elements discussed above, the term flexicurity, as defined by the European Commission, refers to "an integrated strategy for enhancing, at the same time, flexibility and security in the labor market" (European Commission 2007: 5). The strategy was pioneered in Denmark and subsequently began to figure prominently in the policy recommendations of the EU and the OECD (Jorgensen 2005; Viebrock and Clasen 2009). As the name itself suggests, flexicurity policies seek to reconcile employers' increased demands for flexibility with the continuing demands of employees for some measure of job security. On the flexibility side, this involves various measures designed to loosen restrictions on employment, including for example changes to EPL to make it easier or less costly for employers to hire and fire workers, or measures that loosen restrictions on employers' ability to hire workers in various forms of "atypical" (nonstandard) employment (agency work, fixed term contracts, and other forms of irregular (on-demand) employment). On the security side, flexicurity often involves one or more of a bundle of measures designed to support workers in period of unemployment but also – especially – to ease the transition from one job to another – e.g. through assistance with job searches or job placement, or by providing opportunities and support for retraining. Such encouragements and supports are typically accompanied by inducements – e.g. requirements to actively seek alternative employment or to participate in training programs – a kind of activation "stick" to reduce periods of unemployment and dependence on passive (as opposed to active) support.

The idea of flexicurity took hold in some European policy circles in the 1990s as a response to persistently high unemployment, particularly long-term unemployment and unemployment among youth in many countries. From a neoliberal perspective, some economists had long drawn invidious comparisons between Europe's "sclerotic" labor markets and the more flexible labor markets of the US and other "liberal" market economies. While such arguments were often overdrawn, it did appear that high levels of employment protection in some cases contributed to the exclusion of labor market outsiders, "hamper[ing] the transition from employment to work" (Viebrock and Clasen 2009: 7).

While flexibility arguments were thus often brought especially by proponents of deregulation, other critiques emanated from the left, sometimes inspired by the increasing participation of women in the labor market and the growth of various forms of atypical employment. For example, other studies suggested that strong employment protections tend to suppress women's employment (Nelson and Stephens 2013). In this context, social democrats also had their own reasons for questioning the capacity of traditional social protections to protect against new emerging risks in the labor market. As Colin and Palier (2015), for example, pointed out, traditional social policy in many countries organized around the assumption of households headed by male breadwinners enjoying stable careers within a particular firm or industry, was long out of sync with the growing realities of the service and knowledge economies, in which women make up a large proportion of the workforce and in which employment is often less routine and less stable. Adapting social policy to this new reality would require a rethinking of traditional assumptions in which the state would be called upon not just to cover "traditional risks" (above all, occasional spells of unemployment) but to adapt to new emerging risks, including those associated with less continuous career paths, ongoing rapid technological change, and the need to reconcile work and family in a context in which women increasingly participate in the labor market

(Beramendi et al. 2015). This rethinking has been associated with a reorientation of policy initiatives, away from the traditional emphasis on job security toward an increasing focus on employment security – i.e. a retreat from the idea that individuals should be protected against losing a particular job toward facilitating and promoting employability generally – hence the centrality of training and retraining to most conceptions of flexicurity.

Clearly, then, one of the great attractions of flexicurity lies in the appeal it holds for observers and policy-makers on different ends of the ideological spectrum (Viebrock and Clasen 2009). Neoliberals praise the "flexibility" components, i.e. the reductions in traditional employment protections and the activating elements of labor market policy, and urge further moves in this direction. Defenders of social democracy, for their part, stress the "security" aspects and the way the model provides support for those displaced by the market, thus reconciling "adaptability to a changing international environment [with] a solidaristic welfare system [that] protects the citizens from the more brutal consequences of structural change" (Madsen 2002: 243).

The idea of flexicurity first gained traction in the context of the Danish "jobs miracle" of the 1990s. After a decade of soaring joblessness and a suffocating public debt, Denmark succeeded in reducing its unemployment rate dramatically, from over 12 percent to under 5 percent in the late 1990s. Denmark's success has been attributed to a set of policies that have been characterized as involving a "golden triangle" of mutually reinforcing components, namely: flexible labor markets, generous support for the unemployed, and labor market policies that actively underwrite retraining and placement. Some elements of the golden triangle – in particular, relatively low employment protection – were inherited from the past (e.g. Campbell and Hall 2006). Other elements, notably activation and training-based labor market policies were products of policy initiatives in the 1990s (Madsen 2006: 331; also Viebrock and Clasen 2009). Yet even in Denmark, help up as the most successful example of flexicurity, the balance between the "flexibility" and the "security" components continues to be politically contested, as evidence in recent cuts to welfare benefits.

It goes without saying that there is no "one-size-fits-all" flexicurity formula that can simply be copied from one context to another. There is considerable "play" in how policy-makers embrace and implement what travels under the broad banner of flexicurity, and individual countries will have to find their own way. Nonetheless, some of the elements of flexicurity – adapted to local political and institutional conditions – may provide a formula for stabilizing broad political acceptance of enhanced market flexibility while at the same time enhancing the security on which such acceptance ultimately depends.

7.11   Conclusion and Policy Recommendations

7.11.1   Summarizing the Evidence

This chapter aims at summarizing and assessing the global evidence on major factors influencing the future of work. It has become evident that there is a large variation in national developments, yet, there are shared issues of general relevance that make it possible to tell a global story.

Technology and globalization are intimately related forces driving permanent structural change in employment and affecting the global distribution of economic activities and jobs. While there has been permanent technological change, its implications differ with respect to levels of development and speed of adjustment around the globe. Over time, global integration has become stronger, not least facilitated by modern IT and other technological innovation, leading to declining costs of international transactions, but also by political decisions to remove barriers. This all points at the importance of political decisions in shaping the impact globalization can have on the further development of employment patterns. Looking at most recent changes, workers in different parts of the world have been affected quite asymmetrically by technology and globalization. Winners and losers of change can be identified, with a certain tendency toward employment polarization in many developed countries, creating societal and political challenges in compensating for losses while not foregoing the potential wins – and by preparing societies to reap the benefits of technological advancements and global integration through forward-looking, preventive strategies. In addition, demographic change is a major driving force in the world of work around the globe. Diversity in the labor market, induced by demographic factors, is on the increase, with rising employment of women, older workers and migrations, although significant gaps regarding the labor market integration of women, older workers as well as migrants, continue to exist in some regions of the world. Empirical studies into the effects of diversity create a nuanced picture, pointing at the many dimensions of diversity and its consequences.

When looking at different types of employment types we can identify a large variety of contracts, deviating more or less from a permanent, full-time dependent employment status in the formal sector, the standard employment relationship, which is often taken as a benchmark to assess the quality of a job. Part-time work, fixed-term contracts, temporary agency work, but also different forms of self-employment or own-account and crowd work as well as informal employment differ regarding core parameters such as employment stability, earnings and inclusion into social protection from standard employment. Institutional changes, but also changes in the structure of demand and supply for certain skills have opened up this broad diversity of contractual relationships in the world of work around the globe, not least the creation of highly flexible demand patterns and complex value chains in today's economies. Virtually all labor markets exhibit some forms of segmentation, with barriers to mobility between the segments. From a policy perspective, narrowing the regulatory gaps as well as inequality regarding inclusion into social protection between different contract types is a pressing issue, with concrete challenges depending on the national context.

While there is a fragmentation of labor markets characterized by different forms of "external" flexibility, firms have also become more flexible "internally," i.e. as regards their internal processes of working, but in particular regarding working time and mobile working. In general, patterns of working time and workplace flexibility can be in the interest of employers, of workers or both. Over time we have seen many new and diverse arrangements emerging, potentially reconciling productivity and flexibility interests of employers and work/life preferences of workers. There has been an improvement in many cases. Still, there are many issues that can be perceived as problematic from a social progress point of view, in particular very short, very long, and unpredictable working time requirements or ill-designed shift work arrangements that have negative effects on workers' health and families. This is also observed in poorly regulated informal employment or in segments of formal labor markets where working time standards have eroded due to a lack of collective bargaining and appropriate legislation and enforcement.

Moving to the margins of the labor market, different forms of under-, non- or unemployment continue to exist, pointing at a full or partial exclusion of some groups from paid work. Patterns of exclusion and boundaries of the labor market are structured by institutional rules defining certain status forms, and in particular only the existence of a welfare state and social policies make unemployment a useful category and indicator in some regions of the world. This creates measurement issues on the one hand, calling for a multitude of indicators to assess and compare the extent of lack of work, and effective policies to combat unemployment and exclusion on the other hand.

A more heterogeneous workforce can bring about gains in terms of productivity and innovation while requiring additional efforts regarding cohesion and integration. Diversity is also often linked to discrimination. In fact, there is empirical evidence on discrimination in the labor market based on ethnicity, gender, age, disability, sexual, or religious orientation – this is not only creating barriers for individual careers but also implying a loss of productive potentials in the economy. Anti-discrimination rules and systematic awareness raising, monitoring, and enforcement are therefore justified as are positive strategies to change actual practices in the labor market.

Work is a core human activity, and it is intimately related to individual health and well-being. While unemployment is definitively harmful in terms of well-being and health, being employed can help raise individual well-being and health. However, there are also some health risks attached to work. Precarious forms of work can have negative effects on mental health. Industrial work was particularly at risk of physically hazardous working conditions as regards occupational injuries or work-related diseases caused by chemical substances, but as a matter of fact, in many low- and medium-income countries these risks are still very much a present phenomenon. However, in many developed countries recent changes in the modern world of work have created new mental and psychological demands on individuals, creating stressful psychosocial work environments and working-time related stress. These conditions have now been identified using theoretical models and standardized measurements, and respective research evidence indicates that jobs defined by high demands and low control, and by high effort in combination with low reward, increase the risk of stress-related disorders, such as cardiovascular disease or depression. While this evidence has clear implications for work practices within firms so that employers have to meet their responsibilities, there is a role for public policies as regards the prevention of health risks at the workplace, in particular with respect to regulation, monitoring, and support services.

Collective bargaining is an important institutional mechanism to establish negotiated standards regarding pay, working time and other working conditions. It also has a role in settling distributional conflicts. Compared to legislation, collective agreements can be more flexible as they take into account sectoral or firm-specific issues. Empirical research can show that multi-employer collective bargaining can lead to lower earnings inequality and that coordinated or centralized bargaining is beneficial to a positive economic development. Yet, bargaining systems are quite diverse around the globe, with huge differences in bargaining coverage, union density, and employer organization, as well as a tendency to decline in collective bargaining coverage and increased decentralization; similar differences can also be observed inside individual countries. While collective bargaining is a voluntary system, public policies such as extension clauses and minimum wages can also contribute to shape wage structures in systems with low organizational density.

Human capital is a core element of individual life chances and employment potentials. It is also crucial for economic productivity and societal wealth. Empirical research points at the fact that skill formation has a peculiar pattern over the life course with educational investments at different stages building upon each other. Education in early childhood has the strongest returns and a clear potential of reducing ability gaps across children from different backgrounds. Schooling enrolment is far from complete, in particular in medium and low income countries, but is essential in securing individual chances of independent living outside of poverty. Comparative research also gives hints at the specific contribution of vocational education and training for a smooth transition from school to work, in particular if combined with structured learning in firms. Higher education is important for societal progress and innovation. As with schooling also higher education tends to operate under credit constraints so that support through public subsidies is an important measure to mitigate inequality in access to higher education. Finally, continuous training on the job is needed to update skills in a changing economic environment.

Policies regarding employment protection, unemployment protection and reemployment have direct influence on stability and mobility on the labor market. In many countries, institutional rules governing permanent contracts in the formal sector stabilize open-ended employment relationships, but may hamper entry into the core labor market for some groups in the labor force as they tend to reinforce a segmentation of employment. Furthermore, in many countries both formal and effective coverage by unemployment benefits is very limited, leading to a double disadvantage of those in more temporary or informal employment as their access to unemployment protection is also limited. Hence, employment and unemployment protection often privilege certain groups over others, creating gaps in protection for the most vulnerable people. Active labor market policies can help promote the reentry into employment after phases of unemployment, and in fact, there are many options of effective reemployment measures – however, taking a global perspective, the delivery of such policies is quite unequal given institutional, administrative, and fiscal constraints. All in all, relaxing employment protection while strengthening unemployment benefit systems and active labor market policies can help support individuals in a dynamic economic environment where transitions between jobs need to be secured. This, of course, requires fundamental institutional change and capacity building in many countries.

7.11.2   Policy Conclusions

Based on our assessment of the global evidence on core employment issues, some conclusions for supranational, national, and subnational policy-making can be derived.

First, and going much beyond employment policies, opportunities for economic growth should be provided in accordance with ecological sustainability – without such sustainable dynamism good jobs for all can hardly be realized.

Second, in our understanding, full and fair employment in the formal sector should be made a central aim of international institutions and national developmental strategies.

Third, while there is much variation between countries and sectors in terms of development, resources available, and institutional capacities, we think that good jobs can be characterized by a couple of essential features.

Good jobs:
- are free of major characteristics of precariousness, such as a lack of stability and a high risk of job loss, a lack of safety measures and an absence of minimal standards of employment protection;
- enable working persons to exert some control on matters such as the place and the timing of work and the tasks to be accomplished, and these jobs place appropriately high demands on the working person, without overtaxing their resources and capabilities and without harming their health;
- provide fair employment in terms of earnings and of employers' commitment toward guaranteeing job security;
- offer opportunities for skill training, learning, and promotion prospects within a life course perspective, thereby sustaining work ability and stimulating individual development;
- prevent social isolation and any form of discrimination and violence;
- aim at reconciling work and extra-work demands by implementing appropriate rules in day-to-day practices.

Inclusive institutions – ranging from legal and regulatory framework, state welfare provision, collective bargaining coverage, and corporate management to cultural environment – are needed at global and national levels to provide equitable opportunities for a broad cross-section of society and to enhance human development.

Global employment goals embedded in the SDG with a focus on the different aspects of decent work as defined by the ILO, but also regional political strategies such as Europe 2020 have not fully met their ambitions. However, having such global or regional benchmarks is helpful as an ultimate policy orientation, but change is still mainly driven by national if not subnational actors. Here, both economic crises as well as political and fiscal constraints hamper easy progress. Hence, policies toward strengthening full and fair employment and good work

for all may vary according to the level of economic and cultural development in different regions of the world as well as according to institutional arrangements at national level.

We can recognize that technological change and globalization generate new jobs while undercutting existing employment is essential. If programs addressing job displacement are implemented, efforts to facilitate reskilling are preferable to cash compensation, though either must come with access to public and health services. Using public funds to shape technologies that generate more employment than they destroy should be a priority for regions, nation-states, and transnational institutions. And global trade agreements must resist lobbying seeking gains for the few at the expense of the many (Stiglitz 2002). Globalization cannot be framed as a race to the bottom, but rather as a process founded on minimum standards for employment everywhere.

Against this backdrop, we see a core set of policies that are essential:
- Rules regarding employment protection should allow for flexibility while avoiding a deeper segmentation of the labor market; labor laws should neither provide incentives to employers for choosing a particular employment relationship nor create obstacles to mobility on the labor market. Protections should cover all types of work, yielding no particular hidden advantage of choosing one or another type of work. This would expedite the use of different types of employment relations with no mandates prescribing one type of work or another.
- Unemployment protection through social insurance and basic income support should be coupled with appropriate active labor market policies to both replace income losses in phases of unemployment and accelerate reintegration into employment; Social protections should cover all types of work, yielding no particular hidden advantage of choosing one or another type of work.
- Skill formation at different stages of the life course is essential, in particular ensuring the acquisition of skills that can be used in the labor market as well as access to education also for vulnerable groups. Human capital is important for the individual herself and for the society. Early childhood investments should be made available for all since it is the best cost-effective way to reduce inequality of opportunities. Additionally, in order to guarantee the effects of these initial investments, later life human capital investments should be ensured. And for those that reach adulthood with gaps or lags in their human capital accumulation, government should provide policies to remedy them.
- Inclusive labor markets need effective policies to make the most out of diversity and ensure nondiscrimination. Better integration of minority groups and lower segregation and ethnic inequality have been shown to mitigate the conflictual and costly side of ethnic fragmentation. As to birthplace diversity, the results from both cross-country and firm-level studies point to the positive effects of such diversity in the context of advanced economies and industrial sectors. Hence, policies to increase the diversity within immigration, not just its quantity or quality, should also be considered. This is for example the case of the United States and its well-known "Green Card Lottery," in fact a diversity lottery (its official name) in the sense that the odds of winning are manipulated so as to favor immigration of citizens from countries

7

with low levels of past migration to the US. Discrimination in the labor market represents a challenge to equality, social justice, and the notion of "good jobs for all." Its pervasiveness has been clearly demonstrated by a wide range of experimental studies reviewed in this chapter. Discrimination is costly to individuals and for an economy as a whole. A single solution to combating discrimination is not on offer: at best a range of measures operating at societal, firm, and individual level are required. Firstly, a key message is that antidiscrimination legislation is an important basic action for countries, but it is not enough to combat discrimination as it is not "self-enforcing." A combination of proactive policies to promote equal opportunities in employment, and sanctions for noncompliance or discriminatory behavior by companies would increase employer incentives to comply with the legislation and should reduce discrimination. Secondly, there is also the goal of informing both employees, job applicants and employers about both the benefits of diversity and equality, and also the downsides and costs of discrimination. Yet employers operate in social settings, and the salience of group membership varies across time and space. A balanced and fact-based public discourse can help counter negative stereotypes of particular groups, for example immigrants.

- Equally important are legislative and collectively agreed standards regarding working conditions such as remuneration, working time, and health-related aspects of work, ensuring a fair distribution of economic gains as well as working conditions that are compatible with health and extra-work demands. Regarding working time, the first objective is to reduce the incidence of long full-time hours by effective regulation to establish a legally enforced limit on hours of work in conjunction with adequate minimum hourly wage rates. This requires legal rights and social protection to be built which reach beyond the formal workforce to include the most vulnerable workers in the informal economy. The second priority policy area is building reconciliation measures to make it easier for workers to combine employment with the time demands of care responsibilities. This requires investment in maternity and other family-related leave (paternity, parental, leave to care for sick relatives) and an infrastructure of childcare and eldercare services. In some countries the starting point is to implement the ILO Convention on basic maternity rights and extend coverage; for others it is to build on and extend reconciliation measures. The third priority area is to improve the quality of part-time work through equal treatment and other measures. This requires effective implementation of the principle of equal treatment in labor law and social protection, combined with measures to promote the creation of good quality part-time employment opportunities in a wider range of occupations and at higher occupational grades. The fourth priority is to build and effectively implement options for negotiated flexibility at the workplace, such as flexitime arrangements and the statutory individual "right to request" reduced or rescheduled hours, which has been introduced in some countries.

- In this context, to reduce the burden of work-related diseases decent work and employment standards should be enforced for all workers, with special emphasis on vulnerable groups (especially youth unemployment, migrant workers, and persons with disability). To this end, the capacity of occupational safety and health professionals and responsible agencies should be strengthened. Work- and employment-related material and psychosocial adversities should be monitored in a systematic, valid way within companies, based on national legislation, and employers should be motivated to invest in the development of health-conducive work environments.

- All in all, while supranational and national legal rules can establish a broad, but binding framework, particular emphasis lies on collective bargaining between employers and trade unions in establishing suitable arrangements regarding working conditions in certain sectors or regions. Hence, capacities to bargain collectively are seen as a major complement to legislation. Vital social partnership in old and new sectors and forms is therefore important. Institutions to protect workers from insecurity and uncertainty, as well as to facilitate the creation of good jobs, must be created by political forces. In the past, unions played a major role in advocating for workers and establishing labor laws and protections. They still need to play that role, but their decline suggests that it is unlikely that institutions will be created in flexible societies without unions. Hence, these institutions need to be created outside the labor market through public policies.

References

Addison, J.T. 2016. "Collective Bargaining Systems and Macroeconomic and Microeconomic Flexibility: The Quest For Appropriate Institutional Forms In Advanced Economies," *IZA Journal of Labor Policy* 5/19: 1–53.

Addison J.T., P. Teixeira, K. Evers, and L. Bellmann 2014. "Indicative and Updated Estimates of the Collective Bargaining Premium in Germany," *Industrial Relations* 53/1: 125–156.

Adida, C.L., D.D. Laitin, and M.-A. Valfort 2010. "Identifying barriers to Muslim integration in France," *PNAS* 107/52: 384–390.

Alesina, A., and E. La Ferrara 2000. "Participation in Heterogeneous Communities," *Quarterly Journal of Economics* 115(3): 847–904.

Alesina, A., and E. La Ferrara 2002. "Who Trusts Others?" *Journal of Public Economics* 85/2: 207–234.

Alesina, A., and E. La Ferrara 2005. "Ethnic Diversity and Economic Performance," *Journal of Economic Literature* 43/3: 762–800.

Alesina, A., R. Baqir, and W. Easterly 1999. "Public Goods and Ethnic Divisions," *Quarterly Journal of Economics* 114/4: 1243–1284.

Alesina, A., A. Devleeschauwer, W. Easterly, S. Kurlat, and R. Wacziarg 2003. "Fractionalization," *Journal of Economic Growth* 8/2: 155–194.

Alesina, A., J. Harnoss, and H. Rapoport 2016. "Birthplace Diversity and Economic Prosperity," *Journal of Economic Growth* 21: 101.

Alesina, A., S. Michalopoulos, and E. Papaioannou 2016. "Ethnic Inequality," *Journal of Political Economy* 124/2: 428–488.

Anxo, D., J.Y. Boulin, and I. Cebrián 2006. *Working Time Options over the Life Course*. Dublin: European Foundation for the Improvement of Living and Working Conditions, Luxembourg: Office for Official Publications of the European Communities.

Anxo, D., C. Fagan, M.T. Letablier, C. Perraudin, and M. Smith 2007. *Part-Time Work in European Companies. European Foundation for the Improvement of Living and Working Conditions*. Luxembourg: Office for Official Publications of the European Communities.

Arai, M., M. Bursell, and L. Nekby 2016. "The Reverse Gender Gap in Ethnic Discrimination: Employer Stereotypes of Men and Women with Arabic Names," *International Migration Review* 50/2: 385–412.

Arrow, K.J. 1973. "The Theory of Discrimination," in O.A. Ashenfelter and A. Rees (eds.), *Discrimination in Labor Markets*. Princeton, NJ: Princeton University.

Atkinson, A. 2015. *Inequality: What Can Be Done?* Cambridge: Harvard University Press.

Autor, D., D. Dorn, and G.H. Hanson 2016. "The China Shock: Learning from Labor Market Adjustment to Large Changes in Trade," *Annual Review of Economics* 8: 205–240, http://economics.mit.edu/files/11675 (last accessed December 23, 2017).

Autor, D., F. Levy, and R. Murnane 2003. "The Skill Content of Recent Technological Change: An Empirical Exploration," *Quarterly Journal of Economics*, 118/4: 1279–1334.

Azmat, G. and B. Petrongolo 2014. "Gender and the Labor Market: What Have We Learned from Field and Lab Experiments," *Labour Economics* 30: 32–40.

Baert, S. 2016. "Wage Subsidies and Hiring Chances for the Disabled: Some Causal Evidence," *European Journal of Health Economics* 17/1: 71–86.

Bahramitash, R. 2005. *Liberation from Liberalization: Gender and Globalization in Southeast Asia*. London: Zed.

Bail, C. 2008. "The Configuration of Symbolic Boundaries against Immigrants in Europe," *American Sociological Review* 73: 37–59.

Bailyn, L. 2006. *Breaking the Mold Redesigning Work for Productive and Satisfying Lives*. New York: Cornell University Press.

Bannai, A. and A. Tamakashi 2014. "The Association between Long Working Hours and Health: A Systematic Review of Epidemiological Evidence," *Scandinavian Journal of Work, Environment and Health* 40: 5–18.

Barro, R.J. 1997. *The Determinants of Growth. A Cross-Country Analysis*. Boston: The MIT Press.

Barro, R.J. and J.W. Lee 2013. "A New Data Set of Educational Attainment in the World, 1950–2010," *Journal of Development Economics*, 104: 184–198.

Becker, G. 1957. *The Economics of Discrimination*. Chicago: University of Chicago Press.

Becker, G. 1962. "Investment in Human Capital: A Theoretical Analysis," *The Journal of Political Economy* 70/5: 9–49.

Becker, G. 1993. *Human Capital. A Theoretical and Empirical Analysis, with Special Reference to Education*. Chicago: The University of Chicago Press.

Behrman, J. 2010. "Investment in Education – Inputs and Incentives," in D. Rodrik and M. Rosenzweig (eds.), *Handbook of Development Economics, vol. 5*. Amsterdam: Elsevier.

Bell, D.N.F. and D.G. Blanchflower 2011. "Young People and the Great Recession," *Oxford Review of Economic Policy* 27/2: 241–267.

Benach, J., C. Muntaner, and V. Santana 2007. *Employment Conditions and Health Inequalities. Final Report to the WHO Commission on Social Determinants of Health (CSDH)*. Geneva: WHO.

Bendick, Jr. M., C.W. Jackson, and J.H. Romero 1997. "Employment Discrimination against Older Workers: An Experimental Study of Hiring Practices," *Journal of Aging & Social Policy* 8/4: 25–46.

Beramendi, P., S. Häusermann, H. Kitschelt, and H. Kriesi (eds.) 2015. *The Politics of Advanced Capitalism*. Cambridge: Cambridge University Press.

Berg, P., G. Bosch, and J. Charest 2014. "Working-Time Configurations: A Framework for Analyzing Diversity across Countries," *Industrial and Labor Relations Review* 67/3: 805–837.

Berkel, Van R. and I.H. Møller 2002. *Inclusion through Participation*. Bristol: The Policy Press.

Bertrand, M. and E. Duflo 2016. Field Experiments on Discrimination. NBER Working Paper No. 22014.

Bertrand, M. and S. Mullainathan 2004. "Are Emily and Greg More Employable than Lakisha and Jamal? A Field Experiment on Labor Market Discrimination," *American Economic Review* 94/4: 991–1013.

Bescond D., A. Châtaignier, and F. Mehran 2003. "Sept indicateurs pour mesurer le travail décent : une comparaison internationale," *Revue internationale du travail* 142/2 : 195–229.

Blanchard, O. and J. Tirole. 2007. "The Optimal Design of Unemployment Insurance and Employment Protection: A First Pass," *Journal of the European Economic Association* 6/1: 45–77.

Blanchard, O., F. Jaumotte, and P. Loungani 2013. "Labor Market Policies and IMF Advice in Advanced Economies during the Great Recession," *IMF Staff Discussion Note*, SDN/13/02. Washington, DC: International Monetary Fund.

Blanchflower, D. and A. Bryson 2003. "Changes over Time in Relative Union Wage Effects in the UK and the USA Revisited," in J.T. Addison and C. Schnabel (eds.), *International Handbook of Trade Unions*. Cheltenham: Edward Elgar.

Blau, F. and L. Kahn 2007. "The Gender Pay Gap," *The Economists' Voice* 4/4: 1–6.

Blau, F., M. Brinton, and D. Grusky (eds.) 2006. *The Declining Significance of Gender?* New York: Russell Sage Foundation.

Boeri, T., P. Cahuc, and A. Zylberberg 2015. "The Costs of Flexibility-Enhancing Reforms for Individuals: a Literature Review," *OECD Economics Department WP* 2015–2045.

Booth, A., Leigh, A., and E. Varganova 2012. "Does Ethnic Discrimination Vary across Minority Groups? Evidence from a Field Experiment," *Oxford Bulletin of Economics and Statistics* 74/4: 547–573.

Borghans, L., L. Duckworth, J. Heckman, and B. ter Weel 2008. "The Economics and Psychology of Personality Traits," *Journal of Human Resources* 43: 972–1059.

Bourguignon, F. 2015. *The Globalization of Inequality*. Princeton: Princeton University Press.

Bosch, G., P. Dawkings, and F. Michon 1994. *Times Are Changing: Working Time Developments in 14 Industrialised Countries*. Geneva: ILO.

Bowles, S., H. Gintis, and M. Osborne 2001. "The Determinants of Earnings: A Behavioral Approach," *Journal of Economic Literature* 39: 1137–1176.

Bredgaard, T. and F. Larsen 2006. The Transitional Danish Labour Market: Understanding a Best Case, and Policy Proposals for Solving Some Paradoxes. Aalborg: CARMA Research Paper 2.

Brunow, S., M. Trax, and J. Suedekum 2015. "Cultural Diversity and Plant-Level Productivity," *Regional Science and Urban Economics* 53: 85–96.

Brynjolfsson, E. and A. McAfee 2014. *The Second Machine Age: Work, Progress and Prosperity in a Time of Brilliant Technologies*. New York: Norton.

Burchell, B., C. Fagan, C. O'Brien, and M. Smith 2007. *Working Conditions in the European Union: The Gender Perspective*. Luxembourg: Office for Official Publications of the European Communities.

Burchell, B.J., V. Hardy, J. Rubery, and M. Smith 2014. *A New Method to Understand Occupational Gender Segregation in European Labour Markets*. Luxembourg: Publication Office of the European Union.

Bursell, M. 2014. "The Multiple Burdens of Foreign-Named Men. Evidence from a Field Experiment on Gendered Ethnic Hiring Discrimination in Sweden," *European Sociological Review* 30/3: 399–409.

Campbell, J.L. and J.A. Hall 2006. "Introduction: The State of Denmark," in J.L. Campell, J.A. Hall, and O.K. Pedersen (eds.), *National Identities and the Varieties of Capitalism: The Danish Experience*. Montreal: McGill-Queen's University Press.

Cappelli, P. 1999. *The New Deal at Work: Managing the Market-Driven Workforce*. Boston: Harvard Business School Press.

Card, D. 1999. "The Causal Effect of Education on Earnings," in O. Ashenfelter and D. Card (eds.), *The Handbook of Labor Economics*, vol. 3, Amsterdam: Elsevier.

Card, D., J. Kluve, and A. Weber 2010. "Active Labour Market Policy Evaluations: A Meta-Analysis," *Economic Journal, Royal Economic Society* 120/548: F452–F477, http://ideas.repec.org/a/ecj/econjl/v120y2010i548pf452-f477.html (last accessed December 23, 2017).

Card, D., J. Kluve, and A. Weber 2015. What Works? A Meta Analysis of Recent Active Labor Market Program Evaluations. IZA DP No. 9236.

Carling, K., and K. Richardson 2004. "The Relative Efficiency of Labor Market Programs: Swedish Experience from the 1990s," *Labour Economics* 11: 335–354.

Chapman, B. 2006. "Income Contingent Loans for Higher Education: International Reforms," in E. Hanushek and F. Welsch (eds.), *Handbook of the Economics of Education*, vol. 2. Amsterdam: Elsevier.

Chung, H., M. Kerkhofs, and P. Ester 2007. *Working Time Flexibility in European Companies*. European Foundation for the Improvement of Living and Working Conditions. Luxembourg: Office for Official Publications of European Communities.

CIETT 2016. *Economic Report 2016*. International Confederation of Private Employment Services.

Colin, N. and B. Palier 2015. "The Next Safety Net," *Foreign Affairs* 94/4: 29.

Collier, P. 1999. "On the Economic Consequences of Civil War," *Oxford Economic Papers* 51: 168–183.

Collier, P. 2001. "Ethnic Diversity: An Economic Analysis of Its Implications," *Economic Policy* 32: 129–166.

Cooper, C.L., A. Pandey, and J.C. Quick (eds.) 2012. *Downsizing. Is Less Still More?* Cambridge: Cambridge University Press.

Correll, S.J., S. Benard, and I. Paik 2007. "Getting a Job: Is There a Motherhood Penalty?" *American Journal of Sociology* 112/5: 1297–1338.

Cranfield University School of Management and Working Families 2008. *Flexible Working and Performance: Summary of Research*. London: Working Families

Cunha, F. and J. Heckman 2007. "The Technology of Skill Formation," *The American Economic Review Papers & Proceedings* 97/2: 31–47.

Cunha, F., J. Heckman, L. Lochner, and D. Masterov 2006. "Interpreting the Evidence on Life Cycle Skill Formation," in E. Hanushek and F. Welsch (eds.), *Handbook of the Economics of Education*, vol. 1. Amsterdam: Elsevier.

De Stefano, V. 2016. "The Rise of the 'Just-In-Time Workforce': On-Demand Work, Crowdwork and Labour Protection in the 'Gig-Economy'," *Conditions of Work and Employment Series No. 71*. Geneva: International Labour Organization.

Demazière D., N. Guimarães, H. Hirata, and K. Sugita 2013. *Être chômeur à Paris, Sao Paulo, Tokyo. Une méthode de comparaison internationale*. Paris: Presses de Sciences Po.

Desmet, K., I. Ortuño-Ortín, and R. Wacziarg 2012. "The Political Economy of Ethnolinguistic Cleavages," *Journal of Development Economics* 97/2: 322–338.

Dolls, M., C. Fuest, and A. Peichl 2012. "Automatic Stabilizers and Economic Crisis: US vs. Europe," *Journal of Public Economics* 96/3–4: 279–294.

Donkin, A., M. Allen, J. Allen, R. Bell, and M. Marmot 2014. "Social Determinants of Health and the Working Age Population: Global Challenges and Priorities for Action," in S. Leka and R.R. Sinclair (eds.), *Contemporary Occupational Health Psychology: Global Perspectives on Research and Action*, Vol 3. Chichester: Wiley & Sons.

Easterly, W. and R. Levine 1997. "Africa's Growth Tragedy: Policies and Ethnic Divisions," *Quarterly Journal of Economics* 112/4:1203–1250.

Economic Policy Institute. 2015. *Five Social Disadvantages That Depress Student Performance*. Report by Leila Morsy and Richard Rothstein, June 10, 2015. www.epi.org/publication/five-social-disadvantages-that-depress-student-performance-why-schools-alone-cant-close-achievement-gaps/ (last accessed December 23, 2017).

Edgerton, D. 2006. *The Shock of the Old: Technology and Global History Since 1900*. Oxford: Oxford University Press.

Eichhorst, W. 2014. *Fixed-Term Contracts*. IZA World of Labor.

Eichhorst, W., Kaufmann, O., and Konle-Seidl, R. 2008. *Bringing the Jobless into Work?* Berlin: Springer.

Eichhorst, W., P. Marx, and C. Wehner 2016. Labor Market Reforms in Europe: Towards More Flexicure Labor Markets? IZA Discussion Papers No. 8963. Bonn: IZA.

Eichhorst, W., N. Rodriguez-Planas, N. Schmidl, and K. Zimmermann 2015. "A Road Map to Vocational Education and Training in Industrialized Countries," *ILR Review* 68/2: 314–337.

Equality and Human Rights Commission 2016. *Pregnancy and Maternity Related Discrimination and Disadvantage: Summary of Key Findings*. London: Department for Business, Innovation and Skills.

Eurofound 2006. *Working Time Options over the Life Course: New Work Pattern and Company Strategies*. Luxembourg: Publications Office of the European Union.

Eurofound 2007. *Fourth European Working Conditions Survey*. Luxembourg: Publications Office of the European Union.

Eurofound 2012a. *Fifth European Working Conditions Survey*. Luxembourg: Publications Office of the European Union.

Eurofound 2012b. *European Quality of Life Survey*. Luxembourg: Publications Office of the European Union.

Eurofound 2013. *Women, Men and Working Conditions in Europe*. Luxembourg: Publications Office of the European Union.

Eurofound 2015. *First Findings: Sixth European Working Conditions Survey*. Dublin: European Observatory of Working Life.

Eurofound 2016. *Working Time Developments in the 21st Century: Work Duration and Its Regulation in the EU*. Luxembourg: Publications Office of the European Union.

European Commission 2007. *Towards Common Principles of Flexicurity – More and Better Jobs through Flexibility and Security*. Luxembourg.

European Commission 2016a. *Employment and Social Developments in Europe*. Luxembourg.

European Commission 2016b. "Women and Unpaid Work: Recognise, Reduce, Redistribute!" *Employment Social Affairs and Inclusion*, http://ec.europa.eu/social/main.jsp?langId=en&catId=89&newsId=2492&furtherNews=yes; Press release downloaded 07/03/16 (last accessed December 23, 2017).

Evans, J., D. Lippoldt, and P. Marianna 2001. Trends in Working Hours in OECD Countries. Labour Market and Social Policy Occasional Papers, No. 45, OECD. www.oecd-ilibrary.org/social-issues-migration-health/trends-in-working-hours-in-oecd-countries_674061356827 (last accessed December 23, 2017).

Eymann, A. and J. Schweri 2015. Horizontal Skills Mismatch and Vocational Education. IZA Conference Paper, mimeo.

Fagan, C. 2004. "Gender and Working-Time in Industrialized Countries: Practices and Preferences," in J. Messenger (ed.), *Working-Time and Workers' Preferences in Industrialized countries: Finding the Balance*. The Institute for Labour Studies of the International Labour Organization. London: Routledge.

Fagan, C. and B. Burchell 2002 *Gender, Jobs and Working Conditions in the European Union*. Eurofound, Luxembourg: Publications Office of the European Union.

Fagan, C. and P. Walthery 2011. "Individual Working-Time Adjustments between Full-Time and Part-Time Working in European Firms," *Social Politics* 18/2: 269–299.

Fagan, C., C. Lyonette, M. Smith, and A. Saldaña-Tejeda 2012. *The Influence of Working Time Arrangements on Work–Life Integration or 'Balance': A Review of the International Evidence*. Background Report to the International Labour Office for the ILO Tripartite Meeting of Experts on Working time Arrangements, Geneva: International Labour Office. www.ilo.org/travail/whatwedo/publications/WCMS_187306/lang--en/index.htm (last accessed December 23, 2017).

Fagan, C., H. Norman, M. Smith, and M. González Menéndez 2014. *In Search of Good Quality Part-Time Employment*. Geneva: International Labour Office. www.ilo.org/travail/whatwedo/publications/WCMS_237781/lang--en/index.htm (last accessed December 23, 2017).

Fearon, J. 2003. "Ethnic and Cultural Diversity by Country," *Journal of Economic Growth* 8/2: 195–222.

Fearon, J., and D. Laitin 2003. "Ethnicity, Insurgency, and civil war," *American Political Science Review* 97/1: 75–90.

Felbermayr G., D. Baumgarter, and S. Lehwald 2014. *Wachsende Lohnungleichkeit in Deutschland*. Gütersloh: Bertelsmann Stiftung.

Felstead, A., and N. Jewson 2000. *In Work, At Home: Towards an Understanding of Homeworking*. London: Routledge.

Felstead, A., N. Jewson, A. Phizacklea, and S. Walters 2002. "The Option to Work at Home: Another Privilege for the Favoured Few," *New Technology, Work and Employment* 17/3: 188–207.

Galarza, F. and G. Yamada 2014. "Labor Market Discrimination in Lima, Peru: Evidence from a Field Experiment," *World Development* 58: 83–94.

Gallie D. (ed.) 2004. *Resisting Marginalization. Unemployment Experience and Social Policy in European Union*. Oxford: Oxford University Press.

Gallie, D. 2013. *Economic Crisis, Quality of Work, and Social Integration: The European Experience*. Oxford: Oxford University Press.

Ganssmann, H. 2000. "Labor Market Flexibility, Social Protection and Unemployment," *European Societies* 2: 243–269.

Garcia Pérez, J.I. 2015. *Should Severance Pay Be Consistent for All Workers? Single, Open-Ended Contracts with Severance Pay Smoothly Rising with Seniority Can Decrease Both Unemployment and Job Losses*. IZA World of Labor.

George, J., M. Kumar, and D. Ojha (eds.) 2012. *Working Class Movement in India in the Wake of Globalization*. New Delhi: Manohar.

Glewwe, P. and M. Kremer 2006. "Schools, Teachers, and Education Outcomes in Developing Countries," in E. Hanushek and F. Welsch (eds.), *Handbook of the Economics of Education*, vol. 2. Amsterdam: Elsevier.

Golden, L. 2012. *Effects of Working Time on Productivity*. Conditions of Work and Employment Series No. 33, Geneva: International Labour Organisation. www.ilo.org/travail/whatwedo/publications/WCMS_187307/lang--en/index.htm (last accessed December 23, 2017).

Golden, L. and Figart, D.M. 2001. *Working Time: International Trends, Theory and Policy Perspectives*. London: Routledge.

Gordon, R.J. 2016. *The Rise and Fall of American Growth: The US Standard of Living since the Civil War*. Princeton: Princeton University Press.

Graversen, B.K., and J.C. van Ours 2008. "How to Help Unemployed Find Jobs Quickly: Experimental Evidence from a Mandatory Activation Program," *Journal of Public Economics* 92: 2020–2035.

Greenberg, D.H., C. Michalopoulos, and P.K. Robins 2003. "A Meta-analysis of Government-Sponsored Training Programs," *Industrial & Labor Relations Review* 57/1: 31–53.

Groot, W., and H. Maassen van den Brink 2000. "Overeducation in the Labor Market: A Meta-analysis," *Economics of Education Review*, 19/2: 149–158.

Haelermans, C., and L. Borghans 2011. Wage Effects of On-the-Job Training: A Meta-Analysis. IZA Discussion Paper No. 6077, October.

Hambrick, D., T. Seung Cho, M.J. Chen 1996. "The Influence of Top Management Team Heterogeneity on Firms' Competitive Moves," *Administrative Science Quarterly* 41/4: 659–684.

Hamburger, L. 1939. "The Extension of Collective Agreements to Cover Entire Trades and Industries," *International Labour Review* XL/2: 153–194.

Hanushek, E., and L. Woessmann 2015. *The Knowledge Capital of Nations.* Boston: The MIT Press.

Hanushek, E., G. Schwerdt, S. Wiederhold, and S. Woessmann 2015. "Returns to Skills around the World: Evidence from PIAAC," *European Economic Review* 73: 103–130.

Hanushek, E., L. Woessmann, and L. Zang 2011. General Education, Vocational Education, and Labor Market Outcomes over the Life-Cycle. NBER Working Paper Series no. 17504.

Harris, S.D., and A.B. Krueger 2015. A Proposal for Modernizing Labor Laws for Twenty-First-Century Work: The Independent Worker. The Hamilton Project Discussion Paper 2015-10.

Harvey, D. 2005. *A Brief History of Neoliberalism.* New York: Oxford University Press.

Hayter, S. 2015. "Unions and Collective Bargaining," in J. Berg (ed.), *Labour Markets, Institutions and Inequality: Building Just Societies in the 21st Century.* ILO and Edward Elgar.

Hayter, S., and J. Visser 2017. "The Application and Extension of Collective Agreements: Enhancing the Inclusiveness of Labour Protection," *International Labour Review*, forthcoming.

Heath, A., and Cheung, S.Y. 2007. "Unequal Chances: Ethnic Minorities in Western Labour Markets," *Proceedings of the British Academy 137*, Oxford: Oxford University Press

Heth, R., and A. Mushfiq Mobarak 2015. "Manufacturing Growth and the Lives of Bangladeshi Women," *Journal of Development Economics* 115: 1–15.

Heckman, J. 1995. "Lessons from the Bell Curve," *The Journal of Political Economy*, 103: 1091–1152.

Heckman, J.J., and P. Siegelman 1993. "The Urban Institute Audit Studies: Their Methods and Findings," in M. Fix and R. Struyk (eds.), *Clear and Convincing Evidence: Measurement of Discrimination in America.* Washington, DC: The Urban Institute Press.

Heckman, J., J. Stixrud, and S. Urzua 2006. Heckman, J. 1995. "Lessons from the Bell Curve," *The Journal of Political Economy*, 103: 1091–1152.

Heinrich, C.J., P.R. Mueser, K.R. Troske, K. Jeon, and D.C. Kahvecioglu 2013. "Do Public Employment and Training Programs Work?," *IZA Journal of Labor Economics* 2: 6.

Hjort, J. 2014. "Ethnic Divisions and Production in Firms," *Quarterly Journal of Economics* 129/4: 1899–1946.

Hoefinger, H. 2014. *Sex, Love and Money in Cambodia: Professional Girlfriends and Transactional Relations.* New York: Routledge.

Holzer, H. 2010. "Enhancing Diversity through Affirmative Action: What Other Countries Can Learn from the United States' Experience," in OECD, *Equal Opportunities? The Labour Market Integration of the Children of Immigrants.* Paris: OECD Publishing. http://dx.doi.org/10.1787/9789264086395-en (last accessed December 23, 2017).

Hoogendoorn, S. and M. van Praag 2012. Ethnic Diversity and Team Performance: A Field Experiment. IZA Working Paper No. 6731.

Ingre, M., T. Åkerstedt, M. Ekstedt, and G. Kecklund 2012. "Periodic Self-Rostering in Shift Work: Correspondence between Objective Work Hours, Work Hour Preferences (Personal Fit), and Work Schedule Satisfaction," *Scandinavian Journal of Work, Environment and Health* 38/4: 327.

International Labour Organization 2008. *ILO Declaration on Social Justice for a Fair Globalization.* ILO conference, 97th session, Geneva, June.

International Labour Organization 2012. *Statistical Update on Employment in the Informal Economy.* Geneva: ILO. http://laborsta.ilo.org/informal_economy_ E.html (last accessed May 19, 2016).

International Labour Organization 2013a. *Measuring Informality: A Statistical Manual on the Informal Sector and Informal Employment.* Geneva: ILO.

International Labour Organization 2013b. *World of Work Report.* Geneva: ILO.

International Labour Organization 2014. *World Social Protection Report 2014/15.* Geneva: ILO.

International Labour Organization 2015a. *World Employment Social Outlook 2015.* Geneva: ILO.

International Labour Organization 2015b. *World Report on Child Labour 2015.* Geneva: ILO.

International Labour Organization 2015c. *World Employment and Social Outlook, Trends 2015.* Geneva: ILO.

International Labour Organisation 2015d. *ILO Global Estimates on Migrant Workers: Results and Methodology.* Geneva: ILO.

International Labour Organization 2016. *Women at Work: Trends 2016.* Geneva: ILO. www.ilo.org/gender/Informationresources/Publications/WCMS_457317/lang--en/index.htm (last accessed December 23, 2017).

Jacoby, S.M. 1985. *Employing Bureaucracy: Managers, Unions, and the Transformation of Work in the 20th Century.* New York: Columbia University Press.

Jaumotte, F. 2003. Female Labour Force Participation: Past Trends and Main Determinants in OECD Countries. OECD Economics Department Working Papers No. 376.

Jaumotte, F. and Buitron, C.O. 2015. Inequality and Labour Market Institutions. Washington, DC. IMF Staff Discussion Note 15/14.

Jespersen, S.T., J.R. Munch, and L. Skipper 2008. "Costs and Benefits of Danish Active Labour Market Programmes," *Labour Economics* 15: 859–884.

Jorgensen, C. 2005. *Seminar Highlights Flexicurity in the Labour Market.* Dublin: European Industrial Relations Observatory.

Juvani, A., T. Oksanen, P. Salo, M. Virtanen, M. Kivimäki, J. Pentti, and J. Vahtera 2014. "Effort–Reward Imbalance as a Risk Factor for Disability Pension: The Finnish Public Sector Study," *Scandinavian Journal of Work, Environment and Health* 40/3: 266–277.

Kahane, L., N. Longley, and R. Simmons 2013. "The Effect of Coworker Heterogeneity on Firm-Level Output: Assessing the Impacts of Cultural and Language Diversity in the National Hockey League," *Review of Economics and Statistics* 95/1: 302–314.

Kahn, L. 2015. "Skill Shortages, Mismatches, and Structural Unemployment: A Symposium," *ILR Review* 68/2: 247–250.

Kalleberg, A.L. 2000. "Nonstandard Employment Relations: Part-time, Temporary, and Contract Work," *Annual Review of Sociology* 26: 341–365.

Kalleberg, A.L. 2011. *Good Jobs, Bad Jobs: The Growth of Polarized and Precarious Employment Systems in the United States, 1970s to 2000s.* New York: Russell Sage Foundation.

Kalleberg, A.L., and P.V. Marsden 2015. "Transformation of the Employment Relationship," in R. Scott and S. Kosslyn (eds.), *Emerging Trends in the Social and Behavioral Sciences.* Hoboken, NJ: John Wiley and Sons.

Karabarbounis, L., and B. Neiman 2014. "The Global Decline of the Labor Share," *Quarterly Journal of Economics* 129/1: 61–103.

Karamessini, M., and J. Rubery 2014. *Women and Austerity: The Economic Crisis and the Future for Gender Equality.* Abingdon: Routledge.

Karanikolos, M., P. Mladovsky, J. Cylus, S. Thomson, S. Basu, D. Stuckler, J.P. Mackenbach, and M. McKee 2013. "Financial Crisis, Austerity, and Health in Europe," *The Lancet* 381: 1323–1331.

Karasek, R.A., and T. Theorell 1990. *Healthy Work.* New York: Basic Books.

Kelly, E.L.,E.E. Kossek, L.B. Hammer, M. Dunham, J. Bray, K. Chermack, and D. Kaskubar 2008. "Getting There from Here: Research on the Effects of Work–Family Initiatives on Work–Family Conflict and Business Outcomes," *The Academy of Management Annals* 2/1: 305–349.

Kivimäki, M., M. Jokela, S.T. Nyberg, A. Singh-Manoux, E. Fransson, L. Alfredsson, J.B. Bjorner, M. Borritz, H. Burr, A. Casini, E. Clays, D. De Bacquer, N. Dragano, R. Erbel. G.A. Geuskens, M. Hamer, W.E. Hooftman, I.L. Houtman, K.-H. Jöckel, F. Kittel, A. Knutsson, M. Koskenvuo, T. Lunau, I.E.H. Madsen, M.L. Nielsen, M. Nordin, T. Oksanen, J.H. Pejtersen, J. Pentti, R. Rugelies, P. Salo, M.J. Shipley, J. Siegrist, A. Steptoe, S.B. Suominen, T. Theorell, J. Vahtera, P.J.M. Westerholm, H. Westerlund, D. O'Reilly, M. Kumari, G.D. Batty, J.E. Ferrie, and M. Virtanen. 2015. "Long Working Hours and Risk of Coronary Heart Disease and Stroke: A Meta-Analysis for 603 838 Individuals," *The Lancet* 386: 1739–1746.

Kluve, J. 2010. "The Effectiveness of European Active Labor Market Programs," *Labour Economics* 17: 904–918.

Kossek, E.E. 2005. "Workplace Policies and Practices to Support Work and Families: Gaps in Implementation and Linkages to Individual and Organizational Effectiveness," in S. Bianchi, L. Casper, and R. King (eds.), *Workforce/Workplace Mismatch? Work, Family, Health, and Well-being.* Mahwah, NJ: Lawrencce Erlbaum Associates.

Lalive, R., M. Morlok, and J. Zweimüller 2011. Applying for Jobs: Does ALMP Participation Help? Working Paper Series, Department of Economics, University of Zurich, No. 19.

Larsen, F. 2009. How New Governance and Operational Reforms Can Transform Employment Policies towards Work-First – Lessons from the Implementation of Employment Policies in the Danish Municipalities. *Paper for the symposium* at the University of Chicago, May 15, 2009: Welfare States in Transition: Social Policy Transformation in Organizational Practice, Chicago, USA.

Lee, S., and D. McCann 2007. "Working Time Capability: Toward Realizing Individual Choice," in J.-Y. Boulin, M. Lallement, J. Messenger, and F. Michon (eds.), Decent Working Time – New Trends, New Issues. Geneva: International Labour Office.

Lewis, S., D. Anderson, C. Lyonette, N. Payne, and S. Wood (eds.) 2017. Work-Life Balance in Times of Recession, Austerity and Beyond. Routledge.

Linotte D. 1994. "Sur-emploi et chômage déguisé dans les économies planifiées et en transition: une interprétation néo-classique," Revue d'études comparatives Est-Ouest 25/1: 139–156.

Ljungqvist, L. 1993. "Economic Underdevelopment: The Case of Missing Market for Human Capital," Journal of Development Economics 40: 219–239.

Lødemel, I. and H. Trickey (eds.) 2001. An Offer You Can't Refuse – Workfare in International Perspective. Bristol: The Policy Press.

Madsen, P.K. 2002. "The Danish model of flexicurity: A Paradise – with Some Snakes," in H. Sarfati and G. Bonoli (eds.), Labour Market and Social Protections Reforms in International Perspective. UK: Ashgate.

Madsen, P.K. 2006. "Labour Market Flexibility and Social Protection in European Welfare States – Contrasts and Similarities," Australian Bulletin of Labour 32/2: 139.

Marmot, M. 2015. The Health Gap. The Challenge of an Unequal World. London: Bloomsbury Publishing.

Martin, J.P. 2014. Activation and Active Labour Market Policies in OECD Countries: Stylized Facts and Evidence on their Effectiveness. IZA Policy Paper No. 84.

Martin, J.P., and D. Grubb 2001. "What Works and for Whom: A Review of OECD Countries Experiences with Active Labour Market Policies," Swedish Economic Policy Review 8: 9–56.

Maruani, M. (dir.) 2013. Travail et genre dans le monde. Paris: La Découverte.

Maurer-Fazio, M. 2012. "Ethnic discrimination in China's internet job board labor market," IZA Journal of Migration 1: 12.

Mavromaras, K., P.J. Sloane, and Z. And Wei 2012. "The Role of Education Pathways in the Relationship between Job Mismatch, Wages and Job Satisfaction; A Panel Estimation Approach," Education Economics 20/3: 303–321.

Mazzucato, M. 2013. The Entrepreneurial State, London: Anthem.

McGinnity F. and P. Lunn 2011. "Measuring Discrimination Facing Ethnic Minority Job Applicants: An Irish Experiment," Work, Employment and Society 25/4: 693–708.

McKinsey Global Institute (MGI) 2015. The Power of Parity: How Advancing Women's Equality Can Add $12 Trillion to Global Growth. London, San Francisco and Shanghai: McKinsey and Company.

McPherson, M., and M. Schapiro 2006. "US Higher Education Finance", in E. Hanushek and F. Welsch (eds.), Handbook of the Economics of Education vol. 2, Amsterdam: Elsevier.

Messenger, J. (ed.) 2004. Working Time and Workers' Preferences in Industrialized Countries: Finding the Balance. London and New York: Routledge.

Milanovic, B. 2016. Global Inequality: A New Approach for the Age of Globalization, Cambridge: Harvard University Press.

Mincer, J. 1974. Schooling, Experience, and Earnings. New York: Columbia University Press.

Miranda, V. 2011. Cooking, Caring and Volunteering: Unpaid Work Around the World. OECD Social, Employment and Migration Working Papers, No. 116, OECD Publishing. www.oecd.org/berlin/47258230.pdf (last accessed December 23, 2017).

Montano, D. 2014. "Chemical and Biological Work-Related Risks across Occupations in Europe: A Review," Journal of Occupational and Medical Toxicology 9: 28.

Moss, P. (ed.) 2015. 11th International Review of Leave Policies and Related Research 2015, International Network of Leave Policies and Research. Available from: www.leavenetwork.org/lp_and_r_reports/review_2015/

Murnane, R., J. Willett, and F. Levy 1995. "The Growing Importance of Cognitive Skills in Wage Determination," Review of Economics and Statistics 77: 251–66.

Nelson, M., and J.D. Stephens 2013. "The Service Transition and Women's Employment," The Political Economy of the Service Transition, 147–170.

Neumark, D., I. Burn, and P. Button 2015. Is It Harder for Older Workers to Find Jobs? New and Improved Evidence from a Field Experiment. NBER Working Paper No. 21669.

Nijp, H.H., D.G.J. Beckers, S.A.E. Geurts, P. Tucker, and M.A.J. Kompier 2012. "Systematic Review on the Association between Employee Worktime Control and Work–Non-Work Balance, Health and Well-being, and Job-Related Outcomes," Scandinavian Journal of Work, Environment and Health 38/4: 299.

O'Reilly, J., and C. Fagan (eds.) 1998. Part-Time Prospects: An international Comparison of Part-Time Work in Europe, North America and the Pacific Rim. London: Routledge.

O'Reilly, C., D. Caldwell, and W. Barnett 1989. "Work Group Demography, Social Integration, and Turnover," Administrative Science Quarterly 34/1: 21–37.

Odama, J.S., and A.E. Aiyedun (eds.) 2004. Globalization and the Third World Economy: Impacts and Challenges in the 21st Century. Lagos: Malthouse.

Orazem, P. and E. King 2008. "Schooling in Developing Countries: The Role of Supply, Demand and Government Policy," in T.P. Schultz and J. Strauss (eds.), Handbook of Development Economics, vol. 4. Amsterdam: Elsevier.

Organization for Economic Cooperation and Development. 2008. "The Price of Prejudice: Labour Market Discrimination on the Grounds of Gender and Ethnicity," in OECD Employment Outlook 2008, Paris: OECD Publishing, http://dx.doi.org/10.1787/empl_outlook-2008-en (last accessed December 23, 2017).

Organization for Economic Cooperation and Development 2010. Sickness, Disability and Work: Breaking the Barriers. A Synthesis of Findings across OECD Countries. Paris: OECD Publishing.

Organization for Economic Cooperation and Development 2013. "Discrimination against Immigrants – Measurement, Incidence and Policy Instruments," in International Migration Outlook 2013, Paris: OECD Publishing, http://dx.doi.org/10.1787/migr_outlook-2013-7-en (last accessed December 23, 2017).

Organization for Economic Cooperation and Development 2015a. In It Together: Why Less Inequality Benefits All. Paris: OECD Publishing.

Organization for Economic Cooperation and Development 2015b. Perspectives de l'emploi de l'OCDE 2015. Paris: éditions OCDE.

Organization for Economic Cooperation and Development. 2016. Gender Portal 2016: Time Use across the World. www.oecd.org/gender/data/OECD_1564_TUSupdatePortal.xls (last accessed December 23, 2017).

Organization for Economic Cooperation and Development 2017. Employment Outlook 2017. Paris: OECD Publishing.

Pager, D., and H. Shepherd 2008. "The Sociology of Discrimination: Racial Discrimination in Employment, Housing, Credit, and Consumer Markets," Annual Review of Sociology 34: 181–209.

Parrotta, P., Pozzoli, D., and Pytlikova, M. 2014. "Does Labor Diversity Affect Firm Productivity?" European Economic Review 66: 144–179.

Peracchi, F. 2006. "Educational Wage Premia and the Distribution of Earnings: An International Perspective," in E. Hanushek and F. Welsch (eds.), Handbook of the Economics of Education, vol. 1. Amsterdam: Elsevier.

Pessoa, J.P., and J. Van Reenen 2013. Decoupling of Wage Growth and Productivity Growth? Myth and Reality. LSE CEP Discussion Paper No. 1246. http://cep.lse.ac.uk/pubs/download/dp1246.pdf (last accessed December 23, 2017).

Petit, P. 2007. "The Effects of Age and Family Constraints on Gender Hiring Discrimination: A Field Experiment in the French Financial Sector," Labour Economics 14/3: 371–391.

Phelps, E.S. 1972. "The Statistical Theory of Racism and Sexism," American Economic Review 62/4: 659–661.

Pierné, G. 2013. "Hiring Discrimination Based on National Origin and Religious Closeness: Results from a Field Experiment in the Paris Area," IZA Journal of Labor Economics 2/4: 1–15.

Piketty, T. 2014. Capital in the 21st Century. Cambridge: Harvard University Press.

Plantenga, J., and C. Remery 2005. Reconciliation of Work and Private Life: A Comparative Review of Thirty European Countries. Report financed by and prepared for the use of the European Commission Directorate-General for Employment, Social Affairs and Equal Opportunities Unit G.1.

Putnam, R.D. 1995. "Bowling Alone: America's Declining Social Capital," Journal of Democracy 6/1: 65–78.

Rapoport, R., L. Bailyn, K. Fletcher, J. Bettye, and H. Pruitt 2002. Beyond Work-Family Balance: Advancing Gender Equity and Workplace Performance. London, UK: Wiley.

Ray, R. 2008. A Detailed Look at Parental Leave Policies in 21 OECD Countries, Washington D.C.: Center for Economic and Policy Research.

Reynal-Querol, M. 2002. "Ethnicity, Political Systems, and Civil Wars," Journal of Conflict Resolution 46/1: 29–54.

Riach, P.A. and J. Rich 2002. "Field Experiments of Discrimination in the Market Place," *Economic Journal* 112/443: 480–518.

Riach, P.A. and J. Rich 2004. "Deceptive Field Experiments of Discrimination: are they ethical?" *Kyklos* 57/3: 457–470.

Rich, J. 2014. What Do Field Experiments of Discrimination in Markets Tell Us? A Meta Analysis of Studies Conducted since 2000. IZA Discussion Paper No. 8584.

Riedmann, A., H. Bielenski, T. Szczurowska, and A. Wagner. 2006. *Working Time and Work–Life Balance in European Companies.* Luxembourg: Office for Official Publications of the European Communities.

Riedmann, A., G. van Gyes, A. Roman, M. Kerkhofs, and S. Bechmann 2010. *European Company Survey 2009.* Luxembourg: Office for Official Publications of the European Communities.

Robalino, D. 2014. *Designing Unemployment Benefits in Developing Countries.* IZA World of Labor.

Robst, J. 2007. "Education and Job Match: The Relatedness of College Major and Work," *Economics of Education Review* 26/4: 397–407.

Rojer, M.F.P. 2002. *De betekenis van de CAO en het algemeen verbindend verklaren van CAOs.* The Hague: Ministerie van Sociale Zaken en Werkgelegenheid. Werkdocument 271.

Rooth, D.-O. 2014. *Correspondence Testing Studies. What Can We Learn about Discrimination in Hiring?* IZA World of Labor.

Rosholm, M. 2014. *Do Case Workers Help the Unemployed?* IZA World of Labor.

Sarna, M., A. Hegewisch, and H. Hartmann. 2013. *Balancing Working and Family: How Analysing the Costs and Benefits of Work–Family Legislation Supports Policy Change.* Research-in-Brief Institute for Women's Policy Research.

Scarpetta, S. 2014. *Employment Protection.* IZA World of Labor.

Schnall, P., M. Dobson, and P. Landsbergis 2017. "Globalization, Work, and Cardiovascular Diseases," *International Journal of Health Services.* DOI: 10.1177/0020731416664687

Schulte, P.A., R.J. Guerin, A.L. Schill, A. Bhattacharya, T.R. Cunningham, S.P. Pandalai, D. Eggerth, and C.M. Stephenson 2015. "Considerations for Incorporating 'Well-being' in Public Policy for Workers and Workplaces," *American Journal of Public Health* 105: e31–e44.

Schultz, T.W. 1961. "Investment in Human Capital," *The American Economic Review* 51/1: 1–17.

Schweinhart, L., J. Montie, Z. Xiang, W. Barnett, C. Belfield, and M. Nores 2005. *Lifetime Effects: The High/Scope Perry Preschool Study through Age 40.* Ypsilanti, Michigan: High/Scope Press.

Sen, A. 1992. *Inequality Reexamined.* Oxford: Oxford University Press.

Sianesi, B. 2008. "Differential Effects of Active Labour Market Programs for the Unemployed," *Labour Economics* 15: 370–399.

Siegrist, J., E. Rosskam, and S. Leka (eds.) 2015. *Review of Social Determinants of Health and the Health Divide in the WHO European Region: Employment and Working Conditions Including Occupation, Unemployment and Migrant Workers.* Copenhagen: WHO, Regional Office for Europe.

Siegrist, J., and M. Wahrendorf (eds.) 2016. *Work Stress and Health in a Globalized Economy: The Model of Effort–Reward Imbalance.* Dordrecht: Springer.

Smeaton, D., Ray, K., and Knight, G. 2014. *Costs and Benefits to Business of Adopting Work Life Balance Working Practices: A Literature Review.* London, UK: Department for Business Innovation and Skills.

Smith, C., and J. Chan 2015. "Working for Two Bosses: Student Interns as Constrained Labour in China," *Human Relations* 68: 305–326.

Stiglitz, J. 2002. *Globalization and Its Discontents.* New York: Norton.

Stone, K.V.W. and H. Arthurs (eds.) 2013. *Rethinking Employment Regulation: After the Standard Contract of Employment.* New York: Russell Sage Foundation Press.

Takala, J., P. Hämäläinen, K.L. Saarela, L.Y. Yun, K. Manickam, T.W. Jin, P. Heng, C. Tjong, L.G. Kheng, S. Lim, and G.S. Lin 2014. "Global Estimates of the Burden of Injury and Illness at Work in 2012," *Journal of Occupational and Environmental Hygiene* 11: 326–337.

Thelen, K. 2014. *Varities of Liberalization and the New Politics of Social Solidarity.* Cambridge: Cambridge University Press.

Traxler F. 1995. "Farewell to Labour Market Associations? Organized versus Disorganized Decentralisation as a Map for Industrial Relations," in F. Traxler and C.J. Crouch (eds.), *Organized Industrial Relations in Europe. What Future?* Hants: Vermont.

Tucker, P., and S. Folkard 2012. Working Time, Health, and Safety: A Research Synthesis Paper. Conditions of Work and Employment Series No. 31, Geneva: International Labour Organisation.

www.ilo.org/travail/whatwedo/publications/WCMS_181673/lang--en/index.htm

United Nations 2015a. *World Population Prospects: The 2015 Revision.*

United Nations 2015b. *The World's Women 2015: Trends and statistics.* New York: United Nations, Department of Economics and Social Affairs, Statistics Division.

United Nations 2015c. Sustainable Development Goals. https://sustainable development.un.org (last accessed January 4, 2016).

Valfort, M.-A. 2016. Religious Discrimination in Access to Employment: Evidence from a Correspondence Test in France. Working Paper.

Van Oorschot, W. 2004a. "Balancing Work and Welfare: Activation and Flexicurity Policies in The Netherlands, 1980–2000," *International Journal of Social Welfare* 13/1: 15–27.

Van Oorschot, W. 2004b. "Flexible Work and Flexicurity Policies in The Netherlands. Trends and Experiences," *Transfer: European Review of Labour and Research* 10/2: 208–225.

Viebrock, E., and Clasen, J. 2009. "Flexicurity and Welfare Reform: A Review," *Socio-Economic Review* 7/2: 305–331.

Visser, J. 2015. ICTWSS: Database on Institutional Characteristics of Trade Unions, Wage Setting, State Intervention and Social Pacts in 51 Countries between 1960 and 2014. www.uva-aias.net/nl/ictwss (last accessed January 28, 2018).

Visser J., S. Hayter, and R. Gammarano 2015. *The Coverage of Collective Bargaining: Stability, Erosion or Decline.* ILO: Labour Relations and Collective Bargaining Policy Brief No. 1.

Wahrendorf, M. and J. Siegrist 2014. "Proximal and Distal Determinants of Stressful Work: Conceptual Framework and Analysis of Retrospective European Data," *BMC Public Health* 14: 849.

Weichselbaumer, D. 2015. "Testing for Discrimination against Lesbians of Different Marital Status: A Field Experiment," *Industrial Relations: A Journal of Economy and Society* 54/1: 131–161.

Weil, D. 2014. *The Fissured Workplace: Why Work Became So Bad for So Many.* Cambridge: Harvard University Press.

Williams, C.C. 2014. "Out of the Shadows: A Classification of Economies by the Size and Character of their Informal Sector," *Work, Employment and Society* 28/5: 735–753.

Wimmer, A. 2008. "The Making and Unmaking of Ethnic Boundaries: A Multilevel Process Theory," *American Journal of Sociology* 113: 970–1022.

World Health Organization 2008. *Closing the Gap in a Generation: Health Equity through Action on the Social Determinants of Health. Final Report of the Commission on Social Determinants of Health.* Geneva: WHO.

World Health Organization 2013. *International Perspectives on Spinal Cord Injury.* Geneva: WHO.

World Health Organization 2014. *Review of Social Determinants and the Health Divide in the WHO European Region: Final Report,* 2nd edn. Copenhagen: WHO, Regional Office for Europe.

Yotopoulos, P. and D. Romano (eds.) 2007. *The Asymmetries of Globalization,* Routledge Studies in Development Economics, No. 55. London: Routledge.

Zimmermann, K., C. Biavaschi, W. Eichhorst, C. Giulieti, M. Kendzia, A. Muravyev, J. Pieters, N. Podriguez-Planas, and R. Schmidl 2013. "Youth Unemployment and Vocational Training," in K. Zimmermann et al. *Foundations and Trends in Microeconomics* 9/1–2: 1–57.

Zschirnt, E., and D. Ruedin 2016. "Ethnic Discrimination in Hiring Decisions: A Meta-analysis of Correspondence Tests 1990–2015," *Journal of Ethnic and Migration Studies* 42/7: 1115–1134.

8

Social Justice, Well-Being, and Economic Organization*

Coordinating Lead Authors:[1]
Gianluca Grimalda, Kalle Moene

Lead Authors:[2]
Fernando Filgueira, Marc Fleurbaey, Katherine Gibson, Carol Graham, Rubén Lo Vuolo, Reema Nanavaty, Hiroshi Ono, John Roemer, Alain Trannoy

*   Acknowledgments: We thank Amina Simon and Natalie Stelzer for excellent research assistance. We are also grateful to the reviewers of the first draft of our chapter, and to participants in seminars at the OECD, Paris, and at the Institute for International and Development Studies, Geneva. We especially thank Gustaf Arrhenius and the Institute for Future Studies in Stockholm, in whose inspiring environment we developed the key ideas of this chapter. Very warm thanks go to David Schkade, Avner de Shalit and Ingrid Robeyns, who had an invaluable role in the initial phase of this project.
[1]   Affiliations: GG: Kiel Institute for the World Economy, Germany; KM: University of Oslo, Norway.
[2]   Affiliations: FF: CIESU, Uruguay; MF: Princeton University, USA; KG: Western Sydney University, Australia; CG: Brookings, USA; RLV: Centro Interdisciplinario para el Estudio de Políticas Públicas, Argentina; RN: SEWA, India; HO: Hitotsubashi University, Japan and Texas A&M University, USA; JR: Yale University, USA;AT: AMSE and EHESS, France.

Summary

The *average* citizen of the world lives today in a better place than in the past. Income and life expectancy have on average increased, and extreme poverty rates have declined. Nevertheless, the *dispersion* of such a progress has been extremely uneven. In Section 8.2.2 we show that redistribution has been unable to reach the world's poorest people, both globally and nationally. Since the 1980s, both income and wealth have become more concentrated in the hands of the super-rich. The world is drifting toward a new Gilded Age where a global plutocracy becomes more and more dominant. Furthermore, increased material well-being has not translated into increased subjective well-being in rich societies. We discuss the so-called Easterlin paradox highlighting how social comparisons hinder subjective well-being and how individual aspirations dependent on one's social context can perpetuate poverty traps.

Our discussion of economic systems in Section 8.3 starts off observing that markets are indispensable systems for the allocation of productive factors and goods for consumption. Rather than converging to neoliberal forms of economic organizations, a wide variety of capitalistic systems is possible, depending on their system of wage determination and level of income redistribution. Culture adds to this variety. A cooperative social ethos has arguably been instrumental to the establishment of broad-ranging redistributive institutions and safety nets in some countries.

The core of our argument is that equality can serve as a development strategy (Section 8.4). A first cornerstone is wage compression. It stimulates innovation as the profitability of new technology rises, and it drives out of the market firms using inefficient technologies. Empirically, inequality in the US leads to greater productivity dispersion than the more egalitarian Nordic countries. A second cornerstone rests on the expansion of universal welfare programs, including income support, social insurance, and free access to health and education. A third cornerstone concerns asset redistribution. It involves guaranteed basic income, inheritance, and land reform. Taken together, these measures empower workers, who can then escape poverty traps and society as a whole can obtain higher incomes. Exploring forms of ownership and control of productive organizations, we discuss both profit-sharing and cooperative ownership – variants of democratic firms such as the Mondragón cooperatives and the Indian Self-Employed Women's Association. Finally, we make a case for the democratic governance of firms, discussing founding principles, efficiency gains that it permits, and feasible institutional and legal forms that would sustain it.

In Section 8.5 we critically examine the claims that globalization prevents egalitarian policies. Many argue that a "race-to-the-bottom" in tax rates jeopardizes the state's fiscal capacity, and that competition from workers in the "South" reduces unskilled wages in the "North." We note that the share of taxation has never been so large in OECD countries, and that skill-biased technological change has played a larger role than trade in the stagnation of unskilled wages in rich countries. States are far from being powerless in the face of globalization. Nevertheless, we also point out some trends that may constrain states' redistributive action in the future. High-skill workers are migrating toward North America, possibly attracted by low income taxes. Immigration toward the North seems to jeopardize social cohesion and thus compromise redistributive policies, as many voters turn to right-wing parties.

We conclude, in Section 8.6, by indicating policies for the twenty-first century to combat rising global and national inequality. These include a more progressive income tax, a global tax on wealth, and a global basic income. These policies may sound utopian, because they require much stronger global governance than what exists at the moment. Yet they may be achieved progressively, as has happened with many other policies in the past.

8.1 Introduction

The bourgeoisie, during its rule of scarce one hundred years, has created more massive and more colossal productive forces than have all preceding generations together. (Karl Marx and Friedrich Engels, Communist Manifesto, 1848)

"Can capitalism survive? No. I do not think it can," wrote the conservative economist Joseph Schumpeter in his book *Capitalism, Socialism, and Democracy* (1942: 61) – and added, "Can socialism work? Of Course it can" (1942: 167). While many people must have shared this view one hundred years ago, almost nobody holds it today. Instead, capitalism is associated with the end of history.

True or not, even those who believe that global capitalism is particularly ugly, unequal, inhumane, and brute condemn the system without having a clear picture of a possible alternative. The most ardent critics of social injustice under capitalism are perhaps the least precise in prescribing alternatives. To explore feasible alternatives to brute capitalism may therefore seem to be one of the most important issues in the social sciences today.

In the eighteenth and nineteenth century, by contrast, critics saw both the progressive sides of capitalism as well as the ugly ones. Some defended the system – others attacked it. Common for most of them were their sympathies with the poor segments of society. This is actually inherent in modernization theories from the Enlightenment era (Inglehart and Welzel 2005), emphasizing how technological progress gives people more and more control over nature, accompanied by cultural change and new value systems that are conducive to social progress (Marquis de Condorcet 1796).

Adam Smith, of course, saw many benefits of markets and capitalism. Yet he clearly identified the unequal power, social misuse, and the intolerable inequality of income in the capitalist system. In fact, the entire book *Wealth of Nations* can be read as an attack on the commercial system in England. He was morally concerned: "It is but equity, besides," and insisted, "that they who feed, cloath and lodge the whole body of the people, should have such a share of the produce of their own labour as to be themselves tolerably well fed, cloathed and lodged" (Smith 1776, Book I, Ch. VIII, p. 88). Secondly, inequality to Smith was a form of oppression: "For one very rich man there must be at least five hundred poor, and the affluence of the few supposes the indigence of the many" (Smith 1776, Book V, Ch. I, p. 232). Thirdly, Smith was skeptical of governmental interferences – not so much for the reasons that are used today, but simply because interventions tended to favor the rich over the poor. He observed, for instance, that there were "no acts of parliament against combining to lower the price of work; but many against combining to raise it" (Smith 1776, Book I, Ch. VIII, p. 74). Clear defenders of capitalism, like Adam Smith, were also the most serious critics of the system.

Similarly, the most ardent critics of capitalism, such as Karl Marx, also pointed to the social progress and productive improvements that the system offered. Marx was convinced that capitalist dynamics and the political clout of the bourgeoisie led to revolutionary changes in the economy, in politics, and in society at large – as "by the rapid improvement of all instruments of production, by the immensely facilitated means of communication, [capitalism] draws all, even the most barbarian, nations into civilization." Yet, he insisted on the need for a new alternative system – socialism.

Why was he heralding aspects of the system, yet announcing its abrupt end? One reason was that the capitalist mode of production was reaching the end of its progressive period. In his view, the world needed a new system of property relations to foster the further development of technology, labor productivity, and social progress. In the end of their manifesto, Marx and Engels (1848) provide some clues as to what they believed were necessary changes:

1. abolition of property in land and application of all rents of land to public purposes;
2. a heavy progressive or graduated income tax;
3. abolition of all rights of inheritance;
4. confiscation of the property of all emigrants and rebels;
5. centralization of credit in the hands of the state, by means of a national bank with state capital and an exclusive monopoly;
6. centralization of the means of communication and transport in the hands of the state;
7. extension of factories and instruments of production owned by the state; the bringing into cultivation of wastelands, and the improvement of the soil generally in accordance with a common plan;
8. equal liability of all to work; establishment of industrial armies, especially for agriculture;
9. combination of agriculture with manufacturing industries; gradual abolition of all the distinction between town and country;
10. free education for all children in public schools; abolition of children's factory labor in its present form; combination of education with industrial production.

Most of these at the time rather radical suggestions have actually been implemented, much later – many of them during the twentieth century, especially in the period after World War II. The delays teach us an important lesson. Reforms that in one period sound radical and even utopian can easily become politically feasible, and even sound mainstream, in later periods. Indeed, this is the case for agrarian reforms, progressive taxation, inheritance taxes, state property of means of transport and credit, free public education for all children, some national factories, workshops, railroads, and shipyards. Several further reforms, undertaken in the same fashion, were not even considered by the nineteenth-century revolutionaries: public health care, nationally financed pension systems, and state monopoly or dominant position in the production of basic utilities (water, communications, electricity).

The countries that perhaps went furthest in implementing egalitarian reforms and institutional changes are located in the north of Europe and particularly in Scandinavia. Surprisingly to some, their model of social-democratic development actually owes more to Adam Smith than to Karl Marx. The intellectual inspiration from Smith is not direct, but both Smith and social reformers in Scandinavia fought for the interests of the poor and saw modernization and expansion of markets as the key to escaping poverty. Both also saw the primary task as the removal of obstacles to rapid modernization – Adam Smith pointed at the guild privileges and monopolies that limited the size of the market; the social democrats pointed at the strong local unions whose wage premiums restricted the expansion of the most productive sectors (Moene 2011).[3]

What distinguished the social democrats from more conservative followers of Adam Smith like Margaret Thatcher was their solution to the problem of restricting the power of local unions. While Thatcher's solution was to weaken unions as institutions, the social-democratic approach was to strengthen unions as institutions and to structure collective bargaining in a highly centralized manner that reduced the influence of high-paid workers in the wage setting process. Empowering weak groups in the labor market and of course extending the franchise could fix some of the oppressive nature of economic inequality, as Smith saw it.

As reforms were implemented, well-being went up and a more just social order emerged by gradual changes. The twentieth century, especially the 40-odd years after World War II, saw the rise of a welfare state that empowered people, reduced inequality, and transformed society even further. In general, combinations of capitalism and democracy are responsible for most of the twentieth-century advances in well-being and social justice. No other arrangement comes close to achieving the desired goals to the same degree. It does not mean, however, that one size fits all. Capitalism includes countries as different as the US, Sweden, Switzerland, and Japan; useful reforms must fit the circumstances.

Now, however, the heterogeneity of capitalist arrangements is under attack. A renewed ideology, claiming to take inspiration from Adam Smith, has triumphed. It attacks the most progressive arrangements building on a perception where not just self-interest, but also greed, fear, and suffering are the driving forces behind economic prosperity and efficiency. Most countries give in to the quest for deregulation of financial markets, labor markets, housing markets, capital markets – in addition to welfare state retrenchments and less progressive taxes. As a result, inequality rises and the developmental state withers.

We review in Section 8.2.2 the major historical trends in inequality and social justice. We document a failure in helping the poorest, both globally and nationally. Moreover, since the "big U-Turn" of the 1980s, both income and wealth have become more concentrated in the hands of the super-rich. The world is drifting toward a new Gilded Age where a global plutocracy becomes more and more dominant. Global capitalism also faces huge problems in producing material improvements without climate change, and in producing a sense of belonging and happiness in the population.

One lesson from all this is that a small change can make a huge difference – both on the positive and the negative side. It can set forth cumulative changes. A minor regulation or deregulation, for instance, can lay the economic and political foundation for new, more fundamental changes in the same direction. The series of deregulations that we have recently seen in many countries may mirror in impact the step-by-step cumulative changes that once established the local more progressive arrangements.

Another lesson is that we cannot underestimate the role of markets in egalitarian reforms and the capacity of democracy to transform capitalist institutions and production relations. The most progressive and successful social reformers have built on a dual view of capitalism, including both its positive and negative sides. It is not necessarily the reforms that aim at turning the system around that make the most fundamental changes. Rather, those reforms that modify or change certain aspects of the system, and keep other aspects, as we shall return to many times below, are most likely to improve performance and enhance the well-being of the population. Thus both Smith and Marx had it right when heralding some aspects of capitalism and fiercely warning against others.

In any case, the real question is no longer whether capitalism can survive – or whether socialism can work. Rather, we should ask what is the feasible mix of markets and regulation; of social organization and individual autonomy; of social protection and capitalist dynamics; which works best, as measured by well-being and social justice.

There are several ideas of how to combine markets and social empowerment to enhance well-being by creating a more just society. One can:

1. take wage determination out of market competition and place it into a system of collective decision-making;
2. expand the welfare states at the national level, especially the universal welfare programs;
3. provide a national basic income system that frees workers from the slavery of capitalist relationships;
4. transform the structure of property relations and capitalist relations that reclaims the need for collective forms of property;
5. stimulate worker cooperatives where the direct producers in each enterprise make all major decisions and share the revenues;
6. favor the democratic governance of the firm, whereby workers are actively involved in the management of the firm;
7. work for a new global order where international, and possibly global, governance, is used to counter both national and global inequality.

In all these alternatives, there may be a strong complementarity between markets and social intervention, and between equality, participation, and social justice.

The lessons from Karl Polanyi (1944) are relevant in this context. He described the rise of global capitalism from late eighteenth to early twentieth century, emphasizing how modern capitalism came to treat land, labor, and money as natural commodities and not as complex social constructions. Once one has "commodified" these resources, the ideological policy of leaving the markets unregulated seems to follow as a natural result.

---

[3] See Moene (2011) for a discussion of Adam Smith as a social democrat.

The upshot is a disorder with economic and social instability and political unrest. In Polanyi's view, the anti-liberal reactions of fascism and communism, postcolonial wars, and the two world wars followed in essence from markets without social boundaries and state regulations. The national welfare states, the United Nations, and the Bretton Woods agreement were pieces of an imperfect, but far better architecture, than the one that dominated the last years of the nineteenth century and early twentieth century.

We are now at a similar crossroads as the one Polanyi described in the eve of the two great wars. Some of the challenges might be different, but there are enough similarities that we should do well to consider. At the national level, anti-liberal and anti-global political movements have gained momentum. Immigration, capital mobility, and regional and international economic trade are seen as the culprit of all our woes, and populist leaders promise a return to paradise lost through nationalistic policies of borders closed to trade, to capital flows, and especially to immigrants – the new scapegoats for the populist right. Rising inequality fuels populist and authoritarian streaks.

While global capitalism creates uneven growth and environmental crisis, the welfare state is under severe strains from high capital mobility and a more mobile population, potentially eroding its tax base. On top comes a technological revolution that threatens lifelong employment for all. While heightened inequality undermines the solidarity and ethos needed to sustain generous social provisions, the world order gives little hope for international stability. Bretton Woods institutions have long been losing their capacity to regulate. The UN remains underpowered to do its job. We have one declining power (the US) and one emerging power (China) in a world with civil wars in Africa and the Arab States.

Polanyi pointed at how authoritarianism may creep in, how world disorder may turn to open war, and how a dysfunctional global economy may turn threats into harm. Will such catastrophic outcomes be necessary to undertake the needed transformations at the local, national, regional, and global level? Or, will we heed these threats head on knowing that, while we face giant obstacles, inaction will be far worse than trial and error?

The chapter is organized as follows: Section 8.2 reviews the major empirical trends in both subjective and objective well-being, discussing the reasons for the disconnection between the two (greater material well-being has not led to greater subjective well-being in rich countries). Section 8.3 explores the varieties of economic systems around the world. Section 8.4 is the core of our chapter, as it proposes egalitarianism as a development strategy. We discuss the challenges that globalization poses to the welfare state in Section 8.5. Section 8.6 concludes, indicating economic policies to combat inequality and social injustice in the twenty-first century.

8.2   Well-being and Social Justice: Theory and Empirical Evidence

8.2.1   Basic Concepts

We rely on the "compass" of social progress set out in Chapter 2 of this volume, making the important point that it would be ill-advised to put forward a unique notion of social progress that would apply to all societies around the world. Not only is disagreement between academics too large, but also people around the world seemingly hold widely different beliefs on what social justice means (see Online Appendix, Section A8.1, available at www.ipsp.org). In spite of the pluralism of ideas, it is possible to find consensus on at least some basic concepts. For instance, the notion that human beings should be assigned equal dignity regardless of their race, ethnicity, gender, age, talent, and social position can be seen as a nonretractable principle upon which most people around the world would agree.

Chapter 2's authors distinguish between *values* and *principles*. The former refer to individuals' ultimate goals and objectives that make their lives worth living. The latter are the criteria to assess whether the distribution of values across individuals in a society may be considered just.

8.2.1.1   Values

A major distinction may be drawn between *subjective* accounts of well-being, which rely on individuals' own mental states and preferences, and *objective* accounts, which focus on the resources or opportunities that are available to individuals to achieve their goals. Among the accounts of subjective well-being (SWB), *happiness* has received increased attention in the last decades. This approach rests on the long-established utilitarian tradition initiated by Jeremy Bentham, claiming that happiness is simply the absence of pain and occurrence of pleasure – "the two sovereign masters," in Bentham's words (1970).[4] Another subjective account relies on satisfaction, i.e. on an individual's reflective assessment of how close the individual is to satisfying her own life goals or preferences.

Reducing well-being to happiness or satisfaction would lead to paradoxical implications. It may justify the redistribution of resources from a deprived individual to a wealthy individual, if the wealthy individual had expensive tastes – like dining with champagne and caviar – in comparison to the deprived individual. On the other hand, completely ignoring a person's pain and misery would also seem paradoxical. Any balanced notion of well-being should arguably not disregard individual happiness, but also look beyond that (Section 8.2.3.3). Accounts of objective well-being (OWB) do this. Sen (1985) introduces the notion of *functioning* to define the states of "being and doing" that individuals can achieve on the basis of their resources, physical

---

[4]   The notion of happiness as well-being is classified as "objective" in Chapter 2, while the notion of preference satisfaction is classified as subjective. The reason is that the mental states underpinning happiness can, at least in principle, be objectively measured. For the purpose of our concise summary, we conflated the notions of happiness and preference satisfaction into one category, which we refer to as subjective in the sense that it rests on subjective states of mind or preferences.

qualities, and social environments' characteristics. It is worth noting that feelings and satisfaction can appear as "functionings" alongside more objective components. Although this is admitted in theory, the practical applications are rare. Examples of functioning are being well-nourished, having shelter, etc. Sen further defines *capabilities* as the overall set of functioning vectors accessible to a person. The notion of capabilities incorporates individuals' freedom to achieve different states of affairs in their life.

While measurement of SWB typically relies on individuals' answers to research surveys, the measurement of OWB rests on a broader set of observations. Recent approaches to OWB are inherently multidimensional and include both material and nonmaterial components. For instance, the Human Development Index is inspired by the capability approach and includes measures of income, education, and health (see Chapter 1, Section 1.2.2, Chapter 3, Section 3.2.6, and the well-being indicators proposed by OECD 2015). The multidimensional indicators of OWB developed recently include several components that have been proven to be relevant for SWB in empirical research. At the measurement level, therefore, the distance between SWB and OWB seems less big than it might appear theoretically.

8.2.1.2   Principles

The second dimension of social progress consists of principles. Deontological approaches consider a state of affairs as "just" inasmuch as the *process* that brought about that outcome respected certain basic principles. Libertarianism argues that respecting some basic rights, in particular property rights, suffices to warrant the justice of the resulting outcome. Nozick (1974) claims that libertarianism ultimately rests on an inviolable moral right to self-ownership. An individual is entitled to reap the fruits of her own work, acquired abilities, and natural talents, provided that the individual has not infringed upon others' basic rights. Libertarianism can justify large disparities in the distribution of income, as it sees redistribution as a form of "slavery" of the rich toward the poor. This account has been criticized because it reduces the value of liberty to a merely formal assessment, rather than a substantive one (van Parijs 1995). An antithetical account of libertarianism preserves the notion of self-ownership, but argues that natural resources should be considered common property for all. This constitutes one reason to provide a basic income to all (van Parijs 1995; Vallentyne et al. 2005).

Consequentialist approaches only take into account outcomes per se, rather than processes. Utilitarianism represents the most important consequentialist account. In Bentham's original formulation, the utilitarian principle prescribed the maximization of the greatest happiness for the largest number of people.

An intermediate approach is the principle of equality of opportunity. Its basic idea is that the competition between individuals for social and economic positions should start from a *fair* "starting line," where no one enjoys undeserved advantage over others. A very limited form of equality of opportunity sees fairness as being granted by open universal access to careers, thus boiling down to a form of libertarianism.

However, less extreme forms of equality of opportunity argue that some redistribution of material resources should take place. The debate on what defines opportunities is still wide-ranging (see Chapter 2, Section 2.4.3.3). The notion of individual responsibility is central. As Roemer (1998) claims, it seems fair that individuals should be held responsible for their effort to achieve their goals, but not for factors that are beyond their control, i.e. the "circumstances" of their life – their social environment or their family.

Some would argue, however, that even effort is not completely under one's control as the preferences for effort may also be ultimately determined by one's social environment. According to this view, therefore, individuals would be responsible for almost nothing, and justice would boil down to pure equality of outcomes. Principles of justice can thus be used to justify very different positions in the spectrum going from fully libertarian to fully egalitarian positions.

8.2.2   The Evolution of Objective Well-being and Indicators of Social Justice

We believe it is indisputable that the ultimate reason for the *average* progress that human societies have achieved in the course of history is the massive range of technological innovations and productivity and efficiency gains that have been produced (see also Chapter 4, Section 4.2.3). Nonetheless, the *dispersion* of such gains across different groups within the same country can be very large and changeable across time. Such dispersion is the result of how institutions distribute income, wealth, and productivity gains within a society. Hence, social justice is the ultimate factor determining the extent of the disparity. Perhaps even more relevant than the way prosperity is distributed *within* a country is how it is distributed *between* countries. Notions of *global* social justice are even more difficult to establish than notions of national social justice, both for the variety of often conflicting views and for the lack of strong redistributive institutions worldwide (see Chapter 2, Section 2.6.4). The need for global approaches to social justice is nonetheless becoming more important because of the global nature of many problems faced by humankind.

While the list of possible components of OWB may be large (Section 8.2.1.1), here we focus on income, poverty, health, and education. We also focus on income and wealth inequality. Inequality in income and health are recognized by many scholars as general indicators of social justice. Moreover, income inequality at the country level is negatively correlated with the degree of intergenerational mobility (Chapter 3, Sections 3.2.10, 3.2.11, and 3.3.2.4) and, more generally, with inequality of opportunity (Chapter 3, Section 3.5.1.3). Income inequality therefore seems a synthetic indicator of a society's ability to not leave disadvantaged people behind, and to grant fair opportunities to its citizens. Moreover, income inequality is now taken to be one component of OWB (see Section 8.2.1.1), and it negatively affects SWB (Section 8.2.3). In the online Appendix, Section A8.2, we report additional data on the evolution of the Human Development Index, poverty rates, income concentration, and the Miser index. The latter index combines in a single indicator information on both inequality and poverty.

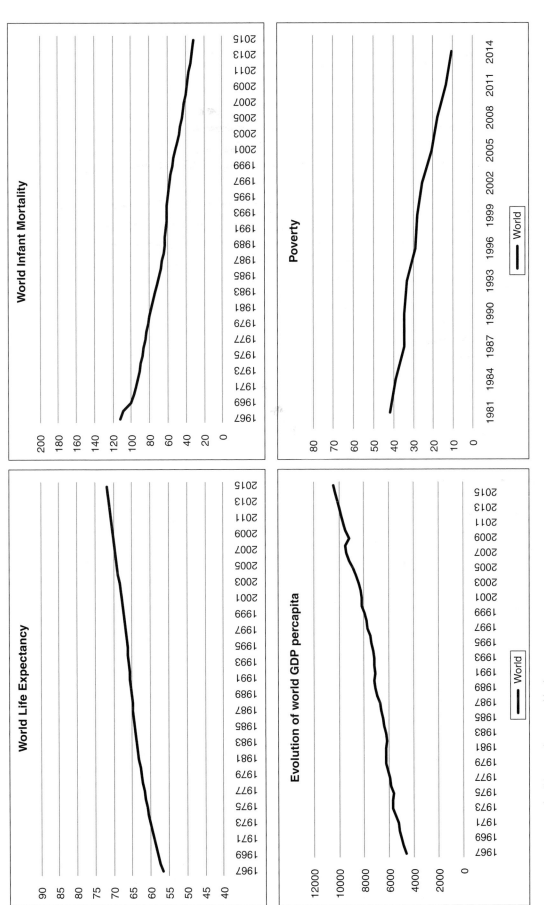

Figure 8.1 | Evolution of well-being indicators worldwide.

Source: Own elaboration based on World Development Indicators (WDI), World Bank

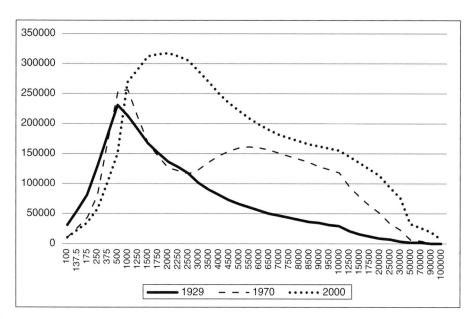

Figure 8.2 | Worldwide income distribution in 1929, 1970, 2000.

Note: The horizontal axis reports different income levels. The vertical axis reports the absolute frequency for each income level, i.e. the number of people owning a certain income. Alternative measures were used to estimate the Gini index for years before 1960 (see references).

Source: Our World in Data (Roser and Ortiz-Ospina 2017)

8.2.2.1   Progress Worldwide

Since World War II, humanity experienced a steady improvement in most indicators of average material well-being worldwide, in spite of the wide variety of socio-economic systems that countries embraced. In the "Global North," "real socialism" frontally opposed capitalist democracies up to the 1990s. In the "Global South," developing countries would either side with the socialist camp or pursue capitalist routes that would usually be far less democratic than in the North. The pursuit of forms of conservative modernization that combined corporatist institutions, authoritarian states, and market-based economies was common in the Global South. In a relatively short span of human history, life expectancy, child mortality, economic growth, and poverty reduction advanced at an unprecedented rate, as shown in Figure 8.1.

Figure 8.2 plots the world income distribution in three different epochs. In 1929, the distribution was highly unequal: the modal global citizen received 500 US dollars (USD) per year, while the median citizen earned around 1000 USD. The distribution in the 1970s shows a bimodal pattern. This suggests that while some countries had been able to catch up with the North, most had not progressed yet. Bimodality of the distribution is typical for the whole 1950–1980 period (Chapter 3, Section 3.4.1). In the year 2000 the world was richer than before, as shown by the shift to right of the distribution. Instances of bimodality virtually disappeared, suggesting that progress had occurred for a substantial number of countries.

The Gini index computed from the world income distribution shows a steady increase from 1820 up to around 1980 (see Chapter 3, Figure 3.3). The reason is that between-country income inequality (BCII) kept on growing from the start of the Industrial Revolution up to the 1950s, a time in which a substantial number of countries

had started industrializing (see Chapter 3 Sections 3.2.2 and 3.4.1, Figures 3.1 and 3.3). In the 2000s we observe, for the first time since the Industrial Revolution, signs of reduction in the global Gini index (Lakner and Milanovic 2013; see also the extensive discussion in Chapter 3, Section 3.4.1 and Figure 3.3). Even with such a reduction, global inequality remains high by any standards. With values slightly lower than 70 percent, it is on a par with inequality in the most unequal country in the world, which is at the time of writing Burkina Faso. Moreover, now that China has moved above the median position in the global income distribution, further growth in China would rather increase world inequality than reduce it – as it has done thus far (Milanovic 2016).

8.2.2.2   Progress by Groups of Countries

When average progress is disaggregated into blocks of countries of high, medium, and low income levels, the general picture is much more mixed than what shown above. The third panel of Figure 8.3 is particularly telling. While middle-income countries have continuously outperformed high-income countries since the 2000s, low-income countries have hardly ever caught up. Poverty reduction has shown progress for low-income countries, but not as fast as middle-income countries; the absolute number of people living in poverty has actually risen in Sub-Saharan Africa (Chapter 1, Section 1.2.2, Chapter 4, Section 4.4.1.1). Conversely, infant mortality and life expectancy show overall convergence.

Milanovic (2016) gives an even starker picture of the unevenness in the process of BCII reduction. He analyzes the growth rate for individual income brackets of the world income distribution between 1988 and 2008 (see Chapter 7, Section 7.2.4, Figure 7.2). Three facts stand out.

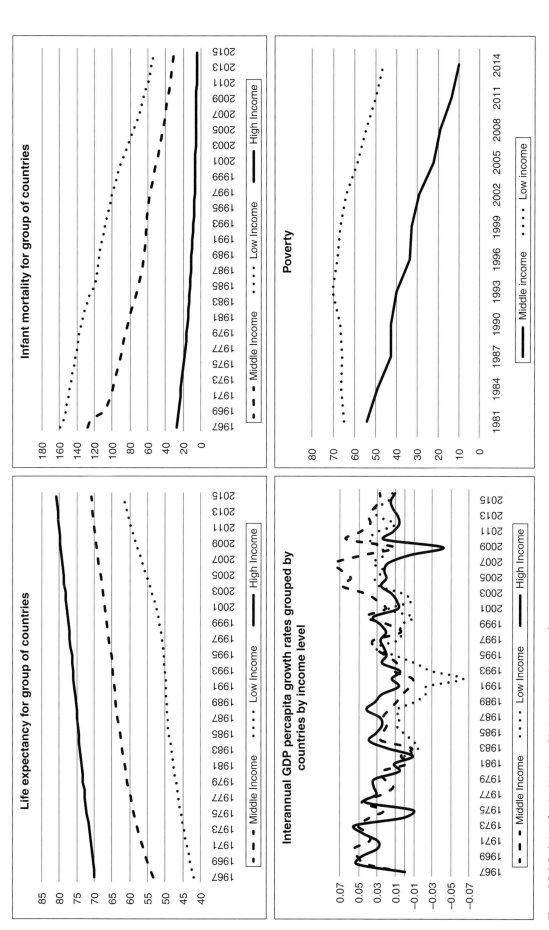

Figure 8.3 | Evolution of main objective well-being indicators by group of countries.
Note: See Figure 8.1.

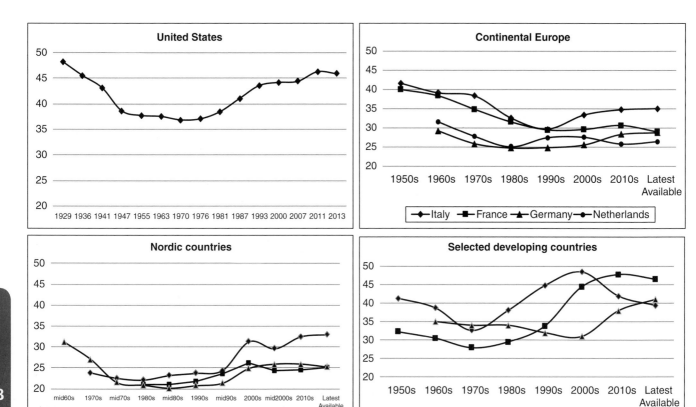

Figure 8.4 | Evolution of within-country inequality, as per Gini index.
Note: Own elaboration based on UNU-WIDER, World Income Inequality Database (WIID3.4), and SWIID (Solt 2016). See note to Figure 8.2.

Table 8.1 | Concentration of wealth in selected countries

	(1)	(2)	(3)	(4)	(5)
	Europe 1910	US 1910	Nordic countries 1970s–1980s	Europe 2010	US 2010
Upper class (top 10%)	90%	80%	50%	60%	70%
"Dominant" (top centile)	50%	45%	20%	25%	35%
"Well-to-do" (2nd–10th percentiles)	40%	35%	30%	35%	35%
Middle class (50th–10th percentiles)	5%	Not available	40%	35%	25%
Lower class (100th–50th percentiles)	5%	Not available	10%	5%	5%
Corresponding Gini coefficient	0.85		0.58	0.67	0.73

Source: Piketty (2014)

The group that experienced the largest income growth is the "global middle-class," mainly formed by skilled workers in strongly developing countries such as China and India. The group whose income grew at the second fastest rate is the top 5 percent of the world income distribution. Such "global plutocrats," as Milanovic calls them, are formed by the rich (meaning top 10 percent) in the US, Europe, Japan, but also by the super-rich (top 1 percent) in Brazil, Russia, and South Africa. In terms of absolute income, this group has amassed the largest gains in the period. Two groups have seen hardly any increase in income in the period: citizens from the middle/low income ranking in rich countries, and most citizens from ex-Communist countries. They occupy the 80th percentile in the world income distribution. The other group of people who have not benefitted is the people lying at the very bottom of the world income distribution. Hence, as much as the world as a whole has *on average* progressed, it has failed to reach out to its poorest people.

8.2.2.3   Within-Country Analysis

The unevenness of the progress concerning income distribution is also apparent looking at WCII. Chapter 3, Sections 3.5 and 3.6, provides an extensive analysis of such patterns for different regions of the world. A decreasing trend in WCII was common in the richest countries during the twentieth century, but this ended in the 1970s and 1980s. WCII then followed a markedly increasing trend, forming the so-called "big U-Turn" in WCII. Figure 8.4 shows how this pattern has been particularly pronounced for the US, although other European countries followed a similar pattern. Panel D of Figure 8.4, shows how WCII patterns in developing countries have been diverse.

The reasons behind such trends are clear. In the period leading up to World War I, markets were largely unregulated, trade unions quite weak, and the welfare state had almost no effect on redistribution. The crises of the 1930s did not increase inequality but actually moderated it; the two world wars had strong inequality-decreasing effects (Piketty 2014; Milanovic 2016). After World War II, an expanding democratic welfare state combined with strong unions to further redistribute income through progressive taxation and a compressed wage distribution. This pattern of growth with redistribution extended beyond the US and Western Europe in the capitalist world, including Japan, Australia, New Zealand, and Canada. The collapse of the world order in the 1970s, with the abandonment of the Bretton Woods monetary system in 1971, the oil crisis of 1973, and the 1974 stock market crash, precipitated economic recessions in the rich Western world and put an end to these redistributive drives.

Wealth inequality is even higher than income inequality (in the Appendix, Section A8.2, we also report data on income concentration). Piketty (2014) divides society into three classes: the "upper class," formed by the top percentile of the distribution, the "middle class," formed by the 40 percent of the population who are richer than the median but poorer than the upper class, and the "lower class," formed by the population's poorest half. The upper class is further broken down into the "dominant" class – the top 1 percent – and the "well-to-do" class, comprised of the remaining 9 percent. The US stands out as being one of the most unequal societies as of 2010, with the upper class owning as much as 70 percent of total wealth (Table 8.1, column 5).

Most continental European countries displayed a more egalitarian distribution in 2010 than the US (Table 8.1, column 4). It is noticeable, though, that the poorest owned the same – 5 percent of the total – in both the US and Europe. The main difference between the US and Europe lies in the European middle class (upper class) being relatively wealthier (less wealthy) than their US counterparts, while the lower class owned the same in the two systems. A helpful reference point is given by the Nordic countries in the 1970s–1980s (Table 8.1, column 3), the least unequal society observed since records began. The share of the upper class amounted to "only" half of total wealth, while the middle class owned 40 percent and the lower class managed to appropriate 10 percent of total wealth. The distribution of wealth in Nordic countries has converged toward continental European levels in the last three decades, although it is still slightly more egalitarian.

One might conclude that the capacity of the welfare state to dent the elites' portfolios is limited. However, this is not completely true. Wealth inequality was even higher in the most unequal society that has ever been observed: Europe in the "belle époque" years, preceding World War I. The European upper class in 1910 had amassed a staggering 90 percent of total wealth (Table 8.1, column 1). The middle class was virtually nonexistent, as people between the median and the 90th percentile owned a meager 5 percent of total wealth, the same share as the poorest half of the population. We need to say that these figures are based on only three European countries – namely, France, the UK, and Sweden – for which comprehensive data are available. However, these three cases yield virtually the same picture. It is particularly interesting that Sweden in 1910 was as inegalitarian as the other two European countries. This shows that the high levels of equality achieved in the course of the twentieth century in Sweden and in the Nordic countries were not a historical legacy, but rather the consequence of robust institutional reforms.

Interestingly, wealth distribution in the US in 1910 was considerably more egalitarian than in Europe (Table 8.1, column 2). The reason, as Piketty (2014) explains, is that it takes time for wealth distribution to become unequal, because large fortunes are accumulated over many generations. US society in 1910 was still relatively "young" for a large concentration of wealth to have taken place, given its markedly egalitarian initial character.

That Europe today is considerably more egalitarian than in 1910 stems in part from the two world wars, which destroyed élites' large fortunes, and in part from the stronger welfare state, constraining the wealth of the upper class (Section 8.5). Yet there are reasons for concern. First, as already noted, the larger European welfare state does not seem to have benefitted the people at the bottom of the distribution. Second, the ongoing trend of increasing concentration of wealth at the top of the distribution tends to take us back to the years of the Belle Epoque in Europe. These are formidable challenges.

The incapacity of the welfare state to empower the neediest people is all the more worrying in the light of digitalization and robotization (see Chapter 7, Section 7.2.2). Although the "end of work" may too pessimistic a scenario, empowering the lower class to own part of productive capital appears to be a necessary arrangement for social justice in the twenty-first century. For instance, Atkinson (2015) recommends the creation of a public Investment Authority to operate a sovereign wealth fund holding investment in companies and in property.

We further reflect on the relationship between OWB, social justice, and technological innovation in the Appendix, Section A8.4.

8.2.3   Subjective Well-being, the Easterlin Paradox, and Other Dimensions of Well-being

8.2.3.1   Subjective Well-being: Its Evolution and Its Paradoxes

Interest in measuring SWB stems in part from the popularization of the so-called Easterlin paradox in economics (Easterlin et al. 2010) and

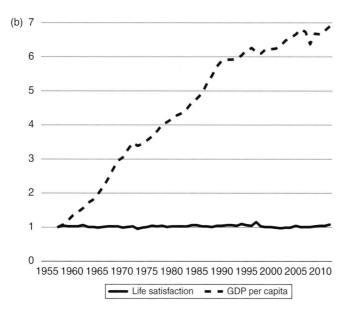

Figure 8.5a | Income and happiness in the United States.
Source: Ono and Lee (2016)

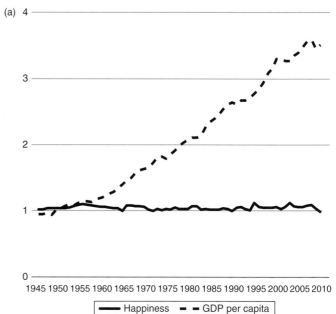

Figure 8.5b | Income and life satisfaction in Japan.
Source: Ono and Lee (2016)

from the theory of hedonic adaptation in psychology (Kahneman et al. 1999). The Easterlin paradox brings out a puzzle: while satisfaction co-varies with one's income level in each period, there is no increase in average life satisfaction over long periods of time – in spite of a tripling of income levels over the period and the improvement in material conditions of life that we reviewed in Section 8.2.2. This puzzle is based on responses to large-scale survey questions conducted in the US and elsewhere, inquiring about individuals' satisfaction with their lives. Figures 8.5a and 8.5b illustrate the paradox in the case of the US and Japan.

The Easterlin paradox points to a disconnect between OWB, as represented by income, and SWB, as measured by survey questions. The paradox has been confirmed in country-level cross-sections as well. Figure 8.6 shows the relationship between gross national product per capita and aggregate happiness from 65 countries based on the World Values Survey (Inglehart and Klingemann 2000). We observe a slightly positive association for incomes above 9000 USD, preceded by a very high – nearly vertical – correlation for incomes below 9000 USD.

One solution to the Easterlin paradox lies in the idea that a substantial portion of individual consumption is "positional" (Layard 2011). That is, individuals derive utility not from consuming a given good (or service) but from consuming it *while others cannot*. A good has positional value when the presence of more owners of similar goods erodes the *social status* of owning it. Social status is by definition a scarce resource, which declines as more people own the good. Clearly, owning a good will bring some utility in addition to the status it confers, but for the sake of the argument we assume here that happiness is only given by the good's positionality. For instance, the owner of a luxurious sport car will be maximally happy when she is the *only* owner of such a car in her neighborhood, but her happiness will decline as more neighbors purchase a car with the same characteristics. When everyone in the neighborhood owns a luxurious car, everyone's happiness will be the same as when *nobody* owned a car. Owning positional goods is a

zero-sum game, where owners' happiness must be balanced out with nonowners' *un*happiness (Clark et al. 2008).

Since it is mainly rich individuals who own positional goods, this account can explain both the positive correlation between happiness and income at one point in time – richer individuals *are* typically happier than poor individuals – and the substantial stability of average happiness over time among rich countries: as consumption of positional goods becomes universal, no individual can gain "status" from higher consumption.

An alternative explanation of the Easterlin paradox hinges on the idea that individuals' happiness adapts to changed circumstances and tends to revert to a constant baseline level (Frederick and Loewenstein 1999). Higher income may tend to have decreasing effects on happiness over time (see also Chapter 4, Section 4.1.1.2). This may be due to either *habituation*, that is, individuals getting used to higher standards of living, or to *contrast*, that is, individuals derive lower satisfaction from previous sources of pleasure (Brickman et al. 1978). Changing aspiration may also reduce happiness. Since aspirations are adjusted upward as income increases, individuals are less happy – and more frustrated – when they do not meet their aspirations.

Easterlin (2003) argues that the real issue is not so much whether adaptation happens or not, but whether it is complete or not. He claims that extant evidence goes against the hypothesis of complete adaptation in domains such as health and marital status, while complete adaptation with respect to income changes is more likely to be the case. Clark et al. (2008) also confirm that the overall long-term effect of income increases may be very small. Empirical evidence is consistent with a model where two-thirds of aggregate income has no effect on average happiness because it is status-related – and thus disappears in a zero-sum game – and where 60 percent of the effect at the individual level vanishes within two years due to

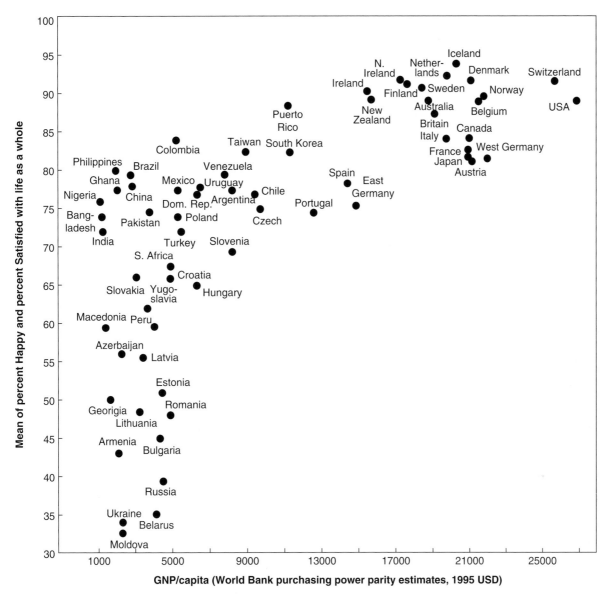

Figure 8.6 | Aggregate happiness by gross national product (GNP) per capita.
Source: Inglehart and Klingemann (2000)

habituation. As a result, only 13 percent of an income increase will survive in the long run at the aggregate level (Clark et al. 2008: 22). Needless to say, this seems a very small gain. Clark et al. (2008) nonetheless add that this is likely to be a lower bound of the actual income effect, because various methodological problems make it difficult to precisely estimate the relationship. First of all, income is only an imperfect proxy for the variable that arguably matters the most in individual happiness: consumption. Secondly, omitted variables or mediating variables such as pollution or education make the relationship between happiness and income somewhat spurious.

In the Appendix we further detail different approaches to the measurement of SWB (Section A8.3.1) and review some methodological controversies surrounding the Easterlin Paradox (Section A8.3.2). In the next section we examine the relationship between safety nets, macroeconomic change, and SWB.

8.2.3.2 Beyond the Easterlin Paradox: Social Safety Nets, Market Liberalization and Individual Well-being

The results described above have been replicated across countries and over time, and patterns in the determinants of SWB are remarkably consistent (see e.g. Helliwell et al. 2013). Psychological, genetic, and other biomarkers of well-being consistently correlate with SWB measures. Income matters within countries, and respondents with means typically score higher than those without sufficient income. Other variables such as health, employment status, stable partnerships, and political freedom are typically as important (Graham 2009). We analyze the beneficial effects that being happy exerts of being happy in the Appendix, Section A8.3.3.

A wide range of studies show that individuals who live in countries with better and more widely shared safety nets and public health systems, among other things, have higher levels of well-being.

Happier individuals with more positive outlooks for the future are not only more productive and healthier, but have better labor market outcomes over time (De Neve et al. 2013). In contrast, several factors associated with persistent poverty not only undermine the productivity of significant sectors of today's labor markets, but also those of the next generation. For example, inferior or inexistent public services, lack of social insurance, and the associated stress due to constant uncertainty and circumstances beyond individuals' control can eventually have negative cognitive effects – which make it difficult for individuals to plan ahead, much less invest in their futures and those of their children.

A prime example that illustrates the linkages between social safety nets and well-being comes from the postcommunist (or transition) countries, namely post-Soviet countries and China. In most transition economies, life satisfaction declined after the transition. The deterioration of social safety nets and the sudden exposure to market uncertainty following the transition are key sources of unhappiness and anxiety in these economies.

Life under communism was predictable and secure. People were guaranteed jobs, and social insurance coverage was universal in its truest form. The transition to market capitalism removed the safety net that had protected the well-being of people and their families. The job market, which had operated at virtually full employment under communism, deteriorated with double-digit declines in employment levels. Exposure to market uncertainty and the privatization of the social safety net in such areas as health insurance and education left the people feeling vulnerable and insecure, their traditional identities being eroded (Ono and Lee 2016). Half of the respondents from 28 transition countries believe that the transition did not bring any gains at all (Guriev and Zhuravskaya 2009).

Interestingly, growing dissatisfaction also emerges in transition economies that experienced a surge in economic growth. Life satisfaction in China actually declined, on average, in the last decades, and this was accompanied by increases in suicide rates and incidence of mental illness (Graham et al. 2015). The deterioration of the social safety net is a key source of unhappiness in China. Like the post-Soviet economies, China's path to market capitalism involved large-scale privatization of public services, such as in the health sector in particular prior to the health care reform of 2011. This weakened the existing institutional setting and destabilized people's lives.

People harbor a deep sense of social injustice following the transition. People had high expectations that the transition was the path to meritocracy. But the transition and its accompanying market reforms fell short of people's expectations, and optimism was replaced by powerlessness followed by hopelessness. As documented by countless testimonies of Russian people in Alexievich (2016)'s seminal book, *Secondhand Time*, the promises of the Gorbachev and Yeltsin eras were left largely undelivered, leaving Russians with a sense of betrayal and resentment for the transition. Increased inequality between the rich and the poor instilled feelings of injustice and unfairness. In the case of China, there is empirical evidence that the transition benefited the rich relative to the poor . Survey responses by income categories taken in 1990 and 2007 show that life satisfaction declined in the bottom two income categories, but increased in the top income category (Easterlin et al. 2012).

Hopes of well-functioning markets were displaced by persistent inequality, widespread corruption, and organized crime. The post-Soviet economies consistently rank among the most corrupt countries in the European Union, according to Transparency International, and among the lowest in interpersonal trust (Putnam 2000). There is a pervasive sense of powerlessness, as they perceive that nothing can be done to overcome these market failures.

While the transition countries provide the most dramatic examples of changes in or deterioration of safety nets, there is a more general relationship between better public goods, environments, and social support and aggregate levels of well-being around the world (Graham 2009; Helliwell et al. 2013).

There is less clarity on the relationship between well-being and the *level* and *nature* of safety nets, however. Different societies have different norms about the relative roles of individual versus collective responsibility in providing social insurance and social support. Some, such as the US, place much more importance on the former, and others, such as most European countries, place more emphasis on the latter. And in other societies, as in many Latin American countries, families play much more of a role in providing social support and help at times of need than they do in others.

Given these differences in social norms and family/social structures, it is not possible to propose a particular form of safety net or social welfare system that will increase aggregate levels of well-being worldwide. Yet societies with inadequate safety nets and/or economic and social systems that accentuate inequalities across socio-economic and racial cohorts clearly have lower levels of SWB than others at comparable income levels.

The US today is a case in point. A significant decline in the availability of low-skilled jobs combined with inadequate social support for the unemployed is increasingly associated with widespread desperation and lack of hope among some cohorts (poor whites in particular). This ill-being is reflected in an increase in preventable deaths (suicide, opioid and drug addiction, and diabetes) and is driving up overall US mortality rates (Case and Deaton 2015; Graham 2017).

Adequate social support for those who fall behind is an essential element of happy and just societies. The nature of that support will vary across societies, reflecting social norms on the one hand and economic and institutional structures on the other. Societies that fail to provide the institutional and economic resources necessary are much more likely to perpetuate or exacerbate injustice and to have significantly lower levels of well-being.

8.2.3.3   Subjective Well-being and Policy

While subjective scores alone cannot serve as a basis for welfare assessments or policy choices, the gaps between objective and subjective indicators provide important and often novel insights which can, for example, help explain persistent poverty and injustice traps, including very unequal distributions of well-being within and across societies.

One of the main findings in social psychology is that people's life goals depend on their aspirations, which in turn are conditioned by the social environment in which one is brought up (Ray 2006; Dalton et al. 2016). Typically, people brought up in relatively disadvantaged social environments set less ambitious life goals than others. This entails that these people will be less willing to take advantage of the opportunities provided to them, and will be, broadly speaking, less successful in life. The upshot is that the condition of disadvantage will be perpetuated across generations, as initially disadvantaged people become locked in to a poverty trap that is ultimately caused by their failure to set higher aspirations. A successful policy of equality of opportunity should therefore take into serious consideration the purely psychological aspect of aspiration failure. Maximizing OWB or equalizing opportunities calls for greater integration between SWB analyses and policies aimed at increasing social justice.

For example, recent research in the US finds significant inequalities in well-being across socio-economic cohorts. A significant percentage of the poor live moment-to-moment, with high levels of stress and other markers of ill-being, and lacking the capacity to plan for or invest in their futures. Wealthy cohorts in the same country, meanwhile, have very high levels of well-being and almost unlimited capacity to invest in their own and their children's futures. The gaps in hope and expectations across these two cohorts makes success seem even less attainable for the poor, adding an additional disincentive to making the necessary investments in education, health, and savings (Graham 2017). Such trends are surely not unique to the US (although they are remarkable for such a wealthy country), and characterize the differences in the lives – and life chances – of the rich and the poor in many developing countries around the world.

The analysis from the previous section also shows that SWB reacted swiftly, and negatively, to badly designed or hastily executed reforms in transition economies. There is little doubt that the sense of dissatisfaction with these policies has fed back negatively on their implementation and further slowed the growth recovery.

More generally, many economic policies pursuing economic growth are implicitly justified by the assumption that they cause greater individual welfare. The finding that SWB reacts modestly to increases in income – for countries richer than a certain income threshold (Section 8.2.3.1; Figure 8.6) – should make one doubtful that economic growth should be the overarching policy goal, especially in rich countries. Layard (2011) goes as far as proposing the taxation of consumption at a fairly high rate. Their rationale is that consumption should be taxed as any good that produces a negative externality on others (e.g. smoking or polluting) in order to reduce the negative impact on others' welfare to optimal levels. Some scholars have even doubted the overall benefits of growth, and have thus called for "degrowth" (see Chapter 4, Section 4.1.1.2). Although these proposals should be evaluated with caution, the bottom line, we believe, is that nonmaterial policy objectives should receive attention alongside material ones.

The considerations in this section highlight how, in our view, SWB and OWB should not be seen as opposing policy objectives, as some in the scholarly debate sometimes portray them. Pursuing SWB does not detract from the need to set out objectively defined objectives of social justice. On the other hand, pursuing OWB-defined objectives will benefit from understanding the psychological mechanisms behind individual behavior, and leaves ample room for taking into account individual SWB when such objectives are reached.

8.3 Varieties of Economic Systems and Their Records on Well-being and Social Justice

8.3.1 Socialism and Communism in the Twentieth Century

Our first step to explore economic organization for the future is to look back at history, in particular at the failure of the Communist experiments in the twentieth century. We believe that there were two principal mistakes that, eventually, destroyed the Soviet-type economies. The first was a system of political dictatorship, which lacked even the imperfect mechanism of political accountability that characterizes capitalist democracies. The second error, which was not clearly visible for a while, was the refusal to introduce markets to organize production and distribution. The fear that markets would bring with them a reappearance of capitalism was sufficiently strong among the leadership of the Soviet Union that markets and freely moving prices were never introduced.

Initial industrialization was successful because it depended mainly upon moving millions of semi-productive farmers into factories and cities, a process that did not require markets. Yet the further problems of organizing complex interfirm trade, providing goods to consumers when and where they are needed, and innovating cannot be organized by centralized allocation – at least in a large, complex modern economy.

Markets perform the function of allocating many kinds of goods and resources from as many as hundreds of thousands of firms to as many as millions of people, in a relatively efficient manner. They do this by providing individuals and firms with material incentives – typically, the firms and entrepreneurs desire to maximize profits, workers desire to earn a decent living, and consumers (who are also workers) desire to meet their household needs within their budgets. There are some caveats concerning the efficiency of markets (Section 8.5.2.1), but these should not obscure the fact that markets are an essential institution, one that has evolved over millennia, that we do not know how to replace. Any complex economy *must use* markets, at least in the foreseeable future (Przeworski 2003. For a detailed analysis of markets as key institution of capitalist systems, see Chapter 6, Section 6.2.1).

The problem is that market systems, unless properly managed, lead to huge inequalities of income and wealth (Section 8.2.2; Chapter 3, Section 3.1.2.3; and Chapter 6, Sections 6.2.2–6.2.3 and 6.3.6–6.3.8). The key question is whether it is possible to have a high standard of living, fairly equally enjoyed in the population, with a large complex economy, where economic activity is organized using markets. The leaders of the Soviet-style societies of the "short twentieth century"

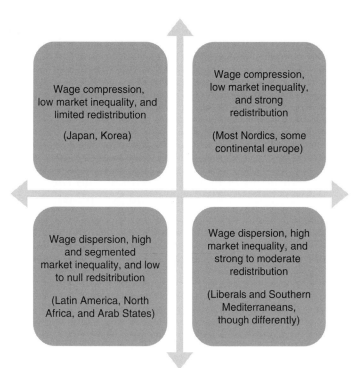

Figure 8.7 | Categorization of capitalist regimes according to their level of wage dispersion (vertical axis) and redistribution (horizontal axis).

(Hobsbawm 1995) elected not to introduce markets because they believed the answer was no. The only way of maintaining a semblance of equality was, they believed, to stick to the system of central allocation. In the end, this engendered economic sclerosis and implosion of the system.

The Chinese Communist leadership, learning from Soviet errors, decided they must transition to a market economy: this was the deduction of Deng Xiao-Ping. They saw Japan, South Korea, Taiwan, Hong Kong, and Singapore leaping ahead of them. In 1979 the Chinese began dissolving the collective farms and leasing land to peasant households on a long-term basis. At the same time, they gradually introduced markets for agricultural produce. Modernization through markets allowed hundreds of millions of Chinese people to exit extreme poverty. This significantly lowered *global* inequality (Section 8.2.2.2), as the Chinese peasantry comprised a large mass of the poorest in the world. However, inequality *within* China is quite severe (Section 8.2.2.3). While the public sector of state-owned firms continues to exist, the private sector is growing rapidly.

So far China's leaders have been unwilling to use tax policy, redistribution, and social empowerment to lead the development toward a more socially just society – perhaps because they believe that such measures are bad for economic growth and development. Or perhaps it is because in authoritarian regimes, where the state has significant amounts of power, it is only natural that a culture of privilege associated with power rather than with innovation will ultimately predominate.

So "real socialism" has either led to stagnation and implosion in authoritarian regimes that also tend to produce nonmarket-based

inequalities linked to power and privilege, or to growth – but highly unequal growth in authoritarian regimes. China's economic success has to do with a particular economic route: that of state capitalism. In doing so, China resembles the choice made by other Asian countries before China embraced markets (Section 8.3.2.4).

Whatever economic model we might ascribe to, it seems obvious that it should be administered through democratic means. It is highly unlikely that authoritarian and even more, totalitarian, political models will produce anything resembling well-being and social justice.

8.3.2   The Varieties of Modern Capitalism

Modern capitalism has many faces and forms. Contrary to the radical convergence thesis that posits that globalization and technological change would lead all countries to resemble one another, countries remain very much distinct in the way they set up markets and capitalist relations. Figure 8.7 offers a rationalization of capitalist systems according to two dimensions: the labor–capital nexus regarding wage dispersion, and the fiscal and welfare state aspect regarding taxation and social spending in transfers and services. Some countries compress wages and also redistribute after such wage compression, others do not compress wages but do redistribute, others compress wages but redistribute very little, and still others neither compress wages nor redistribute.

We reflect more on the interaction between these dimensions in the Appendix, Section A8.5.

8.3.2.1   The Liberal Model

In the comparative literature of economic systems, the liberal model is characterized by its high reliance on markets as transactions mechanisms, and by the limited action space granted to the state in the management of the economy. Although free unregulated markets are clearly an abstraction, as all societies operate some form of regulation of markets, in relative terms the liberal model can be said to come closest to the ideal-type of a free market.

In terms of Esping-Andersen's (1990) analysis of welfare states, the liberal model operates the lowest degree of decommodification. This is defined as *"the degree to which an individual, or families, can uphold a socially acceptable standard of living independently of market participation"* (Esping Andersen 1990: 37). The state is the primary substitute for markets in supporting individuals' standards of living. The state can implement income redistribution and provide social insurance. Both instruments support individuals' incomes in general and in particular under adverse circumstances – such as unemployment, illness, or other factors making an individual unable to participate in the labor market. In some societies, such as in particular Mediterranean societies, the family also acts as a social institution replacing the market to support individuals' incomes, particularly during their youth (Ferrera 1996).

In the liberal model, state intervention is normally limited to providing public goods such as security, law enforcement, and public administration. Health and education normally involve a mixture of private and public intervention. Although the size of the state in the economy, as measured by the ratio between tax revenues and Gross Domestic Product (GDP), is high in absolute terms – around 30 percent of GDP – countries belonging to this model have much lower levels of tax revenues than continental European countries (Figure 8.11 and Section 8.5.3.1). In terms of Figure 8.7, the liberal model is characterized by a high level of wage dispersion. The labor market is left relatively unregulated, therefore there is no capping of high salaries paid to high-skilled individuals (Section 8.5.3.1). At the other side of the spectrum, trade unions are typically weak or nonexistent, so that unskilled workers have little bargaining power. This results in low wages for unskilled workers. The liberal model is also characterized by low levels of income redistribution. This causes high levels of inequality (Section 8.2.2.3). While the US embodies the quintessential form of liberal capitalism, other Anglo-Saxon countries (the UK, Canada, Australia, and New Zealand) are typically grouped into the same model.

High levels of competition among firms and individuals are another aspect characterizing the liberal model. However, competition is not an exclusive characteristic of this model, as the Nordic model also heavily relies on it.

8.3.2.2   The Nordics – Markets with Social Democracy and the Cooperative Social Ethos

The Nordic countries of Denmark, Finland, Iceland, Norway, and Sweden pioneered a model based on political democracy, capitalist property relations (meaning: predominantly private ownership of firms), a market economy, a comprehensive organization of workers in labor unions, and high taxation financing a pervasive welfare state. The political parties that organized this experiment called themselves social-democratic, as opposed to the Communist parties of the Soviet-style countries and China. Rather than dictatorship by a single party, there has been democratic political competition between freely formed parties in these countries. More significantly, there has been a very limited use of public ownership: almost all firms are privately owned by families or shareholders.

Yet, the Nordic countries have achieved what is probably the highest degree of income equality in the world (Section 8.2.2.3), and the greatest security for ordinary people through a large welfare state. As we said, government economic activity is financed by about one-half the GDP of the country, which is collected through various forms of taxation.

The Nordic system rests on a specific social ethos, which has made it possible for these countries to remain egalitarian. The Nordic cooperative social ethos is well summarized by a statement of Per Albin Hansson, a leader of the Swedish social-democratic party in the late 1920s. He said (in a speech in 1928, quoted in Heclo and Madsen 1987):

> The basis of the home is community and togetherness. The good home does not recognize any privileged or neglected members, nor any favorite or stepchildren. In the good home there is equality, consideration, cooperation, and helpfulness. Applied to the great people's and citizens' home this would mean *the breaking down of all the social and economic barriers that now separate citizens into the privileged and the neglected, into the rulers and the dependents, into the rich and the poor, the propertied and the impoverished, the plunderers and the plundered* [italics added]. Swedish society is not yet the people's home. There is a formal equality, equality of political rights, but from a social perspective, the class society remains and from an economic perspective the dictatorship of the few prevails.

The italicized statement defines the kind of solidarity that the social-democratic parties attempted to teach the citizenry, with a great deal of success. This is one of cooperation and reciprocation: I will make my contribution to society, in full expectation that others will do the same. A cooperative ethos is a far cry from the *individualistic ethos*, which is the official creed of capitalism, and values only the individual's advancement – in particular, the increase in his or her material wealth. One's country should be one's home, according to Per Albin Hansson, with all the connotations of mutual aid and respect that characterize a good home.

Now the success of Nordic social democracy, many say, is due to several of the special features of these countries: they are small and at the time their welfare states and social ethos developed, they were homogeneous – linguistically, ethnically, and religiously. Some of this is clearly true, but social and economic cleavages and the inherent conflicts in the Nordic countries at that time are also part of the story.[5]

---

[5]   During the interwar period, Sweden, Norway, and in part Denmark had the world record in strikes and lockouts measured by lost working days. Finland had a civil war in 1918 between the Reds, led by the Social Democratic party, and the Whites, led by the conservative-led Senate. Almost 40,000 people died. The war divided Finland politically for many years.

To appreciate the achievements we also have to recall that the economies that the social democrats inherited in the 1930s were far from affluent. There was open unemployment in the cities and disguised unemployment in the countryside. In Norway around half of the population lived in sparsely populated areas, where most made a living from farming and fishing. The real per capita GDP of Sweden and Norway was below the current real per capita GDP of low middle-income countries today. Thus it is clear that a majority of citizens in the Nordic countries became rich under the social-democratic model of governance, not before. We also mentioned that in 1910 wealth and income distribution in Sweden, for which we have historical data, was as *unequal* as any other industrial society of the time – in particular on a par with France (Section 8.3.2.3). The attainment of equality during the twentieth century was the result of institutional reform and political struggle, rather than a legacy of the past.

The social-democratic model released an impressive development path of modernization and structural change. Over a period of more than 80 years economic growth has been at least on a par with that in the US, but with much more social involvement and egalitarian distribution of the proceeds (Barth et al. 2015). As the system evolved, earnings distribution became more and more compressed. The low wage inequality and the increasing mean level have also induced more egalitarian policies of health, education, and social insurance against income loss and old age.

Throughout, the social equality has been sustained by external pressure on internal behavior. Global economic competition on the outside has led to local cooperation on the inside where the division line is the border of the nation-state. In larger countries, a similar distinction between external and internal could be placed at a lower level than the entire nation. The resulting egalitarian practices and policies have had clear effects on the private sector as well. We will return to this. Policies that make workers more healthy and capable also raise profits from modern technology – and capitalists naturally respond by investing in it more. When this is the case, the productivity of sectors and enterprises becomes less dispersed, reinforcing the initial impact of the egalitarian policy. Some equality creates more equality.

As a result, the Nordic countries not only have the smallest wage differentials and the biggest welfare states, but also the most modern economies and the highest employment rates in the world. Like most countries, the Nordics have also recently experienced raising wage inequality – but the magnitudes are smaller and the level of wage inequality in the Nordic countries is still record low (Section 8.2.2.3).

8.3.2.3 Continental Europe – Markets and Coordinated Capitalism

While social-democratic models rest on wage compression, wage moderation, and a very strong citizenship-based welfare state, continental Europe compresses wages far less, but protects the concrete labor post far more. In welfare terms, continental Europe in general provides social security based on formal employment rather than on citizenship.

At the same time, goods, services, and financial systems are more regulated than in both liberal and social-democratic regimes. Of course, continental European models present wide variations. Germany and Austria have a very precise set of labor institutions and labor capital relations that are closely linked to both their educational systems and their financial systems. Firms engage in "patient capitalism" based on banks' financial backing for long-term projects and long-term expectation of profits. They compete in the world economy based on quality, with strong educational investment in sector-specific skills.

Cooperative labor–capital relations are not only widespread at the sector level but also at the firm level as workers actively participate to differing degrees in firms' management. A robust welfare state based on occupational categories is complemented by wide access to health care, strong unemployment protection, and strong transfers to families with children. The Netherlands and, to a lesser extent, Belgium share some of these traits but have more of a liberal bent to their labor markets with so-called "flexicurity" strategies, whereby workers' turnover across jobs is high, and transition between jobs is covered by unemployment benefits. A citizenship-based welfare state is also more prominent.

France is a case of highly coordinated and regulated capitalism, with a welfare state that combines strong occupational-based social security with very strong family-friendly transfers and services. Labor-capital relations in the private sector are much more adversarial than their German counterparts, but still possess many fine-grained negotiations aimed at job security and wage improvements – though they are highly conflictual when it comes to state employees. The distinction between insiders and outsiders is somewhat more marked than in Germany or the Netherlands and both women, youth, and immigrants face a complex reality. To many, France is a particular form of state-shaped capitalism rather than coordinated capitalism, as it is the state that many times takes the leading role to shape business environments and settle labor and capital disputes. In a similar fashion, many scholars consider the southern Mediterranean countries as a particular form of coordinated capitalism or even, again, as a form of "state-hindered" capitalism. Adversarial labor–capital relations are here part and parcel of a capitalistic model where the state remains a major player not only in regulating the economy, taxing, and spending, but also as an owner of economic enterprises.

A dual labor market in these countries with a sharp division between insiders and outsiders makes wage bargaining a dispersion game – not because of market dynamics, but because of fragmented corporatist privilege and large informal sectors. Global markets, technological change, and financial deregulation have posed major challenges to all coordinated forms of capitalism, but they have been particularly harsh with southern Mediterranean versions and have also eroded much of the success of French "*dirigisme*" in the postwar period.

8.3.2.4 Asian Capitalism: Early and Late Versions of State-Led Capitalism

The key elements of Asian capitalism are the following: First, domestic goods and service markets are highly competitive along both quantity and quality. On the other hand, labor, financial, and export firms belong to highly regulated markets, where the state plays a major role and where nonprice coordination and allocation is dominant. Social protection was weak but has become more important. Basic forms of protection rest in the combined dynamics of large corporations and of families.

In all of these countries history shows that the state was a major developmental player, through educational investments, technological upgrading, tariff protection, export subsidies, wage moderation and compression, control of the consumption of luxury goods, and limits on international financial flows. This is true when we look at the early Japanese miracle, the more recent performance of Thailand or Vietnam, or the peculiar state-led export model of China. It is true that in the more recent experience, inequality and positional consumption have been harder to curb.

Efficiency, innovation, and productivity gains are nurtured by the state, located in large corporations and fueled by an educational system strong on scientific and technological innovation. Wage dispersion is moderated by intrafirm bargaining and state regulatory frameworks. The largest differences in well-being are not so much associated with large income differentials but with the different levels of security that workers have in large corporations and in smaller domestic-oriented firms.

In any case such a nonliberal developmental pattern shows an outstanding record of rapid and sustained economic growth between the 1960s and the twenty-first century. The highest performing economies are often called the "four tigers:" Hong Kong, Korea, Taiwan, and Singapore. Japan is also a member, and in some cases the pioneer of the high-performing Asian economies (Page 1994) alongside the more recent examples of Indonesia, Malaysia, and Thailand. The developmental state is the critical explanation of the Asian miracle.

8.3.2.5   Latin America – Market-Based Divorce between State and Democracy

Social reformers in Latin America have looked at Northern Europe every now and then, but more often than not just to do the opposite of what these small, open economies have done. (A comparative perspective on Latin America and the Nordics is contained in the Appendix, Section A8.6.) In comparison to its European counterparts, Latin America gives us the clearest case of how capitalism can be extremely unequal, hugely inefficient, and largely authoritarian – at the same time.

Historically, the oligarchic period of the late nineteenth century and early twentieth century showed the bad sides of capitalism without democracy in pure form. The entry of this periphery – as many Latin American scholars call their countries – into the world economy was marked by the slave trade and by the expanding production of sugar, cacao, tobacco, salt, and later, cattle. It shaped an anti-liberal variant of capitalism with coerced labor and extreme levels of inequality – with long-term consequences.

The system was not always stagnant. In the early twentieth century, economic growth and the share of exports in GDP were higher than in Europe. Income per capita was similar in Argentina and the UK, in Uruguay and France, in Chile and Norway, in Brazil and Italy and in Mexico and Portugal, Finland, or Greece (Halperin 1997). Hence, development was associated with exports of primary commodities and imports of manufactured goods – both sides divorced from state involvement.

When World War I hampered the flow of imports, however, Latin American firms moved, albeit shyly, to produce replacements. Import substitution was therefore a reality long before it became a home-grown theory of economic development associated with the work of Prebisch (1950). He led the Economic Commission for Latin America from its start in 1948 with an ambition to establish a new school of development economics based on the protection of infant industries, helped by an active state that should provide subsidies, tariff protection, and planning (Montecinos and Markoff's 2009). Most countries adopted Import Substitution Industrialization (ISI) that fit quite well with their emerging populist governance. ISI is a trade and economic policy that advocates replacing foreign imports with domestic production.

Import substitution was based on inefficient market dynamics. The gaps between insiders and outsiders, formal and informal workers, became wider and wider. Economic growth stagnated, inflation soared, and fiscal deficits became increasingly unmanageable. By the 1960s, the easy phase of import substitution was over. Deregulation of finance, commerce, and labor markets followed. The new neoliberal regimes abolished the small welfare state and replaced it with market options for those who could pay.

The result was a catastrophe both economically and socially.[6] The entire transformation took place within a broader epochal change: the end of conservative modernization as defined by Barrington Moore (1966). The triumphs of electoral democracy, urbanization, educational attainment, and increased exposure to new and broader consumption patterns had destroyed the political basis of conservative modernization (Filgueira et al. 2011). While the arenas that can turn expectations into legitimate demands had expanded radically, access to the means to satisfy such demands remained unequal and segmented until the end of the century.

The so-called shift to the left in the region is the political outcome of this second crisis of incorporation. The Washington Consensus was indeed the last attempt at incorporation under conservative modernization dynamics: pushing for democracy, education, and incorporation into market dynamics, but leaving unchanged and at some points even deepening the inequality of opportunity, status, and asset enclosure.

---

[6]   If we compare the ISI rates of growth with the "Washington Consensus" rates of growth, there is no dispute. ISI was better. The only country that showed positive results in average well-being, though not in social justice, was Chile, the darling of the "Chicago Boys" and its most consistent follower. This does bring to the fore the issue of efficiency in today's world and the relevance of market dynamics to foster such efficiency.

Comparing Latin American development to that of Northern Europe, we should notice that in Latin America, inequality and a concentrated landholding pattern allowed for a rentier style of living and an elite who saw no need for innovation. The ISI model allowed for formal, low productivity firms to survive through generous subsidies and protection from international competition. If wages rose too much, more subsidies and protection were granted. Subsidies replaced productivity-enhancing innovations. Rentiers and labor aristocrats constituted, in effect, an anti-Creative-Destruction alliance.

Income differentials grew together with the informal sector. As the welfare state only served workers in formal urban jobs, and never those in rural areas or in informal jobs, the system produced a large mass of uneducated and poverty-stricken citizens. Neither did conservative modernization foster an industrial working class or a middle class that were loyal to democratic ideals. While social insurance in Northern Europe was an act of solidarity, it was in Latin America an act of supporting the privileged. ISI closed markets from external competition and allowed for the survival of low-productivity traditional sectors. The unions that emerged worked to maintain their acquired wage premiums.

In sum, ISI in Latin America allowed large landowners to retain their low wages and productivity and placed wage setting in the hands of small unions, with relatively high wages in line with the subsidies and protection their sectors received.

In sum, ISI in Latin America enabled large landowners to retain their capacity to pay low wages and offer bad quality jobs with low productivity and investment in rural areas. In urban areas, small unions were in charge of wage setting. They set relatively high wages made possible by the subsidies and protection each sector received, rather than by high innovation rates or productivity.

8.3.3 Modernization and Cultural Change

In the Appendix we review the literature on modernization and cultural change (Section A8.7) and studies from experimental economics and psychology on cultural differences in patterns of cooperation (Section A8.8). Using the analysis of cultural values provided by Inglehart and Welzel (2005), we discuss if and how a cooperative social ethos can replace an individualistic ethos, as a fundamental step to establish more just societies. This discussion highlights that culture is not immutable over time. Rather, more secular and self-expressive cultural values are likely to spread in a society as the economy develops. At the same time, past culture engenders a long-lasting influence over a society's cultural trajectory, so that it would be wrong to talk about punctual cultural convergence. This gives some hope to the possibility that a cooperative social ethos will eventually emerge in a society, especially because people seemingly become more concerned with collective values as their material standards of living improve. However, the emergence of such values is not certain, and the amount of time that is required may be very long.

One may then try to instill "social capital" – understood as networks of reciprocity and cooperation instrumental to economic development and well-being (Putnam 2000) – "from above," as many World Bank programs try to do. These programs seem, however, to be rather ineffective. Ostrom (2000) advises not to give up. Social capital springs from the intensification of local social networks, and indeed this process may take a long time. External intervention may have a role in facilitating and directing this process.

8.4 How to Promote Well-being and Social Justice? The Egalitarian Way to Development

Three cornerstones support equality as a development strategy: First, we demonstrate how compressed earnings differences can create high productivity and growth in a way that sustains such compression. Second, we show how better social services can expand human capabilities in an egalitarian manner that also stimulates the political demand for welfare arrangements. Third, we sketch some aspects of how the redistribution of assets, property, and entitlement rights can also reinforce equality of income and opportunities. Finally, we review alternative systems of firm ownership and control, presenting specific case studies.

8.4.1 The First Cornerstone: Wage Compression and Creative Destruction

8.4.1.1 The Dust that Never Settles

Most textbooks exaggerate and simplify. The concept of production, for instance, portrays a supply side with exaggerated flexibility and too little emphasis on dynamics. In real life it is rather the other way around: there is little technological flexibility beyond what is created by the *dynamics* of technological investments and disinvestments. While textbooks focus mostly on competition over costs and prices, competition in real life is much more about the introduction of new things – about innovations, broadly defined. Competitors compete to be the first to introduce profitable new technologies, new work organizations, and new products.

Discarding the typical simplifications and exaggerations in textbook economics, we end up with a perspective on economic change that is simple but perhaps more realistic. Capital comes in vintages. Each vintage of investments embodies the most recent technology that requires the corresponding investments. Ex post, the innovations are not malleable since they are built into fixed capital. Each investment receives falling profits as rivals introduce new and improved designs. Finally, they become economically obsolete and are scrapped. In sum, each unit of production – or each job – is born and then used for a while before it dies by becoming economically obsolete.

This process of creative destruction never rests. It goes on in waves of innovations, an uneven development that constitutes the essence of capitalism. It revolutionizes "the economic structure from within, incessantly destroying the old one, incessantly creating a new one" (Schumpeter 1942: 82).[7]

To capture some important elements in the process, we focus on a specific dynamic production approach, first developed by Johansen (1959). One unit of capital has a certain capacity to produce output when combined with the required inputs. These characteristics remain constant over the life of the capital good. Technical progress and innovations imply that the capacity and productivity of a new vintage are higher than that of an older vintage.[8] Within this set-up, we can explain the persistence of wage inequality where it is sustained by economic investments that reinforce inequality in earnings. Within the set-up we can also explain how *equality* of wages can be sustained by economic investments that reinforce the equality in earnings.

8.4.1.2   Productivity Dispersion, Wage Inequality, and Innovation

How can wage inequality be self-sustaining? There are two links. The first is that inequality in the past creates inequality today. This may happen when wages result from local market forces at the firm level. One characteristic of such an unregulated system of wage determination is that wages are flexible. They adjust to local productivity. Where productivity is high, wages are high, and vice versa. As long as this is the case, a given distribution of productivity gives us a related distribution of wages.

We denote as "flex-wages" those wages that are tied to local productivity. In high-productivity jobs, employers set high flex-wages to make workers obedient. In low-productivity jobs, located in low-productivity surroundings, workers are obedient even at low wages since they have few outside options. In any case, the productivity of the technology limits the ability to raise the lowest wages without raising unemployment.

When wages are taken out of market competition and placed in a system of collective bargaining either at the sector level or at the national level, the resulting wages are anchored to the average productivity of the bargaining level. The overall wage dispersion is thus compressed compared to the distribution of flex-wages. We denote as "fixed-wages" those wages that are in this way tied to average productivity.

The way wages are tied to local productivity also affects the profitability of investment in new technologies and the scrapping of old ones. The key point we want to make is that flex-wages lead to fewer investments in the most recent, most productive technologies, while fixed-wages lead to more investments in these high-productivity technologies. The reason is simple: flex-wages make the most productive technologies more expensive to use compared to fixed-wages.

Take a firm that previously occupied the technological frontier before a new productivity-increasing innovation came about. With flex-wages,

this firm would have to pay higher wages. On the contrary, with fixed-wages this firm would not have to raise their wages as much. This means that the profitability of investing in these activities is lower in a flex-wages system than in a fixed-wages system – even if workers' bargaining power is the same in the two cases. Employers will invest less in new and modern technologies in a flex-wages system compared to a fixed-wages system, and each layer of technology will become thinner.

At the other end of the productivity distribution, the old equipment can live longer with flex-wages than with fixed-wages, because the flex-wages can be adjusted downward. So, although the creation of more productive equipment makes old technologies obsolete, technology upgrade happens later when wages are tied to local productivity.

As a result, a high inequality of wages today generates a high inequality of the distribution of productivity across units in the future via investment decisions. This high dispersion in productivity spills over to high inequality in future earnings. High inequality today, therefore, generates high inequality tomorrow. When wages are tied to average productivity via collective bargaining or in other ways, the result is just opposite. Equality of wages today generates a low dispersion of productivity in the future via investment decisions. This low dispersion in productivity spills over to low inequality in future earnings.

In other words, fixed-wages (tied to average productivity) work just as if there was a subsidy on modern technologies and a tax on old technologies, while flex-wages work as a tax on modern technology and a subsidy on the old. Wage compression therefore stimulates job creation in modern technologies and job destruction in old technologies. It reduces the dispersion of productivity, leading to further reduction in wage inequality.

Even more interesting, the resulting average productivity and average wage under fixed-wages will exceed those under flex-wages. The implicit wage restraint among better-paid workers lowers expected wage costs and speeds up the process of creative destruction. This means that a larger share of the workforce moves to more productive jobs. So, even if wages in the most productive units decline, more workers would move from lower productivity jobs to higher productivity jobs, raising their average wage. More workers are moved up the technology ladder, where even a lower share of value added yields a higher wage. Accordingly, the gap between the most productive and least productive units in operation declines. We can call it a declining productivity gap of wage compression. By productivity gap, or productivity dispersion, we mean across-plant differences in measured productivity levels.

What are the differences across countries? Consider two economies, one (the modern economy) with a high level of previous innovations, and one (the backward economy) with a much lower level of previous innovations in each vintage. The modern economy would have a production structure where workers have jobs with high average

---

[7]   The basic idea of the process of creative destruction stems from Karl Marx. It is associated with Joseph Schumpeter since he gave it the modern form and its name.

[8]   Førsund and Hjalmarsson (1987) give a fine exposition with empirical applications. Our results on the role of equality and inequality for the process of creative destruction build on Moene and Wallerstein (1997) and Barth, Moene, and Willumsen (2015).

productivity affecting their wages. The older vintages are obsolete and scrapped, but since each vintage of modern technology is thick, all workers can be employed there.

In the backward economy with much thinner vintages, the labor force is spread over a wide range of productivity from the most modern to the very backward. When wages are tied to local productivity, the difference in productivity gaps across countries corresponds to comprehensive differences in the distribution of earnings within each country. A technology with low productivity is profitable to use only if the wages at the bottom are low relative to the wages in the most productive units. In the modern economy, in contrast, the gap between the highest and lowest wages would be lower, as workers are employed under much more similar conditions.

8.4.1.3   Productivity Gaps in Reality

Do we find our claimed differences in productivity gaps empirically? We can illustrate the size of the gaps by comparing the distribution of what is denoted the "total factor productivity" in different countries. Total factor productivity is the portion of output not explained by the amount of inputs used in production. We have two claims: (1) poor countries should have higher productivity gaps than richer countries; (2) more egalitarian countries should have smaller productivity gaps than more unequal countries.

To provide the numbers that can illustrate our claims requires some effort and courageous assumptions. Hsieh and Klenow (2010) and Barth et al. (2015) apply methods that err on the safe side by focusing on total factor productivity and not only labor productivity. Comparable numbers for exactly the same years in all countries are not available.

Many observers have thought of the US economy as the most efficient and most modern economy in the world. It is therefore a natural benchmark and starting point. Comparing the US to India, we find that the productivity gap in India is much higher than in the US. This result illustrates the effects of development and of high inequality in developing countries. A jump from the first to the ninth decile in the productivity distribution implies a 330 percent increase in the US (in 1997), while in India (in 1994) a similar jump would imply a 2140 percent increase. In other words, the first decile in India has 4.7 percent of the productivity of the ninth decile, compared to 30 percent in the US. As shown in Table 8.2, other measures show the same pattern: development implies a smaller gap between the most and the least productive technologies in use – and the reduction in the productivity gap can be large. Comparing the US to China confirms the pattern. Developing China has a higher gap between the least and the most productive technology in use – but the gap is less than in India, reflecting the fact that China is more "developed" than India.

What about claim 2? Do developed countries with more compressed distribution of earnings have lower productivity gaps? Comparing the US to Norway illustrates an important feature that appears to be general. Countries with a more egalitarian wage structure have lower productivity gaps. A jump from the first to the ninth decile of the productivity distribution in Norway (in 1998) implies an increase

Table 8.2 | Dispersion of total factor productivity

United States	1977	1987	1997
90–10	1.04	1.01	1.19
72–25	.46	.41	.53
SD	.45	.41	.49
India	1987	1991	1994
90–10	2.97	3.01	3.11
75–25	1.55	1.53	1.60
SD	1.16	1.17	1.23
China	1998	2001	2005
90–10	2.72	2.54	2.44
75–25	1.41	1.34	1.28
SD	1.06	.99	.95
Norway	1997	2001	2005
90–10	.80	.74	.73
75–25	.37	.34	.34
SD	.35	.34	.33

Note: The 90–10 measures the 9th decile relative to the 1st decile, and 75-25 measures the top 25 percentage relative to the lowest 25 percentage. SD is standard deviation.
Sources: The dispersion in the United States, China and India is taken from Table II in Hsieh and Klenow (2010), while the Norwegian figures are calculated in Barth et al. (2015), using Hsieh and Klenow's approach on Norwegian manufacturing data. Industries are weighted by their value-added shares

of 123 percent, while in the US (in 1997) a similar move would imply a 330 percent increase in productivity. The first decile in the productivity distribution in Norway has 80 percent of the productivity of the ninth decile, compared to 30 percent in the US (Barth et al. 2015).

Contrary to what many observers believe, Norway and the Nordics generally have a much lower productivity gap than the US. According to our measure, the US is far from being the most efficient and modern economy in the world. Countries with smaller wage differentials have smaller productivity gaps and – in the case of Norway – higher average productivity. The economies with the most compressed wage structure have the most modern equipment and the highest average productivity, implying that a larger share of the workforce works in high productivity jobs.

Table 8.2 shows that the productivity gaps are highest in developing countries and lowest in countries with small wage differentials among the richer countries – just as our theory predicts. We view all this as a stark illustration of how wage equality and development affect structural change under the process of creative destruction.

8.4.2   The Second Cornerstone: Equality as Capability Expansion via Social Policies

The process of creative destruction can capture changes way beyond markets and firms. It is also relevant in the nonmarket settings of institutional change, public policy-making, collective action, and the evolution of economic systems in general – all decisive for social progress.

Right-wing thinking tends to ignore much of this and may underappreciate the gains of social policy. For conservatives, the welfare state has a double cost: the visible financial burden of welfare spending, plus the cost of distorted – less obedient – behavior as citizens lose the fear of destitution. According to the right wing, poor countries should become rich before they think about the welfare state – redistributive programs and social insurance. But is this right?

The welfare state is in fact *most* needed in developing countries – these arrangements can enhance productivity and growth, to the benefits of the great majority.[9] Actually, we can derive the best arguments for the feasibility of a just society by appealing to the interaction between equality and creative destruction – displayed in social policy for development. As we shall see, some of the countries most exposed to international competition have the most generous social policies and welfare states.

8.4.2.1   What Do Welfare States Do?

In all countries – developing countries in particular – there is a strong link between individual income and, on one side, access to health provisions and insurance and, on the other side, the ability to exercise work effort. Ability and work effort in turn affect a worker's income. Thus, combining ability with the productivity of a worker determines her income (broadly defined), which again shapes her ability to work and her further income possibilities.

In too many instances, the worker has low ability and thus low income, and her low income constrains her ability to acquire education, skills, and equipment to use actual opportunities effectively. Even worse, her vulnerability to shocks can place her household into a persistent low-income trap with low productivity, indebtedness, and other forms of exploitable dependence on others.

Social policies can change some of this. Bad outcomes can become less likely, as the welfare state can enhance a worker's capabilities and incomes beyond the received benefits. The welfare state can heal, train, and take care of workers – and thus reproduce their labor power. It can repair damages and raise workers' capabilities and their functioning. Doing so, it reduces workers' vulnerability to both exogenous shocks and to power abuse by others. When we get more welfare benefits and provisions, workers become more valuable, more secure, and more able producers. Hence, welfare support can enable them to obtain higher levels of sustainable income and productivity. The link from more resources (benefits) to higher ability is as a special case of what is denoted income-based efficiency wages. The notion of efficiency wages was first developed to capture the positive linkages between higher wages, better nutrition for workers, higher productivity, and thus higher efficiency (Dasgupta and Ray 1987; Moene 1992).

If the above is true, a welfare state can free poor producers from their trap and change the self-enforcing cycle of poverty and performance. It can raise worker capability for every level of income. It can provide better education, which again affects productivity in each activity where the better-educated worker participates. A welfare state can also make her more productive for any level of ability, inducing more necessary risk-taking, empowering her to stand up against landowners, employers, and other strongmen, and making her less vulnerable to abuse of power.

A welfare state arrangement can be a highly beneficial investment that not only improves well-being, all else being the same, but also expands the set of feasible opportunities and enhances the ability for individuals to take advantage of them. The link between feasible opportunities and ability may also give rise to two locally stable equilibria – one with low income and low ability, another with higher income and higher ability. The welfare state can engender a shift from the low-income trap to high-income equilibrium.

It first raises the income of a vulnerable group. Next, as group members become more productive, the higher incomes they receive generate additional income growth. Heightened access to resources raises their productivity further, which again leads to a higher income, and so on. Naturally, the process converges to a new and higher level of productivity and income than they had before.

In this way, social policies can help the millions who now go hungry even in good years by raising their productivity and income to capture better opportunities. India has the world's largest (but least known) school feeding program, which raises productivity by providing one meal to every student every day. The child gets better nourishment, and the rest of household gets more to eat – having fewer mouths to feed in the middle of the day – thus raising nutritional standards and school enrolment – in places, by more than 20 percent – and reducing child labor.

India also has the world's most comprehensive rural employment program, yielding higher incomes for each productivity level of the household. The program guarantees 100 days of paid work to every rural adult. Many of the participants in the program are women, who not only obtain better material conditions, but also more power in their villages (Drèze and Kehra 2017).

A welfare state may also change the production relationship. Workers would simply gain more power, and may thus dare to raise their voices against other unfair rules at their workplace. Vulnerable workers can then become less vulnerable when they are net receivers of welfare benefits and support. The consequences for a worker of being fired, or made redundant, become less severe when he is socially insured. The health of his kids is less dependent on their own income when they have access to public health services. Workers become better trained when the education system improves.

Welfare state programs that empower workers and increase their short-term outside options and long-term life chances would also raise the lowest wages that workers are willing to accept. As the lowest wage goes up, the wage distribution changes as well. These

---

[9]   Peter Lindert (2004) offers nice illustrations and explanations of what he denotes as the "Robin Hood paradox," i.e. that the welfare state is least developed where it is most needed.

changes – higher wages and more power to the bottom of the pay scale – work together with what jobs are most profitable to offer.

The profitability of bad jobs is high only when workers are weak and other wages are low. Empowering workers via welfare programs can put an end to this kind of employer dominance that is widespread in developing countries. It may transform bad jobs into good jobs. Again, the changes are most dramatic at the bottom of the wage and skill distribution. All in all, the impact of welfare policies on the pre-tax wage distribution can best be described as compression from below (Barth and Moene 2015).

8.4.2.2   The Political Support for Welfare: Policy Design

Does equality as a development strategy work best when social policies are targeted toward the poor? If the welfare budget had a fixed amount, the answer would obviously be that the most targeted programs are best. The money would then go to those who need the benefits most. But in reality the welfare budget is not fixed. It is endogenous, determined by political support in the voting booth. When this is the case, universal programs that spread welfare benefits widely through the population lead to the highest benefits per capita for the worst-off groups.

As long as the funding of the policy is decided by majority vote, the social policy that will lead to the highest empowerment of the poor and to maximal reduction in poverty may actually be a policy that does not target the poor at all: the least targeted policies benefit the narrowly targeted group the most. A targeted program based on means testing, with benefits that go only to the needy, would garner less support than a universal program unless one can rely on stable and strong altruism in the population.

Universal welfare spending that provides the benefits of health provisions and social insurance to everybody – rich or poor – extends political support way up into the middle class, even among citizens who might pay more into the welfare system in the form of taxes than they expect to get out in the form of benefits. The conservative ideal of a minimalistic welfare state that only provides support to the worst off, either in rich or in poor societies, is not politically sustainable by majority vote (Moene and Wallerstein 2003).

8.4.2.3   The Political Support for Welfare: Inequality

Does the support for equality as a development strategy become highest when inequality is high? How does income distribution affect overall support for social policy? Clearly, as we have alluded to already, the welfare state is nowhere a mechanism of pure redistribution from the rich to the poor. If it were, huge inequality might have generated strong support for more redistribution, as the majority in any country earns less than the average income.

The welfare state has never worked so simply, which is evident from the observation that even in the developed world, it is those countries with the smallest pre-tax income inequality that have the largest and most generous welfare states (see below). Extending the picture to include developing countries, it is even clearer that countries with the most profound inequality and cleavages have almost no welfare arrangements at all.

We can defend a general claim for both rich and poor countries: lower inequality in the distribution of earnings raises political demand for welfare spending. To understand why, one should note that the welfare state is basically a provider of goods and services. Often it is the case that the private sector fails to supply these services equally efficiently. This is the case with social insurance, health care, and education – all "normal goods." People like to have more of them the higher their individual incomes – and when they have to pay higher taxes in order to get them.

To see this, consider a poor woman with some earnings. Keeping all other things constant, just raising her income would raise her demand for welfare provision. Why? Simply because having a higher income, she can afford more of many things that she likes, and also those that the welfare state provides: health services, education, pensions, and social insurance for herself and others. With a lower income, her immediate needs would most likely be so pressing that she would be unable to pay higher taxes to have more welfare provisions.

Less income inequality for a given mean level raises the income for the majority of citizens. When the majority of the population gets higher incomes, a majority of voters demand higher provisions by the welfare state. Welfare spending is therefore one of the clearest examples of how equality creates support for more equality.

8.4.2.4   The Political Support for Welfare: In Practice

The link from low pre-tax inequality to high support for welfare has been tested. There is now a large literature that demonstrates this basic principle from different angles; see for instance Perotti (1996); Moene and Wallerstein (2001, 2003); Iversen and Soskice (2001); Acemoglu (2003); Lindert (2004); Alesina and Glaeser (2004); and Ramcharan (2010).

Figure 8.8 illustrates how the most egalitarian countries (measured by wage inequality) have the most generous welfare arrangements (measured by an index of the rules of the welfare state).

It is not easy to see the causal direction of the link directly. We can use changes in the wage setting system as an indicator of inequality – or what is called an "instrument" in econometrics jargon. Doing that the pattern is clear: wage compression increases welfare spending. There is also a link that goes the other way, capturing how welfare spending empowers weak groups in the labor force, compressing the earnings distribution from below (for details see Barth and Moene 2015).

8.4.2.5   Combining the Mechanisms in the Two Cornerstones

Combining the mechanisms that link equality and welfare with the mechanisms that link equality and productivity, we see the full

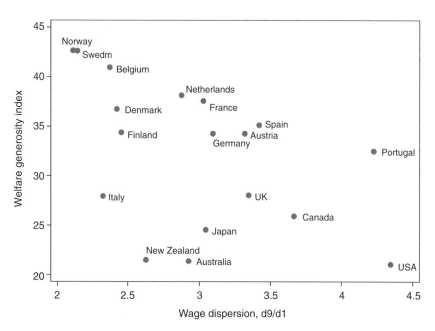

Figure 8.8 | Average values of welfare generosity index over the period 1975–2010 and dispersion of pre-tax hourly wages from OECD.
Sources: Scruggs (2014) for welfare generosity index; OECD for wage dispersion. The figure is reproduced from Barth and Moene (2015)

potential for equality as a development strategy. Earnings compression (in one form or another) induces small productivity gaps across enterprises and sectors that in turn sustain small differences in earnings. The resulting low inequality in the earnings distribution leads again to a high political demand for welfare provisions that empowers weak groups of workers and immediate producers in general. Hence, there are several virtuous circles, working in tandem and reinforcing each other.

None of the circles builds on a redistribution of some given result. On the contrary, it is the basic economic adjustments both in the investments in enterprises and within the labor force that give us a supply side with (1) fewer gaps in productivity across plants and sectors, and (2) a more productive and more empowered labor force. The combination of (1) and (2) leads to an egalitarian dynamic equilibrium of policies, income distribution, and productivity dispersion that can sustain a more egalitarian development path. The combination can also produce a sizeable equality multiplier that magnifies initial changes in an egalitarian direction by as much as 50 percent of the initial change, as estimated in Barth and Moene (2015).

There are various institutions that can help compress earnings. It can be achieved via collective bargaining between unions and employers' associations, via subsidized education and skill-formation, or via direct intervention in wage setting. In the Nordic countries, wage compression has been achieved by a combination of subsidized education and skill formation and collective bargaining. The more coordination there has been in wage bargaining across enterprises, sectors, and types of workers, the more compressed the distribution of earnings. Taking wages out of market competition in this way and placing them within a system of collective decision-making with majority vote lends more power to the lower ranks of the earnings distribution – compressing wages from below and above. Subsidized education and skill formation

have provided a supply of labor that modern enterprises can employ without paying huge wage premiums.

In South Korea, to take another example, wage compression has been achieved basically through subsidized skill-formation and education, making modernization more profitable. As investments in modern enterprises take off, the demand for less qualified workers goes up as well, making it possible to raise their wages without creating higher unemployment. In this way the earnings distribution is compressed both from above and from below. Japan provides similar experiences.

Summing up, both the Nordic countries and South Korea, as different as they are, offer examples that positive development does not necessarily follow the ideal textbook principles of narrow individual solutions and personal incentives. On the contrary, they show how real competition can emphasize cooperation, trust, and long-term cooperative behavior.

In real competition some contestants win and others lose. This creates economic inequalities. Often the winners take all the gains. Real competition therefore requires countervailing power of subsidized education and other welfare state policies to produce good results. Social movements, unions, and other ways of organizing collective interests and sharing devices may also help real competition.

The point here is not to list necessary conditions for implementing equality as a development strategy – conditions that necessarily differ from country to country – but rather to emphasize that the conditions may include collective organizations and behaviors that are deemed counterproductive by defenders of ideal competition.

Yet, collective behavior can share the benefits that arise from the complementarity between market dynamics, fairness, and worker security.

Social organizations, however, do not only have a protective role. They also induce change. It may be difficult to obtain collective gains by individual rewards. Social organization may help in stimulating the process of creative destruction in a positive and egalitarian direction.

Surprisingly perhaps, global competitive forces – when the conditions are right – can also induce equality as a development strategy that revolutionizes the political and economic structure from within. This is at least evident from the observation that most of the countries that have followed such strategies are small open economies that sell half of their output on the world market.

8.4.3   The Third Cornerstone: Assets, Property, and Entitlements Rights

Attempts to redistribute assets and entitlements – rather than flows of earned income – are different in the initial steps of their egalitarian strategy. Yet, as we have emphasized, it is the overall adjustment to an emerging, less unequal path that establishes sustainability. The forms that reduced inequality in income and opportunities takes can nevertheless be important. Another important asset is human capital and education, whose importance we already stressed in the above sections. Space limitations prevent us from further analyzing this topic. The reader can consult Chapter 1 (Sections 1.2.2 and 1.5.6), Chapter 3 (Section 3.6.5.2), Chapter 4 (Section 4.2.2), Chapter 7 (Section 7.9), and Volume 3, Chapter 19, of this Report.

8.4.3.1   Guaranteed Basic Income

Guaranteed basic income is an entitlement to income for all. Such entitlements have a long history and a large variety of analogous names: "basic income," "universal grants," "social dividends," "citizen's wages," and "social income" (Van Trier 1994). All these concepts refer to ways of guaranteeing universal access to an unconditional income for all.

To receive a basic income does not require that one be employed or have made contributions to a social insurance scheme. Universality and unconditionality guarantee that the most disadvantaged groups in society can enjoy a certain level of functioning and that they are able to sustain it over time. In this way people would be free from the anxiety and worry associated with the loss of a minimum income to cover their basic needs.

Basic income is not a substitute for welfare arrangements, but rather a complement. It can also help to raise the political demand for welfare provisions. In practice, the most universal and egalitarian welfare states already have income transfer programs close to basic income guarantees. In the Nordic welfare states, universal family allowance and pension programs function as secure income floors. Similarly, even in Latin America, noncontributive programs for families with dependent children and families in pension systems have features in common with basic income. All forms of basic income function as a universal floor, above which the social insurance schemes would stand (Atkinson 2015).

Basic income is not meant to replace wages or welfare contributions. It diversifies people's income sources in an egalitarian way. It may have many indirect effects, empowering weak groups. The bargaining position of workers, for instance, can become higher with a guaranteed income floor that can function as a continuously provided "strike fund" in labor disputes.

One interesting form is the so-called universal basic share, a commitment to allocate a fixed share of national income as a basic income to all (Moene and Ray 2016; Van Parijs and Vanderborght 2017).

Simply put, the universal basic share is a commitment that is expressed not as a sum of money, but as a share. Specifically, it is a commitment of a fixed fraction of GDP to the provision of a universal basic income for all. The universal basic share is country-neutral. It can be introduced into every country, rich or poor. It scales up or down with country-level income. It works equally well in India as in Norway.

It works as a social dividend, allowing everyone to share in the prosperity of a country. It creates good incentives for collective cohesion. It combines social considerations of fairness with incentives for the collective good.

8.4.3.2   Inheritance

Recently, inheritance taxes have received renewed attention, for instance in works by Piketty (2014) and Atkinson (2015). Atkinson has suggested that receipts of inheritance and gifts should be taxed under "a progressive lifetime capital receipts tax." This means that all inheritance and gifts that a person receives, beyond a certain threshold, should be taxable. The policy can be combined, as Atkinson recommended, by allocating the revenues of the tax to a minimum inheritance for all. Progressive inheritance taxes combined with a minimum inheritance for all can reallocate wealth to the majority of citizens.

Good proposals like Atkinson's can contribute to comprehensive wealth reallocation toward a more egalitarian distribution of capital. It can be given different levels of progressivity and be implemented in different ways for the tax system and welfare arrangements of the country in question. It builds on ideas first proposed by John Stuart Mill in the mid-nineteenth century. It also echoes suggestions that initially had a strong ideological hold in most socialist and social-democratic parties. Today, however, most countries and most social-democratic parties have reduced the incidence and level of inheritance taxes, instead letting private wealth holdings concentrate more and more in the hands of the few.

8.4.3.3   Land Reforms

Land reform is highly debated and emphasized as a necessary intervention in order to improve the economic performance of countries as different as Brazil, Colombia, South Africa, and Zimbabwe. Just as welfare policies can help weak groups to get out of poverty traps, programs for "land to the tiller" can make each smallholder stronger and more productive.

A simple but strong case for land reform can be made by considering a case that emphasizes the actually sad conditions in several countries where rural poverty and malnutrition are unnecessary, but exist yet. In our example, there is just enough land to feed the total rural population at the subsistence level of material consumption. The average productivity with full employment of the rural population is therefore higher or equal to this minimum consumption level. So if all workers work the land, each of them produces an output high enough to sustain the productivity of the household.

If all the land is owned by a small group of landowners, however, the huge concentration of landholdings has counterproductive effects. Each landowner hires agricultural workers until the marginal productivity of labor equals the agricultural wage that covers the subsistence level of consumption. Obviously, landowners cannot pay the workers less than that wage since the workers then receive too little to sustain their productivity. They will not pay more, since there is a surplus of agricultural workers. So what is most profitable for landowners is to hire workers until the marginal productivity equals the subsistence pay.[10]

When this is the case, a substantial part of the landless rural population becomes destitute and unnecessarily undernourished. To prevent this from happening, the country can implement a comprehensive land reform that confiscates all agricultural land and shares it equally with every rural household. Each household can then work their own land and produce a high enough income to maintain their productivity.

This feature of an egalitarian land reform resembles welfare policies, empowering weak groups, enhancing their productivity and capabilities, and generating higher incomes for the great majority. Land reforms can produce results similar to basic income guarantees. To emphasize and maybe exaggerate the similarity, the country can also introduce a system of basic income financed by a tax on the net income to landowners – to achieve the same results. Each landowner can now hire agricultural workers at lower-than-subsistence pay since each worker gets part of his income in the form of a basic wage. Workers can maintain their productivity even though the landowners pay them less than the subsistence wage. In principle this arrangement can lead to full employment of the rural population, as long as the entire surplus of the agriculture is taxed and given back to workers in the form of a universal basic wage.

As is well known, at the end of the eighteenth century there were several proposals for a comprehensive land tax to finance a basic income to all. Among the best-known examples are the proposals by Thomas Paine. The two policies that we have illustrated are extreme variants of his proposals that in our case produce the same result. Both can also be implemented in less extreme forms, and the two can be combined. Yet, our simple extreme illustration highlights the similarity between asset redistribution and income redistribution. It also illustrates the

principle that poverty and malnutrition can be unnecessary and that there are asset reforms that can correct the bad equilibrium.

What is best – land reform or a basic income – does not only depend on economic factors but maybe more on what is politically feasible – and on the endowment effect that ownership of land may provide. In any case, while scholarly debate continues on the need for either asset redistribution or more income redistribution, progressive land reform initiatives are difficult to find in practice – as is very evident from the counterproductive developments in Zimbabwe after independence in 1980 – with periods of more or less spontaneous land reforms and land grabbing.

8.4.4 Ownership and Control: Democratizing Economic Organizations

8.4.4.1 Introduction

Much of the discussion thus far has focused on national-level analysis of social justice and well-being. In the following subsections we look at how social justice outcomes have been produced at the regional scale by nonstate as well as state-led actions. The cases discussed offer strategies for social progress that highlight the emergence of new social norms, noncapitalist economic organizations, and the ethos of solidarity in place, which can be extended to different contexts and be activated at more encompassing scales.

Material wealth is created in a variety of organizational contexts, including capitalist business enterprises, sole proprietorships, cooperatives, and hybrid enterprise forms as well as in households, neighborhoods, and communities. Feminists (Ferguson 2009) have long established that the material stuff of life is not only produced in commercial contexts but also domestic and civic settings. Technologies for inventorying and tracking nonmonetized wealth and its distribution have only recently been developed (Waring 1988) and are as yet not clearly linked to social justice-producing mechanisms.

One set of interventions to create more socially just ways of distributing material well-being has focused on democratizing the appropriation of social surplus within economic organizations involved directly in wealth creation. In this section we provide a review of such schemes.

8.4.4.2 Alternative Pay Schemes of Sharing Profits with Employees

Profit-sharing consists in compensating workers with a share of the profits per worker as part of their pay. The profits that are shared are calculated with a certain fixed base wage, and workers get a share of the profits in addition to this base wage. In its simplest form, profit-sharing means that workers have a contract to obtain part of the surplus created, but without any decision-making rights or democracy at the work place. Whether this actually means that workers obtain

---

10   For more detailed discussions of land reforms and landownership see Dasgupta and Ray (1987), Moene (1992).

higher earnings compared to what they would have achieved with traditional wage labor depends on how high the basic wage is.

Profit-sharing is an old arrangement used in many capitalist enterprises way back into the seventeenth and eighteenth centuries – both in the US and in Europe. For instance, many British coalmines introduced profit-sharing around 1860. The arrangements were popular among workers as long as profits were high and increasing. But when times became bad and the mines had declining profitability, the arrangements became unpopular and the coalmines eventually canceled the system. Recently profit-sharing has been used a lot in Japan and South Korea, where it can constitute around 30 percent of the total pay per worker in large companies.

Weitzman's (1984) work triggered a heated debate about the functionality of profit-sharing as a remuneration system. Weitzman's claim is that profit-sharing in a capitalist market economy would generate a labor market equilibrium that may guarantee stable employment to all. Using the term "suction equilibrium," he describes a state of excess demand, where each profit-sharing firm would hire more workers if it could find them, but where no firm has reason to change wages.

For example, booksellers hired by publishing houses are normally compensated by 30 percent of the value of each book they sell. Accordingly, the publishing houses earn a gross profit of 70 percent of each book sold. Adding an additional seller would only increase profits, and publishing houses would therefore like to hire as many booksellers as possible. Each of the already hired booksellers, however, would not like the entry of new ones, who make it more difficult to sell books. Yet the publishing houses cannot lose anything by hiring an extra seller. She would cost nothing if she does not sell any books, and from every book she sells the publishing house gets 70 percent of the value. It can be easily verified – as done by one of the authors of this chapter – that publishing houses are indeed willing to hire any idle person under the above conditions.

The more interesting question, however, is whether it would work equally well to introduce profit-sharing contracts in all enterprises in the entire economy. Perhaps the suction properties of the macro labor market would persist, guaranteeing a path close to full employment. Yet it would come at a cost. With profit-sharing, workers are invited to bear part of the risk of fluctuations in the output markets, shifting risks from capital owners to workers. The risk borne by workers would also include the risks of management failures. More democratic and participatory models of worker management would correct some of these weaknesses. Yet, it is an open question whether the suction properties of profit-sharing can be maintained with more participatory management.

8.4.4.3 Employee Ownership: Sharing Wealth with Employees

Employee ownership is a much more radical arrangement. It may increase economic justice by broadening the number of business owners through shared enterprise ownership with employees. There are many varieties and grades of employee ownership. In the US, there are extensive employee stockownership plans where employee ownership is highly inegalitarian among the groups of worker owners.

The UK Nutall Review of Employee Ownership (2012) defines employee ownership as "a significant and meaningful stake in a business for all its employees." What is meaningful goes beyond financial participation. The employees' stake must underpin organizational structures that ensure employee engagement. In this way employee ownership can be seen as a business model in its own right (Nutall 2012: 74–75).

Like the case of profit-sharing, there is debate over whether employee ownership is an intervention that promotes radical transformation of the conditions under which social injustice is created. However, it is a strategy that foregrounds the right of employees to claim a share of the profits of business. Employee satisfaction in employee-owned businesses is reportedly higher than in nonemployee owned businesses, and increases in companies that "provide employees with a greater stake and involvement in long-term collaborative goals" (Nutall 2012: 29).

8.4.4.4 The Case of Mondragón Cooperative Corporations and of Kerala

In this section, which is further expanded in the Appendix, Sections A8.9–A8.10, we adopt a Science and Technology Studies perspective (Bijker et al. 2012) to report on cases of socio-economic organization relying on cooperatives or state-based redistributive action to achieve more socially just outcomes. Such a perspective focuses on the coevolution of social practices, technological trajectories, and economic forms of production, over the long run.

The cooperative economy of Mondragón, Spain, began to develop during the 1950s and continues to thrive (Gibson-Graham 2003, 2006; Redondo et al. 2011). The key element of the Mondragón model is direct worker ownership of production and distribution enterprises and indirect ownership of financial (banking, social provision, and insurance) and knowledge (research centers, a university, vocational training, and schools) institutions that support the regional economy. Social justice is embedded in wage structures (no more than 1:6 difference between lowest and highest wage in any business), decision-making (one member, one vote), surplus management (vested in the business or bank to allow for expansion of coops and cooperative employment), welfare provision (access to health and social insurance), and the built environment (a unique urban fabric of co-located high density housing, sociable public spaces, goods and service outlets, and places of employment). A commitment to people before profit lies at the core of the Mondragón economic system.

But how did this model become a shared commitment with the power to shape business practices? Before the first manufacturing plants opened as worker-owned cooperatives, a dense network of community activities and associations had been created under the leadership of the local priest Father Arizmendi-Arrieta, who drew from Catholic teachings and the writings of late nineteenth-century social theorists. These activities built mutual trust and fostered a shared commitment to cooperativism among local people. In the ruins of postwar destruction

8

and in the face of Franco's vindictive economic disenfranchisement of the Basque region, the initial cooperatives used basic technology to produce goods, sold to local consumers. They are now one of the most advanced manufacturers in Europe. A transparent accounting system was developed to manage surplus allocations, and over the decades it has been usefully deployed to facilitate retooling and manage job loss without employment loss (Gibson-Graham et al. 2013).

Temporary workers and noncooperators are encouraged to take up membership as full cooperators when it is financially feasible and economic activities can expand without undermining resilience. Although there are limits to the Mondragón social justice model, it stands out as an example of bottom-up social justice achieved by noncapitalist economic organization.

The creation of an inclusive model of egalitarian justice is also possible at the state level. The Indian state of Kerala stands out for its programs of land reform, food security, and mass health and education targeted to the poor, women, scheduled castes, and rural residents. Such programs started in the 1950s, but their success, arguably, was made possible by the creation of social networks and cultural norms in a much earlier period. Christian Protestant missionaries preached the "equality of humans before God … [and] questioned the creedal bedrock of caste" in Kerala beginning in the early nineteenth century (Singh 2010: 290). In spite of levels of per capita income remaining low, Kerala's citizens attain high levels in relevant dimensions of well-being. Average life expectancy in Kerala is ten years higher than for India as a whole, and comparable with that of the US. The literacy rate is 90 percent. The population growth rate dropped from India's highest, in the 1950s, to below replacement level (less than two children per woman) nowadays. These demographic changes have been achieved without the coercive state practices pursued in China or the rest of India, which have reduced population growth but seen the rise of abnormal female to male sex ratios. In the Appendix, Section 8.10, we provide an account of some of the productive practices that have originated in Kerala, consisting of production cooperatives, credit associations, and decentralized production and consumption. Such practices rests on a sense of shared community, and a focus on women that has arguably achieved gender justice at a regional scale.

8.4.4.5   The Case of Indian Self-Employed Women Association

The Self-Employed Women's Association (SEWA) was born in 1972 of Gandhian principles and trade union tenacity in the same streets that earlier ignited the Indian Independence Movement. For more than four decades, SEWA has been working with poor self-employed women, enrolling them into a union association that helps them improve their livelihoods through various initiatives in training, microfinance, market linkages, and natural resource management, across a number of trades. Today, SEWA is a member-based organization of more than two million poor self-employed women workers spread across fourteen states in India.

The work of SEWA is based on the core beliefs that economic empowerment leads to social justice, that work must contribute to the growth and development of others, and that the decentralization of economic ownership and production creates a more just society.

SEWA focuses on economic empowerment. Its extensive experience in working with marginalized women has shown that the surest way to ensure social justice for an individual is to invest in her economic empowerment. When a marginalized woman gets the support she needs and obtains the ability to increase her income earning potential and uplift her family, she is empowered socially as well. She gains confidence in her dealings with her family, her co-workers and members of her community. She is often able to transcend societal barriers imposed on her on account of tradition, custom, caste, and religion. She is also able to access more and better opportunities. Being able to earn a dignified livelihood has a transformative and sustainable impact on a marginalized woman and her family.

SEWA has a relational view of work. Its interpretation of work is derived from Indian philosophical thought, which conceives the work of an individual in relation to the environment. Whatever we consume is taken from the world, and so something has to be put back into it. In relation to the natural world, this obligation is interpreted as the need to conserve and the need to replenish. If a tree is cut down, one needs to be grown in its place.

In relation to the social environment, it is seen as the need to contribute to the growth and development of others. SEWA's experience has shown that working for others, and especially for the most vulnerable, creates a force that builds a movement that in turn leads to social justice. SEWA's leaders are elected from among the members. To gain leadership positions, the most vulnerable members must accept them. These women are also the ones who become loyal and active, and become the life force of the movement.

A more just society requires that ownership of economic resources be distributed more equitably. Decentralization of ownership and production is one way of achieving this goal. Reaching the poorest has been a major administrative exercise when organized on a national level. SEWA believes that a more efficient system is one where food, clothing and other minimum requirements are distributed locally, possibly with the support of new communication technologies.

The strategy of decentralization is connected to SEWA's idea of "holistic work." In many societies, especially among women, work is satisfying and creative if it is part of communal life. Decentralized production gives communities greater control over what they produce and how it is used. One good example of the holistic nature of decentralized work is found among communities who live in areas rich in natural resources, such as forests. Where communities have a greater control over these resources, they tend to preserve and regenerate them. This holistic perspective requires that the individual give something back to the world, even as she takes away from it for her maintenance. Building such interdependence requires a strong sense of local community and culture that integrates the economic and social realms.

Local production and distribution also strengthen the economic role of women. Much of their work is nonmonetary and meant for use within the family. Women also do much community work that involves maintaining social relationships. Economic decentralization leads to two trends that are beneficial to women: First, it strengthens local markets and local skills, and makes markets more accessible to women. Second, it raises the value of nonmonetary work, including all forms of community and service work. This work acquires a more holistic meaning and comes to be understood as work done for the maintenance of the society.

SEWA's mission to empower its marginalized members and lift them from poverty is driven by two specific goals: bringing full employment to its members, and making them self-reliant. Full employment means that in addition to income, members obtain food, social security, health care, childcare, and shelter. Toward this, SEWA adopts an integrated approach with four specific strategies:

- *Organizing women*: As individuals, poor women have little or no voice. Together they become strong, gain confidence and bargaining power, and become capable of great achievements. SEWA organizes its members into savings groups (federated at the district level), producer groups, cooperatives, and producer companies, and provides continuous handholding support to these entities to achieve their respective objectives.
- *Building new skills and capacities*: SEWA works to continuously build capacities, skills, and leadership, and encourages women to become part of the decision-making process at home and in public. SEWA strives to encourage women to become owners and managers and not just producers and laborers.
- *Encouraging capital formation*: SEWA encourages women to create assets at the household, group, and community levels to fight vulnerability, and improve access to affordable finance.
- *Increasing social security*: To enhance women's well-being and productivity, and reduce the impact of crises on the fragile household economy.

Many of SEWA's economic programs are driven by institutions, and often managed by grassroots women. These institutions include a bank and a manager school. A rural distribution network is SEWA's pioneering initiative to find a sustainable local-economy based solution to address food security, through an institutional model managed by poor, informal sector women. SEWA has also been at the forefront of using information and communication technologies that have vastly improved productive efficiency. Such technologies have for instance been applied to perform economic transactions, thus saving their members precious traveling time, and to give farmers crop futures and spot prices from the commodity exchange. Farmers can thus form better harvest price expectations at the planting stage and thereby make better planting decisions. Over a pilot period of three years, SEWA extended this information system to over 150 villages, linking over 7500 marginal farmers. Community radio programs are also used to broadcast on topics relevant for the community. Finally, SEWA is pioneering tele-medicine and tele-agriculture, with doctors and agriculture experts in cities being linked to members living in remote villages through internet-based conferencing tools.

More details on SEWA's activities can be found in the Appendix, Section A8.11.

8.4.4.6 Democratizing the Firm

Most capitalist firms delegate substantial power to hired workers, in particular their managers, but also to workers' councils (often specialized on specific issues such as working conditions) or union representatives. However, it is fair to say that the typical capitalist firm is controlled by a small subset of its stakeholders, with a strong concentration of power among dominant shareholders and CEOs. This concentration of power has detrimental effects on the general efficiency of the organization by reducing trust, informational flows, and worker motivation. The total surplus created by the firm for the whole set of stakeholders (including workers and local communities) is thus reduced at the benefit of the share of the oligarchy that controls the firm for its own interests (Lazear 1995).

The idea that firms should ideally be democratic and take the form of a partnership between capital and labor, or be governed by labor alone, is as old as capitalism, and was eloquently defended by John Stuart Mill, nineteenth-century socialists like Robert Owen, and more recently, James Meade (1993) and many other economists.

Increasing the power of workers in the organization has been experimented in various forms. Some forms only share power, as in the co-determination that is mandatory in large firms in Germany, with workers having almost half of the seats in the board of directors. Bargaining schemes involving unions share substantial power with workers in several countries, including outside Scandinavia (e.g. Consejos de Salarios in Uruguay), and somehow involve sharing profits on a macro scale. Some forms share power and profit through the transformation of workers into shareholders, as in US Employee Stock Ownership Plans, or in worker cooperatives, discussed previously.

For the sake of diversifying household portfolios, it is worth exploring the possibility for workers to obtain more power without investing their own wealth, since they already engage their careers and future earning possibilities in the firm. It is possible, and it may be optimal, to share power without sharing ownership.

As it has been emphasized in the introduction, from a social justice viewpoint, democratizing firms is intuitively appealing – the stark contrast created by authoritarian and often abusive management in capitalist firms in otherwise democratic societies offers a clear opportunity to reconcile the dignity of individuals qua workers with the level of dignity they enjoy qua citizens. The idea of "democratic firms" raises a number of questions: (1) Do they bring real benefits? (2) If so, how can one explain the current dominance of capitalist firms? (3) Are there ways to encourage the democratization of firms? (4) Is there an optimal form of democratic firm? (5) Is this only for countries in an advanced stage of development, or can it also be implemented in developing countries?

There is now consensus (Dow 2017) that firms dominated by labor power have a more stable work force (adjusting incomes rather than laying off in economic slumps), a more compressed wage distribution, productivity that is at least as high as traditional firms, and greater resilience and survival rates. It is also arguable that they tend to be more environmentally responsible, although one cannot hope that they would fully internalize their costs (Pérotin 2016). They generally provide better working conditions and enhance worker well-being, and if their adoption of new technology is more labor-friendly, the coming digitalization wave might be much smoother with democratic firms than under standard capitalism.

Their greater resilience and productivity is easy to explain due to the workers' commitment, sense of control, and lower fear of opportunistic behavior on the behalf of owners and management (while investors fear the liquidation of assets by worker-controlled firms, workers fear that their specific investments in dedication and know-how may not be rewarded in a traditional firm). Finally, they provide wider social benefits by giving workers civic training and greater self-esteem.

Given these benefits, one may wonder why democratic firms are not more common, since customers should naturally favor the more productive firms while workers should apply for jobs in the more congenial places. Note, however, that owners and managers (including middle management, which tends to be much leaner in democratic firms) represent an important constituency that favors the traditional type.

Three main factors can explain the dominance of the socially inferior traditional firm in a competitive setting. First, the slack labor market strongly reduces the ability of most workers to choose their employers. Second, unlike capital, labor is inalienable as a stock since the abolition of slavery, and can only be sold as a flow. Therefore capital assets are easier to diversify and resell, making it possible for the capitalist firm to keep its productive assets while changing hands. This makes it easy to develop a market in the control rights associated with capital ownership, whereas a membership market for workers is harder to set up; in the absence of such a market, workers cannot capitalize on their efforts for the firm's long-term performance when they leave it.

Also, lenders (banks, bondholders) may be more afraid of opportunistic behavior from firms under worker management than with shareholder control. Third, democracy in the firm, as in the polity, is a public good and therefore it is not viable if it is not protected by the inalienability of control rights. The current labor market does not prevent, and actually considers the norm to be, a relation of subordination rather than partnership between the employer and the employee. Ordinary workers in the labor market are like citizens who would sell their votes to a rich patron. Most firms that start small are actually participatory in the beginning, but it is not in the entrepreneurs' interest to share their power when the firm grows, unless they have strong philanthropic ideals. Even cooperatives often degenerate into capitalist firms when there are no mandatory caps on the proportion of salaried workers in the firm.

These explanations of the dominance of the traditional type suggest ways in which democracy in firms can be promoted. Legal restrictions (similar to the mandatory co-determination laws in Germany) appear ultimately necessary, and must impose partnership status for workers and a certain governance structure. Setting up a membership market for workers may not be needed, since forms of seniority payments and severance bonuses can partly replace it. What is more important is the provision of a favorable financial environment through tax incentives to investors or through dedicated banks, and also encouraging the cooperation of democratic firms in federations like Mondragón (Dow 2017; Section 8.4.4.3). Such federations enable greater workers mobility between firms, depending on their production cycle, and provide a more attractive setting for lenders.

There are interesting questions about how to transition traditional firms to a democratic format. Dow (2003) proposes a referendum among workers and a firm-level profit sharing scheme (a local "Meidner mechanism") building up a control fund for workers. If power, not ownership, is shared, one can simply initiate a change in the norms of corporate governance, either through incentives in the beginning, building on the existing pool of democratic firms from the social and solidarity sector, or directly through regulation. Obviously, the threat of capital flight and, to a lesser extent, CEO flight in the globalized economy (Section 8.5.3.1) should be taken seriously into account when implementing such a transition – and may constrain the full distribution of the benefits of democracy to workers and local communities.

These considerations may also guide the selection of the type of democracy. It may not be optimal to seek full power for the workers, since investors' trust may be better preserved by keeping them in the governance structure. It may be preferable to associate workers to shareholders in bipartite governance bodies (see Volume 3, Chapter 21 of this Report), or even better, to form three colleges by associating other stakeholders (local communities, customers, suppliers) in a third college, preventing either workers or shareholders to separately capture control. This is an area where innovation and experimentation should be encouraged. The optimal form may also depend on the economic, social, and cultural context. Reforming the governance of a firm would go hand in hand with a change in its mission, from maximizing shareholder value to maximizing the total surplus for stakeholders (see Chapter 6).

The democratization of firms does not require a particular level of development and can be experimented in the formal sector of developing economies. Interestingly, the informal sector may also be fertile ground for experimentation in democratic production. Small producers can join forces and form cooperatives, enabling them to preserve their autonomy when external investors arrive and when they modernize their equipment. One example is Conaprole, a dairy cooperative in Uruguay in which both milk production and transformation is organized democratically, and which has been successful enough to become an exporter (see also Section 8.4.4.4).

Democratizing firms without expropriating owners or inducing workers to become shareholders of their own firm, may provide an interesting complement to the Nordic model. It can be done by involvement from below and by participation of union representatives in the board. Compared to standard capitalism, this alternative reduces (but does not eliminate) the need for wage compression and welfare state benefits. Wage compression at the economy level may be obtained via a minimum wage to eliminate low-productivity jobs, without requiring nation-wide bargaining.

8.5   Globalization and Egalitarian Redistribution

What policy space exists to achieve egalitarianism? Many critics of contemporary globalization have raised serious concerns over the possibility of conducting egalitarian redistribution in a global world. Are the arguments ideology-driven rather than evidence-driven? We think that the current state of global affairs requires a rethinking of instruments for the egalitarian-minded policy-maker.

8.5.1   The Three Eras of Globalization

In his paper "National Self-Sufficiency," Keynes (1933: 763) famously stressed the need for national governments to insulate themselves from the interference of what in today's words would be called globalization:

> We do not wish [...] to be at the mercy of world forces working out, or trying to work out, some uniform equilibrium according to the ideal principles, if they can be called such, of laissez-faire capitalism. [...] We wish—for the time at least and so long as the present phase endures – to be our own masters, and to be as free as we can make ourselves from the interferences of the outside world.

Although the world that Keynes faced in the 1930s was different from today's world, his remarks still resonate with the worries expressed by critics of present international integration. Dani Rodrik (2011) identifies three different historical phases of globalization. The first era of globalization occupied the whole century before the start of World War I. It was characterized by:

1.   a rapid increase in world trade, made possible both by reduction in transportation and communication costs and governments' removal of trade restrictions – as epitomized by England's repeal of the Corn Laws in 1846;
2.   a boom in capital flows between countries, particularly after the establishment of the gold standard in the 1870s; and
3.   vast flows of migrants, especially working-class Europeans, moving to other continents.

This era ended with the start of World War I. The interwar period was characterized by protectionist policies and the failure to reestablish the gold standard, which was finally abandoned by most countries after the Great Depression.

The second era of globalization went hand-in-hand with the 1944 Bretton Woods accords, striking a balance between two different and possibly opposing needs: On the one hand, international trade had to be reestablished for countries to reap the benefits of growth and efficiency stemming from trade; protectionist policies had to be discontinued. On the other hand, the laissez-faire policies that had dominated the first era of globalization had to be replaced by government intervention and active management of the economy.

The new consensus viewed markets as incapable of self-regulating and of reaching full employment. There was a need for demand-side policies to achieve the macroeconomic equilibrium. Thus there was also a need for national governments and "self-sufficiency" – which Keynes had advocated a decade earlier. The result was a rather extraordinary piece of international governance, with institutions like the World Bank and the International Monetary Fund seeking to ensure stability in the world economy and the General Agreement on Trade and Tariffs (GATT) regulating international trade. Yet there was ample space for national governments, helped by limited international capital mobility. In this regime of "moderate" globalization the autonomy of national governments was stronger than the independent forces of international trade (Rodrik 2011). In France the period from 1945 through 1975 is still referred to as the *"Trente Glorieuses,"* denoting the unprecedented growth rates in France and other European countries.[11]

The second era of globalization ended with the financial and economic crisis that hit developed economies at the beginning of the 1970s, leading the US government to withdraw the convertibility of the US dollar into gold. The system breakdown led to the third era of globalization, with supply-side policies and a new system that shares many characteristics with the first globalization era. Its pillars are:

1.   tariffs reduction and very low barriers to trade, under the aegis of the World Trade Organization (WTO) as the general arbiter of trade regulation (Chapter 3, Section 3.7.5.1 for a description of trade policies in different countries around the world);
2.   unrestricted capital mobility and deregulation in the financial sector (see Chapter 3, Section 3.7.5.2 for a description of capital account policies around the world); and
3.   rising migration flows.

The volumes of international trade in the current system are close to those in the first globalization era. Global trade as a proportion of global income has only recently exceeded the levels reached in the nineteenth century. Capital is as mobile as in the nineteenth century, but the greater volume of capital today means much larger absolute flows. The main differences are in flexible, rather than fixed, exchange rates, and overall heavier restrictions on people's mobility than in the past.

Rodrik (2011) coined the term "hyper-globalization" to describe the current era. The balance has shifted from national self-sufficiency to the cogency of external constraints. Global governance is weak, if at all present. Each country struggles to reach its desired objectives of growth, redistribution and social protection. Recurrent financial crises – from the crisis in Asia and Argentina in the 1990s to the Great Recession in 2008 – erode growth, employment and

---

[11]   Growth rates in Europe during the 1950–1970 period reached an unprecedented peak of 3.9 percent per capita, which contrasts with growth rates of 0.9 percent in the period 1913–1950, and of 1.9 percent for the period 1970–2012. Growth rates in America were more constant, averaging 1.4 percent in the 1913–1950 period, 1.9 percent in the 1950–1970 spell, and around 1.6 percent over the 1970–2012 period. Source: Piketty (2014), Table 2.5.

well-being (Ayhan Kose et al. 2005; Prasad et al. 2007). High growth countries like India and China have managed globalization by introducing forms of capital controls and restrictions on foreign direct investment.

Are redistribution policies in the current globalization era possible at all? Implicitly we have already presented an optimistic view based on experiences from the small open economies in northern Europe. Many scholars are less optimistic. They point to rising costs of equality under hyper-globalization.

8.5.2 Globalization's Challenges to Egalitarian Redistribution

8.5.2.1 The Efficiency–Equity Tradeoff

According to the standard textbook approach to economic policy, markets and states have distinct roles. Competitive firms allocate resources in production, rational consumers are free to choose, and states redistribute incomes. As long as markets are capable of achieving efficiency, the role of the state is restricted to the correction of unjust inequality.

A theoretical rationale is given by the so-called "theorems of welfare economics" (reviewed in more detail in the online Appendix, Section A8.12). This approach confines the state to a subsidiary role further restricted by the cost of redistribution. Taxing labor incomes to finance redistributive programs is considered to reduce individuals' incentives to work and the size of the pie to be redistributed. This is Okun's (1975) "leaky bucket." Given the efficiency losses of redistribution, the state can only apply second best solutions to the problem of achieving an equitable allocation among citizens.

Nevertheless, as Atkinson (2015), among others, observes: welfare economics rests on flimsy foundations. For one, market competition is best described as monopolistic contest – or by what we have termed "real competition." As such, state-based redistribution can enhance efficiency. Moreover, empirical studies of taxation conclude that the efficiency cost of taxes is rather moderate (Diamond and Saez 2011). Section A8.12 in the Appendix presents further evidence questioning the empirical relevance of such an efficiency-equity tradeoff. Actually, the extent of efficiency losses may in practice be so contained that most economies can afford high levels of just equality – if they so wish. One recipe, called *informed democratic capitalism*, is based on a clear division: the labor market is left to operate without too much intervention; politicians should implement the redistribution levels that satisfy their voters' preferences, and economists and other experts should advise elected representatives to choose the least harmful tax instruments. This recipe may cure the excessive earnings inequality of unregulated markets, ensuring that democracy and capitalism work hand-in-hand to produce a second best outcome. But is it viable under hyper-globalization?

8.5.2.2 The Race to the Bottom

The optimism of informed democratic capitalism during the *Trente Glorieuses* was thwarted with the advent of the third globalization era (Section 8.5.1) and its increasing factor mobility. As argued by Sinn (2003) and others, competition extends to institutions, policies and degrees of market orientation. While it may give rise, in some cases, to more egalitarian institutions with strong unions and generous welfare states, competition may in other cases lead to a race to the bottom in terms of low tax rates, little regulation, and low social standards.

The mechanism for the race to the bottom is simple. People and capital may move to countries where the profitability for their services is higher, taxes are lower and where there are fewer regulations. High-skilled people are more mobile than low-skilled people – they can afford the cost of moving and they more easily obtain work permits. Simula and Trannoy (2010) and Lehmann et al. (2014) argue that the impact of cross-country labor mobility can be rather negative for the extent of redistribution and the degree of progressiveness of taxes.

The race-to-the-bottom seems evident in the case of capital taxation. Estate tax rates sky-rocketed in the years between the 1950s and 1970s, when capital mobility was rather low also in the US and the UK (Piketty 2014). Since then, most taxes on capital have seen a decreasing trend (Devereux and Loretz 2012). The wealth tax has almost disappeared in Europe with the exception of France.

Figure 8.9 shows how the top tax rates on inheritance in four rich countries converge to a historically low value. Interestingly, top tax rates were much higher in the UK and the US over the past century than in France and Germany.

Compared to capital taxes, the race-to-the-bottom seems less severe in taxes on labor. Yet, Figure 8.10 shows how tax rates on top incomes in the US, the UK, France, and Germany converged toward the lowest observed levels since World War II. Yet we do not know how much of this reduction is caused by the option to migrate to countries with lower tax rates. Skilled workers can clearly gain a lot from migration. A Puerto Rican, for instance, can earn almost twice his income by moving to the mainland US.[12] Yet, migration has not emptied the island, as predicted by Anita in *West Side Story*. In 2000, no more than one-third of the Puerto Rico-born population had migrated to the mainland US (Borjas 2008).

There is also a strong belief among policy-makers that migrants respond to wage differences. New tax breaks designed to attract high-income earners prevail (Kleven et al. 2013, 2014). Even Denmark, France, and Sweden have launched specific tax breaks to attract high-skilled workers. For the OECD countries, Grogger and Hanson (2011) show that more educated people are more likely to emigrate and to settle in high-pay destinations.

Almost half of the total emigrant population in the world resides in just eight rich countries – with one-fifth living in the US alone (Docquier

---

[12] Our computations are based on US Census data (See www.census.gov/newsroom/press-releases/2014/cb14-17.html, accessed on 24/8/17).

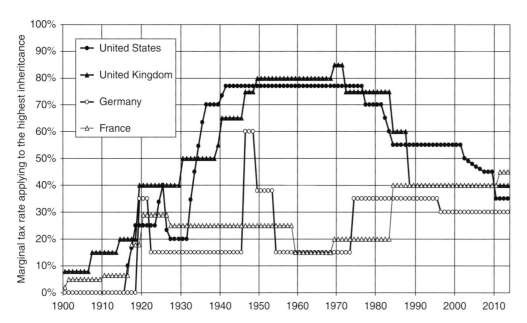

Figure 8.9 | Top inheritance tax rate 1900–2013.
Source: piketty.pse.ens.fr/capital21c (Piketty 2014)

and Raporport 2012). Even though the brain drain in poor countries can be detrimental to development (Bhagwati and Hamada 1974), the picture is less clear when we account for remittances and the frequent instances of emigrants returning to their home countries (Docquier and Rapoport 2012, and Chapter 3, Section 8.7.5.4).

8.5.2.3   Factor Price Equalization and Wage Convergence

The mobility of labor and capital can also contribute to wage equalization across countries, as captured in the so-called "Stolper-Samuelson theorem." The thesis of the theorem is that international trade will reduce wages for low-skilled workers in rich countries, and increase wages for low-skilled workers in poor countries. One implication is that trade liberalization may constrain the possibility for a government to influence its wage-setting policy, and unions may experience lower bargaining power.

But are Western wages actually set in Beijing, as the theory suggests? Focusing on changes in labor demand and prices in China-exposed industries, Freeman (1995) answered negatively, while Wood (1995), using different methods, answered positively. Observing that low-skilled wages fell as much in traded as in nontraded sectors (Berman et al. 1994) led scholars to believe that increased trade was not the main culprit. Rather, skill-biased technological change is a less controversial explanation (see Chapter 3, Section 3.7.5.3, Lee and Vivarelli 2004; Davis and Mishra 2007). Although the view that technology matters more than trade is still dominant, recent work seems to find a larger role for the latter, in particular for what concerns offshoring (Hummels et al. 2014, 2016). Low-skilled wages may in fact fall for the mere threat that firms relocate their activities from rich to poor countries.

8.5.2.4   Immigration and the Decreasing Support for Social Insurance

As indicated in Section 8.4, there are indications that exposition to more global competition may stimulate the political demand for social insurance as countries become more exposed to external risks (Rodrik 1998; Barth and Moene 2015). Can immigration change this positive effect?

A hypothesis that has attracted attention in the comparative literature on the welfare state goes under the name of *ethnic antagonism*. In countries with high heterogeneity, the richest groups – the white majority in the case of the US – may be unwilling to benefit recipients from other groups, such as Afro-Americans (Alesina and Glaeser 2004; Lind 2007). The welfare state tends thus to be smaller in countries with higher ethnic heterogeneity. This may be due to either a direct distaste for other ethnic groups (Alesina and La Ferrara 2002) – similar to the taste for discrimination in the labor market – or to the (possibly misplaced) belief that people from other ethnic groups are less deserving because they lack work ethic and willpower (Gilens 1999). Such negative beliefs may be based on stereotypes stirred by media manipulation or political leaders (Glaeser 2005).

Alesina and Giuliano (2009) find that such explanations matter for preferences for redistribution. As argued by Roemer et al. (2007), in US political debates racial antagonism is often camouflaged under a "libertarian flag." Lower redistribution is justified on the basis of US values being intrinsically libertarian – whereas the real underlying motivation has to do with racial aversion. In fact, empirical analysis based on the US General Social Survey shows that libertarianism has little effect in accounting for racist attitudes. "Authoritarian" values and the insistence on "traditional" values seem more important.

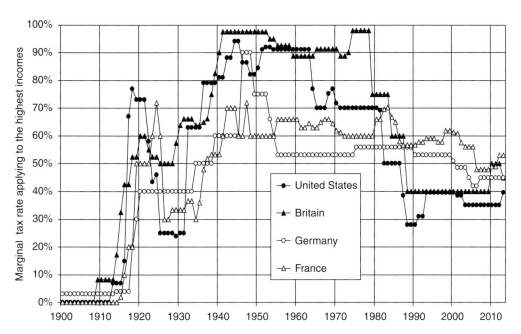

Figure 8.10 | Top income tax rates 1900–2013.
Source: piketty.pse.ens.fr/capital21c (Piketty 2014).

Immigration may be expected to bring about a similar decline in the support for social insurance (Alesina and Glaeser 2004; Roemer et al. 2007). Ethnic antagonism induced by immigration challenges the social contract that rests on shared cultural norms or tolerance of cultural diversity. Immigration may change the networks of solidarity across different socio-economic groups (Brochmann 2003); cultural and religious differences may become more distinct (Brewer 1999).

These rather bleak predictions have some empirical support. Racial/ethnic heterogeneity is negatively related with individual propensities to redistribute, and with public goods provision in different areas within the US (Alesina et al. 1999; Luttmer 2001; Lind 2007) and across countries (Alesina and Glaeser 2004; Alesina and Giuliano 2009). A negative association between ethnic diversity and interpersonal trust has also been identified (Alesina and La Ferrara 2002; Putnam 2007), with negative consequences for economic growth (Knack and Keefer 1997) and social spending (Soroka et al. 2006).

Public opinion tends to oppose immigration. For instance, answers to a 2000 World Value Survey question regarding the necessity to reduce or increase the number of immigrants in one's country reveal that two-thirds were in favor of restricting immigration, while only 8 percent were in favor of expanding it. In all 23 countries surveyed, the anti-immigration block was larger than the pro-immigration one (Scheve and Slaughter 2006).

Borjas (2003) shows that immigration has a negative effect on US workers' real wages. A ten percent higher migration reduces the average native's wage by 3–4 percent. The reduction is larger for unskilled wages and close to zero for the wages to educated workers. Using a different method, Ottaviano and Peri (2012) find only moderate wage losses to unskilled labor and actually a higher average wage as a response to higher immigration. Whatever the direction

of the average effect, the decline in the lowest wages seems minor compared to the strength of anti-immigration sentiments. The case of France is revealing. France's high minimum wage insulates low-skilled workers from the pressure of immigration. Nevertheless, anti-immigrant feelings are rampant. Economics is not the whole story.

8.5.2.5 Globalization and Other Gains from Efficiency

Bowles (2006) discusses how globalization may, in principle, limit governments' effectiveness at carrying out conventional strategies of redistribution. The constraints, however, do not affect a large class of egalitarian interventions that are productivity-enhancing, including land redistribution and ownership reforms at the enterprise level.

Similarly, Bardhan (2006) discusses cases of successes and failure in how globalization affects poverty alleviation in poor and middle-income countries. He shows that many of the problems affecting the poor have little to do with globalization, but rather with domestic institutions, insisting that the poor's material welfare in developing countries would be improved if the trade barriers and subsidies adopted by rich countries were removed. In this sense, more globalization would arguably benefit developing countries and their poor citizens.

8.5.3 The Welfare State in a Global Era

Section 8.5.2 laid out some arguments pointing to a possible weakening of the effectiveness of national welfare states in the current global era. These arguments concerned the loss of tax-raising capacity by governments, the voluntary reduction of support for social insurance as the population becomes more ethnically heterogeneous, and the lack of control over wages as global labor markets become established. We have already commented that the last argument seems to have little empirical relevance, in spite of the often trumpeted negative impact that globalization has on national labor markets in political propaganda. In this section we contend with the first two.

8.5.3.1 A Reassessment of the Race-to-the-Bottom in Tax Rates

That top tax rates have been falling and converging – at least among rich economies – is evident from Figures 8.9 and 8.10. Nevertheless, the argument that such a fall in tax rates would preempt states' financial capacities is simply not supported by macroeconomic data. Figure 8.11 is telling in this respect. It shows the historical evolution of tax revenues as a proportion of GDP in four rich economies, representatives of different "varieties of capitalism" (Section 8.3). Other developed economies would show a similar evolution. No downward trend can be observed since the 1980s. If anything, the weight of the state in the economy has never been as large as today.

The Appendix, Section A8.13 reports data for other OECD countries, for which data are available from 1965 on. It is noteworthy that some countries, such as Ireland and the Netherlands, have experienced sharp drops in their tax revenues since the mid-1980s. Perhaps the race-to-the-bottom is showing some bite for these small open economies. Tax revenues have shown signs of decrease in some Scandinavian countries, such as Sweden and Norway, and a sharp decrease of progressivity in the Swedish income tax is well documented (Bengtsson et al. 2016). Nonetheless, the OECD area shows on average a steady increase in tax revenues.

There are several reasons why the total tax receipts have not been affected by the drop in the tax rates. The first reason has to do with the fact that the graphs we showed concerned the *top* tax rate, rather than the *average* rate. The latter, which is more relevant for the determination of total tax receipts, has gone through lower variation than the top tax rate. In the case of the US, the reduction was in the order of few percentage points (see Saez 2004, for the US). In fact, it can be argued that for the period spanning the end of World War II up to the 1980s, the main function of the top income tax rate was *not* to collect tax revenues per se, but rather to give a signal to the labor market about which income level would be considered socially acceptable.

Top income tax rates were as high as 90 percent in Britain in the 1940s and again in the 1970s, and in the US in the 1950s through the mid-1960s. Tax rates of this magnitude are almost confiscation. They were levied because the dominant "sentiment" in the society was that high incomes were fundamentally undeserved. It is particularly telling that public documents draw a difference between "earned income," such as labor income, and "unearned income," such as capital income. As Figure 8.12 shows, for a limited period within this spell of high taxation in the UK and the US, the tax rates applied to unearned income were higher than those applied to earned income.

It is remarkable that these rather egalitarian sentiments evaporated from both US and UK public debate during the 1980s, and it is an open question what actually determined this profound shift in public opinion. Obviously, the contemporary leadership of Ronald Reagan and Margaret Thatcher played a big role, but it would be difficult to imagine that such leaderships were able to propagate a radically different approach to taxation of high incomes without some underlying social consensus.

Piketty (2014) offers an extensive analysis of the public debate in these two countries over the last century and suggests that US citizens' fear of being overtaken, in terms of standards of living, by Europe and Japan at the end of the 1980s – after a long period of catching-up – was one of the main reasons for the libertarian turn. Incidentally, it would be wrong to say that Europe was committed to inegalitarianism during the *Trente Glorieuses.* Rather than setting high top tax rates, many European countries preferred to apply salary caps to executives, or other forms of control of excessive pays. It is also worth noting that top tax rates on wealth in the US and the UK were similarly confiscatory up to the 1980s, and fell dramatically afterwards. High wealth was seen with as much suspicion as high incomes.

An additional explanation for the declining tax rates can be found in the falling growth rate caused by a secular reduction in the rate of the technical progress (Gordon 2016). When the size of the cake is increasing at a slower pace, the tax sacrifice is less hidden by the increase of the cake. The collapse of communism as a global threat for the affluent also played a part in denting redistributive goals. Atkinson (2015) argues that the vanishing of a collective egalitarian and cooperative ethos which was widespread in the aftermath of World War II played a big role in making redistribution less popular as well as spurring wage inequality.

Average tax rates dropped after the 1980s in most countries, though not as much as top tax rates. Arguably, overall tax revenues did not drop much as top tax rates fell because an increase in incomes compensated for the fall in the tax rates. It is documented that indirect taxation of consumption made up for the drop in income or wealth taxes. It is tempting to conclude that the argument about states losing their tax-raising capabilities does not seem to have much bite.

The consequences of lowering top tax rates on income and wealth, however, go well beyond its impact on government budgets. Brain drain is one. Large numbers of highly educated people from both low-income countries and from rich countries decided to settle in North America. It is open to debate whether the 1 million German university graduates or the 1.4 million UK university graduates who decided to relocate to the US during the 2000s (Docquier and Rapoport 2012) are big enough numbers to slow down the growth of countries where out-migration is taking place, to the advantage of the US. Yet, the migration of the many researchers is noteworthy, given the obvious relevance of scientific research for innovation and growth.

Another obvious consequence of the reduction in the top tax rates is its impact on inequality. The explosion in income inequality and wealth concentration that we witnessed in the US (Section 8.2.2.3) clearly went hand-in-hand with reduction in top tax rates. As discussed in detail by Piketty (2014) and others, the phenomenal rise in the payment of CEOs – partly in salaries and partly in capital incomes – is associated with this trend.

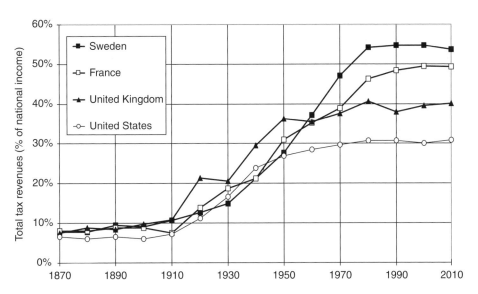

Figure 8.11 | Tax revenues in rich countries 1870–2010.
Source: piketty.pse.ens.fr/capital21c (Piketty 2014)

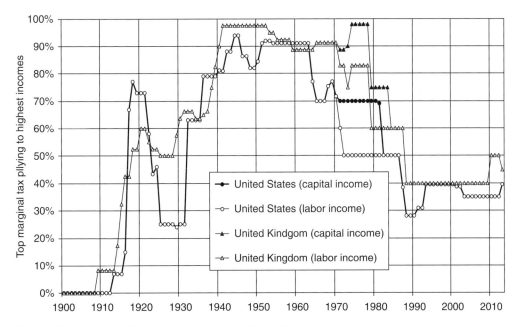

Figure 8.12 | Top tax rates: "Earned income" vs. "unearned income."
Source: piketty.pse.ens.fr/capital21c (Piketty, 2014)

An orthodox explanation of the trend relies holds that the reduction in tax rates raised the productivity and the labor supply of CEOs and managers, and more generally of talented people, who earned much larger quantities of money for their abilities. A related account has to do with the economics of "superstars" (Rosen 1981). Modern communications technology permits firms to reach much larger markets than before. This entails that talented individuals can gain larger profits to their companies. The outcome is the creation of "winner-take-all" markets where the most talented individuals reap huge rewards, even if they are only marginally better in what they do than others. Gabaix and Landier (2008) find very small dispersion in CEO talent, but a high and striking correlation

between CEO pay and firm size. In particular, the six-fold increase of US CEO pay between 1980 and 2003 corresponds to the six-fold increase in large companies' market capitalization over the same period.

Correlation does not mean causation, though. An alternative explanation dismisses the incentive effect on productivity, and points at the incentives of CEOs to exploit their bargaining power. This explanation rests on the idea that CEOs had almost no incentive to bargain for higher pay when the tax rates on top income were at the confiscatory levels of the 1960s. But as soon as tax rates dropped, the incentives of bosses to claim higher pays grew.

Exploring how CEOs' remunerations are set in practice is revealing. Given the complexity of teamwork in large organizations, it is very difficult to ascertain the marginal productivity of each participant. CEOs have large discretionary power in setting their own pay; if their salary is not set by themselves, it is set by a corporate compensation committee whose members are often nominated by the CEO themselves, or expect large remunerations in return.

Which of the two accounts is correct? Both accounts are likely be relevant. Yet the support for the bargaining power account is perhaps most convincing. Neither productivity nor growth rates have shown apparent increases in the US after the fall in the top income tax rate (Piketty 2014). On the contrary, the rate of innovation was higher in the previous decades. This sheds more than a shadow of a doubt on the productivity argument. Piketty, Saez and Stantcheva (2014) show that the elasticity of taxes on "pay from luck" (pay increases derived from a whole sector performing relatively well) exceeds the elasticity of "pay from reward" (pay accruing to managers of companies that outperformed other companies in the same sector). Other pieces of evidence point in the same direction. Firms that were classified as having worse than average governance had managers who achieved the more than average pay rises.

Regardless of whether the correct interpretation is that top managers took advantage of decreasing top tax rates to increase their salaries, or "superstar" CEOs won positional rents, it does not seem that increasing top tax rates would jeopardize government tax-raising capacities.

8.5.3.2   A Reassessment of the Demand for Social Insurance in Open Economies

We already noted how government's size increased in the course of the twentieth century. Prior to 1910 levels of taxation were in the order of 10 percent of GDP. In Piketty's words, the role of the state was in this period confined to its "regalian" duties before the 1910s, namely guaranteeing public order through police and defense, ensuring the rule of law through courts and justice, conducting foreign policy, and little else. It was only during the twentieth century that the welfare state as we know it today was established gradually and reached a plateau after the *Trente Glorieuses*.

One can notice that the government's size is bigger today in France and Sweden compared to the UK and the US. What explains such differences in the size of the government? Political scientist David Cameron (1978) was maybe the first to claim that openness to international trade was a key factor. Larger governments were necessary in countries that were more exposed to international trade, exposing larger risks to their citizens' incomes. The need to stabilize incomes through a state-run system of social insurance had therefore to be regarded as a major cause of the differences in government's size. Rodrik (1998) proposed conclusive evidence of the robustness of this result, which applies to developing economies as well as developed ones. The results stand controlled for a variety of possible confounding factors, including a country's size, geography, or demography. Hence, contrary to the thesis that a state's action space is reduced in a global economy, the opposite seems to be the case.

Atkinson's (2015) historical analysis leads to the same conclusions. He points out that the institutions providing social insurance were built in most countries toward the end of the nineteenth century, in a period of great international economic integration (Section 8.5.1). The Industrial Revolution created new forms of employment relationships that made key institutions of social protection necessary. Programs such as unemployment insurance, industrial injury benefits, sickness insurance, and old-age pensions schemes, were all created between the end of the nineteenth century and the early twentieth century to protect workers from the risk of loss of earnings. It is not incidental that these institutions for social protection were created at a time of high trade openness, because trade fluctuations made such risks even more acute. Germany led the way with Bismarck's reforms. Clearly, other factors were also relevant, such as the need to preserve political and social stability at a time when socialist ideas were spreading and workers' organizations had become stronger.

A significant factor was the need for social protection when jobs stability was threatened by greater competition on international markets. Typically, the coverage and generosity of these institutions was limited at their inception and was enlarged in the interwar period, as governments enlarged their size. Keynes and Beveridge conceived social transfers as automatic stabilizers that would bring an economy back to macroeconomic equilibrium when hit by a negative shock. Writing at the beginning of the 1980s, Abramovitz (1981) still supported income minima, health care, social insurance, and other elements of the welfare state as essential components of the productivity growth process itself. It was only shortly afterward that a major shift in perspective led to social protection being seen as a hindrance, rather than a complement, to economic performance. US Nobel Prize-winning economist Buchanan (1988) strongly advocated that the European social model based on higher social protection than its US counterpart was no longer economically viable under globalization.

This analysis is persuasive in laying down a case for a strong government that protects citizens from the vagaries of international markets. Markets and states should not be seen as substitutes but rather as complements. Stronger states make possible more fruitful market engagements (Rodrik 2011). Nevertheless, this evidence does not address the point raised in Section 8.5.2.3 regarding decreasing support for social insurance under increasing migratory flows, a main hindrance to the stability of the welfare state. The rise of populist parties in many European countries – let alone Donald Trump's election in the US – is a clear signal of how these anti-immigration sentiments are playing a big role. No wonder that raising barriers to trade and restrictions on immigration is seen as an answer to both fears of macroeconomic instability in open economies and anti-welfare sentiments.

8.6   The Road Ahead

8.6.1   Egalitarian Policies for the Twenty-first Century

We have sketched out how equality can be used as a development strategy. Yet there are many hindrances. Even though a better world is economically feasible, there may be strong political forces to prevent its realization. And, as we know, bad policies may be good politics for some rulers.

Many claim that the basic challenge is to fight for the survival of the welfare state under hyper-globalization. In 1998, in an opening speech titled "Worldwide Crisis in the Welfare State: What Is Next in the Context of Globalization?," the then IMF managing director Michel Camdessus stated: *"Welfare systems, based on the best possible motivation of ameliorating hardship and improving human welfare, have come to represent an enormous drain on the resources and the efficiency of many of the so-called welfare states."*

The discussion in Section 8.5.3.1 indicates that Mr. Camdessus's concerns may be unfounded. There is nothing intrinsic in globalization – intended both in general terms and with regard to the specific shape that globalization has taken since the 1980s – that seems to compromise the capacity of the welfare state to operate. Governments have never been as large as today. The race-to-the-bottom seems to affect corporate taxation on mobile assets more than on less mobile personal incomes.

The idea that a marginal rise in taxes above the levels around the world would cause capital to fly to other countries is simply unrealistic. Acting in an open economy adds limitations the government's action space. But such limitations are mere constraints. They do not make governments powerless. Atkinson was clear: states are not passive agents of globalization. They have several useful instruments to deal with it.

Setting policies for the twenty-first century requires insights. We believe that it is unlikely that the system we observe now, based on flexible exchange rates and footloose capital mobility, low barriers to trade, and high barriers to low-skilled migration, will maintain its current shape into the future. The failure and the financial crises that the IMF's "best pupils" – Argentina and the Asian Tigers – suffered when implementing state-of-the-art policy packages made of unbridled markets, government budget surpluses, and monetary contraction are under everyone's gaze.

It is quite noticeable that every change in a policy paradigm has been preceded by a change in the "sentiments" among economists and policy-makers. This was the case for Keynes's (1936) work, which formed the background for the predominance of demand-side policies. To some extent, Milton Friedman's 1962 book *Capitalism and Freedom* had arguably a similar impact in the 1970s as Keynes's *General Theory* in the 1940s. The former set the stage for the "supply-side revolution" that characterizes the current epoch. Nevertheless, maybe we are indeed witnessing today a change of heart within the economics discipline. Many Nobel Prize-winning economists, from Joseph Stiglitz to Paul Krugman, have been vocal in laying bare the shortfalls of the current state of affairs. We do not know whether the dissent toward the current version of globalization has reached the critical mass to determine a regime shift in public policy. If even the IMF nowadays offers advice to countries on how to operate capital controls, maybe we are close to that moment.

Anthony Atkinson and Thomas Piketty have proposed an increase in the progressivity of the income tax, and in particular setting the top

income tax rate to levels around 80 percent. Is this proposal illogical in the light of the race-to-the-bottom? Perhaps not. A level of 65 percent for the top income tax rate is, according to Atkinson, the level that would *maximize* total revenues in the UK. The main counterargument would obviously be whether a process of outgoing brain drain of top income-earners or academics would set in.

This policy would be worth pursuing even in isolation from other countries, if a very simple reform were introduced. A race to the bottom would most likely be avoided if a person were liable to pay taxes not to her country of residence, but to her country of citizenship. In this sense, a German citizen would be liable to pay taxes to the German government even after having migrated to the US. In fact, this arrangement is already in place in the US. Giving up one's citizenship in exchange for financial discounts would, most likely, be too high a price to pay. Moreover, the tax rates computed above already take into account the possibility of people moving abroad.

The second proposal is the well-known proposal by Piketty of instituting a global tax on wealth. The author himself describes the proposal as utopian. But utopian does not mean unimaginable. Clearly, a utopian aspect of the tax lies precisely in ascertaining the tax base for every individual. It requires a level of international cooperation on tax avoidance that comes very close to the institution of an international financial authority.

A perhaps even more utopian piece of global policy regards the institution of a global basic income. In other sections of this chapter we have discussed the advantages of instituting a basic income at the national level. Among the practical problems of implementation is the prospect of migratory inflows into the country, which may put governments under severe financial strain (Van Parijs and Vanderborght 2017). This may either lead to restrictive immigration policies, or to risks of social marginalization and labor market segregation of immigrants. In view of these and other issues, some people argue for a global basic income (Düvell and Jordan 2003). Others propose a gradual approach and designate the European Union or NAFTA as the main distribution units of a supra-state basic income (Schmitter and Bauer 2001; Van Parijs and Vanderborght 2017). Some authors have proposed a global basic income in the form of a Global Resources Dividend aimed at eradicating poverty in the world, as part of a broader strategy that includes radical measures such as a global wealth tax or a Tobin tax (Pogge 2007).

Climate change is also an issue supporting the need for a global basic income (Van Parijs and Vanderborght 2017). The atmosphere's carbon-absorbing capacity is a natural resource to which all human beings have an equal claim. At the same time, all mankind has a right to inherited natural resources and a duty toward the cost of preserving the ecosystem (Section 8.2.1.2). Basic income could be a means to redistribute cost and benefits of the policies need to preserve the ecosystem. The need to slow down the depletion of a valuable natural resource out of fairness to future generations and the need to internalize the negative externalities closely associated with the use of fossil energy can justify a global tax on carbon emission to finance a global basic income.

8

8.6.2   The Cooperative Social Ethos

Human behavior is diverse. The racism, xenophobia, and nativism in many countries show both the need for a cooperative ethos of solidarity and the potential challenges of acquiring it. Yet people have a high ability to cooperate with each other when the circumstances are right. Just look at the many peaceful areas of the world: the big cities, the large corporations, the voluntary organizations, the global markets, and all the other types of interaction and cooperation between strangers. In addition, in many countries citizens trust big governments and allow them to collect high taxes. The social ethos – the guiding belief in society – builds on this kind of trust, but it is more.

We have touched upon how a social ethos of cooperation and reciprocation may lead people to contribute, in the expectation that the other will do the same. Such social ethos may be important for any alternative social arrangement, or economic system, that takes fairness seriously. For instance, this social ethos was crucial for the development of the social and economic society model of Nordic countries. These countries are ranked favorably when it comes to economic and health security, productivity, and equality of income. Clearly there is no obvious way to characterize *necessary* conditions for the development of such a social ethos. It is also obvious that social ethos cannot easily be imported from one country to another (Section 8.3.3).

A cooperative ethos does not require a shared ethnic background and nationality. Neither does it require insulation from competitive pressure. On the contrary, there are clear and maybe surprising differences across countries in how citizens consider the importance of competition and free trade. The strength of a shared cooperative ethos may depend on what else one is sharing. Having a comprehensive welfare state, for instance, means that the gains from trade and globalization are widely shared in society, implying that globalization meets less resistance. Without a welfare state, in contrast, the hostility toward globalization may become strong. In fact, the fraction of people who want protection measures against foreign competition is as high as 61 percent in the US, but as low as 29 percent in Sweden and 35 percent in Denmark and Norway (Melgar et al. 2013). Thus compared to citizens in the US, Nordic citizens have over time acquired much more of a shared belief about the benefits of protection without protectionism, maintained by all governments irrespective of color. In the US, beliefs are clustered on protection and protectionism being two sides of the same thing.

A cooperative social ethos might also involve a commitment not to elude taxation. Citizens from Nordic countries hold among the lowest percentage of wealth in tax havens, less than 5 percent of GDP (Alstadsæter et al. 2017). This compares to 8 percent of wealth held in tax havens by US citizens, 15 percent by continental European citizens, 17 percent by UK citizens, and a staggering 60 percent by Russian citizens.

Also, if civic organizations like unions are weak, capitalists have a relatively uncontested opportunity to develop an individualistic ethos in a nation. It may be in their interests to have individuals worry only about their own material situation and to not organize with others for higher taxes that will be paid disproportionately by the fairly rich; to not provide public goods that the rich can relatively easily substitute with

their private wealth; and to not demand higher wages that directly reduce profits and the income of capitalists and large shareholders. There is no reason to believe that individual preferences for acquiring similar values as the rest of society are not equally strong in all countries. The difference stems from what kind of social ethos they adapt.

8.6.3   What Kind of System?

In our discussion of economic systems in the twentieth century (Section 8.3), three experiments stand out: The first is the Soviet Union, an experiment with political dictatorship and without markets, which failed in both economic provision and social ethos. The second is the Chinese experiment, particularly the form of state capitalism that Deng Xiao-Ping established at the end of the Cultural Revolution. This involves political dictatorship, pervasive markets, and public ownership, and rapid economic growth, but the disappearance of socialist ethos and rapidly growing concentration of income and wealth (Sections 8.3.1 and 8.3.2.4). China's economy has socialist and capitalist features, so it is probably most accurate to say that it is neither capitalist nor socialist at present. It has a large sector of firms that are state-owned, and it has a large and rapidly growing sector of privately owned firms. The ethos in China is much closer to capitalist than socialist. MacFarquhar and Schoenhals (2009) believe the socialist ethos in China was destroyed by the Cultural Revolution, because of which the population lost faith in the Communist Party's ability to lead. The third experiment is the Nordic social democracies, which we illustrated in Section 8.3.2.2.

There are of course many other interesting examples that we have briefly touched upon: northern Europe and Canada are capitalist countries, somewhere between the Nordics and the United States with their welfare states and high taxation, and with a cooperative social ethos that is less developed than in the Nordics. There are South Korea and Japan, racially and linguistically homogeneous, whose ethos might be called Confucian; these countries have achieved rapid economic development. There is no country as egalitarian as Japan that is as large as Japan.

From a scientific viewpoint, we do not possess sufficient evidence to decide how economic systems will evolve in the future, nor even how we would like them to evolve – that is, what variations from capitalism are feasible. Given the failure of the first two experiments in producing what looks like the good society (Section 8.3.1), what can we conclude? Will social democracy of a Nordic type, supported by a cooperative social ethos, eventually spread to other countries that are of larger size and more ethnically heterogeneous? Or is capitalism of the Anglo-Saxon variety – or perhaps the European variety of Germany or France – the necessary future of the world's developing countries? Does the Confucian capitalism of Japan and South Korea show the road forward? Or, is the future likely to be dominated by something else that we have not yet seen? We cannot claim to have the answer to what the feasible economic systems are for the world's developing countries – probably the most important question for social science of our time. But we can use economic theory and psychology to chip away at the problem.

A pessimistic view is based on the fact that the welfare state in the twentieth century developed as a consequence of three catastrophes: the two world wars and the Great Depression. According to Piketty (2014),

Table 8.3 | Toolkit for action

Goals/values	Conjugating earnings equality and socio-economic progress. Implementing wage compression can stimulate a process of Schumpeterian "creative destruction" that stimulates economic development at the same time safeguarding social equality.	Conjugating social justice with socio-economic progress. This will improve workers' capabilities for every income level, thus increasing their productivity.
Policy-makers	Should foster a wage-setting system favoring wage compression and the reduction of skill premia. This will incentivize the replacement of low-paid jobs that use least-productive technologies with better-paid jobs that use most productive ones. As a result the average wage rate will increase.	Should implement welfare policies to provide social insurance, health services and education. By creating a safety net protecting against unemployment or food-shortages, policy-makers can also incentivize risk-taking in economic activities, thus fostering specialization and investment in skills and equipment.
International organizations	One way to ensure wage compression is by increasing education levels, especially of people from the lowest economic brackets. International organizations may develop educational programs especially in developing countries.	Can accompany national governments' action in providing social insurance against risks, health services and education.
NGOs	NGOs may have a role, alongside international organizations, in improving educational levels for people in the lowest economic brackets.	Can accompany national governments' action in providing social insurance against risks, health services and education.
Citizens	Trade unions and entrepreneur organizations should comply with a policy of wage compression. This may be best achieved through a centralized system of wage setting.	Providing social safety nets will empower producers against landowners, employers and the elites.

capital (wealth) was largely destroyed as a result of these catastrophes, and the period of the advance of welfare states coincided with the period when wealth concentration was lowest and the wealthy were, one might conjecture, less powerful than they had been for centuries. Piketty suggests that we are returning to wealth concentrations that look like those of the late nineteenth and early twentieth centuries – a more extreme capitalism, where inheritance will become increasingly important as the manner of wealth transmission across generations. One might conclude that only another Great Depression or world war will bring about sufficient dissatisfaction with current arrangements to induce the kind of transformation we have discussed.

An optimistic view, more in line with most of the discussion in this chapter, posits a rather gradual evolution of economic institutions favoring social justice and inclusiveness, both nationally and globally. These changes may be induced by social movements that occur in a time of peace, and whose victories are implemented through legislation, by the action of enlightened leaders, or both.

We honestly cannot say which of the two scenarios – the pessimistic or the optimistic – is more likely. The third possibility – that capitalism continues to become ever more venal, the concentration of wealth ever greater, the wealthy evermore isolated in their gated communities and private airplanes, with no financial crises sufficiently severe to induce mass social movements – we think is impossible. For such concentrations of wealth will breed capitalist classes with such power and greed that there will be either more financial crises and concomitant depressions, or the increased probability of a great war. One way or the other, capitalism as we now have it is not the end of history.

8.7   Toolkit for Action

Table 8.3 offers guidance about how the relevant actors and decision-makers can promote socio-economic progress.

8.8   Abbreviations

SWB: Subjective Well-Being
OWB: Objective Well-Being

BCII: Between-Country Income Inequality
WCII: Within-Country Income Inequality
ISI: Import Substitution Industrialization
SEWA: Self-Employed Women's Association
GATT: General Agreement on Trade and Tariffs

References

Abramovitz, M. 1981. "Welfare Quandaries and Productivity Concerns." *The American Economic Review* 71/1: 1–17.

Acemoglu, D. 2003. "Cross-Country Inequality Trends." *The Economic Journal* 113/485: 121–149.

Alesina, A.F., and P. Giuliano 2009. "Preferences for Redistribution." *National Bureau of Economic Research*, No. w14825.

Alesina, A.F., and E.L. Glaeser 2004. *Fighting Poverty in the US and Europe: A World of Difference.* Oxford: Oxford University Press.

Alesina, A., and E. La Ferrara 2002. "Who Trusts Others?" *Journal of Public Economics* 85/2: 207–234.

Alesina, A., R. Baqir, and W. Easterly 1999. "Public Goods and Ethnic Divisions" *Quarterly Journal of Economics* 114/4: 1243–1284.

Alstadsæter, A., N. Johannesen, and Zucman, G. 2017. "Who Owns the Wealth in Tax Havens? Macro Evidence and Implications for Global Inequality." *National Bureau of Economic Research*, No. w23805.

Atkinson, A.B. 2015. *Inequality – What Can be Done?* Cambridge, MA: Harvard University Press.

Ayhan Kose, M., E.S. Prasad, and M.E. Terrones 2005. "Growth and Volatility in an Era of Globalization." *IMF Staff Papers* 52: 31–63.

Bardhan, P. 2006. "Globalization and the Limits to Poverty Alleviation," in Bardhan, P.K., Bowles, S., and Wallerstein, M. (eds.), *Globalization and Egalitarian Redistribution*. Princeton, NJ: Princeton University Press.

Barth, E., and K.O. Moene 2015. "The Equality Multiplier. How Wage Compression and Welfare Spending Interact." *Journal of the European Economic Association* 14/5: 1011–1037.

Barth, Erling, K.O. Moene, and F. Willumsen 2015. "Reprint of 'The Scandinavian Model – An Interpretation'," *Journal of Public Economics* 127: 17–29.

Bengtsson, N., B. Holmlund, and D. Waldenström. 2016. "Lifetime versus Annual Tax-and-Transfer Progressivity: Sweden, 1968–2009." *The Scandinavian Journal of Economics* 118/4: 619–645.

Bentham, J. 1970. *An Introduction to the Principles of Morals and Legislation.* Burns, J.H. and Hart, H.L.A. (eds.). Oxford: Oxford University Press.

Berman, E., J. Bound, and Z. Griliches 1994. "Changes in the Demand for Skilled Labor Within US Manufacturing: Evidence from the Annual Survey of Manufactures." *Quarterly Journal of Economics* 109/2: 367–397.

Bhagwati, J., and K. Hamada, K. 1974. "The Brain Drain, International Integration of Markets for Professionals and Unemployment: a Theoretical Analysis." *Journal of Development Economics* 1/1: 19–42.

Bijker, W.E., T.P. Hughes, T. Pinch, and D.G. Douglas 2012. *The Social Construction of Technological Systems: New Directions in the Sociology and History of Technology.* MIT Press: Cambridge.

Borjas, G.J. 2003. "The Labor Demand Curve is Downward Sloping: Reexamining the Impact of Immigration on the Labor Market." *Quarterly Journal of Economics* 118/4: 1335–1374.

Borjas, G.J. 2008. "Labor Outflows and Labor Inflows in Puerto Rico." *Journal of Human Capital* 2/1: 32–68.

Bowles, S. 2006. "Egalitarian Redistribution in Globally Integrated Economies," in P.K. Bardhan, S. Bowles, and M. Wallerstein (eds.), *Globalization and Egalitarian Redistribution.* Princeton, NJ: Princeton University Press.

Brewer, M. 1999. "The Psychology of Prejudice: Ingroup Love or Outgroup Hate," *Journal of Social Issues* 55: 429–444.

Brickman, P., D. Coates, and R. Janoff-Bulman 1978. "Lottery Winners and Accident Victims: Is Happiness Relative?," *Journal of Personality and Social Psychology* 36/8: 917.

Brochmann, G. 2003. "Citizens of Multicultural States: Power and Legitimacy," in G. Brochmann, *Multicultural Challenge*, Emerald Group Publishing Limited.

Buchanan, J.M. 1988. "The Fiscal Crises in Welfare Democracies: with Some Implications for Public Investment," in H. Shibata and T. Ihori (eds.), *The Welfare State, Public Investment, and Growth.* Berlin: Springer.

Cameron, D.R. 1978. "The Expansion of the Public Economy: A Comparative Analysis." *American Political Science Review* 72/4: 1243–1261.

Case, A., and A. Deaton 2015. "Rising Morbidity and Mortality in Midlife among White Non-Hispanic Americans in the 21st Century," *Proceedings of the National Academy of Sciences* 112/49: 15078–15083.

Clark, A. and P. Frijters, and M. Shields 2008. *Relative Income, Happiness, and Utility: An Explanation for the Easterlin Paradox and other Puzzles. Journal of Economic Literature* 46/1: 95–144.

Dalton, P.S., S. Ghosal, and A. Mani 2016. "Poverty and Aspirations Failure," *The Economic Journal* 126/590: 165–188.

Dasgupta, P., and D. Ray 1987. "Inequality as a Determinant of Malnutrition and Unemployment: Policy," *The Economic Journal* 97/385: 177–188.

Davis, D.R., and P. Mishra 2007. "Stolper-Samuelson is Dead: And Other Crimes of Both Theory and Data," in A. Harrison, *Globalization and Poverty*, Chicago: University of Chicago Press.

De Neve, J.E., E. Diener, L. Tay, and C. Xuereb 2013. "The Objective Benefits of Subjective Well-Being," in L. Helliwell and J. Sachs (eds.), *World Happiness Report II.* The Earth Institute, New York.

Devereux, M., and S. Loretz 2012. "What do We Know About Corporate Tax Competition?" *Oxford Center on Business Taxation*, WP 12/29.

Diamond, P., and E. Saez 2011. "The Case for a Progressive Tax: From Basic Research to Policy Recommendations," *Journal of Economic Perspective*, 25/4: 165–190.

Docquier, F., and H. Rapoport 2012. "Globalization, Brain Drain, and Development," *Journal of Economic Literature* 50/3: 681–730.

Dow G. 2003. *Governing the Firm: Workers' Control in Theory and Practice.* Cambridge: Cambridge University Press.

Dow G. 2017. *The Labor-Managed Firm: Theoretical Foundations.* Cambridge: Cambridge University Press.

Drèze, J., and R. Khera. 2017. "Recent Social Security Initiatives in India," *World Development* 98: 555–572.

Düvell, F., and B. Jordan. 2003. *Migration: the Boundaries of Equality and Justice.* Cambridge: Polity Press.

Easterlin, R.A. 2003. "Explaining Happiness," *Proceedings of the National Academy of Sciences* 100/19: 11176–11183.

Easterlin, R.A., L. McVey, M. Switek, O. Sawangfa, and J. Zweig. 2010. "The Happiness-Income Paradox Revisited," *Proceedings of the National Academy of Sciences* 107/53: 22463–22468.

Easterlin, R.A., R. Morgan, M. Switek, and F. Wang. 2012. "China's Life Satisfaction, 1990–2010," *Proceedings of the National Academy of Sciences* 109: 9775–9780.

Esping-Andersen, G. 1990. *The Three Worlds of Welfare Capitalism.* Cambridge: Polity Press and Princeton, NJ: Princeton University Press.

Ferguson, A. 2009 "Feminist Paradigms of Solidarity and Justice," *Philosophical Topics* 37/2: 161–177.

Ferrera, M. 1996. "The 'Southern Model' of Welfare in Social Europe," *Journal of European Social Policy* 6/1: 17–37.

Filgueira, F, L. Reygadas, J.P. Luna, and P. Alegre 2011. "Shallow States, Deep Inequalities and the Limits of Conservative Modernization: the Politics and Policies of Incorporation in Latin America," in M. Blofield and J.P. Luna, *The Great Gap: Inequality and the Politics of Redistribution in Latin America.* University Park, PA: Pennsylvania State University Press.

Førsund, F.R., and L. Hjalmarsson 1987. *Analysis of Industrial Structure. A Putty-Clay Approach.* Stockholm: Almqvist & Wiksell International.

Frederick, S., and G. Loewenstein 1999. "Hedonic Adaptation," in D. Kahneman, E. Diener, and N. Schwarz (eds.), *Well-being: Foundations of hedonic Psychology.* New York: Russell Sage Foundation.

Freeman, R.B. 1995. "Are Your Wages Set in Beijing?" *The Journal of Economic Perspectives* 9/3: 15–32.

Friedman, M. 1962. *Capitalism and Freedom.* University of Chicago Press: 20–21.

Gabaix, X., and A. Landier. 2008. "Why Has CEO Pay Increased so Much?" *The Quarterly Journal of Economics* 123/1: 49–100.

Gibson-Graham, J.K. 2003. "Enabling Ethical Economies: Cooperativism and Class," *Critical Sociology* 29/2: 123–161.

Gibson-Graham, J.K. 2006. *A Postcapitalist Politics.* Minneapolis, MN: University of Minnesota Press.

Gibson-Graham, J.K., J. Cameron, and S. Healy 2013. *Take Back the Economy: An Ethical Guide For Transforming Our Communities.* Minneapolis, MN: University of Minnesota Press.

Gilens, M. 1999. *Why Americans Hate Welfare: Race, Media, and the Politics of Anti-Poverty Policy.* Chicago: Chicago University Press.

Gilens, M. 2009. *Why Americans Hate Welfare: Race, Media, and the Politics of Antipoverty Policy.* Chicago: University of Chicago Press.

Glaeser, E. 2005. "The Political Economy of Hatred," *Quarterly Journal of Economics* 120/1: 45–86.

Gordon, R. 2016. *The Rise and Fall of American Growth: The U.S. Standard of Living Since the Civil War.* Princeton, NJ: Princeton University Press.

Graham, C. 2009. *Happiness around the World: The Paradox of Happy Peasants and Miserable Millionaires.* Oxford: Oxford University Press.

Graham, C. 2017. *Happiness for All? Unequal Lives and Hopes in Pursuit of the American Dream.* Princeton, NJ: Princeton University Press.

Graham, C., A. Eggers, and S. Sukhtankar 2004. "Does Happiness Pay? An Initial Exploration Based on Panel Data from Russia," *Journal of Economic Behavior and Organization* 55/3: 319–342.

Graham, C., S. Zhou and J. Zhang 2015. Happiness and Health in China: The Paradox of Progress. Global Economy and Development Working Paper Series, No. 89. Washington, DC: Brookings Institution.

Grogger, J., and G.H. Hanson 2011. "Income Maximization and the Selection and Sorting of International Migrants," *Journal of Development Economics* 95/1: 42–57.

Guriev, S. and E. Zhuravskaya 2009. "(Un)Happiness in Transition," *Journal of Economic Perspectives* 23/2: 143–168.

Halperin, S. 1997. *In the Mirror of the Third World: Capitalist Development in Modern Europe.* Ithaca, NY: Cornell University Press.

Heclo, H., and H. Madsen 1987. *Policy and Politics in Sweden: Principled Pragmatism.* Philadelphia, PA: Temple University Press.

Helliwell, J., R. Layard, and J. Sachs (eds.) 2013. *World Happiness Report, 2013.* New York: Earth Institute.

Hobsbawm, E.J. 1995. *The Age of Extremes: A History of the World, 1914–1991.* New York: Pantheon Books.

Hsieh, C.T., and P.J. Klenow 2010. "Development Accounting," *American Economic Journal: Macroeconomics* 2/1: 207–223.

Hummels, D., R. Jorgensen, J. Munch, and C. Xian 2014. "The Wage Effects of Offshoring: Evidence from Danish Matched Worker-Firm Data," *American Economic Review* 104/6: 1597–1629.

Hummels, D., J.R. Munch, and C. Xiang 2016. Offshoring and Labor Markets. No. w22041. National Bureau of Economic Research.

Inglehart, R. and H. Klingemann 2000. "Genes, Culture, Democracy and Happiness," in E. Diener and E.M. Suh (eds.), *Culture and Subjective Well-Being.* Cambridge: MIT Press.

Inglehart, R., and C. Welzel 2005. *Modernization, Cultural Change, and Democracy: The Human Development Sequence.* Cambridge: Cambridge University Press.

Iversen, T., and D. Soskice 2001. "An Asset Theory of Social Policy Preferences." *American Political Science Review* 95/4: 875–893.

Johansen, L. 1959. "Substitution versus Fixed Production Coefficients in the Theory of Economic Growth: a Synthesis," *Econometrica* 27/2: 157–176.

Kahneman, D., E. Diener, and N. Schwarz 1999. *Well-Being: The Foundations of Hedonic Psychology.* New York: Russell Sage.

8

Keynes, J.M. 1933. "National Self-Sufficiency," *Studies: An Irish Quarterly Review* 22/86: 177–193.

Keynes, J.M. 1936. *General Theory of Employment, Interest and Money.* Dariya Gang, New Delhi: Atlantic Publishers & Dist.

Kleven, H., C. Landais, and E. Saez 2013. "Taxation and International Migration of Superstars: Evidence from the European Football Market," *American Economic Review* 103/5: 1892–1924.

Kleven, H., C. Landais, E. Saez, and E. Schultz 2014. "Migration and Wage Effects of Taxing Top Earners: Evidence from the Foreigners' Tax Scheme in Denmark," *Quarterly Journal of Economics* 129/1: 333–378.

Knack, S., and P. Keefer 1997. "Does Social Capital Have an Economic Payoff? A Cross-Country Investigation," *The Quarterly Journal of Economics* 112: 1251–1288.

Lakner, C., and B. Milanovic 2015. "Global Income Distribution from the Fall of the Berlin Wall to the Great Recession," *Revista de Economía Institucional* 17/32: 71–128.

Layard, R. 2011. *Happiness: Lessons from a New Science,* 2nd edn. London: Penguin UK.

Lazear E. 1995. *Personnel Economics.* Cambridge, MA: MIT Press.

Lee, E., and M. Vivarelli (eds.) 2004. *Understanding Globalization, Employment, and Poverty Reduction.* New York, NY: Palgrave Macmillan.

Lehmann, E., L. Simula, and A. Trannoy 2014. "Tax Me If You Can: Optimal Non-Linear Income Tax between Competing Governments," *Quarterly Journal of Economics* 129/4: 1995–2030.

Lind, J.T. 2007. "Fractionalization and the Size of Government," *Journal of Public Economics* 91/1: 51–76.

Lindert, P.H. 2004. *Growing Public: Volume 1, the Story: Social Spending and Economic Growth Since the Eighteenth Century.* Cambridge: Cambridge University Press.

Luttmer, E.F. 2001. "Group Loyalty and the Taste for Redistribution," *Journal of Political Economy* 109/3: 500–528.

MacFarquhar, R., and M. Schoenhals 2009. *Mao's Last Revolution.* Cambridge, MA: Harvard University Press.

Marquis de Condorcet (Marie-Jean-Antoine-Nicolas Caritat) 1796. *Outlines of an Historical View of the Progress of the Human Mind, Being a Posthumous Work of the Late M. de Condorcet* (translated from the French).

Marx, K. 1990 (1867). *Capital,* Volume I. Trans. Ben Fowkes (1990). London: Penguin Books.

Marx, K., and F. Engels 1848. *The Communist Manifesto: A Modern Edition.* London: Penguin Classics.

Meade J.E. 1993. *Liberty, Equality, and Efficiency.* New York: New York University Press.

Melgar, N., J. Milgram-Baleix, and M. Rossi 2013. "Explaining Protectionism Support: The Role of Economic Factors," *ISRN Economics Volume 2013.* http://dx.doi.org/10.1155/2013/954071 (last accessed January 28, 2018).

Milanovic, B. 2016. *Global Inequality: a New Approach for the Age of Globalization.* Cambridge, MA: The Belknap Press of Harvard University.

Moene, K.O. 2011. "The Moral Sentiments of Wealth of Nations," *The Adam Smith Review,* Volume 6.

Moene, K.O., and D. Ray 2016. "The Universal Basic Share and Social Incentives," *Ideas for India.* www.ideasforindia.in/article.aspx?article_id=1698 (last accessed December 23, 2017).

Moene, K.O., and M. Wallerstein 1997. "Pay Inequality," *Journal of Labor Economics* 55/3: 403–430.

Moene, K.O., and M. Wallerstein 2001. "Inequality, Social Insurance, and Redistribution" *American Political Science Review,* 95/4: 859–874.

Moene, K.O., and M. Wallerstein 2003. "Earnings Inequality and Welfare Spending" *World Politics,* 55(4), 485–516.

Montecinos, V. and Markoff, J. (eds.) 2009. *Economists in the Americas.* Cheltenham: Edward Elgar Publishing.

Moore, B. 1966. *Social Origins of Dictatorship and Democracy: Lord and Peasant in the Making of the Modern World.* Boston: Beacon Press.

Nozick, R. 1974. *Anarchy, State and Utopia.* New York: Basic Books.

Nutall, G. 2012. *Sharing Success: The Nuttal Review of Employee Ownership.* UK Department for Business, Innovation and Skills.

OECD 2015. *How's Life? 2015: Measuring Well-being.* Paris: OECD Publishing.

Okun, A. 1975. *Equality and Efficiency: The Big Tradeoff.* Washington: The Brookings Institution.

Ono, H., and K.S. Lee 2016. *Redistributing Happiness: How Social Policies Shape Life Satisfaction.* Santa Barbara, CA: Praeger.

Ostrom, E. 2000. "Social Capital: A Fad or a Fundamental Concept?," in P. Dasgupta and I. Serageldin (eds.), *Social Capital: A Multifaceted Perspective.* World Bank.

Ottaviano, G.I., and G. Peri 2012. "Rethinking the Effect of Immigration on Wages," *Journal of the European Economic Association* 10/1: 152–197.

Page, J.M. 1994. "The East Asian Miracle: an Introduction," *World Development* 22/4: 615–625.

Pérotin V. 2016. "Democratic Firms," in J. Gonzalez-Ricoy and A, Gosseries (eds.), *Institutions for Future Generations.* Oxford: Oxford University Press.

Perotti, R. 1996. "Growth, Income Distribution and Democracy: What the Data Say," *Journal of Economic Growth* 1/2: 49–188.

Piketty, T. 2014. *Capital in the Twenty-First Century.* Cambridge, MA: Harvard University Press.

Piketty, T., E. Saez, and S. Stantcheva 2014. "Optimal Taxation of Top Labor Incomes: A Tale of Three Elasticities," *American Economic Journal: Economic Policy* 6/1: 230–271.

Pogge, T. 2007. *Freedom from Poverty as a Human Right: Who Owes What to the Very Poor?* Oxford: Oxford University Press.

Polanyi, K. 1944. *The Great Transformation: The Political and Economic Origin of Our Time.* Boston, MA: Beacon Press.

Prasad, E.S., R.G. Rajan, and A. Subramanian 2007. "Foreign Capital and Economic Growth." *Brookings Papers on Economic Activity* 1: 153–209.

Prebisch, R. 1950. *The Economic Development of Latin America and its Principal Problems.* ECLAC, Santiago de Chile.

Przeworski, A. 2003. *States and Markets: A Primer in Political Economy.* Cambridge: Cambridge University Press.

Putnam, R. 2000. *Bowling Alone: the Collapse and Revival of American Community.* New York: Simon & Schuster.

Putnam, R. 2007. "E Pluribus Unum: Diversity and Community in the Twenty-first Century," *Scandinavian Political Studies* 30/2: 137–174.

Ramcharan, R. 2010. "Inequality and Redistribution: Evidence from U.S. Counties and States, 1890–1930," *Review of Economics and Statistics* 92/4: 729–744.

Ray, D. 2006. "Aspirations, Poverty and Economic Change," in A. Banerjee, R. Benabou, and D. Mookherjee (eds.), *Understanding Poverty.* Oxford: Oxford University Press.

Redondo, G., I. Santa Cruz, and J.M. Rotger 2011. "Why Mondragón? Analyzing What Works in Overcoming Inequalities," *Qualitative Inquiry* 17/3: 277–283.

Rodrik, D. 1998. "Why Do More Open Economies Have Bigger Governments?," *Journal of Political Economy* 106/5: 997–1032.

Rodrik, D. 2011. *The Globalization Paradox: Why Global Markets, States, and Democracy Can't Coexist.* Oxford: Oxford University Press.

Roemer, J.E. 1998. *Theories of Distributive Justice.* Cambridge, MA: Harvard University Press.

Roemer, J.E., W. Lee, and K. Van der Straeten 2007. *Racism, Xenophobia, and Distribution: Multi-issue Politics in Advanced Democracies.* Cambridge, MA: Harvard University Press.

Rosen, S. 1981. "The Economics of Superstars," *The American Economic Review* 71: 845–858.

Roser, M., and E. Ortiz-Ospina 2017. "Income Inequality." Published online at OurWorldInData.org. https://ourworldindata.org/income-inequality (last accessed December 23, 2017).

Saez, E. 2004. "Reported Incomes and Marginal Tax Rates, 1960–2000: Evidence and Policy Implications," *Tax Policy and the Economy* 18: 117–173.

Scheve, K.F., and M.J. Slaughter 2006. "Public Opinion, International Economic Integration, and the Welfare State," in P.K. Bardhan, S. Bowles, and M. Wallerstein (eds.), *Globalization and Egalitarian Redistribution.* Princeton, NJ: Princeton University Press.

Schmitter, P.C., and M.W. Bauer 2001. "A (Modest) Proposal for Expanding Social Citizenship in the European Union," *Journal of European Social Policy* 11/1: 55–65.

Schumpeter J.A. 1942. *Capitalism, Socialism, and Democracy.* New York/London: Harper.

Scruggs, L. 2014. Social Welfare Generosity Scores in CWED 2: A Methodological Genealogy. CWED Working Paper Series.

Sen, A. 1985. *Commodities and Capabilities.* Amsterdam: North-Holland Press.

Simula, L., and A. Trannoy 2010. "Optimal Income Tax Under the Threat of Migration by Top-Income Earners," *Journal of Public Economics* 94: 163–173.

Singh, P. 2010. "We-ness and Welfare: A Longitudinal Analysis of Social Development in Kerala, India," *World Development* 39/2: 282–293

Sinn, H.W 2003. *The New Systems Competition.* Oxford: Basic Blackwell.

Smith, A. 1776. *An Inquiry into the Nature and Causes of the Wealth of Nations*, Volume 1. London: W. Strahan; T. Cadell (2nd edn.).

Solt, F. 2016. "The Standardized World Income Inequality Database," *Social Science Quarterly* 97/5: 1267–1281. SWIID Version 6.0, July 2017.

Soroka, S., K. Banting, and R. Johnston 2006. "Immigration and Redistribution in a Global Era," in P.K. Bardhan, S. Bowles, and M. Wallerstein (eds.), *Globalization and Egalitarian Redistribution.* Princeton, NJ: Princeton University Press.

Vallentyne, P., H. Steiner, and M. Otsuka 2005. "Why Left-Libertarianism Is Not Incoherent, Indeterminate, or Irrelevant: A Reply to Fried," *Philosophy & Public Affairs* 33/2: 201–215.

van Parijs P., and Y. Vanderborght 2017. *Basic Income: A Radical Proposal for a Free Society and a Sane Economy.* Cambridge, MA: Harvard University Press.

van Parijs, P. 1995. *Real Freedom for All: What (If Anything) Can Justify Capitalism?* Oxford: Oxford University Press.

Van Trier, W. 1994. *Every One a King.* Leuven: Department of Sociologie, Katholieke Universiteit Leuven.

Waring, M. 1988. *If Women Counted.* New York: Harper & Row.

Weitzman, M.L. 1984. *The Share Economy: Conquering Stagflation.* Cambridge, MA: Harvard University Press.

Wood, A. 1995. "How Trade Hurt Unskilled Workers," *The Journal of Economic Perspectives* 9/3: 57–80.

Volume **1**

Authors

Introduction

Olivier Bouin, RFIEA
Marie-Laure Djelic, Sciences-Po
Marc Fleurbaey, Princeton University
Ravi Kanbur, Cornell University
Elisa Reis, Federal University of Rio de Janeiro

Chapter 1

Coordinating Lead Authors:
Marcel van der Linden, International Institute of Social History, Amsterdam
Elisa Reis, Federal University of Rio de Janeiro

Lead Authors:
Massimo Livi Bacci, University of Florence
Stephen Castles, University of Sydney
Raul Delgado-Wise, University of Zacatecas
Naila Kabeer, London School of Economics
K.P. Kannan, Centre for Development Studies, Kerala
Ronaldo Munck, Dublin City University
Adrienne Roberts, University of Manchester
Johan Schot, University of Sussex
Göran Therborn, Cambridge University
Peter Wagner, Catalan Institute for Research and Advanced Studies (ICREA) and University of Barcelona

Contributing Authors:
Tim Foxon, University of Sussex
Laur Kanger, University of Sussex

Chapter 2

Coordinating Lead Authors:
Henry S. Richardson, Georgetown University
Erik Schokkaert, University of Leuven

Lead Authors:
Stefano Bartolini, University of Siena
Geoffrey Brennan, Australian National University
Paula Casal, Catalan Institution for Research and Advanced Studies, University of Pompeu Fabra
Matthew Clayton, University of Warwick
Rahel Jaeggi, Humboldt University
Niraja Gopal Jayal, Jawaharlal Nehru University
Workineh Kelbessa, Addis Ababa University
Debra Satz, Stanford University

Contributing Authors:
Gustaf Arrhenius, Institute for Futures Studies Stockholm
Tim Campbell, Institute for Futures Studies Stockholm
Simon Caney, Oxford University
John Roemer, Yale University

Chapter 3

Coordinating Lead Authors:
Stephan Klasen, University of Göttingen, Germany
Giovanni Andrea Cornia, University of Florence, Italy
Rebeca Grynspan, Ibero-American General Secretariat, Madrid, Spain
Luis F. López-Calva, World Bank, Washington, DC, USA
Nora Lustig, Tulane University, USA

Lead Authors:
Augustin Fosu, University of Ghana, Accra, Ghana
Sripad Motiram, University of Massachusetts, Boston, USA and Indira Gandhi Institute of Development Research, Mumbai, India
Flora Myamba, REPOA, Dar es Salaam, Tanzania
Andreas Peichl, ifo institute and University of Munich, Munich, Germany
Eldar Shafir, Princeton University, USA
Ana Sojo, Independent consultant, Santiago, Chile
Ingrid Woolard, University of Cape Town, South Africa

Contributing Authors:
Shai Davidai, The New School, New York, USA
Michael Förster, OECD, Paris, France
Rahul Lahoti, Azim Premji University, Bengaluru, India
Judith Sutz, University of the Republic, Montevideo, Uruguay
Rainer Thiele, Kiel Institute for the World Economy, Germany

Chapter 4

Coordinating Lead Authors:
Purnamita Dasgupta, Institute of Economic Growth, Delhi, India
Ottmar Edenhofer, Mercator Research Institute on Global Commons and Climate Change (MCC) and the Potsdam Institute for Climate Impact Research

Lead Authors:
Adriana Mercedes Avendano Amezquita, Universidad Pedagogica y Tecnologica de Colombia
Antonio Bento, University of Southern California
Simon Caney, University of Warwick
David De la Croix, Université catholique de Louvain
Augustin Fosu, University of Ghana
Michael Jakob, MCC
Marianne Saam, ZEW
Kristin Shrader-Frechette, University of Notre-Dame
John Weyant, Stanford University
Liangzhi You, IFPRI

Contributing Authors:
Gian Carlo Delgado-Ramos, National Autonomous University of Mexico
Marcel J. Dorsch, MCC
Christian Flachsland, MCC and Hertie School of Governance
David Klenert, MCC
Robert Lempert, Rand Corporation
Justin Leroux, HEC Montreal
Kai Lessmann, Potsdam Institute for Climate Impact Research
Junguo Liu, Southern University of Science and Technology, China
Linus Mattauch, University of Oxford
Charles Perrings, Arizona State University
Gregor Schwerhoff, MCC
Kristin Seyboth, KMS Research and Consulting
Jan Steckel, MCC
Jessica Strefler, Potsdam Institute for Climate Impact Research

Chapter Management:
Kristin Seyboth, KMS Research and Consulting

Chapter 5

Coordinating Lead Authors:
Saskia Sassen, Columbia University, USA
Edgar Pieterse, University of Cape Town, South Africa

Lead Authors:
Gautam Bhan, Indian Institute for Humane Studies, India
Max Hirsh, Hong Kong Institute for the Humanities and Social Sciences
Ana Falú, National University of Argentina in Córdoba
Hiroo Ichikawa, Meiji University, Japan
Luis Riffo, CEPAL, Chile
Pelin Tan, Mardin Artukli Üniversity, Turkey
Doris Tarchopulos, Pontificia Universidad Javeriana, Colombia

Chapter 6

Coordinating Lead Authors:
Simon Deakin, University of Cambridge
Fabian Muniesa, Mines ParisTech
Scott Stern, MIT
Lorraine Talbot, University of Birmingham

Lead Authors:
Raphie Kaplinsky, University of Sussex
Martin O'Neill, University of York
Horacio Ortiz, CNRS, Université Paris Dauphine
Kerstin Sahlin, Swedish Research Council
Anke Schwittay, University of Sussex

Chapter 7

Coordinating Lead Authors:
Werner Eichhorst, ZA Institute of Labor Economics (IZA), Germany
André Portela Souza, São Paulo School of Economics, Fundação Getulio Vargas, Brazil

Lead Authors:
Pierre Cahuc, CREST-ENSAE, Malakoff, and Ecole Polytechnique, France
Didier Demazière, Sciences Po CSO, France
Colette Fagan, University of Manchester, UK
Nadya Araujo Guimarães, University of São Paulo, Brazil
Huiyan Fu, Regent's University London, UK
Arne Kalleberg, University of North Carolina, Chapel Hill, USA
Alan Manning, London School of Economics, UK
Frances McGinnity, The Economic and Social Research Institute (ESRI), Ireland
Hillel Rapoport, University of Paris I Panthéon-Sorbonne, Paris School of Economics, France
Phil Scranton, Rutgers University, USA
Johannes Siegrist, University of Duesseldorf, Germany
Kathleen Thelen, Massachusetts Institute of Technology (MIT), USA
Marie-Anne Valfort, University of Paris I Panthéon-Sorbonne, France
Jelle Visser, University of Amsterdam, The Netherlands

Chapter 8

Coordinating Lead Authors:
Gianluca Grimalda, Kiel Institute for the World Economy, Germany
Kalle Moene, University of Oslo, Norway

Lead Authors:
Fernando Filgueira, CIESU, Uruguay
Marc Fleurbaey, Princeton University, USA
Katherine Gibson, Western Sydney University, Australia
Carol Graham, Brookings, USA
Rubén Lo Vuolo, Centro Interdisciplinario para el Estudio de Políticas Públicas, Argentina
Reema Nanavaty, SEWA, India
Hiroshi Ono, Hitotsubashi University, Japan and Texas A&M University, USA
John Roemer, Yale University, USA
Alain Trannoy, AMSE and EHESS, France

Index